Encyclopedia of Finance

Encyclopedia of Finance

Edited by

CHENG-FEW LEE

Rutgers University

and

ALICE C. LEE

San Francisco State University

 Springer

Library of Congress Control Number 2005049962

Encyclopedia of finance / edited by Cheng Few Lee and Alice C. Lee

ISBN-13: 978-0-387-26284-0   ISBN-10: 0-387-26336-5 (e-book)
ISBN-10: 0-387-26284-9

Printed on acid-free paper.

Printed in the United States of America.

9 8 7 6 5 4 3

springer.com

ABOUT THE EDITORS

Cheng-Few Lee is a Distinguished Professor of Finance at Rutgers Business School, Rutgers University and was chairperson of the Department of Finance from 1988–1995. He has also served on the faculty of the University of Illinois (IBE Professor of Finance) and the University of Georgia. He has maintained academic and consulting ties in Taiwan, Hong Kong, China and the United States for the past three decades. He has been a consultant to many prominent groups including, the American Insurance Group, the World Bank, the United Nations and The Marmon Group Inc., etc.

Professor Lee founded the *Review of Quantitative Finance and Accounting* (RQFA) in 1990 and the *Review of Pacific Basin Financial Markets and Policies* (RPBFMP) in 1998, and serves as managing editor for both journals. He was also a co-editor of the *Financial Review* (1985–1991) and the *Quarterly Review of Economics and Business* (1987–1989).

In the past thirty-two years, Dr. Lee has written numerous textbooks ranging in subject matter from financial management to corporate finance, security analysis and portfolio management to financial analysis, planning and forecasting, and business statistics. Dr. Lee has also published more than 170 articles in more than twenty different journals in finance, accounting, economics, statistics, and management. Professor Lee has been ranked the most published finance professor worldwide during 1953–2002.

Alice C. Lee is an Assistant Professor of Finance at San Francisco State University. She has a diverse background, which includes engineering, sales, and management consulting. Her primary areas of teaching and research are corporate finance and financial institutions. She is coauthor of *Statistics for Business and Financial Economics*, 2e (with Cheng-Few Lee and John C. Lee) and Financial Analysis, Planning and Forecasting, 2e (with Cheng-Few Lee and John C. Lee, forthcoming in 2006). In addition, she has co-edited other annual publications including *Advances in Investment Analysis and Portfolio Management* (with Cheng-Few Lee).

TABLE OF CONTENTS

PREFACE

Finance has become one of the most important and popular subjects in management school today. This subject has progressed tremendously in the last forty years, integrating models and ideas from other areas such as physics, statistics, and accounting. The financial markets have also rapidly expanded and changed extensively with improved technology and the ever changing regulatory and social environment. For example, there has been a rapid expansion of financial concepts, instruments, and tools due to increased computing power and seemingly instantaneous information sharing through networks. The internationalization of businesses and economies will continue to impact the field of finance. With all this progress and expansion in finance and society, we thought that it would be useful to put together an updated comprehensive encyclopedia as a reference book for both students and professionals, in an attempt to meet the demand for a key source of fundamental finance terminology and concepts.

This Encyclopedia of Finance contains five parts. Part I includes finance terminology and short essays. Part II includes fifty important finance papers by well know scholars and practitioners such as; James R. Barth, Ren-Raw Chen, Thomas C. Chiang, Quentin C. Chu, Wayne E. Ferson, Joseph E. Finnerty, Thomas S.Y. Ho, C.H. Ted Hong, Cheng Hsiao, Jing-Zhi Huang, Mao-wei Hung, John S. Jahera Jr, Haim Levy, Wilbur G. Lewellen, Joseph P. Ogden, Fai-Nan Peng, Gordon S. Roberts, Robert A. Schwartz, K.C. John Wei, and Gillian Yeo, among others. Topics covered in both Part I and Part II include fundamental subjects such as financial management, corporate finance, investment analysis and portfolio management, options and futures, financial institutions, international finance, and real estate finance. Part III contains appendices which discuss and derive some fundamental finance concepts and models; Part IV lists references; and Part V provides both subject and author indexes.

Fifty papers included in Part II can be classified as eight groups as follows:
a) Investment analysis and portfolio management (papers 3, 7, 10, 12, 19, 21, 29, 31, 34, 40, 45, and 48);
b) Financial management and corporate finance (papers 11, 18, 22, 26, 27, 28, 32, 39, and 42);
c) International finance (papers 4, 6, 15, 30, 33, 41, 42, 47, and 50);
d) Microstructure (papers 16, 17, 20, 30, 35, 36, 37, 38, and 44);
e) Asset pricing (papers 8, 9, 10, 12, and 34);

f) Financial Institutions and Markets (papers 1, 2, 13, 24, and 46);
g) Derivatives (papers 5, 28, and 43);
h) Real estate finance (papers 14, 25, and 49);
i) Risk Management (papers 4, 5, 6, 22, 23, 24, and 39).

For both undergraduate and graduate students, this encyclopedia is a
good supplementary material for above listed finance courses. In addition, this encyclopedia can also be a good supplementary material for
financial accounting courses. We believe that this encyclopedia will not
only be useful to students but also for professors and practitioners in the
field of finance as a reference.

We would like to thank the contributors for willingness to share their
expertise and their thoughtful essays in Part II. We would like to thank
Ms. Judith L. Pforr and Ms. Candace L. Rosa, of Springer for their
coordination and suggestions to this book. Finally, we would also like to
express our gratitude to our secretaries Ms. Mei-Lan Luo, Ms. Sue Wang,
Ms. Ting Yen, and Ms. Meetu Zalani, for their efforts in helping us pull
together this tremendous repository of information.

We hope that the readers will find the encyclopedia to be an invaluable
resource.

By
Cheng-Few Lee
Alice C. Lee

CONTRIBUTORS

James R. Barth, Auburn University and Milken Institute, USA
A. Linda Beyer, Alaska Supply Chain Integrators, USA
Jow-Ran Chang, National Tsing Hua University, Taiwan
Ren-Raw Chen, Rutgers University-New Brunswick, USA
Thomas C. Chiang, Drexel University, USA
Quentin C. Chu, University of Memphis, USA
Chang-Wen Duan, Tamkang University, Taiwan
Wayne Ferson, Boston College, USA
Joseph E. Finnerty, University of Illinois, USA
Jonathan Fletcher, University of Strathclyde, UK
Iraj J. Fooladi, Dalhousie University, Canada
John A. Fox, The Fox Consultant Incorporated, USA
Reto Francioni, The Swiss Stock Exchange, Switzerland
Aron A. Gottesman, Pace University, USA
Tanweer Hasan, Roosevelt University, USA
Yan He, Indiana University Southeast, USA
Randall A. Heron, Indiana University, USA
Thomas S. Y. Ho, Thomas Ho Company, Ltd., USA
C.H. Ted Hong, BeyondBond Inc., USA
Cheng Hsiao, University of Southern California, USA
Chang-Tseh Hsieh, University of South Mississippi, USA
Jing-Zhi Huang, Penn State University, USA
Ken Hung, National Dong Hwa University, Taiwan
Mao-Wei Hung, National Taiwan University, Taiwan
Gady Jacoby, University of Manitoba, Canada
John S. Jahera Jr, Auburn University, USA
Khondkar E. Karim, Rochester Institute of Technology, USA
Richard J. Kish, Lehigh University, USA
Hsein-Chang Kuo, National Chi-Nan University, Taiwan
Alice C. Lee, San Francisco State University, USA
Cheng-Few Lee, Rutgers University-New Brunswick, USA
Cindy Lee, China Trust Bank, USA
Sang Bin Lee, Hanyang University, Korea
Haim Levy, Hebrew University, Israel
Wilbur G. Lewellen, Purdue University, USA
Lin Lin, National Chi-Nan University, Taiwan
William T. Lin, Tamkang University, Taiwan
Melody Lo, University of Southern Mississippi, USA
Chiuling Lu, Yuan Ze University, Taiwan
Dwight B. Means, Dr. Dwight B. Means Jr. Consultant, USA
Shashidhar Murthy, Rutgers University-Camden, USA

Joseph P. Ogden, State University of New York at Buffalo, USA
Lin Peng, City University of New York, USA
Fai-Nan Perng, The Central Bank of China, Taiwan
Triphon Phumiwasana, Milken Institute, USA
Jenifer Piesse, University of London, UK
Deborah N. Pittman, Rhodes College, USA
Gordon S. Roberts, York University, Canada
Lalith P. Samarakoon, University of St. Thomas, USA
Robert A. Schwartz, City University of New York, USA
Suresh Srivatava, University of Alaska Anchorage, USA
Pearl Tan, Nanyang Technology University, Singapore
Nicholas S. P. Tay, University of San Francisco, USA
Khairy Tourk, Illinois Institute of Technology, USA
Geraldo M. Vasoncellos, Lehigh University, USA
Shin-Huei Wang, University of Southern California, USA
Wen-Ching Wang, Robeco Investment Management, USA
Daniel G. Weaver, Rutgers University, USA
K.C. John Wei, Hong Kong University of Science and Technology, HK
Ying Wu, Salisbury University, USA
Chin-Wei Yang, Clarion University of Pennsylvania, USA
Gillian Yeo, Nanyang Technology University, Singapore
Zhaohui Zhang, Long Island University-C. W. Post, USA

PART I: Terminologies and Essays

A

1. Abnormal Return

Return on a stock beyond what would be the expected return that is predicted by market movements alone. [See also **Cumulative abnormal return (CAR)**]

2. Absolute Cost Advantage

Absolute cost advantages can place competitors at a cost disadvantage, even if the scale of operations is similar for both firms. Such cost advantages can arise from an advanced position along the learning curve, where average costs decline as cumulative output rises over time. This differs from economies of scale, which involves the relationship between average costs and the output level per period of time. A firm that enters a market segment early can learn about the production and distribution process first and make more efficient use of assets, technology, raw inputs, and personnel than its competitors. In such cases, the firm can frequently reduce costs and prices and maintain market leadership. Similar advantages can result from possessing proprietary technology that is protected by patents.

Some firms seek to maintain absolute cost advantages by entering foreign market. Early entry can allow the firm to gain experience over its competitors, as it can more efficiently track foreign market trends and technologies and disseminate new methods throughout the firm.

3. Absolute Priority of Claims

In case of liquidation of a firm's assets, the rule requires satisfaction of certain claims prior to the satisfaction of other claims. The priority of claims in liquidation or reorganization typically takes the following order:

1. Special current debt, which includes trustee expenses, unpaid wages that employees have earned in the 90 days preceding bankruptcy (not to exceed $2,000 for any one case), and contributions to employee benefit plans that have fallen due within the 180 days preceding bankruptcy.

2. Consumer claims on deposits not exceeding $900 per claim.

3. Tax claims.

4. Secured creditors' claims, such as mortgage bonds and collateral trust bonds, but only to the extent of the liquidating value of the pledged assets.

5. General creditors' claims, including amounts owed to unsatisfied secured creditors and all unsecured creditors, but only to the extent of their proportionate interests in the aggregate claims of their classes.

6. Preferred stockholders' claims, to the extent provided in their contracts, plus unpaid dividends.

7. Residual claims of common stockholders.

The priority of claims order and amounts are arbitrary, and no conclusions should be drawn about the relative merits of how workers, consumers, the government, creditors, and owners are treated.

4. Absolute Priority Rule (APR)

Establishes priority of claims under liquidation. Once the corporation is determined to be bankrupt, liquidation takes place. The distribution of the proceeds of the liquidation occurs according to the following priority: (1) Administration expenses; (2) Unsecured claims arising after the filing of an involuntary bankruptcy petition; (3) Wages, salaries, and commissions; (4) Contributions to employee benefit plans arising within 180 days before the filing date; (5) Consumer claims; (6) Tax claims; (7) Secured and unsecured creditors' claims; (8) Preferred stockholders' claims; (9)

Common stockholders' claims. APR is similar to absolute priority of claims.

5. Absolute Purchasing Power Parity

Absolute purchasing power parity states that exchange rates should adjust to keep purchasing power constant across currencies. In general, however, absolute purchasing power parity does not hold, in part because of transportation costs, tariffs, quotas, and other free trade restrictions. A more useful offshoot of absolute purchasing power parity is **relative purchasing power parity**. [See also **Relative purchasing power parity**]

6. Accelerated Cost Recovery System (ACRS)

A system used to depreciate accelerated assets for tax purposes. The current system, enacted by the 1986 Tax Reform Act, is very similar to ACRS established in 1981. The current modified accelerated cost recovery system (MACRS) specifies the depreciable lives (recovery periods) and rates for each of several classes of property. It should be noted that this higher level of depreciation is offset by reclassifying individual assets into categories with longer life. [See also **Modified accelerated cost recovery system**]

7. Accelerated Depreciation

A method of computing depreciation deductions for income tax that permits deductions in early years greater than those under straight line depreciation. It includes sums of year's digits, units of production and double decline methods. [See also **Double-declining balance depreciation, Sum-of-the-year's-digits depreciation** and **Unit of production method**]

8. Account Activity

Transactions associated with a deposit account, including home debits, transit checks, deposits, and account maintenance.

9. Account Analysis

An analytical procedure for determining whether a customer's deposit account or entire credit-deposit relationship with a bank is profitable. The procedure compares revenues from the account with the cost of providing services.

10. Account Executive

A representative of a brokerage firm who processes orders to buy and sell stocks, options, etc., for a customer's account.

11. Account Maintenance

The overhead cost associated with collecting information and mailing periodic statements to depositors.

12. Accounting Analytic

The use of financial ratios and fundamental analysis to estimate firm specific credit quality examining items such as leverage and coverage measures, with an evaluation of the level and stability of earnings and cash flows. [See also **Credit scoring model**]

13. Accounting Beta

Project betas can be estimated based on accounting beta. Accounting measures of return, such as EBIT/Total Assets, can be regressed against a profitability index that is based on data for the stocks in the S&P 500 or some other market index:

$$\left[\frac{EBIT}{TA}\right]_{project,\,i,\,t} = \alpha_i + A\beta_i \left[\frac{EBIT}{TA}\right]_{market,\,t} + \varepsilon_{i,\,t},$$

where the slope estimate; $A\beta_i$, is the accounting beta.

Accounting information by product line or division is available in various Securities and Exchange Commission (SEC) filings that are required of publicly traded firms. Although a firm's multidivisional structure may disqualify it from being a pure play comparable, it may include divisional data in its public SEC filing that would be useful for estimating an accounting beta.

14. Accounting Break-Even

Accounting break-even occurs when accounting revenues equal accounting expenses so that pretax income (and hence net income) equals zero. It tells us how much product must be sold so that the firm's overall accounting profits are equal to accounting expenses. Ignoring working capital effects,

$OCF = NI + Depreciation.$

At accounting break-even, net income (NI) is zero, so Operating Cash Flow (OCF) equals the periodic depreciation expense. Substituting this into the general break-even (Q^*) formula, we obtain accounting break-even quantity ($Q_{accounting}^*$) as:

$$Q_{accounting}^* = \frac{FC + Dep}{p - vc},$$

where FC = fixed cost; vc = variable cost per unit; p = price per unit; and Dep = depreciation.

The denominator, (p–vc), is called the contribution margin. The accounting break-even quantity is given by the sum of the fixed cost and depreciation divided by the contribution margin. Accounting break-even tells us how much product must be sold so that the firm's overall accounting profits are not reduced.

15. Accounting Earnings

Earnings of a firm as reported in its income statement. Accounting earnings are affected by several conventions regarding the valuation of assets such as inventories (e.g., LIFO versus FIFO treatment) and by the way some expenditures such as capital investments are recognized over time (such as depreciation expenses).

16. Accounting Income

Income described in terms of accounting earnings, based upon records of transactions in company books kept according to generally accepted principles (GAAP). Accountants generally measure revenues and expenses based on accruals and deferrals rather than cash flows and, in turn, measure the net income of the firm by matching its revenues with the costs it incurred to generate those revenues.

Theoretically, financial analysis should consider **economic income** rather than accounting earnings to determine the value of the firm, since economic income represents the firm's true earnings and cash flows. [See also **Economic income**] However, since economic income is not directly observable, analysts generally use accounting earnings as a proxy. The relationship between economic income and accounting earnings can be related by the following equation:

Accounting Income =
Economic Income (permanent component)
+ Error (Transitory component).

17. Accounting Insolvency

Total book liabilities exceed total book value of assets. A firm with negative net worth is insolvent on the books.

18. Accounting Liquidity

The ease and quickness with which assets can be converted to cash. Current assets are the most liquid and include cash and those assets that will be turned into cash within a year from the date of the balance sheet. Fixed assets are the least liquid type of assets.

19. Accounting Rate of Return (ARR)

The accounting rate of return (ARR) method (which is one of the methods for capital budgeting decision) computes a rate of return for a project based on a ratio of average project income to investment outlay (usually either the total initial investment or the average investment is used). Projects with accounting returns exceeding a management-determined minimum return are accepted; those with returns below the cutoff are rejected. To compute the accounting rate of return, we use the following ratio:

$$ARR = \frac{\text{Average annual net income}}{\text{Total initial investment}}.$$

Similar to the **payback method**, the accounting rate of return method has none of the four desired selection method characteristics. [See also **Payback method**] First, it doesn't even use cash flows; it relies on accounting income. Second, it ignores time value of money concepts. Third, it states no clearly defined, objective decision criterion; like the payback method, its cutoff depends on the discretion of management. Fourth, ARR tells us absolutely nothing about the impact of a project on shareholder wealth.

20. Accounting, Relationship to Finance

The accounting function, quantifies, to a certain extent, the economic relationships within the firm and provides data on which management bases its planning, controlling, and operating decisions. Like accounting, finance deals with value and the monetary resources of the organization. [See also **Finance**]

21. Accounting-Based Beta Forecasting

Elgers (1980) proposed accounting-based beta forecasting. Accounting-based beta forecasts rely upon the relationship of accounting information such as the growth rate of the firm, earning before interest and tax (EBIT), leverage, and the dividend pay-out as a basis for forecasting beta. To use accounting information in beta forecasting, the historical beta estimates are first cross-sectionally related to accounting information such as growth rate, variance of EBIT, leverage, accounting beta, and so on:

$$\beta_i = a_0 + a_1 X_{1i} + a_2 X_{2i} + a_j X_{ji} + \cdots + a_m X_{mi},$$

where β_i is the beta coefficient for ith firm which is estimated in terms of market model. X_{ji} is the jth accounting variables for ith firm, and a_j is the regression coefficient.

22. Accounting-Based Performance Measures

To evaluate firm performance, we can use accounting-based measures such as sales, earnings per share, growth rate of a firm. However, accounting performance measures are vulnerable to distortion by accounting principles, whose application may be somewhat subjective (such as when to recognize revenue or how quickly to depreciate assets). Rather than present an unbiased view of firm performance, accounting statements may be oriented toward the perspective that management wants to present. Additionally, accounting-based performance measures are always *historical*, telling us where the firm has been.

23. Accounts Payable

Money the firm owes to suppliers. These are payments for goods or services, such as raw materials. These payments will generally be made after purchases. Purchases will depend on the sales forecast. Accounts payable is an unfunded short-term debt.

24. Accounts Receivable

Money owed to the firm by customers; the amounts not yet collected from customers for goods or services sold to them (after adjustment for potential bad debts).

25. Accounts Receivable Financing

A secured short-term loan that involves either the assigning of receivables or the factoring of receivables. Under assignment, the lender has a lien on the receivables and recourse to the borrower. Factoring involves the sale of accounts receivable. Then the purchaser, call the factor, must collect on receivables. [See also **Factoring**]

26. Accounts Receivable Turnover

Credit sales divided by average accounts receivable. In general, a higher accounts receivable turnover ratio suggests more frequent payment of receivables by customers. The accounts receivable turnover ratio is written as:

Accounts Receivable Turnover

$$= \frac{Sales}{Accounts\ Receivable}.$$

Thus, if a firm's accounts receivable turnover ratio is larger than the industry average, this implies that the firm's accounts receivable are more efficiently managed than the average firm in that industry.

27. Accreting Swap

A swap where the notional amount increases over the life of the swap. It is used to hedge interest rate risk or agreements with a rising principal value, such as a construction loan.

28. Accrual

The accumulation of income earned or expense incurred, regardless of when the underlying cash flow is actually received or paid.

29. Accrual Bond

A bond that accrues interest but does not pay interest to the investor until maturity when accrued interest is paid with the principal outstanding.

30. Accrual Swap

An interest rate swap where interest on one side accrues only when the floating reference rate is within certain range. The range can be maintained, fixed, or reset periodically during the entire life of the swap.

31. Accrued Interest

Interest income that is earned but not yet received. Alternatively, it refers to pro-rated portion of a bond's coupon payment (c) since the previous coupon date with $(m–d)$ days have passed since the last coupon payment; the accrued interest is $c(m - d)/m$, where m and d represent total days and days left to receive coupon payment, respectively. In a semiannual coupon, if $m = 182$ days, $d = 91$ days and $c = \$60$, then the accrued interest is calculated as:

$$(\$30)\left(\frac{182 - 91}{182}\right) = \$15.$$

32. Accumulated Benefit Obligation (ABO)

FASB Statement 87 specifies that the measure of corporate pension liabilities to be used on the corporate balance sheet in external reports is the accumulated benefit obligation (ABO), which is the present value of pension benefits owed to employees under the plan's benefit formula absent any salary projections and discounted at a nominal rate of interest.

33. Accumulation Phase

During the accumulation phase, the investor contributes money periodically to one or more open-end mutual funds and accumulates shares. [See also **Variable annuities**]

34. Acid-Test Ratio

A measure of liquidity from reported balance sheet figures with targeted minimum value of one. Calculated as the sum of cash, marketable securities, and accounts receivable divided by current liabilities. [See also **Quick ratio**]

35. Acquisition

Assuming there are two firms, Firm A and Firm B. Acquisition is a form of business combination in which Firm B buys Firm A, and they both remain in existence; Firm B as the parent and Firm A as the subsidiary.

Mergers or acquisitions are also ways for a private firm to raise equity capital by selling all or part of the firm to another corporation. [See also **Merger**] Another firm may pay an attractive price for the equity of the private firm, especially if the private firm has a good strategic fit with the buyer's products and plans, or if the purchase offers a foreign corporation easy entry into the US market. Acquisitions can be negotiated to allow the firm's managers to retain their current positions or to receive lucrative consulting contracts.

Another advantage of a merger or acquisition is when the investor is a large corporation with deep pockets and a willingness to help the firm grow. Such a situation can provide financing for the firm's present and foreseeable future needs. Rather than spending time canvassing banks and equity investors for capital, management can concentrate on doing what it presumably does best: managing the firm to make it grow and succeed.

The drawback to a merger or acquisition is a loss of control. Although a seemingly straightforward consequence, this can be a large stumbling block for a business with a tradition of family ownership or for a group of founding entrepreneurs who consider the firm their "baby." Unless the private equity owners get an exceptional deal from the new owner, a merger or sale causes them to give up the return potential of their business. If the company does grow and succeed after the sale, someone else – the new investor – will reap the benefits. If the original owners stay with the new owner, they may become frustrated by the lack of attention from their new partners if the firm is only a small part of the acquirer's overall business.

36. Active Bond Portfolio Management

An investment policy whereby managers buy and sell securities prior to final maturity to speculate on future interest rate movements. In addition, managers can also identify the relative mispricing within the fixed-income market.

37. Active Management

Attempts to achieve portfolio returns more than commensurate with risk, either by forecasting broad market trends or by identifying particular mispriced sectors of a market or securities in a market.

38. Active Portfolio

In the context of the Treynor-Black model (See Treynor and Black, 1973), the portfolio formed by mixing analyzed stocks of perceived nonzero alpha values. This portfolio is ultimately mixed with the passive market index portfolio. [See also **Alpha** and **Active bond portfolio management**]

39. Activity Charge

A service charge based on the number of checks written by a depositor.

40. Activity Ratios

Activity ratios measure how well a firm is using its resources. Four activity ratios are analyzed: (1) **inventory turnover**, (2) **average collection period**, (3) **fixed-asset turnover**, and (4) **total asset turnover**.

Inventory turnover (sales/inventory) measures how well a firm is turning over its inventory. The average collection period (receivables/sales per day) measures the accounts-receivable turnover. The fixed-asset turnover (sales to net fixed assets) measures the turnover of plant and equipment – a measure of capacity utilization. Total-asset turnover (sales/total assets) measures how efficiently total assets have been utilized.

41. Acts of Bankruptcy

Bankruptcy includes a range of court procedures in the US that may result in the firm being liquidated or financially reorganized to continue operations. This may occur voluntarily if the firm permits a petition for bankruptcy, or a creditor's petition may force the firm into the courts. Such a petition by a creditor charges the firm with committing one of the following acts of bankruptcy: (1) committing fraud while legally insolvent, (2) making preferential disposition of firm assets while legally insolvent, (3) assigning assets to a third party for voluntary liquidation while insolvent, (4) failing to remove a lien on the firm within 30 days while insolvent, (5) appointment of a receiver or trustee while insolvent, or (6) written admission of insolvency.

42. Additions to Net Working Capital

A component of the cash flow of the firm, along with operating cash flow and capital spending. These cash flows are used for making investments in net working capital.

Total cash flow of the firm = Operating cash flow
  − Capital spending − Additions to net
  working capital.

43. Add-on Interest

Add-on interest means that the total interest owed on the loan, based on the annual stated interest rate, is added to the initial principal balance before determining the periodic payment. This kind of loan is called an add-on loan. Payments are determined by dividing the total of the principal plus interest by the number of payments to be made. When a borrower repays a loan in a single, lump sum, this method gives a rate identical to annual stated interest. However, when two or more payments are to be made, this method results in an effective rate of interest that is greater than the nominal rate. Putting this into equation form, we see that:

$$PV = \Sigma_{t=1}^{N} \frac{\text{Future Flows}}{(1 + \text{Interest Rate})^t} ,$$

where PV = the present value or loan amount; t = the time period when the interest and principal repayment occur; and N = the number of periods.

For example, if a million-dollar loan were repaid in two six-month installments of $575,000 each, the effective rate would be higher than 15 percent, since the borrower does not have the use of the funds for the entire year. Allowing r to equal the annual percentage rate of the loan, we obtain the following:

$$\$1,000,000 = \frac{\$575,000}{\left(1 + \frac{r}{2}\right)^1} + \frac{\$575,000}{\left(1 + \frac{r}{2}\right)^2} .$$

Using a financial calculator, we see that r equals 19.692 percent, which is also annual percentage return (APR). Using this information, we can obtain the installment loan amortization schedule as presented in the following table.

	Payment	Beginning Balance	Interest (0.19692)/ 2 X (b)	Principal Paid	Ending Loan Balance
	(a)	(b)	(c)	(d)	(e)
Period				(a) − (c)	(b) − (d)
1	$575,000	$1,000,000	$98.460	$476,540	$523,460
2	575,000	523,460	51,540	523,460	0
Biannual payment:				$575,000	
Initial balance:				$1,000,000	
Initial maturity:				One year	
APR:				19.692%	

44. Add-On Rate

A method of calculating interest charges by applying the quoted rate to the entire amount advanced to a borrower times the number of financing periods. For example, an 8 percent add-on rate indicates $80 interest per $1,000 for 1 year, $160 for 2 years, and so forth. The effective interest rate is higher than the add-on rate because the borrower makes installment payments and cannot use the entire loan proceeds for full maturity. [See also **Add-on interest**]

45. Adjustable-Rate Mortgage (ARM)

A mortgage whose interest rate varies according to some specified measure of the current market interest rate. The adjustable-rate contract shifts much of the risk of fluctuations in interest rates from the lender to the borrower.

46. Adjusted Beta

The sample beta estimated by market model can be modified by using cross-sectional market information [see Vasicek, 1973]. This kind of modified beta is called adjusted beta. Merrill Lynch's adjusted beta is defined as:

$$\text{Adjusted beta} = \frac{2}{3} \text{ sample beta} + \frac{1}{3}(1).$$

47. Adjusted Forecast

A (micro or macro) forecast that has been adjusted for the imprecision of the forecast. When we forecast GDP or interest rate over time, we need to adjust for the imprecision of the forecast of either GDP or interest rate.

48. Adjusted Present Value (APV) Model

Adjusted present value model for capital budgeting decision. This is one of the methods used to do capital budgeting for a levered firm. This method takes into account the tax shield value associated with tax deduction for interest expense. The formula can be written as:

$$APV = NPV + T_c D,$$

where APV = Adjusted present value; NPV = Net present value; T_c = Marginal corporate tax rate;

D = Total corporate debt; and $T_c D$ = Tax shield value.

This method is based upon M&M Proposition I with tax. [See also **Modigliani and Miller (M&M) Proposition I**]

49. ADR

American Depository Receipt: A certificate issued by a US bank which evidences ownership in foreign shares of stock held by the bank. [See also **American depository receipt**]

50. Advance

A payment to a borrower under a loan agreement.

51. Advance Commitment

This is one of the methods for hedging interest rate risk in a real estate transaction. It is a promise to sell an asset before the seller has lined up purchase of the asset. This seller can offset risk by purchasing a futures contract to fix the sale price. We call this a long hedge by a mortgage banker because the mortgage banker offsets risk in the cash market by buying a futures contract.

52. Affiliate

Any organization that is owned or controlled by a bank or bank holding company, the stockholders, or executive officers.

53. Affinity Card

A credit card that is offered to all individuals who are part of a common group or who share a common bond.

54. After-Acquired Clause

A first mortgage indenture may include an after-acquired clause. Such a provision states that any property purchased after the bond issue is considered to be security for the bondholders' claim against the firm. Such a clause also often states that only a certain percentage of the new property can be debt financed.

55. Aftermarket

The period of time following the initial sale of securities to the public; this may last from several days to several months.

56. After-Tax Real Return

The after-tax rate of return on an asset minus the rate of inflation.

57. After-Tax Salvage Value

After-tax salvage value can be defined as:

After-tax salvage value = Price − T(Price − BV),

where *Price* = market value; *T*= corporate tax rate; and *BV*= book value.

If *T(Price − BV)* is positive, the firm owes taxes, reducing the after-tax proceeds of the asset sale; if *T(Price − BV)* is negative, the firm reduces its tax bill, in essence increasing the after-tax proceeds of the sale. When *T(Price − BV)* is zero, no tax adjustment is necessary.

By their nature, after-tax salvage values are difficult to estimate as both the salvage value and the expected future tax rate are uncertain.

As a practical matter, if the project termination is many years in the future, the present value of the salvage proceeds will be small and inconsequential to the analysis. If necessary, however, analysts can try to develop salvage value forecasts in two ways. First, they can tap the expertise of those involved in secondary market uses of the asset. Second, they can try to forecast future scrap material prices for the asset. Typically, the after-tax salvage value cash flow is calculated using the firm's current tax rate as an estimate for the future tax rate.

The problem of estimating values in the distant future becomes worse when the project involves a major strategic investment that the firm expects to maintain over a long period of time. In such a situation, the firm may estimate annual cash flows for a number of years and then attempt to estimate the project's value as a going concern at the end of this time horizon. One method the firm can use to estimate the project's going-concern value is the **constant dividend growth model**. [See also **Gordon model**]

58. Agency Bond

Bonds issued by federal agencies such as Government National Mortgage Association (GNMA) and government/government-sponsored enterprises such as Small Business Administration (SBA). An Agency bond is a direct obligation of the Treasury even though some agencies are government sponsored or guaranteed. The net effect is that agency bonds are considered almost default-risk free (if not legally so in all cases) and, therefore, are typically priced to provide only a slightly higher yield than their corresponding T-bond counterparts.

59. Agency Costs

The principal-agent problem imposes agency costs on shareholders. Agency costs are the tangible and intangible expenses borne by shareholders because of the self-serving actions of managers. Agency costs can be explicit, out-of-pocket expenses (sometimes called direct agency costs) or more implicit ones (sometimes called implicit agency costs). [See also **Principal-agent problem**]

Examples of explicit agency costs include the costs of auditing financial statements to verify their accuracy, the purchase of liability insurance for board members and top managers, and the monitoring of managers' actions by the board or by independent consultants.

Implicit agency costs include restrictions placed against managerial actions (e.g., the requirement of shareholder votes for some major decisions) and covenants or restrictions placed on the firm by a lender.

The end result of self-serving behaviors by management and shareholder attempts to limit them is a reduction in firm value. Investors will not pay as much for the firm's stock because they realize that the principal-agent problem and its attendant costs lower the firm's value.

Conflicts of interest among stockholders, bondholders, and managers will rise. Agency costs are the costs of resolving these conflicts. They include the costs of providing managers with an incentive to maximize shareholder wealth and then monitoring their behavior, and the cost of protecting bondholders from shareholders. Agency costs will decline, and firm value will rise, as principals' trust and confidence in their agents rise. Agency costs are borne by stockholders.

60. Agency Costs, Across National Borders

Agency costs may differ across national borders as a result of different accounting principles, banking structures, and securities laws and regulations. Firms in the US and the UK use relatively more equity financing than firms in France, Germany and Japan. Some argue that these apparent differences can be explained by differences in equity and debt agency costs across the countries.

For example, agency costs of equity seem to be lower in the US and the UK. These countries have more accurate systems of accounting (in that the income statements and balance sheets are higher quality reflecting actual revenues and expenses, assets and liabilities) than the other countries, and have higher auditing standards. Dividends and financial statements are distributed to shareholders more frequently, as well, which allows shareholders to monitor management more easily.

Germany, France, and Japan, on the other hand, all have systems of debt finance that may reduce the agency costs of lending. In other countries, a bank can hold an equity stake in a corporation, meet the bulk of the corporation's

borrowing needs, and have representation on the corporate board of directors. Corporations can own stock in other companies and also have representatives on other companies' boards. Companies frequently get financial advice from groups of banks and other large corporations with whom they have interlocking directorates. These institutional arrangements greatly reduce the monitoring and agency costs of debt; thus, debt ratios are substantially higher in France, Germany, and Japan.

61. Agency Problem

Conflicts of interest among stockholders, bondholders, and managers.

62. Agency Securities

Fixed-income securities issued by agencies owned or sponsored by the federal government. The most common securities are issued by the Federal Home Loan Bank, Federal National Mortgage Association, and Farm Credit System.

63. Agency Theory

The theory of the relationship between principals and agents. It involves the nature of the costs of resolving conflicts of interest between principals and agents. [See also **Agency cost**]

64. Agents

Agents are representatives of insurers. There are two systems used to distribute or sell insurance. The direct writer system involves an agent representing a single insurer, whereas the independent agent system involves an agent representing multiple insurers. An independent agent is responsible for running an agency and for the operating costs associated with it. Independent agents are compensated through commissions, but direct writers may receive either commissions or salaries.

65. Aggregation

This is a process in long-term financial planning. It refers to the smaller investment proposals of each of the firm's operational units are added up and in effect treated as a big picture.

66. Aging Accounts Receivable

A procedure for analyzing a firm's accounts receivable by dividing them into groups according to whether they are current or 30, 60, or over 90 days past due. [See also **Aging schedule of accounts receivable**]

67. Aging Schedule of Accounts Receivable

A compilation of accounts receivable by the age of account.

Typically, this relationship is evaluated by using the average collection period ratio. This type of analysis can be extended by constructing an aging-of-accounts-receivable table. The following table shows an example of decline in the quality of accounts receivable from January to February as relatively more accounts have been outstanding for 61 days or longer. This breakdown allows analysis of the cross-sectional composition of accounts over time. A deeper analysis can assess the risk associated with specific accounts receivable, broken down by customer to associate the probability of payment with the dollar amount owed.

Days Outstanding	January Accounts Receivable Range	January Percent of Total	February Accounts Receivable Range	February Percent of Total
0–30 days	$250,000	25.0%	$250,000	22.7%
31–60 days	500,000	50.0	525,000	47.7
61–90 days	200,000	20.0	250,000	22.7
Over 90 days	50,000	5.0	75,000	6.8
Total accounts receivable	$1,000,000	100.0%	$1,100,100	100.0%

68. All-in-Cost

The weighted average cost of funds for a bank calculated by making adjustments for required reserves and deposit insurance costs, the sum of explicit and implicit costs.

69. Allocational Efficiency

The overall concept of allocational efficiency is one in which security prices are set in such a way that investment capital is directed to its optimal use. Because of the position of the US in the world economy, the allocational responsibility of the US markets can be categorized into international and domestic efficiency. Also, since the overall concept of allocational efficiency is too general to test, operational efficiency must be focused upon as a testable concept.

70. Allowance for Loan and Lease Losses

An accounting reserve set aside to equate expected (mean) losses from credit defaults. It is common to consider this reserve as the buffer for expected losses and some risk-based economic capital as the buffer for unexpected losses.

71. Alpha

The abnormal rate of return on a security in excess of what would be predicted by an equilibrium model like CAPM or APT. For CAPM, the alpha for the ith firm (α_i) can be defined as:

$$\alpha_i = (\overline{R}_i - R_f) - \beta_i(\overline{R}_m - R_f),$$

where $\overline{R}_i$ = average return for the ith security, $\overline{R}_m$ = average market rate of return, R_f = risk-free rate, and β_i = beta coefficient for the ith security.

Treynor and Black (1973) has used the alpha value to form active portfolio.

72. Alternative Minimum Tax (AMT)

A federal tax against income intended to ensure that taxpayers pay some tax even when they use tax shelters to shield income.

73. American Depository Receipt (ADR)

A security issued in the US to present shares of a foreign stock, enabling that stock to be traded in the US. For example, Taiwan Semiconductors (TSM) from Taiwan has sold ADRs in the US.

74. American Option

An American option is an option that can be exercised at any time up to the expiration date. The factors that determine the values of American and **European options** are the same except the time to exercise the option; all other things being equal, however, an American option is worth more than a European option because of the extra flexibility it grants the option holder. [See also **European option**]

75. Amortization

Repayment of a loan in installments. Long-term debt is typically repaid in regular amounts over the life of the debt. At the end of the amortization the entire indebtedness is said to be extinguished. Amortization is typically arranged by a **sinking fund**. Each year the corporation places money into a sinking fund, and the money is used to buy back the bond. [See also **Sinking fund**]

76. Amortization Schedule for a Fixed-Rate Mortgage

Amortization schedule for a fixed-rate mortgage is used to calculate either the monthly or the annual payment for a fixed rate mortgage.

The following example is used to show the procedure for calculating annual payment for a fixed-rate mortgage.

Suppose Bill and Debbie have taken out a home equity loan of $5,000, which they plan to repay over three years. The interest rate charged by the bank is 10 percent. For simplicity, assume that Bill and Debbie will make annual payments on their loan. (a) Determine the annual payments necessary to repay the loan. (b) Construct a loan amortization schedule.

(a) Finding the annual payment requires the use of the present value of an annuity relationship:

$$
\begin{aligned}
\text{PVAN} &= (\$CF) \left[\frac{1 - \left(\frac{1}{1+r} \right)^n}{r} \right] \\
&= (\$CF) \left[\frac{1 - \left(\frac{1}{1+.10} \right)^3}{.10} \right] \\
&= \$5000 = (\$CF)(2.48685).
\end{aligned}
$$

This result is an annual payment (CF) of $5,000/2.48685 = $2,010.57.

(b) Below is the loan amortization schedule constructed for Bill and Debbie:

Year (1)	Beginning Balance (2)	Annuity Payments (3)	Interest Paid (2) × 0.10 (4)	Principal Paid (3) − (4) (5)	Ending Balance (2) − (5) (6)
1	$5,000.00	$2,010.57	$500.00	$1,510.57	$3,489.43
2	3,489.43	2,010.57	348.94	1,661.63	1,827.80
3	1,827.80	2,010.57	182.78	1,827.79	0.01

77. Amortize

To reduce a debt gradually by making equal periodic payments that cover interest and principal owed. In other words, it liquidates on an installment basis. [See also **Amortization**]

78. Amortizing Swap

An interest rate swap in which the outstanding notional principal amount declines over time. It generally is used to hedge interest rate risk or mortgage or other amortized loan.

79. Angels

Individuals providing venture capital. These investors do not belong to any venture-capital firm; these investors act as individuals when providing financing. However, they should not be viewed as isolated investors.

80. Announcement Date

Date on which particular news concerning a given company is announced to the public; used in **event studies**, which researchers use to evaluate the economic impact of events of interest. For example, an event study can be focused on a dividend announcement date. [See also **Event studies**]

81. Announcement Effect

The effect on stock returns for the first trading day following an event announcement. For example, an earnings announcement and a dividend announcement will affect the stock price.

82. Annual Effective Yield

Also called the **effective annual rate (EAR)**. [See also **Effective annual rate (EAR)**]

83. Annual Percentage Rate (APR)

Banks, finance companies, and other lenders are required by law to disclose their borrowing interest rates to their customers. Such a rate is called a contract or stated rate, or more frequently, an annual percentage rate (APR). The method of calculating the APR on a loan is preset by law. The APR is the interest rate charged per period multiplied by the number of periods in a year:

$$APR = r \times m,$$

where r = periodic interest charge, and m = number of periods per year.

However, the APR misstates the true interest rate. Since interest compounds, the APR formula will understate the true or effective interest cost. The **effective annual rate (EAR)**, sometimes called the *annual effective yield*, adjusts the APR to take into account the effects of compounded interest over time. [See also **Effective annual rate (EAR)**]

It is useful to distinguish between a contractual or stated interest rate and the group of rates we call yields, effective rates, or market rate. A contract rate, such as the annual percentage rate (APR), is an expression that is used to specify interest cash flows such as those in loans, mortgages, or bank savings accounts. The yield or effective rate, such as the effective annual rate (EAR), measures the opportunity costs; it is the true measure of the return or cost of a financial instrument.

84. Annualized Holding-Period Return

The annual rate of return that when compounded T times, would have given the same T-period holding return as actual occurred from period 1 to period T. If R_t is the return in year t (expressed in decimals), then:

$$(1 + R_1) \times (1 + R_2) \times (1 + R_3) \times (1 + R_4)$$

is called a four-year holding period return.

85. Annuity

An annuity is a series of consecutive, equal cash flows over time. In a regular annuity, the cash flows are assumed to occur at the *end* of each time period. Examples of financial situations that involve equal cash flows include fixed interest payments on a bond and cash flows that may arise from insurance contracts, retirement plans, and amortized loans such as car loans and home mortgages.

The future value of an n-period annuity of $\$C$ per period is

$$FVAN = \$C[1 + (1 + r) + (1 + r)^2 + (1 + r)^3 + \ldots + (1 + r)^{n-1}],$$

which can be reduced to:

$$FVAN = \$C\left[\frac{(1 + r)^n - 1}{r}\right] = \$C \times FVIFA(r,n),$$

where $FVIFA$ (r,n) represents the future value interest factor for an annuity.

To find the present value of an n-period annuity of $\$C$ per period is

$$PVAN = \$C\left[\frac{1}{(1 + r)} + \frac{1}{(1 + r)^2} + \frac{1}{(1 + r)^3} + \ldots + \frac{1}{(1 + r)^n}\right],$$

which can be shown as:

$$PVAN = \$C\left[\frac{1}{r} - \frac{1}{(1 + r)^n}\right] = \$CF \times PVIFA(r,n),$$

where $PVIFA(r,n)$ is the present value interest factor for an annuity.

86. Annuity Due

When a cash flow occurs at the *beginning* of each annuity period, the annuity becomes an annuity due. Since the cash flows in the n-year annuity due occurs at the beginning of each year, they are invested for one extra period of time compared to the n-year regular annuity. This means all the annuity due cash flows are invested at r percent interest for an extra year.

To take this one extra year of compounding into account, the future value interest factor for an annuity [$FVIFA$ (r,n)] can be multiplied by $(1 + r)$ to determine the future value interest factor for an annuity due (FVANDUE):

$$FVANDUE = \$C\left[\frac{(1 + r)^n - 1}{r}\right](1 + r)$$

$$= \$C \times FVIFA(r,n) \times (1 + r).$$

Many situations also require present value calculations for cash flows that occur at the beginning of each time period. Examples include retirement checks that arrive on the first of the month and insurance premiums that are due on the first of the month. Again, the cash flows for the n-year annuity due occur one year *earlier* than those of the n-year regular annuity, making them more valuable. As in determining the FVANDUE, we can adjust for this simply by multiplying the corresponding PVIFA by $(1 + r)$ to reflect the fact that the cash flows are received one period sooner in an annuity due. The formula for the present value of an annuity due (PVANDUE) is

$$PVANDUE = \$C\left[\frac{1 - \left(\frac{1}{1 + r}\right)^n}{r}\right] \times (1 + r)$$

$$= \$C \times PVIFA(r,n) \times (1 + r).$$

87. Annuity Factor

The term used to calculate the present value or future value of the stream of level payments for a fixed period. [See also **Annuity**]

88. Annuity in Advance

An annuity with an immediate initial payment. This is called annuity due. [See also **Annuity due**]

89. Annuity in Arrears

An annuity with a first payment one full period hence, rather than immediately. That is, the first payment occurs on date 1 rather than on date 0.

90. Anticipated Income Theory

A theory that the timing of loan payments should be tied to the timing of a borrower's expected income.

91. Antithetic Variate Method

A technique used in Monte Carlo valuation, in which each random draw is used to create two simulated prices from opposite tails of the asset price distribution. This is one of the variance reduction procedures. Other method is stratified sampling method [See **Stratified sampling**]

92. Applied Research

A research and development (R&D) component that is riskier than **development projects**. [See also **Development projects**] It seeks to add to the firm's knowledge base by applying new knowledge to commercial purposes.

93. Appraisal Ratio

The signal-to-noise ratio of an analyst's forecasts. The ratio of alpha to residual standard deviation. This ratio measures abnormal return per unit of risk that in principle could be diversified away by holding a market index portfolio.

94. Appraisal Rights

Rights of shareholders of an acquired firm that allow them to demand that their shares be purchased at a fair value by the acquiring firm.

95. Appreciation

An increase in the market value of an asset. For example, you buy one share of IBM stock at $90. After one year you sell the stock for $100, then this investment appreciated by 11.11 percent.

96. Appropriation Phase of Capital Budgeting

The focus of the appropriation phase, sometimes called the *development* or *selection phase*, is to appraise the projects uncovered during the identification phase. After examining numerous firm and economic factors, the firm will develop estimates of expected cash flows for each project under examination. Once cash flows have been estimated, the firm can apply time value of money techniques to determine which projects will increase shareholder wealth the most.

The appropriation phase begins with information generation, which is probably the most difficult and costly part of the phase. Information generation develops three types of data: internal financial data, external economic and political data, and nonfinancial data. This data supports forecasts of firm-specific financial data, which are then used to estimate a project's cash flows. Depending upon the size and scope of the project, a variety of data items may need to be gathered in the information generation stage. Many economic influences can directly impact the success of a project by affecting sales revenues, costs, exchange rates, and overall project cash flows. Regulatory trends and political environment factors, both in the domestic and foreign economies, also may help or hinder the success of proposed projects.

Financial data relevant to the project is developed from sources such as marketing research, production analysis, and economic analysis. Using the firm's research resources and internal data, analysts estimate the cost of the investment, working capital needs, projected cash flows, and financing costs. If public information is available on competitors' lines of business, this also needs to be incorporated into the analysis to help estimate potential cash flows and to determine the effects of the project on the competition.

Nonfinancial information relevant to the cash flow estimation process includes data on the various means that may be used to distribute products to consumers, the quality and quantity of the domestic or nondomestic labor forces, the dynamics of technological change in the targeted market, and information from a strategic analysis of competitors. Analysts should assess the strengths and weaknesses of competitors and how they will react if the firm undertakes its own project.

After identifying potentially wealth-enhancing projects, a written proposal, sometimes called a *request for appropriation* is developed and submitted to the manager with the authority to approve. In general, a typical request for appropriation requires an executive summary of the proposal, a detailed analysis of the project, and data to support the analysis.

The meat of the appropriation request lies in the detailed analysis. It usually includes sections dealing with the need for the project, the problem or opportunity that the project addresses, how the project fits with top management's stated objectives and goals for the firm, and any impact the project may have on other operations of the firm.

The appropriation process concludes with a decision. Based upon the analysis, top management decides which projects appear most likely to enhance shareholder wealth. The decision criterion should incorporate the firm's primary goal of maximizing shareholder wealth.

97. Arbitrage

Arbitrage is when traders buy and sell virtually identical assets in two different markets in order to profit from price differences between those markets.

Besides currencies, traders watch for price differences and arbitrage opportunities in a number of financial markets, including stock markets and futures and options markets. In the real world, this process is complicated by trading commissions, taxes on profits, and government restrictions on currency transfers. The vigorous activity in the foreign exchange markets and the number of traders actively seeking risk-free profits prevents arbitrage opportunities based on cross-rate mispricing from persisting for long.

In other words arbitrage refers to buying an asset in one market at a lower price and simultaneously selling an identical asset in another market at a higher price. This is done with no cost or risk.

98. Arbitrage Condition

Suppose there are two riskless assets offering rates of return r and r', respectively. Assuming no transaction costs, one of the strongest statements that can be made in positive economics is that

$$r = r'. \tag{A}$$

This is based on the law of one price, which says that the same good cannot sell at different prices. In terms of securities, the law of one price says that securities with identical risks must have the same expected return. Essentially, equation (A) is a arbitrage condition that must be expected to hold in all but the most extreme circumstances. This is because if $r > r'$, the first riskless asset could be purchased with funds obtained from selling the second riskless asset. This arbitrage transaction would yield a return of $r - r'$ without having to make any new investment of funds or take on any additional risk. In the process of buying the first asset and selling the second, investors would bid up the former's price and bid down the latter's price. This repricing mechanism would continue up to the point where these two assets' respective prices equaled each other. And thus $r = r'$.

99. Arbitrage Pricing Theory (APT)

Ross (1970) derived a generalized capital asset pricing relationship called the arbitrage pricing theory (APT). To derive the APT, Ross assumed the expected rate of return on asset i at time t, $E(R_{it})$, could be explained by k independent influences (or factors):

$$E(R_{it}) = \alpha + \beta_{i1}(\text{factor 1}) + \beta_{i2}(\text{factor 2}) + \cdots \\ + \beta_{ik}(\text{factor } k),$$

where β_{ik} measures the sensitivity of the ith asset's returns to changes in factor k (sometimes called index k). In the terminology of factor analysis, β_{ik}'s are called factor loading.

Using the prior equation, Ross shows that the actual return of the ith security can be defined as:

$$R_i = E(R_i) + [F_1 - E(F_1)]\beta_{i1} + \cdots + [F_k - E(F_k)]\beta_{ik},$$

where $[F_k - E(F_k)]$ represents the surprise or change in the kth factor brought about by systematic economic events.

Like the **capital asset pricing model (CAPM)**, the APT assumes that investors hold diversified portfolios, so only systematic risks affect returns. [See also **Capital asset pricing model (CAPM)**] The APT's major difference from the CAPM is that it allows for more than one systematic risk factor. The APT is a *generalized* capital asset pricing model; the CAPM is a special, one-factor case of the APT, where the one factor is specified to be the return on the market portfolio.

The APT does have a major practical drawback. It gives no information about the specific factors that drive returns. In fact, the APT does not even tell us how many factors there are. Thus, testing the APT is purely empirical, with little theory to guide researchers. Estimates of the number of factors range from two to six; some studies conclude that the market portfolio return is one of the return-generating factors, while others do not. Some studies conclude that the CAPM does a better job in estimating returns; others conclude that APT is superior.

The jury is still out on the superiority of the APT over the CAPM. Even though the APT is a very intuitive and elegant theory and requires much less restrictive assumptions than the CAPM, it currently has little practical use. It is difficult both to determine the return-generating factors and to test the theory.

In sum, an equilibrium asset pricing theory that is derived from a factor model by using diversification and arbitrage. It shows that the expected return on any risky asset is a linear combination of various factors.

100. Arbitrageur

An individual engaging in arbitrage. [See also **Arbitrage**]

101. Arithmetic Average

The risk of an item is reflected in its variability from its average level. For comparison, a stock analyst may want to determine the level of return and the variability in returns for a number of assets to see whether investors in the higher risk assets earned a higher return over time. A financial analyst may want to examine historical differences between risk and profit on different types of new product introductions or projects undertaken in different countries.

If historical, or ex-post, data are known, an analyst can easily compute historical average return and risk measures. If X_t represents a data item for period t, the arithmetic average $\overline{X}$, over n periods is given by:

$$\overline{X} = \frac{\sum_{t=1}^{n} X_t}{n}.$$

In summary, the sum of the values observed divided by the total number of observation—sometimes referred to as the mean. [See also **Geometric average**]

102. Arithmetic Mean

[See **Arithmetic average**]

103. ARM

Adjustable rate mortgage is a mortgage in which the contractual interest rate is tied to some index of interest rates (prime rate for example) and changes when supply and demand conditions change the underlying index. [See also **Adjustable rate mortgage**]

104. Arrears

An overdue outstanding debt. In addition, we use arrearage to indicate the overdue payment.

105. Asian Option

An option in which the payoff at maturity depends upon an average of the asset prices over the life of the option.

106. Asian Tail

A reference price that is computed as an average of recent prices. For example, an equity-linked note may have a payoff based on the average daily stock price over the last 20 days (the Asian tail).

107. Ask Price

The price at which a dealer or market-maker offers to sell a security. Also called the *offer price*.

108. Asset Allocation Decision

Choosing among broad asset classes such as stocks versus bonds. In other words, asset allocation is an approach to investing that focuses on determining the mixture of asset classes that is most likely to provide a combination to risk and expected return that is optimal for the investor. In addition to this, portfolio insurance is an asset-allocation or hedging strategy that allows the investor to alter the amount of risk he or she is willing to accept by giving up some return.

109. Asset Management Ratios

Asset management ratios (also called activity or *asset utilization ratios*) attempt to measure the efficiency with which a firm uses its assets.

Receivables Ratios

Accounts receivable turnover ratio is computed as credit sales divided by accounts receivable. [See also **Accounts receivable turnover ratio**] In general, a higher accounts receivable turnover ratio suggests more frequent payment of receivables by customers. The accounts receivable turnover ratio is written as:

$$\text{Accounts receivable turnover} = \frac{\text{Sales}}{\text{Accounts receivable}}.$$

Thus, if a firm's accounts receivable turnover ratio is larger than the industry average; this implies that the firm's accounts receivable are more efficiently managed that the average firm in that industry.

Dividing annual sales by 365 days gives a daily sales figure. Dividing accounts receivable by daily sales gives another asset management ratio, the **average collection period of credit sales**. In general, financial managers prefer shorter collection periods over longer periods. [See also **Average collection period**]

Comparing the average collection period to the firm's credit terms indicates whether customers are generally paying their accounts on time. The **average collection period** is given by:

$$\text{Average collection period} = \frac{\text{Accounts receivable}}{\text{Sales}/365}.$$

The average collection period (ACP) is easy to calculate and can provide valuable information when compared to current credit terms or past trends.

One major drawback to the ACP calculation, however, is its sensitivity to changing patterns of sales. The calculated ACP rises with increases in sales and falls with decreases in sales. Thus, changes in the ACP may give a deceptive picture of a firm's actual payment history. Firms with seasonal sales should be especially careful in analyzing accounts receivable patterns based on ACP. For instance, a constant ACP could hide a longer payment period if it coincides with a decrease in sales volume. In this case, the ACP calculation would fail to properly signal a deterioration in the collection of payments.

Inventory Ratios

The **inventory turnover ratio** is a measure of how quickly the firm sells its inventory. [See also

Inventory turnover ratio] It is computed as cost of goods sold divided by inventory. The ratio clearly depends upon the firm's inventory accounting method: for example, last-in, first-out (LIFO) or first-in, first-out (FIFO). The inventory turnover ratio is written as:

$$\text{Inventory turnover} = \frac{\text{Cost of goods sold}}{\text{Inventory}}.$$

It is an easy mistake to assume that higher inventory turnover is a favorable sign; it also may signal danger. An increasing inventory turnover may raise the possibility of costly stockouts. Empty shelves can lead to dissatisfied customers and lost sales.

Fixed and Total Assets Ratio

The **total asset turnover ratio** is computed as sales divided by total assets. [See also **Total asset turnover ratio**] The fixed asset turnover ratio is sales divided by fixed assets. Similar to the other turnover ratio, these ratios indicate the amount of sales generated by a dollar of total and fixed assets, respectively. Although managers generally favor higher fixed and total asset turnover ratios, these ratios can be *too* high. The fixed asset turnover ratio may be large as a result of the firm's use of old, depreciated equipment. This would indicate that the firm's reliance on old technology could hurt its future market position, or that it could face a large, imminent expense for new equipment, including the downtime required to install it and train workers.

A large total asset turnover ratio also can result from the use of old equipment. Or, it might indicate inadequate receivables arising from an overly strict credit system or dangerously low inventories.

The asset turnover ratios are computed as:

$$\text{Total asset turnover} = \frac{\text{Sales}}{\text{Total assets}},$$
$$\text{Fixed asset turnover} = \frac{\text{Sales}}{\text{Fixed assets}}.$$

110. Asset Sensitive

A bank is classified as asset sensitive if its GAP is positive. Under this case interest rate sensitive asset is larger than interest rate sensitive liability.

111. Asset Swap

Effectively transforms an asset into an asset of another type, such as converting a fixed rate bond into a floating-rate bond. Results in what is known as a "synthetic security."

112. Asset Turnover (ATO)

The annual sales generated by each dollar of assets (sales/assets). It can also be called as asset utilization ratio.

113. Asset-Backed Debt Securities (ABS)

Issuers of credit have begun following the lead set by mortgage lenders by using asset securitization as a means of raising funds. Securitization meaning that the firm repackages its assets and sells them to the market.

In general, an ABS comes through certificates issued by a grantor trust, which also registers the security issue under the Securities Act of 1933. These securities are sold to investors through underwritten public offerings or private placements. Each certificate represents a fractional interest in one or more pools of assets. The selling firm transfers assets, with or without recourse, to the grantor trust, which is formed and owned by the investors, in exchange for the proceeds from the certificates. The trustee receives the operating cash flows from the assets and pays scheduled interest and principal payments to investors, servicing fees to the selling firm, and other expenses of the trust.

From a legal perspective, the trust owns the assets that underlie such securities. These assets will not be consolidated into the estate of the selling firm if it enters into bankruptcy.

To date, most ABS issues have securitized automobile and credit-card receivables. It is expected that this area will grow into other fields, such as computer leases, truck leases, land and property leases, mortgages on plant and equipment, and commercial loans.

114. Asset-Backed Security

A security with promised principal and interest payments backed or collateralized by cash flows originated from a portfolio of assets that generate the cash flows.

115. Asset-Based Financing

Financing in which the lender relies primarily on cash flows generated by the asset financed to repay the loan.

116. Asset-Liability Management

The management of a bank's entire balance sheet to achieve desired risk-return objectives and to maximize the market value of stockholders' equity. Asset-liability management is the management of the net interest margin to ensure that its level and riskness are compatible with risk/return objectives of the institution.

117. Asset-or-Nothing Call

An option that pays a unit of the asset if the asset price exceeds the strike price at expiration or zero otherwise.

118. Asset-or-Nothing Option

An option that pays a unit of the asset if the option is in-the-money or zero otherwise.

119. Assets

Anything that the firm owns. It includes current, fixed and other assets. Asset can also be classified as tangible and intangible assets.

120. Assets Requirements

A common element of a financial plan that describes projected capital spending and the proposed uses of net working capital. Asset requirements increase when sales increase.

121. Assignment

The transfer of the legal right or interest on an asset to another party.

122. Assumable Mortgage

The mortgage contract is transferred from the seller to the buyer of the house.

123. Asymmetric Butterfly Spread

A butterfly spread in which the distance between strike prices is not equal. [See also **Butterfly spread**]

124. As-You-Like-It Option

[See **Chooser option**]

125. At The Money

The owner of a put or call is not obligated to carry out the specified transaction but has the *option* of doing so. If the transaction is carried out, it is said to have been *exercised*. *At the money* means that the stock price is trading at the exercise price of the option.

126. Auction Market

A market where all traders in a certain good meet at one place to buy or sell and asset. The NYSE is an example for stock auction market.

127. Audit, or Control, Phase of Capital Budgeting Process

The audit, or control, phase is the final step of the capital budgeting process for approved projects. In this phase, the analyst tracks the magnitude and timing of expenditures while the project is progressing. A major portion of this phase is the post-audit of the project, through which past decisions are evaluated for the benefit of future project analyses.

Many firms review spending during the control phase of approved projects. Quarterly reports often are required in which the manager overseeing the project summarizes spending to date, compares it to budgeted amounts, and explains differences between the two. Such oversight during this implementation stage slows top managers to foresee cost overruns. Some firms require projects that are expected to exceed their budgets by a certain dollar amount or percentage to file new appropriation requests to secure the additional funds. Implementation audits allow managers to learn about potential trouble areas so future proposals can account for them in their initial analysis. Implementation audits generally also provide top management with information on which managers generally provide the most accurate estimates of project costs.

In addition to implementation costs, firms also should compare forecasted cash flows to actual performance after the project has been completed. This analysis provides data regarding the accuracy over time of cash flow forecasts, which will permit the firm to discover what went right with the project, what went wrong, and why. Audits force management to discover and justify any major deviations of actual performance from forecasted performance. Specific reasons for deviations from the budget are needed for the experience to be helpful to all involved. Such a system also helps to control intra-firm agency problems by helping to reduce "padding" (i.e., overestimating the benefits of favorite or convenient project proposals). This increases the incentives for department heads to manage in ways that will help the firm achieve its goals.

Investment decisions are based on estimates of cash flows and relevant costs, while in some firms the post-audit is based on accrued accounting and assigned overhead concepts. The result is that managers make decisions based on cash flow, while they are evaluated by an accounting-based system.

A concept that appears to help correct this evaluation system problem is **economic value added (EVA)**. [See also **Economic value added (EVA)**]

The control or post-audit phase sometimes requires the firm to consider terminating or abandoning an approved project. The possibility of abandoning an investment prior to the end of its estimated useful or economic life expands the options available to management and reduces the risk associated with decisions based on holding an asset to the end of its economic life. This form of contingency planning gives decision makers a second chance when dealing with the economic and political uncertainties of the future.

128. Audits of Project Cash Flow Estimated

Capital budgeting audits can help the firm learn from experience. By comparing actual and estimated cash flows, the firm can try to improve upon areas in which forecasting accuracy is poor.

In a survey conducted in the late 1980s, researchers found that three-fourths of the responding *Fortune 500* firms audited their cash flow estimates. Nearly all of the firms that performed audits compared initial investment outlay estimates with actual costs; all evaluated operating cash flow estimates; and two-thirds audited salvage-value estimates. About two-thirds of the firms that performed audits claimed that actual initial investment outlay estimates usually were within 10 percent of forecasts. Only 43 percent of the firms that performed audits could make the same claim with respect to operating cash flows. Over 30 percent of the firms confessed that operating cash flow estimates differed from actual performance by 16 percent or more. This helps to illustrate that our cash flow estimates are merely point estimates of a random variable. Because of their uncertainty, they may take on higher or lower values than their estimated value.

To be successful, the cash flow estimation process requires a commitment by the corporation and its top policy-setting managers; this commitment includes the type of management information system the firm uses to support the estimation process. Past experience in estimating cash flows, requiring cash flow estimates for all projects, and maintaining systematic approaches to cash flow estimation appear to help firms achieve success in accurately forecasting cash flows.

129. Autocorrelation [Serial Correlation]

The correlation of a variable with itself over successive time intervals. The correlation coefficient can be defined as:

$$\rho = \frac{\text{cov}(r_t, r_{t-1})}{\sigma_t \sigma_{t-1}}.$$

It can be defined as where $\text{cov}(r_t, r_{t-1})$ is the covariance between r_t, r_{t-1}, σ_t and σ_{t-1} are standard deviation r_t and r_{t-1}, respectively.

Two useful empirical examples of autocorrelation are:

Interest rates exhibit mean reversion behavior and are often negatively auto correlated (i.e., an up move one day will suggest a down move the next). But note that mean reversion does not technically necessitate negative autocorrelation.

Agency credit ratings typically exhibit move persistence behavior and are positively auto correlated during downgrades (i.e., a downgrade will suggest another downgrade soon). But, for completeness, note that upgrades do not better predict future upgrades.

130. Automated Clearing House System (ACH)

An Automated Clearing House (ACH) system is an information transfer network that joins banks or other financial institutions together to facilitate the transfer of cash balances. An ACH system has a high initial fixed cost to install but requires a very low variable cost to process each transaction. The

Federal Reserve operates the nation's primary ACH, which is owned by the member banks of the Federal Reserve System. Most banks are members of an ACH.

Instead of transferring information about payments or receipts via paper documents like checks, an ACH transfers the information electronically via a computer.

131. Automated Clearinghouse

A facility that processes interbank debits and credits electronically.

132. Automated Loan Machine

A machine that serves as a computer terminal and allows a customer to apply for a loan and, if approved, automatically deposits proceeds into an account designated by the customer.

133. Automated Teller Machines (ATM)

The globalization of automated teller machines (ATMs) is one of the newer frontiers for expansion for US financial networks. The current system combines a number of worldwide communication switching networks, each one owned by a different bank or group of banks.

A global ATM network works like a computerized constellation of switches. Each separate bank is part of a regional, national, and international financial system.

After the customer inserts a credit card, punches a personal identification number (PIN), and enters a transaction request, the bank's computer determines that the card is not one of its own credit cards and switches the transaction to a national computer system. The national system, in turn, determines that the card is not one of its own, so it switches to an international network, which routes the request to the US Global Switching Center. The center passes the request to a regional computer system in the US, which evaluates the request and responds through the switching network. The entire time required for this process, from initiation at the ATM until the response is received, is reassured in seconds. The use, acceptance, and growth of systems like this will revolutionize the way international payments are made well into the 21st century.

134. Availability Float

It refers to the time required to clear a check through the banking system. This process takes place by using either Fed-check collection services, corresponding banks or local clearing houses.

135. Average Accounting Return (AAR)

The average project earnings after taxes and depreciation divided by the average book value of the investment during its life. [See also **Accounting rate of return**]

136. Average Annual Yield

A method to calculate interest that incorrectly combines simple interest and compound interest concepts on investments of more than one year. For example, suppose you invested $10,000 in a five-year CD offering 9.5 percent interest compounded quarterly, you would have $15,991.10 in the account at the end of five years. Dividing your $5,991.10 total return by five, the average annual return will be 11.98 percent.

137. Average Collection Period

Average amount of time required to collect an accounting receivable. Also referred to as days sales outstanding. [See also **Asset management ratios** and **Activity ratios**]

138. Average Cost of Capital

A firm's required payout to the bondholders and the stockholders expressed as a percentage of cap-

ital contributed to the firm. Average cost of capital is computed by dividing the total required cost of capital by the total amount of contributed capital. Average cost of capital (ACC) formula can be defined as:

$$ACC = \frac{S}{V} r_E + \frac{B}{V}(1 - \tau_c)i,$$

where V = total market value of the firm; S = value of stockholder's equity; B = value of debt; r_E = rate of return of stockholder's equity; i = interest rate on debt; and τ_c = corporate tax rate.

Here, r_E is the cost of equity, and $(1 - \tau_c)i$ is the cost of debt. Hence, ACC is a weighted average of these two costs, with respective weights S/V and B/V.

139. Average Daily Sales

Annual sales divided by 365 days.

140. Average Exposure

Credit exposure arising from market-driven instruments will have an ever-changing market-to-market exposure amount. The average exposure represents the average of several expected exposure values calculated at different forward points over the life of swap starting from the end of the first year. The expected exposures are weighted by the appropriate discount factors for this average calculation.

141. Average Price Call Option

The payoff of average price call option = max [0, A(T) − K], where A(T) is the arithmetic average of stock price over time and K is the strike price. This implies that the payoff of this option is either equal to zero or larger than zero. In other words, the amount of payoff is equal to the difference between A(T) and K.

142. Average Price Put Option

The payoff of average price put option = max [0, K − A(T)], where A(T) is the arithmetic average of stock price per share over time and K is the strike price. This implies that the payoff of this option is either equal to zero or larger than zero. In other words, the amount of payoff is equal to the difference between K and A(T).

143. Average Shortfall

The expected loss given that a loss occurs, or as the expected loss given that losses exceed a given level.

144. Average Strike Option

An option that provides a payoff dependent on the difference between the final asset price and the average asset price. For example, an average strike call $= \max[0, S_T - A(T)]$, where A(T) represents average stock price per share over time and S_T represents stock price per share in period T.

145. Average Tax Rate

The average tax rate is the tax bill of a firm divided by its earnings before income taxes (i.e., pretax income). For individuals, it is their tax bill divided by their taxable income. In either case, it represents the percentage of total taxable income that is paid in taxes.

B

1. Back Testing

Testing a value-at-risk or other model using historical data. For example, under the current BIS market risk-based capital requirements, a bank must back test its internal market model over a minimum of 250 past days if it is used for capital requirement calculations. If the forecast VAR errors on those 250 days are too large (i.e., risk is underestimated on too many days), a system of penalties is imposed by regulators to create incentives for bankers to get their models right.

2. Back-to-Back Transaction

A transaction where a dealer enters into offsetting transactions with different parties, effectively serving as a go-between.

3. Backward Equation

[See **Kolmogorov backward equation**]

4. Backwardation

A forward curve in which the futures prices are falling with time to expiration.

5. Backwardization

The situation in which futures prices in futures contracts that expire farther in the future are below prices of nearby futures contracts.

6. Backwards Induction

A procedure for working from the end of a tree to its beginning in order to value an option.

7. Bad Debts

Loans that are due but are uncollectible.

8. Balance Inquiry

A request by a depositor or borrower to obtain the current balance in his or her account.

9. Balance Sheet

The balance sheet provides a static description of the firm's financial position at a fixed point in time. It details the firm's assets and liabilities at the end of the fiscal year for an annual report or at the end of a quarter for a quarterly statement.

The balance comes from a basic accounting equality:

Total assets = Total liabilities + Total equity.

This equation implies that a firm's assets must equal the total of its liabilities and owners' equity. Stated more informally, what the firm owns (assets) equals what it owes (liability claims to creditors plus equity claims to shareholders). The balance sheet shows how all assets are financed, either by borrowing (debt) or owners' investment (equity).

The left-hand side of the balance sheet reports company assets. It divides the total into current assets, plant and equipment, and other assets (which may include such intangible assets as patents and goodwill). The balance sheet lists these categories in order of liquidity. Liquidity is the ability to quickly convert an asset to cash without a loss in value. The most liquid assets, cash and short-term investments of excess cash, such as marketable securities, are listed first; less liquid assets follow.

The right-hand side of the balance sheet shows the claims against company assets. Categories for these claims include current liabilities, long-term debt, common stock, and retained earnings. The liability and equity claims are listed in order of increasing maturity. This order also reflects the general priority of the claims of creditors and equity holders against the firm's cash flows.

10. Balanced Funds

The balanced funds offer a complete investment program to their clients, so far as marketable securities are concerned. Their portfolio are presumably structured to include bonds and stocks in a ratio considered appropriate for an average individual investor given the return outlook for each sector and possibly a risk and volatility constraint.

11. Balloon Loan

A loan that requires small payments that are insufficient to pay off the entire loan so that a large final payment is necessary at termination.

12. Balloon Payment

Large final payment, as when a loan is repaid in installments. For example, (i) most high-quality bond issues establish payments to the sinking fund that are not sufficient to redeem the entire issue. As a consequence, there is the possibility of a large balloon payment at maturity; (ii) if a lease has a schedule of payments that is very high at the start of the lease term and thereafter very low then these early balloon payments would be an evidence that the lease was being used to avoid taxes and not for a legitimate business purpose.

13. Bank Discount Yield

An annualized interest rate assuming simple interest, a 360-day year, and using the face value of the security rather than purchase price to compute return per dollar invested.

14. Bank Drafts

Bank drafts, or bills of exchange, is a basic instrument of foreign trade financing that allow exporters to use their banks as collection agents for foreign accounts. The bank forwards the exporter's invoices to the foreign buyer, either by mail or through a branch or correspondent bank in the buyer's country. When the buyer pays the draft, the exporter's bank converses the proceeds of the collection into the exporter's currency and deposits this money in the exporter's account. Two kinds of bank drafts include **sight drafts** and **time drafts**. [See also **Sight draft** and **Time draft**]

15. Bank Holding Company

Any firm that owns or controls at least one commercial bank.

16. Bank Of Japan Financial Network System

As the Japanese banks have become increasingly more important in international financial flows, their transfer systems also have grown in importance. The Bank of Japan Financial Network System (BOJ-NET) is a cash and securities wire transfer system for yen-denominated payments. The cash wire, an online funds transfer system for banks, is the Japanese counterpart of CHIPS. Financial institutions use BOJ-NET to provide net settlement services for the Japanese clearinghouse system that clears bills and checks. BOJ-NET also provides settlement for the Japanese electronic fund transfer (EFT) system called *Zenguin*. Institutions also can use BOJ-NET to settle yen payments that arise from cross-border transfers and foreign-exchange transactions.

17. Bank-Discount Interest

Bank-discount interest commonly is charged for short-term business loans. Generally, the borrower makes no intermediate payments, and the life of the loan usually is one year or less. Interest is calculated on the amount of the loan, and the life of the loan usually is one year or less. Interest is calculated on the amount of the loan, and the borrower receives the difference between the amount of the loan and the amount of interest. In the example, this gives an interest rate of 15 percent. The interest ($150,000) is subtracted from the $1 million loan amount and the borrower has the use of $850,000 for one year. Dividing the interest payment by the amount of money actually used by the borrower ($150,000 divided by $850,000), we find the effective rate is 17.6 percent.

18. Banker's Acceptance

The banker's acceptance is a comparatively specialized credit source largely confined to financing foreign trade (its only major use within the US has been in financing purchases of raw cotton crops). One of the major difficulties in conducting business overseas is in accessing the creditworthiness of potential customers. This problem is best solved by getting a bank to add its reputation to that of the buyer by accepting, or endorsing, the note payable. The investment attractiveness of banker's acceptances must be stressed because most investors are unfamiliar with this short-term, liquid high-yielding investment.

Banker's acceptances are **time drafts** drawn on and accepted by banks, usually to secure arrangements between unfamiliar firms. [See also **Time draft**] They are frequently used in international trade. After generating a banker's acceptance, a bank typically sells it to an investor at a discount. Maturities range from 30 to 180 days, while denominations vary from $25,000 to over $1 million, depending upon the specific transaction the banker's acceptance was originally created to finance. Banker's acceptances are relatively illiquid compared to T-bills and most carry higher yields than CDs because of the heterogeneous characteristics.

The interest rate on acceptances is quite low, usually at or very slightly above the prime rate. Any bank that performs services of this kind for its customers probably will expect to be compensated in other ways, however, especially through the maintenance of good demand deposit balances.

In sum, Banker's acceptance is an agreement by a bank to pay a given sum of money at a future date. These agreements typically arise when a seller sends a bill or draft to a customer. The customer's bank accepts this bill and notes the acceptance on it, which makes it an obligation of the bank.

19. Bankers Bank

A firm that provides correspondent banking services to commercial banks and not to commercial or retail deposit and loan customers.

20. Bankrupt

The situation in which a borrower is unable to pay obligated debts.

21. Bankruptcy Costs

The major drawback of having debt in the capital structure is its legal requirement for timely payment of interest and principal. As the debt-to-equity ratio rises, or as earnings become more volatile, the firm will face higher borrowing costs, driven upward by bond investors requiring higher yields to compensate for additional risk.

A rational marketplace will evaluate the probability and associated costs of bankruptcy for a levered firm. Bankruptcy costs include explicit expenses, such as legal and accounting fees and court costs, along with implicit costs, such as the use of management time and skills in trying to prevent and escape bankruptcy. It also is difficult to market the firm's products and keep good people on the staff when the firm is teetering on the brink of bankruptcy.

The market will evaluate the present value of the expected bankruptcy costs and reduce its estimate of the value of the firm accordingly. When bankruptcy costs are included in an analysis of M&M Proposition I with taxes, the value of the firm is given as:

$$V_L = V_U + (T)(D) - PV(V_L)$$

This says that the value of the levered firm equals the value of the unlevered firm (V_U) plus the present value of the interest tax shield [$(T)(D)$], minus the present value of expected bankruptcy costs ($PV(V_L)$). Incorporating bankruptcy costs into M&M Proposition I relationship between firm value and debt reduces the debt-to-equity ratio at which the firm's value is maximized to less than 100-percent debt financing. According to the **static tradeoff hypothesis**, increases in debt beyond this optimal level actually reduce firm value, as investors' perceptions of the increased cost of bankruptcy outweigh the tax benefits of additional debt. [See also **Static tradeoff hypothesis**]

In sum, debt puts pressure on the firm, because interest and principal payment are obligations. If these obligations are not met, the firm may risk some sort of financial distress. The ultimate distress is bankruptcy, where ownership of the firm's assets is legally transferred from the stockholders to the bondholders. Bankruptcy costs tend to offset the advantage to debt. [Also see **Financial distress costs** and **Modigliani and Miller (M&M) Proposition I**]

22. Barbell

An investment portfolio in which a large fraction of securities mature near-term and another large fraction of securities mature longer-term.

23. Bargain-Purchase-Price Option

Gives lessee the option to purchase the asset at a price below fair market value when the lease expires.

24. Barrier Option

An option that has a payoff depending upon whether, at some point during the life of the option, the price of the underlying asset has moved pass a reference price (the barrier). Examples are knock-in and knock-out options. [See **Knock-in option** and **Knock-out option**]

25. Base Case

Incremental cash flows are the anticipated changes in cash flow from the base case. [See also **Incremental cash flows**] The firm's base-case projection must assess what the firm's market share and cash flows would be if *no* new projects were implemented; in other words, the after-tax cash flows *without* the project. The firm's planners must recognize that if nothing is done, customers may start buying competitors' products in response to the marketing, new product development, and/or quality efforts of the competition. The base-case estimate should reflect these potential declines in cash flow.

26. Base Rate

An interest rate used as an index to price loans; typically associated with a bank's weighted marginal cost of funds.

27. Basic IRR Rule

This is one of the capital budgeting decision rules. Accept the project if IRR (internal rate of return) is greater that the discount rate; reject the project if IRR is less than the discount tare. [See also **Internal rate of return**]

28. Basic Research

A high-risk/high-reward pursuit component of the research and development (R&D) portfolio. Basic research is research to gain knowledge for its own sake.

29. Basic Swap

A plain vanilla interest rate swap in which one party pays a fixed interest rate and receives a floating rate, while the other party pays a floating rate and receives a fixed rate with all rates applied to the same, constant notional principal amount.

30. Basis

The difference between futures price and the spot price. Basis is one kind of risk in investments.

31. Basis Point

When used to describe an interest rate, a basis point is one hundredth of one percent (= 0.01 percent).

32. Basis Risk

The possibility of unexpected changes in the difference between the price of an asset and the price of the contract hedging the asset. It's the uncertainty that the futures rate minus the cash rate will vary from that expected.

33. Basis Swap

Exchange of floating rate payments between counterparties but with interest rates based on the different indexes.

34. Basket Credit Default Swap

Credit default swap where there are several reference entities.

35. Basket Option

An option that provides a payoff dependant on the value of a portfolio of assets.

36. Baumol's Economic Order Quantity Model

The Baumol's model strives to equate the two opposing marginal costs associated with ordering and holding inventory to minimize total costs. Just as an operations manager sets inventory levels for raw materials and components, a financial manager can treat cash as a manageable inventory and try to minimize the sum of the following costs:

1. Carrying or opportunity costs equal to the rate of return foregone to hold cash, and vice versa; 2. Ordering or transaction costs from converting securities into cash.

The total costs of cash balances can be defined as:

Total costs = Holding costs + Transactions costs

$$= \frac{C}{2}r + \frac{T}{C}F,$$

where C = amount of cash raised by selling marketable securities or borrowing; $C/2$ = average cash balance; r = opportunity cost of holding cash (the foregone rate of return on marketable securities); T = total amount of new cash needed for transaction over entire period (usually one year); T/C = number of transactions; and F = fixed cost of making a securities trade or borrowing money.

The minimum total costs are obtained when C is set equal to C^*, the optimal cash balance. C^* is defined as follows:

$$C^* = \sqrt{\frac{2FT}{r}},$$

where C^* = Optimal amount of cash to be raised by selling marketable securities or by borrowing.

The prior equation represents Baumol's economic order quantity (EOQ) model for determining optimal cash balances. The optimal average cash balance can be defined as $C^*/2$.

In applying Baumol's EOQ model to find an optimal cash balance, the manager must be aware of its underlying assumptions about cash flows:

1. Cash outflows occur at a constant rate.
2. Cash inflows occur periodically when securities are liquidated.
3. Net cash flows also occur at a predictable rate.

EOQ is positively related to F and T and inversely related to r. By taking the square root of FT/r, the relationship with EOQ is less than proportionate. If the value of fixed transaction costs doubles, the EOQ will increase by only 1.41 times.

While the EOQ model offers useful insight into the determination of optimal cash balances, its restrictive assumptions about cash flow behavior are not particularly realistic. Most firms' cash inflows are interspersed with cash outflows. Inflows occasionally exceed flows of outgoing payments. Thus, cash balances over a planning period will move both upward and downward at varying intervals, whereas the EOQ model implicitly assumes demand for cash (inflows) to be positive. Another problem with the EOQ framework is its assumption that inflows (revenue and security sales) are nonrandom and controllable, while outflows (operating costs) are random and uncontrollable. In actuality, control over inflows and outflows is seldom absolute.

37. Bear CD

A bank CD pays the holder a fraction of any fall in a given market index. In other words, the bear CD's payoff increases as the overall level of a particular market index declines. [See also **Bull CD**]

38. Bear Spread

Bear spread is also called short vertical spread. It is simply the reverse of a long vertical spread. Under this case an investor buys a high-exercise-price call (or put) and sells a low-exercise-price call (or put), both having the same time to expiration left. [See also **Bull spread**]

39. Bearer Bond

A bond issued without record of the owner's name. Whoever holds the bond (the bearer) is the owner. There are two drawbacks to bearer bonds; first, they can be easily lost or stolen. Second, because the company does not know who owns its bonds, it cannot notify bondholders of important events.

40. Benchmark Analysis

Financial ratios can be used in *benchmark analysis*, in which the ratios of a specific firm can be com-

pared to a benchmark, such as the industry average or an ideal target or goal determined by management. Data for industry average financial ratios are published by a number of organizations, such as Dun & Bradstreet, Robert Morris Associates, Financial Dynamics, Standard & Poor's, and the Federal Trade Commission. These information sources are readily available at most libraries.

41. Benchmark Error

Use of an inappropriate proxy for the true market portfolio.

42. Benchmark Rate

The key driver rate used in sensitivity analysis or simulation models to assess interest rate risk. Other model rates are linked to the benchmark rate in terms of how they change when the benchmark rate changes.

43. Beneficiary

The recipient of the balance in a trust account upon termination of the trust.

44. Benefit/cost Ratio

A discounted cash flow technique for evaluating capital budgeting projects; more frequently called the **profitability index (PI)**. [See also **Profitability index**]

45. Bermudan Option

An option that can be exercised on specified dates during it life. It is also called as Mid-Atlantic or limited exercise options. This kind of option is a hybrid of American and European options. Instead of being exercised any time before maturity as standard American options, they can be exercised only at a discrete time points before maturity.

46. Best Efforts Offering

A best efforts offering is a less common type of IPO issued by a financially weaker, small, or otherwise risky firm. The investment bank agrees to assist in the marketing of the firm's shares using its best effort and skill but only to sell the shares on a commission basis. The bank buys none of the stock and risks none of its own money. Thus, in a best efforts offering, the issuer bears the risk of price fluctuations or low market demand. If all the shares in a best efforts offering cannot be sold, the issuer may cancel the offering and return all the funds it receives to investors.

Investors should view best efforts offerings with caution. If the knowledgeable investment bank is not willing to risk money to underwrite the firm, why should the investor risk money on the shares.

47. Best-Efforts Underwriting

The underwriter of securities commits to selling as many securities as possible and returns all unsold shares or units to the issuer. [See also **Best efforts offering**]

48. Beta

An estimate of the systematic or market risk of an asset within the capital asset pricing model (CAPM) framework. [See also **Beta coefficient**]

49. Beta Coefficient

We call an asset's or portfolio's systematic risk its beta, denoted by a capital Greek letter β. Beta measures how an asset's returns (R_i) vary with the market portfolio's returns (R_m), compared to the total risk of the market portfolio as:

$$\beta_i = \frac{\text{cov}(R_i, R_m)}{\sigma_m^2},$$

where $\text{cov}(R_i, R_m)$ = Covariance between R_i and R_m; σ_m^2 = variance of R_m.

From this perspective, assets that add to portfolio systematic risk will have a high covariance with the market's returns and will therefore have a large beta. Assets that reduce portfolio systematic risk will have a low covariance and a low beta.

Beta is also equal to:

$$\beta = \frac{\rho_{im}\sigma_i\sigma_m}{\sigma_m^2},$$

where σ_i and σ_m are standard deviation of R_i and R_m, respectively; ρ_{im} is the correlation coefficient between R_i and R_m.

If any asset or portfolio has the same exposure to systematic risk as the market portfolio, its beta equals one. Thus, unlike portfolio variance, beta is not an absolute measure of risk. Rather, beta is a measure of relative risk. Beta measures the volatility or variability of an asset's returns *relative* to the market portfolio.

Yet another way to estimate beta is to use regression analysis. To determine an asset's beta, we need to estimate the following regression equation, called the *market model*:

$$R_{it} = \alpha_i + \beta_i R_{mt} + e_{it},$$

where R_{it} = the return on the ith asset at time t, R_{mt} = the market return at time t, α_i = the intercept term of the regression, β_i = the slope coefficient of the regression, and e_{it} = a random error term.

The estimate of the slope is an estimate of the asset's beta since the slope coefficient measures how volatile an asset's returns are relative to the market's returns. If an asset's returns generally rise (or fall) half as much as those of the market, its beta will be 0.5. Knowing that beta equals 0.5 tells us little about the asset's variance of returns over time, or the asset's expected range of returns. As a relative measure of volatility, beta tells us only how, on average, the asset's returns follow those of the overall market.

Assets that are more volatile than the market or, in other words, assets that are more sensitive to systematic risk than the market, have betas greater than 1.0; whatever the market return is, these assets' average returns are larger in *absolute value*. Assets that are less volatile than the market, or those that have less systematic risk, have betas less than 1.0. These assets' returns, on average, are less in absolute value than those of the market.

50. Bid

An offer to purchase at a specified price.

51. Bid Price

The price at which a dealer is willing to purchase a security.

52. Bid-Ask Spread

The difference between a dealer's bid and asked price. The bid is the highest price anyone has declared that he wants to pay for a security at a given time; ask is the lowest price anyone will take at time same time.

53. Bidder

A firm or person that has made an offer to take over another firm. The bidder offers to pay cash or securities to obtain the stock or assets of another company.

54. Bid-Offer Spread

The amount by which the offer price exceeds the bid price. It is also called bid-ask spread. [See also **Bid-ask spread**]

55. BIF

Bank Insurance Fund that insures deposits at commercial banks. This is one of the two insurance funds under Federal deposit insurance company (FDIC). The other insurance fund is the Sanngs Association Fund (SAIF). [See also **SAIF**]

56. Bill of Lading

The bill of lading (B/L) is a shipping document that governs transportation of the shipper. Essentially it is a shipping document that governs transportation of the exporter's goods to the importer. The seller submits the invoices and the bill of lading to the correspondent bank. The bank, in turn, verifies the paperwork and pays the seller. The correspondent bank then sends the paperwork to the buyer's bank, which pays the correspondent bank and sends the documents to the buyer, who makes the payment.

57. Binary Option

Option with a discontinuous payoff; for example, a cash-or-nothing option or an asset-or-nothing option.

58. Binomial Option-Pricing Model

A model where the price of an asset is monitored over successive short periods of time. In each short period, it is assumed that only two price movements are possible. The binomial option pricing model is the most famous binomial model in finance. [See Rendelman and Bartter, 1979; see also **Appendix G**]

59. Binomial Process

[See **Binomial tree**]

60. Binomial Tree

A representation of possible asset price movements over time, in which the asset price is modeled as moving up or down by a given amount each period. This is a special case of a decision tree analysis. [See also **Decision trees**]

61. Bivariate Normal Distribution

A distribution for two correlated variables, each of which is normal. American option with one dividend payment needs to use this distribution to determine its value.

62. Black's Model (Formula)

A version of Black-Scholes formula in which the underlying asset is a futures price and the dividend yield is replaced with the risk-free rate. The formula is written as:

$$C(F,K,\sigma,r,t,r) = Fe^{-rt}N(d_1) - Ke^{-rt}N(d_2),$$

$$d_1 = \frac{\ln(F/K) + \frac{1}{2}\sigma^2 t}{\sigma\sqrt{t}},$$

$$d_2 = d_1 - \sigma\sqrt{t},$$

where F = futures price; K = exercise price; r = risk-free rate; σ = standard deviation of rates of return; and t = contract period; $N(d_1)$ and $N(d_2)$ are cumulative normal density functions in terms of d_1 and d_2.

The put price is obtained using the parity relationship for options of futures:

$$P(F,K,\sigma,r,t,r) = C(F,K,\sigma,r,t,r) + Ke^{-rt} - Fe^{-rt}.$$

63. Black-Scholes Formula

An equation to value a call option that uses the stock price, the exercise price, the risk-free interest rate, the time to maturity, and the standard deviation of the stock return as:

$$C = SN(d_1) - Xe^{-rt}N(d_2),$$

$$\text{where} \quad d_1 = \frac{\ln(S/X) + (r + \sigma^2/2)t}{\sigma\sqrt{t}},$$

$$d_2 = d_1 - \sigma\sqrt{t},$$

C = current call option value; S = current stock price; $N(d)$ = the probability that a random draw from a standard normal distribution will be less than d, equals the area under the normal curve up to d; X = exercise price; e = 2.71828, the base of the natural log function; r = risk-free interest rate; ln = natural logarithm function; and σ = standard deviation of the annualized continuously compounded rate of return of the stock.

Like most of the models, the Black-Scholes formula is based on some important underlying assumptions:

1. The stock will pay no dividends until after the option expiration date.

2. Both the interest rate, r, and variance rate, σ^2, of the stock are constant.

3. Stock prices are continuous, meaning that sudden extreme jumps such as those in the aftermath of an announcement of a takeover attempt are ruled out.

64. Black-Scholes Option Pricing Model

Black and Scholes came up with a mathematical model to determine the value of an option.

Step 1: Assume the future stock price is constant over time.

Following the equation, $C = \text{Max}(0, S - X)$, where Max denotes the larger of the two bracketed terms, if the stock price is constant over time, then the value of the call, C, is the current price of the stock, S, less the present value of the exercise price, X. Mathematically, the value of the call option, assuming discrete compounding of interest rate is

$$C = S - \frac{X}{(1+r)^t}.$$

If continuous compounding is assumed, then the equation becomes: $V_C = P - Xe^{-rt}$, where e is a constant approximately equal to 2.71828.

Step 2: Assume the price of the stock fluctuates over time.

In this case, we need to adjust the equation for the fluctuation associated with the uncertainty. If we assume that the stock's returns follow a normal distribution, then both S and X in the equation can be adjusted for the uncertainty factor associated with the fluctuation of the stock's price over time. The call option pricing model thus becomes

$$C = SN(d_1) - Xe^{-rt}N(d_2),$$

$$\text{where} \quad d_1 = \frac{\ln(S/X) + (r + \frac{\sigma^2}{2})t}{\sigma\sqrt{t}},$$

$$d_2 = d_1 - \sigma\sqrt{t}, r = \text{risk-free interest rate},$$

and t = time until the option expires (in years).

This equation is the well-known Black-Scholes option pricing model. The adjustment factors $N(d_1)$ and $N(d_2)$ represent the cumulative standard normal distribution function. $N(d_1)$ and $N(d_2)$ are probabilities that a random variable with a standard normal distribution takes on a value less than d_1 and d_2, respectively. The values for $N(d_1)$ and

$N(d_2)$ can be found by using a standardized normal distribution table.

65. Blank Check

A signed check with no amount indicated.

66. Blanket Lien

A loan may specify a blanket lien, or a claim against all work in progress or inventory on hand. For example, if a business mass produces low-value items, it is not practical to give the bank claims against specific items. In other words it refers a secured loan that gives the lender a lien against all the borrower's inventories. [See also **Collateral**]

67. Blanket Mortgage

A blanket mortgage is a claim on all the issuer's real property, including land, buildings, and equipment.

68. Block House

Brokerage firms that help to find potential buyers or sellers of large block trades.

69. Block Sale

A transaction of more than 10,000 shares of stock.

70. Block Transactions

Large transactions in which at least 10,000 shares of stock are bought or sold. Brokers or "block houses" often search directly for other large traders rather than bringing the trade to the stock exchange.

71. Board Broker

Individual who handles limit orders in some exchanges. The board broker makes information on outstanding limit orders available to other traders.

72. Board of Directors

Individuals elected by stockholders to manage and oversee a firm's operations.

73. Board of Governors of the Federal Reserve System

The policy-setting representatives of the Federal Reserve System in charge of setting the discount rate, required reserves, and general policies designed to affect growth in the banking system's reserves and US money supply.

74. Bogey

In portfolio performance analysis, the attribution method explains the difference in returns between a managed portfolio and selected benchmark portfolio is called the bogey. Attribution studies start from the broadest assets allocation choices and progressively focus on ever-finer details of portfolio choice.

75. Bond

A long-term debt of a firm. In common usage, the term *bond* often refers to both secured and unsecured debt. Bonds usually have a face value, it is also called the principal value or the denomination and it is stated on the bond certificate. In addition, the par value (i.e., initial accounting value) of a bond is almost always the same as the face value.

76. Bond Broker

A broker who trades bonds on an exchange.

77. Bond-Equivalent Basis

With bond-equivalent basis, yield calculations use the same number of days for both interest-bearing periods and interest-compounding periods. For example, to figure the annual yield using daily compounding, the annual interest rate might be divided by 365 days, and the result is then compounded for 365 days to get the annual yield.

78. Bond Equivalent Yield of the T-bill

Bond equivalent yield of T-bill (Y_{BEY}) is generally calculated on an annual percentage rate (APR) method as:

$$Y_{BEY} = \frac{10,000 - P}{P} \times \frac{365}{n},$$

where P and n represent market price and the number of days owned the T-bill, respectively. It differs from the effective annual yield method. [See also **APR, Effective annual yield**]

79. Bond Fund

A mutual fund that invests in debt instruments. It is an income fund instead of growth fund.

80. Bond Option

An option where a bond is the underlying asset.

81. Bond Ratings

Most issuers secure bond ratings from one or more agencies such as Standard & Poors (S&P), Moody's, Fitch, and Duff and Phelps. From its analysis and discussions with management, the agency assigns a bond rating. In addition, the rating agency commits to a continual reexamination of the issue's risk. For example, should the financial position of the firm weaken or improve, S&P may place the issue on its *Credit Watch* list, with negative or positive implications. Shortly thereafter, S&P will downgrade, upgrade, or reaffirm the original rating.

Bond rating is another example of an agency cost. [See also **Agency costs**] To show potential investors the credit quality of its bonds, the firm hires a recognized independent third party to rate its bond offering. Even if the bonds receive a lower-than-expected rating and the firm must issue the bonds with a higher coupon to compensate investors for the extra risk, the benefits of a rating in terms of attractiveness to investors and issue liquidity outweigh these extra costs.

Despite the initial cost and the concern that a lower-than-expected rating may cause managers, a bond rating makes it much easier to sell the bonds in the primary market offering, as well as in the secondary market. The rating acts as a signal to the market that an independent agency has examined the qualities of the issuer and the issue and has determined that the credit risk of the bond issue justifies the published rating. An unrated bond issue risks a cool reception in the primary market and thin illiquid, secondary markets (i.e., bond traders and investors are not interested in buying or selling the particular issues). Investors may have good reason to wonder, "What is the firm trying to hide? If this really was an attractive bond issue, the firm would have had it rated." In addition, certain types of investors, such as pension funds and insurance companies, may face restrictions against purchasing unrated public debt. Examples of bond rating categories are presented in the table.

	Moody's	Standard & Poor's	Former Standard & Poor's
Best quality, smallest degree of risk	Aaa	AAA	AAA
High quality, slightly more long-term risk than top rating	Aa1 Aa2 Aa3	AA+ AA AA−	AA
Upper-medium grade, possible impairment in the future	A1 A2 A3	A+ A A−	A

(Continued)

	Moody's	Standard & Poor's	Former Standard & Poor's
Medium-grade, lack outstanding investment characteristics	Baa1 Baa2 Baa3	BBB+ BBB BBB−	BBB
Speculative issues, protection may be very moderate	Ba1 Ba2 Ba3	BB+ BB BB−	BB
Very speculative, may have small assurance of interest and principal payments	B1 B2 B3	B+ B B−	B
Issues in poor standing, may be in default	Caa	CCC	CCC
Speculative in a high degree, with marked shortcomings	Ca	CC	CC
Lowest quality, poor prospects of attaining real investment standing	C	C	C
Default	D	D	D

82. Bond Valuation

Theoretical value of bond is equal to present value of the annuity for future interest payments and the present value of the face value of bond. Suppose that a bond with par (face) value F is purchased today and that the bond matures in N years. Let us assume that interest payments of dollar amount I are to be made at the end of each of the next N years. The bondholders will then receive a stream of N annual payments of I dollars, plus a payment of F dollars at the end of the Nth year. Using the rate of interest r to discount future receipts, the present value of the bond is

$$PV = \sum_{t=1}^{N} \frac{I}{(1+r)^t} + \frac{F}{(1+r)^N}. \tag{A}$$

The first term on the right-hand side of Equation (A) is the present value of the stream of interest payments, while the second term is the present value of the future of the par amount.

83. Bond Yield

Discount rate which, when applied to all the cash flows of a bond, causes the present value of the cash flows to equal the bond's market price. [See also **Yield to maturity**]

84. Book Cash

A firm's cash balance as reported in its financial statements. Also called ledger cash. It is not the same thing as the balance shown in its bank account (bank cash or collected bank cash).

85. Book Value

Under US GAAP, balance sheet items generally are listed at book value, which is the original or historical cost of the items, less calculated depreciation. Frequently, book value fails to accurately represent the current market value of balance sheet items. For example, LIFO (last-in, first-out) inventory accounting may leave items produced years ago on the books even though they were actually sold time ago. On the other hand, for example, last year's fashions or models may be nearly worthless in the current market, while the balance sheet inventory figure values them at their historical cost. Historical cost may grossly undervalue fixed assets such as land or buildings. Likewise, bond issues, valued at par depending upon interest rate or credit risk changes since they were first issued. Similarly, book values of equity claims will differ from current market prices of company stock issues.

86. Book Value Equity

Total assets minus total liabilities reported on the balance sheet. It includes the par value, capital surplus, and accumulated retained earnings.

87. Book Value Per Share

Per-share accounting equity value of a firm. Total accounting equity divided by the number of outstanding shares. The sum of the par value, capital surplus, and accumulated retained earnings is the common equity of the firm, which is usually referred to as the firm's book value. The book value represents the amount contributed directly and indirectly to the corporation by equity investors.

88. Bootstrapping

This term has two meanings. First, it refers to the procedure where coupon bonds are used to generate the set of zero-coupon bond prices. Second, it means the use of historical returns to create an empirical probability distribution for returns.

89. Borrow

To obtain or receive money on loan with the promise or understanding of returning it or its equivalent.

90. Borrowing Portfolio

On the capital market line, assume that the investor can borrow money at the risk-free rate and invest the money in the risky portfolio. The portfolios with a rate of return higher than the return on market portfolio, but with higher risks, along the line contains a negative amount of the risk-free asset and is called borrowing portfolios. The negative amount invested in the risk-free asset can be viewed as borrowing funds at the risk-free rate and investing in risky assets.

91. Bounce a Check

A depositor writes a check which is returned to the bank and by the bank to the depositor because of insufficient funds.

92. Boundary Condition

The value of a derivative claim at a certain time, or at a particular price of the underlying asset. For example, a boundary condition for a zero-coupon bond is that the bond at maturity is worth its promised maturity value.

93. Box Spread

An option position in which the stock is synthetically purchased (buy call, sell put) at one price and sold (sell call, buy put) at a different price. When constructed with European options, the box spread is equivalent to a zero-coupon bond.

94. Branch Banking

An organizational structure in which a bank maintains facilities that are part of the bank in offices different from its home office. Some states allow banks to set up branches through the state, county, or city. Others prohibit branches.

95. Break Point

A break point occurs when raising an additional dollar of funds results in an increase in the weighted average cost of capital.

We know that firms have two sources of equity financing, each with a different cost: the cost of retained earnings (k_{re}) and the cost of new common stock (k_{cs}). In financing a number of attractive projects, the firm may deplete its retained profits from the current year. A need for additional financing creates a need to recalculate a cost of capital that substitutes the cost of new common stock for the cost of retained earnings. The firm must discount additional investments using the new, incremental or *marginal weighed average cost of capital* as a discount rate.

Similarly, a firm may be able to borrow only a limited amount in a year without harming its credit or bond rating. A downgrade would increase the interest rates it pays to borrow funds. Once the firm reaches its debt limit, it must calculate a new cost of capital that incorporates the higher cost of borrowing. Any additional investment then must face a higher cost of capital because of the increase in borrowing costs.

Thus, several break points may exist for a firm. One may arise from depleting current retained profits; another may arise from higher borrowing costs if substantial funds are borrowed in a given year; still others may arise from changes in flotation costs or equity costs should large amounts be raised from these sources in a short time frame. [See also **Capital rationing**]

96. Break-Even Analysis

Analysis of the level of sales at which a project would make zero profit. We calculate the break-even point in terms of both accounting profit and present value. [See also **Break-even point, Accounting break-even, Cash breakeven** and **Financial break-even**]

97. Break-Even Point

A firm's break-even point is where revenues equal total costs. [See also **Accounting break-even** and **Cash breakeven**] Break-even point (Q^*) can be defined as:

$$Q^* = \frac{F + D}{P - V},$$

where F, P, V and D represents total fixed cost, price per unit, variable cost per unit, and depreciation, respectively.

98. Bridge Loan

A loan issued to fund a temporary need from the time a security is redeemed to the time another security is issued.

99. Broker

An individual who executes orders for customers for which she receives a commission.

100. Brokered Deposit

Deposits acquired through a money broker (typically an investment bank) in the national markets.

101. Brokered Market

A market where an intermediary (a broker) offers search services to buyers and sellers.

102. Brownian Motion

A stochastic process in which the random variable moves continuously and follows a random walk with normally distributed independent increments. Named after the Scottish botanist Robert Brown, who in 1827 noticed that pollen grains suspended in water exhibited continual movement. Brownian motion is also called a *Wiener process*. This is a basic concept used to derive the continuous type of option pricing model. [See also **Wiener process**]

103. Bubble Theory (of Speculative Markets)

Bubble refers to security prices that move wildly above their true values and eventually burst. After prices eventually fall back to their original level, causing great losses for investors. The crashes of stock markets of US in 1929, 1987, and 2000 are evidences for the bubble theory.

104. Budget Deficit

The amount by which government spending exceeds government revenues. Fiscal condition for a government can be either budget deficit or budget surplus.

105. Bulge Bracket Firms

Firms in an underwriting syndicate that has the highest commitment to assist in placing the underlying securities.

106. Bull CD

A bull CD pays its holder a specified percentage of the increase in return on a specified market index while guaranteeing a minimum rate of return.

107. Bull Spread

Bull spread is also called long vertical spread. It designates a position for which one has brought a low-exercise-price call (or a low-exercise-price put) and sold a high-exercise-price call (or a high-exercise price put) that both mature in the same month.

108. Bullet Loan

A loan that requires payment of the entire principal at maturity.

109. Bullish, Bearish

Words used to describe investor attitudes. *Bullish* means optimistic; *bearish* means pessimistic. Also used in bull market and bear market for describing the stock market.

110. Bundling, Unbundling

A trend allowing creation of securities either by combining primitive and derivative securities into one composite hybrid or by separating returns on an asset into classes. Both cases are financial engineering techniques. Creative security design often calls for bundling primitive and derivative securities into one composite security. Quite often, creating a security that appears to be attractive requires unbundling of an asset. A mortgage pass-through certificate is unbundled into two classes. Class 1 receives only principal payments from the mortgage pool, whereas class 2 receives only interest payments.

111. Burden

Noninterest expense minus noninterest income for banks. Generally, noninterest expense is larger than the noninterest income.

112. Business Cycle

Repetitive cycles of recession and recovery. Some cyclical indicators for business cycle based upon National Bureau of Economic Research are as follows:

a.   Leading Indicators

Average hourly workweek, production workers, manufacturing.
Average weekly initial claims, state unemployment insurance.
Index of net business formation.
New orders, durable-goods industries.
Contracts and orders, plant and equipment.
Index of new building permits, private housing units.
Change in book value, manufacturing and trade inventories.
Index of industrial materials prices.
Index of stock prices, 500 common stocks.
Corporate profits after taxes (quarterly).
Index: ratio of price to unit labor cost, manufacturing.
Change in consumer installment debt.

b.   Roughly Coincident Indicators

GNP in current dollars.
GNP in 1958 dollars.
Index of industrial production.
Personal income.
Manufacturing and trade sales.
Sales of retail stores.
Employees on nonagricultural payrolls.
Unemployment rate, total.

c.   Lagging Indicators

Unemployment rate, persons unemployed 15 weeks or over.
Business expenditures, new plant and equipment.
Book value, manufacturing and trade inventories.

Index of labor cost per unit of output in manufacturing.
Commercial and industrial loans outstanding in
large commercial banks.
Banks rates on short-term business loans.

Source: US Department of Commerce.

113. Business Failure

It refers to a business that has terminated due to
the loss of creditors. However, it should be noted
that even an all-equity firm can fail.

114. Business Risk

Business risk is determined by the products the firm
sells and the production processes it uses. The effects
of business risk are seen ultimately in the variability
of earnings before interest and taxes (EBIT) over
time. In fact, one popular measure of a firm's business risk is the standard deviation of EBIT. To control for the effects of a firm's size, another popular
method of gauging business risk is to find the standard deviation over time of the firm's operating return on assets, that is EBIT divided by Total assets.

A firm's business risk is affected by three major
influences: unit volume fluctuations, fixed costs (including depreciation expenses), and the relationship
between the firm's selling price and its variable
costs.

115. Business Strategy Matrix

The business strategy matrix model views the firm
as a collection or portfolio of assets grouped into
strategic business units. This technique has been
disparaged by some as a cause of inappropriate
diversification among business units. It has led
firms to acquire or develop unrelated business
units that the firm's officers did not fully understand. For example, the managerial expertise
needed to run a successful electronics firm may be

different from that needed to run a successful bak-
ing company. Nonetheless, this model can still provide some insights into capital budgeting strategy.

The business strategy matrix model emphasizes
market share and market growth rate. Based upon
these attributes, business units are deemed to be
Stars, Cash Cows, Question Marks, or Dogs. Cash
Cows typically are business units with leading market positions in maturing industries; the firm can
direct the cash that these units generate to other
business units that need it, such as Stars and Question Marks. The Stars (units with good market
positions in high growth markets) need funds to
expand and develop competitive advantages, as do
some Question Marks. Proper strategies to build
competitive advantages may turn Question Marks
into Stars; if these strategies are unsuccessful, the
firm may have to divest Question Marks. Dogs
have poor market positions in low-growth industries; unless a turnaround strategy is feasible, these
also are divestment or liquidation candidates.

If an organization uses the business strategy
matrix to assist in planning, management must be
sure to manage the firm's market share in a way
that maximizes shareholder wealth.

116. Butterfly Spread

A position that is created by taking a long position
in a call with strike price K_1, a long position in a
call with strike price K_3, and a short position in
two calls with strike price K_2, where $K_3 > K_2 > K_1$
and $K_2 = 0.5(K_1 + K_3)$. (A butterfly spread can
also be created with put options.)

117. Buying the Index

Purchasing the stocks in the Standard & Poor's
500 in the same proportion as the index to achieve
the same return. An index fund is a good example.

C

1. Calendar Spread

A position that is created by taking a long position in a call option that matures at one time and a short position at a different time. (A calendar spread can also be created using put options.)

2. Calibration

Method for implying a model's parameters from the prices of actively traded options.

3. Call

A call is an option to purchase a fixed number of shares of common stock. It is a right instead of an obligation. Calls can be either buy a call or write a call.

4. Call Deferment Periods

[See **Callable bonds**]

5. Call Loan

A call loan is a loan contract which enables the lender (e.g., the bank) to request repayment of loan in the contract period. For example, most broker loans to investment banks are callable within 24 hours notice.

6. Call Money Rate

It is the rate charged by brokers for the use of margin in common-stock accounts.

7. Call Option

A call option gives the holder the right to buy a particular number of shares of a designated common stock at a specified price, called the **exercise price** (or striking price), on or before a given date, known as the **expiration date**. [See also **Exercise price** and **Expiration date**] On the Chicago Board Options Exchange, options typically are created for three-month, six-month, or nine-month periods. All have the same expiration date: the Saturday following the third Friday of the month of expiration. The owner of the shares of common stock can write, or create, an option and sell it in the options market, in an attempt to increase the return or income on a stock investment.

8. Call Premium

It refers to the price of a call option on common stock. It also refers to the difference between the call price and the face value. [See also **Callable bonds**]

9. Call Price of a Bond

Amount at which a firm has the right to repurchase its bonds or debentures before the stated maturity date. The call price is always set at equal to or more than the par value. [See also **Callable bonds**]

10. Call Protected

Describes a bond that is not allowed to be called, usually for a certain early period in the life of the bond.

11. Call Protection

The feature which does not allow a bond to be called for some (deferment) period.

12. Call Provision

A written agreement between an issuing corporation and its bondholders that gives the corporation the option to redeem the bond at a specified price before the maturity date. A call provision lets the company repurchase or call the entire bond issue at predetermined price over a specific period.

13. Call Risk

[See **Callable bonds**]

14. Callable

Refers to a bond that is subject to be repurchased at a stated call price before maturity. For example, debt may be extinguished before maturity by a call. Historically, almost all publicly issued corporate long-term debt has been callable.

15. Callable Bonds

Callable bonds can be redeemed prior to maturity by the firm. Such bonds will be called and redeemed if, for example, a decline in interest rates makes it attractive for the firm to issue lower coupon debt to replace high-coupon debt. A firm with cash from successful marketing efforts or a recent stock issue also may decide to retire its callable debt.

Callable bonds usually are called away after a decline in interest rates. As rates fall, the bond's price will not rise above its call price. Thus, for callable bonds, the inverse relationship between bond prices and interest rates breaks down once the bond's market price reaches the call price.

Many indentures state that, if called, callable bonds must be redeemed at their **call prices**, typically par value plus a **call premium** of one year's interest.

Investors in callable bonds are said to be subject to **call risk**. Despite receiving the call price, investors usually are not pleased when their bonds are called away. As bonds typically are called after a substantial decline in interest rates, the call eliminates their high coupon payments; they can reinvest the funds only in bonds that offer lower yields.

In order to attract investors, callable bonds must offer higher coupons or yields than noncallable bonds of similar credit quality and maturity. Many indentures specify **call deferment periods** im-

mediately after the bond issue, during which the bonds cannot be called.

16. Call-Loan Money Rate

The rate charged by banks to brokers who deposit securities as collateral.

17. CAMELS

An acronym that refers to the regulatory rating system for bank performance: C = capital adequacy, A = asset quality, M = management quality, E = earnings quality, L = liquidity, and S = sensitivity to market risk.

18. Cancelable Swap

A cancelable swap is a plain vanilla interest rate swap. This kind of swap can be canceled by one side on prespecified dates.

19. Cannibalization

Cannibalization occurs when a project robs cash flow from the firm's existing lines of business. For example, when a soft-drink firm is thinking about introducing a new flavor or a new diet product, the project's incremental cash flows should consider how much the new offering will erode the sales and cash flows of the firm's other product lines.

20. Cap

An options contract that serves as insurance against a high price. [See also **Interest rate cap**]

21. Cap Rate

The rate determining payoffs in an interest rate cap. [See **Interest rate cap**]

22. Capital

Funds subscribed and aid by stockholders representing ownership in a bank. In other words, capital is the stockholder's equity of a bank. Regulatory capital also includes debt components and loss reserves. It can be defined either in book value or market value. The market value of capital is used as an insulation device against credit risk and interest rate risk. [See **Credit risk** and **Interest rate risk**]

23. Capital Allocation Decision

Allocation of invested funds between risk-free assets versus the risky portfolio. [See also **Asset allocation decision**]

24. Capital Allocation Line (CAL)

A graph showing all feasible risk-return combinations of a risky and risk-free asset. [See also **Capital market line**]

25. Capital Asset Pricing Model (CAPM)

An equilibrium asset pricing theory that shows that equilibrium rates of expected return on all risky assets are a function of their covariance with the market portfolio. [See **Sharpe, *Journal of Finance*, September 1964**]

$$E(R_i) = R_F + \beta(E(R_m) - R_F).$$

Thus, expected return on ith security= Risk-free rate + Beta coefficient (Expected return on market portfolio − Risk-free rate). Because the term in parentheses on the right-hand side is positive, this equation says that the expected return on a security is a positive function of its beta.

26. Capital Budgeting

Capital budgeting is the process of identifying, evaluating, and implementing a firm's investment opportunities. Because of their size and time horizon, a firm's capital projects should reflect its strategy for meeting future goals. The typical capital budgeting project involves a large up-front cash outlay, followed by a series of smaller cash inflows and outflows. A project's expected time frame may be as short as one year or as long as 20 or 30 years. But the project's cash flows, including the total up-front cost of the project, are not known with certainty before the project starts. The firm must evaluate the size, timing, and risk of the project's cash flows to determine if it enhances shareholder wealth.

Broadly speaking capital budgeting can be described as a three-phase process that includes a **planning phase**, an **appropriation phase**, and an **audit** or **control phase**. [See also **Planning phase of capital budgeting**, **Appropriation phase of capital budgeting**, and **Audit or Control phase**]

27. Capital Gains

The positive change in the value of an asset. A negative capital gain is a capital loss. It is the change in the price of the stock divided by the initial price. Letting P_t be the purchaser price of the asset and P_{t+1} be the price of the asset at year-end, the capital gain can be computed.

Capital gain = $(P_{t+1} - P_t)/P_t$.

28. Capital Lease

A capital lease or **financial lease** of an asset satisfies any one of the following criteria:

1. The lessee takes ownership of the asset at the end of the lease.

2. The lessee can purchase the asset at the end of the lease at a bargain price (less than fair market value).

3. The length of the lease equals 75 percent or more of the estimated life of the asset.

4. At the beginning of the lease, the present value of the lease payments is 90 percent or more of the fair market value of the property.

Typically, the lessee may not cancel a capital financial lease and is responsible for asset maintenance. In a financial lease, tax law identifies the lessor as the owner of the leased asset, so the lessor can deduct asset depreciation over the life of the lease.

29. Capital Market Line

The efficient set of all assets, both risky and riskless, which provides the investor with the best possible opportunities. The line used in the risk-return trade-off to illustrate the rates of return for efficient portfolios depending on the risk free rate of return and the level of risk (standard deviation) for a particular portfolio.

In sum, formula for capital market line used to describe the trade-off between expected return and total risk is

$$E(R_i) = R_f + [E(R_m) - R_f]\frac{\sigma_i}{\sigma_m},$$

where R_f = risk-free rate, $E(R_m)$ = expected return on the market portfolio, $E(R_i)$ = expected return on the ith portfolio, and σ_i, σ_m = standard deviations of the portfolio and the market, respectively.

30. Capital Market Securities

The classification of a financial instrument as a marketable security typically is based upon maturity and, to a lesser extent, liquidity. Securities with more than one year to maturity, such as stocks, bonds, and mortgages, are called capital market securities.

31. Capital Markets

Financial markets for long-term debt (with a maturity at over one year) and for equity shares. The financial markets are composed of the money markets and the capital markets. The markets where capital, such as stocks and bonds, are traded. Capital markets are used by firms to raise additional funds.

32. Capital Rationing

Capital rationing places an upper limit on the amount of a firm's capital spending over the course of a year. The first break point in a cost of capital schedule usually occurs when a firm runs out of current retained earnings. An easy way to handle the marginal cost of capital problem is to ration capital by setting the upper limit of spending at the point where the firm will run out of retained earnings.

The deficiency in this strategy is rather obvious. To maximize shareholder wealth, the firm should be willing to undertake *any* project with a positive NPV, whether or not total spending exceeds one or more break points.

33. Capital Structure

The mix of debt and equity a firm uses to finance its assets defines the firm's capital structure. A target capital structure is important as it determines the weights in the calculation of a firm's weighted average cost of capital (WACC). There is, however, a second and even more important reason: The firm's *optimum* debt-to-equity mix minimizes the WACC; minimizing the WACC will help the firm to maximize shareholder wealth.

If a nonoptimal capital structure leads to a higher WACC, the firm is likely to reject some capital budgeting projects that could increase its competitive advantage and shareholder wealth under an optimal target financing mix.

34. Capital Structure Ratios

Capital structure ratios (sometimes called *debt utilization* or *leverage ratios*) compare the funds supplied by the owners (equity) with the funds provided by creditors (debt). The **debt-to-assets ratio** is calculated as total debt (i.e., the sum of current and long-term liabilities) divided by total assets; it measures the proportion of assets financed by borrowers. The **debt-to-equity ratio** is computed as total debt divided by stockholders' equity. The two ratios are computed as:

$$\text{Debt-to-assets ratio} = \frac{\text{Total debt}}{\text{Total assets}}$$

$$\text{Debt-to-equity ratio} = \frac{\text{Total debt}}{\text{Total equity}}.$$

The **equity multiplier** is another indicator of a company's use of debt. At first glance, the ratio appears to have little to do with leverage; it is simply total assets divided by stockholders' equity. Recall the accounting identity, however: Assets = Liabilities + Equity. More assets relative to equity suggest a greater use of debt. Thus, larger values of the equity multiplier imply a greater use of leverage by the firm. The equity multiplier is written as:

$$\text{Equity multiplier} = \frac{\text{Total assets}}{\text{Total equity}}.$$

As a rough measure of the firm's ability to service its debt and other fixed obligations, the analyst can calculate the **times interest earned** (TIE) (or **interest coverage) ratio**. The times interest earned ratio is earnings before interest and taxes (EBIT) divided by interest expense. This ratio provides a measure of how well the firm's operations generate funds to pay interest expenses. EBIT can fall by (1–1/TIE) before interest payments are jeopardized. For example, a TIE ratio of 5 indicates that EBIT could fall by (1–1/5) or 80 percent before earnings would fail to cover interest obligations. The times interest earned ratio is given by:

$$\text{Times interest earned ratio} = \frac{\text{EBIT}}{\text{Interest expense}}.$$

An alternative to the TIE ratio, the **fixed charge coverage ratio** is computed as earnings before fixed charges divided by fixed charges. It is more general than TIE, since the denominator includes all fixed charges, such as interest payments, lease payments, bond sinking fund obligations, and so on. However, looking at the fixed charge coverage ratio may give analysts a fuller picture of the firm's ability to pay all of its fixed obligations.

By using appropriate amounts of debt and equity, the firm can minimize its financing costs and thereby maximize shareholder wealth. This suggests that analysts may see danger signals in both high and low ratios. High debt ratios increase the potential of bankruptcy; low debt ratios may indicate that management is not using debt efficiently to maximize shareholder wealth.

35. Capital Surplus

Amounts of directly contributed equity capital in excess of the par value. Equity which cannot otherwise be classified as capital stock or retained earnings. It's usually created from a stock issued at a premium over par value. Capital surplus is also known as share premium (UK), acquired surplus, donated surplus, paid-in surplus, or additional paid-in capital.

36. Capital-Labor Ratio

A production function is a function that can be seen as a function of labor and capital as:

$$Q = f(K, L),$$

where K = capital and L = labor. The capital-labor ratio (K/L) is generally used to measure a firm's degree of capital intensity. Capital intensity results in increased total risks and generally results in an increase in beta. If the capital-labor ratio is greater than one – that is, if K is greater than L – a firm is capital intensive. If the ratio is less than one, then there is a deduction in capital intensity and a shift towards human-resource investment.

37. Caplets

The individual options comprising a cap are sometimes referred to as caplets. An interest rate cap is a series of consecutive long call options (caplets) on a specific interest rate at the same strike price.

38. Capped Option

An option with a maximum payoff, where the option is automatically exercised if the underlying asset reaches the price at which the maximum payoff is attained.

39. Captive Finance Company

A finance company owned by a manufacturer that provides financing to buyers of the firm's products. For example, General Motors Acceptance Corporation is a captive finance company.

40. Car

A loose term sometimes used to describe the quantity of a contract, for example, "I am long a car of bellies." (Derived from the fact that quantities of the product specified in a contract used to correspond closely to the capacity of a railroad car.)

41. CARs

Collateralized automobile receivables (CARs) is a form of asset-backed security in which the collateral is automobile receivables. Other types of account receivable can be used to create asset-backed security also.

42. Card Bank

Bank that administers its own credit card plan or serves as a primary regional agent of a national credit card operation.

43. Cardinal Utility

A cardinal utility implies that a consumer is capable of assigning to every commodity or combination of commodities a number representing the amount or degree of utility associated with it. [See also **Ordinal utility**]

44. Carry

Another term for owning an asset, typically used to refer to commodities. [See also **Carry market** and **Cost of carry**]

45. Carry Market

A situation where the forward price is such that the return on a cash-and-carry is the risk-free rate. Cash-and-carry refers to the simultaneous spot purchase and forward sale of an asset or commodity.

46. Carrying Costs

Costs that increase with increases in the level of investment in current assets. Costs that fall with increases in the level of investment in current assets are called shortage costs. Carrying costs are generally of two types. First, because the rate of return on current assets is low compared with that of other assets, there is an opportunity cost. Second, there is the cost of maintaining the economic value of the item. For example, the cost of warehousing inventory belongs here.

47. Carrying Value

Book value. It is an accounting number based on cost.

48. Carve Outs

[See **Voluntary restructuring**]

49. Cash Basis

The accounting procedure that recognizes revenues when cash is actually received and expenses when cash is actually paid.

50. Cash Breakeven

Cash breakeven occurs when a project's cash inflows equal its cash outflows. Thus, the project's period-by-period operating cash flow is zero. The formula for the cash breakeven point (Q^*_{cash}) is as:

$$Q^*_{cash} = \frac{FC}{p - vc},$$

where FC = fixed costs, VC = variable cost per unit, and P = price per unit.

For any project operating at cash breakeven, net income (ignoring taxes) will equal depreciation expense. This stands to reason. Ignoring working capital for cash flow from operating activities, we know that operating cash flow (OCF) equals net income (NI) plus depreciation (Dep): OCF = NI + Dep. In the case of cash break-even, OCF is zero, so NI = −Dep.

Cash breakeven tells us how much product must be sold so that the firm's overall operating cash flows are not reduced.

51. Cash Budget

A forecast of cash receipts and disbursements expected by a firm in the coming year. It is a short-term financial planning tool. It allows the financial manager to identify short-term financial needs (and opportunities). It will tell the manager the required borrowing for the short term. It is the way of identifying the cash-flow gap on the cash-flow time line. The basic relation is

Ending accounting receivable
= Starting accounting receivable + Sales − Collection.

Collection is not the only source of cash, other sources of cash include sales of assets, investment income, and long-term financing.

52. Cash Budget Process

A cash budget shows the cash flow that the firm anticipates in the upcoming period, given various scenarios. This budget goes beyond a simple summation to cash receipts and disbursements. Rather, it attempts to forecast the actual timing of the cash flows into and out of the business. The precision of the budget depends upon the characteristics of the organization, the degree of uncertainty about the business environment, and the ability of the planner to accurately forecast the future cash flows. The budget process is characterized by five steps:

1. Forecasting sales.
2. Projecting all cash inflows, including forecasted receipts.
3. Projecting all cash outflows.
4. Interrelating the inflows and the outflows, subject to policy decisions of the firm's management.
5. Determining the excess of shortage of cash during the period.

Every cash budget must begin with a forecast of sales, which normally is supplied to the financial planner by the firm's marketing department. The primary source of cash inflow for many firms is not sales, but the collection of accounts receivable. In addition, the firm may raise cash from external sources through short-term or long-term financing or the sales of assets. These inflows also are part of the cash budget.

53. Cash Commodity

The actual physical commodity, as distinguished from a futures commodity. A commodity delivered at the time of sale is a cash commodity while a commodity to be delivered at a specific future date is a future commodity.

54. Cash Concentration Systems

A cash concentration system is designed to move funds from many small accounts into one or several large master accounts as efficiently as possible. A cash concentration network improves the financial manager's control of company cash by accumulating balances in one large account. The manager may be able to forecast total cash flows for the master account with a smaller percentage error than that associated with estimating cash balances of many small accounts. In addition, the manager can invest these funds at higher rates, since pooled funds can buy larger blocks of investment securities or money market instruments that are sold in large denominations. Finally, the cash concentration network can help reduce both excess balances in many small banks and expenses for transferring funds.

A concentration network uses DTCs (depository transfer check), wire transfers, and lockboxes to improve the efficiency of the firm's cash flows and investments. The type of system that a firm employs will depend upon the average dollar volume of its transactions, the number and sophistication of its banks, the timing and type of information that it requires, and the current opportunity cost of float. For example, DTCs are preferable to wire transfers when transferring funds in small dollar amounts through a volume of transactions, since DTCs are much less expensive than wire transfers. However, a high volume of transactions involving disbursements that are known ahead of time (such as payroll) might induce the firm to use an Automated Clearing House (ACH) transfer. ACH transfers often handle high-volume transactions and regular (or batch) transactions, and they usually can make the funds available in one business day. Although the ACH cannot provide the same immediate availability as wire transfer, it is slightly less expensive than a DTC and may serve a useful purpose when handling certain types of payments. Cash concentration systems are improving firms' float management and information gathering. For example, ACH tapes now can be deposited on weekends to help reduce the firm's risk of overdrafts. Future cash concentration systems should continue to make strides in reducing excess balances, administrative costs, and transfer costs while providing the manager with more reliable information to help with

investing cash and arranging appropriate lines of credit.

55. Cash Conversion Cycle

The cash conversion cycle is the net time interval between the actual cash outflow to pay accounts payable and the inflow of cash from the collection of accounts receivable.

The cash conversion cycle reflects the fact that some of the firm's inventory purchases are not immediately associated with cash outflows. Rather, the timeline shows that the firm buys inventories and then pays for them at some later time. Therefore, the cash conversion cycle is the distance on the timeline between payment for inventories and collection of accounts receivable as:

Cash conversion cycle = Operating cycle
$-$Payable deferral period,

where Operating cycle

Receivable collection period = $\left(\dfrac{\text{Accounts receivable}}{\text{sales}/365\ \text{days}}\right)$;

Inventory conversion period
$= \left(\dfrac{\text{Inventory}}{\text{Cost of goods sold}/365\ \text{days}}\right)$.

A shorter cash conversion cycle makes a firm more liquid. This makes it an excellent tool by which to measure the overall liquidity of a firm. The cash conversion cycle helps the manager to model cash flow management decisions on a timeline to clearly show their effects. For example, if the firm introduces a new system to collect accounts receivable more quickly, the manager can compare the cash conversion cycles under the old and new systems to evaluate the effects of the new system. Other financial or operating decisions also can be incorporated into the cash conversion cycle framework to provide a method of analyzing their effects on the firm's cash flows.

The cash conversion cycle quantifies the time it takes for cash to flow out through the working capital accounts and back in to the cash accounts. Essentially, the cycle begins when the organization pays cash for an investment in current assets and ends when cash flows back to the organization as payment for its goods or services. The short-term financial planner's first task is to identify the firm's cash flow cycle. The next step is to focus on how to speed up inflows and slow down outflows in the most cost-effective fashion. If we use average inventory, average accounts receivable (AR), and average accounts payable (AP) to replace inventory, AR, and AP, the cash conversion cycle can be rewritten as:

$$
\begin{aligned}
&\text{Cash conversion cycle} \\
&= \text{Average age of inventory} \\
&\quad + \text{Average age of accounts receivable} \\
&\quad - \text{Average age of accounts payable} \\
&= (\text{No. of days in planning period}) \\
&\quad \times \left[\frac{\text{Average inventory}}{\text{Cash operating expenditures}} \right. \\
&\quad + \frac{\text{Average accounts receivable}}{\text{Sales}} \\
&\quad \left. - \frac{\text{Average accounts payable}}{\text{Cost of goods sold}} \right],
\end{aligned}
$$

where Average inventory = (Beginning inventory + Ending inventory) / 2, Average accounts receivable = (Beginning AR + Ending AR) / 2, and Average accounts payable = (Beginning AP + Ending AP) / 2.

56. Cash Cow

A company that pays out all earnings per share (EPS) to stockholders as dividends (Div). Hence, EPS = Div. The value of the a share of stock becomes: $\frac{EPS}{r} = \frac{Div}{r}$, where r is the discount rate on the firm's stock. Cash cow project represents a strong market share and low market growth project.

57. Cash Cycle

In general, the time between cash disbursement and cash collection. In net working capital man-

agement, it can be thought of as the operating cycle less the accounts payable payment period. The cash cycle begins when cash is paid for materials and ends when cash is collected from receivables. [See also **Cash conversion cycle**]

58. Cash Delivery

The provision of some futures contracts that requires not delivery of the underlying assets (as in agricultural futures) but settlement according to the cash value of the asset.

59. Cash Disbursement Systems

The primary purpose of a disbursement system is to minimize the net cost of delivering payments to a company's employees, suppliers, and stockholders. Such a system must consider several categories of cost:

1. Opportunity costs from investments not made or interest expenses for unnecessary borrowings.
2. Transfer costs associated with moving funds from one location to another.
3. Cost associated with lost discounts, or opportunity costs of late or early payments.
4. Costs associated with vendor/employee ill will.
5. Managerial costs of handling the disbursement system.
6. Costs of any unauthorized disbursements.

To reduce opportunity costs, a firm can design the system to increase disbursement float. [See also **Disbursing float**] This can be accomplished, for example, by mailing checks from a remote disbursement location. The manager must balance the benefit of such a technique against the potential cost in strained relationships with vendors, though. Intentionally late payments or exaggerated mail float might create ill will among vendors and employees and cause the firm problems in the future.

60. Cash Discounts

The most obvious cost of a cash shortage comes from the inability to take advantage of suppliers' cash discounts by paying bills promptly. Most firms buy materials and supplies on terms of "2/10, net 30," which means that the buyer can deduct 2 percent from its bill if it pays within 10 days of receiving it, and that the payment in full is due within 30 days. Now, 2 percent may not sound like very much, but it allows you to use $98 for 20 more days of credit (the difference between 10 days and 30 days). This is an effective rate of 2.04 percent (2/98). To realize the true cost of bypassing the discount, convert the percentage to an annual rate: 20 days is about one-eighteenth of a year, so the true rate is 2.04 percent times 18.25, or 37 percent. In other words, by paying its bills 20 days after the discount date, the company is in effect borrowing money at an annual interest rate of 37 percent.

The annualized cost of foregoing a discount can be found by the following general formula:

$$\text{Annual cost of foregoing a discount} =$$
$$\frac{\text{Percentage cash discount}}{100\% - \text{Percentage cash discount}}$$
$$\times \frac{365 \text{ days}}{\text{Date for net payment} - \text{Date of discount payment}}.$$

It may be argued that when a cash-poor company pays its bills late to stretch out its funds, very probably it will not pay even after 30 days. It will, in fact, pay as late as possible. If we assume that the firm pays suppliers' bills 60 days after receipt rather than 30 days, it exchanges the discount of 2 percent for 50 days of additional credit. This reduces the cost of foregoing discounts from 37 percent to about 15 percent. However, such a policy cannot be maintained indefinitely. It greatly harms the company's relations with its suppliers and possibly with the financial community as well. Additionally, firms paying later may face interest charges imposed by their suppliers. Any such practice should certainly be reserved for real emergencies.

61. Cash Equivalents

Short-term money-market securities. In general, the first item of current assets in a balance sheet is "cash or cash equivalents."

62. Cash Flow after Interest and Taxes

Net income plus depreciation. It is also called net cash inflow in the capital budgeting decision.

63. Cash Flow From Operations

A firm's net cash flow from normal business operating activities used to assess the firm's ability to service existing and new debts and other fixed payment obligations.

64. Cash Flow Mapping

A procedure in which the cash flows of a given claim are assigned-to or mapped-to a set of benchmark claims.

65. Cash Flow Matching

A form of immunization, matching cash flows from a bond portfolio with an obligation. [See also **Dedication strategy**]

66. Cash Flow Timeline

A cash flow timeline can be a useful tool for visualizing and identifying cash flows over time. A cash flow timeline is a horizontal line with up-arrows that represent cash inflows (that is, cash to be received by the decision maker) and down-arrows to indicate cash expenses or outflows. The down arrow at Time 0 represents an investment today; the up-arrow n periods in the future represents $FV, the future value (or compounded value) of the investment. For example, today $100 is invested in a five-year CD that advertises a 10 percent annual interest rate. One year later, an additional $150 will be invested in a four-year

CD that pays 9 percent. How much money will be available when both CDs mature? Note that both CDs mature on the same date.

The cash flow timeline looks like this:

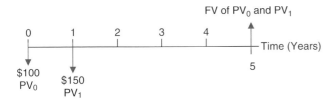

67. Cash Flows

Cash flows deal with the actual transfers of cash into or from the firm. Cash generated by the firm and paid to creditors and shareholders. It can be classified as (1) cash flow from operations, (2) cash flow from changes in fixed assets, and (3) cash flow from changes in net working capital.

68. Cash Letter

Transit letter on tape that lists items submitted between banks for collection.

69. Cash-market

The spot market for the immediate exchange of goods and services for immediate payment.

70. Cash Offer

Selling shares of seasoned equity to the public is called a cash offer. Usually, an investment bank is involved in the sale in one of three ways. A firm can issue seasoned equity using a firm commitment underwriting, by selling all or part of a previously shelf-registered issue, or through a competitive bidding process.

71. Cash Settlement

A procedure where settlement entails a cash payment from one party to the other, instead of delivery of an asset.

72. Cash Transaction

A transaction where exchange is immediate, as contrasted to a forward contract, which calls for future delivery of an asset at an agreed-upon price. It is a contrast to a forward contract. For example, if the book had been on the bookstore's shelf, your purchase of it would constitute a cash transaction.

73. Cash/bond Selection

Asset allocation in which the choice is between short-term cash equivalents and longer–term bonds.

74. Cash-and-Carry

The simultaneous spot purchase and forward sale of an asset or commodity.

75. Cashier's Check

A bank check that is drawn on the bank issuing the check and signed by a bank officer.

76. Cash-or-Nothing Call

An option that pays a fixed amount of cash if the asset price exceeds the strike price at expiration. If the asset price is equal or smaller than the strike price, then the call holder gets nothing.

77. Cashout

Refers to situation where a firm runs out of cash and cannot readily sell marketable securities. It may need to borrow or default on an obligation. Therefore, cash management is very important for a company to avoid the situation. [See also **Baumol's economic order quantity model**]

78. Cash-to-Cash Asset Cycle

The time it takes to accumulate cash, purchase inventory, produce a finished good, sell it, and collect on the sale.

79. Cash-to-Cash Liability Cycle

The length of time to obtain interest-free financing from suppliers in the form of accounts payable and accrued expenses.

80. Cash-to-Cash Working Capital Cycle

The timing difference between the cash-to-cash asset cycle and the cash-to-cash liability cycle.

81. CAT Bond

Bond where the interest and, possibly, the principal paid are reduced if a particular category of "catastrophic" insurance claims exceed a certain amount.

82. CD Basis

CD basis is a method that results in a higher effective yield than the bond-equivalent basis. The math works like this: using daily compounding, the effective yield would be determined by dividing the annual rate by 360, and then compounding for 365 days. [See also **Bond-equivalent basis**]

83. Central Bank

The main bank in a country responsible for issuing currency and setting and managing monetary policy.

84. Central Limit Theorem

One of the most important results in statistics, which states that the sum of independent and identically distributed random variables has a limiting distribution that is normal.

85. Certainty Equivalent

The certain return providing the same utility as the risky return of a risky portfolio in terms of certainty equivalent coefficient (α). In other words, the intercept of an indifference curve that represents the certain return is called the certainty equivalent of the portfolios on that curve and in fact is the utility value of that curve. For example, the certainty equivalent method for capital budgeting under uncertainty has used a certainty equivalent coefficient to convert the risky net cash inflow into risk-free net cash inflow in terms of certainty equivalent coefficient (α). α is

$$\alpha = \frac{certain\ return}{risky\ return},$$

where the value of α ranges from 0 to 1.

86. Certificates of Deposit

Short-term loans to commercial banks. There are active markets in CDs of 3-month, 6-month, 9-month, and 12-month maturities.

87. Certification Effect

As with any other firm commitment offer, the investment bank carries the risk of price fluctuations after the primary market transaction. As with an IPO, this should increase investors' confidence. As an outside third party, the managing investment bank has examined the issuer and found the firm worth. The bank "puts its money where its mouth is" by giving a firm commitment price and underwriting the issue. This certification effect conveys information to the marketplace that the issue is fairly priced. The investment bank is staking its reputation and profits on the attractiveness of the issuer. Investment banking firms with the highest reputations (e.g., Goldman Sachs, Merrill Lynch, and Morgan Stanley) provide the strongest certification effects with respect to security sales. The certification effect provides a signal to the financial markets regarding the quality of the issuer.

88. Certified Check

A check guaranteed by a bank where funds are immediately withdrawn.

89. Certified Financial Planner (CFP)

A designation earned by individuals who have passed the examination sponsored by the Certified Financial Planner Board. Such individuals have studied banking, investment, insurance, estate planning, and tax planning to assist in managing client financial needs.

90. Change in Net Working Capital

Difference between net working capital from one period to another. For example, the change in net working capital in 2005 is the difference between the net working capital in 2005 and 2004. The change in net working capital is usually positive in growing firms.

91. Changes in Fixed Assets

Component of cash flow that equals sales of fixed assets minus the acquisition of fixed assets. For example, when US Composite sold its power systems subsidiary in 2005 it generated $25 in cash flow.

92. Chapter 11

Chapter 11 of the Federal Bankruptcy Reform Act of 1978 tries to allow for a planned restructuring of the corporation while providing for payments to the creditors. Chapter 11 proceedings begin when a petition is filed by the corporation or by three or more creditors. A federal judge either approves or disapproves the petition for protection under Chapter 11. During the petition period, the judge protects the managers and shareholders from the creditors and tries to negotiate a rescue plan between the shareholders and creditors. During this time, the corporation continues to do business.

Once in Chapter 11, the firm's management has 120 days to submit a reorganization plan, which usually includes debt rescheduling and the transfer of equity rights. Anyone has the right to submit such a plan, but only very rarely does anyone but management submit a reorganization plan. The plan must secure the agreement of two-thirds of the shareholders and two-thirds of each class of creditors; for example, senior creditors whose debt is secured and junior creditors whose debt is unsecured are considered separate classes.

After the plan is approved, the judge confirms it. At this point, any payments, property sales, or securities issues or transfers of equity positions take place under the supervision of the court.

Some critics argue that Chapter 11 is flawed and needs reform because it favors shareholders over creditors and junior creditors. They claim it is unfair that shareholders and junior creditors can vote to approve the reorganization plan as equals with the senior creditors.

Also, time works against creditors in Chapter 11. Upon approval of a reorganization plan by the court, interest payments to creditors stop and legal fees begin to erode the remaining value of the firm. Often, senior creditors settle for less than their full debts simply to save time. Shareholders, on the other hand, wish to draw out the reorganization period as long as possible hoping for a turnaround; they have little or nothing left to lose.

In general, this delay is bad for the company. If a firm's managers know they can default on debts and still keep their jobs, they may tend to abuse creditors. This could cause shareholders to require larger returns on their capital and creditors to be less willing to risk their funds.

Critics have presented two basic ideas for reforming Chapter 11: (1) increase the bureaucracy, and (2) allow the market to decide. The first proposes setting time deadlines after which independent arbitrators (more bureaucracy) decide a firm's fate. This would put bankruptcy more firmly in the hands of bureaucrats. The second reform proposal involves creating opportunities for creditors and owners to sell their positions to each other or third parties at prices determined competitively in the market. This market-based solution would encourage whoever ends up with equity control to make the firm as valuable as possible.

93. Chapter 7

Chapter 7 of the Bankruptcy Reform Act of 1978 covers the **liquidation** of a firm. [See also **Liquidation**]

94. Characteristic Line

The line relating the expected return on a security, $E(R_{it})$ to different returns on the market, $E(R_{mt})$. This is a straight line plotting in the dimension with X-axis as percent in return on market, Y-axis as percent return on security. The slope of characteristic line is the beta. [See also **Market model**]

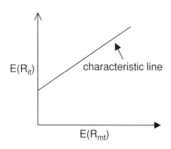

95. Charge-Off

The act of writing off a loan to its present value in recognition that the asset has decreased in value.

96. Charter

A legal document that authorizes a bank to conduct business.

97. Chartered Financial Analyst (CFA)

A designation earned by individuals who have passed a three-part examination sponsored by the Institute of Chartered Financial Analysts. Topics include economics, finance, security analysis, and financial accounting to assist in security analysis and portfolio management.

98. Chartists

Some investors, called chartists or **technicians**, examine graphs of past price movements, number of shares bought and sold, and other figures to try to predict future price movements. [See also **Technicians**]

99. Cheapest to Deliver

When a futures contract permits the seller to select the precise asset or commodity to deliver to the buyer, the cheapest to deliver is the asset that is most profitable for the shorter to deliver.

100. Check Kiting

The process of writing checks against uncollected deposits while checks are in the process of collection, thereby using funds (float) not actually available.

101. Chief Financial Officer (CFO)

In all but the smallest of firms, a top manager with the title chief financial officer (CFO) or vice president of finance usually reports to the president. Managers of two areas usually report to the CFO: the firm's **treasurer** and its **controller**. [See also **Treasurer** and **Controller**]

The CFO serves as the heir apparent for the CEO in many organizations.

102. Chinese Wall

The imaginary barrier that ensures a trust department will manage trust assets for the benefit of the trust beneficiaries, not for other departments in the bank.

103. Chooser Option

An option where the holder has the right to choose whether it is a call or a put at some point during its life. This prespecified date is normally called the choice date. The chooser options can either be a standard simple chooser option or complex chooser option. The former refers to both call and put specified with same price and maturity time. The latter refers to call price and maturity date different from those of put option.

104. Class of Options

A class of options refers to all call and put contracts on the same underlying asset. For example, all AT&T call and put options at various exercise prices and expiration months form one class. [See also **Option class**]

105. Classic Hedge Strategy

The implicit assumption of the classic hedge ratio equal to one is that the prices of the spot commodity (in this case, the stock portfolio) and the futures contract will remain perfectly correlated over the entire hedge period. Then if the stock market does turn down as expected, as losses in the portfolio due to price declines in its composite stocks will be exactly offset by the gain on the futures position. Conversely, if stock prices rise, the portfolio's gain will be offset by equal losses on the future position. Such a strategy implies that the objective of the classic hedge is risk minimization or elimination.

106. Clean Price of Bond

The quoted price of a bond. The cash price paid for the bond (or dirty price) is calculated by adding the accrued interest to the clean price.

107. Clearing

The exchanging of checks and balancing of accounts between banks.

108. Clearing Margin

A margin posted by a member of a clearinghouse.

109. Clearinghouse

The third party of every futures contract, which guarantees that every futures contract will be carried out even if one of the parties defaults. The clearinghouse also facilitates trading of futures contracts before they are due for delivery.

110. Clearinghouse Automated Payment System (CHAPS)

The Clearinghouse Automated Payment System (CHAPS) is a large-value, electronic credit transfer system that provides same-day funds transfers for British pound payments. Located in London, the clearing network is similar to Clearinghouse Interbank Payment System (CHIPS). The 14 CHAPS members operate the system and settle balances at the end of each day through the Bank of England. CHAPS offers transfer services to other banks and customers through its 14 members.

Transfers through CHAPS are considered final; they are guaranteed, irrevocable, and unconditional. Remember, however, that this is a private system, and thus the transfers are guaranteed by the members and not by the Bank of England.

111. Clearinghouse Association

A voluntary association of banks formed to assist the daily exchange of checks among member institutions.

112. Clearinghouse Interbank Payment System (CHIPS)

The Clearinghouse Interbank Payment System (CHIPS) is a private payment-clearing system located in New York City and operated by the New York Clearinghouse Association. The network specialized in international payments denominated in US dollars. It is estimated that CHIPS transfers 90 percent of all international, interbank dollar transactions.

CHIPS tabulates transaction data for all member banks at the end of each day. The system also permits members to review payments online, that is, those in storage awaiting approval. This gives member banks better information about available funds on which to base their credit decisions. A bank officer may be more willing to grant credit knowing that CHIPS will credit a certain account later in the day.

Although the system is highly technical, CHIPS' membership, operating procedures, and efficiency have important economic implications. For one, the role of the US dollar as a world transaction currency is influenced by the relative operating efficiency and safety of its payment mechanism. Further, depending upon CHIPS' handling of failures to settle accounts, such an occurrence can be either an isolated event, or the first link in a chain reaction leading to a worldwide liquidity crisis. Last, but not least, the specific roles of individual banks in the dollar clearing system have important implications for worldwide correspondent banking relationships and, therefore, market share and profits.

113. Clientele Effect

Both federal and state governments tax dividend income at ordinary income tax rates. Any differences between capital gains and income tax rates will lead some investors to prefer one or the other for tax reasons. Another influence on dividend policy will be the composition of the firm's shareholders, commonly called its *clientele*.

Miller and Modigliani introduced the clientele effect as an imperfection of the market that affects dividend policy. M&M observed that each corporation tends to attract a specific type of clientele that favors the firm's established payout ratio. For example, investors in higher tax brackets tend to hold stocks with lower dividend payouts and higher capital gains yields. This way, they can avoid personal taxes on dividend income. On the other hand, retirees, because of their lower tax brackets, tend to invest in companies with larger yields.

Because a firm tends to attract a certain type of investor, management may be reluctant to change its dividend policy. If shareholders have to change their portfolios due to changes in payout ratios, this shift may cause shareholders to incur unwanted transaction costs. In this way, the tax differential favoring capital gains is a systematic imperfection of the market that produces a clientele effect.

114. Closed-End (mutual) Fund

A fund whose shares are traded through brokers at market prices; the fund will not redeem shares at their net asset value. The market price of the fund can differ from the net asset value. For example, a country fund such as Korean fund is a closed-end fund. In addition, REIT is also a closed end fund. [See also **REIT**]

115. CMO

[See **Collateralized mortgage obligation**]

116. Coefficient of Determination

[See **R-squared (R^2)**]

117. Coefficient of Variation

One problem with using the standard deviation as a measure of risk is that we cannot get an intuitive feel for risk by looking at the standard deviation alone. Firm A's profits may have a higher standard deviation than firm B, but because firm A's mean return is much higher, firm A actually may have lower risk. The coefficient of variation allows us to make comparisons because it controls for the size of the average. The coefficient of variation (CV) measures risk-per-unit of return. The coefficient of variation is computed as the standard deviation divided by the mean as:

$$CV = \sigma/\overline{X}.$$

118. Collar

Use of options to place a cap and floor on a firm's borrowing costs. One way to do this is to sell a floor and use the premiums on the floor to pay the premium on the purchase of the cap. [See also **Interest rate collar**]

119. Collar Width

The difference between the strike prices of the two options in a collar.

120. Collateral

One way in which a bank can limit its exposure to risk is by requiring the borrower to pledge some valuable assets as collateral, that is, security for the loan. For example, a company that owns buildings, locomotives, large generating plants, or other major pieces of equipment may pledge these high-value items as security.

121. Collateral Trust Bond

A bond secured by a pledge of common stock held by the corporation.

122. Collateralized Bonds

Collateralized bonds pledge securities to protect bondholders against loss in case of default. An example of collateralized bonds are collateralized mortgage obligations (CMOs) sold by firms and agencies involved in the housing market; the CMO is backed by a pool of mortgages. Other examples of collateralized bonds include bonds backed by credit card receivables and bonds backed by car loans. The issuer pays interest and principal on such a collateralized bond over time as homeowners, credit card users, and car buyers pay off their own loans.

123. Collateralized Debt Obligation

A way of packaging credit risk. Several classes of securities are created from a portfolio of bonds and there are rules for determining how defaults are allocated to classes.

124. Collateralized Mortgage Obligation (CMO)

A security backed by a pool of mortgage that is structured to fall within an estimated maturity range (tranche), based on the timing of allocated interest and principal payments on the underlying mortgages. A CMO services a way to mitigate or reduce prepayment risk of a real estate loan. [See also **Option-adjusted spread (OAS)**]

125. Collected Balances

Ledger balances minus float. [See also **Float**]

126. Collection Float

An increase in book cash with no immediate change in bank cash, generated by checks deposited by the firm that have not cleared [See **Float**]

127. Collection Policy

Procedures and policy followed by a firm in attempting to collect accounts receivable. It is one of the components of credit policy.

128. Collect-on-Delivery Option

An option where the premium is paid only when the option is exercised.

129. Combination

A position involving both calls and puts on the same underlying asset.

130. Combined Leverage

Operating leverage and financial leverage combine to magnify a given percentage change in sales to a potentially much greater percentage change in earnings. Together, operating and financial leverage produce an effect called combined leverage. [See also **Degree of combined leverage**]

131. Commercial Draft

A commercial draft resembles a promissory note, but it works somewhat differently. First, the seller draws a draft ordering payment by the customer and sends this draft to the customer's bank along with any shipping documents. This commercial draft is called a *sight draft* if immediate payment is required; otherwise, it is a *time draft*, on which the customer's signature and the word *accepted* must be added. In either case, the advantage of this trade-credit instrument is that the seller obtains the buyer's formal commitment to pay before goods are delivered. This commitment is the money that the seller receives ahead of time, or the trade acceptance the buyer signs, which the bank then returns to the seller. In sum, commercial draft is a demand for payment.

132. Commercial Loan Theory

A theory suggesting that banks make only short-term, self-liquidating loans that match the maturity of bank deposits.

133. Commercial Paper

Large companies have a very attractive source of short-term funds open to them: they can sell commercial paper, unsecured promissory notes that trade in the organized money market through a number of recognized dealers. The buyers of the paper are primarily commercial banks looking for safe investments that yield higher returns than US Treasury securities. Other buyers include corporations, pension funds, insurance companies, and others that have temporary surplus funds they wish to put to work safely.

Commercial paper is sold in two ways: (1) the issuer may sell the paper directly to the buyer, or

(2) the issuer may sell the paper through a dealer firm. Firms prefer to sell directly to save the dealer's fee of approximately one-eighth of a percentage point (12.5 basis points). One hundred basis points equal 1 percent. Commercial paper is sold on a discount basis. Almost half of commercial paper is issued directly, with most of the direct paper being issued by finance companies. Approximately 75 percent of all paper (both direct and dealer issues) comes from financial companies, including commercial, savings, and mortgage banking firms, finance leasing, insurance underwriting, and other investment activities. The balance of outstanding paper is issued by nonfinancial firms, such as utilities and industrial manufacturers. This paper ordinarily is issued by a dealer.

Beside its relative low cost, commercial paper offers three advantages. First, selling the notes is a fairly simple and informal process, certainly simpler than negotiating a bank loan. While it is not as easy as using trade credit, commercial paper is the simplest of all forms of negotiated credit. Second, the ability to sell unsecured promissory notes gives the issuer a degree of prestige. This, in turn, makes it even easier to sell later issues as the company builds a name for itself in the money market. Third, a commercial paper issue may exceed the legal lending limit of most commercial banks, eliminating the need to combine banks to assemble a financing package.

At first sight, commercial paper may seem to be the obvious choice because of its lower cost, but reliance on commercial paper may be a high-risk policy. A company that finances all of its short-term needs through the sale of notes does not build up a good borrowing relationship with a bank. If economic conditions change and the money market becomes tight, such a company may well find itself in difficulties. The banks will give priority to their regular customers; they may not even have enough loanable funds to meet all the needs of their regular borrowers. The company that has relied on the money market when money was easy will have to continue to rely on it when funds are scarce, and the differential between the interest rates of the two sources is likely to shrink dramatically in such circumstances.

In sum, Commercial paper is a short-term, unsecured promissory note issued by corporations with a high credit standing. Their maturity ranges up to 270 days.

134. Commission Broker

A broker on the floor of the exchange who executes orders for other members.

135. Commitment

A legally binding obligation (subject usually both to conditions precedent and to continuing conditions) to make available loans or other financial accommodation for a specified period; this includes revolving facilities. Even during publicly known credit distress, a commitment can be legally binding if drawn down before it is formally withdrawn for cause.

136. Commitment Fee

Fee charged for making a line of credit available to a borrower.

137. Committed Line of Credit

With the committed line of credit, the borrower pays an up-front fee which then obliges the bank to lend the firm money under the terms of the line of credit. [See also **Revolving credit agreement**]

138. Commodity Futures Trading Commission

A body that regulates trading in futures contracts in the US.

139. Commodity Spread

Offsetting long and short positions in closely related commodities. [See also **Crack spread** and **Crush spread**]

140. Commodity Swap

A swap where cash flows depend on the price of a commodity.

141. Commodity-Indexed Bonds

Several firms have issued commodity-indexed bonds with exposure to prices of commodities such as oil, gold, or silver. In a way, this technique closely resembles the tactic by which a US firm hedges its overseas risk by issuing bonds denominated in a foreign currency. An oil-drilling firm's cash flows are sensitive to the price of oil, as are the cash flows of gold-mining or silver-mining firms to the prices of those commodities. By making coupon interest and/or principal amounts vary along with the commodity price; these firms can reduce their risk of bankruptcy. Falling commodity prices reduce such a firm's cash flows, so its debt service requirements decline, as well.

142. Common Stock

Equity claims held by the "residual owners" of the firm, who are the last to receive any distribution of earnings or assets. It is usually applied to stock that has no special preference either in dividends or in bankruptcy. Owners of common stock in a corporation are referred to as shareholders or stockholders. They receive stock certificates for the shares they own. Owners of common stock are responsible for the election of the Board of Directors, appointment of Senior Officers, the selection of an auditor for the corporate financial statements, dividend policy and other matters of corporate governance.

143. Common Stock Equivalents

Because of the possible dilution in earnings per share (EPS) represented by securities that have the potential to become new shares of common stock, the EPS calculation must account for common stock equivalents (CSEs). CSEs are securities that are not common stock but are equivalent to common stock because they are likely to be converted into common stock in the future. Convertible debt, convertible preferred stock, stock rights, stock options, and stock warrants all are securities that can create new common shares and thus dilute (or reduce) the firm's earnings per share.

144. Common-Base-Year Financial Statements

To see how the ledger items change over item, we can choose a base year balance sheet or income statement and then express each item relative to the base year. Such statements are referred to as common-base-year statements.

145. Common-Size Financial Statements

Common-size financial statements include common-size balance sheets and common-size income statements. A common-size balance sheet expresses all balance sheet accounts as percentages of total assets. A common-size income statement expresses all income statement items as percentages of gross sales.

Common-size statements give an analyst insight into the structure of a firm's financial statements at a particular point in time or during a particular period. They also indicate the percentage of sales consumed by production costs or interest expenses, the proportion of assets that are liquid, or the proportion of liabilities that are short-term obligations.

146. Comparative Static Analysis for Option Pricing Model

It is a sensitive analysis of option pricing model by taking partial derivative with respect to current stock price per share, exercise price and contract period, standard deviation of rates of return, and risk-free rate. [See also **Delta, Theta, Vega, Rho, Gamma,** and **Greeks**]

147. Comparison Universe

The collection of money managers of similar investment style used for assessing relative performance of a portfolio manager.

148. Compensating Balances

A company's cash needs fall into three categories: (1) cash for day-to-day transactions, (2) reserve cash to meet contingencies, and (3) cash for compensating balance requirements. A compensating balance exists when a firm must keep minimum cash balance in a noninterest bearing account at a bank as a condition or a loan or bank service agreement. To determine the appropriate minimum cash balance, a financial manager simply adds together the three segments just estimated. If the cash budget projects a balance significantly higher than the minimum balance, the organization can invest the excess cash in marketable securities. On the other hand, if the cash balance falls below the desired level, the organization can plan to sell marketable securities or to borrow short-term funds. To complete the transition from a cash flow budget to a cash flow plan, the manager must adjust the cash balance to meet the minimum cash balance.

In other words, compensating balance is a deposit that the firm keeps with the bank in a low-interest or non-interest-bearing account to compensate banks for bank loans or service.

149. Competitive Bidding Issue

A competitive bidding issue occurs when a firm announces the size and terms of a proposed security sale and then solicits bids from investment banks to underwrite the issue. Once it accepts a bid, the firm proceeds with the sale just as for a firm commitment underwriting. The competition among banks may reduce the costs of floating the issue. Competitive bid underwriting involves no positive certification effect, as a bank must commit to a price before it can adequately perform its due diligence review and investigate the issuer. Unfortunately, few firms other than US utility companies and French public companies sell seasoned equity by competitive bidding (both of these classes of firms are required by law to seek bids to float security issues).

150. Competitive Offer

Method of selecting an investment banker for a new issue by offering the securities to the underwriter bidding highest. In a competitive bid process, the issuer, usually with the assistance of a financial advisor, structures the bond issue and publishes a notice of sale requesting bids from underwriters. After the bids are received, the bonds are awarded to the underwriting syndicate that submitted the best bid (i.e., the lowest true interest cost to the issuer).

151. Complete Portfolio

The entire portfolio, including risky and risk-free assets.

152. Complex Capital Structure

A corporation that has warrants, convertibles, or options outstanding is said to have a complex capital structure. The complexity comes from the difficulty of measuring the number of shares outstanding. This is a function of a known amount of common shares currently outstanding plus an estimate of the number of shares that may be issued to satisfy the holders of warrants, convertibles, and options should they decide to exercise their rights and receive new common shares.

153. Component Analysis

It is one of the two major approaches to time-series analysis. Component analysis regards the time series as being composed of several influences or components that are generally taken to be trend-cycle, seasonal, and random movement. The seasonal and trend movements are modeled in a deterministic manner. This kind of analysis is easier than the sample-function analysis. [See also **Sample-function analysis**]

154. Composite-Based Beta Forecasting

Lee, Newbold, Chu (1986) proposed composite-based beta forecasting method. The composite-based beta forecasting is the weighted average of the accounting based and market-based beta forecasting. [See also **Accounting-based** and **Market-based beta forecasting**]

155. Composition

Composition is a way a firm can adjust its capital sources. This method involves recomposing the debt of the firm in such a way that the creditors receive partial payment for their claims, say, 60 cents for each dollar. Creditors may find it more expedient to follow this route than to take the troubled firm to court to seek full satisfaction. In court, they would run the risk of receiving less than they would through composition. Moreover, court appearances require various legal costs, which may more than offset the possible gains achieved by going to court.

In sum, composition is a voluntary arrangement to restructure a firm's debt, under which payment is reduced.

156. Compound Interest

Interest that is earned both on the initial principal and on interest earned on the initial principal in previous periods. The interest earned in one period becomes in effect part of the principal in a following period. The longer-lasting the loan, the more important interest on interest becomes.

Future Value of an Investment: $FV = C_0(1 + r)^T$,

where C_0 is the cash to be invested at date 0; r is the interest rate; and T is the number of periods over which the cash is invested.

157. Compound Option

An option that has an option on the underlying asset. There are four main types of compound options: a call on a call, a call on a put, a put on a call and a put on a put. Compound options have two strike prices and two exercise dates.

158. Compound Value

Value of a sum after investing it over one or more periods. Also called future value. [See also **Future value**]

159. Compounding

Compounding involves finding the future value of money invested today. In other words, compounding allows us to determine how money will grow over time. The future value of a cash flow (PV) invested today (PV_0) for n periods at r percent interest per period is given as:

$$FV_n = PV_0(1 + r)^n.$$

Compounding can either be discrete or continuous. [See also **Continuous compounding**]

160. Compounding Frequency

This defines how an interest rate is measured. Frequency can be daily, weekly, monthly, quarterly, annually, or continuously. [See also **Continuous compounding**]

161. Compounding Swap

This kind of option is a variation on the plain vanilla swap. Swap where interest compounds instead of being paid. In other words, the interest is compounded forward until the end of the life of the swap.

162. Concave Function

A concave function is one shaped like the cross section of an upside-down bowl. For example, a function used to describe the relationship between yield to maturity and years to maturity is generally a concave function. This is because the yield to maturity for a long term bond is higher than that of a short-term bond.

163. Concentration Banking

One way to speed up the collection of payments from customers is through concentration banking. In such a system, customers in a particular location make their payments to a local branch office rather than to company headquarters. The branch office then deposits the checks into a local bank account. The firm can then transfer surplus funds periodically to one of the firm's principal banks, called *concentration banks*.

This system reduces mail, processing, and collection float. However, concentration banking involves some additional costs, such as higher administrative costs, compensating balances required by the local bank for its services, and the cost associated with transferring the funds from the local bank to the concentration bank.

In sum, concentration banking is the use of geographically dispersed collection centers to speed up the collection of accounts receivable.

164. Concentration Risk

Portfolio risk resulting from increased exposure to one obligor or groups of correlated (e.g., by industry or location) obligors.

165. Conditional Sales Contract

An arrangement whereby the firm retains legal ownership of the goods until the customer has completed payment. A firm uses it as a credit instrument. Conditional sales contracts usually are paid off in installments and have interest costs built into them.

166. Conditional Value at Risk (C-VaR)

Expected loss during N days conditional on being the (100-X) percent tail of the distribution of profits/losses. The variable N is the time horizon, and X percent is the confidence level.

167. Confidence Index

The confidence index is designed to measure how willing investors are to take a chance in the market. It is the ratio of high-grade bond yields to low-grade bond yields. This ratio is started below one. When bond investors grow more confident about the economy, they shift their holdings from high-grade to lower-grade bonds, lowering their yield relative to high-grade bonds and increasing the confidence index. In other words, the confidence ratio moves close to one.

Confidence-index technicians believe that the confidence index leads the stock market by two to eleven months. An upturn in the confidence index is supposed to foretell of rising optimism and rising prices in the stock market. A fall in the confidence index represents the fact that low-grade bond yields are rising faster or falling more slowly than high-grade yields. This is supposed to reflect increasing risk aversion by institutional money managers who foresee an economic downturn and rising bankruptcies and defaults. Analysts who have examined the confidence index conclude that it conveys some information for security analysis.

168. Confirmation

Contract confirming verbal agreement between two parties to trade in the over-the-counter market.

169. Conflict between Bondholders and Stockholders

These two groups may have interest in the corporation that conflict. Sources of conflict include dividends, dilution, distortion of investment, and underinvestment. Protective covenants work to resolve these conflicts. Stockholders and bondholders have different objective functions, and this can lead to agency problems, where stockholders can expropriate wealth from bondholders.

Because the firm is interested in trying to maximize stockholders wealth, there can develop a conflict of interest between stockholders and bondholders. For instance, stockholders have an incentive to take riskier projects than bondholders do and to pay more out in dividends than bondholders would like them to. This conflict can lead to costly decisions by the firm, which lowers the total value of the firm.

170. Conglomerate Acquisition

Acquisition in which the acquired firm and the acquiring firm are not related, unlike a horizontal or a vertical acquisition. For example, the acquisition of a food-products firm by a computer firm would be considered a conglomerate acquisition.

171. Conglomerate Combination

A conglomerate combination is a type of business combination that may involve firms that have little, if any, product market similarities. A firm that is called a *conglomerate*, however, generally is one that has engaged in several conglomerate combinations.

172. Conservator

An individual or trust department appointed by a court to manage the property of an incapacitated individual.

173. Consol

Consols are bonds that never stop paying a coupon, have no final maturity date, and therefore never mature. Thus, a consol is perpetuity. British bonds are called consols. [See also **Perpetuity**]

174. Consolidated Balance Sheet

A balance sheet showing the aggregate financial condition of a firm and its subsidiaries, netting out all intracompany transactions.

175. Consolidation

Assuming there are originally two firms, Firm A and Firm B. One possible business combination results in the formation of a new firm, Firm C, which has the assets of both Firm A and Firm B. This is called a consolidation.

176. Constant Dividend Growth Model

[See **Gordon model**]

177. Constant Elasticity Variance Model (CEV)

This model allows the variance term to follow a diffusion process in which its elasticity is always constant. It will allow the variance of the rate of return to vary inversely with stock price. In Schroder (1989) shows that this kind of call option model can be defined as

$$
\begin{aligned}
C = \ & (\text{current stock price per share}) \\
& \times (\text{first cumulative} \\
& \text{density function of noncentral } \chi^2) \\
& - (\text{present value of exercise price}) \times \\
& (\text{second cumulative density function} \\
& \text{of noncentral } \chi^2).
\end{aligned}
$$

This kind of option pricing model can be reduced to Black-Scholes option pricing model. [See also **Black-Scholes formula**]

178. Constant Growth Model

A form of the dividend discount model that assumes dividends will grow at a constant rate. [See also **Gordon model**]

179. Constant Maturity Swap (CM Swap)

A swap where a swap rate is exchanged for either a fixed rate or a floating rate on each payment date. For example, an agreement to exchange 6-month LIBOR rate for the 10-year swap rate every six months for next 6 years.

180. Constant Maturity Treasury Swap (CMT Swap)

A swap where yield on a Treasury bond is exchanged for either a fixed rate or a floating rate on each payment date. For example, agreement to exchange a LIBOR rate for Treasury rate (e.g., the 10-year treasury rate).

181. Constructive Sale

A term in tax law describing the owner of an asset entering into an offsetting position that largely eliminates the risk of holding the asset.

182. Consumer Bank

A bank that does not make commercial loans.

183. Consumer Credit

Credit granted to consumers. Trade credit is credit granted to other firms.

184. Consumption Asset

An asset held for consumption rather than investment.

185. Contingent Claim

Claim whose value is directly dependent on, or is contingent on, the value of its underlying assets. For example, the debt and equity securities issued by a firm derive their value from the total value of the firm. When the value of the firm exceeds the amount promised to the debtholders, the shareholders obtain the residual of the firm's value over the amount promised the shareholders, and the debtholders obtain the amount promised. When the value of the firm is less than the amount promised the debtholders, the shareholders receive nothing and the debtholders get the value of the firm.

186. Contingent Immunization

A mixed passive-active investment strategy that immunizes a portfolio if necessary to guarantee a minimum acceptable return but otherwise allows active management.

187. Contingent Liabilities

Items, such as guarantees or related contracts, that may become liabilities if certain developments arise.

188. Contingent Pension Liability

Under Employees Retirement Income Security Act (ERISA), the firm is liable to the plan participants for up to 30 percent of the net worth of the firm.

189. Continuous Compounding

An extreme example of frequent compounding is continuous compounding. Continuous compounding has many financial applications. These range from determining future values on bank accounts that advertise continuous compounding to topics such as the Black-Scholes option pricing model used by most option traders.

We know that $FV_n = PV_0(1 + \frac{r}{m})^{mn}$, that is, the future value (FV) of an investment today is equal to the amount invested multiplied by a future value interest factor that reflects compounded interest. Note that r is the interest rate per period; and m is the number of compounding periods each year, and n is the number of years in the investment horizon.

The future value interest factor $[(1 + r/m)^{mn}]$ rises at a decreasing rate and asymptotically approaches the continuous compounding FVIF of e^{rn}. The FVIF rises as m increases, as the effect of more frequent compounding is to raise the effective annual rate (EAR). Higher EARs result in larger future values.

In sum, continuous compounding implies that interest compounded continuously, every instant, rather than fixed intervals.

190. Continuous Discounting

The present value of interest factor (PVIF) = $[1/(1 + r/m)^{mn}]$ decreases at a decreasing rate and asymptotically approaches the continuous compounding FVIF of e^{-rn}. The PVIF falls as m increases, as the effect of more frequent compounding is to raise EAR. Higher discount rates result in lower present values. [Notation definitions see **Continuous compounding**]

191. Continuously Compounded Interest Rate

A way of quoting an interest rate such that if $1 is invested at a continuously compounded rate of r, the payoff in one year is e^r.

192. Contract Amount

The number of units of the good or service to be delivered.

193. Contract Interest Rate

[See **Annual percentage rate**]

194. Contract Month

The month in which a futures contract is scheduled to mature by making or accepting a delivery.

195. Contract Specification

The precise definition of the good or service to be delivered in the futures contract.

196. Contracting Costs

[See **Transaction costs**]

197. Contribution Margin

Amount that each additional unit produced, such as a jet engine, contributes to after-tax profit of the whole project: (Sales price − Variable cost) × $(1 − T_c)$, where T_c is the corporate tax rate.

198. Control Variate Method

A technique used in Monte Carlo valuation in which simulated asset prices are used to compute two derivatives prices: the price of the derivative that is being valued, and the price of a related derivative for which the value is known. The error in valuing the derivative with a known price is used as a control for that with the unknown price.

199. Controller

The firm's controller traditionally manages accounting, cost analysis, and tax planning and usually reports to the chief financial officer (CFO).

200. Convenience Yield

A measure of the benefits from ownership of an asset that are not obtained by the holder of a long futures contract on the asset.

201. Conventional Mortgage

A mortgage or deed or trust that is not obtained under a government insured program.

202. Convergence Property

The convergence of futures prices and spot prices at the maturity of the futures contract.

203. Conversion

A risk-free position consisting of an asset, a purchased put, and a written call. For example, we can create a risk-free position by buying a stock and a put of the stock and sell the call of the stock to create a Treasury bill.

204. Conversion Factor

A factor used to determine the number of bonds that must be delivered in the Chicago Board of Trade bond futures contract. For example, the Treasury bond futures contract allows a party with the short position to choose to deliver any bond that has a maturity of more than 15 years and that is not callable within 15 years. When a particular bond is delivered, a parameter known as its *conversion factor* defines the price received by the party with the short position.

205. Conversion Fee

Fee charged for converting a loan commitment to a term loan.

206. Conversion Premium

Difference between the conversion price and the current stock price divided by the current stock price. [See also **Conversion price**]

207. Conversion Price

The conversion price, in general, equals

$$\text{Conversion price} = \frac{\text{Par value of bond}}{\text{Conversion ratio}}.$$

It implies that the amount of par value exchangeable for one share of common stock.

208. Conversion Ratio

The number of shares per $1,000 bond (or debenture) that a bondholder would receive if the bond were converted into shares of stock. [See also **Convertible bonds**]

209. Conversion Value

What a convertible bond would be worth if it were immediately converted into the common stock at the current price. [See also **Convertible bonds**]

210. Convertible Bonds

Convertible bonds may vary the amount of money the bondholder ultimately receives. A convertible bond can be converted, as the investor's option, into a specified number of shares of the issuer's common stock (defined as the bond's **conversion ratio**). The conversion ratio is set to make conversion unattractive initially. If the firm meets with success, however, its stock price will rise, and the bond's price will be affected by its **conversion value** (the stock price times the conversion ratio) rather than just its value as a straight bond.

211. Convertible Debt

A bond that may be exchanged for common stock in the same firm. [See also **Common stock**]

212. Convertible Risk

The variability of return caused when one type of security is converted into another type of security. If a bond or a preferred stock is convertible into a stated number of shares of common stock of the corporation issuing the original security, the rate of return of the investment may vary because the value of the underlying common stock has increased or decreased. A convertible security normally has a lower coupon rate, or stated dividend (in the case of preferred stocks), because investors are willing to accept a lower contractual return from the company in order to be able to share in any rise in the price of the firm's common stock.

213. Convertible Securities

A convertible security is a bond or preferred stock issue that typically gives its holder the right to exchange it for a stipulated number of shares of common stock of the issuing corporation during a specified period of time. Therefore, convertible bonds and convertible preferred stock represent options to the security holder. If the price of common stock rises sufficiently, holders of these secur-

ities will find it profitable to exercise their conversion rights. As for a warrant, such a right will have some positive value in the market, so the market will accept a lower coupon rate on the corporation's convertible bonds than it would demand for a bond with no conversion privilege.

Convertible bonds are especially attractive when management prefers to raise capital by issuing equity rather than debt, but believes that transient influences have led the market to temporarily undervalue its common stock. [See also **Convertible bonds**] If this perception is correct, the stock price will rise and, as a result, debt will be converted to equity. A convertible bond issue may offer an advantage over a bond issue with warrants since mangers can predict how much capital the issue will raise.

The exercise of a warrant raises further capital for the firm; conversion simply substitutes equity for debt. The conversion of a bond issue for common stock does not raise new capital, but it does implicitly increase cash flow if the conversion occurs prior to the bond's maturity date, by reducing future coupon payments.

A further distinction between warrants and convertible bonds is that warrants are not callable, while the issuer generally can call a convertible bond. The bondholder can be offered the option of converting it within a short time period or surrendering it at a specific cash price. As with all callable bonds, investors demand higher returns for callable, convertible securities. Firms are willing to pay this higher price in exchange for management flexibility.

We have seen why a corporation might want to issue a hybrid security rather than straight debt and/or equity. What about the investor? These securities may be particularly attractive when investors have trouble assessing the riskiness of a corporation's future business activities. If the corporation embarks on a high-risk enterprise, holders of straight bonds will be in the unappealing position of gaining nothing if the enterprise succeeds and facing greatly increased default risk if it fails.

Warrants or conversion privileges can restore some balance. By exercising a warrant or converting a bond to stock, the bondholder can share in any success resulting from a risky venture. This reduces the importance of assessing the future business risk of a corporation's activities.

214. Convex

Convex shaped like the cross section of a bowl. Convex with shapes such that of price-yield relationship are said to be convex and curvature of the price yield curve is called the convexity of the bond.

215. Convexity

The second derivative of a bond's price with respect to a change in the interest rate, divided by the bond price. In other words, it refers to the degree of curvature of the price-yield curve around some interest level. [See also **Convex**]

216. Convexity Adjustment

There are two possible meanings for this term: (1) it refers to the adjustment necessary to convert a futures interest rate to a forward interest rate. The difference between the expected bond yield and the forward bond yield is known as convexity adjustment. (2) it can also refer to the adjustment to a forward rate that is sometimes necessary when Black's model is used. [See also **Black's model**]

217. Copula Function

A copula function is simply a specification of how the univariate marginal distributions combine to form a multivariate distribution. For example, if we have N-correlated uniform random variables, $U_1, U_2, \ldots, U_N$, then

$$C(u_1, u_2, \ldots, u_N) = \Pr\{U_1 < u_1,\ U_2 < u_2, \ldots, U_N < u_N\}$$

is the joint distribution function that gives the probability that all of the uniforms are in the specified range.

In a similar manner, we can define the Copula function for the default times of N assets

$$C(F_1(T_1), F_2(T_2), \ldots, F_N(T_N)) =$$
$$\Pr\{U_1 < F_1(T_1), U_2 < F_2(T_2), \ldots, U_N < F_N(T_N)\},$$

where $F_i(T_i) = \Pr\{t_i < t\}$.

Li (2000) has shown that how copula function can be used to estimate default correlation. [See also **Default correlation**]

218. Core Capital

Tier 1 capital consisting primarily of stockholder's equity.

219. Core Deposits

A base level of deposits a bank expects to remain on deposit, regardless of the economic environment.

220. Corporate Bonds

Long-term debt issued by private corporations typically paying semiannual coupons and returning the face value of the bond at maturity.

221. Corporate Leverage

Corporate leverage is used to refer to the debt floated by the corporation.

222. Corporations

Proprietorships are the most numerous form of business organization, but in terms of market value, corporations are the dominant form. A corporation is a legal person in the eyes of the law, separate in concept from its owners and managers. As a person, it has rights, duties, privileges, and obligations.

The corporate organizational form has several advantages. As a separate legal entity, its life does not depend on that of its owners. Unlike a proprietorship or partnership, the death of a shareholder does not force the corporation to stop doing business. Shares of ownership in the corporation, especially those listed on stock exchanges such as the New York Stock Exchange, can be traded at easily discernible prices. Issuing shares gives a corporation access to much larger pools of capital than a partnership or proprietorship. As a legal entity, it can borrow money in its own name. Also, as owners of a corporation have limited liability, the most they can lose is their investment.

A major disadvantage of the corporate organizational form is the taxation of earnings. Depending upon the income level, corporate income may be taxed at higher rates than proprietor or partnership income. In addition, corporate dividends are taxed twice. As corporations pay dividends from after-tax earnings, they represent funds that have been taxed once at the corporate level. Investors then pay taxes on these dividends again, as part of their personal income.

Two special forms of corporate organization in the US allow dividends to escape double taxation. [See also **Subchapter S corporation** and **Limited liability company**]

Many countries' laws recognize the corporate form of organization. US corporations may use the suffixes "Inc." or "Corp." to designate themselves. British corporations use the suffix "PLC," for *public limited company*, in which *limited* refers to shareholders' liability in the firm. The suffix "AG" following the same names of firms in Germany, Austria, Switzerland, or Liechtenstein is an abbreviation for *Aktiengesellschaft*, which means *corporation*. Some countries allow corporations to sell bearer shares, which allow the owners to remain anonymous. A history of social upheavals, wars, and high taxation in Europe led to the evolution of bearer shares to allow owners to remain anonymous and thus escape taxation from their governments or identification if their governments were overthrown. Suffixes of "NV" (*Naamioze Venootschap*) in the Netherlands and "SA" (*Societe Anonyme*) in France and Belgium designate such firms.

In sum, a corporation is one type of business organization that is created as a distinct "legal person" composed of one or more actual individuals or legal entities, primary advantages of a corporation include limited liability, ease of ownership, transfer, and perpetual succession.

223. Correlation

Correlation is a statistical concept that relates movements in one set of variables to movements in another. **Covariance** can indicate a positive, zero, or negative relationship between two variables, but little else. [See also **Covariance**] Correlation, however, shows the *strength* of the linear relationship between two sets of variables. The correlation coefficient between two set of numbers, denoted by the small Greek letter rho (ρ), is computed as:

$$\rho_{12} = \frac{\text{cov}(R_1, R_2)}{\sigma_1 \sigma_2},$$

where σ_1 and σ_2 are the standard deviations of the two number series. Mathematically, the correlation will always lie between -1.0 and $+1.0$, inclusively. As correlation approaches $+1.0$, it indicates a stronger *positive* linear relationship between the two series of numbers. As the correlation approaches -1.0, it indicates a stronger *negative* linear relationship between the two series. The greatest reduction in risk occurs when two strongly negatively correlated assets are placed in the same portfolio. Correlations close to zero represent weak linear relationship; a correlation of zero implies that no linear relationship exists.

224. Correlation Coefficient

A statistic in which the covariance is scaled to a value between minus one (perfect negative correlation) and plus one (perfect positive correlation). [See also **Correlation**]

225. Correspondent Bank

A bank that provides services, typically check clearing, to other banks.

226. Cost of Carry

The interest cost of owning an asset, less lease or dividend payments received as a result of ownership; the net cash flow resulting from borrowing to buy an asset.

227. Cost of Common Equity

Unlike debt and preferred stock, cash flows from common equity are not fixed or known beforehand, and their risk is harder to evaluate. In addition, firms have *two* sources of common equity – retained earnings and new stock issues – and thus *two* costs of common equity. It may be clear that there is an explicit cost (i.e., dividends and flotation costs) associated with issuing new common equity. But while the firm pays no extra dividends or flotation costs to use retained earnings, their use is not free; we must consider the opportunity cost of using money that could have been distributed to shareholders.

Retained earnings represent the portion of net income that the firm does not distribute as dividends. From the shareholders' perspective, the opportunity cost of retained earnings is the return the shareholders could earn by investing the funds in assets whose risk is similar to that of the firm. To maximize shareholder wealth, management must recognize that retained earnings have a cost. That cost, k_{re}, is the return that shareholders expect from their investment in the firm.

228. Cost of Debt

The firm's unadjusted cost of debt financing equals the yield to maturity (YTM) on new debt, either a long-term bank loan or a bond issue. The yield to maturity represents the effective annual rate or cost to the firm of borrowing funds in the current market environment. Coupon rates from previously issued bonds reveal little about the firm's present financing costs. The firm's *current* financing costs determine its current cost of capital.

A firm can determine its cost of debt by several methods. If the firm targets an "A" rating (or any other bond rating), a review of the yields to maturity on A-rated bonds can provide an estimate of the firm's current unadjusted borrowing costs. Several additional factors will affect the firm's specific borrowing costs, including convenants and features of the proposed bond issue as well as the number of years until the bond or loan matures or comes due. It is important to examine bonds whose ratings and characteristics resemble those the firm wants to match.

In addition, the firm can solicit the advice of investment bankers on the cost of issuing new debt. Or, if the firm has debt currently trading, it can use public market prices and yields to estimate its current cost of debt. The publicly traded bond's yield to maturity can be found using the techniques for determining the return on an investment. Finally, a firm can seek long-term debt financing from a bank or a consortium of banks. Preliminary discussions with the bankers will indicate a ball-park interest rate the firm can expect to pay on the amount it borrows. [For calculation of YTM see **Yield to maturity**]

229. Cost of Equity Capital

The required return on the company's common stock in capital markets. It is also called the equity holders' required rate of return because it is what equity holders can expect to obtain in the capital market. It is a cost from the firm's perspective. [See also **Cost of common equity**]

230. Cotango

An increment added to a futures price to cover the carrying costs until delivery occurs at the schedule settlement date (also called Forwardation). Therefore, the futures price must exceed the expected future spot price.

231. Counterparties

The buyer and seller of a derivative such as swap are counterparties. Usually, not always, a financial institution serves as an intermediary between the counterparties. When bank and the company agree on an at-the-money forward exchange contract or swap, the company is at risk if the bank fails, just as much as the bank is at risk if the counterparty fails. After inception, swap positions often move in/out-of-the-money and the relative credit risk changes accordingly. [See also **Interest rate swap**]

232. Country Risk

The credit risk that government or private borrowers in a specific country will refuse to repay their debts as obligated for other than pure economic reasons. For example, the repayments from foreign borrowers may be interrupted because of interference from foreign government.

233. Country Selection

A type of active international management that measures the contribution to performance attributable to investing in the better-performing stock markets of the world.

234. Coupon

The stated interest on a debt instrument. In bonds, notes, or other fixed income securities, the stated percentage rate of interest, usually paid twice a year.

235. Coupon Bond

A security that obligates the issuer to make interest payments called coupon payments over the life of the bond, then to repay the face value at maturity.

236. Coupon Interest Rate (Coupon Rate)

The coupon interest rate is the percentage of the par value to be paid annually, as interest, to the bond holder.

237. Coupon-reinvestment Risk

It is the expected yield calculated by assuming that all coupon cash flows would be reinvested at the same yield that exists at the time of purchase. If rates began to fall, it would be impossible to reinvest the coupon at a rate high enough to produce the anticipated yield. If rates increase, the coupon cash flow will be reinvested at higher rates and produce a return above expectation.

238. Covariance

Covariance is a statistical concept that relates movements in one set of variables to movements in another. For example, the covariance between two sets of returns, R_1 and R_2, is

$$\text{cov}(R_1, R_2) = \sum_{t=1}^{N} \left(\frac{(R_{1t} - \overline{R}_1)(R_{2t} - \overline{R}_2)}{N-1}, \right.$$

where N represents the number of joint observations of the assets' returns; R_{1t} and R_{2t} represent the tth observations of R_1 and R_2; and $\overline{R}_1$ and $\overline{R}_2$ represent the average returns on the two assets.

A negative covariance produces a situation where when one set of returns is rising, the other is usually falling, and vice versa. A zero covariance means that the two time series have no linear relationship.

Covariance can indicate a positive, zero, or negative relationship between two variables but little else. To look at the *strength* of the linear relationship between two sets of variables we look at the **correlation**. [See also **Correlation**]

239. Covenants

A bond indenture may include covenants, which can impose restrictions or extra duties on the firm.

Covenants are most effective when they are specific measures that state the acceptable limits for change in the obligor's financial and overall condition. They clearly define what is meant by "significant" deterioration in the obligor's credit quality. Financial covenants are more explicit (and therefore more desirable) than a "material adverse change" clause. Cross default provisions are common: allowing acceleration of debt repayment. These provisions affect the credit rating of the issue and the firm's financing costs. Restrictive covenants designed to protect bondholders and maintain the value of their investment can reduce the issuer's financing costs. The firm must decide if the restrictions and duties are worth the access to lower cost funds. The trustee ensures that the issuer observes any bond covenants. If the issuer violates a covenant, the issue is technically in default and the trustee can pursue a legal remedy, including immediate redemption of the bondholders' principal, in court.

Covenants are an example of a mechanism to control bondholder-firm agency problems. The covenants help ensure that management's actions do not unduly jeopardize the firm's liquidity and the bondholders' security. Examples of covenants include stipulations that the firm must maintain a minimum level of net working capital, maintain a minimum interest coverage ratio, keep pledged assets in good working order, and send audited financial statements to bondholders. Other examples include restrictions on the amount of the firm's debt, its dividend payments, and asset sales.

240. Coverage Ratios

Ratios of company earnings to fixed costs. Low or falling coverage ratios signal possible cash flow difficulties. [See also **Interest coverage ratio**]

241. Covered Call

Covered call is a long position in an asset together with a written call on the same asset. Covered calls are far less risky than naked calls, because the worst can happen is that the investor is required to sell shares already owned at a below their market value.

242. Covered Interest Arbitrage

A zero-investment strategy with simultaneous borrowing in one currency, lending in another, and entering into a forward contract to guarantee the exchange rate when the loans mature.

243. Covered Write

A long position in an asset coupled with sale of a call option on the same asset.

244. Crack Spread

Crude oil is generally refined to make petroleum products, in particular heating oil and gasoline. The split of oil into heating oil and gasoline can be complemented by a process known as "cracking." Hence, the difference between the price of crude oil futures and that of equivalent amounts of heating oil and gasoline is known as crack spread.

245. Credit Bureau

An association that collects and provides information on the credit (payment) histories of borrowers.

246. Credit Check

Efforts by a lender to verify the accuracy of information provided by potential borrowers.

247. Credit Department

The bank department where credit information is collected and analyzed to make credit decisions.

248. Credit Derivatives

A claim where the payoff depends upon the credit rating or default status of a firm. These include credit options, credit swaps, credit forwards and others.

249. Credit Enhancement

A guarantee or letter of credit backing for a loan which improves the creditworthiness of the contract.

250. Credit Exposure

The amount subject to changes in value upon a change in credit quality through either a market based revaluation on the event of an up (down) grade or the application of a recovery fraction in the event of default.

251. Credit File

Information related to a borrower's loan request, including application, record of past performance, loan documentation, and analyst opinions.

252. Credit Instrument

Device by which a firm offers credit, such as an invoice, a promissory note, or a conditional sales contract.

253. Credit Limit

The maximum amount that a borrower is allowed to borrow against a loan commitment or credit line.

254. Credit Period

Time allowed a credit purchaser to remit the full payment for credit purchases. Credit periods vary among different industries. For example, a jewelry store may sell diamond engagement rings for 5/30, net 4 months (the company require final payment within 4 months but offer a 5 percent discount to customers who pay within 30 days). A food wholesaler, selling fresh fruit and produce, might use net 7 months. Generally, a firm must consider three factors in setting a credit period. (1) the probability that the customer will not pay. A firm whose customers are in high-risk businesses may find itself offering restrictive credit terms. (2) the size of the account. If the account is small, the credit period will be shorter. Small accounts are more costly to manage, and small customers are less important. (3) the extent to which the goods are perishable. If the collateral values of the goods are low and cannot be sustained for long periods, less credit will be granted.

255. Credit Quality

Generally meant to refer to an obligor's relative chance of default, usually expressed in alphabetic terms (e.g., Aaa, Aa, A, etc.). In credit metrics analysis, the credit quality includes also the volatility of up (down) grades.

256. Credit Rating

A measure of the creditworthiness of a bond issue. In addition to bond credit rating, there is a growing trend toward the "credit rating" of loans offered for sale. Unlike bonds, a loan credit rating reflects more than the financial soundness of the underlying borrowing corporation. In particular, the value of the underlying collateral can change a loan's credit rating up to one full category above a standard bond rating. As more loans are rated, their attractiveness to secondary market buyers is likely to increase.

257. Credit Ratings Transition Matrix

A table showing the probability that a company will move from one credit rating to another during a certain period of time.

258. Credit Risk

The cash flows to be received by bond market investors are not certain; like individuals, corporate debtors may pay interest payments late or not at all. They may fail to repay principal at maturity. To compensate investors for this credit or **default risk,** rates of return on corporate bonds are higher than those on government securities with the same terms of maturity. Government securities are presumed to be free of credit risk. Generally, as investors perceive a higher likelihood of default, they demand higher default-risk premiums. Since perceptions of a bond's default risk may change over its term, the bond's yield to maturity also may change, even if all else remains constant.

259. Credit Scoring

The use of a statistical model based on applicant attributes to assess whether a loan automatically meets minimum credit standards. The model assigns values to potential borrowers' attributes, with the sum of the values compared to a threshold. More specifically, this is a reference to the application of linear discriminant analysis to combine financial ration to quantitatively predict the relative chance of default. [See also **Credit scoring model**]

260. Credit Scoring Model

Using financial ratio analysis to evaluate credit risk is certainly helpful. Yet, the decision that must be made following the examination of such data can be complicated by the difficulty of interpreting conflicting ratios. Different ratios often imply different predictions for the same firm. To overcome such ambiguity, information from several financial ratios can be combined into a single index. The resulting multivariate financial model will yield a single number for classifying the firm in terms of credit risk. For example, the multivariate financial model developed by Altman (1968) is defined as:

$$Y_i = 0.012X_1 + 0.014X_2 + 0.033X_3 + 0.006X_4 + 0.999X_5,$$

where X_1 = Working capital/Total assets; X_2 = Retained earnings/Total assets; X_3 = EBIT/Total assets; X_4 = Market value of equity/Book value of total debt; and X_5 = Sales/Total assets.

By substituting the financial ratio information for an individual company into this model, we can obtain financial Z-scores. This financial Z-score can be used to determine financial condition of a firm.

261. Credit Sensitive Notes

The coupon rates on credit sensitive notes increase (or decrease) if the issuer's bond rating falls (or rises). This compensates investors for changes in the issuer's credit quality over the life of the note.

262. Credit Spread Option

Option whose payoff depends on the spread between the yields earned on two assets. Options can be written on many spread: bond spreads, credit default swap spreads, and asset swap spreads.

263. Credit Union

A non-profit organization that offers financial services to qualifying members. Credit unions do not pay state and federal income taxes and thus operate at a competitive advantage to other depository institutions.

264. Credit Value at Risk

The credit loss that will not be exceeded at some specified confidence level. [See also **Value at risk**]

265. Credit-Linked Notes (CLNs)

Bonds that have payments determined at least in part by credit events (e.g., default) at a different firm. These also refer to asset-backed securities which were issued against the loan portfolio.

Credit-linked notes exist in a number of forms, but all of them contain a link between the return they pay and the credit-related performance of the underlying asset. A standard CLN is a security, usually issued by an investment-graded entity that has an interest payment and fixed maturity structure similar to a vanilla bond. The performance of the CLN, however, including the maturity value, is linked to the performance of a specified underlying asset or assets as well as that of the issuing entity. CLNs are usually issued at par. They are often used as a financing vehicle by borrowers in order to hedge against credit risk; CLNs are purchased by investors to enhance the yield received on their holdings. Hence, the issuer of the CLN is the protection buyer and the buyer of the note is the protection seller.

266. CreditMetrics Model

CreditMetrics was introduced in 1997 by J.P. Morgan and its co-sponsors (Bank of America, Union Bank of Switzerland) as a value at risk (VAR) framework to apply to the valuation and risk of nontradable assets such as loans and privately placed bonds. Thus, while RiskMetrics seeks to answer the question, "If tomorrow is a bad day, how much will I lose on tradable assets such as stocks and bonds?" CreditMetrics asks, "If next year is a bad year, how will I lose on my loans and loan portfolio?"

267. Creditor

Person or institution that holds the debt issued by a firm or individual. Bond holder is the creditor, creditors do not usually have voting power. The device used by creditors to protect themselves is the loan contracts (that is the indenture).

268. Creditors' Committee

A method of adjusting a capital structure without bankruptcy proceedings involves the operation of the enterprise by a group of creditors, called a creditors' committee. These representatives manage the firm until it gathers sufficient liquid capital to satisfy existing claims or until an acceptable composition is found.

There is no legal compulsion for any creditor to accept an out-of-court adjustment. Any creditor can delay the process if it is dissatisfied with a proposal by the majority (or minority) of creditors to relieve the financial burden on the firm. The unhappy creditor can refuse the arrangement and insist that a claim be met in full; if it is not, the creditor can take the firm to court to be liquidated or reorganized.

269. Cross Rate

An exchange rate may be quoted as a cross-rate, the rate of a non-US dollar currency expressed in terms of another non-US dollar currency.

270. Cross Hedge

Use of a futures contract for a specific asset that differs from the cash asset being hedged. For example, to use index futures to hedge 10-year US government bond. For example IBM hold stocks of GM.

271. Cross Holdings

One corporation holds shares in another firm.

272. Cross-Sectional Analysis

Financial ratios can be used in *cross-sectional analysis*, in which different firms are compared at the same point in time. The best information source for cross-sectional analysis of firm ratios is the firm's financial statements and their footnotes. These materials appear in annual reports as well as 10-Q and 10-K filing with the Securities and Exchange Commission.

273. Crown Jewels

An anti-takeover tactic in which major assets – the crown jewels – are sold by a firm when faced with a takeover threat. This is sometimes referred to as the scorched earth strategy.

274. Crush Spread

Soybean generally can be crushed to produce soybean meal and soybean oil. Therefore, the difference between the price of a quantity of soybeans and that of the soybean meal and oil that can be produced by those soybeans.

275. Cum Dividend

With dividend before the ex-dividend date the stock is said to trade cum dividend.

276. Cumulative Abnormal Return (CAR)

Sum of differences between the expected return on a stock and the actual return that comes from the release of news to the market. The abnormal return on a given stock for a particular day can be calculated by subtracting the market's return (R_m) on the same day – as measured by a broad based index such as the S&P composite index – from the actual return (R) on the stock for the day. $AR = R - R_m$. Cumulative abnormal return (CAR) is the total abnormal return for the period surrounding an announcement on the release of information. The CAR generally can be measured by cumulative average residual. [See also **Cumulative average residual**]

277. Cumulative Average Residual (CAR)

Following Fama, Fisher, Jensen and Roll (1969), the cumulative average residual (CAR) can be defined as:

$$CAR = \sum_{t=1}^{T} AR_t,$$

where $AR_t = \frac{1}{N} \sum_{j=1}^{N} e_{jt};$

$e_{jt} = R_{jt} - \beta_j R_{mt};$

R_{jt} = rate of return for security j in period t; β_j = beta coefficient for j th security; R_{mt} = market rate of return in period t; T = the number of months being summed (T = 1, 2, ..., m); and N = the total number of months in the sample.

278. Cumulative Distribution Function

A function giving the probability that a value drawn from a distribution will be less than or equal to some specified value.

279. Cumulative Dividend

Dividend on preferred stock that takes priority over dividend payments on common stock. Dividends may not be paid on the common stock until all past dividends on the preferred stock have been paid.

280. Cumulative Normal Distribution Function

The cumulative distribution function for the normal distribution; $N(x)$ in the Black-Scholes equation. [See **Black-Scholes option pricing model**]

281. Cumulative Probability

The probability that a drawing from the standardized normal distribution will be below a particular value. For example, the probability for a standardized normal distribution that a drawing will be below 0 is clearly 50 percent because the normal distribution is symmetric. Using statistical terminology, we say that the cumulative probability of 0 is 50 percent. Statisticians also say that N(0) = 50 percent.

282. Cumulative Voting

A procedure whereby a share holder may cast all of his or her votes for one member of the board of directors. The effect of cumulative voting is to permit minority participation. If cumulative voting is permitted. The total number of votes that each shareholder may cast is determined first. The number is calculated as the number of shares (owned or controlled) multiplied by the number of directors to be elected. Each shareholder can distribute these votes as he or she wishes over one or more candidates.

283. Currency Risk

It is also called exchange-rate risk. Securities denominated in a currency other than the currency used by the purchaser have this additional risk. The total return an investor receives will equal the stock return times the change in the currency the security is denominated in relative to the investor's domestic currency.

Total return = Security return × Change in relative exchange rate.

284. Currency Selection

Asset allocation in which the investor chooses among investments denominated in different currencies.

285. Currency Swap

In a currency swap, two firms agree to exchange an equivalent amount of two different currencies for a specified period of time. A fixed rate is paid in one currency while a floating rate is paid in another. Currency swap is generally used to hedge the currency interest rate risk.

As an example of a typical currency swap, suppose a German company would like to borrow US dollars to finance a foreign investment, but the firm is not known outside Germany. Similarly, a US firm needs DMs for its German subsidiary, but the cost of borrowing in the US is cheaper than the cost of borrowing in Germany for this firm. Both firms face a similar problem. They can borrow at favorable rates, but not in the desired currency. In this case, a currency swap presents on solution. A bank acting as an intermediary can bring these two firms together and arrange a swap of deutsche

marks for dollars. The German firm agrees to pay the US company principal and interest on its dollar borrowings in the Untied States, while the US firm agrees to pay the costs of the DM borrowings for its German subsidiaries. Each firm thus obtains the best possible rate and eliminates exposure to exchange rate changes by agreeing to exchange currencies.

286. Currency-Translated Index

An investment in an index denominated in a foreign currency, where the buyer bears both currency and asset risk.

287. Current Account

The difference between imports and exports, including merchandise, services, and transfers such as foreign aid.

288. Current Asset

Asset that is in the form of cash or that is expected to be converted into cash in the next 12 months, such as inventory. Current assets are presented in the balance sheet in order of their accounting liquidity, that is, the ease with which they can be converted to cash at a fair price and the time it takes to do so.

289. Current Exposure

For market-driven instruments, the amount it would cost to replace a transaction today should counterparty default. If there is an enforceable netting agreement with the counterparty, then the current exposure would be the net replacement cost; otherwise, it would be the gross amount. [See also **Exposure**]

290. Current Liabilities

Obligations that are expected to require cash payment within one year or the operating period, whichever is shorter. The three major items found as current liabilities are account payable; accrued wages; and other expenses payable; and note payable. Also, on the balance sheet, Net working capital = cash + other current assets – current liabilities.

291. Current Ratio

Total current assets divided by total current liabilities, used to measure short-term solvency of a firm. [See also **Liquidity ratios**]

292. Current Yield

A bond's annual coupon payment divided by its price. Differs from yield to maturity.

293. Customer Information File

A record of the services used by each customer.

294. Customer Profitability Analysis

A procedure that compares revenues with expenses and the bank's target profit from a customer's total account relationship.

295. Cyclical Liquidity Needs

An estimate of liquid funds needed to cover deposit outflows or loan demand in excess of trend or seasonal factors.

D

1. Date of Payment

Date that dividend checks are mailed.

2. Date of Record

Date on which holders of record in a firm's stock ledger are designated as the recipients of either dividends or stock rights. Dividends will not be paid to those individuals whose notification of purchase is received by the company after this date.

3. Dates Convention

Treating cash flows as being received on exact dates – date 0, date 1, and so forth – as opposed to the end-of-year convention.

4. Day Count

A convention for quoting interest rates.

5. Day Order

A buy order or a sell order expiring at the close of the trading day.

6. Day Trade

A trade that is entered into and closed out in the same day.

7. Daylight Overdrafts

Bank payments from deposits held at a Federal Reserve Bank or correspondent bank in excess of actual collected balances during a day.

8. Days in Receivables

Average collection period. It measures the average amount of time required to collect an account receivable. Suppose in one company, 80 percent of its customers take the discounts and pay on day 20; the rest pay on day 60. The average collection period is 28 days (0.8×20 days $+ 0.2 \times 60$ days). It is also refers to days' sales outstanding.

9. Days Sales Outstanding

Average collection period.

10. Days' Receivables

[See **Average collection period**]

11. De Facto

Existing in actual fact although not by official recognition.

12. De Novo Branch

A newly opened branch.

13. Dealer Market

A market where traders specializing in particular commodities buy and sell assets for their own account. Most debt securities are traded in dealer markets. The many bond dealers communicate with one another by telecommunication equipment-wires, computers, and telephones. Investors get in touch with dealers when they want to buy or sell, and can negotiate a deal. Some stocks are traded in the dealer market. The OTC market is an example.

14. Dealer Reserve

An account established by a bank and dealer used to assign the interest that accrues to dealers as they sell loans to a bank.

15. Debenture

A debenture is an unsecured bond, or a bond that pledges no specific assets as security or collateral. In case of default, debenture holders are treated as general creditors of the firm. The riskiest type of bond is a **subordinated debenture**. [See also **Subordinated debenture**]

16. Debit Card

A plastic card that, when used, immediately reduces the balance in a customer's transactions deposit.

17. Debt

Loan agreement that is a liability of the firm. An obligation to repay a specified amount at a particular time.

18. Debt Capacity

Ability to borrow. The amount a firm can borrow up to the point where the firm value no longer increases. A firm's maximum debt capacity is defined as the point where the advantage derived from an incremental addition of debt to the firm's capital structure is offset by the cost incurred.

19. Debt Displacement

The amount of borrowing that leasing displaces. Firms that do a lot of leasing will be forced to cut back on borrowing.

20. Debt Ratio

Total debt divided by total assets. This ratio is used to determine a firm's capital structure.

21. Debt Service

Interest payments plus repayments of principal to creditors, that is, retirement of debt.

22. Debtor-in-Possession Financing

A loan made to a firm which has filed for Chapter 11 bankruptcy protection.

23. Debt-to-Assets Ratio

[See **Capital structure ratios**]

24. Debt-to-Equity Ratio

[See **Capital structure ratios**]

25. Decision Trees

A graphical representation of alternative sequential decisions and the possible outcomes of those decisions. Decision tree can be used to analyze capital budgeting under uncertainty. It can also be used to analyze the option valuation. [See also **Binomial model**]

26. Declaration Date

Date on which the board of directors passes a resolution to pay a dividend of a specified amount to all qualified holders of record on a specified date.

27. Dedicated Capital

Total par value (number of shares issued multiplied by the par value of each share). Also called dedicated value.

28. Dedication Strategy

Cash flow matching on a multi-period basis is referred to as a dedication strategy. In this case, the manager selects either zero-coupon or coupon bonds that provide total cash flows in each period that match a series of obligations. The advantage of dedication is that it is a once-and-for-all approach to eliminating interest rate risk. Once the cash flows are matched, there is no need for rebalancing. The dedicated portfolio provides the cash necessary to pay the firm's liabilities regardless of the eventual path of interest rates.

29. Deed of Trust

Indenture is sometime referred to as deed of trust. [See also **Indenture**]

30. Deep-Discount Bond

A bond issued with a very low coupon or no coupon and selling at a price far below par value. When the bond has no coupon, it is also called a pure-discount or original-issue-discount bond.

31. Defalcation

The misappropriation of funds or property by an individual.

32. Default

The failure to make obligated interest and principal payments on a loan.

33. Default Correlation

Default correlation is a measurement of the degree to which default of one asset makes more or less likely the default of another asset. One can think of default correlation as being jointly due to (1) a macroeconomic effect which tends to tie all industries into the common economic cycle, (2) a sector-specific effect, and (3) a company-specific effect.

34. Default Premium

A differential in promised yield that compensates the investor for the risk inherent in purchasing a corporate bond that entails some risk of default.

35. Default Probability (DP)

The likelihood that an obligor or counterparty will encounter credit distress within a given time period. "Credit distress" usually leads to either an omitted delayed payment or distressed exchange which would impair the value to senior unsecured debt holders. Note that this leaves open the possibilities that:

(i) Subordinated debt might default without impairing senior debt value, and

(ii) Transfers and clearing might continue even with a senior debt impairment.

This probability can be either marginal default probability (MDP) or cumulative default probability (CDP). The MDP refers the probability that a borrower will default in any given year. The CDP refers the probability that a borrower will default over a specified multiyear period.

36. Default Probability Density

Measures the unconditional probability of default in a future short period of time. As the asset value of a firm increases, the firm is more likely to remain solvent, the default probability drops.

37. Default Risk

The chance that interest or principal will not be paid on the due date and in the promised amount under the loan contract. [See also **Credit risk**]

38. Default Swap

A contract in which the swap buyer pays a regular premium; in exchange, if a default in a specified bond occurs, the swap seller pays the buyer the loss due to the default.

39. Defeasance

A debt-restructuring tool that enables a firm to remove debt from its balance sheet by establishing an irrevocable trust that will generate future cash flows sufficient to service the decreased debt.

40. Deferred Annuities

Tax-advantaged life insurance product. Deferred annuities offer deferral of taxes with the option of withdrawing one's funds in the form of a life annuity.

41. Deferred Availability Credit Items

Checks received for collection for which a bank has not provided credit to the depositor.

42. Deferred Call

A provision that prohibits the company from calling the bond before a certain date. During this period the bond is said to be call protected.

43. Deferred Down Rebate Option

A deferred rebate option for which the current stock price is above the rebate barrier. The payoff to this claim does not depend upon a strike price. The payoff will be done as long as the barrier has been hit.

44. Deferred Nominal Life Annuity

A monthly fixed-dollar payment beginning at retirement age. It is nominal because the payment is fixed in dollar amount at any particular time, up till and including retirement.

45. Deferred Payment Option

An option where the price paid is deferred until the end of the option's life.

46. Deferred Rebate Option

A claim that pays $1 at expiration if the price of the underlying asset has reached a barrier prior to expiration. If a contract that pays $1 at the time of a barrier is reached, it is called rebate option.

Therefore, the deferred rebate option is similar to rebate option.

47. Deferred Swap

A swap with terms specified today, but for which swap payments begin at a later date than for an ordinary swap.

48. Deferred Taxes

It is a noncash expense item. It results from differences between accounting income and true taxable income.

49. Deferred Up Rebate Option

A deferred rebate option for which the current stock price is below the rebate barrier. The payoff to this claim does not depend upon a strike price. The payoff will be done as long as the barrier has been hit.

50. Deferred-Strike Options

Deferred-strike options are also called shout options. As the phrase "deferred-strike" implies, a shout option is an option whose strike price can be specified as an underlying asset price at any time before the maturity of the option. The level of the strike is ultimately set at a specific relationship to the spot, for example, 6 percent or 4 percent below the spot, or 4 percent or 6 percent above, during a period of time normally starting on the trade date and ending on a date agreed upon at the trade time. After the strike is specified according to the terms in the contract or after the shouting time, the shout option becomes a vanilla option until the maturity of the option.

Shout options possess characteristics of American options. Since optimal timing or the "shouting" time is uncertain, there is no straightforward way to price shout options. However, they can be priced using either the binomial tree method or some analytical approximations.

51. Deficit

The amount by which a sum of money is less than the required amount; an excess of liabilities over assets, of losses over profits, or of expenditure over time.

52. Defined Benefit Plans

Pension plans in which retirement benefits are set according to a fixed formula. This plan promises in advance to pay employees a special level of benefit. A major question in the management and regulation of this kind of plan is whether an employer's contribution to the fund is sufficient to meet future pension liability.

53. Defined Contribution Plans

Pension plans in which the employer is committed to making contributions according to a fixed formula. However, benefits paid during retirement are not promised in advance. Instead they depend on contributions and earnings accumulated over time.

54. Degree of Combined Leverage (DCL)

A firm's degree of combined leverage (DCL) is the percentage change in earnings per share (EPS) that results from a 1 percent change in sales volume as:

$$DCL = \frac{\text{Percentage change in EPS}}{\text{Percentage change in sales}}.$$

The relationship between the degrees of operating and financial leverage and the degree of combined leverage is a multiplicative one. DFL times degree of operating leverage (DOL) results in:

$$\frac{\text{Percentage change in EPS}}{\text{Percentage change in EBIT}}$$
$$\times \frac{\text{Percentage change in EBIT}}{\text{Percentage change in sales}}$$
$$= \frac{\text{Percentage change in EPS}}{\text{Percentage change in sales}}.$$

Thus, a firm's degree of combined leverage is simply the product of its degree of operating leverage

and its degree of financial leverage. The DCL represents the impact on earnings per share of the combined effects of operating leverage and financial leverage if profit margins remain constant.

Like the degree of operating leverage and the degree of financial leverage, the DCL is not constant, as the firm's sales rise and fall over time. We know DOL declines as sales increase and DFL declines as EBIT rises. Thus, a firm's degree of combined leverage will fall as its sales and EBIT increase, as long as the firm's margin, fixed operating costs and financial costs remain constant.

The degree of combined leverage uses a firm's operating leverage and financial leverage and the assumption of constant margins to estimate a relationship between changes in sales and changes in earnings. [See also **Appendix B**]

55. Degree of Financial Leverage (DFL)

A firm's financial risk reflects its interest expense, or in financial jargon, its financial leverage. A quick way to determine a firm's exposure to financial risk is to compute its degree of financial leverage. The degree of financial leverage (DFL) measures the sensitivity of EPS to changes in EBIT as:

$$DFL = \frac{\text{Percentage change in EPS}}{\text{Percentage change in EBIT}},$$

This definition clearly suggests that DFL represents the percentage change in earnings per share due to a 1 percent change in earnings before interest and taxes.

There is a more straightforward method to compute a firm's degree of financial leverage that avoids handling percentage changes in variables. This formula is given as:

$$DFL = \frac{\text{EBIT}}{\text{EBIT} - \text{I}} = \frac{\text{EBIT}}{\text{EBT}}.$$

DFL equals the firm's earnings before interest and taxes (EBIT) divided by EBIT minus interest expense (I), or earnings before taxes (EBT).

DFL changes with the level of EBIT for much the same reason that **DOL** changes with sales volume. [See also **Degree of operating leverage**] When EBIT is about the same as the firm's interest expense, EPS is small. A slight change in EBIT can therefore lead to a large percentage change in EPS, resulting in a large DFL. If the firm's interest expense does not change while EBIT continues to grow, the percentage increase in EPS becomes smaller and smaller, resulting in lower values for the firm's degree of financial leverage. [See also **Appendix B**]

56. Degree of Operating Leverage (DOL)

A quick way to approximate a firm's exposure to business risk is to compute its degree of operating leverage. The degree of operating leverage (DOL) is a measure of the sensitivity of EBIT to a change in unit volume in sales, *assuming a constant price-variable cost margin*. Formally,

$$DOL = \frac{Sales\ revenue - Variable\ costs}{Sales\ revenue - Variable\ costs\ - Fixed\ Costs}$$

or, stated with variables, the formula for DOL can be written as:

$$\frac{Q(p-v)}{EBIT} = \frac{Q(p-v)}{Q(p-v)-F},$$

where Q = quantity of goods sold, p = price per unit, v = variable cost per unit, F = total fixed cost, and $EBIT$ = earnings before interest and taxes.

These formulas make computing the degree of operating leverage seem fairly straightforward, but these calculations assume constant margins. Any careful analysis of business risk should include analysis of competitive conditions and other influences on the firm's margins.

Why does a firm's DOL change as its level of unit sales varies? Recall the basic definition of DOL: it is the percentage change in EBIT that corresponds to a 1 percent change in unit sales. For lower levels of sales, EBIT is small. At the firm's **break-even point**, EBIT is zero. [See also

Break-even point] Therefore, any change in sales from the break-even point results in an infinite percentage change in EBIT and a DOL value of infinity. As sales volume grows, the level of EBIT also grows, but the resulting percentage change in EBIT becomes smaller and smaller, leading to reductions in the firm's degree of operating leverage. With constant margins and fixed costs, this implies that firm growth causes business risk to decline. [See also **Appendix B**]

57. Delinquent Account

An account that is past due because the account holder has not made the obligated payment on time.

58. Deliverable Instrument

The asset in a forward contract that will be delivered in the future at an agreed-upon price. A forward contract for foreign exchange currency is a deliverable instrument.

59. Delivery

The tender and receipt of an actual commodity or financial instrument, or cash in settlement of a futures contract.

60. Delivery Date

Specific day that a futures contract expires.

61. Delivery Point

A point designated by a futures exchange at which the financial instrument or commodity covered by futures contract may be delivered in fulfillment of such contract.

62. Delivery Price

Price agreed to (possibly some time in the past) in a forward contract.

63. Delta

The change in the price of a derivative due to a change in the price of the underlying asset. Based upon the call option formula defined in option pricing model [See also **Option pricing equation**]. The mathematic result can be defined as:

$$\frac{\partial C}{\partial S} = N(d_1) > 0.$$

64. Delta Neutral Portfolio

The value of the zero-delta portfolio is not affected by changes in the value of the asset on which the options are written.

65. Delta-Gamma Approximation

A formula using the delta and gamma to approximate the change in the derivative price due to a change in the price of the underlying asset.

66. Delta-Hedging

Hedging a derivative position using the underlying asset, with the amount of the underlying asset determined by the derivative's sensitivity (delta) to the price of the underlying asset.

67. Demand Deposit

Transactions account, payable on demand, that pays no interest to the depositor.

68. Demand Shock

An event that affects the demand for goods and services in the economy.

69. Denomination

Face value or principal of a bond.

70. Depository Transfer Check (DTC)

A depository transfer check (DTC) is an ordinary check restricted "for deposit only" at a designated bank. Hence, the designated collection bank deposits a DTC for the daily deposits into the firm's checking account and then submits the DTC to the collection system. Although the DTC is less expensive than a wire transfer, it is also slower.

71. Depreciation

A non-cash expense, such as the cost of plant or equipment, charge against earnings to write off the cost of an asset during its estimated useful life. It can use straight line method to do the depreciation. [See **Double-declining balance depreciation**]

72. Depreciation Tax Shield

The term T(Dep), the tax rate multiplied by the depreciation expense, is called the depreciation tax shield. It represents the tax savings the firm receives from its noncash depreciation expense. For example, with a 34 percent tax rate, a depreciation expense of $1,000 reduces a firm's tax bill by $340.

73. Derivative

A financial instrument whose value is determined by the specific features of the underlying asset or instrument. [See also **Primitive security**]

74. Derivative Asset/contingent Claim

Securities providing payoffs that depend on or are contingent on the values of other assets such as commodity prices, bond and stock prices, or market index values. Examples are futures and options.

75. Derivative Security

[See **Primitive security**]

76. Detachable Warrant

A warrant entitles the holder to buy a given number of shares of stock at a stipulated price. A detachable warrant is one that may be sold separately from the package it may have originally been issued with (usually a bond).

77. Development Projects

Development projects are attempts to develop projects and technologies that represent small advances of an already established knowledge base. These "sure things" will be low-risk, low-return investments in R&D.

78. DI System

The directional indicator system (DI system) is from a technical family known as momentum oscillators. Oscillators deal with price changes. The logic employed by the directional-indicator system is that any trending period can be characterized as having a significant excess of either positive or negative price movements. Periods when prices are quickly moving upwards will have more upwards price change than downward price change, and vice versa. It is this relative price change that the DI estimates.

79. Diagonal Spread

A position in two calls where both the strike prices and times to maturity are different. It can be regarded as a combination of bull (or bear) and calendar spread. (A diagonal spread can also be created with put options.)

80. Differential Equation

An equation relating a variable to its derivatives and one or more independent variables. The differential equation can be classified into deterministic and stochastic differential equation. Black and Scholes (1973) used stochastic differential equation to derive the option pricing model.

81. Diffusion Process

Generally, a continuous stochastic process in which uncertainty increases with time. Also used to describe the Brownian (random) part of an Itô process. [See also **Differential equation**]

82. Digital Option

Another name for binary option. [See also **Binary option**]

83. Dilution

Loss in existing shareholders' value. There are several kinds of dilution: (1) dilution of ownership, (2) dilution of market value, and (3) dilution of book value and earnings, as with warrants and convertible issues. Firms with significant amounts of warrants or convertible issues outstanding are required to report earnings on a "fully diluted" basis.

84. Direct Agency Costs

[See **Agency costs**]

85. Direct Lease

A lease under which a lessor buys equipment from a manufacturer and leases it to a lessee. In other words, it gives the lessee the use of an asset while the lessor retains title and ownership of the asset.

86. Direct Loan

Loan with terms negotiated directly between the lender and actual user of the funds.

87. Direct Quote

A direct quote states an exchange rate in terms of the amount of US dollars that equal one unit of foreign currency, such as $0.6786/DM. [See also **Indirect quote**]

88. Direct Search Market

Buyers and sellers seek each other direct and transact directly.

89. Dirty Price

The present value of a bond's future cash flows (this implicitly includes accrued interest). For instance, a 7 percent annual coupon bond trading at par would have a dirty price of $107 just prior to coupon payment. CreditMetrics estimates dirty prices since the coupon is paid in non-default states but assumed not paid in default. [See also **CreditMetrics model** and **Accrued interest**]

90. Disbursement Float

A decrease in book cash but no immediate change in bank cash, generated by checks written by the firm. [See also **Float**]

91. Discount Bonds

A bond that sells below par value is said to be selling at a *discount* and is called a discount bond.

The price of a discount bond will rise as it nears maturity if the market rate remains the same, since at maturity its price will equal its par value.

92. Discount Broker

A brokerage firm that offers a limited range of retail services and charges lower fees than full-service brokers.

93. Discount Factor

The term $1/(1+r)^n$ is called a present value interest factor, $PVIF(r,n)$, or discount factor.

When the number of periods n and interest rate r are the same, the future value interest factor $(FVIF)$ and PVIF terms are merely reciprocals of each other. That is,

$$PVIF = 1/FVIF \quad \text{and} \quad FVIF = 1/PVIF.$$

As it is the reciprocal of the compounding future value interest factor, the present value interest factor, $1/(1+r)^n$, will diminish as either the interest rate or the number of years increases. Thus, using the same discount rate, cash flows in the far future are worth less to us than nearer cash flows. Over the same time frame, higher discount rates result in lower PVIFs, meaning future cash flows will be worth less in present value terms.

94. Discount Function

The discounted value of $1 as a function of the time until payment.

95. Discount Instrument

An instrument, such as a Treasury bill, that provides no coupons.

96. Discount on a Currency

The forward rate either will be at a discount or a premium to the spot rate. A currency is selling at a discount if it can be purchased more cheaply in the forward than in the spot market. Or, in other words, using indirect quotes, a dollar that is selling at a discount can buy fewer units of the foreign currency in the forward market than in the spot market.

97. Discount Payback Period Rule

An investment decision rule in which the cash flows are discounted at an interest rate and the payback rule is applied on these discounted cash flows. This method has taken time value of money into account. However, it still does not consider all potential cash flow.

98. Discount Rate

There are two possible meanings for this term as follows:

1. Occasionally, the Fed implements monetary policy by adjusting the discount rate, the interest

rate it charges on its loans to banks. This serves to encourage or discourage banks from borrowing from the Fed to raise loanable reserve. Changes in the discount rate also transmit signals regarding future Fed policy.

2. The interest rate that is used to find a present value often is called a discount rate.

99. Discount Rate for Discount Instrument

The annualized rate of return on a Treasury bill or similar works on 360-days, instead of 365-day year instrument expressed as a percentage of the final face value. It assumes a 360-day, instead of 365-day per year, for calculating this type of rate of return.

100. Discount Window

Interest rate charged by Federal Reserve banks lending to member institutions.

101. Discounted Cash-Flow Valuation Theory

It is the basic tool for determining the theoretical price of a corporate security. The price of a corporate security is equal to the present value of future benefits of ownership. For example, for common stock, these benefits include dividends received while the stock is owned plus capital gains earned during the ownership period.

102. Discounted Dividend Model (DDM)

A formula to estimate the intrinsic value of a firm by figuring the present value of all expected future dividends. [See also **Gordon model**]

103. Discounting

Discounting is the process of determining the present value, or the value as of today, of a future cash flow.

104. Discretionary Account

An account of a customer who gives a broker the authority to make buy and sell decisions on the customer's behalf.

105. Distressing Exchange

During a time of credit distress, debt holders may be effectively forced to accept securities in exchange for their debt claim; such securities being of a lower value than the nominal present value of their original claim. They may have a lower coupon, delayed sinking funds, and/or lengthened maturity. For historical estimation of default probabilities, this would count as a default event since it can significantly impair value.

106. Distribution

A type of dividend paid by a firm to its owners from sources other than current or accumulated retained earnings.

107. Diversifiable Risk

A risk that specifically affects a single asset or a small group of assets. [See also **Unsystematic risk**]

108. Diversification

Diversification occurs when we invest in several different assets rather than just a single one.

Financial theorists commonly assume that the goal of a business is to maximize shareholder wealth. Hence decisions should be evaluated on the basis of how they affect value and, more directly, how they affect the amount and uncertainty of the cash flow stream accruing to the owners.

One line of financial theory has sought to explain conglomerate mergers through the diversification effect. The basic argument follows from portfolio theory: joining together two less than perfectly correlated income streams reduces the relative variability of the streams. However, it has been conversely argued that a perfect capital market allows no economic advantage from a purely conglomerate merger. That is, a merger cannot create diversification opportunities beyond those available to an individual investor before the merger.

109. Divestitures

In a divestiture, one firm sells a segment of its operations to another firm. No new corporate entity is created. The selling firm gives up the operational cash flows associated with the divested assets in exchange for a cash flow from the buyer. Arguably, a decision to divest a segment should be made in a capital budgeting framework.

Tax treatment of a divestiture handles the transaction as an ordinary sale with capital gains or losses recognized normally.

110. Dividend

A payment made to holders of a firm's common stock and/or preferred stock. Cash dividends are paid in cash while stock dividends are paid in stock.

111. Dividend Declaration Date

On the dividend declaration date, the directors of the firm may issue a statement declaring a regular dividend. The statement might be worded something like, "On January 2, 2005, the directors of this corporation met and declared quarterly dividends to be $0.75 per share payable to the holder of record on January 22; payment will be made on February 7, 2005." With this declaration, the dividend becomes a legally binding obligation to the corporation.

112. Dividend Growth Model

A model wherein dividends are assumed to be at a constant rate in perpetuity. [See also **Gorden model**]

113. Dividend Irrelevance

Miller and Modigliani (1961) were the first to present an argument for dividend irrelevance. Miller and Modigliani's theory that the value of the firm is independent of its dividend policy is similar to their analysis of the irrelevance of capital structure. The theory assumes a world without taxes or transaction costs. In addition, investors are assumed to be rational, with homogeneous expectations, and both corporate management and shareholders are assumed to know the same information about the firm.

114. Dividend Payout Ratio

It equals dividend per share divided by earnings per share. [See also **Retention rate**]

115. Dividend Policy

Dividend policy is the decision a firm makes to pay out earnings or retain them for reinvestment in the firm. If it pays out dividends, company policy must determine the amount to retain. Two questions drive a firm's dividend policy: Does dividend policy have an effect upon the firm's value? If so, will the firm try to achieve an optimal payout ratio by attaining an ideal dollar payment per share? These questions have sparked debate between practitioners and academicians for many years. Practitioners see an optimal level of dividend payout, whereas some academic factions have argued that dividend policy does not affect the value of the firm at all.

Still other groups of academics have argued that dividends are the *only* factor that determines firm value. This shows up in Gordon's constant dividend growth model for a share of common stock as:

$$P_0 = \frac{D_1}{r - g},$$

where P_0 = current stock price; D_1 = dividend payout in next period; r = cost of equity capital for the firm; and g = growth rate for the firm.

According to the Gordon model, if the firm increases its cash dividend, the price of its stock will increase. Remember, however, that any increase in the dividend is a reduction in retained earnings, which causes lower growth rate, g, for the firm. According to the model, a lower growth rate reduces the firm's stock price, so the optimal dividend policy must balance the effects of these two variables to maximize the stock price.

116. Dividend Yield

Dividends per share of common stock divided by market price per share.

117. Dividends Per Share

Amount of cash paid to shareholders expressed as dollar per share.

118. DMAC System

The dual moving-average crossover system (DMAC system) employs logic similar to the **MAPB system** by seeking to find when the short-term trend rises above or below the long-term trend. The MAPB represents the short-term trend by the daily price and the long-term trend by the moving average. The DMAC uses a short-term moving average and long-term moving average to represent the short-term and long-term trend. A change in the price trend is signaled when these two moving averages cross. Specifically, a buy signal is generated when the shorter moving average is greater than (above) the longer moving average, and a sell signal when the shorter moving average is less than (below) the longer moving average. The trader always maintains a long or short position in the futures market. [See also **MAPB system**]

119. Dollar-Weighted Return

The internal rate of return on an investment.

120. Dominance Principle

Under the efficient-frontier analysis, the assumption that an investor prefers returns and dislikes risks. For example, an individual is prepared to experience risk associated with the different return, he or she can obtain a higher expected return with two different return portfolios with the same risk. Thus, the higher return portfolio dominates the lower return portfolio and would be preferred. Similarly, if an individual was satisfied with a return, he would select the less risky portfolio.

121. DONCH System

The Donchian system (DONCH system) is part of a family of technical systems known as price channels. The system generates a buy signal any time the daily high price is outside (greater than) the highest price in the specified time interval. A sell signal is generated any time the daily low breaks outside (lower than) the lowest price in the same interval. The system always generates a signal for the trader to take a position, long or short, in the futures market.

122. Double Taxation

Tax law complicates the dividend decision by imposing the burden of double taxation. In effect, income that a firm pays to shareholders as dividends is taxed twice. A corporate income tax is levied on the corporation's profits, and shareholders then pay personal income taxes on the dividends they receive. This is one of the complexities of the US tax laws that affects dividend policy.

The investor has no control over corporate tax effects. It is up to the corporate managers to reduce or defer tax payments as much as possible. However, the investor can influence the amount of personal taxes due on any dividend earnings. Investors can reduce or defer taxes by buying low-dividend, high-growth stocks. Or, if they are tax exempt, investors can buy dividend-paying stocks.

Personal income taxes may affect an investor's preference for dividends or capital gains. When the tax rate on capital gains is substantially lower than the tax rate on personal income, then shareholders should prefer capital gains to dividends. This increases the firm's focus on retained earnings as equity financing. Investors still can realize home-made dividends through capital gains from sales of stock.

Different investors will have different preferences between dividends and capital gains. For example, average investors may prefer dividends because of the need for additional income, while wealthy investors may prefer capital gains because they currently do not need the income. Some large, tax-exempt institutions, such as pension funds, pay no taxes on their investment income, so they may be indifferent between dividends or capital gains. Other tax-exempt institutions, such as foundations and endowments, may favor current income to help meet budget needs.

Investors can defer receiving capital gains by holding stock; gains are received and become taxable only when stock is sold at a profit. Dividends offer less flexibility. Once the firm pays a dividend, the investor must pay taxes on this income. Therefore, the ability to defer taxes on capital gains may bias the investor against cash dividend payments.

123. Double-Declining Balance Depreciation

One of the accelerated depreciation methods. To use the double-declining-balance (DDB) method we first need to find the annual depreciation rate, which is calculated as:

$$\text{Annual depreciation rate} = \frac{1}{N},$$

where N is the number of years used to calculate straight line depreciation method. The annual straight-line rate of depreciation is $1/N$ percent per year; for DDB we need only multiply this

amount by 2. Using this rate, the depreciation over five years for an asset with an initial value of $6,000 is calculated as:

		Depreciation
Year 1 $6,000 (2/5)	=	$2,400
Year 2 ($6,000 – $2,4000)(2/5)	=	1,440
Year 3 ($6,000 – $2,400 – $1,440)(2/5)	=	864
Year 4 ($6,000 – $2,400 – $1,440 – $864)(2/5)	=	518
Year 5 ($6,000 – $2,400 – $1,440 – $864 – $518)(2/5)	=	178 (311)
	TOTAL	$5,400

The maximum depreciation that can be taken is the value of cost minus salvage of $5,400. Thus, $178 of depreciation in year 5 exhausts the depreciation allowed under DDB, even though $311 is available.

Comparison between Straight-line and Double-Declining-balance method

Year	Straight-line	DDB
1	$1,080	$2,400
2	1,080	1,440
3	1,080	864
4	1,080	518
5	1,080	178

124. Doubling Option

A sinking fund provision that may allow repurchase of twice the required number of bonds at the sinking fund call price. This is one aspect of sinking fund call different from conventional bond call.

125. Dow Jones Industrial Average Index (DJIA)

The DJIA is an arithmetic average of the stock prices that make up the index. The DJIA originally assumed a single share of each stock in the index, and the total of the stock prices was divided by the number of stocks that made up the index:

$$DJIA_t = \frac{\frac{\sum_{i-1}^{30} P_{ti}}{30}}{\frac{\sum_{i=1}^{30} P_{0i}}{30}}.$$

Today, the index is adjusted for stock splits and the issuance of stock dividends:

$$DJIA_t = \frac{\sum_{i=1}^{30} \frac{P_{ti}}{AD_t}}{\sum_{i=1}^{30} P_{0i}},$$

where P_{it} = the closing price of stock i on day t, and AD_t = the adjusted divisor on day t. This index is similar to the simple price index except for the stock splits adjusted overtime. The adjustment process is illustrated as:

Adjustment of DJIA divisor to allow for a stock split

Before Split Stock	Price	After 2-for-1 Stock Split by Stock A Price
A	60	30
B	30	30
C	20	20
D	10	10
Sum	120	90

$$\text{Average before split} = \frac{120}{4} = 30$$

$$\text{Adjusted divisor} = \frac{sum\ of\ prices\ after\ the\ split}{Average\ before\ split}$$

$$= \frac{90}{30} = 3$$

$$\text{Average after split} = \frac{90}{3} = 30$$

Before-split divisor = 4 After-split divisor = 3

Alternatively, the average after split can be calculated as:

$$\text{Average} = \frac{30 \times 2 + 30 + 20 + 10}{4} = 30.$$

This average is identical to that obtained by using the adjusted-divisor approach.

As the Table shows, the adjustment process is designed to keep the index value the same as it would have been if the split had not occurred. Similar adjustments have been made when it has been found necessary to replace one of the component stocks with the stock of another company, thus preserving the consistency and comparability of index values at different points in time.

126. Dow Theory

One of the tools used by technical analysts to measure supply and demand and forecast security prices is the Dow theory. The Dow theory is used to indicate reversals and trends in the market as a whole or in individual securities. According to the theory, there are three movements going on in the markets at all times. These movements are (1) daily fluctuations (the narrow movement from day to day), (2) secondary movements (short-run movements over two weeks to a month or more), and (3) primary trends, major movements covering at least four years in duration. The theory asserts that daily fluctuations are meaningless. However, daily asset prices or the market average must be plotted in order to outline the primary and secondary trends. In plotting the asset prices, the Dow theorists search for price patterns indicating market tops and bottoms.

Technical analysts use three basic types of charts: (1) line charts, (2) bar charts, and (3) point-and-figure charts. Bar charts have vertical bars representing each day's price movement. Each bar spans the distance from the day's highest price to the day's lowest price with a small cross on the bar marking the closing price. Lines are used to connect successive day's prices. Patterns indicating market tops or bottoms are then searched for in these line charts by technical analysis. *The Wall Street Journal* uses the bar charts to show daily fluctuations in the Dow Jones Average.

Point-and-figure charts are more complex than line or bar charts. These charts draw the percentage change directly. They are not only used to detect reversals in a trend but are also employed to set actual price forecasts.

The construction of a point-and-figure chart varies with the price level of the stock being charted. Only significant changes are posted to a point-and-figure chart. As a result there are one-point, two-point, three-point, and five-point point-and-figure charts.

To set the price target (forecasted stock price) which a stock is expected to attain, point-and-figure chartists begin by finding a congestion area. A congestion area is a horizontal band created by a series of reversals around a given price level. Congestion areas are supposed to result when supply and demand are equal. A breakout is said to have occurred when a column of price increase rises above the top of a congestion area. Breakout refers to a price rise or fall in which the price rises above or falls below the horizontal band which contained the congestion area. A penetration of the top of a congestion area is a signal for continued price rise. Penetration of the bottom of a congestion area by a column of price declines is a bearish signal.

To establish estimates of the new prices that a security should attain, point-and-figure chartists measure the horizontal width of a congestion area as they watch for a breakout. When a breakout occurs, the chartist projects the horizontal count upward or downward in the same direction as the breakout to establish the new price target.

127. Down-and-In Option

An option that comes into existence when the price of the underlying asset declines to a prespecified level. This option can be classified into down-and-in call and down-and-in put. For example, down-and-in call is a regular call that comes in to existence only if the asset price reaches the barrier level.

128. Down-and-Out Option

An option that ceases to exist when the price of the underlying asset declines to a prespecified level. This option can be classified into down-and-out call and down-and-out put. For example, down-and-out call is a regular call that ceases to exist if the asset price reaches a certain barrier level.

129. Downgrade Trigger

A clause in the contract that states that the contract will be terminated with a cash settlement if the credit rating of one side falls below a certain level.

130. Draft

A written order requesting one party to make payment to another party at a specified point in time.

131. Drift

The expected change per unit time in an asset price.

132. Drift Rate

The average increase per unit of time in a stochastic variable. The drift can be undetectable amid all the up and down movements due to the random terms. [See also **Stochastic process**]

133. Du Pont Analysis

Breaking return on equity into component parts is called Du Pont analysis. [See also **Profitability ratios**]

134. Du Pont System of Financial Control

Highlights the fact that return on asset (ROA) can be expressed in terms of the profit margin and asset turnover. [See also **Profitability ratios**]

135. Dual Banking System

Banking system in the US in which groups trying to obtain a charter to open a bank can apply to the state banking department or the office of the Comptroller of the Currency-the national banking agency. Therefore, charters of US banks can be classified into state bank charter and national charter bank.

136. Dual Funds

Funds in which income and capital shares on a portfolio of stocks are sold separately.

137. Dumbbell Strategy

Dumbbell strategy are characterized by the inclusion of some proportion of short and intermediate term bonds that provide a liquidity buffer to protect a substantial investment in long-term security. The dumbbell portfolio divides its funds between two components. The shortest maturity is usually less than three years, and the longest maturities are more than ten years. The portfolio is weighted at both ends at the maturity spectrum. The logic and mechanics of the dumbbell strategy are straightforward: the short-term treasury notes provide the least risk and highest liquidity, while long-term bonds provide the highest return. The best risk/return portfolio combination may very well be a combination of these extremes. Assuming an upward-sloping yield curve, no intermediate bonds will be held since they have (1) less return than the longest-maturity bonds, and (2) less liquidity and safety than the shortest T-note.

138. Duration

The weighted average time of an asset's cash flows. The weights are determined by present value factors. The formula can be defined as:

$$D = \sum_{t=1}^{T} \frac{(t)(PV_t)}{\sum_{t=1}^{T} PV_t}, \tag{A}$$

where D is the duration of the bond; t is specific point in time; T is the number of years to maturity;

PV_t is the present value of the cash flow received at time t. PV_t is further defined as follows:

$$PV_t = \frac{C_t}{(1+r)^t}, \tag{B}$$

where r is the interest rate, and C_t is the cash payment in period t ($t = 1, 2, 3 \ldots, T$).

If coupon is zero, then duration is equal to maturity, therefore, the duration of zero-coupon bond is equal to maturity.

See table to calculate duration using equations (A) and (B).

Calculation of duration for two bonds

| | | Table A: 6% Coupon Bond | | |
| | | Present value | Proportion of present | Proportion in year X |
Year	Payment	(r = 9.91%)	value	
1	60	54.59	0.0586	0.0586
2	1,060	877.47	0.9414	1.8828
		932.06	1.0000	1.9414
		Table B: 12% Coupon Bond		
		Present value	Proportion of present	Proportion in year X
Year	Payment	(r = 9.82%)	value	
1	120	109.27	0.1053	0.1053
2	1,120	928.66	0.8947	1.7894
		1,037.93	1.0000	1.8947

For the 6 percent coupon bond, we find the duration in terms of equation (A) as:

Duration = $(.0586)(1) + (.9414)(2) = 1.9414$ years.

Similarly, the duration of the 12 percent coupon bond in table B is 1.8947 years. The duration of 6 percent coupon bond is longer then that of 12 percent coupon bond where the maturity for two coupon bonds is equal. In sum, duration refers to the weighted average life of the bond, which also provides a measure of bond's sensitivity of interest rate changes. Two common duration measures are modified and Macaulay duration. The duration discussed here is the Macaulay duration which the yield curve is assumed to be flat.

139. Duration Gap (DUR$_{GAP}$)

The weighted duration of assets (DUR_A) minus the product of the weighted duration of liabilities (DUR_L) and the ratio of total liabilities to total assets (W_L). The formula can be defined as:

$$DUR_{GAP} = DUR_A - (W_L)(DUR_L),$$

where W_L = total liability / total assets.

140. Duration Matching

A procedure for matching the durations of assets and liabilities in a financial institution.

141. Duration Measure

Duration measure is simply a weighted-average maturity, where the weights are stated in present value terms. In the same format as the weighted-average term to maturity, duration is:

$$D = \frac{PVCF_1}{PVTCF}(1) + \frac{PVCF_2}{PVTCF}(2) + \ldots + \frac{PVCF_n}{PVTCF}(n),$$

where $PVCF_t$ = the present value of the cash flow in year t discounted at current yield to maturity; t = the year when cash flow is received; n = maturity; and $PVTCF$ = the present value of total cash flow from the bond discounted at current yield to maturity

142. Dyl Model

Dyl (1975) introduced short selling with margin requirements by creating a new set of risky securities, the ones sold short, which are negatively correlated with the existing set of risky securities. These new securities greatly enhance the diversification effect when they are placed in portfolios. The Dyl model affects the efficient frontier in two ways: (1) If the investor were to combine in equal weight any long position in a security or portfolio with a short position in a security or portfolio, the resulting portfolio would yield zero return and zero variance. (2) Any combination of un-equal weighted long or short positions would yield portfolios with higher returns and lower risk levels.

143. Dynamic Financial Ratio Analysis

In basic finance and accounting courses, industry-average ratios are usually used as a benchmark with which to compare a specific company's ratio at a specific point of time. This is a form of static ratio analysis because the focus is on one point in time. But making static comparisons between ratios does not take full advantage of all the information the ratios provide. Dynamic analysis helps us better compare the ratios between either two firms or between the ratio of individual firm and that of industry average. In addition, this kind of relationship can be used to forecast the future ratios.

The financial manager compares the firm's ratios against same norm, such as the industry's average ratios. Let's take the debt ratio (DR) as an example. By regressing the current year's debt ratio against the industry average of debt ratio, the manager can better analyze the dynamic nature of ratios and determine the adjustment process the firm should undertake to get back on target. If the firm's DR is off target, the manager would attempt to adjust it to meet the mark. Lev (1969) developed the partial adjustment model to define the dynamic financial ratio adjustment process. The equation is:

$$Y_{j,\,t} = Y_{j,\,t-1} + \delta_j \left(Y_{j,\,t}^{\,*} - Y_{j,\,t-1} \right), \qquad (A)$$

where $Y_{j,\,t}^{*}$ = desirable target ratio for firm j; $Y_{j,\,t-1}$ = previous period's ratio for firm j; δ_j = partial adjustment coefficient for firm j reflecting technological and institutional constraints; and $Y_{j,\,t}$ = current year's ratio for the firm.

The partial adjustment model takes the difference between the firm's debt ratio and the target ratio (industry average) and adjusts it by δ. The difference can be only partially adjusted because deviations caused by financial and capacity constraints cannot be completely removed in the short run. Therefore, the coefficient of adjustment reflects the fact that there are limitations to the periodic adjustment of ratios.

144. Dynamic Hedging

A procedure for hedging an option position by periodically changing the position held in the underlying assets. The objective is usually to maintain a delta-neutral position. It can be quite expensive because of the transaction costs involved. Dynamic hedging sometimes referred to as dynamic options replication. [See also **Static option replication**]

145. Dynamic Option Replication

Option replication can be classified into either static or dynamic replication. Dynamic replication requires the position in the hedging assets to be rebalanced frequently and can be quite expensive because of the transaction costs involved. [See also **Static option replication** and **Delta hedging**]

E

1. EAC Method

Equivalent annual cost method is used to do capital decision for projects with unequal lives. It equals to the NPV of cost divided by an annuity factor that has the same life as the investment. However, this method assumes that two alternative projects have same revenue. [For a general case, see **Equivalent annual NPV** and **Appendix D**]

2. EAFE Index

The European, Australian, Far East index, computed by Morgan Stanley, is a widely used index of non-US stocks.

3. Early Exercise

Exercise prior to the maturity date.

4. Early Withdrawal Penalty

An interest penalty a depositor pays for withdrawing funds from a deposit account prior to maturity.

5. Earning Assets

Income-earning assets held by a bank; typically include interest-bearing balances, investment securities, and loans.

6. Earnings Credit (Earnings Credit Rate)

The assumed interest rate at which a bank applied to customer's investable balances to earn interest income. Estimating investment income from balances involves four steps.

1. The bank determines the average *ledger (book) balances* in the account during the reporting period.
2. The average transactions float – uncollected funds that still appear as part of the customer's ledger deposit – is subtracted from the ledger amount. This difference equals *collected balances.*
3. The bank deducts required reserves that must be maintained against collected balances to arrive at investable balances.
4. Management applies an earnings credit rate against investable balances to determine the average interest revenue earned on the customer's account.

7. Earnings Dilution

A decrease in earnings per share after one bank acquires another.

8. Earnings Per Share

Net income divided by the number of outstanding shares of common stock.

9. Earnings Retention Ratio

It equals one minus pay-out ratio. [See also **Plowback ratio**]

10. Earnings Yield

The ratio of earnings to price, E/P.

11. EBIT

Earnings before interest and taxes.

12. EBIT/EPS Analysis

EBIT/EPS analysis allows managers to see how different capital structures affect the earnings and risk levels of their firms. Specifically, it shows the graphical relationship between a firm's operating earnings, or earnings before interest and taxes (EBIT) and its earnings per share (EPS). Scenario analysis with different levels of EBIT can help analysts to see the effects of different capital structures on the firm's earnings per share.

EBIT/EPS analysis is an older tool that was first developed when accounting concepts dominated financial analysis. Also, most managers are familiar with the concept of earnings and are more comfortable discussing the impact of leverage on earnings rather than on cash flow.

Leverage obviously affects earnings per share. For low values of EBIT, the proposed capital structure leads to lower EPS than the current structure. For higher values of EBIT, debt works to the firm's benefit, as EPS is higher under the proposed capital structure than under the current structure.

EBIT/EPS analysis has several practical implications. First, it shows the ranges of EBIT where a firm may prefer one capital structure over another. Second, should the expected EBIT of the firm lie above the indifference EBIT level, the firm's managers should examine the standard deviation of their EBIT forecast. If there is a relatively high probability that the actual EBIT level may fall below the indifference level, management may decide to play it safe and use a more conservative financing strategy with less debt.

Third, a firm's level of business risk will affect its desired exposure to financial risk. Variations in firm sales lead to changes in EPS through the joint effects of operating and financial leverage, as given by the following relationship:

$$DOL \times DFL = DCL,$$

where DOL, DFL, and DCL represent degree of operating leverage, degree of financial leverage and degree of combined leverage, respectively.

A firm's DFL, or degree of financial leverage, is related to its choice of capital structure. Other things being equal, as a firm uses more debt to finance its assets, its degree of financial leverage rises.

There is no evidence that firms adjust their DOLs and DFLs to match some standard degree of com-

bined leverage. This relationship does, however, imply a potential tradeoff between a firm's business and financial risk. Firms with volatile sales, variable price-cost margins, and large amounts of fixed operating expenses may prefer to use less debt in their capital structures. A firm with excessive risk will not attract stock or bond investors.

EBIT/EPS is a simple tool, and so it has a limitation it provides little insight into how financing decision affect shareholder wealth. Still, it provides managers with an idea of how different levels will affect earnings and earnings variability.

13. EBITDA

Earnings before interest, taxes, depreciation, and amortization.

14. Econometric Model

It is based on representations of the underlying economic behavioral system for a particular commodity. These representations attempt to identify and model the relevant supply-and-demand factors that together determine market price and quantity.

15. Economic Assumptions

Economic environment in which the firm expects to reside over the life of the financial plan. The economic condition can be classified as boom, normal, or recession.

16. Economic Earnings

The real flow of cash that a firm could pay out forever in the absence of any change in the firm's productive capacity.

17. Economic Income

Economic income is defined as the maximum value that a firm can consume in a given period and be as well off at the end of the period as it was at the beginning. **Accounting income** measures only the changes in wealth caused by realized or recognized gains and losses, revenues and expenses. [See also **Accounting income**] Economic income measures changes in wealth based upon both realized and unrealized gains and losses. This is why the market value of the firm (its stock price) usually differs from its book value.

Theoretically, financial analysis should consider economic income rather than accounting earnings to determine the value of a firm, since economic income represents the firm's true earnings and cash flows. However, economic income is not directly observable. For that reason, analysts generally use accounting earnings as a proxy. The relationship between economic income and accounting earnings can be related by the following equation:

Accounting Income = Economic Income + Error.

18. Economic Value Added (EVA)

Economic value added (EVA) is a tool by which division managers can correct failures of accounting-driven or sales-driven evaluation systems. EVA addresses the shortcomings of these performance measures while at the same time including a cost most measures omit – the cost of capital, or the cost of financing the firm's operations with debt and equity. EVA is roughly equal to after-tax operating profit minus the firm's dollar cost of capital. If EVA is positive, management has added value to the firm; if it is negative, shareholder wealth has been harmed. In sum, EVA is a measure of financial performance trade-marked by Stern, Stewart & Co. equal to a firm's net operating profit after tax (NOPAT) minus a capital charge representing the required return to shareholders.

19. Economics, Relationship to Finance

The field of economics provides the basic framework within which managers make firm-level decision, since microeconomic decisions are implemented in the context of a dynamic, global macro economy. Like economics, finance employs the

theory of rational decision making; like quantitative management science, finance does use some highly structured models and methods.

20. Economies of Scale and Economies of Scope

Economies of scale and high capital requirements typically go together. Scale economies occur as average production cost declines with rising output per period. Any new entrant must (1) have available financing to construct a large-scale factory and (2) be able to sell in sufficient quantity to be cost-competitive. Entry may be especially unattractive when the entrant considers the impact of added volume on market price; the increase in supply caused by a new entry may lower product prices, making it more difficult for the new entrant to compete in the market. Scale requirements can deter entry and promote positive net present value projects among existing firms. Economies of scope, in particular, refers to financial institution's abilities to generate synergistic cost savings through joint use of inputs in producing multiple products.

21. ECU

European Currency Unit.

22. ECU Swap

Used to transform principal and coupon payments denominated in European Currency Units into another currency, and vice versa.

23. Edge Act Corporation

A specialized organization form open to US domestic banks since 1919 and foreign banks since 1978. These banks specialized in international trade-related banking transactions or investments.

24. Effective Annual Interest Rate

A way of quoting an interest rate such that the quoted rate is the annual percentage increase in an amount invested at this rate. If $1 is invested at an effective annual rate of r, the payoff in one year is $1+r$. [See also **Effective annual rate**]

25. Effective Annual Rate (EAR)

The effective annual rate (EAR) sometimes called the *annual effective yield*, is the true opportunity cost measure of the interest rate, as it considers the effects of periodic compounding. If the periodic interest charge r is known, the EAR is found as:

$$EAR = (1 + r)^m - 1,$$

where $m =$ the number of compounding periods per year.

If the **annual percentage rate (APR)** is known instead, r is found by dividing the APR by m and compounding by m periods. [See also **Annual percentage rate (APR)**]

$$EAR = \left[1 + \frac{APR}{m}\right]^m - 1.$$

It is useful to distinguish between a contractual or stated interest rate and the group of rates we call yields, effective rates, or market rate. A contract rate, such as the annual percentage rate (APR), is an expression that is used to specify interest cash flows such as those in loans, mortgages, or bank savings accounts. The yield or effective rate, such as the effective annual rate (EAR), measures the opportunity costs; it is the true measure of the return or cost of a financial instrument.

26. Effective Annual Yield

Annualized interest rate on a security computed using compound interest techniques. [See also **Effective annual rate**]

27. Effective Convexity

The value for convexity that reflects the price impact of embedded options in different interest rate environments. [See also **Convexity**]

28. Effective Duration

The value for duration reflecting the price impact of embedded options when interest rates rise versus fall. In addition, it can also refer to percentage change in bond price per change in the level of market interest rate.

29. Efficiency Ratio

Noninterest expense divided by the sum of net interest income and noninterest income. This is an aggregate profitability measure for a bank.

30. Efficient Diversification

The organizing principle of modern portfolio theory, which maintains that any risk-averse investor will search for the highest expected return for any level of portfolio risk.

31. Efficient Frontier

Graph representing a set of portfolios that either (i) maximize expected return at each level of portfolio risk or (ii) minimize risk at each level of return.

32. Efficient Market

Unexpectedly good or bad news can cause assets' prices to change. Good news surprises lead market participants either to reduce the risk premium they demand of an asst (thus decreasing its required return) or to increase their expectations for future cash flows. Either reaction leads to an increase in an asset's price. Bad news surprises lead the market to demand a higher risk premium (and required return) or to reduce its expectations for future cash flows; either reaction results in a falling asset price.

If a market adjusts prices quickly and in an unbiased manner after the arrival of important news surprises, it is said to be an efficient market. If the market, for example, for IBM stock is efficient, we should see a quick price change shortly after any announcement of an unexpected event that affects sales, earnings, or new products. A quick movement in the price of a stock such as IBM should take no longer than several minutes. After this price adjustment, future price changes should appear to be random. That is, the initial price reaction to the news should be unbiased, or, on average, fully reflect the effects of the news. Every time IBM's stock price changes in reaction to new information, it should show no continuing tendency to rise or fall after the price adjustment.

Any consistent trend in the same direction as the price change would be evidence of an inefficient market that does not quickly and correctly process new information to properly determine asset prices. Likewise, evidence of price corrections or reversals after the immediate reaction to news implies an inefficient market that overreacts to news.

In an efficient market, it is difficult to consistently find stocks whose prices do not fairly reflect the present values of future expected cash flows. Prices will change only when the arrival of new information indicates that an upward or downward revision in this present value is appropriate.

This means that in an efficient market, investors cannot consistently profit from trades made after new information arrives at the market. The price adjustment occurs so rapidly that no buy or sell order placed after the announcement can, in the long-run, result in returns above the market's average return. An order to buy after the arrival of good news may result in large profits, but such a gain will occur only by chance, as will comparable losses. Stock price trends always return to their random ways after initially adjusting to the new information.

Efficient markets result from interactions among many market participants, all analyzing available information in pursuit of an advantage. Also, the information flows or news they analyze must be random, both in timing and content (i.e., in an efficient market, no one can consistently predict tomorrow's news). The profit motive leads investors to try to buy low and sell high on the basis of new information and their interpretation of it. Hordes of investors analyzing all available information about the economy and individual firms quickly identify incorrectly priced stocks; resulting market pressures immediately push those stocks to their correct prices. In an efficient market, this causes prices to move in a **random walk**, meaning that they appear to fluctuate randomly over time, driven by the random arrival of new information. [See also **Random walk**]

33. Efficient Market Hypothesis (EMH)

The prices of securities fully reflect available information. Investors buying securities in an efficient market should expect to obtain an equilibrium rate of return. Weak-form EMH asserts that stock prices already reflect all information contained in the history of past prices. The semistrong-form hypothesis asserts that stock prices already reflect all past and current publicly available information. The strong-form hypothesis asserts that stock prices reflect all relevant information, including insider information.

34. Efficient Portfolio

If a portfolio is efficient, if there exists no other portfolio having the same expected return at a lower variance of returns. Moreover, a portfolio is efficient if no other portfolio has a higher expected return at the same risk of returns.

35. Efficient Set

Graph representing a set of portfolios that maximize expected return at each level of portfolio risk. Each point on an efficient set represents an efficient portfolio.

36. Elasticity

A measure of the relative quantity response to a change in price, income, interest rate, or other variable.

37. Elasticity (of An Option)

Percentage change in the value of an option accompanying a 1 percent change in the value of a stock.

38. Electronic Trading

System of trading where a computer is used to match buyers and sellers.

39. Electronic Transfer

An electronic transfer is essentially a high-tech, automated **depository transfer check (DTC)**. [See also **Depository transfer check**] To speed the cash transfer, an electronic check image is processed through clearinghouses rather than through a wire network. An electronic transfer is cheaper than a DTC and usually clears in a single business day.

40. Embedding Option

An option that is an inseparable part of another instrument. For example, bond with embedded options. Such bonds are debt exchangeable for common stock (DECS), premium equity participating shares (PEPS) and preferred equity redeemable for common stock (PERCS). All of these instruments are effectively bonds plus some options position.

41. Empirical Research

Research based in historical market data.

42. Employee Stock Ownership Plans

Employee ownership can help align the incentives of *all* the firm's workers with those of the shareholders. Employee stock ownership plans (ESOPs), if correctly implemented, can make all employees think and act like owners. As part of the ESOP, employee participation groups (comprised of members elected by fellow employees) meet regularly to discuss ways to increase productivity and the firm's value and, therefore, the value of the employees' stake. About 10,000 firms, many of them privately owned, currently have ESOPs in place.

ESOPs can be difficult to implement for an international firm. Some countries ban stock options or limit ownership of foreign shares. For a firm residing in such a country, an ESOP plan needs to be designed to meet specific, local requirements.

43. EMU

European Monetary Union. There are eleven eurozone countries. In this union, the European Central bank sets the monetary policy.

44. End-of-Year Convention

Treating cash flows as if they occur at the end of a year (or, alternatively, at the end of a period), as opposed to the date convention. Under the end-of-year convention, the end of year 0 is the present, end of year 1 occurs one period hence, and so on.

45. Endowment Funds

Organization chartered to invest money for specific purposes.

46. Enhancement

Enhancement is less common than **cannibalization**; it reflects an increase in the cash flows of the firm's other products that occurs because of a new project. [See also **Cannibalization**] For example, adding a delicatessen to a grocery store may increase cash flows more than the deli sales alone if new deli customers also purchase grocery items.

47. Enterprise Value

The value of a firm equal to the market capitalization (market value of the equity) plus the market value of outstanding debt.

48. Equilibrium Model

A model for the behavior of interest rates derived from a model of the economy.

49. Equilibrium Rate of Interest

The interest rate that clears the market.

50. Equipment Obligation Bonds
[See **Collateral**]

51. Equipment Trust Certificate

An equipment trust certificate gives the bondholder a claim to specific "rolling stock" (moveable assets), such as railroad cars or airplanes. The serial number of the specific items of rolling stock are listed in the bond indenture and the collateral is periodically examined by the trustee to ensure its proper maintenance and repair.

52. Equity

Ownership interest of common and preferred stockholders in a corporation. Also, total assets minus total liabilities; or net worth.

53. Equity Kicker

Used to refer to warrants because they usually are issued in combination with privately placed bonds.

54. Equity Method

One of the two methods that accounted for stock held as an investment in another corporation. The equity method is used if the investing firm exercises significant control over the other corporation (investee). Under this method the investment is recorded at cost. Any net earnings of the investee are recorded in proportion to the investor's share of ownership as an increase in the investment account of the investor. Dividends or net losses of the investee result in a decrease in the investing firm's investment account.

55. Equity Multiplier

Calculated as assets divided by total equity; the equity multiplier is determined by the firm's financing policy. A firm that uses a larger amount of financial leverage can support a faster sustainable growth rate, when all else remains constant. If actual growth exceeds the sustainable growth rate, a firm can finance the difference by taking on additional debt. Growth below the planned rate may lead to smaller additions to debt and an unplanned reduction in financial leverage. [See also **Capital structure ratios**]

56. Equity Swap

A swap where the return on an equity portfolio is exchanged for either a fixed or a floating rate of interest.

57. Equity-Linked Forward

A forward contract (e.g., for currency) where the quantity to be bought or sold depends upon the performance of a stock or stock index.

58. Equivalent Annual NPV (EANPV)

The net present value of a project divided by an annuity factor that has the same life as the investment.

We will give an example to demonstrate how different lives in capital budgeting needs an annuity factor to deal with this issue. In addition, we will mathematically derive the annuity factor. The traditional NPV technique is suitable for investment projects that have the same life. However it may not be appropriate to select a project from mutually exclusive investment projects, if these projects have different lives. The underlying reason is that, compared with a long-life project, a short-life project can be replicated more quickly in the long run. In order to compare projects with different lives, we can compute the NPV of an infinite replication of the investment project. For example, let Projects A and B be two mutually exclusive investment projects with the following cash flows.

Year	Project A	Project B
0	-100	-100
1	70	50
2	70	50
3		50

By assuming a discount rate of 12 percent, the traditional NPV of Project A is 18.30, and the NPV of Project B is 20.09. This shows that Project B is a better choice than Project A. However, the NPV with infinite replications for Project A and B should be adjusted into a comparable basis.

In order to compare Projects A and B, we compute the NPV of an infinite stream of constant scale replications. Let NPV (N, ∞) be the NPV of an N-year project with NPV (N), replicated forever. This is exactly the same as an annuity paid at the beginning of the first period and at the end of every N years from that time on. The NPV of the annuity is:

$$NPV(N, \textit{infinity}) = NPV(N) + \frac{NPV(N)}{(1+K)^N}$$
$$+ \frac{NPV(N)}{(1+K)^{2N}} + \ldots \quad \text{(A)}$$

In order to obtain a closed-form formula, let $(1/[(1+K)^N]) = H$. Then we have

$$\text{NPV}(N,t) = NPV(N)(1 + H + H^2 + \ldots + H^t). \quad \text{(B)}$$

Multiplying both sides by H, this becomes

$$H[NPV(N,t)] = NPV(N)(H + H^2 + \ldots$$
$$+ H^t + H^{t+1}). \quad \text{(C)}$$

Subtracting Equation (C) from Equation (B) gives

$$NPV(N,t) - (H)NPV(N,t) = NPV(N)(1 - H^{t+1}),$$
$$NPV(N,t) = \frac{NPV(N)(1 - H^{t+1})}{1 - H}.$$

Taking the limit as the number of replications, t, approaches infinity, we obtain:

$$\lim_{t \to \infty} NPV(N,t) = NPV(N,\infty)$$
$$= NPV\left[\frac{1}{1 - [1/(1+K)^N]}\right]$$
$$= NPV(N)\left[\frac{(1+K)^N}{(1+K)^N - 1}\right]. \quad \text{(D)}$$

Equation (D) is the NPV of an N-year project replicated at constant scale an infinite number of times. We can use it to compare projects with different lives because when their cash-flow streams are replicated forever, it is as if they had the same (infinite) life.

For Project A:

$$NPV(2,\infty) = NPV(2)\left[\frac{(1+0.12)^2}{(1+0.12)^2 - 1}\right]$$
$$= (18.30)\left[\frac{1.2544}{0.2544}\right]$$
$$= 90.23.$$

For Project B:

$$NPV(3,\infty) = NPV(3)\left[\frac{(1+0.12)^3}{(1+0.12)^3 - 1}\right]$$
$$= 20.09\left[\frac{1.4049}{0.4049}\right]$$
$$= 69.71$$

Consequently, we would choose to accept Project A over Project B, because, when the cash flows are adjusted for different lives, A provides the greater cash flow.

Alternatively, Equation (D) can be rewritten as an annuity version as:

$$K \times NPV(N,\infty) = \frac{NPV(N)}{Annuity\ factor}, \qquad (E)$$

where the annuity factor is

$$[1 - 1/(1 + K)^N]/K.$$

The decision rule from Equation (E) is equivalent to the decision rule of Equation (D). The left hand side of equation (E) is defined as equivalent annual NPV, which is called the equivalent annual NPV method in capital budgeting decision.

59. Equivalent Loan

The amount of the loan that makes leasing equivalent to buying with debt financing in terms of debt capacity reduction. This concept can be used to determine whether a firm should buy or lease equipments.

60. Equivalent Taxable Yield

The pretax yield on a taxable bond (t) providing an after-tax yield equal to the rate on a tax-exempt municipal bond (r_m).

$$r(1 - t) = r_m$$
$$r = r_m/(1 - t),$$

where t = marginal tax rate.

Thus the equivalent taxable yield (r) is simply the tax-free rate (r_m) divided by $1 - t$.

61. ERISA

Employee Retirement Income Security Act of 1974. This is a federal law that governs the administration of pension plans for nongovernmental employees. The basic provision is that all private corporations fully fund their pension plans.

62. Erosion

Cash-flow amount transferred to a new project from customers and sales of other products of the firm.

63. Estimation Risk

The risk of error in estimating a project's cash flows or required rate of return is called forecasting risk or estimation risk. The following table reviews some source of estimation risk associated with cash flows and required rate return.

Expected Cash Flows	Required Rates of Return
Political risk:	Real risk-free return:
Blocked currencies	Supply/demand for funds
Tariffs, quotas, embargoes	Macroeconomic
Military conflict	consumption patterns
Unstable government	Investor optimism/pessimism
	Long-run real economic growth
Fluctuating exchange rates	
Central bank policy	Expected inflation:
	Monetary policy
Fiscal policy:	Commodity prices
Government spending	
Tax policy	Risk premium:
	Systematic risk
Inadequate or incorrect:	Political risk
Strategic analysis	Exchange rate risk
Market research	Business risk
Pricing policy	Financial risk
Competitor retaliation	
Construction delays	
Delay in R&D, manufacturing, or production	
Work stoppages or strikes	
Technology obsolescence	

64. Euro

The European currency unit introduced in January 1999.

65. Eurobanks

Banks that make loans and accept deposits in foreign currencies.

66. Eurobonds

Eurobonds are bonds denominated in US dollars issued by firms in financial markets outside the US and typically pay interest annually. Eurobonds are an international bond sold primarily in countries other than the country in whose currency the issue is denominated.

67. Eurocurrency

A currency that is outside the formal control of the issuing country's monetary authorities.

68. Eurodollar Bonds

Eurodollar bonds are dollar-denominated bonds that are underwritten by international syndicates of commercial and investment banks. Because these issues are sold outside the US, they escape review by the SEC, somewhat reducing their issue expenses. Eurodollar bonds usually have fixed coupons with annual coupon payments. Most mature in three to ten years, so they are not attractive for firms that want to issue long-term debt. They typically are unsecured, pledging no specific assets to the bondholders in case of default. This is not a major concern to investors, as only the largest and financially strongest firms have access of the Eurobond market. Investors do care that the bonds are sold in bearer form, thus helping bondholders to remain anonymous and evade taxes on coupon income. Some researchers believe that this is the main reason that Eurodollar bond interest rates are low relative to US rates.

69. Eurodollar CD

Deposit of dollars with foreign banks.

70. Eurodollar Futures Contract

A futures contract written on a Eurodollar deposit.

71. Eurodollar Interest Rate

The interest rate on a Eurodollar deposit.

72. Eurodollars

Dollar-denominated deposits at banks of located outside the US. Eurodollar transaction denotes any transaction involving dollars that takes place outside the US.

73. Euroequity

Firms are not limited to domestic financial markets for raising capital. The world's financial markets have become more liquid and more integrated as cross-border restrictions have diminished, and more and more large corporations have begun looking outside their national boundaries to raise financing. US firms can raise money in the Euroequity market by selling equity and debt claims to non-US investors. Changes in tax laws and regulations, as well as lower financing costs, have led US firms to issue more offerings to non-US investors.

A cost advantage of trading in the Euroequity market is that Euroequity is traded over-the-counter in a large, active, cross-border market, so issuing firms need not register their securities on exchanges in many different countries.

74. European Currency Unit (ECU)

An index of foreign exchange which was introduced in eleven European countries in January 2002.

75. European Monetary Unit (EMC)

It is a form of denomination. It is consisted of the currencies of six original European Currency Unit (ECU) members.

76. European Option

A European option is an option that can be exercised only on the expiration date, which makes it simpler to analyze as compared to an **American option** because its term to maturity is known. An American option may be exercised any time up to the expiration date. [See also **American option**] The factors that determine the values of American and European options are the same; all other things being equal, however, an American option is worth more than a European option because of the extra flexibility it grants the option holder.

77. European, Australian, Far East (EAFE) Index

A widely used index of non-US stocks computed by Morgan Stanley.

78. Event Study

Research methodology designed to measure the impact of an event of interest on stock returns.

79. Excess Return

Rate of return in excess of the risk-free rate.

80. Exchange Option

An option permitting the holder to obtain one asset by giving up another. For example, an exchange call maturing t period from today provides the right to obtain one unit of the Nikkei index in exchange for one unit of the S&P index. In addition, standard calls and puts are exchange options in which one of the two assets is cash.

81. Exchange Rate

An exchange rate is the price of one currency in terms of another currency. [See also **Direct quote** and **Indirect quotes**]

82. Exchange Rate Risk

Investors in nondomestic securities face a number of risks beyond those of domestic securities. Exchange rate changes will cause fluctuations in the values of cash flows in terms of US dollars; this is called exchange rate risk.

83. Exchange Ratio for Business Combination

In business combination, two companies agree to exchange shares of common stock. In such a case, the determination of a "price" is actually the determination of an exchange ratio. Larson and Gonedes (1969) have presented a model for exchange ratio determination that involves making assumptions about the precombination and post-combination earnings streams and P/E (price/earnings) ratios.

For example, assume Firm A and Firm B are the acquired firm and the acquiring firm, respectively. Let the exchange ratio (ER) be defined as the number of traded shares of Firm B to be exchanged for the one traded share of Firm A. LG defined the postcombination price (p^*) as

$$p^* = \left[\frac{NI_A + NI_B}{N_B + (ER)(N_A)} \right](PE^*),$$

where NI_A = net income for Firm A, NI_B = net income for Firm B, N_A = number of shares outstanding for Firm A, N_B = number of shares outstanding for Firm B, PE^* = post combination price/earnings ratio.

By comparing p^* with price per share before the combination of Firm A (P_A) and Firm B (P_B), we find the following exchange ratio will affect the shareholders of both Firm A and Firm B as:

(i) The shareholders of Firm A are as well off after the combination as before if

$$ER \geq \frac{N_B P_B}{(NI_A + NI_B)(PE^*) - N_A P_A};$$

(ii) The shareholders of Firm B are as well off after the combination as before if

$$ER \leq \frac{(PE^*)(NI_A + NI_B)}{(N_A)(P_B)} - \frac{N_B}{N_A}.$$

84. Exchanges

National or regional auction markets providing a facility for members to trade securities. A seat is a membership on an exchange. For example, New York exchange and Philadelphia exchanges are national and regional exchange respectively.

85. Exclusionary Self-tender

The firm makes a tender offer for a given amount of its own stock while excluding targeted stockholders. It is the opposite of a targeted repurchase.

86. Ex-Dividend Date

A practical problem arises if a shareholder decides to sell a day to two before the record date. Because the brokerage industry requires some time to process the transaction and enter the name of the buyer on the stockholder list, it has arbitrarily decided that the right to the declared dividend is terminated four business days before the record date. Any sale between this ex-dividend date and the record date leaves the seller with the right to the dividend. The term ex-dividend comes from the Latin *ex* meaning *from*, because the dividend has been taken from anyone who buys the stock after the ex-dividend date.

The extent of the appropriate drop in stock prices associated with dividend payments depends in part on the tax situation of the marginal investor, the individual who at the margin causes an imbalance between supply and demand and therefore causes a price change. If the marginal investor in the marketplace is in the 30 percent tax bracket and the dividend is $1.00 per share, the per-share price of the stock might fall by $0.70 on the ex-dividend date, all else being equal. The price might not fall by a full dollar because the marginal investor realizes only a $0.70 after-tax dividend.

One model has been developed to incorporate tax effects into determining the ex-dividend price as:

$$\frac{P_o - P_x}{D_o} = \frac{1 - T_p}{1 - T_g},$$

where P_o = the price just before the stock goes ex; P_x = the ex-dividend share price; D_o = the amount of the dividend per share; T_p = the relevant marginal personal tax rate; T_g = the effective marginal tax rate on capital gains.

If $T_p = T_g = 0$, or $T_p = T_g$, then $P_x = P_o - D_o$.

Tax laws require the corporation to mail a copy of Form 1099 to every shareholder at the end of the year to report the amount of dividends the firm paid to that person. The firm also sends a copy of this form to the IRS to report the dividend income it paid to each shareholder during the year. This system of informing the taxing authorities is unique to the US. Most other nations of the world require that corporations withhold portions of stockholders' dividends and turn these funds over to the government to settle each individual's tax liability on dividend income.

In sum, ex-dividend date is a date four business days before the date of record for a security. An individual purchasing stock before its ex-dividend date will receive the current dividend.

87. Ex-dividend or Ex-rights

Phrases used to indicate that a stock is selling without a recently declared right or dividend. The ex-rights or ex-dividend date is generally four business days before the date of record.

88. Executive Stock Options

Executive stock options provide stock purchase rights as compensation for corporate employees. For services rendered, the manager or the employee has the right to buy a specific number of shares for a set price during a given period. Unlike warrants and publicly traded options, executive stock options cannot be traded. The option's owner has only two choices: exercise the option or let it expire. Like a warrant, should the owner decide to exercise the option, the corporation receives money and issues new shares.

The use of executive stock options for management compensation raises an interesting agency question. The firm's managers may make investment and financing decisions that increase the firm's risk in order to increase the value of their stock options. Such an action could have a detrimental effect on the bondholders and other creditors of the firm.

89. Executor

An individual or trust department responsible for handling a settlement.

90. Exercise

The exchange of the strike price (or strike asset) for the underlying asset at the terms specified in the option contract.

91. Exercise Price

Price at which the holder of an option can buy (in the case of a call option) or sell (in the case if a put option) the underlying stock. Also called the striking price.

92. Exercise Style

The circumstances under which an option holder has the right to exercise an option. "European" and "American" are exercise styles.

93. Exercising the Option

The act of buying or selling the underlying asset via the option contract.

94. Exotic Option

A derivatives contract in which an ordinary derivative has been altered to change the characteristics of the derivative in a meaningful way. Also called a *nonstandard option*. Most exotic options trade in the over-the-counter market and designed by financial institutions to meet the requirement of their clients. For example, barrier options are exotic options. [See also **Barrier option**]

95. Expectations Hypothesis

The expectations hypothesis assumes that bond investors look ahead and make predictions, or form expectations, about future interest rates. From this perspective, in an efficient market, the return from investing in an N-year bond will be the same as the expected return from rolling over the proceeds (coupons and principal) from maturing one-year bonds into new one-year bonds over the N-year time frame. Thus today's long-term rates reflect expectations about future short-term rates

Although intuitive, the expectations hypothesis does not totally explain the shapes of observed term structures. Historically, the term structure is sloped upward; long-term rates usually are higher than short-term rates. Under the expectations hypothesis the typical upward-sloping term structure implies that the market always expects rising short-term interest rates. This does not agree with the observed behavior of short-term rates over time. Other explanations for the behavior of the term structure have attempted to correct this flaw.

96. Expected Return

Risk arises from the possibility that actual returns may differ from expected returns. Actual returns differ from expected returns whenever there is an unexpected change in an asset's price or cash flow stream. Issuers must compensate investors with an expected return that is greater than the nominal risk-free return; otherwise, investors would have no economic incentive to place their capital at risk. A basic principle of finance is that higher risk leads to higher expected returns, or that *risk drives returns*.

A more complete model of returns is

$$Expected\ return = (1 + Real\ risk\text{-}free\ rate)$$
$$\times (1 + Expected\ inflation\ rate)$$
$$\times (1 + Risk\ premium) - 1.$$

Combining with our nominal risk-free rate gives us

$$Expected\ return = (1 + Nominal\ risk\text{-}free\ rate)$$
$$\times (1 + Risk\ premium) - 1.$$

The term *expected return* on the left-hand side of the equations indicates that the investor may not earn the stated return on an instrument. Because of risk, the actual return may be higher or lower than expected.

97. Expected Return-Beta Relationship

One implication of the capital asset pricing model (CAPM) is that security risk premiums (expected excess returns) will be proportional to beta. This is used to describe relationship between return and systematic risk, as shown in the security market line (SML).

98. Expected Value of a Variable

The average value of the variable obtained by weighting the alternative values by their probabilities.

99. Expiration Date

The time by which the option transaction must be carried out. In other words, it is the maturity date of an option.

100. Expiration-Date Risk

Futures contracts are not usually available for every month. If a hedger needed a futures contract for July and the only contracts that were available were for March, June, September, and December, the hedger would have to select either the June or September contract. Either of these contract would have a different price series than a July contract (if one existed). Hence, the hedger cannot form a perfect hedge and is faced with the chance that the basis may change.

101. Explicit Finite Difference Method

A method for valuing a derivative by solving the underlying differential equation. The value of the derivative at time t is related to three values at time $t + \delta t$. It is essentially the same as the trinomial tree method.

102. Exposure

The amount which would be lost in a default given the worst possible assumptions about recovery in the liquidation or bankruptcy of an obligor. For a loan or used facility it is the full amount of the facility, since the worst assumption is that the borrower draws the full amount and then goes bankrupt. In a credit risk analysis, it is called exposure at default (EAD)

103. Extendable Notes

Notes that have their coupons reset every two or three years to reflect the current interest rate environment and any changes in the firm's credit quality. At each reset, the investor may accept the new coupon rate (and thus effectively extend the maturity of the investment) or put the bonds back to the firm.

104. Extendable Swap

In an extendable swap, one party has the option to extend the life of the swap beyond the specified period.

105. Extension

Voluntary arrangements to restructure a firm's debt, under which the payment date is postponed.

106. Extension Risk

The risk that the holder of a mortgage-backed security will receive outstanding principal payment later than originally anticipated. Later principal payments result from interest rates rising and pre-payments occurring slower than expected.

107. Extinguish

Retire or pay off debt.

F

1. Face Value

The value of a bond that appears on its face. Also referred to as par value or principal.

2. Facility

A generic term which includes loans, commitments, lines, letter, etc: Any arrangement by which a bank accepts credit exposure to an obligor.

3. Facility Fee

Fee imposed for making a line of credit available.

4. Factor

A financial institution that buys a firm's accounts receivables and collects the debt. [See also **Factoring**]

5. Factor Analysis

An analysis aimed at finding a small number of factors that describe most of the variation in a large number of correlated variables. (Similar to a principal components analysis.) [See also **Arbitrage pricing theory**]

6. Factor Model

A model in which each stock's return is generated by common factors, called the systematic sources of risk. [See also **Arbitrage pricing theory**]

7. Factor Portfolio

A well-diversified portfolio constructed to have a beta of 1.0 on one factor and a beta of zero on any other factor. Factor portfolios will serve as the benchmark portfolios for a multifactor security market line.

8. Factoring

Firms can convert accounts receivable to cash by a method called factoring. Factoring essentially involves an outright sale of accounts receivable to a finance company or factoring department of a commercial bank. Factoring differs from **pledging** since it gives the finance company no recourse to the borrower in the case of bad debts. [See also **pledging**] The customer receives notice that the invoice has been sold and is asked to make payment directly to the finance company.

This arrangement clearly increases the lender's risk, as compared to pledging. To reduce this risk, the finance company virtually takes over the work of the borrower's credit department. All new customer orders pass through the finance company, which does a credit appraisal. If the finance company rejects the customer as an unacceptable credit risk, the borrower either must turn down the order or fill it for cash.

Factoring, like pledging, is a fairly costly source of credit. This overall cost has a number of distinct components. The factor charges the borrower a fee between about 1 to 3 percent of the face value of the invoices for credit appraisal. The interest charge depends upon whether the finance company has agreed to forward the funds as soon as the goods are shipped or only on the receivable's due date at the end of the credit period. For payment at shipment, the interest rate may well rise as high as 15 to 25 percent.

The advantages of factoring resemble those of pledging; it is a relatively easy and flexible source of funds once the initial negotiations have been completed, and it provides additional funds as the borrower's scale of operations, and therefore its needs, grow. Factoring always has been widely used by small companies in specific industries, such as textiles, garments, or furniture, which may lack access to bank loans. Factoring allows the smaller company to avoid the cost and trouble of setting up its own credit department; this gives factoring one advantage over pledging. Against this, however, must be set the possible damage to the borrower's reputation when customers learn that their accounts have been sold to a finance company.

Credit-card transactions share some common traits with factoring. In effect, the merchant that accepts a credit card payment is factoring its accounts receivable to the issuer of the card, and the credit-card holder pays the issuer directly.

In sum, factoring is a sale of a firm's accounts receivable to a financial institution known as a factor.

9. Fair Game

Under the fair game, the expected value of a gamble is exactly equal to the cost. Under this situation, there is no way to use "information" available at a point in time (t) to earn return above normal.

10. Fair Game Model

Bases on average returns across a large number of observations, the expected return on an asset equals its actual return that is

$$z_{j,\,t+1} = r_{j,\,t+1} - E(r_{j,\,t+1}|\Phi_t)$$

and $E(z_{j,\,t+1}) = E(r_{j,\,t+1} - E(r_{j,\,t+1}|\Phi_t)) = 0$,

where $z_{j,\,t+1}$ is the error term between the jth stock's actual return $r_{j,\,t+1}$ at time $t+1$ and its expected return $E(r_{j,\,t+1}|\Phi_t)$. The fair-game model is an expected return efficient-market model. In search of a fair game, investors can invest in securities at their current prices and can be confident that these prices fully reflect all available information and are consistent with the risks involved.

11. Fair Market Value

Amount at which common stock would change hands between a willing buyer and a willing seller, both having knowledge of the relevant facts; also called market price.

12. Fair Value

Another name for the theoretical forward price; spot price plus interest less the future value of dividends.

13. Fallen Angels

Obligors having both relatively high percentage risk and relatively large exposure, whose large exposures were created when their credit ratings were better, but who now have much higher percentage risk due to recent downgrades.

14. Fannie Mae

Name referring to the Federal National Mortgage Association (FNMA).

Originally created in 1983, the Federal National Mortgage Association (FNMA), or "Fannie Mae," is the oldest of the three mortgage-backed security sponsoring agencies. While it is now a private corporation owned by shareholders with stock traded on major exchanges, in the minds of many investors it still has implicit government backing that makes it equivalent to a government-sponsored agency. Indeed, supporting this view is the fact that FNMA has a secured line of credit available from the US Treasury should it need funds in an emergency. FNMA is a more active agency than Government National Mortgage Association (GNMA) in creating pass-through securities. GNMA merely sponsors such programs. FNMA actually helps create pass-throughs by buying and holding mortgages on its balance sheet; it also issues bonds directly to finance those purchases.

15. FASB Statement 13

Complicated accounting rules must guide a presentation of the effects of a financial lease on the lessee's balance sheet and income statement. FASB Statement 13 requires the firm to capitalize lease payments and list the leased property as an asset ("leased property under capital lease") and as a liability ("obligations under capital lease"). The rationale for this accounting treatment is straightforward. Since the financing lease is a long-term, fixed obligation to the firm, it should be treated like similar liabilities. The firm's long-term access to the leased asset and liability accounts are amortized to zero over time under the FASB 13 treatment. The income statement deduction includes both the amortization of the liability and an imputed interest expense on the remaining lease liability.

16. Feasible Set

Opportunity set in a portfolio analysis.

17. Fed Wire

The Federal Reserve System operates by Fed Wire to process US-dollar-denominated transactions initiated and received in the US. Since Fed Wire transfers are guaranteed by the US government, the system minimizes users' liquidity and credit risks.

18. Federal Agency Securities

Securities issued by corporations and agencies created by the US government, such as the Federal Home Loan Bank Board and Government National Mortgage Association. [See also **Ginnie Mae**]

19. Federal Deposit Insurance Corporation (FDIC)

The FDIC was created in the Glass-Steagull Act (1933). Fed member bank must be insured by the FDIC. If a bank purchases deposit insurance, it must comply with rules set by FDIC.

20. Federal Financing Bank (FEB)

FEB is a federal agency that borrows from the US Treasury and lends funds to various federal agen-cies. FEB can require the treasury to purchase up to $5 billion of its obligations. The treasury secretary is authorized to purchase any amount of FEB obligations at his or her discretion.

21. Federal Funds

Unsecured short-term loans that are settled in immediately available funds. Federal funds are excess reserves lent by one institution to another institution to meet Fed reserve requirements.

22. Federal Reserve Bank

One of the 12 district federal reserve banks that make up the Federal Reserve System. Typically, regional Federal reserves banks serve as clearing locations where institutions accounts are debited or credited as necessary, and checks are sorted, bundled, and returned to participating depositories.

23. Federal Reserve Board

The Federal Reserve Board (or the Fed) acts as the central bank, or "banker's bank," in the US economy.

The Federal Reserve Board has three basic instruments with which it can affect the money supply to administer its **monetary policy**. [See also **Monetary policy**]

1. **Open market operations** (repurchases or sales of government securities);
2. **Discount rate** changes (adjustment in the interest rate paid by banks when they borrow from the Fed); and,
3. **Reserve requirement** changes (adjustments in the amount of reserves banks must hold either as cash or on deposit at the Fed).

The only interest rate the Fed directly controls is the discount rate. As with any price, demand and supply influences affect all other interest rates. [See also **Open market operations**, **Discount rate**, **Reserve requirement**]

24. FHA

Federal Housing Administration – a federal agency that insures mortgages which target groups that might otherwise be disadvantaged in the housing market, such as low income family.

25. FHLMC

Federal Home Loan Mortgage Corporation (Freddie Mac); a private corporation operating with an implicit federal guarantee; buys mortgages financed largely by mortgage–backed securities. The implicit Federal guarantee can reduce the borrowing cost.

26. Fidelity Bond

A contract that covers losses associated with employee dishonesty, typically embezzlement and forgery at banks.

27. Fiduciary

An individual or trust department responsible for acting in the best interests of a designated third party.

28. Field Warehouse Financing

A form of inventory loan in which a public warehouse company acts as a control agent to supervise the inventory for the lender.

29. Field Warehousing

In field warehousing, the finance company (usually a specialized warehousing organization) takes over the use of a certain part of the borrower's premises. This floor space must be segregated from the borrower's other operations so that it can be kept locked, restricting access only to the warehousing company. The inventory to serve as collateral is transferred to this segregated area, and the warehousing company advances the discounted cash value of the inventory to the borrower. In return,

the warehousing company receives a warehouse receipt, which gives its title to the inventory.

This inventory cannot be sold or used without the warehouse company's permission, and this permission is given only when the borrower repays a corresponding portion of the funds advanced. Thus, the lender can ensure that the collateral always is adequate to secure the loan. The warehousing company locates a member of its own staff, the custodian, on the borrower's premises to ensure that its rights are respected.

30. FIFO

The first-in-first-out accounting method of inventory valuation. In an inflation period, the cost of inventory is lower than that calculated by the last-in-first-out accounting method.

31. Filter Rule

A technical analysis technique stated as a rule for buying or selling stock according to past price movements. The filter rule is usually stated in the following way: Purchase the stock when it rises by X percent from the previous low and hold it until it declines by Y percent from the subsequent high. At this point, sell the stock short or hold cash.

Filter rules are a timing strategy. They show investors when they should be long in a security and when they should sell it short. The alternative to timing is to buy and hold the security. Thus, filter rules are analyzed by comparing them to buy and hold strategy. One further assumption is necessary for the buy and hold strategy to be relevant; namely, the expected return is positive. If the expected return is negative, then the relevant alternative is to hold cash.

32. Finance

Finance is the study of how to manage assets and obtain funds in order to maximize the wealth of the owner. Thus, the broad field of finance deals with such varied topics as designing a personal retirement plan, managing inventory, investing excess cash, borrowing money, or attracting bank depositors. Business operations generate profits when the firm can raise funds at a lower cost than the return generated by the investment of the funds.

Businesses purchase assets with the hope that they will generate future cash flows. The cash flows may be in the form of income, future cost savings, and/or changes in company value. To finance asset purchases, firms sell liability and equity securities, including bonds, stocks, mortgages, and loans. Investors are willing to buy the securities in order to receive future cash flows, which help the investors meet their own future needs. The value of an asset depends on three cash flow characteristics: (1) amount; (2) pattern over time, and; (3) risk.

Investors will pay more for an asset that promises larger cash flows after shorter time periods with lower risks. Values are lower for assets that generate smaller, later, and/or more uncertain cash flows.

33. Finance Charge

As defined by truth-in-lending Regulation Z the finance charge refers to "all charges payable directly or indirectly by the borrower and imposed directly or indirectly by the lender as an incident to or as an extension of credit."

34. Finance Company

A firm that borrows from the money and capital markets to make loans to individuals and commercial enterprises. The services provided by finance companies include consumer lending, business lending and mortgage lending. Finance companies do not accept deposits but instead rely on short and long term debt as a source of funds. Additionally, finance companies often lend money to customers who commercial banks find too risky.

35. Financial Accounting Standards Board (FASB)

The governing body in accounting. FASB issues generally accepted accounting principles (GAAP)

as a guide for financial statement reporting in the US.

36. Financial Analyst

The position of the financial analyst in the corporate structure and the scope of his or her work are interdependent. The financial analyst is a staff member who diagnoses the effects of management proposals and/or decisions on the financial health of the firm. Acting as an internal consultant, the financial analyst examines profitability, cash flows, and operations; conducts studies; interprets information; and designs financial controls. Although some of this analysis is focused entirely within the firm, the analyst also must examine the dynamic economic, social, political, and competitive environments that are external to the firm, in an attempt to gauge their impact on the firm's well-being. This information is used to assist in the process of financial planning and forecasting. The analyst provides this information as input for upper-level management's decisions; generally, he or she does not set policy or make decisions. Major decisions are made by top management, which may include the CFO and treasurer of the firm.

In addition, the financial analyst must perform many tasks on a periodic basis. These activities include analyzing the company's liquidity and profitability and supervising its day-to-day financial operations, including accounts receivable, accounts payable, and cash balances. The analyst must also contribute to longer term projects by analyzing the firm's capital structure and major investment alternatives.

The analyst also completes specific projects that are either self-initiated or, more commonly, requested by others. For example, if the analyst notices a market variation from a normal financial ratio, he or she may try to determine the underlying cause of the variation and report it to management as part of the control function. Also, the analyst may examine the effect of a current economic force on the company, such as how a tax policy change might affect the firm's cash flows and stock value. The financial analyst may assist operations management in determining whether to lease or purchase a specific asset. Some problem analyses are critical to the success of the entire company, such as the decision whether to expand or sell off one of the operating division; others are as commonplace as deciding whether to purchase Treasury bills or certificates of deposit (CDs) with surplus cash.

Within the company's organization structure, the position of financial analyst may be centralized or decentralized or have elements of both. Centralizing the analyst function places it at corporate headquarters, separate from the operational units for which it performs most of its analyses. Decentralizing the position places analysts in each of the firm's divisions to do division-specific work. Centralization allows the firm to pool expertise, promote interaction among the analysts, and maintain objectivity, as the analysis views a divisional issue from a companywide point of view consistent with the firm's overall strategy.

However, certain circumstances create advantages for a decentralized financial analyst function. A decentralized organization is useful: (1) when the analyst's role is to advise the operating manager, who has some independence to make division-level decisions; (2) when the operations of the division are complex and the analyst must possess specialized expertise to make useful recommendations; and (3) when the larger firm is really a holding company for different, independent organization (e.g., one corporation may operate a banking division, another may run an insurance division, and so on).

37. Financial Assets

Financial assets such as stocks and bonds are claims to the income generated by real assets or claims on income from the government.

38. Financial Break-Even

Financial break-even occurs when the project breaks even on a financial basis, that is, when it

has a net present value of zero. To determine a project's financial break-even point, we must first determine the annual operating cash flow, OCF^*, that gives it a zero NPV. The formula for the financial break-even quantity is:

$$Q^*_{financial} = \frac{FC + OCF^*}{p - vc} = Q^*_{cash} + \frac{OCF^*}{p - vc},$$

where FC = fixed costs; VC = variable cost per unit; P = price per unit; OCF^* = annual operating cash flow; and Q^*_{cash} = cash break-even point.

Without any calculations, we know intuitively that this break-even quantity should exceed the cash and accounting break-even quantities. OCF^* must be sufficiently large to both cover depreciation expense *(Dep)* and allow the project to earn its minimum required return. Intuition also tells us that accounting income under financial break-even should exceed that of the accounting break-even point. As OCF^* must exceed the depreciation expense, the firm's net income (*NI*) will be positive (ignoring working capital effects, $OCF = NI + Dep$). Thus, some positive taxable income occurs under financial break-even.

As expected the financial break-even quantity and operating cash flow exceed those of the **cash** and **accounting break-even** analyses. [See also **Cash break-even** and **Accounting break-even**] Note a major difference between financial break-even as compared to cash and accounting break-even: Financial break-even analysis encompasses cash flows from the *entire life* of the project.

39. Financial Distress

Financial distress means that a firm's short-run operating and financial cash inflows are less than its outflows.

Financial distress occurs when the firm's internal rate of return on its investments is less than its cost of capital, either at the present time or in the near future. In terms of sources and uses of funds, financial distress occurs when the inflow of funds from operations is not sufficient to meet required outflows.

In sum, financial distress is the events preceding and including bankruptcy, such as violation of loan contracts.

40. Financial Distress Costs

Legal and administrative costs of liquidation or reorganization (direct costs); an impaired ability to do business and an incentive toward selfish strategies such as taking large risks, underinvesting, and milking the property (indirect costs).

41. Financial Engineering

Creating new financial instruments by combining other derivatives or more generally, by using derivatives pricing techniques.

42. Financial Futures Contract

A commitment between two parties to exchange a standardized financial asset through an organized exchange at a specified price of futures contracts changes prior to delivery, and participants must settle daily changes in contract value.

43. Financial Innovation

The continuous development of new financial products, services and technology to deliver products and services.

44. Financial Intermediaries

An area of finance that deals with financial institutions, such as banks and insurance companies, which collect funds from savers and lend them to or invest them in businesses or people that need cash. Institutions that provide the market function of matching borrowers and lenders or traders. Financial institutions may be categorized as depository, contractual savings, and investment-type. Alternatively, they can be classified into depository institutions, insurance companies securities firms and investment banks, mutual funds and finance companies.

45. Financial Lease

A long-term noncancelable capital lease, generally requiring the lessee to pay all maintenance fees. Tax law identifies lessor as the owner of the leased asset, so the lessor can deduct the depreciation over the life of the lease. [See also **Capital lease**]

46. Financial Leverage

Just as operating leverage arises from fixed operating costs, financial leverage arises from fixed financing costs. Financial leverage magnifies any change in EBIT to produce a percentage change in earnings per share larger than the change in EBIT. Financial leverage defines extent to which a firm relies on debt. Financial leverage is measured by the ratio of long-term debt to long-term plus equity.

47. Financial Management Analysis

Financial management analysis is a field in finance that studies how an organization should manage its assets, liabilities, and equity to produce a good or service.

48. Financial Markets

Markets that deal with cash flows over time, where the savings of lenders are allocated to the financing needs of borrowers. Financial markets are composed of money markets and capital market. [See also **Money and capital markets**]

49. Financial Planning

Financial planning is the process of analyzing alternative investment, financing, and dividend strategies in the context of various potential economic environments. Planning involves forecasting both the outcomes of different strategies and their risks. Thus, financial planning models are tools to help managers improve their forecasts of important accounts of financial statements and better understand the interactions of investment, financing, and dividend decisions.

Planning involves using different economic and sales scenarios and reacting to them with different strategies. Playing what-if games helps managers select an optimal course of action, given managers' risk preferences and beliefs about the most likely scenarios.

In developing a long-term financial plan, these three decisions (policies) can be described more explicitly as follows:

1. *The firm's investment decision.* This refers to the amount of cash needed for the firm's investment in a new asset (it is also called the *capital budgeting decision*). In addition, it also refers to the amount of working capital needed on an ongoing basis (also referred to as the *working capital decision*).

2. *The firm's financing decision.* This refers to new borrowing or new equity issued for financing the firm's investment in new assets. This decision is influenced by the degree of financial leverage the firm chooses to employ and how it plans to raise the necessary new funds.

3. *The firm's dividend decision.* This refers to the amount of cash the firm thinks is necessary and appropriate to pay equity holders as cash dividends.

At the most basic level, a planning model is a tool that uses inputs supplied by managers in the form of economic, accounting, market, and policy information.

50. Financial Requirements

In the financial plan, financing arrangements that are necessary to meet the overall corporate object-ive. The plan will include a section on financing arrangements. This part of the plan should discuss dividend policy and debt policy. Sometimes firms will expect to raise equity by selling new shares of stock. In this case the plan must consider what kinds of securities must be sold and what methods of issuance are most appropriate.

51. Financial Risk

Financial risk measure the additional risk that the firm's stockholders bear when the firm is financed with debt as well as equity.

Financial risk is determined by how the firm decides to finance its assets. Financial risk occurs as a result of fixed costs in a firm's financial structure. A firm's financial structure is the combination of debt and equity that it uses to finance assets. Equity dividends, including preferred stock dividends, are considered to be a variable financing cost, as the firm can reduce the dollar amount of dividends or eliminate them entirely if its cash flow is poor. Shareholders may be unhappy, but even preferred shareholders can do little to force the firm to pay dividends. In sum, financial risk refers to potential variation in income before interest and taxes associated with fixed interest payments on debt and lease payments.

52. Financial Services Holding Company

A parent company that owns a bank holding company plus other subsidiaries, such as a thrift holding company and insurance subsidiary.

53. Financial Z Score

[See also **Credit scoring model**]

54. Finite Difference Method

A method for solving a differential equation. It can be classified into implicit, explicit, or other finite difference method.

55. Firm

A firm is a collection of assets, and the value of those assets depends upon the size, timing, and risk of their cash flows. Of all the possible goals of a firm, only shareholder wealth maximization fully considers the size, timing, and risk of the cash flow generated by the firm's activities.

A firm purchases its assets with funds obtained from sources listed on the right-hand side of the balance sheet – liabilities and owners' equity. Thus, the value of a firm belongs to its creditors and owners. Creditors have a fixed claim on the firm that does not change with variations in the value of the firm's assets over time. As the shareholders have a residual claim on the firm's assets, variations in a firm's value are reflected mainly in the fluctuating value of the owners' or shareholders' wealth in a firm. Alternatives that increase shareholders' wealth should be chosen; alternatives that harm shareholders' wealth should be rejected.

Fluctuations in the value of a firm are most easily seen in fluctuations in the market value of the shareholders' claim on the firm. All else being constant, increases in shareholder value lead to a larger cushion for those with fixed claims on the firm, such as creditors, bondholders, employees, and pensioners.

Economics teaches that the goal of a firm is to maximize its economic profit, which is a function of the difference between the return earned on its assets and the opportunity cost of buying those assets. The workings of the financial markets will ensure that the cost to a firm of raising capital is equal to the capital's opportunity cost; otherwise, available funds will flow to other firms that can offer investors higher expected returns at lower risk. Should returns earned by the firm exceed this cost, the profit belongs to the firm's owners. Thus, the financial goal of maximizing shareholder wealth is similar to the concept of maximizing economic profit.

56. Firm Commitment Offerings

Investment banks distribute most IPOs in firm commitment offerings. With a firm commitment offering, the investment bank commits its capital to purchase IPO shares. Once the offering price is set, the bank purchases the shares at the offer price less a spread, or discount. The bank then sells the securities to investors. In practice, the investment bank lines up a number of investors to purchase the shares before the offering date. The spread represents the investment bank's profit from reselling each share at the offering price.

The issuer has virtually zero price risk in a firm commitment offering once the offer price is set. The issuer receives the proceeds from the sale immediately, which it can then spend as outlined in the prospectus. The investment bank carries, or underwrites, the risk of fluctuating stock prices. Should the market's perception of the issuer change or a macroeconomic event result in a stock market decline, the investment bank carries the risk of loss, or at least the possibility of a smaller than expected spread.

For most firm commitment underwritings, the managing investment bank arranges investment banking **syndicates** to help distribute shares of the newly public firm. The managing investment bank makes a smaller spread, or profit, from selling shares to syndicate members. [See also **Syndicates**]

57. Firm Commitment Underwriting

An underwriting in which an investment banking firm commits to buy the entire issue and assumes all financial responsibility for any unsold shares. [See also **Firm commitment offerings**]

58. Firm-Specific Risk

[See **Diversifiable risk**]

59. First Mortgage Bond

A first mortgage bond has a primary, or senior, claim on assets. In theory, a first mortgage claim means that the underlying asset can be sold and the proceeds distributed to the first mortgage bondholders to satisfy their claims against the firm; any remaining funds from the sale are distributed to satisfy the **second mortgage** holders' claims. [See also **Second mortgage bond**]

60. First-Pass Regression

A time series regression to estimate the betas of securities or portfolios.

61. Fiscal Policy

Fiscal policy involves planning government spending and taxing to influence economic conditions. Both tax laws and government expenditures affect the disposable income of consumers and corporations and, therefore, the level of aggregate demand in the economy. For example, taxes affect the incentives that people have to save and invest, and thus affect future economic growth. Tax laws affect firms' after-tax returns on their investments and thus help determine how a firm will invest today in order to generate future cash flows.

62. Fisher Effect

[See **Nominal risk-free interest rate**]

63. Fisherian Relation

The nominal interest rate in every contract will be equal to the real rate of interest plus the expected future inflation rate is called Fisherian relation:

$$(1 + R_j^t) = (1 + r_j^t)(1 + I_j^t),$$

where r_j^t = the real rate of interest in country j at time t; R_j^t = the nominal rate of interest at time t; and I_j^t = the inflation rate at time t.

The implication of this relationship is that if the real rate of interest is equal everywhere, then the inflation differential between countries is fully reflected in their nominal interest rate.

64. Fixed Annuities

Annuity contracts in which the insurance company pays a fixed dollar amount of money per period.

65. Fixed Asset

Long-lived property owned by a firm that is used by a firm in the production of its income. Tangible fixed assets include real estate, plant, and equipment. Intangible fixed assets include patents, trademarks, and consumer recognition.

66. Fixed Asset Turnover Ratio

[See **Asset management ratios**]

67. Fixed-Charge Coverage Ratio

Ratio of earnings to all fixed cash obligations, including lease payments and sinking fund payments. [See also **Capital structure ratios**]

68. Fixed Costs

Fixed cost is a cost that is fixed in total for a given period of time and for given volume levels. It is not dependent on the amount of goods or services produced during the period.

A factor affecting business risk is the firm's fixed costs. Fixed costs, such as rent, lease payments, and depreciation, remain the same whether the firm's sales, production, or profitability levels rise or fall. The effect of fixed costs on the firm's operating structure is to magnify, or leverage, the impact of a change in sales on EBIT. [See also **Business risk**]

69. Fixed Rate

An interest rate that does not change during a specified period of time. Fixed rate mortgage is a good example for this case.

70. Fixed-Dollar Obligations

Conventional bonds for which the coupon rate is set as a fixed percentage of the par value.

71. Fixed-Income Security

A security such as a bond that pays a specified cash flow over a specified period.

72. Flat Benefit Formula

Method used to determine a participant's benefits in a defined benefit pension plan by multiplying months of service by a flat monthly benefit. [See also **Defined benefit plans**]

73. Flat Volatility

The name given to volatility used to price an interest rate cap when the same volatility is used for each caplet. If different volatility is used for each caplet, then it is called spot volatility.

74. Flex Option

An option traded on an exchange with terms that are different from the standard options trades by the exchange.

75. Flight to Quality

Describes the tendency of investors to require larger default premiums on investments under uncertain economic conditions.

76. Float

Bankers define float as cash obligations that are in the process of collection. Another way to think of float is the difference between the balance shown in a firm's (or an individual's) checkbook and the balance on the bank's books. For instance, suppose that, on average, a firm writes $10,000 worth of checks each day. If it takes five days for these checks to clear and be deducted from the firm's bank account, then the firm's own checking records will show a daily balance of $50,000 lower than the bank's records. Conversely, if the firm, on average, receives $10,000 worth of checks each day but deposits and clears these checks in only three days, the firm's books will show a balance $30,000 higher than the balance on the bank's records. The differ-

ence between the $50,000 negative float and the $30,000 positive float, −$20,000, is called the firm's *net float*. This suggests the possibility that a firm could consistently maintain a negative cash balance on its books, as long as it could accurately forecast its positive and negative clearings.

Float management is an integral component of the cash management system. To understand how to analyze and forecast float, we need to look at the five different types of float:

1. **Invoicing float** is the time it takes for a firm to bill receivables. The efficiency of the company's internal accounting and billing procedures affect this type of float.

2. **Mail float** is the time the firm's bill spends in the mail on its way to the customer and the time the customer's check spends in the mail on its way to the firm.

3. **Processing float** is the time between a firm's receipt of a payment and its deposit of the check for collection.

4. **Collection float** is the time from when the bank accepts a check for deposit to when it makes the funds available in the firm's checking account.

5. **Disbursing float** is the time between when a firm writes a check on available bank account funds and when the bank deducts the corresponding dollar amount from the firm's bank balance.

The first four components of float hinder the firm's ability to turn collection items into cash; these are examples of negative float. The fifth component, disbursing float, is positive float because it increases the amount of cash the firm has to use. High interest rates increase the benefits of reducing negative float or increasing net float.

Mail float generally is hard to control, but it can be controlled to some degree through the use of different collection sites. Processing and invoicing float result from internal company operations, so they can certainly be monitored and fine-tuned for increased efficiency. Collection and disbursement float can be reduced through cash collection and disbursement services provided primarily by the banking system.

In sum, float is the difference between bank cash and book cash. Float represents the net effect of checks in the process of collection, or clearing. *Positive float* means the firm's bank cash is greater than its book cash until the check's presentation. Checks written by the firm generate *disbursement float*, causing an immediate decrease in book cash but no change in bank cash. In *neutral float position*, bank cash equals book cash. Checks written by the firm represent *collection float*, which increases book cash immediately but does not immediately change bank cash. The sum of disbursement float and collection float is *net float*.

77. Floater

Floating-rate bond.

78. Floating Lien

A floating lien gives the lender a claim against all the borrower's inventory without listing or specifying individual items. Such an arrangement makes it difficult, however, for the lender to prevent the borrower from running down inventories to a level that gives no real security for the loan; finance companies, therefore, are usually willing to advance only a small fraction of the estimated market value of the inventory against a floating lien.

79. Floating Rate

An interest rate tied to a base rate that changes over time as market conditions dictate.

80. Floating-Rate Bond

A debt obligation with an adjustable coupon payment.

81. Floating-Rate Note (FRN)

A short-term note whose interest payment varies with a short-term interest rate.

82. Floor

An option position that guarantees a minimum price.

83. Floor Broker

A licensed member of the exchange who is paid a fee for executing orders for clearing members of their customers.

84. Floor Plan Loans

Floor plan loans finance equipment purchases in an arrangement similar to a revolving credit agreement. Many manufacturers or distributors of machine tools, tractors, and similar heavy equipment supply these items to retailers under a floor plan system, which allows the retailer to pay for the merchandise only after actually selling it. The retailer's inventory therefore is financed by the supplier, either a manufacturer or a distributor. The manufacturer or distributor in turn finances this inventory by setting up a credit arrangement with a bank. Under such an arrangement, the bank pays the manufacturer for the equipment as soon as it is shipped. The bank then becomes the official owner of the equipment. When the equipment is sold, the retailer pays the wholesale price plus an interest charge directly to the bank. Alternatively, the retailer many give the manufacturer or distributor a note for the wholesale price of the equipment, which the manufacturer or distributor may then sell to the bank at a discount. This agreement compensates the bank, not by interest payments, but by the difference between the discounted sum it pays to the manufacturer and the full wholesale price it eventually will recover from the retailer.

85. Floor Rate

The rate in an interest rate floor agreement.

86. Floor Trader

An exchange member of the exchange who is paid a fee for executing orders for clearing members or their customers.

87. Floor-Ceiling Agreement

[See **Collar**]

88. Floorlet

One component of a floor.

89. Flotation Costs

The firm cannot costlessly arrange to borrow money, either from a bank or by selling bonds or shares of stock. It costs money to raise money. The costs of issuing securities, flotation costs, include bank application fees; "points" paid on loans; the accounting, legal, and printing costs of offering securities to the public; and any commissions earned by the investment bankers who market the new securities to investors. As a result of these costs, if the firm raises $100 of funds, it actually receives less than $100 to apply to the capital budgeting project. Thus, it must evaluate the cost of financing the project, net of issuing or flotation costs.

90. Flower Bond

Special Treasury bond (no longer issued) that may be used to settle federal estate taxes at par value under certain conditions.

91. FNMA

Federal National Mortgage Association (Fannie Mae); a private corporation operating with an implicit federal guarantee; buys mortgages financed by mortgage-backed securities. [See also **Fannie Mae**]

92. Forced Conversion

If the conversion value of a convertible is greater than the call price, the call can be used to force conversion.

93. Foreclosure

Selling property in order to apply the proceeds in payment of a debt.

94. Foreign Bonds

An international bond issued by foreign borrowers in another nation's capital market and traditionally denominated in that nation's currency.

95. Foreign Currency Futures

A foreign-currency futures contract is similar to other commodity-futures contracts. It promises future delivery of a standard amount of a foreign currency at a specified times, place, and price.

96. Foreign Currency Option

An option on a foreign exchange rate. The valuation model for the European type of currency call option can be defined as:

$$C = Se^{-r_f T} N(d_1) - Xe^{-rT} N(d_2),$$

where S = spot exchange rate; r = domestic risk-free rate; r_f = foreign risk free rate; X = exercise price; σ = standard deviation of spot exchange rate;

$$d_1 = \frac{\left[Ln\left(\frac{S}{X}\right) + \left(r - r_f + \frac{\sigma^2}{2}\right)T \right]}{\sigma\sqrt{T}};$$

$$d_2 = d_1 - \sigma\sqrt{T}.$$

97. Foreign Exchange

Currency of a foreign country acceptable as a medium exchange.

98. Foreign Exchange Market

The foreign exchange market is not a geographic place; it consists of a communications network through which many participants throughout the world agree to buy or sell currencies. The foreign exchange market includes a wide variety of smaller markets for immediate exchanges (spot trading), agreements for later exchanges (forward trading), and contracts based on exchange rates (futures and options trading).

Given the worldwide dispersion of the foreign exchange market, exchange trading never opens or closes. Markets around the world are interconnected by communication links so that it is possible to trade in the foreign exchange market somewhere in the world 24 hours a day, 7 days a week. This interconnection of diverse market segments also provides very competitive prices, which usually are within one-hundredth of a cent of each other.

99. Foreign Exchange Risk

The risk that the value of a position dominated in a foreign currency may decline due to a change in exchange rate. For a financial institution (FI), it refers the risk that foreign exchange rate changes can affect the value of an FI's assets and liabilities located abroad.

100. Foreign Exchange Swap

An agreement to exchange stipulated amounts of one currency for another at one or more future dates.

101. Foreign Tax Credit

Income taxes paid to a foreign country that can be claimed as a tax credit against a domestic tax liability.

102. Forward Contract

A forward contract is an agreement between a commercial bank and a corporate customer to exchange a specific amount of one currency for another on a specific future date at a specific price or exchange rate. At the initiation of the agreement, no money changes hands; the actual exchange of funds takes place on the future date specified in the forward contract. Forward contracts are very useful because they can be tailored to fit any situation, but they are very expensive.

103. Forward Curve

The set of forward or futures prices with different expiration dates on a given date for a given asset.

104. Forward Exchange Rate

The forward price of one unit of a foreign currency. Forward exchange rates can be used to control the risk of fluctuating spot rates over a specified time period. Forward rates allow a participant to "lock in" an exchange rate today for a transaction that will occur sometime in the future. In other words, forward exchange rate is a future day's exchange rate between two major currencies. [See also **Spot exchange rate**]

105. Forward Interest Rate

Rate of interest for a future period that would equate the total return of a long-term bond with that of a strategy of rolling over shorter-term bonds. The forward rate is inferred from the term structure.

106. Forward Parity

The relationship that forward exchange rate (F_{ij}^t) must be equal to the spot exchange rate at some point in time (S_{ij}^{t+1}):

$$S_{ij}^{t+1} = F_{ij}^t.$$

Forward parity must be true given the three relationships (Interest-rate parity, purchasing-power parity, and Fisherian relation).

107. Forward Premium

The annualized percentage difference between the forward price and the spot price.

108. Forward Price

The delivery price in a forward contract that causes the contract to be worth zero.

109. Forward Rate

A forward rate is a rate quoted today on a forward loan that originates at some future period.

110. Forward Rate Agreement (FRA)

Agreement that a certain interest rate will apply to a certain principal amount for a certain time period of the future.

111. Forward Risk-Neutral World

A world is forward risk-neutral with respect to a certain asset when the market price of risk equals the volatility of that asset.

112. Forward Start Option

An option designed so that it will be at-the-money at some time in the future when the option starts.

113. Forward Strip

Another name for the forward curve.

114. Forward Swap

Used when new debt is to be issued at a future date; allows issuer to hedge against an undesirable increase in rates before the securities are issued. [See also **Deferred swap**]

115. Forward Trade

An agreement to buy or sell based on exchange rates established today for settlement in the future. [See also **Spot trade**]

116. Fourth Market

Direct trading in exchange-listed securities between one investor and another without the benefit of a broker.

117. Free Cash Flow

Cash flow available after payment of all taxes and after all positive NPV projects have been provided for.

118. Frequency Distribution

The organization of data to show how often certain values or ranges of values occur. For example, a frequency distribution for either binomial or normal distribution.

119. Full-Service Broker

A brokerage that provides a full range of services to customers including advice in which securities to buy and/or sell.

120. Fully Diluted Earnings Per Share

Earnings per share expressed as if all outstanding convertible securities and warrants have been exercised. [See also **Dilution**]

121. Fundamental Analysis

Research to predict stock value that focuses on such determinants as earnings and dividends prospects, expectations for future interest rates, and risk evaluation of the firm.

122. Fundamental Betas

Fundamental betas are estimates of future betas, based upon both industry-specific and firm-specific balance sheet and income statement data. Researchers have found that the average betas of different industries vary as a result of differences in their business risk. In addition, researchers have discovered that financial statement relationships are useful in predicting a firm's future beta. Betas change over time as a firm's growth, dividend-payout ratio, earnings variability, financial leverage, and size change. Studies have found that increased financial leverage and increased variability in sales and EBIT lead to larger betas, while higher dividend-payout ratios lead to lower betas.

123. Funds Flows

Funds flows reflect changes in various financial statement accounts and transfers of funds from one account to another.

124. Future Value

The future value represents the dollar amount that the current cash flow will come to be worth in the future if it earns interest (or grows) at a given rate over time.

Future Value After One Period

It is very straightforward to calculate the value of, for instance a $100 investment after one year at a 10 percent annual rate of interest. The future value (FV) will be $100 plus 10 percent of $100, or $110.

$$FV_1 = 100 + (0.10)(100) = (100)(1 + 0.10) = 110.$$

Future Value After Two or More Periods

If the money is to be invested for two years, the value of the CD after that time will equal its value after one year plus an additional 10 percent:

$$FV_2 = 110 + (0.10)(110) = (110)(1 + 0.10) = 121$$

or, $FV_2 = (110)(1 + 0.10) = (100)(1 + 0.10)$

$$(1 + 0.10)$$
$$= (100)(1 + 0.10)^2 = 121.$$

During the second year, the $100 principal plus the first periods' interest of $10 *both* earn interest. The $10 of interest earned during the first year earns $1 of interest (10 percent of $10) during the second year. This growth illustrates the effect of compounding. For this reason, future value calculations are often called compound value calculations.

What if our CD can be rolled into a third year? That means the $121 we have at the end of the second year will earn another 10 percent. At the end of the third year the CD will be worth:

$$FV_3 = (121)(1 + 0.10) = (100)(1 + 0.10)^2(1 + 0.10)$$

$$= (100)(1 + 0.10)^3 = 133.10$$

Over three years, the $100 in principal has earned $33.10 in interest.

These equations suggest a general formula for finding the future value (FV) in year n of a sum of money (PV):

$$FV_n = PV(1 + r)^n.$$

The future value of PV is PV multiplied by a future value interest factor, $(1 + r)^n$. The future value interest factor, or FVIF, $(1 + r)^n$, will increase in size as either the interest rate or the number of years increases. It will increase exponentially as n increases, due to the effects of compounding interest. Higher interest rates will have a larger compounding effect.

Future Value of Several Cash Flows

The future values of several amounts are additive *if the amounts are paid at the same future point in time*. If a problem has several present cash flows or investments, we can easily find their total future value simply by adding the individual future values at the same future time.

125. Futures Contract

Unlike a **forward contract**, a futures contract is a standardized financial instrument with a stated amount and specific maturity that is traded on an organized exchange and is resalable up to the close of trading or settlement date. Futures contracts tend to be smaller than forward contracts and are not as flexible in meeting hedging needs. [See also **Forward contract**]

126. Futures Exchange

A futures exchange is the arena for the actual daily trading of futures contracts. The exchange is a nonprofit organization whose members include those allowed to trade on its floor. Members include individual traders, brokerage firms, and other types of institutions.

127. Futures Market

The underlying purpose for futures market is to allow investors to display their uncertainties about the future. Futures markets allow for the transfer of risk from hedgers (risk-averse individuals) to speculators (risk seeking individuals), a key element necessary for the existence of futures market is the balance between the number of hedgers and speculators who are willing to transfer and accept risk.

128. Futures Options

An option on a futures contract.

129. Futures Overlay

Converting an investment in asset A into the economic equivalent of an investment in asset B by entering into a short futures position on asset A and a long futures position on asset B.

130. Futures Price

The delivery price currently applicable to a futures contract.

G

1. GAAP

Generally Accepted Accounting Principles (GAAP) representing the standard rules and procedures that accountants follow when reporting financial information in limited states.

2. Gamma

The change in delta when the price of the underlying asset changes by one unit. Based upon the call option formula defined in option pricing model [see also **Option pricing equation**]. The mathematic result can be defined as

$$\frac{\partial^2 C}{\partial S^2} = \frac{1}{S\sigma\sqrt{T}} N'(d_1) > 0.$$

3. Gamma-Neutral Portfolio

A portfolio with a gamma of zero.

4. GAP

Dollar value of rate-sensitive assets ($RSAs$) minus the dollar value of rate-sensitive liabilities ($RSLs$). Another way of comparing $RSAs$ and $RSLs$ is the $GAP\ Ratio$, defined as:

$$GAP\ Ratio = \frac{RSAs}{RSLs}.$$

5. Gap Option

An option where the option owner has the right to exercise the option at strike price K_1 if the stock price exceeds (or, depending on the option, is less than) the price K_2. For an ordinary option, $K_1 = K_2$.

6. GARCH Model

Generalized autoregressive conditional hetroskedasticity (GARCH) is a model for forecasting volatility where the variance rate follows a mean-reverting process.

7. Garnishment

A court directive authorizing a bank to withhold funds from a borrower.

8. General Break-even Analysis

A generalized formula for break-even quantity, Q^* can be defined as:

$$Q^* = \frac{FC + OCF}{p - vc},$$

where FC = fixed cost; vc = variable cost per unit; p = price per unit; and OCF = operating cash flow.

9. General Cash Offer

A public issue of a security that is sold to all interested investors, rather than only to existing share-holders.

10. General Obligation Bonds

Municipal bonds secured by general fund (i.e., the full faith), credit, and taxing power of the issuing state or local government. [See also **Revenue bond**]

11. General Partnership

Form of business organization in which all partners agree to provide some portion of the work and cash and to share profits and losses. Each partner is liable for the debts of the partnership. [See also **Limited partnership**]

12. Generalized Wiener Process

A stochastic process where the change in a variable in each short time period of length δt has normal distribution with mean and variance, both proportional to δt.

13. Generally Accepted Accounting Principles

In the US, Generally Accepted Accounting Principles (GAAP) are used as guidelines for financial statement reporting. It is a common set of accounting concepts, standards, and procedures by which financial statements are prepared. Besides GAAP, thrifts and insurance companies are also subjected to statutory accounting. [See also **Statutory accounting**]

14. Gentry-De La Garza Model

A way of analyzing receivable balances is to use the Gentry-De La Garza model [see also Gentry and De La Garza (1985)]. This model describes three reasons why accounts receivable balances may increase: sales pattern effects, collection experience effects, and joint effect. Sales pattern effects are increases in receivables due solely to increases in sales.

The increase in accounts receivable is partly a function of increasing sales (the sales pattern effect), partly a function of the deterioration in collections (the collection experience effect), and some combination of both (the joint effect).

The joint effect is explained as the increase in receivables due to a simultaneous deterioration in collections and increase in sales. For instance, some customers may have purchased the product with the assumption that they could pay late; this would both increase sales and slow collection. The joint effect is calculated by taking the difference between the current and past collection experience effects and then multiplying this difference by the difference between the current and past sales levels.

Finally, the sales pattern effect is quantified by taking the difference between the current and past

sales levels multiplied by the prior collection experience effect.

The sum of the sales pattern effect, joint effect, and collection experience effect equals the difference between the receivables balances.

The advantage of the Gentry-De La Garza model is that it separates the increase in receivables into three quantifiable components. A financial manager then can see clearly if an increase in receivables results from faulty credit controls or if the increase is simply consistent with rising sales levels. Deteriorating collections might indicate that credit is granted too freely or that the company is not persistent enough in collecting overdue accounts. Both problems fall under the control of the credit department and are the primary responsibility of the credit manager.

15. Geometric Brownian Motion

A continuous stochastic process, $x(t)$, in which the increments are given as $dx(t)/x(t) = \alpha dt + \sigma dZ$, where dZ is the increment to a Brownian motion driving the process.

16. Geometric Mean (also Called Geometric Average)

If historical, or ex-post, data are known, an analyst can easily compute historical average return and risk measures. If X_t represent a data item for period t, the arithmetic average $\overline{X}$, over n periods is given by:

$$\overline{X} = \frac{\sum\limits_{t=1}^{n} X_t}{n}.$$

The sum of the values observed divided by the total number of observation is sometimes referred to as the mean.

Alternatively, we can use the same data to calculate the geometric average rate of return as:

$$\overline{X}_g = \left[\prod_{i=1}^{N}(1 + X_i)\right]^{\frac{1}{N}} - 1,$$

In general, the geometric average is less than the arithmetic average, and while both measures are intuitively plausible, we are left with the problem of determining which average is more appropriate to calculate. To illustrate, suppose you purchase a stock for $10 per share and at the end of the first year the price is $20 per share; you have experienced a 100 percent return. At the end of the second year, the price has returned to $10 per share; you have experienced a loss of 50 percent. Using the arithmetic average of our yearly returns of $+100$ percent and -50 percent gives an average return of 25 percent, $(+100 - 50)/2$, which is ridiculous. We started with a stock value of $10 per share, and the value of the stock at the end of the second year was $10 per share, so we actually received a return of 0 percent. This is the amount calculated for the geometric average, $\sqrt[2]{(2)(1/2)} - 1$. In fact, viewing these averages as estimates of return that actually result from holding stock, Blume (1974) has shown that a *mixed average* of these two quantities is generally preferable to the individual use of either one. The weights in this compromise estimate depend on the length of time the stock is to be held. Specifically, for a holding period of T years, Blume recommends estimating the annual holding period return by a mixed mean as:

$$\overline{X}_m = \frac{N-T}{N-1}\overline{X}_a + \frac{T-1}{N-1}\overline{X}_g,$$

where N = numbers of periods of data used to calculate the average rates of return and T = number of periods the investment is to be held. Notice that if the stock is to be held for just one year $(T = 1)$, then $\overline{X}_m$ is just the arithmetic average. However, for holding periods longer than one year, some weight is given also to the geometric average. Since it is a weighted average of these quantities, $\overline{X}_m$ must lie between $\overline{X}_a$ and $\overline{X}_g$.

17. Gibson Relation

Gibson relation describes relationship between actual levels of prices and yields as follows:

1. When the price is relatively high, so are interest rates.

2. When prices are low, yields also tend to be low.

18. Gilts

British and Irish government securities.

19. Ginnie Mae

Name referring to the Government National Mortgage Association. [See also **GNMA**]

20. Glass-Steagall Act

The 1933 act that separated lending activities from investment banking activities at commercial banks by prohibiting commercial banks from underwriting corporate securities. Since 1987, the Fed now allows bank holding companies to expand their activities in securities underwriting through the special investment bank subsidiaries of commercial bank.

21. Global Bonds

The international bond market is increasingly ignoring national boundaries. A growing number of debt issues are being sold globally. In 1989, the World Bank was the first issuer of global bonds; in 1993, over $15 billion of global bonds were issued. Global bonds usually are denominated in US dollars. As they are marketed globally, their offering sizes typically exceed $1 billion. In addition to the World Bank, issuers include the governments of Finland and Italy and corporations such as Matsushita Electric Industrial Co., Citicorp, First Chicago Corp., and Korea Electric Power Co.

22. Global Minimum Variance Portfolio

The lowest-variance portfolio achievable, given a population of securities.

23. Globalization

Tendency toward a worldwide investment environment, and the integration of national capital markets.

24. GNMA

Government National Mortgage Association (Ginnie Mae) – a government entity that buys mortgages for low-income housing and guarantees mortgage-backed securities issued by private lenders. GNMA was created by congress in 1968.

GNMA is a government-owned agency with two major functions. The first is sponsoring mortgage-backed securities programs by FIs such as banks, thrifts, and mortgage bankers. The second is acting as a guarantor to investors in mortgage-backed securities regarding the timely pass-through of principal and interest payments on their sponsored bonds. In other words, GNMA provides timing insurance. In acting as a sponsor and payment-timing guarantor, GNMA supports only those pools of mortgage loans whose default or credit risk is insured by one of three government agencies: the Federal Housing Administration (FHA), the Veterans Administration (VA), and the Farmers Home Administration (FMHA). Mortgage loans insured by these agencies target groups that might otherwise be disadvantaged in the housing market, such as low-income families, young families, and veterans. As such, the maximum mortgage under the FHA/VA/FMHA-GNMA securitization program is capped.

25. Going Private

A technique where a **leveraged buyout** (LBO) can be used to take a firm out of public ownership and into private ownership. [See also **Leveraged buyout**]

26. Going Public

Going public offers several advantages to a firm and its current, private shareholders. First, selling stock publicly allows the firm to tap another source of capital: the public equity markets. Managers may decide to make the firm public because they need more capital than a private placement can provide. Or it may be cheaper to raise public equity than to undergo another round of financing from venture capitalists. Studies show that a firm should be profitable and raise at least $10 million for an IPO to be cost-efficient. In addition, once a firm goes public, it can raise money periodically from the public markets by selling additional shares of stock.

Second, a certain prestige and publicity surrounds a firm that goes public and lists its shares on a stock exchange for trading. Third, shareholders may enjoy attractive capital gains if management achieves sales and profit goals. Founding entrepreneurs often purchase shares for pennies when the firm begins operating, but after the IPO, their shares are worth much more. A good time to go public is when investors favor stocks in the firm's industry or when the stock market is in a strong rising trend. The IPO market may be momentarily hot in a certain industry.

A public company enjoys a fourth advantage through its shares' liquidity. Since investors can buy or sell shares easily form each other, investors or managers easily can sell all or part of their investments if they choose. Managers may receive pressure to go public form the firm's private equity holders – especially venture capitalists – who may have a strong desire to liquidate their holdings. Secondary market liquidity eases owners' worries about receiving fair market value for their shares, since an impersonal marketplace, rather than accountants and attorneys, determine the per-share value of the company. Public trading may take the shares even more valuable, by reducing their liquidity risk.

Yet, some firms find going public an undesirable option. First, offering stock to the public is an expensive process. The costs of preparing financial statements, hiring attorneys, and marketing the shares to investors can consume a significant portion of the funds raised.

Another drawback is loss of control over the firm. Unless the firm offers less than 50 percent of its equity to the public, investors who are unknown to current managers and owners will collectively own most of the firm's common stock. Those shareholders will elect a board of directors to ensure that decisions are made in the shareholders' best interests. In addition, shareholders will make other major decisions themselves by voting, as outlined in the corporate charter or as allowed by the board. Additionally, since the former private shareholders will lose control over who buys the publicly traded shares, they may find the firm the target of a hostile takeover sometime in the future. Of course, control can be diluted by selling shares privately as well.

A third potential disadvantage is that a public firm must lay out its finances for all to see. While this reporting requirement allows current and potential investors to examine the firm's strengths and weaknesses and gain insight into management's future plans, it also allows the firm's competitors, both foreign and domestic, to do the same thing. Rivals can factor in the firm's profit margins and product sales as they ploy their marketing and R&D strategies.

Public firms also must submit to regulation by the **Securities and Exchange Commission (SEC)** and the exchange on which their shares are traded. [See also **Securities and exchange commission**]

Finally, having shares listed and traded on an exchange does not always guarantee a dramatic increase in liquidity and share price. If the firm is still relatively small and the market sees no spectacular potential for future growth in sales and profits, investors may ignore the firm after the public offering. This could leave shareholders with shares of a public firm that nobody else really wants to own. The shares can become illiquid quickly if they are not traded frequently, and weak interest can leave them languishing at a low price. The firm may have been better off staying private.

27. Going-Private Transactions

Public owned stock in a firm is replaced with complete equity ownership by a private group. The shares are de-listed from stock exchanges and can no longer be purchased in the open market.

28. Gold Standard

A monetary system where the value of a country's currency is determined by the value of the gold content in the currency.

29. Golden Parachute

Companies often provide their top executives with substantial severance benefits, or golden parachutes, in the event of hostile takeovers. These benefits may have some economic justification because top managers face a dilemma when a hostile threat emerges. If they resist a successful takeover attempt, even if they believe resistance in shareholders' best interests, then they are likely to face dismissal by the new owners. Without the golden parachute, managers may have some incentive to acquiesce too easily to strong, hostile suitors.

30. Goodwill

An intangible asset representing the difference between the book value of an asset or a firm and the actual sales price.

31. Gordon Model

Many firms have sales and earnings that increase over time; their dividends may rise, as well. If we assume that a firm's dividends grow at an annual rate of g percent, next year's dividend, D_1, will be $D_0(1+g)^2$. Generalizing,

$$D_t = D_0(1+g)^t.$$

Substituting this into the equation for the present value of all future dividends, we can show that the price at any future time t can be defined as:

$$P_t = \frac{D_{t+1}}{r-g},$$

where P_t = firm's stock price at time t; $D_{t+1} = D_t(1+g)$, next year's expected dividend (equals the current dividend increased by g percent); g = the expected (constant) dividend growth rate; r = required rate of return.

This result, known as the Gordon model, or the constant dividend growth model, provides a straightforward tool for common stock valuation. The main assumption of constant growth in dividends may not be realistic for a firm that is experiencing a period of high growth or negative growth (that is, declining revenues). Neither will constant dividend growth be a workable assumption for a firm whose dividends rise and fall over the business cycle. The constant dividend growth model also assumes a dividend-paying stock; the model cannot give a value for a stock that does not pay dividends. In addition, in the denominator of the equation, the required rate of return, r, must exceed the estimated growth rate, g. Finally, the constant dividend growth model assumes estimates for r, the required rate of return, and g, the dividend growth rate.

The constant dividend growth model reveals that the following three factors affect stock prices, ceteris paribus: 1) the higher the dividend, the higher the stock price; 2) the higher the dividend growth rate, the higher the stock price; 3) the lower the required rate of return r, the higher the stock price. [See also **Appendix A**]

32. Grace Period

The time period for a credit card statement representing the time from when the statement is generated to the last day full payment can be made and still avoid a finance charge. [See also **Appendix A**]

33. Grandfather Clause

A legislative provision that exempts parties previously engaged in activities prohibited by new legislation.

34. Greeks

A term generally referring to delta, gamma, vega, theta, and rho, all of which measure the change in the price of a derivative when there is a change in an input to the pricing formula.

35. Green Shoe Provisions

Some IPOs contain Green Shoe provisions, named after one of the first firms to include the provision in its underwriting agreement. A Green Shoe provision gives the leading investment bank the right to increase the number of shares sold in the IPO, typically by 10 percent to 20 percent of the original offering. This helps the investment bank satisfy more investors if demand for an issue is particularly hot. This also gives investment banks another way to increase their profits, since they earn the spread on any extra shares they sell.

36. Greenmail

Payments to potential bidders to cease unfriendly takeover attempts. Managers may arrange targeted repurchase to forestall a takeover attempt. In a targeted repurchase, a firm buys back its own stock from a potential bidder, usually at a substantial premium. These premiums can be thought of as payments to potential bidders to delay or stop unfriendly takeover attempts. Critics of such payments label them greenmail.

37. Gross Domestic Product (GDP)

The market value of goods and services produced over a period of time including the sum of consumer expenditures, investment expenditures, government expenditures, and net exports (exports minus imports).

38. Growing Perpetuity

A constant stream of cash flows without end that is expected to rise indefinitely. For example, cash flows to the landlord of an apartment building might be expected to rise a certain percentage each year.

39. Growth Funds

Growth funds are structured to include a well diversified combination of common stock. Basically, three reasons may be cited. First, empirical studies of common stock have almost invariably shown their long-term total return to exceed those on bonds. Second, stock in generally conceded to be a better hedge against inflation risk than bonds. Third, many small investors may prefer to hold obligations of financial institutions as their major fixed-income securities because of their convenience and safety resulting from government insurance programs.

40. Growth Opportunity

Opportunity to invest in profitable projects.

41. Guarantee

Make oneself liable for the debts of another.

42. Guaranteed Insurance Contract

A contract promising a stated nominal rate of interest over some specific time period, usually several years.

43. Guaranteed Investment Contract (GIC)

A financial contract in which the writer of a policy agrees to pay a fixed amount at maturity after receiving a fixed, single premium up front.

44. Guardian

An individual or a trust department appointed by a court to manage a minor's property or personal affairs.

H

1. Haircut

The collateral, over and above the market value of the security, required by the lender when a security is borrowed.

2. Hazard Rate

Measures probability of default in a short period of time conditional on no earlier default.

3. HDD

Heating degree days (HDD). The maximum of zero and the amount by which the daily average temperature is less than $65°$ Fahrenheit. The average temperature is the average of the highest and lowest temperatures (midnight to midnight). The Chicago Mercantile Exchange began trading weather futures and European options on weather futures in September 1999. The contracts are on the cumulative HDD and cooling degree days (CDD) for a month observed at a weather station.

4. Hedge

The forward markets allow users to hedge, or reduce the risk of, adverse currency fluctuations. Hedging is taking a position in two or more securities that are negatively correlated (taking opposite trading positions) to reduce risk.

5. Hedge Fund

Hedge funds are a type of investment pool that solicits funds from (wealthy) individuals and other investors (e.g., commercial banks) and invests these funds on their behalf. Hedge funds, however, are not technically mutual funds in that they are subjected to virtually no regulatory oversight (e.g., by the SEC under the Securities Act and Investment Advisors Act) and generally take significant risk.

6. Hedge Ratio (for An Option)

The number of stocks required to hedge against the price risk of holding on potion. Also called the option's delta. [See also **Delta**].

7. Hedge Ratio (for Futures)

The ratio of the size of a position in a hedging instrument to the size of the position being hedged as:

$$\text{Hedge ratio} = \frac{\text{cov}(\Delta S, \Delta F)}{\text{var}(\Delta F)},$$

where ΔS(Change of spot) $= S_t - S_{t-1}$; ΔF (Change of future) $= F_t - F_{t-1}$.

8. Hedger

A market participant who has or will have a position in the cash commodity and who attempts to eliminate or reduce risk exposure by taking an offsetting position in the futures or forward market.

9. Hedging

Investing in an asset to reduce the overall risk of a portfolio.

10. Hedging Demands

Demands for securities to hedge particular sources of consumption risk, beyond the usual mean-variance diversification motivation.

11. Heston Model

An option pricing model in which the instantaneous variance of the stock return follows a mean-reverting square root process.

12. Highly Leveraged Transaction (HLT)

Transaction in which borrower's debt increases sharply after the asset exchange, such as an LBO.

13. High-Yield Bonds

[See **Junk bonds**]

14. Historical Cost

The value for certain balance sheet items reflecting the original cost or amortized cost.

15. Historical Simulation

A simulation based on historical data.

16. Historical Volatility

The standard deviation of the continuously compounded return on an asset, measured using historical prices.

17. Holder-of-Record Date

The date on which holders of record in a firm's stock ledger are designated as the recipients of either dividends or stock rights. Also called date of record.

18. Holding Company

Besides negotiating terms or making a tender offer, parties to a business combination may form a holding company. A holding company is a corporation that owns sufficient voting stock of another firm (or several firms) to have effective control. This form of organization is quite common in the financial services and banking industries. Typically, the combination forms a new corporation and the shareholders of the firms to be combined exchange their old shares for shares of the new holding company. This type of transaction is ad-

vantageous because it can provide effective control with as little as 10 or 20 percent of the outstanding stock, so a smaller investment is required. The holding company differs from other business combinations in that it can take advantage of legal loopholes in state and federal laws, including tax laws.

19. Holding Period

Length of time that an individual holds a security.

20. Holding-Period Rate of Return

The annualized rate of return expected or realized from holding a security over a specific period of time.

21. Holding-Period Yield

Holding-period yield (HPY) is a measurement of investment performance related to holding period rate of return (HPPR). The HPY is the ratio of the change in the market value of the investment plus cash distributions received during the period divided by the original value of the investment. This is represented as:

$$HPY_t = (r_t) = \frac{(P_t - P_{t-1}) + C_t}{P_{t-1}} = \frac{P_t + C_t}{P_{t-1}} - 1$$
$$= HPRR.$$

From this expression it is easy to see that HPY is equal to $HPR - 1$. The HPY defined in the equation is a discrete type of HPY. It assumes that the cash flows and investments occur at specific points in time.

The frequency of compounding influences the HPR and HPY calculations as:

$$HPY_t^c = \ln\left(\frac{P_t + C_t}{P_{t-1}}\right),$$

where HPY_t^c is the holding-period rate of return with continuous compounding, and ln is the natural logarithm.

More generally, the rate of return with continuous compounding for a given period is expressed by:

$$HPR_t^d = 1 + HPY^d = \exp(HPY^c),$$

where HPR_t^d is the discrete holding-period rate of return and exp(e) is 2.718, the base of natural logarithms. By taking the natural log of both sides of the equation:

$$\ln(1 + HPY^d) = HPY^c.$$

In every case except $HPY^d = 0$, the continuously compounded rate of return is always less than the discrete rate of return

On the other hand, given a continuous rate of return, the discrete rate return can be calculated using:

$$HPY^d = \exp(HPY^c) - 1.$$

22. Holiday Calendar

Calendar defining when days are holidays for the purposes of determining payment dates in a swap.

23. Home Banking

Actions involving the conduct of banking business taking place in customer's homes, including telephone and computer transactions.

24. Home Currency Approach

The home currency approach is a method for evaluating overseas projects. This technique converts foreign currency cash flows to the home currency of the parent firm. Assuming that the home currency is the US dollar, it then discounts the US dollar cash flows at the project's US minimum required return to find the net present value.

The financial analyst can rely on forecasting services that analyze relative economic and political trends to predict future spot rates. Once the foreign cash flows are converted to dollars, the NPV calculation using the project's US required return is straightforward.

The steps in the home currency approach are summarized as:

1. Estimate foreign currency cash flows.
2. Predict future spot exchange rates using forecasts.
3. Convert foreign currency cash flows to home currency cash flows.
4. Compute project NPV using the project's required return.

25. Home Debit

A check drawn on a bank that is presented to the same bank for deposit or payment.

26. Home Equity Loan

Loan secured by an individual's equity in a home.

27. Homemade Dividends

An individual investor can undo corporate dividend policy by reinvesting excess dividends or selling off shares of stock to receive a desired cash flow.

28. Homemade Leverage

Idea that as long as individuals borrow (and lend) on the same terms as the firm. They can duplicate the effects of corporate leverage on their own. Thus, if levered firms are priced too high. Rational investors will simply borrow on personal accounts to buy shares in unlevered firms. [See also **Modigliani & Miller (M&M) proposition I**]

29. Homogeneous Expectations

The assumption that all investors use the same expected returns and covariance matrix or security returns as inputs in security analysis.

30. Horizon Analysis

Interest rate forecasting that uses a forecast yield curve to predict bond prices. Yield curve is a two dimension graph to present the relationship between yield to maturity and maturity. [See also **Yield to maturity**]

31. Horizontal Acquisition

Merger between two companies producing similar goods or service. For example, a steel company buys another steel company.

32. Horizontal Combination

If two firms had performed similar functions in the production or sale of goods and services, then the business combination is said to be *horizontal*. Before a horizontal combination, the firms were, or at least had the potential to be, competitors.

33. Horizontal Spread

[See **Calendar spread**]

34. Hot Money

Funds that move between institutions quickly in search of higher yields or greater safety. The hot money can cause a county's financial crises.

35. Howard-D'Antonio Strategy

Using a mean-variance framework, the Howard-D'Antonio strategy (Howard and D'Antonio, 1984) assumes that the "agent" is out to maximize the expected return for a given level of portfolio risk. A hedge ratio and measure of hedging effectiveness are derived in which the hedger's risk and return are both explicitly taken into account. The strategy can be expressed as:

Hedge ratio $H = \dfrac{(\lambda - \rho)}{\gamma \pi (1 - \lambda \rho)}$,

and hedging effectiveness

$$HE = \sqrt{\frac{1 - 2\lambda\rho + \lambda^2}{1 - \rho^2}},$$

where $\pi = \sigma_f / \sigma_s$ = relative variability of futures and spot returns; $\alpha = \overline{r_f}/(\overline{r_s} - i)$ = relative excess return on futures to that of spot' $\gamma = p_f / p_s$ = current price ration of futures to spot; $\lambda = \alpha / \pi = (\overline{r_f}/\sigma_f)/[\overline{r_s} - i)/\sigma_s]$ = risk-to-excess-return relative of futures versus the spot position; P_s, P_f = the current price per unit for the spot and futures, respectively; ρ = simple correlation coefficient between the spot and futures returns; σ_s = standard deviation of spot returns; σ_f = standard deviation of futures returns; $\overline{r_s}$ = mean return on the spot over some recent past interval; $\overline{r_f}$ = mean return on the futures over some recent past interval; and i = risk-free rate.

36. Hung Convertibles

Convertible bonds that have no chance of being converted are called hung convertibles. The idea here is that if the investors don't wish to convert their bonds into the firm's equity, the conversion process is hung up. The bond is worth more as a bond than it is worth converted into equity. APB No. 15 and FASB No. 55 require a firm to provide EPS information under either circumstance and let the market participant choose which measure is more meaningful.

37. Hybrid Security

A hybrid security is a security which has characteristics of both debt and equity. For example, convertible bond are securities that can be exchanged for a stipulated number of shares of common stock during a specific period.

38. Hypothecation

In a contract, committing property to secure a loan.

39. Hypothesis Testing

Hypotheses are assumptions about a population parameter. Hypothesis testing involves judging the correctness of the hypotheses. In fact, we often rely heavily on sample data in decision making. For example, the results of public opinion polls may actually dictate whether a presidential candidate decides to keep running or to drop out of the primary race.

I

1. Idiosyncratic Risk

An unsystematic risk. This risk can be diversified from a portfolio; hence it is also a diversifiable risk. [See also **Unsystematic risk**]

2. Illiquidity

Illiquidity is the opposite of liquidity; either an asset cannot be converted into cash (e.g., a leased machine cannot be sold to raise cash) or an asset cannot be sold at a reasonable price (e.g., a firm bought a machine for $1 million, but the best offer from another buyer is $100,000). In the latter case, if the firm keeps the asset and uses it, it is worth ten times more than the amount of cash it could raise in a sale in the market.

In the short run, many firms may be illiquid, that is, they may lack cash. They remedy this situation by short-term borrowing. A firm borrows cash to meet its current obligations, knowing that its cash flow will improve in the future. This kind of illiquidity is transitory and is not associated with insolvency or bankruptcy. On the other hand, if a firm faces illiquidity with no expectation of future cash flow improvement, illiquidity may lead to insolvency and bankruptcy.

3. Immunization

A strategy that matches durations of assets and liabilities so as to make net worth unaffected by interest rate movements. If interest rates rise, the present value of assets and liabilities will fall by the same amount. Similarly, if interest rates fall, then the value of the assets and liabilities will rise by the same amount.

4. Immunize

To fully hedge against interest rate risk. Alternatively, it refers that immunization occurs when a financial institution's equity holders are fully protected against interest rate risk.

5. Immunized

It describes a financial institution that is fully hedged or projected against adverse movements in interest rates (or other asset prices).

6. Impairment of Capital Rule

A legal constraint known as the impairment of capital rule is designed to protect the firm's creditors. It stipulates that dividends cannot exceed the amount of retained earnings listed on the balance sheet. This ensures that the firm retains enough capital to pay its legal obligations.

7. Implicit Agency Costs

[See also **Agency costs**]

8. Implicit Contract

It is a long term customer relationship between a borrower and lender based upon reputation. This kind of implicit contract is generally regarding borrowing and repayment that extends beyond the formal explicit legal contract.

9. Implicit Finite Difference Method

A method for valuing a derivative by solving the underlying differential equation. The value of the derivative at time $t + \delta t$ is related to three values at time t. For pricing a stock option, these three values are M = number of stock price; N = number of time maturity; and ΔS = stock of price intervals. For example, values 10, 5 and 3 are chosen for M, N, and ΔS. Thus the option price is evaluated at $3 stock price intervals between $0 and $30 and at half-month time intervals through the life of the option.

10. Implied Distribution

A distribution for a future asset price implied from option prices.

11. Implied Forward Rate

The forward interest rate between t_1 and time t_2 ($t_1 < t_2$) that makes an investor indifferent between, on the one hand, buying a bond maturing at t_2, and, on the other hand, buying a bond maturing at t_1 and reinvesting the proceeds at this forward interest rate.

12. Implied Repo Rate

The repo rate implied from the price of a Treasury bill and a Treasury bill futures price.

13. Implied Tree

A tree describing the movements of an asset price that is constructed to be consistent with observed option prices.

14. Implied Variance (Implied Volatility)

That state of the art method in the market today for estimating the volatility is the implied-variance estimate. Implied variance can generally be regarded as the market's opinion about the future variance of the stock. Originally proposed by Latane and Rendleman (1976), the idea behind the estimation of the implied variance is to equate the Black-Scholes model price to the current market price and solve iteratively for the remaining unknown variance. No closed-form solution is available to compute the implied variance, so a numerical search pro-

cedure such as the Newton-Raphson search or linear least-squares regression must be used. Issues abound concerning the use of implied variance; the first of them is the weighting issue. If the implied variance inherent in the market price for each outstanding option on a stock (underlying asset) were calculated, there would be as many estimates of the stock's implied variance as there are options. Disregarding the possibility of market mispricings for the moment, a number of other factors may also be able to help explain the observed discrepancies.

1. Exercise price (amount in or out of the money) differences
2. Time-to-maturity differences
3. Trading-volume differences among the individual options
4. Market conditions

15. Implied Volatility

The volatility for which the theoretical option price (typically computed using the Black-Scholes formula) equals the observed market price of the option. In other words, the expected volatility in return on an underlying asset or contract derived from an option pricing model.

16. In The Money

The owner of a put or call is not obligated to carry out the specified transaction but has the *option* of doing so. If the transaction is carried out, it is said to have been *exercised*. For example, if you hold a call option on a stock that is currently trading at a price higher than the exercise price, you may want to exercise the option to purchase stock at the exercise price and then immediately resell the stock at a profit. This call option is said to *be in the money*.

17. Inception Profit

Profit created by selling a derivative for more than its theoretical value.

18. Income Beneficiary

One who receives income from a trust.

19. Income Bond

A bond on which the payment of income is contingent on sufficient earnings. Income bonds are commonly used during the reorganization of a failed or failing business.

20. Income Fund

It provides liberal current income from investments. Income fund holds both equity and fixed-income security in a relatively stable proportion.

21. Income Statement

The income statement is an accounting report that summarizes the flow of a firm's revenues and expenses for a specific period. Unlike the balance sheet, it represents flow instead of static information. The income statement affects the balance sheet when the period's net income (or loss) less any dividends, is added to (or subtracted from) retained earnings on the balance sheet. The income statement reports important information about the results of operations and gives reasons for the company's profits or losses.

The income statement may be produced annually, quarterly, or monthly. Company management uses monthly statements primarily for internal purposes, such as estimating sales and profit targets, controlling expenses, and monitoring the progress of long-term targets. Quarterly and annual income statements are especially useful to the firm's shareholders, creditors, and competitors. The top entry of the income statement gives net sales revenue. From this total, subsequent entries subtract expenses, such as the cost of goods sold, selling and administrative expenses, research expense, interest expense, and income tax expense. This gives the famous bottom line: net income.

Alternative accounting methods can also affect the size of reported net income. The methods for calculating depreciation, inventory value, and pension fund liabilities all influence the amount of reported profits. For example, historical cost accounting may understate the cost of goods sold; in an inflationary environment, this can result in an overstatement of sales, taxes, and net income.

Firms generally practice accrual accounting, recognizing revenues and matching corresponding expenses at the time of sale. Unless the firm sells its products only for cash, recognizing revenue does not mean that a cash inflow has occurred; cash will not flow into the firm until some time in the future, when the customer makes a payment on an account. Similarly, matching expenses to revenue distorts the perception of cash outflows. Firms must pay for many matched expenses, including raw materials production costs, and labor expenses, before they sell the corresponding goods. In addition, some income statement expense items do not reflect cash outflows, for example depreciation expense.

Thus, positive net income does not necessarily mean that cash inflows exceed cash outflows; neither does a negative net income figure imply imminent bankruptcy. The analyst needs a better tool than an income statement to determine the cash flows of a firm, which is the purpose of the statement of cash flows. [See also **Statement of cash flows**]

In sum, income statement is a financial report that summarizes a firm's performance over a specified time period.

22. Income-and-Growth Funds

It is one kind of mutual fund. Income-and-growth funds are composed of a combination of common stock and bonds. Whether the emphasis is on income or growth determines what percentage of bonds or common stock is in the portfolio.

23. Incremental After-Tax Operating Cash Flows

For a cost-saving project, it is usually easier to estimate operating cash flows (OCF) by the tax shield approach as:

$$OCF = (S - C)(1 - T) + T(Dep)$$
$$- Change\ in\ NWC,$$

where S = sales revenue, C = cost, T = tax rate, Dep = depreciation, NWC = net working capital.

The incremental sales revenue is expected to be zero for most cost-savings projects, including this one. Operating cash flows depend upon the estimated cost savings, the depreciation, the tax rate, and changes in net working capital.

24. Incremental Cash Flows

The stand-alone principle requires the analyst to examine the incremental cash flows that occur as a result of the project. The cash flows are incremental in that they represent the differences between the firm's after-tax cash flows *with* the project and its **base case**, or the after-tax cash flows *without* the project. [See also **Base case**]

Estimating incremental after-tax cash flows for a project requires a more thorough analysis than just determining the expected change in cash flows from the firm's current condition.

In sum, incremental cash flows are differences between the firm's cash flows with and without a project.

25. Indentures

All bonds will have indentures, which are contracts or agreements between issuing corporations and their bondholders. Such an agreement is supervised by a trustee who acts on the behalf of bondholders to ensure proper execution of the indenture provisions by the corporation. If the issuer violates indenture provisions, it is in default, and the trustee must act to protect the bondholders' interests.

26. Independent Bank

A bank operating in one locality that is not part of a large multibank holding company or group of banks.

27. Independent Projects

Projects are independent projects when acceptance or rejection of any one alternative would have no bearing on the acceptance or rejection of any other. The firm could undertake any or all of a group of independent projects, as long as each accepted project was expected to increase shareholder wealth.

28. Index Amortizing Swap

[See **Indexed principal swap**]

29. Index Arbitrage

An investment strategy that exploits divergences between actual future prices and their theoretically correct parity values to make a profit. [See also **Program trading**]

30. Index Fund

A mutual fund holding shares in proportion to their representation in a market index such as the S&P 500.

31. Index Futures

A futures contract on a stock index or other index.

32. Index Model

A model of stock returns using a market index such as the S&P 500 to represent common or systematic risk factors.

33. Index of Leading Indicators

[See **Business cycle**]

34. Index Option

A call or put option based on a stock market index.

35. Index Rate

The rate that serves as a base rate when pricing certain mortgages and variable rate loans.

36. Indexed Principal Swap

A swap where the principal declines over time. The reduction in the principal on a payment date depends on the level of interest rates. (The lower the interest rate, the greater the reduction in the principal).

37. Indifference Curve

A curve connecting all portfolios with the same utility according to their means and standard deviations.

38. Indirect Loan

Loan in which a retailer takes the credit application and negotiates terms with the actual borrower. The lender then purchases the loan from the retailer under prearranged terms.

39. Indirect Quotes

Exchange rate quotations can easily cause confusion. The market convention is to use indirect quotes; that is, a statement of units of foreign currency per US dollar (for example, DM 1.4736/dollar). Thus, when economists expect the US dollar ($) to strengthen against the yen (¥), they expect the indirect quote (¥/$) of the exchange rate to rise, so the US dollar will purchase more Japanese yen. A weakening US dollar means the dollar will purchase less yen, so the indirect quote will fall.

40. Individual Retirement Account

A retirement account available to individuals to defer income taxes.

41. Industrial Revenue Bond (IRB)

A bond issued by a state government, local government, or political subdivision for the express benefit of a business that will effectively use the proceeds.

42. Inefficient Market

[See **Efficient market**]

43. Inflation

When the economy begins to expand too quickly, demand from consumer and business spending may outstrip supply, driving prices upward; this is inflation. Although many argue that the Fed can best control inflation by slowing the growth of the money supply, others argue for lower levels of government spending and/or higher taxes to reduce aggregate spending in an overheated economy. In the case of economic recessions, some economists favor fiscal policies in the form of higher government spending or lower taxes in order to stimulate demand forces.

Differences in inflation rates between countries will lead to changes in the spot exchange rate over time. Countries with higher inflation rates will face depreciation, or increasing weakness, in their currencies over time.

44. Inflation Differential Risk

Inflation differential risk is the second added dimension of international diversification. Suppose an investor in the US has a security in England whose return is fixed in terms of the pound. Assuming that there is no inflation in the US but that the inflation rate in England is uncertain. The dollar value of the investment at the end of the period is uncertain and hence risky.

45. Inflation-Escalator Clause

A clause in a contract providing for increases or decreases in inflation based on fluctuations in the cost of living, production costs, and so forth.

46. Information Asymmetry

A type of transaction costs relates to the cost of information. Management's inside information is not freely disseminated. If management were to share its secrets and competitive plans with *The Wall Street Journal* or disclose them in mailings to shareholders, that information would quickly arrive in the offices of the firm's competitors.

Because of this information gap or information asymmetry between management and the public financial markets, the firm may need to raise money to take advantage of a competitive opportunity at a time when management feels that the firm's stock is underpriced. If raising equity is not an attractive option because of a low stock price and the firm's debt ratios already are high or are nearing the limits set by covenants in prior bond issues, the firm may miss the investment opportunity. Therefore, firms may avoid issuing excessive amounts of debt in order to maintain financing flexibility in the form of some degree of excess or unused debt capacity. In this way, the firm can maintain its ability to finance good capital budgeting projects by borrowing. This gives the firm another reason not to over-leverage itself; in fact, the firm may try to keep its debt ratio slightly below the optimal ratio in order to ensure that funds will be available if they are needed.

47. Information-Content Effect

Payment of a dividend conveys a signal to the market place. In other words, each divided payment or change in the dividend carries information to investors about the company. In sum, the rise or fall of stock price following the dividend signals is called information-content effect.

48. In-House Processing Float

Refers to the time it takes the receiver of a check to process the payment and deposit it in a bank for collection.

49. Initial Margin

The cash required from a futures trader at the time of the trade.

50. Initial Outlay

The first cash flow estimate is the initial investment in the project. For projects that require designing or modifying equipment and buildings, engineering estimates may be available. Engineers can examine preliminary designs or architectural sketches and estimate the quantities of various materials needed. Estimates of purchases, transportation costs, and construction expenses can be developed based on current market prices.

Another means of estimating the acquisition or construction cost of a project is to solicit bids from various construction or equipment manufacturers based upon a preliminary set of design specifications. An approximate cost can be determined through discussions with bidding firms. If the firm is large enough that it has an in-house engineering or real estate acquisition staff, this expertise also can be tapped to estimate relevant costs.

The expense of developing cost estimates is a sunk cost. That money is spent and gone whether or not the proposed project is accepted; it should not be included in the project's cash flow estimates. However, the initial outlay estimate must consider opportunity costs if the project will use property or equipment presently owned by the firm.

The investment cost estimate may have to be adjusted if the project involves replacing one asset with another, presumably newer and more cost-efficient model. If the old asset is going to be sold, the investment outlay must be reduced by the after-tax proceeds from the sale of the old asset.

Finally, even though a project's initial outlay may directly involve property and equipment (investing cash flows), it also may have implications for net working capital (operating cash flows). For example, if a project affects the firm's production process, inventory levels may change.

New raw materials needs may affect accounts payable. These kinds of expected changes in net working capital must be included as part of the initial outlay.

51. Initial Public Offering

Raising capital privately may fail to raise the necessary funds or the cost of raising funds privately may be too high. When this happens, the firm may choose to go public in an initial public offering (IPO). That is, the firm may sell shares of stock to the general public and allow the shares to trade freely between investors. Many entrepreneurs dream fondly of their firms someday becoming public corporations in this way. [See also **Going public**] IPO is also called an unseasoned new issue.

52. Input List

List of parameters such as expected returns, variances, and covariances necessary to determine the optimal risky portfolio.

53. Inside Information

Nonpublic knowledge about a corporation possessed by corporate officers, major owners, or other individuals, with privileged access to information about a firm.

54. Insider Trading

Some managers may try to use their privileged access to private information about the firm for their own personal gain. By buying shares of stock before good news is announced and selling it prior to the release of bad news, insider trading allows them to profit inordinately as compared to the market as a whole. Such actions are illegal in the US, but it is sometimes difficult to prove that an executive's stock purchases or sales were caused by his or her access to private information.

55. Insolvency

Insolvency means that the firm does not have sufficient cash inflows to meet all of its cash outflows.

Although all businesses expect to succeed, many do not. Various financial indications of serious difficulty often are apparent. Cash shortages may cause illiquidity, borrowing may increase, accounts may be overdrawn, and maintenance of plant and equipment may be delayed. Careful observation of either profit or cash receipt and disbursement trends may signal pending financial troubles. However, frequently occurring illiquidity can make the difficulty so acute that the problem can no longer be ignored.

Cash flow problems can create either **technical** or **legal insolvency**. [See also **Technical insolvency** and **Legal insolvency**]

A firm that finds itself in financial distress due to a state of insolvency or failure to satisfy a bond indenture has several alternatives:

1. Do nothing, but hope something will come along to save the situation.
2. Attempt to sell out. The firm can try to find a buyer, but buyers of troubled firms may be few. Even if one can be found, the seller frequently feels fortunate to walk away with any portion of the original equity.
3. Seek adjustments with creditors outside the judicial process, commonly called a workout. Some arrangements between the firm and its creditors may permit it to keep operating with the hope that it can work its way out of trouble. Such adjustments usually take the form of extensions of repayment schedules and/or compositions of credit.
4. Seek court relief in bankruptcy proceeding in the form of a reorganization or liquidation.
5. Assign assets to a third party for liquidation.
6. Liquidate.

56. Insolvent

The financial position of a firm whose market value of stockholders' equity is less than or equal to zero. A firm is technically insolvent when the book value of stock holders' equity is less than or equal to zero.

57. Installment Loan

A loan that is payable in periodic, partial installments.

58. Instantaneous Forward Rate

Forward rate for a very short period of time in the future.

59. Instruments

Financial securities, such as (i) money market instruments (e.g., commercial paper) or (ii) capital market instruments (e.g., stocks and bonds).

60. Insurance Principle (the Law Of Averages)

The average outcome for many independent trials of an experiment will approach the expected value of the experiment.

61. Interbank Loan

Credit extended from one bank to another.

62. Interest Coverage Ratio

Earnings before interest and taxes divided by interest expense. Used to measure a firm's ability to pay interest. [See also **Capital structure ratios**]

63. Interest on Interest

Interest earned on reinvestment of each interest payment on money invested.

64. Interest Rate Cap

An option that provides a payoff when a specified interest rate is above a certain level. The interest rate is a floating rate that is reset periodically. The

interest rate cap pays the difference between the realized interest rate in a period the interest cap rate.

65. Interest Rate Collar

A combination of an interest rate cap and an interest rate floor. The purchase of an interest rate collar is actually the simultaneous purchase of an interest rate cap and sale of an interest rate floor on the same index for the same maturity and notional principal amount.

66. Interest Rate Derivative

A derivative whose payoffs are dependent on future interest rate.

67. Interest Rate Floor

An option that provides a payoff when an interest rate is below a certain level. The interest rate is a floating rate that is reset periodically.

68. Interest Rate Option

An option where the payoff is dependent on the level of interest rates.

69. Interest Rate Parity

Under interest rate parity, investors are indifferent between investing at home or abroad as far as expected return is concerned; any existing nominal risk-free interest rate disparity is offset by spot and forward exchange rate differentials. When interest rate parity exists, the following relationship is true:

$$S_0 \times (1 + R_{FC})/F_1 = (1 + R_{US}).$$

The left-hand side of the equation reflects the return from converting dollars at the spot rate (S_0), investing them at the foreign rate ($1 + R_{FC}$), and then converting the currency back into dollars at the forward rate (F_1). The right-hand side reflects the return from investing the dollars in the US.

70. Interest Rate Risk

The general level of interest rates in an economy does not remain fixed; it fluctuates. For example, interest rates will change in response to changes in investors' expectations about future inflation rates. From the "**seesaw effect**," a rise in interest rates renders the fixed coupon interest payments on a bond less attractive, lowering its price. [See also **Seesaw effect**] Therefore, bondholders are subject to the risk of capital loss from such interest rate changes should the bonds have to be sold prior to maturity.

A longer term to maturity, all else being equal, increases the sensitivity of a bond's price to a given change in interest rates, as the discount rate change compounds over a longer time period. Similarly, a lower coupon rate also increase the sensitivity of the bond's price to market interest rate changes. This occurs since lower coupon bonds have most of their cash flow occurring further into the future, when the par value is paid.

Because of interest rate risk, investors will demand a larger risk premium for a bond whose price is especially sensitive to market interest rate changes. Hence, we would expect higher yields to maturity for long-term bonds with low coupon rates than for short-term bonds with high coupon rates.

71. Interest Rate Swap

An interest rate swap is a financial transaction in which two borrowers exchange interest payments on a particular amount of principal with a specified maturity. The swap enables each party to alter the characteristics of the periodic interest payments that it makes or receives.

The exchange might involve swapping a fixed-rate payment for a variable payment or the payment of one type of floating rate for another. All swaps trade only interest payments made on underlying note values; no principal payments need to change hands with a simple interest rate swap.

The two primary parties to the swap are called counterparties. Usually, although not always, a financial institution serves as an intermediary between the counterparties. In the typical interest rate swap, the counterparty with the fixed-rate debt pays a premium over the rate the other counterparty initially paid on its variable-rate debt. This premium is based upon factors such as the terms of the swap, the creditworthiness of the counterparties, and the conditions in the market for fixed-rate and variable-rate debt.

It is unusual for two companies to arrange an interest rate swap themselves. In most cases, intermediaries act as brokers, dealers, or principals to the transaction. As a broker or dealer, the intermediary serves to bring the counterparties together and collect an arrangement fee. However, in most swaps, the intermediary acts as a principal to both counterparties, assuming the credit risk in the event that one counterparty defaults. When the intermediary acts as the principal to a swap, its compensation is in the form of an arrangement fee and/or the spread between the terms of the two counterparties.

72. Interest Rates

The level and trend of interest rates play major roles in both financing and the investment decisions made my firms. Changes in interest rates may result in changes in a firm's bond and stock price as well as in the rates charged the firm by banks and other lenders. Such changes may affect the cost of financing enough to make an apparently profitably project turn unprofitable, or vice versa. The difference between long-term and short-term interest rates may influence a firm's decision to issue bonds or seek short-term financing.

Interest rates are the price of money. A borrower uses funds today, promising to repay them over time from future income. A saver forgoes current spending in order to store currency income in the expectation of earning a return that will increase the value of those savings over time.

Thus, interest rates reflect the cost of moving income across time.

As with any price, interest rates rise and fall because of changes over time in demand and supply; in this case, the demand and supply of capital. There is not just one interest rate; there are a myriad of interest rates and therefore, expected investment returns—from rates on short-term certificates of deposit at the bank, to rates offered on bonds issued by multinational corporations, to expected stock markets returns. Interest rates or expected returns on these investments differ because of risk difference between them.

73. Interest Subsidy

A firm's deduction of the interest payments on its debt from its earnings before it calculates its tax bill under current tax law.

74. Intermarket Spread Swap

Switching from one segment of the bond market to another (for example from Treasuries to corporates).

75. Internal Audit

Routine examination of a bank's accounting records.

76. Internal Financing

Net income plus depreciation minus dividends, internal financing comes from internally generated cash flow such as retained earnings.

77. Internal Growth Rate

The internal growth rate measures how quickly a firm can increase its asset base over the next year without raising outside funds. It does not measure divisional growth or break down total growth into domestic or international components. More

detailed analysis must be done to estimate the forces that determine growth rates. The internal growth rate gives a general, companywide value.

The internal growth rate is equal to the ratio of the expected increase in retained earnings (ΔRE) over the next year to the current total asset base (TA_0) as:

$$\frac{\Delta RE}{TA_0}.$$

This also can be written as:

$$\text{Internal growth rate} = \frac{(\text{RR})(\text{ROA})}{1 - (\text{RR})(\text{ROA})}.$$

RR is the firm's retention rate, and ROA is its return on assets. The internal growth rate divides the product of these values by one minus this product.

Most managers plan and think in terms of sales dollars rather than asset size, so it may help to relate the internal growth rate to sales growth. We can roughly estimate a sales growth rate by recalling the total asset turnover ratio, which equals sales divided by total assets. If management can assume that this ratio will remain constant into the foreseeable future, the growth in sales will equal the internal growth rate.

The internal growth rate makes the restrictive assumption that the firm will pursue no outside sources of financing. Should the firm grow at its internal growth rate, its retained earnings account will continually rise (assuming profitable sales), while its dollar amount of debt outstanding will remain constant. Thus, the firm's debt-to-equity ratio declines over time, until debt falls below its correct proportion in management's ideal financing mix.

78. Internal Rate of Return

The internal rate of return (IRR) is a discounted cash flow concept and represents the discount rate at which the present value of a project's cash flows equal the project's cost. This implies that the IRR of a project is the discount rate that sets the project's net present value (NPV) to zero. The internal rate of return can be found by solving for IRR in the following present value relationship as:

$$NPV = \sum_{t=1}^{N} \frac{CF_t}{(1+IRR)^t} - I = 0,$$

where I = initial outlay; CF_t = cash flow in period t; and N = number of periods of project.

If a project has a positive NPV when its cash flows are discounted at the required return, the project's IRR will exceed this required return. Graphically, for any required rate of return below the IRR, the net present value of the project is positive. For any required rate of return greater than the IRR, the NPV is negative.

Thus, the IRR technique has a clearly defined and objective decision rule: accept all projects with IRRs that exceed their minimum required rate of return since those projects will increase shareholder wealth. If the IRR is less than the required return, then the project should be rejected, as it will reduce shareholder wealth. Both the NPV and IRR methods will always agree as to whether a project will increase or decrease shareholder wealth. Although the IRR and NPV are related, the meaning of the IRR is more complex than that of the NPV.

Unlike NPV, IRR does *not* measure the absolute dollar amount by which a project will change shareholder wealth. The IRR tells us nothing about the size of the change in shareholder wealth. Thus, we can say that IRR is a relative, not an absolute, measure of project attractiveness – one project's IRR may be higher, while its NPV is lower, than that of another project.

Thus, IRR satisfies only three of the four capital selections. It considers all cash flows, incorporates the time value of money, and it has an objective decision criterion. But it does not measure the size of the project's impact on shareholder wealth. [See also **Appendix C** for the timing problem of the IRR Method]

79. International Capital Asset Pricing Model

It is being use to test whether assets are best regarded as being traded in segmented (national) or integrated (international) markets, found some evidence that markets are integrated. It can be state as:

$$E(R_i^j) = R_f + \beta_{wi}^j [E(R_w) - R_f],$$

where $E(R_i^j)$ = expected rate of return on ith security (or portfolio) in country j; R_f = the risk-free rate of interest; and $E(R_w)$ = expected rate or return on the world market portfolio;

$\beta_{wi}^j = (\rho_{i,w}\sigma_i\sigma_w)/\sigma_w^2$ or the correlation coefficient between the rate of return on security i in country j and the world market, times the standard deviation of security i, times the standard deviation of the world market, divided by the variance of the world market portfolio. It is also the International system risk of country j.

80. International Fisher Effect

The International Fisher effect shows a) the relationship between the expected exchange rate change and the inflation rate differential, and b) the relationship between the inflation rate differential and the interest rate differential. The equation is as follows:

$$\frac{E(S_1)}{S_0} = \frac{1+h_{FC}}{1+h_{US}} = \frac{1+R_{FC}}{1+R_{US}},$$

where S_0 and $E(S_1)$ are the current spot exchange rate and expected spot rate one year in the future, respectively. R_{US} and R_{FC} are nominal interest rates in US and foreign country, respectively. Finally, h_{US} and h_{FC} are inflation rates for US and foreign country respectively.

If the expected future spot rate, $E(S_1)$, is equal to the forward rate, F_1, then the equation reduces to the interest rate parity relationship:

$$F_1 = S_0 \frac{(1+R_{RC})}{(1+R_{US})}.$$

81. International Monetary Market (IMM)

A division of Chicago mercantile exchange. The Eurodollar futures contracts and associated option are traded at IMM.

82. International System Risk

[See also **International asset pricing model**]

83. Intertemporal Capital Asset Pricing Model

Allowing the investment opportunity set change over time, Merton (1973) develops the intertemporal capital asset pricing model, which introduces a hedge portfolio function into the model.

84. In-the-Money-Option

Either (a) a call option where the asset price is greater than the strike price or (b) a put option where the asset price is less than the strike price.

85. Intrinsic Value

For a call option, this is the greater of the excess of the asset price over the strike price and zero. For a put option, it is the greater of the excess of the strike price over the asset price and zero.

86. Intrinsic Value of an Option

Stock price minus exercise price, or the profit that could be attained by immediate exercise of an in-the-money option.

87. Inventory

A current asset, composed of raw materials to be used in production, work in process, and finished goods.

88. Inventory Conversion Period

The inventory conversion period is defined as inventory divided by cost of goods sold per day as:

$$\text{Inventory conversion period} = \frac{\text{Inventory}}{\text{Cost of goods sold}/365 \text{ days}}.$$

89. Inventory Loan

A secured short-term loan to purchase inventory. The three basic forms are blanket inventory lien, a trust receipt, and field warehouse financing.

90. Inventory Turnover Ratio

Ratio of annual sales to average inventory that measures how quickly inventory is produced and sold. [See **Asset management ratios**]

91. Inverted Market

A market where futures prices decrease with maturity.

92. Inverted Yield Curve

Yield curve with long-term rates below short-term rates.

93. Investable Balances

Ledge balances minus float minus required reserves against associated deposit balances.

94. Investment Asset

An asset held by at least some individuals for investment purposes.

95. Investment Bankers

Financial intermediaries who perform a variety of services, including aiding in the sale of securities, facilitating mergers and other corporate reorganizations, acting as brokers to both individual and institutional clients, and trading for their own accounts.

96. Investment Banking

Activity involving securities underwriting, making a market in securities, and arranging mergers and acquisitions.

97. Investment Company

Firm managing funds for investors. An investment company may manage several mutual funds.

98. Investment Grade Bond

Debt that is rated BBB and above by Standard & Poor's or Baa and above by Moody's. Alternatively, it is lower-rated bonds are classified as speculative-grade or junk bonds.

99. Investment of Different Life

[See **Equivalent annual cost** and **Appendix D**]

100. Investment Opportunity Schedule

An investment opportunity schedule (IOS) is a chart or graph that relates the internal rate of return on individual projects to cumulative capital spending. To set up an investment opportunity schedule, the analyst first computes each project's internal rate of return (or modified internal rate of return). If mutually exclusive projects are part of the analysis, only the highest ranked projects go on to the next step.

After computing the individual modified internal rules of return (MIRR), the projects are ranked from highest to lowest by MIRR, keeping a tally of cumulative project spending.

101. Investment Portfolio

Set of securities chosen by an investor.

102. Investment Quality Bonds

Investment quality bonds have ratings of BBB by Standard & Poor's (or Baa by Moody's) or higher.

They are called investment quality as some institutional investors, such as pension funds and insurance companies, restrict themselves to investing only in these low-default risk issues.

103. Investment Trigger Price

The price of an investment project (or the price of the good to be produced) at which it is optimal to invest in the project.

104. Investments

An area within finance is the study of investments. Students of investments learn how to analyze the investor's stake in stocks, bonds, and other financial instruments. This analysis focuses on evaluating the cash flow from such financial assets to decide whether they represent attractive investments. As in the other fields of finance, the analyst also must plan how to manage the assets in an investment portfolio to meet future liabilities (such as college tuition, a new car or house, or retirement income).

105. Invoice

Bill written by a seller of goods or services and submitted to the purchaser.

106. Invoicing Float

[See also **Float**]

107. IO

Interest Only. A mortgage-backed security where the holder receives only interest cash flows on the underlying mortgage pool.

108. Irrelevance Result

The Miller and Modigliani (1958) theorem that a firm's capital structure is irrelevant to the firm's value when there are no taxes and other assumptions hold.

109. Irrevocable Letter of Credit

International trade often requires banker's acceptances, as well as even more formal arrangements. An exporter that requires even greater certainty of payment may request an irrevocable letter of credit. In this arrangement, the customer's bank sends the exporter a letter stating that it has established a line of credit for the customer with a particular US bank. The exporter then can collect payment from the US bank before making the delivery. The US bank forwards the appropriate documents to the customer's bank to receive reimbursement.

110. ISDA (Institutional Swap Dealers Association)

A committee sponsored by this organization was instrumental in drafting an industry standard under which securities dealers would trade swaps. Including in this draft of a master agreement by which institutions outlined their rights to net multiple offsetting exposures which they might have to counterparty at the time in credit quality.

111. Iso-Expected Return Line

Line, drawn on a mapping of portfolio weights, which shows the combinations of weights all of which provide for a particular portfolio rate of return.

112. Iso-Variance Ellipse

Ellipse, drawn on a mapping of portfolio weights, which shows the combinations of weights all of which provide for a particular portfolio variance.

113. Issuer Exposure

The credit risk to the issuer of traded instruments (typically a bond, but also swaps, foreign exchange, etc.) Labeling credit spread volatility as either market or credit risk is a question of semantics. CreditMetrics addresses market price volatility as it is caused by changes in credit quality. [See also **CreditMetrics**]

114. Itô Process

A stochastic process where the change in a variable during each short period of time of length δt has normal distribution. The mean and variance of the distribution are proportional to δt and are not necessarily constant. [See also **Random Equation**]

J

1. January Effect

Market anomaly whereby stock prices throughout most the world have a propensity to rise sharply during the initial part of the month of January.

2. Jensen's Inequality

If x is a random variable and $f(x)$ is convex, Jensen's inequality states that $E[f(x)] \geq f[E(x)]$. The inequality is reversed if $f(x)$ is concave.

3. Jensen's Measure

The alpha of an investment. It can be defined as:

$$JM = (\overline{R}_i - R_f) - \beta_i[\overline{R}_m - R_f],$$

where $\overline{R}_i$ is an average rate of returns for ith asset or portfolio; R_f = risk-free return; $\overline{R}_m$ = average market rates of return; and β_i is the beta coefficient for the ith asset.

4. Johnson Hedge Model

Developed within the framework of modern portfolio theory. The Johnson hedge model (Johnson, 1960) retains the traditional objective of risk minimization but defines risk as the variance of return on a two-asset hedge portfolio. As in the two-parameter world of Markowitz's (1959), the hedger is assumed to be infinitely risk averse (that is, the investor desires zero variance). Moreover, with portfolio optimization, the risk-minimization objective defined as the variance of return on the combined spot and futures position, the Johnson hedge ratio is expressed in terms of expectations of variance and covariances for price changes in the spot and futures markets. The Johnson hedge model can be expressed in regression from as:

$$\Delta S_t = \alpha + H\Delta F_t + e_t,$$

where ΔS_t = change in the spot price at time t; ΔF_t = change in the futures price at time t; α = constant; H = hedge ratio; and e_t = residual term at time t.

5. Joint Probabilities

In credit risk analysis, stand-alone obligors have some likelihood of each possible credit quality migration. Between two obligors there is some likelihood of each possible joint credit quality migration. The probabilities are commonly influences by the correlation between the two obligors.

6. Joint Venture

A joint venture is a partial business combination. Two or more entities form a new corporation or partnership in order to jointly pursue a business venture. This provides an opportunity to combine resources in optimal proportions rather than in the fixed portfolio proportions dictated by a merger or a tender offer. The participants are partners rather than acquirer and target, and thus the formation of a joint venture does not cast one party as the aggressor, as in a merger or acquisition.

Common reasons for joint venture formation include facilitating technological transfer and developing market structures. International diversification also can give rise to joint ventures because some countries require local investment from any firm operating within their borders; others exempt firms with local participation from government regulations.

Joint ventures also can be used for undertaking certain massive projects. The development of Prudhoe Bay, Alaska, is one such example of a project joint venture.

7. Judgment

Legal ruling regarding the final payment of a court-determined transfer of assets.

8. Judgmental Credit Analysis

Subjective assessment of a borrower's ability and willingness to repay debts.

9. Jumbos

Jumbos are negotiable certificates of deposits (CDs) by thrifts which are large-denomination ($100,000 or greater) time deposits with a minimum maturity of 7 days.

10. Jump-Diffusion Model

A process for an asset price in which the asset most of the time follows an Itô process but can also jump discretely, with occurrence of the jump controlled by a Poisson process.

11. Junior Liens

[See **Second mortgages**]

12. Junk Bonds

Noninvestment quality bonds are called junk bonds or high-yield bonds to reflect their higher risk and higher expected returns.

K

1. Kappa

Another name for *vega*. [See also **Vega**]

2. Keogh Plan

A pension plan for the self-employed which allows them to make contributions and defer taxes until the funds are withdrawn.

3. Key-Person Insurance

Most banks require key-person insurance on the principal officers of the borrowing company to protect their loans. Because the repayment of a loan usually depends upon the managers of the firm running the company profitability, the death or disability of a key manager could jeopardize the safety of the loan. To avoid this uncertainty, the borrower buys a term insurance policy on the life of the key manager for the value of the loan. If he or she should die, the proceeds of the policy would be paid to the bank in settlement of the loan. Key-person insurance is useful in sole proprietorships as well as corporations.

4. Kite

Writing checks against uncollected deposits in the process of clearing through the banking system.

5. Knock-in Option

An option in which there can only be a final payoff if, during a specified period of time, the price of the underlying asset has reached a specified level. This is one of the barrier options; it is attractive to some market participants because they are less expensive than the regular options.

6. Knock-out Option

An option in which there can only be a final payoff if, during a specified period of time, the price of the underlying asset has *not* reached a specified level. This is one of the barrier options; it is attractive to some market participants because they are less expensive than the regular options.

7. Kolmogorov Backward Equation

A partial differential equation that is related to the Black-Scholes equation and that is satisfied by probability distributions for the underlying asset.

8. Kurtosis

Characterizes relative peakedness or flatness of a given distribution compared to a normal distribution. It is the fourth moment of a distribution. Since the unconditional normal distribution has a kurtosis of 3, excess kurtosis is defined as K_{x-3}. Sample kurtosis can be defined as:

$$K_{x-3} = \sum_{i=1}^{n} (X_i - \overline{X})^4 / n - 3.$$

K_{x-3} can either be equal to, larger than, or smaller than 0. [See also **Leptokurtosis**]

L

1. Ladder Option

If the barrier $L > K$ is reached over the life of the option, a ladder option at expiration pays *max* $(0, L - K, S_t - K)$. If the barrier is not reached, the option pays *max* $(0, S_t - K)$.

Ladder options are "more path-dependent" than barrier options. Normally, there are several prespecified ladders or rungs in a ladder option. Whenever the underlying asset price reaches a prespecified higher level in a series of prespecified rungs, the intrinsic value of the option is locked. [See also **Barrier Option**]

2. Ladder Strategy

When investing bonds, allocating roughly equivalent amounts (portions) to different maturities.

3. Lagged Reserve Accounting

System of reserve requirements based on deposits outstanding prior to the reserve maintenance period.

4. Lagging Indicators

[See Business cycle]

5. Lambda

Another name for *vega*. [See **Vega**]

6. Lattice

A binomial tree in which an up move followed by a down move leads to the same price as a down move followed by an up move. Also called a *recombining* binomial tree.

7. Law of One Price (LOP)

A commodity will cost the same regardless of what currency is used to purchase it. The LOP is also the guiding principle behind the Miller & Modigliani arbitrage argument.

8. LBO

[See **Leveraged buyout**]

9. Leading Economic Indicators

Economic series that tend to risk or fall in advance of the rest of the economy. [See also **Business cycle**]

10. Leakage

Release of information to some persons before official public announcement.

11. LEAPS

Long-term Equity Anticipation Securities. These are relatively long term options on individual stocks or stock indices.

12. Lease

A contractual arrangement to grant the use of specific fixed assets for a specified time in exchange for payment, usually in the form of rent. An operating lease is generally a short-term cancelable arrangement, whereas a financial, or capital, lease is a long-term non-cancelable agreement.

13. Lease Rate

The annualized payment required to borrow an asset, or equivalently, the annualized payment received in exchange for lending an asset.

14. Ledger Balances

Dollar value of deposit balances appearing on a bank's books.

15. Ledger Cash

A firm's cash balance as reported in its financial statements. Also called book cash.

16. Legal Insolvency

Legal insolvency is a more serious financial problem than **technical insolvency**. [See also **Technical insolvency**] Legal insolvency exists when a firm's recorded assets amount to less than its recorded liabilities. This condition arises when successive losses create a deficit in the owners' equity account, rendering it incapable of supporting the firm's legal liabilities. The firm may be legally insolvent even when it is liquid and has plenty of cash to pay its current bills. Outsiders may not be aware of the insolvency as long as the liquidity of the firm enables it to meet its cash obligations. A protracted period of legal insolvency usually leads to bankruptcy.

17. Legal Lending Limit

The maximum amount that can be loaned to any one borrower or any group or related borrowers.

18. Lender Liability

Circumstances in which the courts have found lenders liable to their borrowers for fraud, deception, breached fiduciary activities, broken promises, and good faith negotiations.

19. Lending Portfolio

Investors invest in both market portfolio and risk-free asset. When they invest in risk-free asset, it means that they lend money to somebody else. Therefore, this kind of portfolio is called lending portfolio.

20. Leptokurtosis (Fat Tails)

The property of a statistical distribution to have more occurrences far away from the mean than would be predicted by a normal distribution. Since a normal distribution has a kurtosis measure of 3, excess kurtosis (K_x) is defined as $K_x > 3$.

A credit portfolio distribution will typically be leptokurtotic given positive obligor correlations or coarse granularity in the size/number of exposures. This means that a downside confidence interval will be further away from the mean than would be expected given the standard deviation and skewness. [See also **Kurtosis**]

21. Lessee

One that receives the use of assets under a lease. A long term capital or financial lease obligates the lessee to make a series of fixed payments over time.

22. Lessor

One that conveys the use of assets under a lease. If the lessee fails to make payments as scheduled, the lessor, or the owner, can take possession of the leased asset.

23. Letter of Comment

A communication to the firm from the Securities and Exchange Commission that suggests changes to a registration statement. After the changes are made, the 20-day waiting period starts anew.

24. Letter of Credit

Time drafts increase the risk involved in foreign trade. To minimize this risk, an exporter may require the buyer to obtain a letter of credit (L/C) from a specified bank. Sometimes, buyers seek letters of credit themselves to obtain more favorable treatment by exporters. A letter of credit is a guarantee by the buyer's bank to honor the seller's drafts that are drawn on the bank, provided that the drafts comply with the terms specified in the letter of credit and are accompanied by the necessary documents.

A letter of credit affects a trade transaction in the following way. First, the buyer asks the bank to create the letter of credit in favor of the seller. Second, the bank creates the letter of credit and informs its foreign correspondent bank in the seller's country that it has done so. The correspondent bank in the seller's country then notifies the seller about the credit. Next, the seller ships the goods to the buyer and receives a **bill of lading (B/ L)** from the shipper. [See also **Bill of lading**] Finally, the buyer sends the bill of lading to the shipper and receives the merchandise in return.

A letter of credit provides three important benefits to an importer:

1. An importer is safer if it deposits required prepayments with its own bank rather than with the seller in a foreign country. If the seller fails to ship the goods, it is relatively easy for the buyer to recover the deposit from its own bank.

2. If no prepayment is required, the buyer still can finance the purchase through its own bank at a relatively low cost.

3. The buyer can bargain for a lower price and better terms from the seller because it has substituted the bank's credit for its own. Since buyers who obtain letters of credit have eliminated most of the risk for the seller, they are justified in asking for lower prices and better terms.

A letter of credit also offers substantial advantages to the exporter. The exporter receives payment immediately after shipping the merchandise if the letter of credit specifies a sight draft. If the letter of credit calls for a time draft, the exporter receives a note from the bank (a **banker's acceptance**) rather than a note from the buyer; this bank note is virtually risk-free. [See also **Banker's acceptance**] Another advantage to a letter of credit comes from a reduction of the seller's risk of foreign exchange rate fluctuations due to the quick payment schedule.

There are three different types of letters of credit. (a) A *financial* letter of credit (also termed as standby letter of credit) is used to assure access to funding without the immediate need for funds and is triggered at the obligor's discretion. (b) A *project* letter of credit is secured by a specific asset or project income. (c) A *trade* letter of credit is typically triggered by a non-credit related (an infrequent) event. Item (c) is the above-mentioned trade L/C.

25. Level-Coupon Bond

Bond with a stream of coupon payments that are the same throughout the life the bond. The coupon payments are equal to coupon rate times face value of a bond.

26. Leverage Ratio

Ratio of debt to total capitalization of a firm. [See also **Capital structure ratios**]

27. Leveraged Buyout

A method of business combination is the leveraged buyout (LBO). In a leveraged buyout, the buyers borrow a major proportion of the purchase price, pledging the purchased assets as collateral for the loan. The buyers may be an outside group of investors, another company, or the manager of the firm or division that is being sold. Typically, the leverage arises from the payment of the purchase price to the seller (or alternatively, to a lender) using some of the actual earnings of the acquired firm. Once the assets are purchased, the cash flow from their operations is used to pay the principal and interest of the loan. In some cases, an LBO can be used to take a firm out of public ownership and into private ownership, in a technique called **going private**. Any kind of LBO can create an agency problem between the firm's mangers and public shareholders, in that the managers usually have more and better information about the value of the firm than do the shareholders.

The LBO or merger method usually requires the target firm be either cash-rich (generate an abundant cash flow) or sell for less than the separate value of its assets. Additionally, forecasts of future cash flows for the target firm are necessary to estimate the riskiness of the deal over time.

28. Leveraged Equity

Stock in a firm that relies on financial leverage. Holders of leveraged equity face the benefits and cost of using debt. The required rates of return for a leveraged equity is higher than those of un-leveraged equity. [See **Modigliani and Miller (M&M) proposition II**]

29. Leveraged Lease

In a leveraged lease, the lessor borrows money to purchase the asset and the leases out the asset. It is a tax-oriented leasing arrangement that involves one or more third-party lenders. This type of lease is often used in situations while large capital outlay is necessary for the purchase of assets.

30. Liabilities

Debts of the firm in the form of financial claims on a firm's assets. It can be classified as current liability and long-term liability.

31. Liability Management Theory

A theory that focuses in banks issuing liabilities to meet liquidity needs. Liquidity and liability management are closely related. One aspect of liquidity risk control is the buildup of a prudential level of liquid assets. Another aspect is the management of the Deposit institution's (DI) liability structure to reduce the need for large amounts of liquid assets to meet liability withdrawals. However, excessive use of purchased funds in the liability structure can result in a liquidity crisis if investors lose confidence in the DI and refuse to roll over such funds.

32. Liability Sensitive

A bank is classified as liability sensitive if its GAP is negative.

33. LIBID

London Interbank Bid Rate. The rate bid by banks on Eurocurrency deposits (i.e., the rate at which a bank is willing to lend to other banks).

34. LIBOR

London Interbank Offer Rate. A measure of the borrowing rate for large international banks. The British Banker's Association determines LIBOR daily for different currencies by surveying at least eight banks, asking at what rate they could borrow, dropping the top and bottom quartiles of the responses, and computing an arithmetic average of the remaining quotes. Since LIBOR is an average, there may be no actual transactions at that rate. Confusingly, LIBOR is also sometimes referred to as a lending rate. This is because a bank serving as a market maker in the interbank market will offer to lend money at a high interest rate (LIBOR) and borrow money at a low interest rate (LIBID). (The difference between LIBOR and LIBID is the bid-ask spread in the interbank market.) A bank needing to borrow will thus pay LIBOR, and a bank with excess funds will receive LIBID. [See also **LIBID**]

35. LIBOR Curve

LIBOR zero-coupon interest rates as a function of maturity.

36. LIBOR-in-Arrears Swap

Swap where the interest paid on a date is determined by the interest rate observed on that date (not by the interest rate observed on the previous payment date).

37. Lien

Legal right granted by court to attach property until a legal claim is paid.

38. LIFO

The last-in first-out accounting method of valuing inventories. In inflation period, the cost of inventory is higher than that calculated by the first-in-first-out method.

39. Limit Move

The maximum price move permitted by the exchange in a single trading session. There are both upper and lower limit.

40. Limit Order

An order that can be executed only at a specified price or one more favorable to the investor.

41. Limited Branching

Provisions that restrict branching to a geographic area smaller than an entire state.

42. Limited Liability

The fact that shareholders have no personal liability to the creditors of the corporation in the event of bankruptcy.

43. Limited Liability Company

A limited liability company (LLC) is one of two special forms of corporate organizations in the US that allow dividends to escape double taxation. A limited liability company (LLC) organization form has been authorized by the laws of more than 35 states as of the end of 2005. Similar to a **Subchapter S corporation**, it offers owners limited liability and its income is taxed only once as personal income of the shareholder. [See also **Subchapter S corporation**] Unlike a Subchapter S corporation, however, an LLC can have an unlimited number of shareholders, including other corporations. The LLC can sell shares without completing the costly and time-consuming process of registering them with the SEC, which is a requirement for standard corporations that sell their securities to the public. The LLC structure has drawbacks in that, should an owner leave, all others must formally agree to continue the firm. Also, all of the LLC's owners must take active roles in managing the company. To protect partners from unlimited liability, some partnerships, including large accounting firms such as PricewaterhouseCoopers, have changed their organizational forms to LLC.

44. Limited Partnership

Form of business organization that permits the liability of some partners to be limited by the amount of cash contributed to the partnership. [See also **General partnership**]

45. Limited-Liability Instrument

A security, such as a call option, in which all the holder can lose is the initial amount put into it.

46. Line of Credit

A line of credit is an agreement that specifies the maximum amount of unsecured credit the bank will extend to the firm at any time during the life of the agreement. In the past, banks gave lines of credit only to larger, more secure companies. This, too, appears to be changing, however, and some commercial banks now provide lines of credit to small, newly formed companies in which they see good growth potential.

In granting a line of credit, a bank is saying, in effect, "It looks as though your position is sufficiently sound to justify a loan, but when the time comes for you to start borrowing, we shall probably want to talk to you again to make sure that everything is going as expected." For example, a company that expects a rapid increase in sales may arrange a line of credit to finance increases in inventory and receivables. Before allowing the company to begin drawing on the line, however, the bank will want to verify that sales actually have increased. If the company has suffered a drop in sales, the bank is unlikely to allow it to use the line of credit to get out of the resulting financial crisis.

Of course, a line of credit has a cost to the borrower. When the loan actually is used, the borrower must pay interest on the funds borrowed. Even before actually accepting any funds, however, the borrower will probably incur a cost. Most banks require borrowers to keep a specified minimum compensating balance in exchange for being granted a line of credit. The compensating balance essentially compensates the bank for the service it provides. Instead of charging a fee for an additional interest rate, however, the bank obliges the borrower to keep an agree-upon sum in its demand deposit account at all times. Since banks pay no interest on commercial demand deposits, they may then invest the compensating balance in marketable securities or lend them to another borrower; any return the bank earns on these funds is clear profit. In practice, the use of compensating balances has been dwindling. This is especially true for larger firms, which would rather pay fees than hold compensating balances.

47. Linear Programming Approach to Portfolio Analysis

Sharpe (1967) developed a simplified portfolio-analysis model deisgned to be formulated as a linear-programming (LP) problem. Sharpe approaches the problem of capturing the essence of mean-variance portfolio selection in a linear-programming formulation by:

1. making a diagonal transformation of the variables that will convert the problem into a diagonal form, and

2. using a piecewise linear approximation for each of the terms of variance.

The LP that results from the use of market reponsiveness as the risk measure and the imposition of an upper on investment in each security is:

$$MAX\ P = \lambda[\sum_{i=1}^{n} x_i E(R_i)] - (1 - \lambda)[\sum_{i=1}^{n} x_i \beta_i],$$

subject to

$$\sum_{i=1}^{n} x_i = 1 \quad (0 \leq x_i \leq U),$$

where x_i = the fraction of the portfolio invested in security i; $E(R_i)$ = the expected returns on security i; β_i = the beta coefficient of security i; U = the maximum fraction of the portfolio that may be held in any one security; and λ = a parameter reflecting the degree of risk aversion.

48. Linear–Optimization Model

A linear-optimization model is a method of maximizing or minimizing an objective function that is subject to a number of linear constraints. The general form of the problem can be written as:

$Max\ (\alpha_1 x_1 + \alpha_2 x_2),$

subject to

$$-x_1 + 4x_2 \geq 0,$$
$$x_1 + x_2 = 1,$$
$$x_1, x_2 \geq 0,$$

where α_1, α_2 are the percentages of a portfolio invested in securities 1 and 2, respectively; x_1 and x_2 are average rates of return for securities 1 and 2, respectively.

The problem is to maximize the return on the portfolio. As shown by the objective function, with the restriction stated above, the investment in security 2 should be at least 20 percent ($-x_1 + 4x_2 \geq 0$); and, as stated in ($x_1 + x_2 = 1$), the funds of the portfolio should be 100 percent invested. Further, the nonnegative conditions ($x_1, x_2 \geq 0$) preclude the short selling of either security 1 or 2.

49. Lintner's Model

Lintner's model, sometimes referred to as the *partial-adjustment model*, assumes that firms adjust their dividend payouts slowly over time and provides another explanation for a firm's dividend policy. In Lintner's model, a firm is assumed to have a desired level of dividends that is based on its expected earnings. When earnings vary, the firm will adjust its dividend payment to reflect the new level of earnings. However, rather than doing so immediately, a firm will choose to spread (or partially adjust) these variations in earnings over a number of time periods

Lintner (1956) was the first to investigate the partial-adjustment model of dividend behavior. Using this model, Lintner demonstrated how dividend policy decisions can be made by using the following three steps:

Step 1: Compare last period's dividend with the desired level of dividends and adjust the deviation accordingly the next period.

Step 2: Assume the desirable dividend level is $D_t^* = PT_t$, where P is the long-run payout ratio for dividends and E_t is the earnings level for that period.

Step 3: Combining steps 1 and 2, we obtain a dividend decision model:

$$D_t = D_{t-1} + \delta(D_t^* - D_{t-1}) \qquad (A)$$

or,

$$D_t = D_{t-1} + (PE_t - D_{t-1}). \qquad (B)$$

To solve for the variable δ, the partial adjustment coefficient, we use a regression model:

$$D_t = b_0 + b_1 E_t + b_2 D_{t-1} + e_t, \qquad (C)$$

where $b_1 = P\delta$, and $b_2 = (1 - \delta)$. From the estimated b_1 and b_2, we can estimate δ and P as:

$$\delta = 1 - \hat{b}_2 \qquad (D)$$

$$P = \hat{b}_1/(1 - \hat{b}_2). \qquad (E)$$

Here we use the desired dividend payment, D_t, as a function of earnings, whereas with ratio analysis the desired ratio is a function of the industry average.

From this model, we can conclude that firms set their dividend in accordance with their level of current earnings. We can also conclude that changes in dividends over time do not correspond exactly with changes in earnings in the immediate time period, but rather are spread out over several time periods.

Another explanation for the δ coefficient is that it is the average speed of adjustment. We can interpret the quantity $(1 - \delta)$ as a safety factor that management uses to avoid increasing the dividend payment to levels that cannot be maintained.

Equation (C) shows the changes in dividend levels between periods rather than the absolute levels themselves. This allows us to investigate changes in the firm's dividend policy. Of the 28 firms Lintner studied, 26 appeared to have and follow a predetermined target payout ratio, P. On the whole, most of these firms updated their dividend policies annually.

50. Lintner's Observations

Lintner's (1956) work suggested the dividend policy is elated to a target level of dividends and the speed of adjustment of change in dividends. [See also **Lintner's model**]

51. Liquid Yield Option Note

First issued in 1985 after its development by Merrill Lynch, a LYON is a Liquid Yield Option Note. In less fancy terms, LYONs are zero coupon, convertible, callable, putable bonds.

They work this way: prior to maturity, an investor can convert the LYON into a specified number of common shares. As the value of the zero coupon bond approaches par over time, the conversion price increases according to a schedule set in the indenture. On designated dates prior to maturity, an investor can put the bond to the issuer and receive specific prices that increase as the value of the zero coupon bond approaches par over time. Finally, the issuer can call the bonds and pay investors an indenture-specified price that rises over tiem as the bond value accrues to par.

52. Liquidating Dividend

Payment by a firm to its owners from capital rather than from earnings.

53. Liquidation

Bankruptcy law favors reorganization through **Chapter 11**, but if the firm cannot be preserved as a going concern, the law requires liquidation. [See also **Chapter 11**] Liquidation involves selling the firm's assets and distributing the proceeds to the creditors in order of the priority of their claims. Chapter 7 of the Bankruptcy Reform Act of 1978 deals with "straight" liquidation.

In determining whether or not to liquidate a firm, the law asks: Is the firm worth more dead or alive? In other words, is the net present value of the liquidate parts of an enterprise greater than the present value of the firm as a going concern? If the answer is *yes*, the firm's assets are sold and the creditors are paid off. If the answer is *no*, then Chapter 11 proceeding usually are followed.

Once the liquidation of assets has begun, it usually becomes painfully clear that few, if any, assets except cash bring the balance sheet values. Indeed, a significant reduction in asset values is to be expected. Because of this, not all claims on these assets will be satisfied in full; no liquidation generates enough cash to cover all claims.

In this even, available cash must be allocated to the various claims according to a rule called the **absolute priority of claims**. [See also **Absolute priority of claims**]

54. Liquidation Value

Net amount that could be realized by selling the assets of a firm after paying the debt.

55. Liquidity

Refers to the ease and quickness of converting assets to cash. Also called marketability. Current assets have higher liquidity than fixed assets. There are two separate meanings:

(a) At the enterprise level, the ability to meet current liabilities as they fall due; often measures as the ratio of current assets to current liabilitics.

(b) At the security level, the ability to trade in volume without directly moving the market price; often measured as bid/ask spread and daily turnover.

56. Liquidity Preference Hypothesis

The liquidity preference hypothesis argues that long-term rates typically are higher than short-term rates because longer term securities are inherently riskier than shorter term securities; thus, long-term interest rates should incorporate a risk premium over and above the rates predicted by the expectations hypothesis.

Long-term bonds appear to be riskier than short-term bonds for several reasons. First, long-term bonds have greater interest rate risk; their prices change by larger percentages than short-term bond prices for the same change in market interest rates. Second, long-term bonds expose investors to more uncertainty about future inflation and interest rates.

Combining this risk premium perspective with the expectations hypothesis explains the term structure behavior better than the expectations hypothesis alone. [See also **Expectations hypothesis**] The term structure typically should slope upward, presumably due to the liquidity preference-risk premium effect. The term structure may become downward sloping, however, with long-term rates below short-term rates, if substantial declines in future rates are expected.

57. Liquidity Preference Theory

A theory leading to the conclusion that forward interest rates are above expected future spot interest rates.

58. Liquidity Premium

The premium included in longer-term interest rates to compensate investors for price risk associated with volatile interest rates. This premium is due to the belief that most investors find long-term securities to be riskier than short-term securities. This hypothesis is called as liquidity premium hypotheses.

59. Liquidity Ratios

Liquidity ratios measure the ability of a firm to meet its maturing financial obligations and recurring operating expenses. In general, these are short-term obligations, normally due within one year. Several ratios provide evidence of liquidity.

The **current ratio** is defined as current assets (cash, marketable securities, accounts receivable, inventories, and prepaid expenses) divided by current liabilities (typically, accounts payable and short-term bank loans).

Some current assets, such as inventories and prepaid expenses, may not be very liquid. To assess liquidity without these questionable items, another liquidity measure called the **quick**, or **acid-test, ratio** may be used. [See also **Quick (acid-test) ratio**] The numerator of the quick ratio includes only cash, short-term marketable securities, and accounts receivable. The quick ratio is computed as current assets minus inventories and prepaid expenses divided by current liabilities. These two ratios are written as:

$$\text{Current ratio} = \frac{\text{Current assets}}{\text{Current liabilities}},$$
$$\text{Quick ratio} = \frac{\text{Current assets} - \text{Inventory}}{\text{Current liabilities}}.$$

Higher values for the liquidity ratios do not always imply greater liquidity and safety for short-term creditors. The current ratio would increase from one year to the next if the firm undertook an inventory buildup in anticipation of consumer demand that never occurred. The quick ratio helps to control for this distortion.

Still, an increase in accounts receivable could result from either a poor credit check system or slow customer payment on accounts; either scenario could deceive analysts into representing the firm as more liquid than it really was.

A firm is liquid if it has the ability to raise sufficient funds quickly. The statement of cash flows can provide additional insight into the financial flexibility of a company and supplement liquidity ratio analysis.

60. Liquidity Risk

The variation in net income and market value of bank equity caused by a bank's difficulty in obtaining immediately available funds, either by borrowing or selling assets. It also refers the risk that a sudden surge in liability withdrawals may leave a financial institution in a position of having to liquid assets in a very short period of time and at low prices.

61. Load Fund

A mutual fund with a sales commission, or load.

62. Loan Amortization

Individuals often borrow funds through amortized loans, including car loans and home mortgages. Under loan amortization, a loan is repaid by making equal or annuity payments over time. Each payment pays interest and repays some of the principal. The present value interest factor for annuities (PVIFA), which determine annuity payments, aid the analysis of amortized loans.

Interest is a tax-deductible expense for home mortgages and business loans. For tax purposes, it is important to determine how much of each loan payment covers interest and how much constitutes return of principal. A tool to assist this process is a loan amortization schedule, which offers a year-by-year (or period-by-period) summary of the beginning loan balance, the annuity payment, the interest paid, the principal repaid, and the ending balance. The interest paid always equals the beginning periodic balance multiplied by the periodic interest rate. The principal repaid is always the difference between the total payment and the interest paid. The ending balance represents the outstanding principal; it is computed by subtracting the principal repaid from the beginning balance of the period.

63. Loan Commitment

Formal agreement between a bank and borrower to provide a fixed amount of credit for a specified period.

64. Loan Exposure

The face amount of any loan outstanding plus accrued interest plus. [See also **Dirty price**]

65. Loan Participation

Credit extended to a borrower in which members of a group of lenders, each provide a fraction of the total financing; typically arises because individual banks are limited in the amount of credit they can extend to a single customer.

66. Loan Syndication

An arrangement where several lenders make a loan jointly to a borrower.

67. Loan-to-Value Ratio

The loan amount divided by the appraised value of the underlying collateral.

68. Locals

Individuals on the floor of an exchange who trade for their own count rather than for someone else.

69. Location Risk

This is one of the components of the basic risk. The hedger requires delivery of the futures contract in location Y, but the only futures contracts available are for delivery in location X. Hence, the hedger cannot form a perfect hedge because of the transportation costs from X to Y; this may cause the basis to change.

70. Lockbox System

The primary distinguishing feature of a lockbox system is that the firm pays the local bank to take on the administrative chores. Instead of customers mailing their payments to one of the company's offices, they send all payments directly to a post-office box. One or more times a day, the bank collects the checks from the box and deposits them for collection. Among the advantages of a lockbox arrangement is the potential reduction in mail float and a significant reduction in processing float. In some more sophisticated arrangements, banks capture daily invoice data on magnetic tape and forward this data to the company's central office, thereby reducing the burden on the firm's accounts receivable staff.

71. Lock-in Options

A lock-in option is an option that allows its holder to settle the option payoff at a time before the contracted option maturity, but transactions take place only at the expiration date. There are European lock-in options and American lock-in options. Whereas the lock-in time is prespecified in a European lock-in option, it is not contracted *ex ante* but can be chosen by the option holder at any time until the payment date in an American lock-in option.

While European lock-in options are less costly than vanilla options because of smaller time values and delayed payment of option payoffs, American lock-in options permit an investor to fix the option payoff at a more favorable time than merely waiting until the option expires.

72. Lock-up Provisions

IPOs usually contain lock-up provisions that forbid investors (such as corporate officers and directors, or investors such as venture capitalists who own large amounts of the newly public firms' shares) from selling their shares until a certain time after the IPO. By law, insiders must retain their shares for 90 days after the IPO, although some prospectuses required them to hold the shares even longer. The main reason for the lock-up provision is to prevent insiders from selling what may turn out to be overpriced stock immediately after the offering. Insiders can sell their shares as part of the IPO, but his information must be disclosed in the prospectus. Such selling typically is discouraged by the investment bank, however, as insider selling at the IPO sends a bad signal to the market about the insiders' optimism for the firm's future.

73. Lognormal Distribution

A variable has a lognormal distribution when the logarithm of the variable has a normal distribution.

74. London Interbank Offered Rate (LIBOR)

Rate the most creditworthy banks charge one another for large loans of Eurodollars overnight in the London market.

75 Long

A position is long with respect to a price if the position profits from an increase in that price. An owner of a stock profits from an increase in the stock price and, hence, is long the stock. An owner of an option profits from an increase in volatility and, hence, is long volatility.

76. Long Forward

The party to a forward contract who has an obligation to buy the underlying asset.

77. Long Hedge

Protecting the future cost of a purchase by purchasing a futures contract to protect against changes in the price of an asset.

78. Long Position

The purchase of futures contract in anticipation of taking eventual delivery of the commodity (or financial instrument) or an expected increase in the underlying asset's price.

79. Long Run

A period of time in which all costs are variable. It is an economics concept instead of an accounting concept.

80. Long Straddle

A straddle is a simultaneous position in both a call and a put on the same underlying asset. A long straddle involves purchasing both the call and the put. By combining these two seemingly opposing options an investor can get the best risk-return combination that each offers. For a long straddle position. The profit potential is unlimited on upside, limited on downside. The loss potential is limited to the cost of call and put premiums. The effect of time decay is negative. The market sentiment is bullish or bearish. Thus a long straddle is an effective strategy for someone expecting the volatility of the underlying asset to increase in the future.

81. Long Vertical Spread

A spread is a combination of any two or more of the same type of options (two calls or two puts, for instance) on same underlying asset. A vertical spread specifies that the options have the same maturity month. Finally, a long vertical spread designates a position for which one has bought a low-exercise-price call (or a low-exercise put) that both mature in the same month. A long vertical spread is also known as a bull spread because of the bullish market expectation of the investor who enters into it. The investor limits the profit potential in selling the high-exercise-price call (or put). It is a popular position when is expected that the market will more likely go up than down. The profit potential is limited up to the higher exercise price. The loss potential is limited down to the lower exercise price. The effect of time decay is mixed. And the market expectation is cautiously bullish.

82. Long-Term Debt

An obligation having a maturity of more than one year from the date it was issued. Also called funded debt.

83. Long-Term Securities

Securities with maturities in excess of one year.

84. Lookback Call

[See **Lookback option**]

85. Lookback Option

An option that, at maturity, pays off based on the maximum ($\overline{S}_T$) or minimum ($\underline{S}_T$) stock price over the life of the option. A lookback call has the payoff $S_t - \underline{S}_T$, and a lookback put has the payoff $\overline{S}_T - S_t$, where S_t is the sales price of the stock at time t.

86. Lookback Put

[See **Lookback option**]

87. Loss Given Default (LGD)

The loss severity of individual loan. It should take into account any collateral or guarantees. Both LGD and the probability of default (PD) are needed for a two-dimensional internal rating system.

88. Loss Reserve

Both life and property and liability insure estimate expected future claims on the exciting policies. These estimates are called loss reserve.

89. Low Discrepancy Sequence

[See **Quasi-random sequence**]

90. Lower-of-Cost-or-Market Value Method

One of the two methods used to report an investment in another company. This method is used if no evidence of significant control exists. These securities are handled in the same way as marketable security. [See also **Equity method**]

91. Low-Grade Bond

Junk bond.

M

1. Macaulay Duration

The percent change in a bond's price for a given percent change in one plus the bond's yield. This calculation can be interpreted as the weighted average life of the bond, with the weights being the percentage of the bond's value due to each payment. A key assumption to this duration is that the yield curve is flat and that when rate changes, the yield curve shifts in a parallel fashion. [See also **Duration** and **Modified duration**]

2. Macroforecasting

Forecasts of price movements of the general stock market as a whole.

3. Macrohedge

A hedge strategy designed to reduce risk associated with a bank's entire balance sheet position. In other words, a financial institution manager wishes to use futures or other derivative securities to hedge the entire balance sheet duration gap.

4. Mail Float

Refers to the part of the collection and disbursement process where checks are trapped in the postal system [See also **Float**]

5. Maintenance Margin

Due to the difficulty of calling all customers whose margin accounts have fallen in value for the day, a clearing member firm usually will require that a sum of money be deposited at the initiation of any futures position. This additional sum is called a maintenance margin. In most situations, the original margin requirement may be established with a risk-free, interest-bearing security such as a T-bill. However, the maintenance margin, which must be in cash, is adjusted for daily changes in the contract value. [See also **Marking to market**]

6. Make a Market

The obligation of a specialist to offer to buy and sell shares of assigned stocks. It is assumed that this makes the market liquid because the specialist assumes the role of a buyer for investors if they wish to sell and a seller if they wish to buy.

7. Make-Whole Clause

A provision which requires that the borrower make a payment to a lender after a loan is called or prepaid. The amount of the payment equals the net present value of the lost interest and principal payments.

8. Making Delivery

Refers to the seller's actually turning over to the buyer the asset agreed upon in a forward contract.

9. Management Risk

The variability of return caused by bad management decisions; this is usually a part of the unsystematic risk of a stock. Although it can affect the amount of systematic risk.

10. MAPB System

The moving-average with a percentage price band system (MAPB system) belongs to a technical family derived from moving averages. Moving averages come in many forms-that is, simple moving averages, exponentially weighted, linearly weighted, and so on. The MAPB system employs a simple moving average with a band based on a percentage of price centered around it. A signal to initiate a position occurs whenever the closing price breaks outside the band. A signal to exit a position occurs when the price recrosses the moving average. The band creates a neutral zone in which the trader is neither long nor short. [See also **DMAC**]

11. Margin

A cash amount of funds that must be deposited with the broker for each futures contract as a guarantee of its fulfillment.

12. Margin Call

A demand for additional cash funds for each futures position held because of an adverse price movement.

13. Margin Requirement

Whenever someone enters into a contract position in the futures market, a security deposit, commonly called a margin requirement, must be paid. While the futures margin may seem to be a partial payment for the security on which the futures contract is based, it only represents security to cover any losses that may result from adverse price movements.

The minimum margin requirements set by the exchange must be collected by the clearing member firms (members of the exchange involved in the clearinghouse operations) when their customers take positions in the market. In turn, the clearing member firms must deposit a fixed portion of these margins with the clearinghouse. [See also **Marking to market**]

14. Marginal Cost of Funds

The incremental cost of additional funds to finance firm operations. Banks generally use federal funds or negotiable CD rates as marginal cost of funds.

15. Marginal Standard Deviation

Impact of a given asset on the total portfolio standard deviation.

16. Marginal Statistic

A statistic for a particular asset which is the difference between that statistic for the entire portfolio and that for the portfolio not including the asset.

17. Marginal Tax Rate

The marginal tax rate represents the proportion of each additional dollar of income that the government claims as taxes. The firm's marginal tax rate is important in financial decision making. Financial decisions hinge not on the **average tax rate** the firm has paid, but on the tax rate that applies to the additional income to be generated by a project. [See also **Average tax rate**]

One of the marginal costs that businesses must consider is the marginal tax that is paid should expansions or new projects be undertaken.

18. Marked to Market

Describes the daily settlement of obligation on futures positions. [See also **Marking to market**]

19. Market Anomalies

The idea of an efficient market is very important to the study of security analysis and portfolio management. If information is fully reflected in security prices, the market is efficient and it is not worthwhile to pay for information that is already impounded in security prices. The evidence seems to indicate that markets are efficient with respect to most types of information. However, there appears to be certain types of information associated with irregularities in the financial markets. Such irregularities are call market anomalies. Three of the most heavily researched anomalies are the P/E effect, the size effect and the January effect.

20. Market Capitalization

Price per share of stock multiplied by the number of shares outstanding. It is total market value of equity.

21. Market Capitalization Rate

The market-consensus estimate of the appropriate discount rate for a firm's cash flows.

22. Market Clearing

Total demand for loans by borrowers equals total supply of loans from lender. The market clears at the equilibrium rate of interest.

23. Market Conversion Price

[See also **Convertible bond.**]

24. Market Corner

Owning a large percentage of the available supply of an asset or commodity that is required for delivery under the terms of a derivatives contract.

25. Market Exposure

For market-driven instruments, there is an amount at risk to default only when the contract is in-the-money (i.e., when the replacement cost of the contract exceeds the original value). This exposure/uncertainty is captured by calculating the netted mean and standard deviation of exposure(s).

26. Market Interest Rate, Bond

[See also **Yield to maturity**]

27. Market Model

A one-factor model for returns where the index that is used for the factor is an index of the returns on the whole market. It can be defined as:

$$R_{it} = \alpha_i + \beta_i R_{mt} + e_{it},$$

where R_{it} and R_{mt} are rate of return of ith security and market rate of return in period t, respectively. [See also **Beta coefficient and Scatter diagram**]

28. Market or Systematic Risk, Firm-Specific Risk

Market risk is risk attributable to common macroeconomic factors. Firm-specific risk reflects risk peculiar to an individual firm that is independent of market risk.

29. Market Order

A buy or sell order to be executed immediately at current market prices.

30. Market Portfolio

The market portfolio is comprised of all risky assets weighted in proportion to their market value. As such, the market portfolio is a completely diversified portfolio; it has no unsystematic risk. The returns on this portfolio will show only the effects of market wide or systematic risk. Investors who desire complete diversification and who want to eliminate unsystematic risk will want to hold the market portfolio.

Increase and decreases in an asset's value over time will reflect its exposure to both systematic and unsystematic risk factors. One way to measure the systematic risk of an asset or portfolio is to compare its returns over time with those of the market portfolio. Changes in the value of an asset relative to that of the market portfolio will reflect the asset's exposure to systematic risk factors.

31. Market Price

The current amount at which a security is trading in a market. For example, IBM price per share is $95. This is a market price.

32. Market Price of Risk

A measure of the extra return, or risk premium, that investors demand to bear risk. The reward-to-risk ratio of the market portfolio. [See also **Sharpe ratio**]

33. Market Risk

Systematic risk. This term emphasizes the fact that systematic risk influences to some extent all assets in the market. [See also **Systematic risk**]

34. Market Segmentation Hypothesis

The market segmentation hypothesis explains the same phenomenon in terms of differences in supply and demand between segments of the capital markets. Some participants, such as banks, mainly borrow and lend short maturity securities. Others, such as pension funds, are major participants in the long-term portion of the yield curve. If more funds are available to borrow relative to demand in the short-term market than in the long-term market, short-term interest rates will be lower and long-term rates will be higher than predicted by both the expectations and liquidity preference hypothesis. [See also **Expectations hypothesis** and **Liquidity preference hypothesis**]

The drawback to this perspective is that it does not explain very well the usual upward slope of the term structure, nor does it provide a good explanation for the levels of intermediate-term rates. In addition, the financial markets are not strictly segmented; many institutions issue and purchase both short-term and long-term securities.

35. Market Segmentation Theory

The theory that long-maturity and short-maturity bonds are traded in essentially distinct or segmented markets and that prices in one market do not affect those in the other. [See **Market segmentation hypothesis**]

36. Market Stabilization

During the aftermarket, the managing investment bank tries to prevent any significant declines in the price of the issuer's shares; hence, this function by investment banks is sometimes also called market stabilization.

Investment banks do not want to be known for bringing firms public at excessive offering prices, nor do they want to be known for handling IPOs of poor-quality issuers. To help show the market that the bank will stand behind its IPOs, it risks its own money to support the firm by repurchasing any and all shares offered to it at the offering price. This effectively places a floor under the firm's stock price.

The investment bank acts as a signal to market investors. When a highly reputable investment bank places its own capital at risk to underwrite securities, the investing public can have a greater degree of confidence regarding the quality of the issue. If an investment bank is willing to sell shares on a commission basis only, that is a signal of a low-quality, high-risk offering.

37. Market Timer

An investor who speculates on broad market moves rather than on specific securities.

38. Market Timing

Asset allocation in which the investment in the market is increased if one forecasts that the market will outperform T-bills.

39. Market Value

The price at which willing buyers and sellers trade a firm's assets. In general, the market value is different from book value.

40. Market Value Added

A measure to identify successful firms that is growing in popularity is market value added (MVA). MVA measures the value created by the firm's managers; it equals the market value of the firm's stocks and debts minus the amount of money investors paid to the firm (their book value) when these securities were first issued. That is, market value added (MVA) equals:

Market value of stock + Market value of debt
− Book value of stock − Book value of debt.

41. Market Value Ratios

A firm's profitability, risk, quality of management, and many other factors are reflected in its stock and security prices. Hence, market value ratios indicate the market's assessment of the value of the firm's securities.

The price/earnings (P/E) ratio is simply the market price of the firm's common stock divided by its annual earnings per share. Sometimes called the *earnings multiple*, the P/E ratio shows how much investors are willing to pay for each dollar of the firm's earnings per share. Earnings per share comes from the income statement, so it is sensitive to the many factors that affect the construction of an income statement, from the choice of GAAP to management decisions regarding the use of debt to finance assets. The price/earnings ratio is stated as:

$$P/E = \frac{\text{Market price per share}}{\text{Earnings per share}}.$$

Stock prices are determined from the actions of informed buyers and sellers in an impersonal market. Stock prices reflect much of the known information about a company and are fairly good indicators of a company's true value. Although earnings per share cannot reflect the value of patents or assets, the quality of the firm's management, or its risk, stock prices can and do reflect all of these factors. Comparing a firm's P/E to that of the stock market as a whole, or with the firm's competitors, indicates the market's perception of the true value of the company.

While the P/E ratio measures the market's valuation of the firm relative to the income statement value for per-share earnings, the price-to-book-value ratio measures the market's valuation relative to balance sheet equity. The book value of equity is simply the difference between the book values of assets and liabilities appearing on the balance sheet. The price-to-book-value ratio is the market price per share divided by the book value of equity per share. A higher ratio suggests that investors are more optimistic about the market value of a firm's assets, its intangible assets, and the ability of its managers. The price-to-book-value ratio is stated as:

$$\text{Price-to-book-value ratio} = \frac{\text{Market price per share}}{\text{Book value per share}}.$$

Market value indicators reflect the market's perception of the true worth of a firm's *future prospects*. As such, market perceptions of a firm's value are important to the financial analyst. However, the market may not be perfect; investors may become overly optimistic or pessimistic about a firm. The fact that a firm presently has a higher P/E or price-to-book-value ratio than its competition does not automatically imply that the firm is better managed or really deserves its higher valuation. Some firms may have low market value ratios because they truly deserve them; other firms may suffer from extreme and undeserved pessimism on the part of the market. High market value ratios can be similarly deceptive. The analyst must determine whether a firm deserves its market value ratios or not.

42. Marketability

Refers to the ease and quickness of converting an asset to cash. Also called liquidity.

43. Marketability Risk

The variability of return caused by the commissions and price concessions associated with selling an illiquid asset. It is also called liquidity risk. Marketability is made up of two components: (1) the volume of securities that can be bought or sold in a short period of time without adversely affecting the price, and (2) the amount of time necessary to complete the sale of a given number of securities. Other things being equal, the less marketability a security, the lower its price or the higher its yield.

44. Marketable Securities

Some current assets might be called *near cash* or *cash equivalents*. These are marketable securities. They are marketable because they can be readily converted into cash at any time without disrupting the normal routine of business operations. This feature makes these securities almost as liquid as cash, so cash and marketable securities often are combined into a single line item in financial reports and working capital analysis.

45. Market-Based Beta Forecasts

Market-based beta forecasts are based upon market information alone. Historical betas of firms are used as a proxy for their futures betas. This implies that the unadjusted sample beta, $\hat{\beta}_t$, is equal to the population value of future beta:

$$\beta_{t+1} = \hat{\beta}_t.$$

Alternatively, there may be a systematic relationship between the estimated betas for the first period and those of the second period, as shown by Blume (1971):

$$\hat{\beta}_{i,t+1} = a_0 + a_1 \hat{\beta}_{i,t},$$

in which $\hat{\beta}_{i,t+1}$ and $\hat{\beta}_{i,t}$ estimated beta for the ith firm in period $t+1$ and t, respectively.

46. Market-Book Ratio

Market price of a share divided by book value per share. [See also **Tobin's Q**]

47. Market-Driven Instruments

Derivative instruments that are subject to counterparty default (e.g., swaps, forwards, options, etc.). The distinguishing feature of these types of credit exposures is that their amount is only the net replacement cost (the amount the position is in-the-money rather than a full notional amount).

48. Marketed Claims

Claims that can be bought and sold in financial markets, such as those of stockholders and bondholders.

49. Market-Maker

A trader in an asset, commodity, or derivative who simultaneously offers to buy at one price (the bid price) or to sell at a higher price (the offer price), thereby "making a market."

50. Market-to-Book (M/B) Ratio

Market price per share of common stock divided by book value per share. It can be used as approximated measure of Tobin Q. [See also **Market value ratios**]

51. Market-Value-Weighed Index

An index of a group of securities computed by calculating a weighted average of the returns of each security in the index, with weights proportional to outstanding market value. [See also **S&P**]

52. Marking to Market

At the end of each trading day, every futures-trading account is incremented or reduced by the corresponding increase or decrease in the value of all open interest positions. This daily adjustment procedure is applied to the margin deposit and is called marking to market. For example, if an investor is long on a yen futures contract and by the end of the day its market value has fallen $1,000, he or she would be asked to add an additional $1,000 to the margin account. Why? Because the investor is responsible for its initial value. For example, if a futures contract is executed at $10,000 with an initial margin of $1,000 and the value of the position goes down $1,000, to $9,000, the buyer would be required to put in an additional margin of $1,000 because the investor is responsible for paying $10,000 for the contract. If the investor is unable to comply or refuses to do so, the clearing member firm that he or she trades through would automatically close out the position. On the other hand, if the contract's value was up $1,000 for the day, the investor might immediately withdraw the profit if he or she so desired. The procedure of marking to market implies that all potential profits and losses are realized immediately.

53. Markov Process

A stochastic process where the behavior of the variable over a short period of time depends solely on the value of the variable at the beginning of the period, not on its past history. Alternatively it is a finite set of "states" and whose next progression is determinable solely by the current state. A transition matrix model is an example of a Markov process.

54. Markowitz Model

Markowitz (1952) shows how to create a frontier of investment portfolios such that each of them had the greatest possible expected return, given their level of risk.

55. Mark-to-Market

The daily adjustment of a futures trading account to reflect profits or losses due to daily changes in the value of the futures contract. [See also **Marking to market**]

56. Mark-to-Market Swap

Reduces default risk by allowing the fixed rate to be reset when fixed and floating rates diverge substantially after the beginning of the swap.

57. Martingale

A zero-drift stochastic process. [See also **Stochastic process**]

58. Maturity

The date at which the principal of a note, draft, or bond becomes due and payable.

59. Maturity Date

The date on which the last payment on a bond is due.

60. Maturity Gap

It is the difference between the weighted-average maturity of financial institution's asset and liability. The maturity model with a portfolio of assets and liabilities is

$$\text{Maturity Gap} = M_A - M_L,$$

where M_A and M_L represent the weighted average maturity of FI's asset and liability, respectively.

61. Maturity Premium

When the default risk on a class of securities is virtually zero, the risk premium represents a maturity premium that reflects uncertainty about inflation and changes in interest rates over a longer time horizon.

62. Maximum Likelihood Method

A method for choosing the values of parameters by maximizing the probability of a set of observations occurring.

63. MBS

Mortgage-backed security. [See also **Mortage-backed security**]

64. Mean Reversion

The statistical tendency in a time series to gravitate back towards a long term historical level. This is on a much longer scale than another similar measure, called autocorrelation; and these two behaviors are mathematically independent of one another. For example, the tendency of a market variable (such as an interest rate) to revert back to some long-run average level.

65. Mean-Variance Analysis

Evaluation of risky prospects based on the expected value and variance of possible outcomes. [See also **Capital market line**]

66. Mean-Variance Criterion

The selection of portfolios based on the means and variances of their returns. The choice of the higher expected return portfolio for a given level of variance or the lower variance portfolio for a given expected return.

67. Measure

Sometimes also called a probability measure; it defines the market price of risk.

68. Measurement Error

Errors in measuring an explanatory variable in a regression that leads to biases in estimated parameters.

69. Median

The median is defined as the outcome value that exceeds the outcome value for half the population and is exceeded by the other half. Whereas the expected rate of return is a weighted average of the outcomes, the weights being the probabilities, the median is based on the rank order of the outcomes and takes into account only the order of the outcome values.

70. Membership or Seat on an Exchange

A limited number of exchange positions that enable the holder to trade for the holder's own ac-counts and charge clients for the execution of trades for their accounts.

71. Merger

Assuming there are originally two firms, Firm A and Firm B. In one possible business combination, only Firm B survives. This type of combination is known as a merger and Firm B is called the *acquiring firm* while Firm A is called the *acquired* or *target firm*. [See also **Acquisition**]

Many researchers in economics and finance have advanced theories to justify firms' pursuit of mergers. The most recent efforts by academicians in these fields have begun to integrate individual theoretical rationales.

Among the myriad reasons that have been proposed to explain merger activity, the more prominent ones are

1. Economies of scale
2. Market power and market share
3. Diversification
4. Tax and surplus funds motives
5. Undervalued assets
6. Agency problems.

72. Microeconomic Risk

The risk that is diversified away as assets are added to a portfolio is the firm-specific and industry-specific risk, or the "microeconomic" risk. A well-diversified portfolio can reduce the effects of firm-specific or industry-specific events – such as strikes, technological advances, and entry and exit of competitors – to almost zero.

73. Microhedge

A hedge strategy designed to reduce the risk associated with a specific transaction. In other words, a financial institution employs a futures of forward contract to hedge a particular asset or liability risk.

74. Migration

Credit quality migration describes the possibility that a firm or obligor with some credit rating today may move to (or "migrate") to potentially any other credit rating—or perhaps default—by the risk horizon. [See also **Transition matrix**]

75. Migration Analysis

The technique of estimating the likelihood of credit quality migration. [See also **Transition matrix**]

76. Miller-Orr Model

The Miller-Orr model (Miller and Orr, 1966) for cash management improves on Baumol's economic order quantity model (EOQ) methodology in significant ways. Miller and Orr start with the assumption that the firm has only two forms of assets: cash and marketable securities. The model allows for cash balance movement in both positive and negative directions and it can state the optimal cash balance as a range of values, rather than a single-point estimate. This makes the model especially useful for firms with unpredictable day-to-day cash inflows and outflows.

While the Miller-Orr model is an improvement over the **EOQ model**, it too makes some assumptions. [See also **Baumol's economic order quantity model**] The most important is the assumption that cash flows are random, which in many cases is not completely valid. Under certain circumstances and at particular times of the year, consecutive periods' cash flows may be dependent upon one another, the volatility of net cash flows may sharply increase, or cash balances may demonstrate a definite trend. The frequency and extent of these events will affect the Miller-Orr model's effectiveness. Actual tests using daily cash flow for various firms indicate that the model minimizes cash holding costs as wells as or better than the intuitive decisions of these firms' financial managers. However, others studies have shown that simple rules of thumb have performed just as well. Still, the Miller-Orr model is valuable because of the insight it offers concerning the forces that influence a firm's optimal cash balance.

77. Minimum-Variance Frontier

Graph of the lowest possible portfolio variance that is attainable for a given portfolio expected return.

78. Minimum-Variance Portfolio

The portfolio of risky assets with lowest variance. [See also **Appendix E**]

79. Mission Statement

The firm must operate to achieve a purpose or goal; otherwise, decisions will be made carelessly, allowing better informed, more serious competitors to put the firm out of business. Although many firms may have mission statement espousing goals of quality, customer service, fair prices, and so on, such qualitative statements are really only a means to an end. The firm's managers need a definite benchmark against which to evaluate the alternative means for attaining these goals.

80. Mixed Average

[See also **Geometric average**]

81. Mode

The mode is the most likely value of the distribution or the outcome with the highest probability.

82. Modern Portfolio Theory (MPT)

Principles underlying analysis and evaluation of rational portfolio choices based on risk-return trade-offs and efficient diversification. [See also **Markowitz model**]

83. Modified Accelerated Cost Recovery System (MACRS)

MACRS depreciates assets by an accelerated method. In essence, it uses the double declining balance method until it becomes advantageous to use straight-line depreciation over the asset's remaining life.

To ensure some uniformity, MACRS assigns assets to classes, see Table A.

Assets in the 27.5-year or 31.5-year classes must be depreciated using the straight-line method over the appropriate number of years. Additionally, with some exceptions, MACRS follows a half-year convention; the asset receives a half-year's worth of depreciation in the year it is acquired, regardless of when it is actually purchased. Thus, assets in the three-year class are actually depreciated over *four* years; the owner writes off a half-year of depreciation in the Year 1, a full year of depreciation in each of Years 2 and 3, and the remaining half-year of depreciation in Year 4.

Annual accelerated depreciation percentages are given in Table B. To determine an assets' annual depreciation expense, the cost of the asset is multiplied by the percentage for the appropriate asset class and the appropriate year.

For example, for an asset in the three-year class that originally cost $50,000, the first year's depreciation is $50,000 X 0.3333 = $16,665; the second year's depreciation is $50,000 × 0.4445 = $22,225; the third year's depreciation is $50,000 × 0.1482 = $7,410; and the final year's depreciation is $50,000 × 0.0740 = $3,700.

Table A: Depreciation Classes

3-year class	Designated tools and equipment used in research
5-year class	Cars, trucks, and some office equipment, such as computers and copiers
7-year class	Other office equipment and industrial machinery
10-year class	Other long-lived equipment
27.5-year class	Residential real estate
31.5-year class	Commercial and industrial real estate

Table B: MACRS Percentages

	Asset Class			
Year of Ownership	3-Year	5-Year	7-Year	10-Year
1	33.33%	20.00%	14.29%	10.00%
2	44.45	32.00	24.49	18.00
3	14.82	19.20	17.49	14.40
4	7.40	11.52	12.49	11.52
5		11.52	8.93	9.22
6		5.76	8.93	7.37
7			8.93	6.55
8			4.45	6.55
9				6.55
10				6.55
11				3.29

84. Modified Duration

A modification to the standard duration measure so that it more accurately describes the relationship between proportional changes in a bond price and absolute changes in its yield. The modification takes account of the compounding frequency with which the yield is quoted. Modified duration (MD) is Macaulay's duration (D) divided by one plus the prevailing interest rate (R) on the underlying instrument, i.e.,

$$MD = \frac{D}{1+R}.$$

85. Modified Internal Rate of Return

Modified internal rate of return (MIRR) rankings of mutually exclusive projects with comparable sized initial investments will agree with the NPV rankings of those projects. Additionally, the MIRR calculation always gives a single solution.

MIRR is calculated by way of a three-step solution:

1. Using the minimum required rate of return as the discount rate, find the *present* value of all cash outflows (for a conventional project, this will be just the initial cost of the project). This step converts all of the cash outflows into a lump-sum present value at Time 0.

2. Using the required return as the reinvestment or compounding rate, compute the *future* value of each cash inflow as of the end of the project's life. Add the future values together; this sum is sometimes called the terminal value. This step converts all cash inflows into a lump-sum future value at Time *N*.

3. Find the discount rate that allows the present value of the cash outflows to grow equal to the terminal value; this discount rate is the modified internal rate of return.

The decision rule for MIRR is similar to that for IRR: A project is acceptable if its MIRR exceeds the project's minimum required return. A drawback to the MIRR is that it, like the IRR, is a relative measure of attractiveness; it does not indicate the dollar amount by which projects change shareholder wealth.

86. Modigliani and Miller (M&M) Proposition I

Without Taxes

M&M Proposition I (Modigliani and Miller (1958)) makes several assumptions. First, it assumes that the firm pays no taxes. Second, it assumes that investors can borrow and lend money at the same interest rate as corporations. Thus, the firm and its investors can buy and sell securities at zero cost. Third, M&M Proposition I holds the firm's current and future real investment decisions constant. In other words, it assumes that all investors have the same expectations about the firms' future earnings and risk and investors can classify the firm with other corporations of similar business risk. Related to this idea is the assumption that future financing decisions will not affect the firm's investments in assets.

Under these assumptions, the value of the firm is unaffected by its specific capital structure. Through the use of personal borrowing or lending, investors can adjust their exposure to a firm's leverage to reflect their personal preferences.

The guiding force behind M&M is *arbitrage*. Should one strategy result in a higher value, investors will execute that strategy until the resulting supply and demand forces bring the values into line. For example, suppose there are two firms with identical business risk but Firm *L* is levered and Firm *U* has no debt. If Firm *L* were to have a higher value than Firm *U*, investors could use **homemade leverage** by borrowing and purchasing shares of Firm *U* to obtain levered cash flows more cheaply than if they purchased the shares of levered Firm *L* outright. [See also **Homemade leverage**] Investors purchases of the cheaper shares of Firm *U* would cause their price to rise until the value of Firm *U* was equal to that of Firm *L*.

Capital structure does not affect firm value under M&M Proposition I, as individual investors can costlessly adjust the effects of the corporation's leverage to suit themselves. If investors expect the firm to generate an operating profit of $E(EBIT)$ in perpetuity, the value of the levered firm (V_L) or the unlevered firm (V_U) will be that of a perpetuity:

$$V_L = V_U = \frac{E(EBIT)}{WACC} = \frac{E(EBIT)}{k_u}, \qquad (1)$$

where $WACC$ represents the investors' required return (and hence the firm's cost of capital) for firms with this class of business risk; k_u represents a cost of unlevered equity.

The process of homemade leverage also can work in reverse. If a firm increases its debt-to-equity ratio to a level considered too risky by an investor, the investor can reverse the capital structure to receive cash flows identical to those before the firm took on the extra debt.

Under M&M Proposition I's assumptions, the only factors that affect firm value are the firm's level of expected operating income and its business risk, which is measured by the variation in operating income. Firm value is not affected by changes in financing strategy, since whatever the firm does, investors can use homemade leverage (or unleverage) to change the cash flows they receive.

With Tax

When there is a tax, then equation (1) should be redefined as

$$V_L = V_U + (T)(D), \tag{2}$$

where V_L = market value of levered firm, V_U = market value of unlevered firm, T = marginal corporate tax rate, D = total debt, and $(T)(D)$ = tax shield value.

87. Modigliani and Miller (M&M) Proposition II

Without Taxes

M&M Proposition II defines a firms' cost of equity capital (and shareholders' required rate of return) in a world of no taxes, not transaction costs, and constant real investment decisions. The cost of equity capital for an unlevered firm (k_u), or a firm with no debt in its capital structure, is simply its expected level of operating income (EBIT) divided by its assets (TA):

$$k_u = \frac{E(EBIT)}{TA} = \frac{E(EBIT)}{Equity}.$$

M&M show that the cost of equity for a levered firm (k_e) is:

$$k_e = k_u + (k_u - k_d)\left(\frac{D}{E}\right), \tag{1}$$

where k_d is the cost of debt; $(k_u - k_d)(D/E)$ is the financial risk premium; and D/E is the debt equity ratio. The equation says that the cost of levered equity equals the cost of unlevered equity plus a risk premium to compensate shareholders for financial risk.

With Tax

If there exists a tax, then equation (1) should be rewritten as:

$$k_e = k_u + (k_u - k_d)\left(\frac{D}{E}\right)(1-T),$$

where T represents marginal corporate tax rate. [See also **Modigliani and Miller (M&M) propostion I** for variable definitions]

88. Moments (of a Statistical Distribution)

Statistical distributions show the frequency at which events might occur across a range of values. The most familiar distribution is a normal "bell shaped" curve. In general though, the shape of any distribution can be described by its (infinitely many) moments.

a. The *first* moment is the *mean*, which indicates the central tendency.

b. The *second* moment is the *variance*, which indicates the width.

c. The *third* moment is the *skewness*, which indicates any asymmetric "leaning" whether left or right.

d. The *fourth* moment is the *kurtosis*, which indicates the degree of central "peakedness" or, equivalently, the "fatness" of the outer tails.

89. Monetary Policy

Economists believe that money supply growth has broad implications for future economic growth and future levels of inflation. As a consequence, most financial managers are interested in money supply changes over time and the current status of monetary policy. This gives them information about interest rates and inflation rate trends.

Monetary policy involves the use of the **Federal Reserve Board's** powers to affect the money supply, interest rates, and aggregate economic activity. [See also **Federal Reserve Board**]

90. Money Market

In the money market, securities are issued or traded that mature, or come due, in one year or less. Examples of money market securities include US Treasury bills, corporate commercial paper, and negotiable certificates of deposit.

91. Money Market Account

An investment that is initially equal to $1 and increases at the very short-term risk-free interest rate prevailing at that time.

92. Money Market Deposit Account

Small time deposit whose holder is limited to three written checks per month.

93. Money Market Mutual Fund

Mutual fund that accepts customer funds and purchase short-term marketable securities.

94. Money Market Securities

The classification of a financial instrument as a marketable security typically is based upon maturity and, to a lesser extent, liquidity. Investment instruments with maturities of one year or less that are traded to some extent in secondary markets are called money market securities.

95. Money Purchase Plan

A defined benefit contribution plan in which the participant contributes some part and the firm contributes at the same or a different rate. Also called an individual account plan.

96. Money Spread

[See also **Spread (options)**]

97. Money Supply

The federal government's designation of certain liquid assets as money; M1A equals currency outside banks plus demand deposits; M1B equals M1A plus other checkable deposits; M2 equals M1B plus overnight RPs, savings and small time deposits, and money market funds; M3 equals M2 plus large time deposits and term RPs; L equals M3 plus other liquid assets (where RPs are repurchase agreements).

98. Monotinicity

[See also **Rank order**]

99. Monte Carlo Valuation (Simulation)

A procedure for pricing derivative claims by discounting expected payoffs, where the expected payoff is computed using simulated prices for the underlying asset.

100. Moody's Bond Rating

Aaa – bonds of highest quality

Aa – bonds of high quality

A – bonds whose security of principal and interest is considered adequate but may be impaired in the future

Baa – bonds of medium grade that are neither highly protected nor poorly secured

Ba – bonds of speculative quality whose future cannot be considered well assured

B – bonds that lack characteristics of a desirable investment

Caa – bonds in poor standing that may be defaulted

Ca – speculative bonds that are often in default

C – bonds with little probability of any investment value (lowest rating)

101. Mortality Tables

Tables of probability that individuals of various ages will die within a year; created and used by life insurance companies.

102. Mortgage

A contract whereby a borrower provides a lender with a lien on real property as security against a loan.

103. Mortgage Banking

The business of packaging mortgage loans for sale to investors and retaining the servicing rights to the mortgages.

104. Mortgage Bonds

Mortgage bonds pledge real property or specific assets as security. [See also **Collateralized Bonds**]

105. Mortgage Securities

A debt obligation secured by a mortgage on the real property of the borrower.

106. Mortgage Servicing

The process of collecting monthly payments on mortgages, keeping records, paying the associated insurance and taxes, and making monthly payments to holders of the underlying mortgages or mortgage-backed securities.

107. Mortgage-Backed Security

An ownership claim in a pool of mortgages or an obligation that is secured by such a pool. These claims represent securitization of mortgage loans. Mortgage lenders originate loans and then sell packages of these loans in the secondary market. Also called a *pass-through* because payments are passed along from the mortgage originator to the purchaser of the mortgage-backed security.

108. Move Persistence

The statistical tendency in a time series to move on the next step in the same direction as the previous step. [See also **Autocorrelation**]

109. Moving-Average

Moving-average (of rate-of-change) technicians focus on prices and/or moving averages of prices.

The moving average is used to provide a smoothed stable reference point against which the daily fluctuations can be gauged. When the daily prices penetrate above the moving-average line, technicians interpret this penetration as a bearish signal. When the daily prices move downward through the moving average, they frequently fail to rise again for many months.

Moving-average analysts recommend buying a stock when: (1) the 200-day moving average flattens out and the stock's price rises through the moving average, (2) the price of a stock falls below a moving-average line that is rising, and (3) the price of a stock that is above the moving-average line falls but turns around and begins to rise again before it ever reaches the moving-average line.

Moving-average chartists recommend selling a stock when: (1) the moving-average line flattens out and the stock's price drops downward through the moving-average line, (2) a stock's price rises above a moving-average line that is declining, and (3) a stock's price falls downward through the moving-average line and turns around to rise but then falls again before getting above the moving-average line.

110. Multibank Holding Company

A bank holding company that owns controlling interest in at least two commercial banks.

111. Multifactor CAPM

Generalization of the basic CAPM that accounts for extra-market hedging demands.

112. Multiple Rates of Return

More than one rate of return from the same project that make the net present value of the project equal to zero. This situation arises when the IRR method is used for a project in which negative cash flows follow positive ones.

113. Multiples

Another name for price/earnings ratios.

114. Municipal Bonds

Tax-exempt bonds issued by state and local governments, generally to finance capital improvement projects. General obligation bonds are backed by the general taxing power of the issuer. Revenue bonds are backed by the proceeds from the project or agency they are issued to finance.

115. Municipals

Securities issued by states, local governments, and their political subdivisions.

116. Mutual Fund

A pool of funds that is managed by an investment company. Investors in a mutual fund own shares in the fund, and the fund uses the proceeds to buy different assets. Some of the important mutual funds are money market funds, fixed-income funds, balance funds, income funds, asset allocation funds, index funds and growth funds.

117. Mutual Fund Theorem

A result associated with the CAPM, asserting that investors will choose to invest their entire risky portfolio in a market-index mutual fund.

118. Mutual Savings Bank

Firms without capital stock that accept deposits and make loans.

119. Mutually Exclusive Investment Decisions

Investment decisions in which the acceptance of a project precludes the acceptance of one or more alternative projects.

120. Mutually Exclusive Projects

Investment projects are mutually exclusive, or competing projects when they represent different alternatives to meet the same perceived need. Since all of the alternatives seek to meet the same need, the firm will choose only the one that creates the most value for shareholders.

N

1. NAIC

National Association of Insurance Commission, which is an organization with no legal power but with substantial political clout. Commissioners of insurance in each state wield considerable power individually and exert influence collectively through NAIC.

2. Naked Option Writing

The owner of shares of common stock can write, or create, an option and sell it in the options market, in an attempt to increase the return or income on a stock investment. A more venturesome investor may create an option in this fashion without owning any of the underlying stock. This naked option writing exposes the speculator to unlimited risk because he or she may have to buy shares at some point to satisfy the contract at whatever price is reached. This is a serious risk if the value of the underlying asset has a high degree of variability.

3. Naked Options

The writing of a call or put option without owning the underlying asset is known as naked options. Naked options are much riskier than the covered options. [See also **Covered call**]

4. Naked Position

A short position in a call option that is not combined with a long position in the underlying asset. An alternative to a naked position, a financial institution can adopt a covered position which is a short position combining a long position in the underlying asset.

5. Naked Writing

Selling option without an offsetting position in the underlying asset.

6. Nasdaq

It represents the National Association of Securities Dealers Automated Quotation (Nasdaq). This automated quotation system is designed for the OTC market, showing current bid-asked prices for thousands of stocks.

7. Nasdaq Index

This index includes 4,000 over-the-counter (OTC) firms traded on Nasdaq market.

8. Negative Covenant

Part of the indenture or loan agreement that limits or prohibits actions that the company may take.

9. Negative Pledge Clause

A negative pledge clause in a debenture agreement states that any future debt-financed asset purchases also are considered to be security for the bond, even if the assets are financed with first mortgage bonds.

10. Neglected-Firm Effect

Small firms tend to be neglected by large institutional traders. It has been found by Arbel (1985) that investment in stock of this kind in less well-known firms has generated abnormal returns. [See also **January effect**]

11. Negotiable Certificates of Deposit

Negotiable certificates of deposit (CDs) are financial instruments offered by banks to customers who deposit funds for fixed periods at fixed rates of interest. CDs are issued in denominations of

$100,000 or more, with maturities ranging to several years.

Yields on CDs are higher than yields on T-bills for two reasons. First, CDs are substantially less liquid than T-bills (their secondary market is very thin). Second, CDs have higher default risk because the represent unsecured debt obligations of the issuing banks. However, the spread between CD and T-bill yields varies depending upon economic conditions, supply and demand forces, and investor attitudes.

12. Negotiable Order of Withdrawal (NOW)

In 1980, Congress enacted depository institutions deregulation and monetary control act (DIDMCA). Titled III of DIDMCA authorized banks and financial institution offered interest-bearing transactions account. In banks and thrifts, they call this kind of account NOW account.

13. Negotiated Credit

Short-term bank credit is particularly important to the smaller company. Many large, well-established companies make little use of bank credit. When they need working capital above what is available as trade credit – that is, when they need negotiated credit, the term given to all credit that arises from a formal negotiation of funds – they can get attractive terms by borrowing directly from the capital market. This borrowing usually takes the form of selling commercial paper.

14. Negotiated Offer

The issuing firm negotiates a deal with one underwriter to offer a new issue rather than taking competitive bidding.

15. Negotiation

One technique used in business combinations is direct negotiation between the management teams and the boards of directors of the two firms. After negotiations have been worked out, the plans are presented to both shareholder groups for approval.

Negotiation must identify what the firms will exchange, at what prices, and the method of payment. Assume that Firms A and B negotiate so that Firm B acquires all the assets (except cash) of Firm A and pays for these assets with its own cash. Now Firm A has cash as its only asset, and it may pay off its creditors and distribute any remaining cash as a liquidating dividend to its shareholders. If, however, Firm B pays for the assets of Firm A with its own shares of stock, then Firm A may sell off the stock and distribute the cash or distribute the stock directly to its shareholders. Note that the effect of these negotiations on the balance sheet of Firm B is an increase in the assets account, to reflect the acquired assets, and a decrease in cash or an increase in the capital accounts, to reflect the method of payment.

Assume now that Firm B acquires the common stock of Firm A (and not the assets directly). Firm B may acquire the shares for cash, either in exchange for some of its shares or by some more complex plan. In the extreme case in which the shareholders of Firm A surrender all their shares for shares of Firm B, Firm A ceases to exist and Firm B assumes all the assets and liabilities of Firm A. State laws specify that once a certain percentage of A's shareholders agree to an exchange of shares, all shareholders must comply. Holdout shareholders of Firm A may go to the courts to earn a fair price for their shares in the event that they are not satisfied with the negotiated price. In a less extreme case, Firm B may acquire less than all of the shares of Firm A and maintain an interest in Firm A. In this case, the shares of Firm A appear as an investment on the balance sheet of Firm B.

16. Net Cash Balance

Beginning cash balance plus cash receipts minus cash disbursements.

17. Net Float

Sum of disbursement float and collection float. [See also **Float**]

18. Net Interest Margin

Ratio of net interest income to total earning assets; used to evaluate profitability of banks.

19. Net Investment

Gross, or total, investment minus depreciation.

20. Net Operating Losses (NOL)

Losses that a firm can take advantage of to reduce taxes.

21. Net Overhead Burden

Difference between noninterest expense and non-interest income as a fraction of total bank assets.

22. Net Payoff

Another term for profit.

23. Net Present Value

The net benefit, or the net present value (NPV), of an investment is the present value of a project's cash flows minus its cost. The present value of the expected cash flows from a project is found by discounting each cash flow to the present. The *net present value* (NPV) is defined as:

Net present value = Present value of the expected cash flows − Cost of the project

More formally, NPV is:

$$NPV = \frac{CF_1}{(1+r)^1} + \frac{CF_2}{(1+r)^2} + \ldots + \frac{CF_N}{(1+r)^N} - I$$
$$= CF_1[PVIF(r, 1)] + CF_2[PVIF(r, 2)] + \ldots$$
$$+ CF_N[PVIF(r, N)],$$

where CF_t = annual cash flow generated by the project in period t ($t = 1,2,\ldots,N$); $PVIF(r,t)$ = present value factor for r percent in period t; I = initial cost of the project; N = expected life of the project; r = required rate of return used to discount the cash flows.

It is a "net" present value in that it subtracts the project's investment cost form the present value of the project's expected cash flows.

24. Net Present Value Profile

Management may want to assess the sensitivity of a project's NPV to the required rate of return. An NPV profile shows this relationship in a graph of project NPVs for different values of the discount rate. The calculations and graphing of an NPV profile can be handled easily by a spreadsheet program.

If the resulting NPV profile shows a steeply sloped curve, then the NPV of the project under consideration is sensitive to the discount rate assumption. In such a case, management should carefully assess the project's required return. If the NPV profile is sloped gradually, then the project's impact on shareholder wealth is not very sensitive to changes in the discount rate.

25. Net Present Value Rule

An investment is worth making if it has a positive net present value (NPV). If an investment's NPV is negative, it should be rejected.

26. Net Working Capital

Net working capital, the difference between current assets and current liabilities, is a financial indicator that can be used in conjunction with ratio analysis to gauge a firm's liquidity. An increase in net working capital is a net investment in the firm's current assets; and an increase in an asset is considered a use of cash. A decrease in net working capital is a divestment of assets, that is, a source of cash. In general, an abundance of net working capital suggests that the firm has ample liquidity to meet its short-term obligations.

Net working capital = Current assets
– *Current liabilities*

But this may not always be the case. In fact, one of the objectives of short-term financial planning is to reduce excess or redundant working capital to a minimum, since carrying these idle assets has both an explicit and implicit cost.

27. Net Worth

Owner's (stockholders') equity in a firm.

28. Netting

The practice of offsetting promised interest payments with promised interest receipts and transferring the difference with an interest rate swap. [See also **Interest rate swap**] There are at least three types of netting:

(a) *Close-out netting*: In the event of counterparty bankruptcy, all transactions or all contracts of a given type are netted at market value. The alternative would allow the liquidator to choose which contracts to enforce and which to not to (and thus potentially "cherry pick"). There are international jurisdictions where the enforceability of netting in bankruptcy has not been legally tested.

(b) *Netting by novation*: The legal obligation of the parties to make required payments under one or more series of related transactions are canceled and a new obligation to make only the net payment is created.

(c) *Settlement or payment netting*: For cash settled trades, this can be applied either bilaterally or multilaterally and on related or unrelated transactions.

29. Newton-Raphson Method

The Newton-Raphson procedure is designed to solve an equation of the form $f(x) = 0$. *It starts with a guess of the solution: $x = x_0$. It then produces successively better estimates of the solution: $x = x_1$, $x = x_2$, $x = x_3, \ldots$ using the formula $x_{i+1} = x_i - f(x_i)/f'(x_i)$. Usually, x_2 is extremely close to the true solution.*

30. No Loan Fund

A mutual fund that does not charge a regular sales commission or sale charge. In other words, there are no front end sales charges.

31. No-Arbitrage Assumption

The assumption that there are no arbitrage opportunities in market prices.

32. No-Arbitrage Interest Rate Model

A model for the behavior of interest rates that is exactly consistent with the initial term structure of interest rates. [See also **Term structure of interest rates**].

33. Nominal Cash Flow

A cash flow expressed in nominal terms if the actual dollars to be received (or paid out) are given.

34. Nominal Interest Rate

When the bond interest rate is quoted as an APR, it is called a nominal interest rate or **stated annual interest rate**. Given an annual percentage rate, the periodic interest rate is APR/m, where m represents the number of periods or cash flows in a year. Since APR assumes no period-by-period compounding of cash flows, it fails to account for interest-on-interest.

35. Nominal Risk-Free Interest Rate

Potential savers have little incentive to invest unless their expected returns include some protection against expected inflation. To try to protect themselves from a loss of purchasing power, investors will demand a return that reflects inflationary expectations. This return is called the nominal risk-free interest rate; it represents the observed or published return on a risk-free asset.

The nominal risk-free rate depends upon: the **real risk-free rate** and the expected inflation rate. [See also **Real risk-free rate**]

Nominal risk-free interest rate
$$= (1 + \text{Real risk-free interest rate}) \times (1 + \text{Expected inflation rate}) - 1.$$

This equation, known as the Fisher effect, illustrates how the inflation rate determines the relationship between real and nominal interest rates.

Many financial analysts use the interest rate on a one-year Treasury bill to approximate the nominal risk-free rate. The Treasury bill (T-bill) has a short time horizon and the backing of the US government, which give it an aura of safety. The one-year T-bill rate is used because investment returns usually are stated as annual returns.

36. Nonbank Bank

A firm that either makes commercial loans or accepts deposits but does not do both. Thus, it avoids regulation as a commercial bank. In other words, it undertakes many of the activities of a commercial bank without meeting the legal definition of a bank.

37. Nonbank Subsidiary

A subsidiary of a bank holding company that is engaged in activities closely related to banking, such as leasing, data processing, factoring, and insurance underwriting.

38. Noncash Item

Expense against revenue that does not directly affect cash flow, such as depreciation and deferred taxes.

39. Nondebt Tax Shields

If firms pay taxes and interest is tax-deductible, firm value rises as the use of debt financing rises. But this analysis implies that there are limits to the benefits of tax-deductible debt. For example, business risk leads to variations in EBIT over time, which can lead to uncertainty about the firm's ability to fully use future interest deductions. If a firm has a negative or zero operating income, an interest deduction provides little help; it just makes the pretax losses larger. The advantage of tax-deductible interest also is reduced if the firm has tax-loss carry forwards that reduce current and future years' taxable incomes. Also, firms in lower tax brackets have less tax incentive to borrow than those in higher tax brackets.

The present value of future interest tax shields becomes even more uncertain if EBIT is affected by nondebt tax shields. In practice, firms' EBITs are reduced by various expenses, such as depreciation, depletion allowances, amortization, pension contributions, employee and retiree health-care costs, R&D, and advertising expenses. Foreign tax credits, granted by the US government to firms that pay taxes to foreign governments, also diminish the impact of the interest deduction. Thus, the tax deductibility of debt becomes less important to firms with large nondebt tax shields.

40. Nondiversifiable Risk

Risk that remains after a large number of assets are combined in a portfolio. [See also **Systematic risk**]

41. Nonmarketed Claims

Claims that cannot be easily bought and sold in the financial markets, such as those of the government and litigants in lawsuits.

42. Nonnotification Financing

[See **Pledging**]

43. Nonperforming Loan

Loan for which an obligated interest payment is 90 days past due. They are placed on accrual status. Banks have traditionally stopped accruing interest when debt payments were more than 90 days past due.

44. Nonrate Gap

Noninterest-bearing liabilities plus equity minus non-earning assets as a ratio of earning assets.

45. Nonrated Bond

A bond that is not rated by Moody's, S&P, or other rating agency.

46. Nonrecombining Tree

A binomial tree describing asset price moves in which an up move followed by a down move yields a different price than a down move followed by an up move.

47. Nonrecourse

Holder of an obligation has no legal right to force payment on a claim.

48. Nonstandard Option

[See **Exotic option**]

49. Nonstationary Model

A model where the volatility parameters are a function of time.

50. Nonsystematic Risk

Nonmarket or firm-specific risk factors that can be eliminated by diversification. Also called unique risk or diversifiable risk. Systematic risk refers to risk factors common to the entire economy.

51. Normal Backwardation Theory

Normal backwardation is one of the three traditional theories used to explain the relationship between the futures price and the expected value of the spot price of the commodity at some future date. Normal backwardation suggests that the futures price will be bid down to a level below the expected spot price, and will rise over the life of the contract until maturity date. On the maturity date, futures price is equal to spot price. [See also **Expectations hypothesis**]

52. Normal Distribution

System metric bell-shaped frequency distribution that can be defined by its mean and standard deviation. It's a systematic distribution and therefore the skewness of normal distribution is zero. It is a continuous probability distribution that assigns positive probability to all values from $-\infty$ to $+\infty$. Sometimes called the "bell curve."

The probability density function of a normal random variable can be defined as:

$$f(x) = \frac{1}{\sqrt{2\pi}\sigma} e^{-(x-\mu)^2/2\sigma^2}, \quad -\infty < x < \infty,$$

where $\pi = 3.14159$, $e = 2.71828$, and $\mu(-\infty < \mu < \infty)$ and $\sigma^2 (0 < \sigma^2 < \infty)$ are the mean and variance of the normal random variable x. [See also **Central limit theorem**]

53. Normal Market

A market where futures prices increase with maturity.

54. Note

Unsecured debt, usually with maturity of less than 15 years. Note payable is one of the liability items in the balance sheet.

55. Note Issuance Facility

An arrangement in which borrowers can issue short-term securities in their own names.

56. Notional Amount

The dollar amount used as a scale factor in calculating payments for a forward contract, futures contract, or swap.

57. Notional Principal

The principal used to calculate payments in an interest rate swap. The principal is "notional" because it is neither paid nor received.

58. Notional Value

The face value of interest rate swap contracts; a mere reference value to compute obligated interest payments.

59. NPV

Net Present Value = present value of expected cash flow − cost of the project.
[See also **Net present value**]

60. NPVGO Model

A model valuing the firm in which net present value of new investment opportunities is explicitly examined. NPVGO stands for net present value of growth opportunities. This model divided the dividend growth model into two parts as value of share when firm acts as cash cow plus NPV of growth opportunity. [See also **Cash cow** for value of a share]

61. NSF

Not sufficient funds.

62. Numeraire

Defines the units in which security prices are measured. For example, if the price of IBM is the numeraire, all security prices are measured relative to IBM. If IBM is $80 and a particular security price is $50, the security price is 0.625 when IBM is the numeraire.

63. Numerical Procedure

A method of valuing an option when no formula is available.

O

1. Obligor

A party who is in debt to another. It can be either (i) a loan borrower, (ii) a bond issuer, (iii) a trader who has not yet settled, (iv) a trade partner with accounts payable, or (v) a contractor with unfinished performance, etc. [See also **Counterparty**]

2. OCC

Options Clearing Corporation. [See also **Clearinghouse**]

3. Odd Lot

Stock trading unit of less than 100 shares.

4. Odd-lot Theory

The odd-lot theory is one of several theories of contrary opinion. In essence, the theory assumes that the common mean is usually wrong and that it is, therefore, advantageous to pursue strategies opposite to his thinking. In order to find out what the common man is doing, statistics on odd-lot trading are gathered. Most odd-lot purchases are made by amateur investors with limited resources – that is, by the common man, who is the small, unsophisticated investor.

5. Off-Balance Sheet Activities

Commitments, such as loan guarantees, that do not appear on a bank's balance sheet but represent actual contractual obligations. For example, the issuance of standby letter of credit guarantee is also an off-balance-sheet activity.

6. Off-Balance Sheet Financing

Financing that is not shown as a liability on a company's balance sheet. In leasing, lessees needed only to report information on leasing activities in the footnotes of their financial statements. Thus, leasing led to off-balance-sheet financing.

7. Off-Balance Sheet Risk

The risk incurred by a financial institution due to activities related to contingent assets and liabilities.

8. Offer Price

The price that a dealer is offering to sell an asset. It is an ask price.

9. Off-Market Swap

Swaps that have non-standard terms that require one party to compensate another. Relaxing a standardized swap can include special interest rate terms and indexes as well as allowing for varying notional values underlying the swap.

10. One Bank Holding Company

A holding company that owns or controls only one commercial bank.

11. One-Factor APT

A special case of the arbitrage pricing theory (APT) that is derived from the one-factor model by using diversification and arbitrage. It shows the expected return on any risky asset is a linear function of a single factor. The CAPM can be expressed as one-factor APT in which a single factor is the market portfolio.

12. On-the-Run Issue

The most recently issued US Treasury security. It is considered to be the actively traded issue.

13. Open (Good-Till-Canceled) Order

A buy or sell order remaining in force for up to six months unless canceled.

14. Open Account

A credit account for which the only formal instrument of credit is the invoice.

15. Open Contracts

Contracts that have been bought or sold without the transactions having been completed by subsequent sale or purchase, or by making or taking actual delivery of the financial instrument or physical commodity. Measured by "open interest," as reported in the press.

16. Open Interest

The quantity of a derivatives contract that is outstanding at a point in time. (One long and one short position count as one unit outstanding.)

17. Open Market Operation

Open market operations are the Fed's most frequently used monetary policy tool. The Fed buys and sells securities (usually Treasury bills) with other market participants. When it purchases government securities in the open market, the Fed trades dollars for securities. The seller deposits these dollars in a bank, thereby increasing the bank's reserves from which it can make loans. Through a multiplier process, the open market purchase boosts deposits in the US banking system and the money supply rises. An open market sale of securities by the Fed has the opposite effect, reducing the level of loanable funds in the banking system, and therefore the money supply.

18. Open Market Repurchase

A firm can reacquire its stock through an open market repurchase. Acting through a broker, the corporation purchases shares in the secondary market just like any other investor. A corporation usually announces its intention to engage in an open market repurchase in advance, although the exact amount of shares repurchased and the actual days of the transactions are not known.

19. Open Outcry

A system of trading in which buyers and sellers in one physical location convey offers to buy and sell by gesturing and shouting.

20. Open-End (mutual) Fund

A fund that issues or redeems its own shares at their net asset value (NAV). This kind of fund provides opportunities for small investors to invest in financial securities and diversify risk.

21. Operating Activities

Sequence of events and decisions that create the firm's cash inflows and cash outflows. These activities include buying and paying for raw materials, manufacturing and selling a product, and collecting cash.

22. Operating Cash Flow

Earnings before interest and depreciation minus taxes. It measures the cash generated from operations not counting capital spending or working capital requirements.

23. Operating Cycle

When a firm is functioning efficiently, its operating cycle moves through four stages: (1) converting cash to inventory, (2) converting inventory to sales, (3) converting sales to accounts receivable, and (4) converting accounts receivable to cash.

This operating cycle can be very simple or quite complex. A cash flow timeline can depict the most complex as well as the simplest situation.

Two financial ratios, the receivable collection period and the inventory conversion period, help the manager to quantify the operating cycle. The average days of accounts receivable is defined as accounts receivable divided by sales per day as:

$$\text{Receivable collection period} = \frac{\text{Accounts receivable}}{\text{Sales}/365 \text{ days}}.$$

The inventory conversion period is defined as inventory divided by cost of goods sold per day as:

Inventory conversion period

$$= \frac{\text{Inventory}}{\text{Cost of goods sold}/365 \text{ days}}.$$

Adding these two ratios together gives us the length of a firm's operating cycle:

Operating cycle = Receivables collection period
+ Inventory conversion period.

The operating cycle measures conversion of current assets to cash. [See also **Cash conversion cycle**]

24. Operating Income

Sum of interest income and non-interest income for a financial institution. For a non-financial institution, it represents the net sale minus cost of good sold.

25. Operating Lease

An operating lease is a shorter-term lease than for instance, a leveraged lease or a sale and lease-back agreement, which may be cancelled at the lessee's option. An operating lease does not satisfy any of the four financial lease criteria. [See also **Capital lease**] The lessor typically must maintain and service the asset. Computers, photocopiers, and trucks often are acquired under the terms of an operating lease.

26. Operating Leverage

A firm's business risk is affected by its level of fixed costs, or in financial terminology, its operating leverage. Operating leverage magnifies the effect of changing sales to produce a percentage change in EBIT larger than the change in sales, assuming constant profit margins. It is a business risk measure. [See also **Degree of operating leverage**].

27. Opportunity Cost

From economics, we know than an opportunity cost is the cost of passing up the next best alternative. For example, the opportunity cost of a building is its market value. By deciding to continue to own it, the firm is foregoing the cash it could receive from selling it. Economics teaches the TINSTAAFL principle: "There is no such thing as a free lunch." Capital budgeting analysis frequently applies this principle to existing assets.

If a firm is thinking about placing a new manufacturing plant in a building it already owns, the firm cannot assume that the building is free and assign it to the project at zero cost. The project's cash flow estimates should include the market value of the building as a cost of investing since this represents cash flows the firm will not receive from selling the building.

28. Opportunity Set

The possible expected return—standard deviation pairs of all portfolios that can be constructed from a set of assets. Also called a feasible set.

29. Optimal Cash Balance

Based upon Baumol's economic order quantity (EOQ) model the total cost of cash balances can be defined as:

Total costs = Holding costs + Transaction costs
$$= \frac{C}{2}r + \frac{T}{C}F,$$

where C = amount of cash raised by selling marketable securities or borrowing; $\frac{C}{2}$ = average cash balance; r = opportunity cost of holding cash (the foregone rate of return on marketable securities); T = total amount of new cash needed for transaction over entire period (usually one year); $\frac{T}{C}$ = number of transactions; F = fixed cost of making a securities trade or borrowing money.

The minimum total costs are obtained when C is set equal to C^*, the optimal cash balance. C^* is defined as:

$$C^* = \sqrt{\frac{2FT}{r}},$$

where C^* = optimal amount of cash to be raised by selling marketable securities or by borrowing. [See also **Baumal's economic order quantity model**]

30. Optimal Risky Portfolio

An investor's best combination of risky assets to be mixed with safe assets to form the complete portfolio. [See also **Appendix F**]

31. Option

A right – but not an obligation – to buy or sell underlying assets at a fixed price during a specified time period.

32. Option Class

All options of the same type (call or put) on a particular stock.

33. Option Elasticity

The percentage increase in an option's value given a 1 percent change in the value of the underlying security.

34. Option Overwriting

Selling a call option against a long position in the underlying asset.

35. Option Premium

The price of an option. [See also **Option pricing equation**]

36. Option Pricing Equation

An exact formula for the price of a call option. The formula requires five variables: the risk-free interest rate, the variance of the underlying stock, the exercise price, the price of the underlying stock and the time to expiration.

$$C = SN(d_1) - Xe^{-rt}N(d_2),$$

where $d_1 = \dfrac{\ln(S/X) + (r + \sigma^2/2)T}{\sigma\sqrt{T}}$,

$$d_2 = d_1 - \sigma\sqrt{T},$$

C = current call option value; S = current stock price; $N(d)$ = the probability that a random draw from a standard normal distribution will be less than d, in other words, it equals the area under the normal curve up to d; X = exercise price; e = 2.71828, the base of the natural log function; r = risk-free interest rate; $\ln$ = natural logarithm function; σ = standard deviation of the annualized continuously compounded rate of return of the stock.

Like all models, the Black-Scholes formula is based on some important underlying assumptions:

1. The stock will pay no dividends until after the option expiration date.
2. Both the interest rate, r, and variance rate, σ^2, of the stock are constant.
3. Stock prices are continuous, meaning that sudden extreme jumps such as those in the aftermath of an announcement of a takeover attempt are ruled out.

37. Option Series

All options of a certain class with the same strike price and expiration date.

38. Option Theoretic

An approach to estimating the expected default frequency of a particular firm. It applies Robert Merton's model-of-the-firm which states that debt can be valued as a put option of the underlying asset value of the firm. [See also *Credit Monitor Overview*, KMV Corporation, 1993, San Francisco]

39. Option Writer

The party with a short position in the option.

40. Option-Adjusted Spread (OAS)

A procedure for valuing prepayment risk associated with mortgage-backed securities that recognize the magnitude and timing of prepayments and required return to an investor. This kind of model uses option pricing theory to figure the fair yield on pass-throughs and, in particular, the fair yield spread of pass-throughs over treasuries. These so-called option-adjusted spread (OAS) models focus on the prepayment risk of pass-throughs as the essential determinant of the required yield spread of pass-through bonds over treasuries.

Stripped to its basics, the option model views the fair price on a pass-through such as a GNMA (Ginnie) bond as being decomposable into two parts;

$$P_{GNMA} = P_{TBOND} - P_{PREPAYMENT\_OPTION}$$

That is, the value on a GNMA bond to an investor (P_{GNMA}) is equal to the value of a standard noncallable Treasury bond of the same duration (P_{TBOND}) minus the value of the mortgage holder's prepayment call option ($P_{PREPAYMENT\_OPTION}$). Specifically, the ability of the mortgage holder to prepay is equivalent to the bond investor writing a call option on the bond and the mortgagee owning or buying the option. If interest rates fall, the option becomes more valuable as it moves into the money and more mortgages are prepaid early by having the

bond called or the prepayment option exercised. This relationship can also be thought of in the yield dimension:

$$Y_{GNMA} = Y_{TBOND} + Y_{OPTION}.$$

The investors' required yield on a GNMA (Y_{GNMA}) should equal the yield on a similar duration T-bond (Y_{TBOND}) plus an additional yield for writing the valuable call option (Y_{OPTION}). That is, the fair yield spread or *option-adjusted spread (OAS)* between GNMAs and T-bond should reflect the value of this option.

41. Order Book Official

[See **Board broker**].

42. Order Statistics

The n draws of a random variable sorted in ascending order. They are nonparametric statistics.

43. Ordinal Utility

An ordinal utility implies that a consumer needs not be able to assign numbers that represent (in arbitrary unit) the degree or amount of utility associated with commodity or combination of commodity. The consumer can only rank and order the amount or degree of utility associated with commodity. [See also **Cardinal utility**]

44. Organized Exchanges

The organized exchanges have physical locations where brokers act as agents; they help their client buy and sell securities by matching orders. The New York Stock Exchange (NYSE) is the largest organized exchange in the US.

45. Original-Issue-Discount-Bond

A bond issued with a discount from par value. Also called a deep-discount or pure discount bond.

46. Origination Fee

Fee charged by a lender for accepting the initial loan application and processing the loan.

47. Originator

The financial institution that extends credit on a facility which may later be held by another institution through, for instance, a loan sale. Originator can change origination fee. [See also **Facility**]

48. Out of The Money

The owner of a put or call is not obligated to carry out the specified transaction, but has the *option* of doing so. If the transaction is carried out, it is said to have been *exercised*. If the call option is *out of the money* – hat is, the stock is trading at a price below the exercise price – you certainly would not want to exercise the option, as it would be cheaper to purchase stock directly.

49. Out Performance Option

An option in which the payoff is determined by the extent to which one asset price is greater than another asset price, called the benchmark. It is also called exchange option. [See also **Exchange option**]

50. Out-of-the-Money Option

Either (a) a call option where the asset price is less than the strike price or (b) a put option where the asset price is greater than the strike price.

51. Outsourcing

Buying services from third-party vendor. For example, some banks might outsource their data processing.

52. Overdraft

Depositor writing a check for an amount greater than the deposit balance.

53. Overhead

Expenses that generally do not vary with the level of output.

54. Oversubscribed Issue

Investors are not able to buy all the shares they want, so underwriters must allocate the shares among investors. This occurs when a new issue is under priced.

55. Oversubscription Privilege

Allows shareholders to purchase unsubscribed shares in a rights offering at the subscription price. This kind of privilege makes it unlikely that the corporate issuer would need to turn to its underwriter for help.

56. Over-the-Counter Market

The over-the-counter (OTC) market is a telecommunications network of dealers who provide liquidity to investors by their willingness to "make markets" in particular securities. When an investor wants to purchase a security, a dealer firm will sell it (at a price equal to the "ask" price) from its own inventory of securities; if an investor wants to sell, the dealer will purchase the security (at the "bid" price) and hold it in inventory. A source of dealer profit is the spread, or difference between the bid and ask price.

P

1. P/E Effect

Fundamental analysis calls on much wider range information to create portfolios than doe's technical analysis. One of the criteria is to use the price/earnings (P/E) ratio information to formulate portfolios. It has been found that portfolios of low P/E stocks have exhibited higher average risk-adjusted returns than high P/E stocks.

2. P/E Ratio

A firm's stock price per share divided by earnings per share.

3. PAC

Planned amortization class such as collateralized mortgage option (CMO) – A security that is retired according to a planned amortization schedule, while payments to other classes of securities are slowed or accelerated. The objective is to ensure that PACs exhibit highly predictable maturities and cash flows.

4. Package

A derivative that is a portfolio of standard calls and puts, possibly combined with a position in forward contracts and the asset itself.

5. Pac-Man Strategy

In a pac-man strategy, the target firm tries to turn the tables and take over the hostile bidder. [See also **Tender offer**]

6. Par Bond

A bond for which the price at issue equals the maturity value.

7. Par Coupon

The coupon rate on a par bond.

8. Par Value

The face value of a bond is called the par value. Generally, this is the amount of money that the issuer has initially borrowed and promised to repay at a future maturity date. Most US corporate bonds have a par value of $1,000 per bond.

9. Par Yield

The coupon on a bond that makes its price equal the principal.

10. Parallel Shift In The Yield Curve

A change in interest rate where rates at all maturities change by the same amount, in the same direction, at the same time. This never actually occurs.

11. Parent Company

A firm that owns controlling interest in the stock of another firm.

12. Partial Expectation

The sum (or integral) of a set of outcomes times the probability of those outcomes. To understand the calculations of partial expectation, consider a binomial model in which the strike price is $70, and the stock price at expiration can be $20, $40, $60, or $80, with probabilities 1/8, 3/8, 3/8 and 1/8, respectively. If a put is in the money at expiration, the stock price is either $20, $40, or $60. Suppose that for these two values we sum the stock price times the probability. We obtain:

$$\sum_{S_t < 70} PROB(S_t) \times S_t = \left(\frac{1}{8} \times \$20\right) + \left(\frac{3}{8} \times \$40\right) + \left(\frac{3}{8} \times \$60\right) = \$40.$$

The value $40 is clearly not an expected stock price since it is below the expected stock price ($50). We call $40 the *partial expectation* of the stock price conditional upon $S_t < $ ($70).

13. Participating Swap

Allows the fixed rate to be adjusted downward during the life of the swap, depending on the rate for payments indexed to a long-term rate.

14. Partnership

A partnership brings two or more individuals together to invest their time, energy, and talents in the firm. Organizing a partnership is relatively simple, although some legal documents may be needed to spell out the percentage ownership, rights, and duties of each partner. By drawing on the strengths of two or more individuals, each can specialize in his or her own area to help the firm achieve success. Also, the combined financial resources of two or more individuals may increase the firm's ability to raise and borrow capital.

As with a proprietorship, partnership income is taxable to each partner at his or her own personal tax rate. The partnership ends upon the death of any partner; unless other arrangements have been made, firm assets may need to be sold to settle the deceased partner's estate.

As the partners presumably manage their firm, agency costs can be zero, as long as they agree on the firm's goals, work together amicably, and trust and respect each other as professionals. Should intractable differences of opinion or suspicions arise, arguments, and even court battles, can result.

Partnerships suffer from other drawbacks. As with a proprietorship, it is difficult to value and transfer ownership in a partnership. In addition, partners are *jointly and severally liable* for the debts of the partnership. That means each partner may have to pay more than his or her proportional ownership share to settle the firm's debts in case

of failure. Each partner has unlimited liability. Anyone thinking of joining a partnership should seriously consider this risk.

The liability risks just noted describe a *general* partnership. A limited partnership addresses the liability concern by identifying at least one general partner as having unlimited liability; the remaining *limited partners* face liability limited to their investment in the firm, in other words, their personal assets cannot be demanded to settle the firm's debts. However, they also are limited in that they cannot participate in the operations of the firm. Operating decisions may be made only by the general partners.

15. Passbook Savings

Nonnegotiable, small savings account evidenced by a passbook listing the account terms.

16. Passive Investment Strategy

[See also **Passive management**]

17. Passive Management

Buying a well-diversified portfolio to represent a broad-based market index without attempting to search out mispriced securities.

18. Passive Portfolio

A market index portfolio. [See also **Passive portfolio management**]

19. Passive Portfolio Management

An investment policy whereby managers make predetermined securities purchases regardless of the level of interest rates and specific rate expectation. Examples include following a laddered maturity strategy whereby a bank continuously buys 10-year securities as previously owned securities mature.

20. Pass-Through

[See also **Mortgage-back security**]

21. Pass-Through Security

Pools of loans (such as home mortgage loans) sold in one package. Owners of pass-throughs receive all principal and interest payments made by the borrowers.

22. Past-Due Loan

A loan with a promised principal and/or interest payment that has not been made by the scheduled payment data.

23. Path-Dependent Derivative

A derivative where the final payoff depends upon the path taken by the stock price, instead of just the final stock price.

24. Path-Dependent Option

An option whose payoff depends on the whole path followed by the underlying variable-not just its final value. An Asian option is an example of path-dependent option, since Asian option that has a payoff that is based on the average price over some period of time. [See also **Asian option**]

25. Payable Through Drafts

Payable through drafts resemble checks; they are written orders to pay and have the physical appearance of checks. However, they are drawn directly against the issuing firm instead of a bank. The bank receives a draft first; it sends the draft to the issuing firm and awaits approval. The bank releases funds only when the corporate issuer approves specific drafts for payment. In practice, the bank generally withholds payment for one

business day and then covers the payment automatically unless directed otherwise. The issuing firm generally inspects the drafts for inaccuracies in signatures, amounts, and dates, and quickly cancels payments on issued drafts with discrepancies.

Although drafts may increase disbursement float, their main advantage lies in ensuring effective control over payments. Draft payments are popular in the insurance industry, for instance, where they allow field agents to settle claims quickly even though they lack the authority to issue checks. Drafts give the central office the flexibility to improve efficiency in field operations, yet still retain the option to block any payments deemed inappropriate.

26. Payback Method

The payback method calculates a project's payback period as a measure of how long it takes the project to pay for itself. More formally, it is the time necessary for a project to generate cash flows sufficient to recover its cost. Projects with payback periods less than a management-determined cutoff are acceptable. Projects with longer paybacks are rejected.

The payback method has none of the characteristics we want from a project selection method. First, it ignores the time value of money, summing periodic cash flows without regard for the differences in the present values of those dollars. Second, the payback method fails to account for all relevant cash flows, ignoring those that accrue after the payback period. Third, the payback period gives no indication of the absolute change in shareholder wealth due to a particular project. Finally, the decision criterion is quite subjective. The determination of an appropriate payback period is based solely upon management's opinions and perceived needs. It has no relationship to the project's required return.

Some firms use a discounted payback method, in which the payback is computed using the present value of the cash inflows. [See also **Discount payback rule**]

27. Payback Period Rule

An investment decision rule which states that all investment projects that have payback periods equal to or less than a particular cutoff period are accepted, and all of those that pay off in more than the particular cutoff period are rejected. The payback period is the number of years required for a firm to recover its initial investment required by a project from the cash flow it generates.

28. Payer Swaption

A swaption giving the holder the right to be the fixed-rate (or fixed price) payer in the swap.

29. Paylater Strategy

Generally used to refer to option strategies in which the position buyer makes no payments unless the option moves more into the money. This is an exotic option is which the premium is paid only at expiration and only if the option is in the money.

30. Payment Date

The firm mails checks to shareholders on the payment date. [See also **Dividend declaration date**]

31. Payment-in-Kind

Payment-in-kind (PIK) bonds often are issued by cash-strapped firms and firms doing leveraged buyouts. The PIK provision allows the issuer to pay coupon interest in the early years of the issue in the form of either cash or bonds with values equal to the coupon payment. Such bonds help reduce the issuer's cash outflows, but at a cost of increasing the debt. Investors also assume a risky position; unless the issuer's cash situation im-

proves, they find themselves increasing their exposure to the questionable lender.

32. Payments Pattern Approach

Describes the lagged collection pattern of receivables. For instance the probability that a 75-day-old account will still be unpaid when it is 76 days old. [See also **Receivable balance pattern**]

33. Payoff

The cash realized by the holder of an option or other derivatives at the end of its life.

34. Payoff Diagram

A graph in which the value of a derivative or other claim at a point in time is plotted against the price of the underlying asset.

35. Payout Phase

The payout phase usually starts at retirement, when the investor typically has several options, including the following:

1. Taking the market value of the shares in a lump sum payment.
2. Receiving a fixed annuity until death.
3. Receiving a variable amount of money each period that is computed according to a certain procedure.

36. Payout Ratio

Proportion of net income paid out in cash dividends.

37. Peak

The transition from the end of an expansion to the start of a contraction in business cycle.

38. Peak Exposure

For market-driven instruments, the maximum (perhaps netted) exposure expected with 95 percent confidence for the remaining life of a transaction. CreditMetrics does not utilize this figure because it is not possible to aggregate tail statistics across a portfolio, since it is not the case that these "peaks" will all occur at the same time. [See also **Credit-Metrics**]

39. Pecking Order Hypothesis

The pecking order hypothesis is a perspective based upon repeated observations of how corporations seem to raise funds over time. The theory behind this perspective was developed from the **information asymmetry** problem, namely, that management knows more about the firm and its opportunities than the financial marketplace does, and that management does not want to be forced to issue equity when stock prices are depressed. [See also **Information asymmetry**]

Evidence shows that corporations mainly rely on internal funds, especially new additions to retained earnings, to finance capital budgeting projects. If they need outside financing, firms typically issue debt first, as it poses lower risk on the investor than equity and lower cost on the corporation. Should a firm approach its debt capacity, it may well favor hybrid securities, such as convertible bonds, over common stock. As a last resort, the firm will issue common equity. Thus, firms have a financing "pecking order," rather than a goal to maintain a specific target debt-to-equity ratio over time.

Under this pecking order hypothesis, financial theory has come full circle. Like Modigliani and Miller's original work, the pecking order hypothesis implies that firms have no optimal debt-to-equity ratios. Instead, they follow the pecking order, exhausting internal equity (retained earnings) first and resorting to external equity (new issues of common stock) last. Observed debt ratios represent nothing more than the cumulative result of a firm's need to use external financing over time.

Under the pecking order hypothesis, firms with high profitability should have *lower* debt ratios, as these firms' additions to retained earnings reduce their need to borrow. Under the static tradeoff hypothesis, a firm with high profitability ratios should have a lower probability of bankruptcy and a higher tax rate, thus leading to *higher* debt ratios. Most empirical evidence resolves this conflict in favor of the pecking order hypothesis; studies find that more profitable firms tend to have lower debt ratios.

What if the pecking order hypothesis is correct and the firm has no optimal capital structure? Recall that the cost of capital represents the minimum required return on capital budgeting projects. Management must determine the firm's cost of capital regardless of personal beliefs about the existence of an optimal capital structure. Target capital structure weights should reflect management's impression of a capital structure that is sustainable in the long run and that allows for financing flexibility over time. Should a firm fail to earn its cost of capital, shareholder wealth will decline.

The debate over optimal capital structure is not resolved. Empirical studies and surveys of corporate practice have supported both the static tradeoff and the pecking order theories. Part of the uncertainty over which perspective is correct comes from blends between capital structure choices that depart from "plain vanilla" debt and equity. In recent decades, firms have devised myriad financing flavors. Consequently, many firms have several layers of debt and several layers of equity on their balance sheets. Debt can be made convertible to equity; its maturity can be extended, or shortened, at the firm's options; debt issues can be made senior or subordinate to other debt issues. Likewise, equity variations exist. Preferred equity has gained popularity since it increases a firm's equity without diluting the ownership and control of the common shareholders; it also increases future financing flexibility by expanding the firm's capacity for debt issues. Firms can have different classes of common equity, providing holders with differing levels of dividend income or voting rights.

In sum, pecking order in long-term financing is a hierarchy of long-term financing strategies, in which using internally generated cash is at the top and issuing new equity is at the bottom.

40. Peer Group

Sample firms used to generate average reference data for comparison with an individual firm's performance data.

41. Pension Benefit Guarantee Corporation (PBGC)

The Employees Retirement Income Security Act (ERISA) of 1974 established the PBGC, which is a government-run insurance system that ensures that employees of companies that go bankrupt will receive their pension benefits.

42. Percentage of Sales Method

The percentage of sales method is a more complex financial planning model than the internal growth, sustainable growth, or external financing needs models. The percentage of sales method generates a set of *pro forma* or *forecasted balance sheets and income statements* for the firm. The analyst projects what will happen to the firm's accounts over time, which supports an estimate of the firm's external financing needs for a particular period.

The first step of the percentage of sales method is implied by the method's name. Using historical data, the analyst divides each balance sheet and income statement item by sales revenue. The resulting ratios are examined to see which accounts have maintained fairly constant relationships or trends with respect to sales.

The second step of the percentage of sales method is to estimate future sales levels. This estimate can rely on market research studies or on an analysis of internal or sustainable growth rates.

In the third step, the analyst can construct projected financial statements. This process begins by placing the sales forecast at the top of the income statement. To forecast the value of income statement items having a steady or predictable relationship to sales, the analyst assumes this relationship will continue. For items that do not have a consistent relationship to sales, other assumptions will be needed to forecast their values. For example, current credit market conditions may suggest holding interest expense constant or projecting it to grow at a predetermined rate; projected taxes will reflect the firm's tax rate.

Similarly, the analyst projects balance sheet accounts based upon their relationship with sales revenue. Accounts that lack consistent relationships to sales may be assumed to be held constant or to change in a manner consistent with recent trends and future market projections.

The analyst estimates retained earnings by adding the forecasted addition to retained earnings to the existing retained earnings balance. The forecasted addition to retained earnings is the net income on the pro forma (projected) income statement less any dividends, that is:

Projected retained earnings
= *Existing retained earnings*
+ Projected net income
− *Estimated dividend payment.*

The accounting identity requires that total assets equal total liabilities and equity; in the first pass, however, the percentage of sales method will rarely produce this equality. To balance the pro forma balance sheet, the analyst inserts a plug figure, so that:

Total assets = Total liabilities + Stockholders' equity + Plug.

The plug figure, sometimes labeled "external funds needed" or "external funds required," typically represents an addition to or subtraction from notes payable to restore equality to the balance sheet equation. A positive plug figure suggests that additional short-term borrowing will be needed to finance the firm's growth plans. (Of course, this need for funds also can be met by issuing long-term debt or equity.) A negative plug figure suggests that project operating results will generate excess cash which the firm can use to reduce its short-term or long-term borrowing or to repurchase stock.

43. Percentile Level

A measure of risk based on the specified confidence level of the portfolio value distribution (e.g., the likelihood that the portfolio market falls below the 99th percentile number is 1 percent).

44. Perfect Markets

Perfectly competitive financial markets.

45. Perfectly Competitive Financial Markets

Markets in which no trader has power to change the price of goods or services. Perfect markets are characterized by the following conditions: (1) trading is costless, and access to the financial markets is free; (2) information about borrowing and lending opportunities is freely available; (3) there are many traders, and no single trader can have a significant impact of market prices.

46. Performance Shares

Shares of stock given to managers on the basis of performance as measured by earnings per share and similar criteria is a control device used by shareholders to tie management to the self-interest of shareholders.

47. Permanent Working Capital

Some working capital needs persist over time, regardless of seasonal or cyclical variations in sales. The firm will always maintain some minimum level of cash, accounts receivable, or inventory; this is permanent working capital and is usually some target percentage of sales.

48. Perpetual Option

An option that never expires.

49. Perpetual Preferred Stock

Nonmaturing preferred stock.

50. Perpetuity

A constant stream of cash flows without end. A British consol is an example. Consider a consol that pays a coupon of C dollars each year and will do so with a **discount rate** r forever. Simply applying the present value (PV) formula gives us

$$PV = \frac{C}{r}.$$

[See also **Discount rate**]

51. Perquisites

Management amenities such as a big office, a company car, or expense-account meals. "Perks" are agency costs of equity, because managers of the firm are agents of the stockholders.

52. Personal Banker

Individual assigned to a bank customer to handle a broad range of financial services.

53. Personal Trust

An interest in an asset held by a trustee for the benefit of another person.

54. Pie Model of Capital Structure

A model of the debt-equity ratio of the firms, graphically depicted in slices of a pie that represents the value of the firm in the capital markets.

55. Plain Vanilla

A term used to describe a standard deal. The most basic type of interest rate swap is known as a "plain vanilla swap."

56. Planned Amortization Class

A collateralized mortgage obligation (CMO) that receives principal from the underlying mortgages based on a predetermined payment schedule, where the payments vary depending on whether prepayments fall inside or outside some predetermined range.

57. Planning Phase of Capital Budgeting

The planning or identification phase examines areas of opportunity or change that could offer profitable investment.

Over time, managers define and redefine the firm's mission, or "vision," and the strategies they will use to accomplish that mission. This long-term plan provides a foundation for the following 5 to 10 years of operation planning for the firm. The long-term plan is operationalized, or implemented, in the annual capital budget. To develop the capital budget, managers must find investment opportunities that fit within the overall strategic objectives of the firm. In addition, they must consider the firm's position within the various markets it serves and the likely plans of its competitors. Attractive capital budgeting projects are those that take the firm from its present position to a desired future market position. Two popular and well-known methods that managers use to identify potentially attractive capital budgeting projects are the **business strategy matrix** and **SWOT analysis**. [See also **Business strategy matrix** and **SWOT analysis**]

58. Pledged Securities

Bank securities (either treasury or municipal securities) pledged as collateral against deposit liabilities such as Treasury deposits, municipal deposits, and borrowing from Federal Reserve banks. These pledged securities are often held by a third party trustee and cannot be sold without a release.

59. Pledging

In pledging, the firm offers its receivables as security for a cash advance. The lender who accepts and discounts the receivables may be a commercial bank or a specialized industrial finance company.

The first step in setting up a pledging relationship is to negotiate a formal agreement between the borrower and the lender. Once the agreement has been reached and a legal contract signed, the borrower can begin to present its receivables. The lender gives the borrower the face value of the invoices less its own charges. That is, the lender buys the invoices at a discount, paying less than the amount it hopes to collect.

Almost all pledging agreements have two important provisions: the lender's right to recourse, and its right to reject invoices. In the event that the customer defaults and fails to pay the sum invoiced, the borrower is obligated to assume responsibility for the outstanding amount.

The lender also has the right to select only those invoices that it will finance and reject those it considers too risky. It is estimated that the rejection rate could reach as high as fifty percent.

Pledging, or discounting, receivables is not a cheap source of credit. During most of the 1980s, when the commercial bank lending rate varied between 8 and 15 percent, the cost of discounting was about 20 percent. Similar rate differentials exist today. In addition, the lender often charges yet another fee to cover its expenses to appraise credit risks. Consequently, this source of short-term financing is used mostly by companies that have no other source of funds open to them, primarily smaller companies. For such companies, however, this offers two advantages. First, after the initial agreement has been reached, the method is fairly informal and automatic, except for the rejection of invoices for bad risk. Second, the customer being invoiced receives no information that the borrowing company is in financial trouble; he or she simple sends in a check in the normal way and never knows that it has been assigned to a third party. For this reason, pledging receivables is sometimes called nonnotification financing.

60. Plowback Ratio

The proportion of the firm's earnings that is reinvested in the business (and not paid out as dividends). The plowback ratio equals 1 minus the dividend payout ratio.

61. Plug

A variable that handles financial plan. [See also **Percentage of sales method**]

62. PO

Principal Only. A mortgage-backed security where the holder receives only principal cash flows on the underlying mortgage pool.

63. Point

Mortgage lenders customarily charge initial service fees, known as points, at the time of the loan origination. A point is one percent of the principle of the loan.

64. Point of Sale

Electronic terminals that enable customers to directly access deposit accounts.

65. Poison Pill

Strategy by a takeover target company to make a stock less appealing to a company that wishes to acquire it. Examples of such delaying tactics, proxy defenses, or poison pills include

1. Provisions that require super-majorities (for example, two-thirds) of existing share-holders to approve any takeover;
2. The decision to place some, rather than all, board seats up for election every year, thus delaying the ability of an acquirer to control the firm;
3. Provisions to allow the board to authorize and issue large quantities of stock or to repurchase outstanding bonds in the event of a takeover attempt;
4. Provisions that stipulate expensive payouts to existing managers in the face of any successful buyout;
5. The establishment of advance notice requirements, so shareholders must meet deadlines for presenting business or director nominations at shareholder meetings; and
6. Restrictions on the ability of shareholders to call special meetings.

66. Poisson Distribution

A probability distribution that counts the number of events occurring in an interval of time, assuming that the occurrence of events is independent.

67. Poisson Process

A process describing a situation where events happen at random. The probability of an event in time Δ_t is $\lambda \Delta_t$, where λ is the rate (intensity) of the process.

68. Political Risk

Investors in nondomestic securities face a number of risks beyond those of domestic securities. Political risk can affect a bond investor in a number of ways. A foreign government may block currency exchanges, preventing the investor from repatriating coupon income.

69. Pooling of Interests

The general idea motivating the pooling treatment is that the business combination was not a purchase-sale transaction but rather a combining of interests. Hence, the prior accounting valuations are maintained and merely added together for the combined firm. Moreover, from an accounting standpoint, the two firms are considered to have been joined from day one and the accounting reports are restated as if they had been joined.

70. Portfolio Analysis

A portfolio is any combination of assets or investments. A firm can be considered a portfolio of capital budgeting projects.

Expected Return on a Portfolio

The expected rate of return on a portfolio, $E(R_p)$, is simply the weighted average of the expected returns, $E(R_i)$, of the individual assets in the portfolio:

$$E(R_p) = \sum_{i=1}^{n} w_i E(R_i),$$

where w_i is the weight of the ith asset, or the proportion of the portfolio invested in that asset. The sum of these weights must equal 1.0.

$E(R_i)$ is used to stand for the expected return on a risky asset. Whenever risk exists, the actual return is not known beforehand. We know that there is an asset which, for all intents and purposes, is considered risk-free: the Treasury bill or T-bill. Let R_f denote the nominal return on a risk-free asset. Since it has no risk, the expected nominal T-bill return is the same as its actual return.

Variance and Standard Deviation of Return on a Portfolio

The total risk of a portfolio can be measured by its variance or the standard deviation of its returns.

Lower portfolio variability arises from the benefits of **diversification**. [See also **Diversification**] The benefits of diversification are greatest when asset returns are strongly negatively correlated, that is, when they tend to move in opposite directions over time.

Portfolio variance is affected not only by the variance of each asset's return but also by **covariances** between returns. [See also **Covariance**] The variance of a two-asset portfolio is computed by summing the squared weights of each asset times the asset's variance and then adding a term to capture the covariance of the two assets:

$$\sigma_p^2 = w_1^2 \sigma_1^2 + w_2^2 \sigma_2^2 + 2 w_1 w_2 \operatorname{cov}(R_1, R_2),$$

where w_1 and w_2 are weights associated with first and second security respectively. σ_1^2 and σ_2^2 are variance for first and second security, respectively. $\operatorname{Cov}(R_1, R_2)$ represents covariance between R_1 and R_2.

We can also express the portfolio variance in terms of the **correlation** coefficient as [See also **Correlation**]:

$$\sigma_p^2 = w_1^2 \sigma_1^2 + w_2^2 \sigma_2^2 + 2 w_1 w_2 \rho_{12} \sigma_1 \sigma_2,$$

where ρ_{12} represents the correlation coefficient between R_1 and R_2.

The standard deviation of the portfolio's returns is simply the square root of this variance.

71. Portfolio Cushion

In general, portfolio insurance can be thought of as holding two portfolios, the first portfolio can be viewed as the safe or riskless portfolio with value equal to the level of protection desired. This level is called the floor and is the lowest value the portfolio can have. For certain strategies this can be held constant or allowed to change over time as market conditions or needs change. The second portfolio consists of the difference between the total value of the portfolio and the floor, commonly called the portfolio cushion. These assets consist of a leveraged position in risky assets. To insure the portfolio, the cushion should be managed as never to fall below zero in value because of the limited-liability property of common stock.

72. Portfolio Immunization

Making a portfolio relatively insensitive to interest rates.

73. Portfolio Insurance

The practice of using options or dynamic hedge strategies to provide protection against investment losses while maintaining upside potential. In addition, it can use an appropriate mix of treasury bills and security to create a payoff pattern identical to the pattern of an option on the underlying security. This kind of artificial option can be used to perform portfolio insurance. [See also Rubinstein (1985) for details]

74. Portfolio Management

Process of combining securities in a portfolio tailored to the investor's preferences and needs, monitoring that portfolio, and evaluating its performance.

75. Portfolio Opportunity Set

The expected return-standard deviation pairs of all portfolios that can be constructed from a given set of assets.

76. Position Limit

The maximum position a trader (or group of traders acting together) is allowed to hold.

77. Positive Covenant

Part of the indenture or loan agreement that specifies an action that the company must abide by.

78. Positive Float

The firm's bank cash is greater than its book cash until the check's presentation.

79. Post

Particular place on the floor of an exchange where transactions in stocks listed on the exchange occur.

80. Post Audit

The major proportion of control phase for capital budgeting process is the post audit of the project, through which past decisions are evaluated for the benefit of future capital expenditure.

81. Power Option

An option where the payoff is based on the price of an asset raised to a power. For example, a power option for call can be defined as $(S^b - K^b, 0)$, where S and K are stock price per share and exercise price per share respectively; b is the power.

82. Preauthorized Check System

A preauthorized check (PAC) system is a type of cash collection arrangement that may be more useful to firms such as insurance, finance, leasing, and mortgage companies. The PAC is a commercial instrument that is used to regularly transfer funds between demand deposit accounts. Through such a preauthorized indemnification agreement, the collecting firm is authorized to draw a check at specified intervals and in specified amounts on the customer's demand deposit account. An example is a monthly mortgage payment. The PAC reduces mail, processing, and collection float and ensures that the company gets its money by a specified date.

83. Preferred Habitat Theory

Investors prefer specific maturity ranges but can be induced to switch if premiums are sufficient. In other words, markets are not so segmented that an appropriate premium cannot attract an investor who prefers one bond maturity to consider a different one. [See also **Market segmentation theory**]

84. Preferred Stock

A type of stock whose holders are given certain priority over common stockholders in the payment of dividends. Usually the dividend rate is fixed at the time of issue. Preferred stockholders normally do not receive voting rights.

85. Premium Bonds

When a bond's price exceeds its par value, it is said to be selling at a *premium*, and it is called a premium bond. In most cases where the bond sells at a premium, interest rates have fallen after the bond's issue.

The price of a premium bond will fall as it nears maturity if the market rate remains the same, since at maturity its price will equal its par value.

86. Premium on a Bond

Difference between the price of a bond and its par value when the price is higher. When the price is lower than the par value, then this difference is the discount on a bond.

87. Premium on an Option

The forward rate either will be at a discount or a premium to the spot rate. A currency is selling at a premium if it can purchase more units of foreign currency in the forward market than in the spot market. [See also **discount**]

88. Prepaid Forward Contract

A forward contract calling for payment today and delivery of the asset or commodity at a time in the future.

89. Prepaid Forward Price

The price the buyer pays today for a prepaid forward contract.

90. Prepaid Swap

A swap contract calling for payment today and delivery of the asset or commodity at multiple specified times in the future.

91. Prepayment Function and Model

A function estimating the prepayment of principal on a portfolio of mortgages in terms of other variables. Refinancing and housing turnover are two principal sources for prepayment. There are several prepayment models to estimate the rate of prepayment. The most well-known model is the model developed by public security association.

92. Prepayment Penalties

Prepayment penalties, which lender charges borrower for his (or her) prepayment on mortgage, are deigned to compensate for the uncertainty in asset management caused by a prepayment. Lenders face potentially large volumes of prepayments if market yields fall and borrowers with fixed mortgage rates refinance their homes at lower rates.

93. Prepayment Speed

The percentage of the outstanding principal that is prepaid above and beyond normal amortization. [See also **Prepayment function and model**]

94. Present Value

The present value of a cash flow is the amount which, if it were invested today at r percent per year for n years, would grow to equal the future cash flow. The present value (PV) represents the maximum price we are willing to pay today in order to receive the future cash flow, FV.

To solve for PV, the present value, we obtain

$$PV = FV_n \times \left[\frac{1}{(1+r)^n}\right].$$

Like future values, present values are additive as long as the present values occur at the same point in time. If a problem involves several future cash flows, one can easily find their total present value simply by adding the individual present values at time zero.

95. Present Value Factor

Factor used to calculate an estimate of the present value of an amount to be received in a future period. Calculated as $1/(1+r)^n$, where r is the discount rate; and n is the number of compounding periods. [See also **Present value**]

96. Price Participation

The extent to which an equity-linked note benefits from an increase in the price of the stock of index to which it is linked.

97. Price Risk

It is one of the components of the interest rate risk, another component is the coupon-reinvestment risk. Price risk occurs if interest rate change before the target date and the bond is sold prior to maturity. At that time the market price will differ from the value at the time of purchase. If rate increase after the purchase date, the price the bond would be sold at would be below what had been anticipated. If the rate decline, the realized price would be above what had been expected. Increase in interest rates will reduce the market value of a bond below its par value. However it will increase the return from the reinvestment of the coupon interest payment. Conversely, decrease in interest will increase the market value of a bond above its par value but decrease the return on the reinvestment of the coupons. In order for a bond to be protected from the change in interest rate

after the purchase. The price risk and coupon re-investment must offset each other.

98. Price Takers

Individuals who responds to rates and prices by acting as though they have no influence on them.

99. Price Value of a Basis Point

The change in the value of a fixed-income asset resulting from a one basis point change in the asset's yield to maturity. One basis point represents 0.25 percent.

100. Price Volatility

A factor that is the single most important variable affecting the speculative value of the option is the price volatility of the underlying stock. The greater the probability of significant change in the price of the stock, the most likely it is that the option can be exercised at a profit before expiration.

101. Price/Earnings Ratio (P/E Ratio)

The ratio of a stock's price to its earnings per share. Also referred to as the P/E multiple. The P/E ratio tells us how much stock purchasers must pay per dollar of earnings that the firm generates. [See also **Market value ratios**]

102. Price-to-Book-Value Ratio

[See **Market value ratios**]

103. Price-Variable Cost Margin

A factor affecting business risk is the firm's ability to maintain a constant, positive difference between price and per-unit variable cost:

$$Margin = \frac{Price\ per\ unit - variable\ cost\ per\ unit}{Price}.$$

This is one of the factors used to determine the business risk. [See also **Business risk**]

104. Price-Weighted Index

In a price-weighted index the basic approach to sum the prices of the component securities used in the index and divide this sum by the number of components; in other worlds, to compute a simple arithmetic average. The Dow-Jones Industrial Average (DJIA) is the most familiar index of this type. To allow for the impact of stock splits and stock dividends, which could destroy the consistency and comparability of price-weighted index data over time, an adjustment of either the reported price data or the divisor itself is required. [See also **Dow Jones Industrial Average Index**].

105. Pricing Grid

A schedule of credit spreads listed by credit rating that are applied to either a loan or Credit-Sensitive Note (CSN) upon an up(down) grade of the obligor of issuer. If the spreads are specified at market level, then such terms reduce the volatility of the value across all non-default credit quality migrations by keeping the instrument close to par.

106. Primary Capital

The sum of common stock, perpetual preferred stock, surplus, undivided profits, contingency and other capital reserves, valuation reserves, mandatory convertible securities, and minority interest in consolidated subsidiaries at a bank.

107. Primary Market

The primary market is the market for original securities, or first-time issues. For example, a corporation first sells its stock to the public in an initial public offering. Such a sale is a primary market transaction. If, after additional growth, the firm determines that it needs more equity capital, it can sell another new issue of stock in the primary market. In general, whenever a firm raises money by selling shares, bonds, commercial paper, or other securities to investors, it does so in pri-mary market transactions. Government issues of Treasury bills and bonds, as well as state and local government security issues, also occur in the primary market.

108. Prime Rate

The rate of interest charged by commercial banks vary in two ways: the general level of interest rates varies over time, and, at any given time, different borrowers pay different rates because of varying degrees of creditworthiness. The base rate for most commercial banks traditionally has been the prime rate, although in times of soaring market interest rates, some of the larger banks experiment with marginal pricing schemes. The prime rate is the rate that commercial banks charge their most creditworthy business customers for short-term borrowing. The financial press splashes news of any change in this rate across the front page. Congress and the business community speculate about the prime's influence on economic activity, because it is the baseline rate for loan pricing in most loan agreements.

In the latter part of 1971, a large, money-center bank instituted a floating prime rate linked by a formula to the market-determined commercial paper rate. The formula required weekly reviews of the prime rate, with adjustments in minimum steps of one-eighth of a percentage point. The formula kept the prime approximately 50 basis points above the average rate on 90-day commercial paper placed through dealers. The choice of the commercial paper rate reflected the ease of substituting short-term bank loans for commercial paper. Historically, the prime has served as a base line for loan pricing; a loan contract might state its interest rate as "prime plus two" or "120 percent of prime."

However, as the banking industry has begun to price its loans and services more aggressively, the prime rate has become less important. As the use of the prime rate has declined, compensating balances have become less popular, as well. The current trend is to price a loan at a rate above the bank's marginal cost of funds, which typically is reflected by the interest rate on a certificate of deposit. The bank adds an interest-rate margin to this cost of funds, and the sum becomes the rate it charges the borrower. This rate changes daily, in line with the bank's money market rates.

109. Primitive Security, Derivative Security

A *primitive security* is an instrument such as a stock or bond for which payments depend only on the financial status of its issuer. A *derivative security* is created from the set of primitive securities to yield returns that depend on factors beyond the characteristics of the issuer and that may be related to prices of other assets.

110. Principal

The value of a bond that must be repaid at maturity. Also called the face value or the par value.

111. Principal Components Analysis

A multivariate analysis aimed at finding a small number of factors that describe most of the variation in a large number of correlated variables. (Similar to a factor analysis).

112. Principal-Agent Problem

The principals, or owners of the firm hire agents, or managers, to run the firm in the best interests of the principals. But ethical lapses, self-interest, or the owners' lack of trust in the managers can lead to conflicts of interest and suspicions between the two parties. This problem in corporate governance is called the principal-agent problem.

The shareholders of a firm elect a board of directors. In theory, the board's role is to oversee managers and ensure that they are working in the best interests of the shareholders. In practice, however, the board often has a closer relationship with management than with the shareholders. For example, it is not unusual for the firm's top execu-

tives to sit on the firm's board of directors, and the firm's top executives often nominate candidates for board seats. These relationships can obscure loyalties and make the board a toothless watchdog for shareholders' interest.

Managers, acting as agents, may pursue their own self-interest by increasing their salaries, the size of their staffs, or their perquisites (better known as "perks"), which might include club memberships and the use of company planes or luxurious company cars. Management, in conjunction with the Board, may seek to fend off takeovers that would allow shareholders to sell their shares at a price above the current market price, or they may try to preempt such merger or acquisition attempts by seeking changes in the corporate charter that would make such takeovers difficult to pursue.

Other examples of principal-agent relationships that one may relate to: voters (principals) elect officeholders (agents) to work in the best interest of the public; but political action committee (PAC) contributions to political campaigns may affect politician's actions if elected. Investors (principals) trust the advice of stockbrokers (agents) when investing their savings; but many stockbrokers earn their paycheck by generating commissions on trading. Accountants and lawyers (agents) often bill their clients (principals) by the number of hours they work, irrespective of whether the client's tax bill was minimized or the court case was won.

113. Principle of Diversification

Highly diversified portfolios will have negligible unsystematic risks. In other words, unsystematic risks disappear in portfolios, and only systematic risks survive.

114. Private Placement

Firms in the *Fortune* 500 obtain over one-half of their long-term debt from private sources. These private sources include loans from banks and finance companies, as well as private placements of debt. If the largest US firms with access to the public debt market do most of their long-term borrowing in the private market, smaller public and private firms rely on privately arranged loans even more heavily.

A private placement or sale of debt is similar to a private placement of equity. The borrower and lenders negotiate the terms of the placement: the amount of the loan, its interest rate, the timing of cash flows, lender security, and covenants. An investment bank may act as a broker to help place the private debt with accredited investors (those who meet SEC rules regarding net worth and investment experience). Most privately placed debt matures in 5 to 20 years and pays fixed interest rates.

Large insurance companies and pension funds are major purchasers of private debt. These lenders typically have long investment horizons and low liquidity needs, so they are ideal private placement investors.

By avoiding the need to register securities with the SEC, a borrower can save on some of the upfront expenses of issuing debt securities. Lack of registration, however, makes private placements less liquid than publicly issued bonds. Some market participants have attempted to increase the liquidity of the private placement market, such as NASDAQs PORTAL (Private Offering, Resale, and Trading through Automated Linkage) system. Even with such trading, private placements can be bought and sold only among accredited investors. Due to the lack of public disclosure, the investing public is not allowed under SEC rules to trade or invest in private placements.

At year-end 1991, almost every one of the industrial firms with investment-grade S&P bond ratings had total firm assets exceeding $500 million. This statistic suggests that most small firms are shut out of the public capital markets because of those markets' aversion to below-investment-grade issues. Private placements play a major role in financing growth and expansion for many of these small-sized and medium-sized firms. Private placements do this without imposing excessive

interest expenses. The effect of liquidity risk appears to be reduced by a number of different factors, including long investment horizons and little need for immediate liquidity by the investors, such as life insurers; the freer flow of information that occurs during negotiations; the ability to negotiate covenants; and the access that lenders have to firm-specific information (including discussions with top management and on-site plant visits) as they conduct their due diligence analysis. Should default occur, the ability to renegotiate terms and conditions also easier than in the case of a default on a public issue.

115. Private Placement of Equity

A private placement raises funds by allowing outside private investors to purchase shares in the firm. Such a deal may be difficult to arrange, however, as any new investor(s) may suspect the original owners' motives and question their ability to successfully invest the funds to create future value. Arrangements for private placements may be made by a business broker or an investment banker, who earns a commission for finding a qualified investor. To limit the cost and ensure the compatibility of the new owners, current shareholders also may seek additional investors among their friends, relatives, and other contacts.

A private placement of equity can provide needed new capital, but only at the cost of diluting ownership. The original owners now must share control, voting rights, and company profits with additional investors. In addition, there is the problem of placing a value on the firm's privately held common stock. Private firms typically lack audited financial statements and other safeguards that reduce agency costs. Thus, new investors may resist paying what the current owners feel is a fair price for their equity. Equity investments in private firms can impose a great deal of liquidity risk because no well-developed secondary market trades shares in firms that are not publicly owned. In recent years, the Securities and Exchange Commission (SEC) has taken some steps to increase liquidity in the private placement market. Nonetheless, a great deal of liquidity risk still remains for investors in private firms.

116. Pro Forma Financial Statements

Financial statements with projected of forecasted balance sheet and income statement data. In addition, it also includes forecasts of stock price per share, earnings per share, dividend per share, new equity issues and new debt issues. [See also **Percentage of sales method**]

117. Probability Distribution

[See **Normal distribution**]

118. Probability of Default

[See **Default probability**]

119. Probate

Legal act of submitting a will before a court to verify authenticity of the document.

120. Problem Loans

Loan currently in default or expected to obtain default status.

121. Processing Float

[See **Float**]

122. Product Differentiation

Product differentiation can generate positive net present values. Differentiation comes form consumers' belief in a difference between firms' products. Differentiation leads to an imperfect market where a firm can set prices above marginal costs, thus giving the firm some competitive advantage over its rivals. Potential sources of differentiation include advertising and promotion expenditures, marketing skills, brand loyalty, R&D, and quality differences.

123. Profit

The payoff less the future value of the original cost to acquire the position. In accounting, profit refers the net income which is the last item of an income statement.

124. Profit Diagram

A graph plotting the profit on a position against a range of prices for the underlying asset. This diagram is frequently used in analyzing option strategy.

125. Profit Margin

Profits divided by total operating revenue. The net profit margin (net income divided by total operating revenue) and the gross profit margin (earnings before interest and taxes divided by the total operating revenue) reflect the firm's ability to produce a good or service at a high or low cost.

Higher profit margins generate more net income, larger additions to retained earnings, and faster growth, when all else is held constant. Should growth outpace the planned rate, the firm can seek to finance the unexpected growth by raising its prices and/or reducing expenses in an attempt to increase its profit margin. If growth falls short of the planned rate, the firm may have to reduce prices, and therefore its profit margin, to stimulate sales. [See also **Profitability ratios**]

126. Profitability Index

A discounted cash flow technique for evaluating capital budgeting projects is the profitability index (*PI*), also called the *benefit/cost ratio*. The *PI* method computes the ratio between the present values of the cash flows and initial investment as:

$$PI = \frac{Present\ value\ of\ the\ cash\ flows}{Initial\ cost}$$

$$= \frac{\sum_{t=1}^{N} \frac{CF_t}{(1+r)^t}}{I}.$$

The *PI* measures the relative benefits of undertaking a project, namely the present value of benefits received for each dollar invested. A *PI* of 2, for example, means that the project returns $2 for every $1 invested, in present value terms. Since it would be foolish to invest in a project that returns less than a dollar for every dollar invested, the profitability index has a naturally objective decision rule: *The firm should accept a project that has a profitability index greater than 1.0 and reject a project that has a PI less than 1.0.*

The relationship between *PI* and NPV should be clear. Whenever NPV is positive, *PI* exceeds 1.0. Likewise, whenever NPV is negative, *PI* is less than 1.0. Thus, as with the NPV and IRR, the NPV and *PI* always on which projects will enhance shareholder wealth and which will diminish it. Therefore, the NPV, IRR, and *PI* always will agree as to whether a project should be accepted or rejected.

The profitability index considers all relevant cash flows, accounts for the time value of money, and specifies an objective decision criterion. Like IRR, however, *PI* measures *relative* project attractiveness; it indicates which projects add to shareholder wealth, but it gives little insight as to the amount of the change. Thus, like IRR, *PI* rankings of the attractiveness of mutually exclusive projects may differ from NPV rankings.

127. Profitability Ratios

Profitability ratios show the ability of a firm to use its sales, assets, and equity to generate returns. The profit margin, or return on sales, represents the proportion of each sales dollar that becomes profit or net income to the firm. The return on assets ratio, or ROA (sometimes called return on investment, or ROI), measures how efficiently the firm uses its total assets to generate income. Profit margin and return on assets are computed as:

$$Profit\ margin = \frac{Net\ income}{Sales}$$

$$Return\ on\ assets = \frac{Net\ income}{Total\ assets}.$$

The return on assets ratio can be broken into two components; it equals the product of the profit margin and total asset turnover ratio:

$$Return\ on\ assets\ (ROA) = Profit\ margin \\ \times Total\ asset\ turnover$$

$$\frac{Net\ income}{Assets} = \frac{Net\ income}{Sales} \times \frac{Sales}{Total\ assets}.$$

This ratio gives two general strategies by which a firm can generate a high ROA. A firm can have a high profit margin with a low turnover (which is often the case for a jewelry store) or a low profit margin with a high turnover (which is often the case for a supermarket).

The return on equity ratio (ROE) measures profitability with respect to the stockholders' investment in the firm. It is computed as:

$$ROE = \frac{Net\ income}{Total\ equity}.$$

Like return on assets, ROE can be broken down into component parts to improve insight into the means by which the firm generates income. The return on equity is identical to return on assets multiplied by the equity multiplier:

$$\frac{Net\ income}{Total\ equity} = \frac{Net\ income}{Total\ assets} \times \frac{Total\ assets}{Total\ equity}.$$

Since ROA is itself comprised of two other ratios, we obtain:

$$ROE = Profit\ margin \times Asset\ turnover \\ \times Equity\ multiplier;$$

$$\frac{Net\ income}{Total\ equity} = \frac{Net\ income}{Sales} \times \frac{Sales}{Total\ assets} \\ \times \frac{Total\ assets}{Total\ equity}.$$

This analysis shows that a firm's return on equity may change from one year to the next or may differ from a competitor's ROE as a result of differences in profit margin, asset turnover, or leverage. Unlike the other measures of profitability, ROE directly reflects a firm's use of leverage, or debt. If a firm assumes more liabilities to finance assets, the equity multiplier will rise and holding other factors constant, the ROE will increase. This leveraging of a firm's return on equity does not imply greater operating efficiency, only a greater use of debt financing. Setting an optimum proportion of debt is part of the capital structure decision.

Breaking ROE into its component parts is called Du Pont analysis, named after the company that popularized the technique. By examining differences in the components of ROE either over time or across firms, an analyst can gain information about the strengths and weaknesses of firms. Du Pont analysis can break ROE into its components and illustrate how the components can, in turn, be broken into their constituent parts for analysis. Thus, an indication that a firm's ROE has increased as a result of higher turnover can lead to study of the turnover ratio, using data from several years, to determine if the increase has resulted from higher sales volume, better management of assets, or some combination of the two.

It seems obvious that an analyst should prefer higher profitability ratios to lower profitability ratios. Still, the analyst must examine financial statements to determine the reasons for rising profitability and to verify that it represents truly good news about a firm. In an inflationary environment, for example, higher profitability may come from increases in sales revenues due to higher prices, while many expenses (such as FIFO inventory, depreciation, and interest expense) may be based upon historical costs. Higher profits and profitability ratios also could occur because of reductions in R&D spending or advertising expenses; such reductions may benefit the bottom line in the short run, but cutbacks in technological innovation and marketing may hurt the firm in the long run.

Changing from one generally accepted accounting principle to another also may have the effect of raising revenue, reducing expenses, and increasing profit without any real change in firm operations. Higher profits also may arise from extraordinary items, such as a successful lawsuit, or from asset sales; the analysis should remove special items from net income to obtain a clearer picture of firm profitability. The analyst always should compare several consecutive financial reports and, once again, read the financial statement footnotes to confirm that higher profitability really does represent better firm performance, and not inflation, cosmetic expense slashing, changes in GAAP, or nonrecurring items.

128. Program Trading

Coordinated buy orders and sell orders of entire portfolios, usually with the aid of computers, often to achieve index arbitrage objectives. It encompasses several modern investment strategies. The narrowest definition, of program trading is the simultaneous placement of buy and sell orders for group of stock totaling 1 million or more. A common and controversial form of program trading is the simultaneous trading of stock and stock futures to profit from the change in the spread between the two, sometimes called index arbitrage.

129. Project Finance

Project finance is a technique where it is appropriate to use project-specific financing costs as required rates of return. This technique has gained popularity in recent years; it has been used to finance a variety of projects, including oil and gas development projects, R&D partnerships, and factory construction.

Project finance makes sense when a project's accounts are separated from the firm's other asset and cash flow accounts. Additionally, the project's assets must be financed by specific sources of funds whose only recourse in the case of default or project failure is to the assets of the project; in other words, the sponsoring firm is not liable for the debts of the project. Such a project also must have a definite termination time, rather than operating as a going-concern. In such cases, we can compare the project-specific financing costs to the projects returns. Returns in excess of project costs accrue to the parent firm's shareholders.

130. Projected Benefit Obligation (PBO)

PBO is a measure of sponsor's pension liability that includes projected increases in salary up to the expected age of retirement.

131. Promissory Note

Basically, a promissory note is an IOU in which the buyer promises to pay the seller a certain amount by the specified date for a designated order, all in writing and signed by the buyer.

132. Proprietorship

Proprietorships outnumber all other forms of business organizations in the US. A proprietorship is simply a business owned by one person. Setting up a business is fairly simple and inexpensive – seldom more complicated than applying for a city or state license. All income is taxed as personal income to the proprietor. Depending on this person's filing status and income level, this can be an advantage or a disadvantage. For example, depending upon the owner's level of taxable Income, a proprietorship may owe more or less tax than a corporation with the same level of taxable income.

As the firm has one owner, this person's expertise determines much of the success of the firm. If additional expertise is needed, the owner must hire someone. The life of the proprietorship ends when the owner dies; in general, a proprietorship is not an asset that can be easily valued and sold.

Agency costs are nil in proprietorships, as the manager is the owner, and he or she presumably will make decisions that reflect his or her best interests. The ability to raise capital income is limited to the owner's personal wealth and credit line (although generous friends or relatives may help him or her).

Proprietorships have unlimited liability, which makes the proprietor solely responsible for all debts of the business. Should bankruptcy occur, the owner's personal assets – financial holdings, cars, house – may be forfeited to settle any debts. Losses may exceed what the proprietor has invested in the firm.

133. Prospectus

To offer stock for sale, the firm distributes a prospectus, which contains much of the same information that appears in the SEC filing. During the waiting period, the firm can distribute a **red herring** to prospective investors. [See also **Red herring**]

134. Protective Covenant

A provision specifying requirements of collateral, sinking fund, dividend policy, etc., designed to protect the interests of bondholders.

135. Protective Put

Purchase of stock combined with a put option that guarantees minimum proceeds equal to the put's exercise price.

136. Proxy

A grant of authority by the shareholder to transfer his or her voting rights to someone else.

137. Proxy Contest

Attempt to gain control of a firm by soliciting a sufficient number of stockholder votes to replace the existing management.

138. Prudent Man Rule

Requirement that a fiduciary exercise discretion, prudence, and sound judgment in managing the assets of a third party.

139. Public Issue

Sales of securities to the public.

140. Public Offering, Private Placement

A *public offering* consists of bonds sold in the primary market to the general public; a *private placement* is sold directly to a limited number of institutional investors [See also **Private placement**].

141. Public Warehousing

Public warehousing, sometimes called terminal warehousing, is similar to **field warehousing**, except that the physical inventory is transferred to and stored in a warehouse operated by an independent warehousing company instead of in a segregated section of the borrower's premises. [See also **Field warehousing**] The mechanics of the financing arrangement remain the same: no inventory is released to the borrower until it repays the corresponding part of the loan. Warehouse financing is very common in the food and lumber industries. Canned goods, in particular, account for almost 20 percent of all public warehouse loans; however, almost any nonperishable and easily marketable commodity may be used.

142. Publicly Traded Option

A publicly traded option is an agreement between two individuals who have no relationship with the corporation whose shares underlie the option. When a publicly traded option is exercised, money and shares are exchanged between the individuals and the corporation receives no funds. [See also **Warrant**]

143. Pull-to-Par

The reversion of a bond's price to its par value at maturity.

144. Purchase Accounting

An accounting method for acquisitions in which the assets and liabilities of the combined firm reflect a revaluation of assets and liabilities of the subject firms, thus recognizing the value of goodwill and other intangibles. [See also **Purchase method**]

145. Purchase Method

The purchase method of accounting for business combinations corresponds to the basic accounting principles for the acquisition of assets. However, in the case of business combinations, the procedure is complicated because several assets and liabilities may be acquired and more than cash may be given. Also, the excess of the price paid for the acquired asset over its book value is reflected as goodwill on the balance sheet of the acquiring firm and is amortized over a period not exceeding 40 years. Goodwill is not deductible for tax purposes, so the net result of the purchase method is a decrease in accounting earnings without the corresponding tax benefits. Hence, the purchase method is not favored by acquiring firms.

146. Purchased Call

A long position in a call. It refers to buy a call which is available in the market.

147. Purchased Put

A long position in a put. It refers to buy a put which is available in the market.

148. Purchasing Power Parity (PPP)

The purchasing power parity relates the changes in exchange rates to the relative differences in the respective rates of inflation among nations. In other words, it implies that the exchange rate adjusts to keep purchasing power constant among currency. For example, if the expected inflation rate in England is 10 percent and the expected inflation rate in the US is 5 percent, one would expect the interest rate in England to be 5 percent higher than a comparable rate in the US. Likewise, one would expect the English pound sterling to depreciate by 5 percent relative to the US dollar. Without these relationships, an arbitrageur could make a riskless profit by buying or selling a spot currency in the foreign exchange market, investing in the money market with the more favorable interest rate, and hedging these transactions by selling or buying the currency forward for a similar time period. This procedure, called interest rate arbitrage, links the foreign exchange market to the money market. [See also **Interest rate parity**]

149. Purchasing-Power Risk

The variability of return caused by inflation, which erodes the real value of the return. Purchasing power risk is related to the possible shrinkage in the real value of a security even though its normal value is increasing. For example, if the nominal value of a security goes from $100 to $200. The owner of this security is pleased because the investment has doubled in value. But suppose that, concurrent with the value increase of 100 percent, the rate of inflation is 200 percent, that is, a basket of goods costing $100 when the security was purchased now costs $300. The investor has a " money illusion" of being better off in nominal terms. The investment did increase from $100 to $200; nevertheless, in real terms, whereas the $100 at time zero could purchase a complete basket of goods, after the inflation only 2/3 of a basket can now be purchased. Hence, the investor has suffered a loss of value.

150. Pure Discount Bond

Bonds that pay no coupons and only pay back face value at maturity. Also referred to as "bullets" and "zeros." [See also **Discount bond**]

151. Pure Play Method

The pure play method estimates the beta of the proposed project based on information from firms that are in similar lines of business as the project.

If the capital budgeting project involves an expansion to another country, perhaps a firm in that country will qualify as a pure play. The project's systematic risk can be estimated by regressing the foreign firm's stock market returns on those of a US market index. The foreign firm's stock returns should be adjusted for exchange rate fluctuations, so exchange rate risk is included in the analysis.

The main drawback to the pure play method is that the analyst must find one or more publicly traded firms that are close proxies to the project under review. Only for publicly traded firms can the analyst find stock return data from which to estimate beta. The ideal proxy firms are single-product firms so the analysis can focus on the systematic risk of the particular project under consideration. A firm with many different product lines will complicate the comparison, as its betas will reflect the systematic risk of the firm's overall product mix, rather than the project's line of business.

152. Pure Yield Pickup Swap

In a pure yield-pickup swap, there is no expectation of market changes but a simple attempt to increase yield. Basically, two bonds are examined to establish their difference in yield to maturity, with a future adjustment to consider the impact of interim reinvestment of coupons at an assumed rate of return between now and the maturity date.

153. Put

A put is an option to sell a fixed number of shares of common stock. It is a right instead of an obligation.

154. Put Bond

A bond that the holder may choose either to exchange for par value at some date or to extend for a given number of years.

155. Put Option

A put option gives the holder the right to sell a certain number of shares of common stock at a price on or before the expiration date of the option. In purchasing a put, the owner of the shares has bought the right to sell those shares by the expiration date at the exercise price. As with calls, one can create, or write, a put, accepting the obligation to buy shares.

156. Put Provision

Gives holder of a floating-rate bond the right to redeem his or her note at par on the coupon payment date.

157. Putable Bonds

Putable bonds (sometimes called retractable bonds) allow investors to force the issuer to redeem them prior to maturity. Indenture terms differ as to the circumstances when an investor can "put" the bond to the issuer prior to the maturity date and receive its par value. Some bond issues can be put only on certain dates. Some can be put to the issuer in case of a bond rating downgrade. Still others, nicknamed *super poison puts*, are putable only in the case of an event such as a merger, leveraged buyout, or major financial restructuring and subsequent rating downgrade below investment qual-

ity (BBB). In any of these situations, bond investors would suffer a loss of value as the bond's yield would have to rise and its price fall to compensate for the increase in credit risk. The put option allows the investor to receive the full face value of the bond, plus accrued interest. Since this protection is valuable, investors must pay extra for it. Issuers can lower their debt costs by attaching put provisions to their bond issues.

158. Put-Call-parity

A relationship stating that the difference between the premiums of a call and a put with the same strike price and time to expiration equals the difference between the present value of the forward price and the present value of the strike price.

$$C + Xe^{-rT} = P + S,$$

where C is defined as the call price per share; X is the strike price; P is the put price per share; S is the stock price per share; r is the risk-free rate and T is the constant period.

159. Puttable Bond

A bond where the holder has the right to sell it back to the issuer at certain predetermined times for a predetermined price share.

160. Puttable Swap

A swap where one side has the right to terminate the swap early. On the other hand, if a swap which one party has the option to extend the life of swap beyond the specified period is called extendable swap.

Q

1. Q Ratio or Tobin's Q Ratio

Market value of firm's assets divided by replacement value of firm's assets. It can be approximated by market/book ratio.

2. Quality Financial Statements

Analysts sometimes speak of the *quality* of a firm's earnings, or the quality of its balance sheet. In general, quality financial statements are those that accurately reflect reality; they lack accounting tricks and one-time changes designed to make the firm appear stronger than it really is. Financial statements reflect reality when accounting income is a good approximation to economic income.

The Balance Sheet

A quality balance sheet typically shows conservative use of debt or leverage, which keeps the potential of financial distress due to debt service quite low. Limited use of debt also implies the firm has unused borrowing capacity; should an attractive investment opportunity arise, it can draw upon that unused capacity to invest wisely for the shareholders' benefit.

A quality balance sheet shows assets whose market values exceed their book values. In general, inflation and historical cost accounting should keep book values below market values. Beyond these accounting effects, a capable management team and the existence of intangible assets, such as goodwill, trademarks, or patents, will make the market values of firm's assets exceed their book values. Situations that might reduce assets' market values below their book values include: use of outdated, technologically inferior assets; unwanted out-of-fashion inventory; and the presence of non-performing assets on the firm's books (as when a bank writes off a nonperforming loan).

The presence of off-balance sheet liabilities also harms the quality of a balance sheet by hiding economically important information. Such liabilities may include joint ventures and loan commitments or guarantees to subsidiaries.

The Income Statement

High quality earnings are *recurring* earnings that arise from sales to the firm's regular stream of customers. One-time and nonrecurring effects, such as accounting changes, mergers, and asset sales, should be ignored when examining earnings. Also, costs must not appear artificially low as a result of unusual and short-lived input price reductions. Unexpected exchange rate fluctuations that work in the firm's favor to raise revenues or reduce costs also should be viewed as nonrecurring.

Quality earnings are revealed by conservative accounting principles that do not overstate revenues or understate costs. The quality of the income statement rises as its statement of earnings more closely approximates cash. Suppose that a firm sells furniture on credit, allowing customers to make monthly payments. A high-quality income statement should recognize this revenue using the installment principle (i.e., the statement of sales revenue should reflect only the cash collected from sales each month during the year). A low-quality sheet would recognize 100 percent of the revenue from a sale at the time of sale, even though payments may stretch well into the following year. The footnotes to the income statement would tell the analyst which method was used.

3. Quality Risk

The exact standard or grade of the commodity required by the hedger is not covered by the futures contract. Therefore, the price movement of commodity grade A may be different from the price movement of commodity grade B, which will cause the basis to change and prevent the hedger from forming a perfect hedge.

4. Quality Spread

The difference in market yields between yield on risky securities and matched maturity/duration Treasury securities.

5. Quantile

The percentage of data points below a given value. The qth quantile of the distribution F is the smallest value x such that $F(x) \geq q$.

6. Quantity Risk

The exact amount of the commodity needed by the hedger is not available by a single futures contract or any integer multiple thereof. Hence, the amount of the commodity is not hedged exactly; this prevents the hedger from forming a perfect hedge, and the underhedged or overhedged amount is subject to risk.

7. Quanto (Cross Currency Derivative)

A derivative where the payoff is defined in terms of value of variables associated with one currency but is paid in another currency. Therefore, this kind of derivative is a cross-currency derivative.

8. Quasi-Arbitrage

The replacement of one asset or position with another that has equivalent risk and a higher expected rate of return. This is an implicit instead of an explicit arbitrage.

9. Quasi-Random Sequence

A quasi-random sequence (also called a low discrepancy sequence) is a sequence pf representative samples from a probability distribution. Descriptions of the use of quasi-random sequences can be found in Brotherton-Ratcliffe (1994).

Quasi-random sampling is similar to stratified sampling. The objective is to sample representative values for the underlying variables. In stratified sampling it is assumed that we know in advance how many samples will be taken. A quasi-random sampling scheme is more flexible. The samples are taken in such a way that we are always "filling in" gaps between existing samples. At each stage of the simulation the points sampled are roughly evenly spaced throughout the probability space. [See **Stratified sampling**]

10. Quick (Acid-Test) Ratio

A measure of liquidity similar to the current ratio except for exclusion of inventories in the numerator. The formula is:

$$\frac{Cash + Receivables + Marketable\ Securities}{Current\ Liabilities}.$$

The quick ratio is a better measure of liquidity than the current ratio for firms whose inventory is not readily convertible into cash. [See also **Liquidity ratios**]

11. Quick Assets

Current assets minus inventories.

R

1. Rainbow Option

An option that has a payoff based on the maximum or minimum of two (or more) risky assets and cash. For example, the payoff to a rainbow call is max (S_t, Q_t, K), where S_t and Q_t are risky asset prices. This kind of option is often called two-color rainbow option, because the maximum and the minimum prices of two assets look very much like the shape of rainbow in a two-dimensional diagram, with two asset prices as the two axes.

2. Random Equation (Itô Equation)

The *Itô* equation as defined in equation A is a random equation. The domain of the equation is $[0, \infty) \times \Omega$ with the first argument t denoting time and taking values continuously in the interval $[0, \infty)$, and the second argument w denoting a random element taking values from a random set Ω. The range of the equation is the real numbers or real vectors. For simplicity, only the real numbers, denoted by R, are considered as the range of equation.

$$dS(t.w) = \mu[t, S(t, w)]dt + \sigma[t, S(t, w)]dZ(t, w). \qquad (A)$$

3. Random Walk

Theories that stock price changes from day to day are at random; the changes are independent of each other and have the same probability distribution. Mathematically, it is a stochastic process, $X(t)$, in which increments, $e(t)$, are independent and identically distributed:

$$X(t) = X(t - h) + e(t), \qquad (A)$$

where $e(t)$ is the random error. Under the weak-form efficient market, the relationship between stock prices per share in period t (P_t) and that in

period $t-1$ (P_{t-1}) can be defined as:

$$P_t = P_{t-1} + expected\ return + (e_t). \qquad (B)$$

If the stock prices follow equation (B), they are said to follow random walk.

4. Range-Forward Contract

Range-forward contract consists of a long forward contract combined with a long position in a put and a short position in a call. The strike prices are chosen so that the initial value of the call equals the initial value of the put. Since the value of the forward contract is zero initially, the value of the whole package is also zero. A range forward contract has a similar type of payoff pattern to a bull spread. [See also **Bull spread**]

5. Rank Order

A quality of data often found across credit rating categories where values consistently progress in one direction, never reversing direction. Mathematicians term this property of data, *monotonicity*.

6. Rate Anticipation Swap

A switch made in response to forecasts of interest rates.

7. Rate Sensitive

Classification of assets and liabilities that can be repriced within a specific time frame, either because they mature or carry floating or variable rates.

8. Rating

System of assigning letters to security issues indicating the perceived default risks associated with that class of issues. Rating agencies include Standard & Poor's and Moody's etc. [See also **Bond rating**]

9. Ratings Transitions

A change in the credit rating of a bond from one value to another. For example, a rating downgrade is from AAA to AA by Standard and Poor's.

10. Ratio Analysis

Ratio analysis is another means by which to gain insight regarding a firm's strengths and weaknesses. Ratios are constructed by dividing various financial statement numbers into one another. The ratios then can be examined to determine trends and reasons for changes in the financial statement quantities. Ratios are valuable tools, as they standardize balance sheet and income statement numbers; thus, differences in firm size will not affect the analysis.

There are three basic categories of ratio analysis typically are used, **time series analysis**, **cross-sectional analysis**, and **benchmark analysis**. [See also **Time series analysis**, **Cross-sectional analysis**, and **Benchmark analysis**]

There are also many categories of financial ratios. The following list represents the most basic categories:

1. Liquidity ratios
2. Asset management ratios
3. Capital structure ratios
4. Profitability ratios
5. Market value ratios.

11. Ratio Spread

Buying m calls at one strike price and selling n calls at a different strike price, with all options having the same time to maturity and same underlying asset.

12. Real Assets, Financial Assets

Real assets are land, buildings, and equipment that are used to produce goods and services. *Financial* assets are claims such as securities to the income generated by real assets.

13. Real Cash Flow

A future cash flow of capital budgeting decision is expressed in real terms if the current, or date 0, purchasing power of the cash flow is given. In other words, it is the nominal cash flow divided by (1 + inflation rate).

14. Real Interest Rate

Interest rate expressed in terms of real goods; that is, the nominal interest rate minus the expected inflation rate. [See also **Nominal risk-free interest**]

15. Real Option

Option involving real (as opposed to financial) assets. Real assets include land, plant, and machinery. Similar to options on financial securities, real options involve discretionary decisions or rights, with no obligation, to acquire or exchange an asset for a specified alternative price. The ability to value real options (e.g., to defer, expand, contract, abandon, switch use, or otherwise alter a capital investment) has brought a revolution to modern corporate resource allocation.

16. Real Risk-Free Rate of Interest

The real risk-free interest rate is the return investors require on a zero-risk instrument with no inflation. Since no such security or economic environment exists, the real risk-free rate is admittedly a theoretical concept. It forms the basis for all expected returns and observed interest rates in the economy. Although it cannot be observed directly, it can be estimated. Studies indicate that, over time, the real risk-free interest rate in a country is approximately equal to the economy's long-run growth rate. But short-term influences can lead to increase or reductions in the real risk-free rate.

For example, short-term increases in growth above long-term trends (e.g., the business cycle) can cause an economy to have a larger demand for capital than a low-growth or recessionary economy. Larger government budget deficits are an additional source of demand for capital; all else being equal, they lead to higher real risk-free interest rates.

Supply forces can affect the real risk-free rate as well. Changes in national savings affect the pool of funds available for investment. Actions by the Fed can affect the short-term supply of capital and real interest rates. As people typically spend more than they earn when they are young and then earn more than they spend as they grow older, the graying of the baby boomers in the US may boost the supply of capital through a positive influence on personal savings. Legislation offering tax shields or other inducements to save, such as individual retirement accounts (IRAs) and tax-deferred annuities, also increase savings and the supply of capital.

17. Realized Compound Yield

A measure of total return calculated by comparing total future dollars equal to coupon interest or dividends plus reinvestment income and maturity or sale value of the underlying asset, with the initial purchase price, over the appropriate number of compounding periods.

18. Rebalancing

The process of adjusting a trading position periodically. Usually the purpose is to maintain delta neutrality. In the case of options and other more complicated derivatives, the hedge that is set up is only instantaneously riskless. To remain riskless it must be rebalanced continuously. [See also **Delta hedging**]

19. Rebate

The return of a portion of unearned interest to a borrower.

20. Rebate Option

A claim that pays $ 1 at the time the price of the underlying asset reaches a barrier. [See also **Deferred rebate option**]

21. Receivable Balance Pattern

The receivable balance pattern, also known as the **payments pattern approach**, provides a way of monitoring accounts receivable. This technique examines the percentage of credit sales for a given time period (usually one month) that are still outstanding at the end of each subsequent time period.

This approach is not affected by changes in sales levels, as the average collection period (ACP) and aging schedule are, so the receivable balance pattern does not give misleading signals. In addition, this approach can develop predictions of receivable balances and collections as part of a cash flow forecast. [See also **Payments pattern approach**]

22. Receivables

Account receivables which are noninterest bearing short term extensions of credit to customer in the normal course of business. This kind of "*trade credit*" might be at risk to the extent that the customer may not pay his obligation in full.

23. Receivables Turnover Ratio

Total operating revenues divided by average receivables. Used to measure how effectively a firm is managing its accounts receivable. [See also **Asset management ratios**]

24. Receiver Swaption

A swaption giving the holder the right to receive the fixed rate in a swap. Thus, the holder of a receiver swaption would exercise his right when the fixed rate is below the strike price.

25. Recombining Tree

A binomial tree describing asset price moves in which an up move followed by a down move generates the same stock price as a down move followed by an up move. It is also called a lattice. Binomial option pricing model is based upon a lattice.

26. Record Date

The shareholders whose names appear on the corporation's list of shareholders on the record date are entitled to receive the dividend even if they sell their stock before the payment date. [See also **Dividend declaration date**]

27. Recourse

Legal right to enforce a claim against another party.

28. Recoveries

The dollar amount of loans that were previous charge off but now collected.

29. Recovery Rate

It can be defined as 1 minus loss given default (LGD). Recovery rates for individual obligors differ by issuer and industry classification. Rating agencies such as Moody's publish data on the average prices of all defaulted bonds, and generally analysts will construct a database of recovery rates by industry and credit rating for use in modeling the expected recovery rates of assets in the collateral pool.

30. Recovery Value

The percentage of par value received by either a bondholder or a lender in a bankruptcy.

31. Red Herring

A red herring is basically a preliminary **prospectus**. [See also **Prospectus**] The nickname arises from the disclaimer, printed in red on the cover of the prospectus, that the SEC has not yet approved the securities for sale.

32. Redlining

A practice whereby lenders deny loans to residents living in predetermined geographic areas. For example, many lenders were found to be making mortgage loans much more readily available in white neighborhoods than in those with higher proportions of nonwhites. Such a practice is illegal.

33. Reference Price

A market price or rate used to determine the payoff on a derivatives contract.

34. Refunding

The process of replacing outstanding bonds, typically to issue new securities at a lower interest rate than those replaced.

35. Registered Bond

A bond whose issuer records ownership and interest payments. Differs from a bearer bond, which is traded without record of ownership and whose possession is its only evidence of ownership. [See also **Bearer bond**]

36. Registered Trader

A member of the exchange who executes frequent trades for his or her own account.

37. Registration Statement

The registration that discloses all the pertinent information concerning the corporation that wants to make the offering. The statement is filed with the Securities and Exchange Commission.

38. Regression Equation

An equation that describes the average relationship between a dependent variable and a set of explanatory variables. [See also **Scatter diagram** and **Market model**]

39. Regular Cash Dividend

Cash payment by firm to its shareholders, usually four times a year.

40. Regulation A

The securities regulation that exempts small public offerings (those valued as less than $1.5 million) from most registration requirements.

41. Reinvestment Rate Risk

The return that an investor receives from a bond investment equals the bond's yield to maturity or effective annual rate only if the coupon payments can be reinvested at a rate equal to the bond's yield to maturity. Since the form of the interest facto in the bond price equation, $(1 + r)^m$ assumes that all the cash flows are reinvested at the periodic rate r for m periods; should future coupons be reinvested at a lower rate, the investor's actual yield will be less than the bond's yield to maturity. Therefore, reinvestment rate risk occurs when fluctuating interest rates cause coupon payments to be reinvested at different interest rates. Another illustration of reinvestment rate risk occurs when maturing bank CDs are rolled over into new CDs. The risk benefits the investor when the new CD rate is higher than the maturing CD rate; it works against the investor when the new CD rate is lower.

A zero coupon bond, a bond which pays no explicit interest, eliminates reinvestment risk. This is the primary reason for the popularity of zero coupon bonds in the investors.

42. Reinvestment Risk

The risk that future cash flows may be reinvested at rates below those expected or available at present. [See also **Reinvestment rate risk**]

43. REIT

Real estate investment trust, which is similar to a closed-end mutual fund. REIT's invest in real estate or loans secured by real estate and issue shares in such investments. [See also **Closed-end fund**]

44. Relative Price Risk

Relative price risk is one type of the exchange rate risk. It is due to changes in supply-and-demand conditions in various countries.

45. Relative Purchasing Power Parity

A more useful offshoot of **absolute purchasing power parity** is relative purchasing power parity. [See also **Absolute purchasing power parity**] Relative purchasing power parity claims that the exchange rates between countries will adjust over time to reflect their relative inflation rates. If h_{FC} and h_{US} are the inflation rates in a foreign country and the US, respectively, relative purchasing power parity claims that the expected change in the spot rate between the currencies (ΔER) is given as:

$$\Delta ER = \frac{E(S_1)}{S_0} - 1 = \frac{h_{FC} - h_{US}}{1 + h_{US}},$$

which is equivalent to:

$$1 + \Delta ER = \frac{E(S_1)}{S_0} = \frac{1 + h_{FC}}{1 + h_{US}},$$

where S_0 and $E(S_1)$ are the current spot exchange rate and the expected spot rate one year in the future, respectively.

In sum, relative purchasing power parity is the idea that the rate of change in the price level of commodities in one country relative to the price level in another determines the rate of the exchange rate between the two countries' currencies. [See also **International fisher effect**]

46. Remainder Man

One who receives the principal of a trust when it is dissolved.

47. REMIC

A real estate mortgage investment conduit [REMIC] issuing securities collateralized by mortgages and passing on principal and interest payments to investors. REMIC is a new type of Mortgage-backed instrument which is part of the tax reform act of 1986. Like CMOs, REMIC securities represent claims on the underlying cash flows that are prioritized by multiple classes or branches. [See also **Collateralized mortgage obligation (CMO)**]

48. Reorganization

Financial restructuring of a failed firm. Both the firm's asset structure and its financial structure are changed to reflect their true value, and claims are settled. Current law allows the bankrupt firm to be reorganized under chapter 11. The objective of reorganization is to keep the firm alive while settling creditor's claims and attracting new capital into the firm. [See also **Chapter 11**]

49. Replacement Cost

Cost to replace a firm's assets. "Reproduction" cost.

50. Replacement Value

Current cost of replacing the firm's assets.

51. Replacement-Chain Problem

Idea that future replacement decisions must be taken into account in selecting among projects.

52. Repo

Repurchasing agreement. A procedure for borrowing money by selling securities to a counterparty and agreeing to buy them back later at a slightly higher price. [See also **Repurchase agreement**]

53. Repo Rate

The annualized percentage difference between the original sale price and final repurchase price in a repurchase agreement.

54. Repricing

The replacement of an out-of-the-money compensation option with an at-the-money compensation option. This kind of reducing the exercise price of compensation option in response to a decline in stock price is called option repricing.

55. Repurchase Agreements

Repurchase agreements (repos) are not actual securities in themselves, but rather contracts to immediately acquire available funds by selling securities, together with a simultaneous agreement to repurchase those securities at a later date. Most repos are outstanding for only one business day, and nearly all involve Treasury or government agency securities.

For example, suppose a company has $1 million in excess cash available for two days. Instead of buying T-bills and then selling them two days later, the company could create a repurchase agreement with a bank. The company would agree to purchase $1 million worth of T-bills and then sell them back to the bank after two days for the original $1 million plus two days of interest. No actual transfer of physical securities is made; rather, the entire transaction consists of bookkeeping entries on the two parties' accounts.

Repos offer two distinct advantages for investing short-term surplus cash. First, their maturities can be tailored to suit the exact times that the parties have funds available, from overnight to 30 days or more. Second, because repos state the selling price of the securities in the initial agreement between buyer and seller, they eliminate interest rate risk. The yields on repos are similar to, but slightly lower than, those of T-bills.

56. Repurchase of Stock

Device to pay cash to firm's shareholders that provides more preferable tax treatment for shareholders than dividends. Treasury stock is the name given to previously issued stock that has been repurchased by the firm. [See also **Stock repurchase**]

57. Reserve Cash

A company's cash needs fall into three categories: (1) cash for day-to-day transactions, (2) reserve cash to meet contingencies, and (3) cash for compensating balance requirements. To estimate reserve cash requirements, the cash flow manager can tabulate the daily or weekly changes in the cash amount. These changes will range from some very large changes to small fluctuations. Because the major cash flow problem is running short of cash, the financial manager is especially interested in large decreases and thus might select a reserve balance that would meet all but the largest historic cash decreases.

58. Reserve for Bank Debts

Amount appearing on a bank's balance sheet that represents the estimated value of uncollected loans.

59. Reserve Requirement Ratios

Percentages applied to transactions account and time deposits to determine the dollar amount of required reserve assets.

60. Reserve Requirements

In regulating the banking industry, the Fed sets reserve requirements to specify the portion of a bank's total deposits that it must hold as reserves. The Fed hesitates to change the reserve requirement due to the money multiplier effect; small changes in the reserve ratio can have a very large impact on money supply. This makes the tool too coarse for the subtle work of adjusting the economy.

61. Reserve Target

The minimum daily reserve ratio of deposit institution (DI) required by Fed. In general, the DI can either undershooting or overshooting this ratio.

62. Reserves

Qualifying assets to meet reserve requirements, including vault cash and deposit balances help at Federal Reserve Banks.

63. Reset Date

The date in a swap or cap or floor when the floating rate for the next period is set.

64. Residual Claim

Refers to the fact that shareholders are at the bottom of the list of claimants to assets of a corporation in the event of a failure or bankruptcy.

65. Residual Dividend Approach

An approach that suggests that a firm pay dividends if and only if acceptable investment opportunities for those funds are currently unavailable. [See also **Residual theory**]

66. Residual Theory

The most easily understood theory of dividend payment determination is called the residual theory. As the name implies, this theory holds that firms pay dividends out of earnings that remain after it meets its financing needs. These are funds for which the firm has no immediate use. The procedure for a residual dividend policy follows several steps:

1. Determine the firm's optimal capital budget.
2. Determine the amount of equity needed to finance that budget.
3. To the extent possible, use the firm's retained earnings to supply the needed equity.
4. Distribute any leftover earnings as dividends. .

The basic assumption of residual dividend theory is that shareholders want the firm to retain earnings if reinvesting them can generate higher rates of return than the shareholders could obtain by reinvesting their dividends. For example, if a corporation can invest retained earnings in a new venture that generates an 18 percent rate of return, whereas investors can obtain a return of only 10 percent by reinvesting their dividends, then stockholders would benefit more from the firm reinvesting its profits.

Whether firms actually practice the residual theory is a matter of question. Such a theory would imply erratic dividend payments, especially for fast-growth companies. Firms do seem to try to stabilize their dividend-payout rates, so analysts do not place much faith in the residual theory. However, two alternative theories for the dividend behavior of firms have found considerable empirical support.

67. Residual Value

Usually refers to the value of a lessor's property at the time the lease expires.

68. Residuals

Parts of stock returns not explained by the explanatory variable (the market-index return). They measure the impact of firm-specific events during a particular period. [See also **Market model**]

69. Resistance Level

A price level above which it is supposedly difficult for a stock or stock index to rise.

70. Resolution Trust Corporation (RTC)

A government agency (1989–1996) that assisted in the management and savings and loans deemed to be insolvent during the Thrift Crisis. At the time of its dissolution in 1955, RTC had resolved or closed more than 700 saving institutions.

71. Respondent Bank

Bank that purchases services from a correspondent bank.

72. Restrictive Covenants

Provisions that place constraints on the operations of borrowers, such as restrictions on working capital, fixed assets, future borrowing, and payment of dividend.

73. Retained Earnings

Earnings not paid out as dividends. It is one of the items of equity statement. This term also appears in the balance sheet.

74. Retention Rate

The retention rate represents the proportion of every $1 of earnings per share that is retained by the firm; in other words, it is equal to one minus the **dividend payout ratio**. [See also **Dividend payout ratio**]

75. Retention Ratio

Retained earnings divided by net income. It is equal to one minus the dividend payout ratio.

76. Retractable Bonds

[See **Putable bonds**]

77. Return

Profit on capital investments or securities.

78. Return Items

Checks that have not been honored by the drawee bank and have been returned to the check writer.

79. Return on Assets [ROA]

Income divided by average total assets. [See also **Profitability ratios**]

80. Return on Equity (ROE)

Net income after interest and taxes divided by average common stockholders' equity. [See also **Profitability ratios**]

81. Return on Sales (ROS), or Profit Margin

The ratio of operating profits per dollar of sales (EBIT divided by sales). [See also **Profitability ratios**]

82. Revenue Bond

Most of municipal bonds are revenue bonds. They will be repaid out of proceeds from the specific revenue-generating project that they were sold to finance, such as toll roads.

83. Reverse Cash-and-Carry

The simultaneous short-sale and forward purchase of an asset or commodity.

84. Reverse Conversion

A short position in an asset coupled with a purchased call and written put, both with the same strike price and time to expiration. The position is a synthetic short T-bill position.

85. Reverse Mortgage

A mortgage in which the owner of the property can borrow against existing equity in the property.

86. Reverse Purchase Agreement

The purchase of a security coupled with an agreement to sell it at a later date. The opposite of a repurchase agreement.

87. Reverse Repo (RP)

A contract in which a lender provides funds to a borrower for which collateral is provided in the event on nonpayment. Every RP transaction involves both a regular RP and reverse RP depending on whether its viewed from the lender's or borrower's prospective. Most RPs use Treasury or US agency securities as collateral.

88. Reverse Repurchase Agreement

Securities purchased under an agreement to resell them at a later date.

89. Reverse Split

The procedure whereby the number of outstanding stock shares is reduced; for example, two outstanding shares are combined to create one. [See also **Stock split**]

90. Reverse Stock Split

A reverse stock split, as its names implies, is a reduction in the number of shares outstanding, with each share increasing in value to keep the total value of the firm unchanged. As with a **stock split**, theory gives no reason to expect any change in the underlying value of the company that engages in a reverse split. [See also **Stock split**] In fact, many investors regard a reverse split as an admission by management that the company faces financial difficulties. This belief is based primarily on the argument that the market price per share is too low to attract serious investors.

91. Reversible Swap

Allows counterparty to change status from floating-rate payer to fixed-rate payer and vice versa.

92. Reversing Trade

Entering the opposite side of a currently held futures position to close out the position.

93. Reversion Level

The level to which the value of a market variable (e.g., an interest rate) tends to revert.

94. Revolving Commitment (Revolver)

A generic term referring to some facility which a client can use – or refrain from using – without canceling the facility. In other words, it guarantees that funds can be borrowed, repaid and borrowed again over an extended period, perhaps as long as 3 years. [See also **Revolving credit agreement**]

95. Revolving Credit Agreement

Banks usually grant lines of credit for specific lengths of time, usually one year or less. The parties may, of course, renegotiate the loan to provide the funds for a longer time, if needed. Still, the bank usually expects the borrower to clean up the loan – that is, to reduce its debt to the bank to zero – at least once during the year.

A borrower that has a recurring need for funds may instead arrange a revolving credit agreement. This type of loan resembles the line of credit, in that the parties agree to a maximum credit level, and the borrower may draw funds up to that limit. The revolving credit agreement, however, meets the borrower's need to borrow the funds, pay off the loan, and then borrow again, time after time. Such a situation may supply funds for a borrowing company that produces a small number of large, high-value products, such as ships or steam turbines; the firm must borrow to finance the construction of each product until it eventually collects the proceeds of the sale. Moreover, a revolving credit agreement is more likely to be guaranteed by the bank than a line of credit.

Because the bank must commit to the agreement for a much longer time than a conventional line of credit would demand, the negotiation process for a revolving credit agreement tends to be more formal. The bank may specify that the borrower must maintain its working capital above a specified level, forbid any factoring of accounts receivable without the bank's permission, or stipulate that any further borrowing must be subordinated to the revolving credit debt. Commitment fees also are common for large revolving credit agreements. Most banks offer the borrower a choice between a **committed line of credit** and an **uncommitted line of credit**. [See also **Committed line of credit** and **Uncommitted line of credit**.]

96. Revolving Loan

A credit line on which a borrower can both draw and repay many times over the life of the loan contract. [See also **Revolving credit agreement**]

97. Reward-to-Volatility Ratio

Ratio of excess return to portfolio standard deviation. [See also **Sharpe ratio**]

98. Rho

The change in value of a derivative due to a change in the interest rate. Based upon the call option formula defined in option pricing equation [See also **Option pricing equation** for variable definitions]. The mathematical result can be defined as:

$$\frac{\partial C}{\partial r} = TXe^{-rT}N(d_2) > 0.$$

99. Riding the Yield Curve

It is one of the bond portfolio management strategies designed to increase income is called riding the yield curve. To be successful, managers using this approach must be willing to make several rather strong assumptions about the future course of interest rates. To illustrate, suppose that a manager would ordinarily hold 1-year Treasury securities as part of an institution's secondary reserves but now sees an upward-sloping yield curve. The yield on 1-year Treasuries is 3.5 percent, and the yield on 2-year Treasuries is 4.0 percent. *If the manager assumes that the shape and level of the yield curve will remain the same,* the price of 2-year Treasuries must rise so that their yield next year (when they will be 1-year Treasuries) will be 3.5 percent. A manager willing to ride the yield curve would hold 2-year Treasuries this year, then sell them at the end of the year after their price rose to provide additional income on the portfolio. Assuming that the level and shape of the yield curve has, in fact, remained unchanged, the manager would then reinvest the proceeds in 2-year Treasuries and begin the ride again.

In sum, riding the yield curve is an investment strategy the investor buys a security that matures after the investor's assumed holding period. The investor plans to sell the security at the end of the holding period and earn an above-average return because interest rates are expected to remain stable or fall.

100. Rights Issue

An issue to existing shareholders of a security giving them the right to buy new shares at a certain price.

101. Rights Offering

A rights offering allows the firm's current shareholders to purchase additional shares in proportion to their current ownership. This way, the original shareholders maintain control of the firm while raising the needed equity capital among themselves. For example, suppose four shareholders each own 25 percent of a firm whose equity has a value of $4 million. If the firm needs an additional $1 million to finance a plant expansion, it can make a rights offering, allowing each shareholder to invest $250,000. This way, each shareholder can retain 25-percent ownership in the expanded firm.

If a shareholder cannot or declines to invest the full $250,000, the remaining shareholders can invest the difference. Proportionate ownership would change to reflect the overall fraction invested by each shareholder.

The advantage of the rights offering is that the current set of shareholders can maintain control of the firm by each contributing additional funds to meet the firm's needs. This condition creates a practical difficulty, though. As a group, the shareholders may not be able to raise the needed funds, leading to a failure of the rights offering. The firm then must arrange financing from other sources of private equity.

102. Risk Arbitrage

Speculation on perceived mispriced securities, usually in connection with merger and acquisition targets.

103. Risk Class

A partition of the universal set of risk measure so that projects that are in the same risk class can be comparable. M&M propositions have been derived in terms of risk class assumption.

104. Risk Classification

Certain types of projects are inherently more or less risky than other. The firm can use past experience and information from audits of earlier projects to create risk classes or categories for different types of capital budgeting projects. The findings from break-even, scenario, sensitivity, or simulation analysis also can be used to determine risk categories for projects. Each risk category can be given a generic description to indicate the types of projects it should include and a risk-adjusted discount rate or project cost of capital to assign those projects. An example is shown is Table A.

Subjectivity enters this process as management must decide the number of categories, the description of each risk category, and the required rate of return to assign each category.

Differences of opinion or internal firm politics may lead to controversy in classifying a project. Clearly defined category descriptions can minimize such problems.

The process of setting up the risk categories can be made less subjective if the firm audits ongoing and completed capital budgeting projects. Audits can provide fairly objective written records of the firm's experiences with different categories of projects. This paper analysis trail can be used to justify the classifications given to different kinds of projects, as well as the risk premiums assigned to different risk classes.

Table A: Risk Classification Example

Risk categories:	Description
Below-average risk:	Replacement decisions that require no change, or only a minor change, in technology. No change in plant layout required. Discount rate = Cost of capital − 2%.
Average risk:	Replacement decisions involving significant changes in technology or plant layout; all cost-saving decisions; expansions and improvements in the firm's main product lines. Discount rate = Cost of capital.
Above-average risk:	Applied research and development; expansion of production or marketing efforts into developed economies in Europe and Asia. Discount rate = Cost of capital + 2%.
High risk:	Expansion of production or marketing efforts into less-developed and emerging economies; introduction of products not related to any of the firm's current product lines. Discount rate = Cost of capital + 5%.

105. Risk Lover

[See also **Risk averse, risk neutral, risk lover**]

106. Risk Management

The active use of derivatives and other techniques to alter risk and protect profitability.

107. Risk Averse, Risk Neutral, Risk Lover

A *risk-averse* investor will consider risky portfolios only if they provide compensation for risk via a risk premium. A *risk-neutral* investor finds the level of risk irrelevant and considers only the expected return of risky prospects. A *risk lover* is willing to accept lower expected returns on prospects with higher amounts of risk.

108. Risk Neutral

A term describing an investor who is indifferent between receiving amount of x dollar and taking a risky bet with an expected value equal to x dollar. [See also **Risk averse, risk neutral, risk lover**]

109. Risk Premiums

The nominal risk-free return is the same for all investments throughout the market. However, there are as many different interest rates or expected returns as there are time horizons (ranging from one day to many years) and financial instruments (from passbook savings accounts to corporate stocks). The interest rates we observe in the economy differ from the nominal risk-free rate due to risk premiums. With the possible exception of Treasury bills, all investments are risky.

In sum, risk premium is the excess return on the risky asset that is the difference between expected return on risky assets and the return on risk-free assets.

110. Risk-Free Asset

An asset with a certain rate of return; often taken to be short-term T-bills.

111. Risk-Free Investment

A risk-free investment is one in which the investor is sure about the timing and amount of income streams arising from the investment. However, for most types of investments, investors are uncertain about the timing and amount of income of their investments. The types of risks involved in investments can be quite broad, from the relatively riskless **T-bill** to highly risky speculative stock. [See also **Treasury bills**]

112. Risk-Free Rate

The interest rate that can be earned with certainty. It is risk free in terms of default risk instead of inflation risk. [See also **Nominal risk-free interest rate**]

113. Riskless Portfolio

A combination of assets that earns the riskless rate of interest over the chosen investment horizon. The investment horizon is assumed to be one period; the duration of this period can be any length of time, an hour, day, week, and so on.

114. Risk-Neutral Measure

The probability distribution for an asset transformed so that the expected return on the asset is the risk-free rate.

115. Risk-Neutral Probability

In the binomial model, the probability of an up move in the asset price such that the expected return on the asset is the risk-free rate.

116. Risk-Neutral Valuation

The valuation of an option or other derivative assuming the world is risk neutral. Risk-neutral valuation gives the correct price for a derivative in all worlds, not just in a risk-neutral world.

117. Risk-Return Trade-Off

If an investor is willing to take on risk, there is the reward of higher expected returns. Both security market line and capital market line are used to determine the risk return trade off. [See also **Capital market line** and **Security market line**]

118. Risky Asset

An asset with an uncertain rate of return. For example, stocks are risky assets.

119. Risky Corporate Debt

Sometimes, options are used to value risky corporate debt. Because of the limited liability of stockholders, money borrowed by the firm is backed, at most, by the total value of the firm's assets. One way to view this agreement is to consider that stockholders have sold the entire firm to debt holders but hold a call option with an exercise price equal to the face value of the debt. In this case, if the value of the firm exceeds the value of the debt, stockholders exercise the call option by paying off the bondholders. If the value of the firm is less than the value of the debt, shareholders do not exercise the call option, and all assets are distributed to the bondholders.

120. Roll Back

[See also **Backwards induction**]

121. Roth IRA

An individual retirement account introduced in 1998 that allows individuals whose wages and salaries are below a predetermined minimum to contribute after-tax income. The contributions grow on a tax-sheltered basis and thus are not taxed at withdrawal.

122. Round Lot

Common stock trading unit of 100 shares or multiples of 100 shares. When an individual wants to buy fewer than 100 shares, the order is turned over to an odd-lot dealer who will buy or sell from his own inventory.

123. R-Squared (R^2)

Square of the correlation coefficient proportion of the variability explained by the linear model. R^2 for regression for estimating beta is $R^2 = \beta_i^2 \dfrac{\mathrm{var}(R_{mt})}{\mathrm{var}(R_{it})}$. Under this case, R^2 represents the ratio between systematic risk and total risk. [See also **Beta** and **Market model** for variable definitions]

124. Rule 415

In 1983, the SEC passed Rule 415, which allows firms to register security issues (both debt and equity) and then "put them on the shelf" for sale any time over the next two years. Once registered, the securities can be offered for sale by submitting a short statement to the SEC whenever the firm needs the funds or when market conditions are attractive. [See also **Shelf registration**]

125. Rule of 72

Divide 72 by the interest rate at which funds are invested. The value indicates how long it will take for the amount of funds invested to double in value.

126. Run on a Bank

Situation in which a large number of depositors lose confidence in the safety of their deposits and attempt to withdraw their funds.

S

1. S&P 500

[See also **Standard & Poor's 500 composite index (S&P 500)**]

2. Safe Deposit Box

Privacy boxes for storage in a bank vault under lock and key.

3. Safe Harbor Lease

A lease to transfer tax benefits to ownership (depreciation and debt tax shield) from the lessee, if the lessee can not use them, to a lessor that can.

4. SAIF

Savings Association Insurance Fund which insures deposits at savings and loans. This is one of the two insurance funds under FDIC. [See also **BIF**]

5. Sale And Lease-Back Agreement

In a sale and lease-back agreement, the owner of an asset sells it and then leases it back. This method allows cash-strapped firms to sell valuable assets, but still retain their use.

6. Sales Forecast

A key input to the firm's financial planning process. External sales forecasts are based on historical experience, statistical analysis, and consideration of various macroeconomic factors; internal sales forecasts are obtained from internal sources.

7. Sales Terms and Collections

The fastest way to collect receivables is to ask for the money regularly. However, a company also can change its sales terms in an attempt to collect cash more quickly. Such a policy can take several forms, including (i) introduce discounts; (ii) reduce credit terms; (iii) emphasize cash sales; (iv) accept credit cards; and (v) impose penalties for late payment.

8. Sales-Type Lease

An arrangement whereby a firm leases its own equipment, such as IBM leasing its own computers, thereby competing with an independent leasing company.

9. Sallie Mae

Student Loan Marketing Association which guarantees student loans. The asset structure of Sallie Mae is heavily dominated by floating-rate standard loans and advances. Investors supplying funds to Sallie Mae preferred to lock in the high rate prevailing at that time. Therefore, Sallie Mae, pioneered swap program in the US in 1982.

10. Sample-Function Analysis

Sample-function analysis regards a time series as an observed sample function representing a realization of an underlying stochastic process. Complicated parametric statistical-estimation procedures are used to determine the properties of time-series data.

11. Scalper

Speculators are often distinguished by the time they hold their position. They can either be scalper or day trader. Scalper is a trader who holds positions for a very short period of time.

12. Scatter Diagram of a Regression

For example, to estimate beta coefficient, we regress rate of return of company i in period t (R_{it}) on market rate of return in period t (R_{mt}), then the regression model can be defined as:

$$R_{it} = \alpha_i + \beta_i R_{mt} + e_{it} \tag{1}$$

The estimated slope is the beta coefficient (systematic risk). In the regression analysis of equation (1) involving one independent variable (R_{mt}) and one dependent variable (R_{it}), the individual value of R_{it} and R_{mt} are plotted on a two-dimensional graph. In this two-dimensional graph, we can plot the different points in accordance with the pairwise observations of R_{it} and R_{mt} to obtain the scatter diagram as presented in the figure below.

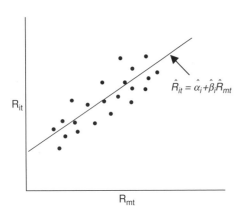

13. Scenario Analysis

Scenario analysis provides a means to evaluate the potential variability in a capital budgeting project's NPV. Scenario analysis computes several net present values for the project based on different scenarios. The initial capital budgeting analysis using the analyst's estimates of expected cash flows is called the *base-case scenario*. From this base case, typically at least two other scenarios are developed – a worst-case scenario and a best-case scenario – and NPVs are computed for each. The worst case NPV and the best case NPV give managers a likely range in which the project's NPV will fall. The purpose of scenario analysis is to examine the joint impact on NPV of simultaneous changes in many different factors.

The worst-case scenario should reflect project results under Murphy's law: "If anything can go wrong, it will." Compared to the base case, the worst-case scenario will have lower sales volume, lower prices, higher costs, shorter product life, lower salvage value, and so on. Rather than being an exercise in disaster forecasting, however, the worst-case scenario should reflect the circumstances that could reasonably be expected should the project be plagued with bad luck or bad analysis. Some of the firm's past failures can be used as models for developing the worst-case scenario. The resulting estimates of cash flows and NPV will reflect this pessimistic perspective.

The best-case scenario should illustrate how the project will turn out if everything works better than expected. The sales figures, prices, costs, and so on should incorporate the upper boundary of *reasonable* optimism. An unrealistic pie-in-the-sky scenario, however, will add little to the analysis. Spreadsheet packages can facilitate the analysis of different scenarios.

The analyst then presents decision makers with three sets of conditions, cash flows, and NPVs. The base-case represents an estimate of the most likely outcome; the worst-case and best-case scenarios illustrate the project's possible extremes. The NPVs of the worst-case and best-case scenarios represent the potential range of the project's impact on shareholder wealth. If the worst-case scenario has a large, negative NPV, management may call for more analysis to see if the project can be modified to reduce its potential for severely decreasing shareholder wealth.

Another possibility is that management may decide that the project's best-case scenario is so attractive that it overcomes the project's downside risk. This may be the case for a project with encouraging engineering or market test results or a project that may propel the firm into a position of industry leadership.

14. Season Dating

Arrangements for credit transactions include special terms for recurrent purchases and seasonal accounts. When a company routinely buys many items, the supplier commonly accounts for all sales during the month as occurring at the end of the month, eliminating the inconvenience of a separate payment for each delivery. These terms are stated as 5/10, EOM, net 60; that is, by paying the bill within 10 days of the end of the month (EOM), the customer will receive a 5-percent discount. Otherwise, full payment is due within 60 days of the invoice date. Manufacturers who produce seasonal goods often encourage customers to take early delivery by allowing them to delay payment until the normal ordering season, a type of credit arrangement known as season dating.

15. Seasonal Liquidity Needs

Cash flow needs that arise from predictable seasonal loan demands and deposit outflows.

16. Seasonal Swap

Notional principal may vary up or down over the life of the swap. Also known as roller coaster swap.

17. Seasoned New Issue

A new issue of stock after the company's securities has previously been issued. A seasoned new issue of common stock can be made by using a cash offer or a rights offer. [See also **Seasoned offering**]

18. Seasoned Offering

Not every public sale of stock by a corporation is an IPO. Corporate growth and/or high debt ratios require some public firms to return to the equity markets to raise funds. A new stock offering by an already public company is called a seasoned offering. Such offerings are easier for the investment

bank and investors to price. Rather than estimating fair market value from accounting data, as in an IPO, investors can refer to daily listings of the market value of the company's shares.

A public company that needs an equity capital infusion faces several choices. It can increase its equity base by selling shares of common or preferred stock, and it can raise money in the US market or issue securities overseas.

Only the US has a public financial market for preferred equity issues; other countries have not developed primary and secondary markets for preferred stock trading. As preferred equity increases a firm's equity base without diluting control, more and more foreign firms are issuing both fixed-rate and adjustable-rate preferred stock in the US markets.

Overseas tax and regulatory environments may make fund-raising cheaper for large US firms. Analysis of the Euroequity and Eurobond markets provides evidence of such cost advantages.

After a firm decides upon the form in which it will raise equity, it can market the new issue in several ways. It can sell the new shares to the public or to current shareholders or place them privately.

19. Seat

Another term for an exchange membership is a seat. A prospective member may buy a full seat, allowing him or her to trade any of the offered futures contracts. To encourage volume on newer or less liquid contracts, most exchanges usually also offer a partial seat. Permitting its owner to trade only a designated number of contracts. Usually, to get onto an exchange to trade, an investor needs to buy or lease a seat from a current owner. The value of an exchange seat can very substantially.

20. SEC

Securities and Exchange Commission, which was established under the authority of the Securities

Act of 1933 and the Securities Exchange Act of 1934. The SEC regulate security firm such as Merrill Lynch and investment banking firm, such as Salomon Smith Barney and Goldman Sachs. [See also **Securities and Exchange Commission**]

21. Second Mortgage Bond

A second mortgage bond has a secondary, or junior, claim on assets. [See also **First mortgage bond**]

22. Secondary Capital

Limited life preferred stock, subordinated debt, and mandatory convertible securities not included as primary capital. Secondary capital is the Tier 2 capital, and primary capital is the Tier 1 capital.

23. Secondary Market

The secondary market is the resale market for securities. The issuing entity (corporation or government) is usually not involved in such transactions. In the secondary market, investors buy and sell securities among themselves. Without the liquidity that the secondary market provides, the primary market would be much less attractive because investors could not easily sell their securities.

The secondary market includes two forums for security trades: **organized exchanges** and an **over-the-counter market**. [See also **Organized exchanges** and **Over-the-counter market**] The New York Stock Exchange (NYSE) is an example of an organized exchange.

24. Second-Pass Regression

A cross-sectional regression of portfolio returns on betas. The estimated slope is the measurement of the reward for bearing systematic risk during the period. This technique was proposed by Fama and Macbeth (1973).

25. Sector Influences

In addition to an overall market factor, various factors related to industry-type indexes are significant in explaining the returns generating process for a particular security. Other potential additional indexes could be related to interest-rate movements and firm capitalization size. Shape (1984) finds quite a wide array of these additional factors, which he classifies as either systematic influences or sector influences. Sector influences includes eight factors: 1. basic industries; 2. capital goods; 3. construction; 4. consumer goods; 5. energy; 6. finance; 7. transportation; 8.utilities.

26. Sector Loadings

For correlation analysis, a firm or industry group is said to be dependent upon underlying economic factors or "sectors" such as: (i) the market as a whole, (ii) interest rates, (iii) oil prices, etc.. As two industries "load" are influenced by common factors, they will have a higher correlation between them. This kind of loading is called sector loading.

27. Securities and Exchange Commission

Public firms must submit to regulation by the Securities and Exchange Commission (SEC) and the exchange on which their shares are traded. Regulation means more paperwork to file and more attorneys' fees to ensure that laws are not unintentionally broken. In the US, public firms must file annual and quarterly reports with the SEC, and corporate insiders who buy and sell the firm's stock must report their transactions to the SEC. The firm must register most public offerings of securities (including the initial public offering) with the SEC and receive SEC approval before selling the securities to the public.

Experts on public policy have known for some time that most employment growth in the US comes from small businesses. To foster future growth, in 1992 the SEC adopted a series of rules to make it easier for small firms to raise public equity financing. The new regulations allow a firm to evaluate the potential market for its shares before committing to the time and expense of preparing a formal offering document.

Firms are allowed to raise up to $1 million without registering the sale with the SEC. They can register securities worth up to $5 million through the simpler and less costly Regulation A process rather than undergoing a full SEC review. The SEC estimates that the new regulations will reduce the cost of raising public equity by smaller firms by up to one-third. In addition, small public firms (by SEC definition, whose with sales less than $25 million and market values of equity below $25 million) will be able to file shorter, less comprehensive quarterly and annual SEC reports, thus reducing management's paperwork time and costs.

28. Securitization

Pooling loans for various purposes into standardized securities backed by those loans, which can then be traded like any other security. In sum, the process of converting assets into marketable securities is called securitization.

29. Security

Collateral which a borrower pledges against a loan or secondary source of repayment in case of default.

30. Security Analysis

Security analysis is used to determine correct value of a security in the marketplace. It is one of the three steps of forming portfolios of securities.

The selection of a portfolio of securities can be thought of as a multi-step process. The first step consists of studying the economic and social environment and the characteristics of individual companies in order to produce a set of forecasts of individual company variables. The second step consists of turning these forecasts of fundamental

data about the corporation and its environment into a set of forecasts of security prices and/or returns and risk measures. This step is often called the valuation process. The third and last step consists of forming portfolios of securities based on the forecast of security returns.

31. Security Characteristic Line

A plot of the excess return on a security over the risk-free rate as a function of the excess return on the market. [See also **Market model**]

32. Security Interest

The legal claim on property that secures a debt or the performance of an obligation.

33. Security Market Line (SML)

A straight line that shows the equilibrium relationship between systematic risk and expected rates of return for individual securities. According to the SML, the excess return on a risky asset is equal to the excess return on the market portfolio multiplied by the beta coefficient. [See also **Capital asset pricing model**]

34. Security Market Plane (SMP)

A plane that shows the equilibrium relationship between expected return and the beta coefficients of more than one factor.

35. Security Selection Decision

Choosing the particular securities to include in a portfolio. In general, the fundamental instead of technical analysis is used to select the particular stock to be in the portfolio.

36. Seesaw Effect

When bonds are originally issued, most sell at prices close to par and offer coupon rates close to the market rates on bonds of similar maturity and risk. Over the life of a bond, its price will vary inversely to, or in the opposite direction of interest rate fluctuations in the economy. As interest rates rise in the economy, bond prices fall; as interest rates fall, bond prices rise. Since one rises as the other falls, we call this relationship between bond prices and interest rates the "seesaw effect."

37. Selection Phase

Because managers want to maximize the firm's value for the shareholders, they need some guidance as to the potential value of the investment projects. The selection phase involves measuring the value, or the return, of the project as well as estimating the risk and weighting the costs and benefits of each alternative to be able to select the project or projects that will increase the firm's value given a risk target.

38. Self-Financing Portfolio

A hedge portfolio that retains specified characteristics (e.g., it is zero-investment and risk-free) without the need for additional investments in the portfolio.

39. Self-Liquidating Loans

In view of high exposure to risk for a comparatively low return, commercial banks have understandably tried to find ways to protect themselves. Until very recently, this effort led them to lend only short-term funds and only in the form of self-liquidating loans – that is, they loaned money only for specific purposes and operations that would produce adequate cash flows to retire the debt quickly. The perfect example of such a self-liquidating situation is a working-capital loan made to a manufacturer or retailer that has a marked seasonal sales pattern.

For example, retail sales of a toy manufacturer's product peak just before Christmas each year. The manufacturer's own sales peak probably comes in August; however, when retailers and toy distributors are building up their inventories for the buying season, to meet this demand, the manufacturer must schedule a high level of production from May through July. In May of each year, therefore, the company takes out a loan from its bank to provide added working capital to finance the build up in inventory. By September, heavy sales draw down the inventory to normal levels. Most of these sales, however, are made on terms of net 30 days, giving the company a large accounts receivable balance, but little cash. Finally, by early November, the customers pay their accounts, and collections of accounts receivable provide enough cash flow to retire the bank loan. Thus, the loan is self-liquidating in six months.

This is a classic bank lending situation. The bank knows before it makes the loan exactly how long the funds will be needed. The relatively short life of the loan increases the bank's liquidity. By making a fairly large number of predictable, short-term loans, a bank feels comfortable lending the highest proportion of its funds that regulations permit. In other words, it will want to lend up to its loan limit, or be fully loaned. If a bank finds little demand for self-liquidating, seasonal loans, it may be forced to lend in longer term, less predictable situations. Caution would probably lead this bank to keep a higher proportion of its funds in marketable securities to preserve its overall liquidity.

This traditional scenario has been transformed by important changes in bank practices during recent years. Commercial banks no longer stress the self-liquidating requirement as strongly as they once did. As the suppliers of short-term financing have become more competitive, banks have become more willing to provide longer term funds in the form of term loans. These new practices are creating an increasingly flexible source of short-term and intermediate-term funds for business organizations.

40. Sell Offs

[See also **Voluntary restructuring**]

41. Semistrong-Form Efficient Market

Different assumptions about information availability give rise to different types of market efficiency. [See also **Efficient market**]

In a semistrong-form efficient market, all *public* information, both past and current, is reflected in asset prices. The US stock market appears to be a fairly good example of a semistrong-form efficient market. For the most part, news about the economy or individual companies appears to produce quick stock price changes without subsequent trends or price reversals.

42. Seniority

The order of repayment; in the event of bankruptcy, senior debt must be repaid before subordinated debt receives any payment.

43. Sensitivity Analysis

Scenario analysis simultaneously modifies many variables that affect cash flows and net present value (NPV) to build different scenarios. [See also **Scenario analysis**] Sensitivity analysis changes one variable at a time from its base-case value; this isolates the effects on NPV of changes in individual variables. If large changes in NPV occur when the product price assumption or exchange rate assumption changes by, for example, 10 percent, then additional research may be warranted to better determine the likely market price or exchange rate. On the other hand, if NPV is relatively stable as the assumed salvage value changes, then great effort should not be expended in order to determine a more accurate estimate of salvage value.

One method for doing sensitivity analysis is to change each individual variable from its base-case value by some amount, say 5 percent or 10 percent, while holding all other variables constant at their base-case values. The resulting NPVs are computed and then recorded or graphed. A steep NPV graph indicates a variable that has a major

impact on project success, especially as the NPV of the project is negative for some reasonable values of the variable. A more gently sloped NPV graph shows that a variable does not have a major influence on NPV, so additional research on likely values of this variable probably is not warranted. Spreadsheet packages allow sensitivity analysis to be done with ease.

Rather than arbitrarily changing each variable by some fixed percentage, the analyst might take a cue from scenario analysis and determine best-case and worst-case values for each variable. NPVs can be computed as each variable is adjusted to its best- and worst-case estimates while all other variables are held at their base-case amounts. This combination of sensitivity analysis can pinpoint which worst-case and best-case values affect NPV by the greatest amount.

44. Separation Property

The property that portfolio choice can be separated into two independent tasks: (1) determination of the optimal risky portfolio, which is a purely technical problem, and (2) the personal choice of the best mix of the risky portfolio and the risk-free asset.

45. Serial Bond Issue

An issue of bonds with staggered maturity dates that spreads out the principal repayment burden over time.

46. Serial Bonds

A series of bonds offered by the same issuer with principal payments that are due at different maturities. Serial bonds are common for municipal bond issuers.

47. Serial Correlation

[See also **Autocorrelation**]

48. Serial Covariance

The covariance between a variable and the lagged value of the variable; the same as autocovariance.

49. Series of Options

A series is a subset of a class and consists of all contracts of the same class (same asset) having the same expiration date and exercise price.

50. Service Charges

Fees imposed for bank services. They are a small portion of operating income for all banks, but they are more important for small banks.

51. Service Corporation

A corporation formed by Saving and Loan Association to conduct diversified line of business.

52. Set of Contracts Perspective

View of corporation as a set of contracting relationships among individuals who have conflicting objectives, such as shareholders or managers. The corporation is a legal contrivance that serves as the nexus for the contracting relationships.

53. Settlement

The time in a transaction at which all obligations of both the buyer and the seller are fulfilled.

54. Settlement Date

The actual exchange of one currency for another occurs on the settlement date. Settlement is handled by an association of 12 New York banks called CHIPS (Clearing House Interbank Payments System).

55. Settlement Price

A figure determined by the closing-price range that is used to calculate daily gains and losses in futures-market accounts (and thus margin calls) and invoice prices for deliveries.

56. Share-Equivalent

The position in shares that has equivalent dollar risk to a derivative. [See also **Delta**]

57. Shareholder

Holder of equity shares. The terms *shareholders* and *stockholders* usually refer to owners of common stock in a corporation.

58. Shareholder Wealth

Shareholder wealth is measurable and observable daily in the financial sections of newspapers (at least for publicly traded firms). Shareholder wealth is nothing more than the market value of a firm's common stock. This market value of the shareholders' claim on a firm is equal to:

Shareholder wealth = (*Common stock price*)

× (*Number of common shares outstanding*).

This relationship allows analysts to keep track of changes in shareholder wealth for competing firms in an industry on a regular basis to see which is most successful at returning value to its shareholders. As long as the number of common stock shares outstanding does not change appreciably, the market's perception of the firm and its management's actions will be reflected in the firm's stock price.

Many possible criteria can be used to evaluate firm performance. Total sales, the growth rate of the firm, market share, management's strategy, or earnings per share frequently are suggested as bases for evaluating and analyzing firms. We argue, however, that shareholder wealth is the best measure of firm performance for several reasons.

First, shareholder wealth is an objective, market-determined measure. It is not subject to manipulation (except in violation of securities laws) or limited to subjective evaluation. The value of a firm's stock is based on the joint decision of many investors, who generally are forward-looking and trade in markets that determine unbiased prices.

Second, any accounting performance measure (such as sales, earnings, or firm growth) is vulnerable to distortion by accounting principles, whose application may be somewhat "subjective (such as when to recognize revenue or how quickly to depreciate assets). Rather than present an unbiased view of firm performance, accounting statements may be oriented toward the perspective that management wants to present. Additionally, accounting-based performance measures are always *historical*. They tell us where the firm has been. In contrast, shareholder wealth is a forward-looking measure) incorporating the market's objective assessment of the firm's prospects for the future.

Third, growth for the sake of growth or merely to increase market share may have dangerous long-run implications. It would be folly to invest scarce capital in plant, equipment, and workers with no plan for how these investments will pay for themselves and return capital (plus interest) to the financial markets. The firm may win the short-term market-share battle but lose the long-term war as poor returns on investments hurt its ability to raise capital, repay loans, and pay bills and workers. The firm may find it difficult to maintain its short-sighted market-share gains as leaner and more financially responsible rivals counterattack at the firm's weak points to reclaim their lost customers. Thus, sacrificing financial value for market share does not lead to successful, long-term business. Maximizing shareholder value does.

Fourth, a shareholder wealth orientation ensures adequate consideration of risk in a firm's decisions. A basic principle of finance is the risk/return tradeoff. Higher risk investments must offer higher expected returns; otherwise, investors will purchase assets that offer the same return with less risk, or a higher return for the same risks. Projects that attempt to increase a firm's earnings or cash flow may favorably affect the *size* and *timing* of cash flows, but they may ignore the *risk* component. Increases in a firm's exposure to risk, even in the face of rising earnings, may lead to a *lower* firm and shareholder value. Attempts to maximize returns without considering risk may harm the firm's long-run viability and value to shareholders, creditors, and employees.

Fifth, shareholder value is the best performance measure because it represents the firm's performance from the perspective of those who have their capital most at risk, namely, its owners. Bondholders or bankers are not owners, but creditors; they receive their interest and principal payments before shareholders receive any cash from the firm. Although a very important component of any successful firm, employees resemble creditors; in exchange for their labor, they receive income from the firm's owners. Overemphasizing customer quality, satisfaction, or service may lead to happy customers, but uncontrolled cost increases to meet these needs without sufficient revenues may ultimately lead to the firm's demise. Lenders, fearing nonpayment, may cut off lines of credit; employees, fearing cutbacks, may leave to take other jobs; and the financial market, upset with the firm's poor use of capital, may downgrade its value, harming its owners.

Focusing on shareholder value rectifies all of these potential problems. Smart managers make decisions to service customers in a cost-efficient manner. They treat and pay employees fairly; otherwise, unmotivated and unhappy employees become unproductive, cost–increasing employees who prevent the firm from satisfying its goals. By focusing on firm value, managers work to maintain stable relationships with financing sources so funds will be available to finance future growth or retrenchment needs.

Some may wonder whether focusing on shareholder wealth may be detrimental to the nonfinancial aspects of the firm. Quite the opposite, focusing on shareholder wealth is the best means of helping the long-term survival of the firm in a dynamic, global economy. Shareholder value simultaneously considers all of the influences on the firm; decisions that are made to maximize shareholder wealth reflect the best interests of all of the firm's constituents or stakeholders.

In particular, decisions to maximize shareholder wealth may benefit employees. Managers realize that a happy, stable work force both increases productivity and reduces costs. Human resource departments of firms often conduct studies to compare the benefits and costs of offering programs to meet workers' needs. For example, an on-site day care center for workers' preschool-aged children can benefit both the employees and shareholders by reducing employee absenteeism and job turnover. Similarly, innovations in flexible worker scheduling and career planning can add value to the firm by reducing employee turnover and the subsequent costs of hiring and training new workers. Wellness programs encourage healthy eating and exercise habits among employees and can reduce both absenteeism costs and health insurance premiums. Workers for some firms periodically leave the factory and visit customers to learn more about customers' needs. This results in better motivated workers who can appreciate the importance of their job to the customer.

Shareholder wealth as a measure of firm performance is objective and forward-looking, and it incorporates all influences on the firm and its stakeholders. No other measure of firm performance is as inclusive and practical as a means for evaluating a firm's strategies.

59. Shark Repellent

Shark repellents are anti-takeover amendments that firms add to their corporate charters to protect themselves from unfavorable takeovers. One such strategy is a supermajority rule that requires 95 percent of a firm's shareholders to approve a **tender offer**. [See also **Tender offer**] Another technique is a fair price amendment, which requires a

suitor to acquire stock at essentially one price. To a certain extent, this protects the shareholders of the firm against two-tier acquisitions, in which the acquiring firm acquires one block of stock at a high price and then the remaining shares at a substantially lower price.

60. Sharpe Ratio

For an asset, the ratio of the risk premium to the return standard deviation (i.e., $\overline{R}_i - R_f/\sigma_i$), where $\overline{R}_i$ is average rate of return for ith security or portfolio; R_f is the risk-free rate, and σ_i is the standard deviation of rates of return for ith security or portfolio.

61. Sharpe's Measure

Reward-to-volatility ratio; ratio of portfolio excess return to standard deviation. [See also **Sharpe ratio**]

62. Shelf Life

Number of days it takes to get goods purchased and sold, or days in inventory.

63. Shelf Registration

The shelf registration process saves issuers both time and money. There is no cost or penalty for registering shelf securities and then not issuing them. Filing fees are relatively low, and the firm can take some securities from the shelf and sell them immediately through one underwriter and then sell more later with another underwriter. This technique allows the issuer to determine which investment bank offers the best service.

Not every firm can use shelf registration. Firms must meet several size, credit quality, and ethics requirements:

1. The market value of the firm's common stock must be at least $150 million.

2. The firm must have made no defaults on its debt in the previous three years.

3. The firm's debt must be investment grade (rated **BBB** or better).

4. The firm must not have been found guilty of violation of the Securities Exchange Act of 1934 in the previous three years.

Despite its attractiveness and lower cost, few firms have chosen to sell seasoned equity through shelf registration; one study found that only 5.6 percent of seasoned equity offerings were shelf registered. As this suggests, shelf registration does have several drawbacks for equity issues. The first is that the securities are sold with no prior due diligence and analysis by an investment bank. An investment bank may assist in selling shelf-registered securities; but its role is limited to marketing the shares, rather than serving as an independent, analytical third party. Consequently, the investment bank can provide little or no certification effect. In fact, the issuer can entirely bypass investment banks when selling shelf-registered stock; it can sell the shares directly to dealers and investors on a stock exchange.

Investors may see a second drawback since the firm can decide when to sell shelf-registered securities. A firm commitment underwriting may take several months. During that time, the firm is at risk of an adverse price move. A shelf offering imposes essentially no delay between submitting the short registration form and selling the shares. This gives the issuer the opportunity to wait for a run-up in the stock price before issuing shares, but smart investors may suspect a shelf sale of equity as a sign that the shares are overpriced.

For a third disadvantage, a shelf registration of common shares leads to uncertainty, which investors do not like. Investors view the shares sitting on the shelf as overhanging the market, ready to be sold at any moment. This potential supply of shares depresses prices and raises investors' concerns about opportunistic stock sales.

64. Short

A position is short with respect to a price if the position profits from a decrease in that price.

A short-seller of a stock profits from a decrease in the stock price and, hence, is short the stock. A seller of an option profits from a decrease in volatility and, hence, is short volatility.

65. Short Call

Selling a call (writing it) has risk-reward characteristics which are the inverse of the long call. However, one major distinction arises when writing calls (or puts) rather than buying them. That is, the writer can either own the underlying asset upon which he or she is selling the option (a **covered write**), or simply sell the option without owning the asset (**naked write**). [See also **Covered write** and **Naked write**]

66. Short Forward

The party to a forward contract who has an obligation to sell the underlying asset.

67. Short Hedge

Sale of a futures contract to protect against a price decline.

68. Short Position or Hedge

The sale of a futures contract in anticipation of a fall in the price of the underlying asset. Also obligates delivery of the commodity of financial instrument (and payment) if the position is left open to maturity.

69. Short Put

A put that has been sold (write a put) can be covered or uncovered.

70. Short Rate

The interest rate applying for a very short period of time.

71. Short Rebate

The rate of return paid on collateral when shares are borrowed.

72. Short Run

That period of time in which certain equipment, resources, and commitments of them are fixed. [See also **Long run**]

73. Short Squeeze

[See also **Squeeze**]

74. Short-Against-the-Box

The short-sale of a stock that the short-seller owns. The result of a short-against-the-box is that the short-seller has both a long and short position and, hence, bears no risk from the stock yet receives the value of the share from the short sale.

75. Short-Run Operating Activities

Events and decisions concerning the short-term finance of a firm, such as how much inventory to order and whether to offer cash terms or credit terms to customers.

76. Short-Sale

A transaction in which an investor borrows a security, sells it, and then returns it at a later date to the lender. If the security makes payments, the short-seller must make the same payments to the lender.

77. Short-Term Debt

An obligation having a maturity of one year or less from the date it was issued. Also called unfunded debt. It includes accounts payable, notes payable etc.

78. Short-Term Risk-Free Rate

T-bill ratio is the short-term risk free rate and T-bond rate is the long-term risk-free rate.

79. Short-Term Securities

Securities that mature in one year or less. These securities include T-bill, commercial paper and other.

80. Short-Term Tax Exempts

Short-term securities issued by states, municipalities, local housing agencies, and urban renewal agencies.

81. Shortage Costs

Costs that fall with increases in the level of investment in current assets.

82. Shout Option

A shout call option expiring at time T has the payoff $\max(0, S_{\hat{t}} - K, S_T - K)$, where $\hat{t}$ is the time; and $S_{\hat{t}}$ is the price at which the option holder "shouted," thereby guaranteeing an expiration payoff at least as great as $S_{\hat{t}} - K$ [See also **Deferred-strike option**]

83. Side Effects

Effects of a proposed project on other parts of the firm. These effects can either be positive or negative.

84. Sight Draft

A sight draft is payable on presentation to the importer and the exporter usually receives the proceeds within one to two weeks. Normally, the exporter's bank (or its correspondent bank in the buyer's country) does not present the draft for payment by the importer until the merchandise has been delivered (usually by ship). When the importer (the buyer) has verified that all the paperwork is in order and that the goods have arrived, it pays the bank and receives title to the merchandise.

85. Sigma

[See also **Vega**]

86. Signaling Approach

Approach to the determination of optimal capital structure asserting that insiders in a firm have information that the market does not; therefore the choice of capital structure by insiders can signal information to outsiders and change the value of the firm. This theory is also called the asymmetric information approach.

87. Simple Interest

Simple interest, unlike compound interest, pays a return only on the principal (the money originally invested) over successive periods. To calculate simple interest, multiply the principal by the interest rate, and multiply again by time. Simple interest does not include any compounding.

88. Simple Linear Regression

Simple linear regression is a statistical technique that fits a straight line to a set of data points, thus providing an expression for a relationship between two variables. One of the more widely used regression techniques is the method of least squares. If x_i is the independent variable and y_i is the dependent variable, the linear equation as:

$$y_i = \alpha + \beta x_i + e_i,$$

can be solved, where α = intercept; β = slope of the least-squares line; e_i = error term.

The values α and β for n observations of x and y can be estimated as:

$$\hat{\alpha} = \frac{(\sum y)(\sum x^2) - (\sum x)(\sum xy)}{n(\sum x^2) - (\sum x)^2} = \bar{y} - \hat{\beta}\bar{x},$$

$$\hat{\beta} = \frac{n(\sum xy) - (\sum x)(\sum y)}{n(\sum x^2) - (\sum x)^2} = \frac{\text{Cov}(x,y)}{\text{Var}(x)}$$

in which $\text{Cov}(x,y)$ stands for the covariance that is

$$\sum_{i=1}^{n} \frac{(y_i - \bar{y})(x_i - \bar{x})}{n},$$

and $\text{Var}(x)$ stands for the variance:

$$\sum_{i=1}^{n} \frac{(x_i - \bar{x})^2}{n}.$$

89. Simple Prospect

An investment opportunity where a certain initial wealth is placed at risk and only two outcomes are possible.

90. Simulation

[See also **Monte Carlo simulation**]

91. Simulation Analysis

In reality, every variable relevant to the capital budgeting decision can be viewed as a random variable. **Scenario analysis** and **sensitivity analysis** limit the randomness aspects of each item by examining only a few values of each variable. [See also **Scenario analysis** and **Sensitivity analysis**] Simulation analysis attempts to realistically portray the relevant inputs to the capital budgeting project as random variables. Each variable, whether it be price, variable cost, project life, or some other item, is assumed to have a probability distribution with a known mean and variance.

In each simulation trial, computer analysis uses a random number generator to select values from each variable's probability distribution as the basis for net present value (NPV) calculation. This process is repeated many times; each time, numbers are randomly drawn from each probability distribution. After replicating the trials several thousand times, the statistical distribution of the computed NPVs is plotted, and the average NPV and its variance are computed. Unlike the NPV point estimates derived from scenario or sensitivity analysis, simulation analysis gives an estimated distribution of potential NPVs.

Of course, the simulation output is only as accurate as the inputs. It is likely that an inaccurate NPV distribution will result if inappropriate probability distributions, means, and variances are used as inputs.

92. Single Index Model

A model of stock returns that decomposes influences on returns into a systematic factor, as measured by the return on a broad market index, and firm-specific factors. This method can be used to simplify the portfolio selection process. [See also **Market model**]

93. Single-Country Funds

Mutual funds that invest in securities of only one country. It is a closed-end fund.

94. Single-Factor Model

A model of security returns that acknowledges only one common factor. [See also **Factor model**]

95. Single-Price Auction (Dutch Auction)

In an important experiment begun in 1992, the Fed instituted a single-price, or Dutch, auction system for selected 2-year and 5-year Treasury notes. In a traditional Treasury auction, securities are allocated to the highest bidders, in descending order of the prices they bid, until all securities to be issued are awarded. Thus, winning bidders for the same security pay different amounts, and the highest bidder pay the same price. Many experts believe that the traditional bidding system encourages primary

dealers, who must bid at every auction, to collude in their efforts to minimize the winner's curse. The traditional system may also encourage cornering: Winning bidders may attempt to compensate for the winner's curse by earning excess profits as they resell securities they have won at the auction.

96. Sinking Fund

It is a procedure that allows for the repayment of principal at maturity by calling for the bond issuer to repurchase some position of the outstanding bonds. An indenture may require the firm to retire specified portions of the bond issue over time through payments to a sinking fund. This provides for an orderly and steady retirement of debt over time. Sinking funds are more common in bonds issued by firm with lower credit ratings; a higher quality issuer may have only a small annual sinking fund obligation due to a perceived ability to repay investors' principal at maturity.

A sinking fund affects the maturity of a bond issue since it allows the firm to retire the issue in bits and pieces over time. After a deferral period following the primary market offering, the sinking fund requirement usually can be satisfied in one of two ways. First, the issuer can select specific bonds for retirement by randomly drawing serial numbers. Investors whose numbers are drawn must return their bonds to the firm in exchange for repayment of principal. The issuer effectively calls in portions of the issue over time.

The second way to meet the sinking fund requirement is to purchase bonds from willing investors in the secondary market. Secondary market purchases become attractive if the bond's market price is less than par.

97. Size Effect

The portfolios of the firm with the smallest market value experienced return that were, both economically and statistically, significantly greater than the portfolios of the firm with large market value.

98. Skewness

A statistical measure which characterizes the asymmetry of a distribution around its mean. Positive skews indicate asymmetric tail extending toward positive values (right-hand side). Negative skewness implies asymmetry toward negative values (left-hand side). It is the third moment of a distribution. To calculate the sample skewness of random variable X as:

$$S_x = \frac{N}{(N-1)(N-2)} \sum_{i=1}^{N} \left(\frac{X_i - \bar{x}}{\sigma_X}\right)^3,$$

where N is the number of observations; and $\bar{x}$ is the sample mean.

The distribution of losses across a credit portfolio will be positively skewed if there is positive correlation between obligors or the size/ number of exposures is coarsely granular. This means that the confidence interval out on the downside tail will be further away from the mean than would be expected given the portfolio's standard deviation alone.

99. Skip-Day Settlement

A convention for calculating yield that assumes a T-bill sale is not settled until two days after quotation of the T-bill price.

100. Small Company Offering Registration

Several states offer programs to ease the process of public equity financing for firms within their borders. A firm in a state that has enacted a SCOR (Small Company Offering Registration) law can raise $1 million by publicly selling shares worth at least $5. This law creates a fairly standardized, fill-in-the blank registration document to reduce a firm's time and cost in preparing an offering. A firm can sell shares from a SCOR offering in other states with minimal notice to the SEC. According to estimates, a SCOR offering can reduce issuing costs by up to one-half for small firms.

101. Small Issues Exemption

Issues of less than $50 million are governed by Regulation A. Under the Regulation A, only a brief offering statement instead of a lengthy regular statement is needed. Securities issues that involve less than $ 1.5 million are not required to file a registration statement with the Securities and Exchange Commission. For Regulation A to be operative, no more than $1.5 million may be sold by insiders.

102. Small-Firm Effect

Market anomaly whereby small companies exhibit a propensity to produce rates of return that are larger than those predicted on the basis of the capital asset pricing model.

103. Society for Worldwide Interbank Financial Telecommunications

The Society for Worldwide Interbank Financial Telecommunications (SWIFT) is not a settlement system, but a communications system that facilitates settlement of wire transfers through banks in different countries. Currently, over 1,600 banks maintain membership in the system, most of them located in the US and Europe. The innovative feature of SWIFT is the standardization of messages so that computer software throughout the world can read SWIFT messages. The SWIFT network handles all types of customers and bank transfers.

104. Soft Dollars

The value of research services that brokerage houses supply to investment managers "free of charge" in exchange for the investment managers' business.

105. Sole Proprietorship

A business owned by a single individual. The sole proprietorship pays no corporate income tax but has unlimited liability for business debts and obligation. [See also **Proprietorship**]

106. Sovereign Risk

[See also **Country risk**]

107. Spark Spread

The difference between the price of electricity and that of the quantity of natural gas required to produce the electricity. Actually the operation cost to produce electricity includes not only gas cost. Therefore, the spark spread is the variable component of the marginal profit.

108. Special Drawing Rights (SDRs)

SDRs are a form of currency related by IMF in the 1970s to increase would liquidity. SDRs are a weighted average of the US dollar, the German mark, the Japanese yen, the French franc, and British pound.

109. Specialist

Individual on the floor of an organized exchange who keeps an inventory of one or more stocks and trades with floor brokers out of that inventory.

110. Speculation

Undertaking a risky investment with the objective of earning a greater profit than an investment in a risk-free alternative (a risk premium). The distinction between hedging and speculation comes not from which side of futures contract one takes but from the motivation for entering into the contract.

111. Speculative-Grade Bond

Bond rate Ba or lower by Moody's, or BB or lower by Standard & Poor's, or an unrated bond.

112. Speculator

A market participant who is willing (for a price) to take on the risk the hedger wishes to eliminate. This trader goes long or short on a contract without having, or intending to take, an opposite position in the cash market. Speculator can be either scalper or day trader. [See also **Scalper**]

113. Spin-Off

In a spin-off, a parent firm distributes all shares in a wholly owned subsidiary to its shareholders, thus creating a new corporate entity (although the same owners have the same percentage of shares in the new firm). A spin-off may involve either the stock of an existing subsidiary or newly created stock representing ownership in the disposed unit.

114. Spontaneous Financing

Short-term financial planning involves much more of the firm's operations than working capital management alone; it extends to management of all of the firm's current assets and current liabilities and their interrelationship. In practice, financial managers make little or no distinction between investment decisions involving current assets and financing decisions involving current liabilities. Current assets and current liabilities often are too closely related for such separate treatment. Both current asset and current liability accounts increase simultaneously, providing financing (at least in the short run) for the investment. For example, when the firm obtains inventory on credit, it generates an account payable. This is called spontaneous financing.

115. Spot Curve

The set of zero-coupon bond prices with different maturities, usually inferred from government bond prices.

116. Spot Exchange Rate

The spot exchange rate represents the exchange rate for an immediate exchange of two currencies. The actual exchange of one currency for another occurs on the settlement date, up to two days later.

117. Spot Interest Rate

Interest rate fixed today on a loan that is made today. In addition, it can also refer to the interest rate on an investment that is made for a period time starting from today and last for n years.

118. Spot Market Transaction

Cash or spot market transaction represent the exchange of any asset between two parties who agree on the asset's characteristic and price, where the buyer tenders payment and take possession of the asset when the price is set. [See also **Forward contract**]

119. Spot Price

The current price of the commodity if purchased in the cash or "spot" market.

120. Spot Rate

The current interest rate appropriate for discounting a cash flow of some given maturity.

121. Spot Trade

There are three types of trade that take place in the foreign exchange market: spot, forward and swap. Spot trade involves an agreement on the exchange rate today for settlement in two days.

122. Spot Volatilities

The volatilities used to price a cap when a different volatility is used for each caplet. [See **Flat volatility**]

123. Spot-Futures Parity Theorem

Describes the theoretically correct relationship between spot and futures prices. Violation of the parity relationship gives rise to arbitrage opportunities.

124. Spread

Refers to the simultaneous purchase and sale of futures contracts for (1) the same commodity or instrument with different maturity months or (2) commodities in different but related markets.

125. Spread (futures)

Taking a long position in a futures contract of one maturity and a short position in a contract of different maturity, both on the same commodity.

126. Spread (options)

A combination of two or more call options or put options on the same stock with different exercise prices or times to expiration. A *money spread* refers to a spread with different exercise price; a *time spread* refers to differing expiration date.

127. Spread Underwriting

Difference between the underwriters's buying price and the offering price. The spread is a fee for the service of the underwriting syndicate.

128. Spreadsheet

A computer program that organizes numerical data into rows and columns on a terminal screen, for calculating and making adjustments based on new data.

129. Squeeze.

The possibility that enough long positions hold their contracts to maturity that supplies of the commodity are not adequate to cover all contracts. A *short squeeze* describes the reverse: short positions threaten to deliver an expensive-to-store commodity.

130. Stable Distribution

A probability distribution for which sums of random variables have the same distribution as the original random variable. Stable distribution can be classified as normal stable distribution and nonnormal stable distribution. The normal distribution is stable because sums of normally distributed random variables are stably distributed.

Nonnormal stable distribution can be further classified into (a) Symmetric stable distribution and (b) non-symmetric stable distribution. This kind of distribution can be used to describe the distribution of the real return of the stock prices.

131. Stable Dividend Policy

The Lintner (1956) study reinforces the notion that dividend policy conveys information to investors. Many financial managers strive to maintain steady or modestly growing dividends and avoid large fluctuations or changes in dividend policies. Reducing dividend fluctuations helps reduce investor uncertainty about future dividends. Lower risk leads to higher stock prices. Managers resist increasing dividends if they do not expect to maintain the increase in the future. This supports a predominant policy of maintaining historical dividends.

If firms hesitate to raise dividends too quickly, they positively abhor the prospect of reducing dividends, for several reasons. First, many individuals and institutions require large cash flows from their investments. For example, retired people in lower tax brackets generally covet high dividend payments. Tax-exempt institutions, such as endowment funds or pension funds, also need high current income and therefore desire high dividends. Miller and Modigliani argue that these in-

dividuals or institutions should ignore a stock's level of dividends because they always can liquidate some of their holdings in order to generate substantial transaction costs, especially brokerage fees. In addition to the time involved in deciding to sell securities, investors may exhaust all of their principal, leaving none for future income requirements.

Second, managers often resist reducing dividends also because a cut in dividends may be interpreted by the investment community as a signal of trouble with the firm or a result of poor management. Even if the reduction is intended to allow the firm to pursue an attractive opportunity, it may adversely affect stock prices.

A third reason that firms resist reducing dividends involves the legal list. Many large, institutional investors are bound by the prudent man rule, or by legislation, to buy only securities that are included on the legal list. One criterion of the list is a long history of continued dividend payments without dividend reductions. Therefore, a firm that reduces or omits a dividend payment faces the risk of being ineligible for purchase by certain institutional investors.

A stable dividend policy can become a sort of self-fulfilling prophecy. An unexpected rise or reduction in dividends can have an announcement effect on the firm's share price. An increase in dividends may lead investors to perceive a promising future and share price may increase. A drop in dividends may lead investors to fear a less promising future, resulting in a drop in share price. These perceptions may be accurate if managers themselves feel it is important to avoid fluctuations, especially cuts. In such a company, investors would be correct in viewing dividend declarations as sources of information.

132. Stack and Roll

A hedging strategy in which an existing stack hedge with maturing futures contracts is replaced by a new stack hedge with longer dated futures contracts.

133. Stack Hedge

Hedging a stream of obligations by entering future contracts with a *single* maturity, with the number of contracts selected so that changes in the *present value* of the future obligations are offset by changes in the value of this "stack" of futures contracts.

134. Staggered-Maturity Plan

A common practice among bond-portfolio managers is to evenly space the maturity of their securities. Under the staggered-maturity plan bonds are held to maturity, at which time the principal is reinvested in another long-term maturity instrument. Little managerial expertise is required to maintain the portfolio and the maturing bonds and regular interest payments provide some liquidity.

135. Stakeholders

Both stockholders and bondholders are stakeholders of a firm.

136. Stand-Alone Percent Standard Deviation

Stand-alone standard deviation expressed as a percentage of the mean value for the given asset.

137. Stand-Alone Principle

To properly estimate the cash flows of a proposed capital budgeting project, the project must be viewed in isolation from the rest of the firm. This stand-alone principle ensures that analysts focus on the project's own cash flows, uncontaminated by cash flows from the firm's other activities.

138. Standard & Poor's Bond Rating

AAA – bonds of highest quality.
AA – high-quality debt obligations.
A – Bonds that have a strong capacity to pay interest and principal but may be susceptible to adverse effects.

BBB – bonds that have an adequate capacity to pay interest and principal, but are more vulnerable to adverse economic conditions or changing circumstances.
BB, B, CCC – primary speculative bonds with great uncertainties and major risk if exposed to adverse conditions.
C – income bonds on which no interest is being paid.
D – bond is in default.

139. Standard and Poor's 500 Composite Index (S&P 500)

The S&P 500 index comprises industrial firms, utilities, transportation firms, and financial firms. Changes in the index are based on changes in the firm's total market value with respect to a base year. Currently, the base period (1941–$1943 = 10$) for the S&P 500 index is stated formally as:

$$\text{S\&P 500 index} = \frac{\sum_{i=1}^{500} P_{ti} Q_{ti}}{\sum_{i=1}^{500} P_{0i} Q_{0i}} \times 10,$$

where P_{0i} = per-share stock price at base year 0; P_{ti} = per-share stock price at index data t; Q_{0i} = number of shares for firm i at base year 0; Q_{ti} = number of shares for firm i at index year t.

The index is multiplied by an index set equal to 10. The specification of this index is identical to that of the value index indicated in the equation.

140. Standard Deviation

The standard deviation, σ, is simply the square root of the **variance**. [See also **Variance**]

$$\sigma = \sqrt{\sigma^2}.$$

The standard deviation formula gives units of measurement that match those of raw data.

Standard deviation can be given a statistical interpretation to help give the analyst an intuitive feel for the possible range of returns that can occur. For example, if the underlying distribution of data is approximately normal, we expect 68 percent of the data terms to fall within one standard deviation of the mean, that is, $\overline{X} \pm \sigma$. About 95 percent of observed returns will fall within two standard deviations of the average $\overline{X} \pm 2\sigma$. Actual returns should fall within three standard deviations of the mean, $\overline{X} \pm 3\sigma$, about 99 percent of the time. Thus, if the mean and standard deviations are known, a rough range for future values can be estimated. [See also **Coefficient of variation**]

141. Standardized Normal Distribution

A normal distribution with an expected value of 0 and a standard deviation of 1. [See also **Standard deviation**]

142. Standby Fee

Amount paid to an underwriter who agrees to purchase any stock that is not subscribed to the public investor in a rights offering.

143. Standby Underwriting

An agreement whereby an underwriter agrees to purchase any stock that is not purchased by the public investor.

144. Standstill Agreements

Contracts where the bidding firm in a takeover attempt agrees to limit its holdings of another firm. These agreements usually lead to cessation of takeover attempts and it has had a negative effect on stock prices.

145. State of the World

It is a credit rating migration outcome; a new credit rating arrived at the risk horizon. This can be either for a single obligor on a stand-alone basis or jointly between two obligors.

146. Stated Annual Interest Rate

The interest rate expressed as a percentage per annum by which interest payment is determined. [See also **Nominal interest rate**]

147. Stated Interest Rate

[See **Annual percentage rate**]

148. Statement of Cash Flows

The statement of cash flows (Financial Accounting Standards Board [FASB] Statement Number 95) can be derived using the balance sheets for two consecutive years and the most recent year's income statement. These inputs give the analyst insight into the firm's cash inflows and outflows; that is, they indicate how the firm raised and spent cash. It shows how income statement items and changes in balance sheet accounts affect the firm's cash position.

The statement of cash flows has three sections: cash flows from operating activities, cash flows from investing activities, and cash flows from financing activities. The sum of the cash flows from these three sections gives the net change in the cash position of the firm. In the language of the accountant, the items in this statement are "reconciled to cash."

The first step in constructing a statement of cash flows is to compute the change in each item between the beginning and ending balance sheets and to classify each as a source or a use of cash. Generally, a source of cash creates a cash inflow: a use of cash generates a cash outflow. A source of cash results when an asset account (except for the cash account) is *decreased* or when a liability or equity account is *increased*. Let's look at this intuitively. A reduction in accounts receivable implies that customers sent cash to the firm to pay their bills;

a reduction in inventory implies that goods have been sold; a decline in fixed assets implies that assets have been sold for cash. Likewise, increases in accounts payable, notes payable, or debt figures imply that the firm has taken on additional financing sources; an increase in a common or preferred stock account implies that the firm has raised funds by a stock issue.

A use of cash leads to a cash outflow; a use of cash occurs when there is an increase in an asset account (except cash) or a reduction in a liability or equity account. Increases in inventory, or fixed assets, for example, imply that the firm used funds to purchase an asset. A reduction in a liability or equity account implies that the firm used cash to pay bills or repurchase securities.

In addition to balance sheet information, we also need the information from the income statement to construct a statement of cash flows. Generally, income is a source of funds and expenses represent a use of funds. However, non-cash expenses, such as depreciation, do not represent a cash outflow and are therefore not a use of funds.

Cash Flows from Operating Activities

This section of the statement of cash flows lists the sources and uses of cash that arise from the normal operations of a firm. In general, the net cash flow from operations is computed as income statement net income plus adjustments for noncash revenues and expenses:

Cash flow from operating activities
  = Net income + Depreciation
    − Change in modified net working capital.

You may recall that net working capital is defined as the difference between current assets and current liabilities:

Net working capital = Current assets
                    − Current liabilities.

Thus, an *increase* in net working capital is a net investment in the firm's current assets; and an increase in an asset is considered a use of cash. A *decrease* in net working capital is a divestment of assets, that is, a source of cash.

A modified net working capital amount is used to compute cash flow from operating activities, as standard definitions of current assets include cash and marketable securities and standard definitions of current liabilities include notes payable. In the statement of cash flows, changes in notes payable are considered a financing flow and thus appear as a component of the cash flows from financing activities. The change in the cash account appears at the bottom of the statement, as the sum of cash flows from operating, investing, and financing activities

Cash Flows from Investing Activities

This section of the statement of cash flows represents the investments a firm makes in both its own fixed assets and the equity of other firms, including subsidiaries or joint ventures. (These holdings are listed in the investment account of the balance sheet.) Increases and decreases in these accounts are considered investment activities. The cash flow from investment activities is the change in gross plant and equipment plus the change in the investment account. The changes are added if they represent a source of funds; otherwise, they are subtracted. The dollar changes in these accounts are computed from the beginning and ending balance sheets.

Cash Flows from Financing Activities.

This section of the statement of cash flows includes cash flows arising from purchases and sales of notes payable and long-term securities and dividend payments to equity holders (recall that interest payments to bond holders help determine the firm's net income, which is part of cash flows from operating activities). Cash flows from financing activities are computed as financing sources minus financing uses. Sources include increases in notes payable and new issues of bonds, preferred stock, and common stock, since these actions result in cash inflows. Uses include principal payments or the repurchase of notes payable, bonds, or stock. Dividend payments to equity holders also are considered in financing use.

The sum of the cash flows from operating, investing, and financial activities is the net increase or decrease in the firm's cash. By detailing changes in important financial statement line items, the statement of cash flows reveals information that the balance sheet and income statement cannot provide.

149. Statewide Branching

Allowing banks to establish branches throughout an entire state.

150. Static Hedge

A hedge that does not have to be changed once it its initiated.

151. Static NPV

The net present value (NPV) of a project at a point in time, ignoring the possibility of postponing adoption of the project.

152. Static Option Replication

The use of options to hedge options, with the goal of creating a hedging portfolio that has a delta that naturally moves in tandem with the delta of the option being hedged. [See Ergener and Kani (1995)] [See also **Dynamic Hedging**]

153. Static Theory of Capital Structure

Theory that the firm's capital structure is determined by a trade-off of the value of tax shields against the costs of bankruptcy.

154. Static Tradeoff Hypothesis

According to the static tradeoff hypothesis, a firm balances the marginal benefits (tax shields) of additional debt financing with its marginal costs, namely the increase in the present value of future expected bankruptcy costs. Any increases in debt beyond this optimal level actually reduces firm value, as investors' perceptions of the increased cost of bankruptcy outweigh the tax benefits of additional debt.

155. Statutory Accounting

Statutory accounting is a combination of cash based and accrual accounting; expenses are recognized when paid but revenues are not recognized until earned. In general, it is a more conservative way of reporting final results than GAAP. Both thrifts and insurers use both generally accepted accounting principles and statutory accounting rule.

156. Step-up Swap

A swap where the principal increases over time in a predetermined way.

157. Stochastic Differential Equation

An equation characterizing the change in a variable in which on or more of the differential terms are increments to stochastic process.

158. Stochastic Process

An equation describing the probabilistic behavior of a stochastic variable is called stochastic process. Stochastic processes can be classified as discrete time or continuous time. A discrete-time stochastic process is one where the value of the variable can change only at certain fixed points in time, whereas a continuous-time stochastic process is one where changes can take place at any time. Stochastic processes can also be classified as continuous variable or discrete variable. In a continuous-variable process, the underlying variable can take any value within a certain range, whereas in a discrete-variable process, only certain discrete values are possible.

159. Stochastic Variable

A variable whose future value is uncertain. A stochastic variable can be classified into either continuous or discrete variable. [See also **Stochastic process**]

160. Stock Dividend

Managers can use stock dividends to change the firm's number of common shares outstanding. A stock dividend is a payout of dividends in the form of stock rather than cash. A stock dividend commonly is expressed as a percentage; for example, a 10-percent stock dividend means that a stockholder receives one new share for every ten shares currently owned.

161. Stock Exchanges

Secondary markets where already-issued securities are bought and sold by members. [See also **Exchanges** and **Secondary market**]

162. Stock Index

An average of the prices of a group of stocks. A stock index can be a simple average of stock prices, in which case it is *equally weighted*, or it can be a weighted average, with the weights proportional to market capitalization, in which case it is *value-weighted*. [See also **Stock market index**]

163. Stock Index Futures

Futures on a stock index. For example, S&P 500 futures and major index futures.

164. Stock Index Options

An option on a stock index. For example, S&P 500 options.

165. Stock Market Index

A stock market index is a statistical measure that shows how the prices of a group of stocks change over time. A stock market index encompasses either all or only a portion of stocks in its market. Stock market indexes employ different weighting schemes, so we can use this basis to categorize the indexes by type. The three most common types of stock market indexes are market-value-weighted indexes, price-weighted indexes, and equally weighted indexes. [See also **Dow Jones Index**, **Standard and Poor's 500 Composite Index (S&P)** and **Wilshire 5000 Equity Index**]

166. Stock Options

One way to help solve the agency problem – to help managers make decisions that are in shareholders' best interests is to relate the managers' personal wealth to shareholder value. Some firms tie managerial compensation to stock performance, often by awarding managers stock options as part of their compensation. The options allow managers to purchase, at a future time, a stated number of the firm's shares at a specific price. If the firm's stock price rises, the value of the shares, and therefore the managers' wealth, also rises. Decisions that detract from the best interest of shareholders will affect management by making the stock options less valuable. More and more firms are basing the compensation of their top managers on the firm's stock price.

167. Stock Repurchase

A stock repurchase occurs when management spends corporate funds to buy back the stock of the company. A stock repurchase can benefit both management and shareholders. The repurchased shares become treasury stock and are then available for reissue to executives under stock option plans, to employees as part of profit sharing plans, and to other firms as part of mergers or acquisitions.

Management gains some defensive benefits by way of a stock repurchase. If managers of a cash-risk, low-debt firm fear a takeover, they may finance the stock purchase with the firm's excess cash or use debt, reducing the attractiveness of the firm as a takeover target. In addition, the repurchase program invites any dissatisfied stockholders to sell their shares back to the firm at a favorable price before a potential takeover company can make an offer for the stock. Management also benefits from the reduction in mailing and processing costs for annual reports, dividend payments, proxy statements, and other materials. Some repurchases are aimed directly at small shareholders for precisely this reason.

Shareholders may also benefit from a stock repurchase. Stockholders who want to sell their shares can do so at a favorable price. Stockholders who choose to hold onto their shares may benefit from the reduction in the number of shares outstanding. For example, suppose someone owns 1,000 shares of a company that has 25,000 shares outstanding. This stock represents a 4-percent (1,000/25,000) stake in the company. If the company repurchases 5,000 of its shares form other investors, then that stockholder's stake in the company increases to 5 percent (1,000/20,000).

Information related to cash dividends paid, repurchases of common stock, and employee compensation and stock option plans can be found in a firm's (consolidated) statement of common stock, retained earnings, and treasury stock.

168. Stock Selection

An active portfolio management technique that focuses on advantageous selection of particular stocks rather than on broad asset allocation choices.

169. Stock Split

Managers can use stock splits to change the firm's number of common shares outstanding. A stock is essentially the same thing as a **stock dividend**, except that a split is expressed as a ratio instead of a percentage. [See also **Stock dividend**] Basically a stock dividend and a stock split increase the number of shares of stock outstanding without any cash flow to the firm or increase in firm value.

170. Stockholder

Holder of equity shares in a firm. The terms *stockholder* and *shareholder* usually refer to owners of common stock.

171. Stockholders' Books

Set of books kept by firm management for its annual report that follows Financial Accounting Standard Board rules. The tax books follow the IRS rules.

172. Stockholders' Equity

The residual claims that stockholders have against a firm's assets, calculated by subtracting total liabilities from total assets; also net worth.

173. Stop Payment

Request by a depositor to stop payment on a previously issued check that has not yet cleared.

174. Stop-Loss Order

A sell order to be executed if the price of the stock, which you already own, falls below a stipulated level. Order can also be differentiated on the basis of allowable time for completion.

175. Storage Costs

The costs of storing a commodity.

176. Straddle

A straddle is a simultaneous position in both a call and a put on the same underlying asset. A long straddle involves purchasing both the call and the put. By combining these two seemingly opposing options an investor can get the best risk-return combination that each offers. A short straddle implies the position risk-return characteristics of the long straddle. A short straddle is a simultaneous position in both a short call and a short put on the same underlying asset. Contrary to the long-straddle position, selling a straddle can be an effective strategy when an investor expects little or no movement in the price of the underlying asset. A similar interpretation of its use would be that the investor expects the future volatility of the underlying asset's price that is currently impounded in the option premiums to decline. Moreover, since the time decay is a positive effect for the value of this position, one appropriate time to set a short straddle might be in the last month before expiration for the combined call and put.

177. Straddle Rules

Tax regulations controlling the circumstances in which a loss on a claim can be realized when a tax payer continues to own related securities or derivatives.

178. Straight Bond

A bond with no option features such as callability or convertibility.

179. Straight Voting

A shareholder may cast all of his or her votes for each candidate for the Board of Directors.

180. Straight–Line Depreciation

A method of depreciation whereby each year the firm depreciates a constant proportion of the initial investment less salvage value. [See also **Double-declining-balance method**]

For example, using the straight-line method, the firm can write off a uniform annual depreciation charge of $1,080, a year, as shown below, when costs are $6,000, and the salvage value is $600:

$$Annual\ depreciation = \frac{cost - salvage}{years}$$
$$= \frac{\$6,000 - \$600}{5} = \$1,080.$$

181. Strangle

The purchase of a put and a call with the same time to expiration and different price. A strangle is a similar strategy to a straddle. The investor is betting that there will be a large price move but is uncertain whether it will be an increase or a decrease. [See also **Straddle**]

182. Strap

A long position in two call options and one put option with the same strike price and expiration date. If a long position in one call and two put with same strike price and expiration date is called strip.

183. Strategic Planning

The process through which managers formulate the firm's mission and goals, and identify strengths, weaknesses, opportunities, and threats.

184. Stratified Sampling

A technique used in Monte Carlo valuation in which random numbers are drawn from each percentile (or other regular interval) of the distribution. [See also **Quasi-random sequence**]

185. Street Name

Describes securities held by a broker on behalf of a client but registered in the name of the firm.

186. Stress Testing

Testing of the impact of extreme market moves in the value of a portfolio. In addition to this, stress testing credit risk models imply to "back test" model to ascertain their predictive accuracy.

187. Striking Price

Price at which the put option or call option can be exercised. Also called the exercise price.

188. Strip

A variant of a straddle. A strip is two puts and one call on a stock, both with the same exercise price and expiration date. [See also **Straddle**]

189. Strip Hedge

Hedging a stream of obligations by offsetting each individual obligation with a futures contract matching the maturity and quantity of the obligation.

190. Stripped Bond

A bond in which individual coupon payments and principal payments are separated (stripped) from the bond and sold as distinct zero coupon securities.

191. Stripped of Coupons

Describes the practice of some investment banks that sell "synthetic" zero coupon bonds by marketing the rights to a single payment backed by a coupon-paying Treasury bond.

192. Stripped Securities

Securities that represent just the coupon interest or principal payments on a loan. The interest-only payment is referred to as an IO, while the principal-only payment is referred to as a PO.

193. STRIPS

An acronym for *Separate Trading of Registered Interest and Principal of Securities*. STRIPS are the interest and principal payments form Treasury bonds and notes traded as individual securities. These securities were introduced by Merrill Lynch and Solomon Brothers in 1982.

194. Strong-Form Efficient Market

Different assumptions about information availability give rise to different types of market efficiency. [See also **Efficient market**]

A market in which prices reflect *all* public and privately available knowledge, including past and current information, is a strong-form efficient market. In such an efficient market, even corporate officers and other insiders cannot earn above-average, risk-adjusted profits from buying and selling stock; even their detailed, exclusive information already is reflected in current stock prices. Few markets can ever pass the test of strong-form efficiency. US laws prohibit *insider trading*, or trading based on important, nonpublic information. These laws reflect a public perception that it is unfair for someone with access to private information to use that position for their own profit. Remember that corporate officers should try to maximize shareholder wealth. Using inside information to benefit themselves at the expense of unknowing shareholders is a violation of the trust that should exist in the principal-agent relationship.

195. Structured Note

A bond that makes payments that, at least in part, are contingent on some variable such as a stock price, interest rates, or exchange rates.

196. Subchapter S Corporation

A Subchapter S corporation is one of two special forms of corporate organizations in the US that allow dividends to escape double taxation. A Subchapter S corporation (named for the section of the tax code that discusses this organization) must have fewer than 35 shareholders, none of which is another corporation. Income from a Subchapter S corporation flows untaxed to the shareholders; thus, it is taxed only once, as personal income of the shareholders.

197. Submartingale Model

A submartingale is a fair-game model where prices in the next period are expected to be greater than prices in the current period. A submartingale model is appropriate for an expanding economy. One with real economic growth,or an inflationary economy, one with nominal price increases.

198. Subordinated Debenture

A subordinated debenture is the riskiest type of bond. [See also **Debenture**] The claims of these bondholders are subordinate, or junior, to the claims of debenture holders. Most "junk bonds," or high-yield bonds, are subordinated debentures.

199. Subordinated Debt

In the case of bankruptcy, the claims of holders of subordinated debt are subordinated to the claims of other debt holders. In banks, insured depositors are paid in full before holders of subordinated debt receive anything.

200. Subordination Clause

A provision in a bond indenture that restricts the issuer's future borrowing by subordinating the new lenders' claims on the firm to those of the existing bond holders. Claims of subordinated or junior debt holders are not paid until the prior debt is paid.

201. Subscription Price

Price that existing shareholders are allowed to pay for a share of stock in a rights offering. A rational

shareholder will only subscribe to the rights offering if the subscription price is below the market price of the stock on the offer's expiration date.

202. Substitution Swap

Exchange of one bond for a bond with similar attributes but more attractively priced.

203. Sum-of-the-Year's-Digits Depreciation

Sum-of-the-year's-digits method is one of the accelerate depreciation methods. The annual depreciation of this method can be calculated as:

$$dep_t = \frac{N - (t - 1)}{\sum\limits_{t=1}^{N} t} \times (cost - salvage\ value),$$

where dep_t = depreciation of the tth period, and N = number of years. For example, if the equipment cost is \$6,000, and the salvage value is \$600 then the sum-of-years' digits for five years are determined as:

Year 1 $\dfrac{5 - (1-1)}{1 + 2 + 3 + 4 + 5} \times (\$6,000 - \$600)$		$= \$1,800$
Year 2 $\dfrac{5 - (2-1)}{15}$	$\times (\$5,400)$	$= 1,440$
Year 3 $\dfrac{5 - (3-1)}{15}$	$\times (\$5,400)$	$= 1,080$
Year 4 $\dfrac{5 - (4-1)}{15}$	$\times (\$5,400)$	$= 720$
Year 5 $\dfrac{5 - (5-1)}{15}$	$\times (\$5,400)$	$= 360$
		$\$5,400$

204. Sunk Cost

A sunk cost is a project-related expense that is not dependent upon whether or not the project is undertaken. For example, assume a firm commissioned and paid for a feasibility study for a project last year. The funds for the study have been spent already; they represent a sunk cost. The study's cost is not an incremental cash flow as its cost is not affected by the firm's decision to either pursue or abandon the project. Therefore, the cost must be excluded from the project's cash flow estimates.

205. Super-Majority Amendment

A defensive tactic that requires 80 percent of shareholders to approve a merger.

206. Supply Shock

An event that influences production capacity and costs in the economy.

207. Support Level

A price level below that which it is supposedly difficult for a stock or stock index to fall.

208. Support Tranche

A class of mortgage-backed securities where the promised principal and interest payments are made after payments to holders of other classes of securities are made.

209. Surplus Funds

Cash flow available after payment of taxes in the project. [See also **Free cash flow**]

210. Sustainable Growth Rate

The sustainable growth rate measures how quickly the firm can grow when it sues both internal equity and debt financing to keep its capital structure steady over time. It is computed as:

$$Sustainable\ growth\ rate = \frac{(RR)(ROE)}{1 - (RR)(ROE)},$$

where RR is the firm's retention rate, which is multiplied by ROE, its return on equity, divided by one minus this product. [See also **Internal growth rate**]

211. Swap

Exchange between two securities or currencies. One type of swap involves the sale (or purchase) of a foreign currency with a simultaneous agreement to repurchase (or sell) it. [See also **Spot trade**]

212. Swap Contract

In addition to using forward, futures, and option contracts to hedge transactions or transaction exposure, many corporation are engaging in what are called *swap transactions* to accomplish this. A swap contract is a private agreement between two companies to exchange a specific cash flow amount at a specific date in the future. If the specific cash flow amount is interest payments, then the contract is an **interest rate swap**; if the specific amount of cash flows is currency payments, then the contract is a **currency swap**. [See also **Interest rate swap** and **Currency swap**] The first swap contract was negotiated between IBM and the World Bank in the early eighties. Since that time, the swap market has grown to over $10 trillion.

213. Swap Rate

The difference between the sale (purchase) price and the price to repurchase (resell) it in a swap. [See also **Spot exchange rate** and **Forward exchange rate**]

214. Swap Spread

The difference between the fixed rate on an interest rate swap and yield on a Treasury bond with the same maturity.

215. Swap Tenor

The lifetime of a swap.

216. Swap Term

Another name for *swap tenor*.

217. Swaption

Swaption represents option on swap. For example, an option to enter into an interest rate swap where a specified fixed bond rate is exchanged for floating-rate bond. Since the floating-rate bond is worth its face value at the start of a swap, swaption can be considered as options on the value of fixed-rate bond with strike price equal to the face value.

218. Swing Option

Swing option is also called take-and-pay option. It is an option created by trading the underlying asset. For example, energy option is which the rate of consumption must be between a minimum and maximum level. There is usually a limit on the number of time the option holder can change the rate at which the energy is consumed.

219. SWOT Analysis

SWOT analysis examines a firm's strengths, weaknesses, opportunities, and threats. It can help managers identify capital budgeting projects that will allow the firm to exploit its competitive advantages or prevent others from exploiting its weaknesses. Strengths and weaknesses arise from the firm's internal abilities, or lack thereof. Opportunities and threats represent external conditions that affect the firm, such as competitive forces, new technologies, government regulations, and domestic and international economic trends.

Strengths give the firm a comparative advantage in the marketplace. Perceived strengths can include good customer service, high-quality products, strong brand image, customer loyalty, innovative R&D efforts, market leadership, and strong financial resources. Managers must continue to develop, maintain, and defend these strengths through prudent capital investment policies or else they will diminish and shareholder wealth will decline as new and existing competitors take advantage of the weakening firm.

A firm's weaknesses give its competitors the opportunity to gain advantages over the firm. Once weakness are identified, the firm should select capital investments to mitigate or correct them. For example, a domestic producer in a global market can try to achieve global economies of scale (that is, achieve "global scale") by making investments that will allow it to export or produce its product overseas. Such a move also may make it easier for the firm to raise money in the future, as it may be able to raise funds in several different financial markets instead of just in its home country.

220. Syndicated Loan

A loan provided by a group of financial institutions (FIs) as opposed to a single lender. A syndicated loan is provided structure by the lead FI (or agent) and the borrower once the terms (rates fees and covenants) are set, pieces of the loan are sold to other FIs.

221. Syndicates

For most firm commitment underwritings, the managing investment bank arranges investment banking syndicates to help distribute shares of the newly public firm. Syndicates serve several purposes. First, a syndicate broadens the market base to include clients from other investment banking firms, thus allowing a broader distribution of the new issue. Second, the syndicate allows the managing investment bank to diversify or spread the risk of underwriting the new issue. Rather than purchasing the entire issue, the managing investment bank actually commits capital to purchase and resell only a portion of the issue; the remainder of the funds comes from members of the syndicate.

222. Synthetic Option

Rubinstein and Leland (1981) suggest a strategy that replicates the returns on a call option by continuously adjusting a portfolio consisting of a stock and a risk-free asset (T-bill, cash). This is called a synthetic call-option strategy; it involves increasing the investment in stock by borrowing when the value of stocks is increasing, and selling stock and paying off borrowing or investing in the risk-free asset when market values are falling.

The key variable in this strategy is the delta value, which measures the change in the price of a call option with respect to the change in the value of the portfolio of risky stocks. For deep-in-the-money options, the delta value will be close to one because a $1 change in the stock value will result in approximately a $1 change in the option value. Thus to replicate the option with cash and stock, almost one share must be purchased and the amount borrowed will be approximately equal to the exercise price. For deep out-of-the-money options, the value of the delta will be close to zero, and the replicating portfolio will contain very few shares and little or no borrowing. Hence in its simplest form the delta value largely depends on the relationship between the exercise price and the stock price. As the market moves to new levels, the value of the delta will change; hence the synthetic option portfolio must be rebalanced periodically to maintain the proper mix between equity and borrowing or cash.

In a similar manner, a portfolio manager can createreplicated put options through a combination of selling short the asset and lending. The amount of stock sold short is equal to the delta value minus one. As the market decreases in value, more of the equity is sold (the short position increases), with the proceeds invested at the risk-free rate. If the market increases in value, money is borrowed to buy the stock and reduce the short position.

223. Systematic Influences

Systematic influences which affect return generating process for a particular security include:

1. Beta (the slope of the regression of excess return for the security against excess return on the S&P index);
2. Dividend yield;
3. Size;
4. Bond beta;
5. Alpha.

[See also **Sector influences**]

224. Systematic Risk

Diversification cannot eliminate risk that is inherent in the macro-economy; this risk is called systematic or **market risk**. [See also **Market risk**] General financial market trends affect most companies in similar ways. Macroeconomic events, such as changes in GDP, rising optimism or pessimism among investors, tax increases or cuts, or a stronger or weaker dollar have broad effects on product and financial markets. Even a well-diversified portfolio cannot escape these effects.

The only risk that should matter to financial markets is an asset's systematic, or market risk that is, the sensitivity of the asset's returns to macroeconomic events. The **unsystematic**, microeconomic component of an asset's total risk disappears in a well-diversified portfolio. [See also **Unsystematic risk**] When financial markets evaluate the tradeoff between risk and expected return, they really focus on the tradeoff between *systematic risk* and expected return.

Systematic risk (or market risk) is the risk that is inherent in the system. As such, it cannot be diversified away. The only way to escape systematic risk is to invest in a risk-free security. A risk-free asset, by definition, will have no systematic risk. In sum, only the systematic portion of risk matters in large, well-diversified portfolios. Thus, the expected returns must be related only to systematic risk.

T

1. TAC

Targeted amortization class (TAC) mortgage-backed securities in which payments are guaranteed for one specific prepayment rate.

2. Tail VaR

The expected loss conditional upon the VaR loss being exceeded. [See also **Value at risk**]

3. Tailing

A reduction in the quantity of an asset held in order to offset future income received by the asset.

4. Take-and-Pay Option

[See **Swing option**]

5. Takedown Risk

In making the loan commitment, the financial institution must always stand ready to provide the maximum of commitment line. The borrower has the flexible option to borrow anything between $0 and the commitment amount ($5 million for example) on any business day in the commit period. This exposes the FI to a degree of future liquidity risk or uncertainty, i.e., takedown risk.

6. Takeover

General term referring to transfer of control of a firm from one group of shareholders to another. Takeover can occur by **acquisition**, **proxy contests**, and going-private transaction. Thus, takeover encompasses a broader set of activities than acquisitions. [See also **Acquisition** and **Proxy contests**]

7. Taking Delivery

Refers to the buyer's actually assuming possession from the seller of the asset agreed upon in a forward contract.

8. Tangible Equity

Total assets minus intangible assets minus total liabilities. In a bank, the largest intangible asset is goodwill, which represents dollar values that may not be realized should the combined institution from merger be forced to liquidate.

9. Target Cash Balance

Optimal amount of cash for a firm to hold, considering the trade-off between the opportunity costs of holding too much cash and the trading costs of holding too little. [See also **Optimal cash balance**]

10. Target Firm

A firm that is the object of a takeover by another firm.

11. Target Payout Ratio

A firm's long-run dividend-to-earnings ratio. The firm's policy is to attempt to pay out a certain percentage of earnings, but it pays a stated dollar dividend and adjusts it to the target as increases in earnings occur. [See also **Lintner's model**]

12. Targeted Repurchase

The firm buys back its own stock from a potential bidder, usually at a substantial premium, to forestall a takeover attempt. This kind of offer will not extend to other shareholders.

13. Tax Anticipation Notes

Short-term municipal debt to raise funds to pay for expenses before actual collection of taxes.

14. Tax Books

Set of books kept by firm management for the IRS that follows IRS rules. The stockholders' books follow Financial Accounting Standards Board (FASB) rules.

15. Tax Credit

Direct reduction in tax liability arising from qualifying expenditures.

16. Tax Deferral Option

The feature of the US Internal Revenue Code that the capital gains tax on an asset is payable only when the gain is realized by selling the asset.

17. Tax Swap

Swapping two similar bonds to receive a tax benefit.

18. Taxable Acquisition

An acquisition in which shareholders of the acquired firm will realize capital gains or losses that will be taxed.

19. Taxable Income

Gross income less a set of deductions. These deductions are expenses items as presented in income statement. It is called earnings before tax.

20. Tax-Deferred Retirement Plans

Employer-sponsored and other plans that allow contributions and earnings to be made and accumulate tax free until they are paid out as benefits.

21. Tax-Equivalent Yield

Tax-exempt interest yield converted to a pretax taxable equivalent by dividing the nominal rate by 1 minus the investor's marginal income tax rate.

22. Tax-Exempts

Tax-exempts are debt obligations of municipalities, states, and federal agencies like the Public Housing Authority. The interest they pay is tax-free. When purchased close to their maturities, these issues have risk characteristics similar to those of other government securities, which depend, of course, on the creditworthiness of the issuers.

23. Tax-Free Acquisition

An acquisition in which the selling shareholders are considered to have exchanged their old shares for new ones of equal value, and in which they have experienced no capital gains or losses.

24. Tax-Timing Option

Describes the investor's ability to shift the realization of investment gains or losses and their tax implications from one period to another.

25. T-Bill

T-bill has a short time horizon and the backing of the US government, which gives it an aura of safety. T-bills, T-notes and T-bonds are liquid assets. Therefore, they are marketable securities, which are parts of current assets. [See also **Treasury bills**]

26. Technical Analysis

Research to identify mispriced securities that focuses on recurrent and predictable stock price patterns. This analysis does not consider the fundamental variables, which are considered by fundamental analysis.

27. Technical Insolvency

Technical insolvency is the inability of the firm to meet cash payments on contractual obligations.

The lack of cash to meet accounts payable, wages, taxes, interest, and debt retirement will constitute technical insolvency, even if the enterprise has adequate assets and generates both economic and accounting profits.

When assets are plentiful in relation to liabilities, a financial manager usually can plan ahead and arrange for sufficient cash through various sources to prevent any embarrassment. Most liquidity problems can be overcome by borrowing or through the planned liquidation of certain assets. A sound, profitable business should have no difficulty in this regard, and reasonable intelligent planning should ward off the danger of technical insolvency. However, if the firm is technically insolvent because of successive losses, poor management, or insufficient investment in working capital, then lenders will be less willing to place fund at its disposal.

The financial manager also should be aware of the potential for variability in the availability of funds. Even a willing lender often is hesitant during periods of tight money, great financial uncertainty, or panic.

28. Technicians

They believe past price change can be used to predict future price movements. Technicians interested in aggregate market forecasting would obviously want to examine past movement of different market indicator series. [See also **Chartists**]

29. Technology and Operation Risks

Technology and operational risks are closely related and in recent years have caused great concern to Financial Institution (FI) managers and regulators alike. The Bank for International Settlements (BIS), the principal organization of Central Banks in the major economies of the world, defines operational risk (inclusive of technological risk) as "the risk of direct or indirect loss resulting from inadequate or failed internal processes, people, and systems or from external events." A number of FIs add reputational risk and strategic risk (e.g., due to a failed merger) as part of a broader definition of operational risk.

30. TED (Treasury Eurodollar) Spread

The difference between the 3-month Eurodollar rate and 3-month Treasury rate.

31. Temporary Working Capital

Some working capital needs persist over time, regardless of seasonal or cyclical variations in sales. In contrast to **permanent working capital**, temporary working capital consists of the additional funds required to meet the seasonal or cyclical variations in sales, over and above permanent working capital. [See also **Permanent working capital**]

32. Tender Offer

In a tender offer, the acquiring firm makes its offer directly to the shareholders of the firm it wishes to acquire. This usually is accomplished through the financial press. The acquiring firm offers to pay a fixed amount per share to each shareholder who tenders shares; this price usually is set far enough above the current market price to entice the shareholders of the target firm.

Tender offers can be made when negotiation breaks down or as a surprise move by one firm to catch the management of the other firm off guard. A tender offer may bid either cash or stock, or some combination, for a block of shares of the target firm. In many large corporations, effective management control can be gained with ownership of less than 50 percent of the shares. Hence, an acquiring firm can make a tender offer, gain control, and then proceed to negotiate for the remainder of the shares.

State and Federal laws impose several legal requirements on tender offers. A bid for shares must remain open for at least 20 days. Moreover, shares that are tendered during this period may be withdrawn during the period. If the bidder raises the original offer price, shares that were tendered under the original offer also are entitled to the higher price. After one firm makes a tender offer, other firms may join the battle for a target firm.

Tender offers have generated a new and colorful vernacular. Some of the frequently encountered terms are **white knight**, **shark repellant**, **pac-man strategy**, and **golden parachute**. [See also **White knight**, **Shark repellant**, **Pac-man strategy**, and **Golden parachute**]

33. Tenor

Time to maturity or expiration of a contract, frequently used when referring to swaps.

34. Term Bonds

Most bonds are term bonds, which mature at some definite point in time. Thus, the price of the bond is

$$PV = \sum_{t=1}^{n} \frac{I_t}{(1+k_b)^t} + \frac{P_n}{(1+k_b)^n},$$

where I_t = the annual coupon interest payment; P_n = the principal amount (face value) of the bond; n = the number of periods to maturity; k_b = discount rate.

35. Term Insurance Policy

It provides a death benefit only, no build-up of cash value for a specified period. The most popular type of term life policy involves a premium that increases with age for a constant amount of death benefits.

36. Term Loan

Loan with a maturity beyond one year, typically repaid from the borrower's future cash flow. Interest and principal are repaid at maturity, the lender must take a more active role in checking the borrower's compliance.

37. Term Premiums

Excess of the yields to maturity on long-term bonds over those of short-term bonds. [See also **Liquidity premium**]

38. Term Repo

A repurchase agreement lasting for a specified period of time longer than one day.

39. Term RPs

Repurchase agreements (RPs or REPOs) with maturity beyond one day. RPs involve a loan between two parties with one either a securities dealer or commercial bank. [See also **Term repo**]

40. Term Structure of Interest Rates

The term structure of interest rates arises from the risk-return relationship among debt securities. The term structure of interest rates is typically described by the yield curve. Typical yield curve diagrams use data for Treasury securities to eliminate risk of default from the analysis. However, similar curves can be constructed using corporate bonds of different maturities with the same credit rating. Over time, the term structure shifts upward or downward and becomes steeper or flatter, depending upon market influences on short-term and long-term interest rates. The term structure generally slopes upward, showing that long-term debt must offer investors a higher return (and borrowers a higher cost) than short-term debt.

The current shape and expected future changes in the shape of the term structure affect the firm's debt financing decision. Low long-term interest rates may convince treasurers to issue long-term debt to lock in low financing costs while they can. As the term structure becomes steeper, however, the temptation rises to issue short-term debt and simply sell new short-term debt issues to replace maturing ones (that is, to roll over maturing short-term debt).

Favoring short-term debt over long-term financing can generate enormous cost savings, boosting the firm's profitability and marketing efforts. [See also **Yield curve**]

41. Terminal Value

The value at maturity.

42. Terms of Sale

Conditions on which firm proposes to sell its goods and services for cash or credit.

43. Theta

The change in the value in the value of a derivative solely due to the passage of time. Based upon the call option formula defined in option pricing model [See also **Option pricing model** for variable definitions]. The mathematical result can be defined as:

$$\frac{\partial C}{\partial T} = \frac{S\sigma}{2\sqrt{T}} N'(d_1) + rXe^{-rT} N(d_2) > 0.$$

44. Third Market

Trading of exchange-listed securities on the OTC market.

45. Thrifts

They include savings and loan associations, savings banks, and mutual savings banks. These institutions traditionally rely upon savings deposits as sources of funds. Hence, they are also called savings institutions. However, they are now able to offer checkable deposits.

46. Tick

Refers to a change in price, either up or down. The amount varies with each contract.

47. Time Decay

Another term for theta. [See also **Theta**]

48. Time Draft

Time drafts are payable after a period of time. These drafts specify that payment is required in 30, 60, or 90 days, or more. A time draft allows the buyer to take title to the merchandise when it promises to pay, rather than when it actually pays the draft.

49. Time Series Analysis of Financial Ratios

Financial ratios can be used in *time series analysis* to evaluate firm performance over time. The best information source for time series analysis of firm ratios is the firm's financial statements and their footnotes. These materials appear in annual reports as well as 10-Q and 10-K filing with the Securities and Exchange Commission.

50. Time Spread

[See **Spread (options)**]

51. Time Value (of an Option)

The part of the value of an option that is due to its positive time to expiration. Not to be confused with present value or the time value of money. [See also **Theta**]

52. Time Value of Money

The time value of money is one of the most important concepts in finance. The time value of money means that a dollar today is worth more than a dollar at any time in the future. The time value of money is a basic building block for much financial analysis. Proper decisions depend upon comparing present cash flows with cash flows in the distant future.

To evaluate the time value of money, four key concepts must be understood: (1) the future value of a single sum; (2) the present value of a single sum; (3) the future value of an annuity; and (4) the present value of an annuity.

53. Times Interest Earned

[See **Interest coverage ratio** and **Capital structure ratios**]

54 Time-Weighted Return

An average of the period-by-period holding-period returns of an investment.

55. Timing Adjustment

Adjustment made to the forward value of a variable to allow for the timing of a payoff from a derivative.

56. TINSTAAFL Principle

Economics teaches the TINSTAAFL principle: "There is no such thing as a free lunch." Capital budgeting analysis frequently applies this principle to existing assets.

57. Tobin's Q

Market value of assets divided by replacement value of assets. A Tobin's Q ratio greater than 1 indicates the firm has done well with its investment decisions. It can be approximated by market value/book value ratio.

58. Tombstone

Tombstone is an advertisement that publicizes a security offering. They are placed in newspapers and magazines by the managing investment bank to advertise its role in forming a syndicate and helping distribute the new issue. The advertisement lists the name of the issuer, the type of security issued, the quantity sold, the offering price, and the members of the investment banking syndicate. The managing investment bank is listed first, for a particularly large or lucrative offering, two or more managing investment banks may share the top position. Members of the syndicate are listed below, in different tiers, with the firms in each tier typically listed in alphabetical order. The most prestigious investment banks are listed in higher tiers; less prestigious banks appear in the lower alphabetized lists. Investment banks sometimes quarrel, and some have even pulled out of deals, over objections to the placement of their name in the tombstone ad. Firms in a tier that are listed out of alphabetical order are less prestigious members of that tier.

59. Total Asset Turnover Ratio

$$\begin{cases} \text{Computed as :} \\ \text{Total asset turnover} = \dfrac{\text{Sales}}{\text{Total Assets}}. \end{cases}$$

More efficient use of assets to generate sales boosts a firm's growth rate, if all else remains constant. A higher turnover allows the firm to increase sales without a large increase in assets. [See also **Asset management ratios**]

60. Total Cash Flow of the Firm

Total cash inflow minus total cash outflow.

61. Total Return Swap

A swap where the return on an asset such as a bond is exchanged for LIBOR plus a spread. The return on the asset includes income such as coupons and the change in value of the asset.

62. Total Risk

Total risk is defined as the sum of systematic and unsystematic risk. Total risk is also equal to the sum of all of the risk components. However, the importance and the contribution to total risk depend on the type of security under consideration. The total risk of bonds contains a much larger fraction of interest-rate risk than the total risk of a stock.

63. Total-Debt-to-Total-Assets Ratio

[See **Leverage ratios**]

64. T-period Holding-Period Return

The percentage return over a T-year period of an investment.

65. Tracking Problem

A perfect hedge is usually not possible because the correlation between the market index and the portfolio may not be perfect. This is called the tracking problem. The greater the correlation between the portfolio and the index, the more effective the hedge, the lower the correlation, the less effective the hedge as a portfolio insurance strategy.

66. Trade Acceptance

Written demand that has been accepted by a firm to pay a given sum of money at a future date.

67. Trade Barrier

Trade barriers reduce import quantities. They prevent domestic consumers from buying all of the foreign goods that they otherwise might buy. This reduced demand for foreign goods reduces demand for foreign currencies; thus, trade barriers can strengthen the currency of the country that erects them. Should two countries place trade barriers against each other, however, their effects may offset one another, with a net impact on exchange rates of zero.

68. Trade Credit (Receivables)

The balance sheet of any company lists accounts receivable on the asset side and accounts payable on the liability side. These categories represent credit extended to other companies (accounts receivable) and credit extended by other companies (accounts payable). These line items measure trade credit, a form of short-term financing provided by a selling company to a buying company. Essentially, the seller provides a loan to the buyer by allowing the buyer to postpone payment while taking immediate possession of goods or services.

The selling company can increase overall sales through trade credit but not without cost. The decision to extend trade credit depends upon the incremental gain per unit of additional risk. Because many firms tie up a lot of capital or assume large obligations in trade credit transactions, decisions involving the management of credit can have a significant impact on cash flow, cost of capital sales growth, and debt capacity.

Trade credit is one of those decisions that affect all aspects of the firm – marketing, production, finance, and so on. Each of these functional areas will have a distinct view of the role of trade credit.

69. Trading Account

Securities debt and equity securities that are bought and hold primarily for the purpose of selling or trading in the neat term. Institutions serving as major dealers in money market assets must keep an inventory of trailing account securities from which to make trade with customers.

70. Trading Costs

Costs of selling marketable securities and borrowing.

71. Trading Range

Price range between highest and lowest prices at which a security is traded. In statistics, it is called range. This measure can be used to measure the variability of a random variable.

72. Trading Volume

Many technical analysts believe that it is possible to detect whether the market in general and/or certain security issues are bullish or bearish by studying the volume of trading. Volume is supposed to be a measure of the intensity of investors' emotions. If high volume occurs on days when prices move up, the overall nature of the market is considered to be bullish. If the high volume occurs on days when prices are falling, this is a bearish sign.

73. Tranche

The principal amount related to a specific class of stated maturities on a collateralized mortgage obligation. [See also **Collateralized mortgage obligation**]

74. Transaction Cash

A company's cash needs fall into three categories: (1) cash for day-to-day transactions, (2) reserve cash to meet contingencies, and (3) cash for compensating balance requirements. The required level of day-to-day transaction cash depends upon the number, frequency, and amount of anticipated transactions. The only requirement for this element of the cash balance is that it be large enough to cover the checks written against the balance.

75. Transaction Costs

Transaction or contracting costs represent the explicit or implicit costs of facilitating exchanges. For example, firms cannot costlessly issue debt and repurchased equity, or negotiate bank loans. Loan covenants may restrict management's discretion in some decision, or even limit returns to shareholders. Covenants also may increase firm expenses by requiring audits or the periodic review of financial statements by the lenders. Real-world firms must pay several different categories of transaction costs such as **flotation costs**, **bankruptcy costs**, **agency costs**, and **information asymmetry**. [See also **Flotation costs**, **Bankruptcy costs**, **Agency costs**, and **Information asymmetry**]

76. Transactions Account

Deposit account on which a customer can write checks. Those accounts include demand deposit and NOWs accounts; NOW represents negotiable order of withdrawal.

77. Transactions Motive

A reason for holding cash that arises from normal disbursement and collection activities of the firm. [See also **Transaction cash**]

78. Transfer Pricing (Financial Institution)

The pricing of funds transferred between organizational units of a bank, such as determining the cost of collecting deposits and borrowed funds to finance a loan.

79. Transfer Pricing (Manufacturing Firm)

It refers to the divisional income determination for deriving the appropriate price at which goods and services should be transferred from one organizational segment to another. The transfer price represents a sales price to the selling segment and a cost price to the buying segment. The transfer price, therefore, significantly affects reported profits of both segments and divisions.

Transfer prices needed for financial reporting purposes may differ from those required for internal decision and management purposes. A particular transfer price base may be excellent for internal performance measurement purposes, for motivating divisional managers, for instituting and maintaining cost control programs, for achieving full utilization of excess capacity, or for the proper allocation of firm resources. However, this same base may be inappropriate for external reporting purposes.

80. Transit Item

Checks drawn on banks outside the community of the bank in which they are deposited. Transit checks deposited are defined as checks drawn on any bank other than the subject bank.

81. Transition Matrix

A square table of probabilities which summarize the likelihood that a credit will migrate from its current credit rating today to any possible credit rating or perhaps default in one period.

82. Treasurer

The firm's treasurer oversees the traditional functions of financial analysis: capital budgeting, short-term and long-term financing decisions, and current asset management and usually reports to the Chief Financial Officer (CFO).

83. Treasury Bill Futures

A futures contract on a Treasury bill. The Treasury bill futures contract promise the future delivery of Treasury bill. These contracts were started in 1972. These contracts are one of the most important future contracts used by the financial institutions to hedge interest rate risk.

84. Treasury Bills

Treasury bills are short-term debt securities issued by the US government. They are perceived to be virtually risk-free; they have essentially no default risk, since investors fully expect the government to pay all interest and principal when it comes due, and their short duration prevents risk due to market movements over time.

T-bills are the most widely traded and, consequently, the most important money market instruments. The Federal Reserve auctions new issues of T-bills with maturities of 91 or 182 days every Monday. Once a month, the Fed offers T-bills with 365-day maturities, as well. Denominations range from $10,000 to $100,000 per bill. All obligations for repayment rests with the US government.

85. Treasury Bond or Note

Debt obligations of the Federal government that make semiannual coupon payments and are sold at or near par value in denominations of $1,000 or more. They have original maturities of more than one year. Treasury notes have initial maturity of 10 years or less and treasury bonds have longer maturity.

86. Treasury Bonds Futures

A futures contract on a Treasury bonds. Financial institutions frequently use this kind of future contract to hedge interest rate risk.

87. Treasury Inflation Protected Securities (TIPS)

On January 29,1997, the US Treasury auctioned a new inflation-indexed security, Treasury Inflation Protected Securities (TIPS) The auction was considered by some to be the biggest news in Treasury debt management since the introduction 20 years ago of the 30-year Treasury security.

Inflation-indexed securities provide a degree of inflation protection for investors and potentially represent cost savings for the US Treasury because it will not have to pay premium for inflation uncertainty. The interest rate paid on these securities (known as the "real rate") provides investors with a guaranteed semiannual return above inflation.

88. Treasury Note

Treasury notes have maturities of less than 10 years. [See also **Treasury bond**]

89. Treasury Note Futures

A futures contract on Treasury notes. It is one of the important futures contracts used by financial institutions to hedge interest rate risk.

90. Treasury Stock

Shares of stock that have been issued and then repurchased by a firm.

91. Tree

A representation of the evolution of the value of a market variable for the purposes of valuing an option or other derivative. [See also **Decision tree**]

92. Trend Analysis

One method that can be used to forecast financial data is known as trend analysis. In trend analysis a regression line is fitted to the financial variable over time. A trend line would be fitted using the method of least squares, this trend line could be used to forecast next year's sales. The following sales model would be estimated as:

$Sales_n = a_0 + a_1 n + \varepsilon_n,$

where $Sales_n$ = sale in year n; n = year; ε_n = error term; and a_0, a_1 = constants to be estimated.

93. Treynor's Measure

Ratio of excess return to beta.

$$\frac{\bar{R}_i - R_f}{\beta_i},$$

where $\bar{R}_i$ = average rates of return for ith security or portfolio; R_f = risk free rate; and β_i = beta coefficient.

94. Triangular Arbitrage

Striking offsetting deals among three markets simultaneously to obtain an arbitrage profit.

95. Trinomial Tree

A tree where there are three branches emanating from each node. It is valuing derivatives. It can be used as an alternative to binomial tree. Under this case, the probabilities is classified into up (P_u), middle (P_m), and down (P_d).

96. Triple-Witching Hour

The four times a year that the S&P 500 futures contract expires at the same time as the S&P 100 index option contract and option contracts on individual stocks. It is called triple-witching hour because of the volatility believed to be associated with the expirations in these three types of contracts.

97. Trough

The transition point between recession and recovery for business cycle. [See also **Business cycle**]

98. Trust Department

Trust refers a property interest held by trust refers one party for the benefit of another. Trust departments are responsible for managing the investments of individuals or institutional clients such as a pension fund.

99. Trust Receipt

Many businesses lack the financial strength and reputation to support unsecured borrowing. These firms may be able to meet their needs for funds by using physical assets to secure the loan. In such cases, the lender takes out a trust receipt— that is, a lien—against these assets. Inventory is the asset most commonly used to secure borrowing in this way.

The lender protects itself against risk by advancing only a portion of the estimated market value of the assets. Where the inventory is readily transferable and saleable, the lender may advance as much as 90 percent. If the inventory is highly specialized, however, the proportion is likely to be considerably lower.

Straightforward borrowing by a trust receipt presents a serious disadvantage in that the physical property that secures the loan must be described in detail in the legal documents. This is clearly difficult if various finished goods are being pledged. An alternative to this is a **floating lien**. [See also **Floating lien**]

100. Trustee

All bonds will have **indentures**. [See also **Indentures**] Such agreements are supervised by a trustee who acts on behalf of bondholders to ensure proper execution of the indenture provisions by the corporation. If the issuer violates indenture provisions, it is in default and the trustee must act to protect the bondholders' interests.

U

1. UBPR

UBPR represents Uniform Bank Performance Report. The UBPR is an analytical tool that is available at no charge through the Financial Institutions Examination Council (FFIEC) at their website www.ffiec.gov. The UBPR is created for bank supervisory, examination, and bank management purposes. The report is produced for each commercial bank in the US that is supervised by the Board of Governors of the Federal Reserve System, Federal Deposit Insurance Corporation, or the Office of the Comptroller of the Currency. UBPRs are also produced for FDIC insured savings banks. This computer generated repot is from a database derived from public and nonpublic sources.

2. Unbundling

[See also **Bundling**]

3. Uncommitted Line of Credit

An uncommitted line of credit does not have an up-front fee payment, and so the bank is not obliged to lend the firm money. If the bank chooses to lend under the terms of the line of credit, it may do so, but it also may choose not to lend. [See also **Revolving credit agreement**]

4. Underlying Asset

The asset whose price determines the profitability of a derivative. For example, the underlying asset for a purchased call is the asset that the call owner can buy by paying the strike price.

5. Underlying Variable

A variable which the price of an option or other derivative depends. [See also **Black-Scholes option pricing model**]

6. Underpricing

Underpricing represents the difference between the aftermarket stock price and the offering price. Underpricing represents money left on the table, or money the firm could have received had the offer price better approximated the aftermarket value of the stock.

7. Underwrite

Purchase securities from the initial issuer and distribute them to investors. [See also **Underwriter**]

8. Underwriter

The investment bank carries, or underwrites, the risk of fluctuating stock prices. Thus, an investment bank is sometimes called an underwriter. Should the market's perception of the issuer change or a macroeconomic event result in a stock market decline, the investment bank carries the risk of loss, or at least the possibility of a smaller than expected spread.

9. Underwriting, Underwriting Syndicate

Underwriters (investment bankers) purchase securities from the issuing company and resell them. Usually a syndicate of investment bankers is organized behind a lead firm. [See also **Syndicates**]

10. Undivided Profits

Retained earnings or cumulative net income not paid out as dividends. It can be used as an internal source of funds.

11. Unearned Interest

Interest received prior to completion of the underlying contract.

12. Unemployment Rate

The ratio of the number of people classified as unemployed to the total labor force. The unemployment rate is used to determine whether a country's economy is in boom, recession, or normal.

13. Unexpected Losses

A popular term for the volatility of losses but also used when referring to the *realization* of a large loss which, in retrospect, was unexpected.

14. Unfunded Debt

Short-term debt, such as account payable is the unfunded debt. Cost of capital of an unfunded debt is the risk-free interest rate.

15. Uniform Limited Offering Registration

Several states offer programs to ease the process of public equity financing for firms within their borders. A firm in a state that has enacted a ULOR (Uniform Limited Offering Registration) law can raise $1 million by publicly selling shares worth at least $5. This law creates a fairly standardized, fill-in-the blank registration document to reduce a firm's time and cost in preparing an offering.

16. Unique Risk

[See **Diversifiable risk**]

17. Unit Banking States

States that prohibit branch banking are called units banking states. Since 1994, most of the states have become branch banking states.

18. Unit Benefit Formula

Method used to determine a participant's retirement benefit plan by multiplying years of service by the percentage of salary.

19. Unit Investment Trust

Money invested in a portfolio whose composition is fixed for the life of the fund. Shares in a unit trust are called redeemable trust certificates, and they are sold at a premium above net asset value.

20. Unit of Production Method

The unit production method is one of the accelerated depreciation methods. This method determines the depreciation in accordance with total production hours for the machines and production hours operate each year. If we assume that a machine is purchased for $ 6,000 and has a salvage value of $ 600, then, the expected useful life of 5,000 hours is divided into the depreciable cost (cost-salvage value) to obtain an hourly depreciation rate of $1.08. If we assume the machine is used 2,000 hours the first year, 1,000 hours the second year, 900 hours the third year, 700 hours the fourth year, and 400 hours the fifth year, then the annual depreciation is determined as follows:

Year 1 $1.08 × 2,000 = $2,160
Year 2 $1.08 × 1,000 = $1,080
Year 3 $1.08 × 900 = $972
Year 4 $1.08 × 700 = $756
Year 5 $1.08 × 400 = $432
Total depreciation $5,400.

21. Unit Volume Variability

Variability in the quantity of output sold can lead to variability in EBIT through variations in sales revenue and total variable costs such as raw material costs and labor costs. The net effect of fluctuating volume leads to fluctuations in EBIT and contributes to business risk. [See also **Business risk**]

22. Universal Financial Institution

A financial institution (FI) that can engage in a broad range of financial service activities. Financial system in US has traditionally been structured along separatist or segmented product lines. Regulatory barriers and restrictions have often inhibited the ability of an FI operating in one area of the financial services industry to expand its product set into other areas. This might be compared with FIs operating in Germany, Switzerland, and the UK, where a more universal FI structure allows individual financial services organizations to offer a far broader range of banking, insurance, securities, and other financial services products. However, the recent merger between Citicorp and Travelers to create Citigroup, the largest universal bank or financial conglomerate in the world, was a sign that the importance of regulatory barrier in the US is receding. Moreover, the passage of the Financial Services Modernization Act of 1999 has accelerated the reduction in the barriers among financial services firms. Indeed, as consolidation in the US and global financial services industry proceeds apace, we are likely to see acceleration in the creation of very large, globally oriented multi-product financial service firms.

23. Universal Life Policy

An insurance policy that allows for a varying death benefit and premium level over the term of the policy, with an interest rate on the cash value that changes with market interest rates. Universal life was introduced in 1979. It combines the death protection features of term insurance with the opportunity to earn market rates of return on excess premiums. Unlike variable life, with its level premium structure, premiums on universal life policies can be changed. The policyholder can pay as high a "premium" as desired, instructing the insurer to invest the excess over that required for death pro-

tection in the insurer's choice of assets. Later, if the policyholder wishes to pay no premium at all, the insurer can deduct the cost of providing death protection for the year from the cash value accumulated in previous years. With other types of policies, skipping a premium would cause the policy to lapse. Unlike whole or variable life policies, the face amount of guaranteed death protection in a universal life policy can be changed at the policyholder's option. Also, unlike variable life, the cash value has a minimum guaranteed rate of return.

24. Unseasoned New Issue

Initial public offering (IPO). It is the first public equity issue that is made by a company. [See also **Initial public offering** and **Going public**]

25. Unsystematic Risk

A well-diversified portfolio can reduce the effects of firm-specific or industry-specific events – such as strikes, technological advances, and entry and exit of competitors – to almost zero. Risk that can be diversified away is known as unsystematic risk or diversifiable risk. Information that has negative implications for one firm may contain good news for another firm. In a well-diversified portfolio of firms from different industries, the effects of good news for one firm may effectively cancel out bad news for another firm. The overall impact of such news on the portfolio's returns should approach zero.

26. Up-and-In

A **knock-in option** for which the barrier exceeds the current price of the underlying asset. [See also **Knock-in option**]

27. Up-and-Out

A **knock-out option** for which the barrier exceeds the current price of the underlying asset. [See also **Knock-out option**]

28. Up-and-Out-Option

An option that comes into existence when the price of the underlying asset increases to a prespecified level.

29. Uptick

A trade resulting in a positive change in a stock price, or a trade at a constant price following a preceding price increase.

30. Usury Ceilings

Usury refers to interest charges in excess of that legally allowed for a specific instrument. Besides disclosure and bankruptcy laws, some sates restrict the rate of interest that may be charged on certain categories of loans, primary consumer loans, but also some agricultural and small business loans. Usury laws establish rate ceilings that a lender may not exceed, regardless of the lender's costs. Usury ceilings apply to lenders of all types, not just to depository institutions.

31. Utility Function

Utility is the measure of the welfare or satisfaction of an investor. The utility function can be defined as $U = f(\overline{R}, \sigma^2)$, where $\overline{R}$ = average rates of return; and σ^2 = variance of rate of return.

32. Utility Theory

Utility theory is the foundation for the theory of choice under uncertainty. Following Henderson and Quandt (1980), cardinal and ordinal theories are the two major alternatives used by economists to determine how people and societies choose to allocate scarce resources and to distribute wealth among one another over time. [See also **Cardinal utility** and **Ordinal utility**]

33. Utility Value

The welfare a given investor assigns to an investment with a particular return and risk. [See also **Utility function**]

V

1. VA Loan

A VA loan is the mortgage which is made by banks and insured by the Veterans Administration (VA), which is a federal agency insuring mortgages.

2. Valuation Reserve

Loan-loss reserve reported on the balance sheet; losses can be charged only against this reserve. In the balance sheet, it is listed as loan and lease loss allowance.

3. Value Additivity (VA) Principle

In an efficient market, the value of the sum of two cash flows is the sum of the values of the individual cash flows. No matter how the payments are divided among claimants, the sum of the values will be the same. Value of bond + value of stock = value of firm.

4. Value At Risk

Value at risk (VaR) is a procedure for estimating the maximum loss associated with a security or portfolio over a specific period of time, associated with a given confidence level. VaR can be used to measure either market risk or credit risk. In a loss distribution, loss can be either expected loss (EL) or unexpected loss (UL). The UL is considered the measure of VaR.

5. Vanilla Option

A standard option or other derivative. For example, ordinary puts and calls are "vanilla" options.

All vanilla options share a few common characteristics: (i) one underlying asset; (ii) the effective starting time is present; (iii) only the price of the underlying asset at the option's maturity affects the payoff of the option; (iv) whether an option is a call or a put is known when sold; and (v) the payoff is always the difference between the underlying asset price and the strike price, and so on. Vanilla options have many limitations resulting from their lack of flexibility. Each kind of exotic options, to some degree, overcomes one particular limitation of vanilla options.

6. Variable Annuities

Annuity contracts in which the insurance company pays a periodic amount linked to the investment performance of an underlying portfolio. Variable annuities are structured so that the investment risk of the underlying asset portfolio is passed through to the recipient, much as shareholders bear the risk of a mutual fund. There are two stages in a variable annuity contract: an **accumulation phase** and a **payout phase**. [See also **Accumulation phase** and **Payout phase**]

7. Variable Cost

A cost that varies directly with volume and is zero when production is zero. For example, if a variable cost is $3/unit, and it has 100 units, its total variable cost is $300. When the number of units becomes 200, the total variable cost is $600.

8. Variable Life Policy

An insurance policy that provides a fixed death benefit plus a cash value that can be invested in a variety of funds from which the policyholder can choose. First introduced in 1975, variable life policies gained popularity after 1980 as an insurance vehicle providing some protection against inflation. Like whole life policies, variable life policies require level premium payments throughout the policyholder's life, but there are important differences. For example, excess premiums that add cash value earn variable, not fixed, rates return, based on the insurer's yield on assets of the *policyholder's choice*. If the selected assets perform well, cash value and death benefits both increase. If not, the cash value may be zero, so the insured bears the entire investment risk. A minimum death benefit is specified in the policy, although there is no maximum. The actual payment to beneficiaries depends on yields earned on excess premiums.

9. Variable Rate Securities

A floating rate security refers to the applicable market interest rate has tied to some index and changes whenever the index changes. In other words, a variable rate security is automatic repricing, usually by changing the interest rate at predetermined intervals. For example a variable rate CD.

10. Variable Universal Life

The newest type of life insurance product is variable universal life, introduced in 1985. So named because it combines the investment flexibility of variable life with the death benefit and premium flexibility of **universal life** [See also **Universal policy**], this new type of policy has gained rapid acceptance among purchasers of life insurance. Variable universal life gives policyholders the greatest freedom to adjust death benefits, premium payments, and investment risk/ expected return as their cash-flow and death protection needs change. (Some sources also use the name flexible premium life for this new policy)

11. Variance

The historical risk of an asset can be measured by its variability of its net income in relation to its **arithmetic average**. [See also **Arithmetic average**] The variance, σ^2, from a sample of data of random variable X is computed by summing the squared deviations and dividing by $n - 1$.

$$\sigma^2 = \frac{\sum_{t=1}^{n}(X_t - \overline{X})^2}{n - 1},$$

where X_t = observation t for random variable X; $\overline{X}$ = arithmetic average of X; and N = number of observations for X.

Squaring the terms can make the variation difficult to interpret. Therefore, analysts often prefer the **standard deviation**, which is simply the square root of the variance. [See also **Standard deviation**]

12. Variance Rate

It represents variance per unit of time. In a generalized Wiener process has two variables: (i) expected drift rate (average drift per unit of time); and (ii) variance rate. [See also **Brownian motion** and **Wiener process**]

13. Variance Reduction Procedures

Procedures for reducing the error in a Monte Carlo simulation. [See also **Antithetic variant method** and **Control variant method**]

14. Variation Margin

An extra margin required to bring the balance in a margin account up to the initial margin when there is a margin call.

15. Vega

The change in the price of a derivative due to a change in volatility. Also sometimes called *kappa* or *lambda*. Based upon the call option formula defined in option pricing model [See also **Option pricing equation** for variable definitions]. The mathematical result can be defined as:

$$\frac{\partial C}{\partial \sigma} = S\sqrt{T}N'(d_1) > 0,$$

where $N'(d) = \frac{2N(d_1)}{2\sigma}$.

16. Vega-Neutral Portfolio

A portfolio with a Vega of zero.

17. Venture Capital

Venture capitalists invest funds in private companies in return for ownership shares. Venture capital comes from a pool of money raised from a variety of limited partners, such as pension funds, insurance companies, and wealthy individuals; the venture capitalists act as the pool's general partners. The venture capitalist generally invests this capital in equity shares of private firms.

Venture capital does not solve the problem of ownership dilution, especially since venture capitalists often demand large ownership shares in exchange for their funds. The arrangement does have advantages, though. Venture capitalists often have expertise in the technology or marketing needs of the firms in which they invest. Venture capitalists frequently sit on their investees' Board of Directors and offer technical, marketing, and financial advice. Thus, they provide both funds and expertise to the growing firm.

Of course, venture capitalists do not provide their time and money simply as a public service. They invest with a future goal of "cashing out," or selling their shares in the company for much more than they paid. A venture capitalist cashes out if the firm goes public, is acquired by another firm, or if the firm's success allows the original owners to repurchase the venture capitalist's shares at a fair price. The venture capitalist returns the investment's profits to the pool's limited partners.

18. Vertical Acquisition

Acquisition in which the acquired firm and the acquiring firm are at different steps in the production process. The acquisition by an airline company of a travel agency would be a vertical acquisition. There are three types of acquisition, which includes **horizontal acquisition**, **vertical acquisition**, and **conglomerate acquisition**. [See also **Horizontal acquisition** and **Conglomerate acquisition**]

19. Vertical Combination

A type of business combination that may involve two firms those are in a supplier-customer relationship. [See also **Vertical acquisition**]

20. Vertical Spread

The sale of an option at one strike price and purchase of an option of the same type (call or put) at a different strike price, both having the same underlying asset and time to expiration.

21. Vested Benefits

These refer to benefits that employees are entitled to even if they leave the firm before retirement. The employee is given a legal claim on his or her pension rights when he or she becomes vested. This means that even if the employee leaves the firm, he or she is still entitled to receive a pension from the firm on retirement. There are various types of vesting formulas, which determine when an employee becomes vested. Most formulas are based on the employee's length of service. For example, if a firm's pension policy states that an employee can become vested after working for the firm for nine years, then after nine years of working for the firm the employee is entitled to receive a pension. From the firm's perspective, the vesting formula may lower the cost of the pension plan because employees who leave the company before they become vested are not entitled to receive any pension benefits.

22. Volatile Deposits

Difference between actual outstanding deposits and core deposits; they represent balances with a high probability of being withdrawn. Implicitly, these are a bank's highly rate sensitive deposit that customers withdraw as interest rates vary.

23. Volatile Funds

For example, negotiable CDs, repurchase agreements, and fed funds purchased are quite volatile. Management assumes that most of these funds could be withdrawn or become unavailable on short notice.

24. Volatility (Options)

The standard deviation of the continuously compounded return on an asset. This measure is one of the five variables used to determine the value of option. [See also **Black-Scholes option pricing model**]

25. Volatility Matrix

A table showing the variation of implied volatilities with strike price and time to maturity.

26. Volatility Risk

The risk in the value of options portfolios due to unpredictable changes in the volatility of the underlying asset.

27. Volatility Skew

Generally, implied volatility as a function of the strike price. Volatility skew refers to a difference in premiums as reflected in differences in implied volatility. Skew is sometimes used more precisely to refer to a difference in implied volatilities between in-the-money and out-of-the-money options. [See also **Constant elasticity variance (CEV) model**]

28. Volatility Smile

A volatility skew in which both in-the-money and out-of-the-money options have a higher volatility than at-the-money options (i.e., when you plot implied volatility against the strike price, the curve looks like a smile.)

29. Volatility Swap

Swap where the realized volatility during an accrual period is exchanged for a fixed volatility. Both percentage volatilities are applied to a notional principal. The payments of volatility swap depends upon the volatility of stocks (or other assets).

30. Volatility Term Structure

A plot the variation of implied volatility with time to maturity.

31. Volume

The number of transactions in a futures contract made during a specified period of time.

32. Voluntary Restructuring

Management has three basic approaches to voluntary restructuring. Carve outs occur when the parent sells a partial interest in a subsidiary through an IPO. The carve out may increase the selling firm's value due to benefits from restructuring the asset composition of the firm. Again, value is enhanced if the manager focuses more on the remaining assets. **Spin-offs** occur when the parent transfers complete ownership of a subsidiary to the existing shareholders. The spin-off allows the shareholders to retain control over a given asset base while allowing management to focus on a smaller segment of the firm's assets. Finally, **sell offs** involve the direct sale of assets to a third party. The selling firm receives cash, which can be used for debt repayment or reinvestment in the remaining assets. Management in this case cannot only refocus on the main line of core business but also now has the wherewithal to finance any necessary changes.

Any of these voluntary approaches may be used by managers of troubled firms in order to fend off the legal complications stemming from bankruptcy. [See also **Spin-offs** and **Voluntary restructuring**]

W

1. Waiting Period

Time during which the Securities and Exchange Commission studies a firm's registration statement. During this time the firm may distribute a preliminary prospectus.

2. Warehousing

A warehousing method of financing can reduce the risk of using inventory as collateral to secure the loan. There are two variations of this method: **field warehousing** and **public warehousing**. [See also **Field warehousing** and **Public warehousing**]

Warehousing, like receivables financing, is a flexible source of short-term credit that automatically grows as the company's working capital needs expand. Also, like receivables financing, its cost is fairly high. Typically, the warehousing company imposes a service charge, usually a fixed minimum plus 1 to 2 percent of the funds loaned, plus an interest rate of 8 to 12 percent or sometimes more. The fixed costs of warehousing – the minimum service charge plus the cost of providing the field warehouse facilities or moving goods to a public warehouse – make it unsuitable for very small firms; the minimum feasible inventory size probably is about $100,000.

3. Warrant

A warrant is a financial instrument issued by a corporation that gives the purchaser the right to buy a fixed number of shares at a set price for a specified period. There usually is a secondary market where existing warrants may be traded.

There are two major differences between a warrant and a **publicly traded option**. [See also **Publicly traded option**] First, the warrant normally matures in three to five years, whereas the maturity of a publicly traded option is normally less than nine months. The second difference is that the warrant is an agreement between the corporation and the warrant's buyer. If the warrant's owner decides to exercise the right to purchase stock, the corporation issues new shares and receives the cash from the sales of those shares.

Typically, a warrant accompanies a bond issue, but it is detachable; it can be traded separately from the bond. A warrant is essentially a call option written by the company that issues the stock. Its value is influenced by the same factors that influence the value of a call option.

In this context, the value of a warrant at expiration (V_W) is defined by the following equation:

$$V_W = Max\ [0, NP - NX],$$

where P and X are the price of the stock and the exercise price of the option, respectively; and N is the number of shares obtainable with each warrant.

4. Wash

A trade in which gains equal losses in stock trading.

5. Weak-Form Efficient Market

Different assumptions about information availability give rise to different types of market efficiency. [See also **Efficient market**]

A weak-form efficient market is a market in which prices reflect all past information, such as information in last year's annual reports, previous earnings announcements, and other past news. Some investors, called *chartists* or *technicians*, examine graphs of past price movements, number of shares bought and sold, and other figures to try to predict future price movements. A weak-form efficient market implies that such investors are wasting their time; they cannot earn above-average, risk-adjusted profits by projecting past trends in market variables. Generally, evidence indicates that historical information is not helpful in predicting stock price performance. [See also **Technicians**]

6. Weather Derivatives

Derivative where the payoff depends on the weather.

7. Weekend Effect

The common recurrent negative average return from Friday to Monday in the stock market.

8. Weighted Average Cost of Capital

The weighted average cost of capital (WACC) represents the firm's minimum required rate of return on its average-risk capital budgeting projects. It is found by multiplying the marginal cost of each capital structure component by its appropriate weight and then summing the terms as:

$$WACC = w_d k_d + w_p k_p + w_e k_e.$$

The weights of debt, preferred equity, and common equity in the firm's capital structure are given by w_d, w_p, and w_e, respectively. The cost of debt, preferred equity, and common equity are k_d, k_p, and k_e, respectively. As the weighed average cost of capital covers all of the firm's capital financing sources, the weights must sum to 1.0. The firm's cost of common equity, k_e, can reflect the cost of retained earnings, k_{re}, or the cost of new common stock, k_{cs}, whichever is appropriate.

The weights represent a specific, intended mix of debt and equity that the firm will try to achieve or maintain over the planning horizon. As much as possible, the target weights should reflect the combination of debt and equity that management feels will minimize the firm's weighted average cost of capital. It is necessary to minimize the WACC in order to maximize shareholder wealth.

The firm should make an effort over time to move toward and maintain its target capital structure mix of debt and equity. There are two ways to measure the mix of debt and equity in the firms' capital structure.

One method uses the firms' book values, or balance sheet amounts, of debt and equity. The actual weight of debt in the firm's capital structure equals the book value of its debt divided by the book value of its assets. Similarly, the actual equity weight is the book value of its stockholders' equity divided by total assets. Once the target weights have been determined, the firm can issue or repurchase appropriate quantities of debt and equity to move the balance sheet numbers toward the target weights.

A second method uses the market values of the firm's debt and equity to compare target and actual weights. The actual weight of debt in the firm's capital structure equals the market value of its debt divided by the market value of its assets. Similarly, the actual equity weight is the market value of the firm's stockholders' equity divided by the market value of its assets. Calculated in this way, bond and stock market price fluctuations, as well as new issues and security repurchases, can move the firm toward – or away from – its target.

Financial theory favors the second method as most appropriate. Current market values are used to compute the various costs of financing, so it stands to reason that market-based costs should be weighted by market-based weights.

The basic capital structure of a firm may include debt, preferred equity, and common equity. In practice, calculating the cost of these components is sometimes complicated by the existence of hybrid financing structures (e.g., convertible debt) and other variations of straight debt, preferred equity, or common equity. A comparison of capital costs between countries also is difficult. What may appear to be lower financing costs in one country may disappear after careful analysis.

9. Weighted Average Life for Mortgage-Backed Securities

The weighted average life (WAL) is a product of the time when principal payments are received and the amount of principal received divided by total principal outstanding. Explicitly, it can be defined as:

$$\text{WAL} = \frac{\sum(\text{Time} \times \text{Expected principal received})}{\text{Total principal outstanding}}.$$

For example, consider a loan with two years to maturity and $100 million in principal. Investors expect $50 million of the principal to be repaid at the end of year 1 and the remaining principal $50 million to be repaid at maturity.

Expected Principal Payments	Principal × Time
$ 50	$ 50 × 1 = $ 50
$ 50	$ 50 × 2 = $ 100
$ 100	$ 150

WAL = 150/100 = 1.5 years

The WAL is presented in mortgage-backed security certificate. In addition to WAL, it also presents: (i) Type of security, (ii) current price, (iii) price change, (iv) spread to average life, (v) spread change, (vi) prepaid speed, and (vii) year to maturity.

10. Weighted Cost of Funds

Weighted average cost of all sources of fund in a depository, including deposits, non-deposits, liabilities, and capital.

11. Weighted Marginal Cost of Fund

Marginal cost of pooled debt funds used in pricing decisions of loans.

12. Weighted Unbiased Estimator

When consideration is given to the types of applications for average rates of return to (1) determine the historical profit rate of an investment and (2) to assess the long-run expected rate of return of some investment instruments, the importance of accuracy and a lack of bias is apparent. Blume (1974)

has investigated the possible bias in using either arithmetic average ($\overline{x}$) or geometric average ($\overline{g}$) to forecast such expected rates of return and has proposed four alternative unbiased estimators: (1) simple unbiased, (2) overlapped unbiased, (3) weighed unbiased, and (4) adjusted unbiased. Blume has also mathematically and empirically shown that the weighted unbiased estimator is the most efficient estimator and is the most robust for nonnormal and nonstationary data.

The definition of the weighted unbiased estimator, $M(W)$, is

$$M(W) = \left(\frac{T - n}{T - 1}\right)\overline{X} + \left(\frac{n - 1}{T - 1}\right)\overline{g},$$

where T = the number of periods used to estimate the historical average returns; and n = the number of investment-horizon periods for which a particular investment is to be held.

13. Well-Diversified Portfolio

A portfolio spread out over many securities in such a way that the weight in any security is close to zero.

14. Whipsawing

Whipsawing occurs when the underlying asset increases enough to trigger rebalancing. After more shares are added, the underlying asset decreases in value and the additional shares are sold at a lower price than what was paid for them. A common remedy for this problem is to use a larger adjustment gap or filter rule; however, the wrong number of shares would be held if the filter rule were increases, particularly if the stock moved in a linear manner. Whipsawed positions commonly occurs when the asset fluctuates around a constant level.

15. White Knight

White knights are alternative suitors (acquirers) that offer friendlier terms to a target firm facing a hostile takeover. [See also **Tender offer**]

16. Whole-Life Insurance Policy

Provides a death benefit and a kind of savings plan that builds up cash value for possible future withdrawal. A whole-life policyholder pays pay fixed amount of premiums in exchange for a known death benefit, the face amount of the policy.

17. Wiener Process

A stochastic process where the change in a variable during each short period of time of length δ_t has a normal distribution with a mean equal to zero and a variance equal to δ_t. [See also **Brownian motion**]

18. Wild Card Play

The right to deliver on a futures contract at the closing price for a period of time after the close of trading.

19. Wilshire 5000 Equity Index

The Wilshire 5000 equity index, which includes about 7,000 stocks, is complied by both market-value-weighted and equally-weighted approaches. This index is being used increasingly because it contains most equity securities available for investment, including all NYSE and AMEX issues and the most active stocks traded on the over-the-counter (OTC) market.

The following formula is used to compute the market-value-weighted Wilshire 5000 equity index:

$$I_t = I_{t-1}\left[\sum_{j=1}^{N}\left(S_{jt}\right)P_{jt}\Big/\sum_{j=1}^{N}\left(S_{jt-1}\right)P_{jt-1}\right],$$

where I_t = index value for the tth period; N = number of stocks in the index; P_{jt} = price of the jth security for the tth period; S_{jt} = shares outstanding of the jth security for the tth period; P_{jt-1} = price of the jth security for the $(t-1)$th period; and S_{jt-1} = shares outstanding of the jth security for the $(t-1)$th period.

20. Window Dressing

The practice in financial reporting in which a firm engages in certain transactions at the end of a reporting period (quarter or fiscal year) to make the financial results appear better or different from that prevailing at the time.

21. Winner's Curse

The average investor wins – that is, gets the desired allocation of a new issue – because those who knew better avoided the issue. Winner's curse is the reason why IPOs have a large average return. To counteract winner's curse and attract the average investor, underwriters underprice issues.

22. Wire Transfers

Wire transfers involve electronic bank-to-bank transfers of funds. A wire transfer can move a large cash balance and make it available to a firm's central finance managers within an hour. While wire transfer is the fastest method available to move funds, it also is the most costly.

23. Working Capital

Working capital is the dollar amount of an organization's current assets, which include cash, marketable securities, accounts receivable, and inventory. These current assets are considered liquid because they can be converted into cash relatively quickly. Each component of working capital is affected by the activities of various parts of the organization. Production, pricing, distribution, marketing, wage contracts, and financing decisions are just a few of the diverse activities within the firm that can affect not only the amount of working capital but also how quickly the individual assets can be converted into cash.

For example, if the firm's union contract requires that the workers be paid weekly, the amount of cash needed to meet the payroll must be available on each payday. This could require the firm to borrow more cash than if the firm paid its workers only once a month.

The external environment in which the firm operates (product markets, investment markets, and financial markets) also can affect the amount and the rate of change of a firm's working capital. In a highly seasonal industry, inventory typically increases dramatically as demand for the product increases. Inventory then decreases as accounts receivable increases and the inventory is shipped. The cycle is completed when the firm collects cash for its accounts receivable. Many organizations must manage their working capital in the face of seasonal and cyclical forces, which can cause a high degree of variability. [See also **Permanent working capital** and **Temporary working capital**]

24. Working Group

The working group gathers the individuals and firms involved in taking the firm public, including investment banks, law firms, and accounting firms. The firm's management team provides the working group with the necessary information and makes the decisions regarding the public offering process. The members of the group work individually and jointly in a number of areas to try to ensure a successful IPO.

The initial planning for an IPO basically involves getting the firm's legal, financial, and organizational details in proper form to minimize the probability of difficulties arising either during or after the IPO. The firm will hire auditors to review its past financial statements and past and current accounting practices. The auditors may require changes in accounting methods and a restatement of past financial data to bring them into regulatory compliance under SEC guidelines.

25. Workout Period

Realignment period of a temporary misaligned yield relationship.

26. World Investable Wealth

The part of world wealth that is traded and is therefore accessible to investors.

27. Writing a Call

Selling a call option.

28. Writing an Option

Selling an option.

29. Written Call

A call that has been sold; a short call.

30. Written Put

A put that has been sold; a short put.

31. Written Straddle

The simultaneous sale of a call and sale of a put, with the same strike price and time to expiration.

X

1. X Efficiency

X efficiencies are those cost savings not directly due to economies of scope or economies of scale. As such, they are usually attributed to superior management skills and other difficult-to-measure managerial factors. To date, the explicit identification of what composes these efficiencies remains to be established in the empirical banking literature.

Y

1. Yankee Bonds

US firms aren't the only issuers of securities outside their national borders. For example, foreign firms can issue securities in the US if they follow US security registration procedures. Yankee bonds are US dollar-denominated bonds that are issued in the US by a non-US issuer. Some issuers also find the longer maturities of Yankees attractive to meet long-term financing needs. While Eurodollar bonds typically mature in ten years or less, Yankees have maturities as long as 30 years. [See also **Eurodollar bonds**]

2. Year End Selling

A popular suggestion of invstment advisors, at year end, is to sell securites for which an investor has incurred substantial losses and purchas an equivalent security. [See also **January effect**]

3. Yield

The return provided by an instrument. For example, yield for investing in stock is equal to dividend yield plus capital gain yield.

4. Yield Curve

Diagram relating market interest rates to term-to-maturity on securities that differ only in terms of maturity. Alternatively it implies the set of yields to maturity for bonds with different times of maturity. [See also **Term structure of interest rates**]

5. Yield Curve Swap

A subset of the basis swap; involves exchange of interest payments indexed to a short-term rate for payments indexed to a long-term.

6. Yield Rate

Tax-equivalent interest income divided by earning assets.

7. Yield to Maturity

The yield to maturity or market interest rate is the effective annual rate of return demanded by investors on bonds of a given maturity and risk. To properly discount the semi-annual coupons, we must determine the periodic interest rate that corresponds to the effective annual rate. We can calculate the effective annual rate for compounding m times per year as:

$$EAR = YTM = (1 + Periodic\ interest\ rate)^m - 1$$

in order to solve for the periodic interest rate

$$Periodic\ interest\ rate = (1 + YTM)^{\frac{1}{m}} - 1.$$

There are two alternatives to calculate yield to maturity.

Alternative 1: Formal Method

Bond price quotes are available in the marketplace, either from bond dealers or from the daily price listings found in secondary sources, such as *The Wall Street Journal*. Both investors and financial managers must calculate the yield to maturity on bonds, given known par values, coupon rates, times to maturity, and current prices. The yield to maturity can be determined from the present value of an annuity factor (*PVIFA*) and present value interest factor (*PVIF*) formulas we used to compute bond price:

$$Price = PVIFA(Coupon) + PVIF(Par\ Value)$$

$$Price = \$CF/2 \left[\frac{1 - \left(\frac{1}{1+r}\right)^n}{r} \right] + Par \left[\frac{1}{(1+r)^n} \right],$$

where r represents the periodic interest rate; and n is the number of semiannual periods until the bond matures. The yield to maturity equals $(1 + r)^2 - 1$; the stated annual rate equals $r \times 2$. But mathematics offers no simple technique for computing r. It is easier to use available technology to solve for the periodic rate. Financial calculators can generally be used to calculate the *YTM*. The *YTM* for a zero coupon bond can be defined as:

$$YTM = \left(\frac{par}{price}\right)^{\frac{1}{n}} - 1.$$

Alternative 2: Approximate Method

For a quick estimate of return, the approximation method can be used. Here, the average annual dollar return to the investor of a bond that matures in n years is the coupon payment plus a straight-line amortization of the bond's premium (or discount):

$$Average\ annual\ dollar\ return = Annual\ coupon + \frac{Par - Price}{n}.$$

The average amount invested in the bond is the average of its purchase price and par value:

$$Average\ investment = \frac{Par + Price}{2}.$$

The approximate yield to maturity

$$= \frac{Annual\ Coupon + \dfrac{Par - Price}{n}}{\dfrac{Par + Price}{2}}.$$

8. Yield-Giveup Swap

The yield-giveup swap version of the intermarket-spread swap works against the investor over time. Therefore, when a swap involves a loss in yield, there is a high premium to be placed on achieving a favorable spread change within a relatively short workout period.

9. Yield-Pickup Swap

In a pure yield-pickup swap, there is no expectation of market changes but a simple attempt to increase yield. Basically two bonds are examined to establish their difference in yield to maturity, with a further adjustment to consider the impact of interim reinvestment of coupons at an assumed rate of return between now and the maturity date.

Z

1. Zero Coupon Bonds

Zero coupon bonds pay no coupon interest and provide only one cash flow: payment of their par value upon maturity. Treasury bills are a form of zero coupon debt. An investor purchases a T-bill at a price below par and receives no interest or other cash flows until maturity. At that time, the investor receives the par value of the T-bill. The return on the security is the difference between its discount price and its par value.

The primary reason for the popularity of zero coupon bonds is that investors do not face any reinvestment rate risk. As these bonds provide no cash flows to reinvest, investors effectively lock in a given yield to maturity. However, under IRS regulations, investors must pay yearly taxes on the *implicit* interest paid by the bonds; the IRS has special rules for determining this value. In essence, investors must pay taxes on income they have not received. Thus, zero coupon bonds are mainly purchased by tax-exempt investors who pay no tax on their investment returns, such as pension funds.

Issuing a zero coupon bond also helps to lower borrowing costs for the firm. The original discount can be expensed for tax purposes on a straight-line basis over the life of the bond. Thus, rather than cash outflows from coupon interest payments, the issuing firm receives annual cash inflows from tax savings. However, the issuer must plan for a large capital requirement at the maturity of these bonds.

2. Zero Gap

Gap can be either positive, negative, or zero. Zero gap implies that rate sensitive asset equal rate sensitive liability.

3. Zero Rate

[See also **Zero-coupon interest rate**]

4. Zero-Balance Accounts

Zero-balance accounts (ZBAs) centralize cash control at the main corporate office. The zero-balance account is a specialized disbursement account on which the firm writes checks against a zero balance. Authorized employees write checks on their departmental accounts, but the firm maintains no funds in these accounts. Instead, these accounts accumulate negative bank balances daily. The cash-control system corrects these daily negative balances by releasing funds from a corporate master account, restoring them to zero balances each day.

A zero-balance account offers a firm with many operating divisions several benefits:

- Greater centralized control over disbursements.
- Elimination of redundant idle bank balances in different banks.
- Reduction of cash transfer expenses.
- More effective cash investments.
- Greater autonomy for local managers.

A ZBA system does require the firm to maintain all accounts at the same concentration bank, however.

5. Zero-Beta Portfolio

The minimum-variance portfolio uncorrelated with a chosen efficient portfolio. This portfolio has beta equal to zero.

6. Zero-Cost Collar

The purchase of a put and sale of a call where the strikes are chosen so that the premiums of the two options are the same.

7. Zero-Coupon Interest Rate

The interest rate that would be earned on a bond that provides no coupons.

8. Zero-Coupon Swap

All cash flows of the swap occur at the end of the life of the agreement; payment obligations are compounded to future maturity.

9. Zero-Coupon Yield Curve

The set of yields to maturity for zero-coupon bonds with different times to maturity. [See also **Yield to maturity** for a discussion of calculations]

10. Zero-Investment Portfolio

A portfolio of zero net value, established by buying and shorting component securities, usually in the context of an arbitrage strategy.

11. Zero-Plus Tick

[See also **Uptick**]

12. Z-Score Model

Z-score is a statistical measure that presumably indicates the probability of bankruptcy. [See also **Credit scoring model**]

13. Z-Tranche

The final class of securities in a CMO exhibiting the longest maturity and greatest price volatility. These securities often accrue interest until all other classes are retired.

PART II: Papers

Chapter 1

DEPOSIT INSURANCE SCHEMES

JAMES R. BARTH, *Auburn University and Milken Institute, USA*
CINDY LEE, *China Trust Bank, USA*
TRIPHON PHUMIWASANA, *Milken Institute, USA*

Abstract

More than two-thirds of member countries of the International Monetary Fund (IMF) have experienced one or more banking crises in recent years. The inherent fragility of banks has motivated about 50 percent of the countries in the world to establish deposit insurance schemes. By increasing depositor confidence, deposit insurance has the potential to provide for a more stable banking system. Although deposit insurance increases depositor confidence, it removes depositor discipline. Banks are thus freer to engage in activities that are riskier than would otherwise be the case. Deposit insurance itself, in other words, could be the cause of a crisis. The types of schemes countries have adopted will be assessed as well as the benefits and costs of these schemes in promoting stability in the banking sector.

Keywords: deposit insurance; banks; regulation, banking crisis; bank runs; banking instability; depositor discipline; moral hazard; bank supervision; financial systems

1.1. Introduction

During the last three decades of the 20th century, more than two-thirds of member countries of the International Monetary Fund (IMF) have experienced one or more banking crises. These crises occurred in countries at all levels of income and in all parts of the world. This troublesome situation amply demonstrates that while banks are important for channeling savings to productive investment projects, they nonetheless remain relatively fragile institutions. And when a country's banking system experiences systemic difficulties, the results can be disruptive and costly for the whole economy. Indeed, the banking crises that struck many Southeast Asian countries in mid-1997 cost Indonesia alone more than 50 percent of its Gross Domestic Product (GDP).

The inherent fragility of banks has motivated many nations to establish deposit insurance schemes. The purpose of such schemes is to assure depositors that their funds are safe by having the government guarantee that these can always be withdrawn at full value. To the extent that depositors believe that the government will be willing and able to keep its promise, they will have no incentive to engage in widespread bank runs to withdraw their funds. By increasing depositor confidence in this particular way, deposit insurance thus has the potential to provide for a more stable banking system.

Although deposit insurance increases depositor confidence, however, it gives rise to what is referred to as "moral hazard" (Gropp and Vesala, 2001). This is a potentially serious problem, which arises when depositors believe their funds are safe. In such a situation they have little, if any, incentive to monitor and police the activities of banks. When this type of depositor discipline is removed because of deposit insurance, banks are freer to engage in activities that are riskier than would otherwise be the case. To the extent that this type of moral hazard is not kept in check by the bank regulatory and supervisory authorities after a country establishes a deposit insurance scheme, its banking system may still be susceptible to a crisis. Deposit insurance itself, in other words, could be the cause of a crisis (Cooper and Ross, 2002; Diamond and Dybvig, 2000).

The establishment of a deposit insurance scheme therefore is not a sinecure. It provides both potential benefits and costs to a society. The difficult issue is maximizing the benefits while simultaneously minimizing the costs. It is for this reason that governments and citizens in countries around the globe need a better appreciation and understanding of deposit insurance. This is particularly the case insofar as ever more countries have been establishing such schemes in recent years. Indeed, since the first national deposit insurance scheme was established by the United States in 1933 (Bradley, 2000), nearly 70 more countries have done so, most within the past 20 years. The IMF, moreover, suggests that every country should establish one (Garcia, 2000).

1.2. The Inherent Fragility of Banks

It is a well known and widely accepted fact that banks are an important part of a nation's financial system. They complement the nonbank financial institutions and the capital markets in promoting economic growth and development. In particular, banks extend credit to business firms for various investment projects and otherwise assist them in coping with various types of financial risk. They also facilitate the payment for goods and services by providing a medium of exchange in the form of demand deposits. But in providing these services, banks create longer-term assets (credit) funded with shorter-term liabilities (deposits). Therein lies the inherent source of bank fragility. Depositors may decide to withdraw their deposits from banks at any time.

The worst-case scenario is one in which depositors nationwide become so nervous about the

safety of their deposits that they simultaneously decide to withdraw their deposits from the entire banking system. Such a systemic run would force banks to liquidate their assets to meet the withdrawals. A massive sale of relatively opaque assets, in turn, would require that they be sold at "fire-sale" prices to obtain the needed cash. This situation could force illiquid but otherwise solvent institutions into insolvency.

The typical structure of a bank's balance sheet is therefore necessarily fragile. Any bank would be driven into insolvency if its assets had to be immediately sold to meet massive withdrawals by its depositors. This would not be a concern if such an event were a mere theoretical curiosity. There have in fact been widespread bank runs in various countries at various points in time. There have even been instances where bank runs in one country have spread beyond its borders to banks in other countries. Unfortunately, bank runs are not benign. They are destructive insofar as they disrupt both the credit system and the payments mechanism in a country. Worse yet, the bigger the role banks play in the overall financial system of a country, the more destructive a banking crisis will be on economic and social welfare. This is typically the situation in developing countries.

1.3. The Benefits of Deposit Insurance Schemes

The primary purpose of a deposit insurance scheme is to minimize, if not entirely eliminate, the likelihood of bank runs. A secondary purpose is to protect small depositors from losses. At the time of the Great Depression in the Unites States, banks had experienced widespread runs and suffered substantial losses on asset sales in an attempt to meet deposit withdrawals. The situation was so devastating for banks that President Roosevelt declared a bank holiday. When banks were re-opened, they did so with their deposits insured by the federal government. This enabled depositors to be confident that their funds were now indeed safe, and therefore there was no need to withdraw them. This action by the government was sufficient to restore confidence in depositors that their funds were safe in banks. By establishing a "safety net" for depositors of banks, bank runs were eliminated in the United States.

Before the establishment of deposit insurance in the United States, it was the responsibility of the Federal Reserve System to prevent bank runs. This goal was supposed to be accomplished by lending funds to those banks which were experiencing liquidity problems and not solvency problems. In other words, the Federal Reserve System was supposed to be a lender of the last resort, always ready to lend to illiquid but solvent banks, when nobody else was willing to do so. Yet, it did not fulfill its responsibility during the 1930s. It was therefore considered necessary to establish an explicit deposit insurance scheme to reassure depositors that their deposits would always be safe and readily available on demand. Deposit insurance thus became a first line of defense against bank runs.

For nearly 50 years after its establishment, the U.S. deposit insurance scheme worked as intended. There were no bank runs and the consensus was that deposit insurance was a tremendous success. But then events occurred that called this view into question. Savings and loans, which had also been provided with their own deposit insurance scheme at the same time as banks, were devastated by interest rate problems at first, and then by asset quality problems during the 1980s. The savings and loan problems were so severe that even their deposit insurance fund became insolvent during the mid-1980s. Ultimately, taxpayers were required to contribute the majority of the $155 billion, the cost for cleaning up the mess. Fortunately, even though the deposit insurance fund for banks became insolvent during the late 1980s, the cleanup cost was only about $40 billion. And taxpayers were not required to contribute to covering this cost.

The fact that several thousand depository institutions – in this case both savings and loans, and banks – could fail, and cost so much to resolve convincingly demonstrated to everyone that deposit insurance was not a panacea for solving banking problems. Despite being capable of addressing the inherent fragility problem of banks, deposit insurance gave rise to another serious problem, namely, moral hazard.

1.4. The Costs of Deposit Insurance Schemes

While instilling confidence in depositors that their funds are always safe, so as to prevent bank runs, deposit insurance simultaneously increases the likelihood of another serious banking problem in the form of moral hazard. By removing all concerns that depositors have over the safety of their funds, deposit insurance also removes any incentive depositors have to monitor and police the activities of banks. Regardless of the riskiness of the assets that are acquired with their deposits, depositors are assured that any associated losses will be borne by the deposit insurance fund, and not by them. This situation therefore requires that somebody else must impose discipline on banks. In other words, the bank regulatory and supervisory authorities must now play the role formerly played by depositors.

There is widespread agreement that regulation and supervision are particularly important to prevent banking problems once countries have established a deposit insurance scheme. Countries doing so must more than ever contain the incentive for banks to engage in excessively risky activities once they have access to deposits insured by the government. The difficult task, however, is to replace the discipline of the private sector with that of the government. Nonetheless, it must and has been done with varying degrees of success in countries around the world. The proper way to do so involves both prudential regulations and effective supervisory practices.

Skilled supervisors and appropriate regulations can help prevent banks from taking on undue risk, and thereby exposing the insurance fund to excessive losses. At the same time, however, banks must not be so tightly regulated and supervised that they are prevented from adapting to a changing financial marketplace. If this happens, banks will be less

able to compete and thus more likely to fail. The
regulatory and supervisory authorities must therefore strike an appropriate balance between being
too lenient and too restrictive, so as to promote a
safe and sound banking industry.

The appropriateness of specific regulations and
supervisory practices necessarily depends upon the
specific design features of a deposit insurance
scheme. Some features may exacerbate moral hazard, whereas others may minimize it. In other
words, it is important for a government to realize
that when designing a scheme, one must take into
account the effects the various features will have
on both depositor confidence and moral hazard. In
this regard, information has recently become available describing many of the important differences
among deposit insurance schemes that have been
established in a large number of countries. It is,
therefore, useful to examine this "menu of deposit
insurance schemes". One can thereby appreciate
the ways in which these schemes differ, and then
try to assess which combination of features seems
to strike a good balance between instilling depositor confidence so as to eliminate bank runs and
yet containing the resulting moral hazard that
arises when depositor discipline is substantially, if
not entirely, eliminated.

1.5. Differences in Deposit Insurance Schemes Across Countries

Of the approximately 220 countries in the
world, about half of them have already established or plans to establish deposit insurance
schemes. Information on selected design features
for the schemes in 68 countries is presented in
Table 1.1. It is quite clear from this information
that there are important differences in key features
across all these countries, which includes both
emerging market economies and mature economies
(Demirgüç-Kunt and Kane, 2002; Demirgüç-Kunt
and Sobaci, 2001; Demirgüç-Kunt and Detragiache, 2000; Garcia, 1999). At the outset it should
be noted that the vast majority of these countries
have only recently established deposit insurance

for banks. Indeed, 50 of the 68 countries have
established their schemes within the past 20 years.
And 32 of these countries established them within
the past decade. More countries are either in the
process or likely in the near future to establish a
deposit insurance scheme. Differences in each of
the other important features noted in the table will
now be briefly described in turn.

One key feature of any deposit insurance scheme
is the coverage limit for insured depositors. The
higher the limit the more protection is afforded to
individual depositors, but the higher the limit the
greater the moral hazard. The limits vary quite
widely for countries, ranging from a low of $183
in Macedonia to a high of $260,800 in Norway.
For purposes of comparison, the limit is $100,000
in the United States. One problem with these comparisons, however, is that there are wide differences in the level of per capita income among
these countries. It is therefore useful to compare
the coverage limits after expressing them as a ratio
to GDP per capita. Doing so one finds that Chad
has the highest ratio at 15, whereas most of the
other countries have a ratio at or close to 1.
Clearly, ratios that are high multiples of per capita
GDP are virtually certain to eliminate any discipline that depositors might have otherwise imposed
on banks.

Apart from coverage limits, countries also differ
with respect to coinsurance, which may or may not
be a part of the deposit insurance scheme. This
particular feature, when present, means that depositors are responsible for a percentage of any
losses should a bank fail. Only 17 of the 68 countries have such a feature. Yet, to the extent that
depositors bear a portion of any losses resulting
from a bank's failure, they have an incentive to
monitor and police banks. Usually, even when
countries adopt coinsurance, the percentage of
losses borne by depositors is capped at 10 percent.
Even this relatively small percentage, however, is
enough to attract the attention of depositors when
compared to the return they can expect to earn on
their deposits, and thereby help to curb moral
hazard.

Table 1.1. Design features of deposit insurance schemes in countries around the world

Countries	Date enacted/ revised	Coverage limit	Coverage ratio limit/ GDP per capita	Coinsurance	Type of fund (Yes = funded; No = unfunded)	Risk-adjusted Premiums	Type of membership
Argentina	1979/1995	$30,000	3	No	Yes	Yes	Compulsory
Austria	1979/1996	$24,075	1	Yes	No	No	Compulsory
Bahrain	1993	$5,640	1	No	No	No	Compulsory
Bangladesh	1984	$2,123	6	No	Yes	No	Compulsory
Belgium	1974/1995	$16,439	1	No	Yes	No	Compulsory
Brazil	1995	$17,000	4	No	Yes	No	Compulsory
Bulgaria	1995	$1,784	1	No	Yes	Yes	Compulsory
Cameroon	1999	$5,336	9	No	Yes	Yes	Voluntary
Canada	1967	$40,770	2	No	Yes	No	Compulsory
Central African Republic	1999	$3,557	13	No	Yes	Yes	Voluntary
Chad	1999	$3,557	15	No	Yes	Yes	Voluntary
Chile	1986	$3,600	1	Yes	No	No	Compulsory
Colombia	1985	$5,500	2	Yes	Yes	No	Compulsory
Croatia	1997	$15,300	3	No	Yes	No	Compulsory
Czech Republic	1994	$11,756	2	Yes	Yes	No	Compulsory
Denmark	1988/1998	$21,918	1	No	Yes	No	Compulsory
Dominican Republic	1962	$13,000	7	Yes	Yes	No	Voluntary
Ecuador	1999	N/A	N/A	No	Yes	No	Compulsory
El Salvador	1999	$4,720	2	No	Yes	Yes	Compulsory
Equatorial Guinea	1999	$3,557	3	No	Yes	Yes	Voluntary
Estonia	1998	$1,383	0	Yes	Yes	No	Compulsory
Finland	1969/1992/1998	$29,435	1	No	Yes	Yes	Compulsory
France	1980/1995	$65,387	3	No	No	No	Compulsory
Gabon	1999	$5,336	1	No	Yes	Yes	Voluntary
Germany	1966/1969/1998	$21,918	1	Yes	Yes	No	Compulsory
Gibraltar	1998		N/A	Yes	No	No	Compulsory
Greece	1993/1995	$21,918	2	No	Yes	No	Compulsory
Hungary	1993	$4,564	1	No	Yes	Yes	Compulsory
Iceland	1985/1996	$21,918	1	Yes	Yes	No	Compulsory
India	1961	$2,355	6	No	Yes	No	Compulsory
Ireland	1989/1995	$16,439	1	Yes	Yes	No	Compulsory
Italy	1987/1996	$125,000	6	No	No	Yes	Compulsory
Jamaica	1998	$5,512	2	No	Yes	No	Compulsory
Japan	1971	N/A	N/A	No	Yes	No	Compulsory
Kenya	1985	$1,757	5	No	Yes	No	Compulsory
Korea	1996	N/A	N/A	No	Yes	No	Compulsory
Latvia	1998	$830	0	No	Yes	No	Compulsory
Lebanon	1967	$3,300	1	No	Yes	No	Compulsory
Lithuania	1996	$6,250	2	Yes	Yes	No	Compulsory

(Continued)

Table 1.1. Design features of deposit insurance schemes in countries around the world (*Continued*)

Countries	Date enacted/ revised	Coverage limit	Coverage ratio limit/ GDP per capita	Coinsurance	Type of fund (Yes = funded; No = unfunded)	Risk-adjusted Premiums	Type of membership
Luxembourg	1989	$16,439	0	Yes	No	No	Compulsory
Macedonia	1996	$183	0	Yes	Yes	Yes	Voluntary
Marshall Islands	1975	$100,000	N/A	No	Yes	Yes	Voluntary
Mexico	1986/1990	N/A	N/A	No	Yes	No	Compulsory
Micronesia	1963	$100,000	N/A	No	Yes	Yes	Voluntary
Netherlands	1979/1995	$21,918	1	No	No	No	Compulsory
Nigeria	1988/1989	$588	2	No	Yes	No	Compulsory
Norway	1961/1997	$260,800	8	No	Yes	No	Compulsory
Oman	1995	$52,630	9	Yes	Yes	No	Compulsory
Peru	1992	$21,160	9	No	Yes	Yes	Compulsory
Philippines	1963	$2,375	3	No	Yes	No	Compulsory
Poland	1995	$1,096	0	Yes	Yes	No	Compulsory
Portugal	1992/1995	$16,439	1	Yes	Yes	Yes	Compulsory
Republic of Congo	1999	$3,557	5	No	Yes	Yes	Voluntary
Romania	1996	$3,600	2	No	Yes	Yes	Compulsory
Slovak Republic	1996	$7,900	2	No	Yes	No	Compulsory
Spain	1977/1996	$16,439	1	No	Yes	No	Compulsory
Sri Lanka	1987	$1,470	2	No	Yes	No	Voluntary
Sweden	1996	$31,412	1	No	Yes	Yes	Compulsory
Switzerland	1984/1993	$19,700	1	No	No	No	Voluntary
Taiwan	1985	$38,500	3	No	Yes	No	Voluntary
Tanzania	1994	$376	2	No	Yes	No	Compulsory
Trinidad & Tobago	1986	$7,957	2	No	Yes	No	Compulsory
Turkey	1983	N/A	N/A	No	Yes	Yes	Compulsory
Uganda	1994	$2,310	8	No	Yes	No	Compulsory
Ukraine	1998	$250	0	No	Yes	No	Compulsory
United Kingdom	1982/1995	$33,333	1	Yes	No	No	Compulsory
United States	1934/1991	$100,000	3	No	Yes	Yes	Compulsory
Venezuela	1985	$7,309	2	No	Yes	No	Compulsory

Source: Demirgüç-Kunt, A. and Sobaci, T. (2001) 'Deposit Insurance Around the World', *The World Bank Economic Review*, 15(3): 481–490. Full database available at *http://econ.worldbank.org/programs/finance/topic/depinsurance/*

Some countries have elected to establish an *ex-ante* funded scheme, whereas others have chosen to provide the funds for any losses from bank failures *ex-post*. Of the 68 countries, only 10 have chosen to establish an *ex-post* or unfunded scheme. In this case, the funds necessary to resolve bank failures are obtained only after bank failures occur. This type of arrangement may provide a greater incentive for private monitoring and policing, because everyone will know that the funds necessary to resolve problems have not yet been collected. And everyone will also know that a way to keep any funds from being collected is to prevent banks from engaging in excessively risky activities. Of course, the degree of monitoring depends importantly on the source of funding. In this regard, there are three alternative arrangements: (1) public funding, (2) private funding, or (3) joint funding. Of these three sources, private funding provides the greatest incentive for private discipline and public funding the least. Although the information is not provided in the table, only 15 of the 68 countries fund their deposit insurance schemes solely on the basis of private sources. At the same time, however, only one country relies solely on public funding. Eleven of the schemes that are privately funded, moreover, are also either privately or jointly administered. No country, where there is only private funding, has decided to have the fund solely administered by government officials.

In addition to the design features already discussed, there are two other important features that must be decided upon when a country establishes a deposit insurance scheme. One is whether in those countries in which premiums are paid by banks for deposit insurance should be risk-based or not (Prescott, 2002). The advantage of risk-based premiums is that they potentially can be used to induce banks to avoid engaging in excessively risky activities. This would enable the banking authorities to have an additional tool to contain moral hazard. Yet, in practice it is extremely difficult to set and administer such a premium structure. Table 1.1 shows that slightly less than one-third of the countries have chosen to adopt risk-based premiums.

The last feature to be discussed is the membership structure of a deposit insurance scheme. A country has to decide whether banks may voluntarily join or will be required to join. A voluntary scheme will certainly attract all the weak banks. The healthy banks, in contrast, are unlikely to perceive any benefits from membership. If this happens, the funding for resolving problems will be questionable for both *ex-ante* and *ex-post* schemes. Indeed, the entire scheme may simply become a government bailout for weak banks. By requiring all banks to become members, the funding base is broader and more reliable. At the same time, when the healthy banks are members, they have a greater incentive to monitor and police the weaker banks to help protect the fund.

1.6. Lessons Learned from Banking Crises

It is quite clear that although many countries at all levels of income and in all parts of the world have established deposit insurance schemes they have not chosen a uniform structure. The specific design features differ widely among the 68 countries for which information is available as already discussed and indicated in Table 1.1. The fact that so many countries around the globe have suffered banking crises over the past 20 years has generated a substantial amount of research focusing on the relationship between a banking crisis and deposit insurance. Although this type of research is still ongoing, there are currently enough studies from which to draw some, albeit tentative, conclusions about deposit insurance schemes that help promote a safe and sound banking industry. These are as follows:

- Even without a deposit insurance scheme, countries have on occasion responded to banking crises with unlimited guarantees to depositors. An appropriately designed scheme that includes a coverage limit may be better able to serve notice to depositors as to the extent of their protection, and thereby enable governments to avoid more costly *ex-post* bailouts.

- The design features of a deposit insurance scheme are quite important. Indeed, recent empirical studies show that poorly designed schemes increase the likelihood that a country will experience a banking crisis.

- Properly designed deposit insurance schemes can help mobilize savings in a country, and thereby help foster overall financial development. Research has documented this important linkage, but emphasizes that it only holds in countries with a strong legal and regulatory environment.

- Empirical research shows that market discipline is seriously eroded in countries that have designed their deposit insurance schemes with a high coverage limit – an *ex-ante* fund – the government being the sole source of funds, and only public officials as the administrators of the fund.

- Empirical research shows that market discipline is significantly enhanced in countries that have designed their deposit insurance schemes with coinsurance, mandatory membership, and private or joint administration of the fund.

All in all, empirical research that has recently been completed indicates that governments should pay close attention to the features they wish to include in a deposit insurance scheme should they decide to adopt one, or to modify the one they have already established (Barth et al., 2006).

1.7. Conclusions

Countries everywhere have shown a greater interest in establishing deposit insurance schemes in the past two decades. The evidence to date indicates that much more consideration must be given to the design features of these schemes to be sure that their benefits are not offset by their associated costs.

REFERENCES

Barth, J.R., Caprio, G., and Levine, R. (2006). *Rethinking Bank Regulation and Supervision: Till Angels Govern.* Cambridge: Cambridge University Press.

Bradley, C.M. (2000). "A historical perspective on deposit insurance coverage" *FDIC-Banking Review,* 13(2): 1–25.

Cooper, R. and Ross, T.W. (2002). "Bank runs: Deposit insurance and capital requirements." *International Economic Review,* 43(1): 55–72.

Demirgüç-Kunt, A. and Kane, E.J. (2002). "Deposit insurance around the globe: Where does it work?" *Journal of Economic Perspectives,* 16(2): 178–195.

Demirgüç-Kunt, A. and Sobaci, T. (2001). "Deposit insurance around the world." *The World Bank Economic Review,* 15(3): 481–490.

Demirgüç-Kunt, A. and Detragiache, E. (2000). "Does deposit insurance increase banking system stability?" International Monetary Fund Working Paper WP/00/03.

Diamond, D.W. and Dybvig, P.H. (2000). "Bank runs, deposit insurance, and liquidity." *Federal Reserve Bank of Minneapolis Quarterly Review,* 24(1): 14–23.

Garcia, G. (2000). "Deposit insurance and crisis management." International Monetary Fund Policy Working Paper WP/00/57.

Garcia, G. (1999). "Deposit insurance: A survey of actual and best practices." International Monetary Fund Policy Working Paper WP/99/54.

Gropp, R. and Vesala, J. (2001). "Deposit insurance and moral hazard: Does the counterfactual matter?" European Central Bank Working Paper No. 47.

Prescott, E.S. (2002). "Can risk-based deposit insurance premiums control moral hazard?" *Federal Reserve Bank of Richmond Economic Quarterly,* 88(2): 87–100.

Chapter 2

GRAMM-LEACH-BLILEY ACT: CREATING A NEW BANK FOR A NEW MILLENIUM

JAMES R. BARTH, *Auburn University and Milken Institute, USA*
JOHN S. JAHERA, *Auburn University, USA*

Abstract

The Gramm-Leach-Bliley Act (GLBA) was signed into law on November 12, 1999 and essentially repealed the Glass-Steagall Act (GSA) of 1933 that had mandated the separation of commercial banking activities from securities activities. It also repealed provisions of the Bank Holding Company Act (BHCA) of 1956 that provided for the separation of commercial banking from insurance activities. The major thrust of the new law, therefore, is the establishment of a legal structure that allows for the integration of banking, securities and insurance activities within a single organization. The GLBA will be explained and discussed, with special emphasis on its importance for U.S. banks in a world of ever increasing globalization of financial services.

Keywords: banking laws; bank regulations; securities; insurance; financial modernization; financial holding companies; Glass-Steagall; globalization; thrifts

2.1. Introduction

The Gramm-Leach-Bliley Act (GLBA) was signed into law on November 12, 1999 and provided for sweeping changes in the allowable activities of banks in the United States (Barth et al., 2000). The GLBA, also known as the Financial Modernization Act, essentially repealed the Glass-Steagall Act (GSA) of 1933 that had mandated the separation of commercial banking activities from securities activities. In addition, the GLBA repealed provisions of the Bank Holding Company Act (BHCA) of 1956 that provided for the separation of commercial banking from insurance activities. While the GLBA formally changed the face of banking, in recent years the regulatory environment had been evolving away from a stringent interpretation of the GSA.

The major thrust of the new law is the establishment of a legal structure that allows for the integration of banking, securities, and insurance activities within a single organization. The GSA was enacted during the Great Depression following the market crash of 1929. The intent was to provide for the separation of banking activities from securities activities based on the view that undue speculation and conflicts of interest had, at least in part, led to the market crash and the subsequent failure of numerous banks. As much as anything, the GSA was supposed to restore confidence in the banking system and securities markets. However, its restrictive provisions eroded gradually over the years, and more rapidly in the past 20 years. In fact, many view the enactment of the GLBA as merely serving to formalize what had already been happening *de facto* in the financial marketplace, as the distinction between different types of financial service firms and their products had become quite blurred.

A particularly important reason to understand the GLBA at this time is globalization. Banks in the United States have operated for decades under some of the most restrictive regulations when compared to banks in most of the other industrial countries around the world. While the GLBA improves the position of banks in terms of global competitiveness, U.S. banks still do not enjoy the same degree of freedom with respect to activities and organizational structure as banks in many other countries.

2.2. Major Provisions of Gramm-Leach-Bliley Act

2.2.1. Financial Holding Companies

The GSA and the BHCA restricted bank affiliations with securities firms and insurance companies. Figure 2.1 provides a schematic of the allowable activities and organizational structure under the prior law and under the new provisions of the GLBA. Essentially, the new law repealed earlier activity restrictions and created new financial holding companies, which are allowed to engage in a wide range of activities, as long as the Federal Reserve determines that the activities do not pose a substantial risk to bank safety or soundness.

The GLBA provides for a new holding company category, the financial holding company. A bank holding company may become a financial holding company provided its depository institutions are adequately capitalized, properly managed, and has a "satisfactory" rating under the Community Reinvestment Act (CRA). The new holding companies may engage in activities deemed to be financial in "nature" or "incidental" to financial activities. The Federal Reserve may also allow activities termed "complementary" to financial activities after determining that the activity does not

impair the safety or soundness of banks. One caveat is that the Federal Reserve may not determine an activity to be financial in nature if the Treasury Department objects. Obviously, this provision may result in disputes regarding the interpretation of the law, and hence add to uncertainty regarding approval of certain activities for banks. The new holding company may own banks as subsidiaries as well as other subsidiaries that engage in other approved financial activities. Activities that the GLBA specifies to be "financial in nature" include underwriting and dealing in securities, insurance underwriting and agency activities, merchant banking, mutual fund sponsorship, and insurance company portfolio investments. Insurance agency activities are regulated solely by the individual states, and therefore may face state imposed restrictions. However, states are precluded from restricting any activity that is specified in the GLBA.

2.2.2. National Bank Financial Subsidiaries

The new law also creates new financial subsidiaries of national banks (and subject to state law, of state banks) that may engage in all the financial activities authorized by the new law. Exceptions include insurance or annuity underwriting, insurance company portfolio investments, real estate investment and development, and merchant banking. These latter activities may only be conducted in financial holding company subsidiaries. Furthermore, there is a limitation of the total assets of all financial subsidiaries of 45 percent of the total assets of the bank or $50 billion.

2.3. Functional Regulation and Equal Treatment for Foreign Banks

The new law generally adheres to the principle of functional regulation, which holds that similar activities should be regulated by the same regulator. Thus, banking regulators regulate bank activities, securities regulators regulate securities activities, and insurance regulators regulate insurance activ-

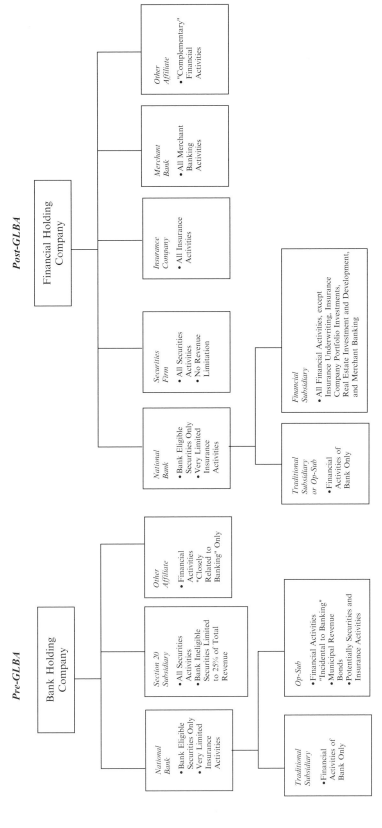

Figure 2.1. Past and new bank permissible activities and organizational structure.

ities. The Federal Reserve, as an umbrella regulator, is authorized to examine financial holding companies and their subsidiaries, but may specifically examine functionally regulated subsidiaries only under limited circumstances. For those entities, the Federal Reserve will generally rely upon the examinations by other federal and state securities and insurance regulatory authorities.

The new law does exempt some banking activities that are deemed to have a "securities" component from the regulatory authority of the Securities and Exchange Commission (SEC). However, the law provides a process that requires the SEC to act by rulemaking before seeking to regulate any bank sale of any new hybrid security product. Finally, if a new product is determined to be an insurance product by the state insurance regulator, then national banks are prohibited from providing it as principal in that state. Any conflicts must be resolved in a court of law.

The GLBA provides for national treatment whereby foreign banks may engage in the newly authorized financial activities on the same basis as domestic banking organizations.

2.3.1. Retention of Thrift Holding Companies

The new law retains the federal savings and loan charter, and allows thrift holding companies to conduct banking, securities, and insurance activities on the same terms as bank holding companies. The law, however, closes a loophole permitting the mixing of banking and commerce by prohibiting thrift holding companies from acquiring commercial firms, or engaging in new commercial activity.

The law also creates new community financial institutions that may obtain long-term federal home loan bank advances for lending to small businesses, small farms, and small agribusinesses. These institutions must be FDIC-insured depository institutions with less than $500 million in assets. Thus, Congress is providing new government directed subsidized lending to selected institutions to induce them to provide credit to businesses favored by it.

2.3.2. Community Reinvestment Act Provisions

The CRA was enacted to ensure that banks do not lend the deposits gathered from individuals in one area to those living in another area in significant proportions. It thus requires banks to make credit available to the communities in which they obtain deposits. Prior to passage, there was concern that the CRA would be weakened. The GLBA therefore required that financial holding companies could not be formed until their insured depository institutions received and maintained a satisfactory CRA rating. Smaller institutions were granted some relief with less frequent CRA examinations. Banks with less than $250 million in assets are to undergo a CRA examination once every five years if they have prior outstanding ratings, and once every four years if they have prior satisfactory ratings. The GLBA further requires than banks and community groups must disclose certain CRA agreements, and provide annual reports on the use of funds and resources utilized in fulfilling such agreements. Financial holdings companies and banks with financial subsidiaries are prohibited from new activities or acquisitions unless each insured institution within the company has earned at least a "satisfactory" CRA rating.

2.3.3. Other Components of the GLBA

Automated teller machines that charge fees must be labeled with a notice of the fee. The machine must also give customers a notice on the screen that a fee will be charged, with the option of canceling the transaction.

The new law also requires the relevant regulators to establish standards for ensuring the privacy of consumers' personal information maintained by financial institutions. Surprisingly, congressional negotiations towards the end was dominated by whether consumer privacy would be adequately protected with the expansion of bank powers In the House of Representatives, shift in a mere 13 votes on the privacy provisions would have defeated the entire legislation.

The law, as passed, requires regulators to establish standards to ensure the privacy of personal financial information held by financial institutions. In addition, consumers must be presented the opportunity to "opt out" of having their financial information shared with nonaffiliated third parties. Further, mandatory disclosure of the institution's privacy policies must be made on an annual basis to all customers.

One other feature designed to benefit consumers is the mandate that federal banking agencies must use "plain" language in all rules made after January 1, 2000 (Banerji et al., 2002; Broome and Markham, 2000; Carow, 2001; Wilmarth, 2002).

2.4. Potential Benefits to Banks and their Customers

Banks potentially benefit from the expanded range of permissible activities through higher average profits resulting from scale and scope economies. The fixed overhead cost of managing a customer relationship can be spread over more services. Banks can also use existing technology, personnel, and delivery channels to distribute securities and insurance services at a relatively low marginal cost. Finally, there may be economies coming from overhead in administration, back-office operations, and information technologies being spread over a bigger base of financial services.

Because of greater opportunities for diversification, a bank with broader powers may also have lower profit variability than a traditional bank. Broad banks will be affected less when firms bypass banks and raise funds directly in the capital markets because a decline in the banks' lending activity will be offset by an increase in their securities activity. In addition, if profits from different financial activities are not highly correlated, then the total profits of a broad bank will be more stable than that of banks specialized in relatively few activities. Customers may also benefit from the broad bank. If a bank achieves greater scale and scope economies, competition should lead to a sharing of these benefits with customers and firms

in the form of lower prices. Also, they may benefit from lower search and transaction costs because of "one-stop" or "one-click" shopping.

2.5. Potential Risk Elements to Banks and their Customers

Two main concerns arise when combining banking, securities, and insurance activities within the same banking organization where the contagion effect of problems in one unit affects other units. The greater range of activities may increase the risk of insolvency to the organization. This might happen if banking organizations encounter unexpected difficulties in the nontraditional activities, due either to a lack of the banks' business experience or because the regulatory authorities might be less able to contain excessive risk-taking in the new activities.

Empirical evidence, however, suggests that the expansion of securities and insurance powers need not put banking organizations at greater risk of insolvency, and may actually reduce the probability of bankruptcy. Policy makers have echoed these views. The FDIC supported the repeal of the GSA on the grounds that this would advance financial modernization without sacrificing safety and soundness (Barth et al., 2004).

The federal safety-net problem is the second concern. It refers to extending the benefits of federal deposit insurance and access to both the payment system and the discount window of the Federal Reserve to a broader range of activities. If banks receive a subsidy from access to the federal safety net and if it can be extended to additional activities, then banks possess an unfair advantage vis-à-vis their nonbank competitors in these activities. Furthermore, such a situation might encourage banks to engage too heavily in additional activities.

Banks, however, also incur special costs associated with the federal safety net. They pay premiums for deposit insurance, hold interest-free reserves, and bear costs to satisfy numerous banking rules and regulations. These costs must be subtracted from any gross subsidy to obtain the net subsidy. Recent estimates of net subsidies indicate that, for most banks, they are either close to zero or zero.

2.6. Implications for the Future

Of all the 19 nonoverlapping G-10 and E.U. countries, Japan and the United States were the most restrictive in their treatment of securities and insurance activities prior to 1999. Japan and the United States were also the most restrictive regarding the mixing of banking and commerce. The majority of the G-10 and E.U. countries place no restrictions on banks owning commercial firms and vice-versa, which was also the case in the United States before 1956. Many other countries also permit banks more latitude to choose the organizational form in which to conduct securities and insurance activities.

An analysis of more than 60 countries has found that tighter the restrictions placed on securities and insurance activities, the more inefficient are banks and greater the likelihood of a banking crisis. The likelihood of a banking crisis is also greater, the tighter the restrictions placed on bank ownership of nonfinancial firms. In fact, none of the securities, insurance, real estate and ownership restrictions produce any beneficial effects with respect to bank development, bank performance, or bank stability.

By permitting banks to engage in banking, securities, and insurance activities, and by providing even broader powers to financial holding companies, the new law will likely rejuvenate banking. While banks held nearly three-fourths of the total assets of all financial intermediaries in 1860, recently their share had declined to less than one fourth. The combined assets of commercial banks, insurance companies, securities firms, and investment companies are almost two-thirds of the assets of all financial intermediaries. Thus, the new broad banks may return to be dominant institutions that they were a century ago.

The importance of capital markets (stocks and bonds) as compared to bank loans is far more important today than in the last century. This shift in the composition of the financial system reflects the fact that financial intermediation based upon a securities-based system is more cost-effective than a bank loan-based system. Today, the cost of intermediation through a bank is about 400 basis points as measured by net interest margin. This compares to less than 100 basis points as measured by the operating expense ratio of mutual funds.

These newer developments have forced banks to transform themselves from traditional spread-income based institutions to nontraditional fee-based institutions. Reflecting these changes, commercial loans are only 16 percent of total assets, while demand deposits are a slightly lower 13 percent. Indeed, non-interest income as a percentage of net operating revenue is 46 percent for banks with more than $1 billion in assets and 27 percent for banks with less than $1 billion in assets. The emphasis of banks is increasingly on asset and risk management, especially for the bigger banks.

Broad banks will therefore not be the banks of the recent past. They will reflect the historic changes brought about mainly by technology and globalization, as well as the corresponding regulations these developments engender. Providing liquidity in the form of deposits and loans to businesses will undoubtedly remain an important service of banks, but it will be subsumed in the broader strategy of asset and risk management using modern information technology.

REFERENCES

Banerji, S., Andrew, H.C., and Sumon, C.M. (2002). "Universal banking under bilateral information asymmetry." *Journal of Financial Services Research*, 22(3): 169–187.

Barth, J.R., Caprio, G., and Levine, R. (2004). "Bank regulation and supervision: what works best?" *Journal of Financial Intermediation*, 13(2): 205–248.

Barth, J.R., Brumbaugh, Jr. R.D., and Wilcox, J.A. (2000). "Glass-Steagall repealed: Market forces compel a new bank legal structure." *Journal of Economic Perspective*, 191–204.

Broome, L.L. and Markham, J.W. (2000). "Banking and insurance: Before and after the Gramm-Leach-Bliley Act." *Journal of Corporation Law*, 25(4): 723–785.

Carow, K.A. and Heron, R.A. (2002). "Capital market reactions to the passage of the Financial Services Modernization Act of 1999." *Quarterly Review of Economics and Finance*, 42(3): 465–485.

Wilmarth, Jr. A.E. (2002). "The transformation of the U.S. Financial Services Industry, 1975–2002: Competition, consolidation and increased risks." *University of Illinois Law Review*, 2: 215–476.

Chapter 3

COMPARATIVE ANALYSIS OF ZERO-COUPON AND COUPON-PRE-FUNDED BONDS

A. LINDA BEYER, *Alaska Supply Chain Integrators, USA*
KEN HUNG, *National Dong Hwa University, Taiwan*
SURESH C. SRIVASTAVA, *University of Alaska Anchorage, USA*

Abstract

Coupon-prefunded bonds have been developed and sold by investment bankers in place of zero-coupon bonds to raise funds for companies facing cash flow problems. Additional bonds are issued and proceeds are deposited in an escrow account to finance the coupon payment. Our analysis indicates that a coupon-prefunded bond is equivalent to a zero-coupon bond only if the return from the escrow account is the same as the yield to maturity of the prefunded issue. In reality, the escrow return is lower than the bond yield. As a result, the firm provides interest subsidy through issuing additional bonds which leads to higher leverage, greater risk, and loss of value compared to a zero-coupon issue.

Keywords: zero-coupon bond; Macaulay duration; escrow account; Treasury STRIPS; junk bonds; coupon collateralization; financial engineering; coupon pre-funded bond; cash flows; and value loss

3.1. Introduction

Coupon-prefunded bonds, new to financial markets, were first issued in 1994 (Doherty, 1997).[1] They were introduced as a means to raise capital for firms unable to generate cash flow to make coupon payments, while still meeting the needs of investors to receive coupon income. With a pre-funded bond structure, additional bonds are issued and an escrow account is established to finance coupon payments over the life of the bond. In this manner, the bond is considered prefunded. The firm is not required to generate cash flow to meet coupon obligations; it is paid out of the escrow account usually collateralized by treasury securities. The risk-free coupon payment allows the firm to set a lower coupon rate on the bond than the yield on a comparable zero-coupon bond. In general, the cost of funding the escrow account is greater than the return of the escrow account. This leads to an interest rate subsidy and the loss of value. In this paper, we compare zero-coupon bonds to prefunded bonds and ascertain conditions under which the two funding options are equivalent. A prefunded issue simultaneously creates an asset and a liability. The net duration of the pre-funded issue is the weighted average of the asset and liability durations. The model of net duration developed in this paper incorporates increased leverage of the pre-funded issue, and appropriately assess its increased risk. In spite of the fact that a prefunded bond is an interesting concept of financial engineering, there is very little academic research on this topic.

The remainder of this paper is made up of four sections. Section 3.2 discusses the options available to a firm interested in issuing debt. In Section 3.3, we derive a mathematical model for Macaulay duration of the prefunded issue to determine the interest rate risk and calculate the loss in value due to interest rate subsidy. A numerical example and its analysis are presented in Section 3.4. Section 3.5 concludes the paper.

3.2. Funding Options

A firm wants to raise funds to finance a new project. The pecking-order theory of capital structure suggests that managers prefer internal equity to external financing (Myers, 1984). In case the internal equity (retained earnings) is not available then issuing new debt is preferred over issuing preferred or additional common stock. Further, firms would like to reduce the interest payment burden. Hence, conventional coupon bond or hybrid financing such as convertible bonds or bonds with warrants are ruled out. The available funding options are (1) zero-coupon bonds, (2) step-up bonds – initially coupon payment is set at a low value and later stepped up, (3) deferred interest bonds – initially there is no interest payment, but it is resumed in 3–7 years, (4) paid-in-kind bonds – issuer has right to pay interest in cash or with similar bonds[2], and (5) prefunded bonds. The focus of the study is to compare zero-coupon and coupon-prefunded bonds.

3.2.1. Zero-Coupon Bonds

Pure discount bonds are often called zero-coupon bonds. It was first issued by J.C. Penney Company Inc. in 1982 (Brigham and Daves, 2004). In recent years, other firms (e.g. IBM, GMAC, Alcoa and Martin-Marietta) have issued zero-coupon bonds. Municipalities started issuing zero-coupon bonds in 1983. These bonds are sold at a deep discount and increase in value as they approach maturity. Zero-coupon bonds do not provide interest or coupon payments at regular intervals like other types of

bonds. Implicit coupons are automatically reinvested by the issuer at yield to maturity. Interest accrues over the life of the bond and a return is earned as the bond appreciates. At maturity its value equals the face value, and the bond holder receives the yield to maturity expected at the time of purchase. If held to maturity, the investor faces no reinvestment risk but high-interest rate risk, as its market price fluctuates considerably with movements in market rates.

Corporate and municipal zero-coupon bonds are usually callable and rated as junk bonds.[3] The financial condition of the company issuing bonds predicates the use of junk bonds, i.e. the firm is unable to generate cash flows to meet coupon payments. Junk bonds are typically rated BB or lower by Standard and Poor's, or BA or lower by Moody's. Junk bonds offer a high-expected return but require investors to take on higher default risk. Covenants on junk bonds are less restrictive, and therefore provide alternatives for firms that may not meet the more restrictive covenants of conventional bonds.

3.2.2. Coupon Pre-Funded Bonds

In raising capital with a prefunded bond issue, additional bonds are issued and an escrow account is established. The firm is not required to generate cash flow to meet coupon obligations over the life of the bond. Bond interests are paid out of an escrow account, which is usually collateralized by treasury securities. In this manner, the bond is considered prefunded. A prefunded bond issue simultaneously creates an asset and a liability. The risk characteristics of prefunded bonds' interest payments are different from that of traditional coupon-bearing bonds because prefunded bonds' coupon payments are asset based. The default free nature of the coupon payment allows the firm to set a lower coupon rate than the yield on a comparable zero-coupon bond. In general, the cost of funding the escrow account is greater than the return from the escrow account. This spread leads to an interest rate subsidy which necessitates issuing more bonds, and hence a loss of value. Greater the spread between the cost of funding the escrow account and the return from the escrow account, the larger the total face value of the prefunded issue and the value loss. With a prefunded bond issue, there are additional flotation costs and cost of establishing the escrow account. However, for this analysis, we consider the escrow costs and additional flotation costs to be negligible.

Market price of prefunded bonds fluctuates with movements in market rates, but it does not move as dramatically as zero-coupon bond prices. The reason for this difference is that zero-coupon bonds do not provide any cash flow until maturity. Coupon payments reduce the impact of interest rate changes on prefunded bonds. Market conditions where interest rate movements are frequent and highly variable make prefunded bonds more attractive than zero-coupon bonds. The risk profiles of zero-coupon and prefunded bonds can be summarized as follows: A zero-coupon bond has no reinvestment risk, higher price elasticity to interest rate changes, and a default risk consistent with its junk bond rating. The prefunded bond has reinvestment risk but lower price elasticity to interest rate changes. For a meaningful analysis of the interest rate risk, one must examine the combined interest rate sensitivity of the escrow asset and the bond liability. The default risk of the prefunded issue should be decomposed into two components: the default risk of the coupon payments and the default risk of the maturity payment. The coupon payments are default free but the default risk of the maturity payments is much higher. This is due to the increased leverage of the prefunded issue compared to zero-coupon financing. In spite of the default-free coupon payments, the prefunded bonds are usually rated as junk bonds.

In the next section, the combined interest rate sensitivity of the escrow asset and the bond liability is examined. A model for the net Macaulay duration of the prefunded issue is developed, and loss of value due to interest rate subsidy is calculated.

3.3. Macaulay Duration and Value Loss

In this section, we calculate the total face value of the prefunded bonds issued, initial balance of the escrow account, interest rate subsidy provided by the firm, effective cost of the prefunded issue, and resulting loss of value. Also, we derive an expression for the net Macaulay duration of the prefunded issue, i.e. the weighted average durations of the coupon bond and the escrow asset

The face values of zero-coupon bonds issued, to raise an amount B, is

$$B_z = B(1 + r_z)^n \qquad (3.1)$$

where r_z is the discount rate for the zero-coupon bond with maturity n. The Macaulay duration of zero-coupon bond is its maturity (Fabbozzi, 2000).

Let B_{pf} be the face value of the prefunded bonds issued to raise an amount B. The annual coupon payment is $B_{pf}(r_{pf})$, where r_{pf} is the prefunded bond yield. The initial balance in the escrow annuity account set up to meet the coupon payments is $B_{pf} - B$. Hence,

$$B_{pf} - B = (B_{pf}r_{pf})(\text{PVIFA}_{r_{es},n})$$
$$B_{pf} = \frac{B}{1 - r_{pf}(\text{PVIFA}_{r_{es},n})} \qquad (3.2)$$

where PVIFA indicates present value interest factor of an annuity, n is the maturity, and r_{es} is the rate of return on the escrow account. Substituting the algebraic expression for PVIFA we get[4]

$$B_{pf} = \frac{r_{es}(1 + r_{es})^n B}{r_{pf} - (r_{pf} - r_{es})(1 + r_{es})^n} \qquad (3.3)$$

The initial balance in the escrow account is

$$B_{pf} - B = \frac{r_{pf}[(1 + r_{es})^n - 1]B}{r_{pf} - (r_{pf} - r_{es})(1 + r_{es})^n} \qquad (3.4)$$

Escrow account is funded at a cost of r_{pf} and provides a return of r_{es}. Consequently, the firm is providing a pre-tax interest subsidy of $(r_{pf}B_{pf})(r_{pf} - r_{es})$ per year, which increases the cost of prefunded issue and leads to loss of value.

The loss of value is:

$$\text{Value Loss} = (r_{pf}B_{pf})(r_{pf} - r_{es})\frac{(1 + r_{pf})^n - 1}{(1 + r_{pf})^n} \quad (3.5)$$

and the effective cost of the prefunded issue is given by:

$$r_{\text{eff}} = \left(\frac{r_{es}(1 + r_{es})^n}{r_{pf} - (r_{pf} - r_{es})(1 + r_{es})^n}\right)^{1/n} - 1 \quad (3.6)$$

The concept of duration was introduced by Macaulay (1938) as a measure of price sensitivity of an asset or liability to a change in interest rates. Working independently, Samuelson (1945) and Redington (1952) developed the same concept about the interest rate risk of bonds. Details of duration computation can be found in any finance text (Fabbozzi, 2000). A prefunded bond issue creates an asset, the escrow account annuity with market value $B_{pf} - B$; and a liability, coupon bonds with market value B_{pf}. The net market value of the prefunded issue is B. Let D_{es} and D_{pf} represent the duration of escrow annuity and the bond liability respectively. Duration D_{es} is the Macaulay duration of an n-year annuity with yield r_{es} and D_{pf} is the Macaulay duration of an n-year coupon bond with yield to maturity r_{pf}. The net duration of the prefunded issue is the weighted average of the durations of the escrow account and the coupon bond. Hence

$$D_{\text{net}} = \frac{B_{pf}}{B} \times D_{pf} - \frac{B_{pf} - B}{B} \times D_{es} \quad (3.7)$$

where (B_{pf}/B) and $(-(B_{pf} - B)/B)$ are the weights of the coupon bond and the escrow annuity respectively. This definition of net duration, D_{net}, captures the increased risk due to additional leverage caused by prefunding of coupon payments and interest subsidy provided by the firm.

3.4. Numerical Example and Analysis

A firm wants to raise $10 million by issuing either zero-coupon bonds or prefunded bonds with five or ten year maturity. We assume that transaction costs are identical for both issues and negligible.[5] Further, we assume that financial market views the zero-coupon and prefunded bonds to be equivalent securities, and prices them with identical yields. Four different yields, 8 percent, 7 percent, 6 percent, and 5 percent,.on zero-coupon and prefunded bonds are considered for this analysis. Later, we modify this assumption and consider the situation where market views prefunded bond to be safer and erroneously prices them with yields lower than the comparable zero-coupon yields by 25, 50, and 75 basis points. In doing so, market overlooks the added default risk associated with increased leverage.

Table 3.1 presents the face value of zero-coupon bonds issued to meet the $10 million funding need. For 5-year maturity with discount rates of 8 percent, 7 percent, 6 percent, and 5 percent, the firm issues zero-coupon bonds with total face values of

Table 3.1. Zero-coupon bond
$B_z = B(1 + r_z)^n$ and $D_z = n$

		Discount rate, r_z			
		8%	7%	6%	5%
Maturity, n 5 years	Funds needed, B	$10,000,000	$10,000,000	$10,000,000	$10,000,000
	Face value of bonds issued, B_z	$14,693,281	$14,025,517	$13,382,256	$12,762,816
	Market value of bonds issued	$10,000,000	$10,000,000	$10,000,000	$10,000,000
	Duration, D_z	5 years	5 years	5 years	5 years
Maturity, n 10 years	Funds needed, B	$10,000,000	$10,000,000	$10,000,000	$10,000,000
	Face value of bonds issued, B_z	$21,589,250	$19,671,514	$17,908,477	$16,288,946
	Market value of bonds issued	$10,000,000	$10,000,000	$10,000,000	$10,000,000
	Duration, D_z	10 years	10 years	10 years	10 years

$14,693,281, $14,025,517, $13,382,256, and $12,762,816 respectively. These values are calculated using Equation (3.1). The Macaulay duration of the 5-year zero-coupon bond is 5 years. For 10-year zero-coupon bonds, an 8 percent, 7 percent, 6 percent, and 5 percent discount rate leads to total face values of $21,589,250, $19,671,514, $17,908,477, and $16,288,946 respectively. The Macaulay duration of the 10-year zero-coupon bond is 10 years.

In Table 3.2, we present the total face value of the prefunded issue, amount of annual coupon payment disbursed from escrow account, and the effective cost of prefunded issue. It provides the following important inferences.

First, when the prefunded bond yield, r_{pf}, is the same as the escrow account return, r_{es}, then (i) the total face value of the pre-funded issued is the same as the total face value of the zero-coupon bonds and (ii) the effective cost of prefunded issue, r_{eff}, is

Table 3.2. Total face value and effective cost of prefunded issue

$$B_{pf} = \frac{r_{es}(1 + r_{es})^n B}{r_{pf} - (r_{pf} - r_{es})(1 + r_{es})^n} \quad \text{and} \quad r_{eff} = \left(\frac{r_{es}(1 + r_{es})^n}{r_{pf} - (r_{pf} - r_{es})(1 + r_{es})^n} \right)^{1/n} - 1$$

			Prefunded bond yield, r_{pf}			
n	r_{es}		8%	7%	6%	5%
5	8%	Face value, B_{pf}	$14,693,281			
		Escrow payment	$1,175,462			
		Effective cost, r_{eff}	8.000%			
	7%	Face value, B_{pf}	$14,881,302	$14,025,517		
		Escrow payment	$1,190,504	$981,786		
		Effective cost, r_{eff}	8.275%	7.000%		
	6%	Face value, B_{pf}	$15,082,708	$14,181,691	$13,382,256	
		Escrow payment	$1,206,617	$992,718	$802,935	
		Effective cost, r_{eff}	8.567%	7.237%	6.000%	
	5%	Face value, B_{pf}	$15,298,893	$14,368,507	$13,509,289	$12,762,816
		Escrow payment	$1,223,912	$1,004,395	$810,557	$638,141
		Effective cost, r_{eff}	8.876%	7.518%	6.201%	5.000%
10	8%	Face value, B_{pf}	$21,589,250			
		Escrow payment	$1,727,140			
		Effective cost, r_{eff}	8.000%			
	7%	Face value, B_{pf}	$22,825,137	$19,671,514		
		Escrow payment	$1,826,011	$1,377,006		
		Effective cost, r_{eff}	8.603%	7.000%		
	6%	Face value, B_{pf}	$24,319,478	$20,627,322	$17,098,477	
		Escrow payment	$1,945,558	$1,443,913	$1,074,509	
		Effective cost, r_{eff}	9.294%	7.509%	6.000%	
	5%	Face value, B_{pf}	$26,160,123	$21,763,801	$18,632,525	$16,288,946
		Escrow payment	$2,092,810	$1,523,466	$1,117,952	$814,447
		Effective cost, r_{eff}	10.094%	8.087%	6.421%	5.000%

r_{es} = escrow return. Maturity = n years. Empty cell represents the improbable case of $r_{pf} < r_z$.

the same as the yield to maturity of the zero-coupon bond, r_z. Second, increase in the spread between r_{pf} and r_{es} increases the total face value of the bonds issued and its effective cost. Finally, for a given spread the total face value of the bonds issued and its effective cost increases with maturity. For example, consider the case when both r_{pf} and r_{es} are equal to 8 percent and the firm wants to issue 5-year maturity bonds to raise $10 million. It can issue either zero-coupon bonds or prefunded-coupon bonds with $14,693,281 face value and 8 percent effective costs. For 10-year maturity, it will have to issue $21,589,250 zero-coupon or prefunded bonds. However, with a 3 percent spread, i.e. $r_{pf} = 8$ percent and $r_{es} = 5$ percent, the firm will have to issue $15,298,893 coupon bonds with ma-

turity 5 years or $26,160,132 coupon bonds with maturity 10 years. The effective cost of 5-year and 10-year prefunded issues will rise to 8.876 percent and 10.094 percent respectively.

Examples of net duration of pre-funded issue, i.e. the weighted average durations of the escrow asset and coupon bond liability are presented in Tables 3.3 and 3.4. In Table 3.3, we present a 5-year bond issue without spread, i.e. both r_{pf} and r_{es} are equal to 8 percent. Firm issues $14,693,281 bonds with annual coupon payment of $1,175,462. Coupon payments are disbursed out of an escrow account with $4,693,281 initial balance. Panel A of Table 3.3 shows that duration of the coupon bond, D_{pf}, is 4.3121 years. Panel B of Table 3.3 shows that the duration of the escrow annuity, D_{es}, is 2.8465 years.

Table 3.3. Net duration of the prefunded issue without spread

$$D_{net} = \frac{B_{pf}}{B} \times D_{pf} - \frac{B_{pf} - B}{B} \times D_{es}$$

Panel A: Bonds issued

Time, t	Cash outflow, CF	PVIF$_{8\%,5}$	CF*PVIF	t*CF*PVIF	Duration, D_{pf}
1	$1,175,462	0.9259	$ 1,088,391	$1,088,391	
2	1,175,462	0.8573	1,007,769	2,015,538	
3	1,175,462	0.7938	933,120	2,799,359	
4	1,175,462	0.7350	864,000	3,455,999	
5	15,868,743	0.6806	10,800,000	53,999,999	
			$14,693,280	$63,359,286	4.3121

Panel B: Escrow annuity

Time, t	Cash inflow, CF	PVIF$_{8\%,5}$	CF*PVIF	t*CF**PVIF	Duration, D_{es}
1	$1,175,462	0.9259	$1,088,391	$1,088,391	
2	1,175,462	0.8573	1,007,769	2,015,538	
3	1,175,462	0.7938	933,120	2,799,359	
4	1,175,462	0.7350	864,000	3,455,999	
5	1,175,462	0.6806	800,000	3,999,998	
			$4,693,280	$13,359,282	2.8465

Panel C: Net durations

Fund raised, B	$10,000,000	Escrow amount, $B_{pf} - B$	$4,693,281
Face value of bond, B_{pf}	$14,693,281	Escrow return, r_{es}	8%
Bond yield, r_{pf}	8.00%	Escrow weight, $(B - B_{pf})/B$	−0.469
Bond weight, B_{pf}/B	1.469	Escrow duration, D_{es}	2.847
Bond duration, D_{pf}	4.312	Net duration, D_{net}	5.000

If escrow return equals the bond yield, i.e. $r_{es} = r_{pf}$, then the net duration equals the maturity.

Panel C of Table 3.3 shows that the weights of bond liability and escrow asset are 1.469 and −.0.469 respectively. Hence, the net duration, D_{net}, of the prefunded issue is 5 years, which is identical to the duration of a zero-coupon bond. The result is understandable because the firm has no net cash outflow for years one to four, the only cash outflow of $14,693,281 is in year five.

In Table 3.4, we present an example of a 5-year prefunded bond issue with 3 percent spread, i.e. $r_{pf} = 8$ percent and $r_{es} = 5$ percent. Firm issues $15,298,250 bonds with annual coupon payment of $1,223,912. Coupon payments are disbursed out of an escrow account with $5,298,250 initial balance. Firm provides the interest subsidy by issuing additional bonds compared to the example in Table 3.3. Panel A of Table 3.4 shows that the

duration of the coupon bond, D_{pf}, is 4.3121 years, same as the example in Table 3.3. But the duration of the escrow annuity, D_{es}, increases to 2.9025 years. The weights of bond liability and escrow asset, reported in Panel C of Table 3.4, are 1.530 and −0.530 respectively. The net duration, D_{net}, of the prefunded issue increases to 5.059 years. The interest subsidy creates the additional leverage, and which stretches the duration beyond its maturity.[6] Because interest subsidy is a realistic condition, the prefunded bond issue has greater interest rate risk than the comparable zero-coupon bond.

Table 3.5 presents net duration, interest subsidy and loss of value associated with a prefunded bond issue for different bond yields and escrow returns. When $r_{pf} = r_{es}$, then there is no interest subsidy or loss of value and the net duration of the pre-funded

Table 3.4. Net duration of the prefunded issue with spread

$$D_{net} = \frac{B_{pf}}{B} \times D_{pf} - \frac{B_{pf} - B}{B} \times D_{es}$$

Panel A: Bonds issued

Time, t	Cash outflow, CF	$PVIF_{8\%,5}$	CF*PVIF	t*CF*PVIF	Duration, D_{pf}
1	$1,223,912	0.9259	$1,133,252	$1,133,252	
2	1,223,912	0.8573	1,049,307	2,098,615	
3	1,223,912	0.7938	971,581	2,914,742	
4	1,223,912	0.7350	899,612	3,598,447	
5	16,522,162	0.6806	11,244,706	56,223,529	
			$15,298,458	$65,968,585	4.3121

Panel B: Escrow annuity

Time, t	Cash inflow, CF	$PVIF_{5\%,5}$	CF*PVIF	t*CF*PVIF	Duration, D_{es}
1	$1,223,912	0.9524	$1,165,630	$1,165,630	
2	1,223,912	0.9070	1,110,124	2,220,249	
3	1,223,912	0.8638	1,057,261	3,171,784	
4	1,223,912	0.8227	1,006,915	4,027,662	
5	1,223,912	0.7835	958,967	4,794,835	
			$5,298,897	$15,380,160	2.9025

Panel C: Net durations

Fund raised, B		$10,000,000	Escrow amount, $B_{pf} - B$	$5,298,250
Face value of bond, B_{pf}		$15,298,250	Escrow return, r_{es}	5%
Bond yield, r_{pf}		8.00%	Escrow weight, $(B - B_{pf})/B$	−0.530
Bond weight, B_{pf}/B		1.530	Escrow duration, D_{es}	2.903
Bond duration, D_{pf}		4.312	Net duration, D_{net}	5.059

If escrow return is less than the bond yield, i.e. $r_{es} < r_{pf}$, then the net duration exceeds maturity.

Table 3.5. Net duration, interest subsidy, and value loss of prefunded bonds

Pre-tax Interest Subsidy $= (r_{pf}B_{pf})(r_{pf} - r_{es})$ per year

$$\text{Value loss} = (r_{pf}B_{pf})(r_{pf} - r_{es})\frac{(1 + r_{pf})^n - 1}{(1 + r_{pf})^n}$$

	Escrow return, r_{es}		Prefunded bond yield, r_{pf}			
			8%	7%	7%	7%
Maturity, n 5 years	8%	Net duration, yrs	5			
		Interest subsidy	0			
		Value loss	0			
	7%	Net duration, yrs	5.019	5		
		Interest subsidy	$11,905	0		
		Value loss	($47,533)	0		
	6%	Net duration, yrs	5.038	5.016	5	
		Interest subsidy	$24,132	$9,927	0	
		Value loss	($96,353)	($40,703)	0	
	5%	Net duration, yrs	5.059	5.037	5.013	5
		Interest subsidy	$36,717	$20,088	$8,106	0
		Value loss	($146,602)	($82,364)	($34,144)	0
Maturity, n 10 years	8%	Net duration, yrs	10			
		Interest subsidy	0			
		Value loss	0			
	7%	Net duration, yrs	10.198	10		
		Interest subsidy	$18,260	0		
		Value loss	($122,527)	0		
	6%	Net duration, yrs	10.433	10.165	10	
		Interest subsidy	$38,911	$14,439	0	
		Value loss	($261,097)	($101,414)	0	
	5%	Net duration, yrs	10.715	10.358	10.135	10
		Interest subsidy	$62,784	$30,469	$11,180	0
		Value loss	($421,288)	($214,004)	($82,282)	0

Empty cell represents the improbable case of $r_{pf} < r_z$.
Zero-coupon and prefunded bonds are priced by market as equivalent securities.

issue is equal to bond maturity. The net duration, interest subsidy, and loss of value increases with the increase in the spread, $r_{pf} = r_{es}$.

Table 3.6 presents the case when prefunded bonds are priced to yield lower than the zero-coupons. The asset-based coupon payments of the prefunded issue are default free, thus market lowers the yield by 25, 50, or 75 basis points from the comparable zero-coupon yield. We recalculate the total face value, net duration, interest subsidy, and loss of value under these conditions. Results in Table 3.6 indicate that the impact of the spread, $r_{pf} - r_{es}$ is still dominant. The total face value and net duration of the prefunded issue is greater than corresponding values for the zero-coupon bond.

3.5. Conclusion

Coupon-prefunded bonds have been developed and sold by investment bankers in place of zero-coupon bonds to raise funds for companies facing cash flow problems. Additional bonds are issued and proceeds are deposited in an escrow account to finance the coupon payment. Our analysis indicates that when the prefunded bond yield is the same as the escrow return then total face value of

Table 3.6. Face value, net duration, interest subsidy, and value loss of prefunded bonds

r_z	B_z		Prefunded bond yield, B_{pf}			
			r_z	$r_z - .25\%$	$r_z - .50\%$	$r_z - .75\%$
8%	$21,589,250	Face value of pre-funded, B_{pf}	$26,160,123	$24,902,535	$23,760,313	$22,718,277
		Duration, D_{net}	10.718 yrs	10.611 yrs	10.516 yrs	10.432 yrs
		Interest subsidy	$62,784	$53,074	$44,551	$37,059
		Value loss	($421,288)	($360,179)	($305,799)	($257,307)
7%	$19,671,514	Face value of pre-funded, B_{pf}	$21,763,801	$20,886,293	$20,076,805	$19,327,721
		Duration, D_{net}	10.358 yrs	10.291 yrs	10.266 yrs	10.181 yrs
		Interest subsidy	$30,469	$24,672	$19,575	$15,100
		Value loss	($214,004)	($175,306)	($140,721)	($109,831)
6%	$13,382,256	Face value of pre-funded, B_{pf}	$18,632,525	$17,985,604	$17,382,097	$16,817,777
		Duration, D_{net}	10.135 yrs	10.094 yrs	10.058 yrs	10.027 yrs
		Interest subsidy	$11,180	$7,756	$4,780	$2,207
		Value loss	($82,282)	($57,769)	($36,030)	($16,839)

r_z = discount rate on zero-coupon bonds, B_z = face value of zero-coupon bonds with 10-year maturity. Escrow account yield = 5%. Prefunded bonds are priced to yield lower than comparable zero-coupon bonds.

the prefunded issued is the same as the total face value of the zero-coupon bonds and the effective cost of prefunded issue is the same as the yield to maturity of the zero-coupon bond. Also, increase in the spread between prefunded bond yield and zero-coupon yield increases the total face value of the bonds issued and its effective cost. The interest subsidy creates additional leverage, which stretches the net duration of the prefunded issue beyond its maturity. Further, an increase in the yield spread between prefunded bonds and zero-coupon bonds increases net duration, interest subsidy, and loss of value. Even when prefunded bonds are priced to yield lower than the zero-coupons, impact of the spread is dominant – total face value and net duration of the prefunded issue is still greater than corresponding values for the zero-coupon bond.

NOTES

1. For the remainder of this paper we will adopt popular finance nomenclature and refer it as prefunded bonds. However, one must keep in mind that only coupon payments are prefunded.
2. See Goodman and Cohen (1989) for detailed discussion of paid-in-kind bonds.
3. U.S. Treasury sells risk-free zero-coupon bonds in the form of STRIPs.
4. See Ross, Westerfield, and Jaffe (2005) for algebraic expression of PVIFA.
5. Alternately, we can assume that all yields are net of transaction costs.
6. This is analogous to a situation in portfolio construction. Consider two assets with standard deviations 10 percent and 20 percent. For an investor who is long on both assets, the portfolio standard deviation will be between 10 percent and 20 percent. However, if the investor is short on the first asset and long on the second asset then portfolio standard deviation will exceed 20 percent.

REFERENCES

Brigham, E.F. and Phillip, R.D. (2004). *Intermediate Financial Management*. Mason, OH: Thomson Southwestern Publishing.

Doherty, J. (1997). "For junk borrowers, pre-funded bonds pick up steam, but they may pose greater risk than zeros." Barrons, MW15.

Fabbozzi, F.J. (2000). *Bond Markets, Analysis and Strategies*. Englewood Cliffs, NJ: Prentice-Hall.

Goodman, L.S. and. Cohen,A.H. (1989). "Payment-in-kind debentures: an innovation." *Journal of Portfolio Management*, 15: 9–19.

Myers, S.C. (1984). "The capital structure puzzle." *Journal of Finance*, 39: 575–592.

Macaulay, F. (1938). *Some Theoretical Problems Suggested by the Movement of Interest Rates, Bond Yields, and Stock Prices in the US since 1856*. New York: National Bureau of Economic Research.

Redington, F.M. (1952). "Review of the principles of life office valuation." *Journal of the Institute of Actuaries*, 78: 286–340.

Ross, S.A., Westerfield, R.W., and Jaffe, J. (2005). *Corporate Finance*. Homewood, IL: Irwin McGraw-Hill.

Samuelson, P.A. (1945). "The effect of interest rate increases on the banking system." *American Economic Review*, 35: 16–27.

Chapter 4

INTERTEMPORAL RISK AND CURRENCY RISK

JOW-RAN CHANG, *National Tsing Hua University, Taiwan*
MAO-WEI HUNG, *National Taiwan University, Taiwan*

Abstract

Empirical work on portfolio choice and asset pricing has shown that an investor's current asset demand is affected by the possibility of uncertain changes in future investment opportunities. In addition, different countries have different prices for goods when there is a common numeraire in the international portfolio choice and asset pricing. In this survey, we present an intertemporal international asset pricing model (IAPM) that prices market hedging risk and exchange rate hedging risk in addition to market risk and exchange rate risk. This model allows us to explicitly separate hedging against changes in the investment opportunity set from hedging against exchange rate changes as well as separate exchange rate risk from intertemporal hedging risk.

Keywords: currency risk; exchange rate risk; hedging risk; inflation risk; international asset pricing; intertemporal asset pricing; intertemporal risk; intertemporal substitution; purchasing power parity; recursive preference; risk aversion

4.1. Introduction

In a dynamic economy, it is often believed that if investors anticipate information shifts, they will adjust their portfolios to hedge these shifts. To capture the dynamic hedging effect, Merton (1973) developed a continuous-time asset pricing model which explicitly takes into account hedging demand. In contrast to the Arbitrage Pricing Theory (APT) framework, there are two factors, which are theoretically derived from Merton's model: a market factor and a hedging factor. Stulz (1981) extended the intertemporal model of Merton (1973) to develop an international asset pricing model. However, an empirical investigation is not easy to implement in the continuous-time model. In a recent paper, Campbell (1993) developed a discrete-time counterpart of Merton's model. Motivated by Campbell's results, Chang and Hung (2000) adopted a conditional two-factor asset pricing model to explain the cross-sectional pricing relationships among international stock markets. In their setup, assets are priced using their covariance with the market portfolio as well as with the hedging portfolio, both of which account for changes in the investment set. Under their proposed international two-factor asset pricing model framework, the international capital asset pricing model (CAPM) is misspecified and estimates of the CAPM model are subject to the omitted variable bias.

If purchasing power parity (PPP) is violated, investors from different countries will have different evaluations for real returns for investment in the same security. This implies that the optimal portfolio choices are different across investors residing in different countries, and any investment in a foreign asset is exposed to currency risk. Therefore, it is reasonable to assume that investors from different countries have different estimations for real returns. This phenomenon clearly shows the existence of currency risk as well as market risk.

There are two goals in this survey. First, we want to know whether hedging demand is important to an international investor. Second, we want to separate currency hedging risk from intertemporal market hedging risk on an international asset pricing model.

The approach we describe here was first proposed by Epstein and Zin (1989, 1991). In their model, the investor is assumed to use a nonexpected utility that distinguishes the coefficient of relative risk aversion and the elasticity of intertemporal substitution. Campbell (1993) applied a log-linear approximation to the budget constraint in order to replace consumption from a standard intertemporal asset pricing model. Chang and Hung (2000) used this model to explain the intertemporal behavior in the international financial markets under no differences in consumption opportunity set.

An important challenge therefore remains – how to build a more realistic intertemporal international asset pricing model (e.g. when the consumption opportunity set is different). This essay surveys the progress that has been made on this front, drawing primarily from Chang and Hung (2000) and Chang et al. (2004).

In Section 4.2, we present a testable intertemporal capital asset pricing model proposed by Campbell. Hence, we can examine whether Campbell's model explains the intertemporal behavior of a number of international financial markets. In Section 4.3, we separate currency hedging risk from intertemporal market hedging risk. This is accomplished by extending Campbell's model to an international framework in which investor's utility depends on real returns rather than on nominal returns and PPP deviation.

4.2. No Differences in Consumption Opportunity Set

This section describes the international asset pricing model we employ to estimate and test the pricing relationships among the world's five main equity markets. The model we use is a two-factor model based on Campbell (1993). We first review the theory of nonexpected utility proposed by Weil (1989) and Epstein and Zin (1991). Then we apply a log-linear approximation to the budget constraint to derive an international asset pricing model, which is used in this chapter.

4.2.1. Asset Pricing Model

4.2.1.1. Nonexpected Utility

We consider an economy in which a single, infinitely lived representative international agent chooses consumption and portfolio composition to maximize utility and uses U.S. dollar as the numeraire and where there is one good and N assets in the economy. The international agent in this economy is assumed to be different to the timing of the resolution of uncertainty over temporal lotteries. The agent's preferences are assumed to be represented recursively by

$$V_t = W(C_t, E_t[V_{t+1}|I_t]), \qquad (4.1)$$

where $W(.,.)$ is the aggregator function, C_t is the consumption level at time t, and E_t is the mathematical expectation conditional on the information set at time t. As shown by Kreps and Porteus (1978), the agent prefers early resolution of uncertainty over temporal lotteries if $W(.,.)$ is convex in its second argument. Alternatively, if $W(.,.)$ is concave in its second argument, the agent will prefer late resolution of uncertainty over temporal lotteries.

The aggregator function is further parameterized by

$$
\begin{aligned}
V_t &= [(1-\delta)C_t^{1-\rho} + \delta(EV_{t+1}^{1-\lambda})^{(1-\rho)/(1-\lambda)}]^{1/(1-\rho)} \\
&= [(1-\delta)C_t^{(1-\lambda)/\theta} + \delta(E_t V_{t+1}^{1-\lambda})^{1/\theta}]^{\theta/(1-\lambda)}
\end{aligned}
\qquad (4.2)
$$

Parameter δ is the agent's subjective time-discount factor and λ is interpreted as the Arrow–Pratt coefficient of relative risk aversion. In addition, $1/\rho$ measures the elasticity of intertemporal substitution. For instance, if the agent's coefficient of relative risk aversion (λ) is greater than the reciprocal of the agent's elasticity of intertemporal substitution (ρ), then the agent would prefer an early resolution towards uncertainty. Conversely, if the reciprocal of the agent's elasticity of intertemporal substitution is larger than the agent's coefficient of relative risk aversion, then the agent would prefer a late resolution of uncertainty. If λ is equal to ρ, the agent's utility becomes an isoelastic, von Neumann–Morgenstern utility, and the agent would be indifferent to the timing of the resolution of uncertainty.

Furthermore, θ is defined as $\theta = (1 - \lambda)/(1 - \rho)$ in accordance with Giovannini and Weil (1989). Three special cases are worth mentioning. First, $\theta \to 0$ when $\lambda \to 1$. Second, $\theta \to \infty$ when $\rho \to 1$. Third, $\theta = 1$ when $\lambda = \rho$. Under these circumstances, Equation (4.2) becomes the von Neumann–Morgenstern expected utility

$$V_t = \left[(1 - \delta)E_t \sum_{j=1}^{\infty} \delta^j \tilde{C}_{t+j}^{1-\gamma} \right]^{1/(1-\lambda)}.\qquad(4.3)$$

4.2.1.2. Log-Linear Budget Constraint
We now turn to the characterization of the budget constraint of the representative investor who can invest wealth in N assets. The gross rate of return on asset i held throughout period t is given by $R_{i,\,t+1}$. Let

$$R_{m,t+1} \equiv \sum_{i=1}^{N} \alpha_{i,t} R_{i,t+1}\qquad(4.4)$$

denote the rate of return on the market portfolio, and $\alpha_{i,t}$ be the fraction of the investor's total wealth held in the ith asset in period t. There are only $N - 1$ independent elements in $\alpha_{i,\,t}$ since the constraint

$$\sum_{i=1}^{N} \alpha_{i,t} = 1\qquad(4.5)$$

holds for all t. The representative agent's dynamic budget constraint can be given by

$$W_{t+1} = R_{m,t+1}(W_t - C_t),\qquad(4.6)$$

where W_{t+1} is the investor's wealth at time t. The budget constraint in Equation (4.6) is nonlinear because of the interaction between subtraction and multiplication. In addition, the investor is capable of affecting future consumption flows by trading in risky assets. Campbell linearizes the budget constraint by dividing Equation (4.6) by W_t, taking log, and then using a first-order Taylor expansion around the mean log consumption/wealth ratio, $\log(C/W)$. If we define the parameter $\beta = 1 - \exp(\overline{c_t - w_t})$, the approximation to the intertemporal budget constraint is

$$\Delta w_{t+1} \cong r_{m,t+1} + k + \left(1 - \frac{1}{\beta}\right)(c_t - w_t),\qquad(4.7)$$

where the log form of the variable is indicated by lowercase letters and k is a constant.

Combining Equation (4.7) with the following equality,

$$\Delta w_{t+1} = \Delta c_{t+1} + (c_t - w_t) - (c_{t+1} - w_{t+1}),\qquad(4.8)$$

we obtain a different equation in the log consumption/wealth ratio, $c_t - w_t$. Campbell (1993) shows that if the log consumption/wealth ratio is stationary, i.e. $\lim_{j\to\infty} \beta^j (c_{t+j} - w_{t+j}) = 0$, then the approximation can be written as

$$c_{t+1} - E_t c_{t+1} = (E_{t+1} - E_t)\sum_{j=0}^{\infty} \beta^j r_{m.t+1+j}$$
$$- (E_{t+1} - E_t)\sum_{j=1}^{\infty} \beta^j \Delta c_{t+1+j}.\qquad(4.9)$$

Equation (4.9) can be used to express the fact that an unexpected increase in consumption today is determined by an unexpected return on wealth today (the first term in the first sum on the right-hand side of the equation), or by news that future returns will be higher (the remaining terms in the first sum), or by a downward revision in expected future consumption growth (the second sum on the right-hand side).

4.2.1.3. Euler Equations

In this setup, Epstein and Zin (1989) derive the following Euler equation for each asset:

$$1 = E_t \left[\left\{ \delta \left(\frac{C_{t+1}}{C_t} \right)^{-\rho} \right\}^\theta \left\{ \frac{1}{R_{m,t+1}} \right\}^{1-\theta} R_{i,t+1} \right] \quad (4.10)$$

Assume for the present that asset prices and consumption are jointly lognormal or apply a second-order Taylor expansion to the Euler equation. Then, the log version of the Euler equation (4.10) can be represented as

$$\begin{aligned} 0 = {} & \theta \log \delta - \theta\rho E_t \Delta c_{t+1} + (\theta - 1)E_t r_{m,t+1} \\ & + E_t r_{i,t+1} + \frac{1}{2}[(\theta\rho)^2 V_{cc} + (\theta - 1)^2 V_{mm} \\ & + V_{ii} - 2\theta\rho(\theta - 1)V_{cm} - 2\theta\rho V_{ci} \\ & + 2(\theta - 1)V_{im}] \end{aligned} \quad (4.11)$$

where V_{cc} denotes $\text{var}(c_{t+1})$, V_{jj} denotes $\text{var}(r_{j,t+1})$ $\forall j = i,m$, V_{cj} denotes $\text{cov}(c_{t+1}, r_{j,t+1})$ $\forall j = i,m$, and V_{im} denotes $\text{cov}(r_{i,t+1}, r_{m,t+1})$.

By replacing asset i by the market portfolio and rearranging Equation (4.11), we obtain a relationship between expected consumption growth and expected return on the market portfolio

$$\begin{aligned} E_t \Delta c_{t+1} = {} & \frac{1}{\rho} \log \delta + \frac{1}{2} \left[\theta\rho V_{cc} + \left(\frac{\theta}{\rho} \right) V_{mm} \right. \\ & \left. - 2\theta V_{cm} \right] + \frac{1}{\rho} E_t r_{m,t+1}. \end{aligned} \quad (4.12)$$

When we subtract Equation (4.11) for the risk-free asset from that for asset i, we obtain

$$E_t r_{i,t+1} - r_{f,t+1} = -\frac{V_{ii}}{2} + \theta(\rho V_{ic}) + (1 - \theta)V_{im} \quad (4.13)$$

where $r_{f,t+1}$ is a log riskless interest rate. Equation (4.13) expresses the expected excess log return on an asset (adjusted for Jensen's inequality effect) as a weighted sum of two terms. The first term, with a

weight θ, is the asset covariance with consumption multiplied by the intertemporal elasticity of substitution, ρ. The second term, with a weight $1 - \theta$, is the asset covariance with the return from the market portfolio.

4.2.1.4. Substituting Consumption out of the Asset Pricing Model

Now, we combine the log-linear Euler equation with the approximated log-linear budget constraint to get an intertemporal asset pricing model without consumption. Substituting Equation (4.12) into Equation (4.9), we obtain

$$\begin{aligned} c_{t+1} - E_t c_{t+1} = {} & r_{m,t+1} - E_t r_{m,t+1} + \left(1 - \frac{1}{\rho} \right) \\ & (E_{t+1} - E_t) \sum_{j=1}^{\infty} \beta^j r_{m,t+1+j} \end{aligned} \quad (4.14)$$

Equation (4.14) implies that the unexpected consumption comes from an unexpected return on invested wealth today or expected future returns.

Based on Equation (4.14), the conditional covariance of any asset return with consumption can be rewritten in terms of the covariance with the market return and revisions in expectations of future market returns which is given by

$$\text{cov}_t(r_{i,t+1}, \Delta c_{t+1}) \equiv V_{ic} = V_{im} + \left(1 - \frac{1}{\rho} \right) V_{ih} \quad (4.15)$$

where $V_{ih} = \text{cov}_t \left(r_{i,t+1}, (E_{t+1} - E_t) \sum_{j=1}^{\infty} \beta^j r_{m,t+1+j} \right)$.

Substituting Equation (4.15) into Equation (4.13), we obtain an international asset pricing model that is not related to consumption:

$$E_t r_{i,t+1} - r_{f,t+1} = -\frac{V_{ii}}{2} + \lambda V_{im} + (\lambda - 1)V_{ih}. \quad (4.16)$$

Equation (4.16) states that the expected excess log return in an asset, adjusted for Jensen's inequality effect, is a weighted average of two covariances—the covariance with the return from the market portfolio and the covariance with news about future returns on invested wealth.

4.2.2. Empirical Evidence

The relationship between risk and return has been the focus of recent finance research. Numerous papers have derived various versions of the international asset pricing model. For example, Solnik (1974) extends the static Capital Asset Pricing Model of Sharpe (1964) and Lintner (1965) to an international framework. His empirical findings reveal that national factors are important in the pricing of stock markets. Furthermore, Korajczyk and Viallet (1989) propose that the international CAPM outperforms its domestic counterpart in explaining the pricing behavior of equity markets.

In a fruitful attempt to extend the conditional version of the static CAPM, Harvey (1991) employs the Generalized Method of Moments (GMM) to examine an international asset pricing model that captures some of the dynamic behavior of the country returns. De Santis and Gerard (1997) test the conditional CAPM on international stock markets, but they apply a parsimonious Generalized Auto-Regressive Conditional Heteroscedasticity (GARCH) parameterization as the specification for second moments. Their results indicate that a one-factor model cannot fully explain the dynamics of international expected returns and the price of market risk is not significant.

On the other hand, recent studies have applied the APT of Ross (1976) to an international setting. For instance, Cho et al. (1986) employ factor analysis to demonstrate that additional factors other than covariance risk are able to explain the international capital market. Ferson and Harvey (1993) investigate the predictability of national stock market returns and its relation to global economic risk. Their model includes a world market portfolio, exchange rate fluctuations, world interest rates, and international default risk. They use multifactor asset pricing models with time-varying risk premiums to examine the issue of predictability. But, one of the drawbacks of the APT approach is that the number and identity of the factors are determined either *ad hoc* or statistically from data rather than from asset pricing models directly.

Several international asset pricing models explicitly take into account currency risk, for example, see

Solnik (1974), Stulz (1981), and Adler and Dumas (1983). But investors in these models are assumed to maximize a time-additive, von Neumann–Morgenstern expected utility of lifetime consumption function. This implies that two distinct concepts of intertemporal substitution and risk aversion are characterized by the same parameter. Another approach examines consumption risk. Cumby (1990) proposes a consumption-based international asset pricing model. Difficulty occurs in the usage of aggregate consumption data, which are measured with error, and are time-aggregated. Chang and Hung (2000) show that estimations of price of market risk obtained from the De Santis and Gerard (1997) conditional CAPM model may be biased downward due to the omission of the hedging risk, which is negatively correlated to the market risk.

4.3. Differences in Consumption Opportunity Set

In this section, we consider the problem of optimal consumption and portfolio allocation in a unified world capital market with no taxes and transactions costs. Moreover, investors' preferences are assumed to be nationally heterogeneous and asset selection is the same for investors in different countries. Consider a world of $M+1$ countries and a set of S equity securities. All returns are measured in the $M+1$st country's currency in excess of the risk-free rate and this currency is referred to as the numeraire currency. Investors are assumed to maximize Kreps–Porteus utility for their lifetime consumption function.

4.3.1. Portfolio Choice in an International Setting

4.3.1.1. Kreps–Porteus Preferences
Define C_t as the current nominal consumption level at time t, and P_t as the price level index at time t, expressed in the numeraire currency. In the setup of Kreps and Porteus (1978) nonexpected utility, the investor's value function can be represented as:

$$V_t = U\left[\frac{C_t}{P_t}, E_t V_{t+1}\right], \qquad (4.17)$$

where V_t is the lifetime utility at time t, E_t is the expected value function conditional on the information available to the investor at time t, $U[.,.]$ is the aggregator function that aggregates current consumption with expected future value. As shown by Kreps and Porteus, the agent prefers early resolution of uncertainty over temporal lotteries if $U[.,.]$ is convex in its second argument. On the other hand, if $U[.,.]$ is concave in its second argument, the agent will prefer late resolution of uncertainty over temporal lotteries.

Furthermore, the aggregator function is parameterized to be homogenous of degree one in current real consumption and in the value of future state-dependent real consumption:

$$U\left[\frac{C_t}{P_t}, E_tV_{t+1}\right] = \left[(1-\delta)\left(\frac{C_t}{P}\right)^{1-\rho}\right.$$
$$\left. +\delta(E_tV_{t+1})^{(1-\rho)/(1-\lambda)}\right]^{(1-\lambda)/(1-\rho)}, \quad (4.18)$$

where λ is the Arrow–Pratt coefficient of relative risk aversion, ρ can be interpreted as the elasticity of intertemporal substitution, and $\delta \in (0,1)$ is the subjective discount factor.

The Kreps–Porteus preference allows the separation of risk aversion from intertemporal substitution. For instance, if the agent's coefficient of relative risk aversion, λ, is greater than the reciprocal of the agent's elasticity of intertemporal substitution, ρ, then the agent prefers early resolution of uncertainty. Conversely, if the reciprocal of the agent's elasticity of intertemporal substitution is larger than the agent's coefficient of relative risk aversion, the agent prefers late resolution of uncertainty. When $\rho = \lambda$, the objective function is the time-separable power utility function with relative risk aversion λ. In addition, when both λ and ρ equal 1, we have standard time-separable log utility function. Hence, the standard time- and state-separable expected utility is a special case under Kreps–Porteus preferences.

4.3.1.2. Optimal Consumption and Portfolio Allocation

We now turn to the characterization of the budget constraint of the representative investor who can invest his wealth in $N(=M+S)$ assets that include M currencies and S equities. Currencies may be taken as the nominal bank deposits denominated in the nonnumeraire currencies. The gross rate of nominal return on asset i held throughout period t is given by $R_{i,t+1}$. Let

$$R_{m,t+1} \equiv \sum_{i-1}^{N} \alpha_{i,t}R_{i,t+1} \quad (4.19)$$

denote the rate of return on the market portfolio, and $\alpha_{i,t}$ be the fraction of the investor's total wealth held in the i th asset in period t. There are only $N-1$ independent elements in $\alpha_{i,t}$, since the constraint

$$\sum_{i=1}^{N} \alpha_{i,t} = 1 \quad (4.20)$$

holds for all t. The representative agent's dynamic budget constraint in terms of real variables can be written as:

$$\frac{W_{t+1}}{P_{t+1}} = R_{m,t+1}\frac{P_t}{P_{t+1}}\left(\frac{W_t}{P_t} - \frac{C_t}{P_t}\right) \quad (4.21)$$

where W_{t+1} is the investor's nominal wealth at time t. The budget constraint in Equation (4.21) is nonlinear because of the interaction between subtraction and multiplication.

Define I_t as the information set available to the representative agent at time t. Denoting by $V(W/P, I)$ the maximum value of Equation (4.17) subject to Equation (4.20), the standard Bellman equations can then be written as:

$$V\left(\frac{W_t}{P_t}, I_t\right) = \max_{C_t, \{\alpha_{i,t}\}_{i=1}^{N}} \left\{(1-\delta)\left(\frac{C_t}{P_t}\right)^{1-\rho}\right.$$
$$\left. +\delta\left[E_tV\left(\frac{W_{t+1}}{P_{t+1}}, I_{t+1}\right)\right]^{(1-\rho)/(1-\lambda)}\right\}^{(1-\lambda)/(1-\rho)}.$$
$$(4.22)$$

Due to the homogeneity of the recursive structure of preferences, the value function can be written in the following functional form:

$$V\left(\frac{W_t}{P_t}, I_t\right) = \Phi(I_t)\left(\frac{W_t}{P_t}\right)^{1-\lambda} \equiv \Phi_t\left(\frac{W_t}{P_t}\right)^{1-\lambda}, \quad (4.23)$$

where $\Phi(.)$ is an unknown function. The homogeneity of degree zero of the recursive utility function implies that $V(W/P, I)$ satisfying Equation (4.22) must be homogeneous of degree zero in W and P.

Let the derivatives with respect to the decision variables C_t equal zero, we then obtain:

$$C_t^{-\rho} = \frac{\delta}{1-\delta}\psi(W_t - C_t)^{-\rho}, \qquad (4.24)$$

where $\psi_t = E_t\left[\Phi_{t+1}\left(R_{m,t+1}\frac{P_t}{P_{t+1}}\right)^{1-\lambda}\right]^{(1-\rho)/(1-\lambda)}$.

Given the structure of the problem, the nominal consumption function is linear in nominal wealth. Hence, we can rewrite Equation (4.24) as:

$$\mu_t^{-\rho} = \frac{\delta}{1-\delta}\psi(1-\mu_t)^{-\rho} \qquad (4.25)$$

where $C(W_t, I_t) = \mu(I_t)W_t \equiv \mu_t W_t$. Combining the Envelope condition with respect to W_t with the first-order condition in Equation (4.25), we obtain the following functional form:

$$\Phi_t = (1-\delta)^{(1-\lambda)/(1-\rho)}\left[\left(\frac{C_t}{W_t}\right)^{-\rho}\right]^{(1-\lambda)/(1-\rho)} \qquad (4.26)$$

Substituting this expression into Equation (4.25), we obtain the following Euler equation for optimal consumption decision:

$$E_t\left\{\left[\delta\left(\frac{C_{t+1}/P_{t+1}}{C_t/P_t}\right)^{-\rho}\right]^{(1-\lambda)/(1-\rho)}\right.$$
$$\left.\left(R_{m,t+1}\frac{P_t}{P_{t+1}}\right)^{(1-\lambda)/(1-\rho)}\right\} = 1, \quad i = 1, \ldots, N$$
$$(4.27)$$

The maximization with respect to the decision variable $\alpha_i(i = 2, \ldots, N)$, given $\alpha_1 = 1 - \sum_{i=2}^{N}\alpha_i$, on the right hand side of Equation (4.22), is equivalent to the following problem:

$$\max_{\{\alpha_{i,t}\}_{i=2}^{N}} E_t\left[\Phi_{t+1}\left(\sum_{i=1}^{N}\alpha_{i,t}R_{i,t+1}\frac{P_t}{P_{t+1}}\right)^{1-\lambda}\right]$$
$$s.t. \sum_{i=1}^{N}\alpha_{i,t} = 1 \qquad (4.28)$$

Using this optimal problem along with Equation (4.26), it is straightforward to show that the necessary conditions can be derived as:

$$E_t\left\{\left[\delta\left(\frac{C_{t+1}/P_{t+1}}{C_t/P_t}\right)^{-\rho}\right]^{1-\lambda/1-\rho}\right.$$
$$\left(R_{m,t+1}\frac{P_t}{P_{t+1}}\right)^{[(1-\lambda)/(1-\rho)]-1} \qquad (4.29)$$
$$\left.(R_{i,t+1} - R_{1,t+1})\frac{P_t}{P_{t+1}}\right\} = 0, \quad i = 1, \ldots, N$$

Taking Equations (4.27) and (4.29) together to represent the Euler equations of the optimal problem defined in Equation (4.22), we obtain a set of N equations that provide a more direct comparison with the traditional expected utility Euler equations. Multiplying Equation (4.29) by $\alpha_{i,t}$, summing up by i, and substituting from Equation (4.27), we obtain:

$$E_t\left\{\left[\delta\left(\frac{C_{t+1}/P_{t+1}}{C_t/P_t}\right)^{-\rho}\right]^{\theta}\left(R_{m,t+1}\frac{P_t}{P_{t+1}}\right)^{\theta-1}\right.$$
$$\left.R_{i,t+1}\frac{P_t}{P_{t+1}}\right\} = 1, \, i = 1, \ldots, N \qquad (4.30)$$

where $\theta = (1-\lambda)/(1-\rho)$. These are the real form Euler equations which are similar to the nominal form Euler equations seen in Epstein and Zin (1989).

When $\rho = \lambda$, the Euler equations of the time additive expected utility model are also obtained in terms of real variables:

$$E_t\left[\delta\left(\frac{C_{t+1}/P_{t+1}}{C_t/P_t}\right)^{-\rho}R_{i,t+1}\frac{P_t}{P_{t+1}}\right] = 1, \quad i = 1, \ldots, N \qquad (4.31)$$

Another special case of this model is the logarithmic risk preferences where $\rho = \lambda = 1$. Then, the real Euler equations are equal to the nominal Euler equations, and can be written in two algebraically identical functional forms:

$$E_t\left[\delta\left(\frac{C_{t+1}}{C_t}\right)^{-1}R_{i,t+1}\right] = 1, \, i = 1, \ldots, N \qquad (4.32)$$

or

$$E_t[R_{i,t+1}/R_{m,t+1}] = 1, \quad i = 1, \ldots, N \quad (4.33)$$

In this case, the parameter ρ governing intertemporal substitutability cannot be identified from these equations. Hence, there is no difference between Euler equations of the nonexpected utility model with logarithmic risk preferences and those of the expected utility model with logarithmic risk preferences.

Assume that asset prices and consumption are jointly lognormal or use a second-order Taylor expansion in the Euler equation when we assume that asset prices and consumption are conditional homoskedastic, then the log-version of the real Euler equation (4.30) can be represented as:

$$
\begin{aligned}
0 = {} & \theta \log \delta - \theta \rho E_t \Delta c_{t+1} + (\theta - 1) E_t r_{m,t+1} \\
& + E_t r_{i,t+1} + \theta(\rho - 1) E_t \Delta \pi_{t+1} \\
& + \frac{1}{2}[(\theta \rho)^2 V_{cc} + (\theta - 1)^2 V_{mm} + V_{ii} \\
& - 2\theta \rho(\theta - 1) V_{cm} - 2\theta \rho V_{ci} + 2(\theta - 1) V_{im}] \\
& + \frac{1}{2}([{\theta(\rho-1)}]^2 V_{\pi\pi} - 2\theta^2 \rho(\rho - 1) V_{\pi c} \\
& + 2\theta(\theta - 1)(\rho - 1) V_{\pi m} + 2\theta(\rho - 1) V_{\pi i}]
\end{aligned}
\quad (4.34)
$$

where V_{cc} denotes $var_t(c_{t+1})$, V_{jj} denotes $var_t (r_{j,t+1}) \forall j = i,m$, V_{cj} denotes $cov_t(c_{t+1},r_{j,t+1}) \forall j = i,m$, V_{im} denotes $cov_t(r_{i,t+1},r_{m,t+1})$, $V_{i\pi} = cov_t (r_{i,t+1}, \pi_{t+1})$, and $\pi_{t+1} = d \ln(P_{t+1}) = \frac{dP_{t+1}}{P_{t+1}}$.

Replacing asset i by market portfolio and undergoing some rearrangement, we are able to obtain a relationship between expected consumption growth and the expected return on the market portfolio:

$$E_t \Delta c_{t+1} = \mu_m + \frac{1}{\rho} E_t r_{m,t+1} + \left(1 - \frac{1}{\rho}\right) E_t \pi_{t+1} \quad (4.35)$$

where

$$
\begin{aligned}
\mu_m = {} & \frac{1}{\rho} \log \delta + \frac{1}{2}\left[\theta \rho V_{cc} + \theta \frac{1}{\rho} V_{mm}\right. \\
& + 2\left(1 - \frac{1}{\rho}\right)\theta(\rho - 1)V_{\pi\pi}\right] \\
& - \frac{1}{2}\left[2\theta V_{cm} + 2\theta(\rho - 1)\right. \\
& V_{\pi c} - 2\theta\left(1 - \frac{1}{\rho}\right)V_{\pi m}\right]
\end{aligned}
$$

When the second moments are conditional homoskedastic, Equation (4.35) indicates that the consumption growth is linearly related to the expected world market return and expected inflation. In addition, the coefficients of these two variables are summed up to 1.

When we subtract the risk free version of Equation (4.34) from the general version, we obtain:

$$
\begin{aligned}
E_t r_{i,t+1} - r_{f,t+1} = {} & -\frac{V_{ii}}{2} + \theta \rho V_{ic} \\
& + (\theta - \theta\rho)V_{i\pi} + (1 - \theta)V_{im}
\end{aligned}
\quad (4.36)
$$

where $r_{f,t+1}$ is a log riskless real interest rate. This result is similar to that of Campbell (1993) except for the inflation term. Equation (4.36) shows that the expected excess log return on an asset is a linear combination of its own variance, which is produced by Jensen's inequality, and by a weighted average of three covariances. The weights on the consumption, inflation, and market are $\theta\rho$, $(\theta - \theta\rho)$, and $(1 - \theta)$, respectively. Moreover, the weights are summed up to 1. This is one of the most important differences between Campbell's model and our real model.

If the objective function is a time-separable power utility function, a real functional form of a log-linear version of the consumption CAPM pricing formula can thus be obtained:

$$E_t r_{i,t+1} - r_{f,t+1} = -\frac{V_{ii}}{2} + \rho V_{ic} + (1 - \rho)V_{i\pi} \quad (4.37)$$

The weights on the consumption and inflation are ρ and $(1 - \rho)$, respectively. These weights are also summed up to 1. However, when the coefficient of relative risk aversion $\lambda = 1$, then $\theta = 0$. The model is reduced to the real functional form of log-linear static CAPM, which is the same as the nominal structure of log-linear static CAPM.

4.3.2. International Asset Pricing Model Without Consumption

In order to get a pricing formula without consumption, we apply the technique of Campbell (1993). Campbell (1993) suggests to linearize the budget constraint by dividing the nominal form of Equation (4.21) by W_t, taking log, and then using a first-order Taylor approximation around the mean log consumption/wealth ratio ($\log(C/W)$). Following his approach, approximation of the nominal budget constraint is:

$$\Delta w_{t+1} \cong r_{m,t+1} + \kappa + \left(1 - \frac{1}{\beta}\right)(c_t - w_t) \quad (4.38)$$

where the log form of the variable is indicated by lowercase letters, $\beta = 1 - \exp(c_t - w_t)$, and κ is a constant.

Combining Equation (4.38) with the following trivial equality

$$\Delta w_{t+1} = \Delta c_{t+1} + (c_t - w_t) - (c_{t+1} - w_{t+1}), \quad (4.39)$$

we obtain a difference equation in the log consumption/wealth ratio, $c_t - w_t$. When the log consumption/wealth ratio is stationary, i.e. $\lim_{j \to \infty} \beta^j(c_{t+j} - w_{t+j}) = 0$, Equation (4.38) implies that the innovation in logarithm of consumption can be represented as the innovation in the discounted present value of the world market return minus the innovation in the discounted present value of consumption growth:

$$c_{t+1} - E_t c_{t+1} = (E_{t+1} - E_t) \sum_{j=0}^{\infty} \beta^j r_{m.t+1+j}$$

$$- (E_{t+1} - E_t) \sum_{j=1}^{\infty} \beta^j \Delta c_{t+1+j}$$

$$(4.40)$$

Now we are ready to derive an international asset pricing model without consumption in terms of real variables by connecting the log-linear Euler equation to the approximation log-linear budget constraint. Substituting Equation (4.35) into Equation (4.40), we obtain:

$$c_{t+1} - E_t c_{t+1} = r_{m,t+1} - E_t r_{m,t+1}$$

$$+ \left(1 - \frac{1}{\rho}\right)(E_{t+1} - E_t) \sum_{j=1}^{\infty} \beta^j r_{m,t+1+j}$$

$$- \left(1 - \frac{1}{\rho}\right)(E_{t+1} - E_t) \sum_{j=1}^{\infty} \beta^j \pi_{m,t+1+j} \quad (4.41)$$

Equation (4.41) implies that an unexpected consumption may come from three sources. The first one is the unexpected return on invested wealth today. The second one is the expected future nominal returns. The direction of influence depends on whether $1/\rho$ is less or greater than 1. When $1/\rho$ is less than 1, an increase (or decrease) in the expected future nominal return increases (or decreases) the unexpected consumption. Conversely, when $1/\rho$ is greater than 1, an increase (or decrease) in the expected future nominal return decreases (or increases) the unexpected consumption. The third one is the inflation in the investor's own country. The direction of influence also depends on whether $1/\rho$ is less or greater than 1. When $1/\rho$ is less than 1, an increase (or decrease) in the inflation decreases (or increases) the unexpected consumption. Conversely, when $1/\rho$ is greater than 1, an increase (or decrease) in the inflation increases (or decreases) the unexpected inflation.

Based on Equation (4.41), the conditional covariance of any asset return with consumption can be rewritten in terms of covariance with market return and revisions in expectations of future market return as:

$$\operatorname{cov}_t(r_{i,t+1}, \Delta c_{t+1}) \equiv V_{ic} = V_{im} + \left(1 - \frac{1}{\rho}\right)$$
$$V_{ih} - \left(1 - \frac{1}{\rho}\right)V_{ih\pi}, \quad (4.42)$$

where

$$V_{ih} = \operatorname{Cov}_t\left(r_{i,t+1}, (E_{t+1} - E_t) \sum_{j=1}^{\infty} \beta^j r_{m,t+1+j}\right)$$

and

$$V_{ih\pi} = \operatorname{Cov}_t\left(r_{i,t+1}, (E_{t+1} - E_t) \sum_{j=1}^{\infty} \beta^j \pi_{t+1+j}\right)$$

Substituting Equation (4.42) into Equation (4.36), we thus obtain an international asset pricing model, which is not related to consumption:

$$E_t r_{i,t+1} - r_{f,t+1} = -\frac{V_{ii}}{2} + \lambda V_{im} + (\lambda - 1) \qquad (4.43)$$
$$V_{ih} + (1 - \lambda)V_{i\pi} + (1 - \lambda)V_{ih\pi}$$

The only preference parameter that enters Equation (4.43) is the coefficient of relative risk aversion (λ). The elasticity of intertemporal substitution ρ is not present under this international pricing model. Equation (4.43) states that the expected excess log return in an asset, adjusted for Jensen's inequality effect, is a weighted average of four covariances. These are the covariance with the market return, the covariance with news about future returns on invested wealth, the covariance with return from inflation, and the covariance with news about future inflation. This result is different from both the international model of Adler and Dumas (1983) and the intertemporal model of Campbell (1993). Adler and Dumas use von Neumann–Morgenstern utility and assume a constant investment opportunity set to derive the international model, and therefore neither V_{ih} or $V_{ih\pi}$ is included in their pricing formula. Since the intertemporal model of Campbell is a domestic model, it does not deal with the issues of inflation and currency that are emphasized in our international asset pricing model.

4.3.3. International Asset Pricing Model When PPP Deviate

Let us now turn to the problem of aggregation across investors. It is true that different investors use different information set and different methods to forecast future world market return and inflation. To obtain the aggregation results, we first superimpose Equation (4.43) by a superscript l to indicate optimal condition for an investor l:

$$E_t r_{i,t+1} - r_{f,t+1} = -\frac{V_{ii}}{2} + \lambda^l V^l_{im} + (\lambda^l - 1) \qquad (4.43)$$
$$V^l_{ih} + (1 - \lambda^l)V^l_{i\pi} + (1 - \lambda^l)V^l_{ih\pi}$$

Then, Equation (4.44) can be aggregated across all investors in all countries.

The operation is to multiply Equation (4.44) by η^l, which indicates risk tolerance where $\eta^l = 1/\lambda^l$ and to take an average of all investors, where weights are their relative wealth. After aggregating all investors, we obtain:

$$E_t r_{i,t+1} - r_{f,t+1} = -\frac{V_{ii}}{2} + \frac{1}{\eta^m} V^m_{im} + \left(\frac{1}{\eta^m} - 1\right) \sum_l \omega^l V^l_{ih}$$
$$+ \left(1 - \frac{1}{\eta^m}\right) \sum_l \omega^l V^l_{i\pi} + \left(1 - \frac{1}{\eta^m}\right) \sum_l \omega^l V^l_{ih\pi}$$

$$(4.45)$$

where $\eta^m = \dfrac{(\sum_l W^l \eta^l)}{(\sum_l W^l)}$ and $\omega^l = \dfrac{(1 - \lambda^l)W^l}{\sum_l (1 - \lambda^l)W^l}$.

There are several interesting and intuitive results in this equation. First, Equation (4.45) shows that an international asset risk premium adjusted for one-half its own variance is related to its covariance with four variables. These are the world market portfolio, aggregate of the innovation in discounted expected future world market returns from different investors across countries, aggregate of the inflation from different countries, and aggregate of the innovation in discounted expected future inflation from different investors across countries. The weights are $1/\eta^m$, $1/\eta^m - 1$, $1 - 1/\eta^m$, and $1 - 1/\eta^m$, respectively. The sum of these weights is equal to 1. Moreover, it is noted that the market hedging risk is a weighted average of world market portfolio for investors from different countries. This is different from the domestic counterpart of Campbell (1993).

Second, an international asset can be priced without referring to its covariance with consumption growth. Rather, it depends on its covariance with world market return, the weighted average of news about future world market return for investors from different countries, inflation, and the weighted average of news about future inflation for investors from different countries.

Third, the coefficient of risk tolerance, η_m, is the only preference parameter that enters Equation (4.45). When consumption is substituted out in this model, the coefficient of intertemporal substitution ρ disappears. Similar results have been documented by Kocherlakota (1990) and Svensson (1989). They show that when asset returns are independently and identically distributed over time, the coefficient of intertemporal substitution is irrelevant for asset returns.

If we are willing to make some more assumptions, we can obtain a more compact result. Namely, if investors are assumed to have the same world market portfolio and use the same method to forecast world market portfolio return, we can multiply Equation (4.44) by λ^l, and take an average of all investors, where weights are their relative wealth, to get a simple version of the international asset pricing model:

$$E_t r_{i,t+1} - r_{f,t+1} = -\frac{V_{ii}}{2} + \lambda^m V_{im} + (\lambda^m - 1) V_{ih}$$
$$+ (1 - \lambda^m) \sum_l \omega^l V_{i\pi}^l + (1 - \lambda^m) \sum_l \omega^l V_{ih\pi}^l$$
$$(4.46)$$

where $\lambda^m = (\sum_l W^l \lambda^l)/(\sum_l W^l)$ and $\omega^l = \frac{(1-\lambda^l) W^l}{\sum_l (1-\lambda^l) W^l}$

Both hedging risk V_{ih} and currency risk $V_{i\pi}^l$ are related to expected return. In addition, they all depend on whether λ^m is different from 1 or not.

Furthermore, when we assume that domestic inflation is nonstochastic, the only random component in π would be the relative change in the exchange rate between the numeraire currency and the currency of the country, where the investor resides. Hence, $V_{i\pi}^l$ is a pure measure of the exposure of asset i to the currency risk of the country, where investor l resides and $V_{ih\pi}^l$ is also a measure of the exposure of asset i to hedge against the currency risk of the country, where investor l resides.

Equation (4.46) also states that the currency risk is different from the hedging risk. However, if V_{ih} and $V_{i\pi}^l$ are large enough, then whether V_{ih} and $V_{i\pi}^l$ and related to expected return depends on whether or not λ^m is different from 1: This may be the reason why Dumas and Solnik (1995) argue that exchange rate risk premium may be equivalent to intertemporal risk premium. But, their conjecture

is based on an empirical "horse race" test between international model and intertemporal model rather than a theoretical derivation.

4.4. Conclusion

The international asset pricing model without consumption developed by Chang and Hung (2004) argues that the real expected asset return is determined by market risk, market hedging risk, currency risk, and currency hedging risk. The weights are related only to relative risk aversion. Moreover, the weights are summed up to 1. Their results may be contrasted with the pioneering work of Adler and Dumas (1983), who assume a constant investment opportunity set, thus their model lacks market hedging risk and currency hedging risk.

In the Chang et al. (2004) model, the price of market hedging risk is equal to the negative price of the currency risk. This may be the reason why Dumas and Solnik (1995) argue that currency risk is equivalent to market hedging risk. But, their conjecture is based on a "horse race" test between international model and intertemporal model rather than on a theoretical derivation.

REFERENCES

Adler, M. and Dumas B. (1983). "International portfolio selection and corporation finance: a synthesis." *Journal of Finance* 38: 925–984.

Chang J.R. and Hung, M.W. (2000). "An International asset pricing model with time-varying hedging risk." *Review of Quantitative Finance and Accounting*, 15: 235–257.

Chang J.R., Errunza,V., Hogan, K., and Hung M.W. (2005). "Disentangling exchange risk from intertemporal hedging risk: theory and empirical evidence", *European Financial Management*, 11: 212–254.

Cho, C.D., Eun, C.S., and Senbet, L.W. (1986). "International arbitrage pricing theory: An empirical investigation." *Journal of Finance*, 41: 313–330.

Campbell, J.Y. (1993). "Intertemporal asset pricing without consumption data." *American Economic Review*, 83: 487–512.

Cumby, R.E. (1990). "Consumption risk and international equity returns: some empirical evidence."

Journal of international Money and Finance, 9: 182–192.

De Santis G. and Gerard, B. (1997). "International asset pricing and portfolio diversification with time-varying risk." *Journal of Finance*, 52: 1881–1912.

Dumas, B. and Solnik, B. (1995). "The world price of foreign exchange risk. *Journal of Finance,* 50: 445–479.

Epstein, L.G. and Zin, S.E. (1989). "Substitution, risk aversion, and the temporal behavior of consumption and asset returns: a theoretical framework." *Econometrica*, 57: 937–969.

Epstein, L.G. and Zin, S.E. (1991). "Substitution, risk aversion, and the temporal behavior of consumption and asset returns: an empirical analysis." *Journal of Political Economy*, 99: 263–286.

Ferson, W.E. and Harvey, R.C. (1993). "The risk and predictability of international equity returns." *Review of Financial Studies*, 6: 527–567.

Giovannini, A. and Weil, P. (1989). "Risk aversion and intertemporal substitution in the capital asset pricing model." *National Bureau of Economic Research*, 2824.

Harvey, R.C. (1991). "The world price of covariance risk." *Journal of Finance*, 46: 111–157.

Kocherlakota, N. (1990). "Disentangling the coefficient of relative risk aversion from the elasticity of intertemporal substitution: an irrelevance result." *Journal of Finance*, 45: 175–190.

Korajczyk, R.A. and Viallet. C. (1989). "An empirical investigation of international asset pricing." *Review of Financial Studie*s, 2: 553–585.

Kreps, D. and Porteus. E. (1978). "Temporal resolution of uncertainty and dynamic choice theory." *Econometrica*, 46: 185–200.

Lintner, J. (1965). "The valuation of risk assets and the selection of risky investments in stock portfolios and capital budgets." *Review of Economics and Statistics*, 47: 13–37.

Merton, R.C. (1973). "An intertemporal capital asset pricing model." *Econometrica*, 41: 867–887.

Ross, S.A. (1976). "The arbitrage theory of capital asset pricing." *Journal of Economic Theory*, 13: 341–360.

Sharpe, W. (1964). "Capital asset prices: a theory of market equilibrium under conditions of risk." *Journal of Finance*, 19: 425–442.

Solnik, B. (1974). "An equilibrium model of the international capital market." *Journal of Economic Theory*, 8: 500–524.

Stulz, R.M. (1981). "A model of international asset pricing." *Journal of Financial Economics*, 9: 383–406.

Svensson, L.E.O. (1989). "Portfolio choice with non-expected utility in continuous time." *Economics Letters*, 30: 313–317.

Weil, P. (1989). "The equity premium puzzle and the risk free rate puzzle." *Journal of Monetary Economic*, 24: 401–421.

Chapter 5

CREDIT DERIVATIVES

REN-RAW CHEN, *Rutgers University, USA*
JING-ZHI HUANG, *Penn State University, USA*

Abstract

Credit derivatives are instruments used to measure, manage, and transfer credit risk. Recently, there has been an explosive growth in the use of these instruments in the financial markets. This article reviews the structure and use of some credit derivative instruments that are popular in practice.

Keywords: credit derivatives; credit risk; default risk; credit spreads; asset swaps; default swaps; credit default swaps; total return swaps; basket default swaps; credit spread options

5.1. Introduction

Recent years have seen a dramatic expansion in the use of credit derivatives in the financial industry. Credit derivatives are used in the diversification and transfer of credit risk, the ability to leverage, and the creation of new asset classes providing yield enhancement. This growth is likely to continue as institutional investors, broker-dealers, hedge funds, and insurance companies all realize the advantages that these instruments have over the traditional alternatives. In the following, we present an overview of the main credit derivatives such as default swaps, total return swaps, and credit spread options.

5.2. Asset Swaps

The most basic building block in the credit world is perhaps the asset swap. An asset swap is a simple structure that enables a counterparty receiving fixed payments on a security to exchange the fixed coupon for a floating rate payment at a fixed spread to London Interbank Offered Rate (LIBOR). Historically, banks have used asset swaps to match their long-term fixed-rate assets with their short-term liabilities, i.e. mortgage loans against depositor accounts. In a par asset swap, one party delivers a risky asset to the other in return for par. They then receive the cash flows of a risky bond in return for regular payments of LIBOR plus a fixed spread (or minus a fixed spread if the asset is better quality than LIBOR, e.g. a U.S. Treasury security). The mechanics of this structure are shown in Figure 5.1.

This fixed spread is known as the Asset Swap Spread. The key point concerning asset swaps is that the fixed coupons being paid are *effectively* guaranteed by the counterparty even if the underlying risky asset defaults. As a result, the payer of the fixed coupon has a credit exposure to the issuer of the defaulting bond. The asset swap spread is therefore the additional return required by the payer of the fixed coupon to compensate for the credit risk incurred and to repay any difference in price if the bond is trading away from par. The par amount paid up front can be used to purchase a par floater. The overall result for counterparty A has been to take fixed cash flows from a risky asset and exchange them for the same cash flows paid by a LIBOR quality counterparty. These fixed coupons can then be exchanged for floating rate payments in another standard interest rate swap.

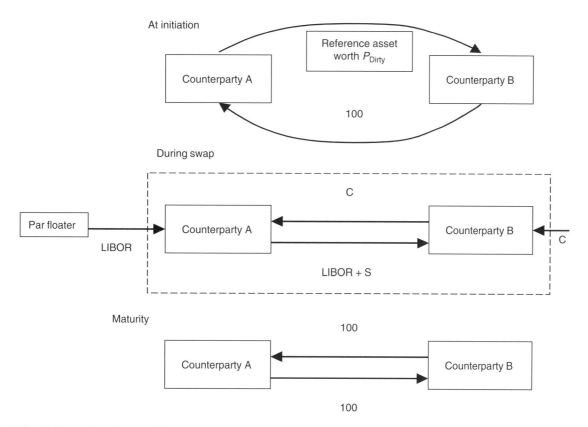

Figure 5.1.   Mechanics of a par floater asset swap

The asset swap is an important measure of default risk as it represents the additional spread that can be locked-in by taking on the risk of an issuer in a fixed-for-floating rate par swap.

5.3. Default Swaps

A default swap is a bilateral contract that allows an investor to buy protection against the risk of default of a specified *reference credit*. The fee may be paid up front, but more often is paid in a "swapped" form as a regular, accruing cash flow.

As a default swap is a negotiated contract, there are several important features that need to be agreed between the counterparties and clearly defined in the contract documentation. First and foremost is the definition of the credit event itself. This is obviously closely linked to the choice of the reference credit and will include such events as bankruptcy, insolvency, receivership, restructuring of debt, and a material change in the credit spread.

This last *materiality* clause ensures that the triggering event has indeed affected the price of the reference asset. It is generally defined in spread terms since a fall in the price of the reference asset could also be due to an increase in the level of interest rates.

Many default swaps define the triggering of a credit event using a *reference asset*. However, in many cases, the importance of the reference asset is secondary as the credit event may also be defined with respect to a class of debt issued by a *reference entity*. In this case, the importance of the reference asset arises solely from its use in the determination of the *recovery price* used to calculate the payment following the credit event.

The contract must specify what happens if the credit event occurs. Typically, the protection buyer will usually agree to do one of the following:

- Deliver the defaulted security to the protection seller in return for par in cash. Note that the contract usually specifies a basket of securities that are ranked *pari passu*, which may be delivered in place of the reference asset. In effect, the protection seller is long a "cheapest to deliver" option.

• Receive par minus the default price of the reference asset settled in cash. The price of the defaulted asset is typically determined via a dealer poll conducted within a few weeks to months of the credit event, the purpose of the delay being to let the recovery price stabilize.

These choices are shown in Figure 5.2. It is often in the interest of the protection seller to choose physical delivery of the asset since the seller may have the view that either by waiting or by entering into negotiations with the issuer of the reference asset, he may be able to receive more than the default price.

For those familiar with option terminology, it may help to think of a default swap as a knock-in option contingent on the credit event. Until the credit event occurs, the default swap is always out-of-the-money. Even a large deterioration in the credit of the reference asset of a default swap that just stops short of the credit event will not be covered by the default swap.

Some default swaps have a different payoff from the standard par minus recovery price. The main alternative is to have a fixed pre-determined

amount that is paid out immediately after the credit event. This is known as a binary default swap. In other cases, where the reference asset is trading at a significant premium or discount to par, the payoff may be tailored to be the difference between the initial price of the reference asset and the recovery price.

The protection buyer automatically stops paying the premium once the credit event has occurred, and this property has to be factored into the cost of the swap payments. It has the benefit of enabling both parties to close out their positions soon after the credit event and so eliminates the ongoing administrative costs that would otherwise occur.

A default swap can be viewed as a form of insurance with one important advantage – efficiency. Provided the credit event in the default swap documentation is defined clearly, the payment due from the triggering of the credit event will be made quickly. Contrast this with the potentially long and drawn out process of investigation and negotiation that may occur with traditional insurance.

In approximate order of importance, the main factors that will determine the cost of the default swap are the shape of the reference asset credit spread curve, the maturity of the protection, the default price of the reference asset, the shape of the LIBOR curve, the credit worthiness of the protection seller, and the correlation of the credit worthiness of the protection seller to the reference asset; default protection bought on the debt of a bank from another closely related bank is probably worthless.

However, it is possible to get a very good idea of the price of the default swap using a simple "static replication" argument. This involves recognizing that buying a default swap on a risky par floating rate asset that only defaults on coupon dates is exactly equivalent to going along a default-free floating rate note and short a risky floating rate note of the same credit quality (see Table 5.1). If no default occurs, the holder of the position makes a net payment equal to the asset swap spread of the

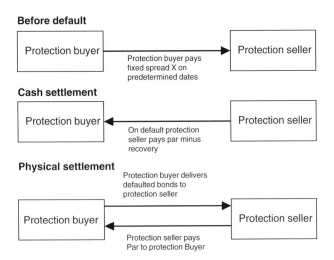

Figure 5.2. Mechanics of a default swap

Table 5.1. Static replication of a default swap on a par floater that can default on coupon dates only

Event	Long riskless FRN	Short risky FRN via asset swap	Default swap
Coupon Payments	+LIBOR	−(LIBOR + ASS)	−ASS
Credit Event occurs on Coupon Date	+100 at Default	−R at Default	(100 − R) at Default
No Credit Event	+100 at Maturity	−100 at Maturity	0

asset on each coupon date until maturity. This spread represents the credit quality of the risky floater at issuance. If default does occur, and we assume that it can only occur on coupon payment dates, the position can be closed out by buying back the defaulted asset in return for the recovery rate and selling the par floater. The net value of the position is equal to the payoff from the default swap.

This argument implies that we would expect the price of the default swap on a par floater to be close to the asset swap spread with the credit quality of the reference credit and the same maturity as the default swap. It also shows that par floaters are a perfect hedge for default swaps.

5.4. Total Return Swaps

A total return swap is a contract that allows an investor to receive all of the cash flow benefits of owning a reference asset without actually possessing the asset itself. The mechanics of this structure are shown in Figure 5.3.

At trade inception, one party, the total return receiver, agrees to make payments of LIBOR plus a fixed spread to the other party, the total return payer, in return for the coupons paid by some specified asset. At the end of the term of the total return swap, the total return receiver must then pay the difference between the final market price of the asset and the initial price of the asset. If default occurs, this means that the total return receiver must shoulder the loss by paying the difference between the initial value of the reference asset and the default value of the reference asset. Standard practice is for cash settlement.

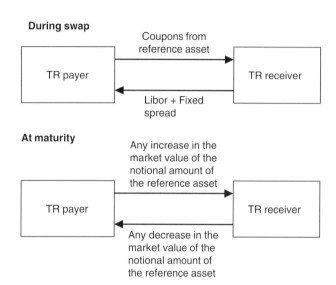

Figure 5.3. Mechanics of a total return swap

It is important to understand that a total return swap has a default swap embedded within it – the payer of the total return has insured himself against the default risk of the asset. Furthermore, he is also protected from the price risk of the asset.

Determination of the fixed spread to LIBOR payable by the total return receiver depends on several factors including the spread curve of the reference asset, the LIBOR curve, the financing cost to the payer of holding the asset on balance sheet, the expected default price of the asset, and counterparty credit quality. In certain circumstances, the price will be close to that of the corresponding default swap.

There are several reasons why an investor would wish to use such a structure. First and foremost is leverage. Using a total return swap, an investor can gain the return of an asset without paying the full price of the asset. The investor only has to make the coupon payments that are paid net. Indeed, if there is no actual transfer of the reference asset, then the limit on the size of the notional depends solely on the amount of risk that the two parties wish to assume.

Another motivation is that it enables investors to obtain off balance sheet exposure to assets that they might otherwise be precluded for tax, political or other reasons. This is especially useful to banks with lower credit ratings and higher funding costs in certain markets. Furthermore, total return swaps are often treated as derivatives and so incur a lower regulatory capital charge.

Total return swaps make it possible to short an asset without actually selling the asset. This may be useful from a point of view of temporarily hedging the risk of the credit, deferring a payment of capital gains tax, or simply gaining confidentiality regarding investment decisions.

As the maturity of the total return swap is not necessarily the same as the maturity of the reference asset, a total return swap effectively creates a new synthetic asset with the required maturity. Credit gaps in a portfolio may therefore be filled.

5.5. Principal Protection

Many loans to developing countries are like investing junk bonds, subject to high default risk. Banks that provide loans to developing countries are fully aware of the high default risk. Buying default swaps would be a natural way to hedge the risk but default swaps of these countries are usually very expensive and will wipe out all the incentive to provide loan to these countries. Furthermore, most banks that provide loan to these countries normally do so due to political and not economic considerations. Hence, protecting the principal and not the interest is the main concern for the lending banks.

A principal protected note (PPN) is developed for this purpose. PPN is similar to a risky floater except that the principal is guaranteed upon default and is similar to a risk-free floater except that the coupons are not guaranteed. As a result, we can value any PPN by either one of the following:

- Risky floater + Principal protection
- Risk-free floater − Risk-free coupons + Risky coupons
- Risk-free zero + Risky coupons

Since the default swaps hedge away coupon risks and the principal is risk-free, a PPN and the default swaps add up to a risk-free floater.

5.6. Credit Spread Options

A spread option is a contract whose payout depends on the credit spread of a reference asset. This reference asset may be either a floating rate note or an asset swap. As with standard options, one must specify whether the option is a call or put, the expiry date of the option, the strike price, and the type of optionality, i.e. American style (exercise at any time), European style (exercise at expiry only), or Bermudan style (exercise on one of several dates). It is also important to define what happens in the event that the underlying asset defaults – one may not want to pay for the right to exercise upon default. On exercise, the option may be settled through cash or physical delivery.

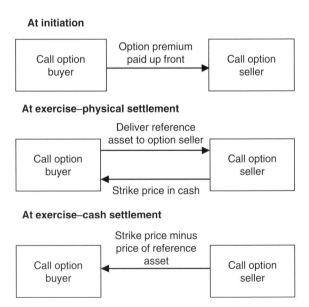

Figure 5.4. Mechanics of a call option on reference asset

Credit spread options are usually quoted in terms of the price of the reference asset. To see how an option on prices translates to an option on spreads, consider the case of a put option on a floating rate note paying LIBOR plus 150 basis points where the strike price is par. As the credit spread of the floating rate note widens, its price falls. If the market asset swap spread widens from 150 basis points to 160 basis points, the price of the floating rate bond falls below par and the put option is now in the money. The sensitivity of the price of the reference asset to changes in the asset swap spread is given by the spread duration. We can therefore view the put option on the price of the reference as a call option on the asset swap spread of the reference asset with an effective notional proportional to the spread duration.

A more complicated version of this is the option on an asset swap shown in Figure 5.5. In this case, the purchaser of a call option pays premium to the option seller to have the right to buy a specific reference asset and enter into a par flat asset swap.

As the asset swap spread of the reference asset widens, the value of the underlying asset swap falls and the buyer is less likely to exercise the call option. Equally, as the value of the underlying asset swap spread rises, the buyer is more likely to exercise the call option. Therefore, the call

option on the asset swap translates into a put option on the asset swap spread and vice versa.

For all practical purposes, default swaps and credit spread options are the same. Indeed the payoff from a credit spread put option (a call on the asset swap spread) struck at par is the same as the payoff from a default swap, which pays par minus the default price. However, there are some differences. First of all, the value of a credit spread option depends on the credit spread volatility. The more volatile the credit spread, the more time-value the option will have and the more the option will be worth. Secondly, the payoff of credit spread option is sensitive to large increases in spread that may not actually constitute formal default. They therefore provide a hedge against price risk as well as default risk. Lastly, they allow the purchaser the right to choose when to exercise.

5.7. Basket Default Swaps

A basket default swap is like a default swap, but the only exception is that it is linked to the default of more than one credit. In the particular case of a first-to-default basket, it is the first asset in a basket whose credit event triggers a payment to the protection buyer. As in the case of a default swap, this payment may involve either cash payment of par minus the default price of the defaulted asset, or physical delivery of the defaulted asset in return for par. In return for protection against the first-to-default, the protection buyer pays a fee to the protection seller as a set of regular accruing cash flows.

To see clearly the mechanics of the structure, consider a deal in which an investor buys first-to-default protection to hedge a $50M notional of each of three credits A, B, and C. Although the total notional amount covered is $150M, it is imperative to note that if one of the credits is defaulted, only the notional size of that credit in the basket gets paid. For example, if credit B defaults, then we receive a payout equal in value to the difference between par and its default price on

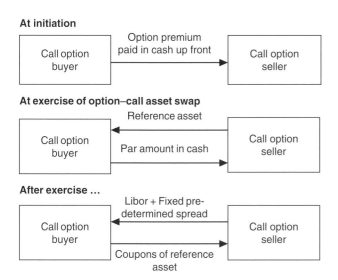

Figure 5.5. Mechanics of a call option on asset swap

a notional of \$50M. See Figure 5.6. The default basket terminates and remaining credits A and C are then left unhedged.

Since there is no simple portfolios that can statically replicate this structure, determining the value of the fixed spread is not an easy task. However, we can easily impose lower and upper limits on the price. Since the structure provides less protection than buying default swaps against *each* of the reference credits individually, it has to be less than this total cost. For a lower bound, we note that the cost of the basket has to be greater than the price of a default swap on the lowest credit quality asset in the basket. The problem is that these bounds may be quite far apart so that in practice we will need a model to get a more accurate price.

The motivation for doing a basket default swap is that it is a cheaper way to buy protection on a group of credits than buying protection individually on each credit. It is therefore an efficient way to reduce credit concentrations at an attractive cost. For the protection seller, the main motivation is that it provides a way to earn a high yield on high-quality securities.

There may also be a regulatory capital advantage to selling protection. For example, an investor may be able to sell protection against five assets, earning a high yield in the process, but only be required to pay the regulatory capital charge against one of the assets in the basket. However, as there is as yet no standard treatment for default baskets, the benefit of this advantage may vary depending upon regulatory framework.

It is important to understand that default baskets are correlation trades. However, there are two types of correlations to think about. First, there is the correlation between the changes in the spreads of the assets in the basket. This captures the fact that as one asset becomes more likely to default, another asset may also become more likely to default. The second type of correlation is the default correlation. This captures the knock-on effect that the default of one asset has on the default of another asset.

This is a subtle issue. To see it more clearly, consider the example of a default basket on two issuers within the same industry sector. We would expect to find a strong positive correlation between the credit spread changes of both issuers. However, if one issuer were to actually default and this was due to idiosyncratic reasons, it has a beneficial effect on the other issuer due to effects such as creating more market share and reducing labor costs. The upshot is that we have positive spread correlation but negative default correlation. A major difficulty is the sheer lack of data available for estimating these correlations. In practice, the credits in most baskets are chosen in such a way that they have low probabilities of default and low correlations with each other.

5.8. Convertible Bonds

Convertible bonds are traditionally regarded as an equity play, i.e. the buyers of convertibles are after potentially high equity value. Some convertible bonds with less likelihood of significant equity appreciation try to attract buyers who try to enhance investment returns. Nowadays, convertibles have become a major credit derivative contract. Institutional investors discover that the credit risk in convertible bonds is significantly mispriced and hence start to arbitrage on high-yield convertibles.

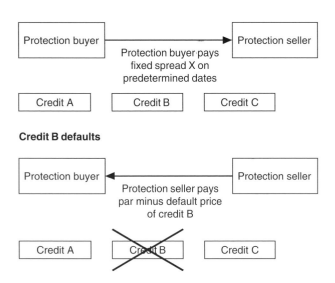

Figure 5.6. A basket default swap on credits A, B and C

A typical credit play of convertibles is to buy an underpriced convertible, engage in an interest rate swap to hedge away the interest rate risk, sell an equity put option to compensate the conversion value paid for, and enjoy the underpriced credit spread. This credit spread can be monetized by selling a spread option, or engaging in a forward asset swap, or buying a default swap.

5.9. Conclusions

What we have presented here constitute the main types of credit derivative instruments. Many of the more exotic structures that are now being traded in the market are simply variations and extensions of these basic building blocks. For example, credit-linked notes may consist simply of a standard bullet bond that has an embedded default swap – the investor receives a coupon plus a spread and loses part of the redemption value if the reference credit defaults.

One important issue in the use of credit derivatives, which is not the focus of this review, is how to price and hedge these instruments. See, for example, Caouette et al. (1998), Saunders and Allen (2002), Duffie and Singleton (2003), and Anson et al. (2004).

Acknowledgement

We would like to thank Dominic O'Kane of Lehman Brothers for helpful comments and suggestions.

REFERENCES

Anson, M., Fabozzi, F., Choudhry, M., and Chen, R.R. (2004). *Credit Derivatives: Instruments, Applications, and Pricing*. New York: John Wiley.

Caouette, J.B., Altman, E.I., and Narayanan, P. (1998). *Managing Credit Risk: The Next Great Financial Challenge*. New York: John Wiley.

Duffie, D. and Singleton, K.J. (2003). *Credit Risk: Pricing, Measurement and Management*. New Jersey: Princeton University Press.

Saunders, A. and Allen, L. (2002). *Credit Risk Measurement*, 2nd edn. New York: John Wiley.

Chapter 6

INTERNATIONAL PARITY CONDITIONS AND MARKET RISK

THOMAS C. CHIANG, *Drexel University, USA*

Abstract

This article presents a set of international parity conditions based on consistent and efficient market behavior. We hypothesize that deviations from parity conditions in international bond, stock, and commodity markets are attributable mainly to relative equity premiums and real interest rate differentials. Testing this hypothesis against four European markets for the recent floating currency period, we gain supportive evidence. Moreover, the deviations of uncovered interest parity, international stock return parity, and purchasing power parity are not independent; the evidence suggests that deviations from the three parities are driven by two common factors: equity premium differential and real interest rate differential.

Keywords: international asset pricing; purchasing power parity; uncovered interest rate parity; exchange rate risk; equity premiums; real interest rate parity; unbiased forward rate hypothesis; Fisher equation; spot exchange rate; forward exchange rate

6.1. Introduction

In the past three decades of floating exchange rates, a substantial amount of research has been devoted to identifying linkages in international markets. The most prominent among these linkages are the uncovered interest parity (UIP), purchasing power parity (PPP), and international stock return parity (ISP).[1] The importance of these conditions stems not only from their significance as building blocks for international finance theory, but also from their application in guiding resource allocation in international money, capital, and goods markets.

Along with theoretical advancements, a large volume of empirical research has spawned an examination of the validity of these parities as applied to various market data. Hodrick (1987), Froot and Thaler (1990), Bekaert and Hodrick (1993), Lothian and Taylor (1997a,b), Engel (1996), and Rogoff (1996) provide summaries for various types of market behavior. A general consensus derived from these studies is that market imperfections, transaction costs, risk premiums, measurement errors, expectations errors, and the lack of more powerful statistical techniques are the main factors that frustrate parity conditions.

It is not our purpose to engage in an exhaustive review of all the parity conditions, nor is it our intention to provide a thorough empirical test. Rather, our goal is to provide a simple theoretical framework within which various asset return relationships can be illustrated and reasoned by established finance theories. From this framework, we are able to identify two common factors that contribute to deviations of the three parity conditions: equity premium differential and real interest rate differential. The evidence based on data derived from four major European markets validates our arguments. Following this introductory section, Section 6.2 provides a simple and yet consistent market behavior to achieve the three parity conditions in the vein of a speculative efficient framework (Roll, 1979). Section 6.3 offers some empirical evidence for each parity condition. Section 6.4 provides a theoretical framework that relates deviations of the parity conditions to equity premiums and real interest rate differentials, and then reports the empirical evidence. Section 6.5 concludes the study. Further empirical evidence for additional parity conditions is offered in an appendix.

6.2. International Parity Conditions

Earlier contributions by Solnik (1978), Roll and Solnik (1979), and Roll (1979) laid a firm foundation for consolidating international parity conditions. Based on a few traditional assumptions, including the premises that both goods and financial markets are perfect and that there is an absence of transactional costs and barriers to trade, the "law of one price" implies that homogeneous goods or assets are expected to trade at the same exchange adjusted price in any two countries. Thus, international parity holds if expected asset returns claimed by investors are equal regardless of whether investments occur in domestic or foreign market.

Consider an economic agent engaging in a one-period investment who expects to claim x_{t+1} in domestic currency when the contract matures in the future. The agent then faces two options: invest in the domestic market or invest in the foreign market. The present values of these two investments are:

$$pv_{j,t} = \frac{x_{t+1}}{1 + R_{j,t+1}^e} \quad \text{and} \quad (6.1)$$

$$pv_{j,t}^* = \frac{x_{t+1}}{(1 + R_{j,t+1}^{*e})(1 + \Delta s_{t+1}^e)}, \quad (6.2)$$

where $R_{j,t+1}^e$ and $R_{j,t+1}^{*e}$ are expected returns in domestic and foreign markets for asset j, respectively; an asterisk denotes a foreign variable and a superscript e refers to an expectation operator; $\Delta s_{t+1}^e > 0$ denotes the expected rate of appreciation of the foreign currency; s_t is the spot exchange rate at time t, expressed as units of domestic currency per unit of foreign currency; and pv stands for the present value. An equilibrium condition leads to:

$$(1 + R_{j,t+1}^e) = (1 + R_{j,t+1}^{*e})(1 + \Delta s_{t+1}^e). \quad (6.3)$$

Applying "the law of one price" and aggregating over the entire market by taking natural logarithms throughout the equation allows us to write a general expression of an international parity relationship as:

$$R_{t+1}^e = R_{t+1}^{*e} + \Delta s_{t+1}^e, \quad (6.4)$$

where $\ln(1 + R_{t+1}^e) \cong R_{t+1}^e$. Notice that the variable x_{t+1}^e may be alternatively denoted by $E(x_{t+1}|I_t)$, indicating an expected value conditional on information available at time t. By defining $R_{t+1}^e = p_{t+1}^e - p_t$ and $\Delta s_{t+1}^e = s_{t+1}^e - s_t$, where p_{t+1}^e, p_t, s_{t+1}^e, and s_t are expressed in natural logarithms, the expected return, R_{t+1}^e, in this economy is simplified by the price appreciation of assets or goods.[2] Applying the indices of p_{t+1}^e and p_t to bond, equity, and commodity markets, Equation (6.4) implies three principal open-parity conditions as:

$$r_t = r_t^* + \Delta s_{t+1}^e, \quad (6.5)$$

$$R_{m,t+1}^e = R_{m,t+1}^{*e} + \Delta s_{t+1}^e, \quad \text{and} \quad (6.6)$$

$$\Delta p_{t+1}^e = \Delta p_{t+1}^{*e} + \Delta s_{t+1}^e, \quad (6.7)$$

where r_t is the short-term interest rate from time t to $t+1$; $R_{m,t+1}^e$ denotes the expected return on the stock market; and Δp_{t+1}^e represents the expected inflation rate. The left-side variables of these equations are domestic expected returns, while the right-side variables are expected returns in foreign instruments plus expected appreciation of currency in the foreign country to engage investments.

The condition in Equation (6.5) is referred to as the uncovered interest rate parity (UIP), which means that the risk-free return from a local investment is equal to the comparable return in a foreign instrument plus an expected appreciation rate of the foreign currency. Since the outcome of the future spot rate is uncertain, an investor with risk aversion tends to sell the total proceeds (principal plus interest earned) in the forward market to hedge the risk. As a result, a covered version of interest rate parity is achieved as follows:

$$r_t = r_t^* + (f_t - s_t), \tag{6.8}$$

where f_t is the natural logarithm of the forward-exchange rate with a maturity that matches that of the instruments r_t and r_t^*. This equation states that a relatively higher interest rate in the domestic market must be offset by its currency discount in the forward market. Since all the parameters in Equation (6.8) are directly assessable, this condition usually holds unless the financial market is imperfect or there are measurement errors for the data.

The parity in Equation (6.6) may be called the international stock return parity condition (ISP) – the return in the domestic equity market is expected to be equal to the exchange rate adjusted return in the foreign market.[3] For instance, an index return in the U.K. market is 10 percent, while the comparable index return in the U.S. market is 8 percent; the excess 2 percent return in the U.K. market will be offset by the same magnitude of dollar appreciation. This condition is more complicated than that of UIP since it involves expectations for both stock returns and exchange rate changes. The expectations formation for stock returns and exchange rates are governed mainly by different sets of economic fundamentals and investor sophistication (Albuquerque et al., 2004), although they might share some common factors. The volatile behavior of stock returns adds an additional risk to the parity condition.

The third condition, expressed in Equation (6.7), is the relative purchasing power parity, which states that the expected return speculated on domestic goods is equal to the expected return

on the foreign goods market plus an expected foreign-currency gain. Alternatively, we can think about the fact that the speculative real return to the domestic economic agent can be achieved by deflating the foreign nominal return $(\Delta p_{t+1}^{*e} + \Delta s_{t+1}^e)$ with the domestic inflation rate (Δp_{t+1}^e), i.e. $(\Delta p_{t+1}^{*e} + \Delta s_{t+1}^e) - \Delta p_{t+1}^e$. This expression is a differenced form of the real exchange rate. In an efficient market, according to Roll (1979), such an excess return from speculation must be zero. In other words, $(\Delta p_{t+1}^{*e} + \Delta s_{t+1}^e) - \Delta p_{t+1}^e = 0$.

A common feature shared by these three principal parities is that linkages between domestic returns and foreign-market returns all go through the channel of the foreign-exchange market. As a result, a shock in the currency market will create an exchange rate risk affecting three markets (goods, bonds, and stocks) simultaneously. Moreover, if we view the exchange rate as an endogenous variable, the change in an exchange rate is seen to be associated with changes in relative returns, as reflected in the relative inflation differential, interest rate differential, and stock return differential. These relative return variables will be determined further by underlying supply and demand conditions in a general equilibrium framework.

Note that the relationships between pairwise variables such as $(\Delta p_{t+1}^e$ and $r_t)$ and $(r_t$ and $R_{m,t+1}^e)$ are well documented in the literature. First, the expected inflation rate in the goods market is linked to the return in the bond market through the Fisher equation. Formally, we write:

$$r_t = \bar{r}_{t+1}^e + \Delta p_{t+1}^e \tag{6.9}$$

and

$$r_t^* = \bar{r}_{t+1}^{*e} + \Delta p_{t+1}^{*e}, \tag{6.10}$$

where $\bar{r}_{t+1}^e$ and $\bar{r}_{t+1}^{*e}$ are expectations of real interest rates for the domestic and foreign countries, respectively. If both PPP and UIP hold, the expected real interest rate parity must be established, i.e.

$$\bar{r}_{t+1}^e = \bar{r}_{t+1}^{*e}. \tag{6.11}$$

The expected real interest rate parity implies that the expected real return on capital must be equal. It is of interest to point out that this condition holds independently of any exchange rate factors. Another implication of this parity condition is that $p_{t+1}^e - p_{t+1}^{*e} = r_t - r_t^*$, i.e. the interest rate differential reflects the expected inflation rate differential as inferred from Fama's efficient interest rate hypothesis (Fama, 1975). Due to the very nature of the information content involved in these markets, Marston (1997) observes that international-parity conditions, represented by a system formed by Equations (6.5), (6.7), and (6.11), are interrelated since their deviations from parity are driven by the same set of information, such as the interest rate differential and inflation rate differential. In particular:

$$\bar{r}_{t+1}^e - \bar{r}_{t+1}^{*e} = \left[r_t - \left(r_t^* + \Delta s_{t+1}^e \right) \right] \\ - \left[\Delta p_{t+1}^e - \left(\Delta p_{t+1}^{*e} + \Delta s_{t+1}^e \right) \right].$$

This equation states that an *ex ante* real interest rate differential is associated with deviations of UIP and PPP[4]; it reveals no direct connection with stock return differentials.

Second, the return in the bond market is linked to the return in the stock market through the Capital Asset Pricing Model (CAPM) and term-structure relationship (Campbell, 1987). In the international context, coexistence of a UIP and ISP must lead to the equity premium parity as:

$$R_{m,t+1}^e - r_t = R_{m,t+1}^{*e} - r_t^*. \tag{6.12}$$

It suggests that excess returns in international equity markets must be equal. Again, exchange rate variations play no explicit role in explaining the equity premium differential unless we want to consider the real term. The international CAPM implies that any divergence in the equity premium differential must reflect the risk differential (betas) associated with two markets. To decompose the equity premium differential, we yield:

$$\left(R_{m,t+1}^e - r_t \right) - \left(R_{m,t+1}^{*e} - r_t^* \right) = \left[R_{m,t+1}^e - \left(R_{m,t+1}^{*e} + \Delta s_{t+1}^e \right) \right] \\ - \left[r_t - \left(r_t^* + \Delta s_{t+1}^e \right) \right]. \tag{6.13}$$

This equation states that the disparity in the equity premiums between two markets is associated with deviations of the stock return parity and the UIP, and has no direct connection with the inflation rate differential.[5]

Before we move to the next section, it is useful to summarize the arguments that we have developed up to this point. Based on consistent market behavior, we have constructed a global financial market system in which international markets are linked through the PPP, UIP, and ISP for goods, bonds, and stocks, while the domestic goods market is linked to bond markets through the Fisher equation by a real interest rate, and the bond market is linked to the stock market via the CAPM by equity premiums. Any shocks to the system could directly or indirectly disturb the equilibrium conditions in the goods, bond, or stock markets through changes in relative asset returns. These changes, in turn, could alter equity premium differentials and real interest rate differentials, causing international capital movements and trade flows. As a result, we observe that deviations of parity conditions are associated with excess-return differentials. Checking into the factors behind the excess-return differentials, we perceive that excess returns reflect mainly compensation for excess risk associated with stock returns, inflation, and exchange rate variations.

6.3. Empirical Evidence

6.3.1. Data

Although a considerable amount of empirical research has been conducted in examining international parity conditions, the approaches utilized have varied in terms of countries, time periods, frequency, model specifications, and underlying theories, among other factors. To obtain a consistent comparison, we shall provide a unified approach by using a consistent data set to examine four major European countries, consisting of the United Kingdom (UK), Germany (GM), France (FR), and Switzerland (SW), and employing the United States (US) as a reference country (with an asterisk in our notation).

In the empirical estimations, we treat the U.S. market as a price maker due to its relatively dominant size and effectiveness in information processing. As such, it allows us to examine the impact of the U.S. market on each of the four European markets. This study uses end-of-the-month spot exchange rates and one-month forward exchange rates, with the exchange rates expressed as prices of the local currency per unit of the U.S. dollar. Short-term interest rates are measured by the one-month euro-currency deposit rates for each country. These euro-currency deposit rates have been widely used in empirical studies due to their homogeneous features and their convenience in comparing across markets. The stock price indices for the five markets are the FTSE 100 (United Kingdom), CAC 40 (France), Dax 30 (Germany), Swiss Market Price (Switzerland), and S&P 500 Index (United States). Inflation rates are measured by the natural log difference of consumer price indices for the countries under investigation. All the rates are measured on a monthly basis, as dictated by the fact that consumer price indices are available only on a monthly basis.

In the meantime, employing monthly observations allows us to construct variables such as forward-exchange rates and short-term interest rates having the same maturity without experiencing a data overlap problem. Since stock indices for France and Switzerland are available only from late 1988 and the Basle Accord was effective at about the same time period, our empirical analysis is confined to the sample period from January 1989 through December 2001.[6] All data were taken from *Data Stream International.*

6.3.2. Evidence on the Parity Conditions

The goal of the empirical exercise in this section is to highlight the main features of each parity condition and to present the findings in a consistent fashion. As noted by Roll (1979), international parity conditions provide no specific guidance to the direction and extent of causation between relative returns and exchange rate changes. Placing the dependent and independent variables on each side of the test equation varies among different researchers. In this section, we shall keep the estimated equation consistent with the model forms expressed by Equations (6.5) through (6.7). In order to achieve a consistent estimator, procedures adopted by White (1980) and Newey and West (1987) have been used in estimating the following set of regressions:

uncovered interest rate parity:

$$r_t = \beta_0 + \beta_1\left(r_t^* + \Delta s_{t+1}\right) + \varepsilon_t, \qquad (6.14)$$

international stock return parity:

$$R_{m,t+1} = \beta_0 + \beta_1\left(R_{m,t+1}^* + \Delta s_{t+1}\right) + \varepsilon_{t+1}, \qquad (6.15)$$

and

purchasing power parity:

$$\Delta p_{t+1} = \beta_0 + \beta_1\left(\Delta p_{t+1}^* + \Delta s_{t+1}\right) + \varepsilon_{t+1}, \qquad (6.16)$$

where β_0 and β_1 are constant coefficients and ε_t is an error term. Since expectations are not directly measurable, we impose a rational expectations framework by using realizations of the variables as proxy.[7] Because our main concern is to examine a parity condition, a joint test to investigate the null hypothesis $(\beta_0\ \beta_1)' = (0\ 1)'$ will also be reported. If the null hypothesis cannot be rejected by the data, a parity condition holds. The estimates for three primary international-parity conditions are reported in Panels A, B, and C of Table 6.1.

Consistent with existing evidence (Solnik, 1982; Mishkin, 1984), none of the test equations gain much support from the data. The joint tests suggest that the null hypothesis of $(\beta_0\ \beta_1)' = (0\ 1)'$ is rejected uniformly. In particular, the estimated slopes of the interest rate parity in Panel A are negligible and statistically insignificant. These results, together with the low R-squares of the test equations, render no supportive evidence for the equality of the two exchange rate adjusted interest rates.

Table 6.1. Estimates of international parity conditions

Country	β_0	β_1	R^2	DW	Joint test

A. Uncovered Interest Rate Parity:

$r_t = \beta_0 + \beta_1(r_t^* + \Delta s_{t+1}) + \varepsilon_t$

Country	β_0	β_1	R^2	DW	Joint test
UK	0.0066***	0.001	0.000	0.010	1.521e+04
	(28.96)	(0.169)		(0.000)	
FR	0.0053***	−0.007	0.008	0.063	1.988e+04
	(27.56)	(0.923)		(0.000)	
GM	0.0046***	−0.007	0.012	0.029	3.044e+04
	(29.42)	(1.190)		(0.000)	
SW	0.0036***	−0.009	0.017	0.041	2.806e+04
	(19.07)	(1.510)		(0.000)	

B. International Stock Return Parity:

$R_{m,t+1} = \beta_0 + \beta_1(R_{m,t+1}^* + \Delta s_{t+1}) + \varepsilon_{t+1}$

Country	β_0	β_1	R^2	DW	Joint test
UK	−0.0001	0.625 ***	0.518	2.160	55.526
	(0.029)	(12.10)		(0.000)	
FR	−0.0001	0.685 ***	0.425	2.233	26.501
	(0.022)	(10.49)		(0.000)	
GM	0.0017	0.683 ***	0.360	2.183	16.139
	(0.395)	(7.837)		(0.000)	
SW	0.0036	0.652 ***	0.475	2.023	24.443
	(1.094)	(9.222)		(0.000)	

C. Purchasing Power Parity:

$\Delta p_{t+1} = \beta_0 + \beta_1(\Delta p_{t+1}^* + \Delta s_{t+1}) + \varepsilon_{t+1}$

Country	β_0	β_1	R^2	DW	Joint test
UK	0.0028***	0.020	0.014	1.492	5206.828
	(7.461)	(1.448)		(0.000)	
FR	0.0015***	0.008	0.014	1.674	3.553e+04
	(8.435)	(1.555)		(0.000)	
GM	0.0019***	0.013	0.017	1.577	1.495e+04
	(7.870)	(1.589)		(0.000)	
SW	0.0017***	0.008	0.007	1.729	1.608e+04
	(6.776)	(1.002)		(0.000)	

a. The *** indicates statistically significant difference from zero at the 1% level.

b. The numbers in parentheses are absolute values of the *t*-statistics.

c. DW denotes the Durbin-Watson statistic.

d. The joint test is to test $(\beta_0\ \beta_1)' = (0\ 1)'$; the joint test is the estimated statistic of χ^2 (2) distribution with 2 degrees of freedom and the numbers in parentheses are the significance levels.

The results for estimating the ISP are presented in Panel B. The estimated coefficients indicate that correlations with the U.S. market are positive and statistically significant.[8] The values of the coefficients vary within a very narrow range, from 0.625 to 0.685 across the different European markets, supporting the efficient aspect of co-movements of international stock returns. However, the test results are still unable to provide supporting evidence for the null hypothesis $((\beta_0\ \beta_1)' = (0\ 1)'$. The rejection of the null hypothesis implies the violation of ISP. This is understandable since, in addition to preference differences and possible asymmetrical information (Frankel and Schmukler, 2000), the index composition varies among the nations, and the underlying industries are subject to their inherent, different volatility and price/interest rate sensibility (Roll, 1992).

Panel C reports estimates of PPP relative to the United States. Again, the estimated slopes are far from unity. None of the R-squares exceed the 2 percent level. This result is very comparable to those reported by Krugman (1978), Roll (1979), Frenkel (1981), Solnik (1982), and Mishkin (1984), among others.[9] This finding is not surprising since our data sample period is relatively short, while most of the evidence in favor of the PPP employs much longer data spans. For example, Abuaf and Jorion (1990), Lothian and Taylor (1997b), Jorion and Sweeney (1996), Cheung and Lai (1993, 1998), Fleissig and Strauss (2000), and Baum et al. (2001) are able to find evidence of mean reversion in deviations from PPP.

The failure of PPP in the short run is perceivable, since in the very nature of price behavior commodity prices are relatively sticky and exchange rates behave more or less like asset prices. Thus, the change in exchange rates as they adjust to news appears to be more sensitive and effective than that of commodity prices. In addition, failure to achieve PPP in the short run may also result from variation in the composition of consumer price indices across different countries (Patel, 1990), differing productivity shocks (Fisher and Park, 1991), and measurement errors in prices from aggregation (Taylor, 1988; Cheung and Lai, 1993).[10]

6.4. Deviations from Parity Conditions and Risk

6.4.1. Sources of Deviations

The analysis in Section 6.2 conveys two important messages: international-parity conditions are inter-related and departure from parity conditions is commonly associated with real interest rate differentials and equity premium differentials. Although some earlier researchers (Korajczyk, 1985; Levine, 1989; Huang, 1990; Chiang, 1991; Korajczyk and Viallet, 1992) recognize these key elements, their studies merely focus on a single parity (Hodrick, 1987) or a smaller set of parity conditions (Mishkin, 1984; Marston, 1997); an explicit role of inter-national stock markets is excluded from their ana-lyses. The current study extends previous research by incorporating the linkage of stock markets into an integrated financial system. This research is bound to provide more insight into a multimarket analysis of international asset allocation, offering a broader spectrum of portfolio behavior in a general equilibrium framework.

To illustrate, assuming that expected changes in spot exchange rates can be predicted by a linear relation of the expected inflation rate differential, short-term interest rate differential, and expected national stock return differential as implied by the three parity conditions, we write:

$$\Delta s_{t+1}^e = \alpha(\Delta p_{t+1}^e - \Delta p_{t+1}^{*e}) + \eta(r_t - r_t^*) + \gamma(R_{m,t+1}^e - R_{m,t+1}^{*e}). \tag{6.17}$$

The arguments on the right side of Equation (6.17) are considered to be the key variables that affect international transactions involving a na-tion's balance of payments. In particular, the variable of the expected inflation differential dic-tates trade flows in a country's current account,[11] while the other two arguments govern capital flows involving bonds and stocks in the capital accounts. The weight of each component will be reflected, respectively, in the parameters α, η, and γ; the restriction $\alpha + \eta + \gamma = 1$ is constrained by the sum of components of the balance of pay-ments. Subtracting $(r_t - r_t^*)$ from both sides of

Equation (6.17) and rearranging the variables yields:[12, 13]

$$\Delta s_{t+1}^e - (r_t - r_t^*) = \gamma[(R_{m,t+1}^e - r_t) - (R_{m,t+1}^{*e} - r_t^*)] + \alpha[(\Delta p_{t+1}^e - r_t) - (\Delta p_{t+1}^{*e} - r_t^*)] \tag{6.18}$$

An important message emerging from Equation (6.18) is that the deviation from UIP is essentially due to the excess relative returns prevailing in stock and goods markets as compared with the risk-free rate in the bond markets. A study by Giovannini and Jorion (1987) finds evidence that foreign exchange-risk premiums are correlated with interest rates. In fact, the information from Equation (6.18) indicates that the sources of uncertainty arise from the stochastic nature of discount factors associated with stock returns and inflation rates relative to interest rates. Using Equations (6.9) and (6.10) and defining $\delta_{t+1}^e = \Delta s_{t+1}^e - (r_t - r_t^*)$, we obtain:

$$\delta_{t+1}^e = \gamma[(R_{m,t+1}^e - r_t) - (R_{m,t+1}^{*e} - r_t^*)] - \alpha(\bar{r}_{t+1}^e - \bar{r}_{t+1}^{*e}). \tag{6.19}$$

The *ex ante* excess depreciation of a national currency beyond its interest rate parity condition, where δ_{t+1}^e is positive, is seen to be associated with relatively higher risk in stock returns and/or infla-tion variations, reflected in a relatively higher equity premium and/or lower expected real inter-est rate differential. These parameters are the main factors that cause international capital flows. Thus, violations of UIP correspond to inter-national capital flows.

Comparing Equation (6.19) with existing litera-ture, it is easy to see that the real interest rate differential hypothesis proposed by Korajczyk (1985) is equivalent to requiring that $\gamma = 0$, while the equity premium differential hypothesis sug-gested by Chiang (1991) is to impose the restriction that $\alpha = 0$. Of course, the UIP holds when $\alpha = \gamma = 0$.

Next, let us consider the deviation of the ISP, defined as $\phi_{t+1}^e = \Delta s_{t+1}^e - (R_{m,t+1}^e - R_{m,t+1}^{*e})$. This expression can be further decomposed as:

$$\phi_{t+1}^e = [\Delta s_{t+1}^e - (r_t - r_t^*)] - [(R_{m,t+1}^e - r_t) - (R_{m,t+1}^{*e} - r_t^*)].$$

Using the information in Equation (6.18), we then derive:

$$\phi_{t+1}^e = -(1-\gamma)[(R_{m,t+1}^e - r_t) - (R_{m,t+1}^{*e} - r_t^*)] \\ - \alpha(\bar{r}_{t+1}^e - \bar{r}_{t+1}^{*e}). \tag{6.20}$$

Equation (6.20) indicates that the deviation of the ISP is attributable to the equity premium differential and real interest rate differential. By the same token, it can be shown that:

$$\theta_{t+1}^e = \gamma[(R_{m,t+1}^e - r_t) - (R_{m,t+1}^{*e} - r_t^*)] \\ + (1-\alpha)(\bar{r}_{t+1}^e - \bar{r}_{t+1}^{*e}), \tag{6.21}$$

where $\theta_{t+1}^e = \Delta s_{t+1}^e - (\Delta p_{t+1}^e - \Delta p_{t+1}^{*e})$, which denotes the *ex ante* value of the deviation of the relative PPP. By checking the right-hand side variables of Equation (6.19) through Equation (6.21), we observe that departures from parity conditions are all attributable to the same factors: the equity premium differential and the real interest rate differential.[14] This is equivalent to saying that the following conditions must be satisfied in order for these parity conditions to hold: expected real returns on bonds are equal across markets and expected excess returns in national equity markets are equal across trading countries. The emphasis on the real interest rate parity to explain the departure of the three parities has been well documented (Mishkin, 1984; Marston, 1997). However, our analysis identifies an additional factor, the equity premium differential, in interpreting the deviations of the three parities.

Another feature of our model is that deviations from parity conditions for the three markets are not independent. The interdependency among them is rooted essentially in the interdependency of financial markets; dynamic adjustments are sensitive to differences in relative asset returns in an integrated and united financial system. From a policy point of view, a parametric change in interest rates made by monetary authorities will create a gap in both the equity premium differential and the real interest rate differential. These would cause investors to reallocate their portfolios, thereby in-

ducing capital and trade flows, and hence disturbing the parity conditions.[15]

6.4.2. Evidence for Deviations from Parity Conditions

In this section, we present evidence for estimating deviations from the three international parity conditions. The estimated equation is written in the following regression form:

$$y_{t+1} = \beta_0 + \beta_1[(R_{m,t+1} - r_t) - (R_{m,t+1}^* - r_t^*)] \\ + \beta_2(\bar{r}_{t+1} - \bar{r}_{t+1}^*) + \varepsilon_{t+1}, \tag{6.22}$$

where y_{t+1} applies to δ_{t+1}, ϕ_{t+1}, or θ_{t+1}; β_0 is an intercept term; β_1 and β_2 are constant parameters; and ε_{t+1} is the random error term. The restrictions of β_1 and β_2 for each parity condition follow the coefficients contained in Equation (6.19) through Equation (6.21).

Utilizing the same set of data presented in Section 6.2.2, the consistent estimates for the four European markets are reported in Table 6.2. As the theory predicts, all the estimated coefficients have the anticipated signs and are statistically significant. The only exception is the variable of the real interest rate differential in PPP for the United Kingdom, where the coefficient is not significant. In terms of explanatory power, the test equations perform reasonably well. The average values of R^2 are: 10 percent, 13 percent, and 56 percent for PPP, UIP, and ISP conditions, respectively. The Durbin–Watson statistics in Table 6.2 do not indicate first-order serial correlation. Taking these statistics together, the null hypothesis that deviations from parity conditions are independent of the equity premium differential and real interest rate differential is decisively rejected.

The results also show that, as the theory predicts, the estimated coefficient of the real interest rate differential, β_2, produces an identical estimated value for both the UIP and ISP equations; it also holds true for the estimated coefficient of the equity premium differential, β_1, in the UIP and PPP equations. The evidence thus suggests that

Table 6.2. Estimates of deviations from parity conditions

Country	β_0	β_1	β_2	R^2	DW
A. Deviation from the Uncovered Interest-Rate Parity					
UK	0.0023	0.297***	−1.088**	0.125	1.838
	(1.024)	(2.993)	(2.424)		
GM	0.0026	0.131***	−2.666***	0.124	1.871
	(1.101)	(2.901)	(3.700)		
FR	0.0048**	0.174***	−2.459***	0.138	2.014
	(1.975)	(3.542)	(3.042)		
SW	0.0002	0.232***	−2.709***	0.145	1.908
	(0.069)	(3.642)	(3.520)		
B. Deviation from the International Stock-Return Parity					
UK	0.0023	−0.703***	−1.088**	0.427	1.838
	(0.960)	(6.328)	(2.336)		
GM	0.0026	−0.869***	−2.666***	0.691	1.871
	(1.085)	(18.28)	(3.729)		
FR	0.0048**	−0.826***	−2.455***	0.607	2.014
	(2.075)	(15.52)	(2.975)		
SW	0.0002	−0.768***	−2.709***	0.503	1.908
	(0.067)	(11.57)	(3.494)		
C. Deviation from the Relative Purchasing-Power Parity					
UK	0.0023	0.297***	−0.088	0.106	1.838
	(1.000)	(2.993)	(0.195)		
GM	0.0026	0.131***	−1.666**	0.079	1.871
	(1.064)	(2.901)	(2.312)		
FR	0.0047**	0.174***	−1.455*	0.096	2.014
	(1.975)	(3.542)	(1.803)		
SW	0.0002	0.232***	−1.709**	0.106	1.908
	(0.063)	(3.642)	(2.221)		

a. Sample period: January 1989–October 2001.
b. Numbers in parentheses are absolute value of the t-statistics. The ***, **, and * indicate statistically significant difference from zero at the 1%, 5%, and 10% levels for the t-ratios, respectively.*
c. DW denotes the Durbin-Watson statistic.

deviations for the three parity conditions are not only interdependent, but also share the same set of information. The results are consistent with the evidence provided by Mishkin (1984) and Marston (1997). However, the information being used in our empirical study is derived directly from the theory. A special feature of this study is that, in addition to real interest rate differentials, depar-

tures from parity conditions are found to be driven by equity premium differentials. It can be concluded that the effect of the risk premium not only presents in pricing domestic equity risk, but is also used in pricing relative risk, and thus is dictating international capital flows.

6.5. Conclusion

This study presents a consistent market behavior framework to establish three parity conditions in bond, stock, and goods markets. Due to the existence of inflation risk and exchange rate risk, earlier studies recognize the significance of a real interest rate differential as a key element in explaining deviations of interest rate parity or PPP. However, the real interest rate differential does not seem adequate to explain capital movements involving the trading of international stocks. On the other hand, the equity premium differential hypothesis highlights the relative risk factor in equity markets; however, inflation rate uncertainty has been ignored. In the current model, both the real interest rate differential and the equity premium differential are used to explain the departures. The statistical results derived from the four European markets relative to the United States validate our argument. The evidence further suggests that deviations from the three international parity conditions are driven by common factors as represented by the equity premium differentials and real interest rate differentials. The intriguing informational content of these differentials is that they reflect not only relative risk across countries, but also relative risk as compared with fixed-income investment.

Appendix

This Appendix provides additional empirical evidence on the popular parity conditions prevailing in international markets. The regression models are:

A. Efficient Interest Rate Parity:
$$s_{t+1} - (r_t - r_t^*) = \beta_0 + \beta_1 s_t + \varepsilon_{t+1}$$

B. Efficient International Stock Parity:

$$s_{t+1} - \left(R_{m,t+1} - R^*_{m,t+1}\right) = \beta_0 + \beta_1 s_t + \varepsilon_{t+1}$$

C. Efficient Purchasing Power Parity:

$$s_{t+1} - \left(\Delta p_{t+1} - \Delta p^*_{t+1}\right) = \beta_0 + \beta_1 s_t + \varepsilon_{t+1}$$

D. International Fama Parity:

$$\left(\Delta p_{t+1} - \Delta p^*_{t+1}\right) = \beta_0 + \beta_1 \left(r_t - r^*_t\right) + \varepsilon_{t+1}$$

E. Real Interest Rate Parity:

$$\bar{r}_{t+1} = \beta_0 + \beta_1 \bar{r}^*_{t+1} + \varepsilon_{t+1}$$

F. Equity Premium Parity:

$$R_{m,t+1} - r_t = \beta_0 + \beta_1 \left(R^*_{m,t+1} - r^*_t\right) + \varepsilon_{t+1}$$

G. Covered Interest Rate Parity:

$$r_t - r^*_t = \beta_0 + \beta_1 (f_t - s_t) + \varepsilon_t$$

H. Unbiased Forward-Rate Hypothesis I:

$$f_t - s_{t+1} = \beta_0 + \beta_1 (f_t - s_t) + \varepsilon_{t+1}$$

I. Unbiased Forward-Rate Hypothesis II:

$$s_{t+1} - s_t = \beta'_0 + \beta'_1 (f_t - s_t) + \varepsilon'_{t+1}$$

Models A through C are efficient versions of the UIP, ISP, and PPP proposed by Roll (1979). An efficient market implies that $\beta_0 = 0$ and $\beta_1 = 1$. The evidence presented in Panels A, B, and C of Table 6.3 is quite consistent with the efficient nature of the spot exchange rate, suggesting that all

Table 6.3. Estimates of international parity conditions

Country	β_0	β_1	R^2	DW	Joint Test
A. Efficient Interest-Rate Parity:					
$s_{t+1} - (r_t - r^*_t) = \beta_0 + \beta_1 s_t + \varepsilon_{t+1}$					
UK	−0.0315	0.933***	0.858	1.692	2.556
	(1.553)	(20.87)			(0.279)
FR	0.0452	0.975***	0.934	1.848	1.558
	(1.128)	(43.14)			(0.459)
GM	0.0123	0.980***	0.941	1.774	1.153
	(1.027)	(45.83)			(0.562)
SW	0.0162	0.958***	0.993	1.721	3.065
	(1.678)	(40.19)			(0.216)
B. Efficient International-Stock Parity:					
$s_{t+1} - \left(R_{m,t+1} - R^*_{m,t+1}\right) = \beta_0 + \beta_1 s_t + \varepsilon_{t+1}$					
UK	−0.0281	0.943***	0.857	1.716	3.100
	(1.359)	(20.68)			(0.212)
FR	0.0316	0.982***	0.932	1.800	0.594
	(0.770)	(42.42)			(0.743)
GM	0.0097	0.984***	0.939	1.747	0.667
	(0.800)	(45.37)			(0.716)

Table 6.3. (*Continued*)

Country	β_0	β_1	R^2	DW	Joint Test
SW	0.0167	0.958***	0.912	1.679	3.026
	(1.706)	(39.35)			(0.220)
C. Efficient Purchasing Power Parity:					
$s_{t+1} - \left(\Delta p_{t+1} - \Delta p^*_{t+1}\right) = \beta_0 + \beta_1 s_t + \varepsilon_{t+1}$					
UK	−0.0357**	0.918***	0.789	2.095	6.127
	(2.221)	(26.52)			(0.047)
FR	0.1003*	0.945***	0.853	2.317	3.677
	(1.833)	(30.59)			(0.159)
GM	0.0226	0.961***	0.841	2.207	1.879
	(1.365)	(31.36)			(0.391)
SW	0.0160	0.954***	0.857	2.088	1.823
	(1.264)	(28.22)			(0.402)
D. International Fama Parity:					
$\left(\Delta p_{t+1} - \Delta p^*_{t+1}\right) = \beta_0 + \beta_1 \left(r_t - r^*_t\right) + \varepsilon_{t+1}$					
UK	−0.0003	0.339	0.021	1.898	20.754
	(0.587)	(1.517)			(0.000)
FR	−0.0009***	0.070	0.007	2.103	335.354
	(5.056)	(1.055)			(0.000)
GM	−0.0005**	0.384***	0.081	1.760	25.218
	(2.040)	(3.106)			(0.000)
SW	−0.0004	0.311***	0.058	2.057	57.229
	(1.357)	(3.015)			(0.000)
E. Real Interest-Rate Parity:					
$\bar{r}_{r+1} = \beta_0 + \beta_1 \bar{r}^*_{t+1} + \varepsilon_{t+1}$					
UK	0.0032***	0.249	0.013	1.660	28.741
	(5.267)	(1.478)			(0.000)
FR	0.0032***	0.217**	0.028	1.014	91.299
	(9.547)	(2.092)			(0.000)
GM	0.0021***	0.253**	0.032	1.570	42.080
	(5.404)	(2.192)			(0.000)
SW	0.0012***	0.263***	0.035	1.869	57.168
	(3.958)	(2.672)			(0.000)
F. Equity-Premium Parity:					
$R_{m,t+1} - r_t = \beta_0 + \beta_1 \left(R^*_{m,t+1} - r^*_t\right) + \varepsilon_{t+1}$					
UK	−0.0038***	0.793***	0.525	2.028	32.905
	(2.579)	(13.78)			(0.000)
FR	−0.0024	0.907***	0.401	2.092	2.010
	(0.667)	(10.75)			(0.366)
GM	−0.0000	0.921***	0.357	2.051	0.495
	(0.001)	(7.827)			(0.781)
SW	0.0021	0.937***	0.477	1.957	0.639
	(0.650)	(9.600)			(0.726)
G. Covered Interest Rate Parity:					
$r_t - r^*_t = \beta_0 + \beta_1 (f_t - s_t) + \varepsilon_t$					
UK	0.0002	1.018***	0.810	1.847	11.045
	(1.300)	(28.52)			(0.004)
FR	0.0001	1.025***	0.887	2.015	8.607
	(0.997)	(56.17)			(0.014)

Table 6.3. (*Continued*)

Country	β_0	β_1	R^2	DW	Joint Test
GM	0.0000	1.004***	0.854	2.001	0.075
	(0.161)	(28.24)			(0.963)
SW	0.0000	0.988***	0.830	1.679	0.144
	(0.124)	(25.63)			(0.931)

H. Unbiased Forward-Rate Hypothesis I:
$f_t - s_{t+1} = \beta_0 + \beta_1(f_t - s_t) + \varepsilon_{t+1}$

Country	β_0	β_1	R^2	DW	Joint Test
UK	0.0007	0.510	0.001	1.737	0.127
	(0.217)	(0.369)			(0.938)
FR	0.0007	1.057	0.008	1.902	0.065
	(0.219)	(0.875)			(0.968)
GM	0.0005	1.210	0.010	1.818	0.064
	(0.184)	(1.007)			(0.969)
SW	0.0017	2.182*	0.026	1.742	6.455
	(0.486)	(1.704)			(0.040)

I. Unbiased Forward-Rate Hypothesis II:
$s_{t+1} - s_t = \beta_0' + \beta_1'(f_t - s_t) + \varepsilon_{t+1}$

Country	β_0	β_1	R^2	DW	Joint Test
UK	−0.0007	0.490	0.001	1.737	0.881
	(0.287)	(0.372)			(0.644)
FR	−0.0007	−0.057	0.000	1.902	1.074
	(0.219)	(0.047)			(0.584)
GM	−0.0005	−0.210	0.000	1.818	1.042
	(0.184)	(0.175)			(0.594)
SW	−0.0017	−1.182	0.008	1.742	2.942
	(0.486)	(0.923)			(0.230)

a. The numbers in parentheses are absolute values of the *t*-statistics.
b. The ***, **, and *indicate statistically significant difference from zero at the 1%, 5%, and 10% levels for the *t*-ratios, respectively.
c. DW denotes the Durbin-Watson statistic.
d. The joint test is to test $(\beta_0\ \beta_1)' = (0\ 1)'$; the joint test is the statistics of the χ^2 (2) distribution with 2 degrees of freedom and the numbers in parentheses are the significance levels.

information concerning future exchange rate adjusted return differentials is incorporated into the current spot exchange rate. The supportive evidence holds true for all three parity conditions. However, it should be pointed out that specifying the model in this form tends to lead to not rejecting the efficient-market hypothesis. In particular, Roll's specification is more or less to test spot exchange rate efficiency rather than to test parity conditions. If we check the estimated equations, the series of return differentials is stationary and its magnitude is rather small as compared

with the level of exchange rates. As a result, the dominance of the lagged exchange rate variable in the test equation gives rise to a high R-square.

Next let us consider the efficient-market hypothesis for U.S. Treasury bills. Fama (1975) argues that the one-month nominal interest rate can be viewed as a predictor of the inflation rate. Applying this notion in international markets implies that the nominal interest rate differential can be used to predict the inflation rate differential. The evidence in Panel D does provide some predictive evidence for the German and Swiss markets. However, the efficient-market hypothesis is rejected in the international context. This also casts doubt on the validity of real interest rate parity. The results from Panel E confirm this point; the correlations of real interest rates for three of the four markets are positive and statistically significant, but the parity condition still fails. The reasons advanced by Koraczyk (1985) are the existence of risk premiums and market imperfections.

In the text as well as in the finance literature, we are concerned with the relationship between stock equity premiums. The evidence derived from Panel F indicates that the correlation for each country is highly significant, although we are unable to find strong support for the parity condition. If we view the U.S. equity premium as a proxy for the world-portfolio premium, the slope coefficient for each estimated equation can be treated virtually as a beta coefficient in light of the CAPM framework.[16]

Panel G contains the results for testing covered interest rate parity. Since all the variables in this equation are directly observable and readily assessed by economic agents, the estimated equation is closest to the parity condition. It is generally recognized that arbitrage profit derived from this equation is very negligible, if there is any. Thus, any gap in this equation must reflect country risk (Frankel and MacArthur, 1988), transaction costs (Fratianni and Wakeman, 1982), or simply data errors.

The forward premium (or discount) has been commonly used to predict foreign-exchange risk premiums as well as currency depreciation as denoted by the equations in Panels H and I. The unbiasedness hypothesis in Panel H requires that $\beta_0 = \beta_1 = 0$; however, the unbiasedness hypothesis in Panel I implies that $\beta_0' = 0$ and $\beta_1' = 1$ (Hansen and Hodrick, 1980; Cornell, 1989; Bekaert and Hodrick, 1993). Fama (1984) notes the complementarity of the regressions in Panels H and I and suggests that $\beta_0 = -\beta_0'$, that $\beta_1 = 1 - \beta_1'$, and that $\varepsilon_{t+1} = -\varepsilon_{t+1}'$. Consistent with the existing literature, the evidence presented in Panel H and Panel I apparently rejects the unbiasedness hypothesis.[17] However, the complementary nature of the coefficients appears consistent with Fama's argument. The puzzle entailed in this set of equations is that the estimated slope in the Panel I equation is typically negative. This interpretation has been attributable to risk premium (Fama, 1984; Giovannini and Jorion, 1987; Hodrick, 1987; Mark, 1988; and Jiang and Chiang, 2000), forecast errors (Froot and Thaler, 1990), and regime shifting (Chiang, 1988; Bekaert and Hodrick, 1993).

NOTES

1. Other parity conditions, including an unbiased forward-rate hypothesis, covered interest rate parity, and real interest rate parity will be discussed at a later point. A formal derivation of these parity conditions can be achieved by employing a consumption-based approach in the Lucas framework (Lucas, 1982; Roll and Solnik, 1979; Chiang and Trinidad, 1997; Cochrane, 2001).

2. In order to simplify the analysis, we ignore the coupon payment (c_{t+1}) to the bond and the dividend payment (d_{t+1}) to the stock by assuming $c_{t+1} = d_{t+1} = 0$. Different tax effects are also abstracted from the calculations. We can link the current model to a Lucas – Cochrane framework by setting $pv_{jt} = p_t$. Thus, $p_t = E(m_{t+1}x_{t+1})$, where p_t is the current asset price; m_{t+1} is the stochastic discount factor; and x_{t+1} is the payoff at time $t + 1$. By setting $x_{t+1} = p_{t+1}$, we have:

$$p_t = \frac{1}{R_{t+1}^e} E_t(p_{t+1}).$$

3. An equilibrium relationship between asset returns based on a continuous-time model can be found in Stulz (1981).

4. Frankel and MacArthur (1988) further decompose UIP into two parts: the covered interest differential and the currency risk premium. Thus, Equation (6.11) becomes:

$$\bar{r}_{t+1}^e - \bar{r}_{t+1}^{*e} = \left[(r_t - r_t^*) - (f_t - s_t)\right] + \left[(f_t - s_t) - \Delta s_{t+1}^e\right] + \left[\Delta s_{t+1}^e - \left(\Delta p_{t+1}^e - \Delta p_{t+1}^{*e}\right)\right].$$

The first term on the right-hand side of this expression is a deviation of the covered interest rate, which is considered a country premium; the second term is the currency risk premium; and the third term is the change in the real exchange rate. Branson (1988) interprets these three components as the measure of a lack of integration of the bond, currency, and goods markets, respectively.

5. A systematic relationship between stock returns and inflation can be found in Stulz's study (1986).

6. The Basle Accord was a landmark regulatory agreement affecting international banking. The agreement was reached on July 12, 1988. Its goals were to reduce the risk of the international banking system, and to minimize competitive inequality due to differences among national banking and capital regulations (Wagster, 1996).

7. Using realizations to proxy expectations could generate an error-in-the-variables problem. In fact, the formation of expectations has long been a challenging issue in empirical estimations. Expectations range from rational expectations, distributed lag expectations, adaptive expectations, regressive expectations, and random walk to expert expectations based on survey data (Frankel and Froot, 1987).

8. In the finance literature, expected returns are related to risk, which can be modeled by ARCH or GARCH in mean (Baillie and Bollerslev, 1990). Also, many recent studies incorporate conditional variance and covariance into various models to examine the relationship between excess returns and risk (Domowitz and Hakkio, 1985; Hodrick, 1987; Bekaert and Hodrick, 1993; Hu, 1997; De Santis and Gerard, 1998; Jiang and Chiang, 2000; Cochrane, 2001). In this chapter, we do not intend to explore these types of models.

9. Our test here follows the traditional approach by focusing on examining whether the slope coefficient differs significantly from unity. Rogoff (1996) provides a good review. Recent research pays particular attention to the stochastic properties of dynamics of adjustments toward PPP, and employs more powerful statistical techniques. Cheung and Lai (1993, 1998), Jorion and Sweeney (1996), Lothian and

Taylor (1997b), and Baum et al. (2001) present evidence in favor of PPP.

10. Roll's efficient estimations and other parity conditions are provided in the Appendix.

11. Expected inflation rate differentials can also affect the capital account through their effects on real interest rate differentials (Frankel, 1979).

12. As mentioned earlier, Frankel and MacArthur (1988) decomposed UIP into two parts: the covered-interest differential and the currency risk premium, while Gokey (1994) decomposed UIP into a real interest rate differential and an *ex ante* deviation from relative PPP as:

$$\Delta s_{t+1} - \left(r_t - r_t^*\right) = \left[\Delta s_{t+1}^e - \left(\Delta p_{t+1}^e - p_{t+1}^{*e}\right)\right] + \left[\bar{r}_{t+1}^{*e} - \bar{r}_{t+1}^e\right].$$

Basically, Frankel and MacArthur's decomposition (1988) is achieved by subtracting and adding the forward premium, $(f_t - s_t)$, into the UIP as we showed in Note 4, while Gokey's decomposition (1994) is obtained by subtracting and adding the expected inflation rate differential, $(\Delta p_{t+1}^e - \Delta p_{t+1}^{*e})$, into the equation.

13. The long-term interest rate differential can also be added to the right side of Equation (6.17) as an independent argument. As a result, difference in long – short rate spreads will be shown on the right side of Equation (6.18) to capture the information of relative liquidity risk, as implied by the expectations hypothesis of the term-structure of interest rates.

14. Using Equations (6.19) through (6.21), we obtain the following two equations as:

$$\bar{r}_{t+1}^e - \bar{r}_{t+1}^{*e} = \theta_{t+1}^e - \delta_{t+1}^e, \text{ and}$$

$$\left(R_{m,t+1}^e - r_t\right) - \left(R_{m,t+1}^{*e} - r_t^*\right) = \delta_{t+1}^e - \phi_{t+1}^e.$$

15. A precise process and speed of adjustment to restore a new equilibrium can be very complicated, and so cannot be answered without having a complete specification of the model, which is beyond the scope of the current study.

16. Cumby (1990) tests whether real stock returns from four countries are consistent with consumption-based models of international asset pricing. The hypothesis is rejected by including a sample that began in 1974. However, the null cannot be rejected when only the 1980s are considered.

17. Estimates of the unbiasedness hypothesis are based on the sample period from 1989.1 to 1998.12 due to unavailability of FR, GM, and SW forward markets and the switch to the euro starting in January 1999.

REFERENCES

Albuquerque, R., Bauer, G., and Schneider, M. (2004). "International equity flows and returns: A quantitative equilibrium approach." Working Paper, National Bureau of Economic Research.

Abuaf, N. and Jorion, P. (1990). "Purchasing power parity in the long run." *Journal of Finance*, 45: 157–174.

Baillie, R.T. and Bollerslev, T. (1990). "A multivariate generalized ARCH approach to modeling risk premia in forward foreign exchange rate markets." *Journal of International Money and Finance*, 9: 309–324.

Baum, C.F., Barkoulas, J.T. and Caglayan, M. (2001). "Nonlinear adjustment to purchasing power parity in the post-Bretton Woods era." *Journal of International Money and Finance*, 20: 379–399.

Bekaert, G. and Hodrick, R.J. (1993). "On biases in the measurement of foreign exchange risk premiums." *Journal of International Money and Finance*, 12: 115–138.

Branson, W.H. (1988). "Comments on political vs. currency premia in international real interest differentials: a study of forward rates for 24 countries." by J.A. Frankel and A.T. MacArthur. *European Economic Review*, 32: 1083–1114.

Campbell, J.Y. (1987). "Stock returns and the term structure." *Journal of Financial Economics*, 18: 373–399.

Cheung, Y.W. and Lai, K.S. (1993). "Long-run purchasing power parity during the recent float." *Journal of International Economics*, 34: 181–192.

Cheung, Y.W. and Lai, K.S. (1998). "Parity reversion in real exchange rates during the post-Bretton Woods period." *Journal of International Money and Finance*, 17: 597–614.

Chiang, T.C. (1988). "The forward rate as a predictor of the future spot rate – a stochastic coefficient approach." *Journal of Money, Credit and Banking*, 20: 210–232.

Chiang, T.C. (1991). " International asset pricing and equity market risk." *Journal of International Money and Finance*, 10: 349–364.

Chiang, T.C. and Trinidad, J. (1997). "Risk and international parity conditions: a synthesis from consumption-based models." *International Economic Journal*, 11: 73–101.

Cochrane, J.H. (2001). *Asset Pricing*. Princeton and Oxford: Princeton University Press.

Cornell, B. (1989). "The impact of data errors on measurement of the foreign exchange risk premium." *Journal of International Money and Finance*, 8: 147–157.

Cumby, R. (1990). "Consumption risk and international equity returns: some empirical evidence." *Journal of International Money and Finance*, 9: 182–192.

De Santis, G. and Gerard, B. (1998). "How big is the premium for currency risk?" *Journal of Financial Economics*, 49: 375–412.

Domowitz, I. and Hakkio, C.S. (1985). "Conditional variance and the risk premium in the foreign exchange market." *Journal of International Economics*, 19: 47–66.

Engel, C. (1996). "The forward discount anomaly and the risk premium: a survey of recent evidence." *Journal of Empirical Finance*, 3: 123–192.

Fama, E.F. (1975). "Short-term interest rates as predictors of inflation." *American Economic Review*, 65: 269–282.

Fama, E.F. (1984). "Forward and spot exchange rates." *Journal of Monetary Economics*, 14: 319–338.

Fisher, E. and Park, J. (1991). "Testing purchasing power parity under the null hypothesis of cointegration." *Economic Journal*, 101: 1476–1484.

Fleissig, A.R. and Strauss, J. (2000). "Panel unit root tests of purchasing power parity for price indices." *Journal of International Money and Finance*, 19: 489–506.

Frankel, J.A. (1979). "On the mark: a theory of floating exchange rates based on real interest differential." *American Economic Review*, 69: 610–622.

Frankel, J.A. and Froot, K.A. (1987). "Using survey data to test standard propositions regarding exchange rate expectations." *American Economic Review*, 77: 133–153.

Frankel, J.A. and MacArthur, A.T. (1988). "Political vs. currency premia in international real interest differentials: a study of forward rates for 24 countries." European Economic Review, *32: 1083–1114.*

Frankel, J.A. and Schmukler, A.L. (2000). "Country funds and asymmetric information." *International Journal of Finance and economics*, 5: 177–195.

Fratianni, M. and Wakeman, L.M. (1982). "The law of one price in the Eurocurrency market." *Journal of International Money and Finance*, 3: 307–323.

Frenkel, J.A. (1981). "The collapse of purchasing power parities during the 1970s." *European Economic Review*, 16: 145–165.

Froot, K.A. and Thaler, R.H. (1990). "Anomalies: foreign exchange." *Journal of Economic Perspective*, 4: 179–192.

Giovannini, A. and Jorion P. (1987). "Interest rates and risk premia in the stock market and in the foreign exchange market." *Journal of International Money and Finance*, 6: 107–124.

Gokey, T.C. (1994). "What explains the risk premium in foreign exchange returns." *Journal of International Money and Finance*, 13: 729–738.

Hansen, L.P. and Hodrick, R.J. (1980). " Forward exchange rates as optimal predictors of future spot rates: an econometric analysis." *Journal of Political Economy*, 88: 829–853.

Hodrick, R.J. (1987). *The Empirical Evidence on the Efficiency of Forward and Futures Foreign Exchange Markets*. New York: Harwood Academic.

Hu, X. (1997). "Macroeconomic uncertainty and the risk premium in the foreign exchange market." *International Journal of Finance and Finance*, 16: 699–718.

Huang, R.D. (1990). "Risk and parity in purchasing power." *Journal of Money, Credit and Banking*, 22: 338–356.

Jiang, C. and Chiang, T.C. (2000). "Do foreign exchange risk premiums relate to the volatility in the foreign exchange and equity markets?" *Applied Financial Economics*, 10: 95–104.

Jorian, P. and Sweeney, R.J. (1996). "Mean reversion in real exchange rates." *International Journal of Finance and Economics*, 15: 535–550.

Korajczyk, R.A. (1985). "The pricing of forward contracts for foreign exchange." *Journal of Political Economy*, 93: 346–368.

Korajczyk, R.A. and Viallet, C.J. (1992). "Equity risk premia and the pricing of foreign exchange risk." *Journal of International Economics*, 33: 199–220.

Krugman, P. (1978). "Purchasing power parity and exchange rate, another look at the evidence." *Journal of International Economics*, 8: 397–407.

Levine, R. (1989). "The pricing of forward exchange rates." *Journal of International Money and Finance*, 8: 163–180.

Lothian, J.R. and Taylor, M.P. (1997a). "The recent float from the perspective of the past two centuries." *Journal of Political Economy*, 104: 488–509.

Lothian, J.R. and Taylor, M.P. (1997b). "Real exchange rate behavior." *Journal of International Money and Finance*, 16: 945–954.

Lucas, R.E., Jr. (1982). "Interest rates and currency prices in a two-country world." *Journal of Monetary Economics*, 10: 335–360.

Mark, N.C. (1988). "Time-varying betas and risk premia in the pricing of forward foreign exchange contracts." *Journal of Financial Economics*, 22: 335–354.

Marston, R.C. (1997). "Tests of three parity conditions: distinguishing risk premia and systematic forecast errors." *Journal of International Money and Finance*, 16: 285–303.

Mishkin, F.S. (1984). "Are real interest rates equal across countries: an empirical investigation of international parity conditions." *Journal of Finance*, 39: 1345–1357.

Newey, W.K. and West, K.D. (1987). "A simple, positive semi-definite, heteroskedasticity and autocorrelation consistent covariance matrix." *Econometrica*, 55: 703–708.

Patel, J. (1990). "Purchasing power parity as a long run relation." *Journal of Applied Econometrics*, 5: 367–379.

Rogoff, K. (1996). "The purchasing power parity puzzle." *Journal of Economic Literature*, 34: 647–668.

Roll, R. (1979). "Violations of purchasing power parity and their implications for efficient international commodity markets," in M. Sarnat and G.P. Szego (eds.) *International Finance and Trade*. Cambridge, MA: Ballinger.

Roll, R. and Solnik, B. (1979). "On some parity conditions encountered frequently in international economics." *Journal of Macroeconomics*, 1: 267–283.

Roll, R. (1992). "Industrial structure and the comparative behavior of international stock market indexes." *Journal of Finance*, 47: 3–41.

Solnik, B. (1978). "International parity conditions and exchange risk." *Journal of Banking and Finance*, 2: 281–293.

Solnik, B. (1982). "An empirical investigation of the determinants of national interest rate differences." *Journal of International Money and Finance*, 3: 333–339.

Stulz, R.M. (1981). "A model of international asset pricing." *Journal of Financial Economics*, 9: 383–406.

Stulz, R.M. (1986). "Asset pricing and expected inflation." *Journal of Finance*, 41: 209–223.

Taylor, M. (1988). "An empirical examination of long run purchasing power parity using cointegration techniques." *Applied Economics*, 20: 1369–1381.

Wagster, J.D. (1996). "Impact of the 1988 Basle Accord on international banks." *Journal of Finance*, 51: 1321–1346.

White, H. (1980). "A heteroscedasticity–consistent covariance matrix estimator and a direct test for heteroscedasticity." *Econometrica*, 48: 55–68.

Chapter 7

TREASURY INFLATION-INDEXED SECURITIES

QUENTIN C. CHU, *The University of Memphis, USA*
DEBORAH N. PITTMAN, *Rhodes College, USA*

Abstract

In January 1997, the U.S. Treasury began to issue inflation-indexed securities (TIIS). The new Treasury security protects investors from inflation by linking the principal and coupon payments to the Consumer Price Index (CPI). This paper discusses the background of issuing TIIS and reviews their unique characteristics.

Keywords: treasury inflation-indexed securities; consumer price index; real interest rate; inflation risk premium; phantom income; reference CPI; dutch auction; competitive bidders; noncompetitive bidders; bid-to-cover ratio; Series-I bonds.

Eleven issues of Treasury inflation-indexed securities (TIIS) have been traded in the U.S. market as of December 2003. Inflation-indexed securities are intended to protect investors from inflation by preserving purchasing power. By linking value to the Consumer Price Index (CPI), TIIS provide investors with a "real" rate of return. This security can be viewed as one of the safest financial assets due to its minimal exposure to default risk and uncertain inflation.

The fundamental notion behind inflation protection is to preserve the purchasing power of money. Today, inflation protection may be accomplished by linking investment principal to some form of a price index, such as the Consumer Price Index (CPI) in the United States, Canada, the United Kingdom, and Iceland; the Wholesale Price Index (WPI) in Finland, Brazil, and Argentina; and equities and gold in France.

In essence, investors purchasing inflation-indexed securities are storing a basket of goods for future consumption. Fifteen countries, including the United States have issued inflation-indexed securities, starting from the 1940s.[1] Some of the countries had extremely high inflation, such as Mexico and Brazil (114.8 percent and 69.2 percent in the year prior to the introduction of inflation-indexed securities), and others had moderate inflation like Sweden and New Zealand (4.4 percent and 2.8 percent).

The United Kingdom. has the largest and oldest market for inflation-indexed securities. As of 1997, there were £55 billion index-linked gilts outstanding, constituting about 20 percent of all government bonds in the United Kingdom. The United States is the most recent country to issue inflation-indexed securities to the public. The treasury announced its intention to issue inflation-indexed bonds on May 16, 1996. The first U.S. Treasury inflation-indexed securities were $7 billion of 10-year notes issued in January 1997.

There are many motivations for the issue of inflation-indexed securities. First, governments can reduce public financing costs through reducing the interest paid on public debt by the amount of an inflation risk premium. Rates on Treasury securities are usually taken to represent the nominal risk-free rate, which consists of the real rate plus expected inflation and an inflation risk premium. By linking value to the price index, inflation-indexed securities provide investors with a real rate of interest. This return is guaranteed, whatever the course of inflation. When there is no risk of inflation, the inflation risk premium is reduced, if not eliminated completely. Benninga and Protopapadakis (1983) revised the Fisher equation to incorporate an inflation risk premium.

Second, the issue of inflation-indexed securities is an indication of a government's intention to fight inflation. A government can keep inflation low through its fiscal and monetary policies. According to the Employment Act of 1946, one of the four primary goals of the U.S. federal government is to stabilize prices through a low-inflation rate. Inflation-indexed securities provide a way for the public to evaluate the government's performance in controlling inflation. For a constant level of expected inflation, the wider the yield spread between nominal and real bonds, the higher the inflation risk premium, and presumably lower the public's confidence in the monetary authorities.

Moreover, a government promises investors a real rate of return through the issue of inflation-indexed securities. Any loss of purchasing power due to inflation, which investors experience during the investment period, will be offset by inflation-adjusted coupon payments and principal. In an environment with high inflation, the government's borrowing costs will be high. Reducing borrowing costs provides an incentive for a government to control inflation. The willingness of the government to bear this risk shows its determination to fight inflation.

Inflation-indexed securities also provide a direct measure of expected real interest rates that may help policymakers make economic decisions. According to economic theory, most savings, consumption, and investment decisions depend critically on the expected real rate of interest, the interest rate one earns after adjusting the nominal interest rate for the expected rate of in-flation. Real interest rates measure the real growth rate of the economy and the supply and demand for capital in the market.

Before the trading of inflation-indexed securities, there was no security in the United States, which was offering coupon and principal payments linked to inflation, and therefore enabling measurement of the expected real rate. Empirical studies testing the relationship between expected real rates and other macroeconomic variables have relied instead on indirect measures of the expected real rate such as *ex post* real rates estimated by subtracting actual inflation from realized nominal holding-period returns (Pennachi, 1991). Inflation-indexed securities permit the direct study of the real interest rate. Wilcox (1998) includes this as one benefit, which has motivated the Treasury to issue these new securities.

Finally, inflation-indexed securities offer an alternative financial vehicle for portfolio management. Since the returns on nominal bonds are fixed in nominal terms, they provide no hedge against uncertain inflation. Kaul (1987) and Chu et al. (1995) have documented a negative correlation between equity returns and inflation in the United Kingdom as in the case of investors in equity markets, who suffer during periods of unexpected high inflation. Inflation-indexed securities, by linking returns to the movement of a price index, provide a hedge for investors who have a low-risk tolerance for unexpected inflation. Investors most averse to inflation will purchase inflation-indexed securities, and those less sensitive to inflation will purchase the riskier nominal bonds.

The design of the U.S. inflation-indexed securities underwent considerable discussion in determining the linking price index, the cash flow structure, the optimal length of maturity, the auction mechanism, and the amount of issuance. TIIS are auctioned through the Dutch auction method used by other Treasury securities. Participants submit bids in terms of real yields. The highest accepted yield is used to price the newly issued TIIS for all participants (Roll, 1996).

Both principal and coupon payments of TIIS are linked to the monthly nonseasonally adjusted U.S. City Average-All Items Consumer Price Index for All Urban Consumers (CPI-U). The Bureau of Labor Statistics compiles and publishes the CPI independently of the Treasury. The CPI-U is announced monthly. Inflation-indexed securities provide a guarantee to investors that at maturity investors will receive the inflation-adjusted amount or the par value whichever is greater. The coupon payments and the lump-sum payment at maturity are adjusted according to inflation rates. With a fixed coupon rate, the adjustment to a nominal coupon payment is accomplished by multiplying the principal value by one plus the inflation rate between the issuance date and the coupon payment date. Inflation-indexed securities set a floor (par value), an implicit put option, guaranteeing the bond's value will not fall below its face value if the United States experiences cumulative deflation during the entire life of the TIIS, which is a highly unlikely event.

TIIS are eligible for stripping into their principal and interest components in the Treasury's Separate Trading of Registered Interest and Principal of Securities Program. Since March 1999, the U.S. Treasury Department has allowed all TIIS interest components with the same maturity date to be interchangeable (fungible). Fungibility is designed to improve the liquidity of stripped interest components of TIIS, and hence increase demand for the underlying inflation-indexed securities. Other Treasury securities are strippable as well.

Since first issue in 1997, TIIS have constituted only a small portion of total Treasury securities issuance. At the end of 2002, the market capitalization of the TIIS was $140 billion, while the total Treasury market capitalization was $3.1 trillion. There are only 11 issues of TIIS outstanding, with original maturities running from 5 to 30 years. The issuance of TIIS was increased from two to three auctions of 10-year TIIS per year, along with a statement from the U.S. Treasury that they actively intend to promote trading in the 10-year note. Limited issuance prevents full coverage for various in-vestment horizons and constrains trading volume in the new security. TIIS have not been closely followed by financial analysts, nor well understood by the investment public.

Since the inception of the TIIS in 1997, actual inflation has been very low by historical standards, and there has not been strong interest in hedging against inflation. Although the Federal Reserve remains concerned about potential inflation, higher inflation levels have not materialized. In more recent years, the government has been retiring Treasury debt due to government surpluses, which makes significant new issues of TIIS less likely.

One disadvantage of TIIS is the potential for tax liability on phantom income. Although the securities are exempt from state and local taxes, they are subject to federal taxation. Positive accrued inflation compensation, if any, is reportable income, even though the inflation-adjusted principal will not be received until maturity. Some taxable investors may thus hesitate to invest in TIIS, while others with nontaxable accounts such as retirement accounts might find this market attractive. Consequently, investor tax brackets may affect decisions about including TIIS in a portfolio. The emergence of pension funds specializing in TIIS should attract more individual investment in the form of IRA and 401(k) savings, although these investors are more likely to buy and hold.

One feature of the TIIS that impedes its use as a perfect measure of the *ex ante* real rate is the CPI indexing procedure. There is a three-month lag in the CPI indexing system for TIIS. Figure 7.1 indicates how the reference CPI is calculated on May 15, 2000. The reference CPI for May 1, 2000, is the CPI-U for the third-previous calendar month, i.e. the announced CPI for February 2000. The Bureau of Labor Statistics surveys price information for the February CPI between January 15 and February 15, and then announces the February CPI on March 17, 2000. The reference CPI for any other day of May is calculated by linear interpolation between the CPIs of February and March (the CPI for March becomes available on April 14, 2000). Once the March CPI is announced, the

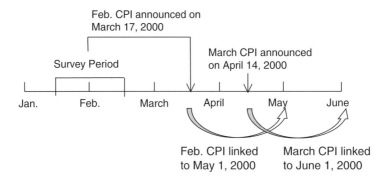

Figure 7.1. Calculation of reference CPI. This figure illustrates the lag effect in indexing the CPI. Due to CPI-U reporting procedures, the reference CPI for May 1, 2000, is linked to the February CPI-U, and the reference CPI for June 1, 2000, is linked to the March CPI-U.

reference CPI for any day in May 2000 is known. The reference CPI for May 15, 2000 can be calculated according to the following formula:

$$RCPI_{May15} = CPI_{Feb} + (14/31)\,(CPI_{March} - CPI_{Feb})$$
$$= 169.7 + (14/31)(171.1 - 169.7)$$
$$= 170.33226,$$

where *RCPI* represents the reference CPI for a particular day.[2]

The principal value of TIIS on any particular day is determined by multiplying the face value at the issuance by an applicable index ratio. The index ratio is defined as the reference CPI applicable to the calculation date divided by the reference CPI applicable to the original issuing date.

Table 7.1 shows the percentage holdings of TIIS for competitive bidders, noncompetitive bidders, the Federal Reserve, and foreign official institutions. The total dollar amount tendered by competitive bidders is 2.24 times the total dollar amount accepted. The bid-to-cover ratio of 2.24 indicates the intensity of demand for the TIIS.

The first TIIS was issued in January 1997, which offered a real coupon rate of 3.375 percent and 10 years to maturity. The first maturity of TIIS occurred on July 15, 2002. There are eight 10-year TIIS and three 30-year TIIS currently outstanding. Maturities range from 2007 to 2032. Ten-year TIIS original issuances are scheduled in July each year, with a reopening in October and the following January. Each issue has a unique CUSIP number

Table 7.1. TIIS distribution among investment groupsThe numbers in this table represent auction results of TIIS between October 1998 and July 2001. Information on new issuance and reopening are summarized for the 11 auctions held during this period of time. Amounts are in millions of dollars.

	Tendered		Accepted	
Competitive	153,446	98.13	68,410	95.90
Noncompetitive	601	0.38	601	0.84
Federal Reserve	2,202	1.41	2,202	3.09
Foreign Official Institutions	125	0.08	125	0.18
Total	156,374	100.00[a]	71,338	100.00[a, b]

[a] Numbers are in percentage.
[b] Does not add to 100.00 percent because of rounding.

for identification purposes, which is also used in the case of reopening. All 11 issues have been reopened at least once after the original issue date.

The average annual return on the 10-year TIIS, since inception in 1997, was 7.5 percent, compared to a return on the 10-year nominal Treasury of 8.9 percent. The comparable annual volatility has been 6.1 percent for the TIIS compared to 8.2 percent for the Treasury. Issue size varies from $5 billion to $8 billion. For all 11 issues, the amounts tendered by the public have been consistently higher than offering amounts. The average daily trading volume of the TIIS was $ 2 billion, compared to $300 billion for the Treasury market.

The U.S. Treasury also issues Series-I Bonds, usually called I-Bonds, whose values are linked to the CPI as well. Unlike TIIS, I-Bonds are designed to target individual investors. The motivation for such a security is to encourage public savings. Investors pay the face value of I-Bonds at the time of purchase. The return on I-Bonds consists of two separate parts: a fixed rate of return, and a variable inflation rate. As inflation rates evolve over time, the value of I-Bonds also varies. Values will be adjusted monthly, while interest is compounded every six months. Interest payments are paid when the bond is cashed. As in the TIIS, there is an implicit put option impounded in I-Bonds that protects investors from deflation.

There are differences between I-Bonds and TIIS. First, I-Bonds are designed for individual investors with long-term commitments. Although investors can cash an I-Bond any time 6 months after issuance, there is a 3-month interest penalty if the bond is cashed within the first 5 years. TIIS, on the other hand, can be traded freely without penalty.

The real rates of return on I-Bonds and TIIS are different. The Treasury announces the fixed rates on I-Bonds every 6 months, along with the rate of inflation. Both the fixed rate and the inflation rate remain effective for only 6 months until the next announcement date. The real coupon rate on a TIIS, however, is determined through an auction mechanism involving all market participants on the original issue date. TIIS principal is linked to the daily reference CPI, and its value can be adjusted daily instead of monthly as in the case of I-Bonds.

The tax treatment of I-Bonds and TIIS is also different. While there is phantom income tax on TIIS, federal income taxes can be deferred for up to 30 years for I-Bonds. If there is early redemption, taxes are levied at the time I-Bonds are cashed. Investors can purchase I-Bonds through retirement accounts, but there is a limit on the amount one can purchase. An investor can purchase up to $30,000 worth of I-Bonds each calendar year, a limit that is not affected by the purchase of other bond series.

NOTES

1. According to the date of introduction of inflation-indexed securities, these countries are Finland, France, Sweden, Israel, Iceland, Brazil, Chile, Colombia, Argentina, the United Kingdom, Australia, Mexico, Canada, New Zealand, and the United States.
2. The U.S. Treasury posts the reference CPI for the following month around the 15th of each month on its web site at http://www.publicdebt.treas.gov.

REFERENCES

Benninga, S. and Protopapadakis, A. (1983). "Nominal and real interest rates under uncertainty: The Fisher theorem and the term structure." *The Journal of Political Economy,* 91(5):856–867.

Chu, Q.C., Lee, C. F., and Pittman, D.N. (1995). "On the inflation risk premium." *Journal of Business, Finance, and Accounting,* 22(6):881–892.

Kaul, G. (1987). "Stock returns and inflation: The role of the monetary sector." *Journal of Financial Economics,* 18(2): 253–276.

Pennachi, G. G. (1991). "Identifying the dynamics of real interest rates and inflation: Evidence using survey data." *Review of Financial Studies,* 4(1):53–86.

Roll, R. (1996). "U.S. Treasury inflation-indexed bonds: The design of a new security." *The Journal of Fixed Income* 6(3):9–28.

Wilcox, D. W. (1998). "The introduction of indexed government debt in the United States." *The Journal of Economic Perspectives,* 12(1):219–227.

Chapter 8

ASSET PRICING MODELS

WAYNE E. FERSON, *Boston College, USA*

Abstract

The asset pricing models of financial economics describe the prices and expected rates of return of securities based on arbitrage or equilibrium theories. These models are reviewed from an empirical perspective, emphasizing the relationships among the various models.

Keywords: financial assets; arbitrage; portfolio optimization; stochastic discount factor; beta pricing model; intertemporal marginal rate of substitution; systematic risk; Capital Asset Pricing Model; consumption; risk aversion; habit persistence; durable goods; mean variance efficiency; factor models; arbitrage pricing model

Asset pricing models describe the prices or expected rates of return of financial assets, which are claims traded in financial markets. Examples of financial assets are common stocks, bonds, options, and futures contracts. The asset pricing models of financial economics are based on two central concepts. The first is the "no arbitrage principle," which states that market forces tend to align the prices of financial assets so as to eliminate arbitrage opportunities. An arbitrage opportunity arises if assets can be combined in a portfolio with zero cost, no chance of a loss, and a positive probability of gain. Arbitrage opportunities tend to be eliminated in financial markets because prices adjust as investors attempt to trade to exploit the arbitrage opportunity. For example,

if there is an arbitrage opportunity because the price of security A is too low, then traders' efforts to purchase security A will tend to drive up its price, which will tend to eliminate the arbitrage opportunity. The arbitrage pricing model (APT), (Ross, 1976) is a well-known asset pricing model based on arbitrage principles.

The second central concept in asset pricing is "financial market equilibrium." Investors' desired holdings of financial assets are derived from an optimization problem. A necessary condition for financial market equilibrium in a market with no frictions is that the first-order conditions of the investor's optimization problem are satisfied. This requires that investors are indifferent at the margin to small changes in their asset holdings. Equilibrium asset pricing models follow from the first-order conditions for the investors' portfolio choice problem, and a market-clearing condition. The market-clearing condition states that the aggregate of investors' desired asset holdings must equal the aggregate "market portfolio" of securities in supply.

Differences among the various asset pricing models arise from differences in their assumptions about investors' preferences, endowments, production and information sets, the process governing the arrival of news in the financial markets, and the types of frictions in the markets. Recently, models have been developed that emphasize the role of human imperfections in this process. For a review of this "behavioral finance" perspective, see Barberis and Shleifer (2003).

Virtually all asset pricing models are special cases of the fundamental equation:

$$P_t = E_t\{m_{t+1}(P_{t+1} + D_{t+1})\}, \qquad (8.1)$$

where P_t is the price of the asset at time t and D_{t+1} is the amount of any dividends, interest or other payments received at time $t + 1$. The market wide random variable m_{t+1} is the "stochastic discount factor" (SDF). By recursive substitution in Equation (8.1), the future price may be eliminated to express the current price as a function of the future cash flows and SDFs only: $P_t = E_t\{\Sigma_{j>0} (\Pi_{k=1}, \ldots, j \, m_{t+k})D_{t+j}\}$. Prices are obtained by "discounting" the payoffs, or multiplying by SDFs, so that the expected "present value" of the payoff is equal to the price.

We say that a SDF "prices" the assets if Equation (8.1) is satisfied. Any particular asset pricing model may be viewed simply as a specification for the stochastic discount factor. The random variable m_{t+1} is also known as the benchmark pricing variable, equivalent martingale measure, Radon–Nicodym derivative, or intertemporal marginal rate of substitution, depending on the context. The representation in Equation (8.1) goes at least back to Beja (1971), while the term "stochastic discount factor" is usually ascribed to Hansen and Richard (1987).

Assuming nonzero prices, Equation (8.1) is equivalent to:

$$E_t (m_{t+1} \mathbf{R}_{t+1} - \mathbf{1}) = 0, \qquad (8.2)$$

where $\mathbf{R}_{t+1}$ is the vector of primitive asset gross returns and $\mathbf{1}$ is an $\mathbf{N}$-vector of ones. The gross return $R_{i,t+1}$ is defined as $(P_{i,t+1} + D_{i,t+1})/P_{i,t}$, where $P_{i,t}$ is the price of the asset i at time t and $D_{i,t+1}$ is the payment received at time $t + 1$. Empirical tests of asset pricing models often work directly with asset returns in Equation (8.2) and the relevant definition of m_{t+1}.

Without more structure the Equations (8.1,8.2) have no content, because it is always possible to find a random variable m_{t+1} for which the equations hold. There will be some m_{t+1} that "works," in this sense, as long as there are no redundant asset returns. For example, take a sample of asset gross returns with a nonsingular covariance matrix and let m_{t+1} be $.[\mathbf{1}'(E_t\{\mathbf{R}_{t+1}\mathbf{R}_{t+1'}\}) - \mathbf{1}]\mathbf{R}_{t+1}$ Substitution in to Equation (8.2) shows that this SDF will always "work" in any sample of returns. The ability to construct an SDF as a function of the returns that prices all of the included assets, is essentially equivalent to the ability to construct a minimum-variance efficient portfolio and use in as the "factor" in a beta pricing model, as described below.

With the restriction that m_{t+1} is a strictly positive random variable, Equation (8.1) becomes equivalent to the no arbitrage principle, which says that all portfolios of assets with payoffs that can never be negative but are positive with positive probability, must have positive prices (Beja, 1971; Rubinstein, 1976; Ross, 1977; Harrison and Kreps, 1979; Hansen and Richard, 1987.)

While the no arbitrage principle places restrictions on m_{t+1}, empirical work more typically explores the implications of equilibrium models for the SDF based on investor optimization. A representative consumer–investor's optimization implies the Bellman equation:

$$J(W_t, s_t) \equiv \max E_t\{U(C_t, .) + J(W_{t+1}, s_{t+1})\}, \qquad (8.3)$$

where $U(C_t, .)$ is the utility of consumption expenditures at time t, and $J(.)$ is the indirect utility of wealth. The notation allows that the direct utility of current consumption expenditures may depend on other variables such as past consumption expenditures or the current state variables. The state variables, s_{t+1}, are sufficient statistics, given wealth, for the utility of future wealth in an optimal consumption–investment plan. Thus, the state variables represent future consumption–investment opportunity risk. The budget constraint is: $W_{t+1} = (Wt - C_t)\mathbf{x}' \mathbf{R}_{t+1}$, where $\mathbf{x}$ is the portfolio weight vector, subject to $\mathbf{x}'\mathbf{1} = 1$.

If the allocation of resources to consumption and investment assets is optimal, it is not possible to obtain higher utility by changing the allocation. Suppose an investor considers reducing consumption at time t to purchase more of (any) asset. The expected utility cost at time t of the foregone consumption is the expected product of the marginal utility of consumption expenditures, $Uc(C_t,.) > 0$ (where a subscript denotes partial derivative), multiplied by the price of the asset, and which is measured in the same units as the consumption expenditures. The expected utility gain of selling the investment asset and consuming the proceeds at time $t + 1$ is $E_t\{(P_{i,t+1} + D_{i,t+1}) J_w (W_{t+1}, s_{t+1})\}$. If the allocation maximizes expected utility, the following must hold: $P_{i,t} E_t\{U_c (C_t,.)\} = E_t\{(P_{i,t+1} + D_{i,t+1}) J_w(W_{t+1}, s_{t+1})\}$ which is equivalent to Equation (8.1), with

$$m_{t+1} = \frac{J_w(W_{t+1}, s_{t+1})}{E_t\{U_c (C_t,.)\}}. \tag{8.4}$$

The m_{t+1} in Equation (8.4) is the "intertemporal marginal rate of substitution" (IMRS) of the consumer–investor.

Asset pricing models typically focus on the relation of security returns to aggregate quantities. It is therefore necessary to aggregate the first-order conditions of individuals to obtain equilibrium expressions in terms of aggregate quantities. Then, Equation (8.4) may be considered to hold for a representative investor who holds all the securities and consumes the aggregate quantities. Theoretical conditions that justify the use of aggregate quantities are discussed by Gorman (1953), Wilson (1968), Rubinstein (1974), and Constantinides (1982), among others. When these conditions fail, investors' heterogeneity will affect the form of the asset pricing relation. The effects of heterogeneity are examined by Lintner (1965), Brennan and Kraus (1978), Lee et al. (1990), Constantinides and Duffie (1996), and Sarkissian (2003), among others.

Typically, empirical work in asset pricing focuses on expressions for expected returns and excess rates of return. The expected excess returns are modeled in relation to the risk factors that create variation in m_{t+1}. Consider any asset return $R_{i,t+1}$ and a reference asset return, $R_{0,t+1}$. Define the excess return of asset i, relative to the reference

asset as $r_{i,t+1} = R_{i,t+1} - R_{0,t+1}$. If Equation (8.2) holds for both assets it implies:

$$E_t\{m_{t+1} r_{i,t+1}\} = 0 \text{ for all i.} \tag{8.5}$$

Use the definition of covariance to expand Equation (8.5) into the product of expectations plus the covariance, obtaining:

$$E_t\{r_{i,t+1}\} = \frac{\text{Cov}_t(r_{i,t+1}; -m_{t+1})}{E_t\{m_{t+1}\}}, \text{ for all i,} \tag{8.6}$$

where $\text{Cov}_t(.;.)$ is the conditional covariance. Equation (8.6) is a general expression for the expected excess return from which most of the expressions in the literature can be derived.

Equation (8.6) implies that the covariance of return with m_{t+1}, is a general measure of "systematic risk." This risk is systematic in the sense that any fluctuations in the asset return that are uncorrelated with fluctuations in the SDF are not "priced," meaning that these fluctuations do not command a risk premium. For example, in the conditional regression $r_{it+1} = a_{it} + b_{it} m_{t+1} + u_{it+1}$, then $\text{Cov}_t(u_{it+1}, m_{t+1}) = 0$. Only the part of the variance in a risky asset return that is correlated with the SDF is priced as risk.

Equation (8.6) displays that a security will earn a positive risk premium if its return is negatively correlated with the SDF. When the SDF is an aggregate IMRS, negative correlation means that the asset is likely to return more than expected when the marginal utility in the future period is low, and less than expected when the marginal utility and the value of the payoffs, is high. For a given expected payoff, the more negative the covariance of the asset's payoffs with the IMRS, the less desirable the distribution of the random return, the lower the value of the asset and the larger the expected compensation for holding the asset given the lower price.

8.1. The Capital Asset Pricing Model

One of the first equilibrium asset pricing models was the Capital Asset Pricing Model (CAPM), developed by Sharpe (1964), Lintner (1965), and Mossin (1966). The CAPM remains one of the foundations of financial economics, and a huge number of theoretical papers refine the assumptions and provide derivations of the CAPM. The CAPM states that expected asset returns are given by a linear function of the assets' "betas," which are their regression coefficients against the market portfolio. Let R_{mt} denote the gross return for the market portfolio of all assets in the economy. Then, according to the CAPM,

$$E(R_{it+1}) = \delta_0 + \delta_1 \beta_i, \qquad (8.7)$$

where $\beta_i = \mathrm{Cov}(R_i, R_m)/\mathrm{Var}(R_m)$.

In Equation (8.7), $\delta_0 = E(R_{0t+1})$, where the return R_{0t+1} is referred to as a "zero-beta asset" to R_{mt+1} because the condition $\mathrm{Cov}(R_{0t+1}, R_{mt+1}) = 0$.

To derive the CAPM, it is simplest to assume that the investor's objective function in Equation (8.3) is quadratic, so that $J(W_{t+1}, S_{t+1}) = V\{E_t(R_{pt+1}), \mathrm{Var}_t(R_{pt+1})\}$ where R_{pt+1} is the investor's optimal portfolio. The function $V(.,.)$ is increasing in its first argument and decreasing in the second if investors are risk averse. In this case, the SDF of Equation (8.4) specializes as: $m_{t+1} = a_t + b_t R_{pt+1}$. In equilibrium, the representative agent must hold the market portfolio, so $R_{pt+1} = R_{mt+1}$. Equation (8.7) then follows from Equation (8.6), with this substitution.

8.2. Consumption-based Asset Pricing Models

Consumption models may be derived from Equation (8.4) by exploiting the envelope condition, $U_c(.) = J_w(.)$, which states that the marginal utility of current consumption must be equal to the marginal utility of current wealth, if the consumer has optimized the tradeoff between the amount consumed and the amount invested.

Breeden (1979) derived a consumption-based asset pricing model in continuous time, assuming that the preferences are time-additive. The utility function for the lifetime stream of consumption is $\Sigma_t \beta^t U(C_t)$, where β is a time preference parameter

and $U(.)$ is increasing and concave in current consumption, C_t. Breeden's model is a linearization of Equation (8.1), which follows from the assumption that asset values and consumption follow diffusion processes (Bhattacharya, 1981; Grossman and Shiller, 1982). A discrete-time version follows Lucas (1978), assuming a power utility function:

$$U(C) = [C^{1-\alpha} - 1]/(1 - \alpha), \qquad (8.8)$$

where $\alpha > 0$ is the concavity parameter of the period utility function. This function displays constant relative risk aversion equal to α. "Relative risk aversion" in consumption is defined as: $Cu''(C)/u'(C)$. Absolute risk aversion is defined as: $u''(C)/u'(C)$. Ferson (1983) studied a consumption-based asset pricing model with constant absolute risk aversion.

Using Equation (8.8) and the envelope condition, the IMRS in Equation (8.4) becomes:

$$m_{t+1} = \beta(C_{t+1}/C_t)^{-\alpha}. \qquad (8.9)$$

A large body of literature in the 1980s tested the pricing Equation (8.1) with the SDF given by the consumption model (Equation (8.9)). See, for example, Hansen and Singleton (1982, 1983), Ferson (1983), and Ferson and Merrick (1987).

More recent work generalizes the consumption-based model to allow for "nonseparabilities" in the $U_c(C_t,.)$ function in Equation (8.4), as may be implied by the durability of consumer goods, habit persistence in the preferences for consumption, nonseparability of preferences across states of nature, and other refinements. Singleton (1990), Ferson (1995), and Cochrane (2001) review this literature; Sarkissian (2003) provides a recent empirical example with references. The rest of this section provides a brief historical overview of empirical work on nonseparable-consumption models.

Dunn and Singleton (1986) and Eichenbaum et al. (1988) developed consumption models with durable goods. Durability introduces nonseparability over time, since the actual consumption at a given date depends on the consumer's previous expenditures. The consumer optimizes over the current expenditures C_t, accounting for the fact that durable goods purchased today increase consumption at future dates, and thereby lower future marginal utilities. Thus, $U_c(C_t,.)$ in Equation (8.4) depends on expenditures prior to date t.

Another form of time nonseparability arises if the utility function exhibits "habit persistence." Habit persistence means that consumption at two points in time are complements. For example, the utility of current consumption may be evaluated relative to what was consumed in the past, so the previous standard of living influences the utility derived from current consumption. Such models are derived by Ryder and Heal (1973), Becker and Murphy (1988), Sundaresan (1989), Constantinides (1990), and Campbell and Cochrane (1999), among others.

Ferson and Constantinides (1991) model both durability and habit persistence in consumption expenditures. They show that the two combine as opposing effects. In an example based on the utility function of Equation (8.8), and where the "memory" is truncated at a single-lag, the derived utility of expenditures is:

$$U(C_t,.) = (1 - \alpha)^{-1}\Sigma_t \, \beta_t \, (C_t + bC_{t-1})^{1-\alpha}, \quad (8.10)$$

where the coefficient b is positive and measures the rate of depreciation if the good is durable and there is no habit persistence. Habit persistence implies that the lagged expenditures enter with a negative effect ($b < 0$). Empirical evidence on similar habit models is provided by Heaton (1993) and Braun et al. (1993), who find evidence for habit in international consumption and returns data.

Consumption expenditure data are highly seasonal, and Ferson and Harvey (1992) argue that the Commerce Department's X-11 seasonal adjustment program may induce spurious time series behavior in the seasonally adjusted consumption data that most empirical studies have used. Using data that are not adjusted, they find strong evidence for a seasonal habit model.

Abel (1990) studied a form of habit persistence in which the consumer evaluates current consump-

tion relative to the aggregate consumption in the previous period, and which the consumer takes as exogenous. The idea is that people care about "keeping up with the Joneses." Campbell and Cochrane (1999) developed another model in which the habit stock is taken as exogenous (or "external") by the consumer. The habit stock in this case is modeled as a highly persistent weighted average of past aggregate consumptions. This approach results in a simpler and more tractable model, since the consumer's optimization does not have to take account of the effects of current decisions on the future habit stock In addition, by modeling the habit stock as an exogenous time series process, Campbell and Cochranes' model provides more degrees of freedom to match asset market data.

Epstein and Zin (1989, 1991) consider a class of recursive preferences that can be written as: $J_t = F(C_t, \text{CEQ}_t \, (J_{t+1}))$. $\text{CEQ}_t(.)$ is a time t "certainty equivalent" for the future lifetime utility J_{t+1}. The function $F(., \text{CEQ}_t(.))$ generalizes the usual expected utility function and may be nontime-separable. They derive a special case of the recursive preference model in which the preferences are:

$$J_t = \left[(1 - \beta)C_t^p + \beta \, E_t \, (J_{t+1}^{1-\alpha})^{p/(1-\alpha)}\right]^{1/p}. \quad (8.11)$$

They show that the IMRS for a representative agent becomes (when $p \neq 0$, $1 - \alpha \neq 0$):

$$m_{t+1} = [\beta(C_{t+1}/C_t)^{p-1}]^{(1-\alpha)/p} \, \{R_{m,t+1}\}^{((1-\alpha-p)/p)}. \quad (8.12)$$

The coefficient of relative risk aversion for timeless consumption gambles is α and the elasticity of substitution for deterministic consumption is $(1 - p)^{-1}$. If $\alpha = 1 - p$, the model reduces to the time-separable power utility model. If $\alpha = 1$, the log utility model of Rubinstein (1976) is obtained. Campbell (1993) shows that the Epstein–Zin model can be transformed to an empirically tractable model without consumption data. He used a linearization of the budget constraint that makes it possible to substitute for consumption in terms of the factors that drive the optimal consumption function. Expected asset returns are then determined by their covariances with the underlying factors.

8.3. Multi-Beta Asset Pricing Models

Beta pricing models are a class of asset pricing models that imply the expected returns of securities are related to their sensitivity to changes in the underlying factors that measure the state of the economy. Sensitivity is measured by the securities' "beta" coefficients. For each of the relevant state variables, there is a market-wide price of beta measured in the form of an increment to the expected return (a "risk premium") per unit of beta.

The CAPM represented in Equation (8.7) is the premier example of a single-beta pricing model. Multiple-beta models were developed in continuous time by Merton (1973), Breeden (1979), and Cox et al. (1985). Long (1974), Sharpe (1977), Cragg and Malkiel (1982) and Connor (1984). Dybvig (1983), Grinblatt and Titman (1983), and Shanken (1987) provide multi-beta interpretations of equilibrium models in discrete time. Multiple-beta models follow when m_{t+1} can be written as a function of several factors. Equation (8.3) suggests that likely candidates for the factors are variables that proxy for consumer wealth, consumption expenditures, or the state variables – the sufficient statistics for the marginal utility of future wealth in an optimal consumption–investment plan. A multi-beta model asserts that the expected return is a linear function of several betas, i.e.

$$E(R_{it+1}) = \delta_0 + \Sigma_{j=1,\ldots,K} \beta_{ij} \, \delta_j, \qquad (8.13)$$

where the $\beta_{ij}, j = 1, \ldots, K$, are the multiple regression coefficients of the return of asset i on K economy-wide risk factors, $f_j, j = 1, \ldots, K$. The coefficient δ_0 is the expected return on an asset that has $\beta_{0j} = 0$, for $j = 1, \ldots, K$, i.e. it is the expected return on a zero-(multiple) beta asset. If

there is a risk-free asset, then δ_0 is the return for this asset. The coefficient δ_k, corresponding to the k'th factor has the following interpretation: it is the expected return differential, or premium, for a portfolio that has $\beta_{ik} = 1$ and $\beta_{ij} = 0$ for all $j \neq k$, measured in excess of the zero-beta asset's expected return. In other words, it is the expected return premium per unit of beta risk for the risk factor, k.

A multi-beta model, under certain assumptions, is equivalent to the SDF representation of Equation (8.2). This equivalence was first discussed, for the case of the CAPM, by Dybvig and Ingersoll (1982). The general multifactor case is derived by Ferson (1995) and Ferson and Jagannathan (1996), who show that the multi-beta expected return model of Equation (8.13) is equivalent to Equation (8.2), when the SDF is linear in the factors: $m_{t+1} = a_t + \Sigma_j b_{jt} \, f_{jt+1}$.

The logic of the equivalence between multi-beta pricing and the SDF representation of asset pricing models is easily seen using a regression example. Consider a regression of asset returns onto the factors, f_j of the multi-beta model. The regression model is $R_{it+1} = a_i + \Sigma_j \beta_{ijt} \, f_{jt} + u_{it+1}$. Substitute the regression equation into the right hand side of Equation (8.6) and assume that $\text{Cov}_t(u_{i,t+1}, m_{t+1}) = 0$. The result is:

$$E_t(R_{it+1}) = \delta_{0t} + \Sigma_{j=1,\ldots K} \, \beta_{ijt}$$
$$[\text{Cov}_t\{f_{jt+1}, -m_{t+1}\}/E_t(m_{t+1})], \qquad (8.14)$$

which is a version of the multi-beta Equation (8.13). The market-wide risk premium for factor j is $\delta_{jt} = [\text{Cov}_t\{f_{jt+1}, -m_{t+1}\}/E_t(m_{t+1})]$. In the special case where the factor f_{jt+1} is a traded asset return, Equation (8.14) implies that $\delta_{jt} = E_t(f_{j,t+1}) - \delta_{0t}$; the expected risk premium equals the factor portfolio's expected excess return.

Equation (8.14) is useful because it provides intuition about the signs and magnitudes of expected risk premiums for particular factors. The intuition is essentially the same as in Equation (8.6). If a risk factor f_{jt+1} is negatively correlated with m_{t+1}, the model implies that a positive risk premium is associated with that factor beta. A factor that is negatively related to marginal utility should carry a positive premium, because the big payoffs disappointingly come when the value of payoffs is low. This implies a low present value, and thus a high expected return. With a positive covariance the opposite occurs. If the factor is high when payoffs are highly valued, assets with a positive beta on the factor have a payoff distribution that is "better" than risk free. Thus, the expected return premium is negative, and such assets can have expected returns below that of a risk-free asset.

8.4. Relation to Mean–Variance Efficiency

The concept of a "minimum-variance portfolio" is central in the asset pricing literature. A portfolio R_{pt+1} is minimum variance if and only if no portfolio with the same expected return has a smaller variance. Roll (1977) and others have shown that a portfolio is minimum variance if and only if a single-beta pricing model holds, using the portfolio as the risk factor.[1] According to the CAPM, the market portfolio with return R_{mt+1} is minimum variance. If investors are risk averse, the CAPM also implies that R_{mt+1} is on the positively sloped portion of the minimum-variance frontier, or "mean–variance efficient." This implies that the coefficient δ_1 in Equation (8.7) is positive, which says that there is a positive tradeoff between market risk and expected return when investors are risk averse.

Multiple-beta asset pricing models imply that combinations of particular portfolios are minimum-variance efficient. Equation (8.13) is equivalent to the statement that a combination of K factor-portfolios is minimum-variance efficient, when the factors are traded assets. This result is proved by Grinblatt and Titman (1987), Shanken (1987), and Huberman et al. (1987). The correspondence between multi-beta pricing and mean variance efficiency is exploited by Jobson and Korkie (1982), Gibbons et al. (1989), Kandel and Stambaugh (1989), and Ferson and Siegel (2005), among others, to develop tests of multi-beta models based on mean variance efficiency.

8.5. Factor Models

A beta pricing model has no empirical content until the factors are specified, since there will almost always be a minimum-variance portfolio which satisfies Equation (8.13), with $K = 1$. Therefore, the empirical content of the model is the discipline imposed in selecting the factors. There have been four main approaches to finding empirical factors. The first approach is to specify empirical proxies for factors specified by the theory. For example, the CAPM says that the "market portfolio" of all capital assets is the factor, and early studies concentrated on finding good measures for the market portfolio. A second approach is to use factor analytic or principal components methods. This approach is motivated by the APT, as described below. A third approach chooses the risk factors as economic variables or portfolios, based on intuition such as that provided by Equations (8.3) and (8.4). With this approach, likely candidates for the factors are proxies for consumer wealth, consumer expenditures, and variables that may be sufficient statistics for the marginal utility of future wealth in an optimal consumption–investment plan. For examples of this approach, see Chen et al. (1986), Ferson and Harvey (1991), Campbell (1993), and Cochrane (1996). A fourth approach to factor selection forms portfolios by ranking stocks on firm characteristics that are correlated with the cross-section of average returns. For example, Fama and French (1993, 1996) use the ratio of book value to market price, and the relative market value (size) of the firm to form their "factors."

Lo and MacKinlay (1990), MacKinlay (1995), and Ferson et al. (1999) provide critiques of the approach of sorting stocks on empirically motivated characteristics in order to form asset pricing factors. Lo and MacKinlay examine the approach as a version of data mining. MacKinlay argues that the factors generated in this fashion by Fama and

French (1993, 1996) are statistically unlikely to reflect market risk premiums. Ferson, Sarkissian, and Simin show that a hypothetical characteristic, bearing an anomalous relation to returns, but completely unrelated to risk, can be repackaged as a spurious "risk factor" with this approach. Berk (1995) emphasizes that the price of a stock is the value of its future cash flows discounted by future returns, so an anomalous pattern in the cross-section of returns would produce a corresponding pattern in ratios of cash flow to price. Some of the most empirically powerful characteristics for the cross-sectional prediction of stock returns are ratios, with market price per share in the denominator. However, patterns that are related to the cross-section of asset risks are also likely to be captured by sorting stocks on such ratios. Thus, the approach of sorting stocks on patterns in average returns to form factors is potentially dangerous, because it is likely to "work" when it "should" work, and it is also likely to work when it should not. At the time this chapter was written the controversy over such empirically motivated factors was unresolved.

8.6. Factor Models and the Arbitrage Pricing Model

The Arbitrage Pricing Model based on the APT of Ross (1976) is an example of a multiple-beta asset pricing model, although in the APT Equation (8.13) is an approximation. The expected returns are approximately a linear function of the relevant betas as the number of securities in the market grows without bound. Connor (1984) provided sufficient conditions for Equation (8.13) to hold exactly in an economy with an infinite number of assets, in general equilibrium. This version of the multiple-beta model, the exact APT, has received wide attention in the finance literature. See Connor and Korajczyk (1988), Lehmann and Modest (1988), Chen, (1983) and Burmeister, and McElroy (1988) for discussions on estimating and testing the model when the factor realizations are not observable, under auxiliary assumptions.

This section describes the Arbitrage Pricing Theory (APT) of Ross (1976), and how it is related to factor models and to the general SDF representation for asset pricing models, as in Equation (8.2). For this purpose, we suppress the time subscripts and related notation. Assume that the following data-generating model describes equity returns in excess of a risk-free asset:

$$r_i = E(r_i) + \beta'_{if} f + e_i, \quad (8.15)$$

where $E(f) = 0 = E(e_{if})$, all i, and $f_t = F_t - E(F_t)$ are the unexpected factor returns. We can normalize the factors to have the identity as their covariance matrix; the β_i absorb the normalization. The $N \times N$ covariance matrix of the asset returns can then be expressed as:

$$\mathrm{Cov}(R) \equiv \Sigma = BB' + V, \quad (8.16)$$

where V is the covariance matrix of the residual vector, $\mathbf{e}$, B is the $N \times K$ matrix of the vectors, β_i, and Σ is assumed to be nonsingular for all N. An "exact" factor structure assumes that V is diagonal. An approximate factor model, as described by Chamberlain (1983) and Chamberlain and Rothschild (1983), assumes that the eigenvalues of V are bounded as $N \to \infty$, while the K nonzero-eigenvalues of BB' become infinite as $N \to \infty$. Thus, the covariance matrix Σ has K unbounded and N–K bounded eigenvalues, as N becomes large.

The factor model represented in Equation (8.16) decomposes the variances of returns into "pervasive" and "nonsystematic" risks. If $\mathbf{x}$ is an N-vector of portfolio weights, the portfolio variance is $\mathbf{x}'\Sigma\mathbf{x}$, where $\lambda_{\max}(\Sigma)\mathbf{x}'\mathbf{x} \geq \mathbf{x}'\Sigma\mathbf{x} \geq \lambda_{\min}(\Sigma)\mathbf{x}'\mathbf{x}$, $\lambda_{\min}(\Sigma)$ being the smallest eigenvalue of Σ and $\lambda_{\max}(\Sigma)$ being the largest. Following Chamberlain (1983), a portfolio is "well diversified" if $\mathbf{x}'\mathbf{x} \to 0$ as N grows without bound. For example, an equally weighted portfolio is well diversified; in this case $\mathbf{x}'\mathbf{x} = (1/N) \to 0$. The bounded eigenvalues imply that V captures the component of portfolio risk that is not pervasive or systematic, in the sense that this part of the variance vanishes in a well-diversified portfolio. The exploding eigen-values of BB' imply that the common factor risks are pervasive, in the sense that they remain in a large, well-diversified portfolio.

The arbitrage pricing theory of Ross (1976) asserts that $\alpha'\alpha < \infty$ as N grows without bound, where α is the N vector of "alphas," or expected abnormal returns, measured as the differences between the left and right hand sides of Equation (8.13), using the APT factors in the multi-beta model. The alphas are the differences between the assets' expected returns and the returns predicted by the multi-beta model, also called the "pricing errors." The Ross APT implies that the multi-beta model's pricing errors are "small" on average, in a large market. If $\alpha'\alpha < \infty$ as N grows, then the cross-asset average of the squared pricing errors, $(\alpha'\alpha)/N$ must go to 0 as N grows.

The pricing errors in a beta pricing model are related to those of a SDF representation. If we define $\alpha_m = E(m\mathbf{R} - 1)$, where m is linear in the APT factors, then it follows that $\alpha_m = E(m)\alpha$; the beta pricing and stochastic discount factor alphas are proportional, where the risk-free rate determines the constant of proportionality. Provided that the risk-free rate is bounded above 100 percent, then $E(m)$ is bounded, and $\alpha'\alpha$ is bounded above if and only if $\alpha_m'\alpha_m$ is bounded above. Thus, the Ross APT has the same implications for the pricing errors in the SDF and beta pricing paradigms.

The "exact" version of the APT derived by Connor (1984) asserts that $\alpha'\alpha \rightarrow 0$ as N grows without bound, and thus the pricing errors of all assets go to zero as the market gets large. Chamberlain (1983) shows that the exact APT is equivalent to the statement that all minimum-variance portfolios are well diversified, and are thus combinations of the APT factors. In this case, we have $E(m\mathbf{R}-1) = 0$ when m is linear in the APT factors, and a combination of the factors is a minimum-variance efficient portfolio in the large market.

8.7. Summary

The asset pricing models of financial economics are based on an assumption that rules out arbitrage opportunities, or they rely on explicit equilibrium conditions. Empirically, there are three central representations. The first is the minimum-variance efficiency of a portfolio. The second is the beta pricing model stated in terms of risk factors, and the third is the SDF representation. These three representations are closely related, and become equivalent under anciliary assumptions. Together they provide a rich and flexible framework for empirical analysis.

NOTE

1. It is assumed that the portfolio R_{pt+1} is not the global minimum-variance portfolio; that is, the minimum variance over all levels of expected return. This is because the betas of all assets on the global minimum-variance portfolio are identical.

REFERENCES

Abel, A.B. (1990). "Asset prices under habit formation and catching up with the Joneses." *American Economic Review,* 80: 38–42.

Barberis, N. and Shleifer, A. (2003). "Behavioral Finance," in G.M. Constantinides, M. Harris and R.M. Stulz (eds.) *Handbook of the Economics of Finance*. North Holland: Elsevier.

Becker, G. and Murphy, K.M. (1988). "A theory of rational addiction." *Journal of Political Economy*, 96: 675–700.

Beja, A. (1971). "The structure of the cost of capital under uncertainty." *Review of Economic Studies,* 4: 359–369.

Berk, J. (1995). "A critique of size-related anomalies." *Review of Financial Studies*, 8: 275–286.

Bhattacharya, S. (1981). "Notes on multiperiod valuation and the pricing of options." *Journal of Finance*, 36: 163–180.

Burmeister, E. and McElroy, M.B. (1988). "Joint estimation of factor sensitivities and risk premia for the Arbitrage Pricing Theory." *Journal of Finance*, 43(3): 721–733.

Braun, P., Ferson, W.E., and Constantinides, G.M. (1993). "Time nonseparability in aggregate consumption: international evidence." *European Economic Review*, 37: 897–920.

Breeden, D. (1979). "An intertemporal asset pricing model with stochastic consumption and investment opportunities." *Journal of Financial Economics*, 7: 265–296.

Brennan, M.J. and Kraus, A. (1978). "Necessary Conditions for Aggregation in Securities Markets." *Journal of Financial and Quantitative Analysis*, 407–418.

Campbell, J.Y. (1993). "Intertemporal Asset Pricing without consumption data." *American Economic Review*, 83: 487–512.

Campbell, J.Y. and Cochrane J.H. (1999). "By force of habit: a consumption-based explanation of aggregate stock market behavior." *Journal of Political Economy*, 107: 205–251.

Chamberlain, G. (1983). "Funds, factors and diversification in arbitrage pricing models." *Econometrica*, 51: 1305–1324.

Chamberlain, G. and Rothschild, M. (1983). "Arbitrage, factor structure and mean variance analysis on large asset markets." *Econometrica*, 51: 1281–1304.

Chen, N.F. (1983). "Some empirical tests of the theory of arbitrage pricing." *Journal of Finance*, 38: 1393–1414.

Chen, N., Roll, R., and Ross, S. (1986). "Economic forces and the stock market." *Journal of Business*, 59: 383–403.

Cochrane, J.H. (1996). "A cross-sectional test of a production based asset pricing model, working paper." *Journal of Political Economy*, 104: 572–621.

Cochrane, J.H. (2001). *Asset Pricing*. Princeton, NJ: Princeton University.

Connor, G. (1984). "A unified beta pricing Theory." *Journal of Economic Theory*, 34: 13–31.

Connor, G. and Korajczyck, R. (1988). "Risk and return in an equilibrium APT: application of a new test methodology." *Journal of Financial Economics*, 21: 255–290.

Constantinides, G.M. (1982). "Intertemporal Asset Pricing with heterogeneous consumers and without demand Aggregation." *Journal of Business*, 55: 253–267.

Constantinides, G.M. (1990). "Habit formation: a resolution of the equity premium puzzle." *Journal of Political Economy*, 98: 519–543.

Constantinides, G.M. and Duffie, D. (1996). "Asset pricing with heterogenous consummers." *Journal of Political Economy*, 104: 219–240

Cox, J.C., Ingersoll, J.E., and Ross, S.A. (1985). "A theory of the term structure of interest rates." *Econometrica*, 53: 385–408.

Cragg, J.G. and Malkiel, B.G. (1982). *Expectations and the Structure of Share Prices*. Chicago: University of Chicago Press.

Dunn, K.B. and Singleton, K.J. (1986). "Modelling the term structure of interest rates under non-separable utility and durability of goods." *Journal of Financial Economics*, 17: 27–55.

Dybvig, P.H. (1983). "An explicit bound on individual assets' deviations from APT pricing in a finite economy." *Journal of Financial Economics*, 12: 483–496.

Dybvig, P. and Ingersoll, J. (1982). "Mean variance theory in complete markets." *Journal of Business*, 55: 233–252.

Eichenbaum, M.S., Hansen, L.P., and Singleton, K.J. (1988). "A time series analysis of representative agent models of consumption and leisure choices under uncertainty." *Quarterly Journal of Economics*, 103: 51–78.

Epstein, L.G. and Zin, S.E. (1989). "Substitution, risk aversion and the temporal behavior of asset returns: a theoretical approach." *Econometrica*, 57: 937–970.

Epstein, L.G. and Zin, S.E. (1991). "Substitution, risk aversion and the temporal behavior of asset returns." *Journal of Political Economy*, 99: 263–286.

Fama, E.F. and French, K.R. (1993). "Common risk factors in the returns on stocks and bonds." *Journal of Financial Economics*, 33: 3–56.

Fama, E.F. and French, K.R. (1996). "Multifactor explanations of asset pricing anomalies." *Journal of Finance*, 51: 55–87.

Ferson, W.E. (1983). "Expectations of real interest rates and aggregate consumption: empirical tests." *Journal of Financial and Quantitative Analysis*, 18: 477–497.

Ferson, W.E. (1995). "Theory and empirical testing of asset pricing models," in J. Maksimovic, and Ziemba (eds.) *Handbooks in Operations Research and Management Science*. Amsterdam: Elsevier.

Ferson, W.E. and Constantinides, G.M. (1991). "Habit persistence and durability in aggregate consumption: empirical tests." *Journal of Financial Economics*, 29: 199–240.

Ferson, W.E. and Harvey, C.R. (1991). "The Variation of Economic Risk Premiums." *Journal of Political Economy*, 99: 385–415.

Ferson, W.E. and Harvey, C.R. (1992). "Seasonality and consumption based Asset Pricing Models." *Journal of Finance*, 47: 511–552.

Ferson, W.E. and Jagannathan, R. (1996). "Econometric evaluation of Asset Pricing Models," in G.S. Maddala and C.R. Rao (eds.) *Handbook of Statistics: volume 14: Statistical Methods in Finance*. Amsterdam, the Netherlands.

Ferson, W.E. and Merrick, J.J. (1987) "Non-stationarity and stage of the business cycle effects in consumption-based asset pricing relations." *Journal of Financial Economics*, 18: 127–146.

Ferson, W.E., Sarkissian, S., and Simin, T. (1999). "The alpha factor Asset Pricing Model: a parable." *Journal of Financial Markets*, 2: 49–68.

Ferson, W.E. and Siegel, A.F. (2005). "Testing portfolio efficiency with conditioning information," Working paper, Boston College.

Gibbons, M.R., Ross, S.A., and Shanken, J. (1989). "A test of the efficiency of a given portfolio." *Econometrica*, 57: 1121–1152.

Gorman, W.M. (1953). "Community Preference Fields." *Econometrica*, 21: 63–80.

Grinblatt, M. and Titman, S. (1983). "Factor pricing in a finite economy." *Journal of Financial Economics*, 12: 497–508.

Grinblatt, M. and Titman, S. (1987). "The relation between mean-variance efficiency and arbitrage pricing." *Journal of Business*, 60: 97–112.

Grossman, S. and Shiller, R.J. (1982). "Consumption correlatedness and risk measurement in economies with nontraded assets and heterogeneous information." *Journal of Financial Economics*, 10: 195–210.

Hansen, L. P. and Richard, S. F. (1987). "The role of conditioning information in deducing testable restrictions implied by dynamic asset pricing models." *Econometrica*, 55: 587–613.

Hansen, L.P. and Singleton, K.J. (1982). "Generalized instrumental variables estimation of nonlinear rational expectations models." *Econometrica*, 50: 1269–1285.

Hansen, L.P. and Singleton, K.J. (1983). "Stochastic consumption, risk aversion and the temporal behavior of asset returns." *Journal of Political Economy*, 91: 249–266.

Harrison, M. and Kreps, D. (1979). "Martingales and arbitrage in multi-period securities markets." *Journal of Economic Theory*, 20: 381–408.

Heaton, J. (1993). "The interaction between time-nonseparable preferences and time aggregation." *Econometrica*, 61(2): 353–385.

Huberman, G., Kandel, S.A., and Stambaugh, R.F. (1987). "Mimicking portfolios and exact arbitrage pricing." *Journal of Finance*, 42: 1–10.

Jobson, J.D. and Korkie, R. (1982). "Potential performance and tests of portfolio efficiency." *Journal of Financial Economics*, 10: 433–466.

Kandel, S. and Stambaugh, R.F. (1989). "A mean variance framework for tests of asset pricing models." *Review of Financial Studies*, 2: 125–156.

Lee, C.F., Wu, C., and Wei, K.C.J. (1990). "The heterogeneous investment horizon and the capital asset pricing model: theory and implications." *Journal of Financial and Quantitative Analysis*, 25: 361–376.

Lehmann, B.N. and Modest, D.M. (1988). "The empirical foundations of the arbitrage pricing theory." *Journal of Financial Economics*, 21: 213–254.

Lintner, J. (1965)."The valuation of risk assets and the selection of risky investments in stock portfolios and capital budgets." *Review of Economics and Statistics*, 47: 13–37.

Lo, A.W. and MacKinlay, A.C. (1990). "Data snooping in tests of financial asset pricing models." *Review of Financial Studies*, 3: 431–467.

Long, J. (1974). "Stock prices, inflation, and the term structure of interest rates." *Journal of Financial Economics*, 1: 131–170.

Lucas, Jr. R.E. (1978). "Asset prices in an exchange economy." *Econometrica*, 46: 1429–1445.

MacKinlay, A.C. (1995). "Multifactor models do not explain deviations from the CAPM." *Journal of Financial Economics*, 38: 3–28.

Merton, R. C. (1973). "An intertemporal capital asset pricing model." *Econometrica*, 41: 867–887.

Mossin, J. (1966). "Equilibrium in a capital asset market." *Econometrica*, 34(4): 768–783.

Roll, R. (1977). "A critique of the asset pricing theory's tests -part 1: On past and potential testability of the theory." *Journal of Financial Economics*, 4: 129–176.

Ross, S. A. (1976). "The arbitrage pricing theory of capital asset pricing." *Journal of Economic Theory*, 13: 341–360.

Ross, S. (1977). "Risk, return and arbitrage," in I. Friend and J. Bicksler (eds.) *Risk and Return in Finance Ballinger*. Cambridge: Mass.

Rubinstein, M. (1974). "An aggregation theorem for securities markets." *Journal of Financial Economics*, 1: 225–244.

Rubinstein, M. (1976). "The valuation of uncertain income streams and the pricing of options." *Bell Journal of Economics and Management Science*, 7: 407–425.

Ryder, Jr. H.E. and Heal, G.M. (1973). "Optimal growth with intertemporally dependent preferences." *Review of Economic Studies*, 40: 1–31.

Sarkissian, S. (2003). "Incomplete consumption risk sharing and currency premiums." *Review of Financial Studies*, 16: 983–1005.

Shanken, J. (1987). "Multivariate Proxies and Asset Pricing Relations: Living with the Roll Critique." *Journal of Financial Economics*, 18: 91–110.

Sharpe, W. F. (1964). "Capital asset prices: a theory of market equilibrium under conditions of risk." *Journal of Finance*, 19: 425–442.

Sharpe, W. F. (1977). "The capital asset pricing model: a multi-beta interpretation," in H. Levy and M. Sarnat, (eds.) *Financial Decision making under uncertainty*. New York: Academic Press.

Singleton, K.J. (1990). "Specification and estimation of intertemporal Asset Pricing Modelas," in E. Friedman and F. Hahn (eds.) *Handbook of Monetary Economics*. North Holland: Elsevier.

Sundaresan, S. M. (1989). "Intertemporally dependent preferences and the volatility of consumption and wealth." *Review of Financial Studies*, 2: 73–89.

Wilson, R. B. (1968). "The theory of syndicates." *Econometrica*, 36: 119–131.

Chapter 9

CONDITIONAL ASSET PRICING

WAYNE E. FERSON, *Boston College, USA*

Abstract

Conditional asset pricing studies predictability in the returns of financial assets, and the ability of asset pricing models to explain this predictability. The relation between predictability and asset pricing models is explained and the empirical evidence for predictability is summarized. Empirical tests of conditional asset pricing models are then briefly reviewed.

KeyWords: stochastic discount factors; financial asset returns; predictability; rational expectations; conditional expectations; discount rates; stock prices; minimum-variance portfolios; mean variance efficiency; latent variables; capital asset pricing models; market price of risk; multiple-beta models

9.1. Introduction

Conditional Asset Pricing refers to a subset of Asset Pricing research in financial economics. (See Chapter 8.) Conditional Asset Pricing focuses on predictability over time in rates of return on financial assets, and the ability of asset pricing models to explain this predictability.

Most asset pricing models are special cases of the fundamental equation:

$$P_t = E_t\{m_{t+1}(P_{t+1} + D_{t+1})\}, \qquad (9.1)$$

where P_t is the price of the asset at time t, and D_{t+1} is the amount of any dividends, interest or other payments received at time $t + 1$. The market-wide random variable m_{t+1} is the "stochastic discount factor" (SDF). By recursive substitution in Equation (9.1), the future price may be eliminated to express the current price as a function of the future cash flows and SDFs only: $P_t = E_t\{\sum_{j>0} (\prod_{k=1,\ldots,j} m_{t+k})D_{t+j}\}$. Prices are obtained by "discounting" the payoffs, or multiplying by SDFs, so that the expected "present value" of the payoff is equal to the price. A SDF "prices" the assets if Equation (9.1) is satisfied, and any particular asset pricing model may be viewed as a specification for the stochastic discount factor.

The notation $E_t\{.\}$ in Equation (9.1) denotes the conditional expectation, given a market-wide information set, Ω_t. Empiricists don't get to see Ω_t, so it is convenient to consider expectations conditional on an observable subset of instruments, Z_t. These expectations are denoted as $E(.|Z_t)$. When Z_t is the null information set, we have the unconditional expectation, denoted as $E(.)$.

Empirical work on conditional asset pricing models typically relies on "rational expectations," which is the assumption that the expectation terms in the model are mathematical conditional expectations. This carries two important implications. First, it implies that the "law of iterated expectations" can be invoked. This says that the expectation, given coarser information, of the conditional expectation given finer information, is the conditional expectation given the coarser information. For example, taking the expected value of Equation (9.1), rational expectations implies that versions of Equation (9.1) must hold for the expectations $E(.|Z_t)$ and $E(.)$. Second, rational expectations implies that the differences between realizations of the random variables and the expectations in the model, should be unrelated to the information that the expectations in the model are conditioned on. This leads to implications for the predictability of asset returns.

Define the gross asset return, $R_{it+1} = (P_{it+1} + D_{it+1})/P_{it}$ The return of the asset i may be predictable. For example, a linear regression over time of R_{it+1} on Z_t may have a nonzero slope coefficient. Equation (9.1) implies that the conditional expectation of the product of m_{t+1} and R_{it+1} is the constant, 1.0. Therefore, $1 - m_{t+1}R_{it+1}$ should not be predictably different from 0 using any information available at time t. If there is predictability in a return R_{it+1} using any lagged instruments Z_t, the model implies that the predictability is removed when R_{it+1} is multiplied by the correct m_{t+1}. This is the sense in which conditional asset pricing models are asked to "explain" predictable variation in asset returns.

If a conditional asset pricing model fails to explain predictability as described above, there are two possibilities (Fama, 1970, 1991). Either the specification of m_{t+1} in the model is wrong, or the use of rational expectations is unjustified. The first instance motivates research on better conditional asset pricing models. The second possibility motivates research on human departures from rationality, and how these show up in asset market prices. For a review of this relatively new field, "behavioral finance," see Barberis and Shleifer (2003).

Studies of predictability in stock and long-term bond returns typically report regressions that attempt to predict the future returns using lagged variables. These regressions for shorter horizon (monthly, or annual holding period) returns typically have small R-squares, as the fraction of the variance in long-term asset returns that can be predicted with lagged variables over short horizons is small. The R-squares are larger for longer-horizon (two- to five-year) returns, because expected returns are considered to be more persistent than returns themselves. Thus, the variance of the expected return accumulates with longer horizons faster than the variance of the return, and the R-squared increases (Fama and French, 1988).

Because stock returns are very volatile, small R-squares can mask economically important variation in the expected return. To illustrate, consider a special case of Equation (9.1), the simple Gordon (1962) constant-growth model for a stock price: $P = kE/(R - g)$, where P is the stock price, E is the earnings per share, k is the dividend payout ratio, g is the future growth rate of earnings, and R is the discount rate. The discount rate is the required or expected return of the stock. Stocks are long "duration" assets, so a small change in the expected return can lead to a large fluctuation in the asset value. Consider an example where the price-to-earnings ratio, $P/E = 15$, the payout ratio, $k = 0.6$, and the expected growth rate, $g = 3$ percent. The expected return, R, is 7 percent. Suppose there is a shock to the expected return, *ceteris paribus*. In this example a change of 1 percent in R leads to approximately a 20 percent change in the asset value.

Of course, it is unrealistic to hold everything else fixed, but the example suggests that small changes in expected returns can produce large and economically significant changes in asset values. Campbell (1991) generalizes the Gordon model to allow for stochastic changes in growth rates, and estimates that changes in expected returns through time may account for about half of the variance of equity index values. Conditional Asset Pricing models focus on these changes in the required or expected rates of return on financial assets.

9.2. The Conditional Capital Asset Pricing Model

The simplest example of a conditional asset pricing model is a conditional version of the Capital Asset Pricing Model (CAPM) of Sharpe (1964):

$$E(R_{it+1}|Z_t) = \gamma_0(Z_t) + \beta_{imt}\gamma_m(Z_t), \qquad (9.2)$$

where R_{it+1} is the rate of return of asset i between times t and $t + 1$, and β_{imt} is the market beta at time t. The market beta is the conditional covariance of the return with the market portfolio divided by the conditional variance of the market portfolio; that is, the slope coefficient in a conditional regression of the asset return on that of the market, conditional on the information at time t. Z_t is the conditioning information, assumed to be publicly available at time t. The term $\gamma_m(Z_t)$ represents the risk premium for market beta, and $\gamma_0(Z_t)$ is the expected return of all portfolios with market betas equal to zero. If there is a risk-free asset available at time t, then its rate of return equals $\gamma_0(Z_t)$.

Sharpe (1964) did not explicitly put the conditioning information, Z_t, into his derivation of the CAPM. The original development was cast in a single-period partial equilibrium model. However, it is natural to interpret the expectations in the model as reflecting a consensus of well-informed analysts' opinion – conditional expectations given their information – and Sharpe's subsequent writings indicated this intent (e.g. Sharpe, 1984). The multiple-beta intertemporal models of Merton (1973) and Cox–Ingersoll–Ross (1985) accommodate conditional expectations explicitly. Merton (1973, 1980) and Cox–Ingersoll–Ross also showed how conditional versions of the CAPM may be derived as special cases of their models.

Roll (1977) and others have shown that a portfolio is "minimum variance" if and only if a model like Equation (9.2) fits the expected returns for all the assets i, using the minimum-variance portfolio as R_{mt+1}. A portfolio is minimum variance if and only if no portfolio with the same expected return has a smaller variance. According to the CAPM, the market portfolio with return R_{mt+1} is minimum variance. If investors are risk averse, the CAPM also implies that the market portfolio is "mean-variance efficient," which says that $\gamma_m(Z_t)$ in Equation (9.2) is positive. In the CAPM, risk-averse investors choose portfolios that have the maximum expected return, given the variance. This implies that there is a positive tradeoff between market risk, as measured by β_{imt}, and the expected return on individual assets, when investors are risk averse. In the conditional CAPM, mean–variance efficiency is defined relative to the conditional expectations and conditional variances of returns. Hansen and Richard (1987) and Ferson and Siegel (2001) describe theoretical relations between conditional and "unconditional" versions of mean–variance efficiency.

The conditional CAPM may be expressed in the SDF representation given by Equation (9.1) as: $m_{t+1} = c_{0t} - c_{1t}R_{mt+1}$. In this case, the coefficients c_{0t} and c_{1t} are specific measurable functions of the information set Z_t, depending on the first and second conditional moments of the returns. To implement the model empirically, it is necessary to specify functional forms for c_{0t} and c_{1t}. Shanken (1990) suggests approximating the coefficients using linear functions, and this approach is followed by Cochrane (1996), Jagannathan and Wang (1996), and other authors.

9.3. Evidence for Return Predictability

Conditional asset pricing presumes the existence of some return predictability. There should be instruments Z_t for which $E(m_{t+1}|Z_t)$ or $E(R_{t+1}|Z_t)$ vary over time, in order for $E(m_{t+1}R_{t+1} - 1|Z_t) = 0$ to have empirical bite. At one level, this is easy. Since $E(m_{t+1}|Z_t)$ should be the inverse of a risk-free return, all we need for the first condition to bite is observable risk-free rates that vary over time. Indeed, a short-term interest rate is one of the most prominent of the lagged instruments used to represent Z_t in empirical work. Ferson (1977) shows that the behavior of stock returns and short-term interest rates, as documented by Fama and Schwert (1977), imply that conditional covariances of returns with m_{t+1} must also vary over time.

Interest in predicting security returns is probably as old as the security markets themselves. Fama (1970) reviews the early evidence and Schwert (2003) reviews anomalies in asset pricing based on predictability. It is useful to distinguish, following Fama (1970), predictability based on the information in past returns ("weak form") from predictability based on lagged economic variables that are public information, not limited to past prices and returns ("semi-strong" form).

A large body of literature studies weak-form predictability, focusing on serial dependence in returns. High-frequency serial dependence, such as daily or intra-day patterns, are often considered to represent the effects of market microstructure, such as bid–ask spreads (e.g. Roll, 1984) and non-synchronous trading of the stocks in an index (e.g. Scholes and Williams, 1977). Serial dependence may also represent predictable changes in the expected returns.

Conrad and Kaul (1989) report serial dependence in weekly returns. Jegadeesh and Titman (1993) find that relatively high-return recent "winner" stocks tend to repeat their performance over three- to nine-month horizons. DeBondt and Thaler (1985) find that past high-return stocks perform poorly over the next five years, and Fama and French (1988) find negative serial dependence over two- to five-year horizons. These serial dependence patterns motivate a large number of studies, which attempt to assess the economic magnitude and statistical robustness of the implied predictability, or to explain the predictability as an economic phenomenon. For a summary of this literature subsequent to Fama (1970), see Campbell et al. (1997). Research in this area continues, and it's fair to say that the jury is still out on the issue of predictability using lagged returns.

A second body of literature studies semi-strong form predictability using other lagged, publicly available information variables as instruments. Fama and French (1989) assemble a list of variables from studies in the early 1980s, which as of this writing remain the workhorse instruments for conditional asset pricing models. In addition to the level of a short-term interest rate, as mentioned above, the variables include the lagged dividend yield of a stock market index, a yield spread of long-term government bonds relative to short-term bonds, and a yield spread of low-grade (high-

default risk and low liquidity) corporate bonds over high-grade corporate bonds. In addition, studies often use the lagged excess return of a medium-term over a short-term Treasury bill (Campbell, 1987; Ferson and Harvey, 1991). Additional instruments include an aggregate book-to-market ratio (Pontiff and Schall, 1998) and lagged consumption-to-wealth ratios (Lettau and Ludvigson, 2001a). Of course, many other predictor variables have been proposed and more will doubtless be proposed in the future.

Predictability using lagged instruments remains controversial, and there are some good reasons the measured predictability could be spurious. Studies have identified various statistical biases in predictive regressions (e.g. Hansen and Hodrick, 1980; Stambaugh, 1999; Ferson et al., 2003), and have questioned the stability of predictive relations across economic regimes (e.g. Kim et al., 1991; or Paye and Timmermann, 2003) and raised the possibility that the lagged instruments arise solely through data mining (e.g. Lo and MacKinlay, 1990; Foster et al., 1997).

A reasonable response to these concerns is to see if the predictive relations hold out-of-sample. This kind of evidence is also mixed. Some studies find support for predictability in step-ahead or out-of-sample exercises (e.g. Fama and French, 1989; Pesaran and Timmerman, 1995). Similar instruments show some ability to predict returns outside the United States, where they were originally studied (e.g. Harvey, 1991; Solnik, 1993; Ferson and Harvey, 1993, 1999). However, other studies conclude that predictability using the standard lagged instruments does not hold in more recent samples (e.g. Goyal and Welch, 2003; Simin, 2002). It seems that research on the predictability of security returns will always be interesting, and conditional asset pricing models should be useful in framing many future investigations of these issues.

9.4. Tests of Conditional CAPMs

Empirical studies have rejected versions of the CAPM that ignore lagged variables. This evidence, and mounting evidence of predictable variation in the distribution of security returns led to empirical work on conditional versions of the CAPM starting in the early 1980s. An example from Equation (9.2) illustrates the implications of the conditional CAPM for predictability in returns. Rational expectations implies that the actual return differs from the conditional expected value by an error term, u_{it+1}, which is orthogonal to the information at time t. If the actual returns are predictable using information in Z_t, the model implies that either the betas or the premiums ($\gamma_m(Z_t)$ and $\gamma_0(Z_t)$), are changing as functions of Z_t, and the time variation in those functions should track the predictable components of asset returns. If the time variation in $\gamma_m(Z_t)$ and $\gamma_0(Z_t)$ can be modeled, the conditional CAPM can be tested by examining its ability to explain the predictability in returns.

The earliest empirical tests along these lines were the "latent variable models," developed by Hansen and Hodrick (1983) and Gibbons and Ferson (1985), and later refined by Campbell (1987) and Ferson et al. (1993). These models allow time varying expected returns, but maintain the assumption that the conditional betas are fixed parameters over time.

Consider the conditional representation of the CAPM. Let $r_{it+1} = R_{it+1} - R_{0t+1}$, and similarly for the market return, where R_{0t+1} is the gross, zero beta return. The conditional CAPM may then be stated for the vector of excess returns r_{t+1}, as $E(\mathbf{r}_{t+1}|Z_t) = \boldsymbol{\beta} E(r_{mt+1}|Z_t)$, where $\boldsymbol{\beta}$ is the vector of assets' betas. Let r_{1t} be any reference asset excess return with nonzero beta, β_1, so that $E(r_{1t+1}|Z_t) = \beta_1 E(r_{mt+1}|Z_t)$. Solving this expression for $E(r_{mt+1}|Z_t)$ and substituting, we have $E(\mathbf{r}_{t+1}|Z_t) = \mathbf{C}E(r_{1t+1}|Z_t)$, where $\mathbf{C} = (\boldsymbol{\beta}/\beta_1)$. and ./ denotes element-by-element division. The expected market risk premium is now a latent variable in the model, and $\mathbf{C}$ is the $\mathbf{N}$-vector of the model parameters. Gibbons and Ferson (1985) argued that the latent variable model is attractive in view of the difficulties associated with measuring the true market portfolio of the CAPM, but Wheatley (1989) emphasized that it remains neces-

sary to assume that ratios of the betas measured with respect to the unobserved market portfolio, are constant parameters.

Campbell (1987) and Ferson and Foerster (1994) show that a single-beta latent variable model is rejected by the data. This rejects the hypothesis that there is a conditional minimum-variance portfolio such that the ratios of conditional betas on this portfolio are fixed parameters. Therefore, the empirical evidence suggests that conditional asset pricing models should be consistent with either (1) a time varying beta, or (2) more than one beta for each asset.

Conditional CAPMs with time varying betas are examined by Harvey (1989), replacing the constant beta assumption with the assumption that the ratio of the expected market premium to the conditional market variance is a fixed parameter: $E(r_{mt+1}|Z_t)/\text{Var}(r_{mt+1}|Z_t) = \gamma$. Then, the conditional expected returns may be written according to the conditional CAPM as $E(r_{t+1}|Z_t) = \gamma \ \text{Cov}(r_{t+1}, r_{mt+1}|Z_t)$. Harvey's version of the conditional CAPM is motivated from Merton's (1980) model, in which the ratio γ, called the "market price of risk," is equal to the relative risk aversion of a representative investor in equilibrium. Harvey also assumes that the conditional expected risk premium on the market (and the conditional market variance, given fixed γ) is a linear function of the instruments: $E(r_{mt+1}|Z_t) = \boldsymbol{\delta}_m{}'Z_t$, where $\boldsymbol{\delta}_m$ is a coefficient vector. He rejects this version of the conditional CAPM for monthly data in the United States. In Harvey (1991), the same formulation is rejected when applied to a world market portfolio and monthly data on the stock markets of 21 developed countries.

Lettau and Ludvigson (2001b) examine a conditional CAPM with time varying betas and risk premiums, using rolling time-series and cross-sectional regression methods. They condition the model on a lagged, consumption-to-wealth ratio, and find that the conditional CAPM works better for explaining the cross-section of monthly stock returns.

9.5. Multi-beta Conditional Asset Pricing Models

A multi-beta asset pricing model essentially expands Equation (9.2) to allow for multiple sources of risk and expected return. Such a model asserts that the expected return is a linear function of several betas, i.e.

$$E_t(R_{it+1}) = \lambda_{0t} + \Sigma_{j=1,\ldots,K}\beta_{ijt}\lambda_{jt}, \qquad (9.3)$$

where the $\beta_{ijt}, j = 1, \ldots, K$, are the conditional multiple regression coefficients of the return of asset i on K risk factors, $f_{jt+1}, j = 1, \ldots, K$. The coefficient λ_{0t} is the expected return on an asset that has $\beta_{0jt} = 0$, for $j = 1, \ldots, K$; i.e. it is the expected return on a zero-(multiple-) beta asset. If there is a risk-free asset, then λ_{0t} is the return of this asset. The coefficient λ_{kt}, corresponding to the k'th factor has the following interpretation: it is the expected return differential, or premium, for a portfolio that has $\beta_{ikt} = 1$ and $\beta_{ijt} = 0$ for all $j \neq k$, measured in excess of the zero-beta asset's expected return. In other words, it is the expected return premium per unit of beta risk for the risk factor, k. Multiple-beta models follow when m_{t+1} can be written as a conditional linear function of the K factors, as shown by Ferson and Jagannathan (1996).

Bansal and Viswanathan (1993) developed conditional versions of the CAPM and multiple-factor models in which the stochastic discount factor m_{t+1} is a nonlinear function of the market or factor returns. Using nonparametric methods, they find evidence to support the nonlinear versions of the models. Bansal et al. (1993) compare the performance of nonlinear models with linear models, using data on international stocks, bonds, and currency returns, and they find that the nonlinear models perform better. Farnsworth et al. (2002) compared the empirical performance of a large set of conditional asset pricing models using the SDF representation.

Conditional multiple-beta models with constant betas are examined empirically by Ferson and Harvey (1991), Evans (1994), and Ferson and Korajczyk (1995), who find that while such models are rejected using the usual statistical tests, they still capture a large fraction of the predictability of stock and bond returns over time. Allowing for time varying betas, these studies find that the time variation in betas contributes a relatively small amount to the time variation in expected asset returns, while time variation in the risk premium are relatively more important.

While time variation in conditional betas is not as important as time variation in expected risk premiums, from the perspective of modeling predictable time variation in asset returns, this does not imply that beta variation is empirically unimportant. From the perspective of modeling the cross-sectional variation in "unconditional" expected asset returns, beta variation over time may be empirically very important. This idea was first explored by Chan and Chen (1988). To see how this works, consider the unconditional expected excess return vector, obtained from the model as $E\{E(\mathbf{r}|Z)\} = E\{\lambda(Z)\boldsymbol{\beta}(Z)\} = E(\lambda)E(\boldsymbol{\beta}) + \text{Cov}(\lambda(Z),\boldsymbol{\beta}(Z))$. Viewed as a cross-sectional relation, the term $\text{Cov}(\lambda(Z),\boldsymbol{\beta}(Z))$ may differ significantly in a cross-section of assets. Therefore the implications of a conditional version of the CAPM for the cross-section of unconditional expected returns may depend importantly on common time variation in betas and expected market risk premiums.

Jagannathan and Wang (1996) used the conditional CAPM to derive a particular "unconditional" 2-factor model. They show that $m_{t+1} = \alpha_0 + \alpha_1 E(r_{mt+1}|\Omega_t) + R_{mt+1}$, where Ω_t denotes the information set of investors and a_0 and a_1 are fixed parameters, is a valid SDF in the sense that $E(R_{i,t+1}m_{t+1}) = 1$ for this choice of m_{t+1}. Assuming that $E(r_{mt+1}|Z_t)$ is a linear function of Z_t, they find that their version of the model explains the cross-section of unconditional expected returns better than an unconditional version of the CAPM.

New empirical tests of the conditional CAPM and multiple-beta models, using the multi-beta representation and SDF representations, continue to appear regularly in the literature. Future studies will continue to refine the relationships among the various empirical specifications. Research on the predictability of security returns will always be interesting, and Conditional Asset Pricing Models should be useful in framing many future investigations of these issues.

REFERENCES

Bansal, R. and Viswanathan, S. (1993). "No arbitrage and arbitrage pricing: a new approach." *Journal of Finance*, 48: 1231–1262.

Bansal, R., Hsieh, D., and Viswanathan, S. (1993). "A new approach to international arbitrage pricing." *Journal of Finance*, 48: 1719–1747.

Barberis, N. and Shleifer, A. (2003). "A survey of behavioral finance," in R. Stulz (ed.) *Handbook of the Economics of Finance*. North Holland: Elsevier.

Campbell, J.Y. (1987). "Stock returns and the term structure." *Journal of Financial Economics*, 18: 373–399.

Campbell, J.Y. (1991). "A variance decomposition for stock returns." *Economic Journal*, 101: 157–179.

Campbell, J.Y., Lo, A., and MacKinlay, A.C. (1997). *The Econometrics of Financial Markets*. Princeton: Princeton University Press.

Chan, K.C. and Chen, N.F. (1988). "An unconditional test of asset pricing and the role of firm size as an instrumental variable for risk." *Journal of Finance*, 63: 431–468.

Cochrane, J.H. (1996). "A cross-sectional test of a production based asset pricing model." *Journal of Political Economy*, 104(3): 572–621.

Conrad, J. and Kaul, G. (1989). "Mean reversion in short-horizon expected returns." *Review of Financial Studies*, 2: 225–240.

Cox, J.C., Ingersoll, J.E., and Ross, S.A. (1985). "A theory of the term structure of interest rates." *Econometrica*, 53: 385–408.

DeBondt, W. and Thaler, R. (1985). "Does the stock market overreact?" *Journal of Finance*, 40: 793–805.

Evans, M.D.D. (1994). "Expected returns, time-varying risk and risk premia." *Journal of Finance*, 49(2): 655–679.

Fama, E.F. (1970). "Efficient capital markets: a review of theory and empirical work." *Journal of Finance*, 25: 383–417.

Fama, E.F. (1991). "Efficient capital markets II." *Journal of Finance*, 46: 1575–1618.

Fama, E. and French, K. (1988). "Permanent and temporary components of stock prices." *Journal of Political Economy*, 96: 246–273.

Fama, E. and French, K. (1989). "Business conditions and expected returns on stocks and bonds." *Journal of Financial Economics*, 25: 23–49.

Fama, E.F. and Schwert, G.W. (1977). "Asset returns and inflation." *Journal of Financial Economics*, 5: 115–146.

Farnsworth, H., Ferson, W.E., Jackson, D., and Todd, S. (2002). "Performance evaluation with stochastic discount factors." *Journal of Business*, 75: 473–504.

Ferson, W.E. (1989). "Changes in expected security returns, risk and the level of interest rates." *Journal of Finance*, 44: 1191–1217.

Ferson, W.E. and Foerster, S.R. (1994). "Finite sample properties of the generalized methods of moments tests of conditional asset pricing models." *Journal of Financial Economics*, 36: 29–56.

Ferson, W.E. and Harvey, C.R. (1991). "The variation of economic risk premiums." *Journal of Political Economy*, 99: 385–415.

Ferson, W.E. and Harvey, C.R. (1993). "The risk and predictability of international equity returns." *Review of Financial Studies*, 6: 527–566.

Ferson, W.E. and Harvey, C.R. (1999). "Economic, financial and fundamental global risk in and out of EMU." *Swedish Economic Policy Review*, 6: 123–184.

Ferson, W.E. and Jagannathan, R. (1996). "Econometric evaluation of Asset Pricing Models," in G.S. Maddala and C.R. Rao (eds.) *Handbook of Statistics*. 14 Chapter 1, 1–30, Amsterdam, the Netherlands.

Ferson, W.E. and Korajczyk, R.A. (1995). "Do arbitrage pricing models explain the predictability of stock returns?" *Journal of Business*, 68: 309–349.

Ferson, W.E. and Siegel, A.F. (2001). "The efficient use of conditioning information in portfolios." *Journal of Finance*, 56: 967–982.

Ferson, W.E., Foerster, S.R., and Keim, D.B. (1993). "General tests of latent variable models and mean variance spanning." *Journal of Finance*, 48: 131–156.

Ferson, W.E., Sarkissian, S., and Simin, T. (2003). "Spurious regressions in financial economics?" *Journal of Finance*, 58: 1393–1414.

Foster, D., Smith, T., and Whaley, R. (1997). "Assessing goodness-of-fit of asset pricing models: the distribution of the maximal R-squared." *Journal of Finance*, 52: 591–607.

Gibbons, M.R. and Ferson, W.E. (1985). "Testing asset pricing models with changing expectations and an unobservable market portfolio." *Journal of Financial Economics*, 14: 217–236.

Gordon, M. (1962). *The investment, financing and valuation of the firm*. Homewood, IL: Irwin.

Goyal, A., and Welch, I. (2003). "Predicting the equity premium with dividend ratios." *Management Science*, 49(5).

Hansen, L.P. and Hodrick, R. (1980). "Forward exchange rates as optimal predictors of future spot rates: An econometric analysis." *Journal of Political Economy*, 88: 829–853.

Hansen, L.P. and Hodrick, R.J.(1983). "Risk averse speculation in the forward foreign exchange market," in J. Frenkel (ed.) *An econometric analysis of linear models, exchange rates and international macroeconomics*. Chicago, IL: University of Chicago Press.

Hansen, L.P. and Richard, S.F. (1987). "The role of conditioning information in deducing testable restrictions implied by dynamic asset pricing models." *Econometrica*, 55: 587–613.

Harvey, C.R. (1989). "Time-varying conditional covariances in tests of asset pricing models." *Journal of Financial Economics*, 24: 289–318.

Harvey, C.R. (1991). "The world price of covariance risk." *Journal of Finance*, 46: 111–157.

Jagannathan, R. and Wang, Z. (1996). "The conditional CAPM and the cross-section of expected returns." *Journal of Finance*, 51: 3–54.

Jegadeesh, N. and Titman, S. (1993). "Returns to buying winners and selling losers: implications for stock market efficiency." *Journal of Finance*, 48: 65–91.

Kim, M., Nelson, C.R., and Startz, R. (1991). "Mean reversion in stock returns? a reappraisal of the statistical evidence." *Review of Economic Studies*, 58: 515–528.

Lettau, M. and Ludvigson, S. (2001a). "Consumption, aggregate wealth and expected stock returns." *Journal of Finance*, 56: 815–849.

Lettau, M. and Ludvigson, S. (2001b). "Resurrecting the (C)CAPM: A Cross-Sectional Test when Risk Premia are Time-Varying." *Journal of Political Economy*, 109(6): 1238–1287.

Lo, A. and MacKinlay, A.C. (1990). "Data snooping biases in tests of financial asset pricing models." *Review of Financial Studies*, 3: 431–468.

Merton, R.C. (1973). "An intertemporal capital asset pricing model." *Econometrica*, 41: 867–887.

Merton, R.C. (1980). "On estimating the expected return on the market: an exploratory investigation." *Journal of Financial Economics*, 8: 323–362.

Paye, B. and Timmermann, A. (2003). "How stable are financial prediction models? Evidence from US and International Stock Market Data." Working Paper, University of California at San Diego.

Pesaran, M.H. and Timmermann, A. (1995). "Predictability of stock returns: Robustness and economic significance." *Journal of Finance*, 50: 1201–1228.

Pontiff, J. and Schall, L. (1998). "Book-to-market as a predictor of market returns." *Journal of Financial Economics*, 49: 141–160.

Roll, R. (1977). "A critique of the asset pricing theory's tests -part 1: On past and potential testability of the theory." *Journal of Financial Economics*, 4: 129–176.

Roll, R. (1984). "A simple implicit measure of the effective bid-ask spread in an efficient market." *Journal of Finance*, 39: 1127–1140.

Scholes, M. and Williams, J. (1977). "Estimating beta from nonsynchronous data." *Journal of Financial Economics*, 5: 309–327.

Schwert, G.W. (2003). "Anomalies and market efficiency," in G.M. Constantinides, M. Harris and R.M. Stulz (eds.) *Handbook of the Economics of Finance*. North Holland: Elsevier.

Shanken, J. (1990). "Intertemporal asset pricing: an empirical investigation." *Journal of Econometrics*, 45: 99–120.

Sharpe, W.F. (1964). "Capital asset prices: a theory of market equilibrium under conditions of risk." *Journal of Finance*, 19: 425–442.

Sharpe, W.F. (1984). "Factor models, CAPM's and the APT." *Journal of Portfolio Management*, 11: 21–25.

Simin, T. (2002). "The (poor) predictive performance of asset pricing models." Working Paper, The Pennsylvania State University.

Solnik, B. (1993). "The unconditional performance of international asset allocation strategies using conditioning information." *Journal of Empirical Finance*, 1: 33–55

Stambaugh, R.S. (1999). "Predictive regressions." *Journal of Financial Economics*, 54: 315–421.

Wheatley, S. (1989). "A critique of latent variable tests of asset pricing models." *Journal of Financial Economics*, 23: 325–338.

Chapter 10

CONDITIONAL PERFORMANCE EVALUATION

WAYNE E. FERSON, *Boston College, USA*

Abstract

Measures for evaluating the performance of a mutual fund or other managed portfolio are interpreted as the difference between the average return of the fund and that of an appropriate benchmark portfolio. Traditional measures use a fixed benchmark to match the average risk of the fund. Conditional performance measures use a dynamic strategy as the benchmark, matching the fund's risk dynamics. The logic of this approach is explained, the models are described and the empirical evidence is reviewed.

Keywords: security selection; market timing; investment performance; benchmark portfolio; alpha; market efficiency; conditional alpha; risk dynamics; stochastic discount factor; conditional beta; portfolio weights; mutual funds; pension funds

10.1. Conditional Performance Evaluation

Conditional Performance Evaluation is a collection of empirical approaches for measuring the investment performance of portfolio managers, adjusting for the risks and other characteristics of their portfolios. A central goal of performance evaluation in general, is to identify those managers who possess investment information or skills superior to that of the investing public, and who use the advantage to achieve superior portfolio returns. Just as important, we would like to identify and avoid those managers with poor performance. Since the risks and expected returns of financial assets are related, it is important to adjust for the risks taken by a portfolio manager in evaluating the returns. In order to identify superior returns, some model of "normal" investment returns is required, i.e. an asset pricing model is needed (see the entries on Asset Pricing Models and Conditional Asset Pricing).

Classical measures of investment performance compare the average return of a managed portfolio to that of a "benchmark portfolio" with similar risk. For example, Jensen (1968) advocated "alpha" as a performance measure. This is the average return minus the expected return implied by the Capital Asset Pricing Model (Sharpe, 1964). The CAPM implies that the expected return is a fund-specific combination of a safe asset and a broad market portfolio, and so this combination is the benchmark. Chen et al. (1987), Connor and Korajczyk (1986), and Lehmann and Modest (1987) extended this idea to multi-beta asset pricing models, where several returns are combined in the benchmark to adjust for the fund's risk.

It is traditional to distinguish between investment ability for security selection and ability for market timing. Security selection refers to an ability to pick securities that are "undervalued" at current market prices, and which therefore may be expected to offer superior future returns.

Market timing refers to an ability to switch the portfolio between stocks and bonds, anticipating which asset class will perform better in the near future. The classical performance measures are "unconditional," in the sense that the expected returns in the model are unconditional means, estimated by past averages, and the risks are the fixed unconditional second moments of return. If expected returns and risks vary over time, the classical approach is likely to be unreliable. Ferson and Schadt (1996) showed that if the risk exposure of a managed portfolio varies predictably with the business cycle, but the manager has no superior investment ability, then a traditional approach will confuse common variation in the fund's risk and the expected market returns with abnormal stock picking or market timing ability. "Conditional Performance Evaluation" (CPE) models the conditional expected returns and risk, attempting to account for their changes with the state of the economy, thus controlling for any common variation.

The problem of confounding variation in mutual fund risks and market returns has long been recognized (e.g. Jensen, 1972; Grant, 1977), but these studies tend to interpret such variation as reflecting superior information or market timing ability. A conditional approach to performance evaluation takes the view that a managed portfolio whose return can be replicated by mechanical trading, based on readily available public information, should not be judged to have superior performance. CPE is therefore consistent with a version of market efficiency, in the semi-strong form sense of Fama (1970).

In the CPE approach a fund's return is compared with a benchmark strategy that attempts to match the fund's risk dynamics. The benchmark strategy does this by mechanically trading, based on predetermined variables that measure the state of the economy. The performance measures, the "conditional alphas," are the difference between a fund's return and that of the benchmark dynamic strategy. This generalizes the classical performance measures, such as Jensen's alpha, which compare a fund's return with a fixed benchmark that carries the same average risk. Since CPE uses more information than traditional performance measures, it has the potential to provide more accuracy. In practice, the trading behavior of managers overlays portfolio dynamics on the dynamic behavior of the underlying assets that they trade. For example, even if the risk of each security were fixed over time, the risk of a portfolio with time-varying weights, would be time varying. The desire to handle such dynamic behavior motivates a conditional approach. Investors may wish to understand how funds implement their investment policies dynamically over time. For example, how is a fund's bond–stock mix, market exposure, or investment style expected to react in a time of high-interest rates or market volatility? CPE is designed to provide a rich description of funds' portfolio dynamics in relation to the state of the economy.

A conditional approach to performance evaluation can accommodate whatever standard of superior information is held to be appropriate, by the choice of the lagged instruments, which are used to represent the public information. Incorporating a given set of lagged instruments, managers who trade mechanically in response to these variables get no credit for superior performance. To represent public information, much of the empirical literature to date has focused on a standard set of lagged variables. Examples include the levels of interest rates and interest rate spreads, dividend-to-price ratios, and dummy variables indicating calendar-related patterns of predictability. More recent studies expand the analysis to consider a wider range of indicators for public information about the state of the economy (e.g. Ferson and Qian, 2004).

10.2. Examples

Implementations of Conditional Performance Evaluation have typically used either simple linear regression models or "stochastic discount factor" methods. (See the entry on Asset Pricing.) Ferson and Schadt (1996) used simple linear regressions. To illustrate, let r_{mt+1} be the return on a market or benchmark index, measured in excess of a short-term Treasury return. For example, the benchmark index could be the Standard & Poor's 500, a "style" index such as "small cap growth," or a vector of excess returns. The traditional regression for Jensen"'s alpha is:

$$r_{pt+1} = \alpha_{pJ} + \beta_p r_{mt+1} + \varepsilon_{pt+1}, \qquad (10.1)$$

where r_{pt+1} is the return of the fund in excess of a short term "cash" instrument and α_{pJ} is Jensen's alpha. Ferson and Schadt (1996) proposed the conditional model:

$$r_{pt+1} = \alpha_p + \beta_o r_{mt+1} + \boldsymbol{\beta}'[r_{mt+1} \otimes \mathbf{Z}_t] + u_{pt+1},$$
$$(10.2)$$

where $\mathbf{Z}_t$ is the vector of lagged conditioning variables and α_p is the conditional alpha. The coefficient β_o is the average beta of the fund, and $\boldsymbol{\beta}'\mathbf{Z}_t$ captures the time-varying part of the conditional beta. The interaction terms $[r_{mt+1} \otimes \mathbf{Z}_t]$ in the Ferson and Schadt regression model control for common movements in the fund's "beta", and the conditional expected benchmark return. The conditional alpha, α_p, is thus measured net of these effects.

To see more explicitly how Equation (10.2) compares the fund's return to a benchmark strategy with the same risk dynamics, recall that the excess returns are $r_{pt+1} = R_{pt+1} - R_{ft+1}$ and $r_{mt+1} = R_{mt+1} - R_{ft+1}$, where R_{ft+1} is the gross return of a risk-free asset. The benchmark strategy is to invest the fraction $\beta_0 + \boldsymbol{\beta}'\mathbf{Z}_t$ of the portfolio in the market index with return R_{mt+1}, and the fraction $1 - \beta_0 - \boldsymbol{\beta}'\mathbf{Z}_t$ in the risk-free investment. This benchmark strategy has a time-varying beta equal to $\beta_0 + \boldsymbol{\beta}'\mathbf{Z}_t$, the same as that ascribed to the fund. The conditional alpha is just the difference between the fund's average return and the average return of the benchmark strategy.

Christopherson et al. (1998) propose a refinement of Equation (10.2) to allow for a time-varying conditional alpha:

$$r_{p,t+1} = \alpha_{p0} + \boldsymbol{\alpha}_{1_p}'\mathbf{Z}_t + \beta_o r_{m,t+1}$$
$$+ \boldsymbol{\beta}'[r_{m,t+1} \otimes \mathbf{Z}_t] + u_{pt+1}. \qquad (10.3)$$

In this model, the term $\alpha_{p0} + \boldsymbol{\alpha}_{1p}'\mathbf{Z}_t$ captures the time-varying conditional alpha.

An alternative approach to Conditional Performance Evaluation uses "SDF" models, as developed by Chen and Knez (1996), Dalhquist and Soderlind (1999), Farnsworth et al. (2002) and Ferson et al. (2006). With this approach, abnormal performance is measured by the expected product of a fund's returns and a SDF. (See the entry on Asset Pricing Models for a discussion of stochastic discount factors.) Specifying the stochastic discount factor corresponds to specifying an asset pricing model. For a given SDF, denoted by m_{t+1}, we can define a fund's "conditional SDF alpha" as:

$$\alpha_{pt} \equiv E(m_{t+1}R_{pt+1}|Z_t) - 1, \qquad (10.4)$$

where one dollar invested with the fund at time t returns R_{pt+1} dollars at time $t+1$. In the case of an open-end, no-load mutual fund, we may think of R_{pt+1} as the net asset value return. More generally, if the fund generates a payoff V_{pt+1} for a cost $c_{pt} > 0$, the gross return is $R_{pt+1} \equiv V_{pt+1}/c_{pt}$. A SDF is said to price the vector of underlying primitive assets with returns $\mathbf{R}_{t+1}$ if their gross returns satisfy the equation $E_t\{m_{t+1}\mathbf{R}_{t+1}\} = \mathbf{1}$.

If the SDF prices the primitive assets, α_{pt} will be zero when the fund (costlessly) forms a portfolio of the primitive assets, provided the portfolio strategy uses only the public information at time t. In that case $R_{p,t+1} = \mathbf{x}(Z_t)'\mathbf{R}_{t+1}$, where $\mathbf{x}(Z_t)$ is the portfolio weight vector. Then Equation (10.3) implies that $\alpha_{pt} = [E(m_{t+1}\mathbf{x}(Z_t)'\mathbf{R}_{t+1}|Z_t)] - 1 = \mathbf{x}(Z_t)'[E(m_{t+1}\mathbf{R}_{t+1}|Z_t)] - 1 = \mathbf{x}(Z_t)'\mathbf{1} - 1 = 0$.

When the SDF alpha of a fund is not zero, this is interpreted to indicate "abnormal" performance relative to the model that provides the specification of m_{t+1}. The economic intuition is simple when $m_{t+1} = \rho u'(C_{t+1})/u'(C_t)$ in the consumer choice problem: Maximize the expected utility function $E_t\{\Sigma_{j \geq 0}\rho^j u(C_{t+j})\}$. Then, the condition $E_t\{m_{t+1}\mathbf{R}_{t+1}\} = \mathbf{1}$ is the necessary first-order condition of the maximization. If the consumer–investor in this problem can invest in a fund with a given SDF alpha, the consumer–investor would wish to hold more of the fund with $\alpha_{pt} > 0$, and less of the fund with $\alpha_{pt} < 0$.

10.3. Conditional Market Timing

A classical market timing regression, when there is no conditioning information, is the quadratic regression:

$$r_{pt+1} = a_p + b_p r_{mt+1} + \gamma_{tmu}[r_{m,t+1}]^2 + v_{pt+1}. \quad (10.5)$$

Treynor and Mazuy (1966) argue that $\gamma_{tmu} > 0$ indicates market timing ability. The logic is that a market timing manager will generate a return that has a convex relation to the market. When the market is up, the fund will be up by a disproportionate amount. When the market is down, the fund will be down by a lesser amount. However, a convex relation may arise for a number of other reasons. Chen et al. (2005) provide an analysis of various nonlinear effects unrelated to true-timing ability. One of these is common time variation in the fund's risk and the expected market return, due to public information on the state of the economy. In a market timing context, the goal of conditional performance evaluation is to distinguish timing ability that merely reflects publicly available information, from timing based on better information. We may call such informed timing ability "conditional market timing."

Admati et al. (1986) describe a model in which a manager with constant absolute risk aversion in a normally distributed world, observes at time t a private signal equal to the future market return plus noise, $r_{mt+1} + \eta$. The manager's response is to change the portfolio beta as a linear function of the signal. They show that the γ_{tmu} coefficient in regression in Equation (10.5) is positive, if the manager increases market exposure when the signal about the future market return is favorable. Bhattacharya and Pfleiderer (1983), and Lee and Rahman (1990) show how to use the squared re-

siduals of the regression to separate the manager's risk aversion from the signal quality, measured by its correlation with the market return.

In a conditional model, the part of the correlation of fund betas with the future market return, which can be attributed to the public information, is not considered to reflect conditional market timing ability. Ferson and Schadt (1996) developed a conditional version of the Treynor–Mazuy regression:

$$
\begin{aligned}
r_{pt+1} = {} & a_p + b_p r_{mt+1} + \mathbf{C}_p'(\mathbf{Z}_t r_{mt+1}) \\
& + \gamma_{tmc}[r_{m,t+1}]^2 + v_{pt+1},
\end{aligned} \quad (10.6)
$$

where the coefficient vector $\mathbf{C}_p$ captures the linear response of the manager's beta to the public information, $\mathbf{Z}_t$. The term $\mathbf{C}_p'(\mathbf{Z}_t r_{mt+1})$ controls the public information effect, which would bias the coefficients in the original Treynor–Mazuy model. The coefficient γ_{tmc} measures the sensitivity of the manager's beta to the private market timing signal, purged of the effects of the public information.

Merton and Henriksson (1981) and Henriksson (1984) described an alternative model of market timing in which the quadratic term in Equation (10.5) is replaced by an option payoff, $\max(0, r_{m,t+1})$. This reflects the idea that market timers may be thought of as delivering (attractively priced) put options on the market index. Ferson and Schadt (1996) developed a conditional version of this model as well.

Becker et al. (1999) developed conditional market timing models with explicit performance benchmarks. In this case, managers maximize the utility of their portfolio returns in excess of a benchmark portfolio return. The model allows separate identification of the manager's risk aversion and skill, as measured by the signal quality. Performance benchmarks often represent an important component of managers' incentive systems, but they have been controversial, both in practice and in the academic literature. Starks (1987), Grinblatt and Titman (1989a,b), and Admati and Pfleiderer (1997) argue that benchmarks don't properly align managers' incentives with those of the investors in the fund. Carpenter et al. (2000) provide a theoretical justification of benchmarks, used in combination with investment restrictions.

10.4. Conditional weight-based Performance Measures

Returns-based measures of performance compare the return earned by the fund with a benchmark return over the evaluation period. The benchmark is designed to control for risk, and it may also control for style, investment constraints, and other factors. The manager who performs better than the benchmark has a positive "alpha." In some situations, information on the manager's investment positions or portfolio weights is also available. In these situations, weight-based measures of performance are attractive. With weight-based measures the manager's choices are directly analyzed for evidence of superior ability. The idea is that a manager, who increases the fund's exposure to a security or asset class before it performs well, or who avoids "losers" ahead of time, is seen to add investment value.

Cornell (1979) was among the first to propose the usage of portfolio weights to measure the performance of trading strategies. Copeland and Mayers (1982) modify Cornell's measure and use it to analyze Value Line rankings. Grinblatt and Titman (1993) proposed a weight-based measure of mutual fund performance. A number of studies have used the Grinblatt and Titman measure, including Grinblatt and Titman (1989); Grinblatt et al. (1995); Zheng (1999); and Wermers (1997). These studies combine portfolio weights with unconditional moments of returns to measure performance.

Ferson and Khang (2002) consider conditioning information in weight-based measures of performance. The idea is similar to that of conditional, returns-based measures. Any predictive ability in a manager's portfolio weights that merely reflects the lagged, public information is not considered to represent superior ability. By using lagged instru-

ments and portfolio weight data, conditional weight-based measures should provide more precision in measuring performance.

The use of portfolio weights may be especially important in a conditional setting. When expected returns are time varying and managers trade between return observation dates, returns-based approaches are likely to be biased. Even conditional returns-based methods are affected. This bias, which Ferson and Khang call the "interim trading bias," can be avoided by using portfolio weights in a conditional setting.

The following stylized example illustrates the idea. Suppose that returns can only be measured over two periods, but a manager trades each period. The manager has neutral performance, but the portfolio weights for the second period can react to public information at the middle date. By assumption, merely reacting to public information does not require superior ability. You have to trade "smarter" than the general public to generate superior performance. If returns were independent over time there would be no interim trading bias, because there would be no information at the middle date about the second-period return.

Suppose that a terrorist event at the middle date increases market volatility in the second period, and the manager responds by shifting into cash at the middle date. If only two-period returns can be measured and evaluated, the manager's strategy would appear to have partially anticipated the higher volatility. For example, the fund's two-period market exposure would reflect some average of the before- and after-event positions. Measured from the beginning of the first period, the portfolio would appear to partially "time" the volatility increasing event because of the move into cash. A returns-based measure over the two periods will detect this as superior information.

In this example, since only two-period returns can be measured and evaluated, a Conditional Weight-based Measure (CWM) would examine the ability of the manager's choices at the beginning of the first period to predict the subsequent two-period returns. To record abnormal ability under the CWM, the manager would have to anticipate the higher volatility and adjust the portfolio prior to the event. If the manager has no information beyond the public information, the CWM is zero. The ability of the manager to trade at the middle period thus creates no interim trading bias in a CWM.

The CWM is the conditional covariance between future returns and portfolio weights, summed across the asset holdings:

$$\text{CWM} = E\{\Sigma_j w_j(Z, S)[r_j - E(r_j|Z)]|Z\}. \quad (10.7)$$

The symbol $w_j(Z,S)$ denotes the portfolio weight in asset j at the beginning of the period and $r_j - E(r_j|Z)$ denotes the unexpected or abnormal excess return. The expectation is taken from the perspective of an investor, who only sees the public information Z at the beginning of the period. As viewed by an investor with this information, the sum of the conditional covariances between the weights, measured at the end of December, and the subsequent abnormal returns for the securities in the first quarter, is positive for a manager with superior information, S. If the manager has no superior information, S, then the covariance is zero.

It is important to recognize that weight-based measures do not avoid the issue of specifying a performance benchmark. For example, Equation (10.7) can also be written as

$$\text{CWM} = E\{\Sigma_j w_j(Z, S)r_j - \Sigma_j E(w_j(Z, S)|Z)]r_j\}. \quad (10.8)$$

This shows that the measure is the expected difference between the portfolio return and the return of a portfolio that uses the weights that would have been expected on the basis of the public information. The latter portfolio may be interpreted as the benchmark.

In a portfolio with abnormal performance, the covariance between the weights and subsequent abnormal returns need not be positive for every security. Consider two securities, which are highly correlated with each other. A manager with superior ability may buy one and sell the other as a result of hedging considerations. However, under certain assumptions the sum of the covariances across securities will be positive (Grinblatt and Titman, 1993).

Ferson and Khang (2002) introduce an explicit "external" benchmark with weights, $w_{jb}(Z)$, which are in the public information set Z at the beginning of the period. Their empirical measure is then:

$$\text{CWM} = E\{\Sigma_j[w_j(Z, S) - w_{jb}(Z)][r_j - E(r_j|Z)]|Z\}. \quad (10.9)$$

Because w_b is assumed to be known given Z, it will not affect the conditional covariance in theory. However, in practice it is desirable to measure performance relative to an external benchmark. One reason is statistical: the weights w_j may be highly persistent over time, while the deviations from benchmark are better behaved. The benchmark also helps the interpretation. Equation (10.9) is the difference between the unexpected return of the fund and the unexpected return of the benchmark.

In Ferson and Khang, the benchmark at time t is formed from the actual lagged weights of the fund at $t - k$, updated using a buy-and-hold strategy. With the buy-and-hold benchmark, the measure examines the deviations between a manager's weights and a strategy of no trading during the previous k periods. This takes the view that a manager with no information would follow a buy-and-hold strategy.

10.5. Empirical Evidence Using Conditional Performance Evaluation

There is a large body of empirical literature on the performance of mutual funds. Equity-style mutual funds have received the most attention. There are fewer studies of institutional funds such as pension funds, and a relatively small number of studies focus on fixed-income-style funds. Research on the performance of hedge funds has been accumulating rapidly over the past few years.

Traditional measures of the average abnormal performance of mutual funds, like Jensen's alpha, are found to be negative more often than positive across many studies. For example, Jensen (1968) concluded that a typical fund has neutral performance, only after adding back expenses. Traditional measures of market timing often find that any significant market timing ability is perversely "negative," suggesting that investors could time the market by doing the opposite of a typical fund. Such results make little economic sense, which suggests that they may be spurious.

The first conditional performance evaluation studies, by Chen and Knez (1996), Ferson and Schadt (1996), and Ferson and Warther (1996) found that conditioning on the state of the economy is both statistically and economically significant for measuring investment performance. Ferson and Schadt (1996) find that funds' risk exposures change in response to public information on the economy, such as the levels of interest rates and dividend yields. Using conditional models, Ferson and Schadt (1996), Kryzanowski et al. (1997), Zheng (1999), Becker et al. (1999), and Mamaysky et al. (2003) find that the distribution of mutual fund alphas shifts to the right, and is centered near zero. Farnsworth et al. (2002) use a variety of conditional SDF models to evaluate performance in a monthly sample of U.S. equity mutual funds, using a simulation approach to control for model biases. They find that the conditional performance of the average mutual fund is no worse than a hypothetical random stock-picking fund.

Ferson and Warther (1996) attribute differences between unconditional and conditional alphas to predictable flows of public money into funds. Inflows are correlated with reduced market exposure, at times when the public expects high returns, due to larger cash holdings in response to inflows at such times. In pension funds, which are not subject to high-frequency flows of public money, no overall shift in the distribution of fund alphas is found when moving to conditional models (Christopherson et al., 1998). A similar result is found for hedge funds, which often use lockup periods and notification periods to control the flows of funds (e.g. Kazemi, 2003).

Henricksson (1984), Chang and Lewellen (1984), Grinblatt and Titman (1989a), Cumby and Glen (1990), Ferson and Schadt (1996), and others estimated unconditional models to assess market timing ability for equity mutual funds. They find a tendency for negative estimates of the timing coefficients. Ferson and Schadt (1996) found that this result does not occur in conditional models. Becker et al. (1999) simultaneously estimate the fund managers' risk aversion for tracking error and the precision of the market timing signal, in a sample of more than 400 U.S. mutual funds for 1976–1994, including a subsample with explicit asset allocation objectives. The estimates suggest that U.S. equity mutual funds behave as risk averse benchmark investors, but little evidence of conditional timing ability is found. Chen (2003) finds a similar result in a sample of hedge funds, using a variety of market indexes. Jiang (2003) presents a nonparametric test of mutual fund timing ability, and again finds no evidence of ability after the effect of lagged public information variables is accounted for. Thus, controlling for public information variables, there seems to be little evidence that mutual funds have conditional timing ability for the level of the market return.

Busse (1999) asks whether fund returns contain information about market volatility. He finds evidence using daily data that funds may shift their market exposures in response to changes in second moments. Laplante (2003) presents a model of market timing funds that accomodates timing in response to signals about both the first and second moments of return. Given the prevalence of market timing funds and the dearth of evidence that such funds can time the first moments of returns, further research on the higher moments is clearly warranted.

Ferson and Khang (2002) study the conditional weight-based approach to measuring performance. Using a sample of equity pension fund managers (1985–1994), they find that the traditional returns-based alphas of the funds are positive, consistent with previous studies of pension fund performance. However, these alphas are smaller than the potential effects of interim trading bias. The conditional weight-based measures indicate that the pension funds have neutral performance.

In summary, conditional performance measures are superior to traditional measures, both on theoretical and statistical grounds. Conditional measures eliminate the perverse, negative timing coefficients often observed with unconditional measures, and in some cases are found to deliver more precise performance measures. Overall, the empirical evidence based on conditional performance measures suggests that abnormal fund performance, after controlling for public information, is rare.

REFERENCES

Admati, A. and Pfleiderer, P. (1997). "Performance benchmarks: Does it all add up?" *Journal of Business*, 70(3): 323–350.

Admati, A., Bhattacharya, S., Ross, S., Pfleiderer, P. (1986). "On timing and selectivity." *Journal of Finance*, 41: 715–730.

Becker, C., Ferson, W., Myers, D. and M. Schill. (1999). "Conditional market timing with benchmark investors." *Journal of Financial Economics*, 52: 119–148.

Bhattacharya, S. and Pfleiderer, P. (1983). "A note on performance evaluation," Technical Report 714, Stanford University Graduate School of Business.

Busse, J. (1999). "Volatility timing in mutual funds: Evidence from daily returns." *Review of Financial Studies*, 12(5): 1009–1041.

Carpenter, J., Dybvig, P.H., and Farnsworth, H. (2000). "Portfolio performance and agency." Working Paper, Washington University, St Louis.

Chang, E.C. and Lewellen, W.G. (1984). "Market timing and mutual fund investment performance." *Journal of Business*, 57: 55–72.

Chen, Y. (2003). "On conditional market timing of hedge fund managers." Working Paper, Boston College.

Chen, Z. and Knez.,P.J. (1996). "Portfolio performance measurement: theory and applications." *Review of Financial Studies*, 9: 511–556.

Chen, N-fu, Copeland T., and Mayers, D. (1987). "A comparison of single and multifactor performance methodologies." *Journal of Financial and Quantitative Analysis*, 224: 1–17.

Chen, Y., Ferson, F. and Peters, H. (2005). "Measuring the timing ability of fixed-income mutual funds." Working Paper, Boston College

Christopherson, J.A., Ferson, W., and Glassman, D.A. (1998). "Conditioning manager alpha on economic information: another look at the persistence of performance." *Review of Financial Studies*, 11: 111–142.

Connor, G. and Korajczyk, R. (1986). "Performance measurement with the arbitrage pricing theory: A new framework for analysis." *Journal of Financial Economics*, 15: 373–394.

Copeland, T.E. and Mayers, M. (1982). "The value line enigma (1965–1978): A case study of performance evaluation issues." *Journal of Financial Economics*, 10: 289–321.

Cornell, B. (1979). "Asymmetric information and portfolio performance measurement." *Journal of Financial Economics*, 7: 381–390.

Cumby, R. and Glen, J. (1990). "Evaluating the performance of international mutual funds." *Journal of Finance*, 45: 497–521.

Dahlquist, M. and Soderlind, P. (1999). "Evaluating portfolio performance with stochastic discount factors." *Journal of Business*, 72: 347–384.

Fama, E. F. (1970). "Efficient capital markets: A review of theory and empirical work." *Journal of Finance*, 25: 383–417.

Farnsworth, H., Ferson, W., Jackson, D., and Todd, S. (2002). "Performance evaluation with stochastic discount factors." *Journal of Business*, (July) 75: 473–504.

Ferson, W.E. and Khang, K. (2002). "Conditional performance measurement using portfolio weights: evidence for pension funds." *Journal of Financial Economics*, 65: 249–282.

Ferson, W. and Qian, M. (2004). "Conditional Performance Evaluation revisited," Research Foundation Monograph. Charlottesville, VA: CFA Institute.

Ferson, W. and Schadt, R. (1996). "Measuring fund strategy and performance in changing economic conditions." *Journal of Finance,* 51: 425–462.

Ferson, W. and Warther, V.A. (1996). "Evaluating fund performance in a dynamic market." *Financial Analysts Journal*, 52(6): 20–28.

Ferson, W., Henry, T., and Kisgen, D. (2006). "Evaluating government bond fund performance with stochastic discount factors," Review of Financial Studies (forthcoming).

Grant, D. (1977). "Portfolio performance and the "cost" of timing decisions." *Journal of Finance*, 32: 837–846.

Grinblatt, M. and Titman, S. (1989a). "Portfolio performance evaluation: old issues and new insights." *Review of Financial Studies*, 2: 393–416.

Grinblatt, M. and Titman, S. (1989b). "Mutual fund performance: an analysis of quarterly portfolio holdings." *Journal of Business*, 62: 393–416.

Grinblatt, M. and Titman, S. (1993). "Performance measurement without benchmarks: an examination of mutual fund returns." *Journal of Business*, 60: 97–112.

Grinblatt, M., Titman, S., and Wermers, R. (1995). "Momentum strategies, portfolio performance and herding: a study of mutual fund behavior." *American Economic Review*, 85: 1088–1105.

Henriksson, R.D. (1984). "Market timing and mutual fund performance: an empirical investigation." *Journal of Business*, 57: 73–96.

Jensen, M. (1968). "The performance of mutual funds in the period 1945-1964." *Journal of Finance*, 23: 389-346.

Jensen, M. (ed.) (1972). *Studies in the Theory of Capital Markets*. New York: Praeger Publishers.

Jiang, W. (2003). "A nonparametric test of market timing.' *Journal of Empirical Finance*, 10: 399–425.

Kazemi, H. (2003). "Conditional Performance of Hedge Funds." Working Paper, University of Massachusetts at Amherst.

Kryzanowski, L., Lalancette, S., and To, M.C. (1997). "Performance atribution using an apt with prespecified factors." *Journal of Financial and Quantitative Analysis,* 32.

Laplante, M. (2003). "Mutual fund timing with information about volatility." Working Paper, University of Texas at Dallas.

Lee, C.F and Rahman, S. (1990). "Market timing, selectivity and mutual fund performance: An empirical investigation." *Journal of Business*, 63: 261–287.

Lehmann, B. and Modest, D. (1987). "Modest mutual fund performance evaluation: a comparison of benchmarks and benchmark comparisons." *Journal of Finance*, 42: 233-265.

Mamaysky, H., Spiegel, M. and Zhang, H. (2003). "Estimating the dynamics of mutual fund alphas and betas." Working Paper, Yale School of Organization and Management.

Merton, R.C. and Henriksson, R.D. (1981). "On market timing and investment performance II: Statistical procedures for evaluating forecasting skills." *Journal of Business*, 54: 513–534.

Sharpe, W.F. (1964). "Capital asset prices: a theory of market equilibrium under conditions of risk." *Journal of Finance*, 19: 425-442.

Starks, L. (1987). "Performance incentive fees: an agency theoretic approach." *Journal of Financial and Quantitative Analysis*, 22: 17–32.

Treynor, J. and Mazuy, K. (1966). "Can mutual funds outguess the market?" *Harvard Business Review*, 44: 131–136.

Wermers, R. (1997). "Momentum investment strategies of mutual funds, performance persistence, and survivorship bias." Working Paper, University of Colorado.

Zheng, L. (1999). "Is money smart? A study of mutual fund investors' fund selection ability." *Journal of Finance* 54, 901–933.

Chapter 11

WORKING CAPITAL AND CASH FLOW

JOSEPH E. FINNERTY, *University of Illinois, USA*

Abstract

One of the everyday jobs of the treasurer is to manage the cash, and flow of funds through the organization. If the amount or receipt and collection activities are out of control, the entire firm may face bankruptcy. There is an old saying, "If you pay attention to the pennies, the dollars will take care of themselves." In this spirit, this paper looks at taking care of the daily amounts of cash flowing through the firm in a systematic fashion. The purpose is to understand the importance of the interrelationships involved and to be able to measure the amount and speed of the cash flow. Once something can be measured, it can be managed.

Keywords: working capital; accounts receivable; accounts payable; inventory; cash flow; cash management; flow of funds; marketable securities; cash flow cycle; matching principle

11.1. Introduction

The management of cash flow is essential to the success of every enterprise, whether it be public or private. In fact, cash management is probably more critical to the success of an enterprise than making an individual sale or providing a service for a period of time. A business can lose a single customer or can suspend services for a short period without irreparable damage. However, let an imbalance in cash flow occur that forces a cash manager to miss a payroll, a debt payment, or a tax deadline and, quite possibly, the company is entirely out of business. This is a rather harsh penalty for one mistake or oversight on the part of the cash manager.

During the 1960s and 1970s, when we were experiencing high rates of inflation and attendant high-interest rates, the idea of cash management became well accepted, and integrated into the financial function of the firm. This was caused by the high costs of idle cash balances. With the recession and attendant drop in inflation and lower interest rates during the 1980s, the management of cash was still important, but for different reasons. During this period even though rates were low, credit standards were tightened and cash became scarce. Again idle cash balances were undesirable. During the economic boom of the 1990s with the advent of the New Economy (Information), the changing economy caused the focus to shift from manufacturing and production to service and information. As these changes took place, the silo approach to cash management as part of the traditional treasury function shifted to a totally integrated approach focusing on creation of shareholder value. Cash management became the development and implementation of integrated financial strategies for the entire organization. During the recession (2000–2003), the economy faced low-interest rates and at the same time credit standards are tightening in the context of the new information economy, thus giving reasons for paying close attention to cash balances. In October 2004, the Federal Regulations of the U.S. Banking System for the first time were allowing all check payments to be processed electronically. This change has sped up the flow of cash through the system, and made it more important for treasurers to keep track of cash balances.

The purpose of cash flow and working capital management has become an indispensable part of the entire organization. The objective is no longer to maximize cash flow or minimize idle cash but rather to ensure the availability of cash in the form and amount required for the continuing operation of the enterprise and to ensure an addition to shareholder value.

Standard texts on the subject include: Gallinger and Healey(1991) and Maness and Zietlow (1998).

11.2. Definitions

11.2.1. Working Capital

The following terms are those more commonly used in connection with working capital.

Working capital is the dollar amount or the total of a firm's current assets. Current assets include cash, marketable securities, investments, accounts receivable, and inventories. These assets are considered liquid because they can be converted into cash within a year. The dollar amount of these assets varies from time to time because of seasonal variations in sales and cyclical variations in general business conditions. Hence, the level of working capital held by a company is not constant.

Working capital can be thought of consisting two parts – permanent and temporary. Permanent working capital is the dollar amount of working capital that remains fairly constant over time, regardless of fluctuations in sales. Temporary working capital is the additional assets required to meet the seasonal or cyclical variations in sales above the permanent level.

11.2.2. Working Capital Management

Working capital management is a much broader concept than working capital because it involves the management of current assets, current liabilities, and the interrelationship between them. In practice, we tend to make no distinction between the investment decisions regarding current assets and the financing decisions regarding current liabilities. In fact, quite often these two are so closely related that we talk about spontaneous financing of assets – for example, a firm buying some inventory on credit. In such a situation, both assets and liabilities are increased simultaneously thereby providing, at least in the short run, the financing for the investment.

11.2.3. Net Working Capital

Net working capital is the difference between current assets and current liabilities. It is a financial indicator that can be used in conjunction with ratios to gauge the liquidity of a company. In general, an abundance of net working capital is considered desirable because it suggests that the firm has ample liquidity to meet its short-term obligations. As we shall see, this may not always be the case. In fact, one of the objectives of cash management is to reduce excess or redundant net working capital to a minimum, and thereby reduce the cost of holding idle assets.

11.3. An Overview of Corporate Working Capital

11.3.1. Money

The subject of this paper is cash flow, or in other words, how money moves through a business enterprise. Everyone has a general understanding of what money is and how it can be used. A simple definition of money, one used by the Federal Reserve, is: Money is made up of the currency in circulation and checking account balances. The characteristics that must be present for something to serve as money are, first, a store of value; second, ready acceptance; and third, easy transferability.

Throughout history, we have seen various things serve as money – for example, the giant stone of the Yap Islanders, the tobacco currency of early American colonists, gold, silver, shells, and even paper. The key feature that these diverse things have in common is that the participants in the economy were willing to use them for transaction purposes, or to represent the accumulation of wealth. In the new age of the internet, money has taken the form of information. There is no physical representation of value, i.e. dollar bills, credit cards, etc, but rather information with respect to account numbers and the ability to transfer value from one account to another. Such things as digital cash, digital wallets, and virtual credit cards are being used as e-money. This new approach will have an impact on working capital with respect to time and costs. From this understanding of the function that money serves, we can move to a much more sophisticated concept – that of the flow of funds.

When financial managers talk of the flow of funds or working capital, they are referring to the fact that money as we know it – corporate cash checking account and e-money – is actually increasing or decreasing as a result of management actions or decisions. However, they are also referring to factors or accounts that are not really money, but which serve as close substitutes. Such things as inventory, accounts receivable, financial instruments, and other types of marketable securities are all affected by economic or corporate activity. As these accounts change, the ultimate effect is a change in the level of corporate cash. But before these so-called near monies are actually turned into money, we can keep track of them by observing the corporate flow of funds.

11.3.2. Cash Management

Maximum cash generation is usually the primary objective of the financial manager. This objective is based on the assumption that any business is only as sound as the management of its cash flow. However, cash flow management is not an isolated task in the normal operation of a business. Instead, managing cash flow means being deeply involved with every aspect of business operations. Consequently, any and all management effort must be directed to at least satisfying cash flow requirements while managers try to achieve the other objectives of the company. To be more specific, cash flow must be considered to achieve survival, profitability, growth, creation of shareholder value, and finally, the efficient use of corporate resources.

No one objective or goal predominates at all times. The goals are interrelated to such a degree that it is in the best interest of management to work toward attaining all the goals simultaneously. At any given time, priorities may vary as to which objective is most crucial, but all of them must ultimately be achieved to run a successful enterprise.

Keynes' famous statement "In the long run, we're all dead" does not necessarily apply to the corporate form of business. Survival becomes one of the primary objectives for any business. Temporary illiquidity, or lack of money, or financial resources may lead to suspending payments of corporate obligations. As long as creditors accept deferred or rescheduled payments, the short-run problems may be worked out and the business may survive. The ultimate threat of creditors is to drive a business into bankruptcy, which is in effect the admission by management that the cash values from dissolving the business is worth more than trying to keep the business going.

From the cash flow manager's perspective, the desire for survival demands that the firm be managed in such a way as to guarantee the maximum cash flow possible. Thus, management seeks to convert the company's investment in inventories and receivables into cash as quickly as possible. Remember that this desire to speed up cash inflow must be balanced against growing revenues, increasing profits, and the creation of shareholder wealth. In the extreme case, a company could make every product on an order basis and demand cash payment. This would eliminate inventories and receivables. No doubt, the competitive structure of any industry would reduce this strategy to a very unprofitable one in short order.

Other things being equal, the higher the profits a company generates, the more successful it is in achieving its other goals. However, as a business seeks to maximize profits, it must take greater risks. As the risk increases, the need for careful cash management becomes much more important. As a business strives to become more profitable by becoming more competitive, there is a cost in terms of higher inventories, more efficient production equipment, and more liberal credit policies to encourage sales. Competitive strategies increase the firm's need for cash flow by slowing down the rate at which working capital is converted into cash and by increasing the amount of resources tied up in each of the working capital components. Indeed, the cash manager will constantly be forced to balance profitability, growth, and survival as the manager tries to ensure that the company not only has sufficient funds but also uses those funds in an efficient fashion.

Rapid expansion in revenue and increase in market share make marketing management an exciting profession. Marketing-oriented individuals measure their success not by increased profits, but by the increase in the year's market share or by the percentage of market share a given product line has achieved. In striving for these objectives, quite often the risks of rapid growth are overlooked. The major problems begin to surface when the cash management system has not kept up with the rapid growth and its attendant increase in risk.

The efficient use of leverage is of primary importance to sustaining rapid growth. The owners of a company do not have the liquid resources to provide all of the cash necessary to finance the growth, and so external funding must be sought. Usually this external funding is in the form of debt, which increases the overall risk for the company.

In and of itself, leverage is neither good nor bad. However, the misuse of leverage can place severe drains on the cash flow of a firm at a time when the company can least afford these drains.

An effective financial manager must balance the multiple objectives of the firm, and keep in mind that there are many ways to achieve these objectives ,and use the firm's resources efficiently. Too much emphasis on any one of these goals can lead to very severe cash flow problems. The effective management of cash flow is necessary to achieve the multiple objectives simultaneously.

11.3.3. The Components of Working Capital

The components of working capital are the current assets listed on a firm's balance sheet – cash, marketable securities, accounts receivable, and inventory. We can envision the flow of funds through a company as the process of continuously converting one asset into another. Cash is used to buy the necessary raw material that will be used in the production of goods and services. These goods are sold to customers. This increases accounts receivable. As customers pay their bills, accounts receivable are once again turned into cash. If there is a temporary surplus of cash, it may be used to purchase marketable securities. By holding marketable securities, a firm can earn interest on surplus funds, but can quickly convert these funds back into cash when needed. The company then repeats the cycle. The amount of funds and the speed at which the funds move from one account to another are the essential elements of cash flow management.

11.4. Flow of Funds

The flow of funds through an organization encompasses all segments of the corporation and is related to all decisions within the firm. This flow of cash, or flow of funds, is one of the main concerns of the cash manager. The flow of funds diagram below illustrates how funds flow through a company. Because the flow is circular and continuous, it is possible to start anywhere in the diagram.

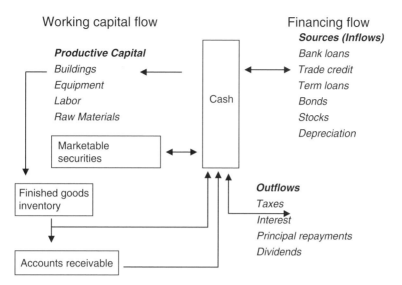

Figure 11.1. Flow of funds

11.4.1. Cash

Cash is listed first on the balance sheet because it is the most liquid shortest term asset. In the flow of funds diagram, it is at the heart of the process. A company may keep a small amount of actual currency on hand as petty cash, but this quantity of cash is usually very small compared to the company's demand deposits, checking account balances, or lines of credit. Demand deposits are the principal way in which a corporation pays its bills, both by issuing a check or electronic funds transfer.

The main problem that financial managers face is maintaining the cash account at an appropriate level. If they hold too little cash, they run the risk of not being able to pay the bills, or take advantage of opportunities that arise. On the other hand, holding too much cash is not good, because the interest that would have been earned if the funds had been properly invested is lost. The process of balancing too little versus too much cash demands most of a cash manager's attention.

11.4.2. Marketable securities

Marketable securities are closely related to cash. In fact, they are often called cash equivalents and may

be combined with cash on the company's balance sheet. Investing in marketable securities involves purchasing money market instruments. These include treasury bills, commercial paper, certificates of deposit, and other short-term investments. A ready secondary market exists for such securities because most companies regularly buy and sell them before they mature. Because such a large market exists, any company can easily sell these instruments at a price close to their true value. This is why they are called marketable securities.

Most firms invest excess cash balances in marketable securities because they earn interest.

The financial manager is faced with two problems when managing the marketable securities account. First, how much money should he invest? And second, what is the appropriate maturity? When making this decision, other things being equal, the longer the maturity, the higher the yield on the investment.

11.4.3. Accounts Receivable

Accounts receivable consist of the money owed to the company by customers. Accounts receivable exist because most firms sell on credit. Customers buy now and pay later.

Accounts receivable usually constitute a very large component of a company's working capital. Thousands, even millions, of dollars can be tied up in a firm's accounts receivable. Why do companies make such a large commitment? The answer is, of course, that most companies extend credit to customers. This is primarily for marketing reasons. Customers are more willing to buy on credit, and very often competitors are willing to offer credit. In most businesses, credit terms are determined by traditional industry practice and competitive conditions. The automobile industry is a great example of using credit terms to sell cars.

Many financial managers work very closely with the marketing department to determine credit terms. This is because financial managers are responsible for obtaining the funds needed to finance accounts receivable. However, financial managers do have some control over the level of accounts receivable by ensuring prompt billing and collection.

11.4.4. Inventories

Inventories are the physical materials that company uses to make its products, or to sell directly to its customers. Companies maintain inventories for two main reasons: first, it is more efficient and less expensive to buy from suppliers in large quantities; and second, many customers demand a wide selection of products and fast delivery. If a company is not able to offer its customers wide choice and fast delivery, it will lose sales to competitors.

We have discussed the four components of working capital – cash, marketable securities, accounts receivable, and inventory. Associated with each of these components is too small or too large.

Too much cash has an opportunity cost of forgone interest, which will hurt profitability. Too little cash may lead to a situation in which the company is unable to meet its commitments and is forced into bankruptcy despite profitable operations. An excess of funds tied up in marketable securities can lead to slower company growth because the funds have not been efficiently used for expansion. Insufficient funds in marketable securities may lead to an inadequate safety margin when cash is needed in an emergency.

Too little cash tied up in accounts receivable may indicate a noncompetitive credit policy, a business downturn, or a dwindling market for the company's products. Too large an amount in accounts receivable may indicate an overgenerous credit policy, which in turn, could lead to collection and bad-debt problems, and inefficient use of the firm's resources.

Finally, too much inventory incurs the risk of obsolescence as well as additional costs of storage, insurance, and handling. On the other hand, too little inventory may place the firm in a noncompetitive position for failing to have the products to sell when the consumer wants them.

11.4.5. The Accounting Perspective Versus the Financial Perspective

A manufacturer or wholesaler seldom generates a sale directly in exchange for cash. Instead, the firm exchanges a product for the IOU of the customer according to predetermined selling terms. When a company purchases inventory, the cash payment typically follows the actual receipt of the inventory by 30 days.

From the accounting perspective, no distinction is made between an actual transaction and a cash transaction. Thus, on the seller's side, a transaction requires a record of the sale on the day it occurs, even though no cash actually changes hands. The buyer's side also records the purchase, and at the same time, records an increase in inventory and accounts payable. But the actual transaction has no immediate effect on the cash account of either company. This is known as accrual accounting. We can define accrual basis accounting as the recognition of revenue when it is earned and the recognition of expense in the period in which it is incurred, without regard to the time of receipt or payment of cash.

Financial accounting enables a manager to measure the financial performance of a firm by properly matching the firm's revenues and expenses as they occur. At the same time, however, accrual accounting does not provide the proper picture of the cash flow through the company. Although it is well known that corporate managers seek to maximize profit and maintain corporate liquidity, accounting theory focuses almost exclusively on measuring and reporting profitability. Any use of an accrual accounting system to measure cash flow is just as foolhardy as the use of a cash budget to measure profitability. These diverse systems were designed to measure different types of activity.

One very important financial statement presented by firms is the cash flow statement. Basically it provides information about cash flows from three areas of firm activity: 1) cash flow from operating activity, 2) cash flow from investing activity, and 3) cash flow from financing activity. The cash flow from operations is merely the reported net income plus a minus the change in net working capital plus depreciation. The cash flow from investing activity is any purchase or sale of fixed assets needs a plant, equipment or land, and the cash flow from financing activities considers the issuance of equity or debt as well as the repayment of debt, the repurchase of equity, and the payment of preferred and common dividends. Using these classifications of cash flow, we can identify "free cash flow." The firm's free cash flow is defined as cash provided by operating activities minus capital expenditures net of depositions minus preferred dividends. The amount of free cash flow available to management will allow for flexibility in making decisions about the firm's future.

It must be noted that the accounting perspective (net income) and the financial perspective (free cash flow) are very different. Each serves a different function and uses different forms of analysis to give different perspectives on a given firm's performance.

11.4.6. The Reasons for Holding Cash

As we have already said, cash is listed first on a company's balance sheet and is considered a com-

ponent of working capital. Cash is made up of demand deposits and currency. Now, let's examine the reasons for holding cash.

There are three principal reasons for holding cash. First, a company needs cash for transactions. This cash is used to pay bills, wages, taxes, and meet other company obligations. We have already seen that having a positive net income does not guarantee that a company has enough cash on hand to meet all of its obligations.

The second reason for keeping a supply of cash is to have it available as a reserve. The old rule of saving for a rainy day is just as applicable for corporations as it is for individuals. Financial managers cannot predict exactly what future cash needs will be. Therefore, managers must have some cash in serve to meet unexpected needs. The exact amount of cash held in reserve depends on the degree of uncertainty about these needs. If there is a great deal of uncertainty about day-to-day cash needs, the company will have to maintain a large cash reserve. The necessity for maintaining a large cash reserve is lessened if the company has fast, dependable, and easy access to short-term credit. For example, if a bank extends a line of credit that can be used during times of cash shortages, lower cash reserves can be maintained.

Finally, holding cash is an essential part of many lending indentures. When a firm borrows money, the lender requires certain conditions (covenants) that must be adhered to, for example, a certain level of cash must be maintained in a bank account. In order to be in legal compliance with the lending agreement, the firm must maintain a minimum level of cash or working capital

11.4.7. Investing in Marketable Securities

Most cash held in demand deposits earns no interest. Therefore, once the basic corporate needs for cash are satisfied, the financial manager should invest extra cash in the most productive manner possible. Many cash managers invest at least a part of this surplus money in marketable securities. As mentioned earlier, marketable securities earn a reasonable rate of return and offer the advantage of being quickly convertible into cash.

There are four criteria that should be considered when evaluating marketable securities: safety, marketability or liquidity, yield, and taxability. Safety refers to the probability that the full principal will be returned without any loss. Financial managers require a very high degree of safety in marketable securities. Marketability refers to how quickly and easily a security can be converted into cash. This factor is especially important if the security is being held as a reserve for the cash account, because it may have to be sold on very short notice. Yield is the interest or the price appreciation received from holding the security. Some securities pay interest; some may have tax-free interest; other securities sell at a discount and pay full face value at maturity. The effect is the same as paying interest. Some securities may have tax-free interest; discount securities may be taxed at a different rate than interest paying securities; and so on. Therefore, a cash manager must be aware of the corporation's tax situation in order to select the best type of marketable security.

There are three main reasons for investing in marketable securities. One is that they act as a reserve for the cash account. In other words, marketable securities are held to meet unexpected cash needs. Therefore, as noted earlier, their marketability is very important because they may have to be sold quickly.

Securities can also be used to meet known cash outflows. Frequently the need for certain cash outflows can be predicted. One example is taxes. Every company regularly withholds taxes from employees' paychecks. This money is paid to the government on a monthly or quarterly basis. The cash manager knows the exact amount and the due dates of these payments in advance and can purchase securities that mature at the correct time.

A third reason for investing in marketable securities is that company profits benefit. Cash managers describe funds not needed for cash reserves or taxes as "free" because such funds are not constrained by specific liquidity requirements. There-fore, cash managers can invest free cash for a higher yield after considering taxes, even though such investments are less liquid and may be a bit more risky.

11.4.8. Creating an Integrated Cash Management System

There are two main benefits to be derived from a cash management program – first, incremental profits that will augment net income, and second, freed-up resources (namely cash) that can be used for other corporate purposes. Both of these benefits are worthwhile, but the most important benefit is probably an effective cash management system. Such a system will not only pay for itself but should also have a positive effect on net income.

Reviewing the cash management cycle from beginning to end is the best approach to integrating cash management with overall company planning. The objective of the review is to find all the ways (that are consistent with the firm's other objectives) to speed up inflows and slow down outflows. The emphasis should be on evaluating all corporate functions that, from a financial executive's standpoint, can potentially affect cash flow.

An integrated cash management analysis involves reviewing the firm's billing and collection procedures in light of industry practice and competition. The purpose of the review is to shorten the time it takes for payments to be put to some useful purpose.

Many banks offer cash management services to both corporate and individual clients. The relationship the company has with its bank and the form and amount of bank compensation must be reviewed carefully. In addition, an in-depth review of forecasting and planning procedures must be done to ensure that management has a good understanding of the company's cash flow cycle. Both the timing and the amounts of flows must be taken into consideration so that the firm's short-term investment performance will produce an acceptable rate of return.

A total review of a cash management system should also look beyond cash mobilization to information mobilization. This ensures that the decision maker receives information quickly so excess funds can be invested or short-term liabilities reduced. Clearly, it makes no sense to mobilize a company's cash if productive uses for the additional funds are not exploited.

The next step in a cash management system is to integrate it with the financial management information system. This means setting up a planning and budgeting system that identifies projected financial needs, forecasts surpluses or deficits of funds, and then makes coordinated decisions to use those funds most effectively. Systematically coordinating short- and long-term activity allows a financial executive to know at all times what is happening at the bank, in the firm's marketable security portfolio, to the firm's capital budget plans, and to overall corporate liquidity needs.

The benefits of using cash more efficiently are readily apparent. But if all of the financial functions are combined, the overall cost of managing such a system is reduced. Thus, from both income-generating and cost-reduction perspectives, a cash management system can be self-sustaining.

To develop and implement broader integrated systems, cash managers must take more responsibility for coordinating and working with executives in other functional areas of the firm. It is also important to review corporate policies and procedures, to determine whether there is full interaction in the cash management function.

As a result of the wide-ranging impact of cash management on the entire firm, financial executives have a more complex job than ever before. Such executives must broaden their interests and interactions while at the same time performing the traditional financial functions. For example, they have to interact with the purchasing department and with the materials management staff. They also must play a much larger role in contract negotiations. Too often, contracts are left to the legal department, and some important financial considerations may be overlooked, especially as these

considerations relate to the firm's cash management policies. Costs, payments, disbursement schedules, progress payments, and other financial considerations are of concern to financial executives. They should be involved in negotiations before contracts are finalized.

The idea of taking a company-wide view rather than looking specifically at individual operations makes eminent sense. Cash managers should broaden their perspective and think of cash management as an activity that is affected by all components of the company's operations. All decisions that are made and actions taken through the company affect cash flow, and hence cash management. This includes everything from production scheduling and inventory control to marketing and credit policy – from tax policy, negotiation, accounting, and control to personnel and payroll. The effects of cash management have an impact on all areas of a company.

The simple statement that cash management speeds up inflows and slows down outflows must be put into perspective for it to be effective and useful. Emphasis should be placed on evaluating how well the organization performs in all cash management areas, and how effectively the concepts as a whole.

11.4.9. Cash Flow Cycle

The flow of funds or cash flow refers to the movement of money through the business. The time it takes for these funds to complete a full-cycle reflects the average duration that a firm's cash is invested in inventory and accounts receivable, both of which are non-earning assets. Therefore, it is in a company's best interest to keep the cash cycle as short as possible.

To see the relationship between the various accounts and the cash cycle refer to the cash cycle chart below.

The table below shows how cash, accounts receivable, inventory, and accounts payable will be affected by each of the four steps in the cash cycle.

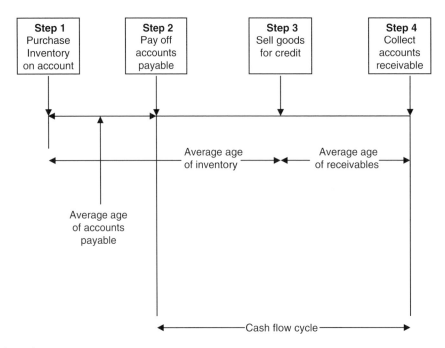

Figure 11.2.   Cash cycle

11.5. Calculating the Cash Flow Cycle

The cash flow cycle is defined as the average age of inventory plus the average accounts receivable less the average age of accounts payable. Or as the cash cycle chart indicates, the cash flow cycle is the average time it takes for a company to pay out cash, and receive a cash inflow that completes the transaction.

The cash flow cycle can be calculated using the following equation:

$$
\begin{aligned}
\text{Cash flow Cycle} = &\ \text{Average age of inventory}\\
&+ \text{Average age of accounts receivable}\\
&- \text{Average age of accounts}\\
= &\ \frac{360\ \text{Days}}{\text{Cost of goods sold}/\text{Inventory}}\\
&+ \frac{\text{Accounts receivable}}{\text{Net credit sales}} \times 360\ \text{Days}\\
&- \frac{\text{Accounts payable}}{\text{Credit purchases}} \times 360\ \text{Days}
\end{aligned}
$$

To illustrate how this equation can be put to use, let us look at a Company ABC, where:

Cost of goods sold   = $470,570
Inventory   = $345,420

Table 11.1.   Changes in accounts

Account	Step 1	Step 2	Step 3	Step 4
Cash	0	−	0	+
Accounts receivable	0	0	+	−
Inventory	+	0	−	0
Accounts payable	+	−	0	0

Accounts receivable   = $ 70,820
Net credit sales   = $575,460
Accounts payable   = $ 26,890
Credit purchases   = $352,927

Substituting these figures in our equation, we calculate the cash flow cycle of ABC Company as:

$$
\begin{aligned}
\text{Cash flow cycle} &= \frac{360}{470,475/345,420} + \frac{70,820}{575,460}\\
&\quad \times 360 - \frac{26,890}{352,927} \times 360\\
&= 265 + 44 - 27\\
&= 282\ \text{days}
\end{aligned}
$$

In the above example, ABC's cash cycle is 282 days. It is not possible to decide at this point if this amount of time is too long or too short because it represents a lot of factors that need to be considered. Calculating your company's cash flow cycle is the starting point of any analysis that you will have to perform to answer the question: Is cash being effectively managed in my company?

11.6. The Matching Principle

One of the fundamental principles of finance is matching the cash inflows from assets with the cash outflows from their respective sources of financing. The technique of hedging can be used when trying to accomplish this objective.

Financing temporary current assets with short-term sources of funds and financing fixed assets and permanent current assets with long-term sources of funds illustrates how the matching principle is put to work. The basic strategy of the perfect hedge is to match the expected inflows and outflows of funds. This is fundamentally sound financing because the inflows of funds from the sale of assets are being used to repay the loans that financed these acquisitions. When the cash inflow is in excess of the required cash outflow, the situation is considered to be more conservative than the opposite case in which the cash outflow is greater than the cash inflow. This imbalance must be met by rolling over short-term financing or seeking other sources of funds. This is considered to be an aggressive approach.

The company, DEF, demonstrates the trade-off that exists between risk and return when using different approaches to the matching principle. The trade-off should be kept in mind when a company is considering a change in its sources of funds in response to changing conditions. The aggressive approach should be used when firms are expanding their working capital during the recovery and prosperity phases of the business cycle. Alternatively, during the recessionary phase, a more conservative approach may be more appropriate.

11.7. A Conservative Versus an Aggressive Approach to the Matching Concept

The figures below illustrate the results DEF Company would achieve by employing an aggressive approach or a conservative approach to matching its cash inflows with its cash outflows.

11.8. Summary

The purpose of this paper is to put working capital into the proper perspective for managers

Table 11.2. DEF Company (dollars in millions)

Assets		
Current assets	$100	
Fixed assets	100	
Total assets	$200	

Liabilities		
	Conservative	Aggressive
Short-term liabilities (at 7%)	$25	$100
Long-term debt (at 12%)	125	50
Equity	50	50
Total liabilities plus equity	$200	$200

Income statement		
Earnings before interest and taxes	$50.00	$50.00
Less:		
Interest	(16.75)	(13.00)
Taxes (at 40%)	(13.30)	(14.80)
Net income	$19.95	$22.20
Current ratio $\left(\dfrac{\text{Current assets}}{\text{Current liabilities}}\right)$	4.0	1.0
Net working capital $\left(\text{Current assets}-\text{Current liabilities}\right)$	$75.00	$0.00
Rate of return on equity $\left(\dfrac{\text{Net income}}{\text{Equity}}\right)$	39.9%	44.4%

concerned with managing the cash flow of their firms. They must realize that planning and managing cash flow are more than just managing the cash account. Although the cash account is one of the major assets that affects cash flow, other current assets and current liabilities, and quite often long-term assets and financing, it also has an impact on the cash cycle of the firm.

The concept of working capital and management's philosophy of trying to maintain it at a particular level are also important. If management is aggressive, it may take one approach to the matching principle that will have direct impact on the cash flow planning process. If management tends to be more conservative, other options may be available. Above all, when we are dealing with the cash flow planning process, it must be remembered that we are involved with a very dynamic situation that is closely related to the character of the decision maker. Therefore, given the exact same situation, two different managers can reach satisfactory solutions that may be entirely different from one another.

REFERENCES

Gallinger, G.W. and Healey, P.B. (1991). *Liquidity Analysis and Management*, 2nd edn. Reading, MA: Addison-Wesley.

Maness, T.S. and Zietlow, J.T. (1998). *Short Term Financial Management*, Fort Worth, TX: The Dryden Press.

Chapter 12

EVALUATING FUND PERFORMANCE WITHIN THE STOCHASTIC DISCOUNT FACTOR FRAMEWORK

J. JONATHAN FLETCHER, *University of Strathclyde, United Kingdom*

Abstract

The stochastic discount factor (SDF) approach to fund performance is a recent innovation in the fund performance literature (Chen and Knez, 1996). A number of recent studies have used the stochastic discount factor approach to evaluate the performance of managed funds. In this paper, I present an overview of the use of the stochastic discount approach to evaluate the unconditional and conditional performance of the fund. I also discuss estimation issues and provide a brief survey of empirical evidence.

Keywords: stochastic discount factor (SDF); fund performance; generalized method of moments; asset pricing models; unconditional performance; conditional performance; law of one price; no arbitrage; benchmark model; mutual funds

12.1. Introduction

Evaluating the performance of a managed fund has a long and illustrious history since the seminal studies of Sharpe (1966) and Jensen (1968). There have been numerous performance measures developed and used in the literature during the past thirty-five years. A partial list of these measures includes the unconditional Jensen measure (extended by Connor and Korajczyk, 1986), the selectivity and market timing measures of Treynor and Mazuy (1966) and Hendriksson and Merton (1981), the period weighting measure of Grinblatt and Titman (1989), the portfolio weight measures of Cornell (1979), Grinblatt and Titman (1993), Daniel et al. (1997), and Ferson and Khang (2002), and the conditional performance measure of Ferson and Schadt (1996). A recent innovation in the fund performance literature has been the development of performance measures within the stochastic discount factor (SDF) approach. A major attraction of the stochastic discount factor approach is that most asset pricing models can be written as a candidate model of the SDF.

Chen and Knez (1996) present a general framework to evaluate fund performance within the SDF approach[1]. Chen and Knez also explore the minimal conditions under which valid performance measures exist. The SDF approach to fund performance has been used and developed in a number of recent studies such as Dahlquist and Soderlind (1999), Farnsworth et al. (2002), Ferson et al. (2003), Fletcher and Forbes (2004), and Lynch et al. (2004) among others. The SDF performance measures of Chen and Knez have also been used to examine the profitability of momentum trading strategies (Ahn et al.,

2003c) and seasoned equity offerings (Ahn et al., 2003b).

In this paper, I present an overview of the SDF approach to fund performance and discuss a number of estimation issues in using the SDF approach. The paper is organized as follows. Section 12.2 provides an overview of the SDF approach to fund performance. Section 12.3 discusses estimation issues. Section 12.4 presents a summary of empirical findings. The final section concludes.

12.2. Evaluating Performance

Ross (1978), Harrison and Kreps (1979), and Hansen and Richard (1987), among others, show that if the law of one price holds in financial markets, then there exists a stochastic discount factor m_t such that:

$$E_{t-1}(m_t x_{it}) = p_{it-1} \quad \text{for } i = 1, \ldots, N, \qquad (12.1)$$

where x_{it} is the payoff of asset i at time t, p_{it-1} is the price of asset i at time $t-1$, N is the number of primitive assets, and E_{t-1} is the expected value conditional on the information available to investors at time $t-1$. Where the payoff of asset i is equal to the gross return of asset i, the payoff equals 1. Where the payoff of asset i is an excess return, the price equals 0. Equation (12.1) states that the expected value of the risk-adjusted payoff of asset i at time t conditional on information available at time $t-1$ has a price equal to p_{it-1}. Under the assumption of no arbitrage, m_t will be positive in every state of nature (Cochrane, 2001). In complete markets, m_t will be unique.

Equation (12.1) can be written in terms of excess returns as:

$$E_{t-1}(m_t r_{it}) = 0, \qquad (12.2)$$

where r_{it} is the excess return of asset i in period t. Where there is no conditioning information, Equation (12.2) implies that:

$$E(m_t r_{it}) = 0 \qquad (12.3)$$

Equation (12.3) can be rearranged using the definition of covariance as:

$$E(r_{it}) = \frac{-\text{cov}(m_t r_{it})}{E(m_t)} \qquad (12.4)$$

Equation (12.4) states that the expected excess return of asset i depends upon the covariance between the SDF and excess return ($\text{cov}(m_t r_{it})$). The $\text{cov}(m_t r_{it})$ captures the risk adjustment implied by the SDF model. Assets with a negative covariance with the SDF have higher expected excess returns.

Chen and Knez (1996) present a general framework to evaluate fund performance using a candidate model of the SDF. Define y_t as a candidate model of the SDF. Chen and Knez (1996) show that the unconditional performance of the fund can be written as:

$$\alpha_p = E(y_t r_{pt}), \qquad (12.5)$$

where α_p is the performance of the fund and r_{pt} is the excess return of the fund in period t. The performance of the fund (α_p) measures the difference between the expected risk-adjusted excess return of the fund and its price (0). If performance is positive (negative), the fund offers a higher (lower) risk-adjusted excess returns than expected, which signifies superior (inferior) performance.

The conditional performance of the fund is given by:

$$\alpha_{pt} = E_{t-1}(y_t r_{pt}). \qquad (12.6)$$

The conditional performance of the fund α_{pt} measures the difference between the expected risk-adjusted excess return of the fund at time t conditional on information available at time $t-1$ minus its price. The conditional performance of the fund varies over time as a function of conditioning information.

What is the goal of a performance measure? Chen and Knez (1996) point out that a performance measure seeks to measure the value added by a professional portfolio manager. Does the portfolio manager enlarge the investment opportunity set of investors? This question can be addressed by using unconditional performance measures or conditional performance measures. An unconditional framework assumes that the investment opportunity set of uninformed investors is spanned by passive trading strategies in the N primitive assets. A conditional framework allows for uninformed investors to follow dynamic trading strategies in the N primitive assets based on publicly available information.

Grinblatt and Titman (1989) and Chen and Knez (1996) point out that a good performance measure should have two characteristics. First, any trading strategy that can be achieved by uninformed investors should be given zero performance. Second, trading strategies followed by portfolio managers with superior information should be given positive performance. If a performance measure satisfies the first characteristic, it is defined as an admissible performance measure. Chen and Knez show that the first characteristic is met if there exists a SDF that correctly prices the set of primitive assets that uninformed investors can trade in. This result implies that an admissible performance measure is equivalent to using a valid SDF model. Such SDFs will exist if the law of one price (LOP) holds in financial markets (Chen and Knez, 1996). Admissible performance measures can also be consistent with no arbitrage (NA) opportunities in financial markets.

The use of the conditional performance framework provides a greater challenge to the portfolio manager because valid SDF models will be able to price not only the N primitive assets but also dynamic trading strategies in the primitive assets. Portfolio managers who trade on the use of public information will not be rewarded superior performance within the conditional framework. In contrast, the portfolio manager can be rewarded superior performance by trading on public information in an unconditional framework (see Ferson and Schadt, 1996; Ferson and Khang, 2002; Ferson, 2003, for further discussion).

Chen and Knez (1996) and Farnsworth et al. (2002) show that portfolio managers who trade in the N primitive assets (without superior information and trading costs) will be assigned zero performance by all admissible performance measures. For admissible unconditional measures, the performance of the fund will be zero when the manager does not trade on any information and for admissible conditional measures, the performance of the fund will be zero when the manager only trades on public information. The ambiguity in fund performance for admissible performance measures is when the portfolio manager's return cannot be perfectly replicated by the primitive assets. In this situation, the fund performance will be sensitive to the SDF model used. Chen and Knez show that there are different SDF models that price the primitive assets correctly, but can give the same fund positive and negative performance. This result holds even for admissible performance measures that satisfy the no arbitrage condition. However, Chen and Knez point out that if a fund is given positive performance by one admissible no arbitrage performance measure, then the fund adds value for at least one investor.

The sensitivity of fund performance to the SDF model used is related to the literature that shows the sensitivity of the Jensen (1968) performance measure to the benchmark portfolio used (Roll, 1978; Lehmann and Modest, 1987). Much of the debate about how sensitive the Jensen performance of the fund is to the benchmark portfolio stems from the use of inappropriate benchmarks i.e. inadmissible performance measures. The analysis in Chen and Knez (1996) is more serious in that fund performance is sensitive to the SDF model used even for admissible measures.

Ahn et al. (2003a) build on the earlier work of Chen and Knez (1996) to derive the upper and lower performance bounds for a given fund under the conditions that the SDF model prices the primitive assets and satisfies the no arbitrage condition. Ahn et al. show that for a given set of primitive assets, all admissible performance measures for a given fund will lie within these bounds. The performance of the fund will only be unambiguous when the lower bound lies above zero (positive performance) or the upper bound lies below zero (negative performance). When the bounds straddle zero, admissible performance measures can give the same fund positive or negative performance.

12.3. Estimation Issues

The estimation of fund performance, within the SDF framework, is conducted using Generalized Method of Moments[2] (GMM) (Hansen, 1982). One approach is to use a two-step approach. First, the coefficients in the candidate SDF model are estimated. Second, the performance of the fund is estimated as in Equation (12.5) by multiplying the fund's excess return by the SDF model and taking the average. An alternative approach is to estimate the coefficients in the SDF model and the performance measure jointly. Farnsworth et al. (2002) advocate this approach, as it is more efficient than a two-step approach. I will discuss the estimation of the unconditional performance measure first, and then move on to the conditional measures.

Define the following set of residuals for a given candidate model of the stochastic discount factor y_t:

$$u_{it} = r_{it} y_t - 0 \quad \text{for } i = 1, \ldots, N \tag{12.7}$$

$$u_{pt} = alpha_p - y_t r_{pt},$$

where $alpha_p$ is the unconditional performance of the fund. The sample mean of the residuals are the moment conditions in GMM estimation. The first N moment conditions identify the K parameters in the SDF model y_t. These moment conditions are also the pricing errors of the N primitive assets. The last moment condition identifies the performance of the fund. There are $N + 1$ moment conditions and $K + 1$ parameters in the system of Equations in (12.7). When $N + 1 = K + 1$, the system of equations is exactly identified and there are no over identifying restrictions. Under the null hypothesis of no abnormal performance $alpha_p$ should be equal to zero.

Define g as the $(N + 1)^* 1$ vector of the sample mean of residuals (moment conditions). GMM estimates the $K + 1$ parameters to minimize the quadratic form $g'Wg$, where W is an $(N + 1)^*(N + 1)$ arbitrary weighting matrix. Hansen (1982) shows that the estimates have an asymptotic normal distribution for any arbitrary weighting matrix. Hansen also shows that the most efficient weighting matrix is S^{-1}, where S is the covariance matrix of the moment conditions. The advantage of the GMM approach is that it is valid under general distributional assumptions and we can incorporate the effects of serial correlation and heteroskedasticity.

When we estimate the performance of more than one fund, the number of moment conditions increase sharply. However, Farnsworth et al. (2002) show that the estimated performance and standard error of the fund is invariant to the number of funds used in the estimation. This result implies there are no biases in the performance (or standard error) for a given fund by excluding other funds from the estimation. This finding is encouraging given the number of funds used in empirical studies. Ferson et al. (2003) generalize this result to conditional time-varying performance measures.

We can include additional moment conditions to the system of Equations in (12.7) to incorporate additional restrictions implied by SDF models. Dahlquist and Soderlind (1999) and Farnsworth et al. (2002) show that it is important to add a moment condition for the gross risk-free return. The expected value of the SDF should be just below one (see Cochrane, 2001). By including this moment condition, the expected value of the SDF model has more sensible values. Farnsworth et al. also point out that for linear factor models of the SDF, where the factors are portfolio returns, it is important to impose the restriction that the model correctly prices the factors.

Two issues arise using GMM to estimate the unconditional performance of the fund. First, the researcher must choose the set of N primitive assets. This set should capture the investment opportunity set that investors can trade in. The number of primitive assets should also be small. Cochrane (2001) recommends that the number of moment conditions should be at most one-tenth of the number of time-series observations because the estimate of S can become unstable and near singular, when the number of moment conditions is too high. Different sets of primitive assets have been used in the literature. Chen and Knez (1996), Dahlquist and Soderlind (1999), and Ahn et al. (2003a) all use industry portfolios in their set of primitive assets. Dahlquist and Soderlind also add a short-term Treasury Bill to the set of primitive assets. Farnsworth et al. (2002) use two bond portfolios, one-month Treasury Bill, and six stock portfolios that capture small cap/large cap, value/growth, and momentum/contrarian investment strategies. One issue that arises is whether fund performance is sensitive to the choice of the primitive assets. Ahn et al. (2003d) propose further discussion of this issue in an asset pricing context, and propose a novel approach to form the set of primitive assets.

Second, what weighting matrix should be used in estimating the system of Equations in (12.7). The issue of the weighting matrix can be important whenever the number of parameters is less than the number of moment conditions. A major problem in using the optimal weighting matrix S^{-1} is that in small sample sizes the optimal weighting matrix can perform poorly (Lettau and Ludvigson, 2001). The optimal weighting matrix can suffer from two other problems whenever we want to consider how well different models of y_t price the N primitive assets. First, the optimal weighting matrix is different across each model, and so cannot be used to compare the pricing performance of different models. Using the optimal weighting matrix, improvements in model performance can come from lower pricing errors and a more volatile weighting matrix. Second, the optimal weighting matrix evaluates the ability of SDF models to price the primitive assets in terms of how well the model prices portfolios of large, long, and short positions (Cochrane, 2001). Cochrane and Chretien and Cliff (2001) show that the optimal weighting matrix estimates the parameters in the SDF to

price the sample global minimum variance portfolio as well as possible.

The two most popular alternative weighting matrixes that can be used to evaluate fund performance are the ones proposed in the asset pricing literature. Cochrane (1996) advocates the use of the identity weighting matrix and Hansen and Jagannathan (1997) advocate the use of the inverse of the second moment matrix of asset payoffs. Since the same weighting matrix is used across models, we can evaluate how well different models price the primitive assets. The identity weighting matrix places an equal weight on each moment condition. In terms of evaluating asset pricing models, the identity matrix estimates the parameters to minimize the sum of squared pricing errors. This approach is most useful whenever the researcher wants to examine how well models price a given set of assets rather than complex long/short portfolios of assets. However, the use of the identity weighting matrix can lead to more volatile estimates of the parameters (Hodrick and Zhang, 2001).

The use of the Hansen and Jagannathan (1997) weighting matrix in the GMM minimization $g'Wg$ is equal to the squared Hansen and Jagannathan distance measure under the LOP assumption. The distance measure captures the smallest distance between a given candidate model of the SDF and the true set of discount factors that price the primitive assets. The distance measure is also the most mispriced portfolio of the primitive assets with unit norm. Asset pricing models that are more able to price the primitive assets should have lower distance measures. Given the choice of weighting matrixes available, an interesting study would be to explore whether fund performance is sensitive to different weighting matrixes.

The GMM framework can be extended to estimate the conditional performance measures. To estimate the average conditional performance as in Farnsworth et al. (2002), we can add additional moment conditions to capture the unconditional implications of conditioning information as in Cochrane (1996, 2001). Define z_{lt-1} as the value of the lth information variable at time $t-1$. Cochrane shows that if we multiply both sides of Equation (12.2) by z_{lt-1}, and take unconditional expectations that:

$$E(m_t r_{it} z_{lt-1}) = 0 \qquad (12.8)$$

The payoff $r_{it} z_{lt-1}$ is the payoff of a dynamic trading strategy that has a zero price. Cochrane shows that this approach is sufficient to test all the implications of conditioning information. The approach has the attractive feature that it is still valid even if the researcher uses smaller information set than observed by investors. Using less information variables than observed by investors reduces the power of the tests (Cochrane, 1996).

For every information variable z_{lt-1} used by the researcher, there are N additional moment conditions. The restrictions from Equation (12.8) imply the following residuals:

$$u_{lit} = y_t r_{it} z_{lt-1} - 0 \quad \text{for } i = 1, \ldots N$$
$$\text{and } l = 1, \ldots, L, \qquad (12.9)$$

where L is the number of common information variables. We can estimate the average conditional performance as in Farnsworth et al. (2002) by adding the L^*N extra moment conditions from Equation (12.9) to the system of Equations in (12.7). In this situation, the $alpha_p$ coefficient is the average conditional performance of the fund.

We can estimate time-varying conditional performance by assuming that the performance of the fund is a linear function of the common information variables[3] as in Dahlquist and Soderlind (1999) and Lynch et al. (2004). The extra parameters in the conditional performance function can be estimated by adding additional moment conditions to the system of Equations in (12.7) and (12.9). An alternative approach to the linear functional form followed by Ferson et al. (2003) who use a small number of conditioning dummy variables that capture different states of the term structure.

The SDF approach is a very general approach to fund performance and a wide range of alternative

models can be used. The models include different versions of the consumption asset pricing model or production based asset pricing models can be used. The most popular models used in the evaluation of fund performance are linear factor models such as the capital asset pricing model (CAPM) or arbitrage pricing theory (APT).

Models such as the CAPM and APT imply a linear model of the SDF (see Cochrane, 2001; Ferson, 2003, for a review). In the unconditional versions of the models where the coefficients in the model are assumed constant through time, the SDF can be written as:

$$y_t = a + \sum_{k=1}^{K} b_k f_{kt}, \qquad (12.10)$$

where f_{kt} is the value of factor k in period t, a is the constant in the linear model, b_k is the slope coefficient relative to the kth factor (for $k = 1, \ldots, K$), and K are the number of factors in the model. The slope coefficients b_k capture the importance of each factor in the SDF model. The factors f_{kt} can be excess returns on portfolios or zero-cost portfolios, or aggregate macroeconomic variables, or state variables that predict changes in the investment opportunity set. Unconditional models assume that the betas and factor risk premiums are constant through time. Conditional versions of the models can be used by assuming that the coefficients in the model are a linear function of the common information variables as in Cochrane (1996) and Lettau and Ludvigson (2001) among others[4].

An alternative approach is not to rely on an asset pricing model at all, and use nonparametric performance measures such as in Chen and Knez (1996) or the numeraire portfolio of Long (1990). The Chen and Knez measures rely on less restrictive assumptions than an asset pricing model such as the LOP. The SDF used by Chen and Knez under the LOP builds on the earlier work of Hansen and Jagannathan (1991). Hansen and Jagannathan show that there exists under the LOP, an unique SDF that correctly prices the primitive assets and is also a portfolio payoff. This unique SDF is a linear function of the N primitive assets. This approach can be modified to impose the no arbitrage condition.

12.4. Empirical Evidence

There have been numerous empirical studies evaluating fund performance during the past three decades. The number of studies using the SDF is small. Chen and Knez (1996) use their LOP and NA measures to evaluate the performance of a sample of 68 U.S. mutual funds between 1968 and 1989. Chen and Knez find little support of superior performance by funds and the average fund performance is -0.09 percent using the unconditional LOP and NA measures. Dahlquist and Soderlind (1999) use the Chen and Knez measures to evaluate the small sample properties of the performance tests and the performance of Swedish mutual funds using weekly data. Dahlquist and Soderlind find that the asymptotic tests can perform poorly in small samples and reject the null hypothesis of zero performance too often when there is no abnormal performance. In addition, the power of the tests can be low because detecting true superior performance requires a large abnormal return and a long sample period. Dahlquist and Soderlind find that the average Swedish mutual fund provides small positive performance, but is not statistically significant.

Ahn et al. (2003a) estimate the upper and lower performance bounds for 320 U.S. mutual funds between 1984 and 1997 using the set of admissible performance measures under the no arbitrage condition. Ahn et al. find that for 80 percent of the funds, the performance is sensitive to the SDF model used. There are valid SDF models that assign the same fund positive or negative performance. Where the valid SDF models agree on the performance of the fund, the results support the existence of inferior performance.

Ahn et al. (2003a) also use the performance bounds to conduct diagnostic tests on different performance measures used in the academic litera-

ture. Ahn et al. consider the Jensen (1968) and Ferson and Schadt (1996) measures using the CAPM, the three-factor Fama and French (1993) model, and the four-factor model used in Ferson and Schadt (1996), two consumption-based models using the standard time-separable power utility function and an external habit function, and the Chen and Knez (1996) LOP and NA measures. Among the linear factor models, Ahn et al. find that the conditional Fama and French model have the smallest proportion of funds that have performance measures that lie outside the bounds. The two consumption models perform poorly with a substantial number of funds having performance measures outside the bounds. The performance of the funds using the Chen and Knez LOP measure falls out with the bounds in only 0.62 percent of cases.

Farnsworth et al. (2002) provide a comprehensive examination of fund performance across a wide class of SDF models. The models used are five linear factor models (CAPM, Fama and French (1993), three-factor APT, three-factor model using traded factors, and four-factor model using macroeconomic variables), the Chen and Knez (1996) LOP model, the numeraire portfolio of Long (1990), and the Bakashi and Chen (1998) model. Conditional and unconditional versions of the models are used. Farnsworth et al. examine the performance of the different models to price the primitive assets using the Hansen and Jagannathan (1997) distance measure, and also consider how well the models capture the time-series predictability of the pricing errors of the primitive assets. Farnsworth et al. find that conditional models are better able to capture the time-series predictability in pricing errors and have lower Hansen and Jagannathan distance measures in most cases when dynamic trading strategies of the primitive assets are included. However, this improved performance of the conditional model comes at the expense of higher unconditional Hansen and Jagannathan distance measure.

Farnsworth et al. (2002) use hypothetical trading strategies to examine whether the different models assign zero performance for strategies with no skill, and if the models can detect significant superior performance. The trading strategies allow for varying levels of stock selection and market timing skill. Farnsworth et al. find that there is a small downward bias in performance for the stock selection strategies with no skill of the order of −0.19 percent for unconditional models and −0.12 percent for conditional models. Most of the models are able to detect significant superior performance for strategies with varying degrees of stock selection and market timing ability. The poorest performing models at detecting superior performance are the numeraire portfolio model of Long (1990) and the four-factor linear model using macroeconomic variables. Performance findings are similar across the remaining models.

When the models are used to evaluate the performance of a sample of U.S. mutual funds, Farnsworth et al. (2002) find that the average fund performance across models is −0.06 percent for unconditional models and −0.09 percent for conditional models. Adding back annual expenses and trading costs, the average mutual fund earns better performance than the hypothetical trading strategies with no skill. There is little evidence of superior performance by U.S. mutual funds. Fletcher and Forbes (2004) also find little evidence of superior performance by U.K. unit trusts using a wide range of SDF models.

Lynch et al. (2004) evaluate the conditional performance of U.S. mutual funds between 1977 and 1993. Lynch et al. use the CAPM, Fama and French (1993), and Carhart (1997) models to evaluate fund performance, and use the dividend yield on the market index as the information variable. The dividend yield is used to track the variation in the business cycle. Lynch et al. finds that conditional performance of funds varies over time. There are also interesting patterns in the conditional performance across different fund investment sectors. The abnormal performance of growth funds rises during booms and falls during downturns. The converse is true of the other investment sectors[5].

Ferson et al. (2003) use the SDF approach to evaluate the conditional performance of U.S. government bond mutual funds between 1986 and 2000. The models used are based on continuous-time term structure models. Ferson et al. use reduced form SDF models for the one-factor affine model, the two-factor affine model, the three-factor affine model, and the two-factor Brennan and Schwartz (1979) model. The empirical versions of the models include additional time-averaged factors due to using the models over discrete periods of time. This approach has the advantage of dealing with the interim trading bias of Goetzmann et al. (2000) and Ferson and Khang (2002). Ferson et al. (2003) use conditioning dummy variables to estimate fund performance over different states of the term structure.

Ferson et al. (2003) conduct a number of diagnostic tests of the different term structure models. Ferson et al. find that the additional empirical factors play an important role in explaining bond returns. The one-factor affine model has the poorest performance in pricing different bond portfolio strategies. The two-factor models perform better than the one-factor affine model, and the three-factor affine model has the best performance. Ferson et al. find that government bond performance varies across states of the term structure. Although there is little evidence of superior performance, some types of funds perform better in certain states of the term structure. In low-short rates, young funds, low turnover, low loads, low expenses, and low total costs all have significant positive performance.

12.5. Conclusions

The SDF approach to evaluate fund performance is a recent innovation in the fund performance literature. The SDF approach has a number of attractive features in that most asset pricing models imply a candidate model of the SDF and the approach can be applied to conditional performance evaluation. A small number of studies have evaluated fund performance within the SDF approach, and find little support for superior performance. It would be interesting to compare the SDF approach to fund performance to the more traditional Jensen (1968) and Ferson and Schadt (1996) measures based on linear-beta models. There has been a lively debate in the academic literature recently about the relative merits of the two alternative approaches in testing asset pricing models (see Kan and Zhou, 1999; Jagannathan and Wang, 2002). There is also wide scope for using the SDF approach to examine the conditional performance of different types of funds.

NOTES

1. Cochrane (2001) and Ferson (2003) provide excellent reviews of the stochastic discount factor approach to asset pricing. Ferson also includes an excellent discussion of the different approaches to conditional performance evaluation.
2. See Jagannathan et al. (2002) for a review of GMM in financial applications.
3. Christopherson et al. (1998) assume a linear functional form of conditional performance using linear beta models.
4. However, conditional factor models are untestable because we do not observe the full information set used by investors (Hansen and Richard, 1987).
5. See Kosowksi (2001) for an alternative approach to examine whether mutual fund performance varies over the business cycle.

REFERENCES

Ahn, D.H., Cao, H.H., and Chretien, S. (2003a). "Portfolio performance measurement: a no arbitrage bounds approach." Working paper, University of Alberta.

Ahn, D.H., Cliff, M., and Shivdasani, A. (2003b). "Long-term returns of seasoned equity offerings: bad performance or bad models?" Working paper, Purdue University.

Ahn, D.H., Conrad, J., and Dittmar, R.F. (2003c). "Risk adjustment and trading strategies." *Review of Financial Studies*, 16: 459–485.

Ahn, D.H., Conrad, J., and Dittmar, R.F. (2003d). "Basis assets." Working Paper, University of North Carolina.

Bakashi, G. and Chen, Z. (1998). "Asset pricing without consumption or market portfolio data." Working Paper, University of Maryland.

Brennan, M.J. and Schwartz, E.S. (1979). "A continuous time approach to the pricing of bonds." *Journal of Banking and Finance*, 3: 133–155.

Carhart, M.M. (1997). "On persistence in mutual fund performance." *Journal of Finance*, 52: 57–82.

Chen, Z. and Knez, P.J. (1996). "Portfolio performance measurement: theory and applications." *Review of Financial Studies*, 9: 511–555.

Chretien, S. and Cliff, M. (2001). "Assessing asset pricing models with a returns decomposition." Working paper, Purdue University.

Christopherson, J.A., Ferson, W.E., and Glassman, D. (1998). "Conditioning manager alphas on economic information: another look at the persistence in performance." *Review of Financial Studies*, 11: 111–142.

Cochrane, J.H. (1996). "A cross-sectional test of an investment based asset pricing model." *Journal of Political Economy*, 104: 572–621.

Cochrane, J.H. (2001). *Asset Pricing*. Princeton, NJ: Princeton University Press.

Connor, G. and Korajczyk, R.A. (1986). "Performance measurement with the arbitrage pricing theory: a new framework for analysis." *Journal of Financial Economics*, 15: 373–394.

Cornell, B. (1979). "Asymmetric information and portfolio performance measurement." *Journal of Financial Economics*, 7: 381–390.

Dahlquist, M. and Soderlind, P. (1999). "Evaluating portfolio performance with stochastic discount factors." *Journal of Business*, 72: 347–383.

Daniel, K., Grinblatt, M., Titman, S., and Wermers, R. (1997). "Measuring mutual fund performance with characteristic based benchmarks." *Journal of Finance*, 52: 1035–1058.

Fama, E.F. and French, K.R. (1993). "Common risk factors in the returns on bonds and stocks." *Journal of Financial Economics*, 33: 3–53.

Farnsworth, H., Ferson, W.E., Jackson, D., and Todd, S. (2002). "Performance evaluation with stochastic discount factors." *Journal of Business*, 75: 473–505.

Ferson, W.E. (2003). "Tests of multifactor pricing models, volatility bounds and portfolio performance," in G.M. Constantinides, M. Harris, and R. Stulz (eds.) *Handbook of the Economics of Finance*. Amsterdam: Elsevier Science.

Ferson, W.E. and Khang, K. (2002). "Conditional performance measurement using portfolio weights: evidence for pension funds." *Journal of Financial Economics*, 65: 249–282.

Ferson, W.E. and Schadt, R.W. (1996). "Measuring fund strategy and performance in changing economic conditions." *Journal of Finance*, 51: 425–461.

Ferson, W.E., Henry, T., and Kisgen, D. (2003). "Evaluating government bond performance with stochastic discount factors." Working Paper, Boston University.

Fletcher, J. and Forbes, D. (2004). "Performance evaluation of UK unit trusts within the stochastic discount factor approach." *Journal of Financial Research*, 27: 289–306.

Goetzmann, W.N., Ingersoll, J., and Ivkovic, Z. (2000). "Monthly measurement of daily timers." *Journal of Financial and Quantitative Analysis*, 35: 257–290.

Grinblatt, M. and Titman, S. (1989). "Portfolio performance evaluation: old issues and new insights." *Review of Financial Studies*, 2: 393–421.

Grinblatt, M. and Titman, S. (1993). "Performance measurement without benchmarks: an examination of mutual fund returns." *Journal of Business*, 60: 97–112.

Hansen, L.P. (1982). "Large sample properties of generalized method of moments estimators." *Econometrica*, 50: 1029–1054.

Hansen, L.P. and Jagannathan, R. (1991). "Implications of security market data for models of dynamic economies." *Journal of Political Economy*, 99: 225–262.

Hansen, L.P. and Jagannathan, R. (1997). "Assessing specification errors in stochastic discount factor models." *Journal of Finance*, 52: 591–607.

Hansen, L.P. and Richard, S.F.R. (1987). "The role of conditioning information in deducing testable restrictions implied by dynamic asset pricing models." *Econometrica*, 55: 587–613.

Harrison, M. and Kreps, D. (1979). "Martingales and arbitrage in multi-period securities markets." *Journal of Economic Theory*, 20: 381–408.

Hendriksson, R. and Merton, R.C. (1981). "On market timing and investment performance. II. Statistical procedures for evaluating forecasting skills." *Journal of Business*, 54: 513–533.

Hodrick, R. and Zhang, X. (2001). "Evaluating the specification errors of asset pricing models." *Journal of Financial Economics*, 62: 327–376.

Jagannathan, R. and Wang, Z. (2002). "Empirical evaluation of asset pricing models: a comparison of SDF and beta methods." *Journal of Finance*, 57: 2337–2367.

Jagannathan, R., Skoulakis, G., and Wang, Z. (2002). "Generalized method moments: applications in finance." *Journal of Business and Economic Statistics*, 20: 470–481.

Jensen, M.C. (1968). "The performance of mutual funds in the period 1945–1964." *Journal of Finance*, 23: 389–416.

Kan, R. and Zhou, G. (1999). "A critique of the stochastic discount factor methodology." *Journal of Finance*, 54: 1221–1248.

Kosowksi, R. (2001). "Do mutual funds perform when it matters most to investors? US mutual fund performance and risk in recessions and booms 1962–1994." Working paper, London School of Economics.

Lehmann, B.N. and Modest, D.M. (1987). "Mutual fund performance evaluation: a comparison of benchmarks and benchmark comparisons." *Journal of Finance*, 42: 233–265.

Lettau, M. and Ludvigson, S. (2001). "Resurrecting the (C)CAPM: a cross-sectional test when risk premia are time-varying." *Journal of Political Economy*, 109: 1238–1287.

Long, J. (1990). "The numeraire portfolio." *Journal of Financial Economics*, 26: 29–70.

Lynch, A.W., Wachter, J., and Boudry, W. (2004). "Does mutual fund performance vary over the business cycle." Working paper, New York University.

Roll, R. (1978). "Ambiguity when performance is measured by the securities market line." *Journal of Finance*, 33: 1051–1069.

Ross, S.A. (1978). "A simple approach to the valuation of risky streams." *Journal of Business*, 51: 153–475.

Sharpe, W.F. (1966). "Mutual fund performance." *Journal of Business*, 39: 119–138.

Treynor, J. and Mazuy, K. (1966). "Can mutual funds outguess the market?" *Harvard Business Review*, 44: 131–136.

Chapter 13

DURATION ANALYSIS AND ITS APPLICATIONS

IRAJ J. FOOLADI, *Dalhousie University, Canada*
GADY JACOBY, *University of Manitoba, Canada*
GORDON S. ROBERTS, *York University, Canada*

Abstract

We discuss duration and its development, placing particular emphasis on various applications. The survey begins by introducing duration and showing how traders and portfolio managers use this measure in speculative and hedging strategies. We then turn to convexity, a complication arising from relaxing the linearity assumption in duration. Next, we present immunization – a hedging strategy based on duration. The article goes on to examine stochastic process risk and duration extensions, which address it. We then examine the track record of duration and how the measure applies to financial futures. The discussion then turns to macrohedging the entire balance sheet of a financial institution. We develop a theoretical framework for duration gaps and apply it, in turn, to banks, life insurance companies, and defined benefit pension plans.

Keywords: duration; fixed-income securities; immunization; hedging interest rate risk; macrohedging; bond price volatility; stochastic process risk; financial institution management; pension funds; insurance companies;banks

13.1. Introduction

Duration Analysis is the key to understanding the returns on fixed-income securities. Duration is also central to measuring risk exposures in fixed-income positions.

The concept of duration was first developed by Macaulay (1938). Thereafter, it was occasionally used in some applications by economists (Hicks, 1939; Samuelson, 1945), and actuaries (Redington, 1952). However, by and large, this concept remained dormant until 1971 when Fisher and Weil illustrated that duration could be used to design a bond portfolio that is immunized against interest rate risk. Today, duration is widely used in financial markets.

We discuss duration and its development, placing particular emphasis on various applications. The survey begins by introducing duration and showing how traders and portfolio managers use this measure in speculative and hedging strategies. We then turn to convexity, a complication arising from relaxing the linearity assumption in duration. Next, we present immunization – a hedging strategy based on duration. The article goes on to examine stochastic process risk and duration extensions, which address it. We then examine the track record of duration and how the measure applies to financial futures. The discussion then turns to macrohedging the entire balance sheet of a financial institution. We develop a theoretical framework for duration gaps and apply it, in turn, to banks, life insurance companies and defined benefit pension plans.

13.2. Calculating Duration

Recognising that term-to-maturity of a bond was not an appropriate measure of its actual life, Macaulay (1938) invented the concept of duration as the true measure of a bond's "longness," and applied the concept to asset/liability management of life insurance companies.

Thus, duration represents a measure of the time dimension of a bond or other fixed-income security. The formula calculates a weighted average of the time horizons at which the cash flows from a fixed-income security are received. Each time horizon's weight is the percentage of the total present value of the bond (bond price) paid at that time. These weights add up to 1. Macaulay duration uses the bond's yield to maturity to calculate the present values.

$$\text{Duration} = D = \frac{\sum_{t=1}^{N} \frac{tC(t)}{(1+y)^t}}{P_0} = \sum_{t=1}^{N} tW(t), \quad (13.1)$$

where $C(t)$ = cash flow received at time t, $W(t)$ = weight attached to time t, cash flow, $\sum_{t=1}^{N} W(t) = 1$, y = yield-to-maturity, and P_0 = current price of the bond,

$$P_0 = \sum_{t=1}^{N} \frac{C(t)}{(1+y)^t}.$$

A bond's duration increases with maturity but it is shorter than maturity unless the bond is a zero-coupon bond (in which case it is equal to maturity). The coupon rate also affects duration. This is because a bond with a higher coupon rate pays a greater percentage of its present value prior to maturity. Such a bond has greater weights on coupon payments, and hence a shorter duration.

Using yield to maturity to obtain duration implies that interest rates are the same for all maturities (a flat-term structure). Fisher and Weil (1971) reformulated duration using a more general (non-flat) term structure, and showed that duration can be used to immunize a portfolio of fixed-income securities.

$$D = \frac{\sum_{t=1}^{N} \frac{tC_{(t)}}{(1+r_t)^t}}{P_0} = \sum_{t=1}^{N} tW_{(t)}, \quad (13.2)$$

where r_t = discount rate for cashflows received at time t.

Their development marks the beginning of a broader application to active and passive fixed-income investment strategies, which came in the 1970s as managers looked for new tools to address the sharply increased volatility of interest rates.[1] In general, duration has two practical properties.

1 Duration represents the "elasticity" of a bond's price with respect to the discount factor $(1+y)^{-1}$. This was first developed by Hicks (1939). This property has applications for active bond portfolio strategies and evaluating "value at risk."

2 When duration is maintained equal to the time remaining in an investment planning horizon, promised portfolio return is immunized.

13.3. Duration and Price Volatility

In analyzing a series of cash flows, Hicks (1939) calculated the elasticity of the series with respect to the discount factor, which resulted in re-deriving Macaulay duration. Noting that this elasticity was defined in terms of time, he called it "average period," and showed that the relative price of two series of cash flows with the same average period is unaffected by changes in interest rates. Hicks' work brings our attention to a key mathematical property of duration. "The price elasticity of a bond in response to a small change in its yield to maturity is proportional to duration." Following the essence of work by Hopewell and Kaufman (1973), we can approximate the elasticity as:

$$\text{Duration} = D = -\frac{dP}{dr}\frac{(1+r)}{P} \cong -\left[\frac{\Delta P/P}{\Delta r/(1+r)}\right],$$

$$(13.3)$$

where P denotes the price of the bond and r denotes the market yield. Rearranging the term we obtain:

$$\Delta P \cong -D \left[\frac{\Delta r}{(1+r)} \right] P. \qquad (13.4)$$

When interest rates are continuously compounded, Equation (13.4) turns to:

$$\Delta P \cong -D[\Delta r]P.$$

This means that if interest rates fall (rise) slightly, the price increases (decreases) in different bonds are proportional to duration.

The intuition here is straightforward: if a bond has a longer duration because a greater portion of its cash flows are being deferred further into the future, then a change in the discount factor has a greater effect on its price. Note again that, here, we are using yield instead of term structure, and thus strictly speaking, assuming a flat-term structure.

The link between bond duration and price volatility has important practical applications in trading, portfolio management, and managing risk positions. For the trader taking a view on the movement of market yields, duration provides a measure of volatility or potential gains. Other things equal, the trader will seek maximum returns to a rate anticipation strategy by taking long or short positions in high-duration bonds. For derivative strategies, price sensitivity for options and futures contracts on bonds also depends on duration. In contrast with traders, bond portfolio managers have longer horizons. They remain invested in bonds, but lengthen or shorten portfolio average duration depending on their forecast for rates.

13.4. Convexity – A Duration Complication

Equation (13.4) is accurate for small shifts in yields. In practice, more dramatic shifts in rates sometimes occur. For example, in its unsuccessful attempt to maintain the U.K. pound in the European monetary snake, the Bank of England raised its discount rate by 500 basis points in one day! In cases where interest rate changes involve such large shifts, the price changes predicted from the duration formula are only approximations. The cause of the divergence is convexity. To understand this argument better, note that the duration derived in Equation (13.3) can be rewritten as:

$$D \cong - \left[\frac{\Delta P/P}{\Delta(1+r)/(1+r)} \right] = - \frac{\Delta \ln P}{\Delta \ln(1+r)}. \qquad (13.5)$$

However, the true relationship between $\ln P$ and $\ln(1+r)$ is represented by a convex function. Duration is the absolute value of the slope of a line, which is tangent to the curve representing this true relationship. A curve may be approximated by a tangent line only around the point of tangency.

Figure 13.1 illustrates convexity plotting the "natural log of bond price" on the y-axis and the "natural log of 1 plus interest rate" on the x-axis. The absolute value of the slope of the straight line that is tangent to the actual relationship between price and interest rate at the present interest rate represents the duration. Figure 13.1 shows that the duration model gives very accurate approximations of percentage price changes for small shifts in yields. As the yield shifts become larger, the approximation becomes less accurate and the error increases. Duration overestimates the price decline resulting from an interest rate hike and underestimates the price increase caused by a decline in yields. This error is caused by the convexity of the curve representing the true relationship.

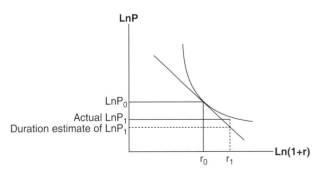

Figure 13.1. Actual versus duration estimate for changes in the bond price

Thus, convexity (sometimes called positive convexity) is "good news" for an investor with a long position: when rates fall, the true price gain (along the curve) is greater than predicted by the duration line. On the other hand, when rates rise, the true percentage loss is smaller than predicted by the duration line.

Note that the linear price-change relationship ignores the impact of interest rate changes on duration. In reality, duration is a function of the level of rates because the weights in the duration formula all depend on bond yield. Duration falls (rises) when rates rise (fall) because a higher discount rate lowers the weights for cash flows far into the future. These changes in duration cause the actual price-change curve to lie above the tangent line in Figure 13.1. The positive convexity described here characterizes all fixed-income securities which do not have embedded options such as call or put features on bonds, or prepayment, or lock-in features in mortgages.

Embedded options can cause negative convexity. This property is potentially dangerous as it reverses the "good news" feature of positive convexity, as actual price falls below the level predicted by duration alone.

13.5. Value At Risk

Financial institutions face market risk as a result of the actions of the trader and the portfolio manager. Market risk occurs when rates move opposite to the forecast on which an active strategy is based. For example, a trader may go short and will lose money if rates fall. In contrast, a portfolio manager at the same financial institution may take a long position with higher duration, and will face losses if rates rise.

Value at risk methodology makes use of Equation (13.4) to calculate the institution's loss exposure[2]. For example, suppose that the net position of the trader and the portfolio manager is $50 million ($P = \$50$ million) in a portfolio with a duration of 5 years. Suppose further that the worst-case scenario is that rates, currently at 6 percent, jump by 50

basis points in one day ($\Delta r = .005$). The risk management professional calculates the maximum loss or value at risk as:

$$dp = -5[.005/(1 + .06)]\$50 \text{million}$$
$$= \$ - 1.179 \text{ million}$$

If this maximum loss falls within the institution's guidelines, the trader and the portfolio manager may not take any action. If, however, the risk is excessive, the treasury professional will examine strategies to hedge the interest rate risk faced by the institution. This leads to the role of duration in hedging.

13.6. Duration and Immunization

Duration hedging or immunization draws on a second key mathematical property. "By maintaining portfolio duration equal to the amount of time remaining in a planning horizon, the investment manager can immunize locking in the original promised return on the portfolio." Note that immunization seeks to tie the promised return, not to beat it. Because it requires no view of future interest rates, immunization is a passive strategy. It may be particularly attractive when interest rates are volatile.[3]

Early versions of immunization theory were offered by Samuelson (1945) and Redington (1952). Fisher and Weil (1971) point out that the flat-term structure assumption made by Redington and implied in Macaulay duration is unrealistic. They assume a more general (nonflat) term structure of continuously compounded interest rates and a stochastic process for interest rates that is consistent with an additive shift, and prove that "a bond portfolio is immune to interest rate shifts, if its duration is maintained equal to the investor's remaining holding horizon."

The intuition behind immunization is clearly explained by Bierwag (1987a, Chapter 4). For investors with a fixed-planning period, the return realized on their portfolio of fixed-income securities could be different than the return they expected at the time of investment, as a result of interest rate shifts. The realized rate of return has two components: interest accumulated from re-investment of coupon income and the capital gain or loss at the end of the planning period. The two components impact the realized rate of return in opposite directions, and do not necessarily cancel one another. Which component dominates de-pends on the relationship between portfolio dur-ation and the length of the planning horizon. When the portfolio duration is longer than the length of the planning period, capital gains or losses will dominate the effect of reinvestment re-turn. This means that the realized return will be less (greater) than promised return if the rates rise (fall). If the portfolio duration is less than the length of the planning period, the effect of reinvest-ment return will dominate the effect of capital gains or losses. In this case, the realized return will be less (greater) than promised return if the rates fall (rise). Finally, when the portfolio dur-ation is exactly equal to the length of the planning period, the portfolio is immunized and the realized return will never fall below that promised rate of return.[4]

Zero-coupon bonds and duration matching with coupon bonds are two ways of immunizing interest rate risk. Duration matching effectively creates synthetic zero-coupon bonds. Equating duration to the planed investment horizon can easily be achieved with a two-bond portfolio. The duration of such a portfolio is equal to the weighted average of the durations of the two bonds that form the portfolio as shown in Equation (13.6).

$$D_P = W_1 D_1 + W_2 D_2, \qquad (13.6)$$

where $W_2 = 1 - W_1$. Setting the right-hand side of Equation (13.6) equal to the investment horizon, this problem is reduced to solving one equation with one unknown.

The preceding argument is consistent with the view presented in Bierwag and Khang (1979) that immunization strategy is a maxmin strategy: it maximizes the minimum return that can be obtained from a bond portfolio. Prisman (1986)

broadens this view by examining the relationship between a duration strategy, an immunization strategy, and a maxmin strategy. He concludes that, for a duration strategy to be able to maximize the lower bound to the terminal value of the bond portfolio, there must be constraints on the bonds to be included.

13.7. Contingent Immunization

Since duration is used in both active and passive bond portfolio management, it can also be used for a middle-of-the-road approach. Here fund man-agers strive to obtain returns in excess of what is possible by immunization, at the same time, they try to limit possible loss from incorrect anticipa-tion of interest rate changes. In this approach, called contingent immunization, the investor sets a minimum acceptable Holding Period Return (HPR) below the promised rate, and then follows an active strategy in order to enhance the HPR beyond the promised return. The investor con-tinues with the active strategy unless, as a result of errors in forecasting, the value of the portfolio reduces to the point where any further decline will result in an HPR below the minimum limit for the return. At this point, the investor changes from an active to immunizing strategy[5].

13.8 Stochastic Process Risk – Immunization Complication

Macaulay duration uses yield to maturity as the discount rate as in Equation (13.1). Because yield to maturity discounts all bond cash flows at an identical rate, Macaulay duration implicitly as-sumes that the interest rates are generated by a stochastic process in which a flat-term structure shifts randomly in a parallel fashion so that "all" interest rates change by the same amount. When we assume a different stochastic process, we obtain a duration measure different from Macaulay dur-ation (Bierwag, 1977; Bierwag et al., 1982a). If the actual stochastic process is different from what we assume in obtaining our duration measure, our computed duration will not truly represent the portfolio's risk. In this case, equating the duration measure to the investment horizon will not immunize portfolio, and there will be stochastic process risk. Although immunization is a passive strategy, which is not based on an interest rate forecast, it is necessary to predict the stochastic process governing interest rate movements.

A number of researchers have developed strategies for minimizing stochastic process risk and its consequences (for example, Fong and Vasicek, 1983, 1984; Bierwag et al., 1987, 1993; Prisman and Shores, 1988; Fooladi and Roberts, 1992).

In a related criticism of Macaulay duration, Ingersoll et al. (1978) argue that the assumed stochastic process in the development of single-factor duration models is inconsistent with equilibrium conditions. The source of arbitrage opportunities is the convexity of the holding period return from immunized portfolios with respect to interest rate shifts. Total value is a convex function of interest rate changes, which for the immunized funds has its minimum at the point of the original rate, r_0. This means that holding period return is also a convex function of interest rate shifts with the minimum at the original rate. Thus, the larger the shift, the greater the benefit from an interest rate shock. Therefore, in particular in the presence of large shocks to interest rates, and or for high-coupon bonds, risk-less arbitrage would be possible by investors who short zero-coupon bonds for a return of r_0, and invest in other bond portfolios without taking an extra risk.

Although, this argument is sound, it does not mar the validity of immunization strategies. Bierwag et al. (1982a) develop an additive stochastic process that is consistent with general equilibrium, and for which the holding period return is not a strictly convex function of interest rate shifts. Further, Bierwag (1987b) shows that there is no one-to-one correspondence between a particular duration measure and its underlying stochastic process. Duration measures derived from some disequilibrium processes such as the Fisher–Weil process, the Khang process, and additive and

multiplicative processes of Bierwag also correspond to equilibrium processes. Additionally, Bierwag and Roberts (1990) found examples of equilibrium stochastic processes give rise to duration measures that have been previously derived from disequilibrium stochastic processes such as Fisher–Weil duration.

On the practical side, the risk-less-arbitrage argument seemed hypothetical to many practitioners who were aware of the difficulties in taking a large short position in bonds. Practitioners were more concerned that the reality of nonparallel shifts in sloping yield curves could impair the hedges constructed based on Macaulay duration.

The current generation of models incorporates the term structure so that it is no longer the case that duration users must assume a flat-term structure. Bierwag et al. (1983b, 1987, 1993) and Brennan and Schwartz (1983) are a few examples. Current models also allow for nonparallel shifts in the yield curve. These include multifactor models (Chambers et al., 1988; Nawalka and Chambers, 1997) in which the short and long ends of the yield curve are allowed to shift in opposite directions.[6]

13.9. Effectiveness of Duration-Matched Strategies

Given that duration extensions are numerous, how effective is basic Macaulay duration in the design and implementation of active and passive strategies? Bierwag and Roberts (1990) test the key implication of duration theory for active managers – portfolios with higher durations are predicted to have greater price sensitivity when rates change. Constructing portfolios with constant durations using Government of Canada bonds, they measure monthly holding period returns over the period of 1963–1986. They find that, as predicted, higher duration portfolios had greater return volatility and that Macaulay duration explained around 80 percent of the variance in holding period returns.

A number of studies examine the effectiveness of immunization over sample sets of government bonds for the United States, Canada, and Spain, among others. Fooladi and Roberts (1992) use actual prices for Government of Canada bonds over the period 1963–1986, setting the investment horizon to five years, and rebalancing every six months to maintain duration equal to the time remaining in the investment horizon. Their performance benchmark consists of investing in a bond with maturity matched to the horizon. This maturity-bond strategy involves buying and holding a bond with an initial five year maturity. Due to stochastic process risk, there will always be cases in which the duration hedging strategy falls short or overshoots the promised return, which brings the target proceeds. Their test measures hedging performance so that the better strategy is the one that comes closer most often to the original promised return. They conclude that duration matching allowed the formation of effective hedges that outperformed nonduration-matched portfolios. These results validate the widespread use of Macaulay duration in measuring risk and in immunization. They also support similar results obtained for U.S. Treasury Securities by Bierwag and coworkers (1981, 1982b).

Beyond establishing the credibility of duration matching as a hedging technique, empirical research has also probed the hedging effectiveness of alternative duration-matching strategies in the face of stochastic process risk. Fong and Vasicek (1983, 1984) propose hedging portfolios designed by constraining M-squared, a measure of cashflow dispersion. Prisman and Shores (1988) and Bierwag et al. (1993) show that the Fong–Vasicek measure does not offer a general solution to minimizing hedging error. The latter paper reinforces results in tests of duration effectiveness discussed earlier which find that stochastic process risk is best controlled by constraining the portfolio to include a maturity bond. This result is replicated for immunization in the Spanish government bond market by Soto (2001).

Going beyond Macaulay duration, Soto (2001) and Nawalkha and Chambers (1997), among others, examine the increase in hedging effective-

ness offered by multi-factor duration models. They establish that a three-factor model controlling for the level, slope and term structure curvature works best in the absence of the maturity bond constraint.

13.10. Use of Financial Futures

The basics of duration analysis can be combined with the use of futures markets instruments for hedging purposes. An investor can hold a long position in a certain security (for example, three month bankers acceptances) and a short position in a futures contract written on that security, and reduce overall exposure to interest rate risk. This is because, as interest rates change, prices of the security and the futures contract move in the same direction and gains and losses in the long and short positions largely cancel out. The durations of the security held long and of the security underlying the futures contract determine the hedge ratio. When we combine the cash and futures positions, the duration of the overall portfolio may be expressed as:

$$D_P = D_C + D_F(V_F/V_C), \qquad (13.7)$$

where, D_C, D_F, and D_P denote durations of the cash portfolio, futures portfolio, and the overall portfolio, respectively, and V_F and V_C are the values of futures and cash positions, respectively. It should be noted that $V_F = hF$ where F denotes the futures price and h is the number of future contracts per unit of cash portfolio (the hedge ratio).

Bierwag (1987a) shows that, for a perfect hedge, in general the hedge ratio (h) is determined by:

$$h = \frac{1 + r_o^f}{1 + r_o^c} \times \frac{-D_C}{D_F} \times \frac{V(r_o^c)}{F(r_o^f)a}, \qquad (13.8)$$

where $V(r_o^c) =$ the value of the long position, $F(r_o^f) =$ the future price for one unit of contract, $r_o^c =$ the current yield to maturity of the long asset, $r_o^f =$ the current yield to maturity of the asset underlying the futures contract, and $a =$ the derivative r^f with respect to r^c.

If the underlying asset is the same and the maturities of asset and future contract are identical, it may be reasonable to assume $a = 1$. Equation (13.7) shows how an investor can use futures contracts to alter duration of a bond portfolio.

13.11. Duration of Corporate Bonds

Our review of immunization research has so far concentrated on government bonds, and ignored default risk. In practice, bond portfolio managers often hold corporate, state, and municipal bonds to enhance yields. This raises the question of how to apply immunization to such portfolios. Simply using Macaulay (or Fisher–Weil) duration for each bond to find portfolio weights will be misleading. Ignoring default risk is equivalent to assuming that we have locked in a higher yield than is possible immunizing with government bonds alone. The promised return must be adjusted to an expected return reflecting the probability of default.

As Bierwag and Kaufman (1988) argue, in computing duration for nondefault-free bonds, in addition to the stochastic process governing interest rate shifts, we must also consider the stochastic process governing the timing of the losses from default. Default alters both a bond's cash flows and their timing. Thus, we cannot immunize a portfolio of nondefault-free bonds at its promised rate of return. An interesting question follows. Is it possible to immunize such a portfolio at its (lower) risk-adjusted return using a single-factor duration model?

Fooladi et al. (1997) answer affirmatively but contend that Macaulay duration is not a true measure of interest rate sensitivity for bonds with default risk. Assuming risk-averse investors, they derive a general expression for duration, which includes terms for default probabilities, expected repayment, and the timing of repayment. They illustrate that, under certain circumstances, their general single-factor duration measure is an immunizing measure. They conclude that practical application of duration analysis in immunization calls for employing duration measures that are adjusted for default risk.

Jacoby (2003) extends the model of Fooladi et al. (1997), by representing bondholders' preferences with a log-utility function. Accounting for default risk, his duration measure is the sum of the Fisher–Weil duration and the duration of the expected delay between the time of default and actual recovery caused by the default option. Using historical long-term corporate bond default and recovery rates, he numerically simulates his duration measure. His conclusion is that failing to adjust duration for default is costly for high-yield bonds, but appears to be trivial for investment-grade bonds.

In an earlier paper, Chance (1990) draws on Merton's (1974) option pricing bond valuation. Chance shows that the duration of a zero-coupon bond is the weighted average of the duration of a corresponding risk-less discount bond and that of the limited liability option. Chance finds that his duration is lower than the bond's Macaulay duration (maturity for a zero-coupon bond).

Since many corporate bonds are callable, Acharya and Carpenter (2002) also use option pricing technology to derive a valuation framework of callable defaultable bonds. In their model, both interest rates and firm value are stochastic and the call and default decisions are endogenized. With respect to interest rate sensitivity, as in Chance's model, their model implies that default risk alone reduces the bond's duration. They further show that, everything else being equal, call-risk will also shorten bond duration.

The theoretical work of Chance (1990) and Acharya and Carpenter (2002) emphasizes the significance of adjusting Macaulay duration for both default and call-risks. Jacoby and Roberts (2003) address the question of the relative importance for duration of these two sources of risk. Using Canadian corporate data, they estimate and compare the default-and call-adjusted duration with its Macaulay counterpart. In general, their results support the need for callability adjustment, but fail to uncover any significant impact of default risk for investment-grade callable and defaultable bonds. Their results provide some support for the Acharya and Carpenter (2002) model, that predicts an interaction between call and default risks. Jacoby and Roberts demonstrate that during a recessionary period (1991–1994), the call adjustment is less important (but still significant) relative to other periods. This is because bond prices are depressed during recessionary periods, and therefore the incentive to call these bonds arising from lower interest rates is significantly reduced.

13.12. Macrohedging

This section broadens the application of duration to "macrohedging" addressing interest rate exposure at the macro level of a corporate entity, in particular, a financial institution. Macrohedging or balance sheet hedging considers the entire balance sheet and treats both sides as variable. Without a macro approach to hedging, we are forced to take the liability side as given, and cannot address asset/liability management.

As with its micro counterpart, macrohedging can be a tool for either passive or active strategies. In a passive ("routine hedging") strategy, immunization for example, hedging seeks to eliminate interest rate risk completely. In contrast, an active ("selective hedging") approach leaves some interest rate exposure unhedged seeking to achieve superior returns based on a view of future rates.

13.13. Duration Gap

A "duration gap" measures the mismatch between assets and liabilities. When the duration gap is zero, the assets and liabilities are perfectly matched so that the financial institution's net worth is immunized against shifts in interest rates. We illustrate duration gap using a simple example involving "one" discount rate for all assets and a financial institution with a single asset, which is financed partly by equity and partly by liabilities. The balance sheet identity requires:

$$A = E + L, \tag{13.9}$$

where A denotes assets, E denotes equity, and L denotes liabilities. Taking the derivative of Equation (13.9) with respect to the interest rate (single discount rate) and rearranging the terms we obtain:

$$\frac{dE}{dr} = \frac{dA}{dr} - \frac{dL}{dr}. \tag{13.10}$$

For the equity to be unaffected by changes in interest rates, the right hand side of Equation (13.10) must be zero. Multiplying both sides of Equation (13.10) by a fixed quantity, $(1 + r)/A$, and noting the definition of duration, we obtain

$$\frac{E}{A}D_E = D_A - \frac{L}{A}D_L = D_{\text{Gap}} \tag{13.11}$$

where D_A, D_L, and D_E denote the durations of assets, liabilities, and equity, respectively. The right hand side of Equation (13.11) is called duration gap, D_{Gap}. A zero duration gap tells us that the equity has zero interest rate exposure.

Restating the equation for duration of equity in terms of Equation (13.3), replacing P (for price) with E (for equity), results in Equation (13.12).

$$D_E \cong -\left[\frac{\Delta E/E}{\Delta r/(1 + r)} \right] \tag{13.12}$$

Substituting for D_E from Equation (13.12) into Equation (13.11), and rearranging the terms results in the following formula for changes in the value of equity as a function of duration gap[7]:

$$\Delta E \cong -D_{\text{Gap}} \left[\frac{\Delta r}{(1 + r)} \right] \times A \tag{13.13}$$

This highly useful formula shows how a shift in interest rates impacts the market value of an Financial Institution equity.[8] It is set up so that duration gap mathematically plays the same role as duration in the corresponding formula for fixed-income securities in Equation (13.4). When duration gap is zero, the shares of the FI will not be affected by interest rate shocks; the FI's shares will behave like floating rate bonds with zero duration. The shares of an FI with a positive duration gap will rise when rates fall analogously to a long position in a bond. If an FI has a negative duration gap, its shares will increase in value when rates rise. Holding the shares of such an FI is like taking a short position in a bond.[9]

It follows that, in parallel with fixed-income securities, the formula (Equation 13.13) has practical implications both for passive management (immunization) and for active management (interest rate speculation). To illustrate, suppose that the management of an FI regards future interest rate movements as highly uncertain. In this case, the FI should immunize by setting the duration gap to zero. On the other hand, if senior executives predict that rates will fall, the FI should expand its portfolio of longer term loans financed by short term deposits increasing D_{Gap}.[10]

Central to this strategy is the implied assumption that the difference between convexity of assets and convexity of liabilities (adjusted for capital structure and the ratio of return on assets over return on liabilities) is non-negative. Fooladi and Roberts (2004) show that if this difference which they call "convexity gap" is not nonnegative, satisfying duration condition is not sufficient for hedging against interest rate risk.

To reduce adjustment time, and to save on transactions costs, FIs adjust duration gaps using off-balance-sheet positions in derivative securities such as interest rate futures, interest rate options and swaps. Bierwag (1997) shows that to find the proper hedge ratio for futures hedging, we simply substitute D_{Gap} for D_c in Equation (13.8) (that is used for constructing hedged positions in bond portfolios).

13.14. Other Applications of Duration Gaps

Duration gap also has applications to managing the balance sheets of life insurance companies and pension funds, and even to nonfinancial corporations and governments.

Life insurance companies were the first class of financial institutions to implement duration matching.[11] Policy reserves are the main liability of a life company and represent the expected present value of future liabilities under life policies.

The typical life insurance company invests the bulk of its assets in bonds and mortgages. This leads to a constitutionally negative duration gap as future policy liabilities generally have a longer duration than bonds and mortgages. To address the resulting interest rate exposure, during the 1980s life companies increased their investments in mortgages and other positions in real estate. The recession and real estate collapse of the early 1990s led to the insolvency of several life companies. Today, well-managed life insurance companies recognize that off-balance sheet positions in futures and other derivatives offer an attractive way to hedge an imbalanced duration gap without the risks that come with large positions in real estate.

Pension plans come in two types: defined benefit and defined contribution. The balance sheet of a defined benefit pension plan, like that of a life insurance company, has a constitutional imbalance in duration. Given that an average employee may retire 20 years from today, and then live for another 20 years, the duration of the pension liability is generally longer than the duration of the asset portfolio invested in equities and bonds. As a result, in the 1990s, many defined benefit pension plans were increasing their equity exposures and taking equity positions in real estate.[12] Bodie (1996) shows that this leaves pension funds exposed to mismatched exposures to interest rate and market risks. Beginning in 2000, sharp declines in both stock prices and long-term interest rates created a "Perfect Storm" for defined benefit pension funds (Zion and Carache, 2002). As a result, a number of plans are seeking to switch to the defined contribution format.

Many pension plans offer some form of indexation of retirement benefits to compensate for inflation that occurs after employees retire. To address inflation risk, pension funds can immunize all or part of their liabilities against interest rate risk using macro or micro hedging, and then add an inflation hedge. The portfolio shifts to equities and real estate investments discussed earlier offer a potential inflation hedge. Another attractive possibility is Treasury Inflation Protected Securities

(TIPS). These bonds offer indexation of principal and interest, and thus have approximately zero nominal (inflation) duration.

Duration gaps can also be used to hedge the equity of nonfinancial corporations and governments against interest rate fluctuations. For example, in a highly innovative application of duration analysis, the New Zealand government explored how this tool could help guide the recent restructuring of its liabilities.[13]

Acknowledgment

The authors gratefully acknowledge the support of the Social Sciences and Humanities Research Council of Canada. Iraj Fooladi also acknowledges support from Douglas C. Mackay Fund at Dalhousie. Iraj Fooladi also acknowledges support from Douglas C. Mackay Fund at Dalhousie.

NOTES

1. Bierwag (1987a, 1997) provide excellent reviews of duration analysis.
2. For more on market risk see J.P. Morgan (1994) and Saunders (2000, Chapter 9).
3. This discussion of immunization begins by assuming default and option free securities in order to separate interest rate risk from other risks.
4. Bierwag and Kaufman (1977) maintain that, for the duration matched portfolios, these two effects (unexpected gains and losses resulting from interest rate shifts) cancel out, unless the stochastic process is not consistent with the equilibrium conditions, in which case the unexpected gain will be greater than the unexpected loss.
5. For more details on contingent immunization see: Bierwag (1987a) and Leibowitz and Weinberger (1981, 1982, 1983).
6. Detailed discussion of these modelling issues is in Bierwag (1987a, 1997).
7. For simplicity, the derivation assumes away any difference between rates of return for assets and liabilities, r_A and r_L. This may not be strictly true because interest earned on assets is higher than interest paid on liabilities. However, the essence of the argument is not affected by this assumption. In practice, duration gap implementation uses the average of the rates on assets and liabilities.

8. Following prior research, we chose the change in the market value of equity (E) as the target because maximizing equity value is most likely to be the goal of management and shareholders. Another possible target is E/A (the capital ratio) particularly in the case in which E/A is at the regulatory minimum of 8 percent and management wishes to immunize against any fall in the ratio. In practice, a financial institution likely targets equity along with other variables. Further discussion of this issue is in Kaufman (1984) and Bierwag and Kaufman (1996).
9. Some readers may be familiar with the concept of "funding gap." Funding gap is defined as rate sensitive assets minus rate sensitive liabilities. It differs from duration gap in two fundamental respects. First, funding gap relates interest rate shifts to the "book value of net income," duration gap relates rate shifts to the "market value of equity." Second, funding gap ignores the repricing of long-term assets when rates change. Because of these differences, a positive funding gap corresponds to a negative duration gap.
10. More generally, academic research supports the view that FI shares move in the direction expected by the theory of duration gaps. For an example, see Flannery and James (1984).
11. Early researchers on duration (Macaulay, 1938; Redington, 1952, for example) were actuaries who published their results in actuarial journals.
12. A related trend is for companies to switch their plans from defined benefit to defined contribution.
13. While coupons are fully indexed, the principal of TIPS is only indexed for inflation. In case of deflation the principal amount cannot be indexed to a level lower than its unadjusted principal.
14. In the early 1990s, New Zealand became the first country in the world to engage an accounting firm to state its balance sheet according to Generally Accepted Accounting Principles. Going one step further, the Treasury sought advice from academic researchers on how to apply macrohedging. In particular, a major privatization program provided the government with cash to reduce its outstanding debt and this raised the question of how the remaining debt should be structured to hedge the government's balance sheet assets (see Falloon, 1993).

REFERENCES

Acharya, V.V. and Carpenter, J.N. (2002). "Corporate bond valuation and hedging with stochastic interest rates and endogenous bankruptcy." *Review of Financial Studies*, 15: 1355–1383.

Bierwag, G.O. (1977). "Immunization, duration, and the term structure of interest rates." *Journal of Financial and Quantitative Analysis*, 12, 5, 725–741.

Bierwag, G.O. (1987a). *Duration Analysis, Managing Interest Rate Risk*. Cambridge, MA: Ballinger Publishing Company.

Bierwag, G.O. (1987b). "Bond returns, discrete stochastic processes, and duration." *Journal of Financial Research*, 10(Autumn), 10, 3, 191–209.

Bierwag, G.O. (1997). *Duration Analysis: A Historical Perspective Document*. School of Business, Miami International University, 12, 5, 725–741.

Bierwag, G.O. and Kaufman, G.G. (1977). "Coping with the risk of interest-rate fluctuations: a note." *Journal of Business* 50(3): 364–370.

Bierwag, G.O. and Kaufman, G.G. (1988). "Duration of non-default free securities." *Financial Analysts Journal*, 44(4): 39–46; published as a monograph to members of the Institute of Chartered Financial Analysis.

Bierwag, G.O. and Kaufman, G.G. (1996). "Managing interest rate risk with duration gaps to achieve multiple targets." *Journal of Financial Engineering*, March, 5, 53–73.

Bierwag, G.O. and Khang, C. (1979). "An immunization strategy is a maximin strategy." *Journal of Finance*, May: 389–399.

Bierwag, G.O. and Roberts, G.S. (1990). "Single factor duration models: Canadian tests." *Journal of Financial Research*, 13: 23–38.

Bierwag, G.O., Kaufman, G.G., Schweitzer, R., and Toevs, A. (1981). "The art of risk management in bond portfolios." *Journal of Portfolio Management*, 7: 27–36.

Bierwag, G.O., Kaufman, G.G., and Toevs, A. (1982a). "Single factor duration models in a discrete general equilibrium framework." *The Journal of Finance*, 37: 325–338.

Bierwag, G.O., Kaufman, G.G., and Toevs, A. (1982b). "Empirical tests of alternative single factor duration models." Paper presented at Western Finance Association, Portland, Oregon (June).

Bierwag, G.O., Kaufman, G.G., and Toevs, A. (1983). "Immunization strategies for funding multiple liabilities." *Journal of Financial and Quantitative Analysis*, 18: 113–124.

Bierwag, G.O., Kaufman, G.G., and Latta, C. (1987). "Bond portfolio immunization: tests of maturity, one- and two-factor duration matching strategies." *Financial Review*, 22, 2, 203–219.

Bierwag, G.O., Fooladi, I., and Roberts, G. (1993). "Designing and immunization portfolio: is M-squared the key?" *Journal of Banking and Finance*, 17: 1147–1170.

Brennan, M.J. and Schwartz, E.S. (1983). "Duration, bond pricing, and portfolio management, in innovations in bond portfolio management, duration analysis and immunization," in G.G. Kaufman, G.O. Bierwag, and A. Toevs (eds.) *Proceedings from the Ashland Conference, 1981*. Greenwich, Conn.: Jai Press.

Bodie, Z. (1996). "What the pension benefit guarantee corporation can learn from the federal savings and loan insurance corporation." *Journal of Financial Services Research*, 10(March): 83–100.

Chambers, D.R., Carleton, W.T., and McEnally, R.W. (1988). "Immunizing default-free bond portfolios with a duration vector." *Journal of Financial and Quantitative Analysis*, 23(1): 89–104.

Chance, D.M. (1990). "Default risk and the duration of zero coupon bonds." *Journal of Finance*, 45(1): 265–274.

Falloon, W. (1993). "Southern exposure." *Risk* 6(September): 103–107.

Fisher, L. and Weil, R.L. (1971). "Coping with the risk of market-rate fluctuations: returns to bondholders from naive and optimal strategies." *Journal of Business* (October): 408–431.

Flannery, M.J. and James, C.M. (1984). "The effect of interest rate changes on the common stock returns of financial institutions." *The Journal of Finance*, 39: 1141–1153.

Fong, H.G. and Vasicek, O. (1983). "Return maximization for immunized portfolios, in innovations in bond portfolio management, duration analysis and immunization," in G.G. Kaufman, G.O. Bierwag, and A. Toevs (eds.) *The Ashland Conference, 1981*. Greenwich, CT: Jai Press.

Fong, H.G. and Vasicek, O.A. (1984). "A risk minimizing strategy for portfolio immunization." *Journal of Finance*, 34(December): 1541–1546.

Fooladi, I. and Roberts, G. (1992). "Portfolio immunization: Canadian tests." *Journal of Economics and Business*, 44(1): 3–17.

Fooladi, I. and Roberts, G. (2004). "Macrohedging for financial institutions: beyond duration." *Journal of Applied Finance*, 14(1): 11–19.

Fooladi, I., Roberts, G., and Skinner, F. (1997). "Duration for bonds with default risk." *Journal of Banking and Finance*, 21(1): 1–16.

Hicks, J.R. (1939). *Value and Capital*, 2nd edn, 1946. Oxford: Clarendon Press.

Hopewell, M.H. and Kaufman, G.G. (1973). "Bond price volatility and term to maturity: a generalized respecification." *American Economic Review*, September: 749–753.

Ingersoll, J.E., Skelton, J., and Weil, R.L. (1978). "Duration forty years later." *Journal of Financial and Quantitative Analysis*, November: 621–650.

Jacoby, G. (2003). "A duration model for defaultable bonds." *Journal of Financial Research*, 26: 129–146.

Jacoby, G. and Roberts, G. (2003). "Default- and call-adjusted duration for corporate bonds." *Journal of Banking and Finance*, 27: 2297–2321.

Kaufman, G.G. (1984). "Measuring and managing interest rate risk: a primer," in *Economic Perspective*. Federal Reserve Bank of Chicago (8): 16–29.

Leibowitz, M.L. and Weinberger, A. (1981). "The uses of contingent immunization." *Journal of Portfolio Management* (Fall): 51–55.

Leibowitz, M.L. and Weinberger, A. (1982). "Contingent immunization, Part I: Risk control procedures." *Financial Analysts Journal* (November–December): 17–32.

Leibowitz, M.L. and Weinberger, A. (1983). "Contingent immunization, Part II: Problem areas." *Financial Analysts Journal* (January–February): 35–50.

Macaulay, F.R. (1938). "Some theoretical problems suggested by the movement of interest rates, bonds, yields, and stock prices in the United States since 1856." National Bureau of Economic Research, New York, Columbia University Press, pp. 44–53.

Merton, R.C. (1974). "On the pricing of corporate debt: the risk structure of interest rates." *Journal of Finance*, 29: 449–470.

Morgan, J.P. (1994). *Introduction to Riskmetrics*. New York: J.P. Morgan.

Nawalkha, S.K. and Chambers, D.R. (1997). "The M-vector model: Derivation and testing of extensions to M-square." *Journal of Portfolio Management*, 23(2): 92–98.

Prisman, E. (1986). "Immunization as a MaxMin strategy: a new look." *Journal of Banking and Finance*, 10(December): 493–504.

Prisman, E.Z. and Shores, M.R. (1988). "Duration measures for specific term structure estimations and applications to bond portfolio immunization." *Journal of Banking and Finance*, 12(3): 493–504.

Redington, F.M. (1952). "Review of the principle of Life-Office Valuations." *Journal of the Institute of Actuaries*, 78: 286–340.

Samuelson, P.A. (1945). "The effects of interest rate increases on the banking system." *American Economic Review* (March): 16–27.

Saunders, A. (2000). *Financial Institutions Management*, 3rd edn. Boston: Irwin McGraw Hill, Chapters 8, 9 and 18.

Soto, G.G. (2001). "Immunization derived from a polynomial duration vector in the Spanish bond market." *Journal of Banking and Finance*, 25: 1037–1057.

Zion, D. and Carache, B. (2002). *The Magic of Pension Accounting*. Boston: Credit Suisse First.

Chapter 14

LOAN CONTRACT TERMS

ARON A. GOTTESMAN, *Pace University, USA*

Abstract

Loan contract terms refer to the price and nonprice terms associated with a corporate loan deal between a borrower and a lender or a syndicate of lenders. The specification of loan contract terms differs across loans. These differences are attributable to the tradeoffs between values of loan contract terms that the borrower chooses when negotiating the loan contract, as well as the purpose of the loan and borrower and lending syndicate characteristics. Methodological issues that arise when investigating the relations between loan contract terms include allowing for loan contract terms that are determined simultaneously and accurately estimating credit risk.

Keywords: loan contract terms; corporate loans; syndicated loans; loan pricing corporation; maturity; collateral; credit spread; syndicate size; simultaneity; credit risk

14.1. Introduction

Loan Contract Terms refer to the price and nonprice terms associated with a corporate loan deal between a borrower and a lender or a syndicate of lenders.[1] Corporate loan deals are composed of one or more loans, designated *loan facilities*, and loan contract terms can vary across facilities. Price terms include the rate spread over the risk-free rate, typically the prime rate or LIBOR, and fees

such as upfront, annual, cancellation, and commitment fees. Nonprice terms include deal and facility size, maturity, collateral, financial and nonfinancial covenants, and performance pricing covenants. Other characteristics across which loans differ include whether the loan is a revolver or term loan, the seniority of the loan, and the size and concentration of the lending syndicate, among others.[2]

The specification of loan contract terms differs across loans. These differences are attributable to the tradeoffs between values of loan contract terms that the borrower chooses when negotiating the loan contract, as well as the purpose of the loan and borrower and lending syndicate characteristics.[3] Melnik and Plaut (1986) model loan commitment contracts as a "package" of negotiated terms.[4] In their model, the loan commitment contract is described by the vector $B[L^*, T, m, k, C]$, where L^* is the amount of credit the lender is willing to provide, T is the maturity of the contract, m is the rate spread, k is the loan commitment fee rate, and C is the collateral. Borrowers can choose to tradeoff less favorable specification of some contract terms in exchange for more favorable specification of other contract terms. Melnik and Plaut (1986) empirically test for the existence of such tradeoffs through investigating whether loan commitment size is related to other loan contract features, and find support for the hypotheses that lenders are willing to provide a larger loan commitment in exchange for a higher spread or more collateral. They also find support for the hypothesis that lenders are willing to provide larger loan commitments in exchange for a continuing customer relationship. As well, Melnik and Plaut (1986) identify a positive relation between loan commitment size and firm characteristics such as proxies for firm credit rating and firm size.

While Melnik and Plaut's (1986) study provides important early insight into the relation between loan contract terms, subsequent studies contribute to a more complete understanding. One relation that has received attention is the relation between loan spreads and maturity. Two competing hypotheses explain the nature of the relation. The *tradeoff hypothesis* forecasts a positive relation between corporate loan spreads and maturity, while the *credit quality hypothesis* forecasts a negative relation. The positive relation forecasted by the tradeoff hypothesis is based on the observation that, *ceteris parabis*, borrowers prefer to borrow for longer periods to avoid the costs associated with liquidation at maturity, while lenders prefer to lend for shorter periods to avoid agency problems.[5] The negative relation forecasted by the credit quality hypothesis is based on the argument that lenders direct riskier borrowers to shorter-maturity loans, and less-risky borrowers to longer-maturity loans. Because less-risky borrowers are less likely to default, the corporate loan spreads they pay are lower than the spreads paid by riskier borrowers, hence the relation between loan spreads and maturity is forecasted to be negative.[6]

Some empirical evidence identifies a negative relation between loan spreads and maturity, which supports the credit quality hypothesis. Strahan (1999) performs regression estimation of measures of spread against maturity and other regressors, and identifies a statistically significant negative coefficient associated with his measure of maturity for both lines of credit and term loans. Dennis et al. (2000) identify a negative relation as well.[7] But there is also evidence that longer maturity loans are associated with higher spreads (Hel-

wege and Turner, 1999; Coleman et al., 2002), supportive of the tradeoff hypothesis. Gottesman and Roberts (2004) argue that both hypotheses can coexist: the credit quality hypothesis at the portfolio level, and the tradeoff hypothesis at the individual firm level. Gottesman and Roberts (2004) test a matched pair sample consisting of longer and shorter maturity loan facilities between identical lender syndicates and individual borrowers. Both loan facility elements of each matched pair are segments of identical larger loan deals; hence firm and temporal characteristics are controlled. Through the use of these controls any effects associated with the credit quality hypothesis are eliminated, as both elements of each matched pair are associated with the same firm, and, therefore, are characterized by identical credit quality. Gottesman and Roberts (2004) identify a positive relation between loan spreads and maturity using their methodology, and argue that the tradeoff hypothesis is supported at the firm level, while the credit quality hypothesis describes reality at the loan portfolio level.

Another relation that has received attention is the relation between loan spreads and collateralization. There is extensive evidence that loans that are collateralized are associated with higher spreads than noncollateralized loans (Berger and Udell, 1990, 1995; Dennis et al., 2000; John et al., 2003; Gottesman and Roberts, 2005). Superficially, these finding are odd: shouldn't collateralization reduce the risk associated with the loan, and therefore lead to lower spreads? One explanation for the existence of higher spreads for collateralized loans is that riskier borrowers are more likely to be forced by lenders to collateralize than less risky borrowers, as suggested in theoretical models and empirical papers.[8] Hence, the higher spreads associated with collateralized loans arise because of the riskier nature of these borrowers, even after the risk-reducing effects of collateralization (Berger and Udell, 1990; Pozzolo, 2002). An alternative explanation for the higher spreads associated with collateralized loans is unrelated to the risk characteristics of the borrower; instead, John et al.'s

(2003) management-consumption hypothesis argues that the higher spreads are the result of agency problem associated with collateralized debt. Support for this hypothesis comes from empirical evidence of higher *ex ante* spreads (e.g. John et al., 2003; Gottesman and Roberts, 2005).

Empirical tests identify a number of additional relations between loan contract terms. For example, there is evidence that larger and less leveraged firms are more likely to borrow revolving loans rather than term loan (Coleman, A.D.F., Esho, N., and Sharpe, I.G. 2002). Further, loans that include a performance-pricing covenant have significant lower spreads than loans without such a covenant (Asquith et al., 2002), though there is also evidence that this result is limited to accounting-based performance pricing covenants (Panyagometh et al., 2004). Accounting-based performance-pricing covenants are associated with collateralization, longer maturity, and riskier loans (Doyle, 2003). There is evidence of a complementary pattern between performance pricing and other covenant provisions, though performance-pricing covenants are designed to deal with the scenario where the borrower's credit improves, while other covenants are designed for scenarios where credit deteriorates (Beatty et al., 2002).

14.2. Characteristics of the Lending Syndicate

Corporate loans are provided by either a sole lender or by a syndicate of lenders; indeed, syndicates of lenders provide a large proportion of corporate loans. The characteristics of the lending syndicate are important to both the lender and the borrower, and a lending syndicate structure that is optimal for the lenders maybe suboptimal for the borrower. We therefore expect tradeoffs between the syndicate structure and other loan contract terms. The arranging bank in a syndicate plays an important role in influencing syndicate size, concentration, and negotiated loan contract terms. As Lee and Mullineaux (2001) discuss, arranging banks control the size and concentration of the syndicate in a number of ways. First, the

arranger chooses which lenders to invite into the syndicate. Second, the arranger specifies participation bracket size and fee. Third, the arranger can close the syndication before the end of the offering period.

Lee and Mullineaux (2001) provide arguments as to why syndicate size is important. Larger syndicates can be costly, as unanimous agreement by all participants is required to permit change to the original loan agreement. Hence, should the borrower face financial distress, larger syndicates require costlier renegotiations and are more likely to result in failure to reach unanimous agreement. Because riskier firms are more likely to face financial distress, smaller syndicates are highly desirable for loans to riskier borrowers. Yet the arranging bank may prefer larger syndicates as it allows them to provide participation opportunities to other lenders.

Borrowers may prefer syndicated loans to avoid situations where a sole-lender monopolizes proprietary information about the borrower. As Boot (2000) notes, banks can use their monopoly over proprietary information about the borrower to charge a higher rate than would be expected in a competitive environment (the hold-up problem).[9] One solution for the borrower is to engage in multiple bank relationships and to ensure the availability of competing sources of loans (von Thadden, 1992).[10] Syndicated loans can be perceived as a source of multiple relationships. Note, however, that the more the lenders, the more likely that the proprietary information will be leaked. Therefore, Bhattcharya and Chiesa (1995) contend that a firm will form less relationships if it holds valuable proprietary information that it does not wish to leak.[11] Hence, there are tradeoffs associated with multiple banking relationships as well. Empirical evidence suggests that a relationship with a single lender is associated with superior credit availability. There is also mixed empirical evidence regarding the interaction between loan rates and the number of bank relationships in which the borrower is engaged.[12] As for concentration, concentrated loan share gives participants the incentives to monitor and renegotiate in good faith, and is less likely to result in free riding. This suggests that concentrated syndicates are particularly desirable when there are information asymmetries and potential agency issues that require monitoring. Yet participants may wish to limit their exposure, particularly for loans to risky borrowers.

Lee and Mullineaux (2001) perform empirical tests and find that syndicate size is positively related to the information available about the borrower, the term to maturity, and the arranging bank's reputation. Syndicate concentration is positively related to information asymmetry and to the presence of security. Concentration is negatively related to borrower credit quality and lead bank reputation. As well, syndicate size is larger when resale activities are limited and less concentrated. Dennis and Mullineaux (2000) and Jones et al. (2000) find that the share of the syndicated loan held by the arranging bank is negatively related to loan quality. Esty and Megginson (2003) find that syndicate size is larger and more diffused in countries where lenders cannot rely on legal enforcement mechanisms.

14.3. Methodological Issues

14.3.1. Simultaneity

Dennis et al. (2000) criticize the empirical literature on loan contract terms, arguing that studies that focus on single contract features ignore the econometric issues that arise if contract features are determined simultaneously. For example, Dennis et al. (2000) note that maturity and collateral may be related to common exogenous factors such as credit quality or agency costs. While the simultaneity issue can be resolved through excluding other loan contract terms from OLS estimation, such an approach does not permit analysis of the tradeoff across loan contract terms. To account for simultaneity, Dennis et al. (2000) perform their tests through estimating a simultaneous equation model using two-stage least squares (2SLS) estimation, for a sample of revolver loans, specified as follows:

$$\text{Duration} = \gamma_{DS}\text{Secured} + \beta_1 X_1 + e_1 \qquad (14.1)$$

$$\text{Secured} =_{\gamma SD} \text{Duration} + \beta_2 X_2 + e_2 \qquad (14.2)$$

$$\text{All-In-Spread} = \gamma_{AD}\text{Duration} + \gamma_{AS}\text{Secured} + \gamma_{AC}\text{Comfee} + \beta_3 X_3 + e_3 \qquad (14.3)$$

$$\text{Comfee} = \gamma_{CD}\text{Duration} + \gamma_{CS}\text{Secured} + \gamma_{CA}\text{All-In-Spread} + \beta_4 \mathbf{X}_4 + e_4 \qquad (14.4)$$

where *duration* is maturity; *secured* is a collateralization dummy; *all-in-spread* is the basis point coupon spread over LIBOR plus the annual fee and upfront fee, spread over the life of the loan; *comfee* is the commitment fee; and $\mathbf{X}$ is a vector of other control variables that measure firm characteristics such as risk and size, and loan characteristics such as loan purpose and structure. This model captures the tradeoffs suggested by Melnik and Plaut (1986) through two bi-directional relations: between duration and security, and between spreads and fees. It also allows the values of duration and security to influence spreads and fees.

The 2SLS estimation performed by Dennis et al. (2000) provides evidence of a positive relation between maturity and collateralization, and between all-in-spreads and commitment fees. As noted earlier, they also find evidence that spreads are negatively related to maturity and positively related to collateralization. To demonstrate that accounting for simultaneity is critical, Dennis et al. (2000) repeat their estimation using single equation estimation and fail to find evidence of the relation between maturity and collateralization. Further, single equation estimation results in evidence of a positive relation between commitment fee and both maturity and collateralization. These results differ from the results when 2SLS estimation is used. Dennis et al. (2000) use the differences between the results for single equation and 2SLS estimation as evidence that ignoring simultaneity can "…produce potentially biased and inconsistent estimates of the relationships." (p. 107).

14.3.2. Measures of Risk

The credit riskiness of the borrower strongly influences the negotiated package of terms. Most obviously, we expect a lender to demand a higher spread from a borrower with a higher probability of default, to compensate for the additional risk with which the lender is burdened. Riskiness also influences important loan contract terms such as maturity and collateralization, as discussed earlier. The influence of credit riskiness on loan contract terms requires that it be controlled when relating loan contract terms to each other; yet riskiness of the borrower is often difficult to estimate.

One measure that is frequently used to control for the borrower's riskiness is the borrower's credit rating. However, credit ratings are an inadequate control for risk, as they do not provide useful information about short-and medium-term likelihood of default. Ratings tend to overestimate risk when the economy is strong and underestimate risk when the economy is weak, due to systematic variations in the relation between ratings and risk. This effect is further exacerbated by change in the risk-free rate of interest as the economy changes.[13] Other measures of credit risk based on long-term averages, such as the variance of earnings, are also inadequate for similar reasons.

One alternative is to use an options theoretic approach to estimate default risk in the spirit of Merton (1974). A relatively easy-to-implement method of estimating the implied probability of default is described by Saunders and Allen (2002, Chapter 4) and Allen and Peristiani (2004). The implied default probability is $N(-\mathbf{DD}_{it})$, where

$$\mathbf{DD}_{it} = \frac{\ln\left(\frac{V_{Ait}}{L_{it}}\right) + \mathbf{T}\left(\mathbf{r}_t + 0.5\sigma^2_{Ait}\right)}{\sigma_{Ait}\sqrt{\mathbf{T}}}. \tag{14.5}$$

In this equation, borrower i's asset value and asset volatility at time t, V_{Ait} and σ_{Ait}, are identified through solving the following system of nonlinear equations:

$$\mathbf{V}_{Eit} = \mathbf{V}_{Ait}N(\mathbf{DD}_{it}) - e^{-r_t T}L_{it}N(\mathbf{DD}_{it} - \sigma_{Ait}\sqrt{\mathbf{T}}), \tag{14.6}$$

$$\sigma_{Eit} = \frac{V_{Ait}}{\mathbf{V}_{Eit}}N(\mathbf{DD}_{it})\sigma_{Ait}, \tag{14.7}$$

where $\mathbf{V}_{Eit}$ is the market value of borrower i's equity at time t, $\mathbf{L}_{it}$ the borrower's debt, $\mathbf{r}_t$ the risk-free rate, σ_{Eit} the borrower i's equity volatility at time t, T the period, and $N(\ )$ the normal distribution. Allen and Peristiani note that the implied default probability estimated using the above methodology does not exactly correspond to the actual probability due to the normality assumption. However, they argue that this measure reflects variations in the probability of default. These characteristics make it a useful companion to measures of average long-term risk such as credit ratings.

NOTES

1. We primarily focus on the literature related to private loans in this discussion.
2. Many studies use data from the Loan Pricing Corporation's (LPC) Dealscan database, which details price and nonprice loan contract terms associated with syndicated loans. The LPC Dealscan database reports a number of measures of spread for each loan facility including the prime spread; the LIBOR spread; and measures that combine spread and fees.
3. The values of loan contract terms can also be influenced by macroeconomic factors, as well as loan market factors such as regulation and competitiveness. For example, see Berger and Hannan (1989), Petersen and Rajan (1995), Hannan (1997), Covitz and Heitfield (1999), Boot and Thakor (2000), Beck et al. (2004), among many others.
4. Other early papers that relate demand for credit to loan contract terms include Azzi and Cox (1976), Arzac et al. (1981), and Koskela (1983).
5. Agency problems associated with longer maturity loans include asset substitution and underinvestment. See Myers (1977) and Barnea et al. (1980). Also see signaling arguments in Flannery (1986) and Kale and Noe (1990), which suggest that less risky borrowers will choose shorter loans.
6. Dennis et al. (2000) review and develop a number of hypotheses that relate maturity and collateral to other borrower characteristics besides credit quality; for example, their tax hypothesis predicts that maturity is inversely related to the firm's marginal tax rate, and positively related to the slope of the yield curve.

7. Also see Berger and Udell (1990) and Guedes and Opler (1996).
8. See Boot et al. (1991), Bester (1994), Coco (1999), Hester (1979), Berger and Udell (1990, 1995), Carey et al. (1998), and Harhoff and Korting (1998). Note that others argue that less risky borrowers are more likely to collateralize. See Bester (1987, 1985), Chan and Kanatas (1985) and Besanko and Thakor (1987).
9. Also see Rajan (1992).
10. Degryse and Ongena (2001) empirically investigated publicly listed Norwegian firms, and found that firm profitability is negatively related to the number of relationships that the firm has with banks. They interpret this to suggest that young firms begin with bilateral relationships, and remain with the bank if successful. Mediocre firms, on the other hand, develop multiple banking relationships.
11. Also see Bolton and Scharfstein (1996) and Detragiache et al. (2000).
12. See Degryse and Ongena (2001).
13. See Standard and Poor's (2004) and Treacy and Carey (1998).

REFERENCES

Allen, L. and Peristiani, S. (2004). "Conflicts of interest in merger advisory services." Working Paper, Baruch College, May.

Arzac, E.R., Schwartz, R.A., and Whitcomb, D.K. (1981). "A theory and test of credit rationing: some further results." *American Economic Review*, 71: 735–777.

Asquith, P., Beatty, A., and Weber, J. (2002). "Performance pricing in debt contracts." Working Paper, Penn State University and MIT.

Azzi, C.F., and Cox, J.C. (1976). "A theory and test of credit rationing: comment." *American Economic Review*, 66: 911–917.

Barnea, A., Haugen, R., and Senbet, L. (1980). "A rationale for debt maturity structure and call provisions in an agency theoretic framework." *Journal of Finance*, 35: 1223–1234.

Beatty, A., Dichev, I.D., and Weber, J. (2002). "The role and characteristics of accounting-based performance pricing in private debt contracts." Working Paper, Penn State University, University of Michigan, and MIT.

Beck, T., Demirguc-Kunt, A., and Maksimovic, V. (2004). "Bank competition and access to finance: international evidence." *Journal of Money, Credit, and Banking*, 36: 627–649.

Berger, A.N. and Hannan, T.H. (1989). "The price–concentration relationship in banking." *The Review of Economics and Statistics*, 71: 291–299.

Berger, A.N. and Udell, G.F. (1990). "Collateral, loan quality and bank risk." *Journal of Monetary Economics*, 25: 21–42.

Berger, A.N. and Udell, G.F. (1995). "Relationship lending and lines of credit in small firm finance." *Journal of Business*, 68: 351–381.

Besanko, D. and Thakor, A.V. (1987). "Collateral and rationing: sorting equilibria in monopolistic and competitive credit markets." *International Economic Review*, 28: 671–690.

Bester, H. (1985). "Screening vs. rationing in credit markets with imperfect information." *American Economic Review*, 57: 850–855.

Bester, H. (1987). "The role of collateral in credit markets with imperfect information." *European Economic Review*, 31: 887–899.

Bester, H. (1994). "The role of collateral in a model of debt renegotiation." *Journal of Money, Credit, and Banking*, 26: 72–86.

Bhattcharya, S. and Chiesa, G. (1995). "Proprietary information, financial intermediation, and research incentives." *Journal of Financial Intermediation*, 4: 328–357.

Bolton, P. and Scharfstein, D. (1996). "Optimal debt structure and the number of creditors." *Journal of Political Economy*, 104: 1–25.

Boot, A.W. (2000). "Relationship banking: what do we know?" *Journal of Financial Intermediation*, 9: 7–25.

Boot, A.W. and Thakor, A.V. (2000). "Can relationship banking survive competition?" *Journal of Finance*, 55: 679–713.

Boot, A.W., Thakor, A.V., and Udell, G.F. (1991). "Collateralized lending and default risk: equilibrium analysis, policy implications and empirical results." *Economic Journal*, 101: 458–472.

Carey, M., Post, M., and Sharpe, S.A. (1998). "Does corporate lending by banks and finance companies differ? Evidence on specialization in private debt contracting." *Journal of Finance*, 53: 845–878.

Chan, Y. and Kanatas, G. (1985). "Asymmetric valuations and the role of collateral in loan agreements." *Journal of Money, Credit, and Banking*, 17: 84–95.

Coco, G. (1999). "Collateral and heterogeneity in risk attitudes and credit market equilibrium. *European Economic Review*, 43: 559–574.

Coleman, A.D.F., Esho, N., and Sharpe, I.G. (2002). "Do bank characteristics influence loan contract terms." Australian Prudential Regulation Authority Working Paper.

Covitz, D. and Heitfield, E. (1999). "Monitoring, moral hazard, and market power: a model of bank lending." Finance and Economics Discussion Series 37, Board of Governors of the Federal Reserve System.

Degryse, H. and Ongena, S. (2001). "Bank relationships and firm profitability." *Financial Management*, 30: 9–34.

Dennis, S.A. and Mullineaux, D.J. (2000). "Syndicated loans." *Journal of Financial Intermediation*, 9: 404–426.

Dennis, S., Nandy, D., and Sharpe, I.G. (2000). "The determinants of contract terms in bank revolving credit agreements." *Journal of Financial and Quantitative Analysis*, 35: 87–110.

Detragiache, E., Garella, P.G., and Guiso, L. (2000). "Multiple versus single banking relationships, theory and evidence." *Journal of Finance*, 55: 1133–1161.

Doyle, J.T. (2003). "Credit risk measurement and pricing in performance pricing-based debt contracts." Working Paper, University of Michigan.

Esty, B. and Megginson, W. (2003). "Creditor rights, enforcement, and debt ownership structure: evidence from the global syndicated loan market." *Journal of Financial and Quantitative Analysis*, 38(1): 37–59.

Flannery, M. (1986). "Asymmetric information and risky debt maturity choice." *Journal of Finance*, 41: 18–38.

Gottesman, A.A. and Roberts, G.S. (2004). "Maturity and corporate loan pricing." *Financial Review*, 38: 55–77.

Gottesman, A.A. and Roberts, G.S. (2005). "Loan rates and collateral." Working Paper, York University.

Guedes, J. and Opler, T. (1996). "The determinants of the maturity of new corporate debt issues." *Journal of Finance*, 51: 1809–1833.

Hannan, T.H. (1997). "Market share inequality, the number of competitors, and the HHI: an examination of bank pricing." *Review of Industrial Organization*, 12: 23–35.

Harhoff, D. and Korting, T. (1998). "Lending relationships in Germany: empirical evidence from survey data." *Journal of Banking and Finance*, 22: 1317–1353.

Helwege, J. and Turner, C.M. (1999). "The slope of the credit yield curve for speculative-grade issuers." *Journal of Finance*, 54: 1869–1884.

Hester, D.D. (1979). "Customer relationships and terms of loans: evidence from a pilot survey." *Journal of Money, Credit, and Banking*, 11: 349–357.

John, K., Lynch, A.W., and Puri, M. (2003). "Credit ratings, collateral and loan characteristics: implications for yield." *Journal of Business*, 76(3): 371–410.(July).[0]

Jones, J., Lang, W., and Nigro, P. (2000). "Recent trends in bank loan syndications: evidence for 1995 to 1999." Working Paper, Office of the Controller of the Currency.

Kale, J. and Noe, T.H. (1990). "Risky debt maturity choice in a sequential game equilibrium." *Journal of Financial Research*, 13: 155–166.

Koskela, E. (1983). "Credit rationing and non-price loan terms." *Journal of Banking and Finance*, 7: 405–416.

Lee, S.W. and Mullineaux, D.J. (2001). "The size and composition of commercial lending syndicates." Working Paper, University of Kentucky.

Melnik, A. and Plaut, S. (1986). "Loan commitment contracts, terms of lending, and credit allocation." *Journal of Finance*, 41: 425–435.

Merton, R.C. (1974). "On the pricing of corporate debt: the risk structure of interest rates." *Journal of Finance*, 29: 449–470.

Myers, S. (1977). "The determinants of corporate borrowing." *Journal of Financial Economics*, 5: 147–176.

Panyagometh, K., Roberts, G.S., and Gottesman, A.A. (2004). "The relation between performance pricing covenants and corporate loan spreads." Working Paper, York University.

Peterson, M.A. and Rajan, R.G. (1995). "The effect of credit market competition on lending relationships." *Quarterly Journal of Economics*, 110: 403–444.

Pozzolo, A.F. (2002). "Collateralized lending and borrowers' riskiness." Working Paper, Banca d' Italia.

Rajan, R.G. (1992). "Insiders and outsiders: the choice between informed and arm's-length debt." *Journal of Finance*, 47: 1367–1400.

Saunders, A. and Allen, L. (2002). *Credit Risk Measurement: New Approaches to Value at Risk and Other Paradigms*, 2nd edition., New York: John Wiley and& Sons.

Standard and Poor's. (2004). "Corporate defaults in 2003 recede from recent highs." *Standard and Poor's*, January.

Strahan, P.E. (1999). "Borrower risk and the price and nonprice terms of bank loans." Working Paper, Federal Reserve Bank of New York.

Treacy, W.F. and Carey, M.S. (1998). "Credit risk rating at large US banks." *Federal Reserve Board Bulletin*, (November): 897–921.

von Thadden, E.L. (1992). "The commitment of finance, duplicated monitoring, and the investment horizon." ESF-CEPR Working Paper No. 27 in Financial Markets, 27 London.

Chapter 15

CHINESE A AND B SHARES

YAN HE, *Indiana University Southeast, USA*

Abstract

A and B shares exist in the Chinese stock markets. A shareholders are domestic investors and B shareholders are foreign investors. During the early-and mid-1990s, B shares were traded at a discount relative to A shares, and B-share returns were higher than A-share returns. It is found that B-share market has persistent higher bid-ask spreads than the A-share market and traders in the B-share market bear higher informed trading and other transaction costs. In addition, the higher volatility of B-share returns can be attributed to the higher market making costs in the B-share market.

Keywords: Chinese A shares; Chinese B shares; stock; return; volatility; asymmetric information; bid-ask spread; transaction costs; stock ownership; Shanghai stock exchange; Shenzhen stock exchange

The development of equity markets in China started in early 1990s. Open for business in December 1990, the Shanghai Stock Exchange (SHSE) and the Shenzhen Stock Exchange (SZSE) are the two major securities exchanges in China. By 1998, the SHSE had raised a total of RMB140.814 billion for listed companies and the SZSE had raised a total of RMB 128 billion for listed companies. The two exchanges played an important role in promoting the restructuring of state-owned enterprises.

Stock shares in China are divided into two broad categories: untradable and tradable. By the end of 1998, the total untradable equity of the listed companies was 166.484 billion shares (i.e. 65.89 percent of the total equity of the listed companies), allocated as follows: (1) shares owned by government, 86.551 billion; (2) shares owned by legal persons, 71.617 billion; (3) shares owned by employees and others, 8.317 billion. Outstanding tradable shares totaled 86.193 billion shares (i.e. 34.11 percent of the total equity of the listed companies), allocated as follows: (1) Class A shares, 60.803 billion; (2) Class B shares, 13.395 billion; and (3) Class H shares, 11.995 billion. Class A shares are owned by domestic investors and traded in the domestic markets. Class B shares are owned by foreign investors but traded in the domestic markets. Class H shares are listed on the Hong Kong Stock Exchange.

China has tightly restricted foreign stock ownership throughout the 1990s. The ownership restriction creates two distinct groups of investors: the domestic and foreign investors. Class A shares are domestic shares and class B shares are foreign shares. In 1991, the Shanghai Stock Exchange (SHSE) and Shenzhen Stock Exchange (SZSE) began to offer B shares, providing foreign investors with a legal channel to invest in China's equity markets. B shares are also known as Renminbi Special Shares. B shares are issued in the form of registered shares and they carry a face value denominated in Renminbi. B shares are subscribed and traded in foreign currencies, but they are listed and traded in securities exchanges inside China. The B share market has attracted a considerable amount of foreign investors. The Market provides an additional channel for foreign capital to invest in China.

Since March 2001, China has opened its B-share market – previously reserved for overseas investors – to Chinese individuals with foreign currency deposits. However, the impact of the opening up of the B-share market to Chinese is limited, because that market is small compared to the number of Chinese people and institutions' foreign currency holdings. Despite the rising foreign currency deposits in China, Chinese people who have foreign currency holdings still account for a very small proportion of investors.

Tables 15.1 to 15.3 are obtained from the China Securities Regulatory Committee.

During the early- and mid-1990s, B shares were traded at a discount relative to A shares, and B-share returns were higher than A-share returns. Su (1999) explains the return premiums on the foreign-owned B shares in the Chinese stock markets by testing a one-period capital asset-price model (CAPM). He concludes that foreign inves-

tors are more risk-averse than domestic investors. Sun and Tong (2000) explain the price discount of the B shares by differential demand elasticity. They document that when more H shares and red chips are listed in Hong Kong, the B-share discount becomes larger. In addition, Chui and Kwok (1998) show that the returns on B shares lead the returns on A shares, which induces an asymmetric positive cross-autocorrelation between the returns on B and A shares. They argue that A- and B-share investors have different access to information, and information often reaches the B-share market before it reaches the A-share market.

The Chinese stock markets have grown very rapidly during the late 1990s and early 2000s. A number of studies investigate the return and risk in the newly developed markets. For example, Lee et al. (2001) examine time-series features of stock returns and volatility, as well as the relation between return and volatility in four of China's stock exchanges. On the one hand, test results provide strong evidence of time-varying volatility and show volatility is highly persistent and predictable. On the other hand, the results do not show any relation between expected returns and expected risk.

Table 15.1. Trading summary of A and B shares during 11/2000–11/2001

	A or B share listed No. of companies	Total market capitalization (100 000 000 Yuan)	Stock turnover (100 000 000 Yuan)	Stock trading volume (100 000 000)	No. of transactions (10 000)
2000/11	1063	46061.78	5012.27	365.02	5013
2000/12	1088	48090.94	3737.6	271.35	3719
2001/01	1100	48497.99	3013.63	220.08	3082
2001/02	1110	46228.75	1950.05	151.92	2197
2001/03	1122	50908.44	5095.17	488.33	4335
2001/04	1123	51006.9	5395.87	422.43	4720
2001/05	1129	53205.49	4452.16	328.33	3739
2001/06	1137	53630.58	4917.12	355.5	4449
2001/07	1140	46440.83	3100.68	228.25	2983
2001/08	1151	48054.63	2490.85	221.31	2507
2001/09	1154	45831.36	1766.64	154.67	1858
2001/10	1152	43742.14	1951.5	181.03	1914
2001/11	1153	45431.59	2092.26	200.31	2374

Table 15.2. A and B shares offering (1987–1998)

	87	88	89	90	91	92	93	94	95	96	97	98	Total
Shares issued (100MM)	10	25	7	4	5	21	96	91	32	86	268	102	746
A share	10	25	7	4	5	10	43	11	5	38	106	79	343
H share							40	70	15	32	137	13	307
B share						11	13	10	11	16	25	10	96
Capital raised (RMB 100MM)	10	25	7	4		94	375	327	150	425	1,294	837	3,553
A share	10	25	7	4		50	195	50	23	224	655	440	1,687
H share							61	89	31	84	360	38	763
B share						44	38	38	33	47	81	26	307
Rights offering of A and B shares							82	50	63	70	198	335	797

Table 15.3. Number of listed companies (1990–1998)

Companies	1990	1991	1992	1993	1994	1995	1996	1997	1998
Issuing A share	10	14	35	140	227	242	431	627	727
Issuing B share	0	0	0	6	4	12	16	25	26
Issuing A and B shares	0	0	18	34	54	58	69	76	80
Issuing A and H shares	0	0	0	3	6	11	14	17	18
Total	10	14	53	183	291	323	530	745	851

The development in the Chinese markets may affect the risk and return of A- and B-share classes. He and Wu (2003) provide two interesting findings: (1) the daily returns of domestic shares (A shares) and foreign shares (B shares) were almost identical in the late 1990s, while the B-share returns were much higher than the A-share returns during the mid-1990s; (2) the volatility of B-share daily returns was higher than that of A shares, while previous studies have often documented higher return volatility for A shares. (For example, Su and Fleisher (1999) report that A shares have higher volatility than B shares based on the data of mid-1990s.)

Since A and B shares are entitled to the same cash flows of a firm and have similar returns, the higher return volatility of B shares is puzzling. The market microstructure theory suggests that both volatility and bid-ask spreads are positively related to asymmetric information (see Kyle, 1985; Easley et al., 1996). According to this theory, higher volatility is caused by higher degree of information

asymmetry and participation rate of informed traders in the market, which, in turn, lead to higher trading costs. Thus, the higher volatility of B shares may be due to a more severe asymmetric information problem in the B-share market. If so, we should observe higher trading costs for B shares. Furthermore, Easley et al. (1996) show that spreads and volatility are negatively related to liquidity. Since the order processing cost is the cost of providing liquidity and immediacy, lower liquidity results in higher order processing cost and higher volatility. A recent study by Green et al. (2000) on the London Stock Exchange shows that changes in transaction costs have a significant effect on share price volatility. Moreover, Chordia et al. (2002) document that return volatility is significantly related to quoted spreads. These findings confirm the theoretical prediction that volatility and trading costs are positively correlated.

Therefore, the higher volatility in the B-share market may reflect higher idiosyncratic risk (rather than higher systematic risk) of B-share stocks. The trading risk associated with asymmetric information can be diversified away and therefore it is not systematic risk (see Chordia et al. 2001). Asset-pricing models (e.g. CAPM and APT) suggest that expected returns should be determined by systematic risk. Since higher volatility does not necessarily imply higher systematic risk, it may not be accompanied with higher returns. Su (1999) finds that market risk (measured by market betas) can explain returns of A and B shares, but nonmarket risk variables, such as the variance of returns and firm size, do not systematically affect returns. Thus, the difference in return volatility between the A- and B-share markets may be caused by the difference in idiosyncratic risk. Trading cost, which reflects asymmetric information and liquidity of trading, may explain the B-share market anomaly. For example, if B-share investors incur higher trading costs than A-share investors, the return volatility of B shares would be higher than that of A shares, other things being equal. In line with the above arguments, He and Wu (2003) examine whether the difference in trading costs (or market making costs) between the Chinese A and B shares can explain the difference in return volatility between the two classes of shares. They estimate the end-of-day bid-ask spread and its informed trading and noninformed trading cost components for each stock using daily data in the late 1990s. Their results show that the B-share market has persistent higher bid-ask spreads than the A-share market, and traders in the B-share market bear higher informed trading and other transaction costs. Furthermore, they find that the higher volatility of B-share returns can be attributed to the higher market making costs in the B-share market.

REFERENCES

Chordia, T., Roll, R., and Subrahmanyam, A. (2002). "Order imbalance, liquidity, and market returns." *Journal of Financial Economics*, 65: 111–131.

Chui, A. and Kwok, C. (1998). "Cross-autocorrelation between A shares and B shares in the Chinese Stock Market." *Journal of Financial Research*, 21: 333–354.

Easley, D., Kiefer, N., O'Hara, M., and Paperman, J. (1996). "Liquidity, information, and infrequently traded stocks." *Journal of Finance*, 51: 1405–1436.

Green, C.J., Maggioni, P., and Murinde, V. (2000). "Regulatory lessons for emerging stock markets from a century of evidence on transactions costs and share price volatility in the London Stock Exchange." *Journal of Banking and Finance*, 24: 577–601.

He, Y., Wu, C., and Chen, Y.-M. (2003). "An explanation of the volatility disparity between the domestic and foreign shares in the Chinese Stock Markets." *International Review of Economics and Finance*, 12: 171–186.

Kyle, A. (1985). "Continuous auctions and insider trading." *Econometrica*, 53: 1315–1335.

Lee, C.F., Chen, G., and Rui, O.M. (2001). "Stock returns and volatility on China's stock markets." *The Journal of Financial Research*, 24: 523–544.

Su, D. (1999). "Ownership restrictions and stock prices: evidence from Chinese markets." *Financial Review*, 34: 37–56.

Su, D. and Fleisher, B.M. (1999). "Why does return volatility differ in Chinese stock markets?" *Pacific-Basin Finance Journal*, 7: 557–586.

Sun, Q. and Tong, W. (2000). "The effect of market segmentation on stock prices: the China syndrome." *Journal of Banking and Finance*, 24: 1875–1902.

Chapter 16

DECIMAL TRADING IN THE U.S. STOCK MARKETS

YAN HE, *Indiana University Southeast, USA*

Abstract

All NYSE-listed stocks were switched from a fractional to a decimal trading system on January 29, 2001 and all NASDAQ stocks followed suit on April 9, 2001. The conversion to decimal trading in the U.S. markets has significantly reduced bid–ask spreads. This decline is primarily due to the drop in market makers' costs for supplying liquidity. In addition, rounding becomes less salient after the decimalization. The decrease in bid–ask spreads can be ascribed to the decrease in price rounding, when controlling for the changes in trading variables.

Keywords: decimal trading; decimalization; NYSE; NASDAQ; clustering; rounding; bid–ask spread; volatility; fractional trading; price improvement

The minimum increment of trading prices varies substantially with market and location. For instance, pricing of stock, bond, and options markets in the U.S. and Canada had traditionally been denominated in eighths, while in European and Asian markets decimal prices are more common. During the later half of 1990s, the U.S. and Canadian markets underwent substantial changes. Canadian stocks switched from fractions to decimals in April 1996. In the U.S. markets, the minimum tick size was reduced from one-eighth of a dollar to one-sixteenth of a dollar in June 1997. At the beginning of year 2000, the U.S. equity markets were the only major financial markets in the world that traded in fractional increments. This fractional trading practice puts U.S. markets at a competitive disadvantage with foreign markets trading the same securities. In addition, individual investors may have a difficulty in determining the differences between increasingly smaller fractions.

To make the U.S. securities markets more competitive globally and their prices easier to decipher, the Securities Industry Association and the Securities and Exchange Commission decided to convert the U.S. equity and exchange-traded options markets from fractional to decimal trading. The NYSE selected seven pilot securities for a decimal pricing test on August 28, 2000, another 57 securities were added to the pilot program on September 25, 2000, and another 94 were added on December 4, 2000. The NASDAQ market began its decimal test with 14 securities on March 12, 2001, and another 197 securities were added on March 26, 2001. All NYSE-listed stocks were switched to a decimal trading system on January 29, 2001 and all NASDAQ stocks followed suit on April 9, 2001.

Recently, a number of studies have generated interesting findings about the effects of decimalization on return volatility and bid–ask spreads. They report that decimalization affects bid–ask spreads, volatility, quote size, and price improvement frequency (or the probability of trades within the quoted bid–ask spreads). First of all, it was shown that the recent conversion to decimal trading in the

U.S. markets has significantly reduced bid–ask spreads (see NYSE, 2001; NASDAQ, 2001; Chakravarty et al., 2001a,b; Chung et al., 2001; Gibson et al., 2002). These findings coincide with two earlier studies (Ahn et al., 1998; Bacidore, 1997) on the Toronto Stock Exchange (TSE). Bacidore et al., (2001b) examine a wide range of market quality issues on the NYSE post-decimalization, and find that an increase in the aggressiveness of limit order pricing results in narrower bid–ask spreads. Chung et al. (2004) examine the relationship between NASDAQ trading costs and the extent of order preferencing. They document lower order preferencing and a positive relationship between the bid–ask spread and the proportion of internalized volume on NASDAQ after decimalization. Second, Bessembinder (2003) and NASDAQ (2001) show that intraday return volatility has declined, and there is no evidence of systematic reversals in quotation changes. Thus, it appears that the NYSE and NASDAQ markets are able to supply sufficient liquidity in the wake of decimalization. Third, Bessembinder (2003) presents that quote size decreases after decimalization. Jones and Lipson (2001) and Goldstein and Kavajecz (2000) report decreases in limit-order book depth after an earlier NYSE tick size reduction, and Bacidore et al. (2001a) report decreases in limit-order book depth after the decimalization on the NYSE. Finally, Bacidore et al. (2001b) and Bessembinder (2003) find evidence that the percentage of orders experiencing price improvement (i.e. executed within the quotes) increases on the NYSE after decimalization, though the dollar amount of price improvement falls. According to Coughenour and Harris (2003), decimal trading effectively relaxes the public order precedence rule and gives specialists more price points within the bid–ask spread on which to quote aggressively. This allows specialist trading firms of all size to trade more often inside the current quote and so the probability that a trade occurs inside the quotes becomes higher.

Almost all the above studies document the changes in "total" return volatility and spreads of transactions. He and Wu (2004) examine the composition of return volatility, serial correlation, and trading costs before and after the decimalization on the NYSE. Specifically, they decompose the variance of price changes into components associated with public news, rounding errors, and market-making frictions (asymmetric information and liquidity costs). First, the test results show that both variance components due to market-making frictions (or bid–ask spreads) and rounding errors decline considerably after decimalization, while the variance component due to public news shocks remains unchanged. Second, the serial correlation of price changes is significantly reduced after decimalization, indicating a weakened bid–ask bounce effect as a result of decimal trading. Finally, bid–ask spreads decline substantially after decimalization and this decline is primarily due to the drop in market makers' costs for supplying liquidity.

In addition to volatility and transaction costs, the recent decimalization also provides an opportunity to revisit the issue of price rounding. Since traders often choose to use a larger price increment than the minimum tick, prices tend to cluster on certain fractions or decimals even when the tick is small. (See Ball et al. (1985) for gold trading; Brown et al. (1991) for silver; Goodhart and Curcio (1992) for foreign exchange; and Aitken, et al. (1995) for Australian stocks.) Harris (1999) predicts that the conversion to decimal trading would lead to lower execution costs. Bessembinder (2002) shows that bid–ask spreads have declined after the decimalization.

He and Wu (2003) investigate the pattern of price rounding before and after decimal trading and its effect on bid–ask spreads for NYSE stocks by using the second pilot sample which includes 57 NYSE securities. Prior to September 25, 2000, these stocks were traded on sixteenths. Since then, they have been traded on pennies. First, since decimal trading leads to a finer price grid or a set of less discrete prices, it is expected to observe a decline in frequencies of rounding on integers, halves, and quarters. Second, although frequencies of rounding on integers, halves, and quarters may decline after decimalization, it is expected that cross-sectionally the relationship between rounding and trading variables and the relationship between execution costs and rounding will stay the same. That is, the sensitivity of trading variables to rounding and the sensitivity of execution costs to rounding should remain unchanged because the fundamentals of the market do not change as a result of decimalization. Finally, consistent with the arguments of Harris (1997, 1999), it is expected to find a significant relationship between the decrease in execution costs and the decrease in rounding after decimalization, when controlling for the changes in stock features. If fractional pricing indeed allows market makers to keep bid–ask spreads artificially high to earn a positive rent, a conversion to decimal trading should reduce price rounding, decrease market makers' rents, and cause a fall in bid–ask spreads.

The empirical results of He and Wu (2003) show that although rounding is pervasive in transaction prices, bids, and asks in both the pre- and post-decimalization periods, it has become less salient after the decimalization. The cross-sectional relationship between rounding and trading variables is similar before and after the decimalization, and so is the relationship between execution costs and rounding when trading variables are held constant for each stock. More importantly, the quoted and effective bid–ask spreads decrease after the decimalization, and this decrease can be ascribed to the decrease in price rounding when controlling for the changes in trading variables.

REFERENCES

Ahn, H.-J., Cao, Q.C., and Choe, H. (1998). "Decimalization and competition among stock markets: Evidence from the Toronto stock exchange cross-listed securities." *Journal of Financial Markets,* 1: 51–87.

Aitken, M., Brown, P., Buckland, C., Izan, H.Y., and Walter, T. (1995). "Price clustering on the Australian stock exchange." Working Paper, University of Western Australia.

Bacidore, J. (1997). "The impact of decimalization on market quality: an empirical investigation of the Toronto Stock Exchange." *Journal of Financial Intermediation,* 6: 92–120.

Bacidore, J., Battalio, R., and Jennings, R. (2001a). "Order submission strategies, liquidity supply, and trading in pennies on the New York Stock Exchange," Working Paper, Indiana University.

Bacidore, J., Battalio, R., Jennings, R., and Farkas, S. (2001b). "Changes in order characteristics, displayed liquidity, and execution quality on the NYSE around the switch to decimal pricing," Working Paper, The New York Stock Exchange.

Ball, C.A., Torous, W.N., and Tshoegl, A.E. (1985). "The degree of price resolution: the case of the gold market." *Journal of Futures Markets,* 5: 29–43.

Bessembinder, H. (2003). "Trade execution costs and market quality after decimalization." *Journal of Financial and Quantitative Analysis*, 13: 19–42.

Brown, S., Laux, P., and Schachter, B. (1991). "On the existence of an optimal tick size." *Review of Futures Markets,* 10: 50–72.

Chakravarty, S., Harris, S., and Wood, R. (2001a). "Decimal trading and market impact," Working Paper, University of Memphis.

Chakravarty, S., Harris, S., and Wood, R. (2001b). "Decimal trading and market impact: The Nasdaq experience." Working Paper, University of Memphis.

Chung, K., Van-Ness, B., and Van-Ness, R. (2001). "Are Nasdaq stocks more costly to trade than NYSE stocks? Evidence after decimalization." Working Paper, Kansas State University.

Chung, K., Chuwonganant, C., and McCormick, T. (2004). "Order preferencing and market quality on Nasdaq before and after decimalization." *Journal of Financial Economics,* 71: 581–612.

Coughenour, J. and Harris, L. (2003). "Specialist profits and the minimum price increment." Working Paper.

Gibson, S., Singh, R., and Yerramilli, V. (2002). "The effect of decimalization on the components of the bid-ask spreads." Working Paper, Cornell University.

Goldstein, M. and Kavajecz, K. (2000). "Eighths, sixteenths and market depth: Changes in tick size and liquidity provision on the NYSE." *Journal of Financial Economics*, 56: 125–149.

Goodhart, C. and Curcio, R. (1992). "Asset price discovery and price clustering in the foreign exchange market." Working Paper, London School of Business.

Harris, L. (1997). "Decimalization: a review of the arguments and evidence." Working Paper, University of Southern California.

Harris, L. (1999). "Trading in pennies: A survey of the issues." Working Paper, University of Southern California.

He, Y. and Wu, C. (2003). "The effects of decimalization on return volatility components, serial correlation, and trading costs." Working Paper.

He, Y. and C. Wu. (2004). "Price rounding and bid-ask spreads before and after the decimalization." *International Review of Economics and Finance*, 13: 19–42.

Jones, C. and Lipson, M. (2001). "Sixteenths: direct evidence on institutional trading costs." *Journal of Financial Economics*, 59: 253–278.

NASDAQ. (2001). "The impact of decimalization on the NASDAQ stock market," prepared by NASDAQ Research Department.

NYSE. (2001). "Comparing bid-ask spreads on the NYSE and NASDAQ immediately following NASDAQ decimalization," prepared by NYSE Research Department.

Chapter 17

THE 1997 NASDAQ TRADING RULES

YAN HE, *Indiana University Southeast, USA*

Abstract

Several important trading rules were introduced in NASDAQ in 1997. The trading reforms have significantly reduced bid–ask spreads on NASDAQ. This decrease is due to a decrease in market-making costs and/or an increase in market competition for order flows. In addition, in the post-reform period, the spread difference between NASDAQ and the NYSE becomes insignificant with the effect of informed trading costs controlled.

Keywords: NASDAQ; trading rules; reforms; bid–ask spread; SEC order handling rules; the sixteenths minimum increment rule; the actual size rule; NYSE; informed trading costs; SEC

The National Association of Securities Dealers (NASD) was established in 1939. Its primary role was to regulate the conduct of the over-the-counter (OTC) segment of the securities industry. In the middle of 1960s, the NASD developed an electronic quote dissemination system, and in 1971, the system began formal operation as the National Association of Securities Dealers Automated Quotations (NASDAQ) system. By the mid-1980s, timely last-sale price and volume information were made available on the terminals. Through the late 1980s and the early 1990s, more functions were added to the system. For instance, the Small Order Execution System (SOES) was introduced in 1988, and the Electronic Communi-

cation Networks (ECN) was introduced in the 1990s. Services provided by the NASDAQ network include quote dissemination, order routing, automatic order execution, trade reporting, last sale, and other general market information.

NASDAQ is a dealer market, and it is mainly quote driven. On NASDAQ, the bid–ask quotes of competing dealers are electronically disseminated to brokers' offices, and the brokers send the customer order flow to the dealers who have the best quotes. In comparison, the New York Stock Exchange (NYSE) is an auction market, and it is mainly order driven.

Several important trading rules were introduced in NASDAQ in 1997, including the SEC Order Handling Rules, the Sixteenths Minimum Increment Rule, and the Actual Size Rule. The experimentation of the new rules started on January 20, 1997. The SEC Order Handling Rules were applied to all the NASDAQ stocks in October 1997. The Actual Size Rule was applied to 50 NASDAQ stocks on January 20, 1997 and 104 additional stocks on November 10, 1997. The Sixteenths Minimum Increment Rule was applied to all the stocks in NASDAQ on June 2, 1997. The following table provides a detailed implementation schedule for the new trading rules.

NASDAQ implemented the Order Handling Rules according to a phased-in schedule. On January 20, 1997, the first group of 50 stocks became subject to the Order Handling Rules. The SEC Order Handling Rules include the Limit Order

Table 17.1. New trading rules' implementation schedule

Date	Number of stocks affected by the rules	Rules implemented
01/20/1997	50 NASDAQ stocks	The SEC Order Handling Rules
		The Actual Size Rule
	The same 50 NASDAQ stocks	The Relaxation of the Excess Spread Rule
	All the NASDAQ stocks	
02/10/1998	51 NASDAQ stocks added	The SEC Order Handling Rules
02/24/1997	52 NASDAQ stocks added	The SEC Order Handling Rules
04/21/1997–07/07/1997	563 NASDAQ stocks added	The SEC Order Handling Rules
06/02/1997	All NASDAQ stocks with bid price not less than $10	The Sixteenths Minimum Increment Rule
08/04/1997	250 NASDAQ stocks added	The SEC Order Handling Rules
08/11/1997	251 NASDAQ stocks added	The SEC Order Handling Rules
09/08/1997–10/13/1997	800 NASDAQ stocks /week added	The SEC Order Handling Rules
10/13/1997	All NASDAQ stocks	The SEC Order Handling Rules
11/10/1997	104 stocks added	The Actual Size Rule

Display Rule, the ECN Rule, and the Relaxation of the Excess Spread Rule.

The Limit Order Display Rule requires displaying customer limit orders that are priced better than a market maker's quote, or adding them to the size associated with a market maker's quote when it is the best price in the market. Before the new trading rules, limit orders on NASDAQ were only offered to the market makers. The Limit Order Display Rule promotes and facilitates the public availability of quotation information, fair competition, market efficiency, the best execution of customer orders, and the opportunity for investors' orders to be executed without the participation of a dealer. By virtue of the Limit Order Display Rule, investors now have the ability to directly advertise their trading interests to the marketplace, thereby allowing them to compete with market maker quotations, and affect bid–ask spreads.

The ECN Rule requires market makers to display in their quotes any better-priced orders that the market maker places into an ECN. The ECN Rule was implemented partially because market participants had increasingly been using ECNs to display different prices to different market participants. In particular, NASDAQ was concerned that the reliability and completeness of publicly available quotations were compromised because market makers could widely disseminate prices through ECNs superior to the quotation information they disseminate on a general basis through NASDAQ. Accordingly, the ECN Rule was adopted to require the public display of such better-priced orders.

Prior to January 20, 1997, NASDAQ continuously calculated for each stock the average of the three narrowest individual spreads among all dealers' spreads. The Excess Spread Rule (ESR) forced all dealers to keep their spreads within 125 percent of this average. On January 20, 1997, the ESR was amended for all NASDAQ stocks to stipulate that each dealer's average spread during the month could not exceed 150 percent of the three lowest average spreads over the month. The new ESR defines compliance on a monthly basis rather than continuously, placing no limits on the market makers' ability to vary their spreads during the month as long as their monthly average is in compliance.

The Actual Size Rule is a by-product of the Order Handling Rules. This rule repeals the regulatory minimum quote size (1000 shares). With the implementation of the SEC's Order Handling Rules, the 1000 share minimum quote size requirements impose unnecessary regulatory burdens on market makers. Since the investors are allowed to display their own orders on NASDAQ according to the Limit Order Display Rule, the regulatory justification for the 1000 share minimum quote size requirements is eliminated. So, it is appropriate to treat NASDAQ market makers in a manner equivalent to exchange specialists, and not subject them to the 1000 share minimum quote size requirements. On January 20, 1997, 50 pilot stocks became subject to the Actual Size Rule. These 50 stocks also became subject to the SEC Order Handling Rules. On November 10, 1997, the pilot program was expanded to an additional 104 stocks. After 1997, the Rule was implemented to all stocks on NASDAQ.

The Sixteenths Minimum Increment Rule requires that the minimum quotation increment be reduced from one-eighth to one-sixteenth of a dollar for all securities with a bid price of $10 or higher. On June 2, 1997, NASDAQ reduced the minimum quotation increment from one-eighth to one-sixteenth of a dollar for all NASDAQ securities with a bid price of $10 or higher. The reduction is expected to tighten quoted spreads and enhance quote competition. Furthermore, it complements the Order Handling Rules by allowing orders to be displayed in increments finer than one-eighth of a dollar. Specifically, the opportunity is increasing for small customers and ECN limit orders to drive the inside market.

Overall, all these new rules were designed to enhance the quality of published quotation, promote competition among dealers, improve price discovery, and increase liquidity. Under these rules, NASDAQ is transformed from a pure quote driven market to a more order driven market. Successful implementation of these rules should result in lower bid–ask spreads by either reducing order execution costs or dealers' profits.

Before 1997, a host of studies compared trading costs between NASDAQ and the NYSE based on the old trading rules. It is documented that bid–ask spreads or execution costs are significantly higher on NASDAQ than on the NYSE. Researchers debate whether NASDAQ bid–ask spreads are competitive enough to reflect market-making costs. Christie and Schultz (1994) find that NASDAQ dealers avoid odd-eighth quotes. This evidence is interpreted as consistent with tacit collusion, due to which bid–ask spreads are inflated above the competitive level. Moreover, Huang and Stoll (1996) and Bessembinder and Kaufman (1997) contend that higher spreads on NASDAQ cannot be attributed to informed trading costs.

Since the Securities and Exchange Committee (SEC) changed some important trading rules on NASDAQ in 1997, studies attempt to assess the effect of these reforms on market performance. Barclay et al. (1999) report that the reforms have significantly reduced bid–ask spreads on NASDAQ. Bessembinder (1999) finds that trading costs are still higher on NASDAQ than on the NYSE even after NASDAQ implemented new trading rules. Weston (2000) shows that the informed trading and inventory costs on NASDAQ remain unchanged after the reforms, and that the reforms have primarily reduced dealers' rents and improved competition among dealers on NASDAQ. He and Wu (2003a) report further evidence of the difference in execution costs between NASDAQ and the NYSE before and after the 1997 market reforms. In the prereform period the NASDAQ–NYSE disparity in bid–ask spreads could not be completely attributed to the difference in informed trading costs. However, in the postreform period the spread difference between these two markets becomes insignificant with the effect of informed trading costs controlled. In addition, He and Wu (2003b) examine whether the decrease in bid–ask spreads on NASDAQ after the 1997 reforms is due to a decrease in market-making costs and/or an increase in market competition for order flows. Their empirical results show that lower market-making costs and higher competition significantly reduce bid–ask spreads.

REFERENCES

Barclay, M.J., Christie W.G., Harris J.H., Kandel E., and Schultz P.H. (1999). "Effects of market reform on the trading costs and depths of NASDAQ stocks." *Journal of Finance*, 54: 1–34.

Bessembinder, H. (1999). "Trade execution costs on NASDAQ and the NYSE: A post-reform comparison." *Journal of Financial and Quantitative Analysis*, 34: 387–407.

Bessembinder, H. and Kaufman H. (1997). "A comparison of trade execution costs for NYSE and NASDAQ-listed stocks." *Journal of Financial and Quantitative Analysis*, 32: 287–310.

Christie, W.G. and Schultz, P.H. (1994). "Why do NASDAQ market makers avoid odd-eighth quotes?" *Journal of Finance*, 49: 1813–1840.

He, Y. and Wu, C. (2003a). "The post-reform bid-ask spread disparity between NASDAQ and the NYSE." *Journal of Financial Research*, 26: 207–224.

He, Y. and Wu, C. (2003b). "What explains the bid-ask spread decline after NASDAQ reforms?" *Financial Markets, Institutions & Instruments*, 12: 347–376.

Huang, R.D. and Stoll, H.R. (1996). "Dealer versus auction markets: a paired comparison of execution costs on NASDAQ and the NYSE." *Journal of Financial Economics*, 41: 313–357.

Weston, J. (2000). "Competition on the NASDAQ and the impact of recent market reforms." *Journal of Finance*, 55: 2565–2598.

Chapter 18

REINCORPORATION

RANDALL A. HERON, *Indiana University, USA*
WILBUR G. LEWELLEN, *Purdue University, USA*

Abstract

Under the state corporate chartering system in the U.S., managers may seek shareholder approval to reincorporate the firm in a new state, regardless of the firm's physical location, whenever they perceive that the corporate legal environment in the new state is better for the firm. Legal scholars continue to debate the merits of this system, with some arguing that it promotes contractual efficiency and others arguing that it often results in managerial entrenchment. We discuss the contrasting viewpoints on reincorporations and then summarize extant empirical evidence on why firms reincorporate, when they reincorporate, and where they reincorporate to. We conclude by discussing how the motives managers offer for reincorporations, and the actions they take upon reincorporating, influence how stock prices react to reincorporation decisions.

Keywords: incorporation; reincorporation; Delaware; corporate charter; director liability; antitakeover; takeover defenses; contractual efficiency; managerial entrenchment; corporate law; shareholders

18.1. Introduction

Modern corporations have been described as a "nexus of contractual relationships" that unites the providers and users of capital in a manner that is superior to alternative organizational forms. While agency costs are an inevitable consequence of the separation of ownership and control that characterizes corporations, the existence of clearly specified contractual relationships serves to minimize those costs. As Jensen and Meckling (1976, p. 357) noted:

> The publicly held business corporation is an awesome social invention. Millions of individuals voluntarily entrust billions of dollars, francs, pesos, etc., of personal wealth to the care of managers on the basis of a complex set of contracting relationships which delineate the rights of the parties involved. The growth in the use of the corporate form as well as the growth in market value of established corporations suggests that, at least up to the present, creditors and investors have by and large not been disappointed with the results, despite the agency costs inherent in the corporate form.
>
> Agency costs are as real as any other costs. The level of agency costs depends among other things on statutory and common law and human ingenuity in devising contracts. Both the law and the sophistication of contracts relevant to the modern corporation are the products of a historical process in which there were strong incentives for individuals to minimize agency costs. Moreover, there were alternative organizational forms available, and opportunities to invent new ones. Whatever its shortcomings, the corporation has thus far survived the market test against potential alternatives.

Under the state corporate chartering system that prevails in the U.S., corporate managers can affect the contractual relationships that govern their organizations through the choice of a firm's state of incorporation. Each state has its own distinctive corporate laws and established court precedents that apply to firms incorporated in the state. Thus, corporations effectively have a menu of choices for the firm's legal domicile, from which they may select the one they believe is best for their firm and/or themselves. The choice is not constrained by the physical location either of the firm's corporate headquarters or its operations. A firm whose headquarters is in Texas may choose Illinois to be its legal domicile, and vice versa. Corporations pay fees to their chartering states, and these fees vary significantly across states, ranging up to $150,000 annually for large companies incorporated in Delaware. State laws of course evolve over time, and managers may change their firm's legal domicile – subject to shareholder approval – if they decide the rules in a new jurisdiction would be better suited to the firm's changing circumstances. This is the process referred to as *reincorporation*, and it is our topic of discussion here.

18.2. Competition Among States for Corporate Charters

There has been a long-running debate among legal and financial scholars regarding the pros and cons of competition among states for corporate charters. Generally speaking, the proponents of competition claim that it gives rise to a wide variety of contractual relationships across states, which allows the firm to choose the legal domicile that serves to minimize its organizational costs and thereby maximize its value. This "Contractual Efficiency" viewpoint, put forth by Dodd and Leftwich (1980), Easterbrook and Fischel (1983), Baysinger and Butler (1985), and Romano (1985), implies the existence of a determinate relationship between a company's attributes and its choice of legal residency. Such attributes may include: (1) the nature of the firm's operations, (2) its ownership structure, and (3) its size. The hypothesis fol-

lowing from this viewpoint is that firms that decide to reincorporate do so when the firm's characteristics are such that a change in legal jurisdiction increases shareholder wealth by lowering the collection of legal, transactional, and capital-market-related costs it incurs.

Other scholars, however, argue that agency conflicts play a significant role in the decision to reincorporate, and that these conflicts are exacerbated by the competition among states for the revenues generated by corporate charters and the economic side effects that may accompany chartering (e.g. fees earned in the state for legal services). This position, first enunciated by Cary (1974), is referred to as the "Race-to-the-Bottom" phenomenon in the market for corporate charters. The crux of the Race-to-the-Bottom argument is that states that wish to compete for corporate chartering revenues will have to do so along dimensions that appeal to corporate management.

Hence, states will allegedly distinguish themselves by tailoring their corporate laws to serve the self-interest of managers at the expense of corporate shareholders. This process could involve creating a variety of legal provisions that would enable management to increase its control of the corporation, and thus to minimize the threats posed by outside sources. Examples of the latter would include shareholder groups seeking to influence company policies, the threat of holding managers personally liable for ill-advised corporate decisions, and – perhaps most important of all – the threat of displacement by an alternative management team. These threats, considered by many to be necessary elements in an effective system of corporate governance, can impose substantial personal costs on senior managers. That may cause managers to act in ways consistent with protecting their own interests – through job preservation and corporate risk reduction – rather than serving the interests of shareholders. If so, competition in the market for corporate charters will diminish shareholder wealth as states adopt laws that place restrictions on the disciplinary force of the market for corporate control (see Bebchuk, 1992; Bebchuk and Ferrell, 1999; Bebchuk and Cohen, 2003).

Here, we examine the research done on reincorporation and discuss the support that exists for the contrasting views of both the Contractual Efficiency and Race-to-the-Bottom proponents. In the process, we shall highlight the various factors that appear to play an influential role in the corporate chartering decision.

18.3. Why, When, and Where to Reincorporate

To begin to understand reincorporation decisions, it is useful to review the theory that relates a firm's choice of chartering jurisdiction to the firm's attributes, the evidence as to what managers *say* when they propose reincorporations to their shareholders, and what managers *actually do* when they reincorporate their firms.

Central to the Contractual Efficiency view of competition in the market for corporate charters is the notion that the optimal chartering jurisdiction is a function of the firm's attributes. Reincorporation decisions therefore should be driven by changes in a firm's attributes that make the new state of incorporation a more cost-effective legal jurisdiction. Baysinger and Butler (1985) and Romano (1985) provide perhaps the most convincing arguments for this view.

Baysinger and Butler theorize that the choice of a strict vs. a liberal incorporation jurisdiction depends on the nature of a firm's ownership structure. The contention is that states with strict corporate laws (i.e. those that provide strong protections for shareholder rights) are better suited for firms with concentrated share ownership, whereas liberal jurisdictions promote efficiency when ownership is widely dispersed. According to this theory, holders of large blocks of common shares will prefer the pro-shareholder laws of strict states, since these give shareholders the explicit legal remedies needed to make themselves heard by management and allow them actively to influence corporate affairs. Thus, firms chartered in strict states are likely to remain there until owner-

ship concentration decreases to the point that legal controls may be replaced by market-based governance mechanisms.

Baysinger and Butler test their hypothesis by comparing several measures of ownership concentration in a matched sample of 302 manufacturing firms, half of whom were incorporated in several strict states (California, Illinois, New York, and Texas) while the other half had reincorporated out of these states. In support of their hypothesis, Baysinger and Butler found that the firms that stayed in the strict jurisdictions exhibited significantly higher proportions of voting stock held by major blockholders than was true of the matched firms who elected to reincorporate elsewhere. Importantly, there were no differences between the two groups in financial performance that could explain why some left and others did not. Collectively, the results were interpreted as evidence that the corporate chartering decision is affected by ownership structure rather than by firm performance.

Romano (1985) arrived at a similar conclusion from what she refers to as a "transaction explanation" for reincorporation. Romano suggests that firms change their state of incorporation "at the same time they undertake, or anticipate engaging in, discrete transactions involving changes in firm operation and/or organization" (p. 226). In this view, firms alter their legal domiciles at key times to destination states where the laws allow new corporate policies or activities to be pursued in a more cost-efficient manner. Romano suggests that, due to the expertise of Delaware's judicial system and its well-established body of corporate law, the state is the most favored destination when companies anticipate legal impediments in their existing jurisdictions. As evidence, she cites the high frequency of reincorporations to Delaware coinciding with specific corporate events such as initial public offerings (IPOs), mergers and acquisitions, and the adoption of antitakeover measures.

In their research on reincorporations, Heron and Lewellen (1998) also discovered that a substantial portion (45 percent) of the firms that reincorporated in the U.S. between 1980 and 1992 did so immediately prior to their IPOs. Clearly, the process of becoming a public corporation represents a substantial transition in several respects: ownership structure, disclosure requirements, and exposure to the market for corporate control. Accordingly, the easiest time to implement a change in the firm's corporate governance structure to parallel the upcoming change in its ownership structure would logically be just before the company becomes a public corporation, while control is still in the hands of management and other original investors. Other recent studies also report that the majority of firms in their samples who undertook IPOs reincorporated in Delaware in advance of their stock offerings (Daines and Klausner, 2001; Field and Karpoff, 2002).

Perhaps the best insights into why managers choose to reincorporate their firms come from the proxy statements of publicly traded companies, when the motivations for reincorporation are reported to shareholders. In the process of the reincorporations of U.S. public companies that occurred during the period from 1980 through 1992, six major rationales were proclaimed by

management (Heron and Lewellen, 1998): (1) takeover defenses; (2) director liability reduction; (3) improved flexibility and predictability of corporate laws; (4) tax and/or franchise fee savings; (5) conforming legal and operating domicile; and (6) facilitating future acquisitions.

A tabulation of the relative frequencies is provided in Figure 18.1. As is evident, the two dominant motives offered by management were to create takeover defenses and to reduce directors' legal liability for their decisions. In addition, managers often cited multiple reasons for reincorporation. The mean number of stated motives was 1.6 and the median was 2. In instances where multiple motives were offered, each is counted once in the compilation in Figure 18.1.

18.4. What Management Says

It is instructive to consider the stated reincorporation motives in further detail and look at examples of the statements by management that are contained in various proposals, especially those involving the erection of takeover defenses and the reduction of director liability. These, of course,

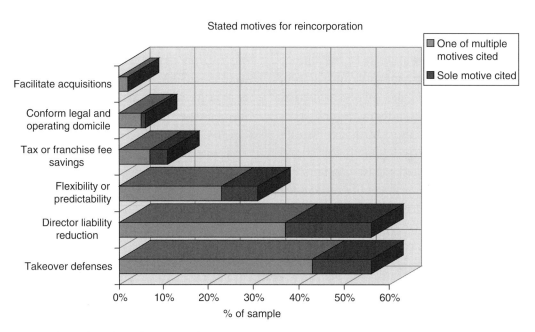

Figure 18.1. Stated motives for reincorporation

represent provisions that may not be in the best interests of stockholders, as a number of researchers have argued. The other motives listed are both less controversial and more neutral in their likely impact on stockholders, and can be viewed as consistent with Contractual Efficiency arguments for reincorporations. Indeed, reincorporations undertaken for these reasons appear not to give rise to material changes in firms' stock prices (Heron and Lewellen, 1998).

18.4.1. Reincorporations that Strengthen Takeover Defenses

Proponents of the Race-to-the-Bottom theory contend that the competition for corporate chartering may be detrimental if states compete by crafting laws that provide managers with excessive protection from the market for corporate control – i.e. from pressures from current owners and possible acquirers to perform their managerial duties so as to maximize shareholder wealth. Although takeover defenses might benefit shareholders if they allow management to negotiate for higher takeover premiums, they harm shareholders if their effect is to entrench poorly performing incumbent managers.

The following excerpts from the proxy statement of Unocal in 1983 provides an example of a proposal to reincorporate for antitakeover reasons:

> In addition, incorporation of the proposed holding company under the laws of Delaware will provide an opportunity for inclusion in its certificate of incorporation provisions to discourage efforts to acquire control of Unocal in transactions not approved by its Board of Directors, and for the elimination of shareholder's preemptive rights and the elimination of cumulative voting in the election of directors.
>
> The proposed changes do not result from any present knowledge on the part of the Board of Directors of any proposed tender offer or other attempt to change the control of the Company, and no tender offer or other type of shift of control is presently pending or has occurred within the past two years.

Management believes that attempts to acquire control of corporations such as the Company without approval by the Board may be unfair and/or disadvantageous to the corporation and its shareholders. In management's opinion, disadvantages may include the following:

> a nonnegotiated takeover bid may be timed to take advantage of temporarily depressed stock prices;
>
> a nonnegotiated takeover bid may be designed to foreclose or minimize the possibility of more favorable competing bids;
>
> recent nonnegotiated takeover bids have often involved so-called "two-tier" pricing, in which cash is offered for a controlling interest in a company and the remaining shares are acquired in exchange for securities of lesser value. Management believes that "two-tier" pricing tends to stampede shareholders into making hasty decisions and can be seriously unfair to those shareholders whose shares are not purchased in the first stage of the acquisition;
>
> nonnegotiated takeover bids are most frequently fully taxable to shareholders of the acquired corporation.
>
> By contrast, in a transaction subject to approval of the Board of Directors, the Board can and should take account of the underlying and long-term value of assets, the possibilities for alternative transactions on more favorable terms, possible advantages from a tax-free reorganization, anticipated favorable developments in the Company's business not yet reflected in stock prices, and equality of treatment for all shareholders.

The reincorporation of Unocal into Delaware allowed the firm's management to add several antitakeover provisions to Unocal's corporate charter that were not available under the corporate laws of California, where Unocal was previously incorporated. These provisions included the establishment of a Board of Directors whose terms were staggered (only one-third of the Board elected each year), the elimination of cumulative voting (whereby investors could concentrate their votes on a small number of Directors rather than spread them over the entire slate up for election), and the requirement of a "supermajority" shareholder vote to approve any reorganizations or mergers not approved by at least 75 percent of the Directors then in office. Two years after its move to Delaware, Unocal was the beneficiary of a court ruling in the *Unocal vs. Mesa* case [493 A.2d 946 (Del. 1985)], in which the Delaware Court upheld Unocal's discriminatory stock repurchase plan as a legitimate response to Mesa Petroleum's hostile takeover attempt.

The Unocal case is fairly representative of the broader set of reincorporations that erected takeover defenses. Most included antitakeover charter amendments that were either part of the reincorporation proposal or were made possible by the move to a more liberal jurisdiction and put to a shareholder vote simultaneously with the plan of reincorporation. In fact, 78 percent of the firms that reincorporated between 1980 and 1992 implemented changes in their corporate charters or other measures that were takeover deterrents (Heron and Lewellen, 1998). These included eliminating cumulative voting, initiating staggered Board terms, adopting supermajority voting provisions for mergers, and establishing so-called "poison pill" plans (which allowed the firm to issue new shares to existing stockholders in order to dilute the voting rights of an outsider who was accumulating company stock as part of a takeover attempt).

Additionally, Unocal reincorporated from a strict state known for promoting shareholder rights (California) to a more liberal state (Delaware) whose laws were more friendly to management. In fact, over half of the firms in the sample studied by Heron and Lewellen (1998), that cited antitakeover motives for their reincorporations, migrated *from* California, and 93 percent migrated *to* Delaware. A recent study by Bebchuk and Cohen (2003) that investigates how companies choose their state of incorporation reports that strict shareholder-right states that have weak antitakeover statutes continue to do poorly in attracting firms to charter in their jurisdictions.

Evidence on how stock prices react to reincorporations conducted for antitakeover reasons suggests that investors perceive them to have a value-reducing management entrenchment effect. Heron and Lewellen (1998) report statistically significant (at the 95 percent confidence level) abnormal stock returns of -1.69 percent on and around the dates of the announcement and approval of reincorporations when management cites only antitakeover motives. In the case of firms that actually *gained* additional takeover protection in their reincorporations (either by erecting specific new takeover defenses or by adopting coverage under the antitakeover laws of the new state of incorporation), the abnormal stock returns averaged a statistically significant -1.62 percent. For firms whose new takeover protection included poison pill provisions, the average abnormal returns were fully -3.03 percent and only one-sixth were positive (both figures statistically significant). Taken together with similar findings in other studies, the empirical evidence therefore supports a conclusion that "defensive" reincorporations diminish shareholder wealth.

18.4.2. Reincorporations that Reduce Director Liability

The level of scrutiny placed on directors and officers of public corporations was greatly intensified as a result of the Delaware Supreme Court's ruling in the 1985 *Smith vs. Van Gorkom* case [488 A.2d 858 (Del. 1985)]. Prior to that case, the Delaware Court had demonstrated its unwillingness to use the benefit of hindsight to question decisions made by corporate directors that turned out after the fact to have been unwise for shareholders. The court provided officers and directors with liability protection under the "business judgment" rule, as long as it could be shown that they had acted in good faith and had not violated their fiduciary duties to shareholders. However, in *Smith vs. Van Gorkom*, the Court held that the directors of Trans-Union Corporation breached their duty of care by approving a merger agreement without sufficient deliberation. This unexpected ruling had an immediate impact since it indicated that the Delaware Court would entertain the possibility of monetary damages against directors in situations where such damages were previously not thought to be applicable. The ruling contributed to a 34 percent increase in shareholder lawsuits in 1985 and an immediate escalation in liability insurance premiums for officers and directors (Wyatt, 1988).

In response, in June of 1986, Delaware amended its corporate law to allow firms to enter into indemnification agreements with, and establish provisions to limit the personal liability of, their officers and directors. Numerous corporations rapidly took advantage of these provisions by reincorporating into Delaware. Although 32 other states had established similar statutes by 1988 (Pamepinto, 1988), Delaware's quick action enabled it to capture 98 percent of the reincorporations, which were cited by management as being undertaken to reduce directors' liability, with more than half the reincorporating firms leaving California.

The 1987 proxy statement of Optical Coatings Laboratories is a good illustration of a proposal either to change its corporate charter in California or to reincorporate – to Delaware – for liability reasons, and documents the seriousness of the impact of liability insurance concerns on liability insurance premiums:

> During 1986, the Company's annual premium for its directors' and officers' liability insurance was increased from $17,500 to $250,000 while the coverage was reduced from $50,000,000 to $5,000,000 in spite of the Company's impeccable record of never having had a claim. This is a result of the so-called directors' and officers' liability insurance crisis which has caused many corporations to lose coverage altogether and forced many directors to resign rather than risk financial ruin as a result of their good faith actions taken on behalf of their corporations.
>
> This year at OCLI, we intend to do something about this problem. You will see included in the proxy materials a proposal to amend the Company's Articles of Incorporation, if California enacts the necessary legislation, to provide the Company's officers and directors with significantly greater protection from personal liability for their good faith actions on behalf of

the Company. If California does not enact the necessary legislation by the date of the annual meeting, or any adjournment, a different proposal would provide for the Company to change its legal domicile to the State of Delaware, where the corporation law was recently amended to provide for such protection.

Although it was a Delaware Court decision that prompted the crisis in the director and officer liability insurance market, Delaware's quick action in remedying the situation by modifying its corporate laws reflects the general tendency for Delaware to be attentive to the changing needs of corporations. Romano (1985) contends that, because Delaware relies heavily upon corporate charter revenues, it has obligated itself to be an early mover in modifying its corporate laws to fit evolving business needs. It is clear that this tendency has proven beneficial in enhancing the efficiency of contracting for firms incorporating in Delaware.

In contrast to the reaction to the adoption of antitakeover measures, investors have responded positively to reincorporations that were undertaken to gain improved director liability protection. Observed abnormal stock returns averaging approximately +2.25 percent (again, at the 95 percent confidence level) are reported by Heron and Lewellen (1998). In a supplemental analysis, changes in the proportions of outside directors on the Boards of firms that reincorporated for director liability reasons were monitored for two years subsequent to the reincorporations, as a test of the claim that weak liability protection would make it more difficult for firms to attract outsiders to their Boards. The finding was that firms that achieved director liability reduction via reincorporation did in fact increase their outside director proportions by statistically significant extents, whereas there was no such change for firms that reincorporated for other reasons.

18.4.3. Other Motives for Reincorporations

Reincorporations conducted solely to gain access to more flexible and predictable corporate laws, to save on taxes, to reconcile the firm's physical and legal domicile, and to facilitate acquisitions fall into the Contractual Efficiency category. Researchers have been unable to detect abnormal stock returns on the part of firms that have reincorporated for these reasons. The bulk of the reincorporations where managers cite the flexibility and predictability of the corporate laws of the destination state as motivation have been into Delaware. Romano (1985) argues that Delaware's responsive corporate code and its well-established set of court decisions have allowed the state to achieve a dominant position in the corporate chartering market. This argument would be consistent with the evidence that a substantial fraction of companies that reincorporate to Delaware do so just prior to an IPO of their stock. Indeed, Delaware has regularly chartered the lion's share of out-of-state corporations undergoing an IPO: 71 percent of firms that went public before 1991, 84 percent that went public between 1991 and 1995, and 87 percent of those that have gone public from 1996 (Bebchuk and Cohen, 2002).

The language in the 1984 proxy statement of Computercraft provides an example of a typical proposal by management to reincorporate in order to have the firm take advantage of a more flexible corporate code:

> The Board of Directors believes that the best interests of the Company and its shareholders will be served by changing its place of incorporation from the State of Texas to the State of Delaware. The Company was incorporated in the State of Texas in November 1977 because the laws of that state were deemed to be adequate for the conduct of its business. The Board of Directors believes that there is needed a greater flexibility in conducting the affairs of the Company since it became a publicly owned company in 1983.
>
> The General Corporation Law of the State of Delaware affords a flexible and modern basis for a corporation action, and because a large number of corporations are incorporated in that state, there is a substantial body of case law, decided by a judiciary of corporate spe-

cialists, interpreting and applying the Delaware statutes. For the foregoing reasons, the Board of Directors believes that the activities of the Company can be carried on to better advantage if the Company is able to operate under the favorable corporate climate offered by the laws of the State of Delaware.

The majority of reincorporations which are done to realize tax savings or to reconcile the firm's legal domicile with its headquarters involve reincorporations out of Delaware – not surprisingly, since Delaware is not only a very small state with few headquartered firms but also has annual chartering fees which are among the nation's highest. The following excerpt from the 1989 proxy statement of the Longview Fibre Company illustrates the rationale for such a reincorporation:

> Through the Change in Domicile, the Company intends to further its identification with the state in which the Company's business originated, its principal business is conducted, and over 64% of its employees are located. Since the Company's incorporation in the State of Delaware in 1926, the laws of the State of Washington have developed into a system of comprehensive and flexible corporate laws that are currently more responsive to the needs of businesses in the state.
>
> After considering the advantages and disadvantages of the proposed Change in Domicile, the Board of Directors concluded that the benefits of moving to Washington outweighed the benefits and detriments of remaining in Delaware, including the continuing expense of Delaware's annual franchise tax (the Company paid $56,000 in franchise taxes in fiscal year 1988, whereas the "annual renewal fee" for all Washington corporations is $50.00). In light of these facts, the Board of Directors believes it is in the best interests of the Company and its stockholders to change its domicile from Delaware to Washington.

Note in particular the issue raised about the annual franchise tax. Revenues from that source currently account for approximately $400 million of Delaware's state budget (Bebchuk and Cohen, 2002).

18.5. Summary and Conclusions

Distinctive among major industrialized countries, incorporation in the U.S. is a state rather than a federal process. Hence, there are a wide variety of legal domiciles that an American firm can choose from, and the corporation laws of those domiciles vary widely as well – in areas such as the ability of shareholders to hold a firm's managers accountable for their job performance, the personal liability protection afforded to corporate officers and directors, and the extent to which management can resist attempts by outsiders to take over the firm. The resulting array of choices of chartering jurisdictions has been characterized by two competing views: (1) the diversity is desirable because it enables a firm to select a legal domicile whose laws provide the most suitable and most efficient set of contracting opportunities for the firm's particular circumstances; (2) the diversity is undesirable because it encourages states to compete for incorporations – and reincorporations – by passing laws that appeal to a firm's managers by insulating them from shareholder pressures and legal actions, and making it difficult for the firm to be taken over without management's concurrence. Thus, the choice of legal domicile can become an important element in the governance of the firm, and a *change* of domicile can be a significant event for the firm.

As for many other aspects of corporate decision-making, a natural test as to which of the two characterizations are correct is to observe what happens to the stock prices of companies who reincorporate, on and around the time they do so. The available evidence indicates that reincorporations which result in the firm gaining additional takeover defenses have negative impacts on its stock price – apparently, because investors believe that a takeover and its associated premium price for the firm's shares will thereby become less likely. Conversely, reincorporations that occasion an increase in the personal liability protection of officers and directors have positive stock price effects. The inference is that such protection makes it easier for the firm to attract qualified directors who can then help management improve the firm's financial performance. These effects are accentuated when the reincorporation is accompanied by a clear statement from management to the firm's shareholders about the reasons for the proposed change. There is, therefore, some support for both views of the opportunity for firms to "shop" for a legal domicile, depending on the associated objective. Other motives for reincorporation seem to have little if any impact on a firm's stock price, presumably because they are not regarded by investors as material influences on the firm's performance.

REFERENCES

Baysinger, B.D. and Butler, H.N. (1985). "The role of corporate law in the theory of the firm." *Journal of Law and Economics*, 28: 179–191.

Bebchuk, L. (1992). "Federalism and the corporation: the desirable limits on state competition in corporate law." *Harvard Law Review*, 105: 1435–1510.

Bebchuk, L.A. and Cohen, A. (2002). "Firms' decisions where to incorporate," Discussion Paper No. 351. Cambridge, MA: Harvard Law School, Olin Center for Law, Economics, and Business, February 2002. www.law.harvard.edu/programs/olin_center

Bebchuk, L.A. and Cohen A. (2003). "Firms' decisions where to incorporate." *Journal of Law and Economics*, 46: 383–425.

Bebchuk, L.A. and Ferrell A. (1999). "Federalism and corporate law: the race to protect managers from takeovers." *Columbia Law Review*, 99: 1168–1199.

Cary, W. (1974). "Federalism and corporate law: reflections upon Delaware." *Yale Law Journal*, 83: 663–707.

Daines, R. and Klausner, M. (2001). "Do IPO charters maximize firm value? An empirical examination of antitakeover defenses in IPOs." *Journal of Law Economics and Organization*, 17: 83–120.

Dodd, P. and Leftwich, R. (1980). "The market for corporate charters: 'Unhealthy Competition' versus federal regulation." *Journal of Business*, 53: 259–282.

Easterbrook, F.H. and Fischel, D.R (1983). "Voting in corporate law." *Journal of Law and Economics*, 26: 395–427.

Field, L. and Karpoff, J. (2002). "Takeover defenses of IPO firms." *Journal of Finance*, 57: 1857–1889.

Heron, R. and Lewellen, W. (1998). "An empirical analysis of the reincorporation decision." *Journal of Financial and Quantitative Analysis*, 33: 549–568.

Jensen, M. and Meckling, W. (1976). "Theory of the firm: managerial behavior, agency costs, and ownership structure." *Journal of Financial Economics*, 3: 305–360.

Pamepinto, S. (1988). "Reincorporation: 1988 background report," Investor Responsibility Research Center Report, Washington, DC.

Romano, R. (1985). "Law as a product: Some pieces of the reincorporation puzzle." *Journal of Law, Economics, and Organization*, 225–283.

Wyatt Company. (1988). "Directors and officers liability survey," Chicago, IL: Wyatt.

Chapter 19

MEAN VARIANCE PORTFOLIO ALLOCATION

CHENG HSIAO, *University of Southern California, USA*
SHIN-HUEI WANG, *University of Southern California, USA*

Abstract

The basic rules of balancing the expected return on an investment against its contribution to portfolio risk are surveyed. The related concept of Capital Asset Pricing Model asserting that the expected return of an asset must be linearly related to the covariance of its return with the return of the market portfolio if the market is efficient and its statistical tests in terms of Arbitraging Price Theory are also surveyed. The intertemporal generalization and issues of estimation errors and portfolio choice are discussed as well.

Keywords: mean–variance efficiency; covariance; capital asset pricing model; arbitrage pricing theory; Sharpe ratio; zero-beta portfolio; volatility; minimum variance portfolio; value at risk; errors of estimation

19.1. Introduction

Stock prices are volatile. The more volatile a stock, the more uncertain its future value. Investment success depends on being prepared for and being willing to take risk. The insights provided by modern portfolio theory arise from the interplay between the mathematics of return and risk. The central theme of modern portfolio theory is: "In constructing their portfolios investors need to look at the expected return of each investment in relation to the impact that it has on the risk of the overall portfolio" (Litterman et al., 2003).

To balance the expected return of an investment against its contribution to portfolio risk, an investment's contribution to portfolio risk is not just the risk of the investment itself, but rather the degree to which the value of that investment moves up and down with the values of the other investments in the portfolio. This degree to which these returns move together is measured by the statistical quantity called "covariance," which is itself a function of their correlation along with their volatilities when volatility of a stock is measured by its standard deviation (square root of variance). However, covariances are not observed directly; they are inferred from statistics that are notoriously unstable.

In Section 19.2, we summarize the Markowitz (1952, 1959) mean–variance allocations rule under the assumption that the correlations and volatilities of investment returns are known. Section 19.3 describes the relationship between the mean variance efficiency and asset pricing models. Section 19.4 discusses issues of estimation in portfolio selection.

19.2. Mean–Variance Portfolio Selection

The basic portfolio theory is normative. It considers efficient techniques for selecting portfolios based on predicted performance of individual securities. Marschak (1938) was the first to express preference in terms of indifference curves in a mean–variance space. Von Neumann and Morgenstern (1947) provided an axiomatic framework to study the theory of choice under uncertainty. Based on these developments, Markowitz (1952, 1959) developed a mean–variance approach of asset allocation.

Suppose there are N securities indexed by i, $i = 1, \ldots, N$. Let $R' = (R_1, \ldots, R_N)$ denote the return of these N securities. Let $\mu = ER$ and Σ be the mean and the nonsingular covariance matrix of R. A portfolio is described by an allocation vector $X' = (x_1, \ldots, x_N)$ of quantity x_i for the ith security. In the mean–variance approach, an investor selects the composition of the portfolio to maximize her expected return while minimizing the risk (i.e. the variance) subject to budget constraint. Since these objectives are contradictory, the investor compromises and selects the portfolio that minimizes the risk subject to a given expected return, say d. A portfolio X is said to be the minimum-variance portfolio of all portfolios with mean (or expected) return d if its portfolio weight vector is the solution to the following constrained minimization:

$$\min_x X'\Sigma X \qquad (19.1)$$

subject to

$$X'\mu = d, \qquad (19.2)$$

and

$$X'i = 1, \qquad (19.3)$$

where i is an $N \times 1$ vector of ones. Solving the Lagrangian

$$L = X'\Sigma X + \lambda_1[d - X'\mu] + \lambda_2(1 - X'i), \qquad (19.4)$$

yields the optimal portfolio

$$X_p = \frac{1}{D}\left\{\left[\left(\mu'\Sigma^{-1}\mu\right)\Sigma^{-1}i - \left(i'\Sigma^{-1}\mu\right)\Sigma^{-1}\mu\right]\right.$$
$$\left. + d\left[\left(i'\Sigma^{-1}i\right)\Sigma^{-1}\mu - \left(i'\Sigma^{-1}\mu\right)\Sigma^{-1}i\right]\right\},$$
$$(19.5)$$

where

$$D = \left(\mu\Sigma^{-1}\mu\right)\left(i'\Sigma^{-1}i\right) - \left(i'\Sigma^{-1}\mu\right)^2. \qquad (19.6)$$

From Equation (19.5), we have:

Proposition 1: *Any two distinct minimum-variance portfolios can generate the minimum variance frontier.*

Proposition 2: *Let portfolio o as the portfolio with the smallest possible variance for any mean return, then the global minimum variance portfolio has*

$$X_0 = \frac{1}{\left(i'\Sigma^{-1}i\right)}\Sigma^{-1}i,$$

$$\mu_0 = ER_0 = EX_0'R = \frac{i'\Sigma^{-1}\mu}{i'\Sigma^{-1}i},$$

$$= \frac{1}{i'\Sigma^{-1}i} \qquad (19.7)$$

Proposition 3: *The covariance of the return of the global minimum-variance portfolio o with any portfolio p is*

$$Cov\left(R_o, R_p\right) = \frac{1}{i\Sigma^{-1}i}. \qquad (19.8)$$

that is, the correlation of them is positive, $corr(R_0, R_p) > 0$ *for any portfolio p.*

Proposition 4: *If the covariance of the returns of two portfolios p and q equal to 0, $Cov(R_p, R_q) = 0$, then portfolios p and q are called orthogonal portfolios and the portfolio q is the unique portfolio which is orthogonal to p.*

Proposition 5: *All portfolios on positively slope part of mean–variance frontier are positively correlated.*

When a risk-free asset with return R_f is present, the expected return of investing in the $N + 1$ assets will be

$$\mu_\alpha = (1 - \alpha)R_f + \alpha X'\mu, \qquad (19.9)$$

where $0 < \alpha < 1$ is the proportion of investment in the risky assets. The minimum-variance portfolio with the expected return of investing in both N

risky assets and the risk-free asset equal to d, $\mu_\alpha = d$, is the solution of

$$\alpha^2 X' \Sigma X \qquad (19.10)$$

subject to Equations (19.3) and (19.9) equal to d,

$$X_p^* = \frac{1}{i'\Sigma^{-1}(\mu - R_f i)} \Sigma^{-1}(\mu - R_f i), \qquad (19.11)$$

$$\alpha = \frac{i'\Sigma^{-1}(\mu - R_f i)}{(\mu - R_f i)\Sigma^{-1}(\mu - R_f i)}(d - R_f). \qquad (19.12)$$

Thus, when there is a risk-free asset, all minimum-variance portfolios are a combination of a given risky asset portfolio with weights proportional to X_p^* and the risk-free asset. This portfolio of risky assets is called the tangency portfolio because X_p^* is independent of the level of expected return. If we draw the set of minimum-variance portfolios in the absence of a risk-free asset in a two-dimensional mean-standard deviation space like the curve GH in Figure 19.1, all efficient portfolios lie along the line from the risk-free asset through portfolio X_p^*.

Sharpe (1964) proposes a measure of efficiency of a portfolio in terms of the excess return per unit risk. For any asset or portfolio with an expected return μ_a and standard deviation σ_a, the *Sharpe ratio* is defined as

$$sr_a = \frac{\mu_a - R_f}{\sigma_a} \qquad (19.13)$$

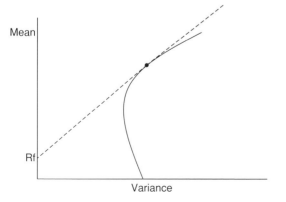

Figure 19.1. Mean–Variance frontier with risk-free asset

The tangency portfolio X_p^* is the portfolio with the maximum *Sharpe ratio* of all risky portfolios. Therefore, testing the mean–variance efficiency of a given portfolio is equivalent to testing if the *Sharpe ratio* of that portfolio is maximum of the set of *Sharpe ratios* of all possible portfolios.

19.3. Mean–Variance Efficiency and Asset Pricing Models

19.3.1. Capital Asset Pricing Models

The Markowitz mean–variance optimization framework is from the perspective of individual investor conditional on given expected excess returns and measure of risk of securities under consideration. The Capital Asset Pricing Model (CAPM) developed by Sharpe (1964) and Lintner (1965) asks what values of these mean returns will be required to clear the demand and supply if markets are efficient, all investors have identical information, and investors maximize the expected return and minimize volatility.

An investor maximizing the expected return and minimizing risk will choose portfolio weights for which the ratio of the marginal contribution to portfolio expected return to the marginal contribution to risk will be equal. In equilibrium, expected excess returns are assumed to be the same across investors. Therefore, suppose there exists a risk-free rate of interest, R_f, and let $Z_i = R_i - R_f$ be the excess return of the ith asset over the risk-free rate (R_f) then the expected excess return for the ith asset in equilibrium is equal to

$$E[Z_i] = \beta_{im} E[Z_m], \qquad (19.14)$$

and

$$\beta_{im} = \frac{\mathrm{Cov}(Z_i, Z_m)}{\mathrm{Var}(Z_m)}, \qquad (19.15)$$

where Z_m is the excess return on the market portfolio of assets, $Z_m = R_m - R_f$, with R_m being the return on the market portfolio.

In the absence of a risk-free asset, Black (1971) derived a more general version of the CAPM. In the Black version, the expected return of asset i in equilibrium is equal to

$$E[R_i] = E[R_{om}] + \beta_{im}\{E[R_m] - E[R_{om}]\}, \quad (19.16)$$

and

$$\beta_{im} = \frac{\text{Cov}(R_i, R_m)}{\text{Var}(R_m)}, \quad (19.17)$$

where R_{om} is the return on the *zero-beta portfolio* associated with m. The *zero-beta* portfolio is described as the portfolio that has the minimum variance among all portfolios that are uncorrelated with m.

Closely related to the concept of trade-off between risk and expected return is the quantification of this trade-off. The CAPM or *zero-beta* CAPM provides a framework to quantify this relationship. The CAPM implies that the expected return of an asset must be linearly related to the covariance of its return with the return of the market portfolio and the market portfolio of risky assets is a mean–variance efficient portfolio. Therefore, studies of market efficiency have been cast in the form of testing the Sharpe–Lintner CAPM and the *zero-beta* CAPM.

Under the assumption that returns are independently, identically (IID) multivariate normally distributed, empirical tests of the Sharpe–Lintner CAPM have focused on the implication of Equation (19.14) that the regression of excess return of the ith asset at time t, $Z_{it} = R_{it}-R_{ft}$ on the market excess return at time t, $Z_{mt} = R_{mt}-R_{ft}$, has intercept equal to zero. In other words for the regression model

$$Z_{it} = c_{im} + \beta_{im}Z_{mt} + \varepsilon_{it}, \substack{i=1, ..., N, \\ t=1, ..., T.} \quad (19.18)$$

The null hypothesis of market portfolio being mean–variance efficient is:

$$H_0: c_{1m} = c_{2m} = ... = c_{Nm} = 0. \quad (19.19)$$

Empirical tests of Black (1971) version of the CAPM model note that Equation (19.15) can be rewritten as

$$E[R_i] = \alpha_{im} + \beta_{im}E[R_m], \\ \alpha_{im} = E[R_{om}](1 - \beta_{im}) \; \forall i. \quad (19.20)$$

That is, the Black model restricts the asset-specific intercept of the (inflation adjusted) real-return market model to be equal to the expected *zero-beta* portfolio return times one minus the asset's beta. Therefore, under the assumption that the real-return of N assets at time t, $R_t = (R_{it}, ..., R_{Nt})'$ is IID (independently identically distributed) multivariate normal, the implication of the Black model is that the intercepts of the regression models

$$R_{it} = \alpha_{im} + \beta_{im}R_{mt} + \varepsilon_{it}, \substack{i=1, ..., N, \\ t=1, ..., T,} \quad (19.21)$$

are equal to

$$\alpha_{im} = (1 - \beta_{im})\gamma, \quad (19.22)$$

where the constant γ denotes the expected return of *zero-beta portfolio*.

19.3.2. Arbitrage Pricing Theory

Although CAPM model has been the major framework for analyzing the cross-sectional variation in expected asset returns for many years, Gibbons (1982) could not find empirical support for the substantive content of the CAPM using stock returns from 1926 to 1975. His study was criticized by a number of authors from both the statistical methodological point of view and the empirical difficulty of estimating the unknown zero beta return (e.g. Britten-Jones, 1999; Campbell et al., 1997; Gibbons et al., 1989; Shanken, 1985; Stambaugh, 1982; Zhou, 1991). Ross (1977) notes that no correct and unambiguous test can be constructed because of our inability to observe the exact composition of the true market portfolio. Using arbitrage arguments, Ross (1977) proposes the Arbitrage Pricing Theory (APT) as a testable alternative. The advantage of the APT is that it allows for multiple risk factors. It also does not require the identification of the market portfolio.

Under the competitive market the APT assumes that the expected returns are functions of an unknown number of unspecified factors, say $K(K < N)$:

$$R_i = E_i + \beta_{i1}\delta_{1t} + \ldots + \beta_{iK}\delta_{Kt} + \varepsilon_{it}, \begin{matrix} i=1, \ldots, N, \\ t=1, \ldots, T, \end{matrix}$$

$$(19.23)$$

where R_{it} is the return on asset i at time t, E_i is its expected return, β_{ik} are the factor loadings, δ_{kt} are independently distributed zero mean common factors and the ε_{it} are zero mean asset-specific disturbances, assumed to be uncorrelated with the δ_{kt}.

As an approximation for expected return, the APT is impossible to reject because the number of factors, K, is unknown. One can always introduce additional factors to satisfy Equation (19.23). Under the additional assumption that market portfolios are well diversified and that factors are pervasive, Connor (1984) shows that it is possible to have exact factor pricing. Dybvig (1985) and Grinblatt and Titman (1987), relying on the concept of "local mean–variance efficiency", show that given a reasonable specification of the parameters of an economy, theoretical deviations from exact factor pricing are likely to be negligible. Thus, the factor portfolios estimated by the maximum likelihood factor analysis are locally efficient if and only if the APT holds (Roll and Ross, 1980, Dybvig and Ross, 1985).

19.3.3. Intertemporal Capital Asset Pricing Model (ICAPM)

The multifactor pricing models can alternatively be derived from an intertemporal equilibrium argument. The CAPM models are static models. They treat asset prices as being determined by the portfolio choices of investors who have preferences defined over wealth after one period. Implicitly, these models assume that investors consume all their wealth after one period. In the real world, investors consider many periods in making their portfolio decisions. Under the assumption that consumers maximize the expectation of a time-separable utility function and use financial assets to transfer wealth between different periods and states of the world and relying on the argument that consumers' demand is matched by the exogen-

ous supply, Merton (1973) shows that the efficient portfolio is a combination of one of mean–variance efficient portfolio with a hedging portfolio that reflects uncertainty about future consumption-investment state. Therefore, in Merton Intertemporal Capital Asset Pricing Model (ICAPM) it usually lets market portfolio serve as one factor and state variables serve as additional factors.

The CAPM implies that investors hold a mean–variance portfolio that is a tangency point between the straight line going through the risk-free return to the minimum-variance portfolios without risk-free asset in the mean-standard deviation space. Fama (1996) shows that similar results hold in multifactor efficient portfolios of ICAPM.

19.4. Estimation Errors and Portfolio Choice

The use of mean variance analysis in portfolio selection requires the knowledge of means, variances, and covariances of returns of all securities under consideration. However, they are unknown. Treating their estimates as if they were true parameters can lead to suboptimal portfolio choices (e.g. Frankfurther et al., 1971; Klein and Bawa, 1976; Jorion, 1986) have conducted experiments to show that because of the sampling error, portfolios selected according to the Markowitz criterion are no more efficient than an equally weighted portfolio. Chopra (1991), Michaud (1989), and others have also shown that mean–variance optimization tends to magnify the errors associated with the estimates.

Chopra and Zemba (1993) have examined the relative impact of estimation errors in means, variances, and covariances on the portfolio choice by a measure of percentage cash equivalent loss (CEL). For a typical portfolio allocation of large U.S. pension funds, the effects of CEL for errors in means are about 11 times as that of errors in variances and over 20 times as that of errors in covariances. The sensitivity of mean–variance efficient portfolios to changes in the means of individual assets was also investigated by Best and Grauer (1991) using a quadratic programming approach.

The main argument of these studies appears to be that in constructing an optimal portfolio, good estimates of expected returns are more important than good estimates of risk (covariance matrix). However, this contention is challenged by De Santis et al. (2003). They construct an example showing the estimates of Value at Risk (VaR), identified as the amount of capital that would be expected to be lost at least once in 100 months, using a $100 million portfolio invested in 18 developed equity markets to the sensitivity of different estimates of covariance matrix. Two different estimates of the covariance matrix of 18 developed equity markets are used – estimates using equally weighted 10 years of data and estimates giving more weights to more recent observations. They show that changes in estimated VaR can be between 7 and 21 percent.

The main features of financial data that should be taken into account in estimation as summarized by De Santis et al. (2003) are:

(i)   Volatilities and correlations vary over time.

(ii) Given the time-varying nature of second moments, it is preferable to use data sampled at high frequency over a given period of time, rather than data sampled at low frequency over a longer period of time.

(iii) When working with data at relatively high frequencies, such as daily data, it is important to take into account the potential for autocorrelations in returns.

(iv) Daily returns appear to be generated by a distribution with heavier tails than the normal distribution. A mixture of normal distributions appear to approximate the data-generating process well.

(v)   Bayesian statistical method can be a viable alternative to classical sampling approach in estimation (e.g. Jorion, 1986).

REFERENCES

Best, M.J. and Grauer, R.R. (1991). "On the sensitivity of mean variance efficient portfolios to changes in asset means: some analytical and computational results." *The Review of Financial Studies*, 4(2): 315–342.

Black, F. (1971). "Capital market equilibrium with restricted borrowing." *Journal of Business*, 45: 444–454.

Britten-Jones, M.. (1999). "The sampling error in estimates of mean efficient portfolio weight." *The Journal of Finance*, 54(2): 655–671.

Campbell, J.Y., Lo, A.W., and MacKinley, A.C. (1997). *The Econometrics of Financial Markets*. Princeton, NJ: Princeton University Press.

Chopra, Vijay K. (1991). "Mean variance revisited: near optimal portfolios and sensitivity to input variations." *Russell Research Commentary*.

Chopra, V.K. and Ziemba, W.T. (1993). "The effect of errors in mean, variances, and covariances on optimal portfolio choice." *Journal of Portfolio Management*, Winter, 6–11.

Connor, G. (1984). "A unified beta pricing theory." *Journal of Economic Theory*, 34: 13–31.

De Santis, G., Litterman, B., Vesval, A., and Winkelmann, K. (2003). "Covariance Matrix Estimation," in *Modern Investment Management*, B. Litterman and the Quantitative Resources Group, Goldman Sachs Asset Management (ed.) Hoboken, NJ: Wiley.

Dybvig, P.H. (1985). "An explicit bound on individual assets' deviation from APT pricing in a finite economy." *Journal of Financial Economics*, 12: 483–496.

Dybvig, P.H. and Ross, S.A. (1985). "Yes, the APT is testable." *Journal of Fiance*, 40: 1173–1183.

Fama, E.F. (1996). "Multifactor portfolio efficiency and multifactor asset pricing." *Journal of Financial and Quantitative Analysis,* 31(4): 441–465.

Frankfurter, G.M., Phillips, H.E., and Seagle, J.P. (1971). "Portfolio selection : the effects of uncertain means, variances, and covariances." *Journal of Financial and Quantitative Analysis*, 6(5): 1251–1262.

Gibbons, M.R. (1982). "Multivariate tests of financial models: a new approach." *Journal of Financial Economics*, 10: 3–27.

Gibbons, M.R., Ross, S.A., and Shanken, J. (1989). "A test of efficiency of a given portfolio." *Econometrica*, 57: 1121–4152.

Grinblatt, M. and Titman, S. (1987). "The relation between mean-variance efficiency and arbitrage pricing." *Journal of Business*, 60(1): 97–112.

Jorion, P. (1986). "Bayes-Stein estimation for portfolio analysis." *Journal of Financial and Quantitative Analysis*, 21(3): 279–292.

Klein, R.W. and Bawa,V.S. (1976). "The effect of estimation risk on optimal portfolio choice." *Journal of Financial Economics*, 3: 215–231.

Lintner, J. (1965). "The valuation of risk assets and the selection of risky investments in stock portfolios and capital budgets." *Review of Economics and Statistics*, 47(1): 13–37.

Litterman, B. and the Quantitative Resources Group, Goldman Sachs Asset Management (2003). *Modern Investment Management*. Hoboken, NJ: John Wiley.

Markowitz, H.M. (1952). "Portfolio selection." *The Journal of Finance*, 7: 77–91.

Markowitz, H.M. (1959). *Portfolio Selection: Efficient Diversification of Investments*, New York: John Wiley.

Marschak, J. (1938). "Money and the theory of assets." *Econometrica*, 6: 311–325.

Merton, R.C. (1973). "An intertemporal capital asset pricing model." *Econometrica*, 41: 867–887.

Michaud, R.O. (1989). "The Markowitz optimization enigma: Is 'optimized' optimal ?" *Financial Analysis Journal*, 45: 31–42.

Roll, R. and Ross, S.A. (1980). "An empirical investigation of the arbitrage pricing theory." *Journal of Finance*, 33: 1073–1103.

Ross, R. (1977). "A critique of the asset pricing theory's tests, part 1: One past and potential testability of the theory." *Journal of Financial Economics,* 4: 129–176.

Stambaugh, R.F. (1982). " On the exclusion of assets from tests of the two parameter model." *Journal of Financial Economics*, 10: 235–268.

Shanken, J. (1982). "The arbitrage pricing theory: Is it testable?" *Journal of Finance*, 37(5): 1129–1140.

Shanken, J. (1985). "Multivariate tests of the zero-beta." *Journal of Financial Economics*, 14: 327–348.

Sharpe, W.F. (1964). "Capital asset prices: a theory of market equilibrium under conditions of risk." *Journal of Finance*, 19: 425–442.

Von Neumann, J. and Morgenstern, O. (1947). *Theory of Games and Economic Behavior*, 2nd edn. Princeton: Princeton University Press.

Zhou, G. (1991). "Small samples tests of portfolio efficiency." *Journal of Financial Economics*, 30: 165–191.

Chapter 20

ONLINE TRADING

CHANG-TSEH HSIEH, *University of Southern Mississippi, USA*

Abstract

The proliferation of the Internet has led to the rapid growth of online brokerage. As the Internet now allows individual investors access to information previously available only to institutional investors, individual investors are profiting in the financial markets through online trading schemes. Rock-bottom fees charged by the online brokers and the changing attitude toward risk of the Internet-literate generation prompt the practitioners to question the validity of the traditional valuation models and statistics-based portfolio formulation strategies. These tactics also induce more dramatic changes in the financial markets. Online trading, however, does involve a high degree of risk, and can cause a profitable portfolio to sour in a matter of minutes. This paper addresses the major challenges of trading stocks on the Internet, and recommends a decision support system for online traders to minimize the potential of risks.

Keywords: Internet; day trading center; web-based brokers; online trading; valuation models; decision support systems; risks management; portfolio formulation strategies; financial market; stock investment; institutional investors

20.1. Introduction

In the past decade, one of the most phenomenal changes in investment markets is the burgeoning number of online brokers, and its subset, the so-called day-trading centers. Instead of doing busi-ness using the old style face-to-face approach, or over the phone with stockbroker, investors have been using the Web to explore a wealth of free information and have been making investment decisions with a new fleet of Internet-based brokers. Concepts of online trading have been around for quite some time. Before the proliferation of the Internet, however, online trading was primarily used as a vehicle for trading by institutional investors. With the help of the Internet, individual investors are now able to access the stock markets in ways similar to those of the major players, the institutional investors (Barnett, 1999b; Smith, 1999a). The direct use of the Internet to trade stocks also raises doubt among investors about the validity of the traditional stock valuation models as well as portfolio formulation strategies.

Inspired by the successful story of E*Trade, the pioneering Internet-based broker, many Web-based brokers have joined the throng that has forced traditional full-service firms to respond with bigger changes. Although, by the end of 1998, online brokers still controlled only $400 billion of assets in customer accounts as compared with $3,200 billion managed by full-service brokers, transactions done through online traders now represent more than 15 percent of all equity trades, a two-fold increase in just two years. And the online brokerage industry has doubled customer assets to more than $420 billion, and doubled accounts managed to 7.3 million by early 1999.

The Internet has revolutionized the way in which consumers perform research and participate in the buying and selling of securities. As of January 2003, there are an estimated 33 million U.S. consumer online trading accounts that control roughly $1.6 trillion in customer assets (Mintel International Group, 2002). The convenience of online trading has introduced millions of new consumers to the possibilities of online money management. At the same time, the Internet and wireless devices have transformed the way in which capital markets operate and have made it possible for individual investors to have direct access to a variety of different markets, and to tools that were at one time reserved only for the investment professional.

20.2. The Issues

The proliferation of online trading sites has created major changes in the ways stocks are traded. Traditionally, an investor who wants to purchase a stock has to go through a broker. The broker will send a buy order to a specialist on the exchange floor, if the stock is listed on the NYSE. The specialist then looks for sellers on the trading floor or in his electronic order book. If the specialist finds enough sellers to match his offer price, the specialist completes the transaction. Otherwise, the specialist may purchase at a higher price, with customer permission, or sell the stock to the customer out of his own inventory.

If the stock is listed on the NASDAQ, the broker consults a trading screen that lists offers from the market makers for the said stock. The broker then picks up the market maker with the best price to complete the transaction. On the other hand, for buying stock online, the broker such as E*Trade simply collects order information, and completes the transaction through the electronic communication network (ECN).

For traditional brokerage services, the broker usually charges hefty fees. For example, Morgan Stanley Dean Witter charges $40 per trade for customers with at least $100,000 in their accounts and if they make at least 56 trades per year. Merrill Lynch charges $56 per trade for a $100,000

account, with 27 trades per year. Typically, fees for a single trade at the full-service brokerage can be anywhere from $100 to $1000 depending upon the services involved. Charles Schwab, however, charges $29.95 per trade up to 1000 shares, and the champion of the online trader, E*Trade, charges merely $14.95 per market-order trade up to 5000 shares. Alternatively, the investor can choose unlimited number of trades and access to exclusive research and advice for a yearly fee (Thornton, 2000).

The reduced cost offered by online trading has encouraged investors to increase the frequency of trading. Since the fee paid to complete a transaction through traditional brokerage is enough to cover fees of many trades charged online, the investor can afford to ride the market wave to try and realize a windfall caused by the price fluctuation on a daily basis. Perhaps, this helps explain why in two short years, Island, Instinet, and seven other ECNs, now control a whopping 21.6 percent of NASDAQ shares and nearly a third of the trades and are seeking to expand their operations to include NYSE company shares (Vogelstein, 1999a; Reardon, 2000).

Although investors of all sizes could use online brokers, the most noteworthy change in financial markets is the increasing number of individual investors. These are the new breed of investors armed with the knowledge of information technology and a very different attitude toward risk in the investment market place (Pethokoukis, 1999). Their changing attitudes have contributed to several major changes in stock market strategies (Becker, 1998; Barnett, 1999a; Gimein, 1999; Pethokoukis, 1999; Vogelstein, 1999b; Sharma, 2000).

1. *Webstock frenzies.* Although day traders represent a small percentage of all active traders on a daily market, the industry makes up about 15 percent of NASDAQ's daily volume (Smith, 1999b). The aggressive trading behavior of day traders, fueled by margin loans supplied by day-trading centers, is one of the

driving forces behind the runaway price of many Internet-related stocks. Since the beginning of 1999, for example, Yahoo stock rose $40 in one day. eBay shares fell $30. Broadcast.com gained $60 a share, and then lost $75 two days later. Webstocks as a whole gained 55 percent in the first days of trading in 1999, then a free-fall started in the early summer. Since April 1999, American Online stock price has dropped almost 67 percent. And the Goldman Sachs Internet Index currently stands nearly 43 percent below its all-time high in April. By Spring 2000, many of the tech stocks have recorded more than 80 percent of share price corrections. Some of these corrections actually happened in just a matter of few days (Cooper, 2001). These stocks have taught the online/day traders the real meaning of "volatility" (McLean, 1999).

2. *Changing goals of investment.* The easy money mentality has led to new goals for formulating investment portfolios. Traditional portfolio models have been based on a mean-variance modeling structure, and for years numerous variations of such models have filled the academic journals. Today, however, investment professionals have been forced to abandon the investment strategies developed by academics, focusing instead on strategies that achieve instant profits. As Net stocks became the horsepower to help pump the DJ index near to the 11,000 mark by early 2000, investors have renounced traditional buy-and-hold strategies and have switched to holding stocks for minutes at a time. In addition, the changing investment goals are partially caused by the change in the valuation system.

3. *Different valuation models.* Many of today's hot stocks are not worth anywhere near where they trade.. For example, Netstock Amazon.com, one of the hottest, sold just $610 million in books and CDs in 1999 and is yet to make its first penny. However, its $20 billion market value makes it worth $5 billion

more than Sears. In fact, with the exception of Yahoo, all Webstocks have infinite P/E ratios. This anomaly prompts practitioners to question traditional models of valuing the stock, and forecasters everywhere concede that old models are suspect (Weber, 1999).

Online trading also engenders some changes in the traditional investing scenario. First, the wide variation in investor knowledge of the stock market and of trading is crucial in the online setting. The costs to investors of bad judgment are likely to be borne by new entrants to the world of individual investing; these investors are pleased with the simplicity of the interactive user-friendly formats of e-brokerages, but are seldom proficient in the mechanisms and arrangements beyond the interface. Experienced investors can better identify the benefits and costs of choosing specific e-brokerages.

Second, the frequency of online investor trading deserves special attention. Many market analysts suggest that the growing U.S. economy and the low commissions charged by e-brokerages influence investors to trade more often. For example, an average Merrill Lynch (full-service broker) customer makes four to five trades per year while the core investors in an e-brokerage such as E*Trade make an average of 5.4 trades per quarter. Frequent trading is generally contrary to the recommendations of financial theory. Ultimately, it is possible for an e-brokerage to allow investors to trade frequently at very low or even zero costs per trade while earning large profits on the fraction of the increasingly large bid–ask spread that is pushed back by the market maker. At the same time, the investor may be unaware of the indirect costs incurred with each trade.

Third, the evolution of electronic trading may increase market fragmentation in the short run. E-brokerages may increasingly channel trades away from exchanges and toward market makers to compensate for lost revenue resulting from low direct commissions. Market fragmentation may have a negative impact on prices, increasing the bid–ask spread and potential for arbitrage opportunities (e.g. buy low in one market and sell high in another market within a short period of time). This is contrary to the belief that electronic markets may force centralization and increase liquidity (i.e. the ability to buy and sell securities quickly).

Clearly, people's attitudes toward risk have been changing constantly. Many behavioral factors that have not been successfully incorporated into traditional quantitative models have now become decisive factors in valuing investments. Several new models have thus been developed in an effort to better explain why all of a sudden investors do not see the stock market as the dangerous place they once did.

20.3. Some New Portfolio Structure Models

Among the new models, which overturn statistical relationships that have held true for decades, the major ones are (Glassman,and Hassett, 1998):

1. *Fed model*. Edward Yardeni, an economist at the Deutsche Bank, developed this model. The model relates earnings yield on stocks to interest rates. When the earnings yield is equal to the current yield on a 10-year U.S. Treasury bond, stocks are at fair value. If the earnings yield is above the interest rate, stocks are a buy; if below, stocks are overvalued.
   For example, over the next 12 months, the consensus earnings forecast of industry analysts for the S&P 500 is $52.78 per share. This is a 19.1 percent increase over the latest available four-quarter trailing sum of earnings. The fair value of the S&P 500 Index was 1011.11, derived as the 12-month forward earnings divided by the 10-year Treasury bond yield, assuming at 5.22 percent. If the S&P 500 closed at 1318.31, then the market would be 30.4 percent overvalued. Individual investors can enter their projected bond yield and estimated growth in corporate earnings to check the valuation of the stocks at Yardeni's Web site.

2. *Campbell–Shiller model*. The valuation model developed by John Y. Campbell of Harvard

University and Robert J. Shiller of Yale University looks at price earnings ratios over time to determine a long-term market average (Campbell, 1987, 1996; Campbell and Shiller, 1991). When the current P/E exceeds that average, the market is overvalued. For example, the long-term average of P/E is 15. Therefore, at its current ratio of over 33, the stock price is overvalued.

3. *Cornell model*. This model discounts future cash flows and compares that to the current market level. The discount factor is a combination of the risk-free interest rate and a risk premium to compensate for the greater volatility of stocks. When the value of the discounted cash flows is above the current price, the market is cheap. Otherwise, it is overvalued.

4. *Glassman–Hassett model*. Similar to the Cornell model with one major exception, Glassman and Hassett argue that the risk premium, historically at 7 percent, is heading toward 0 percent. This means the discount factor that applies to stocks drops sharply, thus raising the fair value of the market.

The Internet has drastically changed the way investors make investment decisions. Technology empowers individual investors through many inventions and innovated services. Much information traditionally available only to institutional investors is now accessible to individual investors through the World Wide Web. For example, the Thomson Investors site allows individual traders to view the institutional pre-trade activity and get a bird's eye view of the activity on the NYSE floor. One very useful source of information is from StarMine. Investors can use this Web site to identify experts worth listening to, then use Multex to get the full detail of the relevant information (Mullaney, 2001). At Bestcalls.com, visitors can examine conference call information, and in the near future, individuals will be able to see corporate officers deliver the bullet points of their business models to institutions at www.eoverview.com, Net Roadshow's Web site.

These services may not bring individual investors up to par with institutional investors. However, they are now able to make investment decisions based on information with similar quality and currency as the big investors. The saved costs of trading through online brokers might provide individual investors an edge over their big counterparts. Since the individual investors' activity usually involves only small volumes of a given stock, their decisions will not likely cause a great fluctuation in the price. This will enable them to ride the market movement smoothly. Nevertheless, online traders must be aware that not all online brokers are competent. It is very important to sign up services with reputed brokers, who are backed with solid Internet infrastructure to minimize the frustration with those brokers (Gogoi, 2000).

Trading online, however, involves an unusually high degree of risks. Since most online traders are looking for profits in a relatively short period of time, their investing targets are primarily in tech-concentrated NASDAQ markets where volatility is the rule (McNamee, 2000; Opiela, 2000). Yet, many online investors forget that online or off, disciplines for managing portfolio to minimize risk are still indispensable (Campbell 1996; Brockman and Chung, 2000; Farrell, 2000).

20.4. Conclusion

Online trading provides convenience, encourages increased investor participation, and leads to lower upfront costs. In the long run, these will likely reflect increased market efficiency as well. In the short run, however, there are a number of issues related to transparency, investors' misplaced trust, and poorly aligned incentives between e-brokerages and market makers, which may impede true market efficiency.

For efficiency to move beyond the user interface and into the trading process, individual investors need a transparent window to observe the actual flow of orders, the time of execution, and the

commission structure at various points in the trading process. In this regard, institutional rules, regulations, and monitoring functions play a significant role in promoting efficiency and transparency along the value chain in online trading markets.

REFERENCES

Barnett, M. (1999a). "Day trading can damage your wealth." *The Industry Standard*, 5: 19.

Barnett, M. (1999b). "Individual investors are becoming institutions." *Industry Standard*, 19–26, 33–34.

Becker, G. (1998). "You want high returns? Brace yourself for high risk." *Business Week*, 19: 15.

Brockman, P. and Chung, D. (2000). "Informed and uninformed trading in an electronic, order-driven environment." *Financial Review*, 125–146.

Campbell, J. (1987). "Stock returns and the term structure." *Journal of Financial Economics*, 18: 373–399.

Campbell, J. (1996). "Understanding risk and return." *Journal of Political Economy*, 104: 298–345.

Campbell, J. and Shiller, R. (1991). "Yield spreads and interest rate movements: a bird's eye view." *Review of Economic Studies*, 58: 495–514.

Cooper, J. (2001). "Hey, chicken littles, the sky isn't falling." *Business Week*, 12: 43.

Farrell, C. (2000). "Online or off, the rules are the same." *Business Week*, 22: 148–149.

Gimein, M. (1999). "Playing the net stock game." *The Industry Standard*, 25: 20–21.

Glassman, J. and Hassett, K. (1998). "Are stocks overvalued? Not a chance." *The Wall Street Journal*, 30.

Gogoi, P. (2000). "Rage against online brokers." *Business Week*, 20: EB98–EB102.

McLean, B. (1999). "Net stocks have their seasons too." *Fortune*, 6: 305–308.

McNamee, M. (2000). "Trading online: It's a jungle out there." *Business Week*, 22: 168–169.

Mintel International Group Ltd. (2002). "Online trading market – US report," 1.

Mullaney, T. (2001). "What's an investor to do?" *Business Week*, 19: EB14–EB15.

Opiela, N. (2000). "Online trading: Opportunity or obstacle?" *Journal of Financial Planning*, 54–60.

Pethokoukis, J. (1999). "The young and the fearless." *Business Week*, 1: 63–64.

Pethokoukis, J. (1999). "Forget the cyclone. The net ride is scarier." *US News & World Report*, 22: 55.

Reardon, T. (2000). "The price is right." *Accountancy*, 81.

Sharma, M. (2000). "The growth of web-based investment." *Information Systems Management*, Spring, 58–64.

Smith, G. (1999a). "Day of reckoning for day-trading firms?" *Business Week*, 18: 88–89

Smith, G. (1999b). "Valuing those Internet stocks." *Business Week*, 8: 87.

Thornton, E. (2000). "Take that, cyber boy." *Business Week*, 10: 58–59.

Vogelstein, F. (1999a). "Online traders beware!" *US News & World Report*, 18: 41–42.

Vogelstein, F. (1999b). "A virtual stock market." *US News & World Report*, 26: 47–48.

Weber, J. (1999). "The market: Too high? Too low?" *Business Week*, 5: 92–93.

Chapter 21

A NOTE ON THE RELATIONSHIP AMONG THE PORTFOLIO PERFORMANCE INDICES UNDER RANK TRANSFORMATION

KEN HUNG, *National Dong Hwa University, Taiwan*
CHIN-WEI YANG, *Clarion University, USA*
DWIGHT B. MEANS, Jr., *Consultant, USA*

Abstract

This paper analytically determines the conditions under which four commonly utilized portfolio measures (the Sharpe index, the Treynor index, the Jensen alpha, and the Adjusted Jensen's alpha) will be similar and different. If the single index CAPM model is appropriate, we prove theoretically that well-diversified portfolios must have similar rankings for the Treynor, Sharpe indices, and Adjusted Jensen's alpha ranking. The Jensen alpha rankings will coincide if and only if the portfolios have similar betas. For multi-index CAPM models, however, the Jensen alpha will not give the same ranking as the Treynor index even for portfolios of large size and similar betas. Furthermore, the adjusted Jensen's alpha ranking will not be identical to the Treynor index ranking.

Keywords: Sharpe index; Treynor index; Jensen alpha; Adjusted Jensen alpha; CAPM; multi-index CAPM; performance measures; rank correlation; ranking; rank transformation

21.1. Introduction

Measurement of a portfolio's performance is of extreme importance to investment managers. That is, if a portfolio's risk-adjusted rate of return exceeds (or is below) that of a randomly chosen portfolio, it may be said that it outperforms (or underperforms) the market. The risk–return relation can be dated back to Tobin (1958), Markowitz (1959), Sharpe (1964), Lintner (1965), and Mossin (1966). Evaluation measures are attributed to Treynor (1965), Sharpe (1966), and Jensen (1968, 1969). Empirical studies of these indices can be found in the work by Friend and Blume (1970), Black et al. (1972), Klemkosky (1973), Fama and MacBeth (1974), and Kim (1978). For instance, the rank correlation between the Sharpe and Treynor indices was found by Sharpe (1966) to be 0.94. Reilly (1986) found the rank correlation to be 1 between the Treynor and Sharpe indices; 0.975 between the Treynor index and Jensen alpha; and 0.975 between the Sharpe index and Jensen alpha.

In addition, the sampling properties and other statistical issues of these indices have been carefully studied by Levy (1972), Johnson and Burgess (1975), Burgess and Johnson (1976), Lee (1976), Levhari and Levy (1977), Lee and Jen (1978), and Chen and Lee (1981, 1984, 1986). For example, Chen and Lee (1981, 1986) found that the statistical relationship between performance measures and their risk proxies would, in general, be affected by the sample size, investment horizon, and market conditions associated with the sample period. Notwithstanding these empirical findings, an analytical study of the relationship among these measures is missing in the literature. These performance measures may well be considered very "similar" owing to the unusually high rank correlation coefficients in the empirical studies. However, the empirical findings do not prove the true relationship. These measures can theoretically yield rather divergent rankings especially for the portfolios whose sizes are substantially less than the market. A portfolio size about 15 or more in which further decreases in risk is in general not possible (Evans and Archer, 1968; Wagner and Lau, 1971; Johnson and Shannon, 1974) can generate rather different rankings. In the case of an augmented CAPM, a majority of these performance measures, contrary to the conventional wisdom, can be rather different regardless of the portfolio sizes!

In this note, it is our intention to (1) investigate such relationship, (2) clarify some confusing issues, and (3) provide some explanations as to the empirically observed high rank correlations among performance measures. The analysis is free from the statistical assumptions (e.g. normality) and may provide some guidance to portfolio managers.

21.2. The Relationship between Treynor, Sharpe, and Jensen's Measures in the Simple CAPM

Given the conventional assumptions, a typical CAPM formulation can be shown as[1]

$$y_i = \alpha_i + \beta_i x \qquad (21.1)$$

where $y_i = \pi_p - \pi_f$, which is the estimated excess rate of return of portfolio i over the risk-free rate, $x = \pi_m - \pi_f$, which is the excess rate of return of the market over the risk-free rate.

The Treynor index is a performance measure which is expressed as the ratio of the average excess rate of return of a portfolio over the estimated beta or

$$T_i = \frac{\bar{y}_i}{\beta_i} \qquad (21.2)$$

Similarly, the Sharpe index is the ratio of the average excess rate of return of a portfolio over its corresponding standard deviation or

$$S_i = \frac{\bar{y}_i}{Sy_i} \qquad (21.3)$$

A standard deviation, which is significantly larger than the beta, may be consistent with the lack of complete diversification. While the Sharpe index uses the total risk as denominator, the Treynor index uses only the systematic risk or estimated beta. Note that these two indices are relative performance measures, i.e. relative rankings of various portfolios. Hence, they are suitable for a nonparametric statistical analysis such as rank correlation.

In contrast to these two indices, the Jensen alpha (or α) can be tested parametrically by the conventional t-statistic for a given significance level. However, the absolute Jensen alpha may not reflect the proper risk adjustment level for a given performance level (Francis, 1980). For instance, two portfolios with the identical Jensen's alpha may well have different betas. In this case, the portfolio with lower beta is preferred to the one with higher beta. Hence, the adjusted Jensen alpha can be formulated as the ratio of the Jensen alpha divided by its corresponding beta (see Francis, 1980) or

$$AJ_i = \frac{\alpha_i}{\beta_i} \qquad (21.4)$$

The close correlation between the Treynor and Sharpe indices is often cited in the empirical work of mutual fund performances. Despite its popular acceptance, it is appropriate to examine them analytically by increasing the portfolio size (n) to the number of securities of the market (N), i.e. the portfolio risk premium x approaches the market risk premium y. Rewriting the Treynor index, we have

$$T_i = \frac{\bar{y}_i}{\beta_i} = y_i^* \left[\frac{\text{Var}(x)}{\text{Cov}(x, \bar{y}_i)} \right] = \left[\frac{\bar{y}_i}{\text{Var}(y_i)} \right] \cdot \text{Var}(x)$$

$$= \frac{\bar{y}_i}{Sy_i} \left[\frac{\text{Var}(x)}{Sy_i} \right] = S_i \cdot s_x \qquad (21.5)$$

since $\mathrm{Cov}(x \cdot y_i) = \mathrm{Var}(y_i) = \mathrm{Var}(x)$ for $x = y_i^2$.

Equation (21.5) indicates that the Treynor index, in general, will not equal the Sharpe index even in the case of a complete diversification, i.e. $n = N$. It is evident from (21.5) that these two indices are identical only for $s_x = 1$, a highly unlikely scenario. Since neither the Treynor nor Sharpe index is likely to be normally distributed, a rank correlation is typically computed to reflect their association. Taking rank on both sides of Equation (21.5) yields

$$\mathrm{Rank}(T_i) = \mathrm{Rank}(S_i) \cdot s_x \qquad (21.6)$$

since s_x in a given period and for a given market is constant. As a result, the Treynor and the Sharpe indices (which must be different values) give identical ranking as the portfolio size approaches the market size as stated in the following propositions:

Proposition #1: *In a given period and for a given market characterized by the simple CAPM, the Treynor and Sharpe indices give exactly the same ranking on portfolios as the portfolio size (n) approaches the market size (N).*

This proposition explains high rank correlation coefficients observed in empirical studies between these indices. Similarly, Equation (21.5) also indicates that parametric (or Pearson Product) correlation between the Treynor and Sharpe indices approaches 1 as n approaches N for a constant s_x, i.e. T_i is a nonnegative linear transformation of S_i from the origin. In general, these two indices give similar rankings but may not be identical.

The Jensen alpha can be derived from the CAPM for portfolio i:

$$J_i = \alpha_i = \bar{y}_i - \beta_i \bar{x} \qquad (21.7)$$

It can be seen from Equation (21.7) that as $n \to N$, $y_i \to x$, and $\beta_i \to 1$. Hence α_i approaches zero. The relationship of the rankings between the Jensen alpha and the Treynor index ranking are equal can be proved as β_i approaches 1 because:

$$\begin{aligned}\mathrm{Rank}(J_i) &= \mathrm{Rank}(\alpha_i) \\ &= \mathrm{Rank}\left(\frac{\alpha_i}{\beta_i}\right) \\ &= \mathrm{Rank}(\bar{y}_i) - \mathrm{Rank}(\beta_i \bar{x}) \qquad (21.8)\\ &= \mathrm{Rank}\left(\frac{y_i}{\beta_i}\right) - \mathrm{Rank}(\bar{x}) \\ &= \mathrm{Rank}(T_i)\end{aligned}$$

Since $\bar{x}$ is a constant; $y_i/\beta_i \to y_i$ and $\beta_i \bar{x} \to \bar{x}$. We state this relationship in the following proposition.

Proposition #2: *In a given period and for a given market characterized by the simple CAPM, as the portfolio size n approaches the market size N, the Jensen alpha ranking approaches the Treynor index ranking.*

However, the Jensen alpha will in general be dependent on the average risk premium for a given beta value for all portfolios since

$$\begin{aligned}\mathrm{Rank}(\alpha_i) &= \mathrm{Rank}(\bar{y}_i) - \beta_i \mathrm{Rank}(\bar{x}) \\ &= \mathrm{Rank}(\bar{y}i) - \text{constant} \qquad (21.9)\end{aligned}$$

for a constant β_i (for all i). In this case the Jensen alpha will give similar rank to the Treynor index for a set of portfolios with similar beta values since

$$\mathrm{Rank}\left(\frac{y_i}{\beta_i}\right) = \mathrm{Rank}(\bar{y}_i) = \mathrm{Rank}(\alpha_i)$$

for a fairly constant set of β_i's. Hence, we state the following proposition.

Proposition #3: *In a given period and for a given market characterized by the simple CAPM, the ranking of the Jensen alpha and that of the Treynor index give very close rankings for a set of fairly similar portfolio betas regardless of the portfolio size.*

Next, we examine the relationship between the adjusted Jensen alpha and the Treynor index in the form of the adjusted Jensen alpha (*AJ*). Since

$$\alpha_i = \bar{y}_i - \beta_i \bar{x}$$

hence

$$AJ = \frac{\alpha_i}{\beta_i} = \frac{\bar{y}_i}{\beta_i} - \bar{x} \qquad (21.10)$$

It follows immediately from Equation (21.10) that

$$\text{Rank}(AJ) = \text{Rank}(T) - \text{Rank}(\bar{x}) \qquad (21.11)$$

The result is stated in the following proposition.

Proposition #4: *In a given period and for a given market characterized by the simple CAPM, the adjusted Jensen alpha gives precisely identical rankings as does its corresponding Treynor index regardless of the portfolio size.*

Clearly, it is the adjusted Jensen alpha that is identical to the Treynor index in evaluating portfolio performances in the framework of the simple CAPM. The confusion of these measures can lead to erroneous conclusions. For example, Radcliffe (1990, p. 209) stated that "the Jensen and Treynor measures can be shown to be virtually identical." Since he used only the Jensen alpha in his text, the statement is not correct without further qualifications such as Proposition #3. The ranking of the Jensen alpha must equal that of the adjusted Jensen alpha for a set of similar betas, i.e. $\text{Rand}(\alpha_i/\beta_i) = \text{Rank}(\alpha_i)$ for a constant beta across all *i*. All other relationships can be derived by the transitivity property as shown in Table 21.1. In the next section, we expand our analysis to the augumented CAPM with more than one independent variable.

21.3. The Relationship Between the Treynor, Sharpe, and Jensen Measures in the Augmented CAPM

An augumented CAPM can be formulated without loss of generality, as

$$y_i = \alpha_i + \beta_i x + \sum c_{ij} z_{ij} \qquad (21.12)$$

where z_{ij} is another independent variable and c_{ij} is the corresponding estimated coefficient. For instance, z_{ij} could be a dividend yield variable (see Litzenberger and Ramaswami, 1979, 1980, 1982). In this case again, the Treynor and Sharpe indices have the same numerators as in the case of a simple CAPM, i.e. the Treynor index still measures risk premium per systematic risk (or β_i) and the Sharpe index measures the risk premium per total risk or (s_y). However, if the portfolio beta is sensitive to the additional data on z_{ij} due to some statistical problem (e.g. multi-collinearity), the Treynor index may be very sensitive due to the instability of the beta even for large portfolios. In this case, the standard deviations of the portfolio returns and portfolio betas may not have consistent rankings. Barring this situation, these two measures will in general give similar rankings for well-diversified portfolios.

Table 21.1. Analytical rank correlation between performance measures: Simple CAPM

	Sharpe Index (S_i)	Treynor Index (T_i)	Jensen Alpha (J_i)	Adjusted Jensen Alpha AJ_i
Sharpe Index (S_i)	1			
Treynor Index (T_i)	$\text{Rank}(T_i) = \text{Rank}(S_i) \cdot S_X$ Identical ranking as $n \to N$	1		
Jenson Alpha (J_i)	As $n \to N$ $\text{Rank}(J_i) \to \text{Rank}(S_i)$	$\text{Rank}(J_i) \to \text{Rank}(T_i)$ as $n \to N$ or $\beta \to 1$ or $\text{Rank}(J_i) \to \text{Rank}(T_i)$ for similar β_i's	1	
Adjusted Jenson Alpha (AJ_i)	As $n \to N$ $\text{Rank}(AJ_i) \to \text{Rank}(S_i)$	$\text{Rank}(AJ_i) = \text{Rank}(T_i)$ regardless of the portfolio size	$\text{Rank}(\alpha_i/\beta_i) = \text{Rank}(\alpha_i)$ for similar β_i's	1

However, in the augmented CAPM framework, the Jensen alpha may very well differ from the Treynor index even for a set of similar portfolio betas.

This can be seen from reranking (α_i) as:

$$\text{Rank}(\alpha_i) = \text{Rank}(\bar{y}_i) - \beta_i \, \text{Rank}(\bar{x}) - \sum_j \text{Rank}(c_{ij}\bar{z}_{ij})_j$$

(21.13)

It is evident from Equation (21.13) that the Jensen alpha does not give same rank as the Treynor index, i.e. Rank (α_i) $\neq$ Rank $\bar{y}_i/\beta_i$ = Rank ($\bar{y}_i$) for a set of constant portfolio beta β_i's. This is because $c_{ij}\bar{z}_{ij}$ is no longer constant; they differ for each portfolio selected even for a set of constant β_i's (hence $\beta_i^* \text{Rank}(\bar{x})$) for each portfolio i as stated in the following proposition.

Proposition #5: *In a given period and for a given market characterized by the augmented CAPM, the Jensen alpha in general will not give the same rankings as will the Treynor index, even for a set of similar portfolio betas regardless of the portfolio size.*

Last, we demonstrate that the adjusted Jensen alpha is no longer identical to the Treynor index as shown in the following proposition.

Proposition #6: *In a given period and for a given market characterized by the augmented CAPM, the adjusted Jensen alpha is not identical to the Treynor index regardless of the portfolio size.*

We furnish the proof by rewriting Equation (21.12) for each portfolio i as:

Since $\alpha_i = \bar{y}_i - \beta_i \bar{x} - \sum_j c_{ij}\bar{z}_{ij}$ implies

$$\frac{\alpha_i}{\beta_i} = \frac{\bar{y}_i}{\beta_i} - \bar{x} - \sum_j \left(\frac{c_{ij}}{\beta_i}\right)\bar{z}_{ij}$$

We have

$$\text{Rank}(AJ_i) = \text{Rank}(T_i) - \text{Rank}(\bar{x}) - \sum_j \text{Rank}\left(c_{ij}/\beta_i\right)\bar{z}_{ij}$$

(21.14)

It follows immediately that Rank (AJ) $\neq$ Rank (T) in general since the last term of Equation (21.14) is not likely to be constant for each estimated CAPM regression. It is to be noted that contrary to the case of the simple CAPM, the adjusted Jensen alpha and the Treynor index do not produce identical rankings. Likewise, for a similar set of β_i's for all i, the rankings of the Jensen and adjusted Jensen alpha are closely related. Note that the property of transitivity, however, does not apply in the augmented CAPM since the pairwise rankings of T_i and J_i or AJ_i do not

Table 21.2. Analytical rank correlation between performance measures: Augmented CAPM

	Sharpe Index S_i	Treynor Index T_i	Jensen Alpha J_i	Adjusted Jensen Alpha AJ_i
Sharpe Index S_i	1			
Treynor Index T_i	Rank (T_i) and Rank (S_i) are similar barring severe multicollinearity or an unstable beta	1		
Jenson Alpha J_i	Rank(J_i) $\neq$ Rank (S_i)	Rank(J_i) $\neq$ Rank (T_i) even for a similar beta and regardless of the portfolio size	1	
Adjusted Jenson Alpha AJ_i	Rank(AJ_i) $\neq$ Rank(S_i)	Rank(AJ_i) $\neq$ Rank (T_i) regardless of the portfolio size	Rank (AJ_i) $\rightarrow$ Rank (J_i) for a set of similar β_i's	1

converge consistently (Table 21.2) even for large porfolios.

21.4. Conclusion

In this note, we first assume the validity of the single index CAPM. The CAPM remains the foundation of modern portfolio theory despite the challenge from fractal market hypothesis (Peters, 1991) and long memory (Lo, 1991). However, empirical results have revalidated the efficient market hypothesis and refute others (Coggins, 1998). Within this domain, we have examined analytically the relationship among the four performance indices without explicit statistical assumptions (e.g. normality). The Treynor and Sharpe indices produce similar rankings only for well-diversified portfolios. In its limiting case, as the portfolio size approaches the market size, the ranking of the Sharpe index becomes identical to the ranking of the Treynor index. The Jensen alpha generates very similar rankings as does the Treynor index only for a set of comparable portfolio betas. In general, the Jensen alpha produces different ranking than does the Treynor index. Furthermore, we have shown that the adjusted Jensen alpha has rankings identical to the Treynor index in the simple CAPM. However, in the case of an augmented CAPM with more than one independent variable, we found that (1) the Treynor index may be sensitive to the estimated value of the beta; (2) the Jensen alpha may not give similar rankings as the Treynor index even with a comparable set of portfolio betas; and (3) the adjusted Jensen alpha does not produce same rankings as that of the Treynor index. The potential difference in rankings in the augmented CAPM suggests that portfolio managers must exercise caution in evaluating these performance indices. Given the relationship among these four indices, it may be necessary in general to employ each of them (except the adjusted Jensen alpha and the Treynor index are identical in ranking in the simple CAPM) since they represent different measures to evaluate the performance of portfolio investments.

NOTES

1. We focus our analysis on the theoretical relationship among these indices in the framework of a true characteristic line. The statistical distributions of the returns (e.g. normal or log normal), from which the biases of these indices are derived, and other statistical issues are discussed in detail by Chen and Lee (1981, 1986). We shall limit our analysis to a pure theoretical scenario where the statistical assumptions are not essential to our analysis. It is to be pointed out that the normality assumption of stock returns in general has not been validated in the literature.

2. This condition is guaranteed if the portfolio y_i is identical to the market (x) or if n is equal to N. In this special case, if the portfolio is weighted according to market value weights, the portfolio is identical to the market so $Cov(x, y_i) = Var(y_i) = Var(x)$.

REFERENCES

Black, F., Jensen, M.C., and Scholes, M. (1972). "The Capital Asset Pricing Model: Some empirical tests," in M.C. Jensen (ed.) *Studies in the Theory of Capital Markets*, New York: Praeger Publishers Inc.

Burgess, R.C. and Johnson, K.H. (1976). "The effects of sampling fluctuations on required inputs of security analysis." *Journal of Financial and Quantitative Analysis*, 11: 847–854.

Chen, S.N. and Lee, C.F. (1981). "The sampling relationship between sharpe's performance measure and its risk proxy: sample size, investment horizon, and market conditions." *Management Science*, 27(6): 607–618.

Chen, S.N. and Lee, C.F. (1984). "On measurement errors and ranking of three alternative composite performance measures." *Quarterly Review of Economics and Business*, 24: 7–17.

Chen, S.N. and Lee, C.F. (1986). "The effects of the sample size, the investment horizon, and market conditions on the validity of composite performance measures: a generalization." *Management Science*, 32(11): 1410–1421.

Coggin, T.D. (1998). "Long-term memory in equity style index." *Journal of Portfolio Management*, 24(2): 39–46.

Evans, J.L. and Archer, S.H. (1968). "Diversification and reduction of dispersion: an empirical analysis." *Journal of Finance*, 23: 761–767.

Fama, E.F. and MacBeth, J.D. (1973). "Risk, return and equilibrium: empirical tests." *Journal of Political Economy*, 81: 607–636.

Francis, J.C. (1980). *Investments: Analysis and Management,* 3rd edn, New York: McGraw-Hill Book Company.

Friend, I. and Blume, M.E. (1970). "Measurement of portfolio performance under uncertainty." *American Economic Review*, 60: 561–575.

Jensen, M.C. (1968). "The performance of mutual funds in the period 1945–1964." *Journal of Finance*, 23(3): 389–416.

Jensen, M.C. (1969). "Risk, the pricing of capital assets, and the evaluation of investment portfolio." *Journal of Business*, 19(2): 167–247.

Johnson, K.H. and Burgess, R.C. (1975). "The effects of sample sizes on the accuracy of E-V and SSD efficient criteria." *Journal of Financial and Quantitative Analysis*, 10: 813–848.

Johnson, K.H. and Shannon, D.S. (1974). "A note on diversification and reduction of dispersion." *Journal of Financial Economics*, 4: 365–372.

Kim, T. (1978). "An assessment of performance of mutual fund management." *Journal of Financial and Quantitative Analysis*, 13(3): 385–406.

Klemkosky, R.C. (1973). "The bias in composite performance measures." *Journal of Financial and Quantitative Analysis*, 8: 505–514.

Lee, C.F. (1976). "Investment horizon and functional form of the Capital Asset Pricing Model." *Review of Economics and Statistics*, 58: 356–363.

Lee, C.F. and Jen, F.C. (1978). "Effects of measurement errors on systematic risk and performance measure of a portfolio." *Journal of Financial and Quantitative Analysis*, 13: 299–312.

Levhari, D. and Levy, H. (1977). "The Capital Asset Pricing Model and investment horizon." *Review of Economics and Statistics*, 59: 92–104.

Levy, H. (1972). "Portfolio performance and investment horizon." *Management Science*, 18(12): B645–B653.

Litner, J. (1965). "The valuation of risk assets and the selection of risky investment in stock portfolios and capital budgets." *Review of Economics and Statistics*, 47: 13–47.

Litzenberger, R.H. and Ramaswami, K. (1979). "The effects of personal taxes and dividends on capital asset prices: theory and empirical evidence." *Journal of Financial Economics*, 7(2): 163–196.

Litzenberger, R.H. and Ramaswami, K. (1980). "Dividends, short selling restriction, tax induced investor clienteles and market equilibrium." *Journal of Finance*, 35(2): 469–482.

Litzenberger, R.H. and Ramaswami, K. (1982). "The effects of dividends on common stock prices tax effects or information effect." *The Journal of Finance*, 37(2): 429–443.

Lo, A.W. (1991) "Long-term memory in stock market prices." *Econometrica*, 59(5): 1279–1313.

Markowitz, H.M. (1959). *Portfolio Selection Cowles Monograph 16*. New York: Wiley, Chapter 14.

Mossin, J. (1966). "Equilibrium in a capital market." *Econometrica*, 34: 768–783.

Peters, E.E. (1991). *Chaos and Order in the Capital Markets: A New View of Cycles, Prices and Market Volatility*. New York: John Wiley.

Radcliffe, R.C. (1990). *Investment: Concepts, Analysis, and Strategy*, 3rd edn. Glenview, IL: Scott, Foresman.

Reilly, F.K. (1986). *Investments,* 2nd edn. Chicago, IL: The Dryden Press.

Sharpe, W.F. (1964). "Capital asset price: A theory of market equilibrium under conditions of risk." *The Journal of Finance*, 19(3): 425–442.

Sharpe, W.F. (1966). "Mutual fund performance." *Journal of Business Supplement on Security Prices*, 39: 119–138.

Tobin, J. (1958). "Liquidity preference as behavior toward risk." *The Review of Economic Studies*, 26(1): 65–86.

Treynor, J.L. (1965). "How to rate management of investment funds." *Harvard Business Review*, 43: 63–75.

Wagner, W.H. and Lau, S.T. (1971). "The effect of diversification on risk." *Financial Analysts Journal*, 27(5): 48–53.

Chapter 22

CORPORATE FAILURE: DEFINITIONS, METHODS, AND FAILURE PREDICTION MODELS

JENIFER PIESSE, *University of London, UK and University of Stellenbosch, South Africa*
CHENG-FEW LEE, *National Chiao Tung University, Taiwan and Rutgers University, USA*
HSIEN-CHANG KUO, *National Chi-Nan University and Takming College, Taiwan*
LIN LIN, *National Chi-Nan University, Taiwan*

Abstract

The exposure of a number of serious financial frauds in high-performing listed companies during the past couple of years has motivated investors to move their funds to more reputable accounting firms and investment institutions. Clearly, bankruptcy, or corporate failure or insolvency, resulting in huge losses has made investors wary of the lack of transparency and the increased risk of financial loss. This article provides definitions of terms related to bankruptcy and describes common models of bankruptcy prediction that may allay the fears of investors and reduce uncertainty. In particular, it will show that a firm filing for corporate insolvency does not necessarily mean a failure to pay off its financial obligations when they mature. An appropriate risk-monitoring system, based on well-developed failure prediction models, is crucial to several parties in the investment community to ensure a sound financial future for clients and firms alike.

Keywords: corporate failure; bankruptcy; distress; receivership; liquidation; failure prediction; Discriminant Analysis (DA); Conditional Probability Analysis (CPA); hazard models; misclassification cost models

22.1. Introduction

The financial stability of firms is of concern to many agents in society, including investors, bankers, governmental and regulatory bodies, and auditors. The credit rating of listed firms is an important indicator, both to the stock market for investors to adjust stock portfolios, and also to the capital market for lenders to calculate the costs of loan default and borrowing conditions for their clients. It is also the duty of government and the regulatory authorities to monitor the general financial status of firms in order to make proper economic and industrial policy. Further, auditors need to scrutinize the going-concern status of their clients to present an accurate statement of their financial standing. The failure of one firm can have an effect on a number of stakeholders, including shareholders, debtors, and employees. However, if a number of firms simultaneously face financial failure, this can have a wide-ranging effect on the national economy and possibly on that of other countries. A recent example is the financial crisis that began in Thailand in July 1997, which affected most of the other Asia-Pacific countries. For these reasons, the development of theoretical bankruptcy prediction models, which can protect the market from unnecessary losses, is essential. Using these, governments are able to develop policies in time to maintain industrial cohesion and minimize the damage caused to the economy as a whole.

Several terms can be used to describe firms that appear to be in a fragile financial state. From standard textbooks, such as Brealey et al. (2001) and Ross et al. (2002), definitions are given of distress, bankruptcy, or corporate failure. Pastena and Ruland (1986, p. 289) describe this condition as when

1. the market value of assets of the firm is less than its total liabilities;
2. the firm is unable to pay debts when they come due;
3. the firm continues trading under court protection.

Of these, insolvency, or the inability to pay debts when they are due, has been the main concern in the majority of the early bankruptcy literature. This is because insolvency can be explicitly identified and also serves as a legal and normative definition of the term "bankruptcy" in many developed countries. However, the first definition is more complicated and subjective in the light of the different accounting treatments of asset valuation. Firstly, these can give a range of market values to the company's assets and second, legislation providing protection for vulnerable firms varies between countries.

22.2. The Possible Causes of Bankruptcy

Insolvency problems can result from endogenous decisions taken within the company or a change in the economic environment, essentially exogenous factors. Some of the most common causes of insolvency are suggested by Rees (1990):

- Low and declining real profitability
- Inappropriate diversification: moving into unfamiliar industries or failing to move away from declining ones

- Import penetration into the firm's home markets
- Deteriorating financial structures
- Difficulties controlling new or geographically dispersed operations
- Over-trading in relation to the capital base
- Inadequate financial control over contracts
- Inadequate control over working capital
- Failure to eliminate actual or potential loss-making activities
- Adverse changes in contractual arrangements.

Apart from these, a new company is usually thought to be riskier than those with longer history. Blum (1974, p. 7) confirmed that "other things being equal, younger firms are more likely to fail than older firms." Hudson (1987), examining a sample between 1978 and 1981, also pointed out that companies liquidated through a procedure of creditors' voluntary liquidation or compulsory liquidation during that period were on average two to four years old and three-quarters of them less than ten years old. Moreover, Walker (1992, p. 9) also found that "many new companies fail within the first three years of their existence." This evidence suggests that the distribution of the failure likelihood against the company's age is positively skewed. However, a clear-cut point in age structure has so far not been identified to distinguish "new" from "young" firms in a business context, nor is there any convincing evidence with respect to the propensity to fail by firms of different ages. Consequently, the age characteristics of liquidated companies can only be treated as an observation rather than theory.

However, although the most common causes of bankruptcy can be noted, they are not sufficient to explain or predict corporate failure. A company with any one or more of these characteristics is not certain to fail in a given period of time. This is because factors such as government intervention may play an important role in the rescue of distressed firms. Therefore, as Bulow and Shoven (1978) noted, the conditions under which a firm goes through liquidation are rather complicated. Foster (1986, p. 535) described this as "there need not be a one-to-one correspondence between the non-distressed/distressed categories and the non-bankrupt/bankrupt categories." It is noticeable that this ambiguity is even more severe in the not-for-profit sector of the economy.

22.3. Methods of Bankruptcy

As corporate failure is not only an issue for company owners and creditors but also the wider economy, many countries legislate for formal bankruptcy procedures for the protection of the public interest, such as Chapter VII and Chapter XI in the US, and the Insolvency Act in the UK. The objective of legislation is to "[firstly] protect the rights of creditors ... [secondly] provide time for the distressed business to improve its situation ... [and finally] provide for the orderly liquidation of assets" (Pastena and Ruland, 1986, p. 289). In the UK, where a strong rescue culture prevails, the Insolvency Act contains six separate procedures, which can be applied to different circumstances to prevent either creditors, shareholders, or the firm as a whole from unnecessary loss, thereby reducing the degree of individual as well as social loss. They will be briefly described in the following section.

22.3.1. Company Voluntary Arrangements

A voluntary arrangement is usually submitted by the directors of the firm to an insolvency practitioner, "who is authorised by a recognised professional body or by the Secretary of State" (Rees, 1990, p. 394) when urgent liquidity problems have been identified. The company in distress then goes through the financial position in detail with the practitioner and discusses the practicability of a proposal for corporate restructuring. If the practitioner endorses the proposal, it will be put to the company's creditors in the creditors' meeting, requiring an approval rate of 75 percent of attendees. If the restructuring report is accepted, those notified will thus be bound by this agreement and the

practitioner becomes the supervisor of the agreement. It is worth emphasizing that a voluntary arrangement need not pay all the creditors in full but a proportion of their lending (30 percent in a typical voluntary agreement in the UK) on a regular basis for the following several months. The advantages of this procedure are that it is normally much cheaper than formal liquidation proceedings and the creditors usually receive a better return.

22.3.2. Administration Order

It is usually the directors of the insolvent firm who petition the court for an administration order. The court will then assign an administrator, who will be in charge of the daily affairs of the firm. However, before an administrator is appointed, the company must convince the court that the making of an order is crucial to the survival of the company or for a better realization of the company's assets than would be the case if the firm were declared bankrupt. Once it is rationalized, the claims of all creditors are effectively frozen. The administrator will then submit recovery proposals to the creditors' meeting for approval within three months of the appointment being made. If this proposal is accepted, the administrator will then take the necessary steps to put it into practice.

An administration order can be seen as the UK version of the US Chapter XI in terms of the provision of a temporary legal shelter for troubled companies. In this way, they can escape future failure without damaging their capacity to continue to trade (Counsell, 1989). This does sometimes lead to insolvency avoidance altogether (Homan, 1989).

22.3.3. Administrative Receivership

An administration receiver has very similar powers and functions as an administrator but is appointed by the debenture holder (the bank), secured by a floating or fixed charge after the directors of the insolvent company see no prospect of improving their ability to honor their debts. In some cases, before the appointment of an administration receiver, a group of investigating accountants will be empowered to examine the real state of the company. The investigation normally includes the estimation of the valuable assets and liabilities of the company. If this group finds that the company has no other choices but to be liquidated, an administration receiver will work in partnership with the investigation team and thus be entitled to take over the management of the company. The principal aim is to raise money to pay debenture holders and other preferential creditors by selling the assets of the businesses at the best price. The whole business may be sold as a going concern if it is worth more as an entity. As in an administration order, the receiver must advise creditors of any progress through a creditors' meeting, which is convened shortly after the initial appointment.

22.3.4. Creditors' Voluntary Liquidation

In a creditors' voluntary liquidation, the directors of the company will take the initiative to send an insolvency practitioner an instruction that will lead to the convening of a creditors' and shareholders' meetings. In a shareholders' meeting, a liquidator will be appointed and this is ratified in a subsequent creditors' meeting. Creditors have the right to determine who acts as liquidator. A liquidator will start to find potential purchasers and realise the assets of the insolvent firm in order to clear its debts. Unlike receivers who have wide ranging powers in the management of the businesses, the liquidator's ability to continue trading is restricted. This is the most common way to terminate a company (Rees, 1990).

22.3.5. Members' Voluntary Liquidation

The procedure for a member's voluntary liquidation is similar to that of the creditors' voluntary liquidation. The only difference is that in a members' voluntary liquidation the directors of the firm must swear a declaration of solvency to clear debts with fair interest within 12 months and creditors are not involved in the appointment of a liquidator. Therefore, a company's announcement of a members' voluntary liquidation by no means signals its insolvency, but only means closure with diminishing activity, purely a necessity to remain in existence.

22.3.6. Compulsory Liquidation

A compulsory liquidation is ordered by the court to wind up a company directly. This order is usually initiated by the directors of the insolvent firm or its major creditors. Other possible petitioners include the Customs and Excise, the Inland Revenue, and local government (Hudson, 1987, p. 213). The entire procedure is usually started with a statutory demand made by creditors who wish to initiate a compulsory liquidation. If the firm fails to satisfy their request in a stated period of time, this failure is sufficient grounds to petition the court to wind up the firm. Once the order is granted, the Official Receiver will take control of the company immediately or a liquidator will be appointed by the Official Receiver. The company then must cease trading and liquidation of assets begins. However, an interesting phenomenon is that many valuable assets may be removed or sold prior to the liquidator taking control, or even during the delivery of the petition to the court, leaving nothing valuable for the liquidator to deal with. In this sense, the company initiating a compulsory liquidation has been terminated in practical terms far before a court order is granted.

22.4. Prediction Model for Corporate Failure

Because corporate failure is not simply the closure of a company but has wider implications, it is important to construct models of corporate failure for assessment and prediction. If bankruptcy can be predicted accurately, it may be possible for the firm to be restructured, thus avoiding failure. This would benefit owners, employees, creditors, and shareholders alike.

There is an established literature that supports the prediction of corporate failure using financial ratio analysis. This is because by using financial performance data it is possible to control for the systematic effect of firm size and industry effects (Lev and Sunder, 1979, pp.187–188) in cross-section models to determine if there are signs of corporate failure. Thus, there is a history of financial ratio analysis in bankruptcy prediction research.

22.4.1. Financial Ratio Analysis and Discriminant Analysis

The earliest example of ratio analysis in predicting corporate failure is attributed to Patrick (1932), although it attracted more attention with the univariate studies of Beaver (1966). This work systematically categorized 30 popular ratios into six groups, and found that some ratios, such as cash flow/total debt ratio, demonstrated excellent predictive power in corporate failure models. These results also showed the deterioration of the distressed firms prior to failure, including a fall in net income, cash flow, and working capital, as well as an increase in total debt. Although this was a useful beginning, univariate analysis was later found to be limited and better results were obtained from including a number of ratios that combined to give a more robust model with improved predictive power.

With the increased popularity of the multi-ratio analysis, multivariate discriminant analysis (MDA) began to dominate the bankruptcy prediction literature from the 1980s. MDA determines the discriminant coefficient of each of the characteristics chosen in the model on the basis that these will discriminate efficiently between failed and nonfailed firms. A single score for each firm in the study is generated and a cut-off point determined that minimizes the dispersion of scores associated with firms in each category, including the probability of overlap between them. An intuitive advantage of MDA is that the model considers the entire profile of characteristics and their interaction.

Another advantage lies in its convenience in application and interpretation (Altman, 1983, pp. 102–103).

One of the most popular MDA applications is the Z-score model developed by Altman (1968). Because of the success of the Z-score in predicting failure, 22 selected financial ratios were classified into five bankruptcy-related categories. In a sample of 33 bankrupt and 33 nonbankrupt manufacturing companies between 1946 and 1965, the final specification model determined the five variables, which are still frequently used in the banking and business sectors. The linear function is

$$Z\text{-score} = 1.2Z_1 + 1.4Z_2 + 3.3Z_3 + 0.6Z_4 + 0.999Z_5$$

$$(22.1)$$

where

> Z-score = overall index;
> Z_1 = working capital/total assets;
> Z_2 = retained earnings/total assets;
> Z_3 = earnings before interest and taxes/total assets;
> Z_4 = market value of equity/book value of total debt;
> Z_5 = sales/total assets.

Altman (1968) also tested the cut-off point to balance Type I and Type II errors, and found that in general, it was possible for a company with a Z-score smaller than 1.8 to fail during the next few years whereas one with a Z-score higher than 2.99 was much more likely to succeed. The Z-score model remains popular as an indicator of credit risk for banks and other lenders.

Although these statistical discrimination techniques are popular in predicting bankruptcy, there are a number of methodological problems associated with them. Some are a function of the properties of financial ratios, for example, proportionality and zero-intercept assumptions are both critical to the credibility of the ratio analysis. The basic ratio form is assumed to be $y/x = c$, where y and x are two accounting variables that are different but linearly related and c is the value of the ratio. This raises three questions. First, is there an error term in the relationship between the two accounting variables? Second, is an intercept term likely to exist in this relationship? And finally, supposing the numerator and denominator are not linearly related?

With respect to the first question, Lev and Sunder (1979) proved that if there is an additive error term in the relationship between y and x suggested by the underlying theory, that is, $y = \beta x + e$ or $y/x = \beta + e/x$, the comparability of such ratios will be limited. This is because "the extent of deviation from perfect size control depends on the properties of the error term and its relation to the size variable, x" (Lev and Sunder, 1979, p. 191). The logic is as follows: Where the error term is homoscedastic, e/x is smaller for large firms than for small ones because x as a size variable for large firms will, on average, be greater than that of small firms. Therefore, the ratio y/x for large firms will be closer to the slope term β than that for small firms. Then, since the variance of the ratio y/x for smaller firms is greater than that of larger firms, it proves that the ratio y/x of two groups (large and small firms) are statistically drawn from two different distributions. This weakens the validity of the comparison between ratios. Furthermore, to include an additive error term in the relationship between the numerator and the denominator is not adequate as a size control.

However, if y is heteroscedastic, it may result in the homoscedasticity of y/x. But it is also possible that this heteroscedastic problem of y/x remains unchanged. Lev and Sunder (1979) note that this problem may be ameliorated only when the error term is multiplicative in the relationship, that is, $y = \beta x e$ or $y/x = \beta e$. This is because the deviation of y/x now has no mathematical relationship with the size variable x. As a result, this form of the ratio is more appropriate for purposes of comparison.

The same argument can be applied where an intercept term exists in the relationship between two ratio variables, represented by $y = \alpha + \beta x$ or $y/x = \beta + \alpha/x$. It is clear that the variance of y/x for smaller firms will be larger than that for larger firms under the influence of the term α/x. Again,

this is not appropriate in comparisons of corporate performance.

If two variables are needed to control for the market size of y, such as $y = \alpha + \beta x + \delta z$, or $y = \alpha + \beta x + \delta x^2$ if the underlying relationship is nonlinear, the interpretation of the ratios can be ambiguous. All those problems cast doubt on the appropriateness of ratios in a number of situations. Theoretically, use of ratios is less problematic if and only if highly restrictive assumptions are satisfied. Empirically, Whittington (1980) claimed that violation of the proportionality assumption of the ratio form is the most common problem in research using financial data, especially in a time-series analysis at firm level. McDonald and Morris (1984, p. 96) found that the proportionality assumption is better satisfied when a group of firms in a simple homogeneous industry is analyzed, otherwise some amendment of the form of the ratios will be necessary. However, the replacement of the basic form of the ratio with a more sophisticated one is not a solution. On the contrary, on average, the basic form of the ratio performed quite satisfactorily in empirical studies. Keasey and Watson (1991, p. 90) also suggested that possible violations of the proportionality assumptions can be ignored, and since no further theoretical advances have been made on the topic, basic ratio analysis is still common in bankruptcy research.

In addition to the flaws in the design of financial ratios, there are other methodological problems associated with the use of MDA. Of these, nonnormality, inequality of dispersion matrices across all groups, and nonrandom sampling are the most prevalent. The violation of the normality assumption has been extensively discussed in the literature since the 1970s (Kshirsagar, 1971; Deakin, 1976; Eisenbeis, 1977; Amemiya, 1981; Frecka and Hopwood, 1983; Zavgren, 1985; Karels and Prakash, 1987). Non-normality results in biased tests of significance and estimated error rates. Studies on univariate normality of financial ratios found that these distributions tended to be skewed (Deakin, 1976; Frecka and Hopwood, 1983; Karels and

Prakash, 1987). If the ratios included in the model are not perfectly univariate normal, their joint distribution will, a priori, not be multivariate normal (Karels and Prakash, 1987). Therefore, data used in bankruptcy modeling should seek to minimize multivariate non-normality problems. The traditional stepwise procedure does not satisfy this requirement. However, despite several complementary studies on data transformation and outlier removal for ratio normality (Eisenbeis, 1977; Ezzamel et al., 1987; Frecka and Hopwood, 1983), this is rarely used in MDA models (Shailer, 1989, p. 57). Because all these techniques are imperfect, McLeay (1986) advocated that selecting a better model is more straightforward than the removal of outliers or data transformations.

Given the problems of non-normality, inequality of dispersion matrices across all groups in MDA modeling is trivial by comparison. In theory, the violation of the equal dispersion assumption will affect the appropriate form of the discriminating function. After testing the relationship between the inequality of dispersions and the efficiency of the various forms of classification models, a quadratic classification rule seems to outperform a linear one in terms of the overall probability of misclassification when the variance–covariance matrices of the mutually exclusive populations are not identical (Eisenbeis and Avery, 1972; Marks and Dunn, 1974; Eisenbeis, 1977). More importantly, the larger the difference in dispersion across groups, the more the quadratic form of the discriminating function is recommended.

One of the strict MDA assumptions is random sampling. However, the sampling method used in bankruptcy prediction studies is choice-based, or state-based, sampling which results in an equal or approximately equal draw of observations from each population group. Because corporate failure is not a frequent occurrence (Altman et al., 1977; Wood and Piesse, 1988), such sampling technique will cause a relatively lower probability of misclassifying distressed firms as nondistressed (Type I Error) but a higher rate of misclassifying nondistressed firms as distressed (Type II Error) (Lin and

Piesse, 2004; Kuo et al., 2002; Palepu, 1986; Zmijewski, 1984). Therefore, the high predictive power of MDA models claimed by many authors appears to be suspect. Zavgren (1985, p. 20) commented that MDA models are "difficult to assess because they play fast and loose with the assumptions of discriminant analysis." Where there is doubt about the validity of the results of MDA models, a more robust approach such as conditional probability analysis (CPA) is an alternative.

22.4.2. Conditional Probability Analysis

Since the late 1970s, the use of discriminant analysis has been gradually replaced by the CPA. This differs from MDA in that CPA produces the "probability of occurrence of a result, rather than producing a dichotomous analysis of fail/survive as is the norm with basic discriminant techniques" (Rees, 1990, p. 418). CPA primarily refers to logit and probit techniques and has been widely used in bankruptcy research (Keasey and Watson, 1987; Martin, 1977; Mensah, 1983; Ohlson, 1980; Peel and Peel, 1987; Storey et al., 1987; Zavgren, 1985, 1988). The major advantage of CPA is that it does not depend on the assumptions demanded by MDA (Kennedy, 1991, 1992). However, logit CPA is not always preferred under all conditions. If the multivariate normality assumption is met, the MDA Maximum Likelihood Estimator (LME) is more asymptotically efficient than MLE logit models. In all other circumstances, the MLE of MDA models may not be consistent, unlike that of logit models (Amemiya, 1981; Judge et al., 1985; Lo, 1986). However, as the rejection of normality in bankruptcy literature is very common, the logit model is appealing. Empirically, the logit analysis is most robust in the classification of distress.

The most commonly cited example of CPA research in this field is Ohlson (1980). The sample used included 105 bankrupt and 2058 nonbankrupt industrial companies during 1970–1976, contrasting with earlier studies that used equal numbers of bankrupts and nonbankrupts (Altman, 1968). The CPA logit analysis results in prediction failure with an accuracy rate of over 92 percent and included financial ratios to account for company size, capital structure, return on assets, and current liquidity, among others. This model was specified as:

$$Y = -1.3 - 0.4Y_1 + 6.0Y_2 - 1.4Y_3 + 0.1Y_4$$
$$\quad - 2.4Y_5 - 1.8Y_6 + 0.3Y_7 - 1.7Y_8 - 0.5Y_9$$

$$(22.2)$$

where:

   Y = overall index;
   Y_1 = log(total assets/GNP price-level index);
   Y_2 = total liabilities/total assets;
   Y_3 = working capital/ total assets;
   Y_4 = current liabilities/current assets;
   Y_5 = one if total liabilities exceed total assets, zero otherwise;
   Y_6 = net income/total assets;
   Y_7 = funds provided by operations/total liabilities;
   Y_8 = one if net income was negative for the last two years, zero otherwise;
   Y_9 = change in net income.

It is interesting to note that Ohlson (1980) chose 0.5 as the cut-off point, implicitly assuming a symmetric loss function across the two types of classification errors. The cut-off point was calculated using data beyond the estimation period, although the characteristics of the CPA model, and the large sample size, neutralized any problems (Ohlson, 1980, p. 126). It is important to note that while this was a valid approach for cross-section comparisons, it could not be transferred to comparisons across different time periods. With respect to predictive accuracy rates, Ohlson (1980) found that the overall results of the logit models were no obvious improvement on those from the MDA. Hamer (1983) tested the predictive power of MDA and logit CPA, and concluded that both performed comparably in the prediction of business failure for a given data set. However, given the predictive accuracy rates were overstated in previous MDA papers, mainly due to the use of choice-based sampling, this comparison may be biased and the inferences from them could favor CPA. Apart from this, other

factors discussed in this literature question these comparisons, citing differences in the selection of predictors, the firm matching criteria, the lead time, the estimation and test time periods, and the research methodology. Unless these factors are specifically controlled, any claim about the comparative advantages between CPA and MDA in terms of the predictive ability will not be robust.

In conclusion, CPA provides all the benefits of other techniques, including ease of interpretation, but also has none of the strict assumptions demanded by MDA. Thus, CPA can be claimed to be the preferred approach to bankruptcy classification.

22.4.3. Three CPA Models: LP, PM, and LM

Three commonly cited CPA models are: the linear probability model (LP), the probit model (PM), and the logit model (LM). This technique estimates the probability of the occurrence of a result, with the general form of the CPA equation stated as

$$\Pr(y = 1) = F(x, \beta)$$
$$\Pr(y = 0) = 1 - F(x, \beta)$$

$$(22.3)$$

In this specification, y is a dichotomous dummy variable which takes the value of 1 if the event occurs and 0 if it does not, and $Pr()$ represents the probability of this event. $F()$ is a function of a regressor vector x coupled with a vector β of parameters to govern the behavior of x on the probability. The problem arises as to what distribution best fits the above equation. Derived from three different distributions, LP, PM, and LM are then chosen to determine the best fit.

LP is a linear regression model, which is simple but has two main problems in application. The first is the heteroscedastic nature of the error term. Recall the form of an ordinary LP, $Y = X'\beta + \varepsilon$, where Y is the probability of an outcome and X is a column of independent variables, β is the parameter vector, and ε is the error term. When an event occurs, $Y = 1$, $\varepsilon = 1 - X'\beta$;

but when it does not occur, $Y = 0$, $\varepsilon = (-X'\beta)$. The second error term is not normally distributed, so Feasible General Least Squares Estimation Procedure (FGLS) should be used to correct heteroscedasticity (Greene, 1997, p. 87).

A more serious problem is that LP cannot constrain Y to lie between 0 and 1, as a probability should. Amemiya (1981, p. 1486) then suggested the condition that $Y = 1$ if $Y > 1$ and $Y = 0$ if $Y < 0$. But this can produce unrealistic and nonsensical results. Therefore, LP is rarely used and is discarded in the present study.

In the discussion of qualitative response models, there is a lively debate about the comparative benefits of logit and probit models. Although logit models are derived from a logistic density function and probit models from a normal density function, these two distributions are almost identical except that the logistic distribution has thicker tails and a higher central peak (Cramer, 1991, p. 15). This means the probability at each tail and in the middle of the logistic distribution curve will be larger than that of the normal distribution. However, one of the advantages of using logit is its computational simplicity, shown here in the relevant formulae:

$$\text{Probit Model: Prob}\,(Y = 1) = \int_{-\infty}^{\beta'x} \frac{1}{\sqrt{2\pi}} e^{-t^2/2} \mathrm{d}t$$
$$= \Phi(\beta'x)$$
$$(22.4)$$

$$\text{Logit Model: Prob}\,(Y = 1) = \frac{\exp(\beta'x)}{1 + \exp(\beta'x)}$$
$$= \frac{1}{1 + \exp(-\beta'x)}$$
$$(22.5)$$

where function $\Phi(\,)$ is the standard normal distribution. The mathematical convenience of logit models is one of the reasons for its popularity in practice (Greene, 1997, p. 874).

With respect to classification accuracy of CPA models, some comparisons of the results produced from these two models suggest that they are actually indistinguishable where the data are not heavily concentrated in the tails or the center (Amemiya, 1981; Cramer, 1991; Greene, 1997). This finding is consistent with the difference in the shape of the two distributions from which PM and LM are derived. It is also shown that the logit coefficients are approximately $\pi/\sqrt{3} \approx 1.8$ times as large as the probit coefficients, implying that the slopes of each variable are very similar. In other words, "the logit and probit model results are nearly identical" (Greene, 1997, p. 878).

The choice of sampling methods is also important in CPA. The common sampling method in the bankruptcy literature is to draw a sample with an approximately equal number of bankrupts and nonbankrupts, usually referred to as the state-based sampling technique, and is an alternative to random sampling. Although econometric estimation usually assumes random sampling, the use of state-based sampling has an intuitive appeal. As far as bankruptcy classification models are concerned, corporate failure is an event with rather low probability. Hence, a random sampling method may result in the inclusion of a very small percentage of bankrupts but a very high percentage of nonbankrupts. Such a sample will not result in efficient estimates in an econometric model (Palepu, 1986, p. 6). In contrast, state-based sampling is an "efficient sample design" (Cosslett, 1981, p. 56), which can effectively reduce the required sample size without influencing the provision of efficient estimators if an appropriate model and modification procedure are used. Thus, in bankruptcy prediction, the information content of a state-based sample for model estimation is preferred to that of random sampling. A state-based sample using CPA resulted in an understatement of Type I errors but an overstatement of Type II errors (Palepu, 1986; Lin and Piesse, 2004).

Manski and McFadden (1981) suggested several alternatives that can minimize the problems of state-based sampling. These include the weighted exogenous sampling maximum likelihood estimator (WESMLE) and the modified version by Cosslett (1981), the nonclassical maximum likelihood estimator (NMLE), and the conditional maximum likelihood estimator (CMLE). They compare and report these estimation procedures, which can be summarized as follows:

- All these estimators are computationally tractable, consistent, and asymptotically normal.
- The weighted estimator and conditional estimator avoid the introduction of nuisance parameters.
- The nonclassical maximum likelihood estimators are strictly more efficient than the others in large samples.
- In the presence of computational constraints, WESMLE and CMLE are the best; otherwise, NMLE is the most desirable.

Thus, by using any of these modifications, the advantages of using state-based sampling technique can be retained, while the disadvantages can be largely removed. The inference from this comparison is that the selection of modification method depends upon two factors: the sample size and the computational complexity. The modification cited in the bankruptcy literature is CMLE for three main reasons. Firstly, it has been extensively demonstrated in logit studies by Cosslett (1981) and Maddala (1983). Secondly, it was the model of choice in the acquisition prediction model by Palepu (1986), the merger/insolvency model by BarNiv and Hathorn (1997), and the bankruptcy classification models by Lin and Piesse (2004). Finally, because CMLE only introduces a change to the constant term that normally results from MLE estimation, while having no effects on the other parameters, this procedure is relatively simple. Without bias caused by the choice of sampling methods, modified CPA can correct all the methodological flaws of MDA.

22.5. The Selection of an Optimal Cut-Off Point

The final issue with respect to the accuracy rate of a bankruptcy classification model is the selection of an optimal cut-off point. Palepu (1986) noted that traditionally the cut-off point determined in

most early papers was arbitrary, usually 0.5. This choice may be intuitive, but lacks theoretical justification. Joy and Tollefson (1975), Altman and Eisenbeis (1978), and Altman et al. (1977) calculated the optimal cut-off point in the ZETA model. Two elements in the calculation can be identified, the costs of Type I and Type II errors and the prior probability of failure and survival, both of which had been ignored in previous studies. However, Kuo et al. (2002) uses fuzzy theory methods to improve a credit decision model.

Although their efforts were important, unsolved problems remain. The first is the subjectivity in determining the costs of Type I and Type II errors. Altman et al. (1977, p. 46) claimed that bank loan decisions will be approximately 35 times more costly when Type I errors occurred than for Type II errors. This figure is specific to the study and is not readily transferred and therefore a more general rule is required. The second problem is the subjectivity of selecting a prior bankruptcy probability. Wood and Piesse (1988) criticized Altman et al. (1977) for choosing a 2 percent higher failure rate than the annual average failure rate of 0.5 percent, suggesting spurious results from Altman et al. and necessitating a correction that was taken up in later research. The final problem is that the optimal cut-off score produced may not be "optimal" when multinormality and equal dispersion matrices assumptions are violated, which is a common methodological problem in this data analysis (Altman et al. 1977, p. 43, footnote 17).

The optimal cut-off equation in Maddala (1983, p. 80) is less problematic. It begins by developing an overall misclassification cost model:

$$C = C_1 P_1 \int_{G_2} f_1(x)\mathrm{d}x + C_2 P_2 \int_{G_1} f_2(x)\,\mathrm{d}x \qquad (22.6)$$

where

C = the total cost of misclassification;
C_1 = the cost of mis-classifying a failed firm as a non-failed one (Type I error);
C_2 = the cost of mis-classifying a non-failed firm as a failed one (Type II error);

P_1 = the proportion of the failed firms to the total population;

P_2 = the proportion of the non-failed firms to the total population;

G_1 = the failed firm group;

G_2 = the non-failed firm group;

x = a vector of characteristics $x = (x_1, x_2, \ldots, x_k)$;

$f_1(x)$ = the joint distribution of the characteristics x in the failed group;

$f_2(x)$ = the joint distribution of x in the non-failed group.

$P_1 + P_2 = 1$

However,

$$\text{Given} \quad \int_{G_2} f_1(x)\mathrm{d}x + \int_{G_1} f_1(x)\mathrm{d}x = 1 \qquad (22.7)$$

Combining (22.6) and (22.7) gives

$$
\begin{aligned}
C &= C_1 P_1 \left(1 - \int_{G_1} f_1(x)\mathrm{d}x\right) + C_2 P_2 \int_{G_1} f_2(x)\mathrm{d}x \\
&= C_1 P_1 + \int_{G_1} [C_2 P_2 f_2(x) - C_1 P_1 f_1(x)]\mathrm{d}x
\end{aligned}
$$

$$(22.8)$$

then to minimize the total cost of misclassification, min C, it is necessary for

$$C_2 P_2 f_2(x) - C_1 P_1 f_1(x) \leq 0 \qquad (22.9)$$

or

$$\frac{f_1(x)}{f_2(x)} \geq \frac{C_2 P_2}{C_1 P_1} \qquad (22.10)$$

If it is assumed that the expected costs of Type I error and Type II error are equal, $C_2 P_2 = C_1 P_1$, the condition to minimize the total misclassification cost will be

$$\frac{f_1(x)}{f_2(x)} \geq 1 \qquad (22.11)$$

This result is consistent with that proposed by Palepu (1986), assuming equal costs of Type I and II errors. Therefore, the optimal cut-off point is the probability value where the two conditional mar-

ginal densities, $f_1(x)$ and $f_2(x)$, are equal. In this equation, there is no need to use the prior failure rate to calculate the optimal cut-off point, the *ex post* failure rate (that is, the sample failure rate). Palepu (1986) illustrates this more clearly using Bayes' theorem.

Instead of using the costs of Type I and Type II errors, the expected costs of these errors are still unknown. Unfortunately, the subjectivity of deciding the relationship between the two types of expected costs still remains. There is no theoretical reason why they should be the same. However, compared to the previous arbitrary 50 percent cut-off point, this assumption is neutral and therefore preferred. Examples of applications using this method to determine the cut-off probability can be found in Palepu (1986) and Lin and Piesse (2004).

22.6. Recent Developments

While MDA and CPA are classified as static analyses, dynamic modeling is becoming more common in the bankruptcy literature. Shumway (2001) criticized static bankruptcy models for their examination of bankrupt companies 1 year prior to failure, while ignoring changes in the financial status of the firm year to year and proposed a simple dynamic hazard model to assess the probability failure on a continuous basis. Given the historical infrequency of corporate failure, the hazard model avoids the small sample problem because it requires all available time series of firm information. Because the hazard model takes the duration dependence, time-varying covariates, and data sufficiency problems into consideration, it is methodologically superior to both the MDA and CPA family of models. More empirical evidence is needed on its predictive power. Similar studies are in Whalen (1991) and Helwege (1996).

22.7. Conclusion

There are many reasons why a firm may fail and corporate insolvency *does not necessarily* include the inability to pay off financial obligations when they mature. For example, a solvent company can also be wound up through a member's voluntary liquidation procedure to maximize the shareholders' wealth when the realized value of its assets exceeds its present value in use. Bulow and Shoven (1978) modeled the potential conflicts among the various claimants to the assets and income flows of the company (for example, bondholders, bank lenders, and equity holders) and found that a liquidation decision should be made when "the coalition of claimants with negotiating power can gain from immediate liquidation" (Bulow and Shoven, 1978, p. 454). Their model also considered the existence of some asymmetric claims on the firm. This emphasizes the complex nature of bankruptcy decisions and justifies the adoption of members' voluntary liquidation procedure to determine a company's future (see Brealey and Myers, 2001, p. 622; Ross and Westerfield, 2002, p. 857).

The evolution and development of failure prediction models have produced increasingly superior methods, although an increase of their predictive power does not necessarily correlate with complexity. In addition, the costs of bankruptcy vary with different institutional arrangements and different countries (Brealey and Myers, 2001, pp. 439–443; Ross and Westerfield, 2002, p. 426). This implies that a single bankruptcy prediction model, with a fixed cut-off probability that can be used for all time periods and in all countries, does not exist. This paper has raised some of the problems with modeling corporate failure and reviewed some empirical research in the field.

Acknowledgements

We would like to thank many friends in University of London (U.K.) and National Chi Nan University (Taiwan) for valuable comments. We also want to thank our research assistant Chiu-mei Huang for preparing the manuscript and proofreading several drafts of the manuscript. Last, but not least, special thanks go to the Executive Editorial Board of the *Encyclopedia in Finance* in Springer, who expertly managed the development process and superbly turned our final manuscript into a finished product.

REFERENCES

Altman, E.I. (1968). "Financial ratios, discriminant analysis and the prediction of corporate bankruptcy." *Journal of Finance*, 23(4): 589–609.

Altman, E.I. (1983). *Corporate Financial Distress: A Complete Guide to Predicting, Avoiding, and Dealing with Bankruptcy.* New York: John Wiley.

Altman, E.I. and Eisenbeis, R.O. (1978). "Financial applications of discriminant analysis: a clarification." *Journal of Quantitative and Financial Analysis*, 13(1): 185–195.

Altman, E.I., Haldeman, R.G., and Narayanan, P. (1977). "Zeta analysis: a new model to identify bankruptcy risk of corporations." *Journal of Banking and Finance*, 1: 29–54.

Amemiya, T. (1981). "Qualitative response models: a survey." *Journal of Economic Literature*, 19(4): 1483–1536.

BarNiv, R. and Hathorn, J. (1997). "The merger or insolvency alternative in the insurance industry." *Journal of Risk and Insurance*, 64(1): 89–113.

Beaver, W. (1966). "Financial ratios as predictors of failure." *Journal of Accounting Research*, 4 (Supplement): 71–111.

Blum, M. (1974). "Failing company discriminant analysis." *Journal of Accounting Research*, 12(1): 1–25.

Brealey, R.A., Myers, S.C., and Marcus, A.J. (2001). *Fundamentals of Corporate Finance*, 3rd edn. New York: McGraw-Hill.

Bulow, J. and Shoven, J. (1978). "The bankruptcy decision." *The Bell Journal of Economics*, 9(2): 437–456.

Cosslett, S.R. (1981). "Efficient estimation of discrete-choice models," 51–111, in C.F. Manski and D. McFadden (eds.) *Structural Analysis of Discrete Data with Econometric Applications*. London: MIT Press.

Counsell, G. (1989). "Focus on workings of insolvency act." *The Independent*, 4th April.

Cramer, J.S. (1991). *The Logit Model: An Introduction for Economists*. Kent: Edward Arnold.

Deakin, E.B. (1976). "Distributions of financial accounting ratios: some empirical evidence." *Accounting Review*, 51(1): 90–96.

Eisenbeis, R.A. (1977). "Pitfalls in the application of discriminant analysis in business, finance, and economics." *The Journal of Finance*, 32(3): 875–900.

Eisenbeis, R.A. and Avery, R.B. (1972). *Discriminant Analysis and Classification Procedure: Theory and Applications.* Lexington, MA: D.C. Heath and Company.

Ezzamel, M., Cecilio M.M., and Beecher, A. (1987). "On the distributional properties of financial ratios." *Journal of Business Finance and Accounting*, 14(4): 463–481.

FitzPatrick, P.J. (1932). "A comparison of ratios of successful industrial enterprises with those of failed firms." *Certified Public Accountant*, October, November, and December, 598–605, 656–662, and 727–731, respectively.

Foster, G. (1986). *Financial Statement Analysis*, 2nd edn. New Jersey: Prentice-Hall.

Frecka, T.J. and Hopwood, W.S. (1983). "The effects of outliers on the cross-sectional distributional properties of financial ratios." *The Accounting Review*, 58(1): 115–128.

Greene, W.H. (1997). *Econometric Analysis*, 3rd edn. New Jersey: Prentice-Hall.

Hamer, M.M. (1983). "Failure prediction: sensitivity of classification accuracy to alternative statistical methods and variable sets." *Journal of Accounting and Public Policy*, 2(4): 289–307.

Helwege, J. (1996). "Determinants of saving and loan failures: estimates of a time-varying proportional hazard function." *Journal of Financial Services Research*, 10: 373–392.

Homan, M. (1989). *A Study of Administrations under the Insolvency Act 1986: The Results of Administration Orders Made in 1987*. London: ICAEW.

Hudson, J. (1987). "The age, regional and industrial structure of company liquidations." *Journal of Business Finance and Accounting*, 14(2): 199–213.

Joy, M.O. and Tollefson, J.O. (1975). "On the financial applications of discriminant analysis." *Journal of Financial and Quantitative Analysis*, 10(5): 723–739.

Judge, G.G., Griffiths, W.E., Hill, R.C., Lutkepohl, H., and Lee, T.C. (1985). *The Theory and Practice of Econometrics*. New York: John Wiley.

Karels, G.V. and Prakash, A.J. (1987). "Multivariate normality and forecasting of business bankruptcy." *Journal of Business Finance and Accounting*, 14(4): 573–595.

Keasey, K. and Watson, R. (1987). "Non-financial symptoms and the prediction of small company failure: a test of the Argenti Hypothesis." *Journal of Business Finance and Accounting*, 14(3): 335–354.

Keasey, K. and Watson, R. (1991). "Financial distress prediction models: a review of their usefulness." *British Journal of Management*, 2(2): 89–102.

Kennedy, P. (1991). "Comparing classification techniques." *International Journal of Forecasting*, 7(3): 403–406.

Kennedy, P. (1992). *A Guide to Econometrics*, 3rd edn, Oxford: Blackwell.

Kshirsagar, A.M. (1971). *Advanced Theory of Multivariate Analysis*. New York: Marcel Dekker.

Kuo, H.C., Wu, S., Wang, L., and Chang, M. (2002). "Contingent Fuzzy Approach for the Development of Banks' Credit-granting Evaluation Model." *International Journal of Business*, 7(2): 53–65.

Lev, B. and Sunder, S. (1979). "Methodological issues in the use of financial ratios." *Journal of Accounting and Economics*, 1(3): 187–210.

Lin, L. and Piesse, J. (2004). "The identification of corporate distress in UK industrials: a conditional probability analysis approach." *Applied Financial Economics*, 14: 73–82.

Lo, A.W. (1986). "Logit versus discriminant analysis: a specification test and application to corporate bankruptcies." *Journal of Econometrics*, 31(3): 151–178.

Maddala, G.S. (1983). *Limited-dependent and Qualitative Variables in Econometrics*. Cambridge: Cambridge University Press.

Manski, C.F. and McFadden, D.L. (1981). "Alternative estimators and sample designs for discrete choice analysis," 2–50, in C.F. Manski and D.L. McFadden (eds.) *Structural Analysis of Discrete Data with Econometric Applications*. London: MIT Press.

Marks, S. and Dunn, O.J. (1974). "Discriminant functions when covariance matrices are unequal." *Journal of the American Statistical Association*, 69(346): 555–559.

Martin, D. (1977). "Early warning of bank failure: a logit regression approach." *Journal of Banking and Finance*, 1(3): 249–276.

McDonald, B. and Morris, M.H. (1984). "The functional specification of financial ratios: an empirical examination." *Accounting And Business Research*, 15(59): 223–228.

McLeay, S. (1986). "Students and the distribution of financial ratios." *Journal of Business Finance and Accounting*, 13(2): 209–222.

Mensah, Y. (1983). "The differential bankruptcy predictive ability of specific price level adjustments: some empirical evidence." *Accounting Review*, 58(2): 228–246.

Ohlson, J.A. (1980). "Financial ratios and the probabilistic prediction of bankruptcy." *Journal of Accounting Research*, 18(1): 109–131.

Palepu, K.G. (1986). "Predicting takeover targets: a methodological and empirical analysis." *Journal of Accounting and Economics*, 8(1): 3–35.

Pastena, V. and Ruland, W. (1986). "The merger bankruptcy alternative." *Accounting Review*, 61(2): 288–301.

Peel, M.J. and Peel, D.A. (1987). "Some further empirical evidence on predicting private company failure." *Accounting and Business Research*, 18(69): 57–66.

Rees, B. (1990). *Financial Analysis*. London: Prentice-Hall.

Ross, S.A., Westerfield, R.W., and Jaffe, J.F. (2002). *Corporate Finance*, 6th edn. New York: McGraw-Hill.

Shailer, G. (1989). "The predictability of small enterprise failures: evidence and issues." *International Small Business Journal*, 7(4): 54–58.

Shumway, T. (2001). "Forecasting bankruptcy more accurately: a simple hazard model." *Journal of Business*, 74(1): 101–124.

Storey, D.J., Keasey, K., Watson, R., and Wynarczyk, P. (1987). *The Performance of Small Firms*. Bromley: Croom-Helm.

Walker, I.E. (1992). *Buying a Company in Trouble: A Practical Guide*. Hants: Gower.

Whalen, G. (1991). "A proportional hazard model of bank failure: an examination of its usefulness as an early warning tool." *Economic Review*, First Quarter: 20–31.

Whittington, G. (1980). "Some basic properties of accounting ratios." *Journal of Business Finance and Accounting*, 7(2): 219–232.

Wood, D. and Piesse, J. (1988). "The information value of failure predictions in credit assessment." *Journal of Banking and Finance*, 12: 275–292.

Zavgren, C.V. (1985). "Assessing the vulnerability to failure of American industrial firms: a logistic analysis." *Journal of Business, Finance and Accounting*, 12(1): 19–45.

Zavgren, C.V. (1988). "The association between probabilities of bankruptcy and market responses – a test of market anticipation." *Journal of Business Finance and Accounting*, 15(1): 27–45.

Zmijewski, M.E. (1984). "Methodological issues related to the estimation of financial distress prediction models." *Journal of Accounting Research*, 22(Supplement): 59–82.

Chapter 23

RISK MANAGEMENT*

THOMAS S.Y.HO, *Thomas Ho Company, Ltd, USA*
SANG BIN LEE, *Hanyang University, Korea*

Abstract

Even though risk management is the quality control of finance to ensure the smooth functioning of the business model and the corporate model, this chapter takes a more focused approach to risk management. We begin by describing the methods to calculate risk measures. We then describe how these risk measures may be reported. Reporting provides feedback to the identification and measurements of risks. Reporting enables the risk management to monitor the enterprise risk exposures so that the firm has a built-in, self-correcting procedure that enables the enterprise to improve and adapt to changes. In other words, risk management is concerned with four different phases, which are risk measurement, risk reporting, risk monitoring, and risk management in a narrow sense. We focus on risk measurement by taking a numerical example. We explain three different methodologies for that purpose, and examine whether the measured risk is appropriate based on observed market data.

Keywords: value at risk; market risk; delta-normal methodology; delta-gamma methodology; volatility; component VaR; historical simulation; Monte Carlo simulation; back testing; risk reporting

In recent years, a subject called risk management quickly established an indispensable position in finance, which would not surprise us, because finance has studied how to deal with risk and we have experienced many catastrophic financial accidents resulting in much loss such as Orange County and Long Term Capital Management.

Risk management as a broad concept consists of four phases: risk measurement, risk reporting, risk monitoring, and risk management in a narrow sense. We will discuss the four phases one by one mainly focusing on risk measurement.

23.1. Risk Measurement

Risk measurement begins with identifying all the sources of risks, and how they behave in terms of the probability distribution, and how they are manifested. Often, these sources of risk are classified as market risk, credit risk, liquidity risk, and legal risk. More recently, there are operational risks and business risks.

23.1.1. Market Risk

Market risk is often defined as the losses that arise from the mark to market of the trading securities. These trading securities may be derivatives such as swaps, swaptions, caps, and floors. They can be securities such as stocks and bonds. Market risk is referred to as the potential loss of the portfolio due to market movements.

While this is the basic idea of the market risk, the measure of the "value" is a subject of concern. Market risk is concerned with the fall in the mark to market value. For an actively trading portfolio that is managed at a trading desk, the value is defined as the sell price of the portfolio at normal market conditions. For this reason, traders need to mark their portfolio at their bid price at the end of the trading day, the mark to market value. Traders often estimate these prices based on their discussions with counter-parties, or they can get the prices from market trading systems.

We need to extend the mark to market concept to determine the risk measure, which is the potential loss as measured by the "mark to market" approach.

23.1.2. Value at Risk (VaR)

To measure the risks, one widely used measure is the Value at Risk (VaR). So far, risk in finance has been measured depending on which securities we are concerned with. For example, beta and duration have been the risk measures for stocks and bonds, respectively. The problem with this approach is that we cannot compare the stock's risk with the bond's risk. To remedy this drawback, we need a unified measure for comparison purposes, which has prompted the birth of VaR risk measure. Value at Risk is a measure of potential loss at a level (99 percent or 95 percent confidence level) over a time horizon, say, 7 days. Specifically 95 percent-1-day-VaR is the dollar value such that the probability of a loss for 1 day exceeding this amount is equal to 5 percent. For example, consider a portfolio of $100 million equity. The annualized volatility of the returns is 20 percent. The VaR of the portfolio over 1 year is $46.527 million (i.e.100–53.473) and $32.8971 million (i.e.100–67.1029), for 99 percent or 95 percent confidence levels, respectively. If we imagine a normal distribution which has a mean of $100 million and a 20 percent standard deviation, the probabilities that the normally distributed variable has less than $53.473

million and $67.1029 million are 1 percent and 5 percent, respectively. In other words, the probability of exceeding the loss of $46.527 million over a 1-year period is 1 percent when the current portfolio value is $100 million, and the annualized volatility of the returns is 20 percent. Therefore, we have a loss exceeding $46.527 million only once out of 100 trials. A critical assumption to calculate VaR here is that the portfolio value follows a normal distribution, which is sometimes hard to accept.

The risk management of financial institutions measures this downside risk to detect potential loss in their portfolio. The measure of risk is often measured by the standard deviation or the volatility. A measure of variation is not sufficient because many securities exhibit a bias toward the upside (profit), as in an option, or the downside (loss), as in a high-yield bond, which is referred to as a skewed distribution, as compared to a symmetric distribution such as a normal distribution. These securities do not have their profits and losses evenly distributed around their mean. Therefore the variation as a statistic would not be able to capture the risk of a position. Volatility is a measure of variability, and may not correctly measure the potential significant losses of a risky position.

VaR has gained broad acceptance by regulators, investors, and management of firms in recent years because it is expressed in dollars, and consistently calculates the risk arising from the short or long positions and different securities. An advantage of expressing VaR in dollars is that we can compare or combine risk across different securities. For example, we have traditionally denoted risk of a stock by beta and risk of a bond by duration. However, if they have different units in measuring the stock and the bond, it is hard to compare the risk of the stock with that of the bond, which is not the case in VaR.

There are three main methodologies to calculate the VaR values: Delta-normal methods, Historical simulation, and the Monte Carlo simulation.

23.1.2.1. Delta-Normal Methodology

The delta-normal methodology assumes that all the risk sources follow normal distributions and the VaR is determined assuming that the small change of the risk source would lead to a directly proportional small change of the security's price over a certain time horizon.

VaR for single securities: Consider a stock. The delta-normal approach assumes that the stock price itself is the risk source and it follows a normal distribution. Therefore, the uncertainty of the stock value over a time horizon is simply the annual standard deviation of the stock volatility adjusted by a time factor. A critical value is used to specify the confidence level required by the VaR measure. Specifically, the VaR is given by:

$$\text{VaR} = \alpha \times \text{time factor} \times \text{volatility} \quad (23.1)$$

α is called the critical value, which determines the one-tail confidence level of standard normal distribution. Formally, α is the value such that the confidence level is equal to the probability that X is greater than α, where X is a random variable of a standard normal distribution.

Time factor is defined as $\sqrt{t}$, where t is the time horizon in measuring the VaR. The time-measurement unit of the time factor should be consistent with that of the volatility. For example, if the volatility is measured in years, t is also measured in years.

Volatility is the standard deviation of the stock measured in dollars over 1 year.

The problem for a portfolio of stocks is somewhat more complicated. In principle, we can use a large matrix of correlation of all the stock returns, and calculate the value. In practice, often this is too cumbersome. The reason for this is that, since we treat each stock as a different risk source, we have the same number of risk sources as that of the stocks constituting the portfolio. For example, if we have a portfolio consisting of 10 stocks, we have to estimate 10 variances and 45 co-variances. One way to circumvent it is to use the Capital Asset Pricing Model. Then the portfolio return distribution is given by:

$$E[R_P] = r_f + \beta_P(E[R_M] - r_f). \quad (23.2)$$

The distribution of the portfolio is therefore proportional to the market index by a beta. By using the CAPM, we have only one risk source regardless of the size of a portfolio, which makes it much simpler to calculate portfolio VaR.

The VaR calculation for bonds requires an extra step in the calculation. The risk sources for default-free bonds are interest rate risks. These risks, per se, do not directly measure the loss. In the case of stocks, the fall in stock price is the loss. But for bonds, we need to link the rise in interest rates to the loss in dollar terms.

By the definition of duration, we have the following equation

$$\Delta P = -\$\text{Duration} \times \Delta r, \quad (23.3)$$

where $Duration is the dollar duration defined as the product of the price and duration.

$$\$\text{Duration} = P \times \text{Duration}. \quad (23.4)$$

Δr is the uncertain change in interest rates over the time horizon for the VaR measure. We assume that this uncertain movement has a normal distribution with zero mean and standard deviation σ. The interest rate risk is described by a normal distribution. For the time being, we assume that the interest rate risk is modeled by the uncertain parallel movements of the spot-yield curve and the yield curve is flat at r.

Given these assumptions, it follows from Equation (23.3) that the price of the bond, or a bond position, has a normal distribution given by:

$$\widetilde{\Delta P} = -\$\text{Duration} \times \widetilde{\Delta r}$$

The means of calculating the critical value for a particular interval of a normal distribution is therefore given by:

$$\text{VaR(bond)} = \alpha \times \text{time factor} \times \$\text{Duration} \times \sigma \times r$$
$$\sigma = \text{SD}\left(\frac{\Delta r}{r}\right) \quad (23.5)$$

Since the standard deviation in Equation (23.5) is based on a proportional change of interest rates, we should multiply by r to get the standard deviation of a change of interest rates.

The above formula assumes that the spot-yield curve makes a parallel shift movement and is flat, because \$duration is derived based on the same assumptions. Further, the above formula assumes that the uncertain changes in interest rates follow a normal distribution, because we use the standard deviation to measure risk. More generally, we can assume that the yield curve movements are determined by n key rates $r(1), r(2), \ldots, r(n)$. These key rate uncertain movements are assumed to have a multivariate normal distribution over the time horizon t of the VaR measure with the variance–covariance Ω. Given this multiple risk factor model, the bond price uncertain value is a multivariate normal distribution given by:

$$\widetilde{\Delta P} = - \sum_{i=1}^{n} \$KRD(i) \, \widetilde{\Delta r}(i),$$

where $\$KRD(i)$ is the dollar key rate duration given by the $P \times KRD(i)$. $KRD(i)$ is the key rate duration. It is the bond price sensitivity to the ith key rate movement. Then it follows that the VaR of the bond is given by:

$$VaR(bond) = \alpha \times \text{time factor}$$
$$\times \left(\sum_{i=1}^{n} \sum_{j=1}^{n} \$KRD(i) \$KRD(j) \Omega_{ij} \right)^{0.5}, \quad (23.6)$$

where the dollar key rate durations of the bond are denoted by \$KRD. P is the bond price, or the value of the bond position. Ω_{ij} is the ith and jth entry of the variance–covariance matrix Ω, i.e. it is the covariance of the distribution of the ith and jth key rate movements. Here, we calculate the variance–covariance of key rates. Therefore, we do not have to multiply by r.

VaR for a Portfolio: Now, we are in the position to determine the VaR of a portfolio of these types of assets. Suppose the portfolio has n securities. Let P_i be the price of the ith security, which may be the bond price or a stock price. Let x_i be the number of the securities in the portfolio. Then the portfolio value is given by:

$$P = \sum_{i=1}^{n} x_i \cdot P_i. \quad (23.7)$$

The risk of the portfolio may be measured by the VaR of the portfolio value as defined by Equation (23.7). Let $\Delta \theta_i$ for $i = 1 \ldots n$ be the risk sources, with Ω the variance–covariance of these risks. Let $\$Duration(i)$ be the dollar duration (or sensitivity) of the portfolio to each risk source $\Delta \theta_i$. The portfolio uncertain value is given by:

$$\widetilde{\Delta P} = - \sum_{i=1}^{n} \$Duration(i) \, \widetilde{\Delta \theta}_i, \quad (23.8)$$

where P is the portfolio value. Following the above argument, the VaR of the portfolio is given by:

$$VaR(portfolio) = \alpha \times \text{time factor}$$
$$\times \left(\sum_{i=1}^{n} \sum_{j=1}^{n} \$Duration(i) \$Duration(j) \Omega_{ij} \right)^{0.5} \quad (23.9)$$

We can now calculate the contribution of risk for each risk source to the portfolio VaR. Let us define $VaR\beta_i$ (also called the component VaR) to the ith risk source θ_i to be:

$$VaR\beta_i(portfolio) = \alpha \times \text{time factor}$$
$$\times \sum_{j=1}^{n} \$Duration(i) \$Duration(j) \Omega_{ij}$$
$$\times \left(\sum_{i=1}^{n} \sum_{j=1}^{n} \$Duration(i) \$Duration(j) \Omega_{ij} \right)^{-0.5}$$

$VaR\beta_i$ is the contribution of risk by ith risk source to the VaR measure. It is clear from the definition that

$$\sum_{i=1}^{n} VaR\beta_i = VaR \quad (23.10)$$

This means the sum of the component VaR ($VaR\beta_i$) is equal to the VaR of the portfolio.

Since the risk sources are correlated with each other, we have to appropriately identify the effect of correlations and diversifications on the risks to measure the risk contribution of each risk source to the VaR of the portfolio. VaRβ_i is a way to isolate all these effects.

A Numerical Example: To calculate the VaR of a portfolio of three different stocks (GE, CITI, and HP), we calculate the daily rate of returns for each stock and estimate the variance–covariance matrix of the stocks' returns. The sample period is from January 3, 2001 to May 2, 2002. The number of total observations is 332. For the purpose of calculating VaR, we assume that the expected proportional changes in the stock prices over 1 day are equal to 0. To calculate the daily rates of return and the variance–covariance matrix, we use the following formulas:

$$r_{i,t} = \frac{S_{i,t} - S_{i,t-1}}{S_{i,t-1}}, \quad \forall i = \text{GE, CITI, and HP}$$

$$\bar{r}_i = 0$$

$$\sigma_i^2 = \frac{1}{m} \sum_{t=1}^{m} (r_{i,t} - \bar{r}_i)^2$$

$$\sigma_{i,j} = \frac{1}{m} \sum_{t=1}^{m} (r_{i,t} - \bar{r}_i)(r_{j,t} - \bar{r}_i),$$

where m is the number of days in the estimation period.

We first calculate the individual stock VaR, and then the stock portfolio VaR to measure the diversification effect. We assume the size of the portfolio position to be \$100 and the invested weights to be equal. Further, we assume that the significance level is 1 percent and the horizon period is 5 days.

First, we calculate the variance–covariance matrix assuming that the expected means are 0. From the variance–covariance matrix, we can get standard deviations of each individual stock as well as the standard deviation of the portfolio with equal weights. To get the standard deviation of the portfolio, we premultiply and postmultiply the variance–covariance matrix with the weight vector. The variance–covariance matrix $\mathbf{\Omega}$, the correlation

matrix $\mathbf{\Sigma}$ of three stocks, and the variance of the portfolio consisting of three stocks are given below.

$$\mathbf{\Omega} = \begin{pmatrix} 0.00060272 & 0.00038256 & 0.00034470 \\ 0.00038256 & 0.00047637 & 0.00032078 \\ 0.00034470 & 0.00032078 & 0.00126925 \end{pmatrix}$$

$$\mathbf{\Sigma} = \begin{pmatrix} 1.00000000 & 0.71396050 & 0.39410390 \\ 0.71396050 & 1.00000000 & 0.41253223 \\ 0.39410390 & 0.41253223 & 1.00000000 \end{pmatrix}$$

$$\mathbf{w}^{\mathrm{T}} = \left(\frac{1}{3}, \frac{1}{3}, \frac{1}{3} \right)$$

$$\sigma_{\text{Portfolio}}^2 = \mathbf{w}^{\mathrm{T}} \mathbf{\Omega} \mathbf{w} = (1/3 \; 1/3 \; 1/3)$$
$$\begin{pmatrix} 0.00060272 & 0.00038256 & 0.00034470 \\ 0.00038256 & 0.00047637 & 0.00032078 \\ 0.00034470 & 0.00032078 & 0.00126925 \end{pmatrix} \begin{pmatrix} 1/3 \\ 1/3 \\ 1/3 \end{pmatrix}$$
$$= 0.00049382$$

Second, since we have the equal weight portfolio, the amount that has been invested in each individual stock is 33.33 dollars. Furthermore, since the significance level is assumed to be 1 percent, $\alpha = 2.32635$.

The detailed derivation of the individual VaR as well as the portfolio **VaR** is given as follows.

$$\text{VaR}_i = \text{total invest} \times w_i \times \sigma_i \times \alpha \times \sqrt{\text{days}}$$

$$\text{VaR}_P = \text{total invest} \times \sigma_P \times \alpha \times \sqrt{\text{days}},$$

$$(23.11)$$

where

$$i = \{\text{GE, CITI, HP}\}$$

$$\sigma_P = \sqrt{\mathbf{w}^{\mathrm{T}} \mathbf{\Omega} \mathbf{w}}$$

$$= \sqrt{\sum_i \sum_j \omega_i \omega_j \sigma_{i,j}}$$

$$= \sqrt{\sum_i \omega_i^2 \sigma_i^2 + 2 \sum_i \sum_{j \neq i} \omega_i \omega_j \sigma_{i,j}}$$

By plugging the appropriate numbers in Equation (23.11), we can get three individual stock VaRs and the portfolio VaR.

$$\text{VaR}_{\text{GE}} = \text{total invest} \times w_{\text{GE}} \times \sigma_{\text{GE}} \times \alpha$$
$$\times \sqrt{\text{days}} = \frac{100}{3} \times \sqrt{0.00060272}$$
$$\times 2.32635 \times \sqrt{5} = 4.25693$$

$$\text{VaR}_{\text{CITI}} = \text{total invest} \times w_{\text{CITI}} \times \sigma_{\text{CITI}} \times \alpha$$
$$\times \sqrt{\text{days}} = \frac{100}{3} \times \sqrt{0.00047637}$$
$$\times 2.32635 \times \sqrt{5} = 3.78451$$

$$\text{VaR}_{\text{HP}} = \text{total invest} \times w_{\text{HP}} \times \sigma_{\text{HP}} \times \alpha$$
$$\times \sqrt{\text{days}} = \frac{100}{3} \times \sqrt{0.00126925}$$
$$\times 2.32635 \times \sqrt{5} = 6.17749$$

$$\text{VaR}_P = \text{total invest} \times \sigma_P \times \alpha \times \sqrt{\text{days}} = 100$$
$$\times \sqrt{0.00049382} \times 2.32635$$
$$\times \sqrt{5} = 11.55968$$

Once we have calculated the VaRs, we are concerned with how much each individual stock contributes to the portfolio risk. To this end, we calculate the betas of individual stocks. We define the beta of the stock here taking the portfolio as "market portfolio" of the CAPM. The method of determining the beta (the systematic risk) of a stock within the portfolio is given by the formula below. The numerator is the covariance of each stock with the market portfolio and the denominator is the variance of the market portfolio, which is the variance of the portfolio consisting of GE, CITI and HP.

$$\text{Beta}_{\text{Delta-Normal Method}} = \begin{pmatrix} \beta_{\text{GE}} \\ \beta_{\text{CITI}} \\ \beta_{\text{HP}} \end{pmatrix} = \frac{\Omega w}{\mathbf{w}^{\mathbf{T}} \Omega \mathbf{w}}$$

$$= \frac{\Omega \cdot \begin{pmatrix} 1/3 \\ 1/3 \\ 1/3 \end{pmatrix}}{(1/3 \ 1/3 \ 1/3) \cdot \Omega \cdot \begin{pmatrix} 1/3 \\ 1/3 \\ 1/3 \end{pmatrix}}$$

$$= \begin{pmatrix} 0.89775 \\ 0.79631 \\ 1.30595 \end{pmatrix}.$$

Component VaR is a product of three parts, which are weight ω_i, β_i, and portfolio VaR. The reason to get the β is that β represents the systematic risk or the marginal contribution of each stock's risk to the portfolio risk.

$$\text{Component VaR}_i = \omega_i \times \beta_i \times \text{VaR}_{\text{Portfolio}} \ \forall i$$
$$= \text{GE, CITI, and HP}$$

For example, the GE component VaR is that

$$\text{Component VaR}_{\text{GE}} = \omega_{\text{GE}} \times \beta_{\text{GE}} \times \text{VaR}_{\text{Portfolio}}$$
$$= \frac{1}{3} \times 0.89775 \times 11.55968$$
$$= 3.45922$$

Since the component VaR is the individual stock's contribution to the portfolio risk, the sum of three component VaRs should be the portfolio VaR. Mathematically, since the sum of each beta multiplied by its corresponding weight is equal to 1, the sum of three component VaRs should be the portfolio VaR.

The final results have been summarized in Table 23.1.

Portfolio effect is defined as the individual stock VaR net of the component VaR, measuring the effect of diversification on the risk of the individual asset risk. When there are many uncorrelated assets in the portfolio, then portfolio effect can be significant. The portfolio effect can also measure the hedging effect within the portfolio if one asset has a negative correlation to another asset.

The advantage of the methodology above is its simplicity; it exploits the properties of a normal

Table 23.1. VaR calculation output by delta-normal method

5-day VaR	GE	CITI	HP	Total
Weight	1/3	1/3	1/3	1
Individual stock VaR	4.25693	3.78451	6.17749	14.21893
Portfolio VaR	–	–	–	11.55968
Beta	0.89775	0.79631	1.30595	–
Beta*Weight	0.29925	0.26544	0.43532	1
Component VaR	3.45922	3.06835	5.03212	11.55968
Portfolio Effects	0.79771	0.71616	1.14537	2.65924

distribution. Specifically, we can use the additive property of the distribution. In doing so, we can build up the VaR of a portfolio from each single security and we can aggregate the information. Finally, we can calculate the contribution of the risk of each security to the portfolio risks. However, the simplicity comes with a cost.

The main drawback is that the normality assumption precludes other distributions that have skewed distribution as the main source of risks. For example, a short position of a call or put option would be misleading with the use of the delta-normal methodology, because the distribution is not normal and the potential losses are much higher than assuming the normal distribution when the time horizon is not sufficiently short. One way to ameliorate the problem is to extend the methodology to incorporate skewness in the measurement. It is important to point out that if security returns are highly skewed (e.g. out of the money options), there will be significant model risks in valuing the securities. In those situations, the error from a delta-normal methodology is only part of the error in the estimation. For this reason, in practice, those securities usually have to be analyzed separately in more detail and they require specific methodologies in managing their risks. Another problem of the normality assumption is the fat-tail effect of stocks, where there is a significant probability for the stock to realize high or low returns. Kurtosis of the stock returns, a measure of the fatness of the tails, is empirically significant.

Another drawback of the delta-normal method comes from the assumption that the risk is measured by the first derivative called delta. When we cannot adequately measure the risk by the first derivative, we should extend to the second deri-vative called gamma to measure the risk. This method is called the delta-gamma methodology.

However, for the most part, delta-normal does provide a measure of risks enabling risk managers to evaluate the risks of a portfolio.

23.1.4. Historical Simulation Methodology
Historical simulation is another VaR measuring methodology. The method uses a historical period of observed movement of the risk sources: stock returns, interest rate shifts, and foreign exchange rate changes. It simulates the portfolio returns over that period, as if the portfolio were held unchanged over that period of time. The VaR of the portfolio returns is then computed.

This is a simple methodology, particularly for trading desks. The reason is that for most trading desks; the trading books have to be marked to market daily. The modeling technologies are in place to value the securities and aggregate the reports. Simulating the historical scenarios is a fairly straightforward procedure. As in Figure 23.1, we sort the historical return data in an increasing order and locate $x$percent percentile to calculate VaR.

Using the historical return data set of each of the stocks, in Table 23.2, we can find α percent percentile value of their daily returns to calculate the VaR of each stock and portfolio. We also use their historical returns to determine their variance and covariance matrix. With the estimation of this variance and covariance matrix, we can then determine the securities's beta and the component VaR[1]. The results are summarized in Table 23.3.

In comparing Tables 23.1 and 23.3, the results suggest that the two methods do not provide the same VaR numbers, but they are reasonably close

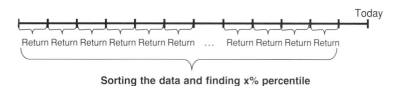

Sorting the data and finding x% percentile

Figure 23.1. The historical simulation methodology

Table 23.2. Historical return data set

Date	(1) GE	(2) CITI	(3) HP	(1)+(2)+(3) Portfolio
2001,01,03	3.0933	2.9307	4.1983	10.2224
2001,01,04	0.1743	0.4550	0.5578	1.1872
2001,01,05	−0.5202	−1.1971	−3.8599	−5.5771
2001,01,08	−1.2330	−0.1925	0.8165	−0.6090
2001,10,29	−1.2431	−1.4958	−0.8403	−3.5793
2001,10,30	−0.9707	−0.6106	−0.8238	−2.4051
2001,10,31	0.0642	−0.0220	−0.2750	−0.2327
2002,04,30	0.7563	0.3265	0.2554	1.3382
2002,05,01	0.1585	0.5081	−0.4678	0.1987
2002,05,02	−0.1052	0.7507	0.4547	1.1003
1% percentile	−4.88495	−4.05485	−6.60260	−12.47086
1% VaR	4.88495	4.05485	6.60260	12.47086[a]

[a]12.47086 is not equal to the sum of three numbers (4.88495, 4.05485, 6.60260) because of the diversification effect.

Table 23.3. VaR calculation output by historical simulation method

5-day VaR	GE	CITI	HP	Total
Weight	1/3	1/3	1/3	1
Individual stock VaR	4.88495	4.05485	6.60260	15.54241
Portfolio VaR	–	–	–	12.47086
Beta	0.89775	0.79631	1.30595	–
Beta*Weight	0.29925	0.26544	0.43532	1
Component VaR	3.73188	3.31021	5.42877	12.47086
Portfolio Effects	1.15306	0.74465	1.17384	3.07155

within 10 percent error. One source of error can be the normality distribution assumption. To the extent that in the sample period, the stock returns exhibited significant fat-tail behavior, then the discrepancies between the two measures can be significant.

23.1.5. Monte Carlo Simulation Methodology

The Monte Carlo simulation refers to a methodology, where we randomly generate many scenarios and calculate the VaR of the portfolio. The method is similar to the historical simulation method, but the difference is that we now simulate many scenarios using a forward-looking estimate of volatilities and not the historical volatilities over a period of time.

We use a multivariate normal distribution with the given variance–covariance matrix based on the delta-normal method and zero means of the stocks to simulate the stock returns 100,000 times. These returns are then used to calculate the VaR of each stock and the VaR of the portfolio. The variance–covariance matrix of stock returns generated by Monte Carlo simulation is as follows:

$$\Omega_{\text{Monte Carlo}} = \begin{pmatrix} 0.00139246 & 0.00130640 & 0.00156568 \\ 0.00130640 & 0.00124862 & 0.00148949 \\ 0.00156568 & 0.00148949 & 0.00207135 \end{pmatrix}$$

$$\begin{aligned}
\text{Monte Carlo VaR}_{\text{GE}} &= 0.01 \text{ Percentile of Scenario}_{\text{GE}} \\
&\quad \times \text{total invest} \times w_{\text{GE}} \times \sqrt{\text{day}} \\
&= 0.08577711 \times \frac{100}{3} \times \sqrt{5} \\
&= 6.39345
\end{aligned}$$

$$\begin{aligned}
\text{Monte Carlo VaR}_{\text{CITI}} &= 0.01 \text{ Percentile of Scenario}_{\text{CITI}} \\
&\quad \times \text{total invest} \times w_{\text{CITI}} \times \sqrt{\text{day}} \\
&= 0.08126864 \times \frac{100}{3} \times \sqrt{5} \\
&= 6.05741
\end{aligned}$$

$$\begin{aligned}
\text{Monte Carlo VaR}_{\text{HP}} &= 0.01 \text{ Percentile of Scenario}_{\text{HP}} \\
&\quad \times \text{total invest} \times w_{\text{HP}} \times \sqrt{\text{day}} \\
&= 0.11359961 \times \frac{100}{3} \times \sqrt{5} \\
&= 8.46722
\end{aligned}$$

$$\begin{aligned}
\text{Monte Carlo VaR}_P &= 0.01 \text{ Percentile of Scenario}_P \\
&\quad \times \text{total invest} \times \sqrt{\text{day}} \\
&= 0.09362381 \times 100 \times \sqrt{5} \\
&= 20.93492.
\end{aligned}$$

Using the variance and covariance matrix of the stocks, which we can calculate from the randomly generated returns, we can then determine the component VaR as we have done in the examples above. VaR by the Monte Carlo Simulation Method is given in Table 23.4.

Table 23.4. VaR calculation output by Monte Carlo simulation method

5-day VaR	GE	CITI	HP	Total
Weight	1/3	1/3	1/3	1
Individual stock VaR	6.39345	6.05741	8.46722	20.91807
Portfolio VaR	–	–	–	20.93492
Beta	0.95222	0.90309	1.14469	–
Beta*Weight	0.31741	0.30103	0.38156	1
Component VaR	6.64489	6.30204	7.98799	20.93492
Portfolio Effects	−0.25144	−0.24464	0.47923	−0.01685

The results show that the VaR numbers are similar in all three approaches. This is not too surprising, since the three examples use the same model assumptions: the variance–covariance matrix of the stocks. Their differences result from the use of normality in the delta-normal and the Monte Carlo simulation approaches, whereas the historical simulation is based on the historical behavior of the stocks. Note that while we use the assumption of multivariate normal distributions of the stock in the Monte Carlo example here, in general this assumption is not required, and we can use a multivariate distribution that models the actual stock returns behavior best. Another source of error in this comparison is the model risks. The number of trials in both the historical simulation and the Monte Carlo simulations may not be sufficient for the results to converge to the underlying variances of the stocks.

23.2. Risk Reporting

The sections above describe the measurement of VaR. We can now report the risk exposure and we illustrate it with a bank's balance sheet below[2]. VaR is defined in this report with 99 percent confidence level over a 1-month time horizon.

The report shows the market value (or the fair value) of each item on a bank's balance sheet and the VaR value of each item. VaR/MV is the ratio of VaR to the market value, measuring the risk per dollar, and $VaR\beta_i$ is the marginal risk of each item to the VaR of the bank (the VaR of the equity).

Table 23.5. VaR table: Aggregation of risks to equity ($million.)

Items	Market value	VaR	VaR/MV (%)	Component VaR
Prime rate loans	3,286	11.31	0.34	4.5
Base rate loans	2,170	4.92	0.23	−4.3
Variable rate mortgages	625	5.47	0.87	−4.8
Fixed-rate loans	1,231	30.49	2.50	−22.5
Bonds	2,854	33.46	1.17	−28.2
Base-rate time deposits	1,959	5.83	0.30	3.24
Prime-rate time deposits	289	1.56	0.54	0.98
Fixed-rate time deposits	443	11.69	2.64	9.55
Demand deposits	5,250	44.62	0.85	36.89
Long-term market funding	1,146	19.85	1.73	15.16
Equity	1,078	10.59	0.98	10.59

Note that the sum of the VaR values of all the items is not the same as the VaR of the equity. This is because the sum of the VaR values does not take diversification or hedging effects into account. However, the sum of the component VaR is equal to the VaR of the equity, because the component VaR has already reflected the diversification effect or hedging effects. VaR/MV measures the risk of each item per dollar. The results show that the fixed rate loans and the fixed rate time deposits are the most risky with the VaR per dollar being 2.5 percent and 2.64 percent respectively.

The results of the component VaR show that the demand deposit, while not the most risky item on the balance sheet, contributes much of the risk to equity. All the items on the asset side of the balance sheet (except for the prime rate loans) become hedging instruments to the demand deposit position.

One application of this overview of risks at the aggregated and disaggregated level is that we can identify the "natural hedges" in the portfolio. The risk contribution can be negative. This occurs when there is one position of stocks or bonds that is the main risk contributor. Then any security that is negatively correlated with that position would lower the portfolio total risk. The report will show that the risk contribution is negative, and that security is considered to offer a natural hedge to the portfolio. This methodology can extend from a portfolio of securities to a portfolio of business units. These units may be trading desks, a fund of funds, or multiple strategies of a hedge fund.

23.3. Risk Monitoring: *Back testing*[3]

The purpose of the back testing is to see whether the methods to calculate VaR are appropriate in the sense that the actual maximum loss has exceeded the predetermined VaR within an expected margin. The expected margin depends on which significance level we select when we calculate the VaR.

The basic idea behind the back test is to compare the actual days when the actual loss exceeds the VaR with the expected days, based on the significance level. We calculate the expected number of VaR violation days and actual VaR violation days.

23.4. Risk Management

In the previous sections, we have discussed the risk measurement, reporting, and monitoring. Now, we discuss the actions that we can take in managing the risks.

Much of the impetus of risk management started in the aftermath of the series of financial debacles for some funds, banks, and municipalities. In a few years, much progress has been made in research and development. More financial institutions have put in place a risk management team and technologies, including VaR calculations for the trading desks and the firm's balance sheets.

In reviewing the methodologies and technologies developed in these years, one cannot help noticing that most risk management measures and techniques focus on banks and trading floors, in particular. These management techniques are

precise about the risk distributions and the characteristics of each security.

Risk management can increase shareholders' value if the risk management can reduce transaction costs, taxes, or affect investment decisions. With real options, the cost of capital can change, the strategic investments can be affected by default and other factors, and the firm value can be affected.

NOTES

1. Since we use the same stock prices as the delta-normal method, we have the same variance–covariance matrix, which means that we have the same betas.
2. The example is taken from Thomas S.Y. Ho, Allen Abrahamson, and Mark Abbott 1996 "Value at Risk of a Bank's Balance Sheet," *International Journal of Theoretical and Applied Finance*, vol. 2, no. 1, January 1999.
3. Jorion, P., 2001, *Value at Risk*, 2nd edition, McGraw Hill. "For more information, see"
4. 12.47086 is not equal to the sum of three numbers (4.88495, 4.05485, 6.60260) because of diversification effect.

BIBLIOGRAPHY

Bruce, M.C. and Fabozzi, F.J. (1999). "Derivatives and risk management." *The Journal of Portfolio Management*, Special Theme: Derivatives and Risk Management, 16–27.
Chow, G. and Kritzman, M. (2002). "Value at risk portfolio with short positions." *The Journal of Portfolio Management*, 28(3): 73–81.
Ho, Thomas S.Y. and Lee, S.B. (2004). *The Oxford Guide to financial Modeling*. Oxford University Press: New York.
Jorion, P. (2001). *Value at Risk*. McGraw Hill. 2nd edn.
Kupiec, P.H. (1998). "Stress testing in a value at risk framework." *The Journal of Derivatives*, 6(1): 7–24.
Smith, C.W. and Smithson, C. (1998). "Strategic Risk Management," in Donald Chew, Jr (ed) *The New Corporate Finance: Where Theory Meets Practice*, 2nd edn. Irwin/McGraw-Hill: Boston. pp. 460–477.

Chapter 24

TERM STRUCTURE: INTEREST RATE MODELS*

THOMAS S.Y. HO, *Thomas Ho Company, Ltd, USA*
SANG BIN LEE, *Hanyang University, Korea*

Abstract

Interest movement models are important to financial modeling because they can be used for valuing any financial instruments whose values are affected by interest rate movements. Specifically, we can classify the interest rate movement models into two categories: equilibrium models and no-arbitrage models. The equilibrium models emphasize the equilibrium concept. However, the no-arbitrage models argue that the term-structure movements should satisfy the no-arbitrage condition. The arbitrage-free interest rate model is an extension of the Black–Scholes model to value interest rate derivatives. The model valuation is assured to be consistent with the observed yield curve in valuing interest rate derivatives and providing accurate pricing of interest rate contingent claims. Therefore, it is widely used for portfolio management and other capital market activities.

Keywords: lognormal versus normal movements; mean reversion; interest correlation; term structure volatility; Cox, Ingersoll and Ross model; Vasicek model; Brennan and Schwartz two-factor model; Ho and Lee model; Black, Derman, and Toy model; Hull and White model

24.1. Introduction

There are many examples of interest rate derivatives that are actively traded in over-the-counter markets and in organized exchanges. Caps, floors, Treasury bond options, Treasury bond futures options, Euro-dollar futures options, and swaption are just some examples of this important class of derivatives in our financial markets. They are classified as "interest rate derivatives" because their stochastic movements are directly related to the interest rate movements in a way that is analogous to the stock option price that moves in step with the underlying stock price.

We first present an empirical analysis of historical yield curve movements, which conveys its relationship to interest rate models. Then we provide an overview of the interest rate models.

24.2. Interest Rate Movements: Historical Experiences

Interest rate movements refer to the uncertain movements of the Treasury spot yield curve. Each STRIPS bond is considered a security. When the daily closing price is reported, the bond's yield-to-maturity can be calculated. The observed Treasury

spot yield curve is the scattered plot of the yield to
maturity against the maturity for all the STRIPS
bonds. Since the spot yield curve is a representation of the time value of money, and the time value
of money is related to the time-to-horizon in a
continuous fashion, the scattered plots should be
a continuous curve. Hence, we call the scattered
plot a yield curve.

What are the dynamics of the spot yield curve?
Let us consider the behavior of spot yield curve
movements in relation to interest rate levels, historically. The monthly spot yield curves from the
beginning of 1994 until the end of 2001 are
depicted in the figure below.

As Figure 24.1 shows, the spot yield curves can
take on a number of shapes. When the yields of the
bonds increase with the bonds' maturities, the yield
curve is said to be upward sloping. Conversely,
when the yield decreases with maturity, the spot
curve is called downward sloping. Although not
shown in Figure 24.1, the early 1980s displayed a
yield curve that was downward sloping. In 1998,
the yield curve was level or flat. In the early part of
2001, the yield curve was humped, with the yields
reaching the peak at the one-year maturity. Historically, the spot yield curve has changed its shape
as well as the level continually.

The yield curve movement is concerned with the
change of the yield curve shape over a relatively

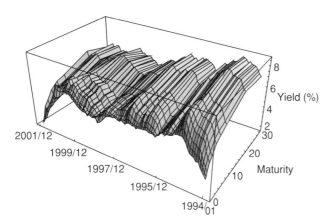

Figure 24.1. A time-series diagram of monthly
spot yield curve movements (1994.01 ∼ 2001.12). *Data
Source*: http://www.economagic.com/

short time interval, say, one month. Describing
yield curve movements is slightly more complicated than describing a stock movement. To describe the movement of stocks, we can decompose
the stock movement into two parts: the expected
drift or expected returns and the uncertain movement. The model is represented by:

$$dS = \mu S dt + \sigma S dZ \qquad (24.1)$$

where dS represents a small movement for a short
time interval dt. μ is called the instantaneous returns of the stock, σ is the instantaneous standard
deviation (or volatility) of the stock. dZ represents
a small uncertain movement specified by a normal
distribution. The mean and the standard deviation
of the normal distribution is 0 and $\sqrt{dt}$, respectively. The first term is called the drift term. It
represents the expected movement of the stock
price. If the first term is zero, then the future
stock price is *expected* to remain the same as the
present observed price. Of course, the realized
stock price in the future can deviate from the initial
stock price because of the uncertain stock price
movement specified by the second term. The random term dZ can be viewed as a unit of risk, a
normal distribution over an (infinitely) short time
interval. The coefficient of the dZ term represents
the volatility of the process. If this coefficient is
zero, then the process has no risk, and the stock
price movement has no uncertainty.

But to specify the movement of the yield curve,
in a way that is similar to Equation (24.1), is more
problematic. Since a yield curve is determined by
all the U.S. STRIPS bonds, the movement of the
yield curve should be represented by the movements of all the bond prices. But the movements
of all the bond prices are not independent of each
other. They have to be correlated. The following
empirical evidence may suggest how the yield curve
movements may be best specified.

24.2.1. Lognormal Versus Normal Movements

The movements (often referred to as the *dynamics*)
of each interest rate of the spot yield curve can be

specified as we have done for a stock. We can rewrite Equation (24.1), replacing the stock price with a rate that is the yield to maturity of a zero coupon bond of a specific maturity "t". Thus we have:

$$dr = \mu(r,t)rdt + r\sigma dZ \qquad (24.2)$$

When a t year rate is assumed to follow the process specified by Equation (24.2), we say that the interest rate follows a *lognormal process* and Equation (24.2) is called a *lognormal model*. In comparing Equation (24.2) with Equation (24.1), note that the drift term of the interest rate model is any function of the short-term interest rate r and time, while the lognormal model for stock tends to assume that the instantaneous stock return is a constant number. Therefore, the research literature of interest rate models has somewhat abused the language in calling Equation (24.2) a lognormal model. The important point is that, in a lognormal process, the volatility term is proportional to the interest rate level $r(t)$. When the interest rate level is high, we experience high interest rate volatility. When the interest rate level is low, we experience low interest rate volatility.

There is an alternative specification of the interest rate process, which research literature calls the *normal process*. In the normal process, the volatility is independent of the interest rate level, and it is given below:

$$dr = \mu(r,t)dt + \sigma dz \qquad (24.3)$$

Equation (24.3) is called the *normal model*. Note that the distinction made between the lognormal model and the normal model depends only on the volatility term and not on the drift term. For a normal model, the interest rate fluctuates with a volatility independent of the interest rate level over a short time interval. For a lognormal model, the interest rate has a volatility related to the interest rate level, in particular, when the volatility becomes arbitrarily small as interest rate level approaches zero. This way, the interest rates can never become negative. And a lognormal process is written as:

$$\frac{dr}{r} = \mu(r,t)dt + \sigma dZ \qquad (24.3a)$$

Based on historical observations, the yield curve movements have been shown to be both normal and lognormal depending on the interest rate levels. Which model is more appropriate to describe interest rate movements, the normal or lognormal model? We need to evaluate the model from an empirical perspective. Using U.S. historical interest rates, the squared change of the interest rate over a one-month period could be plotted against the interest rate level. Then we can see that the interest rate volatility has no relationship between the interest rate levels. If there were a positive relationship, we would see the higher volatility values related to higher interest rates. This result is consistent with Cheyette (1997), where he shows that the positive correlation between the interest rate volatility and the interest rate level is weak when the interest rate level is below 10 percent. However, when interest rate level was high in the late 1970s and early 1980s, the interest rate volatility was also high then, showing positive correlations only during that period.

24.2.2. Interest Rate Correlations

We have discussed the dynamics of interest rates. Now, let us consider the co-movements of interest rates. Do interest rates move together in steps, such that they all rise or fall together?

While the yield curve in principle can take many shapes historically, all the interest rates along the yield curve are positively correlated. But the interest rates do not shift by the same amount. The co-movements of the interest rates can be investigated by evaluating the correlations of the interest rates, as presented in Table 24.1.

The results show that all the correlations are positive, which suggests that all the interest rates tend to move in the same direction. The long rates, which are the interest rates with terms over 10 years, are highly correlated, meaning that the segment of the yield curve from a 10- to 30-year range

Table 24.1. Correlation matrix of the interest rates

	0.25	0.5	1	2	3	5	7	10	20	30
0.25	1.000	0.936	0.837	0.701	0.630	0.533	0.443	0.377	0.087	0.083
0.5	0.936	1.000	0.938	0.832	0.770	0.675	0.587	0.509	0.224	0.154
1	0.837	0.938	1.000	0.940	0.895	0.816	0.731	0.654	0.379	0.291
2	0.701	0.832	0.940	1.000	0.989	0.950	0.898	0.832	0.573	0.426
3	0.630	0.770	0.895	0.989	1.000	0.980	0.945	0.887	0.649	0.493
5	0.533	0.675	0.816	0.950	0.980	1.000	0.982	0.946	0.736	0.595
7	0.443	0.587	0.731	0.898	0.945	0.982	1.000	0.976	0.821	0.670
10	0.377	0.509	0.654	0.832	0.887	0.946	0.976	1.000	0.863	0.750
20	0.087	0.224	0.379	0.573	0.649	0.736	0.821	0.863	1.000	0.867
30	0.083	0.154	0.291	0.426	0.493	0.595	0.670	0.750	0.867	1.000

tends to move up and down together. The interest rates that are closer together along the yield curve have higher correlations.

24.2.3. Term Structure of Volatilities

Interest rate volatility is not the same for all interest rates along the yield curve. By convention, based on the lognormal model, the uncertainty of an interest rate is measured by the annualized standard deviation of the proportional change in a bond yield over a time interval (dt). For example, if the time interval is a one-month period, then dt equals 1/12 year. This measure is called the interest rate volatility and it is denoted by $\sigma(t,T)$, the volatility of the T-th year rate at time t. More precisely, the volatility is the standard deviation of the proportional change in rate over a short time interval, and it is given by:

$$\sigma(t,T) = Std\left(\frac{\Delta r(t,T)}{r(t,T)}\right) / \sqrt{\Delta t} \qquad (24.4)$$

where $r(t, T)$ is the yield-to-maturity of the zero-coupon bond with time-to-maturity T at time t and Std.($\cdot$) is a standard deviation over dt. We can relate Equation (24.4) to (24.3a) by the following algebraic manipulations. For a small time step, Equation (24.3a) can be written as:

$$\frac{\Delta r(t,T)}{r(t,T)} \cong \mu\Delta t + \sigma(t,T)\Delta Z$$

For sufficiently small Δt, we have:

$$\sigma\left(\frac{\Delta r(t,T)}{r(t,T)}\right) \cong \sigma(t,T)\sqrt{\Delta t}$$

Rearranging the terms, we can express σ as Equation (24.4) requires. Similarly, based on the normal model, the term structure of volatilities is given by

$$\sigma(t,T) = \sigma(\Delta r(t,T)) / \sqrt{\Delta t} \qquad (24.5)$$

The relationship of the volatilities with respect to the maturity is called *the term structure of volatilities*. The interest rate volatilities can be estimated using historical monthly data ($\Delta t = 1/12$). Below is the standard deviation of the rates for 0.25, 0.5, 1, 2, 3, 5, 7, 10, 20, 30 years.

The historical term structure of volatilities shows that the short-term rates tend to have higher volatilities than the long-term rates, falling from

Table 24.2. Historical term structure of volatilities; $\sigma(\Delta r(t)/r(t)) \cdot \sqrt{12}$

0.25	0.5	1	2	3	5	7	10	20	30
0.1906	0.1908	0.1872	0.1891	0.1794	0.1632	0.1487	0.1402	0.1076	0.1137

19.06 percent for the 0.25-year rate to 11.37 percent for the 30-year rate. The empirical results suggest that we cannot think of interest rate volatility as one number. The volatility has to depend on the term of the interest rate in question.

24.2.4. Mean Reversion

Thus far the discussion focuses on the volatility term of the dynamics of the interest rates. Now we investigate the drift term of interest rate movements. Research tends to argue that the yield curve cannot follow a random walk like a stock, as in Equation (24.1). The yields of the Treasury bonds cannot rise and fall with the expected drift, yet to be constant or at a certain fixed proportion to the interest rate level. Since the nominal interest rate, which is what we are concerned with here, is decomposed into the real interest rate and the expected inflation rate as stated in the Fisher equation, the movements of the nominal rates can be analyzed by considering the movements of the real rates and the inflation rate. One may argue that the real rate cannot follow a random walk because the real rate is related to all the individuals' time value of money in real terms. We tend to think the real interest rate is quite stable and that the real rate does not follow a random walk like a stock. To the extent that we believe the government seeks to control the inflation rate of an economy, the inflation rate cannot follow a random walk either. Therefore, we cannot assume that the (nominal) interest rate follows a random walk.

One may conclude that the interest rates tend to fall when the interest rates are high. Conversely, the interest rates tend to rise when interest rates are low. This is a somewhat imprecise description of a yield curve behavior, but we will provide a more precise description of this behavior later in the chapter, where we will provide alternative interest rate models in specifying this behavior. Research literature calls the dynamics that describe this behavior of interest rates a *mean reversion process*.

24.3. Equilibrium Models

Interest rate models seek to specify the interest rate movements such that we can develop a pricing methodology for an interest rate option.

24.3.1. The Cox-Ingersoll-Ross Model

The Cox, Ingersoll, and Ross (CIR) (1985) interest rate model is based on the productive processes of an economy. According to the model, every individual has to make the decision of consuming and investing with their limited capital. Investing in the productive process may lead to higher consumption in the following period, but it would sacrifice consumption today. The individual must determine the optimal trade off.

Now assume that the individual can also borrow and lend capital to another individual. Each person has to make economic choices. The interest rates reach the market equilibrium rate when no one needs to borrow or lend. The model can explain the interest rate movements in terms of an individual's preferences for investment and consumption as well as the risks and returns of the productive processes of the economy.

As a result of the analysis, the model can show how the short-term interest rate is related to the risks of the productive processes of the economy. Assuming that an individual requires a premium on the long-term rate (called term premium), the model continues to show how the short-term rate can determine the entire term structure of interest rates and the valuation of interest rate contingent claims.

The CIR model

$$dr = a(b - r)dt + \sigma\sqrt{r}\,dZ \qquad (24.6)$$

Cox et al. (1985) offer one of the earlier attempts at modeling interest rate movements. The proposed equilibrium model extends from economic principles of interest rates. It assumes mean reversion of interest rates. As we have discussed in the previous section, mean reversion of interest rates means that when the short-term interest rate (r) is higher than the long-run interest rates (b), the short-term rate would fall adjusting gradually to the long-run interest rate. Conversely, when the short-term interest rate is lower than the long-run interest rate, the short-term rate would rise gradually to the long-run interest rate. Note that the long-run interest rate is not the long-term interest rate. Long-term interest rates continuously make stochastic movements, while the long-run interest rate is a theoretical construct, hypothesizing that the economy has a constant long-run interest rate that interest rates converge to over time. The constant (a) determines the speed of this adjustment. If the constant (a) is high/low, the adjustment rate to the long-term rate would be high/low. The CIR model is a lognormal model since the interest rate volatility is positively related to the interest rate level. The classification of lognormal and normal is based on the uncertain movement of the interest rate over a short period of time as described above.

24.3.2. The Vasicek Model

The second model is called the Vasicek model (1977). This model is similar to the CIR model such that the model assumes that all interest rate contingent claims are based on short-term interest rates. The only difference is that the volatility is not assumed to be dependent on the interest rate level, and therefore it is a normal model.

The Vasicek model

$$dr = a(b - r)dt + \sigma dZ, \ (a > 0) \tag{24.7}$$

These models assume that there is only one source of risk and the models are referred to as *one-factor models*. This assumption implies that all bond prices depend on the movements of the rate (r), and that all bond prices move in tandem because of their dependence on one factor. At first, this assumption seems to be unrealistic because, as we have discussed, the yield curve seems to have many degrees of freedom in its movements, and therefore, how can we confine our yield curve to exhibit a one-factor movement?

24.3.3. The Brennan and Schwartz Two-Factor Model

For many purposes the one-factor model may not be appropriate to use as valuation models. An interest rate spread option is one example that a one-factor model may not be adequate to value. The values of some securities depend on the changing interest rate spreads between the two-year rate and the ten-year rate. The one-factor model assumes that all the interest rates that move in tandem would eliminate the risk of the spread between the two-year and the ten-year rates.

One extension asserts that all the bond prices of all maturities are generated by the short-term interest rate and a long-term rate – the long-term rate being the consol bond, which has no maturity and whose rate represents the long-term rate. Different versions of the two-factor models have been proposed in the following papers: Brennan and Schwartz (1982), Richard (1978), and Longstaff and Schwartz (1992). The Brennan and Schwartz model is given below:

$$\begin{aligned} dr &= a_1 + b_1(l - r)dt + r\sigma_1 dZ \\ dl &= l(a_2 + b_2 r + c_2 l)dt + l\sigma_2 dW \end{aligned} \tag{24.8}$$

where r is the short-term rate and l is the consol rate, and where a consol bond is a bond that pays a fixed coupon periodically into the future on a notional amount with no maturity. σ_1 and σ_2 are the standard deviations of the short-term and consol rate, respectively. dZ and dW represent the risks which may be correlated. All the parameters a_1, b_1 and a_2, b_2, c_2 are estimated from the historical data.

24.4. Arbitrage-Free Models

From the standard economic theory perspective, arbitrage-free modeling takes a departure from the CIR approach. The main point of the departure is sacrificing the economic theory in providing a model of the term structure of interest rates for a more accurate tool for valuing securities. Since the yield curve measures the agents' time value of money, the standard economic theory relates the interest rate movements to the dynamics of the economy. By way of contrast, arbitrage-free modeling assumes the yield curve follows a random movement much like the model used to describe a stock price movement. We can show that stock prices are assumed to be random and such an assumption does not incorporate the modeling of the agent's behavior and the economy.

24.4.1. The Ho–Lee model

Ho–Lee (1986) takes a different approach in modeling yield curve movements as compared to CIR and Vasicek. The arbitrage-free interest rate model uses the relative valuation concepts of the Black–Scholes model. This concept of relative valuation becomes a more complex concept to accept in the interest rate theory. Arbitrage-free modeling, like the Black–Scholes model, argues that the valuation of interest rate contingent claims is based solely on the yield curve. Economic research focuses on understanding the inferences made from the yield curve shape and its movements. The arbitrage-free model omits all these fundamental issues, apparently ignoring part of the economic theory behind interest rate research. The model assumes that the yield curve moves in a way that is consistent with the arbitrage-free condition.

Let us assume that there is a perfect capital market in a discrete time world. But this time, the binomial model is applied to the yield curve movements. We assume:

(1) Given the initial spot yield curve, the binomial lattice model requires that the yield curve can move only up and down.

(2) The one period interest rate volatility (the instantaneous volatility) is the same in all states of the world.

(3) There is no arbitrage opportunity in any state of the world (at any node point on the binomial lattice).

Assumption (1) is a technical construct of the risk model. Assumption (2) is made simply for this example. This assumption can be altered. Assumption (3) is the most interesting and important, called the "arbitrage-free condition". This arbitrage-free condition imposes constraints on the yield curve movements.

Thus far it seems that the extension is directly from the Black–Scholes model. But there is one problem: interest rate is not a security. We cannot buy and sell the one-period rate, though we can invest in the rate as the risk-free rate. Moreover, we cannot use the one-period rate to form an arbitrage argument as the Black–Scholes model does with stock, since the one-period rate is the risk-free rate, which obviously cannot be the "underlying asset" as well. In equity option, the stock is both the underlying instrument as well as the risk source or the risk driver.

A. Arbitrage-free hedging: The conceptual extension of the interest rate arbitrage-free model from the Black–Scholes model is to introduce the short-term interest rate as the risk source (or risk drive or state of the world). The Black–Scholes model's risk neutral argument requires an underlying security and the risk-free rate. However, in the interest rate model, the risk-free rate is the risk source. One condition we want to impose on the interest rate movement is arbitrage-free, that is, the interest rate movements do not allow any possible arbitrage opportunity in holding a portfolio of bonds at any time. Research shows that the interest rate movements are arbitrage-free if the following two conditions hold (Harrison and Kreps 1979): (1) all the bonds at any time and state of the world have a risk-neutral expected return of the prevailing one period rate and (2) any bond on the initial yield curve has the risk-neutral expected return of the one-period interest rate of the initial yield curve. That is, for an interest rate movement to be arbitrage-free, there must be a probability assigned to each node of a tree such that all interest rate contingent claims have an expected "risk-free return," which is the one-period rate. Note that this probability is the "risk neutral," where the market probability can be quite different.

B. Recombining condition: For tractability of the model, we require the discount function to recombine in a binomial lattice. This requirement is similar to the Black–Scholes model. Namely, the yield curve making an up movement and then a down movement must have the same value as the yield curve that makes a down movement and then an up movement. The difference between the yield curve movement and the stock movement is that we need the entire discount function (or the yield curve), and not just one bond price, to be identical when they recombine.

Under these restrictions, we can derive all the possible solutions. Let us consider the simplest solution for us to gain insight into these arbitrage-free models. Suppose the spot yield curve is flat. The spot curve can shift in a parallel fashion up and down. The binomial lattice represented is called "normal" (or arithmetic) because the parallel shift of the curve is a fixed amount and not a proportion of the value at the node. The movements of the discount function can be represented by the binomial movements.

The purpose of the arbitrage-free model is not to determine the yield curve from any economic theory or to hypothesize that the yield curve should take on particular shapes. The arbitrage-free model takes the yield curve (or the discount function) as given, and then hypothesizes the yield curve (or the discount function) movements in order to relatively value other interest rate derivatives. Using a dynamic hedging argument similar to the Black–Scholes model, the argument shows that we can assume the local expectation hypothesis to hold: the expected return of all the bonds over each time step is the risk-free rate, the one-period interest rate.

The Ho–Lee model is similar to the Vasicek model in that they are both normal models. The main difference of course is that the Ho–Lee model is specified to fit the yield curve, whereas the Vasicek model is developed to model the term structure of

interest rates. For this reason, the Vasicek model has the unobservable parameter called term premium, and the yield curve derived from the Vasicek model is not the same as the observed yield curve in general. Unlike the Vasicek model, the arbitrage-free interest rate model does not require the term premium, which cannot be directly observed. Instead, the arbitrage-free interest model only requires the given observed yield curve to value bonds. Hence, the theoretical bond prices would be the same as those observed.

Specifically, let the initial discount function, prices of zero-coupon bonds with a face value of $1 and with maturity T, be denoted by $P(T)$. The discount function $P(T)$, for example, may be observed from the STRIPS market. The yield of the bond $P(T)$ is denoted by $r(T)$. Let σ be the volatility of the interest rate. Interest rate volatility may be estimated from historical data. Then the price of a one-period bond $P_i^n(1)$ in time n and state i on the binomial lattice is given by:

$$P_i^n(1) = 2\left[\frac{P(n+1)}{P(n)}\right] \cdot \frac{\delta^i}{(1+\delta^n)} \tag{24.9}$$

where

$P_i^n(1) =$ a one-period bond price at time period n and state i,

$\delta = e^{-2r(1)\sigma}$,

$\sigma = \text{Std}\left(\frac{\Delta r(1)}{r(1)}\right).$

$-0.5 \ln \delta$ is the standard deviation of the change of the interest rate over each step size, while σ is the standard deviation of the proportional change of the interest rate.

While Equation (24.9) provides the bond price for one period at any state i and time n, the model also has closed form solutions for bonds with any maturity at any node point on the lattice.

The basic idea of the derivation is quite simple, though the manipulation of the algebra is somewhat laborious. To derive the model, we need to determine the close form solution for $P_i^n(T)$, the price of a T year zero-coupon bond, at time n and state i, such that, under the risk-neutral probability 0.5, the expected return of a zero-coupon bond with any maturity, at any node point, equals the one-period risk-free rate. That is:

$$P_i^n(T) = 0.5P_i^n(1)\{P_i^{n+1}(T-1) + P_{i+1}^{n+1}(T-1)\}$$
(24.10)

and we need to satisfy the initial observed yield curve condition:

$$P(T) = 0.5P(1)\{P_0^1(T-1) + P_1^1(T-1)\} \quad (24.11)$$

The above equations hold for any i, n, and T. Then the model is assumed to be arbitrage-free in that all bonds have the expected returns and the bond pricing consistent with the initial spot yield curve (or the discount function $P(T)$).

Equation (24.9) specifies the one-period bond price (and hence the one-period interest rate) on each node of the binomial lattice. For this reason, we say that the model is an interest rate model, as the model specifies how the short-term interest rate movements are projected into the future.

We can show that once we can specify the one-period rate on a lattice, we can determine all the bond prices at each node point on the lattice by a backward substitution procedure similar to that used by the Black–Scholes model.

We can define the one period rate to be

$$r_i^n(1) = -\ln P_i^n(1) \quad (24.12)$$

Using Equation (24.12), we see that the $r_i^n(1)$ can be expressed in three terms:

$$r_i^n(1) = \ln \frac{P(n)}{P(n+1)} + \ln\left(0.5(\delta^{-(n/2)} + \delta^{n/2})\right) + \left(\frac{n}{2} - i\right)\ln\delta$$
(24.13)

The first term is the one-period forward rate. That means that under the arbitrage-free interest rate movement model, we can think of the movement of the short-term rate as based on the forward rates. When there is no interest rate

uncertainty, ($\delta = 1$), both the second and third terms are equal to zero, and therefore, the one-period forward rates define the future spot rate arbitrage-free movements.

The last term specifies the cumulative upward and downward shifts of the rates after n periods. It is important to note that the sizes of all the shifts are the same, $\ln\delta$. That means the interest rate risk is independent of the level of interest rate, and the interest rate follows a normal distribution.

The second term is more difficult to explain as well as important. Let us consider a two-year bond. Assume that the yield curve is flat at 10 percent. The bond price is therefore 0.826446. After one year, the interest rate shifts to 20 percent or 0 percent with equal probability, just to exaggerate the problem a little bit. The expected price of the bond is now

$$0.916607\left(=\frac{1}{2}\times\left(\frac{1}{1.2}\right) + \frac{1}{2}\times\left(\frac{1}{1.0}\right)\right).$$

The expected return of the bond over the first year is $10.9095 (= (0.916607/0.826446) - 1)$. Therefore, even with a yield curve that is flat at 10 percent, the yield curve makes the shifts of up or down with the same probability, and the expected return of the bond exceeds 10 percent. The reason is straightforward: When the interest rate moves, the bond price does not move in step with the interest rates. This is simply a matter of bond arithmetic of the yield calculation, where the yield is in the denominator. We can show that bonds have positive convexity. When the yield curve makes a parallel shift up or down with equal probability, the expected bond price is higher than the prevailing bond price. After all, it is the positive convexity of a bond that motivates the barbell trades.

Since bonds have positive convexity, if the interest rate shifts up or down by the same amount (with equal probability) relative to the forward rate, the expected returns of the bonds would exceed the one-period interest rate. To maintain the arbitrage-free condition, such that the local

Maturity (years)	1	2	3	4	5
Yield (%)	6.0	7.0	8.0	9.5	10.0
Forward volatility (%)	15.0	14.0	13.0	11.0	

expectation hypothesis holds, we require the interest rate to shift higher in both up and down movements, so that the expected bonds' returns are equal to the one-period interest rate. That is, the interest rate movements must be adjusted upwards to correct for this convexity effect. This correction is the second term. Note that the second term, the convexity adjustment term, increases with the volatility as one may expect.

Thus far, we have discussed a set of interest rate models that exhibit normal distributions, which does not reflect the relationship between the interest rate uncertain movements and the interest rate levels. The lognormal model ensures that the interest rate uncertain movement increases or decreases with interest rate level. In particular, when interest rates continue to fall, the interest rate movement will continue to become smaller. In this case, the interest rates cannot become negative, while the normal model often has scenarios where the interest rates can become negative. An example of a lognormal model is the Black–Derman–Toy model.

24.4.2. The Black–Derman–Toy Model

The Black–Derman–Toy (BDT) (1990) model is a binomial lattice model. This model assumes that the short-term interest rate follows a lognormal process. The model does not have a closed form solution and can best be explained by describing the procedure to construct the short-term interest rate movements.

The Black–Derman–Toy model uses a recombining lattice to determine a lognormal interest rate model. Further, the model can take the initial term structure of interest rate as input, as well as the term structure of volatilities, as in the extended Ho–Lee model. The model is specified by an iterative construction that can be best illustrated with an example:

As inputs to the model, we begin with the given term structure of interest rates and term structure of forward volatilities:

On the lattice, initially we have a one-period rate, say, 6 percent. The lognormal model is determined by the following random walk at a node:

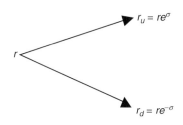

Note that, using the definition of r_u and r_d, we know

$$r_u = r_d e^{2\sigma}. \qquad (24.14)$$

Step 1. Construct the lowest short-term rate for each period in the lattice.

These rates are r, $r \cdot \exp[-\sigma(1)]\mu(1)$, $r \cdot \exp[-\sigma(2)]\mu(2)$. Note that we do not know μ, the only parameter unknown at this point.

Step 2. Specify the short-term rates at all the nodes using Equation (24.14).

We need to iteratively calculate the rate r_u, applying Equation (24.14) repeatedly.

Step 3. Determine μ by a "bootstrap" approach.

Search for the value $\mu(1)$ such that a two-year bond, given by the discount function $P(T)$, can be priced according to the market. Then, we determine $\mu(2)$ such that $\mu(2)$ can price the three-year bond exactly according to the observed (or given) three-year bond price. This iterative procedure, called the bootstrap approach, can determine the lattice as desired.

We calculate the short rates by following the BDT procedure given the yields and the instantaneous forward volatilities in the table above.

24.4.3. The Hull–White Model

The Hull–White model (1990) is a normal model that has an explicit term to capture the mean reversion of interest rates. It is similar to the Vasicek model with the difference of being arbitrage-free. This approach enables the model to capture the term structure of volatilities by adjusting the adjustment rate of the short-term rate to the long-term equilibrium rate. The lattice model they propose is not a binomial model but a trinomial model. The trinomial model enables the model to adjust for the speed of adjustment and it can be constructed such that the model has no negative interest rates in all scenarios.

The Hull–White model can also be extended to a two-factor model (1994) that is arbitrage-free in a form similar to the Brennan and Schwartz model. Specifically, the model is specified by two simultaneous equations:

$$dr = [\theta(t) + u - ar]dt + \sigma_1 dW \quad (24.15)$$

$$du = -bu\, dt + \sigma_2 dZ \quad (24.16)$$

In this case, the short-term rate makes partial adjustments to the long-term rate, while the long-term rate follows a random movement. Using normal model properties, these models can derive closed form solutions for many derivatives in the continuous time formulation.

REFERENCES

Black, F. (1995). "Interest rates as options." *Journal of Finance*, 50(5):1371–1376.

Black, F., Derman, E., and Toy, W. (1990). "A one-factor model of interest rates and its application to treasury bond options." *Financial Analysts Journal*, 46: 33–39.

Black, F. and Karasinski, P. (1991). "Bond and option pricing when short rates are lognormal." *Financial Analysts Journal*, 47: 52–59.

Brennan, M.J. and Schwartz, E.S. (1979). "A continuous time approach to the pricing of bonds." *Journal of Banking and Finance*, 3: 135–155.

Brennan, M.J. and Schwartz, E.S. (1982). "An equilibrium model of bond pricing and a test of market efficiency." *Journal of Financial and Quantitative Analysis*, 17: 301–329.

Cheyette, O. (1977). "Interest rate models," in Advances in fixed income valuation, modeling and risk management, edited by Frank J. Fabozzi, Frank J. Fabozzi Associates, New Hope, Pennsylvania.

Cox, J.C., Ingersoll, J.E. Jr., and Ross, S.A. (1985). "A theory of the term structure of interest rates." *Econometrica*, 53: 385–407.

Dothan, U.L. (1978). "On the term structure of interest rates." *Journal of Financial Economics*, 6: 59–69.

Harrison, M.J. and Kreps, D.M. (1979). "Martingales and arbitrage in multi-period securities markets." *Journal of Economic Theory*, 20: 381–408.

Ho, T.S.Y. and Lee, S. (1986). "Term structure movements and pricing of interest rate contingent claims." *Journal of Finance*, 41: 1011–1029.

Ho, T.S.Y. and Lee, S. (1990). "Interest rate futures options and interest rate options." *The Financial Review*, 25(3): 345–370.

Ho, T.S.Y and Lee, S.B. (2004). *The Oxford Guide to Financial Modeling*. New York: Oxford University Press.

Hull, J. and White, A. (1990). "Pricing interest-rate-derivative securities." *The Review of Financial Studies*, 3(4): 573–592.

Hull, J. and White, A. (1993). "one-factor interest-rate models and the valuation of interest-rate derivative securities." *Journal of Financial and Quantitative Analysis*, 28(2): 235–254.

Hull, J. and A. White, (1994), "Numerical Procedures for Implementing Term Structure Model II: Two-Factor Models," *Journal of Derivatives*, 37–48, Winter.

Litterman, R. and Scheinkman, J.A. (1991). "Common factors affecting bond returns." *Journal of Fixed Income*, 1(1): 54–61.

Longstaff, F.A., and E.S. Schwartz, (1992), "Interest rate volatility and the term structure: A two factor general equilibrium model," *Journal of Finance*, 47(4): 1259–1282.

Richard, S.F., (1978), "An arbitrage model of the term structure of interest rates," *Journal of Financial Economics*, 6: 33–57.

Vasicek, O. (1977). "An equilibrium characterization of the term structure." *Journal of Financial Economics*, 5: 177–188.

Chapter 25

REVIEW OF REIT AND MBS

CHENG-FEW LEE, *National Chiao Tung University, Taiwan and Rutgers University, USA*
CHIULING LU, *Yuan Ze University, Taiwan*

Abstract

In this article, the history and the success of Real Estate Investment Trusts (REITs) and Mortgage-Backed Securities (MBS) in the U.S. financial market are discussed. Both securities are derived from real estate related assets and are able to increase the liquidity on real estate investment. They also provide investors with the opportunity to diversify portfolios because real estate assets are relatively less volatile and less correlated to existing investment instruments. Therefore, REITs and MBS enhance the width and the depth of the financial market.

Keywords: REIT; MBS; real estate; mortgage; FHA; VA; Fannie Mae; Ginnie Mae; Freddie Mac; prepayment; public securities association

25.1. Introduction

The revolution in the American real estate market was enhanced by securitization. For real properties, public listed Real Estate Investment Trusts (REITs) create tradable and standardized securities for individuals and institutional investors while providing alternative investments for diversification. Through the capital market, real estate practitioners have more reliable funds, and no longer limit themselves to bank loans. For real estate related loans, Mortgage-Backed Securities (MBS) establish a capital conduit linking borrowers and lenders directly, bypassing financial intermediaries. MBS also release the burden of the bank from holding long-term mortgage debt and bearing credit risk. In addition, MBS create a secondary market of mortgage debt, and provide an alternative investment.

Although, REITs and MBS are generated under different backgrounds and developed under different circumstances, they play a significant role in real estate financing. Nevertheless, challenges in real estate securitization have been important issues for the past four decades and will continue to do so in the future.

In this chapter, the development of REITs and MBS for the past forty years in the United States is described. In addition, empirical findings in the literature are also examined.

25.2. The REIT Background

A REIT is a creation of the federal tax code that permits an entity to own real properties and mortgage portfolios. REITs incur no corporate tax on transfers of profits to holders of beneficial interest given certain provisions within the Internal Revenue Code are met. To qualify as a REIT for tax purposes, the trust must satisfy many requirements including asset, income, distribution, and ownership restrictions. For example, a REIT must have a minimum of 100 shareholders; invest at least 75 percent of the total assets in real estate assets; derive at least 75 percent of gross income from rents, or interest on mortgages on real property;

and pay at least 90 percent of the taxable income in the form of shareholder dividends. Basically, if any company fails to qualify as a REIT, the company cannot be taxed as a REIT until five years from the termination date. To know REITs better, this study begins with the origin of REITs, then discusses the related regulation changes and current development, and finally examines relevant accounting and financial issues.

REITs were created by the U.S. Congress in 1960 to enable small investors to become involved in real estate development which was previously limited to the affluent. However, for the first three decades, REITs were recognized as passively managed firms, and were not competitive with real estate limited partnerships. Until the Tax Reform Act of 1986, REITs were empowered to not only own, but also operate and manage their own assets. In addition, the Act reduced tax shelter opportunities for real estate partnerships. Thereafter, it was possible for REITs to be self-managed rather than managed by external advisors, and became more attractive to investors. For the distribution rule, REITs were required to distribute at least 95 percent of taxable income as dividends. However, in 1999, the REIT Modernization Act changed the minimum requirement to 90 percent, which was consistent with the rules from 1960 to 1980.

According to the National Association of REIT (NAREIT), there are over 800 REITs and 171 of them were traded on the NYSE, AMEX, and NASDAQ during 2003. The market capitalization and the number of publicly traded REITs from 1971 to 2003 are illustrated in Figure 25.1. Since inception, REITs played a limited role in the capital market until the end of 1980s. At the end of 1980s, the combined effect of overbuilding, the savings and loan crisis, and the impact of the Tax Reform Act of 1986 led to the expansion of REITs. Investors realized that tradable and liquid real estate investment is crucial during recessions and REITs happened to fit these needs. Figure 25.1 shows that the total market capitalization of REITs amounted to more than US$224 billion as of December 31, 2003.

Because real estate maintains greater residual value than other assets such as computers or machinery, and real estate may appreciate at the same time, applying depreciation used in normal earnings measures resulted in underestimated cash flows for REITs. Bradley et al. (1998) observed that REITs' depreciation expenses are roughly equal to net income, and cash flow available for distribution is about twice the required payout. Consequently, agency problems caused by free cash flows arise (see Lu and Shen, 2004). In order

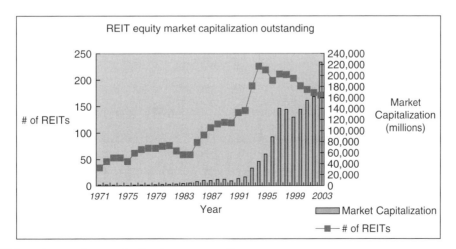

Figure 25.1.   REIT equity market capitalization outstanding
Source: NAREIT

to estimate cash flows and evaluate REITs' performance more accurately, Funds From Operations (FFO) is designed to be another supplemental measure relative to Earnings Per Share (EPS). The NAREIT defines FFO as net income excluding gains or losses from sales of property or debt restructuring, and adds back the depreciation of real estate.

A high dividend yield (7 percent on average in 2002) is one attraction for investors to invest in REITs. Figure 25.2 shows the dividend payout ratios as a percentage of the FFO. This ratio decreased in the 1990s, but has increased since 2000. This trend indicates that REITs reserved more cash at the end of 1990s. At the end of 2000, only 63 percent of the FFO was distributed to shareholders. This ratio increased to 81 percent at the end of 2003. Basically, the dividend policy of REITs is quite different from that of nonfinancial firms (see Lee and Kau, 1987) and is highly regulated by the IRS.

Compared to income-producing commercial real estate, REITs are financed on a more conservative basis. Generally, REITs finance their pro-jects with about half debt and half equity. According to the NAREIT, the average debt ratio for equity REITs is 41.8 percent as of the fourth quarter of 2003 and about two-thirds of REITs with senior unsecured debt ratings are investment grade. Figure 25.3 shows that the average leverage ratio of REITs has increased from 1996 to 2003, but not more than 55 percent. The coverage ratios defined as dividing EBITDA by interest expenses is over 3, from 1996 to 2003. The valuation of REITs depends on several criteria including management quality, dividend coverage from FFO, anticipated growth in FFO, and economic outlook. Fortunately, because public REITs are traded everyday, stock prices reflect real time pricing. Therefore, a capital asset pricing model could be employed to calculate REITs' expected returns and systematic risk. According to previous research, REITs underperform in the market on a nominal basis and earn fair returns on a risk-adjusted basis. Glascock and Hughes (1995) found that the REIT betas are consistently below the market ($= 1$) and equal to 0.377 for the entire period from 1972 to 1991. Figure 25.4 compares

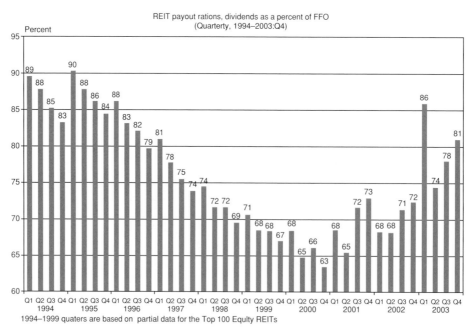

Figure 25.2. REIT payout ratios, dividends as percent of FFO
Source: NAREIT

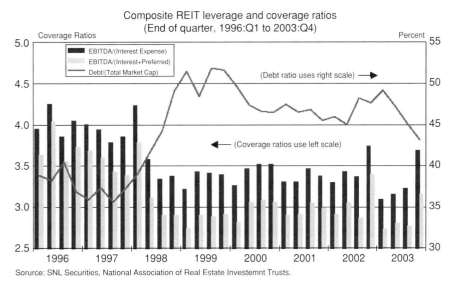

Figure 25.3. Composite REIT leverage and coverage ratios

the dividend yield of REITs with a 10-year constant maturity treasury yield and indicates that the former was higher for most of time during the past 15 years. In addition, the difference between these two yields has increased in the 2000s. Real estate investment has been considered good for hedging inflation. Fortunately, REITs investment still preserves this function. Figure 25.5 shows the trend of

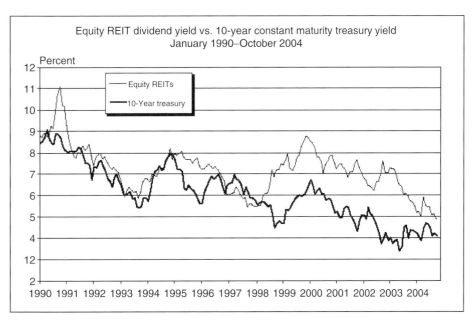

Figure 25.4. Equity REIT dividend yield vs. 10-year constant maturity treasury yield
Source: NAREIT

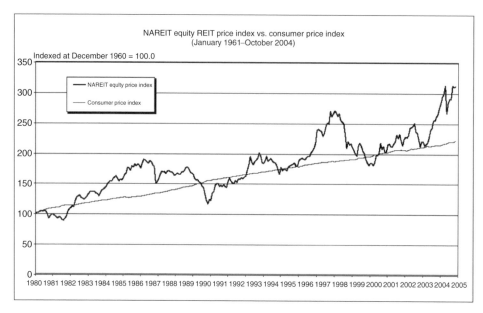

Figure 25.5. NAREIT equity REIT price index vs. consumer price index
Source: NAREIT

the NAREIT equity REIT price index versus the Consumer Price Index from 1990 to 2004. In the long run, the equity REIT price index was higher than the Consumer Price Index. Consequently, REITs are a viable inflation hedge instrument.

REITs have helped increase the liquidity of the real estate market and have become viable investments for diversification purposes by institutional and individual investors. It is anticipated that this industry will continue to expand, and more countries will follow this track.

25.3. The MBS Story

The secondary mortgage market has evolved and grown in the United States for the last three decades. MBS provide mortgage originators with liquidity and facilitate a geographic flow of funds from places with a surplus of savings to where home mortgages are needed.

The strong support of the federal government has played the most important role in the development of the MBS market. Therefore, the government's sponsorship in the process and then the market structure and participants are examined. The MBS pricing and related risk will also be illustrated.

25.3.1. The Special Contributions of the Government-Sponsored Enterprises

The three most important events in the evolution of the secondary mortgage market were the creation of Federal Housing Administration (FHA) in 1934, the chartering of the Federal National Mortgage Association (FNMA or Fannie Mae) in 1938, and the origination of Veterans Administration (VA) in 1944.

The FHA and the VA helped set up the mortgage underwriting standard and provided mortgage default insurance or guarantees. The FNMA was transformed into a privately owned and managed organization under the Housing and Urban Development Act of 1968. After that, government ownership was eliminated and the FNMA became solely owned by private investors. This Act also created the Government National Mortgage Association (GNMA or Ginnie Mae) to deal with subsidized mortgage purchases for special federal housing programs.

Though the secondary mortgage market based on pools of FHA or VA home mortgages was well established, a market for conventional loans did not exist. The Federal Home Loan Mortgage

Corporation (FHLMC or Freddie Mac) chartered under Title III of the Emergency Home Finance Act of 1970 provided liquidity for conventional loans as well as for FHA–VA mortgages.

25.3.2. Market Participants

Basically, there are four entities involved in the operation of the secondary mortgage market. The first entity is the mortgage originator such as mortgage bankers, thrifts, and commercial banks. They perform loan underwriting and establish loan terms in the primary market, and then sell mortgages to replenish funds. The second entity involved is the FHA and the VA, which perform credit enhancement functions by providing insurance or guarantees. The third entity in the process is the mortgage buyers. Prior to the mid-1950s, buyers were life insurance companies or thrifts. However, after the mid-1950s, both the FNMA and the FHLMC became the predominant purchasers. The FNMA and the FHLMC in turn created mortgage pools for securitization. The fourth entity is the end investors such as REITs, pension funds, mutual funds, IRAs, life insurance companies, or even the mortgage originators themselves.

25.3.3. MBS Pricing

According to Bartlett (1989), MBS are a hybrid investment in which a portfolio holding of an MBS consists of one part a standard-coupon bond and one part a short-call option. Since the homeowner has the right to call (prepay) the mortgage at any time, the MBS investor is in effect short the implied call. Therefore, Bartlett defines the MBS price as follows:

$$\text{MBS Value} = \textit{Non-callable Bond Value} \\ - \textit{Call Option Value.}$$

Unlike traditional debt securities, the cash flow of MBS is unpredictable due to unexpected delayed payment, prepayment, or default. Because borrowers hold options, not only is the expected

maturity of MBS more difficult to estimate relative to the other straight bond investments, but also the exact timing and amount of the cash flow is unknown in advance. Therefore, the valuation of the MBS turns out to be more complicated.

The factors related to the pricing of MBS include but are not limited to interest rate risk, default risk, risk of delayed payment, and prepayment risk. Prepayment ratios most significantly effect the predication of cash flow. Therefore, several models have been developed to estimate this rate. Those models include the 12-year prepaid life (based on FHA data assumption), constant prepayment rate (CPR) assumption, FHA prepayment experience, the Public Securities Association (PSA) model, and the econometric prepayment models (see Brueggeman and Fisher, 2001). Kau et al. (1985, 1987, 1990a, 1990b, 1992, 1993, 1995) have developed several models to analyze different mortgages and MBS. The research is continuing on prepayment estimation, but no conclusive model has been developed as of yet.

Figure 25.6 presents the outstanding volume of public and private bond market debt from 1985 to 2003. The outstanding level of mortgage related debt was US\$5.309 trillion in 2003. US\$3.526 trillion (66.4 percent) was debt related to Freddie Mae, Fannie Mae, and Ginnie Mae. The outstanding level of corporate debt and U.S. Treasury bonds was US\$4.462 trillion and US\$3.575, respectively. Obviously, MBS market-related securities were higher than the corporate bond and U.S. Treasury bond markets. This trend indicates the success and need for the mortgage secondary market.

Figure 25.7 shows the Commercial MBS yield spread defined as the difference between AAA-rated 10-year CMBS and 10-year Treasuries. The spread once reached more than 200 basis points, but has declined to less than 80 basis points in 2004. The yield on CMBS is still higher than that of Treasuries even though the number had declined. Given similar risk level, mortgage-related securities do provide investors with better alternative investment.

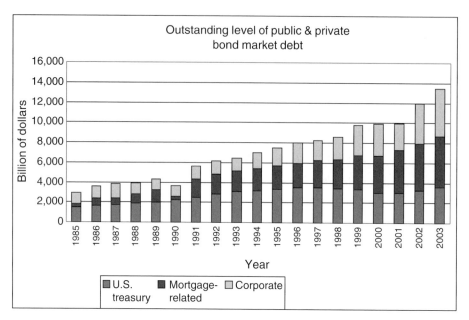

Figure 25.6. Outstanding level of public and private bond market debt
Source: The Bond Market Association

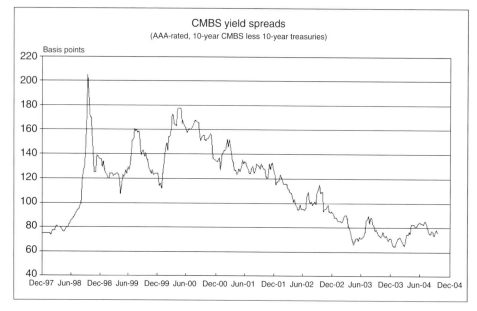

Figure 25.7. CMBS yield spreads
Source: Morgan Stanley

25.4. The Impact of Securitization on Financial Institutions

The process of mortgage securitization helps financial institutions to manage their asset portfolios, interest rate exposure, capital requirement, and deposit insurance premiums. Saunders and Cornett (2003) state that asset securitization provides a mechanism for financial institutions to hedge the interest rate risk. They point out that the process of securitization not only makes asset portfolio of financial institutions more liquid, but also provides an important source of fee income. Saunders and Cornett (2004) indicate that by increasingly relying on securitization, banks and thrifts have begun to move away from being asset transformers to become asset brokers. Therefore, the differences between commercial banking and investment banking began to diminish as asset securitization expanded.

25.5 Conclusion

Equity securities, debt instruments, and derivatives have become popular investment or hedging vehicles during the past century. However, real estate, which is the most conventional investment asset, lost favor to liquid and tradable securities among investors. Not until the 1970s did institutional investors start to show an interest in real estate in the United States (see Bernstein, 2003). The creation of REITs and MBS has changed the way of real estate financing in the United States and has also facilitated investment in real estate market. REITs and MBS were developed to complete the market, and indeed fulfill the objectives of an affordable housing policy for government and that of an asset allocation for the portfolio management purpose.

REFERENCES

Bartlett, W.W. (1989). *Mortgage-Backed Securities: Products, Analysis, Trading.* Englewood Cliffs, NJ: Prentice Hall.

Bernstein, P. (2003). "Real estate matters." *The Journal of Portfolio Management: Special Real Estate Issue*, 1.

Bradley, M., Capozza, D., and Seguin, P. (1998). "Dividend Policy and Cash-flow Uncertainty." *Real Estate Economics*, 26: 555–580.

Brueggeman, W. and Fisher, J. (2001). *Real Estate Finance and Investments.* Irwin: McGraw-Hill.

Glascock, J. and Hughes, W.T. (1995). "NAREIT identified exchange listed REITs and their performance characteristics, 1972–1990." *Journal of Real Estate Literature*, 3(1): 63–83.

Kau, J.B., Keenan, D.C., Muller, III W.J., and Epperson, J.F. (1985). "Rational pricing of adjustable rate mortgages." *AREUEA Journal*, 13(2): 117–128.

Kau, J.B., Keenan, D.C., Muller, III W.J., and Epperson, J.F. (1987). "The valuation and securitization of commercial and multifamily mortgages." *Journal of Banking and Finance*, 11: 525–546.

Kau, J.B., Keenan, D.C., Muller, III W.J., and Epperson, J.F. (1990a). "Pricing commercial mortgages and their mortgage-backed securities." *Journal of Real Estate Finance and Economics*, 3(4): 333–356.

Kau, J.B., Keenan, D.C., Muller, III W.J., and Epperson, J.F. (1990b). "The valuation and analysis of adjustable rate mortgages." *Management Science*, 36: 1417–1431.

Kau, J.B., Keenan, D.C., Muller, III W.J., and Epperson, J.F. (1992). "A generalized valuation model for fixed-rate residential mortgages." *Journal of Money, Credit, and Banking*, 24(3): 279–299.

Kau, J.B., Keenan, D.C., Muller, III W.J., and Epperson, J.F. (1993). "Option theory and floating rate securities with a comparison of adjustable- and fixed-rate mortgages." *Journal of Business,* 66(4): 595–617.

Kau, J.B., Keenan, D.C., Muller, III W.J., and Epperson, J.F. (1995). "The valuation at origination of fixed-rate mortgages with default and prepayment." *Journal of Real Estate Finance and Economics*, 11: 5–36.

Lee, C.F. and Kau, J.B. (1987). "Dividend payment behavior and dividend policy of REITs." *The Quarterly Review of Economics and Business*, 27: 6–21.

Lu, C. and Shen, Y. (2004). "Do REITs pay enough dividends?" Unpublished working paper, Department of Finance, Yuan Ze University.

Saunders, A. and Cornett, M.M. (2003). *Financial Institutions Management.* Irwin: McGraw-Hill, 733–768.

Saunders, A. and Cornett, M.M. (2004). *Financial Markets and Institutions,* Irwin: McGraw-Hill, 645–667.

Chapter 26

EXPERIMENTAL ECONOMICS AND THE THEORY OF FINANCE

HAIM LEVY, *Hebrew University, Israel*

Abstract

Experimental findings and in particular Prospect Theory and Cumulative Prospect Theory contradict Expected Utility Theory, which in turn may have a direct implication to theoretical models in finance and economics. We show growing evidence against Cumulative Prospect Theory. Moreover, even if one accepts the experimental results of Cumulative Prospect Theory, we show that most theoretical models in finance are robust. In particular, the CAPM is intact even if investors make decisions based on change of wealth, employ decision weights, and are risk-seeking in the negative domain.

Keywords: decision weights; prospect theory; cumulative prospect theory; certainty effect; expected utility; stochastic dominance; prospect stochastic dominance; value function; Markowitz stochastic dominance; configural weights

26.1. Introduction

Theoretical models in finance are based on certain assumptions regarding the investors' characteristics and their investment behavior. In particular, most of these models assume rational investors who always prefer more than less consumption (money), and who maximize von Neumann–Morgenstern (1944) expected utility.

The main models in finance that we relate to in this paper are:

(1) The Modigliani–Miller (1958) relationship between the value of the firm and its capital structure.
(2) Black–Scholes (1973) option pricing.
(3) Ross's (1976) Arbitrage Pricing Model (APT).
(4) The Sharpe–Lintner (1964 and 1965, respectively) Capital Asset Pricing Model (CAPM).
(5) Stochastic Dominance—the various investment decision rules (for a review, see Levy 1992, 1998).
(6) Market Efficiency – though recently some empirical studies reveal (short term) autocorrelations, most academic research still assumes that the market is at least "weakly efficient," namely one cannot employ *ex-post* rates of return to establish investment rules that provide abnormal returns. Of course, if this is the case, there is no room for "technicians" and charterists who try to predict the market based on past rates of return. (For the market efficiency hypotheses see Fama, 1965, 1991).

In this paper, we analyze the impact of recent experimental finding, and particularly the implication of Prospect Theory (PT) (see Kahneman and Tversky, 1979) (K&T), Cumulative Prospect Theory (CPT) (see Tversky and Kahneman, 1992

(T&K), and Rank-Dependent Expected utility (RDEU) (see Quiggin 1982, 1993) on each of these subjects that are cornerstones in finance and in decision making under uncertainty.

The structure of this paper is as follows: In Section 26.2, we deal with the main findings of PT and their implication regarding the above mentioned topics. In Section 26.3, we cover experimental studies in finance focusing on some recent studies, which cast doubt on some of the results and claims of PT and CPT. In Section 26.4, we analyze the implication of the experimental findings to the theory of finance. Concluding remarks are given in Section 26.5.

26.2. Allias Paradox, PT, CPT, and RDEU: Claims and Implication to the Theory of Finance

26.2.1. Probability Distortions (or Decision Weights)

Most models in economics and finance assume expected utility maximization. Probably the most famous example contradicting the expected utility paradigm is provided by Allias, and is known as the Allias paradox (1953). Table 26.1 provides two

Table 26.1. Allias paradox. All outcomes are in million $

Part I			
	A		B
Outcome	Probability	Outcome	Probability
1	1	0	0.01
		1	0.89
		5	0.10
Part II			
	C		D
Outcome	Probability	Outcome	Probability
0	0.89	0	0.90
1	0.11	5	0.10

choices in both part I and part II. In part I most subjects would typically choose A, while in part II most of them choose D. Such choices constitute a contradiction to the classic EU paradigm because from the choice in part I we can conclude that:

$$u(1) > 0.01u(0) + 0.89u(1) + 0.10\ u(5)$$

This inequity can be rewritten as

$$0.11u(1) > 0.01\ u(0) + 0.10\ u(5), \qquad (26.1)$$

and the choices in part II implies that

$$0.89u(0) + 0.11u(1) < 0.9u(0) + 0.10u(5)$$

The last inequality can be rewritten also as

$$0.11u(1) < 0.01u(0) + 0.10u(5) \qquad (26.2)$$

As Equations. (26.1) and (26.2) contradict each other for any preference u, we have an inconsistency in the choices in part I and II. How can we explain this result? Does it mean that the EU paradigm is completely wrong? And if the answer is positive, do we have a better substitute to the EU paradigm?

The preference of D over C is not surprising. However, the preference of A over B in Part I seems to induce the paradox. The choice of A is well-known as the "certainty effect," (see Kahneman and Tversky, 1979), i.e. the "one bird in the hand is worth more than two in the bush" effect. The explanation for the contradiction in Equations (26.1) and (26.2) is due to the "certainty effect," or alternatively, due to probability distortion in the case where probabilities are smaller than 1. Indeed, experimental psychologists find that subjects tend to subjectively distort probabilities in their decision making. To be more specific, one makes a decision using a weight $w(p)$ rather than the objective probability p. In our specific case, $w(0.01) > 0.01$ – hence the attractiveness of B relative to A decreases, which explains the choice of A in this case. However, in such a case, the classical von Neuman–Morgenstern expected utility is rejected once decision weight $w(p)$ is employed rather than objective probability p.

Probability distortions or decision weights is a subject of many experimental studies conducted mainly by psychologists. Probably the earliest experiments showing that subjects distort probabilities were conducted by Preston and Baratta (1948) and Edwards (1955, 1962). However, the publication of Prospect Theory (PT) by Kahneman and Tversky in 1979 in *Econometrica* has exposed this issue widely to economists, and hence has strongly influenced research in economics and finance. Though decision weights is an old notion, it is still currently occupying researchers (see for example, Prelec, 1998).

In their original paper, Kahneman and Tversky argue that probability p is changed to decision weight $w(p)$ in some systematic manner. However, probability distortion as suggested by Kahneman and Tversky (1979) as well as in the previous studies mentioned above may violate First degree Stochastic Dominance (FSD) or the monotonicity axiom, a property that most economists and psychologists alike are not willing to give up, because violation of FSD essentially means preferring less over more money. Before we illustrate this property, let us first define FSD.

FSD: Let F and G be the cumulative distributions of the returns on two uncertain prospects. Then F dominates G by FSD if $F(x) \leq G(x)$ for all x, and there is at least one strict inequity. Moreover,

$F(x) \leq G(x)$ for all $x \Leftrightarrow E_F u(x) \geq E_G u(x)$

for all utility function $u \in U_1$ where

U_1 is the set of all nondecreasing utility functions ($u' \geq 0$) (see Hanoch and Levy, 1969; Hadar and Russell, 1969). For a survey and more details, see Levy, 1992, 1998.

Let us illustrate with an example why the decision weights framework of PT may lead to a violation of FSD.

Example: Consider two prospects x and y. Suppose that x gets the values 3 and 4 with equal probability, and y gets the value 4 with certainty. It is obvious that y dominates x by FSD. Yet, with possible decision weights $w(1/2) = 3/4$ and $w(1) = 1$, we may find a legitimate preference showing a higher expected value for x, i.e. x is preferred to y despite the fact that y dominates x by FSD. For example, for the function $u(x) = x$ (the same is true for many other utility functions), we have

$$EU(x) = \left(\frac{3}{4}\right)3 + \left(\frac{3}{4}\right)4 = \frac{21}{4} = 5\frac{1}{4} > EU(y)$$
$$= 1 \times 4 = 4$$

Thus, the FSD inferior prospect is selected, which is an undesired result.

Fishburn (1978) shows that this distortion of probability may contradict FSD, or the monotonicity property, which is considered as a fatal flaw of such a probability distortion framework (see also Machina, 1994, p. 97). Quiggin (1982) offers a remedy to this problem. He suggests that the probability distortion should be done as a function of the cumulative distribution rather than as a function of the individual probabilities (for more studies along this line, see also Wakker et al., 1994; Yaari, 1987; Machina 1994).

According to Quiggin, a given probability p may be distorted in different ways depending on the ranking of the outcome it corresponds to. Thus, the probability $p = 1/4$ may be distorted to different values $w_i(p)$, depending on the rank of the ith outcome. For example, take the following prospect:

$x = 1, 2, 3, 4$
$P(x) = 1/4 \ 1/4 \ 1/4 \ 1/4$

Then $w(1/4)$ corresponding to $x = 1$ may be larger than $1/4$ and $w(1/4)$ corresponding to $x = 2$ may be smaller than $1/4$ (the opposite relationship is also possible). Thus, the probability distortion is not only a function of the probability p_i but also on the rank of the corresponding outcome, hence the name Rank-Dependent Expected Utility (RDEU). This is in sharp contrast to the decision weights suggested by Kahneman and Tversky in 1979, because by the original PT, $w(1/4)$ is the same for all values and does not depend on the rank of the outcome. Realizing the possible FSD violation, Quiggin (1982) suggests a modification to PT where a transformation of the cumulative distribution is employed. This idea is the basis for Cumulative Prospect Theory (CPT). By this model, the decision weight is also a function of the rank of the outcome. However, unlike Quiggin, Tversky and Kahneman distinguish between negative and positive outcomes. To be more specific, in the CPT framework, the decision weights are given as follows. Consider a prospect $(x_1, p_1; \ldots; x_n, p_n)$, where p_i denote the objective probabilities and x_i denote the outcomes. Assume, without loss of generality, that $x_1 \leq \ldots \leq x_k \leq 0 \leq x_{k+1} \leq \ldots \leq x_n$. The decision weights, which are employed in CPT are given by

$$\pi_1 = w^-(p_1), \quad \pi_n = w^-(p_n),$$
$$\pi_i = w^-(p_1 + \ldots + p_i) - w^-(p_1 + \ldots + p_{i-1})$$
$$\text{for } 2 \leq i \leq k,$$
$$\pi_i = w^+(p_i + \ldots + p_n) - w^+(p_{i+1} + \ldots + p_n)$$
$$\text{for } k+1 \leq i \leq n-1,$$

where w^- and w^+ are weighting functions, which Tversky and Kahneman (1992) experimentally estimate by the functions,

$$w^+(x) = \frac{x^\gamma}{(x^\gamma + (1-x)^\gamma)^{1/\gamma}} \text{ and}$$
$$w^-(x) = \frac{x^\delta}{(x^\delta + (1-x)^\delta)^{1/\delta}}$$

(26.3)

Given these formulas, Tversky and Kahneman find the following estimates: $\hat{\gamma} = 0.61$ and $\hat{\delta} = 0.69$ (see Tversky and Kahneman, 1992, pp. 309–312). It can be easily shown that for $\gamma < 1$ and $\delta < 1$, the weighting functions have a reverse S-shape, implying the overweighing of small probabilities. The probability distortion as suggested by Kahneman and Tversky is illustrated in Figure 26.1.

Several researchers argue that in cases of equally likely outcomes, which we call here "uniform" probability distribution, probabilities are not distorted. Quiggin (1982), who was the first one to propose that cumulative probabilities are distorted

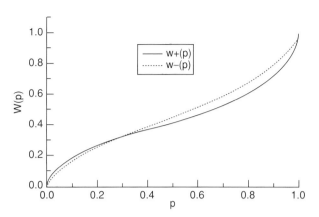

Figure 26.1. CPT decision weights

rather than the raw individual probabilities, argues that for "two equally likely" outcomes ($p = 0.50$) there will be no distortion of probabilities. This argument contradicts Equation (26.3), which suggests a distortion even in this case. Though Quiggin does not extend his argument beyond 50:50 bet (actually by his method any other uniform bet, e.g. with 3 or more equally likely outcomes, is distorted) we hypothesized that the probability of a uniform bet (with a $1/n$ probability for each of the n outcomes) should not be distorted as long as the outcomes are not extreme. This is also the result of Viscusi's (1989) "Prospective Reference Theory" with a symmetric reference point, for which he finds experimental support. However, not all authors agree with the fact that uniform probability distributions are undistorted. Nevertheless, recall that if probabilities are distorted even with a uniform distribution, it has a devastating impact on all reported empirical studies in finance and economics (see below).

The RDEU of Quiggin transforms probabilities in the following manner. Instead of comparing the cumulative distributions F and G, the subjects compare the distributions F^* and G^* where $F^* = T(F)$ and $G^* = T(G)$, where T is the distortion function with $T' > 0$. It can be easily shown that using CPT or RDEU decision weights does not violate FSD. Namely,

$$F^* \leq G^* \Leftrightarrow T(F^*) \leq T(G^*)$$

(26.4)

(See Levy and Wiener, 1998. For a survey of SD rules, PT, and the impact of decision weights on choices, see Levy, 1998).

In PT and CPT frameworks, probabilities are also distorted in the uniform case. However, the advantage of PT over CPT is that with PT all probabilities with the same size, e.g. $p_i = 1/4$ are distorted in an identical way, hence the choices in a uniform bet are not affected by the probability distortion as suggested by PT. The advantage of CPT over PT is that FSD is not violated. Recalling that CPT decision weights is a technical method which was invented to avoid FSD violations, and that FSD violations do occur experimentally (see Birnbaum, 1997) leads one to question the benefit of introducing CPT decision weights.

26.2.2. Change of Wealth Rather than Total Wealth

Expected utility is defined on total wealth, i.e. $u(w + x)$ where w is the initial wealth and x is the change of wealth. Experimental studies reveal that subjects make decisions based on change of wealth, i.e. $u(x)$, rather than $u(w + x)$. It is interesting to note that though the change of wealth argument has been shown experimentally by Kahneman and Tversky, this idea appeared in the literature as early as 1952. Markowitz (1952b) claims that investors make decisions based on change of wealth rather than total wealth. It is easy to construct an example showing that

$$Eu(w + x) > Eu(w + y) \text{ and } Eu(x) < Eu(y)$$

when x and y are the returns on two risky projects. As we shall see later on in this paper, ignoring the initial wealth may indeed affect the choice of the "optimum" portfolio from the efficient set. However, it does not affect the division of the feasible set of portfolios to the efficient and inefficient sets.

26.2.3. Integration of cash flows

Expected utility maximization and portfolio selection advocate that one should select a portfolio of assets that maximizes expected utility and one should not consider each asset in isolation. Therefore, correlations should play an important role in portfolio selection. Tversky and Kahneman experimentally find that this is not the case, hence conclude that subjects have difficulties in integrating cash flows from various sources. Let us illustrate this idea with the experiment conducted by Tversky and Kahneman in 1981 with the following two tasks.

Task I: Imagine that you face a pair of concurrent decisions. First, examine both decisions, then indicate the option you prefer.

Decision 1: Choose between A and B given below:

(A) A sure gain of \$2,400.
(B) 25 percent chance to gain \$10,000 and 75 percent chance to gain nothing.

Decision 2: Choose between C and D given below:

(C) A sure loss of \$7,500.
(D) 75 percent chance to lose \$10,000 and 25 percent to lose nothing.

A large majority of people choose A in decision 1 and D in decision 2.

Task II: Choose between E and F given below:

(E) 25 percent chance to win \$2,400 and 75 percent chance to lose \$7,600
(F) 25 percent chance to win \$2,500 and 75 percent chance to lose \$7,500.

In Task II, everybody correctly preferred option F over option E. Indeed, F dominates E by FSD. Note that if you return to Task I, however, you get that the inferior option E in Task II is obtained by choosing A and D. The dominating option F in Task II is obtained by combining the two options that most people reject in Task I (i.e. $F = B + C$). Thus, a fully rational decision maker who knows to integrate cash flows from various sources should incorporate the combined decisions, and realize that the combined cash flows of $B + C$ dominate those of $A + D$ in Task I.

From this and other examples, Tversky and Kahneman conclude that investors consider decision problems one at a time instead of adopting a broader frame. Such a procedure induces a reduction in expected utility because the investors miss an opportunity to diversify, hedge, or self-insure. The "narrow framing" of investors arises from the common practice of maintaining multiple "mental accounts." Thus, the main finding is that the subjects – at least those who participated in the study – are limited in their capability to integrate cash flows from various sources even in a relatively simple case let alone in more complicated cash flows from many sources. If these findings are relevant, not only to subjects in an experiment but also to the investors in practice, this is a severe blow to diversification theory of Markowitz (1952a, 1959, 1987) and Tobin (1958).

26.2.4. Risk Seeking Segment of Preferences

Most models in economics and finance assume risk aversion, i.e. a preference u with $u' > 0$ and $u'' < 0$ (see for example Arrow, 1965, 1971; Pratt, 1964). However, as early as 1948, Friedman and Savage, based on observed peoples' behavior, suggested a risk-seeking segment of the preference. Markowitz (1952b) modified this preference and suggested another function, which also contains a risk-seeking segment. Both of these studies rely on positive economics arguments. Kahneman and Tversky, on the other hand, base their argument on experimental findings (see also Swalm, 1966).

Figure 26.2 provides the main utility functions advocated in the literature.[1] Figure 26.2a depicts the classical utility function which is concave everywhere, in accordance with the notion of decreasing marginal utility. Such a function implies risk aversion, meaning that individuals would never accept any fair bet (let alone unfair bets). Friedman and Savage (1948)] claim that the fact that investors buy insurance, lottery tickets, and both insurance and lottery tickets simultaneously, plus the fact that most lotteries have more than one big prize, imply that the utility function must have

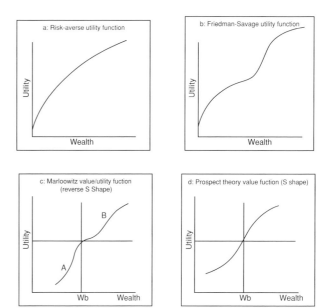

Figure 26.2. Alternaive shapes of the utility/value function

two concave regions with a convex region in between, as represented in Figure 26.2b.

Markowitz (1952b) points out several severe problems with the Friedman and Savage utility function[2]. However, he shows that the problems are solved if the first inflection point of the Friedman and Savage utility function is exactly at the individual's current wealth. Thus, Markowitz introduces the idea that decisions are based on "change" in wealth. Hence, Markowitz's utility function can be also considered as a "value function" (as later suggested by Kahneman and Tversky in 1979). By analyzing several hypothetical gambles, Markowitz suggests that individuals are risk-averse for losses and risk-seeking for gains, as long as the possible outcomes are not very extreme. For extreme outcomes, Markowitz argues that individuals become risk-averse for gains, but risk-seeking for losses. Thus, Markowitz suggests a utility function, which is characterized by three inflection points, as shown in Figure 26.2c. Notice that the central part of this function (the range between Points A and B in Figure 26.2c) has a reversed S-shape.

Based on their experimental results, with bets which are either negative or positive, Kahneman and Tversky (1979) and Tversky and Kahneman (1992) claim that the value function is concave for gains and convex for losses, yielding an S-shaped function, as shown in Figure 26.2d.

26.3. Experimental Studies In Finance

Experimental studies in finance lagged behind experimental studies in economics. Yet, the whole November/December 1999 issue of the *Financial Analyst Journal* is devoted to behavioral finance and discusses issues such as arbitrage, overconfidence, momentum strategies, market efficiency in an irrational world, and equity mispricing. In this section we discuss a few experimental studies in finance.

26.3.1. *Portfolio diversification and Random Walk*

In the last three decades, there has been a growing interest of economists in experimental economics. The Nobel prize committee recognized this important field by awarding the Nobel Prize in 2002 to Vernon Smith and Daniel Kahneman. On the importance of experimental research in economics, Vernon Smith asserts: "It is important to economic science for theorists to be less own-literature oriented, to take seriously the data and disciplinary function of laboratory experiments, and even to take seriously their own theories as potential generators of testable hypotheses." (See Smith, 1982, p. 924). (See also, Plott, 1979; Smith, 1976, 1982; Wilde, 1980).

While laboratory experiments are widely used in economics research, finance research is well behind in this respect. Probably, the first serious experiment in finance was done by Gordon et al. (1972), who studied portfolio choices experimentally. They indicate that to study the investors' preference, there is an advantage to the experimental method over the empirical method simply because it is difficult, if not impossible, to obtain empirically the relevant data (For a similar argument, see

Elton and Gruber, 1984). The first experimental studies in finance in diversification and portfolio choices focused on the allocation of money between the riskless asset and one risky asset as a function of various levels of wealth (see Gordon et al., 1972, Funk et al., 1979 and Rapoport, 1984).

Kroll et al. (1988a) study the choice between risky assets whose returns are normally distributed, where the riskless asset (borrowing and lending) is allowed. The subjects were undergraduate students who did not study finance or investment courses. The main findings of this experiment are:

(1) The subjects selected a relatively high percentage of mean-variance "inefficient" portfolios.
(2) The errors involved do not decrease with practice.
(3) The subjects requested a lot of useless information, i.e. they asked for historical rates of returns when the parameters were known and the returns were selected randomly (information given to the subjects). Thus, the subjects presumably believed that there are some patterns in rates of return, though such patterns do not exist.

Odean (1998) in his analysis of many individual transactions reports that there is a tendency of investors to hold losing investments too long and to sell winning investments too soon (a phenomenon known as the disposition effect). This result is consistent with the results of Kroll et al. (see (3) above). He finds that when individual investors sold a stock and quickly bought another, the stock they sold outperformed on average the stock they bought by 3.4 percentage points in the first year. This costly overtrading may be explained by the fact that investors perceive patterns where none exist or do not want to admit their errors in selection of their investments. Perceiving patterns when they do not exist is exactly as reported by KL&R.

In a subsequent paper, Kroll et al.(1988b) experimentally test the Separation Theorem and the Capital Asset Pricing Model (CAPM). In this experiment the 42 subjects were undergraduate students who took a course in statistics. They had to select portfolios from three available risky assets and a riskless asset. This experiment reveals some negative and some positive results. The results are summarized as follows:

(1) As predicted by the M-V rule, the subjects generally diversified between the three riskless assets.

(2) A tenfold increase in the reward to the subject significantly improved the subjects' performance. This finding casts doubt on the validity of the results of many experiments on decision making under uncertainty which involves a small amount of money.

(3) Though the subjects were told that rates of return are drawn randomly, as before, they, again, asked for (useless) information. This finding may explain why there are "chartists" and "technical analysts" in the market even if indeed rates of returns are randomly distributed over time. Thus, academicians may continue to claim the "random walk" property of returns and practitioners will continue to find historical patterns and employ technical rules for investment based on these perceived patterns.

(4) Changing the correlation (from -0.8 to 0.8), unlike what Markowitz's theory advocates, does not change the selected diversification investment proportions.

(5) The introduction of the riskless asset does not change the degree of homogeneity of the investment behavior. Thus, at least with these 42 subjects the Separation Theorem (and hence the CAPM) does not hold in practice.

In the study of KL&R, the subjects were undergraduate students with no background in finance and they could not lose money. These are severe drawbacks as the subjects may not represent potential investors in the market. To overcome these drawbacks, Kroll and Levy (K&L) (1992) conducted a similar experiment with the same parameters as in KL&R but this time with second year MBA students and where financial gains and

losses were possible. The results improved dramatically in favor of Markowitz's diversification theory. Figure 26.3 shows the average portfolio with and without leverage selected in the KL&R study and in the K&L study. In the K&L study, the selected portfolios are L and U (for levered and unlevered portfolios) while in KL&R they are $\hat{U}$ and $\hat{L}$. As can be seen U and L are much closer to the optimum solution (in particular, L is much closer to line rr' than $\hat{L}$), indicating that when real money is involved and MBA students are the subjects, much better results are achieved. Also, as predicted by portfolio theory, the subjects, unlike in KL&R study, change the investment proportions when correlation changes.

Finally, the investment proportions selected were similar to those of the optimum mean variance portfolio. Therefore, K&L conclude that the subjects behave *as if* they solve a quadratic programming problem to find the optimum portfolio even though they did not study this tool at the time the experiment was conducted.

26.3.2. The Equity Risk Premium Puzzle

The difference between the observed long-run average rate of return on equity and on bonds cannot be explained by well behaved risk averse utility function; hence the term equity risk premium puzzle. Benartzi and Thaler (1995) suggest the loss aversion preference as suggested by PT S-shape function to explain the existing equity risk premium. They show that if investors weight loses 2.5 more heavily than possible gains the observed equity risk premium can be explained. However, Levy and Levy (2002b) have shown that the same conclusion may be drawn with a reverse S-shape utility function as suggested by Markowitz, as long as the segment corresponding to $x < 0$ is steeper than the segment corresponding to $x > 0$.

Levy and Levy (2002c) (L&L) analyze the effect of PT and CPT decision weights on Arrow (1965) and Pratt (1964) risk premium. They show that a positive risk premium may be induced by decision weights $w(p)$ rather than probabilities p even in the absence of

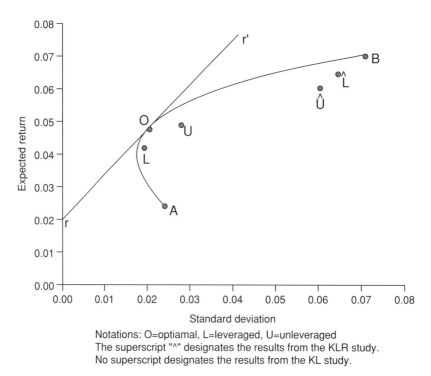

Notations: O=optiamal, L=leveraged, U=unleveraged
The superscript "^" designates the results from the KLR study.
No superscript designates the results from the KL study.

Figure 26.3. The efficient frontier and the actual portfolios selected by the subjects

risk aversion. In their experiment a large proportion of the choices contradicts risk aversion but this does not contradict the existence of a positive equity risk premium. Thus, one does not need loss aversion to explain Arrow's risk premium because it can be induced by the use of decision weights. Unlike the case of Arrow's risk premium, with Pratt's risk aversion measure or with historical data, which is composed of more than two values, the risk premium may increase or decrease due to the use of decision weights. To sum up, the equity risk premium puzzle can be explained either by loss aversion, which is consistent both with an S-shape function and a reverse S-shape function, or by decision weights, even in the absence of loss aversion.

26.3.3. The Shape of Preference

Risk aversion and a positive risk premium are two important features of most economic and finance models of assets pricing and decision making under uncertainty. Are people risk averse? As shown in Figure 26.1, Friedman and Savage, Mar-

kowitz, and K&T claim that this is not the case. So what can we say about preference? In a series of experiments with and without financial rewards, Levy and Levy (2002a,b) have shown that a major portion of the choices contradict risk-aversion. L&L conducted several experiments with 328 subjects. To test whether the subjects understood the questionnaire and did not fill it out randomly just to "get it over with," they first tested FSD which is appropriate for risk-seekers and risk averters alike. They found that 95 percent of the choices conform with FSD (i.e. with the monotonicity axiom), which validates the reliability of their results. They find that in Experiment 1 *at least 54 percent* of the choices contradict risk aversion, in Experiment 2 *at least 33 percent* of the subjects contradict risk aversion and in Experiment 3 *at least 42 percent* of the choices contradict risk aversion. It is interesting to note that the subjects in these three experiments were business school students, faculty, Ph.D students and practitioners (financial analysts and funds managers).

In these three experiments, L&L also tested the effect of the subjects characteristics, the size of the outcomes as well as the framing of the bet. The results are very similar across all these factors with the exception that Ph.D. students and faculty members choose more consistently with risk aversion (71–78 percent correct second degree stochastic dominance (SSD) choices). But there may be a bias here because these subjects are more familiar with SSD rules, and it is possible that they mathematically applied it in their choices. However, even with these sophisticated subjects at least 22 percent–29 percent of them selected inconsistently with risk aversion, implying trouble for theoretical models, which rely on risk aversion.

The fact that 33 percent–54 percent of the subjects behave "as if" they are not risk averse, implies that they choose "as if" the utility function is not concave in the whole range. For example, K&T, Friedman and Savage and Markowitz utility functions are consistent with L&L findings. Note that L&L findings do not imply risk seeking in the whole range, but rather no risk-aversion in the entire range. Therefore, their finding does not contradict the possibility that with actual equity distribution of rates of return corresponding to the US market the risk premium may even increase due to decision weights.

Rejecting risk aversion experimentally is repeated in many experiments (see for example L&L, 2001, 2002a). Hence, the remainder contrasts K&T S-shape function and Markowitz's reverse S-shape function. Employing prospect stochastic dominance (PSD) and Markowitz's stochastic dominance (MSD) L&L contrast these two utility functions. Let us first present these two investment criteria:[3]

Prospect stochastic dominance (PSD):
Let U_s be the set of all S-shape preferences with $u' > 0$ for all $x \gtrless 0$ and $u'' > 0$ for $x < 0$ and $u'' < 0$ for $x > 0$. Then

$$\int_y^x [G(t) - F(t)] \geq 0 \text{ for all } x > 0, y < 0 \quad (26.5)$$

$$\Leftrightarrow E_F u(x) \geq E_G u(x) \text{ for all } u \in U_s.$$

Markowitz Stochastic Dominance (MSD):
Let U_M be the set of all reverse S-shape preferences with $u' > 0$ for all $x \gtrless 0$ and $u'' < 0$ for $x < 0$ and $u'' > 0$ for $x > 0$. Define F and G as above. Then F dominates G for all reverse S-shaped value functions, $u \in U_M$, if and only if

$$\int_{-\infty}^y [G(t) - F(t)]dt \geq 0 \text{ for all } y$$

$$\leq 0 \text{ and } \int_x^\infty [G(t) - F(t)]dt$$

$$\geq 0 \text{ for all } x \geq 0 \quad (26.6)$$

(with at least one strict inequality). And (5) holds iff $E_F u(x) > E_G u(x)$ for all $u \in U_M$. We call this dominance relation MSD–Markowitz Stochastic Dominance.

Table 26.2.   The choices presented to the subjects

Suppose that you decided to invest $10,000 either in stock F or in stock G. Which stock would you choose, F, or G, when it is given that the *dollar gain or loss* one month from now will be as follows:
TASK I:

	F Gain or loss	Probability	G Gain or loss	Probability
	−3,000	1/2	−6,000	1/4
	4,500	1/2	3,000	3/4
Please write F or G				

TASK II:
Which would you prefer, F or G, if the dollar gain or loss one month from now will be as follows:

	F Gain or loss	Probability	G Gain or loss	Probability
	−500	1/3	−500	1/2
	+2,500	2/3	2,500	1/2
Please write F or G				

(Continued)

Table 26.2.   The choices presented to the subjects
(*Continued*)

TASK III:

Which would you prefer, F or G, if the dollar gain or loss one
month from now will be as follows:

F Gain or loss	Probability	G Gain or loss	Probability
+500	3/10	−500	1/10
+2,000	3/10	0	1/10
+5,000	4/10	+500	1/10
		+1,000	2/10
		+2,000	1/10
		+5,000	4/10

Please write
F or G

TASK IV:

Which would you prefer, F or G, if the dollar gain or
loss one month from now will be as follows:

F Gain or loss	Probability	G Gain or loss	Probability
−500	1/4	0	1/2
+500	1/4		
+1,000	1/4	+1,500	1/2
+2,000	1/4		

Please write
F or G

Source: Levy and Levy, (2002a).

Table 26.3.   The results of the experiment*

Task	F	G	Indifferent	Total
I(Gϕ_{PSD}F,Fϕ_{MSD}G)	71	27	2	100
II(Fϕ_{FSD}G)	96	4	0	100
III(Fϕ_{FSD}G)	82	18	0	100
IV(Gϕ_{SSD}F)	47	51	2	100

Number of subjects: 260
*Numbers in the tables are in percent, rounded to the nearest
integer. The notations ϕ_{FSD}, ϕ_{SSD}, and ϕ_{MSD} indicate
dominance by FSD, SSD, PSD, and MSD, respectively.
Source: Levy and Levy, (2002a).

Table 26.2 presents the four Tasks while Table
26.3 presents the results of the experimental study of
Levy and Levy (2002a). Note that in Task I G dominates F by PSD, but F dominates G by MSD. As can

be seen from Table 26.3, in Task I, 71 percent of the
subjects choose F despite the fact that G dominates F
by PSD. Thus, *at least* 71 percent of the choices are
in contradiction to PSD, and supporting MSD, i.e. a
reverse S-shape preference as suggested by Markowitz. Note also that 82–96 percent of the choices (see
Tasks II and III) are consistent with FSD. Once
again, by the results of Task IV we see that about
50 percent of the choices reject the assumption of
risk aversion (SSD). Table 26.4 taken from Levy and
Levy (2002b) reveals once again the results of another experiment showing that at least 62 percent of
the choices contradict the S-shape preference of PT.

Wakker (2003) in his comment on Levy and
Levy's (2002a) paper claims that the dominance
by PSD (or by MSD) also depends on probability
weights. Generally, his claim is valid. However, if a
uniform distribution ($p_i = 1/4$ for all observations)
is considered, his criticism is valid only if indeed
probabilities are distorted in such a case. Are probabilities distorted in such a case? And if the answer
is positive, can we blindly use the distortion formula suggested by T&K? There is evidence that in
the case of uniform distributions probabilities are
not distorted, or are distorted as recommended by
PT but not by CPT (hence do not affect choices).
Thus, Wakker's claim is invalid. Let us elaborate.
In Viscusi's (1989) *Prospective Reference Theory*
there is also *no* probability distortion in the symmetric case. Also, in the original PT framework
(Kahneman and Tversky, 1979), in which the
probabilities are transformed directly, the choice
among prospects is unaffected by subjective probability distortion in the case of equally likely outcomes. Thus, as the study reported in Table 26.4
was conducted with uniform probabilities and
moderate outcomes, it is safe to ignore the effects
of subjective probability distortion in this case.
Wakker (2003) argues that by CPT probabilities
are distorted even in the bets given in Table 26.4,
hence the conclusion against the S-shape function
by Levy and Levy is invalid. If one uses the distortion formula [see eq. (3)] of T&K also in the
uniform case, Wakker is correct. However, recall
that the formula of T&K is based on aggregate

Table 26.4a. The choices presented to the subjects

Suppose that you decided to invest $10,000 either in stock F or in stock G. Which stock would you choose, F, or G, when it is given that the *dollar gain or loss* one month from now will be as follows:

F		G	
Gain or loss	Probability	Gain or loss	Probability
−1,600	1/4	−1,000	1/4
−200	1/4	−800	1/4
1,200	1/4	800	1/4
1,600	1/4	2,000	1/4

Please write F or G

Table 26.4b. The results of experiment 2*

	F	G	Indifferent	Total
(F φ PSD G, G φ MSD F)	38%	62%	0%	100%

Number of subjects: 84.
*Numbers in the tables are in percent, rounded to the nearest integer. The notations φ PSD, and φ MSD indicate dominance by PSD, and MSD, respectively.
Source: Levy and Levy, (2002b).

data of nonsymmetrical probability distributions and with no financial reward or penalty. So why should one think it is appropriate to apply it to the uniform probability case? Moreover, as we see in section IVe, formula (3) suggests decision weights which are hard to accept if indistinguishability is employed in all cases.

Yet, even if one adheres to T&K distortion weights formula, even in the equally likely outcomes case, the S-shape preference is rejected and Wakker is wrong in his criticism. Indeed, Levy and Levy (2002b) conduct a direct confrontation of PSD and MSD where probability distortion is taken into account exactly as suggested by K&T's CPT and exactly as done by Wakker (2003). Table 26.5 presents the two choices *F* and *G*, the objective probabilities as well as the decision weights as recommended by CPT [see eq. (3)].

Note that with the data of Table 26.5, *G* dominates *F* by PSD with objective as well as subjective

probabilities. Yet 50 percent of the subjects selected *F*. This implies that *at least* 50 percent (it may be much larger than 50 percent but this cannot be proven) of the subjects' choices do not conform with an S-shape preference, rejecting this important element of PT and CPT (see Table 26.5).

To sum up, with objective probabilities the S-shape preference is rejected. With PT the S-shape is also rejected by the decision weights $w(1/4)$ which is identical for all outcomes (For a proof, see Levy and Levy, 2002b). Table 26.5 reveals that the S-shape function is rejected also when decision weights are taken into account exactly as recommended by CPT's formula.

Thus, more than 50 percent of the choices contradicts risk aversion and more than 50 percent of the choices contradicts the S-shape function – the preference advocated by PT and CPT. The experiments' results yield most support Markowitz's reverse-Shape preference. From this above analysis we can conclude that investors are characterized by a variety of preferences and that there is no one dominating preference.

26.3.4. Asset Allocation and the Investment Horizon

Benartzi and Thaler (1999) (B&T) present subjects with a gamble reflecting a possible loss. The subjects could choose to gamble or not in an experiment which contains N repetitions. The subjects were reluctant to take the gamble. However, where the multi-period distributions of outcome induced by the N repetitions was presented to

Table 26.5. G dominates F by PSD even with CPT decision weights (task II of experiment 3 in levy and levy 2002b)

F			G		
Gain or loss	Probability	CPT decision weights	Gain or loss	Probability	CPT decision weights
−875	0.5	0.454	−1,000	0.4	0.392
2,025	0.5	0.421	1,800	0.6	0.474

Source: Levy and Levy, (2002b).

them, more subjects were willing to take the gamble. This shows that the subjects either have difficulties to integrate cash flows from various trials or they have "narrow framing." These results also have strong implications to asset allocation and the investment horizon. B&T found the subjects willing to invest a substantially higher proportion of their retirement funds in stocks (risky assets) once they were shown the distributions of the long-run return relative to the investment proportion when the distribution of return is not shown to them. The results of B&T shed light on the debate between practitioners and academicians regarding the relationship between the portfolio composition and the investment horizon. While Samuelson (1994) and others correctly claim that for myopic (power) utility functions, the investment horizon should not have any effect on asset allocation, practitioners claim that the longer the horizon, the higher the proportion of assets that should be allocated to stocks. The results of B&T support the practitioners' view provided that the subjects observe the multi-period distribution, i.e. overcoming the "narrow framing" effect. Ruling out irrationality or other possible biases, this finding means that the subjects in B&T's experiment do not have a myopic utility function. It is interesting that Leshno and Levy (2002) have shown that as the number of period N increases, stocks "almost" dominate bonds by FSD, when "almost" means for almost all preferences, not including the myopic function. Thus, this theoretical result is consistent with B&T's experimental results.

26.3.5. Diversification: the 1/n rule

Let us open this section by the following old assertion:

Man should always divide his wealth into three parts: one third in land, one third in commerce and one third retained in his own hands.

                                                    Babylonian Talmud

Two interesting conclusions can be drawn from this 1500-year-old recommendation, which is probably the first diversification recommendation. The first conclusion is consistent with what Markowitz recommended and formalized about fifty years ago: diversification pays. The second conclusion is in contrast to Markowitz's recommendation: invest 1/3 in each asset and ignore the optimum diversification strategy, which is a function of variances, correlations, and means.

It is interesting that Benartzi and Thaler (2001) experimentally find that this is exactly what investors do. Presented with n assets (e.g. mutual funds) the subject is inclined to invest $1/n$ in each fund. This is true regardless of the content of funds. If one fund is risky (stocks) or riskless, this does not change the $1/n$ choice, implicitly implying that the Talmud's recommendation is intact as correlations, means and variances are ignored. From this we learn that investors believe that "a little diversification goes a long way," but mistakenly ignore the optimal precise diversification strategy.

26.3.6. The CAPM: Experimental Study

One of the cornerstones of financial theory is asset pricing, as predicted by the CAPM. The problem with testing the CAPM empirically is that the *ex-ante* parameters may change over time. However, while the CAPM cannot be tested *empirically* with *ex-ante* parameters, it can be tested *experimentally* with *ex-ante* parameters. The subjects can provide buy-sell orders and determine collectively equilibrium prices of risky assets when the future cash flow (random variables) corresponding to the various assets are given. Levy (1997) conducted such an experiment with potential financial loss and reward to the subjects. Thus, like in Lintner's (1969) approach for given distributions of end-of-period returns, the subjects collectively determine, exactly as in an actual market, the current market values P_{io}. Therefore, the means μ_i, variances σ_i^2 and correlations, R_{ij} are determined simultaneously by the subjects. Having these parameters one can test the CAPM with *ex-ante* parameters. Lintner (1969) found that subjects typically diversify in only 3–4 assets (out of the 20 available risky assets), yet the CAPM, or the $\mu - \beta$ linear relationship was as predicted by the CAPM with an R^2 of about 75 percent. Thus, Levy found a strong support to the CAPM with *ex-ante* parameters.

26.4. Implication of the Experimentalfindings to Finance

26.4.1. Arbitrage Models

Let us first analyze the arbitrage-based models like Modigliani and Miller (M&M) (1958), Black and Scholes (1973) model and the APT model of Ross (1976). Let us first illustrate M&M capital structure with no taxes. Denoting by V_U and V_L the value of the unlevered and levered firms, respectively, M&M claim that $V_U = V_L$ further, if $V_U \neq V_L$, one can create an arbitrage position such that the investor who holds return $\tilde{y}$ will get after the arbitrage $\tilde{y} + a$ when $a > 0$. Thus, an FSD position is created and as the two returns are fully correlated, the FSD dominance implies an arbitrage position. Thus, arbitrage is achieved by selling short the overpriced firm's stock and holding long the underpriced firm's stock. If probability is distorted, this will not affect the results as the investor ends up with the same random variable. If preference is S-shaped, it does not affect the results as FSD position is created, which holds for all $u \in U_1$ and the S-shape functions are included in U_1. Making decisions based on change of wealth rather than total wealth also does not affect these results (recall that FSD is not affected by initial wealth). However, the fact that investors have difficulties in integrating cash flows from various sources may affect the result. The reason is that before the arbitrage, the investor holds, say, the stock of the levered firm. If $V_L > V_U$ the investor should sell the levered firm, borrow and invest in the unlevered firm. However, the investor should be able to *integrate* the cash flows from

these two sources and realize that the levered firm's return is duplicated. According to prospect theory, "mental departments" exists and the subjects may be unable to create this cash flow integration. However, recall that to derive the condition $V_L = V_U$, it is sufficient that *one* investor will be able to integrate cash flows to guarantee this equilibrium condition and not that all investors must conduct this arbitrage transaction ("money machine" argument).

Black and Scholes (B&S) equilibrium option pricing is based on the same no-arbitrage idea. Whenever the call option deviates from B&S equilibrium price economic forces will push it back to the equilibrium price until the arbitrage opportunity disappears. This is very similar to M&M case; hence it is enough that there is one sophisticated investor in the market who can integrate cash flows.

Thus, a "money machine" is created whenever the market price of an option deviates from its equilibrium price. The same argument holds for all theoretical models which are based on an arbitrage argument, e.g, Ross's (1976) arbitrage pricing theory (APT). Thus, for arbitrage models, the integration of cash flows issue may induce a problem to some investors but luckily, in these models, *one* sophisticated investor who knows how to integrate cash flows is sufficient to guarantee the existence of an asset price as implied by these models.

Despite this argument, in a multiperiod setting, when the investment horizon is uncertain, in some cases we do not have a pure arbitrage as the gap in the price of the two assets under consideration (e.g. $V_L > V_U$) may even (irrationally) increase over time (see Thaler, 1993). Thus, while in a one-period model where all assets are liquidated at the end of the period, the above argument is valid; this is not necessarily the case in a multi-period setting.

26.4.2. Stochastic Dominance (SD) Rules

It is easy to show that prospect F dominates prospect G in terms of total wealth $(W + x)$ if only F

dominates G with change in wealth (x). Thus, shifting from *total* wealth to *change* of wealth does not affect the dominance result. The same is true with the Mean-Variance rules. SD rules deal mainly with two distinct options and not with a mix of random variables, hence generally the issues of integration of cash flows does not arise with the application of SD rules (it is relevant, however, to the Mean-Variance rule). If preference is an S-shaped or reverse S-shape, FSD is intact as it is defined for all $u \in U_1(u' > 0)$. If probabilities are distorted by a distortion function $T(\cdot)$ where $F^* = T(F)$ and $T' > 0$, the FSD relationship is also unaffected by the distortion. Let us turn now to SSD and TSD. If preference is S-shape, SSD or TSD rules which assumes $u'' < 0$ are irrelevant. However, even with risk aversion, with probability distortion $T(F)$ ($T' > 0$), the SSD and TSD dominance relationships are affected. Thus, FSD is unaffected by the experimental findings of probability distortion, but SSD and TSD are affected. With probability distortion one should first transform probabilities and only then compare F^* and G^* when $F^* = T(F)$ or $G^* = T(P)$. However, as the kth individual is characterized by probability distortion T_k, each investor has his subjective SD efficient set and therefore the classical two-step portfolio selection (i.e. determining the efficient set in its first step and selecting the optimal portfolio from the efficient set in the second step) is meaningless as there is no one efficient set for all investors. To sum up, FSD efficiency analysis is intact and SSD and TSD are not. If, however, in SSD analysis, it is assumed that $T' > 0$ and $T'' < 0$, SSD analysis also remains intact (see Levy and Wiener, 1998).

26.4.3. Mean-Variance (M-V) Rule and PT

If the utility function is S-shaped or reverse S-shaped the Mean-Variance rule does not apply and hence it is not an optimal investment decision rule even in the face of normal distributions. Probability distortion is even more devastating to the M-V efficiency analysis. The whole idea of the M-V efficient set is that all investors face the same efficient set which depends on mean, variances and correlations. Now if the kth investor distorts F_i to $T_k(F_i)$ when F_i is the cumulative distribution of the ith asset, then we have K subjective efficient sets (composed of the individual assets) and the idea of M-V efficiency analysis breaks down. Nevertheless, as we shall see below, the M-V efficiency analysis surprisingly is intact in the presence of mutual funds, or if the probability distortion is done on portfolios but not on each individual asset.

26.4.4. Portfolios and Mutual Funds: Markowitz's M-V Rule and PT – A Consistency or a Contradiction?

It is interesting that in the same year (1952) Markowitz, published two seminal papers that seem to contradict one another. One of these papers deals with the M-V rule (Markowitz, 1952a) and the other with the reverse S-shape function (Markowitz, 1952b). The Mean-Variance rule implies implicitly or explicitly risk aversion, while the reverse S-shape function, and for that matter also the S-shape function of PT, imply that risk aversion does not hold globally. Do we have here a contradiction between these two articles of Markowitz?

To analyze this issue we must first recall that the M-V rule is intact in two alternate scenarios: (1) a quadratic utility function; and (2) risk aversion and normal distributions of return. Obviously, under S-shape or reverse S-shape preference, scenario (1) does not hold. What about scenario (2)? Generally, if one compares two assets X and Y, indeed it is possible that X dominates Y by the M-V rule, but the expected utility of Y is greater than the expected utility of X for a given S-shape function even if X and Y are normally distributed. Hence, for such a comparison of any two arbitrary prospects, the two papers of Markowitz are indeed in contradiction. However, when diversification among all available assets is allowed, Levy and Levy (2004) have shown that the two articles do not contradict each other but conform with each other. Let us be more specific. Figure 26.4 illustrates the M-V efficient frontier. It is possible that asset a dominates b by M-V rule but not for all S-shape or reverse S-shape functions. However, and that is the important point, for any interior asset like asset b, there is an asset b′ on the frontier which dominates b by the M-V rule as well as by EU for all monotonically increasing utility functions, including the S-shape and reverse S-shape functions. To see this claim, recall that under scenario (2) normal distributions are assumed. Regarding assets b and b' we have $\mu(b') > \mu(b)$ and $\sigma(b') = \sigma(b)$; hence portfolio b', dominates portfolio b by FSD, or $Eu(b') > Eu(b)$ for all utility functions, including the S-shape and reverse S-shape preferences (For FSD in the normal distribution case see Levy, 1998). Thus, Markowitz's M-V diversification analysis is intact for all $u \in U_1$ including $u \in U_M$ and $u \in U_{PT}$ as $U_M \subset U_1$ and $U_{PT} \subset U_1$. To sum up, the quadratic utility function does not conform with the experimental findings regarding preferences. Assuming normality and risk aversion is also not justified in light of the experimental findings regarding preferences. However, allowing investors to diversify (with nor-

mal distributions), the M-V efficient frontier is the efficient one also is EU framework, without the need to assume risk aversion. Also, as the FSD efficient set is invariant to change in wealth instead of total wealth, looking at the change of wealth rather than the total wealth does not change our conclusion. Thus, the two papers of Markowitz are not in contradiction as long as diversification is allowed, an assumption which is well accepted. Thus, while portfolio a dominates b with risk aversion, such dominance does not exist with other preferences with a risk seeking segment. But a vertical comparison (e.g. b and b′) allows us to conclude that Markowitz's M-V inefficient set is inefficient for all $u \in U_1$ and not only to risk averse utility functions (see Figure 26.4).

So far, we have dealt only with the factors of preferences and change of wealth rather than total wealth. Let us now see how the other findings of PT and CPT affect the M-V analysis. First, if individual investors fail to integrate cash flows from various assets, the M-V efficiency analysis and the Separation Theorem collapse. However, we have mutual funds and in particular indexed funds which carry the integration of cash flows for the investors. If such mutual funds are available – and in practice they are – the M-V analysis is intact also when one counts for the "mental departments" factor. To see this, recall that with a normal distribution mutual fund b' dominates mutual fund (or asset) b by FSD with objective distributions because $F_{b'}(X) \leq F_b(X)$ for all values x (see Figure 26.4). As FSD is not affected by CPT probability distortion, also $T(F_{b'}(X)) \leq T(F_b(X))$, hence the M-V efficient set (of mutual funds) is efficient also in CPT framework. Thus, change of wealth (rather than total wealth), risk-seeking segment of preference and probability distortion (as recommended by CPT), do not affect Markowitz's M-V efficiency analysis and the Separation Theorem. Hence, under the realistic assumption that mutual funds exist, the CAPM is surprisingly intact even under the many findings of experimental economics which contradict the CAPM assumptions.

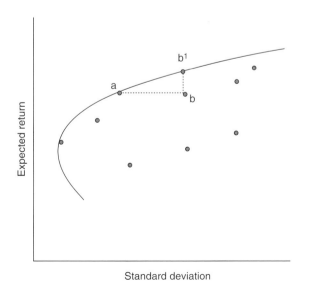

Figure 26.4. Mean–variance dominance and FSD dominance

26.4.5. The Empirical Studies and Decision Weights

Though we discuss above the probability distortion in the uniform case, we need to return to this issue here as it has a strong implication regarding empirical studies in finance.

Nowadays, most researchers probably agree that probability distortion takes place at least at the extreme case of low probabilities (probability of winning in a lottery, probability that a fire breaks out, etc.). Also probability distortion may take place when extreme gains or losses are incurred. Also the "certainty effect" is well documented. However, if one takes probability distortion too seriously and adopts it exactly as recommended by T&K (1992) [see eq. (3) above], paradoxes and absurdities emerge. For example, take the following two prospects:

x:	−$2,000	−$1,000	+$3,000	+$4,000
p(x)	1/4	1/4	1/4	1/4
y:	−$10^6	−$1,000	+$10^{12}	$10^{24}
p(y)	1/4	1/4	1/4	1/4

Employing the distortion of T&K [see eq. (3) above] for probability distortion implies the following decision weights:

x:	−$2,000	−$1,000	+$3,000	+$4,000
w (x)	0.29	0.16	0.13	0.29
y:	−$10^6	−$1,000	+$10^{12}	+$10^{24}
p(y)	0.29	0.16	0.13	0.29

Does it make sense? With x, the probability of $x = -2{,}000$ increases from 0.25 to 0.29, and the probability of $x = -1{,}000$ drops from 0.25 to 0.16. And similar is the case with y. Thus, the magnitudes of the outcomes are not important and the probabilities are distorted by the same formula regardless of whether the outcome is -10^6 or only $-2{,}000$. This type of probability distortion which is insensitive to the magnitude of the out-

comes, has been employed by Wakker (2003). Not everyone agrees with CPT weighting function [see eq. (3)]. Birnbaum and McIntosh (1996), finds that the probability distortion depends on the configuration of the case involved, hence suggests a "configurational weighting model." Moreover, Birnbaum experimentally shows that in some cases, FSD is violated. Note that FSD was the main reason why CPT and RDEU were suggested as substitutes to PT. Thus, if FSD is indeed violated, CPT is losing ground and PT may be a better description of investors' behavior. Similarly, Quiggin (1982) suggests that in cases where there are two equally likely outcomes with a 50:50 chance, probability is not distorted, which contradicts eq. (3). Viscusi (1989) shows that with probability $p_i = 1/n$ with n possible outcome, $w(1/n) = 1/n$, i.e. probability is not distorted. Also, the original PT of K&T implies that in case of an equally likely outcome, the choices are not affected by the decision weights. We emphasize this issue because the issue whether probability is distorted or not in equally likely outcomes has important implications to empirical studies.

In virtually all empirical studies in finance and economics where distribution is estimated, n observations are taken and each observation is assigned an equal probability. For example, this is the case in the calculation of σ^2, β, etc. If probabilities are also distorted in the uniform case, namely, $w(1/n) \neq 1/n$ as suggested by CPT of T&K, all the results reported in the empirical studies are questionable, including all the numerous empirical studies which have tested the CAPM. The implicit hypothesis in these studies is that in the uniform probability case, with no extreme values, probabilities are not distorted. We cannot prove this, but recall that the distortion formula of T&K is also obtained in a very limited case; an experiment with some specific lotteries when the S-shaped preference and the weighting function are tested simultaneously. Hence, the parametric assumptions concerning both functions are needed. Also, T&K report aggregate rather than individual results. Therefore, the burden of the proof that probabilities are distorted in the uniform case is on the advocates of PT and CPT. Finally, as mentioned above, if one employs PT (1979), decision weights where $w(1/n) = p_0$ for all observations, the decision maker who maximizes EU will not change his decision also in the uniform case (for a proof see, Levy and Levy, 2002b). However, with decision weight p_0 rather than $1/n$, the empirical results may change, despite the fact that choices are unchanged. This issue has to be further investigated.

26.5. Conclusion

Experimental research is very important as it allows us to control variables and sometimes to study issues that cannot be studied empirically, e.g. testing the CAPM with *ex-ante* parameters. Experimental findings and in particular Prospect Theory and cumulative Prospect Theory (PT and CPT, respectively) contradict expected utility theory (EUT) which, in turn, may have a direct implication to financial and economic decision making theory and to equilibrium models.

Taking the PT and CPT implication to the extreme, we can assert that virtually all models in finance and in particularly all empirical studies results and conclusions are incorrect. However, this conclusion is invalid for two reasons: (a) subjects in the experiments are not sophisticated investors who in practice risk a relatively large amount of their own money; and (b) one cannot conclude from a specific experiment (or from a few of them), conducted with no real money and with unequal probabilities that probabilities are distorted also in the uniform case, i.e. with equally likely outcomes. Therefore, PT and CPT do not have an unambiguous implication regarding the validity of the empirical studies in economics and finance which implicitly assume equally likely outcomes. Let us elaborate.

Drawing conclusions from the "average subject behavior" and assuming that also sophisticated investors behave in a similar way may be misleading. For example, for all arbitrage models it is possible that most subjects and even most investors

in practice do not know how to integrate cash flows, but it is sufficient that there are some sophisticated investors who integrate cash flows correctly to obtain the arbitrage models' equilibrium formulas (e.g. APT, M&M and B&S models). Probability distortion, various preference shapes and change of wealth rather than the total wealth, do not affect these arbitrage models. There are exceptions however. If the gap between the prices of the two assets increases irrationally rather than decreases over time, the arbitrage profit is not guaranteed (see Thaler, 1999). To sum up, in a one-period model where the assets are liquidated at the end of the period, the arbitrage models are intact, but this is not necessarily the case in a multi-period setting with irrational asset pricing.

The capacity of investors to carry cash-flows integration is crucial in particular for M-V portfolio selection. However, in this case we may divide the group of investors into two subgroups. The first group is composed of sophisticated investors who diversify directly; hence presumably do not conduct the common mistakes done by subjects in experiments. This group includes also the financial consultants and advisers who know very well how to take correlations of returns (integration of cash flows) into account. For example, professional advisers recommend that, "You don't want more than one company in an industry, and you don't want companies in related industries."[4]

This advice is quite common and one can document numerous other similar assertions made by practitioners. Therefore, it is obvious that cash-flows integration and correlations are well taken into account by this segment of investors. The other group of investors who may be exposed to all deviations from rationality are composed of the less sophisticated investors. These investors who cannot integrate cash flows from various sources may buy mutual funds managed by professional investors. Thus, if the M-V efficient set contains these mutual funds the Separation Theorem and the CAPM hold even with S-shape (or reverse S-shape) utility function, with change of wealth rather than total wealth and with CPT probability distortion. Thus, the CAPM is theoretically intact in the Rank Dependent Expected Utility (RDEU) framework. While the CAPM may not hold due to other factors (transaction codes, market segmentation, etc.), the experimental findings by themselves do not cause changes in the M-V efficiency analysis and the CAPM, as long as mutual funds exist in the market.

To sum up, though experimental findings open a new way of thinking on financial theory, most financial models, albeit not all of them, are robust even with these experimental findings. However, in some extreme cases, experimental evidence may explain phenomena, which cannot be explained by rational models. If investors follow some bounded rational behavior, booms and crashes in the stock market may be obtained (see Levy et al., 2000) even though there is no classical economic explanation for such a stock market behavior.

Acknowledgment

The author acknowledges the financial support of the Krueger Center of Finance.

NOTES

1. The analysis of the various alternate preferences of Figure 26.2 is taken from Levy and Levy, (2002).
2. For example, Markowitz argues that individuals with the Friedman and Savage utility function and wealth in the convex region would wish to take large symmetric bets, which is in contradiction to empirical observation.
3. For PSD see Levy and Weiner (1998) and Levy (1998) and Levy (1998). For MSD see Levy and Levy (2002a).
4. A quote from Mr. Lipson, a president of Horizon Financial Advisers, see *Wall Street Journal*, 10 April 1992 (an article by Ellen E. Schultz).

REFERENCES

Allais, M. (1953). "Le Comportement de l'homme rationnel devant le risque: Critique des postulates et axioms de l'école Americaine." *Econometrica*, 21: 503–564.

Arrow, K. (1965). *Aspects of the Theory of Risk Bearing.* Helsinki: Yrjo Jahnssonin Sattio.

Arrow, K.J. (1971). *Essays in the Theory of Risk Bearing.* Chicago: Markham Publishing Company.

Benartzi, S. and Thaler, R. (1995). "Myopic loss aversion and the equity premium puzzle." *The Quarterly Journal of Economics*, 110(1): 73–92.

Benartzi, S. and Thaler, R. (1999). "Risk aversion or myopia? Choices in repeated gambles and retirement investments." *Management Science,* 45(3): 364–381.

Benartzi, S. and Thaler, R. (2001). "Naive diversification strategies in retirement savings plans." *American Economic Review*, 91(1): 79–98.

Birnbaum, M.H. and McIntosh, W.R. (1996). "Violations of branch independence in choices between gambles." *Organizational Behavior and Human Decision Processes*, 67: 91–110.

Birnbaum, M.H. (1997). "Violations of monotonicity in judgment and decision making.," In A.A.J. Marley (Eds.), *Choice, decision, and measurement: Essays in honor of R. Duncan Luce* (pp. 73–100), Mahwah, NJ: Erlbaum.

Black, F. and Scholes, M. (1973). "The pricing of options and corporate liabilities." *Journal of Political Economy*, 81: 637–654.

Edwards, W. (1955). "The prediction of decisions among bets." *Journal of Experimental Psychology*, 50: 201–214.

Edwards, W. (1962). "Subjective probabilities inferred from decisions." *Psychology Review*, 69: 109–135.

Elton, E.J. and Gruber, M.J. (1984) *Modern Portfolio Theory and Investment Analysis,* 2nd edn. New York: Wiley.

Fama, E.F. (1965). "The behavior of stock market prices." *Journal of Business*, 38: 34–105.

Fishburn, P.C. (1978). "On Handa's 'new theory of cardinal utility' and the maximization of expected return." *Journal of Political Economy*, 86: 321–324.

Friedman, M. and Savage, L.J. (1948). "The utility analysis of choices involving risk." *Journal of Political Economy*, 56: 279–304.

Funk, S.G., Rapoport, A., and Jones, L.V. (1979). "Investing capital on safe and risky alternatives: an experimental study." *Journal of Experimental Psychology: General*, 108: 415–440.

Gordon, M.J., Paradis, G.E., and Rorke, C.H. (1972). "Experimental evidence on alternative portfolio decision rules." *The American Economic Review,* 52: 107–118.

Hadar, J. and Russell, W. (1969). "Rules for ordering uncertain prospects." *American Economic Review*, 59: 25–34.

Hanoch, G. and Levy, H. (1969). "The efficiency analysis of choices involving risk." *Review of Economic Studies*, 36: 335–346.

Kahneman, D. and Tversky, A. (1979). "Prospect theory of decisions under risk." *Econometrica*, 47(2): 263–291.

Kroll, Y. and Levy, H. (1992). "Further tests of separation theorem and the capital asset pricing model." *American Economic Review*, 82: 664–670.

Kroll, Y., Levy, H., and Rapoport, A. (1988a). "Experimental tests of mean-variance model for portfolio selection." *Organizational Behavior and Human Decision Processes*, 42: 388–410.

Kroll, Y., Levy, H., and Rapoport, A. (1988b). "Experimental tests of the separation theorem and the capital asset pricing model." *American Economic Review*, 78: 500–519.

Leshno, M. and Levy, H. (2002). "Preferred by 'All' and preferred by 'Most' decision makers: almost stochastic dominance." *Management Science*, 48: 1074–1085.

Levy, H. (1992). "Stochastic dominance and expected utility: survey and analysis." *Management Science*, 38(4): 555–593.

Levy, H. (1997). "Risk and return: an experimental analysis." *International Economic Review*, 38: 119–149.

Levy, H. (1998). *Stochastic Dominance: Investment Decision Making under Uncertainty*. Boston, MA: Kluwer Academic Publishers.

Levy, M. and Levy, H. (2001). "Testing the risk-aversion: a stochastic dominance approach." *Economics Letters*, 71: 233–240.

Levy, M. and Levy, H. (2002a). "Prospect theory: much ado about nothing?" *Management Science*, 48: 1334–1349.

Levy, M. and Levy, H. (2002b). "Experimental test of prospect theory value function." *Organizational Behavior and Human Decision Processes*, 89: 1058–1081.

Levy, H. and Levy, M. (2002c). "Arrow-Pratt risk aversion, risk premium and decision weights." *The Journal of Risk and Uncertainty,* 25: 265–290.

Levy, H. and Levy, M. (2004). "Prospect Theory and Mean-Variance Analysis." *The Review of Financial Studies*, 17: 1015–1041.

Levy, H. and Wiener, Z. (1998). "Stochastic dominance and prospect dominance with subjective weighting functions." *Journal of Risk and Uncertainty*, 16: 147–163.

Levy, M. Levy, H., and Solomon, S. (2000). *Microscopic Simulation of Financial Markets: from Investor Behavior to Market Phenomena*. San Diego, CA: Academic Press.

Lintner. J. (1965). "Security prices, risk, and maximal gains from diversification." *Journal of Finance*, 20: 587–615.

Machina, M.J. (1994). "Review of generalized expected utility theory: the rank-dependent model." *Journal of Economic Literature*, 32: 1237–1238.

Markowitz, H.M. (1952a). "Portfolio selection." *Journal of Finance*, 7: 77–91.

Markowitz, H.M. (1952b). "The utility of wealth." *Journal of Political Economy*, 60: 151–156.

Markowitz, H.M. (1959). *Portfolio selection*. New York: John Wiley.

Markowitz, H.M. (1987). *Mean Variance Analysis, Portfolio Choice and Capital Markets*. New York: Basil Blackwell.

Modigliani, F. and Miller, M.H. (1958). "The cost of capital corporation finance and the theory of investment." *American Economic Review*, 48: 261–297.

Odean, T. (1998). "Are investors reluctant to realize their losses." *Journal of Finance*, 53: 1775–98.

Plott, C.R. (1979). "The application of laboratory experimental methods to public choice," in C.S. Russell (ed.) *Collective Decision Making*. Washington: Resources for the Future.

Pratt, J.W. (1964). "Risk aversion in the small and in the large." *Econometrica*, 32: 122–136.

Prelec, D. (1998). "The probability weighting function." *Econometrica*, 66: 497–527.

Preston, M.G. and Baratta, P. (1948). "An experimental study of the auction-value of uncertain outcomes." *American Journal of Psychology*, 61: 183–193.

Quiggin, J. (1982). "A theory of anticipated utility." *Journal of Economic Behavior and Organization*, 3: 323–343.

Quiggin, J. (1993). *Generalized Expected Utility Theory: The Rank Dependent Model*. Boston, MA: Kluwer Academic Publishers.

Rapoport, A. (1984). "Effects of wealth on portfolio under various investment conditions." *Acta Psychologica,* 55: 31–51.

Ross, S.A. (1976). "The arbitrage theory of capital asset pricing." *Econometrica*.

Samuelson, P.A. (1994). "The long term case for equities." *Journal of Portfolio Management*, 21: 15–24.

Smith, V.L. (1976). "Experimental economics: induced value theory." *American Economic Review Proceedings,* 66: 274–279.

Smith, V.L. (1982). "Microeconomic systems as an experimental science." *The American Economic Review,* 72: 923–955.

Swalm, R.O. (1966). "Utility theory – Insights into risk taking." *Harvard Business Review*, 44: 123–136.

Thaler, H. (1993) *Advances in behavioral finance*; New York: Russell Sage Foundation, 1993.

Thaler, R.H. (1999). "The end of behavioral finance." *Financial Analysts Journal*, 55(6): 12–17.

Tobin, J. (1958). "Liquidity preferences as behavior toward risk." *Review of Economic Studies*, 25: 65–86.

Tversky, A. and Kahneman, D. (1981). "The framing of decisions and the psychology of choice." *Science*, 211: 453–480.

Tversky, A. and Kahneman, D. (1992). "Advances in prospect theory: cumulative representation of uncertainty." *Journal of Risk and Uncertainty*, 5: 297–323.

Viscusi, W.K. (1989). "Prospective reference theory: toward an explanation of the paradoxes." *Journal of Risk and Uncertainty*, 2: 235–264.

von Neuman, J. and Morgenstern, O. (1944). *Theory of games and economic behavior*. Princeton, NJ: Princeton University Press.

Wakker, P.P. (2003). "The data of Levy and Levy, 'Prospect theory: Much ado about nothing? actually support prospect theory.' *Management Science*, 48: 1334–1349.

Wakker, P.P., Erev, I., and Weber, E.U. (1994). "Comonotonic independence: the critical test between classical and rank-dependent utility theories." *Journal of Risk and Uncertainty*, 9: 195–230.

Wilde, L. (1980). "In the case of laboratory experiments in economics," in J. Pitt (ed.) *The Philosophy of Economics*. Dordrect, Holland: Reidel.

Yaari, M. (1987). "The dual theory of choice under risk." *Econometrica*, 55(1): 95–115.

Chapter 27

MERGER AND ACQUISITION: DEFINITIONS, MOTIVES, AND MARKET RESPONSES

JENIFER PIESSE, *University of London, UK and University of Stellenbosch, South Africa*
CHENG-FEW LEE, *National Chiao Tung University, Taiwan and Rutgers University, USA*
LIN LIN, *National Chi-Nan University, Taiwan*
HSIEN-CHANG KUO, *National Chi-Nan University and Takming College, Taiwan*

Abstract

Along with globalization, merger and acquisition has become not only a method of external corporate growth, but also a strategic choice of the firm enabling further strengthening of core competence. The mega-mergers in the last decades have also brought about structural changes in some industries, and attracted international attention. A number of motivations for merger and acquisition are proposed in the literature, mostly drawn directly from finance theory but with some inconsistencies. Interestingly, distressed firms are found to be predators and the market reaction to these is not always predictable. Several financing options are associated with takeover activity and are generally specific to the acquiring firm. Given the interest in the academic and business literature, merger and acquisition will continue to be an interesting but challenging strategy in the search for expanding corporate influence and profitability.

Keywords: merger; acquisition; takeover; LBO; synergy; efficiency; takeover regulations; takeover financing; market reaction; wealth effect

27.1. Introduction

Merger and acquisition (M&A) plays an important role in external corporate expansion, acting as a strategy for corporate restructuring and control. It is a different activity from internal expansion decisions, such as those determined by investment appraisal techniques. M&A can facilitate fast growth for firms and is also a mechanism for capital market discipline, which improves management efficiency and maximises private profits and public welfare.

27.2. Definition of "Takeover", "Merger", and "Acquisition"

Takeover, merger, and acquisition are frequently used synonymously, although there is clearly a difference in the economic implications of takeover and a merger (Singh, 1971: Conventions and Definitions). An interpretation of these differences defines takeover and acquisition as activities by which acquiring firms can control more than 50% of the equity of target firms, whereas in a merger at least two firms are combined with each other to form a "new" legal entity. In addition, it has been suggested that imprudent takeovers accounted for more than 75% of corporate failure in listed manufacturing firms in the United Kingdom over the periods 1948–1960 and 1954–1960 (Singh, 1971). In contrast, conglomerates resulting from mergers increased industry concentration during the same periods. Because of the different economic outcomes, distinguishing between these may be useful.

Other writers too have required a more careful definition of terms. Hampton (1989) claimed that "a merger is a combination of two or more businesses in which only one of the corporations survives" (Hampton, 1989, p. 394). Using simple algebra, Singh's (1971) concept of merger can be symbolized by $A + B = C$, whereas Hampton's (1989) can be represented by $A + B = A$ or B or C. What is important is the different degrees of negotiating power of the acquirer and acquiree in a merger. Negotiating power is usually linked to the size or wealth of the business. Where the power is balanced fairly equally between two parties, a new enterprise is likely to emerge as a consequence of the deal. On the other hand, in Hampton's (1989) definition, one of the two parties is dominant.

The confusion worsens when the definition replaces the word 'negotiating power' with 'chief beneficiary' and 'friendliness' (Stallworthy and Kharbanda, 1988). This claim is that the negotiating process of mergers and acquisitions is usually 'friendly' where all firms involved are expected to benefit, whereas takeovers are usually hostile and proceed in an aggressive and combative atmosphere. In this view, the term 'acquisition' is interchangeable with 'merger', while the term 'takeover' is closer to that of Singh's (1971).

Stallworthy and Kharbanda (1988, p. 26, 68) are not so concerned with the terminology and believed that it is meaningless to draw a distinction in practice. They also claim that the financial power of firms involved is the real issue. If one party is near bankruptcy, this firm will face very limited options and play the role of target in any acquisition activity. Rees (1990) disagrees and argues that is unnecessary to distinguish between terms because they arise from a similar legal framework in the United Kingdom.

27.3. Motives for Takeover

The rationale for takeover activity has been discussed for many years (see Brealey et al., 2001,

p. 641; Ross et al., 2002, p. 824). Unfortunately, no single hypothesis is sufficient to cover all takeovers and it is because the motives for takeovers are very complicated that it is useful to develop some framework to explain this activity. Of the numerous explanations available, the following are the most common in the literature, which has prompted the development of some hypotheses to explain takeover activities. Of these, eight broad reasons for takeover have emerged:

- Efficiency Theory
- Agency Theory
- Free Cash Flow Hypothesis
- Market Power Hypothesis
- Diversification Hypothesis
- Information Hypothesis
- Bankruptcy Avoidance Hypothesis
- Accounting and Tax Effects

Each are discussed in the next section, and clearly many are not mutually exclusive.

27.3.1. Efficiency Theories

Efficiency theories include differential efficiency theory and inefficiency management theory. Differential efficiency theory suggests that, providing firm A is more efficient than firm B and both are in the same industry, A can raise the efficiency of B to at least the level of A through takeover. Inefficiency management theory indicates that information about firm B's inefficiency is public knowledge, and not only firm A but also the controlling group in any other industry can bring firm B's efficiency to the acquirer's own level through takeover. These two theories are similar in viewing takeover as a device to improve the efficiency problem of the target firm. However, one difference is that firm B is not so inefficient that it is obvious to the firms in different industries in the first, but it is in the second. Thus, Copeland and Weston (1988) concluded that differential efficiency theory provides a theoretical basis for horizontal takeovers while inefficiency management theory supports conglomerate take-overs.

In the economics literature, efficiency assumes the optimal allocation of resources. A firm is Pareto efficient if there is no other available way to allocate resources without a detrimental effect elsewhere. However, at the organizational level, a firm cannot be efficient unless all aspects of its operations are efficient. Therefore, in this literature a simplified but common definition of efficiency is that 'a contract, routine, process, organization, or system is efficient in this sense if there is no alternative that consistently yields unanimously preferred results' (Milgrom and Roberts, 1992, p. 24). According to this definition, to declare a firm inefficient requires that another is performing better in similar circumstances, thus avoiding the problem of assessing the intangible parts of a firm as part of an efficiency evaluation.

The idea of efficiency in the takeover literature arises from the concept of synergy, which can be interpreted as a result of combining and coordinating the good parts of the companies involved as well as disposing of those that are redundant. Synergy occurs where the market value of the two merged firms is higher than the sum of their individual values. However, as Copeland and Weston (1988, p. 684) noted, early writers such as Myers (1968) and Schall (1972), were strongly influenced by Modigliani–Miller model (MM) (1958), who argued that the market value of two merged companies together should equal the sum of their individual values. This is because the value of a firm is calculated as the sum of the present value of all investment projects and these projects are assumed to be independent of other firms' projects. But this Value Additivity Principle is problematic when applied to the valuation of takeover effects. The main assumption is very similar to that required in the MM models, including the existence of a perfect capital market and no corporate taxes. These assumptions are very unrealistic and restrict the usefulness of the Value Additivity Principle in practice. In addition, the social gains or losses are usually ignored in those studies. Apart from those problems, the value creation argument has been supported by empirical studies. For example, Seth (1990) claimed that in both unrelated and related takeovers, value can be created to the same degree.

Synergy resulting from takeover can be achieved in several ways. It normally originates from the better allocation of resources of the combined firm, such as the replacement of the target's inefficient management with a more efficient one (Ross et al., 2002, p. 826) and the disposal of redundant and/or unprofitable divisions. Such restructuring usually has a positive effect on market value. Leigh and North (1978) found that this post-takeover and increased efficiency resulted from better management practices and more efficient utilisation of existing assets.

Synergy can also be a consequence of "operational" and "financial" economies of scale through takeovers (see Brealey et al., 2001, p. 641; Ross et al., 2002, p. 825). Operational economies of scale brings about the 'potential reductions in production or distribution costs' (Jensen and Ruback, 1983, p. 611) and financial economies of scale includes lower marginal cost of debt and better debt capacity. Other sources of synergy are achieved through oligopoly power and better diversification of corporate risk. Many sources of synergy have been proposed and developed into separate theories to be discussed in later sections.

Finally, efficiency can be improved by the introduction of a new company culture through takeover. Culture may be defined as a set of secret and invisible codes that determines the behavior patterns of a particular group of people, including their way of thinking, feeling, and perceiving everyday events. Therefore, it is rational to speculate that a successful takeover requires the integration of both company cultures in a positive and harmonious manner. Furthermore, the stimulation of new company culture could itself be a purpose of takeover, as Stallworthy and Kharbanda (1988) noted, and the merger of American Express and Shearson Loeb Rhoades (SLR) is a good example of this.

However, disappointing outcomes occur when a corporate culture is imposed on another firm following takeover conflict. This can take some time and the members of both organisations may take a while to adjust. Unfortunately, the changing business environment does not allow a firm much time to manage this adjustment and this clash of corporate cultures frequently results in corporate failure. Stallworthy and Kharbanda (1988, p. 93) found that, "it is estimated that about one-third of all acquisitions are sold off within five years... the most common cause of failure is a clash of corporate cultures, or 'the way things are done round here'."

27.3.2. Agency Theory

Agency theory is concerned with the separation of interests between company owners and managers (Jensen and Meckling, 1976). The main assumption of agency theory is that principals and agents are all rational and wealth-seeking individuals who are trying to maximize their own utility functions. In the context of corporate governance, the principal is the shareholder and the agent is the directors/senior management. The neoclassical theory of the firm assumes profit maximization is the objective, but more recently in the economics literature other theories have been proposed, such as satisficing behavior on the part of managers, known as behavioral theories of the firm. Since management in a diversified firm does not own a large proportion of the company shares, they will be more interested in the pursuit of greater control, higher compensation, and better working conditions at the expense of the shareholders of the firm. The separation of ownership and control within a modern organization also makes it difficult and costly to monitor and evaluate the efficiency of management effectively. This is known as "moral hazard" and is pervasive both in market economies and other organizational forms. Therefore, managing agency relationships is important in ensuring that firms operate in the public interest.

A solution to the agency problem is the enforcement of contractual commitments with an incentive scheme to encourage management to act in shareholders' interests. It can be noted that management compensation schemes vary between firms as they attempt to achieve different corporate goals. One of the most commonly used long-term remuneration plans is to allocate a fixed amount of company shares at a price fixed at the beginning of a multiyear period to managers on the basis of their performance at the end of the award period. By doing so, managers will try to maximize the value of the shares in order to benefit from this bonus scheme, thereby maximizing market value of the firm. Therefore, the takeover offer initiated by the firm with long-term performance plans will be interpreted by the market as good news since its managers' wealth is tied to the value of the firm, a situation parallel to that of shareholders. Empirically, it can be observed that "the bidding firms that compensate their executives with long-term performance plans, experience a significantly favorable stock market reaction around the announcements of acquisition proposals, while bidding firms without such plans experience the opposite reaction" (Tehranian et al., 1987, p. 74). Appropriate contracting can certainly reduce agency problems.

However, contracting may be a problem where there is information asymmetry. Managers with expertise can provide distorted information or manipulate reports to investors with respect to an evaluation of their end of period performance. This phenomenon is "adverse selection" and reflects information asymmetry in markets, a problem that is exacerbated when combined with moral hazard. Milgrom and Roberts (1992, p. 238) concluded that "the formal analysis of efficient contracting when there is both moral hazard and adverse selection is quite complex."

Another solution may be takeover. Samuelson (1970, p. 505) claimed that "takeovers, like bankruptcy, represent one of Nature's methods of eliminating deadwood in the struggle for survival." An inefficient management may be replaced following takeover, and according to Agrawal and Walkling (1994), encounters great difficulty in finding an equivalent position in other firms without considerable gaps in employment. In this way, takeover is regarded as a discipline imposed by the capital markets. Jensen and Ruback (1983) claimed that the threat of takeover will effectively force managers to maximize the market value of the firm as shareholders wish, and thus eliminate agency problems, or their companies will be acquired and they will lose their jobs. This is consistent with the observations of some early writers such as Manne. (1965).

Conversely, takeover could itself be the source of agency problems. Roll's (1986) hubris hypothesis suggests that the management of the acquirer is sometimes over-optimistic in evaluating potential targets because of information asymmetry, and in most cases, because of their own misplaced confidence about their ability to make good decisions. Their over-optimism eventually leads them to pay higher bid premiums for potential synergies, unaware that the current share price may have fully reflected the real value of this target. In fact, acknowledging that takeover gains usually flow to shareholders, while employee bonuses are usually subject to the size of the firm, managers are encouraged to expand their companies at the expense of shareholders (Malatesta, 1983). The hubris theory suggests that takeover is both a cause of and a remedy for agency problems. Through takeover, management not only increase their own wealth but also their power over richer resources, as well as an increased view of their own importance. But a weakness in this theory is the assumption that efficient markets do not notice this behavior. According to Mitchell and Lehn (1990), stock markets can discriminate between "bad" and "good" takeovers and bad bidders usually turn to be good targets later on. These empirical results imply that takeover is still a device for correcting managerial inefficiency, if markets are efficient. Of course, good bidders may be good targets too, regardless of market efficiency. When the market is efficient, a growth-oriented company can become an attract-

ive target for more successful or bigger companies who wish to expand their business. When firms are inefficient, a healthy bidder may be mistaken for a poor one and the resulting negative reaction will provide a chance for other predators to own this newly combined company. In these cases, the treatment directed towards target management may be different since the takeover occurs because of good performance not poor. In either case, Mitchell and Lehn (1990) admitted on the one hand that managers' pursuit of self-interest could be a motive for takeover but on the other they still argue that this situation will be corrected by the market mechanism.

27.3.3. Free Cash Flow Hypothesis

Closely connected to agency theory is the free cash flow hypothesis. Free cash flow is defined as "cash flow in excess of that required to fund all projects that have positive net present values when discounted at the relevant cost of capital (Jensen, 1986, p. 323)." Free cash flow is generated from economic rents or quasi rents. Jensen (1986) argued that management is usually reluctant to distribute free cash flow to shareholders primarily because it will substantially reduce the company resources under their control while not increasing their own wealth since dividends are not their personal goal but bonus schemes. However, the expansion of the firm is a concern in management remuneration schemes so that free cash flow can be used to fund takeover, and thus grow the company. In addition, because fund-raising in the market for later investment opportunities puts management under the direct gaze of the stock market, there is an incentive for management to hold some free cash flow or internal funds for such projects (Rozeff, 1982; Easterbrook, 1984). Consequently, managers may prefer to retain free cash to grow the company by takeover, even though sometimes the returns on such projects are less than the cost of capital. This is consistent with the empirical results suggesting that organizational inefficiency and over-diversification in a firm are normally the result of managers' intention to expand the firm beyond its optimal scale (Gibbs, 1993). Unfortunately, according to agency theory, managers' behaviors with respect to the management of free cash flow are difficult to monitor.

Compared with using free cash in takeovers, holding free cash flow too long may also not be optimal. Jensen (1986) found that companies with a large free cash flow become an attractive takeover target. This follows simply because takeover is costly and acquiring companies prefer a target with a good cash position to reduce the financial burden of any debt that is held now or with the combined company in the future. Management would rather use up free cash flow (retention) for takeovers than keep it within the firm. However, Gibbs (1993, p. 52) claims that free cash flow is only a "necessary condition for agency costs to arise, but not a sufficient condition to infer agency costs". In practice, some methods such as reinforcement of outside directors' power have also been suggested as a way to mitigate the potential agency problems when free cash flow exists within a firm. Apart from this legal aspect, management's discretion is also conditioned by fear of corporate failure. In a full economic analysis, an equilibrium condition must exist while the marginal bankruptcy costs equal the marginal benefits that management can gain through projects. Again, the disciplinary power of the market becomes a useful weapon against agency problem regarding the management of free cash flow.

27.3.4. Market Power Hypothesis

Market power may be interpreted as the ability of a firm to control the quality, price, and supply of its products as a direct result of the scale of their operations. Because takeover promises rapid growth for the firm, it can be viewed as a strategy to extend control over a wider geographical area and enlarge the trading environment (Leigh and North, 1978, p. 227). Therefore the market power hypothesis can serve as an explanation for horizontal and vertical takeovers.

Economic theory of oligopoly and monopoly identifies the potential benefits to achieving market power, such as higher profits and barriers to entry. The market power hypothesis therefore explains the mass of horizontal takeovers and the increasing industrial concentration that occurred during the 1960s. For example, in the United Kingdom, evidence shows that takeovers "were responsible for a substantial proportion of the increase in concentration over the decade 1958–1968 (Hart and Clarke, 1980, p. 99)."

This wave of horizontal takeovers gradually decreased during recent years, primarily because of antitrust legislation introduced by many countries to protect the market from undue concentration and subsequent loss of competition that results. Utton (1982, p. 91) noted that tacit collusion can create a situation in which only a few companies with oligopolistic power can share the profits by noncompetitive pricing and distorted utilization and distribution of resources at the expense of society as a whole. In practice, antitrust cases occur quite frequently. For example, one of the most famous antitrust examples in the early 1980s was the merger of G.Heileman and Schlitz, the sixth and fourth largest companies in the US brewing industry. The combined company would have become the third largest brewer in the United States, but this was prohibited by the Department of Justice on anti-competitive grounds. Similarly, in the United Kingdom, GEC's bid for Plessey was blocked by the Monopolies and Mergers Commission (MMC) in 1989 on the grounds of weakening price competition and Ladbroke's acquisition of Coral in 1998 was stopped for the same reason. At an international level, the US and European antitrust authorities were ready to launch detailed investigations in 1998 into the planned takeover of Mobil, the US oil and gas group, by Exxon, the world's largest energy group. More recently, irritated by antitrust lawsuits against him, Bill Gates of Microsoft accused the US government of attempting to destroy his company. However, horizontal takeovers are not the only target of the antitrust authorities and vertical and conglomerate takeovers are also of concern. This is because a "large firm's power over prices in an individual market may no longer depend on its relative size in that market but on its overall size and financial strength (Utton, 1982, p. 90)."

27.3.5. The Diversification Hypothesis

The diversification hypothesis provides a theoretical explanation for conglomerate takeovers. The diversification of business operations, i.e. the core businesses of different industries has been broadly accepted as a strategy to reduce risk and stabilise future income flows. It is also an approach to ensure survival in modern competitive business environments. In the United Kingdom, Goudie and Meeks (1982) observed that more than one-third of listed companies experiencing takeover in mainly manufacturing and distribution sectors during 1949–1973 could be classified as conglomerates. Since then, conglomerate takeover has become widespread as an approach to corporate external growth (Stallworthy and Kharbanda, 1988; Weston and Brigham, 1990).

Although different from Schall's (1971, 1972) Value Additivity Principle, Lewellen's (1971, 1972) coinsurance hypothesis provides a theoretical basis for corporate diversification. This argues that the value of a conglomerate will be greater than the sum of the value of the individual firms because of the decreased firm risk and increased debt capacity (see also Ross et al., 2002, pp.828–829, 830–833). Appropriate diversification can effectively reduce the probability of corporate failure, which facilitates conglomerate fund raising and increases market value. Kim and McConnell (1977) noted that the bondholders of conglomerates were not influenced by the increased leverage simply because the default risk is reduced. This result remains valid even when takeovers were financed by increased debt. Takeover can also result in an increased debt capacity as the merged firm is allowed to carry more tax subsidies, and according to the MM Proposition (1958, 1963), the tax shield provided by borrowings is a dominant factor in

firm valuation. In summary, the potentially higher tax deductions, plus the reduced bankruptcy costs, suggest that conglomerates will be associated with higher market values after takeovers.

Corporate diversification can also improve a firm's overall competitive ability. Utton (1982) stated that large diversified firms use their overall financial and operational competence to prevent the entry of rivals. One way to achieve this is through predatory pricing and cross subsidization, both of which can effectively form an entry barrier into the particular industry, and force smaller existing competitors out of the market. Entry via takeover reveals the inefficiency of incumbents as entry barriers are successfully negotiated. McCardle and Viswanathan (1994, p. 5) predicted that the stock prices of such companies should suffer. In fact, many writers had discussed this "build or buy" decision facing potential entrants (Fudenberg and Tirole, 1986; Harrington, 1986; Milgrom and Roberts, 1982). McCardle and Viswanathan (1994) used game theory to model the market reaction to direct/indirect entry via takeover. From these game theoretic models, there are indications that corporate diversification will not cause an increase in market value for the newly combined firm as opposed to Lewellen's (1971, 1972) coinsurance hypothesis, weakening the justification of diversification as a motive for takeover.

27.3.6. The Information Hypothesis

The information hypothesis stresses the signaling function of many firm-specific financial policies and announcements. It argues that such announcements are trying to convey information still not publicly available to the market and predict a revaluation of the firm's market value, assuming efficient markets. Takeovers have the same effect. Both parties release some information in the course of takeover negotiations and the market may then revalue previously undervalued shares.

This hypothesis has been supported by numerous event studies, demonstrating substantial wealth changes of bidders and targets (see the summary paper of Jensen and Ruback, 1983). Sullivan et al. (1994, p. 51) also found that the share prices of the firms involved in takeover "are revalued accordingly as private information is signaled by the offer medium that pertains to the target firm's stand-alone value or its unique synergy potential". Bradley et al. (1983) proposed two alternative forms of the information hypothesis. The first is referred to as the "kick-in-the-pants" hypothesis, which claims that the revaluation of share price occurs around the firm-specific announcements because management is expected to accept higher-valued takeover offers. The other is the "sitting-on-a-gold-mine" hypothesis asserting that bidder management is believed to have superior information about the current status of targets so that premiums would be paid. These two explanations both stress that takeover implies information sets which are publicly unavailable and favor takeover proposals. It is also noted that these two forms of information hypothesis are not mutually exclusive, although not all empirical research supports the information hypothesis (Bradley, 1980; Bradley et al., 1983; Dodd and Ruback, 1977; Firth, 1980; Van Horne, 1986).

Finally, the information hypothesis is only valid where there is strong-form market efficiency. Ross's signaling hypothesis (1977) points out that management will not give a false signal if its marginal gain from a false signal is less than its marginal loss. Therefore, it cannot rule out the possibility that management may take advantage of investors' naivety to manipulate the share price. The information hypothesis only suggests that takeover can act as a means of sending unambiguous signals to the public about the current and future performance of the firm, but does not take management ethics into account.

27.3.7. The Bankruptcy Avoidance Hypothesis

The early economic literature did not address bankruptcy avoidance as a possible motivation for takeover, largely because of the infrequent examples of the phenomenon. However, some writers

(for example, Altman, 1971) suggest the potential link between takeover and bankruptcy in financial decisions. Stiglitz (1972) argued that enterprises can avoid the threat of either bankruptcy or takeover through appropriately designed capital structures and regards takeover as a substitute for bankruptcy. Shrieves and Stevens (1979) also examined this relationship between takeover and bankruptcy as a market disciplining mechanism and found that a carefully timed takeover can be an alternative to bankruptcy.

However, intuition suggests that financially unhealthy firms are not an attractive target to potential predators. One way to resolve this dilemma is to consider the question from the bidder and target perspectives separately. To acquirers, the immediate advantages of a distressed target are the discounted price and lack of competition from other predators in the market. Much management time and effort is involved in searching and assessing targets, as well as the negotiation and funding process. This is much less for a distressed target than for a healthy one (Walker, 1992, p. 2). In addition, there may be tax benefits as well as the expected synergies. From the target shareholders' viewpoint, the motivation is more straightforward. Pastena and Ruland (1986, p. 291) noted that "with respect to the merger/bankruptcy choice, shareholders should prefer merger to bankruptcy because in a merger the equity shareholders receive stock while in bankruptcy they frequently end up with nothing."[1] However, while the bankruptcy avoidance hypothesis can be justified from the bidder and target shareholder perspectives, it fails to take the agency problem into account. Ang and Chua (1981) found that managers of a distressed company tended to stay in control if there was a rescue package or the firm was acquired.

However, not all distressed firms welcome acquisition as a survival mechanism and Gilson (1989) suggested that agency problems may not be the reason for the management of a distressed firm to reject a takeover offer. Managers dismissed from failing firms that filed for bankruptcy or private debt restructuring during 1979–1984, were still unemployed three years later, while those still in post were on reduced salary and a scaled-down bonus scheme (Gilson and Vetsuypens, 1993). Clearly, bankruptcy is costly to managers as well as other stakeholders.

If takeover can serve as a timely rescue for distressed companies, bankrupt firms present similar characteristics as distressed targets. In a two-country study, Peel and Wilson (1989, p. 217) found that in the United Kingdom, factors associated with corporate failure are similar to those in acquired distressed firms. These include longer time lags in reporting annual accounts, a going-concern qualification, and a high ratio of directors' to employees' remuneration, while neither company size or ownership concentration was important. However, in the United States, different factors were identified, with the differences attributed to the variation between the UK and US business environment.

Finally, although the benefits of acquiring distressed companies have been identified, Walker (1992) argued that there are economic advantages to acquiring distressed firms after their insolvency, as many problems will be solved by receivers at the time they are available for sale. Clearly, this weakens the validity of the bankruptcy avoidance hypothesis.

27.3.8. Accounting and Tax Effects

Profiting from accounting and tax treatments for takeover could be another factor influencing the takeover decision. Two accounting methods are at issue: the pooling of interests and the purchase arrangements. Copeland and Weston (1988) defined them as follows,

In a pooling arrangement the income statements and balance sheets of the merging firms are simply added together. On the other hand, when one company purchases another, the assets of the acquired company are added to the acquiring company's balance sheet along with an item called goodwill . . . [which is] the difference between the purchase price and the book value

of the acquired company's assets . . . [and, by regulation, should] be written off as a charge against earnings after taxes in a period not to exceed 40 years. (Copeland and Weston, 1988, p. 365)

Thus, the difference between the pooling and purchase methods lies in the treatment of goodwill, which is not recognized in the former but is in the latter. Not surprisingly, these two accounting treatments have different effects on company's postmerger performance. It is observed that "when the differential is positive (negative), the pooling (purchase) method results in greater reported earnings and lower net assets for the combined entity . . . the probability of pooling (purchase) increases with increases (decreases) in the differential (Robinson and Shane, 1990, p. 26)." After much debate, the pooling method was prohibited in the United States in 2001, which abolishes the accounting effects as a reason for merger and acquisition.

However, takeover can be motivated by tax considerations on the part of the owner. For example, a company paying tax at the highest rate may acquire an unsuccessful company in an attempt to lower its overall tax payment (Ross et al., 2002, p. 827). This may extend to country effects in that a firm registered in a low-corporate tax region will have a reduced tax liability from assets transferred associated with a takeover. The globalization of business increases the opportunity for cross-border takeovers, which not only reflect the tax considerations but have longer-term strategic implications.

27.4. Methods of Takeover Financing and Payment

A takeover can be financed through borrowings (cash) or the issue of new equity, or both (see Brealey et al., 2001, pp. 645–648; Ross et al., 2002, pp. 835–838). The sources of debt financing include working capital, term debt, vendor takeback, subordinated debt, and government contributions, while equity financing consists of mainly preferred and common shares, and also retained earnings (Albo and Henderson, 1987). The financing decision is specific to the acquiring firm and considerations such as equity dilution, risk policy, and current capital structure. Of course, the interrelation between the participants in the capital markets and the accessibility of different sources of financing is critical to any financing decision.

In debt financing, borrowers' credibility is the main concern of the providers of capital in determining the size and maturity of the debt. Some additional investigation may be conducted before a particular loan is approved. For example, lenders will be interested in the value of the underlying tangible assets to which an asset-based loan is tied or the capacity and steadiness of the cash flow stream of the borrower for a cash flow loan.

Equity financing can be divided into external and internal elements. External equity financing through the stock market is bad news as issuing new equity implies an overvalued share price, according to the signaling hypothesis. In contrast, debt financing is regarded as good news because increasing the debt-to-equity ratio of a firm implies managers' optimism about future cash flows and reduced agency problems. Therefore, debt financing is welcomed by the stock market as long as it is does not raise gearing levels too much.

Reserves are an internal source of equity financing, and is the net income not distributed to shareholders or used for investment projects, which then become part of owners' future accumulated capital. Donaldson (1961) and Myers (1984) suggest that a firm prefers reserves over debt and external equity financing because it is not subject to market discipline. This ranking of preferences is called the "the pecking order theory". However, given possible tax advantages, debt financing increases the market value of the firm to the extent that the marginal gain from borrowings is equal to the marginal expected loss from bankruptcy. The contradictory implications arising from these hypotheses results from the fundamentally different assumptions on which they are based. The pecking order theory of funding preference emphasizes agency theory, while the static trade-off argument that determines optimal capital structure assumes that managers' objectives are to maximize the market value of the firm. As to external equity financing, since this is a negative signal to the market and subject to unavoidable scrutiny, it is the last choice of funding for predators.

However, distressed acquirers have fewer options. Firstly, they may not have sufficient reserves for a takeover and may have to increase their already high gearing levels. They are also unwilling to issue new stocks, as this will jeopardize the current share price. Alternatively, they can initiate takeovers after resolving some problems through a voluntary debt restructuring strategy. Studies on the relationship between troubled firms and their debt claimants suggest that distressed firms have a better chance of avoiding corporate failure if the restructuring plan fits their current debt structure (Asquith et al., 1994; Brown et al., 1993; Gilson et al., 1990; John et al., 1992). Finally, distressed acquirers can finance takeovers by selling off part of the firm's assets. Brown et al. (1994) noted that such companies can improve the efficiency of their operations and management and repay their debts by partial sale of assets.

A growing literature on method of takeover payment shows the existence of a relationship between methods of takeover payment and of financing for takeover. Most of the research focuses on the common stock exchange offer and cash offer (Sullivan et al., 1994; Travlos, 1987). Those studies imply that wealthy firms initiate a cash offer but distressed ones prefer an all-share bid. However, it is not only the users that differentiate cash offers from all-share offers. As Fishman (1989, p. 41) pointed out, "a key difference between a cash offer and a (risky) securities offer is that a security's value depends on the profitability of the acquisition, while the value of cash does not." Therefore, it is reasonable to assume that the "costs" of using a cash offer are lower than those using an all-share offer, given conditions of information asymmetry. In addition, cash offers are generally accepted in "preempt competition," in which high premiums must be included in cash offers to "ensure that sufficient shares are tendered to obtain control (Hirshleifer and Titman, 1990, p. 295)."

27.5. Market Reaction to Acquiring Firms

Compared to research on the wealth effects of takeover on target shareholders, research on the effects on bidder shareholders is limited. Moreover, the results for target shareholders are more consistent (see Brealey et al., 2001, p. 652, 657; Ross et al., 2002, pp. 842–845) whereas those for bidder shareholders are still inconclusive. Halpern (1983, pp. 306–308) noted

> *The one consistent finding for all merger and takeover residual studies is the presence of large and significant positive abnormal returns and CAR's for the target firm's shareholders regardless of the definition of the event date... From the discussion of the abnormal returns to bidders it appears that tender offers are wealth maximising events. For mergers, the results are more ambiguous but leaning toward to the same conclusion.*

Jensen and Ruback (1983), Langetieg (1978), Bradley (1980), Dodd (1980), and Malatesta (1983) use using event study methods to examine the market reaction to acquiring firms and concur with this result. More recently, Lin and Piesse (2004) argue that such ambiguities result from ignorance of the distortion effects of distressed acquirers in many samples and find the stock market reacts differently to nondistressed and distressed bidders, given semi-strong efficiency. Therefore, a sample that does not separate the two groups properly will inevitably result in confusing results, despite the noise that frequently accompanies takeover activity.

The long-term performance of acquiring firms is also a concern. Agrawal et al. (1992) found that after a failed bid, shareholders in the United States generally suffered a significant loss of about 10%

over the following 5 years. Gregory (1997) came to the same conclusion despite known differences in the US and UK business environments, claiming this supported Roll's (1986) hubris hypothesis and agency theory.

27.6. Conclusion

Corporate mergers and acquisitions in industrialized economies are frequent and it is accepted that large mergers in particular have huge wealth redistribution effects as well as raising concerns for corporate governance and takeover codes. This activity is an useful corporate strategy, used by organizations to achieve various goals, and also acts as a mechanism for market discipline. A number of motivations for takeover have been discussed, although these are not mutually exclusive, while others are omitted altogether.

This paper has reviewed studies on merger motives, financing and payment methods, wealth creation, and distribution between bidders' and target shareholders and the impact of takeovers on the competitors of predator and target companies (Chatterjee, 1986; Song and Walkling, 2000). The growing scope for studies on takeover activity suggests that acquisition is an increasingly importance corporate strategy for changing business environments, and has implications for future industrial reorganization and the formation of new competitive opportunities.

Acknowledgements

We would like to thank many friends in University of London (U.K.) and National Chi Nan University (Taiwan) for valuable comments. We also want to thank our research assistant Chiumei Huang for preparing the manuscript and proofreading several drafts of the manuscript. Last, but not least, special thanks go to the Executive Editorial Board of the *Encyclopedia in Finance* in Springer, who expertly managed the development process and superbly turned our final manuscript into a finished product.

NOTES

1. Especially in a competitive bidding situation, target shareholders usually receive a premium on the market price of their shares, although competition for distressed companies is rare

REFERENCES

Agrawal, A. and Ralph A.W. (1994). 'Executive Careers and Compensation Surrounding Takeover Bids', *Journal of Finance*, 49(3): 985–1014.

Agrawal, A., Jaffe, J., and Mandelker, G.N. (1992). "The post-merger performance of acquiring firms: a re-examination of an anomaly." *Journal of Finance*, 47(4): 1605–1621.

Albo, W.P. and Henderson, R.A. (1987). *Mergers and Acquisitions of Privately-held Businesses*, Canadian Cataloguing in Publication Data.

Altman, E.I. (1971). *Corporate Bankruptcy in America*. New York: Lexington Books.

Ang, J.S. and Chua, J.H. (1981). "Corporate bankruptcy and job losses among top level managers." *Financial Management*, 10(5): 70–74.

Asquith, P., Gertner, R., and Scharfstein, D. (1994). "Anatomy of financial distress: an examination of junk bond issuers." *Quarterly Journal of Economics*, 109(3): 625–658.

Bradley, M. (1980). "Interfirm Tender Offers and the Market for Corporate Control." *Journal of Business*, 53(4): 345–376.

Bradley, M., Desai, A., and Kim, E.H. (1983). "The rationale behind interfirm tender offers: information or synergy." *Journal of Financial Economics*, 11(4): 183–206.

Brealey, R.A., Myers, S.C., and Marcus, A.J. (2001). *Fundamentals of Corporate Finance*, 3rd edn. New York: McGraw-Hill.

Brown, D.T., James, C.M., and Mooradian, R.M. (1993). "The information content of distressed restructurings involving public and private debt claims." *Journal of Financial Economics*, 33(1): 93–118.

Brown, D.T., James, C.M., and Mooradian, R.M. (1994). "Asset sales by financially distressed firms." *Journal of Corporate Finance*, 1(2): 233–257.

Chatterjee, S. (1986). "Types of synergy and economic value: the impact of acquisitions on merging and rival firms." *Strategic Management Journal*, 7(2): 119–139.

Copeland, T.E. and Weston, J.F. (1988). *Financial Theory and Corporate Policy*, 3rd edn. Reading: Addison-Wesley.

Dodd, P. and Ruback, R. (1977). "Tender offers and stockholder returns: an empirical analysis." *Journal of Financial Economics*, 5(3): 351–374.

Dodd, P. (1980). "Merger proposals, management discretion and stockholder wealth." *Journal of Financial Economics*, 8: 105–137.

Donaldson, G. (1961). *Corporate Debt Capacity: A Study of Corporate Debt Policy and the Determination of Corporate Debt Capacity*. Boston: Division of Research, Harvard Graduate School of Business Administration.

Easterbrook, F.H. (1984). "Two agency-cost explanations of dividends." *American Economic Review*, 74(4): 650–659.

Firth, M. (1980). "Takeovers, shareholder returns, and the theory of the firm." *Quarterly Journal of Economics*, 94(2): 235–260.

Fishman, M.J. (1989). "Preemptive bidding and the role of the medium of exchange in Acquisitions." *Journal of Finance*, 44(1): 41–57.

Fudenberg, D. and Tirole, J. (1986). "A 'signal-jamming' theory of predation." *RAND Journal of Economics*, 17(3): 366–376.

Gibbs, P.A. (1993). "Determinants of corporate restructuring: the relative importance of corporate governance, takeover threat, and free cash flow." *Strategic Management Journal*, 14(special issue): 51–68.

Gilson, S.C. (1989). "Management turnover and financial distress." *Journal of Financial Economics*, 25(2): 241–262.

Gilson, S.C. and Vetsuypens, M.R. (1993). "CEO compensation in financially distressed firms: an empirical analysis." *Journal of Finance*, 48(2): 425–458.

Gilson, S.C., John, K., and Lang, L.H.P. (1990). "Troubled debt restructurings: an empirical study of private reorganisation of firms in default." *Journal of Financial Economics*, 27(2): 315–353.

Goudie, A.W. and Meeks, G. (1982). "Diversification by Merger." *Economica*, 49(196): 447–459.

Gregory, A. (1997). "An examination of the long run performance of uk acquiring firms." *Journal of Business Finance*, 24(7 and 8): 971–1002.

Halpern, P. (1983). "Corporate acquisitions: a theory of special cases? a review of event studies applied to acquisitions." *Journal of Finance*, 38(2): 297–317.

Hampton, J.J. (1989). *Financial Decision Making: Concepts, Problems, and Cases*, 4th edn. New Jersey: Prentice-Hall.

Harrington, J.E. (1986). "Limit pricing when the potential entrant is uncertain of its cost function." *Econometrica*, 54(2): 429–438.

Hart, P.E. and Clarke, R. (1980). *Concentration in British Industry 1935–75*. London: Cambridge University Press.

Hirshleifer, D. and Titman, S. (1990). "Share tendering strategies and the success of hostile takeover bids." *Journal of Political Economics*, 98(2): 295–324.

Jensen, M.C. (1986). "Agency costs of free cash flow, corporate finance, and takeovers." *American Economic Review*, 76(2): 323–329.

Jensen, M.C. and Meckling, W.H. (1976). "Theory of the firm: managerial behaviour, agency cost and ownership structure." *Journal of Financial Economics*, 3: 305–360.

Jensen, M.C. and Ruback, R.S. (1983). "The market for corporate control: the scientific evidence." *Journal of Financial Economics*, 11(1–4): 593–638.

John, K., Lang, L.H.P., and Netter, J. (1992). "The voluntary restructuring of large firms in response to performance decline." *Journal of Finance*, 47(3): 891–917.

Kim, H. and McConnell, J. (1977). "Corporate mergers and co-insurance of corporate debt." *Journal of Finance*, 32(2): 349–365.

Langetieg, T.C. (1978). "An application of a three-factor performance index to measure stockholder gains from merger." *Journal of Financial Economics*, 6: 365–383.

Leigh, R. and North, D.J. (1978). "Regional aspects of acquisition activity in british manufacturing industry." *Regional Studies*, 12(2): 227–245.

Lewellen, W.G. (1971). "A pure financial rationale for the conglomerate merger." *Journal of Finance*, 26(2): 521–537.

Lewellen, W.G. (1972). "Finance subsidiaries and corporate borrowing capacity." *Financial Management*, 1(1): 21–31.

Lin, L. and Piesse, J. (2004). "Financial risk assessment in takeover and the change of bidder shareholders' wealth." *International Journal of Risk Assessment and Management*, 4(4): 332–347.

Malatesta, P.H. (1983). "The wealth effect of merger activity and the objective functions of merging firms." *Journal of Financial Economics*, 11: 155–181.

Manne, H.G. (1965). "Mergers and the market for corporate control." *Journal of Political Economy*, 73(2): 110–120.

McCardle, K.F. and Viswanathan, S. (1994). "The direct entry versus takeover decision and stock price performance around takeovers." *Journal of Business*, 67(1): 1–43.

Milgrom, P. and Roberts, J. (1982). "Limit pricing and entry under incomplete information: An equilibrium analysis." *Econometrica*, 50(2): 443–460.

Milgrom, P. and Roberts, J. (1992). *Economics, Organisation and Management*. New Jersey: Prentice-Hall.

Mitchell, M.L. and Lehn, K. (1990). "Do bad bidders become good targets?" *Journal of Political Economy*, 98(2): 372–398.

Modigliani, F. and Miller, M.H. (1958). "The cost of capital, corporation finance, and the theory of investment." *American Economic Review*, 48(3): 261–297.

Modigliani, F. and Miller, M.H. (1963). "Corporate income taxes and the cost of capital." *American Economic Review*, 53(3): 433–443.

Myers, S.C. (1968). "Procedures for capital budgeting under uncertainty." *Industrial Management Review*, 9(3): 1–19.

Myers, S.C. (1984). "The capital structure puzzle." *Journal of Finance*, 39(3): 575–592.

Pastena, V. and Ruland, W. (1986). "The merger bankruptcy alternative." *Accounting Review*, 61(2): 288–301.

Peel, M.J. and Wilson, N. (1989). "The liquidation/merger alternative: some results for the UK corporate sector." *Managerial and Decision Economics*, 10(3): 209–220.

Rees, B. (1990). *Financial Analysis*. London: Prentice-Hall.

Robinson, R.J and Shane, P.B. (1990). "Acquisition accounting method and bid premia for target firms." *The Accounting Review*, 65(1): 25–48.

Roll, R. (1986). "The hubris hypothesis of corporate takeovers." *Journal of Business*, 59(2): 197–216.

Ross, S.A. (1977). "The determination of financial structure: the incentive signalling approach." *Bell Journal of Economics*, 8(1): 23–70.

Ross, S.A., Westerfield, R.W., and Jaffe, J.F. (2002). *Corporate Finance*, 6th edn, New York: McGraw-Hill.

Rozeff, M. (1982). "Growth, beta and agency costs as determinants of dividend payout ratios." *Journal of Financial Research*, 5: 249–259.

Samuelson, P. (1970). *Economics*, 8th edn. New York: McGraw-Hill.

Samuelson, R.J. (1986). "How Companies Grow Stale." *Newsweek*, 8: 45.

Schall, L.D. (1971). "Firm financial structure and investment." *Journal of Financial and Quantitative Analysis*, 6(3): 925–942.

Schall, L.D. (1972). "Asset valuation, firm investment, and firm diversification." *Journal of Business*, 45(1): 11–28.

Seth, A. (1990). "Value creation in acquisitions: a re-examination of performance issues." *Strategic Management Journal*, 11: 99–115.

Shrieves, R. and Stevens, D. (1979). "Bankruptcy avoidance as a motive for merger." *Journal of Financial and Quantitative Analysis*, 14(3): 501–515.

Singh, A. (1971). *Take-overs: Their Relevance to the Stock Market and the Theory of the Firm.* Cambridge: Cambridge University Press.

Song, M.H. and Walking, R.A. (2000). "Abnormal returns to rivals of acquisition targets: a test of 'Acquisition Probability Hypothesis'." *Journal of Financial Economics*, 55: 143–171.

Stallworthy, E.A. and Kharbanda, O.P. (1988). *Takeovers, Acquisitions and Mergers: Strategies for Rescuing Companies in Distress.* London: Kogan Page.

Stiglitz, J. (1972). "Some aspects of the pure theory of corporate finance: bankruptcies and takeover." *The*

Bell Journal of Economics and Management Science, 3(2): 458–482.

Sullivan, M.J., Jensen, M.R.H., and Hudson, C.D. (1994). "The role of medium of exchange in merger offers: examination of terminated merger proposal." *Financial Management*, 23(3): 51–62.

Tehranian, H. Travlos, N., and Waegelein, J. (1987) "The effect of long-term performance plans on corporate sell-off induced abnormal returns." *Journal of Finance*, 42(4): 933–942.

Travlos, N.G. (1987). "Corporate takeover bids, methods of payment, and bidding firms' stock returns." *Journal of Finance*, 42(4): 943–963.

Utton, M.A. (1982). *The Political Economy of Big Business.* Oxford: Martin Robertson.

Van Horne, J.C. (1986). *Financial Management and Policy*, 7th edn. New Jersey: Prentice-Hall.

Walker, I.E. (1992). *Buying A Company in Trouble: A Practical Guide.* Hants: Gower.

Weston, J.F. and Brigham, E.F. (1990). *Essentials of Managerial Finance*, 9th edn. London: Dryden Press.

Chapter 28

MULTISTAGE COMPOUND REAL OPTIONS: THEORY AND APPLICATION

WILLIAM T. LIN, *Tamkang University, Taiwan*
CHENG-FEW LEE, *National Chiao Tung University, Taiwan and Rutgers University, USA*
CHANG-WEN DUAN, *Tamkang University, Taiwan*

Abstract

We explore primarily the problems encountered in multivariate normal integration and the difficulty in root-finding in the presence of unknown critical value when applying compound real call option to evaluating multistage, sequential high-tech investment decisions. We compared computing speeds and errors of three numerical integration methods. These methods, combined with appropriate root-finding method, were run by computer programs Fortran and Matlab. It is found that secant method for finding critical values combined with Lattice method and run by Fortran gave the fastest computing speed, taking only one second to perform the computation. Monte Carlo method had the slowest execution speed. It is also found that the value of real option is in reverse relation with interest rate and not necessarily positively correlated with volatility, a result different from that anticipated under the financial option theory. This is mainly because the underlying of real option is a nontraded asset, which brings dividend-like yield into the formula of compound real options.

In empirical study, we evaluate the initial public offering (IPO) price of a new DRAM chipmaker in Taiwan. The worldwide average sales price is the underlying variable and the average production cost of the new DRAM foundry is the exercise price. The twin security is defined to be a portfolio of DRAM manufacturing and packaging firms publicly listed in Taiwan stock markets. We estimate the dividend-like yield with two methods, and find the yield to be negative. The negative dividend-like yield results from the negative correlation between the newly constructed DRAM foundry and its twin security, implying the diversification advantage of a new generation of DRAM foundry with a relative low cost of investment opportunity. It has been found that there is only a 4.6 percent difference between the market IPO price and the estimated one.

Keywords: average sales price; CAPM; closed-form solution; critical value; dividend-like yield; DRAM chipmaker; DRAM foundry; Fortran; Gauss quadrature method; investment project; IPO; Lattice method; management flexibility; Matlab; Monte Carlo method; multivariate normal integral; non-traded asset; real call option; secant method; strategic flexibility; twin security; vector autoregression; uncertainty.

28.1. Introduction

Since Brennan and Schwartz (1985) applied the options theory to the evaluation of natural resources investment projects, further researches in this area have focused on valuing specific forms of managerial or project flexibility and on determining how to optimally capture the full value of such flexibility, ignoring the net present value (NPV) framework. The biggest difference between real option and financial option models is that the underlying of real option is a nontraded asset, which is not reproducible. Thus, we cannot compute the value of real option under a risk-neutral framework.

McDonald and Siegel (1984, 1985) noted if the object of investment is a nontraded asset, its expected return will be lower than the equilibrium total expected rate of return required in the market from an equivalent-risk traded security. Thus there exists a rate of return shortfall. (d) in the real option pricing model, which is the difference between the security's expected rate of return (α_s) and the real growth rate of the underlying asset (α_v), rendering the pricing of nontraded assets and traded assets somewhat different. Trigeorgis (1993a, b) also observed that regardless of whether the underlying asset under valuation is traded or not, it may be priced in the world of systematic risk by substituting the real growth rate with certainty-equivalent rate.

In the rapidly developing economic environment, information acquired by the management of a business or investor is oftentimes incomplete. Management often needs to make investment decision under high uncertainty. In real world, a business frequently adjusts its investment decision in response to the uncertainty in the market. Traditional evaluation models for investment do not offer full management flexibility, which however may be remedied by the approach of real options. Keeley et al. (1996) indicate that a proper evaluation model must reflect the "high risk" and "multistage" nature of an investment project and capture the prospective profit growth of the firm. Trigeorgis (1994), Amram and Kulatilaka (1999), Copeland and Antikarov (2001), and McDonald (2002) suggested the use of real options approach for evaluation of investment decision. Relative to the net present value (NPV) approach, which employs the "one-dimensional" thinking of NPV being greater than zero or not, real options is a "two-dimensional" approach that concurrently captures the NPV of the hi-tech investment opportunity and the volatility contained in the uncertainty.

According to the economic growth theory of Schumpeter (1939), a normal and healthy economic system does not grow steadily along some fixed path, and creative destruction is the main reason for the disintegration of a fixed normal economic system. Schumpeter further observed that such creative destruction is brought about by technological innovations. Therefore, in a new industry, technological innovations, which induce more inventions, are the main cause of economic cycle. Innovations tend to attract investment activities that give the technology market effect and bring new profit opportunities. In industrialized countries, many studies have demonstrated that technological innovations drive long-run economic growth, improve productivity, and introduce new products to the market. It is no doubt that innovations bring growth and profit opportunities for businesses. In the U.S., the earnings of a high-tech firm often do not have a direct bearing on its stock price. More often than not, earnings and stock price of a firm move in opposite directions, indicating the value of a high-tech firm lies in innovations, and not in physical assets such as equipment and plant. Hence the valuation of the investment project of a continuously innovating high-tech firm with high profit is an interesting study. This chapter intends to explore whether innovations do bring big profit opportunities that coincide with the theory of Schumpeter (1939).

In the case study of ProMos, the company's main product is DRAM. The DRAM products have strict requirements for process equipment and technology. For the DRAM industry, technological innovations are often illustrated in the process technology and equipment. The new DRAM foundry project of ProMos in 1996 fits the approach of real options. The costs of plant construction, operation, and R&D are very high. It is a capital-intensive investment project and the plant building will take several years. Thus, it involves a sequential multistage capital budgeting process

(Trigeorgis, 1994), characterized by the cash flow in initial stage of the project being small and that in later stages big. This project targets primarily in-the-money opportunity presented when the market undergoes rapid growth. A single-stage model is inadequate for this kind of project, while multistage real option is more appropriate for depicting the value of decision points throughout the project.

The model should be able to reflect the multistage and high-risk nature of high-tech investment. In simulation, we assume that the investment decision in each stage is made at the beginning of the stage, that when the value of real options is higher than the planned investment amount for the stage, the project will be implemented and continue until the end of the stage when the decision for the next stage is made. Thus, the real option for each stage is European style. As discussed above, the model used to evaluate an investment project involving high-tech industry must also remedy the fact that the investment project is a nontraded asset. Trigeorgis (1993) handled the property of a nontraded asset with dividend-like yield, which is defined as the rate of return short fall. In the dividend-like yield, there exists a positive correlation between the underlying asset and twin security; if the dividend-like yield is positive, it suggests the positive correlation between the underlying asset and twin security, implying poor diversification and high-opportunity costs of the new investment project; conversely, it implies diversification advantage and low-opportunity costs of the new investment project.

We extend the closed-form solution of Geske (1979) for two-stage compound financial options to a closed-form solution for multistage compound real options to depict the multistage, sequential nature of a high-tech investment project. We also examine the difference in valuation algorithm brought about by the inclusion of nontraded assets into the options theory. We also tackle the difficulty encountered in closed-form solution of multivariate normal integration and the nonlinear root-finding of critical value, and compare the computing speed and the degree of error reduction of different multivariate normal integration numer-ical procedures in combination with various critical value root-finding methods.

Finally, we study the new DRAM foundry investment case of ProMos to discuss how to select the underlying variable and twin security in an investment project that is a nontraded asset under the framework of real options. We will also estimate the exercise price and dividend-like yield, based on which, to determine of value of ProMos at the time of initial public offering (IPO) and carry out sensitivity analysis.

28.2. Real Options

The concept of real options was first proposed by Myers (1977), who observed that the assets of many firms, in particular investment projects with growth opportunity may be expressed as a call option. Real options apply the analytical framework of financial options, which take into account management flexibility and strategic flexibility overlooked in the traditional NPV approach, and consider the irreversibility and deferability of investment decision. Trigeorgis and Mason (1987) pointed out that corporate management frequently adopts decision mechanism with considerable flexibility when dealing with highly uncertain, large investment project. Thus the valuation of such project should include the traditional NPV_3 plus the options value derived from management flexibility, which is termed "*expanded NPV*":

$$\text{Expanded NPV} = \text{Static NPV} + \text{Value of Real Option} \quad (28.1)$$

Thus, the higher the uncertainty and the longer the investment period, the greater the discount rate and the smaller the NPV, but the drop in NPV will be offset by the *value of real option* derived from management flexibility. That is why discount cash flow (DCF) based evaluation methods[4] are often questioned by researchers. The NPV approach is suitable for the valuation of fixed cash flow investments, such as bonds, but does not express well when the investment project has uncertain factors, such as strategic moves and subsequent investment opportunities. The real options approach can capture the value of latent profit opportunities brought about by such uncertainties.

In high-tech industries like biotechnology and semiconductor, the risks are high and cash flow is small, which may be even negative in the initial development of a new generation of technology. But when the product is accepted by the market and enters the mass production stage, cash flow is high and the stock price of the company often rises sharply. It is as if these businesses are out-of-money in their initial stage and become in-the-money in the mass production stage, bringing substantial prospective profit opportunity for investors who put money into the firm at the initial stage. Therefore the evaluation model for the high-tech investment project is different from the NPV method, which follows the theory of the higher the risk, the greater the discount rate and the smaller the NPV.

Luehrman (1998a,b) indicated that information required for evaluation of investment project using real options method is just expanded information for the traditional model and not difficult to obtain. Luehrman (1998a,b) also suggested that NPV method is a "one-dimensional" thinking that evaluates whether the NPV of the underlying asset is greater than zero, while real options method is a "two-dimensional" thinking, which takes into account the NPV of the underlying and the opportunity presented by uncertainties. Thus in the evaluation of investment project with high uncertainty, the latter offers a better decision-making approach than other methods. Through the concept of flexibility in American options, real options approach allows the selection of optimal time point for exercise. The traditional evaluation techniques do not offer such flexible decision-making.

Given the high uncertainty in the high-tech industry, investors or management not only need to consider the R&D and manufacturing capabilities of the business, but also the impact the product will be subjected to in the market. Amram and

Kulatilaka (1999) suggested that management should evaluate the extent of its ability to bear the uncertainty to explain the interaction between investment opportunity and uncertainty so as to make the optimal investment decision. Figure 28.1 is a perfect interpretation of the relationship between the value of investment opportunity and uncertainty as presented by Amram and Kulatilaka (1999); from the traditional viewpoint, an investment with high uncertainty will see its value fall. But under the viewpoint of real options, the value of an investment opportunity increases with the decisions made by the management as degree of uncertainty rises. For high-tech industry characterized by high growth, timely actions taken by the management in response to the uncertain condition can create greater value for the entire investment project. Such view is consistent with the suggestion of Trigeorgis (1996) that real options approach offers management flexibility and strategic flexibility.

Lurhrman (1998a,b) used option space[5] created by two option-value metrics of value-to-cost (NPV_q) and volatility[6] to illustrate the technique of real options and locate the investment opportunity in the space for decision-making. Setting $NPV_q = 1$ as the center of abscissa, Lurhrman (1998a,b) divided the option space into six regions as shown in Figure 28.2, each representing a different "level" of investment opportunity, which are respectively invest now, maybe now, probably later, invest never, probably never, and maybe

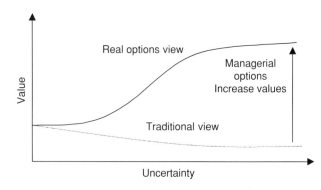

Figure 28.1. Uncertainty increases value (Amram and kulatilaka 1999)

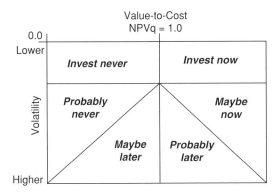

Figure 28.2. Lurhrman's option space

later. Such classification fully depicts the spirit of decision-making.

In the option space presented by Luehrman, the greater the NPV_q, the higher the cumulative variance ($\sigma^2 t$) and the higher the value of the investment project; if $NPV_q > 1$, the cumulative variance is small, indicating that other changes will be small in the future and the investment project may proceed right away. Alternately, projects with $NPV_q > 1$ and small cumulative variance should not go ahead, while projects with large cumulative variance and relatively high uncertainty may be decided later after the inflow of new information. Projects with $NPV_q > 1$ should not be executed immediately, but wait for situation to clear up before making the decision. Using option-value metrics for investment decision-making captures the NPV of the project and the value of opportunity under high risk. The two-dimensional model of real options is perfectly interpreted in the option space of Lurhrman (1998a,b).

28.2.1. Treatment of Nontraded Assets

The partial differential equation (PDE) for the pricing of derivative products derived under arbitrage-free argument may be applied regardless of whether the underlying asset is traded or not. Hull (1997) indicated that the Black–Scholes–Merton's PDE does not contain the variable of risk preferences, that is, it assumes that the risk attitude of the investors is irrelevant to the underlying. Hence,

the use of risk-neutral evaluation method is meaningless in the evaluation of nontraded assets. In the real world, underlying assets to be valued are mostly nontraded assets that make the risk attitude of the investor an important factor. If the expected growth rate of the underlying asset is adjusted, it amounts to pricing the asset in a risk-neutral world.

Constantinides (1978) priced underlying asset with market risk in a world where the market price of risk is zero. He utilized the certainty equivalence approach to adjust the parameters in the model to effective value, that is, deducting risk premium and discounting the expected cash flows at the risk-free rate. The Constantinides model lets $\tilde{x}$ be cash flow, realized at the end of period, hence the risk-adjusted NPV given by capital asset pricing model (CAPM) under the assumption of single period is:

$$RANPV(\tilde{x}) = \frac{\bar{x} - (\bar{r}_m - r_f)\mathrm{cov}(\tilde{r}_m, \tilde{x})/\sigma_m^2}{1 + r_f} \quad (28.2)$$

where r_m, r_f, and σ_m are, respectively, market rate of return, risk-free return, and rate of market return shortfall. Under the assumption of zero market price of risk, $\bar{x} - (\bar{r}_m - r_f)\mathrm{cov}(\tilde{r}_m, \tilde{x})/\sigma_m^2$ depicts the expected cash flow ($\bar{x}$), which is adjusted to certainty-equivalent cash flows and discounted at the risk-free rate of return.[7] Merton (1973) showed that the equilibrium security returns satisfy the basic CAPM relationship. The derivation process of Constantinides (1978) was based on the equilibrium model, while the traditional PDE-based pricing models admit no arbitrage framework. These two models have different processes, but derive consistent results.

In handling the risk factors of uncertainty, Cox et al. (1985) suggested the use of certainty equivalent cash flows, not risk-adjusted discount rate. Trigeorgis (1993) also indicated that the contingent claim of asset can be priced in the real world of systemic risk by substituting real growth rate with certainty equivalent rate. Certainty equivalent rate is obtained by deducting risk premium from the original growth rate of the asset. Such an approach is the same as pricing in a risk-neutral environment. The expected return of all assets in risk-neutral environment is risk-free return. But when the investor has certain risk preferences, the expected growth rate in equilibrium will differ from the original growth rate. Such risk adjustment approach amounts to discounting certainty equivalent cash flows at the risk-free rate of return, instead of adjusting the expected cash flows at the risk-adjusted rate.

28.2.2. Dividend-like Yield

McDonald and Siegel (1984, 1985) discussed that since the rate of return derived from an option pricing equation should be consistent with capital market equilibrium, the results derived from the Black–Scholes equation are independent of and irrelevant to the consideration of capital market equilibrium and there exists a shortfall between the expected return and the required return. It is like dividend yield, i.e. only when the underlying asset does not pay any dividend and the expected return is equal to the market required equilibrium return will the Black–Scholes equation be satisfied. The presence of this shortfall derived from CAPM consists of the conclusion of Constantinides (1978). Trigeorgis (1993) defined the shortfall as dividend-like yield (δ). Hence, if an investment project valued by real options model involves nontraded assets, the pricing model will contain a dividend-like yield, which differs from the pricing models for traded assets.

Real options pricing models apply mostly in cases of nontraded assets. In a perfect market, we assume the existence of twin security, which is a traded asset having equivalent risk as the nontraded asset and paying fixed dividend and satisfies CAPM. In such a case, the value of nontraded asset using PDE pricing model is determined under risk-neutral environment. Thus if there exists a twin security having the same financial risk as that for the nontraded asset, the real option can be priced.

Lin (2002) took into account the dividend-like yield in his real options model in the valuation of venture capital projects. Although his model simulated value of the project based on assumed parameters, the paper had comprehensive discussion of dividend-like yield. Thus under the assumption of perfect market, CAPM may be used for the estimation of dividend-like yield. Duan et al. (2003) proposed in case study that dividend-like yield can be estimated using cost of carry model that frees the estimation method from the restriction of perfect market assumption. In case study using real data, the dividend-like yields of the underlying as estimated by two different methods are close.

28.3. Hi-tech Value as a Call Option

Technological innovations and progression play an important role in driving the economic development. Countries around the world endeavor in technological innovation to maintain their competitiveness. According to the economic growth theory of Schumpeter (1939), the innovation process is the core to understanding the economic growth and the innovation process can be divided into five patterns: production of new products, use of new technologies, development of new markets, acquisition of new materials, and establishment of any new organization. The innovation process is filled with uncertainties in every stage, from the research and development of product, to its testing, volume production, and successful entry into the market.

In the observation of old firms in the market, their competitors mostly come out of old firms in the field who either started their own business or joined other firms in the same industry. That is because the managers of older firms tend to reject innovation for the fear that it will accelerate the phase-out of existing products or that the existing production lines cannot be used for the manufacture of new products. So innovators have to leave the firm to start their own business in order to realize their innovative ideas. As a result, older firms lose many profit opportunities. According to the report by Bhide (2000), 71 percent of successful entrepreneur cases made it through replication or revision of prior work experience, that is, the results of innovation. For example, Cisco is facing the threat of losing market share to Juniper; Microsoft publicly expressed in 1998 that its operating system was threatened by Linux; the microprocessors produced by Transmeta featuring low power consumption, excellent heat radiation, and low price are poised to threaten Intel and AMD. These competitors were mostly former employees of older firms. Their examples demonstrate that no matter how long a company has been established or how high its market share is, it might be replaced by new venture businesses with new ideas if it does not have webs of innovation.

The decision process for the development and investment of a new venture capital project until its IPO is a multistage investment process, which may be generally divided into seed stage, start up, growth stage, expansion stage, and bridge stage. Each stage has its missions and uncertainties, while one stage is linked to the next. In the example of Lucent New Ventures Group (LNVG) established in 1997, its investment process involved four stages: identification of opportunity, market qualifications, commercialization, and acquisition of value. The Nokia Group, founded in 1967, following merger divides its investment and development stages into production factors, investment, and innovation. From these traditional venture cases, the development and investment of a new venture business before its listing do not proceed in one stage, but in multiple stages.

In fact, the investment project involving a new venture business may be viewed as a sequential investment project. Majd and Pindyck (1987) indicated that an investment project usually possesses three properties: (1) the investment decisions and cash outflow are sequential; (2) it takes a period of time to build the project; and (3) there is cash inflow only after the project is completed. Such description fits the development stages of a venture capital project. Many Internet, biotechnology, semiconductor, and information technology companies illustrate the characteristics of negative cash flow in the initial stage, high reinvestment rate, and

high uncertainty in future operations, but their IPO prices are higher than those of traditional firms. In the example of Amazon.com that had seen widening losses from 1996 to 1998, the company stock flew through the roof to US$300; the market value of Yahoo! once surpassed that of Boeing, the aircraft giant; Nokia lost US$80 million in 1992, but the company enjoyed a net profit of US$2.6 billion in 2000 after it formed the Nokia Venture Partners Fund in 1998 and its stock price once reached a P/E ratio of 100 in May 2000. The aforementioned firms are all typical venture businesses.

In recent years, venture capitalists turn their attention to biotechnology business. A large venture capital firm in Taiwan is seriously considering putting money in a biotech company in Gaithersburg, Maryland that develops immunotherapy. Analysis of its financial statements shows that the company has not been profitable in recent years. If the venture capital firm decides to invest or not based on the customary indicators, such as internal rate of return (IRR), P/E ratio, P/S ratio, and P/B ratio, it might miss a profit opportunity. When examining a venture business, investors should look at the value of infinite possible business opportunities. Referring only to numbers obtained from traditional analytic methods might result in missed investment opportunities with good profit potential.

A venture capital business usually does not focus on the sale of product or service and develops a multistage investment process. The input of funds at one investment stage begets the right to determine whether to invest in the next stage. Thus, the right of management to determine whether to invest at each stage is an American call option. After exercising the right, the management acquires the call option on strategy and management in the next stage that renders the entire investment process a multistage compound call option.

Myers (1984) suggested that the value of capital and R&D input in the initial stage of an investment project does not lie in the cash flows expected in future, but in the future growth opportunity. Therefore the investment process from the time a venture business is conceived to its mature stage or public listing may be expressed as a multistage compound option. Management can make pertinent flexible decision in response to market uncertainty in every stage to sidestep the risks brought about by uncertainty and accurately evaluate the execution of investment.

28.4. Two-Stage Compound Option

To understand the meaning of compound option, we first discuss the theory of two-stage compound option. The two-stage compound option was initiated and applied by Black–Scholes (1973), Cox and Ross (1976), Geske (1977), Roll (1977), and Myers (1987), among others.

Consider the constituents of a firm's capital structure are stocks (S) and bonds (B) and the firm has discount bonds outstanding with face value M and a maturity of T years, and suppose the firm plans to liquidate in T years and pay off the bonds. If the value of the firm V is less than M at the time of liquidation, the bondholders will get assets V and stockholders get nothing; and if V is greater than M, bondholders get M and stockholders receive $V - M$, where the payment to stockholders is $\max(V - M, 0)$. Hence, a call on the firm's stock is an option or a compound option.

According to Geske (1979), the compound option is written as

$$C(V,t) = f(S,t) = f(g(V,t),t) \qquad (28.3)$$

Therefore, change of call value may be expressed as a function of changes in the value of the firm and time, and the dynamic stochastic process of V and C may be expressed as follows:

$$dV = \alpha_v V \, dt + \sigma_v V \, dz_v \qquad (28.4)$$

and

$$dC = \alpha_c C \, dt + \sigma_c C \, dz_c \qquad (28.5)$$

where $\alpha_v, \alpha_c, \sigma_v$, and σ_c are instantaneous expected rates of return on the firm (on the call) and instantaneous volatility of return on the firm (on the call), respectively. By applying Itô's lemma or Taylor's series expansion, the dynamics of the call option can be expressed as follows:

$$dC = \frac{\partial C}{\partial t} dt + \frac{\partial C}{\partial V} dV + \frac{1}{2} \frac{\partial^2 C}{\partial V^2} V^2 \sigma_v^2 dt \qquad (28.6)$$

According to Merton, a multiposition, zero net investment having three-security hedge portfolio (H) consisting of the firm, a call, and a risk-free asset may be created by way of short sales and financing. Let n_1 be the dollars invested in the firm, n_2 the dollars invested in the call, and n_3 the dollars invested in risk-free debt. If dH is the instantaneous return to the hedge portfolio, then

$$dH = n_1 \frac{dV}{V} + n_2 \frac{dC}{C} + r_f n_3 dt \qquad (28.7)$$

Substituting for the stochastic return on the firm and the call yield, we can eliminate the Weiner term of V, which implies $dH = 0$. Thus we can simplify the equation above into the familiar partial differential equation below:

$$\frac{\partial C}{\partial t} = r_f C - r_f V \frac{\partial C}{\partial V} - \frac{1}{2} \frac{\partial^2 C}{\partial V^2} V^2 \sigma_v^2 \qquad (28.8)$$

On expiration date t^*, the value of call option is either zero or intrinsic value, subject to the boundary condition of

$$C_{t^*} = max(0, \ S_{t^*} - K) \qquad (28.9)$$

The boundary condition implies that the level of stock price will be determined by the level of call option on the value of the firm. In fact, we can learn from (28.8) that the variable that determines the value of option is V, not S. However, since stock is an option on V, it follows a related diffusion and again its dynamics can be expressed as a function of V and t as:

$$\frac{\partial S}{\partial t} = r_f S - r_f V \frac{\partial S}{\partial V} - \frac{1}{2} \frac{\partial^2 S}{\partial V^2} V^2 \sigma_v^2 \qquad (28.10)$$

Subject to the boundary condition of $S_T = \max(V_T - M, 0)$, the solution to Equation (28.10) is the B–S equation:

$$S = V\Phi_1(h_2 + \sigma_v\sqrt{T - t}) - Me^{-r_f(T-t)}\Phi_1(h_2)$$

(28.11)

and

$$h_2 = \frac{\ln(V/M) + (r_f - 0.5\sigma_v^2)(T - t)}{\sigma_v\sqrt{T - t}}$$ (28.12)

When the option expires, the decision to exercise or not depends on the relationship between S and K; thus, at date $t = t^*$, the value of the firm, V^{cr}, that makes the holder of an option on the stock indifferent between exercising or not is the solution of the integral equation $S_\tau^* - K = 0$ where $\tau = T - t^*$ and S_τ^* is given by Equation (28.11). If the value of firm is less than V^{cr}, the call on the stock remains unexercised.

Based on Equations (28.8) and (28.10) as well as their boundary conditions, the two-stage compound option value given by Geske (1979) is:

$$C = V\Phi_2\left(h_1 + \sigma_v\sqrt{\tau_1}, h_2 + \sigma_v\sqrt{\tau_2}, \sqrt{\frac{\tau_1}{\tau_2}}\right)$$

$$- Me^{-r_f\tau_2}\Phi_2\left(h_1, h_2, \sqrt{\frac{\tau_1}{\tau_2}}\right)$$

$$- Ke^{-r_f\tau_1}\Phi_1(h_1)$$ (28.13)

and

$$h_1 = \frac{\ln(V/V^{cr}) + (r_f - 0.5\sigma_v^2)\tau_1}{\sigma_v\sqrt{\tau_1}}$$ (28.14)

$$h_2 = \frac{\ln(V/M) + (r_f - 0.5\sigma_v^2)\tau_2}{\sigma_v\sqrt{\tau_2}}$$ (28.15)

where $\Phi_2(\bullet, \bullet, \rho)$ stands for the bivariate cumulative normal distribution. The value V^{cr} is calculated using the following equation:

$$S_\tau - K = V\Phi_1(h_2 + \sigma_v\sqrt{\tau}) - Me^{-r_f\tau}\Phi(h_2) - K = 0$$

(28.16)

with $\tau = T - t^*$, $\tau = t^* - t$, and $\tau = T - t$. Note that when $M = 0$ or $T = \infty$, the stockholder's

option to repurchase the firm from the bond-holders disappears and the formula reduces to that of B–S applied to a call written on the equity of an all-equity finance firm.

28.5. Multistage Real Compound Call Option and Dividend-like Yield

Since Geske (1979) proposed the closed-form solution of compound options, the concepts of compound options have been widely applied to financial models. Kemna (1993) divided capital budgeting into the pioneer venture stage and the trial-run stage prior to commercial venture and used two-stage compound call options to assess the value of strategic flexibility of the investment projects. In Kemna's model, the underlying variable is a forward contract, while forward price is the projected value of the commercial venture at the conclusion of the trial-run stage. Because there is no cost of carry in the forwards pricing models, the problem of dividend-like yield of nontraded asset is avoided (Trigeorgis, 1993).

Keeley et al. (1996) illustrated the multistage and high-risk nature of the investment projects with a three-dimensional tree, multistage compound call option model. This model adopted the algorithm for financial option valuation in the evaluation of an investment project. It assumed the expected return of a twin security is the risk-free interest rate, which ignored the fact that the investment project is a nontraded asset, and utilized numerical method to sidestep the difficulty of closed-form solution.

Lin (2002) employed the multistage compound call options to evaluate the multistage investment nature of high-tech firms. Lin (2002) took into account dividend-like yield for nontraded assets and compared a number of numerical solutions, but did not discuss the selection of the underlying variable and twin security. Duan et al. (2003) approached the choice problem of the underlying variable and twin security using case discussion. Their paper utilized the more efficient numerical method and proposed techniques for the setting and estimation of important parameters for multistage compound call options. It also depicted rather comprehensively the application of real options in the valuation of nontraded assets.

Thus, a perfect valuation model for high-tech investment project must take into consideration the dividend-like yield for nontraded assets and is able to reflect the uncertainty and multistage nature of the investment project and provide a complete parameter model and estimation method. In this section, we will develop a multistage compound call option equation for nontraded asset and further discuss the estimation of dividend-like yield.

28.5.1. Multistage Real Compound Call Option

Hull (1997) points out that the use of risk-neutral evaluation model is meaningless when the underlying is a nontraded asset. Constantinides (1978) used certainty-equivalence approach to shift the underlying with market risk to a scenario where the market price of risk is zero. By referring to the paper of Merton (1973), he pointed out that an expected return of a security must satisfy the basic equation of CAPM:

$$\alpha_i - r_f = \lambda_m \sigma_{im}/\sigma_m = \lambda_m \rho_{im}\sigma_i \qquad (28.17)$$

$$\lambda_m = (\alpha_m - r_f)/\sigma_m \qquad (28.18)$$

where ρ, σ, and λ are correlation, standard deviation, and market price of risk, respectively. The i and m are ith security and market portfolios. Following the discussion above, if the price of any derivative is dependent on ζ and t, it should satisfy

$$\mu - r_f = \lambda\sigma \qquad (28.19)$$

and

$$r_f = \alpha_i - \lambda_m \rho_{im}\sigma_i = \alpha_i - \lambda_i\sigma_i \qquad (28.20)$$

Under a complete market, assuming that there exists a twin-traded security, S, having the same risk as the investment project, V, and an expected rate of return $(\alpha_s = r + \lambda_m \rho_{vm}\sigma_v)$. There is a shortfall (δ), between the expected return and

required return, i.e. $\delta = \alpha_s - \alpha_v = r_f + \lambda_m \rho_{vm}\sigma_v - \alpha_v$. This traded twin-traded-security must satisfy $(\alpha_v + \delta) - r_f = \lambda\sigma_v$. Thus, $(\alpha_v - \lambda\sigma_v) = r_f - \delta$ and the original PDE equation (28.8) for call option evaluation will be transformed into the following valuation model for real call options:

$$\frac{1}{2}\sigma_v^2 V^2 \frac{\partial^2 C_{t_{n-1},t_n}}{\partial V^2}dt + (r_f - \delta)V\frac{\partial C_{t_{n-1},t_n}}{\partial V}dV$$
$$+ \frac{\partial C_{t_{n-1},t_n}}{\partial t}dt - r_f C_{t_{n-1},t_n} = 0 \qquad (28.21)$$

The constraint is $C_{t_n,t_n} = \max(V_{t_n} - I_{t_n},0)$, denoting only when the company value is not less than the pre-IPO investment, total I_{t_n}, is the implementation of the IPO plan meaningful.

We can follow the approach of Geske (1979) to obtain the closed-form solution of multistage compound real call option as shown below:

$$C_{(t_n-t_1)} = Ve^{-\delta(t_n-t_1)}\Phi_{(n-1)}(\mathbf{H};\boldsymbol{\Sigma})$$
$$- \sum_{J=1}^{n-i} e^{-r_f\Phi_J}I_{t_{J+1}}\Phi_J(\mathbf{K};\boldsymbol{\Sigma}) \qquad (28.22)$$

where

$i = 1, 2, \ldots\ldots, n.$

$$\mathbf{H} = \left(h_{i1}, h_{i2}, \ldots h_{i(n-i)}\right)^T$$

$$\boldsymbol{K} = \mathbf{H} - \sigma_v\sqrt{\boldsymbol{\Psi}}^T$$

$$\boldsymbol{\Psi} = \left((t_{i+1} - t_i), (t_{i+2} - t_i), \ldots (t_n - t_i)\right)^T$$

$$\boldsymbol{\Sigma} = \sqrt{\psi_i/\psi_j},\ i < j.$$

$$h_{ij} = \frac{\ln\left(\dfrac{V}{V^{cr}}\right) + \left(r_f - \delta + \dfrac{1}{2}\sigma_v^2\right)(t_{i+1} - t_i)}{\sigma_v\sqrt{t_{i+1} - t_i}}$$

$$h_{i(n-i)} = \frac{\ln\left(\dfrac{V}{I_{t_n}}\right) + \left(r_f - \delta + \dfrac{1}{2}\sigma_v^2\right)(t_n - t_i)}{\sigma_v\sqrt{t_n - t_i}}$$

$$V^{cr} = \left(V_{i+1}^{cr}, V_{i+2}^{cr}, \ldots V_{n-1}^{cr}\right)^T$$

$$\exists\ V^{cr} \ni C_{n-i-1}^{cr} - I_{t_{i+1}} = 0$$

and

$$\Phi_n(\mathbf{H};\Sigma) = \Pr\left[\bigcap_{j=1}^{n}(x_j \le h_j)\right] = \frac{1}{\sqrt{|\Sigma|(2\pi)^n}}$$

$$\int_{-\infty}^{h_1}\int_{-\infty}^{h_2}L\int_{-\infty}^{h_n}e^{-(1/2)\mathbf{x}^T\Sigma^{-1}\mathbf{x}}dx \qquad (28.23)$$

In seeking the value of compound options in Equation (28.22), we would encounter two numerical methods. One is the solution for the approximation value of the multivariate normal integral, $\Phi(\bullet)$, and the other is the root-finding in nonlinear equation for critical value, V^{cr}. These two methods will be explored in the sections below.

28.5.2. Estimation of the Dividend-like Yield

The estimation of dividend-like yield is important. In this section, we apply two methods – CAPM and cost of carry model for the estimation of dividend-like yield. In the CAPM approach, market risk premium and beta risk in the model are estimated first. But given that these risk values are hard to observe in the market, their estimations have many constraints. If the underlying asset has a forward contract or futures contract, the net cost of carrying the underlying can be used to estimate dividend-like yield. These two estimation methods are derived from different theories, but they reach consistent conclusions.

28.5.2.1. CAPM Method
Based on the CAPM, the expected return (α_s) to the twin security is shown as below:

$$\alpha_s = r_f + beta \times (r_m - r_f) \qquad (28.24)$$

where r_m is rate of market return. To estimate the required rate of return, we can compute the drift term through the dynamics of the logarithm value of underlying, and then we can obtain the drift, α_v. Andersson (1999) employed this approach to obtain the dividend-like yield and then applied it for evaluating a pulp industry with real options.

28.5.2.2. Cost of Carry Model
The reason why we estimate the dividend-like yield with the other method is because the risk premium

is hard to observe in the market, and we can check how well the resulting δ is estimated by CAPM. To overcome the restriction of the perfect market assumption in CAPM, Pickles and Smith (1993) applied the formal of the future price to calculate the dividend-like yield. Their method was based on the equivalence of the expected return for the holders of an inventory and the holders of products with potential growth possibilities. The expected return for the holder of a growth product is:

$$\alpha_s = \alpha_v + \delta \qquad (28.25)$$

where δ also equals the payout rate representing the opportunity cost of keeping the option to construct the new chipmakers. From a holding inventory point of view, the expected return is:

$$\alpha_s = \alpha_v - c + \gamma \qquad (28.26)$$

where c is the storage cost of the commodity, γ the convenience yield of the commodity. From Equations (28.25) and (28.26), the dividend-like yield can be derived as:

$$\delta = \gamma - c \qquad (28.27)$$

For two forward contracts with different expiration dates, their cost of carry differs. Without arbitrage opportunity, the difference, termed as CC, can be shown to be as follows:

$$CC = r_f + c - \gamma \qquad (28.28)$$

where c is the cost of storage and γ the convenience yield. From Equation (28.27) and (28.28), we can obtain:

$$\delta = r_f - CC \qquad (28.29)$$

The role of the dividend-like yield on the project represents the opportunity cost of keeping the option alive. The holder of an asset such as a stock expects to obtain a payout in the form of a dividend plus capital appreciation. Furthermore, it also implies that the expected net cash flows accruing from producing project, or diversification advantage of the project. The greater the dividend-like yield on the project, greater is the cost of holding the options, which also means that the investment project offers poor diversification advantage. If the dividend-like yield is relatively low or negative, this indicates that there is a lower or zero cost of holding options, or more diversification advantage.

28.6. Algorithms for Computing Multivariate Normal Integrals and Solving the Root of Nonlinear Model

Multidimensional integration is usually solved using numerical method. This paper examines and compares three methods: Gauss quadrature method, Monte Carlo method, and Lattice method. The integration equation of cumulative distribution function is Equation (28.23). Where $\mathbf{H} = (h_1, h_2, \ldots, h_n)^T$, h_i are finite numbers, $x = (x_1, x_2, \ldots, x_n)$, Σ is symmetrical covariance matrix with positive definite eigenvalue. The multivariate normal integral cannot be obtained directly, but often computed by numerical method.

Monte Carlo method is frequently used in computing the value of multivariate normal integral. Genz (1992) successfully applied this method in solving multivariate normal integration. But the computer runtime of this method is relatively long. Gauss quadrature method is another frequently used method. Its computation becomes rather straightforward after Drezner (1992) improved upon it. This method can also be conveniently executed using the Fortran code provided by Scherish (1984). However, it needs the substitutions of numbers in the Gauss Integral Weights and Abscissae Table developed by Steen et al. (1969) to compute multivariate normal integral. Errors that might occur in the process are related to the order in the aforementioned tables used. Usually the higher the order, the less the error. However, the short point of this method is that as the dimension of the integration increases, so does the computer runtime. According to the examination results of Genz (1999) on a number of integration methods, Lattice method is more efficient in terms of runtime and error reduction when applied to computation of multivariate normal integral.

We utilized three numerical methods — Drezner-improved Gauss quadrature method (referred to as Drezner method[8] below), Monte Carlo method, and Lattice method to compute multivariate normal integral so as to obtain the value of multistage, sequential compound options. We also compared the computer runtime of these three methods.

28.6.1. Monte Carlo method

To apply Monte Carlo method, Genz (1992) suggests converting the $(-\infty, h_i)$ in multivariate normal integration equation to $(0, 1)$ and covariance matrix x in equation (28.23) to Y to break n-variate normal integral into n products of one-dimensional normal integral. First one must multiply the covariance matrix X by diagonal matrix c to convert into y, then $x^T \Sigma^{-1} x = y^T y$, i.e. $c^T c = \Sigma^{-1}$, and Equation (28.23) can be transformed into Equation (28.30):

$$\Phi_n(\mathbf{H}) = (2\pi)^{-(n/2)} \int_{\mathbf{H}} e^{-(1/2)y^T y} d\mathbf{y} \qquad (28.30)$$

Equation (28.30) can be further developed into (28.31):

$$\Phi_n(\mathbf{H}) = (2\pi)^{-(n/2)} \int_{a_1'(y_1)}^{b_1'(y_1)} e^{-(y_1^2/2)} \ldots$$
$$\int_{a_n'(y_1,\ldots,y_{n-1})}^{b_n'(y_1,\ldots,y_{n-1})} e^{-(y_n^2/2)} d\mathbf{y} \qquad (28.31)$$

where

$$a_i'(\mathbf{y}) = \left(a_i - \sum_{j=1}^{i-1} c_{ij} y_j \right) / c_{i,i}$$

and

$$b_i'(\mathbf{y}) = \left(b_i - \sum_{j=1}^{i-1} c_{ij} y_j \right) / c_{i,i}.$$

Let $y_i, = \Phi^{-1}(z_i)$, $i = 1, 2 \ldots n$ then

$$z_i = \Phi(y_i) = \frac{1}{\sqrt{2\pi}} \int_{-\infty}^{y_i} e^{-(t^2/2)} dt.$$

So

$$\frac{1}{\sqrt{2\pi}} e^{-(y_i^2/2)} dy_i = dz_i.$$

Then Equation (28.31) may be transformed into the following:

$$\Phi_n(\boldsymbol{H}) = \int_0^{e_1} \int_0^{e_2(z_1)} \cdots \int_0^{e_n(z_1, z_2, \ldots, z_{n-1})} dz \qquad (28.32)$$

where

$$e_i(z_1, z_2, \ldots z_{i-1}) = \Phi\left[\left(b_i - \sum_{j=1}^{i-1} c_{ij}\Phi^{-1}(z_j)\right)/c_{i,i}\right]$$

Finally, let $z_i = e_i w_i$, $i = 1, \ldots, n$, so $dz_i = e_i dw_i$, which may switch this integral interval to [0,1] interval. The product of n one-dimensional integrals is shown in Equation (28.33):

$$\Phi_n(\boldsymbol{H}) = \int_0^1 \int_0^1 \cdots \int_0^1 f(w_1, w_2, \ldots w_{n-1}) d\boldsymbol{w}$$
$$= e \int_0^1 e_2(w) \ldots \int_0^1 e_n(w) \int_0^1 d\boldsymbol{w} \qquad (28.33)$$

where

$$e_i(w) = \Phi\left[\left(b_i - \sum_{j=1}^{i-1} c_{ij}\Phi^{-1}(e_j(w)w_j)\right)/c_{i,i}\right],$$

$$f(\boldsymbol{w}) = e_1(w)e_2(w)\ldots e_n(w).$$

To solve the one-dimensional integrals and their product in Equation (28.33), first set the computation of initial value as $e_1 = \Phi(b_1/c_{1,1})$ and $f_1 = e_1$ to generate a set of evenly distributed random variables w_i from random sampling. The interval of even distribution is $(0, 1)$, where $i = 1, \ldots, n-1$, then

$$y_{i-1} = \Phi^{-1}[w_{i-1}(e_{i-1})] \qquad (28.34)$$

$$e_i = \Phi\left[\left(b_i - \sum_{j=1}^{i-1} c_{ij} \times y_j/c_{i,i}\right)\right] \qquad (28.35)$$

$$f_i = e_i \times f_{i-1} \qquad (28.36)$$

After obtaining $\bar{f}$, the average of f_i, repeat the aforementioned steps to obtain multiple $\bar{f}$ of different values and to acquire the approximation of multivariate normal integral computed by Monte Carlo method.

28.6.2. Drezner Method

Drezner's (1992) method is an improved Gauss quadrature method. In computing the multivariate normal integral, it first converts the interval in the equation from $(-\infty, h_i)$ to $(0, \infty)$, then extracts appropriate order K^9 from the Gauss integral weight A_i and abscissae x_i table developed by Steen et al. (1969) using $W(x) = \exp(-x^2)$ as weight function and substitutes it in the equation to obtain multivariate normal integral.

In the n-dimensional integration equation (28.23), let Σ be the matrix of correlation coefficients corresponding to $\boldsymbol{x}$. Then $\Phi_n(\boldsymbol{H};\Sigma)$ may be expressed as follows:

$$\Phi_n(H;\Sigma) = \Phi_{n-1}(H^i;\Sigma_1) - \Phi_n(H^{-i};\Sigma_2) \qquad (28.37)$$

where $\boldsymbol{H}^{-i} = (h_1, \ldots, h_{i-1}, -h_i, h_{i+1}, \ldots, h_n)$ and $\boldsymbol{H}^i = (h_1, \ldots, h_{i-1}, h_{i+1}, \ldots, h_n)$. If all $\boldsymbol{H}$ are nonpositive values, the multivariate normal integral may be computed with the following equation:

$$\boldsymbol{\Phi}_n(\boldsymbol{H};\boldsymbol{\Sigma}) \cong \boldsymbol{C} \sum_{i_1=1}^{K} \cdots \sum_{i_n=1}^{K} A_{i_1} \ldots A_{i_n} f(x_{i_1}, \ldots, x_{i_n}) \qquad (28.38)$$

where K is the order[10] of weight A_i and abscissae x_i in the Gauss integral weight A_i and abscissae x_i table, while $\boldsymbol{C}$ and $f(\cdot)$ are as follows:

$$\boldsymbol{C}^2 = \prod_{i=1}^{n} [2/\mathbf{r}_{ii}]/[(2\pi)^n|\boldsymbol{\Sigma}|] \qquad (28.39)$$

$$f(\mathbf{u}_1, \ldots, \mathbf{u}_n) = \exp\{\mathbf{x}^T\mathbf{x} - (\mathbf{h}'' - \mathbf{x})^T\boldsymbol{\Sigma}''(\mathbf{h}'' - \mathbf{x})\} \qquad (28.40)$$

where $\mathbf{u}_i = (\mathbf{h}_i - \mathbf{x}_i)[\mathbf{r}_{ii}/2]^{1/2}$
$$\boldsymbol{\Sigma}^{-1} = \{\boldsymbol{r}_{ij}\}$$
$$\mathbf{h}_i'' = \mathbf{h}_i[\mathbf{r}_{ii}/2]^{1/2}$$
$$\boldsymbol{\Sigma}'' = \{\boldsymbol{r}_{ij}''\} = \{\mathbf{r}_{ij}/[\mathbf{r}_{ii}\mathbf{r}_{jj}]^{1/2}\}$$

28.6.3. Lattice Method

Equation (28.33) is an n-dimensional integration equation. Lattice method first uses p-point rule to transform it into the following equation:

$$\Phi(\mathbf{H}) = \frac{1}{p} \sum_{k=1}^{p} f\left(\left\{\frac{k}{p}\mathbf{a}\right\}\right) + E \qquad (28.41)$$

The above equation is Korobov filter, where $\mathbf{a} = a_1, a_2, \ldots, a_n$. Then $f(w)$ may be expressed as follows using Fourier expansion:

$$f(w) = \sum_{\mathbf{m}} \mathbf{C_m} e^{2\pi i m \bullet w} \qquad (28.42)$$

The coefficients being given by $C_m = \int_0^1 dw_1 \ldots \int_0^1 dw_n f(w) e^{-2\pi i m \bullet w}$, where $\mathbf{m}$ is the vector of Fourier indices $(m_1, m_2, \ldots, m_n)$ each being an integer in $(-\infty, \infty)$, C_m is the Fourier coefficient corresponding to $\mathbf{m}$. The error of equation (28.41) can be expressed as:

$$E = \sum_{\mathbf{m}}{}' \mathbf{C_m} \Delta_p(\mathbf{m} \bullet \mathbf{a}) \qquad (28.43)$$

where Σ_m denotes multiple summation over $(-\infty, \infty)$ in each Fourier index. The prime attached to the summation in $\sum'_m$ denotes exclusion of $(0, 0, \ldots, 0)$ from the summation. The quantity $\Delta_p(\mathbf{m} \bullet \mathbf{a})$ is defined by:

$$\Delta p(\mathbf{m} \bullet \mathbf{a}) = 1 \quad \text{if } \mathbf{m} \bullet \mathbf{a} = 0 \qquad (28.44)$$
$$\Delta p(\mathbf{m} \bullet \mathbf{a}) = 0 \quad \text{otherwise}$$

The method described above is the number theoretic method of Korobov. But since the Lattice method primarily purports to choice $\mathbf{a}$ value for minimization of error term E, Hlawka (1962) and Zaremba (1966) suggested that optimal $\mathbf{a}$ was chosen when the first Fourier coefficient contribution to Equation (28.43) was minimized, that is,

$$\rho(\mathbf{a}) = m_1^* m_2^* L m_n^* \qquad (28.45)$$

where

$$m_i^* = \max(1, |m_i|)$$

But Lyness and Gabriel (1969) reckoned that this approach was the lack of an easily computable

and realistic error estimate for Equation (28.41). Subsequently Cranley and Paterson (1976) suggested the use of randomization to enhance the solution efficiency. Let $\boldsymbol{\beta}$ be a random vector with distribution $G(\boldsymbol{\beta})$ defined in domain of integration. Hence equation (28.45) may be rewritten as $\int R(f, \boldsymbol{\beta}) dG(\boldsymbol{\beta})$, in which when $R(f, \boldsymbol{\beta})$ may be construed, it may be randomized using the quadrature rule. In the randomized integrating range, Korobov filter may modify formula (28.41) into the following with the use of quadrature rules:

$$\Phi_n(\mathbf{H}) = \frac{1}{p} \sum_{k=1}^{p} f\left(\frac{k}{p}\mathbf{a} + \boldsymbol{\beta}\right) + E_p(\boldsymbol{\beta}) \qquad (28.46)$$
$$= K_p(\boldsymbol{\beta}) + E_p(\boldsymbol{\beta})$$

The error term can be expressed as:

$$E_p(\boldsymbol{\beta}) = \sum_{\mathbf{m}}{}' \mathbf{C_m} \Delta_p(\mathbf{m} \bullet \mathbf{a}) e^{2\pi i m \bullet \boldsymbol{\beta}} \qquad (28.47)$$

Equation (28.46) is used to compute integral using the p-point Lattice method of Korobov.

In the process of solving multivariate normal integrals in Equation (28.22) to find the value of compound option, there exists a problem where the lower limit[11] of interval is unknown, that is, we need to find critical value V^{cr}. We will discuss and compare three numerical methods for solving critical values – Newton–Raphson method, Dekker method, and Secant method. V^{cr} involves a nonlinear solving process that becomes more difficult and hard to converge as the dimension of multivariate integration increases. Frequently applied, Newton–Raphson method sometimes cannot meet the convergence requirements for finding the critical value V^{cr}. This is because Newton–Raphson method uses first-order derivative and divergence occurs when the first-order derivative is zero. The choice of critical value solver is important and should be prudent, especially if the equation contains partial derivative and other unknown factors, such as convergence requirements.

The coding of Newton–Raphson method is not difficult and easy to comprehend. But when integration also requires differentiation in the root-finding process, the coding will become more difficult. The zero method of Dekker (1969) can better satisfy the multivariate nature in computing multistage compound options. Brent (1971) further expanded on the Dekker method by combining inverse quadratic interpolation and bisection to solve the problem of zero one-dimensional partial derivative in Newton–Raphson method. It uses the method of repeatedly deducting bisections to result in faster convergence and find the root after the correct interval is defined. The computing speed of this method is also much faster.

As mentioned above, when an equation has both integration and differentiation, the Dekker method (1969) does not necessarily produce faster computing speed. Using the simple secant method instead of complicated functions offers accuracy and computer execution speed not inferior to those of Dekker's (1969) method and Brent's (1971) method. The difference between quadrature method and secant method is that the former entails repeatedly dividing the interval into bisections and approximates the root by keeping on switching the sign of function between two intervals. The latter entails using an approximating line to determine two-point interval and finding the root with this line. Their theories are similar.

28.7. Simulative Analysis

To compare the computation speed and error of three different numerical integration methods combined with two critical company value root-finding methods, we ran them with two computer programs, Fortran 4.0 and Matlab 5.3, and performed sensitivity analysis of important parameters, such as volatility and interest rate. Table 28.1 depicts the presumptions of parameter values required for the computation, where the project value, V, is the presumed present value of the current stage and the presumed investment in each stage is the present value of the current stage. To examine the effect of same total investment, but different distributions to each stage on the model, we classify the investment pattern into

Table 28.1. Parameter value for the simulative analysis

Parameter	Symbol	Parameter value
Company value at time t_1	V	85
The investment of stage 2	I_{t_2}	5 and 10
The investment of stage 3	I_{t_3}	5, 10 and 15
The investment of stage 4	I_{t_4}	5 and 15
The total pre-IPO investments	I_{t_5}	30
Risk-free rate	r_f	[5% 13%]
Volatility of the company value	σ_v	[0.1 0.9]
Required rate of return	α_v	0.05
Market price of risk	λ_m	0.4
Correlation coefficient	ρ_{vm}	0.1 and 0.4
Maturity (year)	T	6

four modes: up-sloping, down-sloping, up, then down, and down, then up.

The market price of risk $\lambda_m = (r_m - (r_f)/\sigma_m$, where $r_{m \text{ and }} \sigma_m$ denote the expected return and market volatility, respectively. According to the empirical results of Pindyck (1993) based on the data of New York Stock Exchange between 1926 and 1988, $r_m - r_f = 0.08$ and $\sigma_m = 0.2$. Thus, the market price of risk $\lambda_m = 0.4$, which is also presumed in the simulation computation stated below. It took an average of six years, $T = 6$, for a high-tech company defined in different ages to go from setup to IPO. Suppose these companies go through four stages in the process,[12] we let the beginning of each stage being the major investment decision-making point and each stage have an equal duration of 1.5 years.

28.7.1. Comparing Numerical Methods for Multivariate Normal Integral and Critical Value

We compared three numerical methods for the multivariate normal integral in terms of speed and error. We also employed two computer programs to compare the computing speed of these three methods. When testing the Drezner method for multivariate normal integral, we applied the finding a zero method of Dekker (1969) in Matlab 5.3 to find critical value, V^{cr}; when testing Lattice and Monte Carlo methods, we used the double-precision method in MS-Fortran 4.0 to solve critical value, V^{cr}. These three integration methods were coded in Matlab and Fortran languages, respectively.

Given the enormity of equations involved, we only present the results of single sensitivity. Both of two program languages used here provided built-in values[13] for direct computation of one-dimensional normal integral. But for a two-dimensional normal integration, only Fortran provides[14] built-in values while Matlab does not. Based on the fact that the speeds and errors of one-dimensional and two-dimensional integration are nearly identical, we applied the Gauss integration to further compare the speeds and errors in computing three-dimensional and four-dimensional integrals. From Table 28.2, one can see that the computer runtime of Monte Carlo method is markedly more than that of Drezner and Lattice methods. Moreover, when combining Drezner method for solving multivariate normal integral and Dekker's (1969) critical value solver, executed with the code pro-

vided in Matlab tool box, the runtime for computing three-dimensional critical value was on an average 60 seconds. On the other hand, running Lattice method for solving multivariate normal integral combined with secant method for solving critical value with Fortran took only 1 second.

In comparison, running the Monte Carlo method for solving multivariate normal integral combined with secant method for solving critical value with Fortran codes took on an average as high as 120 seconds to compute to the three-dimensional critical value. In the process of finding the critical value, V^{cr}, both Monte Carlo and Lattice methods had errors in control range and their resulting integrals are almost identical. But in terms of computing speed, there is a significant difference between them.

28.7.2. Critical Values, Company Values Against Investment Modes

The Appendix illustrates the critical values and the values of real call options.[15] We find that all critical values in stage i are influenced by the planned investment outlay for stage i and stages thereafter. The higher the investment amount, the higher the critical value. But when the company goes for IPO,

Table 28.2. Computing speed for critical value (V_i^{cr}) and real call values

| | Drezner's improved Gauss | | | | | | | | Lattice | | Monte-Carlo | |
| | V_4 | | V_3 | | V_2 | | V_1 | | V_2 | V_1 | V_2 | V_1 |
σ_v	second	flops	second	flops	second	flops	second	flops	second	second	second	second
0.1	0.11	1323	0.98	153663	28.79	5346997	8.13	10163317	0.090	0.016	137.35	67.95
0.2	0.00	1487	1.21	165478	36.47	6006569	8.12	11697490	0.093	0.018	129.74	61.77
0.3	0.00	1776	1.32	188458	40.21	6636759	8.19	13231663	0.091	0.019	139.92	59.04
0.4	0.00	1873	1.53	211306	45.81	7568574	8.19	14765721	0.110	0.019	132.19	58.32
0.5	0.05	2435	1.65	234300	49.22	8153987	8.13	16299756	0.101	0.013	134.86	63.88
0.6	0.05	2676	1.81	257362	46.96	7794794	8.13	17833791	0.102	0.015	129.07	61.53
0.7	0.05	2524	1.81	256948	52.01	8640625	6.42	19049349	0.105	0.018	133.51	58.39
0.8	0.06	2917	2.09	291705	51.96	8658105	5.55	20111421	0.103	0.019	140.82	59.77
0.9	0.06	2765	1.98	279963	51.85	8629144	5.55	21173469	0.120	0.015	142.93	66.21
Sum	0.38		14.38		403.28		66.41		0.915	0.152	1220.39	556.86

Note: dividend-like yield, $\delta = r_f + \lambda_m \rho_{vmx} \sigma_v - \alpha_v$, $r_f = 0.08$ and $\rho = 0.1$ (Up-sloping investment mode.)

its value does not affect the critical values in stage 1 and stages thereafter. Thus the company value at the time of IPO does not affect the investment decision made at each stage. From Figures 28.3 and 28.4, one can see that investment mode affects the values of real call options. If the mode is up-sloping, the value of real call option is at the highest, followed by in sequence down-then-up mode, up-then-down mode, and down-sloping mode. These results are consistent in the three numerical integration methods described above. A down-sloping investment mode will result in the lowest value for the entire project, while up-sloping investment mode will give the entire project maximum value. These results indicate that down-sloping mode offers less decision flexibility than up-sloping mode and are consistent with the suggestions of Trigeorgis (1993) for the use of real options in evaluating management and strategic flexibility.

28.7.3. Sensitivity Analysis

28.7.3.1. Sensitivity Analysis of Dividend-Like Yield

The dividend-like yield is the shortfall between the expected rate of return of a twin security (α_s) and the required rate of return to the company value (α_v). It is a function of risk-free rate (r_f), the correlation coefficient (ρ), the volatility, α_v, and the required rate of return. The smaller the ρ, the less correlation between the new investment project and the existing market portfolio and the greater diversification advantage the project offers; the greater the ρ, the less diversification advantage.

Panel A in Figure 28.3 depicts the sensitivity of δ to the changes of ρ and σ. It shows that the relationship between σ and δ depends on the value of ρ; when $\rho > 0$, σ and δ move together; when $\rho < 0$, σ increases and δ decreases. We can also show how the change of r_f and σ will affect the δ value. The results show a positive correlation between r_f and δ.

We will perform sensitivity analysis of σ and r_f, respectively, under the circumstances where ρ is equal to zero and greater than zero.

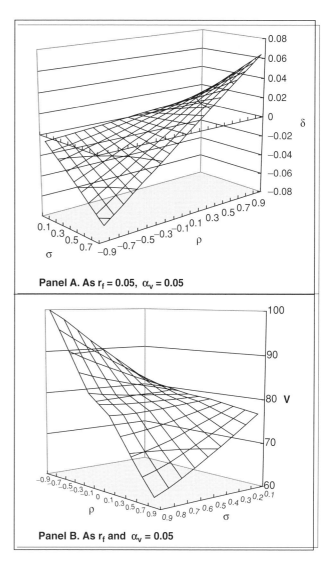

Panel A. As r_f = 0.05, α_v = 0.05

Panel B. As r_f and α_v = 0.05

Figure 28.3. Sensitivity analysis of dividend-like yield and real call values

28.7.3.2. Sensitivity Analysis of Volatility

The derived closed-form solution of real call options has one difference from that of traditional financial call options. The dividend in the solution for the latter has nothing to do with volatility or interest rate, and the value of financial call option increases along with rising volatility or interest rate. But in the closed-form solution we derived for real options, dividend-like yield is an increasing function of volatility and interest rate. Therefore, real call option is not necessarily an increasing function of volatility.

The effect of correlation coefficient of up-sloping investment mode and volatility on the value of real call option under the assumption that r and α_v equal to 0.05 is shown in Panel B of Figure 28.3. The results show that the greater the positive value of ρ, decreasing σ drives up the real call value, and when ρ turns negative, σ and real call value move together. It is similar to financial options framework. Figure 28.4 illustrates the two-dimensional graph of σ versus value of real call option in four investment modes based on the results of three numerical integration methods under the assumption of $\rho = 0$ and 0.1, respectively.

When $\rho = 0$, $\delta = 0.03$ and $r = 0.08$, indicating that the value of real call option increases with rising volatility. But the magnitude of increase is associated with the investment mode. Up-sloping mode showed the biggest increase, implying that decision-makers adopt an up-sloping investment approach in response to the future uncertainty of the investment project, which gives greater value on decision flexibility than the other three invest-

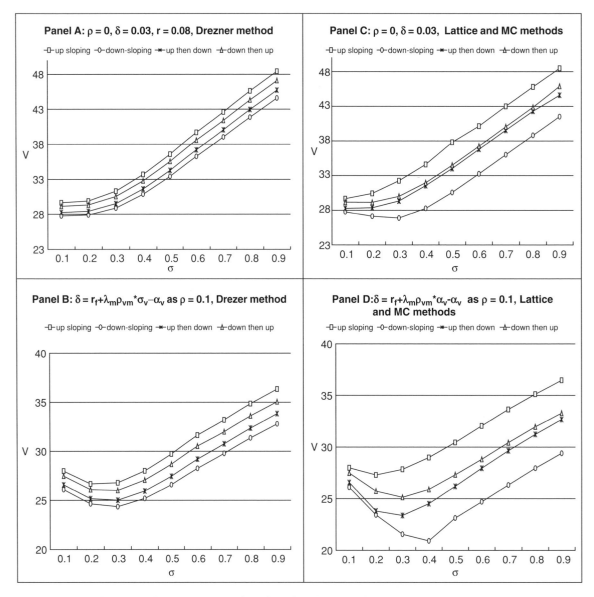

Figure 28.4.   Sensitivity analysis : Real call option function for volatility

ment modes. This outcome is consistent in all three numerical integration methods used here. However, the integral computed by Drezner method is lower than those computed by Monte Carlo and Lattice methods under an up-sloping mode and higher under a down-sloping mode.

When $\rho > 0$, δ and σ_v move together, given that rising volatility will boost the expected rate of return to a twin security, dividend-like yield, δ, rises along with it. Under a constant r_f, the linkage between σ_v and δ becomes $\partial\delta/\partial\sigma_v = \lambda_m\rho_{vm}$.

Figure 28.4 shows that suppose $\rho = 0.1$, the results obtained by Drezner method show that the relationship between σ_v and real call options was akin to a J-curve. The reflection point on the curve occurred when σ_v was 0.25, meaning real call option is a decreasing function of σ_v when $\sigma_v < 0.25$ and is an increasing function of σ_v when $\sigma_v > 0.25$. Real call option is not necessarily an increasing function of volatility. The effect of volatility on the value of investment project may not be positive. The same relationships between volatility and real call option are observed under Lattice and Monte Carlo methods that they also show a J-curve. But the value of σ_v varies at the turning point of the J-curve under different investment modes. It is approximately 0.2 under up-sloping mode and 0.4 under down-sloping mode. The result that the reflection point of J-curve also raises when investment mode switches from up-sloping to down-sloping is consistent with the finding of Dias (1998). Rising volatility raises the value of option. But if we assume the investment project proceeds under a risk-aversion economic system, the required rate of return for the investors will rise with volatility, which leads to rising dividend-like yield and lowers the value of investment project. But the net effect depends on the relative magnitude of these two influences.

When the correlation coefficient of the investment project and the market portfolio gets higher, the diversification advantage the project brings to the investment portfolio is less. Figure 28.3 shows that after ρ rises to 0.4, σ_v has a decreasing relationship with real call options, a phenomenon to-

tally different from the positive relationship observed between financial options and volatility. But such phenomenon becomes less apparent as risk-free rate increases. With respect to the results obtained from the Drezner method, when $\rho = 0.4$, the value of real options decreases as σ_v increases, but stays practically unchanged after $\sigma_v > 0.3$. Under both Lattice and Monte Carlo methods, the values of real call options are hardly affected by σ_v when $\sigma_v > 0.4$. It indicates that when the new project produces little diversification advantage for the market, the project is adverse to the value of the company when interest rate rises, meaning the company will have less desire to proceed with the investment.

28.7.3.2. Sensitivity Analysis of Risk-Free Rate

In the financial option model of Black–Scholes (1973), the value of call option increases when r_f rises. But in real options model, the effect of linkage between risk-free rate, r_f, and dividend-like yield (δ) must be taken into account when evaluating the effect of risk-free rate on the investment project. Dividend-like yield (δ) increases when r_f rises and the two have the following relationship:

$$\frac{\partial\delta}{\partial r_f} = 1 + \frac{\partial\lambda_m}{\partial r_f}\rho_{vm}\sigma_v \qquad (28.48)$$

Under the circumstance where the effect of r_f fluctuation on λ_m is ignored, i.e. $\partial\delta/\partial_r = 1$, rising r will result in drop of the project value under various values of σ_v as shown in Figure 28.5 under $\rho > 0$,[16] The same conclusion is observed in all three numerical integration methods discussed here. It is contrary to the theory that the value of a financial call options rise with increasing r_f. Nevertheless, it is consistent with the phenomenon where higher interest rate lowers the desire of businesses to invest in new plants.

28.8. The Case Study: ProMos Technologies Inc.

ProMos Technologies Inc.[17], a joint venture of Siemens Co. of Germany and Mosel Vitelic Inc., was founded in 1996 as the first plant to manufacture

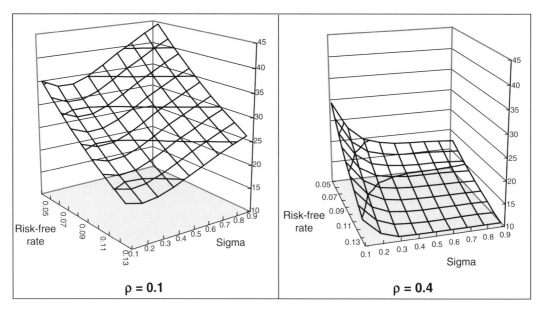

Figure 28.5. Sensitivity analysis: Real call option function for σ and r_f as $\rho > 0$

new generation 64 Megabytes (Mb) DRAM products in Taiwan. Today DRAM is the largest single product in the semiconductor industry and as modern technology continues to advance, more electronic products will use higher-density DRAM. For these reasons, we are interested in the value analysis of ProMos Technologies Inc.

The ProMos prospectus shows that the company mainly attempts to produce 8-inch wafer of 64 Mb DRAM chips manufactured on 0.35 to 0.2 μm. However, the technology[18] and good ratio[19] are strongly correlated to the number of chips manufactured. By this correlation, ProMos projected its monthly production to be 1550 pieces in 1997 and to reach 17,300 pieces per month by 1998, and 22,000 pieces by the time its IPO is announced.

28.8.1. The Model

With the IPO prospectus of ProMos, it took three years to complete the investment project – the foundry construction started in 1996 and the IPO was launched in 1999. We assume that there were four investment stages, with an investment decision being made at the beginning of each stage.

The dynamics of underlying variable spot ASP (V_t) of DRAM follows a geometric Brownian motion. The unit production cost (I_t) is set to be the exercise price at time t, where $t = 1996, 1997, 1998$, and 1999. Hence the decision-making point for the sequential capital investments can be viewed as options on options shown in Figure 28.6.

28.8.2. Finding the Underlying Variable and Twin Securities

We cannot construct a synthetic real option using the DRAM foundry because the foundry is a non-traded asset. In the DRAM markets, as the integration density of DRAM increases, the minimum feature size of DRAM decreases. Therefore, many novel process technologies have been developed in order to overcome the limitations originating in small feature-sized device and to meet the better performances in new DRAM. The competitiveness of the DRAM market drives chipmakers to keep developing higher-density chips. The density of DRAM has been approximately quadrupled every three years by virtue of advances of DRAM technology. Therefore, a key factor that affects the profitability of a firm depends on the successful

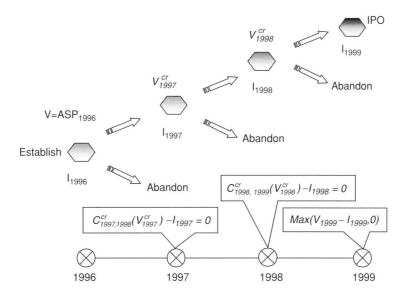

Figure 28.6. Decision-making point of ProMos construction started in 1996 with the IPO in 1999

launch of a new generation product. Figure 28.7 illustrates the relationship between the number of units of DRAM chips of various densities sold and the stock price for Winbond Electronics Corporation from 1993 to 2001. Figure 28.7 also shows that the 64 Mb DRAM products was the major product to decide the business performance of DRAM chipmakers from 1996 to 2000. The chip-

maker's profitability depends mainly on DRAM sale prices and chipmaker's revenues. However, as the prospects of the semiconductor industry is closely linked to the prosperity of the DRAM industry, so a bullish electronic industry is reflected by a prospering semiconductor industry, resulting in the growth in value of prospective stock prices of the DRAM chipmakers. Therefore, if the

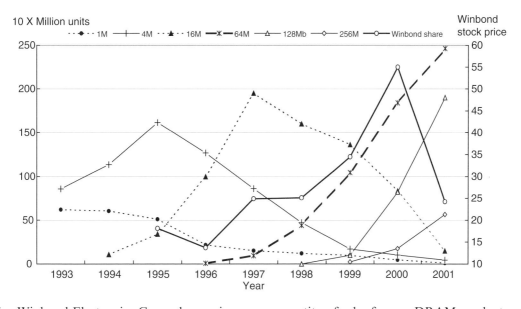

Figure 28.7. Winbond Electronics Corp. share price versus quantity of sales for any DRAM product

change of stock price would influence DRAM-average sales price, the consumption goods[20] can replace the twin security of investment goods.[21]

The common use of vector autoregressions (VARs) has been in testing for the causality between variables. Causality in the sense defined by Granger (1969) and Sims (1980) inferred that when lagged values of an independent variable have explanatory power in a regression of a dependent variable on lagged values of the dependent variable and the independent variables, the VAR can be used to test the hypothesis. Tests of the restrictions can be based on simple F-test in the single equation of the VAR model. The fact that the unrestricted equations have identical regressions means that these tests can be based on the results of simple ordinary least square (OLS) estimates. In Table 28.3, we show the causality test between the stock portfolio return (R_p)[22] of the old DRAM chipmakers[23] and return of DRAM ASP (ASP-R) by the VAR model, where the estimation formula of stock portfolio return is:

$$R_p = \sum w_i \times R_i \qquad (28.49)$$

$$w_i = \frac{MV_i}{\sum MV_i} \qquad (28.50)$$

where w_i is weight and MV_i is the market capitalization of a DRAM public company i. Models 1 and 2 in Table 28.1 are the VAR models derived from the stock portfolio return and DRAM ASP return as independent variables, respectively. Tests reveal that only Model 1 is statistically significant (F-statistic is 4.8606) and R-squared is 0.4581. It indicates that the stock portfolio return of the existing DRAM chipmakers is the cause of DRAM ASP return and that DRAM ASP return is the result of stock portfolio return.

In 1996 ProMOS's main product was 64 Mb DRAM. As each density DRAM had a limited life cycle and in a world of rapid growth of the total bit, the DRAM price was greatly affected by cycles of new generation product. The 64 Mb DRAM was eventually overtaken by the products with higher-density levels. Therefore, the under-

Table 28.3. Causality test between twin securities (stock portfolio) and DRAM ASP with VAR model

Variable	Model 1 ASP-R	Model 2 R_P
Intercept	−0.0034	0.0344
	(−0.2646)	(1.4041)*
$ASP - R_{(-1)}$	0.4201	0.3391
	(3.0507)***	(1.2994)
$ASP - R_{(-2)}$	0.4161	−0.1449
	(2.9406)***	(−0.5407)
$ASP - R_{(-3)}$	−0.4034	−0.1307
	(−2.8884)***	(−0.4939)
$ASP - R_{(-4)}$	−0.0822	0.3252
	(−0.5933)	(1.2387)
$R_{P(-1)}$	0.0046	0.1460
	(0.0601)	(1.0052)
$R_{P(-2)}$	0.0643	0.2074
	(0.8552)	(1.4550)
$R_{P(-3)}$	0.0474	−0.0932
	(0.6259)	(−0.6501)
$R_{P(-4)}$	−0.1643	−0.1112
	(−2.1241)**	(−0.7584)
R-squared	0.4581	0.1329
F-statistic	4.8606***	0.8813

1. *ASP-R* and R_p are the rate of return for DRAM ASP and stock portfolio, respectively; in which the lag term is indicated in the brackets.
2. The rate of return for stock portfolio includes the semiconductor manufacture firms announced by the Taiwan Semiconductor Industry Association (TSIA) and which are already established in 1996. They include United Microelectronics Corp., Orient Semiconductor Electronics, Ltd., Taiwan Semiconductor Manufacturing Co., Ltd., Macronix International Co., Ltd., Mosel Vitelic Inc. and Winbond Electronics Corp.
3. ***, **, * Significant at the 0.01, 0.05, and 0.1 levels, respectively.

lying of the new DRAM foundry investment project of ProMos can be used as the worldwide ASP of the DRAM market. Kelly (1998) takes the spot gold price as the underlying variable for a gold-mining investment project. We applied that the worldwide ASP as the underlying asset is different from Kelly's (1998) approach, since gold has no life cycle. The unit production cost of 64 Mb DRAM is set to be the exercise price. The options will be exercised if the spot price of DRAM goes higher than the predetermined exercise price, the new investment project is deep in the money.

28.8.3. Exercise Price

The unit cost changes over years had being set as the exercise prices shown in Table 28.4. The table shows that the unit cost decreases over the years since the DRAM chips were manufactured on improved technology, with $0.35\,\mu m$ technology down to $0.2\,\mu m$ technology from 1996 to 1999.

28.8.4. Dividend-Like Yield

Based on the CAPM, the expected return (α_s) to the twin security,[24] which is a portfolio of DRAM manufacturing firms publicly listed on Taiwan stock markets, is shown as Equation (28.24). According to the yearbook of Ibbotson and Sin-

quefield in 1999, the risk premium of market is 8 percent. It is similar to the conclusion of the empirical results in Pindyck (1993) based on the data of New York Stock Exchange between 1926 and 1988. The beta is estimated to be -0.5485 against the market of Taiwan Stock Exchange (TSE). The expected return of the twin security is derived to be 0.797 percent, with a given the annual average risk-free rate of 5.185 percent from 1996 to 1999. Therefore, we can compute the dividend-like yield to be -0.37203.

In the market of DRAM exchange, sales price of DRAM consists of the contract and the spot price. The pricing is the result of a negotiation between the buyer and seller. No agreement or negotiation is carried out in the trade of the spot market. Since the market trade manners differ, the response in supply–demand relationship of the two kinds of market also varies. In the buyer market, the

Table 28.4. Case study of ProMos

Panel A. Estimation of Average Unit Production Cost					
Estimator	Symbol	1996	1997	1998	1999
Total cost $(1000 \times \text{NT\$})^{(a)}$	–	–	253683	6796358	10676556
64Mb DRAM manufactured on (μm)	–	–	0.35	0.25	0.25–0.2
Production technology (DRAM unit/chip)$^{(b)}$	–	–	30	175	406
Production (pieces of wafer)$^{(c)}$	–	–	18500	207168	264000
Production (1,000DRAM units)$^{(d)=(b)\times(c)}$	–	–	571	36292	107184
Unit cost $(\text{NT\$})^{(e)=(a)/(d)}$	–	–	444.28	187.27	99.61
Exchange rate $(\text{NT\$/US\$})^{(f)}$	–	27.46	28.69	33.46	32.27
Units cost $(\text{US\$})^{(g)=(e)/(f)}$	–	–	15.480	5.597	3.08
Worldwide ASP (US\$)	–	9.690	5.909	4.101	6.415
64 Mb DRAM ASP (US\$)	–	99.42	45.82	10.19	6.59
Panel B. Estimation of the parameter					
Unit cost (exercise price)	I_t	–	15.48	5.597	3.08
Average of annual exchange rate	e_t	–	28.69	33.46	32.27
Risk-free interest rate	r_{ft}	–	5.78%	5.72%	4.14%
Volatility of the underlying	σ_v	–		37.36%	
Dividend-like yield	δ_1	–		-0.38	
	δ_2	–		-0.37203	
Worldwide DRAM ASP at 1996	V	–		9.69	
Risk-free interest rate at 1996	r_f	–		5.1%	

1. The δ_1 and δ_2 estimated by the CAPM approach and the cost of carry method respectively.
2. The 64 Mb DRAM ASP is US\$99.42 in 1996.

contract price will be higher than the spot price; and the vice versa is true in the seller market. Further, due to the trade cycle of the DRAM product, the response of spot price to supply–demand is rather flexible, and therefore it would take the lead in contract price fluctuations. However, the spread differences between spot price and contract price can respond to the elasticity of supply–demand and the trading cost in the two types of trading markets.

The DRAM market is usually a buyer's market, where contract price is higher than spot price, and firms complete the trading in the contract market. Therefore, most operation revenue comes from the contract market. It is sufficient to perceive the importance of DRAM contract market in a firm's cost of carry (CC). According to a report provided by DRAMeXchange Co., the average annual percentage difference between contract price and spot price is about 10 to 40 percent. ProMos data also show that the average annual difference between contract price and spot price is approximately 20 percent. The study conducted by ICIS–LOR in 1999 reports that the average contract price of DRAM in the Asian market in September 1999 was US$7.501, while the DRAM spot ASP of the same period was US$6.769. Thus the CC amounts to 10.8 percent. Since an average maturity of contract takes three months, the annual cost of carry is 43.2 percent, which is also consistent with the survey of DRAMeXchange. With a risk-free interest rate of 4.41 percent,[25] the dividend-like yield in Equation (28.29) is computed as −0.3906. This result differs not much from the dividend-like yield obtained by the mentioned CAPM approach. The difference between the dividend-like yields estimated by those two methods is 1.857 percent, and therefore the computed real option is almost same.

It is important to identify whether the dividend-like yield is positive or negative. The expected return of a newly constructed DRAM foundry is obtained through the CAPM. Since the DRAM chips manufactured by old generation of technology do not have a pricing advantage, their sales prices of DRAM products always decline and the relative costs of investment opportunity will also rise. On the contrary, the price of a new generation DRAM chips is expected to rise. Therefore, the sales prices of the two different generation DRAM chips experience a negative correlation[26], resulting in a negative value of beta. The resulting negative value of beta implies that the diversification advantage of the newly constructed foundry contributes to the company. If the volatility is high and the risk-free interest rate is low, then a new DRAM chipmaker manufacturing higher-density DRAM with marketing strength tends to have a higher expected return and a negative dividend-like yield would occur.

28.8.4. Volatility

The worldwide ASP of the DRAM market is the basis for the new DRAM foundry investment project of ProMos. Therefore, we also employ worldwide ASP of DRAM to estimate volatility in order to avoid the calculation from being affected by the DRAM life cycle. Kelly (1998) takes the spot gold price as the underlying variable for a gold-mining investment project. We applied that the worldwide ASP as the underlying asset is different from Kelly's (1998) approach, since gold has no life cycle. Based on the ASP calculated by Dataquest of Gartner for the worldwide DRAM spot market from 1990 to 1997, the volatility of W.W. ASP was computed to be 37.36 percent. These parameter estimation results are shown in Table 28.4.

28.8.5. Valuation of ProMos

ProMos was constructed in 1996 and IPO was made in 1999. We can obtain two critical values of V_{1997}^{cr} and V_{1998}^{cr}. If we take the worldwide ASP of DRAM in 1996 as its underlying asset, we can obtain the intrinsic value of IPO for the new DRAM foundry when it is constructed. In Table 28.5, we use two methods to estimate the dividend-like yield. We also place the worldwide DRAM ASP in 1996 into the model to solve for

Table 28.5. IPO's value of ProMos

Method	CAPM approach	Cost of carry approach
δ	−0.38	−0.37203
Worldwide ASP at 1996 (US$)	9.69	
V^{cr} at 1998	5.83	5.87
V^{cr} at 1997	11.03	11.2
Value of Real call options at 1996	9.0339	8.4383
IPO's value (US$million)	2710.17	2531.49
IPO's value (NT$million)	74416.47	69510.23
Price/share (NT$)	38.16	35.65

1. The critical value V^{cr} is derived from function $C^{\mathrm{cr}}_{t_i,t_{i+1}}(V^{\mathrm{cr}}_{t_i}) - I_{t_i} = 0$.
2. δ is dividend-like yield.
3. Firm IPO's value is calculated as a value of real call options to multiply expected output.
4. The share price is calculated as IPO's value divided by outstanding share when IPO.

the unit value of DRAM manufactured by the DRAM chipmaker.

We find that all critical values are influenced by the unit producing cost of ProMos for stage t and stages thereafter. The higher the unit producing cost, the greater the critical value. But when ProMos goes for IPO, the W.W. ASP of DRAM does not affect the critical value. In Table 28.5, the V^{cr}_{1998} values are 5.83 and 5.87, respectively. It indicates that as the ASP of spot market is higher than V^{cr}_{1998}, the newly constructed DRAM foundry would exercise in 1998. Similarly, as the ASP of spot market is higher than the V^{cr}_{1997}, and it would exercise in 1997. In the table, we show that the real options values of the construction stage of the firm are US$9.0339 and US$8.4383, respectively. It expresses the intrinsic values of manufacturing each unit of DRAM by the firm when it is constructed.

According to the expectation of ProMos, the DRAM chips are manufactured on improved technology, 0.35 to 0.2 μm, and after the time of IPO, it may reach 50,000 pieces per month, as each contains 500 DRAM chips. By then, the paid-in capital of the firm may reach NT$19.5 billion (amounts to issuing 1950 million ordinary shares).[27] Therefore, by timing the estimated unit real options value of DRAM with the expected productivity of the firm, we can obtain the value

of the firm at the time of IPO. We can also evaluate the value of shares of the firm in IPO according to the first issue of its ordinary shares. Table 28.5 shows the analysis of share price in IPO. It illustrates, as the underlying variable is worldwide DRAM ASP, the value per share is NT$38.16 with $\delta = -0.38$, which is close to the listing price of NT$40.01 of ProMos in IPO as on May 13, 1999. Since worldwide DRAM ASP already contains the price of low-density DRAM, this average would cause worldwide DRAM ASP to plunge. The value of real call options would decline. However, if the firm can upgrade its manufactured product on improved technology and actively promote the sale of higher-density DRAM in order to reduce the production cost, then the exercise price in the options model will decrease, and the product market value of the DRAM chipmaker will increase.

28.9. Conclusion

We employed the closed-form solution for multistage compound real call option of Lin (2002) to evaluate a sequential investment project. In consideration of the dividend-like yield of nontraded asset, we revised Lin's model, which did not discuss the selection of underlying variable and twin security, and referred to the method of Duan et al.

(2003) for the estimation of dividend-like yield. Finally in a case study, the value of newly built DRAM foundry of ProMos was assessed.

In the process of solving multivariate normal integrals, there exists a root-finding problem for critical value at each stage where the lower limit of interval is unknown. This critical value is an at-the-money finite value. We used three numerical methods for simulating the approximation value of the multivariate normal integral and found that lattice method was the best method in terms of execution efficiency and the Monte Carlo method was the worst. But the values obtained from those two methods were close to each other. The Gauss quadrature method improved by Drezner (1992) was easy to learn and easy to apply. But it was too straightforward and ran into the selection problem at order k, resulting in critical value that differed somewhat from that obtained from the other two numerical integration methods. In the process of root-finding, we found that focus on improving the Newton–Raphson method, while ignoring the basic numerical solver tended to complicate the root-finding process.

In the simulation analysis of investment modes, it is found that the real call value of up-sloping mode was the highest among the four modes, indicating that the strategy of up-sloping investment offers more decision flexibility and provides the highest value. Such finding supports the suggestions of Trigeorgis (1993a, b) for the use of real options in evaluating management and strategic flexibility.

In volatility and interest rate sensitivity analysis, we found that the valuation result of an investment project derived from real call option differed from financial call option, mainly because an investment project a nontraded asset that is subjected to the influence of dividend-like yield. In the formula for dividend-like yield, there exists ρ; when the value of ρ is large or positive, it indicates the high correlation of the new investment project with the current market status; hence poor diversification advantage of the project and higher investment risks. That is when σ increases, the value of decision flexibility brought by the new project declines, and hence the real call value

drops. Conversely, when ρ is small or negative, the project offers more diversification advantage and the real call value rises with the increase of σ. Regardless of the value of ρ, when interest rate increases, the real call value drops. In addition, when ρ is large under high interest rate market, that is when the project offers poor diversification advantage, its value is subjected to the influence of interest rate only and nearly totally unrelated to σ.

In the case study, we first identified the underlying variable and twin security for the model and then applied VAR to test the causality between underlying variable and twin security. The result indicated that the use of DRAM ASP as underlying variable in the case of ProMos was appropriate. The result of dividend-like yield estimation showed that yields obtained from CAPM and cost of carry model was close, differed by only 1.857 percent and both values were negative, indicating the negative correlation between the new DRAM foundry of ProMos and existing portfolio of representative chipmakers. It indicates that the new investment offered diversification advantage and carried lower opportunity cost.

Based on the investment prospectus of ProMos for its new foundry that planned different process technologies in different stages, we estimated the unit manufacturing cost of DRAM and set the exercise price to find the critical value of the company and its IPO price. It is found that the at-the-money critical value decreased by the year, indicating the competitiveness of ProMos products. The manufacturing process followed the Moore's law. Finally we estimated the share price of the company at the time of IPO based on the projected capacity and its outstanding shares at the time of IPO. The result showed that the share value at the time of IPO was close to the listing price in IPO.

NOTES

We acknowledge the financial support from National Science Council of R.O.C.

1. Also termed dividend-like yield.

2. "Certainty-equivalent rate" means deducting risk premium from the original growth rate of underlying, which is the same as pricing in a risk neutral world.

3. Referring to static NPV.

4. Such as NPV and IRR.

5. Lurhrman (1998a,b) estimated value-to-cost (NPV_q) by discounting the exercise price (X) at risk-free rate (r_f), which is defined as $PV(X) = X/(1 + r_f)^t$ and then as "modified" NPV after deducting the present value of exercise price from the value of the underlying (S). The value-to-cost (NPV_q) is the value of underlying asset divided by present value of exercise price, $NPV_q = S/PV(X)$; when $NPV_q > 1$, it represents the modified NPV being greater than zero; conversely, when $NPV_q < 1$, the modified NPV is less than zero. The cumulative variance ($\sigma^2 t$) is the variance of investment value multiplied by time.

6. Defined as cumulative variance.

7. Cox, Ingersoll, and Ross (1985) used certainty equivalent approach for risk adjustment, not risk-adjusted discount rate, that is modifying the real expected growth rate to certainty equivalent growth rate by deducting discount premium from real expected growth rate.

8. Extend the use of bivariate normal integral computation by Drezner (1978).

9. Very low order will result in greater error. $K = 15$ is also the optimum choice from tables developed by Steen et al. (1969).

10. The order K used in this paper is 15 (see appendices).

11. The lower limit of interval for the multivariate normal integral in the model has unknown critical value. After transformation into standard normal distribution, the critical value is transformed into the upper limit of interval.

12. A company typically goes through four stages from setup to IPO – seed, start up, expansion, and growth up. Thus our model incorporates these four stages, which form five decision points.

13. Matlab tool box provides NORCDF($\square$).

14. DBNRDF($\square$).

15. Referring to Lin (2002).

16. Referring to Duan et al. (2003) under $\rho < 0$.

17. The ProMos expect total investment capital of US\$1,700 million in three years.

18. The technology of manufacturing 8-inch wafer is, when manufactured on $0.35\,\mu m$, the chip ratio is 50 percent; when manufactured on $0.25\,\mu m$, and the chip ratio is 100 percent.

19. The good ratio for 64 Mb DRAM is 20 percent at the start of mass production (1997), and it takes one year of production time for the good ratio to reach 80 percent.

20. It can be DRAM product.

21. It can be stock.

22. The weight of portfolio return is the ratio between the market value of individual stocks of six listed semiconductor firms and the total market value of the portfolio. The six listed semiconductor firms include United Microelectronics Corp., Orient Semiconductor Electronics, Ltd., Taiwan Semiconductor Manufacturing Co., Ltd., Macronix International Co., Ltd., Mosel Vitelic Inc. and Winbond Electronics Corp.

23. The sampling firms are the semiconductor manufacture firms published by The Taiwan Semiconductor Industry Association (TSIA) since 1996.

24. The rate of return on twin security can be expressed as $\alpha_s = r_f + \lambda \rho_{vm} \sigma_v$, where λ and ρ_{vm} are the market price of risk and the correlation between the underlying asset and on the twin security, respectively.

25. For risk-free interest rate, we employ Government-bond average interest rate of 4.14 percent in 1999.

26. The correlation can be computed by $\rho_{vm} = beta \times (\sigma_m/\sigma_v)$, where σ_v and σ_m are volatility of underlying asset and market portfolio, respectively.

27. In Taiwan, the face value of per share is NT\$10.

REFERENCE

Amram, M.H. and Kulatilaka, N.H. (1999). "Real options." *Harvard Business School Press* 11: 11–31.

Andersson, H. (1999). "Capital budgeting in a situation with variable utilization of capacity – an example from the pulp industry." Working Paper, *SSE/EFI*.

Bhide, A.V. (2000). "The Origin and Evolution of New Business." England: Oxford University Press.

Black, F. and Scholes, M. (1973). "The pricing of options and corporate liabilities." *Journal of Political Economics*, 81: 637–659.

Brennan, M.J. and Schwartz, E.S. (1985). "Evaluating natural resource investment." *Journal of Business*, 58: 135–157.

Brent, R.P. (1971). "Algorithms for Minimization without Derivatives." New Jersey: Prentice-Hall.

Constantinides, G.M. (1978). "Market risk adjustment in project valuation." *Journal of Finance*, 33: 603–616.

Copeland, T.E. and Antikarov, V. (2001). "Real Options: A Practitioner's Guide." New York: Texere, LLC.

Cox, J.C. and Ross, S.A. (1976). "The valuation of options for alternative stochastic processes." *Journal of Financial Economics*, 3: 145–166.

Cox, J.C., Ingersoll, J.E. Jr., and Ross, S.A. (1985). "An inter-temporal general equilibrium model of asset prices." *Econometrica*, 53: 363–384.

Cranley, R. and Patterson, T.N.L. (1976). "Randomization of number theoretic methods for multiple integration." *SIAM Journal of Numerical Analysis*, 13: 904–914.

Dekker, T.J. (1969). "Finding a zero by means of successive linear interpolation," in Dejon and Henrici (eds.) *Constructive Aspects of the Fundamental Theorem of Algebra*. New York: Wiley.

Drezner, Z. (1978). "Computation of the Bivariate Normal Integral." *Mathematics of Computation*, 32: 277–279.

Drezner, Z. (1992). "Computation of the multivariate normal integral." *ACM Transactions on Mathematical Software*, 18: 470–480.

Duan, C., Lin, W.T. and Lee, C. (2003). "Sequential capital budgeting as real options: the case of a new dram chipmaker in Taiwan." *Review of Pacific Basin Financial Markets and Policies*, 6: 87–112.

Genz, A. (1992). "Numerical computation of the multivariate normal probabilities." *Journal of Computational and Graphical Statistics*, 1: 141–150.

Genz, A. (1999). "Comparison of methods for the computation of multivariate normal probabilities." Working Paper.

Geske, R. (1977). "The valuation of corporate liabilities as compound options." *Journal of Financial and Quantitative Analysis*, 12: 541–552.

Geske, R. (1979). "The valuation of compound options." *Journal of Financial Economics*, 7: 63–81.

Granger, C.W.J. (1969). "Investigating causal relations by econometric models and cross-spectral methods." *Econometrica*, 37: 424–438.

Hlawka, E.M (1962). "Zur angenäherten berechnung mehrfacher integrale." *Monatshefte Fur Mathematik*, 66: 140–151.

Hull, J.C (1997). *Options, Futures, and Other Derivatives*, 3rd edn. Prentice-Hall.

Ibbotson, R.G. and Sinquefield, R.A. (1999). "Stocks Bonds, Bills, and Inflation Yearbook." Chicago: Ibbotson Associates.

Keeley, R.H., Punjabi, S., and Turki, L. (1996). "Valuation of early-stage ventures: option valuation models vs. traditional approach." *Entrepreneurial and Small Business Finance*, 5: 115–138.

Kelly, S. (1998) "A Binomial Lattice Approach for Valuing a Mining Property IPO." *Quarterly Review of Economics and Finance*, 38: 693–709.

Kemna, A.G.Z (1993). "Case studies on real options." *Financial Management*, 22: 259–270.

Korobov, N.M. (1957). "The approximate calculation of multiple integral using number-theoretic methods." *Doklady Akademmi Nauk SSSR*, 115: 1062–1065.

Lin, W.T. (2002). "Computing a multivariate normal integral for valuing compound real options." *Review of Quantitative Finance and Accounting*, 18: 185–209.

Luehrman, T.A. (1998a). "Strategy as Portfolio of Real Options." *Harvard Business Review*, 89–99.

Luehrman, T.A (1998b). "Investment opportunities as real options: getting started on the numbers." *Harvard Business Review*, 51–67.

Lyness, J.N, and Gabriel, J.R. (1969). "Comment on a new method for the evaluation of multidimensional integrals." *The Journal of Chemical Physics*, 50: 565–566.

Majd, S. and Pindyck, R.S. (1987). "Time to build, option value, and investment decisions." *Journal of Financial Economics*, 18: 7–27.

McDonald, R. (2002). *Derivatives Markets*. Addison Wesley.

McDonald, R. and Siegel, D. (1984). "Option pricing when the underlying asset earns a below-equilibrium rate of return: a note." *Journal of Finance*, 39: 261–265.

McDonald, R. and Siegel, D. (1985). "Investment and the valuation of firms when there is an option to shut down." *International Economic Review*, 26: 331–349.

Merton, R.C. (1973) "An intertemporal capital asset pricing model." *Econometrica*, 41: 867–887.

Myers, S.C. (1977). "Determinants of corporate borrowing." *Journal of Financial Economics*, 5: 147–176.

Myers, S.C. (1984). "Finance theory and financial strategy." *Interface*, 14: 126–137.

Myers, S.C. (1987). "Finance theory and financial strategy." *Midland Corporate Finance Journal*, 5: 6–13.

Pickles, E. and Smith, J.L. (1993). "Petroleum property valuation: a binomial lattice implementation of option pricing theory." *Energy Journal*, 14: 1–26.

Pindyck, R.S. (1993). "Investments of uncertain cost." *Journal of Financial Economics*, 34: 53–76.

Roll, R. (1977). "An analytic valuation formula for unprotected american call options on stocks with known dividends." *Journal of Financial Economics*, 5: 251–258.

Schumpeter, J.A. (1939). *Business cycles: A Theoretical, Historical, and Statistical Analysis of the Capitalist Process*. New York: McGraw-Hill.

Sims, C.hristopher A. (1980). "Macroeconomics and Reality." *Econometrica*, 48: 1–48.

Steen, N.M., Byrne, G.D. and Gelbard, E.M. (1969). "Gaussian quadratures for integrals." *Mathematics of Computation*, 23: 169–180.

Trigeorgis, L. (1993a). "The nature of option interactions and the valuation of investment with multiple real options." *Journal of Financial and Quantitative Analysis*, 28: 1–20.

Trigeorgis, L. (1993b). "Real options and interactions with financial flexibility." *Financial Management*, 25: 202–224.

Trigeorgis, L. (1994). "Options in capital budgeting: managerial flexibility and strategy in resoure allocation." Cambridge, MA: MIT Press.

Trigeorgis, L. (1996). "Real options: managerial flexibility and strategy in resource allocation." Cambridge, MA: MIT Press.

Trigeorgis, L. and Mason, S.P. (1987). "Valuing managerial flexibility." *Mildland Corporate Journal*, 5: 14–21.

Zaremba, S.K. (1966). "Good lattice points, discrepancy and numerical integration." *Annali di Matematica Pura ed Applicata*, 73: 293–318.

Appendix

The firm's critical value V_i^{cr} and real call options value given δ is constant and $r_f = 0.08$.

Investment mode	σ_v	V_4^{cr}	V_3^{cr}	V_2^{cr} Drezner	Lattice	MC	Real call options value Drezner	Lattice	MC
Up-sloping	0.1	43.52	51.27	52.61	52.65	52.65	29.67	29.67	29.67
	0.2	43.41	50.18	49.20	49.22	49.22	29.92	30.42	30.42
	0.3	42.77	47.85	44.45	44.50	44.50	31.30	32.25	32.25
	0.4	41.63	44.82	39.41	39.84	39.84	33.68	34.60	34.60
	0.5	40.15	41.53	34.62	34.80	34.80	36.58	37.96	37.96
	0.6	38.48	38.25	30.30	30.47	30.47	39.70	40.14	40.14
	0.7	36.74	35.13	26.54	26.56	26.56	42.62	43.00	43.00
	0.8	35.01	32.25	23.31	23.44	23.44	45.60	45.80	45.80
	0.9	33.32	29.64	20.59	20.62	20.62	48.42	48.50	48.50
Down-sloping	0.1	32.92	41.60	55.77	55.79	55.79	27.78	27.77	27.77
	0.2	31.70	40.93	55.34	55.34	55.34	27.91	27.12	27.12
	0.3	29.76	39.14	53.60	53.72	53.72	28.90	26.87	26.87
	0.4	27.57	36.74	50.87	51.06	51.06	30.87	28.27	28.27
	0.5	25.36	34.13	47.67	47.84	47.84	33.41	30.58	30.58
	0.6	23.23	31.54	44.38	44.57	44.57	36.25	33.26	33.26
	0.7	21.26	29.08	41.21	41.47	41.47	39.04	36.00	36.00
	0.8	19.45	26.84	38.27	38.33	38.33	41.87	38.82	38.82
	0.9	17.82	24.81	35.61	35.72	35.72	44.59	41.50	41.50
Up, then down	0.1	32.92	47.09	55.06	55.13	55.13	28.28	28.28	28.28
	0.2	31.70	46.82	53.78	53.85	53.85	28.43	28.36	28.36
	0.3	29.76	45.63	51.01	51.75	51.75	29.54	29.35	29.35
	0.4	27.57	43.69	47.39	47.53	47.53	31.63	31.54	31.54
	0.5	25.36	41.38	43.51	43.76	43.76	34.28	34.03	34.03
	0.6	23.23	38.95	39.70	39.83	39.83	37.20	36.80	36.80
	0.7	21.26	36.55	36.16	36.35	36.35	40.06	39.53	39.53
	0.8	19.45	34.27	32.95	33.06	33.06	42.95	42.28	42.28
	0.9	17.82	32.16	30.11	30.13	30.13	45.72	44.59	44.59

(*Continued*)

The firm's critical value V_i^{cr} and real call options value given δ is constant and $r_f = 0.08$. (*Continued*)

Investment mode	σ_v	V_4^{cr}	V_3^{cr}	V_2^{cr}			Real call options value		
				Drezner	Lattice	MC	Drezner	Lattice	MC
Down, then up	0.1	43.52	45.37	53.90	53.90	53.90	29.17	29.18	29.18
	0.2	43.41	42.92	52.24	52.36	52.36	29.35	29.14	29.14
	0.3	42.77	39.47	48.94	49.06	49.06	30.56	30.00	30.00
	0.4	41.63	35.69	44.94	44.97	44.97	32.78	31.96	31.96
	0.5	40.15	31.99	40.83	40.90	40.90	35.56	34.49	34.49
	0.6	38.48	28.54	36.92	37.19	37.19	38.59	37.25	37.25
	0.7	36.74	25.44	33.38	33.58	33.58	41.41	40.06	40.06
	0.8	35.01	22.70	30.25	30.26	30.26	44.32	42.85	42.85
	0.9	33.32	20.31	27.51	27.83	27.83	47.08	45.88	45.88

Chapter 29

MARKET EFFICIENCY HYPOTHESIS

MELODY LO, *University of Southern Mississippi, USA*

Abstract

Market efficiency is one of the most fundamental research topics in both economics and finance. Since Fama (1970) formally introduced the concept of market efficiency, studies have been developed at length to examine issues regarding the efficiency of various financial markets. In this chapter, we review elements, which are at the heart of market efficiency literature: the statistical efficiency market models, joint hypothesis testing problem, and three categories of testing literature.

Keywords: market efficiency; security returns; information; autocorrelation; serial correlation (tests); random walk model; (sub)martingale; hypothesis testing; (speculative) profits; trading rules; price formation

29.1. Definition

The simplest but economically reasonable statement of market efficiency hypothesis is that security prices at any time fully reflect all available information to the level in which the profits made based on the information do not exceed the cost of acting on such information. The cost includes the price of acquiring the information and transaction fees. When the price formation in equity market satisfies the statement, market participants cannot earn unusual profits based on the available information. This classical market efficiency definition was formally intro-

duced by Fama (1970), and developed at length by researchers in the field.

29.2. The Efficient Market Model

Much of work on this line of research is based on an assumption that the condition of market equilibrium can be stated in terms of expected returns. Although there exists diversified expected return theories, they can in general be expressed as follows:

$$E(\hat{p}_{i,t+1}) = [1 + E(\hat{r}_{i,t+1}|I_t)] \times p_{i,t}, \qquad (29.1)$$

where E is the expected value operator; $p_{i,t}$ is the price of security i in period t, $r_{i,t+1}$ is the one-period rate of return on security i in the period ending at $t+1$, and $E(r_{i,t+1}|I_t)$ is the expected rate of return conditional on information (I) available in period t. Also, variables with hats indicate that they are random variables in period t. The market is said to be efficient, if the actual security prices are identical to their equilibrium expected values expressed in Equation (29.1). In other words, if the actual security price formation follows the market efficiency hypothesis, there would be no expected returns/profits in excess of equilibrium expected returns. For a single security, this concept can be expressed as follows:

$$\begin{aligned} E(\hat{Z}_{i,t+1}|I_t) &= 0, \text{ and} \\ Z_{i,t+1} &= r_{i,t+1} - E(\hat{r}_{i,t+1}|I_t), \end{aligned} \qquad (29.2)$$

where $Z_{i,t+1}$ is the return at $t+1$ in excess of the equilibrium expected returns anticipated at t. This concept can also apply to the entire security market. Suppose that market participants use information, I_t, to allocate the amount, $\lambda_i(I_t)$, of funds available to each of n security that makes up the entire security market. If the price formation of each of n security follows Equation (29.2), then the total excess market value at $t+1(\hat{V}_{t+1})$ equals to zero, i.e.

$$E(\hat{V}_{t+1}|I_t) = \sum_{i=1}^{n}\lambda_i(I_t)E(\hat{Z}_{i,t+1}|I_t) = 0. \qquad (29.3)$$

The general efficient market models of Equations (29.2) and (29.3) are the foundations for empirical work in this area. Researchers in the field largely agree that security prices "fully reflect" all available information has a direct implication: successive returns (or price changes) are independent. Consequently, researchers tend to conclude market is efficient if there are evidences that demonstrate $E(\hat{Z}_{i,t+1}|I_t) = 0$ and $Z_{i,t}$ is uncorrelated with $Z_{i,t+k}$ for any value of k. Similarly, if $E(\hat{V}_{t+1}|I_t) = 0$ and $V_{i,t}$ is uncorrelated with $V_{i,t+k}$ for any value of k, market is evident to be efficient.

Based on efficiency models in Equations (29.2) and (29.3), two special statistical models, submartingale and random walk, are closely related to the efficiency empirical literature. The market is said to follow a submartingale when the following condition holds:

$$E(\hat{Z}_{i,t+1}|I_t) \geq 0 \text{ for all } t \text{ and } I_t. \qquad (29.4)$$

The expected returns conditional on I_t is nonnegative and has an important implication on trading rule. This means investors should hold the security once it is bought during any future period, because selling it short cannot generate larger returns. More importantly, if Equation (29.4) holds as equality, the market is said to follow a martingale. Researchers usually conclude that security prices follow "patterns" and market is inefficient when the empirical evidences are toward rejection of a martingale model.

The security prices exhibit the random walk statistical property if not only that the successive returns are independent but also that they are identically distributed. Using f to denote the density function, the random walk model can be expressed as follows:

$$f(r_{i,t+1}|I_t) = f(r_{i,t+1}) \text{ for all } t \text{ and } I_t. \qquad (29.5)$$

The random walk property indicates that the return distributions would repeat themselves. Evidences on random walk property are often considered to be a stronger supportive of market efficiency hypothesis than those on (sub)martingale property.

29.3. The Joint Hypothesis Problem

The continuing obstacle in this line of empirical literature is that the market efficiency hypothesis *per se* is not testable. This is because one cannot test market efficiency hypothesis without imposing restrictions on the behavior of expected security returns. For example, the efficiency models of Equations (29.2) and (29.3) are derived based on a joint hypothesis: (i) the market equilibrium returns (or prices) are assumed to be some functions of the information set and (ii) the available information is assumed to be fully utilized by the market participants to form equilibrium returns, and thereby current security prices. As all empirical tests of market efficiency are tests of a joint hypothesis, a rejection of the hypothesis would always lead to two possible inferences: either (i) the assumed market equilibrium model has little ability to capture the security price movements or (ii) the market participants use available information inefficiently. Because the possibility that a bad equilibrium model is assumed to serve as the benchmark can never be ruled out, the precise inferences about the degree of market efficiency remains impossible to identify.

29.4. Three Categories of Testing Literature

The empirical work on market efficiency hypothesis can be categorized into three groups. First, weak-form tests are concerned with how well past security returns (and other explanatory variables) predict future returns. Second, semi-strong-form tests focus on the issue of how fast security price responds to publicly available information. Third, strong-form tests examine whether security prices fully reflect private information.

29.4.1. Weak-Form Tests

Controversy about market efficiency centers on the weak-form tests. Many results from earlier works on weak-form tests come directly from the submartingale expected return model or the random walk literature. In addition, much of the earlier works consider information set as just past historic returns (or prices). The most frequently used procedure to test the weak form of efficient markets is to examine whether there is statistically significant autocorrelation in security returns using serial correlation tests. A pattern of autocorrelation in security returns is interpreted as the possibility that market is inefficient and market participants are irrational, since they do not fully exploit speculative opportunities based on the price dependence. The serial correlation tests are tests of a linear relationship between current period's returns (R_t) and past returns (R_{t-1}):

$$R_t = \alpha_0 + \alpha_1 R_{t-1} + \varepsilon_t, \qquad (29.6)$$

where R_t is the rate of return, usually calculated as the natural logarithm first differences of the trading price (i.e. $R_t = \ln P_t - \ln P_{t-1}$; P_t and P_{t-1} are the trading prices at the end of period t and of period $t-1$, respectively.), α_0 is the expected return unrelated to previous returns, and α_1 is the size of first-order autocorrelation in the rate of returns. For market efficiency hypothesis to hold, α_1 needs to be statistically indifferent from 0.

After conducting serial correlation analysis, Kendall (1953) concluded that market is efficient because weekly changes in 19 indices of British industrial share prices and in spot prices for cotton and wheat exhibit the random walk property. Roberts (1959) notes that similar statistical results can be found when examining weekly changes in

Dow Jones Index. (See also Moore, 1962; Godfrey et al., 1964; and Fama, 1965.) Some researchers later argued that the size of serial correlation in returns offers no precise implications on the extent of speculative profits available in the market. They propose that examining the profitability of various trading rules can be a more straightforward methodology for efficiency tests. A representative study that adopted this methodology was done by Alexander (1961), where he examines the profitability of various trading rules (including the well-known y% filter rule). Despite a positive serial correlation in return series, he also discovers that y% filter rule cannot outperform buy-and-hold rule. He thus concludes that the market is still an efficient one. Similarly, Fama and Blume (1966) find positive dependence in very short-term individual stock price of the Dow Jones Industrial index. Yet, they also suggest that market is efficient because the overall trading costs from any trading rule, aiming to utilize the price dependence to profit, is sufficiently large to eliminate the possibility that it would outperform the buy-and-hold rule. In general, results from earlier work (conducted before the 1970s) provide no evidence against efficient market hypothesis since they all report that the autocorrelations in returns are very close to 0.

As more security data becomes available, the post-1970 studies always claim that there is significant (and substantial) autocorrelation in returns. Lo and MacKinlay (1988) report that there is positive autocorrelation in weekly returns on portfolios of NYSE stocks grouped according to size. In particular, the autocorrelation appears to be stronger for portfolios of small stocks. According to Fisher's (1966) suggestion, this result could be due to the nonsynchronous trading effect. Conrad and Kaul (1988) investigate weekly returns of size-based portfolios of stocks that trade on both Wednesdays to somehow alleviate the nonsynchronous trading effect. However, as in Lo and MacKinlay (1988), they find positive autocorrelation in returns and that this pattern is stronger for portfolios of small stocks.

On another note, the post-1970 weak-form test studies focus on whether variables other than past returns can improve return predictability. Fama and French (1988) use dividend yield to forecast returns on the portfolios of NYSE stock. They find that dividend yield is helpful for return predictability. On the other hand, Compbell and Shiller (1988) report that earnings/price ratio increases the return predictability. In summary, recent studies suggest that returns are predictable when variables other than past returns are used and the evidences seem to be against the market efficiency hypothesis that was well supported before the 1970s.

29.4.2. Semi-strong-Form Tests

Each of the semi-strong-form tests is concerned with the speed of price adjustment to a particular public information event. The event can be macroeconomic announcement, companies' financial reports, or announcement on stock split. The initial work in this line of research was by Fama et al., (1969), in which they studied the speed of price adjustment to the stock-split announcement. Their results show that the informational implications of a stock split are fully reflected in the price of a share at least by the end of the month, or most probably almost immediately after the day of the stock-split announcement. They therefore conclude that the stock market is efficient because the prices respond quite speedily to new public information. Waud (1970) uses residual analysis to study how fast market reacts to the Federal Reserve Bank's announcement on discount rate changes. The result suggests that market responds rapidly to the interest-rate announcement even when the Federal Reserve Board is merely trying to bring the discount rate in line with other market rates. Ball and Brown (1968) investigate the price reactions to the annual-earnings announcement. They conclude that market participants seem to have anticipated most information by the month's end, after the annual-earnings announcement. These earlier studies (prior to the 1970s), focusing on different events of public announcement, all find supportive evidences of market efficiency hypothesis. Since the 1970s, the

semi-strong-form test studies have been developed at length. The usual result is that stock price adjusts within a day of the announcement being made public. Nowadays, the notation that security markets are semi-strong-form efficient is widely accepted among researchers.

29.4.3. Strong-Form Tests

The strong-form tests are concerned with whether prices fully reflect all available information so that no particular group of investors have monopolistic access to some information that can lead to higher expected returns than others. It is understandable that as long as some groups of investors in reality do have monopolistic access to the information, the strong-form market efficiency hypothesis is impossible to hold. In fact, both groups of specialists, NYSE (see Niederhoffer and Osborne, 1966) and corporate insiders (see Scholes, 1969), have monopolistic access to information, and which has been documented. Since the strong-form efficiency model is impossible to satisfy, the main focus in this line of work is to assess if private information leads to abnormal expected returns, and if some investors (with private information) perform better than others because they possess more private information. The most influential work before the 1970s was by Jensen (1968, 1969) where he assessed the performance of 115 mutual funds. Jensen (1968) finds that those mutual funds under examination on average were not able to predict security prices well enough to outperform the buy-and-hold trading rule. Further, there appears no evidence suggesting that individual mutual fund performs significantly better than what we expect from random chances. Using Sharpe–Lintner theory (see Sharpe, 1964; Lintner, 1965), Jansen (1969) developed a model to evaluate the performance of portfolios of risk assets. Most importantly, he manages to derive a measure of portfolio's "efficiency". The empirical results show that on average the resources spent by the funds managers to better forecast security prices do not generate larger portfolio returns than what could have been earned by equivalent risk portfolios selected either by random selection trading rule or by combined investments in market portfolios and government bonds. Jansen further interprets his results that probably mutual fund managers do not have access to private information. These results are clear in line with strong-form market efficiency models because evidence suggests that current security prices have fully reflected the effects of all available information. After the 1970s, there is less of new research examining investors' access to private information that is not reflected in security prices. Representative studies were done by Henriksson (1984) and Chang and Lewellen (1984). In tests of 116 mutual funds, Henriksson (1984) reports that there is difference between mutual fund returns and Sharpe–Lintner market line. Similarly, Chang and Lewellen (1984) note that examination of mutual fund returns show no supportive evidence of fund managers' superior selection abilities. In short, recent studies largely agree to prior literature's view that investors with private information are unable to outperform a passive investment strategy. Evidences are still in favor of the existence of market efficiency hypothesis.

29.5. Conclusion

This review has been brief and so various issues related to market efficient model have not been considered. Volatility tests of market efficiency, and cross-sectional return predictability based on various asset pricing models are just some of the omitted issues. For more details, readers are referred to two excellent market efficiency survey papers by Fama (1970, 1991).

REFERENCES

Alexander, S.S. (1961). "Price movements in speculative markets: trends or random walks." *Industrial Management Review*, 2: 7–26.

Ball, R. and Brown, P. (1968). "An empirical evaluation of accounting income numbers." *Journal of Accounting Research*, 6: 159–178.

Chang E.C., and Lewellen, W.G. (1984). "Market timing and mutual fund investment performance." *Journal of Business*, 57: 57–72.

Campbell J.Y. and Shiller, R. (1988). "Stock prices, earnings and expected dividends." *Journal of Finance*, 43: 661–676.

Conrad, J. and Kaul, G. (1988). "Time-variation in expected returns." *Journal of Business*, 61(4): 409–425.

Fama, E.F. (1965). "The behavior of stock market price." *Journal of Business*, 38(1): 34–105.

Fama, E.F. (1970). "Efficient capital markets: a review of theory and empirical work." *Journal of Finance*, 25(2): 383–417.

Fama, E.F. (1991). "Efficient capital markets: II." *Journal of Finance*, 46(5): 1575–1617.

Fama, E.F. and Blume, M. (1966). "Filter rules and stock market trading profits." *Journal of Business (Special Supplement)*, 39: 226–241.

Fama, E.F. and French, K.R. (1988). "Dividend yields and expected stock returns." *Journal of Financial Economics*, 22: 3–25.

Fama, E.F., Fisher, L., Jensen, M.C., and Roll, R. (1969). "The Adjustment of Stock Prices to New Information." *International Economic Review*, 5: 1–21

Fisher, L. (1966). "Some new stock-market indexes." *Journal of Business*, 39(1), Part 2: 191–225.

Godfrey, M.D., Granger, C.W.J., and Morgenstern, O. (1964). "The random walk hypothesis of stock market behavior." *Kyklos*, 17: 1–30.

Henriksson, R.T. (1984). "Market timing and mutual fund performance: an empirical investigation." *Journal of Business*, 57: 73–96.

Jensen, M.C. (1968). "The performance of mutual funds in the period 1945–64." *Journal of Finance*, 23: 389–416.

Jensen, M.C. (1969). "Risk, the pricing of capital assets, and the evaluation of investment portfolios." *Journal of Business*, 42: 167–247.

Kendall, M.G. (1953). "The analysis of economic time-series, Part I: Prices." *Journal of the Royal Statistical Society*, 96 (Part I): 11–25.

Lintner, J. (1965). "Security prices, risk, and maximal gains from diversification." *Journal of Finance*, 20: 587–615.

Lo, A.W. and MacKinlay, A.C. (1988). "Stock market prices do not follow random walks: evidence from a simple specification test." *Review of Financial Studies*, 1(1): 41–66.

Moore, A. (1962). "A Statistical Analysis of Common Stock Prices." PhD thesis, Graduate School of Business, University of Chicago.

Niederhoffer, V. and Osborne, M.F.M. (1966). "Market making and reversal on the stock exchange." *Journal of the American Statistical Association*, 61: 897–916.

Roberts, H.V. (1959). "Stock market 'patterns' and financial analysis: methodological suggestions." *Journal of Finance*, 14: 1–10.

Scholes, M. (1969). "A test of the competitive hypothesis: the market for new issues and secondary offering." PhD thesis, Graduate School of Business, University of Chicago.

Sharpe, W.F. (1964). "Capital assets prices: a theory of market equilibrium under conditions of risk." *Journal of Finance*, 19: 425–442.

Waud, R.N. (1970). "Public interpretation of federal discount rate changes: evidence on the 'Announcement Effect'." *Econometrica*, 38: 231–250.

Chapter 30

THE MICROSTRUCTURE/ MICRO-FINANCE APPROACH TO EXCHANGE RATES

MELODY LO, *University of Southern Mississippi, USA*

Abstract

The vast empirical failure of standard macro exchange rate determination models in explaining exchange rate movements motivates the development of microstructure approach to exchange rates in the 1990s. The microstructure approach of incorporating "order flow" in empirical models has gained considerable popularity in recent years, since its superior performance to macro exchange rate models in explaining exchange rate behavior. It is shown that order flow can explain about 60 percent of exchange rate movements versus 10 percent at most in standard exchange rate empirical models. As the microstructure approach to exchange rates is an active ongoing research area, this chapter briefly discusses key concepts that constitute the approach.

Keywords: microstructure approach; order flow; exchange rates; macroexchange rate models; heterogeneous information; private information; asset market approach; goods market approach; currency; divergent mappings; transaction

30.1. Definition

The microstructure approach to exchange rates is considered to be a fairly new but active research area. This line of research emerged in the early 1990s mostly due to the vast empirical failure of standard macro exchange rate determination models. In more recent years (the late 1990s), there was considerably a large amount of published work regarding the microstructure approach to exchange rates, suggesting order flow is evident to be the missing piece in explaining exchange rate behavior. The following definition of the microstructure approach to exchange rates comes directly from its pioneer, Richard Lyons (See Lyons, 2001).

The microstructure approach is a new approach to exchange rates whose foundations lie in microeconomics (drawing particularly from microstructure finance). The focus of the approach is dispersed information and how information of this type is aggregated in the marketplace. By dispersed information, we mean dispersed bits of information about changing variables like money demands, risk preferences, and future inflation. Dispersed information also includes information about the actions of others (e.g. about different trading responses to commonly observed data). The fact that the private sector might be solving a problem of dispersed information is not considered in traditional macro models. Rather, macro models assume that information about variables like money demands, risk preferences, and inflation is either symmetric economy-wide, or in some models, asymmetrically assigned to a single player – the central bank. In reality, there are many types of dispersed information that exchange rates need to impound. Understanding the nature of this information problem and how it is solved is the essence of this micro-based research agenda.

30.2. Empirical Failure of Traditional Approaches To Exchange Rates

The literature has documented extensively the little ability traditional/standard exchange rate determination models have to explain exchange rate behavior. Meese and Rogoff (1983) show that a random walk model outperforms the standard international-finance models in forecasting exchange rates. In that respect, Meese (1990) writes that "...the proportion of (monthly or quarterly) exchange rate changes that current models can explain is essentially zero...This result is quite surprising, since exchange rate changes would be entirely unpredictable only in very special cases of the theoretical models discussed." More recently, a survey paper by Frankel and Rose (1995) also notes that "To repeat a central fact of life, there is remarkably little evidence that macroeconomic variables have consistent strong effects on floating exchange rate, except during extraordinary circumstances such as hyperinflations."

Two most frequently discussed standard exchange rate determination approaches are (1) goods market approach and (2) asset market approach. The goods market approach suggests that exchange rates move to reflect necessary changes in excess demand/supply of foreign currency resulting from international trades. A domestic economy necessarily demands for more foreign currencies when its citizens consume more imported goods. The general prediction of goods market approach is that an increase in domestic trade deficit must lead to the depreciation of domestic currency against foreign currency. However, existing studies find no empirical evidence to

support any specific relation between current account imbalance and exchange rate movements.

In open economies, domestic citizens can purchase not only foreign goods but also foreign financial assets. The asset market approach suggests that demand for foreign currency increases when domestic citizens increase their possessions on foreign assets, and this in turn would cause domestic currency to depreciate against foreign currency. Different from the goods market approach, the asset market approach also concerns the market efficiency issue. Specifically, the theoretical models on asset market approach determine equilibrium exchange rate at the level that no public information can lead to excess returns.

In general, the empirical model specification for asset market approach is as follows (Lyons, 2001):

$$\Delta E_t = f_1(i,m,z) + \varepsilon_{1t}, \qquad (30.1)$$

where ΔE_t is changes in nominal exchange rate (usually monthly or weekly data is used), the function $f_1(i,m,z)$ includes the current and past values of domestic and foreign interest rates (i), money supply (m), and all other macro variables (z). Similar to the low predictability of goods market approach, the majority of asset market empirical studies report that macro variables in Equation (30.1) explain 10 percent only, at most, of exchange rate movements. Further details on the empirical failure of various standard exchange rate determination models are well documented by Taylor (1995).

The disappointing results from the existing exchange rate models motivated researchers to look for sources responsible for the empirical failure. They attribute the general empirical failure to the unrealistic assumptions shared among standard exchange rate determination models. In detail, these models assume that every market participant learns new information at the same time when macroeconomic information/news is made public. Further, all market participants are assumed to have the ability to impound macro information into prices to the same level. However, both assumptions can easily be argued. In reality, not only market participants' information set is heterogeneous, but also their mapping ability from available information to price is impossible to be the same. The heterogeneity in information set is evident from the fact that foreign exchange traders, working for different banks, each have their own customers to deal with. Transactions with different customers offer each trader "private" information that he may not intend to share with others. In addition, it is understandable that different people tend to interpret the market impact of new information on exchange rate differently, regardless whether the information is made available to all of them at the same time. This idea of divergent mappings from information to prices is discussed by Isard (1995, pp. 182–183) who states that "economist's very limited information about the relationship between equilibrium exchange rates and macroeconomic fundamentals,... it is hardly conceivable that rational market participants with complete information about macroeconomic fundamentals could use that information to form precise expectations about the future market-clearing level of exchange rates."

30.3. Why Microstructure Approach?

The unrealistic assumptions in standard exchange rate models mentioned above have been relaxed in the literature that aims to explain why the financial market crashed. It is important to note that despite events such as stock market crash and currency crisis appear to be macro issues, they can be largely explained by microstructure approach that considers the existence of heterogeneous information among market participants (see Grossman, 1988; Romer, 1993; Carrera, 1999). For the same token, Lyons argues that adopting microstructure approach to investigate the trading process of exchange rates may help our understanding on when and how exchange rates move. Lyons (2001, p. 4) notes that the microstructure approach is an approach that relaxes three of the assets approach's most uncomfortable assumptions. First, on the aspect of information, microstructure

models recognize that some information relevant to exchange rates is not publicly available. Second, on the aspect of players, microstructure models recognize that market participants differ in ways that affect prices. Last, on the institutional aspect, microstructure models recognize that trading mechanism differs in ways that affect prices.

30.4. The Information Role of Order Flow

The central variable that takes the fundamental role in microstructure approach, but has never been presented in any of previous exchange rate models, is order flow. Order flow is cumulative flow of signed transaction volume. A simple example on how order flow is counted for individual transaction can be helpful. Suppose that a dealer decides to sell 5 units of U.S. dollars via a market order (one unit usually represents a transaction worth $1 million), then order flow is counted as –5. The negative sign is assigned for this $5 million transaction because it is a seller-initiated order. Each transaction is signed positively or negatively depending on whether the initiator of the transaction is buying or selling. Over time, order flow gives us a relative number of buyer-initiated versus seller-initiated orders in a market. Thus, order flow provides information to dealers about the relative demand for currencies at any time in the market. Since market participant must make buy-or-sell decisions according to available information (including their private information), it is presumed that order flow is at certain level driven by market fundamentals.

Order flow plays a fundamental role in exchange rate movements because it has the function to transmit information that is not known by everyone in the market. In fact, this concept of order flow transmitting information is intuitionally appealing. As an example to describe the intuition, consider two traders (referred to dealer A and dealer B) in the foreign exchange market, and each of them trades for a particular bank. Each bank of course has its own customers from whom it buys and sells foreign exchange. When dealer A trades with his own customers, he obtains private information, such as the customers' view of the current market (price), and which, is not known to dealer B. However, when dealer A puts orders in the inter-dealer market in an attempt to balance out positions with outside customers (for inventory concern), dealer A's private information is learned by dealer B. An alternative example is related to the idea of divergent mappings from (public) information to prices. Suppose dealer A hears a macro announcement at the same time as dealer B. Although they do not know how each other would interpret the announcement's effect on prices, they can learn this information by watching how each other trades.

A related question that is frequently asked is "does order flow really contain (market) information?" The answer is positive. The direct evidences come from dealers themselves. In surveys conducted by Cheung and Wong (2000), about 50 percent of dealers who responded to the survey claim that they believe banks with larger customer base have information advantage. This is because they get to trade with more customers, and more transactions ensure more private information, which leads to better speculative opportunities. Further evidence is from empirical analysis, which examine whether order flows have a permanent effect on prices. The rationale behind this empirical analysis is if order flow does not contain any information about market fundamentals, it can only have transitory effect on prices. French and Roll (1986) have used this methodology to identify the information arrival. Using vector auto-regression models, Evans (2001) and Payne (1999) found that order flow innovation has long-run effect on prices. This result provides evidence that order flow does contain information related to market fundamentals.

The general empirical model specification for microstructure approach to exchange rates can be written as follows (Lyons, 2001):

$$\Delta E_t = f_2(X,I,Z) + \varepsilon_{2t}, \qquad (30.2)$$

where ΔE_t is changes in nominal exchange rate between two transactions, function $f_2(X,I,Z)$ includes the order flow (X), dealers' inventory (I), and all other micro variables (Z). The microstructure models predict that an upward move in price is associated with a situation in which buyer-initiated trades exceed seller-initiated trades. In other words, to support microstructure approach to exchange rate, there needs to be a positive relation between order flows and prices. Lyons (2001) and Evans and Lyons (2002) have shown the considerably strong positive impact of order flow on exchange rates. More precisely, they have shown that order flow can explain about 60 percent (versus 10 percent at most in standard exchange rate empirical models expressed in Equation (30.1)) of exchange rate movement.

30.5. Conclusion

The high explanatory power of order flow for exchange rate movements is exciting news for researchers in the area. So far, all empirical evidences have suggested order flow is indeed the important missing piece in exchange rate determination. Lyons (2001) thus claims that order flows help solve three exchange rate puzzles: (1) the determination puzzle, (2) the excess volatility puzzle, and (3) the forward-bias puzzle. Yet, there is not much agreement toward this claim (see Dominguez, 2003). Clearly, more research needs to be done before these puzzles may be solved.

REFERENCES

Carrera, J.M. (1999). "Speculative attacks to currency target zones: a market microstructure approach." Journal of Empirical Finance, 6: 555–582.
Cheung, Y.W. and Wong, C.Y.P. (2000). "A survey market practitioners' view on exchange rate dynamics." Journal of International Economics, 51: 401–423.
Dominguez, K.M.E. (2003). "Book Review: Richard K. Lyons, The microstructure approach to exchange rates, 2001, MIT Press" Journal of International Economics, 61: 467–471.

Evans, M. (2001). "FX trading and exchange rate dynamics." Working Paper No. 8116, National Bureau of Economic Research.

Evans, M. and Lyons, R.K. (2002). "Order flow and exchange rate dynamics." *Journal of Political Economy*, 110: 170–180.

Frankel, J. and Rose, A. (1995). "Empirical research on nominal exchange rates," in *Handbook of International Economics*. Amsterdam, New York and Oxford: Elsevier, North-Holland, p. 3, 1689–1729.

French, K.R. and Roll, R. (1986). "Stock return variances: the arrival of information and the reaction of traders." *Journal of Financial Economics*, 17: 5–26.

Grossman, S.J. (1988). "An analysis of the implications for stock and futures price volatility of program trading and dynamic hedging strategies." *Journal of Business*, 61: 275–298.

Isard, P. (1995). "Exchange Rate Economics." Cambridge: Cambridge University Press.

Lyons, R.K. (2001). "The Microstructure Approach to Exchange Rates." Cambridge: MIT Press.

Meese, R. (1990). "Currency Fluctuations in the Post-Bretton Woods Era." *The Journal of Economic Perspectives*, 4(1): 117–134.

Meese, R. and Rogoff, K. (1983). "Empirical exchange rate models of the seventies." *Journal of International Economics*, 14: 3–24.

Payne, R. (1999). "Informed trade in spot foreign exchange markets: an empirical investigation." Typescript, London School of Economics.

Romer, D. (1993). "Rational asset-price movements without news." *American Economic Review*, 83: 1112–1130.

Taylor, M.P. (1995). "The economics of exchange rates." *Journal of Economic Literature*, 83: 13–47.

Chapter 31

ARBITRAGE AND MARKET FRICTIONS

SHASHIDHAR MURTHY, *Rutgers University, USA*

Abstract

Arbitrage is central to finance. The classical implications of the absence of arbitrage are derived in economies with no market frictions. A recent literature addresses the implications of no-arbitrage in settings with various market frictions. Examples of the latter include restrictions on short sales, different types of impediments to borrowing, and transactions costs. Much of this literature employs assumptions of continuous time and a continuous state space. This selected review of the literature on arbitrage and market frictions adopts a framework with discrete states. It illustrates and discusses a sample of the principal results previously obtained in continuous frameworks, clarifying the underlying intuition and enabling their accessibility to a wider audience.

Keywords: arbitrage; frictions; asset pricing; review; short sales constraints; sublinear pricing functional; super martingales; discrete state space; transactions costs; borrowing constraints

31.1. Introduction

The concept of arbitrage and the requirement that there be no arbitrage opportunities is central to finance. Essentially, an arbitrage opportunity is an investment where one can get something for nothing: a trading strategy with zero or negative current cost that is likely to yield a positive return and sure to not entail a future liability. Thus, the requirement that there be no arbitrage is a minimal desired attribute of a properly functioning securities market.

The implications of the absence of arbitrage are central to much of finance, simultaneously illuminating many areas and giving rise to new fields of inquiry. From early developments of the spot-forward parity relationships to the fundamental irrelevance propositions of Modigliani and Miller (1958), many arguments have at least implicitly used the main intuition of no-arbitrage that close substitutes must obey the law of one price, viz. two securities with the same payoffs must have the same price. Modern day application of this intuition came to the fore with the Black and Scholes (1973) model of option pricing. A first systematic analysis of the implications of no arbitrage was then carried out by Ross (1976, 1978). The principal question in such analysis is: given a set of some primitive assets, how much can one infer about the valuation of other assets if there are to be no arbitrage opportunities? Both the analysis of Ross (1976, 1978) and its generalization by Harrison and Kreps (1979) assume that investors are able to trade in frictionless markets.

A recent, burgeoning literature addresses the implications of no-arbitrage in settings with various market frictions. Examples of the latter include restrictions on short sales, different types of impediments to borrowing, and transactions costs. This paper reviews a selected portion of this literature and surveys the principal results obtained. Much of this literature employs the assumption of continuous time or an infinite dimensional state space. Here, a discrete framework is adopted in the interest of clarifying the intuition behind previously obtained results and rendering them accessible to a wider audience.

The principal implication of no-arbitrage in a frictionless setting may be summarized by what is sometimes known as the Fundamental Theorem of Asset Pricing (Dybvig and Ross, 1987). This theorem states that the absence of arbitrage is equivalent to the existence of both a strictly positive linear pricing rule and a solution to the choice problem of some investor who prefers more to less. Apart from implying that the law of one price holds, this result has several alternative representations and implications. One of the best known is that the no-arbitrage value of a claim is the cost of a portfolio that exactly replicates or hedges the claim's payoff. A second is that relative prices of assets must be martingales under a "risk-neutral" probability measure.

Rather than purport to be an exhaustive survey, this paper reviews a sample of the main results from the literature on arbitrage and market frictions.[1] One striking result is that the cheapest way to hedge a given liability may be to hedge a larger liability. This was first shown by Bensaid et al. (1992) in a transactions costs setting. An implication of this is that pricing may fail to be linear and instead be sublinear: the value of the sum of payoffs may be less than the sum of the values of the individual payoffs. Thus, there may be room for financial innovation, or departures from Modigliani–Miller (1958) type irrelevance, where an intermediary pools securities, and then strips them; see Chen (1995) for a discussion. When there are no frictions, the price paid when buying a claim is also the amount received in going short or writing the claim. Market frictions which result in sublinearity of the valuation or pricing rule can lead to bid–ask spreads on derivative securities even when there are no transactions costs (i.e. bid–ask spreads) in trading the primary securities, as shown by Luttmer (1996).

Furthermore, departures from the law of one price and the martingale property may occur under frictions. In the presence of a short sales constraint that changes elastically depending on the collateral posted, Hindy (1995) showed that an asset's value depends not only on its dividends but also on the collateral services it provides. When investors face short sales or borrowing constraints, Jouini and Kallal (1995a,b) show that asset prices may be super martingales.

The rest of this paper is organized as follows. A basic framework is set out in the next section, following which the benchmark case of no frictions is discussed in Section 31.3. Due to limitations of space, we formally illustrate the above results considering primarily the case of no short sales in Sections 31.4 and 31.5. However, we also briefly outline the impact of other types of frictions such as constraints on portfolio weights that permit some short sales (such as that under a leverage constraint or margin restriction), and transactions costs in Section 31.6. We conclude with some remarks relating to the consistency with equilibrium of results obtained from the no-arbitrage approach under frictions.

31.2. A Basic Framework

Consider an economy over dates $t = 0$ and T. Uncertainty is described by a discrete state space Ω with typical member $\omega \in \{1, \ldots, N\}$ denoting the final state of nature realized at date T where $N < \infty$. The probabilities of these states are $\{p(\omega)\}$ corresponding to an underlying probability measure P.

Investors trade a set of primitive assets which are in positive net supply, and whose prices are taken as given. Asset $j = 1, \ldots, J$ has price $S_j(0)$ at date 0 and the future price $S_j(\omega) \equiv D_j(\omega)$ in state ω at date T, where D_j is a given random dividend or payoff. Asset $j = 1$ is taken to be a risk-free bond with current price of unity; (one plus) its constant interest rate is denoted R. A portfolio choice is $z \equiv (z_1, \ldots, z_J)$, comprising holdings of shares of the various assets at date 0. Investors choose portfolios to maximize their preferences that are strictly increasing in consumption at dates 0 and T.

Trading in assets is subject to market frictions that take the form of a constraint on short sales and/or borrowing. The formulation we will consider for most of this paper restricts holdings of shares of some or all assets to be at least as large as exogenously given lower bounds: $z_j \geq -\underline{z}_j$, where $\underline{z}_j \geq 0$.[2] In the case of no short sales of asset j, $\underline{z}_j = 0$; if instead some limited but fixed amount of short sales is permitted, $\underline{z}_j > 0$. Similarly, note that the no borrowing case corresponds to $\underline{z}_1 = 0$, since asset $j = 1$ is the risk-free bond. A portfolio that satisfies the short sales constraint is termed admissible.

Investors can use the primitive assets to create, i.e. exactly replicate, various payoffs using admissible portfolios. Every such payoff $x \equiv \{x(\omega)\}$, where $x(\omega) = \sum_j z_j S_j(\omega)$ is hence said to be marketed, i.e. available for purchase and/or sale. In the presence of market frictions, the set of marketed payoffs is not limited to those payoffs that can be explicitly replicated. For instance, consider a payoff x of 1 in some state ω' and 0 in other states whose replication require a portfolio that involves a short position in asset j (and positions in other securities). Suppose, the latter short position is equal to the maximum amount permitted of $\underline{z}_j > 0$. Then, the payoff $2x$ cannot be exactly replicated because it would require a short position of $2\underline{z}_j$ shares. However, the payoff $2x$ may still be termed marketed if there exists a portfolio that produces *at least* 2 in state ω' and 0 elsewhere; i.e. if the payoff can be *super-replicated*.

Thus, it is natural to define a price for an arbitrary payoff x as the minimum cost

$$\phi(x) \equiv \left\{ \sum_j z_j S_j(0) : x(\omega) \leq \sum_j z_j S_j(\omega), \forall \omega \right\}$$

(31.1)

at which it can be exactly replicated or superreplicated by an admissible portfolio, where the associated functional $\phi(.)$ is termed a pricing or valuation rule.[3]

An arbitrage opportunity is an admissible portfolio z that either has (i) a nonpositive cost $\sum_j z_j S_j(0)$ when initiated and a date T payoff

$x \equiv \{x(\omega)\}$, where $x(\omega) = \sum_j z_j S_j(\omega)$, which is positive in some states and nonnegative in others, or (ii) a negative current cost and a nonnegative future payoff in all states.

31.3. Exact Replication and Prices under no Frictions

At this stage, it is useful to present the principal result on the implications of the absence of arbitrage for the benchmark case where there are no market frictions. This result, known as the Fundamental Theorem of Asset Pricing, is due to Ross (1976, 1978). Given the definition of the pricing or valuation operator $\phi(.)$, it is clear that there are no arbitrage opportunities in this frictionless setting only if every nonnegative marketed payoff x (which is also positive in some state) has price $\phi(x) > 0$. The result below establishes a further property: that of linearity. See Dybvig and Ross (1987) for a proof of the result below.

Proposition 1: Suppose there are no market frictions, i.e. $\underline{z}_j = \infty, \forall j$. Then there are no arbitrage opportunities if and only if the pricing rule in Equation (31.1), denoted $\phi^*(.)$ here, is positive and linear.

Apart from implying that the law of one price must hold, the linearity property means that $\phi^*(\lambda x) = \lambda \phi^*(x)$ for all λ, i.e. the price functional is homogeneous. It is useful to further interpret the above result in terms of an implicit state price vector $\xi \equiv \{\xi(\omega)\}$, where $\xi(\omega)$ is the price of a state security that pays 1 unit in state ω, and 0 elsewhere. The linearity and positivity of $\phi^*(.)$ are equivalent to $\phi^*(x) = \sum_\omega \xi(\omega) x(\omega)$ and $\xi(\omega) > 0$, respectively. The pricing rule $\phi^*(.)$ values every marketed payoff precisely because the latter can be exactly replicated, or hedged, using a portfolio of existing assets: it assigns a value equal to the cost of the replicating portfolio.

Another useful interpretation of the linearity of $\phi^*(.)$ is that there exists a ("risk-neutral") probability measure Q^* that is equivalent to the underlying measure P under which relative or normalized asset prices are martingales. Thus, every primitive asset's current price relative to, say, the price of the bond (which is 1), is equal to the expectation under Q^* of its future payoffs relative to that of the bond: $S_j(0) = E^{Q^*}[D_j R^{-1}]$. Equivalently, the value of every payoff satisfies $\phi(x) = \sum_\omega q^*(\omega)x(\omega)R^{-1}$, where $q^*(\omega)$ denotes the risk-neutral probability of state ω under Q^*. These well known implications of no-arbitrage in frictionless markets provide the basis of most option pricing models, following Black and Scholes (1973), Merton (1973), and Cox and Ross (1976).

31.4. No Short Sales

We now return to the economy with frictions of Section 31.2, and consider the case of no short sales. As in the frictionless case, it is clear that there are no arbitrage opportunities in this setting only if every nonnegative marketed payoff x (which is positive in some state) has price $\phi(x) > 0$. We proceed by recording a result below that is the counterpart to Proposition 1.

Proposition 2.: Suppose the only friction is that the short sales of some assets is prohibited, i.e. $\underline{z}_j = 0$ for some j, and $\underline{z}_j = \infty$ for the rest. Then there are no arbitrage opportunities if and only if the pricing rule in Equation (31.1), denoted $\phi^{NS}(.)$ here, is positive and sublinear. Furthermore, there exist underlying positive hypothetical linear pricing rules $\phi(.)$ such that $\phi^{NS}(x) \geq \phi(x)$, for all marketed payoffs x. Also, there exists a new probability measure associated with $\phi^{NS}(.)$ under which the (normalized) price process of an asset is a super martingale if the asset cannot be sold short, and a martingale if the asset can be sold short.[4]

The proof follows from Garman and Ohlson (1981), Chen (1995), Jouini and Kallal (1995a,b), and Luttmer (1996), and rather than reproduce it here, we will shortly present a simple binomial example where the result is explicitly illustrated. (Also note that while some of these papers consider transactions costs, their results apply here). But first, a few implications of the sublinearity property and the supermartingale property are discussed.

Observe that, in contrast to Proposition 1, the pricing rule $\phi^{NS}(.)$ is not linear but sublinear. The sublinearity implies that the value of a portfolio of two payoffs x and y may be less than the sum of the values of the payoffs, i.e. $\phi^{NS}(x+y) \leq \phi^{NS}(x) + \phi^{NS}(y)$.

It also implies that $\phi^{NS}(\lambda x) = \lambda \phi^{NS}(x)$ for all $\lambda \geq 0$, i.e. the price functional is positively homogeneous.

Chen (1995) discusses the role of financial innovation in such a context. He shows that an innovator (who is assumed to not face any short sales constraint, unlike other investors) can earn profits by purchasing a "pooled" payoff $x+y$ at a cost $\phi^{NS}(x+y)$, stripping it into individual components x and y, and selling (i.e. issuing) the latter at prices $\phi^{NS}(x)$ and $\phi^{NS}(y)$, respectively. Other investors cannot earn the same profits because they cannot short-sell (i.e. issue) the individual component securities x and y. In a frictionless economy, in contrast, the linearity of the pricing rule $\phi^*(.)$ leaves no role for such financial innovation; i.e. the Modigliani–Miller (1958) invariance proposition holds.

Next, consider the relationship between the value of a security with payoff x and another security with payoff $-x$. In a frictionless world, the values of these two securities (the second security is essentially equivalent to going short the first) are the negative of each other, i.e. their values sum to 0. This follows from the linearity (homogeneity) of the valuation rule ϕ^*. Under no short sales, the valuation rule $\phi^{NS}(.)$ is only positively homogeneous, and thus $\phi^{NS}(-x)$ may differ from $-\phi^{NS}(x)$. The intuition is just that the cost of super-replicating a payoff x will in general differ from that for the payoff $-x$. Also note that since the value of a zero payoff must be zero, $\phi^{NS}(x) + \phi^{NS}(-x)$ is at least as large as $\phi^{NS}(x + (-x)) = \phi^{NS}(0) = 0$; i.e. the sum of the values of both securities may be positive. Consequently, the ask price $\phi^{NS}(x)$ of the payoff x may exceed the bid price $-\phi^{NS}(-x)$. Thus, as Jouini and Kallal (1995a,b) and Luttmer (1996) show, a derivative security's price may exhibit a bid–ask spread even where there are no transactions costs (i.e. bid–ask spreads) in trading the primitive assets.

As we noted in Section 31.3, asset prices (normalized by, say, the bond) in frictionless economies are martingales under the risk-neutral probability measure. In other words, one cannot expect to earn more than the risk-free rate after correcting for risk. In sharp contrast, Proposition 2 shows that there exists a risk-neutral probability measure, say Q^{NS}, under which (normalized) prices of assets subject to short sales constraints are super martingales. In other words, $S_j(0)/R^{-1} \ge E^{Q^{NS}}[D_j]$ for such assets: their prices after correcting for risk and the risk-free return are expected to be nonincreasing. This is compatible with the absence of arbitrage opportunities from the perspective of a risk-neutral investor because an asset whose price is expected to decrease relative to the bond cannot be sold short. This super martingale property was proved by Jouini and Kallal (1995a,b) in a model with short sales constraints (and transactions costs).

31.5. A Simple Binomial Model

As an example of a simple model that explicitly illustrates the results of Proposition 2 and their significance, we now consider a one-period binomial model. A stock and bond are traded with the constraint that no short sales of the stock is permitted, but borrowing (short sales of the bond) is allowed. The stock's current price is S and its end-of-period price is uS in state u, and dS in state d. The bond has current price of unity and one plus a risk-less return of R where $d < R < u$.

Consider a payoff $x \equiv (x_d, x_u)$ comprised of x_d in state d and x_u in state u. Hedging any such payoff requires a portfolio of z_s shares of the stock and z_b units of the bond that satisfies

$$z_s \omega S + z_b R \ge x_\omega \quad \text{and} \quad z_s \ge 0, \tag{31.2}$$

where $\omega \in \{d, u\}$ denotes both the future state and the return of the stock. Note from Equation (31.2) we allow for the possible super-replication of the payoff; also observe that z_s must satisfy the no-short-sales constraint. Since the cost of the hedge portfolio is $z_s S + z_b$ it follows, using Equations (31.1) and (31.2), that the value of the payoff is

$$\phi^{NS}(x) \equiv Min \{z_s S + z_b : z_s \omega S + z_b R \ge x_\omega;$$
$$z_s \ge 0; \tag{31.3}$$
$$\omega \in \{d,u\}\},$$

i.e. it equals the cost of the cheapest hedge portfolio.

Denote the risk-neutral probability of state u in the frictionless counterpart to the above example by $q^* \equiv (R-d)/(u-d)$. It is then easy to verify that the solution to (31.3) is:

$$\phi^{NS}(x) = [q^* x_u + (1-q^*) x_d] R^{-1} \text{ if } x_u \ge x_d \tag{31.4}$$

and

$$\phi^{NS}(x) = x_d R^{-1} \quad \text{if } x_u < x_d. \tag{31.5}$$

In other words, for a payoff such as that of a call option, where $x_u > x_d$, the value is given by (31.4) and is no different from what it would be in a frictionless world. This is because exact replication, or an exact hedge, of the call entails a long position in the stock and borrowing. In contrast, for a security such as a put option, where $x_u < x_d$, the value in Equation (31.5) is just the discounted value of the payoff in the "down" state discounted at the risk-free return. The reason is that an exact hedge or replication of the put would require short sales of the stock and is hence infeasible due to the no-short-sales constraint. Instead, the cheapest super-replication of the put involves a long bond position with face value x_d.

To see that the valuation functional ϕ^{NS} in Equations (31.4) and (31.5) is sublinear, compare the value of the payoff (dS, uS) from the stock with the sum of the values $\phi^{NS}(dS, 0)$ and $\phi^{NS}(0, uS)$. The former is obviously $\phi^{NS}(dS, uS) = [q^* uS + (1-q^*)dS]R^{-1} = S$. However, the latter sum, $\phi^{NS}(dS, 0) + \phi^{NS}(0, uS) = dSR^{-1} + [q^* uS + (1-q^*)0] R^{-1} = S + dSR^{-1}q^*$, exceeds the current stock price, and this proves the sub-linearity. The intuition is that the cost of hedging the combined payoff (dS, uS) is less than the sum of the costs of hedging $(dS, 0)$ and $(0, uS)$ because hedging $(dS, 0)$ entails super-replication.

Finally, we show how the super martingale property of Proposition 2 comes about. Recall that with no frictions, $q^* \equiv (R-d)/(u-d)$ is the risk-neutral probability of state u under which the stock, bond, and all other payoffs (i.e. options) are martingales. Now define the probability $q \in [0, q^*]$ and the associated hypothetical linear valuation rule $\phi^q(x) = [qx_u + (1-q)x_d]R^{-1}$. It is easy to verify that the actual sublinear valuation rule $\phi^{NS}(.)$ of the economy with short sales constraints in Equations (31.4) and (31.5) is related to the sets $\{q\}$ and $\{\phi^q(.)\}$ by:

$$\phi^{NS}(x) = \text{Max}\{\phi^q(x): q \in [0, q^*]\}. \quad (31.6)$$

Compared to the probability q^*, every other probability $q \in [0, q^*)$ places less weight on the "up" state and more weight on the "down" state. Hence, under each of these probabilities $q \in [0, q^*)$, the stock's (normalized) current value exceeds its expected future value, i.e. $S/R^{-1} > [quS + (1-q)dS]$. In other words, the stock has a price process which is a super martingale because it cannot be sold short.

31.6. Other Types of Frictions

Due to limitations of space, we have so far considered primarily the case of no short sales. In this section, we briefly outline the impact of other types of frictions.

Consider an alternative formulation of a short sales constraint where the admissible extent of short sales of an individual asset varies with the value of the investor's portfolio and with any collateral pledged. Such a constraint recognizes that some assets (such as a very liquid, short-term Treasury bill) are judged to have "high" value as collateral, and thus better afford the ability to maintain a short position than is the case with other assets (such as an illiquid, off-the-run Treasury bond) deemed to have "low" collateral value. In such a setting, Hindy (1995) proved that the absence of arbitrage implies that every asset's price admits a decomposition into a dividend-based value and a residual that depends on the

asset's "collateralizability." Thus, the law of one price may not hold: asset k may sell at a higher price than asset l even if their payoffs are the same if a one dollar worth of asset k allows investors the ability to short more of a third asset j than does a dollar worth of asset l.[5]

Transactions costs in trading some or all assets constitute yet another type of market friction. In a binomial stock price model with proportional transactions costs, Bensaid, et al. (1992), showed that even when an option's payoff can be exactly replicated, it can be cheaper to hedge an option with a strategy that results in a payoff that dominates that of the option when there are transactions costs. This result is foreshadowed in Boyle and Vorst (1992) who derive the cost of exactly hedging an option in an identical framework, and show that their hedge portfolio's cost is increasing in the number of trading periods for a high enough transaction cost parameter, and for options close to at-the-money–i.e. those which have a lot of convexity and whose exact replication requires a lot of rebalancing. Thus, the intuition from these papers is essentially that the benefits of exact replication can be traded off against savings on transactions costs. It should also be intuitively clear that in such settings that the cost of super-replicating a pool of payoffs may be cheaper than the sum of the costs of super-replicating the individual payoffs. In other words, the sublinearity result of Proposition 2 will continue to hold.

31.7. Conclusion

We have provided a review of the principal results which obtain when there are no arbitrage opportunities in a world where investors have to contend with market frictions. We conclude with some remarks about the consistency of these results with equilibrium.

One of the advantages of the no-arbitrage approach to valuation is that it allows one to make predictions about prices that are independent of particular investor attributes such as risk aversion, endowments etc. The reason is that the prices of the existing primitive assets effectively subsume the risk preferences of the marginal investor. Furthermore, in the absence of frictions, all investors' marginal utility-based valuations of all traded assets coincide: i.e. any investor may be taken to be the marginal agent supporting prices.

When there are frictions, investors' valuations may be heterogeneous, and hence differ from that predicted by the no-arbitrage approach. For instance, when there are short sales constraints, Chen (1995) showed that the price of a security derived from the no-arbitrage condition may be lower than the price that the seller of the security can actually receive by selling it to the investor who values it most. Furthermore, as Detemple and Murthy (1997) showed, the introduction of what may otherwise be considered redundant securities can upset a given equilibrium in the presence of constraints on portfolio weights. More recently, Hara (2000) shows that even when introduction of a new security does not change utility-maximizing consumption choices it may give rise to a multiplicity of each investor's security demands which in turn raises subtle equilibrium issues.

Thus, while routine application of the no-arbitrage approach in the presence of market frictions is not necessarily as useful as in a frictionless world, it nevertheless presents exciting new challenges for future research in asset pricing.

NOTES

1. Some other papers relevant to arbitrage and market frictions, which we do not discuss are Dybvig and Ross (1986), Jarrow and O'Hara (1989), and Prisman (1986).
2. Other important types of market frictions include (i) a constraint on portfolio weights (such as that under a leverage constraint or margin restriction) where the permitted amount of short sales or borrowing varies with the value of the portfolio, (ii) unlimited short sales at a cost that increases with the extent of short sales, and (iii) transactions costs that have either or both a fixed component and a variable component.
3. Given the availability of a risk-free bond, every payoff has such a minimum cost. Also note that each primitive asset must satisfy $\phi(D_j) = S_j(0)$, $j = 1, \ldots, J$, for

if this were not true, they would not be held by any investor (which is incompatible with the fact that they are in positive net supply).
4. In this finite dimensional setting, the new probability measure associated with $\phi^{NS}(.)$ need not be equivalent to P; i.e. the new measure need not assign positive probabilities to the same states that P does. However, limiting arguments can be used in an infinite state space to establish equivalency.
5. Note that such a violation of the law of one price does not occur in Sections 31.4 and 31.5 where we considered a simpler type of short sales constraint.

REFERENCES

Bensaid, B., Lesne, J.P., Pages, H., and Scheinkman, J. (1992). "Derivative asset pricing with transactions costs." *Mathematical Finance*, 2: 63–86.

Black, F. and Scholes, M. (1973). "The pricing of options and corporate liabilities." *Journal of Political Economy*, 81: 637–654.

Boyle, P. and Vorst, T. (1992). "Option pricing in discrete time with transactions costs." *Journal of Finance*, 47: 271–293.

Chen, Z. (1995). "Financial innovation and arbitrage pricing in frictional economies." *Journal of Economic Theory*, 65: 117–135.

Cox, J. and Ross, S. (1976). "The Valuation of options for alternative stochastic processes." *Journal of Financial Economics*, 3: 145–166.

Detemple, J. and Murthy, S. (1997). "Equilibrium asset prices and no-arbitrage with portfolio constraints." *Review of Financial Studies*, 10: 1133–1174.

Dybvig, P. and Ross, S. (1986). "Tax clienteles and asset pricing." *Journal of Finance*, 41: 751–762.

Dybvig, P. and Ross, S. (1987). "Arbitrage," in J. Eatwell, M. Milgate and P. Newman (eds.) *The New Palgrave: A Dictionary of Economics*, volume 1. New York: Stockton Press, pp. 100–106.

Garman, M. and Ohlson, J. (1981). "Valuation of risky assets in arbitrage-free economies with transactions costs." *Journal of Financial Economics*, 9: 271–280.

Hara, C. (2000). "Transaction costs and a redundant security: divergence of individual and social relevance." *Journal of Mathematical Economics*, 33: 497–530.

Harrison, M. and Kreps, D. (1979). "Martingales and arbitrage in multiperiod security markets." *Journal of Economic Theory*, 20: 381–408.

Hindy, A. (1995). "Viable prices in financial markets with solvency constraints." *Journal of Mathematical Economics*, 24: 105–136.

Jarrow, R. and O'Hara, M. (1989). "Primes and scores: an essay on market imperfections." *Journal of Finance*, 44: 1263–1287.

Jouini, E. and Kallal, H. (1995a) "Martingales and arbitrage in securities markets with transaction costs." *Journal of Economic Theory*, 66: 178–197.

Jouini, E. and Kallal, H. (1995b). "Arbitrage in securities markets with short-sales constraints." *Mathematical Finance*, 5: 197–232.

Luttmer, E. (1996). "Asset pricing in economies with frictions." *Econometrica*, 64: 1439–1467.

Merton, R. (1973). "Theory of rational option pricing." *Bell Journal of Economics and Management Science*, 4: 141–83.

Modigliani, F. and Miller, M. (1958). "The cost of capital, corporation finance and the theory of investment." *American Economic Review*, 48: 261–297.

Prisman, E. (1986). "Valuation of risky assets in arbitrage free economies with frictions." *Journal of Finance*, 41: 293–305.

Ross, S. (1976). "Return, risk and arbitrage," in I. Friend and J. Bicksler (eds.) *Risk and Return in Finance*. Cambridge, MA: Ballinger, pp. 189–218.

Ross, S. (1978). "A simple approach to the valuation of uncertain income streams." *Journal of Business*, 51: 453–475.

Chapter 32

FUNDAMENTAL TRADEOFFS IN THE PUBLICLY TRADED CORPORATION

JOSEPH P. OGDEN, *University at Buffalo, USA*

Abstract

This article discusses some fundamental cost-benefit tradeoffs involving publicly traded corporations from a corporate finance viewpoint. The fundamental benefits include greater access to capital at a lower cost and economies of scale. The potential costs are associated with two fundamental problems: principal–agent conflicts of interest and information asymmetry. Various mechanisms have evolved in the United States to mitigate these problems and their costs, so that the bulk of the fundamental benefits can be realized.

Keywords: cost of capital; liquidity; economies of scale; conflicts of interest; information asymmetry; disclosure; monitoring; intermediaries; contract devices; signaling

32.1. Introduction

This article discusses, from a corporate finance perspective, the fundamental benefits and costs associated with the publicly traded corporation as a form of business organization. The fundamental benefits are two-fold. First, by incorporating and attaining public-trading status a firm gains access to a large pool of capital, which it can use to pursue capital investment projects that take advantage of economies of scale. Second, a firm's cost of capital is reduced because public investors will accept a lower cost of capital, and this is so because

investors are diversified and the firm's securities are more liquid.

Costs relate to two fundamental problems that beset the publicly traded corporation, both of which are consequences of the separation of ownership and control. The first problem involves "principal–agent conflicts of interest." The second problem is "information asymmetry." This article discusses these fundamental problems, their potential costs, and various mechanisms that have evolved in the United States to mitigate these problems and their costs, so that the bulk of the fundamental benefits can be realized.

31.2. Fundamental Benefits of the Publicly Traded Corporation

The fundamental benefits of the publicly traded corporation are two-fold. First, by attaining public-trading status, a firm gains access to the large pool of equity capital that is available in the public equity markets, and also enhances its access to credit markets for debt capital. Large amounts of capital allow a firm to pursue capital investment projects that take advantage of economies of scale, and thus are more profitable. Second, as many corporations emerge, secondary markets develop that allow investors to trade corporate securities and become diversified. In addition, secondary markets increase the value of corporate securities by increasing their liquidity and decreasing the cost of debt and equity capital, which in turn increase the assessed profitability of corporate projects.

32.2.1. Economies of Scale

All for-profit businesses are established to create value. The corporation is specially designed to create value on a large scale. A corporation is a separate legal entity, tethered to its owners by shares of stock. The two basic legal characteristics that distinguish a corporation from other forms of business (e.g. a sole proprietorship) are "limited liability" and the "separation of ownership and control." Regarding the first, the extent of stockholders' financial responsibility for the liabilities of a corporation that they collectively own is limited to the corporation's assets, and does not extend to the stockholders' personal assets. Regarding the second, in most corporations ownership is vested in one group, stockholders, while control is vested in another group, management (though, of course, managers may hold some of the firm's shares).

These two legal characteristics allow a corporation to create value efficiently and on a large scale. Limited liability allows many individuals to pool their capital without concern for legal complexities and inefficiencies that would be involved if the personal assets of each individual were involved. As Jensen and Meckling (1976) explain, with unlimited liability individual stockholders would need to monitor each other's wealth in order to estimate their own liability, which would be very costly if the firm's shares were widely held.

The separation of ownership and control allows the two basic inputs in any economy, capital and expertise, to be contributed by separate individuals. Some individuals have expertise to develop and undertake profitable real investments, but lack capital, whereas other individuals have capital, but lack the time and/or expertise to undertake profitable real investments. The corporation combines these two factors of production under a formal efficient structure.

Moreover, economies of scale are present in virtually all business activities, and are generally very large. Scale economies allow a larger firm, at least potentially, to create substantial value by reducing the cost of production. A corporation has the potential to amass large amounts of capital, which in turn allows it to pursue capital investment projects that take advantage of economies of scale, and thus are more profitable.

32.2.2. Reducing the Cost of Capital: Diversification and Liquidity

Two additional important benefits are associated with the publicly traded corporation: diversification and liquidity. To see these benefits, note that each firm in the economy can amass a large amount of capital by appealing to many investors to become stockholders. In turn, each investor can invest only a small portion of his or her investable wealth in any given firm, and therefore can invest in the equities of many firms simultaneously. Thus, investors can reduce the risk of their portfolios by diversifying across many firms. Risk-averse investors will accept a lower expected return on the equity of each firm because they can eliminate much of the risk of these investments via diversification. Consequently, each firm's cost of equity capital will be lower than would be the case if investors were not diversified. In turn, if all firms in the economy face a lower cost of equity capital, more projects will be deemed profitable (i.e., value-creating).

A security is liquid to the extent that an investor can quickly buy or sell the security at or near a fair price and at a low transaction cost. Liquidity is important to an investor because the ultimate purpose of investment is to provide for future consumption, either sooner or later. Investors will accept a lower expected return on equity (and thus firms will enjoy a lower cost of equity capital) if equities are liquid. The liquidity of securities naturally follows from investors' desire to become diversified. This is so because secondary markets will develop to allow trading in securities. (For additional discussion, see Ogden et al., 2003, pp. 76–77).

32.3. Fundamental Costs of the Publicly Traded Corporation

According to Modern Corporate Finance Theory, two fundamental problems beset the publicly traded corporation: "principal–agent conflicts of interest and information asymmetry." These problems are important because they can potentially impose costs that are sufficiently large as to threaten the fundamental benefits discussed in the previous section. This section discusses these problems and their costs. The next section discusses various mechanisms designed to alleviate these problems, and thus to mitigate their costs.

32.3.1. Principal–Agent Conflicts of Interest

The first fundamental problem concerns the relationship between a principal and an agent. In general, a principal hires an agent to act in the principal's interest by performing a specified task. A problem arises in that the agent is hired to act in the principal's interest and yet, as a self-interested human being, the agent cannot be expected to subordinate his or her own interests. Thus, a conflict of interest naturally arises between the principal and the agent. In corporate finance, two types of principal–agent conflicts of interest are paramount: (1) conflicts between a firm's stockholders (as principals) and its management (as agents); and (2) conflicts between the firm (as an agent) and its creditors (as principals).

Regarding conflict (1), a firm's management is hired to act in the stockholder's interest, which is generally assumed to maximize the market value of the firm's equity. However, managers are ultimately interested in maximizing their own welfare and they control the firm. As noted earlier, an important feature of the corporation is the separation of ownership and control, and this feature is critical to capturing the stated fundamental benefits.

Managers have a self-serving incentive to capture "private benefits of control." The following are among the activities that management might employ to capture such benefits: (a) excessive consumption of "perquisites," (b) manipulating earnings and dividends, (c) maximizing the size of the firm, rather than the market value of its equity, (d) siphoning corporate assets, (e) excessive diversification at the corporate level, (f) a bias toward investments with near-term payoffs, (g) underemployment of debt, (h) entrenching their positions, and (i) packing the firm's board of directors with cronies. (For a discussion of these activities, see Ogden et al., 2003, pp. 83–88.) In the absence of mechanisms (discussed later) to offset management's private incentives, the costs to stockholders of such activities can be sufficiently large as to negate the stated fundamental benefits of the publicly traded corporation.

In addressing conflict (2), we generally assume that the conflict of interest between stockholders and management is resolved. Instead, we focus on a conflict of interest between the firm and its creditors. In this context, a creditor can be seen as a principal who "hires" the firm as an agent (i.e. by paying money up-front in the form of a loan) to act in the creditor's interest (i.e. to operate the firm in a manner that ensures that timely interest and principal payments will be made to the creditor.)

A conflict arises in that the firm's management, who will be controlling the firm, is hired to act in the stockholders' interest, rather than the creditor's interest. In the absence of mechanisms (discussed later) to protect the creditor's interest, management may engage in any of the following activities that serve to expropriate wealth from a creditor to stockholders: (a) increasing leverage, especially by subsequently issuing additional debt that has equal priority to the firm's original debt, (b) increasing the riskiness of the firm's operations (the "asset substitution" or "risk-shifting" problem), and (c) paying dividends. (For a discussion of these activities, see Ogden et al., 2003, pp. 88–93.)

In addition, Myers (1977) identifies an important deadweight cost of debt called the "underinvestment problem" or the "debt overhang problem." If a firm has default-risky debt outstanding and a profitable investment opportunity that must be financed with equity, the firm's management might forego the investment even though it is profitable *per se*. This can occur if a sufficient portion of the net present value (NPV) of the project transfers to the creditors (i.e. creditors are made better off by the adoption of the project) such that the net benefit to stockholders (i.e. net of their cash contribution) is negative.

32.3.2. Information Asymmetry

The second fundamental problem is called the "information asymmetry" problem. Akerlof (1970) is generally credited with recognizing information asymmetry as a general problem in a market, though its application to corporate finance was quickly recognized. To illustrate the problem, Akerlof refers to the market for used automobiles. The crux of the problem is that the quality of a particular used make and model of automobile varies across the units for sale, and sellers know more about the quality of their unit than do potential buyers. Sellers of low-quality units have an incentive to make minimal repairs and otherwise exaggerate the quality of their unit to mimic the better-quality units in the market. As a result, in equilibrium all units will share a common price, which reflects the (true) average quality of units for sale. However, this equilibrium is unsustainable because some or all of the sellers of (truly) better-quality units will exit the market. After they exit, the true average quality of units in the market is lower, and thus so must the common price. This process will continue until only the "lemons" remain in the market. In short, the market for used automobiles can collapse under the weight of information asymmetry. (See Ogden et al., 2003, pp. 101–102.)

The markets for corporate securities are also naturally beset by information asymmetry because of product market competition and the separation of ownership and control. A firm's management

(assumed to be acting in the stockholders' interest) must devise strategic plans to compete in its chosen product market. These plans cannot be divulged to the firm's diffuse stockholders for the simple reason that this would be tantamount to revealing the information to the firm's competitors, who could surreptitiously become stockholders in order to gain access to such plans, and then thwart them with counter-strategies.

Consequently, a firm's management generally and necessarily has more information about the firm's operations, and thus its true value, than do the firm's actual or potential stockholders. In the absence of mechanisms (discussed below) to mitigate this information asymmetry problem, the market for corporate securities may be very poor,- and could even collapse àla Akerlof's argument.

32.4. Mitigating the Costs

A wide variety of mechanisms have emerged in the U.S. and other markets to mitigate costs associated with both the agency and information asymmetry problems discussed above. This section briefly discusses such mechanisms, following a top-down approach. (For an in-depth discussion of each of these mechanisms, see Ogden et al., 2003, Chapter 5.)

32.4.1. Government Laws and Regulations

The most fundamental services that government provides are for establishment of property rights through legislation and the enforcement of legal contracts through a judicial system. In addition, government generally regulates the financial markets, such as with the US Securities Act of 1933 and the Securities Exchange Act of 1934, the latter of which established the Securities and Exchange Commission (SEC). The SEC requires all firms with publicly traded securities to register such securities, to file periodic financial statements, etc. The 1934 act also requires publicly traded firms to provide stockholders the opportunity to vote on matters such as the election of board directors. The SEC also prohibits insider trading, requires major owners of a firm's equity to disclose their owner-ship, etc. The regulations imposed by the SEC most obviously help to reduce information asymmetry and associated costs. In addition, these regulations curb the self-serving activities of managers, and thus help to mitigate costs associated with principal–agent conflicts of interest.

32.4.2. Securities Traders, Analysts, and the Press

Securities traders, analysts, and the press all generate important information about the values of securities and the efficacy of firms' managements. Their efforts help to reduce information asymmetry. In addition, they serve as indirect monitors of each firm's management, which curbs management's opportunities to engage in self-serving activities, and thus mitigates costs associated with stockholder–management conflicts of interests.

32.4.3. Ownership Structure

A firm's stockholders can promote their own interest through "activism," specifically, by voting on major management-initiated proposals, submitting their own proposals, and monitoring management's decisions. Unfortunately, if a firm's ownership is diffuse, activism is generally thwarted by the "free-rider problem," whereby stockholders have an incentive to freely benefit from the costly efforts of others to monitor and reform management.

One means of mitigating the free-rider problem is for a firm's equity to be closely held (i.e. by nonmanagement stockholders), so that most or all of a firm's stockholders have a sufficient financial incentive to monitor management. However, close ownership is costly because it reduces the benefits of the corporate form discussed earlier. Alternatively, a firm may require management to own a substantial number of the firm's shares (or to hold stock options), which serves to align stockholders' and management's interests. However, this mechanism is also imperfect. For instance, if the bulk of a manager's personal portfolio is invested in the manager's own firm, his or her financial policies (i.e. real investment and financial decisions) may be distorted in a way that reduces the value of the firm's shares.

32.4.4. Board Oversight

Board directors are hired to protect and promote the interests of a firm's stockholders. The existence of boards of directors is perhaps the most obvious indication of a potential conflict of interest between stockholders and management. An independent board can be an effective advocate of stockholders' interests because the board generally has powers to: (1) require board approval of major capital expenditures, acquisitions, divestitures, and security offerings, (2) control the firm's capital structure, (3) hire outside consultants to scrutinize major projects, and (4) as necessary, fire senior management.

However, senior management has an incentive to "pack the board" with its cronies. If management is successful in doing so, the board becomes little more than a "rubber stamp" for management's decisions. To avoid this, stockholders should insist on an independent board, consisting of mostly outsiders who are not beholden to management.

32.4.5. Financial Institutions

A wide variety of financial institutions exist in the United States, including commercial banks, finance companies, insurance companies, venture capital firms, and securities firms (i.e. underwriters). According to theory, one of the most fundamental services provided by financial institutions is to mitigate costs associated with the information asymmetry problem in the market for corporate securities. Sellers of valuable proprietary information work through a financial institution that acts as an "intermediary" between the firm and investors. The intermediary is in a position to verify the value of the proprietary information, and yet can be trusted to keep such information confidential.

32.4.6. Contract Devices

Finally, firms employ a variety of contract devices to mitigate principal–agent conflicts of interest and/or information asymmetry problems. To illustrate, we briefly discuss two types of contracts that can alleviate conflicts: executive compensation contracts and debt contracts.

For a firm with diffuse ownership, devising a contract with senior management is problematic because managers have private incentives to maximize their own welfare, as discussed earlier. In order to align the interests of stockholders and management, a firm may include performance-based provisions in the executive's compensation contract, such as an annual earnings-based bonus or grants of stock or stock options. Such provisions may serve the intended purpose reasonably well, but could also backfire by causing management to distort the firm's capital investment program, its capital structure, its dividend policy, etc.

We also mentioned earlier that a conflict of interest arises between a borrowing firm and its creditors, whereby the firm has an incentive to take actions to expropriate wealth from creditors. Creditors can mitigate these incentives by including various provisions and covenants in the debt contract. For instance, a creditor may demand collateral to mitigate the asset substitution problem. Creditors may also restrict the firm's ability to issue additional debt and to restrict or prohibit the payment of dividends.

32.4.7. Signaling

Finance theory also suggests that firms can provide "signals" of true value to the market in order to mitigate the information asymmetry problem. In the finance literature, authors have suggested each of the following signaling mechanisms: ownership structure, leverage, dividends, and stock repurchases. (For discussion, see Ogden et al., 2003, Chapter 4.)

32.5. Summary

This article discusses fundamental tradeoffs associated with the publicly traded corporation. On the positive side, corporations allow for the concentration of large quantities of capital, which can be used for investing in large capital investment projects that capture valuable economies of scale. In addition, the corporate form allows investors to diversify and to trade securities, which reduces the cost of capital. On the negative side, the separation of ownership and control engenders two fundamental and potentially costly problems: principal–agent conflicts of interest and information asymmetry. Various mechanisms have evolved at various levels to mitigate these problems and their costs, so that more of the fundamental benefits of the publicly traded corporation can be realized.

REFERENCES

Akerlof, G. (1970). "The market for 'lemons,' qualitative uncertainty and the market mechanism." *Quarterly Journal of Economics*, 84: 488–500.

Jensen, M.C. and Meckling, W. (1976). "Theory of the firm: managerialbehavior, agency costs, and ownership structure." *Journal of Financial Economics*, 1: 305–360.

Myers, S.C. (1977). Determinants of corporate borrowing. *Journal of Financial Economics*, 5: 146–175.

Ogden, J.P., Jen, F.C., and O'Connor, P.F. (2003). *Advanced Corporate Finance: Policies and Strategies*. Upper Saddle River, NJ: Prentice-Hall.

Chapter 33

THE MEXICAN PESO CRISIS

FAI-NAN PERNG, *The Central Bank of China, Taiwan*

Abstract

The Mexican Peso Crisis was the byproduct of various developments including large inflows of short-term foreign capital, prolonged current account deficit, and political instability. Between 1990 and 1993, investors in the United States were particularly eager to provide loans, many of them short-term, to the Mexican government and to Mexican corporations. Throughout this period, the share of foreign capital inflows exceeded the current account deficit. However, political instability and U.S. interest rate hikes soon changed the optimism for Mexico's economic outlook. At the beginning of 1994, this did not affect the value of the peso, for Mexico was operating with a target zone exchange rate and its central bank stood ready to accept pesos and pay out dollars at the fixed rate. Yet Mexico's reserves of foreign currency were too small to maintain its target zone exchange rate. When Mexico ran out of dollars at the end of 1994, the Mexican government announced a devaluation of the peso. As a result, investors avoided buying Mexican assets, adding to downward pressure on the peso.

Overall, the Mexican meltdown of 1994–1995 had many facets. Yet couple of lessons are particularly clear: while foreign capital can make up for the shortfall in domestic saving, only long-term capital – in the forms of foreign direct investment or long-term debt – is conducive to domestic investment; large and abrupt movements of capital across national borders can cause excessive financial market volatility and undermine economic stability in the countries involved. Last and most importantly, prolonged current ac-count deficit should be remedied by allowing the domestic currency to depreciate, promoting savings, or cutting back government expenditure rather than financed by foreign capital inflows. Countries with protracted current account deficits such as Argentina, the Philippines, Indonesia, Thailand, and Saudi Arabia, with Thailand in particular, should heed Mexico's experience.

Keywords: foreign capital inflow; current account deficit; foreign exchange reserves; target zone exchange rate; short-term debt; long-term debt.

Mr. Perng, the Governor of Taiwan's central bank, noted the long running current account deficits for a number of Asian countries in his article published in the Commercial Times *on 23 February 1995. He stated that the situation in Thailand was especially worrisome as its current account deficit was mainly financed by short-term financial capital inflows. Fifteen months after the publication of this article, the Asian financial crisis broke out with Thailand at the front line of the crisis.*
Fai-nan Perng (*Commercial Times*, 23 February 1995)

The Mexican government stopped repaying external debt obligations in August 1982 due to a shortfall of its foreign exchange reserves. Brazil, Argentina, and Chile followed suit, which triggered what came to be known as the Latin American Debt Crisis. Later, following a series of economic and financial reforms, conditions in Mexico gradually improved sufficiently to start attracting inward in-

THE MEXICAN PESO CRISIS

vestment again. The debt relief initiative put forth by U.S. Treasury Secretary Nicholas Brady in 1990 eventually put Mexico more firmly back on her feet. Thereafter, Mexico engaged in several rounds of negotiations with the United States with the intent of securing the North American Free Trade Agreement and eventually won the U.S. Congress over toward the end of 1993. It is fair to say that in the years between 1990 and 1993, most foreign investors were bullish about the outlook of the Mexican economy.

In a separate development, the advancement of telecommunications and computer technology has sped and immensely reduced the cost of transferring capital. Moreover, a growing number of households started to entrust their savings with professional fund managers. Portfolios managed by fund managers tend to be well diversified with assets invested in multiple currencies (huge sums of money can literally be moved from one currency to another or one financial product to the next at the push of a button), a practice that further hastened the speed and amplified the magnitude of international capital movements (the combined value of cross-border portfolio investment in Europe, America, and Japan reached $2500 billion in 1991). While this was taking place, the U.S. economy was mired in a protracted downturn. The Federal Reserve rightly countered with a monetary stimulus. The interest rate on the three-month fixed deposits was slashed from 10.25 percent in March 1989 to 3.1875 percent in January 1994. Against the backdrop of highly efficient international financial markets, U.S. investors moved a huge chunk of their capital abroad. A significant portion of this outflow was absorbed by emerging markets in Latin America including, of course, Mexico.

Owing to the various developments outlined in the preceding paragraphs, substantial foreign capital began to flow into Mexico in 1990. The size of foreign capital inflow ballooned from $8.441 billion in 1990 to $32.06 billion by 1993. Altogether, some $92.647 billion of foreign capital swamped Mexico's financial markets in those four years (Table 33.1).

Among the first to be affected by this foreign capital inflow was, not surprisingly, the Peso. At that time, Mexico's exchange rate system was one of target zone. The lower bound of the Peso/USD exchange rate had been set at 3.05 since November 1991 when foreign exchange controls were removed. The upper bound had been raised gradually at a rate of 0.0004 Peso per day, beginning on 21 October 1992. The idea was to allow the Peso/USD exchange rate to adjust within a band wide enough to properly reflect supply and demand in the foreign exchange market (Figure 33.1).

Before the end of 1993, the Peso/USD exchange rate was relatively stable due to large and sustained foreign capital inflows that more than offset current account deficits. Under this arrangement, the integrity of Mexico's target zone exchange rate regime was not put to test. At the same time, the Mexican inflation rate was running at a significantly higher level than that of the United States. Between 1990 and September 1994, the U.S. CPI rose by only 4 percent. During the same period, the Mexican CPI jumped by 61.3 percent. In a parallel development, the Peso depreciated from 2.9454 to 3.4040 to a dollar. According to the purchasing power parity, the Peso/USD exchange rate should have been 4.5682 in September 1994. In other words, the Peso was overvalued by 34 percent (Table 33.2 and Figure 33.2).

Maintaining a stable Peso/USD exchange rate helped to push the Mexican inflation down, as American prices were stable. Mexican CPI inflation was 23.3 percent in 1990, which dropped to 8.4 percent by September 1994. An overvalued Peso, however, undermined the competitiveness of Mexican exports. It's a small wonder that the position of the current account continued to worsen. A deficit of $7.451 billion in 1990 swelled to $23.391 billion in 1993, a figure approaching 6 percent of Mexico's GDP. For 1994, this figure was projected to rise to $28 billion or 8 percent of Mexico's GDP (Table 33.1).

Throughout this period, the share of foreign capital inflows that exceeded the current account deficit was bought by the central bank. This would

Table 33.1. Mexico's balance of payments (1990–1994)

Items	1990	1991	1992	1993	1994[2]		
Current Account	−7,451	−14,888	−24,806	−23,391	−7,020 (Jan. – Nov.)		
Trade balance	−4,433	11,329	20,677	18,891			
Services	−6,993	−6,305	−7,150	−7,187			
Transfers	3,975	2,746	3,021	2,687			
Capital Account	8,441	25,139	27,008	32,059	14,600 (Jan. – Nov.)		
Direct Investment	2,549	4,742	4,393	4,901			
Portfolio Investment	−3,985	12,138	19,175	27,867			
Other Investment	9,877	8,259	3,440	−709			
Government borrowings	1,657	−1,454	−5,867	−1,136			
Net errors and omissions	1,228	−2,278	−5,867	−1,436			
Reserves and related items[1]	−2,218	−7,973	−1,745	−7,232			
change in reserve assets (−: increase)	−3,479	−7,834	−1,118	−6,129			
Foreign exchange reserves (year end)	9,446	17,140	18,394	24,886	16 Dec. 94	11,150	
					13 Jan. 95	3,480	
Exchange rate (year end, Peso/US$)	2.9454	3.0710	3.1154	3.1059	19 Dec. 94	3.4647	22 Dec. 94 4.7000
					31 Jan. 95	6.3500	6 Feb. 95 5.3350

Note: 1. A plus sign indicates a reduction in assets or an increase in liabilities; a minus sign indicates the opposite.

2. As published by Mexico's central bank in its monetary policy report on 25 January 1995.

Source: International Financial Statistics, published by IMF on Jan. 1995.

Table 33.2. Peso/US$ exchange rate and inflation comparison

	1990	1991	1992	1993	1994/9
Nominal exchange rate (Peso/US$)	2.9454	3.0710	3.1154	3.1059	3.4040
PPP exchange rate (Peso/US$)	2.9454	3.5421	3.9944	4.2842	4.5682
Whole Sale Price Index (WPI)	100.0	120.5	136.7	148.8	163.3
Mexico	(23.3)	(20.5)	(13.4)	(8.9)	(8.4)
Producer Price Index (PPI) US	100.0	100.2	100.8	102.3	104.0

Note: Annual growth rate % in brackets

explain why Mexico's foreign exchange reserves rose from $5.946 billion in 1989 to $24.886 billion by the end of 1993 (Table 33.1).

At the beginning of 1994, for a variety of reasons, investor confidence began to wane. External factors include U.S. interest rate hikes that started from February 1994 and the resulting rise in the rate of return from investing in the dollar, which were inarguably the most important. Explanations that

had roots at home include the January 1994 riot in the southern province of Chiapas, the assassination of Señor Colosios, the ruling party's presidential candidate in March, and the deterioration of the current account deficit. No longer upbeat about the prospect of the Mexican economy and recognizing that the Peso/USD exchange rate had become unstable, foreign capital inflow dried up to a level that could no longer sustain the current account

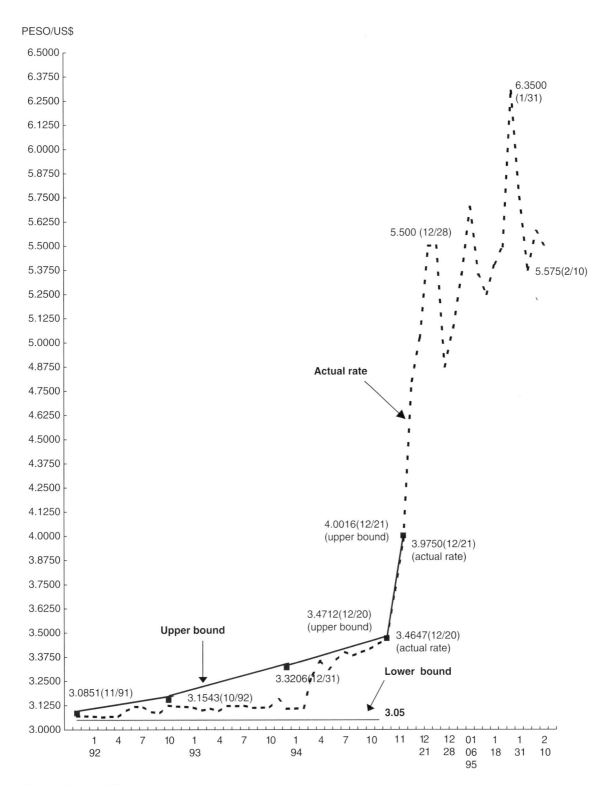

Figure 33.1. Peso/US$ exchange rate

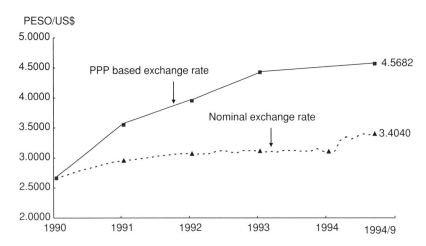

Figure 33.2. Nominal exchange rate and purchasing power parity (PPP) based exchange rate

deficit. Demand for the U.S. dollar far exceeded the supply in the foreign exchange market; the Peso sapped. In order to keep the Peso exchange rate within the upper bound of the target zone, the Mexican government intervened heavily by selling the dollar, a process that quickly depleted precious foreign exchange reserves. In order to replenish official reserves that were running at a dangerously low level, Mexico issued the Tesobonos, a U.S. dollar-denominated short-term debt payable in Peso at maturity. In retrospect, Mexico's central bank should have tightened its monetary stance. But instead, it acted like an innocent bystander, fearing such measures would dampen economic growth and hoping that foreign investors will return in droves after the presidential election in August. Although the ruling party did get re-elected, its secretary general, Señor Masssieu, was assassinated in September. When the newly elected President Zedillo was sworn into office on December 1, Mexico's financial markets were on the brink of collapse.

Among the many forces that were weighing on Mexico's financial markets, the overvalued Peso and the accompanying deterioration in the current account deficit were the most obvious. Another key feature of the Mexican debacle was that foreign capital inflows had predominantly been invested in short-term debts. Of the $32 billion worth of capital inflow in 1993, $27.9 billion was invested in such instruments (Table 33.1). The source of this type of

foreign capital inflow can be traced to mutual funds (Fidelity alone had $8 billion invested in emerging markets in 1994), and hedge and pension funds. All it took was one telephone call for the funds to be shifted out of Mexico once the fund managers convinced themselves that the Peso exchange rate was unstable or when the sentiment on the outlook of the Mexican economy suddenly turned bearish.

With the current account position worsening and the inflow of foreign capital reduced to a trickle, the Mexican government resorted to financing the current account deficit with official reserves in addition to issuing short-term dollar debts and the Tesobonos. Mexico's foreign exchange reserves declined from $24.886 billion at the end of 1993 to $11.15 billion on 16 December 1994. Although Señor Serra, the finance minister, repeatedly reassured foreign investors that the upper bound of the peso exchange rate would not be breached, that very ceiling was hastily raised from 3.4712 to 4.0016 on 20 December. The Peso exchange rate fell sharply from 3.4647 at the close of the business day on December 20 to 3.9750 the next day, getting uncomfortably close to the 4.0016 mark. Unable to stem the tide of foreign capital outflow and with the level of foreign exchange reserves running precariously low, the Mexican government had little choice but to let the Peso float (Figure 33.1). The Peso fell to an all-time low of 5.5 to a dollar on 28 December.

The exodus of foreign capital not only exerted a severe downward pressure on the Peso exchange rate but also depressed stock prices. The Mexican stock index fell from 2857.5 on 23 September 1994 to 1935.32 on 9 February 1995, or 32 percent in four months (Figure 33.3).

For a variety of reasons, the United States came to Mexico's rescue and brought the international financial community to the negotiating table. Possible explanations for the action taken by the U.S. government include:

1. As much as $53 billion of debt was about to become due at the end of 1995. Unaided, Mexico was in eminent danger of repeating the 1982 crisis.

2. Mexico had become United States' third largest trading partner, with bilateral trade amounting to $100 billion per annum. A further deterioration in the Mexican economy was more than likely to have a negative impact on the United States; the number of illegal immigrants waiting to cross the border could rise considerably.

3. The contagion effect of the Mexican crisis was beginning to be felt by other large Latin American debtors such as Brazil and Argentina. Helping Mexico would prevent the contagion from spreading further afield.

4. The aid package included broad based economic stabilization measures (putting a 7 percent cap on wage increases, cutting back government expenditure, and curbing the expansion of bank credits and money supply).

President Bill Clinton's proposal to provide a $40 billion loan guarantee that would have enabled Mexico to raise fresh capital in international financial markets and resume debt repayment was rejected by the U.S. Congress on 30 January. The Peso took the hit and tumbled to 6.35 to a dollar the next day. By then, Mexico had only enough foreign exchange reserves to last two more days. In an emergency session, the United States, Germany, and France finally agreed to provide Mexico with a $48.8 billion refinancing package, the details of which are as follows:

1. The U.S. government would establish a $20 billion credit line (with $1.4 billion coming from the Exchange Stabilization Fund of the Department of Treasury) made up of:

   (a) A Peso/dollar swap line for maturities that fall within 12 months or between 3 to 5 years

   (b) Guarantee for debts with maturities up to 10 years designed to help Mexico to raise new debts in international markets.

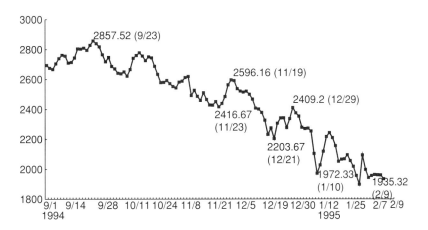

Figure 33.3. Mexican stock index

The remaining $600 million came in the form of a temporary short-term swap credit line set up by the U.S. Federal Reserve.

2. The IMF offered a $17.8 credit line of which $7.8 billion came in the form of emergency credits and a $10 billion stand-by credit facility financed by emerging market economies with ample foreign exchange reserves.

3. The Bank for International Settlements chipped in with a $10 billion credit line consisting of swap facilities offered by its 29 member central banks (including the United States, Japan, Germany, UK, and France).

4. Argentina, Mexico, Chile, and Colombia collectively offered a $1 billion credit line.

The combined value of the four credit lines listed above summed to $48.8 billion. Meanwhile, a consortium of private sector financial institutions headed by Citibank and JP Morgan negotiated for a syndication loan worth $3 billion.

The following lessons can be learnt from the Mexican financial crisis:

I. Capital formation can promote economic growth, but the most reliable source of fund is domestic savings. While foreign capital can make up for the shortfall in domestic savings, only long-term capital, in the forms of foreign direct investment or long-term debt, is conducive to domestic investment. Foreign portfolio investment channels funds into secondary markets, resulting in the transfer of ownership, but brings little direct benefit to domestic capital formation.

II. The size of global portfolio investment has grown exponentially. Fund managers make investment decisions based on predictions about future exchange rates, interest differentials, and stock prices. Large and abrupt movements of capital across national borders can cause excessive financial market volatility and undermine economic stability in the countries involved. These adverse effects would be especially acute in small but highly open economies. For this reason, capital account liberalization should follow a gradual and orderly approach.

III. Prolonged current account deficit should be remedied (by allowing the domestic currency to depreciate, promoting saving, or cutting back government expenditure) rather than financed by foreign capital inflows. A country cannot rely on external financing indefinitely. Interestingly enough, countries like Argentina, the Philippines, Indonesia, Thailand, and Saudi Arabia have all been running current account deficits since 1987. It is worth pointing out that Thailand, in particular, relies almost exclusively on short-term capital inflows to finance her current account deficit.

IV. The IMF should acquire in-depth knowledge of member economies, work with them to establish an early warning system, and make policy recommendations that would prevent the outbreak of future crises.

Chapter 34

PORTFOLIO PERFORMANCE EVALUATION

LALITH P. SAMARAKOON, *University of St. Thomas, USA*
TANWEER HASAN, *Roosevelt University, USA*

Abstract

The portfolio performance evaluation involves the determination of how a managed portfolio has performed relative to some comparison benchmark. Performance evaluation methods generally fall into two categories, namely conventional and risk-adjusted methods. The most widely used conventional methods include benchmark comparison and style comparison. The risk-adjusted methods adjust returns in order to take account of differences in risk levels between the managed portfolio and the benchmark portfolio. The major methods are the Sharpe ratio, Treynor ratio, Jensen's alpha, Modigliani and Modigliani, and Treynor Squared. The risk-adjusted methods are preferred to the conventional methods.

Keywords: performance; evaluation; standard deviation; systematic risk; conventional methods; benchmark comparison; style comparison; risk-adjusted measures; Sharpe measure; Treynor measure; Jensen measure; alpha; Modigliani-Modigliani measure; Treynor squared

34.1. Introduction

The portfolio performance evaluation primarily refers to the determination of how a particular investment portfolio has performed relative to some comparison benchmark. The evaluation can indicate the extent to which the portfolio has outperformed or under-performed, or whether it has performed at par with the benchmark.

The evaluation of portfolio performance is important for several reasons. First, the investor, whose funds have been invested in the portfolio, needs to know the relative performance of the portfolio. The performance review must generate and provide information that will help the investor to assess any need for rebalancing of his investments. Second, the management of the portfolio needs this information to evaluate the performance of the manager of the portfolio and to determine the manager's compensation, if that is tied to the portfolio performance. The performance evaluation methods generally fall into two categories, namely conventional and risk-adjusted methods.

34.2. Conventional Methods

34.2.1. Benchmark Comparison

The most straightforward conventional method involves comparison of the performance of an investment portfolio against a broader market index. The most widely used market index in the United States is the S&P 500 index, which measures the price movements of 500 U.S. stocks compiled by the Standard & Poor's Corporation. If the return on the portfolio exceeds that of the benchmark index, measured during identical time periods, then the portfolio is said to have beaten the benchmark index. While this type of comparison with a passive index is very common in the investment world, it creates a particular problem. The level of risk of the investment portfolio may not be the same as that of the benchmark index portfolio. Higher risk should lead to commensurately higher returns in the long term. This means if the investment portfolio has performed better than the benchmark portfolio, it may be due to the investment portfolio being more risky than the benchmark portfolio. Therefore, a simple comparison of the return on an investment portfolio with that of a benchmark portfolio may not produce valid results.

34.2.2. Style Comparison

A second conventional method of performance evaluation called "style-comparison" involves comparison of return of a portfolio with that having a similar investment style. While there are many investment styles, one commonly used approach classifies investment styles as value versus growth. The "value style" portfolios invest in companies that are considered undervalued on the basis of yardsticks such as price-to-earnings and price-to-book value multiples. The "growth style" portfolios invest in companies whose revenue and earnings are expected to grow faster than those of the average company.

In order to evaluate the performance of a value-oriented portfolio, one would compare the return on such a portfolio with that of a benchmark portfolio that has value-style. Similarly, a growth-style portfolio is compared with a growth-style benchmark index. This method also suffers from the fact that while the style of the two portfolios that are compared may look similar, the risks of the two portfolios may be different. Also, the benchmarks chosen may not be truly comparable in terms of the style since there can be many important ways in which two similar style-oriented funds vary.

Reilly and Norton (2003) provide an excellent disposition of the use of benchmark portfolios and portfolios style and the issues associated with their selection. Sharpe (1992), and Christopherson (1995) have developed methods for determining this style.

34.3. Risk-adjusted Methods

The risk-adjusted methods make adjustments to returns in order to take account of the differences in risk levels between the managed portfolio and the benchmark portfolio. While there are many such methods, the most notables are the Sharpe ratio (S), Treynor ratio (T), Jensen's alpha (α), Modigliani and Modigliani (M^2), and Treynor Squared (T^2). These measures, along with their applications, are discussed below.

34.3.1. Sharpe Ratio

The Sharpe ratio (Sharpe, 1966) computes the risk premium of the investment portfolio per unit of total risk of the portfolio. The risk premium, also known as excess return, is the return of the portfolio less the risk-free rate of interest as measured by the yield of a Treasury security. The total risk is the standard deviation of returns of the portfolio. The numerator captures the reward for investing in a risky portfolio of assets in excess of the risk-free rate of interest while the denominator is the variability of returns of the portfolio. In this sense, the Sharpe measure is also called the "reward-to-variability" ratio. Equation (34.1) gives the Sharpe ratio:

$$S = \frac{r_p - r_f}{\sigma_p} \tag{34.1}$$

where S is the Sharpe ratio, r_p the return of the portfolio, r_f the risk-free rate, and σ_p the standard deviation of returns of the portfolio.

The Sharpe ratio for an investment portfolio can be compared with the same for a benchmark portfolio such as the overall market portfolio. Suppose that a managed portfolio earned a return of

20 percent over a certain time period with a standard deviation of 32 percent. Also assume that during the same period the Treasury bill rate was 4 percent, and the overall stock market earned a return of 13 percent with a standard deviation of 20 percent. The managed portfolio's risk premium is (20 percent − 4 percent) = 16 percent, while its Sharpe ratio, S, is equal to 16 percent/32 percent = 0.50. The market portfolio's excess return is (13 percent − 4 percent) = 9 percent, while its S equals 9 percent/20 percent = 0.45. Accordingly, for each unit of standard deviation, the managed portfolio earned a risk premium of 0.50 percent, which is greater than that of the market portfolio of 0.45 percent, suggesting that the managed portfolio outperformed the market after adjusting for total risk.

34.3.2. Treynor Ratio

The Treynor ratio (Treynor, 1965) computes the risk premium per unit of systematic risk. The risk premium is defined as in the Sharpe measure. The difference in this method is in that it uses the systematic risk of the portfolio as the risk parameter. The systematic risk is that part of the total risk of an asset which cannot be eliminated through diversification. It is measured by the parameter known as 'beta' that represents the slope of the regression of the returns of the managed portfolio on the returns to the market portfolio. The Treynor ratio is given by the following equation:

$$T = \frac{r_p - r_f}{\beta_p} \qquad (34.2)$$

where T is the Treynor ratio, r_p the return of the portfolio, r_f the risk-free rate, and β_p the beta of the portfolio.

Suppose that the beta of the managed portfolio in the previous example is 1.5. By definition, the beta of the market portfolio is equal to 1.0. This means the managed portfolio has one-and-half times more systematic risk than the market portfolio. We would expect the managed portfolio to earn more than the market because of its higher

risk. In fact, in the above example, the portfolio earned an excess return of 16 percent whereas the market earned only 9 percent. These two numbers alone do not tell anything about the relative performance of the portfolio since the portfolio and the market have different levels of market risk. In this instance, the Treynor ratio for the managed portfolio equals (20 percent − 4 percent)/1.5 = 10.67, while that for the market equals (13 percent − 4 percent)/1.00 = 9.00. Thus, after adjusting for systematic risk, the managed portfolio earned an excess return of 10.67 percent for each unit of beta while the market portfolio earned an excess return of 9.00 percent for each unit of beta. Thus, the managed portfolio outperformed the market portfolio after adjusting for systematic risk.

34.3.3. Jensen's Alpha

Jensen's alpha (Jensen, 1968) is based on the Capital Asset Pricing Model (CAPM) of Sharpe (1964), Lintner (1965), and Mossin (1966). The alpha represents the amount by which the average return of the portfolio deviates from the expected return given by the CAPM. The CAPM specifies the expected return in terms of the risk-free rate, systematic risk, and the market risk premium. The alpha can be greater than, less than, or equal to zero. An alpha greater than zero suggests that the portfolio earned a rate of return in excess of the expected return of the portfolio. Jensen's alpha is given by.

$$\alpha = r_p - [r_f + \beta_p(r_m - r_f)] \qquad (34.3)$$

where α is the Jensen's alpha, r_p the return of the portfolio, r_m the return of the market portfolio, r_f the risk-free rate, and β_p the beta of the portfolio.

Using the same set of numbers from the previous example, the alpha of the managed portfolio and the market portfolio can be computed as follows. The expected return of the managed portfolio is 4 percent + 1.5 (13 percent − 4 percent) = 17.5 percent. Therefore, the alpha of the managed portfolio is equal to the actual return less the expected return, which is 20 percent − 17.5 percent = 2.5 percent. Since we are measuring the expected return as a function of the beta and the market risk premium, the alpha for the market is always zero. Thus, the managed portfolio has earned a 2.5 percent return above that must be earned given its market risk. In short, the portfolio has a positive alpha, suggesting superior performance.

When the portfolio is well diversified all three methods – Sharpe, Treynor, and Jensen – will give the same ranking of performance. In the example, the managed portfolio outperformed the market on the basis of all three ratios. When the portfolio is not well diversified or when it represents the total wealth of the investor, the appropriate measure of risk is the standard deviation of returns of the portfolio, and hence the Sharpe ratio is the most suitable. When the portfolio is well diversified, however, a part of the total risk has been diversified away and the systematic risk is the most appropriate risk metric. Both Treynor ratio and Jensen's alpha can be used to assess the performance of well-diversified portfolios of securities. These two ratios are also appropriate when the portfolio represents a sub-portfolio or only a part of the client's portfolio. Chen and Lee (1981, 1986) examined the statistical distribution of Sharpe, Treynor, and Jensen measures and show that the empirical relationship between these measures and their risk proxies is dependent on the sample size, the investment horizon and market conditions. Cumby and Glen (1990), Grinblatt and Titman (1994), Kallaberg et al. (2000), and Sharpe (1998) have provided evidence of the application of performance evaluation techniques.

34.3.4. Modigliani and Modigliani Measure

The Sharpe ratio is not easy to interpret. In the example, the Sharpe ratio for the managed portfolio is 0.50, while that for the market is 0.45. We concluded that the managed portfolio outper-

formed the market. The difficulty, however, is that the differential performance of 0.05 is not an excess return. Modigliani and Modigliani (1997) measure, which is referred to as M^2, provides a risk-adjusted measure of performance that has an economically meaningful interpretation. The M^2 is given by

$$M^2 = r_{p^*} - r_m \tag{34.4}$$

where M^2 is the Modigliani-Modigliani measure, r_{p^*} the return on the adjusted portfolio, r_m the return on the market portfolio.

The adjusted portfolio is the managed portfolio adjusted in such a way that it has the same total risk as the market portfolio. The adjusted portfolio is constructed as a combination of the managed portfolio and risk-free asset, where weights are specified as in Equations (34.5) and (34.6).

$$w_{r_p} = \frac{\sigma_m}{\sigma_p} \tag{34.5}$$

$$w_{r_f} = 1 - w_{r_p} \tag{34.6}$$

where w_{r_p} represents the weight given to the managed portfolio, which is equal to the standard deviation of the market portfolio (σ_m) divided by the standard deviation of the managed portfolio (σ_p). w_{r_f} is the weight on the risk-free asset and is equal to one minus the weight on the managed portfolio. The risk of the adjusted portfolio (σ_{p^*}) is the weight on the managed portfolio times the standard deviation of the managed portfolio as given in Equation (34.7). By construction, this will be equal to the risk of the market portfolio.

$$\sigma_{p^*} = w_{r_p} \times \sigma_p = \frac{\sigma_m}{\sigma_p} \times \sigma_p = \sigma_m \tag{34.7}$$

The return of the adjusted portfolio (r_{p^*}) is computed as the weighted average of the returns of the managed portfolio and the risk-free rate, where the weights are as in Equations (34.5) and (34.6) above:

$$r_{p^*} = w_{r_f} \times r_f + w_{r_p} \times r_p \tag{34.8}$$

The return on the adjusted portfolio can be readily compared with the return on the market portfolio since both have the same degree of risk. The differential return, M^2, indicates the excess return of the managed portfolio in comparison to the benchmark portfolio after adjusting for differences in the total risk. Thus, M^2 is more meaningful than the Sharpe ratio.

In the example, the standard deviation of the managed portfolio is 32 percent and the standard deviation of the market portfolio is 20 percent. Hence, the $w_{r_p} = 20/32 = 0.625$, and $w_{r_f} = 1 - 0.625 = 0.375$. The adjusted portfolio would be 62.5 percent invested in the managed portfolio and 37.5 percent invested in Treasury bills. Now the risk of the adjusted portfolio, $\sigma_{p^*} = 0.625 \times 32$ percent $= 20$ percent, is the same as the risk of the market portfolio. The return on the adjusted portfolio would be $r_{p^*} = 0.375 \times 4$ percent $+ 0.625 \times 20$ percent $= 14$ percent. The $M^2 = 14$ percent $- 13$ percent $= 1$ percent. Thus, on a risk-adjusted basis, the managed portfolio has performed better than the benchmark by 1 percent.

34.3.5. Treynor Squared

Another performance measure, called T^2 analogous to M^2, can be constructed. This is a deviant of the Treynor measure, and the rationale is the same as that of M^2. T^2 is defined as

$$T^2 = r_{p^*} - r_m \qquad (34.9)$$

where T^2 is the Treynor-squared measure, r_{p^*} the return on the adjusted portfolio, and r_m the return on the market portfolio.

The adjusted portfolio is the managed portfolio adjusted such that it has the same degree of systematic or market risk as the market portfolio. Since the market risk or beta of the market portfolio is equal to one, the adjusted portfolio is constructed as a combination of the managed portfolio and risk-free asset such that the adjusted portfolio has a beta equal to one. The weights are specified as in equations below.

$$w_{r_p} = \frac{\beta_m}{\beta_p} \qquad (34.10)$$

$$w_{r_f} = 1 - w_{r_p} \qquad (34.11)$$

where w_{r_p} represents the weight given to the managed portfolio, which is equal to the beta of the market portfolio (β_m) divided by the beta of the managed portfolio (β_p). w_{r_f} is the weight on the risk-free asset and is equal to one minus the weight on the managed portfolio. The beta of the adjusted portfolio (β_{p^*}) is the weight on the managed portfolio times the beta of the managed portfolio, and this will be equal to the risk of the market portfolio as shown in the following equation:

$$\beta_{p^*} = w_{r_p} \times \beta_p = \frac{\beta_m}{\beta_p} \times \beta_p = \beta_m \qquad (34.12)$$

The return of the adjusted portfolio (r_{p^*}) is computed as the weighted average of the returns of the managed portfolio and the risk-free rate, where the weights are as determined above in equations (34.10) and (34.11):

$$r_{p^*} = w_{r_f} \times r_f + w_{r_p} \times r_p \qquad (34.13)$$

The return on the adjusted portfolio can be readily compared with the return on the market portfolio since both have the same level of market risk. The differential return, T^2, indicates the excess return of the managed portfolio in comparison to the benchmark portfolio after adjusting for differences in the market risk.

In the example, the beta of the managed portfolio is 1.5. Hence, $w_{r_p} = 1.0/1.5 = 0.67$ and $w_{r_f} = 1 - 0.67 = 0.33$. The adjusted portfolio would be 67 percent invested in the managed portfolio and 33 percent invested in Treasury bills. The beta of the adjusted portfolio, $\sigma_{p^*} = 0.67 \times 1.5 = 1.00$, which is equal to the beta of the market portfolio. The return on the adjusted portfolio would be $r_{p^*} = 0.33 \times 4$ percent $+ 0.67 \times 20$ percent $= 14.72$ percent. $T^2 = 14.72$ percent $- 13.00$ percent $= 1.72$ percent. Thus, after adjusting for market risk, the managed portfolio has performed better than the benchmark by 1.72

percent. T^2 is a better measure of relative performance when the market risk of a managed portfolio is the relevant risk metric.

REFERENCES

Chen, S.N. and Lee, C.F. (1981). "The sampling relationship between Sharpe's performance measure and its risk proxy: sample size, investment horizon and market conditions." *Management Science*, 27: 607–618.

Chen, S.N. and Lee, C.F. (1986). "The effects of the sample size, the investment horizon and market conditions on the validity of composite performance measures: A generalization." *Management Science*, 32: 1410–1421.

Christopherson, J.A. (1995). "Equity style classifications." *Journal of Portfolio Management*, 21: 32–43.

Cumby, R.E. and Glen, J.D. (1990). "Evaluating the performance of international mutual funds." *Journal of Finance*, 45: 497–521.

Grinblatt, M. and Titman, S. (1994). "A study of monthly mutual fund returns and performance evaluation techniques." *Journal of Financial and Quantitative Analysis*, 29: 419–444.

Jensen, M.C. (1968). "The performance of mutual funds in the period 1945–1964." *Journal of Finance*, 23: 389–416.

Kallaberg, J.G., Lin, C.L., and Trzcinka, C. (2000). "The value added from investment managers: an examination of funds of REITs." *Journal of Financial Quantitative Analysis*, 35: 387–408.

Lintner, J. (1965). "The valuation of risk assets and the selection of risky investments in stock portfolios and capital budgets." *Review of Economics and Statistics*, 47: 13–47.

Modigliani, F. and Modigliani, L. (1997). "Risk-adjusted performance: how to measure it and why." *Journal of Portfolio Management*, 23: 45–54.

Mossin, J. (1966). "Equilibrium in the capital market." *Econometrica*, 34: 768–783.

Reilly, F.K. and Norton, E.A. (2003). *Investments*, 6th edn. Mason, Ohio: Thompson-Southwestern.

Sharpe, W.F. (1964). "Capital asset prices: a theory of market equilibrium under conditions of risk." *Journal of Finance*, 19: 425–442.

Sharpe, W.F. (1966). "Mutual fund performance." *Journal of Business*, 39(1): 119–138.

Sharpe, W.F. (1992). "Asset allocation: management style and performance measurement." *Journal of Portfolio Management*, 18: 7–19.

Sharpe, W.F. (1998). "Morningstar's risk-adjusted ratings." *Financial Analysts Journal*, 54: 21–33.

Treynor, J.L. (1965). "How to rate management of investment funds." *Harvard Business Review*, 43: 63–75.

Chapter 35

CALL AUCTION TRADING[1]

ROBERT A. SCHWARTZ, *Baruch College, USA*
RETO FRANCIONI, *Swiss Stock Exchange, Switzerland*

Abstract

A call auction is an order driven facility which, in contrast with continuous trading, batches multiple orders together for simultaneous execution in a multilateral trade, at a single price, at a predetermined point in time, by a predetermined matching algorithm. The chapter describes how orders are handled and clearing prices set in call auction trading, contrasts call auctions with continuous trading, and identifies different types of call auctions (including price scan auctions, sealed bid auctions, and open limit order book auctions). Attention is given to the use of information technology in call market design, the integration of an auction in a market's microstructure, and to the facility's ability to deal with market quality issues such as containing intra-day price volatility, sharpening price discovery, and catering to participant demands for immediacy. To produce robust results, a call auction must attract sufficient critical mass order flow; the paper concludes by noting that, because large traders in particular are reluctant to enter their orders early in the auction process, book building cannot be taken for granted.

Keywords: book building; continuous trading; critical mass order flow; hybrid markets; information technology; intra-day price volatility; order driven facility; open limit order book auction; price and time priority; price discovery; price improvement; price scan auction; sealed bid auction

A call auction is an order driven facility that batches multiple orders together for simultaneous execution in a multilateral trade, at a single price, at a predetermined point in time. This contrasts with continuous trading where a trade can occur whenever a buy and a sell order cross in price. Our discussion of call auction trading is implicitly in the context of equity trading, but the concepts involved apply to a far greater array of financial instruments and nonfinancial resources.

The call auction form of trading died out in the precomputer age but has made its re-entrance today as an electronic marketplace. An electronic call auction has been incorporated in recent years in a number of market centers around the world, most notably Deutsche Börse, Euronext (the Paris, Amsterdam, Brussels and Lisbon, exchanges), the London Stock Exchange, and the NASDAQ Stock Market. These electronic calls are not being used as standalone systems, but have been combined with continuous trading to create hybrid markets. When it comes to trading, one size does not fit all. With a hybrid system, an investor can select among alternative trading venues depending on the size of the order, the liquidity of the stock being traded, and the investor's own motive for trading.

A pure "order driven" market is a trading environment where all of the participants are investors seeking to buy or to sell shares for their own portfolio purposes. The environment is called "order driven" because limit orders that are placed by some participants set the prices at which others can trade by market order. Most order driven markets are not "pure," but allow for market making. Even without imposing specific obligations or offering incentives, large market participants often choose to make markets as a specific business line. There is a need for market making services, and these services get paid for.

An order driven market can be structured in two fundamentally different ways. With a "continuous" market, a trade can be made at any moment in continuous time that a buy order and a sell order meet in price. In the continuous market, trading is generally a sequence of bilateral matches. Alternatively, in a "call auction," orders are batched together for a simultaneous execution. At the time of a call, a market clearing price is determined, and buy orders at this price and higher execute, as do sell orders at this price and lower.

Call auctions and continuous trading both have their advantages and their shortcomings. In most exchanges, both methods are combined, as are order driven and quote driven facilities[2] so as to form an optimum structure for all kinds of users. In principle, an auction appears to be the ideal way of defining the equilibrium market price at a specific point in time. Continuous trading is more apt to resemble a never ending crawl around a dynamically evolving equilibrium price.

Many retail customers are accustomed to trading with immediacy. Nevertheless, if there were only retail orders, periodic calls would probably be the better way to provide fair and equitable treatment to every investor. However, markets must also cope with the problem of handling big block orders. A lot of interaction with the market is needed to trade large orders. That is where some see the advantage of continuous trading. It offers a special kind of interaction between the market participants, opportunities to test the market, and to get information from the market. For big orders, periodic calls may not provide the kind of flexibility that some participants want.

On both sides of the Atlantic, this has led to combinations of both call and continuous systems. Call auctions are typically used at the beginning of

each trading session to open their continuous order driven markets. The opening price has special importance because orders that have come in during the overnight trading halt are normally considered to have an equal right to get filled, at least partly, at the opening price. Setting the opening price should, therefore, be done carefully – be it by a well-structured auction or through a less formalized process. Calls can also be used to close the market. The major European equity markets and NASDAQ in the United States do this to sharpen the accuracy of price determination at this critical time of the trading day, and in recognition of the multiplicity of uses to which the closing prices are put (at index rebalancings and derivative expirations, as well as for marking-to-market in derivative markets, share valuations for various other legal purposes, etc.). Some exchanges also run periodic calls during a trading session (Deutsche Börse's market model includes one intra-day call). The intra-day calls are important particularly for securities with low trading volume.

35.1. Order Handling

Orders are handled differently in call auctions than in continuous trading, and the time clock is used differently. With a call auction, trades are made at specific points in time rather than whenever, in continuous time, a buy and a sell order cross. To accomplish this, orders submitted to a call auction that could otherwise have been matched and executed are batched together for a multilateral clearing. The clearings are generally held at predetermined points in time (at the open, at the close, and/or at set times during the trading day).

As noted, at the time of a call, the batched orders are matched, and a single clearing price is established. The single clearing price reflects the full set of orders submitted to the call. Buy orders at this value and higher execute, as do sell orders at this value and lower. Because all executed orders clear at the same price, there is no bid–ask spread in call auction trading. Further, with single price clearing, buy orders priced above the single clearing value and sell orders priced below it receive price improvement.

35.2. Alternative Call Auction Designs

Many variations in auction design exist. Calls can be held "on request" instead of at predetermined regular intervals. Multiple (discriminatory) pricing in a call is possible. The amount of precall pricing information to reveal is a decision variable. Traders may be free to change their orders/quotes quotes until the last moment, or there may be restrictions of various kinds. And so forth.

Taking an aerial view, we identify four basic types of call auctions (with several variations in between).

35.2.1. Price Scan Auctions

In a price scan auction, a sequence of prices is "called out" until a value is found that best balances the buy and sell orders. The NYSE call auction opening best fits into this category. The exchange specialists periodically announce indicated opening price ranges, traders respond with their orders, and as they do, the specialists adjust their indicated opening prices.[3]

35.2.2. Sealed Bid Auctions

In a sealed bid auction, participants submit their orders in sealed envelopes that are not opened until the time of the auction. These auctions are totally "closed book" (nontransparent) during the preopen phase, and consequently no participant knows what orders the others are submitting. The term may also be applied more broadly when orders are submitted electronically or by other means if pre-trade orders and indicated clearing prices are not revealed to participants. The U.S. Treasury's new issues market is a good example of the sealed bid auction.

In an electronic trading environment, the auction can be set up with various degrees of preauction transparency that allows traders to react to an indicated clearing price that is continuously displayed as the market forms. This functionality characterizes the third category of call auctions:

35.2.3. Open Limit Order Book

With an open limit order book, posted orders are displayed to the public in the precall order entry period. As the time of the call approaches, the procedure also identifies and updates an indicated clearing price, which at each instant, is the value that would be set in the call if the call were to be held at that instant. At the time of the call, the book is frozen and the indicated clearing price becomes the actual clearing price. The open limit order book call is used in most electronic order driven trading platforms around the world.

The fourth category is not, strictly speaking, a call because it does not undertake price discovery. However, because it is based on the principle of order batching, we include it here:

35.2.4. Crossing Networks

A crossing network does not discover price. Rather, buy and sell orders are matched in a multilateral trade at a price that is set elsewhere. Generally, the value used at a cross is either the last transaction price or the midpoint of the bid–ask spread set in a major market center. In the United States, ITG's Posit crosses and Instinet's cross are good examples of this facility.

35.3. Order Batching and Price Determination

Figures 35.1–35.4 describe order batching and price determination in a call. In each of these figures, share price is shown on the vertical axis, and the number of orders is shown on the horizontal axis. The number of shares sought for purchase or offered for sale is conventionally displayed on the horizontal axis, but the exposition is simplified by assuming that all orders are for the same number of shares (e.g. one round lot). The following legend is used in the diagrams:

. Individual buy order

● Cumulative buy orders at the price or better

○ Individual sell order

Ⓞ Cumulative sell order at the price or better

Figure 35.1 displays the individual buy and sell orders. The horizontal axis gives the total number of orders (buys plus sells) that have been placed at each price. At each price, the orders are arrayed according to the sequence in which they have arrived. At the price of 52, just one sell order has been placed. At 51, a sell order arrived first, and then a buy order. At 50, two buy orders arrived followed by one sell order. And so on.

Figures 35.2 and 35.3 show how the individual buy and sell orders are aggregated. The buy orders only (both individual and aggregated) are shown in Figure 35.2. Because the price limit on a buy order

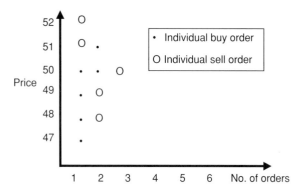

Figure 35.1. Batching of customer orders

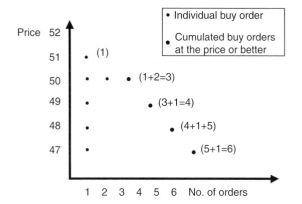

Figure 35.2. Cumulation of the buy orders

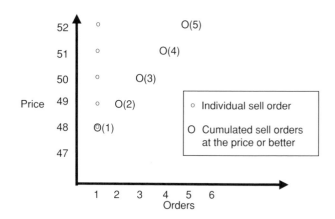

Figure 35.3. Cumulation of the sell orders

is the highest price at which the order is to be executed, the buy orders are cumulated from the highest price (in this case 51) down to the lowest (47). At 51, there is just one order to buy. Two additional buy orders have been entered at 50, and thus at 50, there is a total of three buy orders. At yet lower prices, one order has been placed at each of the prices, 49, 48, and 47. Thus, the cumulative number of orders at these prices is four, five, and six, respectively.

The sell orders only (both individual and aggregated) are shown in Figure 35.3, and they are also cumulated. Because the price limit on a sell order is the lowest price at which the order is to be executed, the sell orders are cumulated from the lowest price (48) up to the highest price (52). There is only one sell order at each of the prices, and the cumulative number of sell orders increases by one order as we move from the single order at 48 to the five orders at 52.

The cumulative buy and sell orders are matched together in Figure 4 to determine the clearing price at which they execute and the specific orders that execute. At the intersection of the two curves, price is 50 and the number of orders is three. Thus, three buy orders execute (the one placed at 51 and the two at 50) and three sell orders execute (the one placed at 48, the one at 49, and the one at 50). Note that three is the maximum number of orders that can execute: at the higher price of 51 there is only one buy order, and at the lower price of 49 there are only two sell orders. For this reason, the clearing price in a call auction is typically identified as the value that maximizes the number of shares that execute (and, in the special case presented here, the number of orders that execute).

Note that the most aggressive buy orders are matched with the most aggressive sell orders. This is because orders receive price priority. Namely, the most aggressive orders (on either side) are executed first. As we discuss below, if several orders have the same price limits, the order that was input first gets executed first (time priority). In the example depicted in Figure 4, three of the executed orders receive price improvement (the buy at 51, the sell at 49, and the sell at 48). The less aggressive orders (the buys at 49, 48, and 47, and the sells at 51 and 52) remain unexecuted. These orders may be rolled into the continuous market, held for the next call, or cancelled, depending on the wishes of the investor.

In Figure 4, at the market-clearing price of 50, the cumulated sell orders match the cumulated buy orders exactly. What if no price exists that gives an exact match? For instance, what would happen if, everything else constant, three buy orders rather than two were entered at 50? The decision rule would still pick 50 to be the price (this value would still maximize the number of orders that execute), but with a cumulative of only three sell

orders at 50, only three of the four buy orders can be executed.

A further decision rule is needed to specify which three of the four orders to pick. The rule commonly used is the "time priority rule:" orders execute according to the sequence in which they were placed, with the first to arrive being the first to execute. Time priority is valuable in call auction trading as it gives participants an incentive to place their orders earlier in the precall, order entry period.[4]

35.4. Relationship Between Limit and Market Orders

Limit orders and market orders are very different order types in continuous trading, but are virtually the same in call auction trading. For continuous markets, limit orders set the prices at which market orders execute, and limit orders sitting on the book provide immediacy to the market orders (i.e. the market orders execute upon arrival). Limit order traders are willing to wait patiently for an execution and they are the liquidity providers. In a continuous market, market order traders demand immediate liquidity.

In contrast, market orders in the call environment are nothing more than extremely aggressively priced limit orders. Specifically, a market order to buy has an effective price limit of infinity and a market order to sell has an effective price limit of zero. Participants in a call auction all wait until the next call for their orders to execute, and thus market orders in a call auction do not receive immediacy as they do in continuous trading. The distinction in continuous trading that limit order placers supply liquidity while market order placers demand liquidity, does not apply to call auction trading. In a call auction, all participants supply liquidity to each other. However, with an open book call, those participants who place their orders early in the precall order entry period are key to the book building process. As we discuss further below, early order placers are the catalysts for liquidity supply.

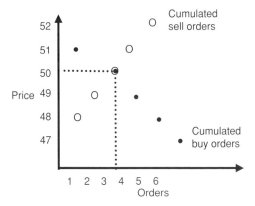

Figure 35.4. Matching of the cumulated buy & sell orders

35.5. The Electronic Call Auction

Over 100 years ago, the New York Stock Exchange was a call market (nonelectronic, of course). In some respects, the nonelectronic call was a fine system for participants on the exchange floor but it had deficiencies for anybody away from the floor. Investors not physically present had little knowledge of what was happening (the calls offered no transparency), and access to trading was limited because shares of a stock could be exchanged only periodically (when the market for the stock was called). On May 8, 1869, the call procedure was abandoned when the NYSE merged with a competing exchange, the Open Board of Brokers, and became a continuous trading environment.

The Tel-Aviv Stock Exchange through the 1970s and the Paris Bourse before the 1986 introduction of its electronic market, CAC (the acronym stands for "Cotation Assistée en Continu"), were also nonelectronic call auctions that did not survive.

Call auction trading had been very popular with continental European exchanges in the earlier days when they still had floor trading. But with growing competition among exchanges, continuous trading became increasingly popular. This went hand-in-hand with extended trading hours. Both developments meant that the volume at the opening call got thinner and its importance was reduced. The widespread trend to fully automated trading of most European exchanges, however, has allowed for new solutions and combinations.

In recent years, tremendous advances in information technology and a slew of other developments in the industry have paved the way for the call's reentry. With an electronic open limit order book, participants anywhere around the globe are able to see the auction as it forms, and can enter their own orders with electronic speed. Compared to traditional floor trading, electronic trading offers new flexibilities for fine-tuning market architecture. Automated order book trading usually starts with an opening call and uses a call to resume trading after any halt. As noted, the major European exchanges and NASDAQ have also introduced closing electronic calls, particularly to provide "better" closing prices. For securities with little liquidity and less frequent trading, one or two calls per day may suffice.

While information technology (IT) can be used advantageously in continuous trading, it is essential for efficient call auction trading. Moreover, the call auction is an extremely good environment for the application of IT. In a continuous market, IT speeds up the rate at which orders can be submitted, displayed, and turned into trades, and in so doing, it accentuates the importance of nanoseconds. In an electronic call auction environment, on the other hand, IT is used to sort and cumulate orders, and to find the clearing prices. In a call auction, the computer is used to do one thing in particular that it was created to do, namely, to compute.

The electronic call auction is appealing for small and mid-cap stocks because order batching augments the efficiency of liquidity provision by focusing liquidity at specific points in time. The procedure also has particular appeal for the large cap stocks, because it caters to the needs of institutional participants whose portfolios are mostly comprised of these issues. Market impact is reduced for the institutional investor because the call is a point in time meeting place, and as noted, batching orders in a multilateral trade focuses liquidity. For all stocks, commissions may be lower due to the greater ease of handling orders and clearing trades in the call auction environment.

For the broad market, electronic call auctions can reduce short-period (e.g. intra-day) price volatility, unreliable pricing, unequal access to the market, and various forms of manipulation and abuse.[5] Further, the electronic call auction is an explicit price discovery facility. That is, batching many orders together for simultaneous execution at a single price produces a consensus value that better reflects the broad market's desire to hold shares. Consequently, the electronic call auction is a good opening facility for the continuous order driven market. Moreover, because it is an explicit price discovery facility, call auction trading can be used to dampen short-period (e.g. intraday) price volatility.

One feature of call auction trading that has been thought by some to be a drawback is that it does not provide transactional immediacy (participants have to wait for a call). With call and continuous trading combined in a hybrid market structure, this limitation ceases to be a deficiency. And, in any event, immediacy involves a cost (bid–ask spreads and market impact costs) that not all investors wish to pay. Retail and institutional customers who place limit orders are not looking for immediate executions and many institutional customers are more concerned with anonymity and keeping trading costs low than with obtaining immediate executions.

To deliver its promise of being a highly efficient trading environment, a call auction must attract sufficient volume. To accomplish this, some order placers must be incented to enter their orders early in the precall order entry period. The early stages of book building cannot be taken for granted, however, especially for an auction that opens the market at the start of a trading day. Some participants, particularly big institutional customers, are reluctant to post orders, an act that may reveal their trading intentions when the book is thin. Nevertheless, early order placers, the catalysts for liquidity supply, are needed. Two incentives for early order placement are (1) the use of time priorities and (2) reduced commission rates for early order entry. The inclusion of retail customers who are less concerned that their small orders will have any meaningful impact on the clearing price also helps. Lastly, a market maker could play an important role in animating book building during the precall order entry period.

NOTES

1. Adapted from Robert A. Schwartz and Reto Francioni (2004), *Equity Markets in Action: The Fundamentals of Market Structure and Trading,* John Wiley (Copyright © 2004 Robert A. Schwartz and Reto Francioni; This material is used by permission of John Wiley); and Robert A. Schwartz, (2003) "The Call Auction Alternative," In Robert A. Schwartz, John Aidan Byrne and Antoinette Colaninno (eds.) *Call Auction Trading: New Answers to Old Questions,* Kluwer Academic Publishers (Springer).

2. In a quote driven market, the quotes of a dealer or market maker establish the prices at which others can trade by market order.

3. The Paris Stock Exchange's market, before the Bourse introduced electronic trading in 1986, was a classic price scan call auction. When the market for a stock was called, an auctioneer would cry out one price after another, scanning the range of possibilities, until an acceptable balance was found between the buy and sell orders.

4. Further situations can be described that require more complex rules of order execution. As is typically the case, the set of decision rules required for an actual operating system is far more complicated than those we need consider to achieve a basic understanding of a system.

5. For further discussion of the properties of call auction trading, see Cohen and Schwartz (1989), Economides and Schwartz (1995), and Schwartz, Francioni and Weber (2006), Chapter 4.

REFERENCES

Cohen, K.J. and Schwartz, R.A. (1989). "An electronic call market: its design and desirability," in H. Lucas and R.A. Schwartz (eds.) *The Challenge of Information Technology for the Securities Markets: Liquidity, Volatility, and Global Trading.* Homewood, IL: Dow Jones-Irwin, pp. 15–58.

Economides, N. and Schwartz, R.A. (1995). Electronic call market trading. *Journal of Portfolio Management,* 22: 10–18.

Francioni, R., Schwartz, R. and Weber, B., ?The Equity Trader Course,? John Wiley & Sons, forthcoming, 2006.

Chapter 36

MARKET LIQUIDITY[1]

ROBERT A. SCHWARTZ, *City University of New York, USA*
LIN PENG, *City University of New York, USA*

Abstract

Liquidity, which is integrally related to trading costs, refers to the ability of individuals to trade at reasonable prices with reasonable speed. As such, liquidity is a major determinant, along with risk and return, of a company's share value. Unfortunately, an operational, generally accepted measure of liquidity does not exist. This entry considers the following proxy measures: the bid–ask spread, the liquidity ratio (which relates the number or value of shares traded during a brief interval to the absolute value of the percentage price change over the interval), and the variance ratio (which relates the volatility of short-term price movements to longer-term price movements). The determinants of liquidity considered are the size of the market for a stock and market structure. The paper concludes by stressing that illiquidity increases the cost of equity capital for firms, but that trading costs can be reduced and liquidity enhanced by the institution of a superior trading system.

Keywords: bid–ask spread; cost of equity capital; liquidity; liquidity ratio; market structure; risk and return; share value; trading costs; trading system; variance ratio

Liquidity refers broadly to the ability of individuals to trade quickly at prices that are reasonable in light of underlying demand/supply conditions. Liquidity, risk, and return are the major determinants of a company's share value. Risk constant and expected return must be higher and a company's cost of capital greater, if the market for its shares is less liquid. A number of authors have studied the cross-sectional relationship between liquidity and asset prices (see, for example, Amihud and Mendelson, 1986; Brennan and Subrahmanyam, 1996; Easley et al., 2002; Pastor and Stambaugh, 2003), as well as the time series relationship (Jones, 2002). However, a comprehensive understanding of the impact and determinants of liquidity is still lacking. The problem is that an operational, generally accepted measure of liquidity does not exist.

Liquidity is often described by the depth, breadth, and resiliency of the market for an asset. A market has depth and breadth if orders exist at an array of prices in the close neighborhood above and below the values at which shares are currently trading, and if the buy and sell orders exist in substantial volume. A market is resilient if temporary price changes due to order imbalances quickly attract new orders that restore reasonable share values.

Liquidity (and its converse, illiquidity) can also be defined in terms of the transaction costs incurred to obtain a fast execution. Transaction costs include an explicit component such as commissions, and an implicit component such as a bid–ask spread and market impact. The ask quotation is the price at which shares can be purchased with immediacy, and the bid quotation is the price at which shares can be sold with immediacy. The difference, known as the bid–ask spread, is the cost of a round-trip, and half of the spread is typically viewed as the cost of buying or selling shares immediately.

Market impact exists when a buy order drives the ask up, or a sell order drives the bid down. This occurs because the volume of shares at the quotes may be small relative to the size of the order, and/or because of the dissemination of the information that a large trader has arrived in the market. The spread and market impact are large if a market lacks depth and breadth.

Bid–ask spreads are directly quantifiable, but market impact is very difficult. The problem is two-fold. First, because of information leaks and front-running, an order can impact prices before it reaches the market. Second, prices are constantly changing due to news and liquidity trading, and thus a reasonable benchmark against which to assess the implicit cost components of a transaction price is not readily available.

Prices are also distorted due to the difficulty of finding equilibrium values in the marketplace. Errors in price discovery occur because prices depend on the order flow while simultaneously orders are priced with imperfect information about the underlying consensus values. Analogous to the market impact effect, transaction prices can be pushed up if impatient buyers outnumber impatient sellers, or can be pushed down if impatient sellers outnumber impatient buyers (Ho et al., 1985). In a resilient market, errors in price discovery are quickly corrected.

None of the attributes of liquidity thus far discussed provide an unambiguous measure of the concept. One commonly used measure is the bid–ask spread (Amihud and Mendelson, 1986). Another is the liquidity ratio, which relates the number or value of shares traded during a brief time interval to the absolute value of the percentage price change over the interval. The larger the ratio of shares traded to the percentage price change, the more liquid the market is presumed to be. This view underlies measures of specialist performance that have been used by various stock exchanges, and characterizes the approach taken by some researchers to measure and to contrast the liquidity of different market centers (Cooper et al., 1985; Hui and Heubel, 1984).

The liquidity ratio, however, can be misleading. If news causes prices to change, a large liquidity ratio that is attributed to heavy trading volume would suggest that prices have adjusted too slowly in response to the informational change. This is because a bid that is too high attracts market orders to sell, and an ask that is too low attracts market orders to buy. Consequently, to the extent that trading is triggered by informational change (rather than by idiosyncratic investor needs), trading volume is less, and the liquidity ratio is smaller (not larger) in a more efficient market.

Another measure of liquidity is the variance ratio, which relates the volatility of short-term price movements to the volatility of longer-term price movements. Transaction prices jump up and down as executions bounce between the bid and the ask, as large orders impact prices, and as transaction prices fluctuate around equilibrium values due to price discovery errors. Thus, implicit execution costs increase the volatility of short-term price movements. Because the effect attenuates as the interval over which price changes are measured is lengthened, it is possible to proxy liquidity by the variance ratio. Hasbrouck and Schwartz (1988), for example, find that an appropriately adjusted ratio of two-day to half-hour returns variance is predominantly less than unity (the value expected for a perfectly liquid market) for a large sample of NYSE, Amex and OTC stocks. Ozenbas et al. (2002) report an accentuation of intra-day volatility that is most pronounced in the first half-hour of a trading day in five markets – the New York Stock Exchange and NASDAQ in the United States, and the London Stock Exchange, Euronext Paris and Deutsche Börse in Europe.

A primary determinant of liquidity is the size of the market for a stock (or inversely, thinness). Size can be measured as the number or value of shares outstanding, the number or value of shares traded, and/or the number of shareholders. Empirical studies have shown that spreads are wider, market impact greater, and price discovery less accurate for thinner issues (Cohen et al., 1986; Schwartz and

Francioni, 2004). But even for larger issues, markets can be thin, particularly for big, institutional investors. This is because, during any trading session, only a relatively small number of individuals actually seek to trade. For small-cap and mid-cap stocks, the problem may be particularly striking within a trading day: at any given moment, only a handful of individuals (if any) may be actively looking to buy or to sell shares.

Market structure also affects the liquidity of individual issues, and the U.S. Securities and Exchange Commission has required that execution venues report their execution quality on multiple dimensions (see SEC, 2000). The primary market makers in certain market centers are dealers and specialists, whose role is to supply immediacy to public traders. In this context, the provision of immediacy is essentially synonymous with the provision of liquidity, the ability to transact quickly at reasonable prices. Liquidity may also be enhanced by other market structure mechanisms. One important approach would be to increase the depth and breadth of a market by encouraging public traders to place more limit orders. The imposition of rules to prevent destabilizing trades (i.e. tick-test rules) and the time bunching of orders are two other ways to increase liquidity. In 2001, the NYSE and NASDAQ completed a conversion from fractional to decimal prices under pressure from the SEC. The switch has resulted in sharply reduced quoted spreads. However, there is evidence that the inside market depth has been reduced for the large traders (Sofianos, 2001).

Public orders generally execute at inferior prices in illiquid markets. As a consequence, expected returns on securities traded in less liquid markets must be higher and the cost of capital for the listed companies is greater. The important insight is that the costs of trading can be decreased by the institution of a superior trading system. In the limit, as a market becomes frictionless, the issues traded in it become perfectly liquid.

NOTE

1. This material is modified from an equivalent entry from: *The New Palgrave Dictionary of Money and Finance,* by: Newman, Peter. Reprinted with permission of Palgrave Macmillan. Copyright © Newman, Peter.

REFERENCES

Amihud, Y. and Mendelson, H. (1986). "Asset pricing and the bid-ask spread." *Journal of Financial Economics,* 17(2): 223–49.

Beebower, G., Kamath, V. and Surz, R. (1985). "Commission and transaction costs of stock market trading." Working paper, SEI Corporation, July.

Bernstein, P. (1987). "Liquidity, stock markets, and market makers." *Financial Management,* 16: 54–62.

Brennan, M.J. and Subrahmanyam, A. (1996). "Market microstructure and asset pricing: on the compensation for illiquidity in stock returns." *Journal of Financial Economics,* 41(3): 441–464.

Cohen, K., Maier, S., Schwartz, R.A., and Whitcomb, D. (1986). *The Microstructure of Securities Markets.* Englewood Cliffs, New Jersey: Prentice-Hall.

Cooper, K., Groth, J., and Avera, W. (1985). "Liquidity, exchange listing, and common stock performance." *Journal of Economics and Business,* 37(1): 19–33.

Easley, D., Hvidkjaer, S., and O'Hara, M. (2002). "Is information risk a determinant of asset returns?" *Journal of Finance,* 57: 2185–2221.

Economides, N. and Siow, A. (1988). "The division of markets is limited by the extent of liquidity." *American Economic Review,* 78: 108–121.

Grossman, S.J. and Miller, M. (1988). "Liquidity and market structure." *Journal of Finance,* 43: 617–633.

Hasbrouck, J. and Schwartz, R.A. (1988). "Liquidity and execution costs in equity markets." *Journal of Portfolio Management,* 14(3): 10–17.

Ho, T., Schwartz, R.A., and Whitcomb, D. (1985). "The trading decision and market clearing under transaction price uncertainty." *Journal of Finance,* 40(1): 21–42.

Hui, B. and Heubel, B. (1984). "Comparative liquidity advantages among major US stock markets." DRI Financial Information Group Study Series No. 84081.

Jones, C.M. (2002). "A century of stock market liquidity and trading costs." Working Paper, Columbia University.

Lippman, S.A. and McCall, J.J. (1986). "An operational measure of liquidity." *American Economic Review*, 76(1): 43–55.

Ozenbas, D., Schwartz, R.A., and Wood, R. (2002). "Volatility in US and European equity markets: an assessment of market quality." *International Finance*, 5(3): 437–461.

Pastor, L. and Stambaugh, R.F. (2003). "Liquidity risk and expected stock returns." *Journal of Political Economy*, 111(3): 642–685.

Schwartz, R.A. and Francioni, R. (2004). *Equity Markets In Action: The Fundamentals of Market Structure and Trading*. New Jersey: John Wiley.

Sofianos, G. (2001). Trading and market structure research, Goldman Sachs.

US Securities and Exchange Commission (SEC) (2000). "Disclosure of order routing and execution practices." Release No. 34-43084, 28 July.

Chapter 37

MARKET MAKERS[1]

ROBERT A. SCHWARTZ, *City University of New York, USA*
LIN PENG, *City University of New York, USA*

Abstract

The primary focus of this entry is on market maker services, revenues, and costs. A market maker's basic function is to service the public's demand to trade with immediacy by continuously standing ready to buy shares from customers who wish to sell, and to sell shares to customers who wish to buy. Additionally, the market maker helps to stabilize prices and to facilitate a reasonably accurate price discovery. Further, a special type of market maker – a stock exchange specialist – fulfills the role of an auctioneer. The bid–ask spread is the classic source of market maker profits, while the costs of market maker operations include: order-processing, risk-bearing (the cost of carrying an unbalanced portfolio), and adverse selection (the cost of trading with a better-informed participant). The paper further considers the competitive environment that market makers operate within, and concludes with the thought that institutionalization, the advent of electronic trading, deregulation, and globalization of the equity markets have led to major changes in market maker operations in the recent past, and will continue to do so in the coming years.

Keywords: adverse selection; bid–ask spread; competitive environment; electronic trading; exchange specialist; immediacy; market maker; order-processing; price stabilization; price discovery; risk-bearing

Market makers play a central role in many equity markets by buying and selling shares to service the public's demand to trade immediately (the classic service provided by a dealer). Market makers are also responsible for stabilizing prices (making a market "fair and orderly") and facilitating price determination. Some market makers, such as stock exchange specialists, also perform the role of auctioneer.

Demsetz (1968) was one of the first to analyze the supply of immediacy. Buyers and sellers arrive sporadically at the market, and it is not a simple matter for them to find each other in time. The market maker provides a solution by continuously standing ready to trade from his or her own inventory of shares. The service is not free, however. The dealer sells to buyers at higher ask prices, and buys from sellers at lower bid prices. The bid–ask spread is the market maker's compensation (sometimes referred to as "the dealer's turn").

Market makers are not necessary for immediacy to be provided to a market. Public traders can post limit orders with commission brokers acting as middlemen. However, immediacy is not the only marketability service provided by a market maker.

The liquidity provided by market makers also helps to stabilize prices. Most participants in the securities markets prefer prices that, all else equal, are less volatile. They care about this as investors because they are generally assumed to be risk-averse. They care about this as traders because they are averse to transaction price uncertainty. Market maker intervention helps to stabilize price fluctuations in the short run. The U.S. exchange specialist in particular has an "affirmative obligation" to make a fair and orderly market.

Market makers also facilitate the determination of accurate prices. First, their own quotes directly set market prices. Second, their quotes are signals that public traders react to in writing their orders; therefore, market makers indirectly affect market prices by influencing the public order flow. Third, exchange specialists establish market-clearing prices at the opening of the trading day and at the resumption of trading after halts caused by the advent of news.

Price stabilization and price discovery are both consistent with the provision of immediacy. This is because "immediacy" means not only the ability to trade promptly, but also the ability to trade in reasonable amounts at prices that properly reflect current market conditions. (Smidt, 1971 emphasizes the supply of liquidity in depth, namely the ability of investors to trade quickly and in size, at the market maker's quotes.) Consequently, transactional immediacy, price stability and accurate price discovery are all attributes of markets that are "fair and orderly."

As auctioneers in an agency market, market makers also organize and oversee trading. Stock exchange specialists do so by maintaining the limit order books and by assuring that trading rules are not violated. On some exchanges (such as the Tokyo Stock Exchange), market makers act only in the clerical bookkeeping and regulatory oversight capacities, and are not allowed to trade the stocks assigned to them.

The bid–ask spread set by the market maker reflects the following components: order-processing costs, risk premium or inventory costs, adverse selection costs, and profit (Stoll, 1989). The order-processing costs compensate market makers for their time and effort, cost of paperwork, etc. Risk bearing is central to the dealership function (Amihud and Mendelson, 1980; Ho and Stoll, 1981). The market maker trades to make a

market rather than for his or her own investment motives. If buyers appear, a market maker must be willing to assume a short position; if sellers arrive, the market maker must be willing to assume a long position. As a result, the market maker generally acquires an unbalanced portfolio. The market maker is then subject to uncertainty concerning the future price and the future transactions volume in the asset. Not knowing when transactions will be made, the market maker does not know for how long an unbalanced inventory position will have to be maintained. An unbalanced inventory position implies the existence of diversifiable risk. Thus, the market maker requires a risk premium on the inventory risk, which other investors can eliminate by proper portfolio diversification (the expected return on a stock compensates all investors and market makers for accepting nondiversifiable risk).

Market makers also protect themselves against adverse selection. Public orders to purchase or to sell securities are motivated by either idiosyncratic liquidity reasons or informational change. The market maker typically does not know whether an order has originated from an informed trader or from a liquidity trader. If a public trader receives news and transmits the order before the market maker has learned of the informational change, the public trader profits at the market maker's expense (Bagehot, 1971; Copeland and Galai, 1983; Glosten and Milgrom, 1985). The market maker responds to the cost of ignorance by increasing the ask quote and lowering the bid so that the expected loss to the informed traders is compensated by the expected gain from the liquidity traders. The market maker cannot achieve total protection, however, by sufficiently widening the spread. Regardless of how much the offer is raised and/or or the bid is lowered, any informationally motivated trade would be at the market maker's expense.

And the defensive maneuver is not costless. The market maker profits from liquidity trades, and in the process of widening the spread to guard against informed traders, increases the cost of transacting and so loses an increasing number of liquidity traders. Yet, there must be investors who trade for noninformational reasons. Without the liquidity traders, the dealer market would collapse (Grossman and Stiglitz, 1980).

The competitive environment of a market maker firm differs depending on whether it operates in an agency/auction environment or in a dealer market. In an agency/auction market, limit order traders and floor traders provide competition for the single market maker (stock exchange specialist). In contrast, a dealer market is competitive only if the order flow for a security is directed to more than one dealer firm. This competition for marketability services fragments the informational content of the order flow, however. In other words, each dealer firm knows what buy and sell orders it receives, but does not observe the flow of orders to competing dealer firms. However, in a screen-based system, each dealer firm does see the quotes posted by others. In addition, information is transferred by transaction price reporting and via inter-dealer trading.

The online reporting of large transactions, however, can signal information about a dealer's inventory position to its competitors. And, when the order flow is dominated by institutional investors, as on the London Stock Exchange, other problems can arise (see Neuberger and Schwartz, 1990). These include fair-weather market making (taking the privileges but failing to meet the obligations of market making), preferencing (the diversion of order flow to a market maker firm that is not necessarily posting the best quotes, but that has guaranteed best-price execution nonetheless), handling a lumpy order flow (few trades but of large size), and coping with one-way markets (buyers only or sellers only). All told, market making is a complex, multifaceted operation.

Institutionalization, the advent of electronic trading, deregulation, and globalization of the equity markets are having a profound impact on securities trading and price determination. These forces have led to major changes in market maker operations in the recent past, and will continue to do so in the coming years.

NOTE

1. This material is modified from an equivalent entry from *The New Palgrave Dictionary of Money and Finance*, by Newman, Peter. Reprinted with permission of Palgrave Macmillan. Copyright © Newman, Peter.

REFERENCES

Amihud, Y., Ho, T., and Schwartz, R.A. (eds.) (1985). *Market Making and the Changing Structure of the Securities Industry*. Lexington, MA: Lexington Books.
Amihud, Y. and Mendelson, H. (1980). "Dealership market: market making with inventory." *Journal of Financial Economics*, 8: 31–53.
Bagehot, W. (1971). "The only game in town." *Financial Analysts Journal*, 27: 12–14, 22.
Cohen, K., Maier, S., Schwartz, R.A., and Whitcomb, D. (1979). "Market makers and the market spread: a review of recent literature." *Journal of Financial and Quantitative Analysis*, 14: 813–835.
Copeland, T. and Galai, D. (1983). "Information effects on the bid-ask spread." *Journal of Finance*, 38: 1457–1469.
Demsetz, H. (1968). "The cost of transacting." *Quarterly Journal of Economics*, 82: 33–53.
Garman, M. (1976). "Market microstructure." *Journal of Financial Economics*, 3: 257–275.
Glosten, L. and Milgrom, P. (1985). "Bid, ask, and transaction prices in a specialist market with heterogeneously informed traders." *Journal of Financial Economics*, 14: 71–100.
Grossman, S.J. and Stiglitz, J. (1980). "On the impossibility of informationally efficient markets." *American Economic Review*, 70: 393–408.
Ho, T. and Stoll, H. (1981). "Optimal dealer pricing under transaction and return uncertainty." *Journal of Financial Economics*, 9: 47–73.
Ho, T. and Stoll, H. (1983). "The dynamics of dealer markets under competition." *Journal of Finance*, 38: 1053–1074.
Neuberger, A. and Schwartz, R.A. (1990). "Current developments in the London equity market." *Finanzmarkt und Portfolio Management*, 3: 281–301.

O'Hara, M. and Oldfield, G.S. (1986). "The microeconomics of market making." *Journal of Financial and Quantitative Analysis,* 21: 361–376.

Schwartz, R.A. and Francioni, R. (2004). *Equity Markets in Action: The Fundamentals of Market Structure and Trading*. New York: John Wiley.

Smidt, S. (1971). "Which road to an efficient stock market: free competition or regulated monopoly?" *Financial Analysts Journal,* 27: 18–20, 64–69.

Stoll, H. (1985). "Alternate views of market making," in Amihud, Ho and Schwartz (eds.) *Market Making and the Changing Structure of the Securities Industry*. Lexington Books, pp.67–92.

Stoll, H. (1989). "Inferring the components of the bid-ask spread: theory and empirical tests." *Journal of Finance,* 44: 115–134.

Tinic, S.M. and West, R. (1972). "Competition and the pricing of dealer services in the over-the-counter stock market." *Journal of Financial and Quantitative Analysis,* 7: 1707–1727.

Chapter 38

STRUCTURE OF SECURITIES MARKETS[1]

ROBERT A. SCHWARTZ, *City University of New York, USA*
LIN PENG, *City University of New York, USA*

Abstract

The entry reviews essential elements of market structure – the systems, procedures, and protocols that determine how orders are handled, translated into trades, and transaction prices determined. There are various contrasting alternatives, such as order-driven and quote-driven markets; consolidated vs fragmented markets; human intervention vs electronic trading; and continuous markets vs periodic call auctions. A major objective of market design noted in the discussion is to enhance the accuracy with which prices are discovered in a dynamic, uncertain environment. Lastly, the entry points out that market structures are rapidly changing, and that much remains to be learned about how best to structure a technologically sophisticated, hybrid market that efficiently services the varied needs of diverse participants.

Keywords: call auctions; consolidated markets; continuous markets; electronic trading; fragmented markets; hybrid market; market structure; order-driven markets; price discovery; quote-driven markets

The structure of a securities market refers to the systems, procedures, and protocols that determine how orders are handled, translated into trades, and transaction prices determined. To date, theoretical security valuation models have generally not considered the effect of a market's structure on asset prices. Formulations such as the Capital Asset Pricing Model and the Arbitrage Pricing Theory, for example, address the risk and return dimensions of a security, but ignore considerations such as liquidity, trading costs, information costs, and transaction uncertainty. When these realities are taken into account, it is apparent that market structure matters, that it does affect the price and size of trades.

Market structures differ significantly among major international equity market centers (see Schwartz and Francioni, 2004). The New York Stock Exchange (NYSE) and other U.S. exchanges are agency/auction markets where the market maker (specialist) acts as both dealer and broker's broker. Examples of a dealer market include the Nasdaq market in the United States and the London Stock Exchange (LSE) before they introduced their electronic order-driven trading systems (Supermontage for Nasdaq and SETS for the LSE). The Tokyo Stock Exchange (TSE) is an agency/auction market where the market maker (saitori) handles the orders but does not take a dealership position. Markets also differ in the way in which orders are consolidated or fragmented, in the way in which information is disseminated, and in the degree to which trading is computerized.

Whether investors trade through an intermediary, as in a dealer market, or directly with each other, as in an agency/auction market, is one of the most important distinctions in market structure. In a dealer market, the market maker initiates trades by posting bid and ask quotations that are publicly disseminated. The bid is the price at which public traders can sell to a dealer, and the ask is the price at which they can buy from a dealer. The bid–ask spread is the dealer's compensation for providing marketability services. To achieve a trade in a dealer market, a customer (usually via a broker) contacts a dealer by telephone or electronically and accepts his or her quotation.

In an agency/auction market, public participants trade with each other, and floor professionals in an agency market such as the NYSE act in a brokerage (agency) capacity. When trading is active in a stock, floor traders gather in a "crowd," and trading truly takes place in an auction environment. In the U.S. exchanges, orders are consolidated at the posts of specialists, who are market professionals who function as both principals and as agents. Specialists have an affirmative obligation to buy and to sell shares so as to make "a fair and orderly market" when counterpart orders do not provide sufficient liquidity. They also have a negative obligation: when a public order and a specialist's quote are at the same price, the specialist must step aside and let the public order execute first.

Two types of orders are commonly used in an agency/auction market: limit orders and market orders. A limit order states the maximum price at which a public investor is willing to *buy*, or the minimum price at which the public investor is willing to *sell*, a specified number of shares. A market order is unpriced; it states the number of shares the investor wishes to trade "at market," namely the price prevailing when the order is received by the market center. To execute a market order, limit orders must exist; for limit orders to exist, there must be a facility for maintaining public orders in a file (limit order book). This file characterizes agency/auction exchanges. Handa and Schwartz (1996) have examined the costs and returns to placing limit orders.

Trades may also be negotiated if they are difficult to handle because of their size. In an agency/auction environment such as the NYSE, a buyer or seller may give a not held (NH) order to a floor trader who uses his or her discretion to negotiate with other floor traders or to expose the order to the limit order book. The floor trader is "not held to the price" if the order executes at a price inferior to that which existed at the time of its arrival. Large orders are also negotiated in the "upstairs market," a network of trading desks of securities dealers and institutional investors who bring buyers and sellers together at mutually acceptable prices. Trades may also be negotiated with a dealer and/or electronically through a facility such as Liquidnet or Pipeline. Institutional investors commonly negotiate with the market makers to obtain larger sizes than the market makers are quoting and/or prices that are within the bid–ask spread. Large orders are also commonly broken up (sliced and diced) and brought to the market in smaller tranches for execution over an extended period of time.

A major function of a market center is to find the prices at which shares are traded. This process is known as "price discovery." The accuracy of price discovery depends on the systems used for handling orders, disseminating information, and making trades. If an issue is traded in more than one market center, intermarket linkages including information systems and arbitrage operations must be implemented to ensure both adequate price protection for investors and price consistency across markets. Intermarket linkages also connect equity markets and derivative product markets (for example, the futures and options markets for stock indices in Chicago and the cash market for shares in New York).

Another feature of market structure is the means by which information concerning current market conditions (floor information) is transferred among participants. The informational signal transmitted by a quote differs significantly from that transmitted by a transaction price. A quote reflects an individual's willingness to trade; it is firm only up to its stated size and may be improved on in terms of price and/or quantity. Quotes may also reflect trading strategy and gaming by market participants. A transaction price has actually been accepted by both counterparties to a trade, but relates to the past and does not necessarily represent the price at which one can trade in the present. Nonetheless, latest transaction prices do reflect current market conditions when transactions occur frequently. For this reason, transaction price reporting has been introduced in both the U.S. and London dealer markets (see Seguin, 1991).

The extent to which orders are fragmented or consolidated in trading also defines a market's structure (see Cohen et al., 1986). A competitive dealer market is naturally fragmented in the sense that orders are routed to one of several dealer firms. This may be desirable because of the competition for marketability services that fragmentation implies. Most apparent is that bid–ask spreads are tightened in a competitive dealer environment compared to a monopoly dealer environment (see Ho and Stoll, 1983). However, given the fragmented nature of a dealer market, dealers may not be as closely regulated as the specialists in the agency/auction market. This may create incentives for dealers to collude (see Christie and Schultz, 1994a,b). In 1996, the justice department settled with the Nasdaq dealers on accusations of spread collusion.

Another problem of the dealer market is that fragmenting the order flow across different dealer firms can obscure information and impair the accuracy of price determination (see Neuberger and Schwartz, 1990). However, in a screen-based system such as the US Nasdaq market, each dealer firm does see the quotes posted by the others. A dealer market with fragmented orders may also reduce the opportunity for the interaction of all buying and selling interest in that security and thus reduce price competition. In 1997, the U.S. Securities and Exchange Commission enacted the Order-Handling Rules (OHRs), which required that public limit orders be exposed in the national best bid and offer (NBBO). The rules set in motion the transition of the Nasdaq market from a predominantly quote-driven, dealer market towards an order-driven, agency market.

Order flow in an agency/auction environment is by its nature more consolidated than in a competitive dealer market. Consolidation is desirable because it allows orders to be matched against each other with a minimum of broker–dealer intervention. Furthermore, the consolidation of orders facilitates the enforcement of order exposure and trading priority rules. The primary priority rule is price; highest-priced bids and lowest-priced asks have precedence. A secondary priority rule specifies the sequence in which orders at the same price execute; usually, the first order entered at the price is the first to execute (time priority). However, too much consolidation may lead to monopoly power for a single market center, which may lead it to lose its incentive to reduce transaction costs and to innovate.

An agency/auction market is fragmented when shares are listed on more than one exchange, traded in-house by a brokerage firm, on an Alternative Trading System (ATS) and/or on an Electronic Communications Network (ECN) . This fragmentation may be desirable if it truly represents competition between market centers. It is not desirable if one market center free-rides on the prices discovered by another market center. For example, a satellite market may guarantee trades at the best price quoted in a major market center and charge lower commissions for the service.

Order consolidation facilitates the consolidation and transference of floor information. For example, NYSE specialists are in a unique position from which to observe the order flow and to set prices that are reasonable given the current demand for shares. But, like the saitori in Tokyo, specialists are not permitted to receive orders directly from customers, which restricts their access to information. In contrast, both dealers can receive orders directly from customers, including institutional traders. This contact enables them to obtain further information about market conditions.

In addition to being spatially (geographically) consolidated, orders can be consolidated temporally (over time). Orders are temporally consolidated when they are bunched together in call auction trading. In continuous trading, orders are executed whenever they cross during trading hours and, in a continuous market, trades are generally bilateral. In contrast, in call auction trading, orders are stored for simultaneous execution in multilateral trades at predetermined times when the market is "called."

Call market trading has certain advantages (see Schwartz and Francioni, 2004). In particular, dependence on the intermediation of dealers and brokers is lessened and trading costs are reduced. Since everyone trades at the same price, at the same time and under the same conditions, call market trading is fairer, and the procedure can produce prices that are more accurate and less volatile. But, traditional call market trading has had its limitations. Accessibility to the market was restricted and the dissemination of floor information poor in the old call markets of Europe. These limitations can be overcome with the use of computer technology. Pagano and Schwartz (2003) have found that the introduction of electronic call auctions at market closings on the Paris Bourse (now Euronext Paris) reduced transaction costs and improved price discovery.

One of the more striking changes in market structure that occurred as the twentieth century drew to a close was the advent of electronic trading. At its inception, electronic systems tended to mimic existing systems; now they are more commonly developing their own distinctive functionality. The first electronic exchange, the Computer Assisted Trading System (CATS), was introduced by the Toronto Stock Exchange in 1977. CATS is based on the principle of continuous trading in an agency/auction environment. The success of CATS has led to the implementation of similar systems in Tokyo (1982), Paris (1986), and elsewhere. Small order execution systems were also introduced in the U.S. and London dealer markets in the 1980s. Now most national equity markets around the globe provide floorless, electronic trading platforms. The major exceptions, the New York Stock Exchange in the U.S., is in the process of converting to a hybrid structure that integrates an electronic platform (Direct+) with its trading floor.

Electronic technology has strong advantages: it gives participants direct access to markets and control over their orders regardless of geographic location; it provides direct access to information concerning current market conditions; it provides anonymity; it enables the investors to trade without a broker and thus reduce transaction costs; and, as systems become increasingly sophisticated, the computational power of the computer facilitates the handling of institutional-sized orders and the negotiation of trades. Investors in the 1990s have witnessed a proliferation of fourth-market organizations. Electronic facilities such as Instinet and Archipelago allow members to post orders and to match that of other traders in the system. Crossing systems such as Posit and Instinet's Crossing Network allow investors to trade portfolios directly without a bid–ask spread. Liquidnet and Pipeline allow participants to find each other on their screen and negotiate their trades electronically.

Electronic technology solves the major problems associated with call market trading: restricted accessibility to a market and inadequate dissemination of floor information (see Pagano and Schwartz, 2003). Reciprocally, a call market environment may be more suitable than the continuous market for the use of electronic technology. In particular, the submission and handling of institutional-sized orders can be accommodated in an electronic call (see Schwartz and Francioni, 2004).

Because of strong vested interests, technological inertia, and the ability of an established market center to retain order flow, the superiority of a new system may not ensure its acceptance. Market structure has evolved slowly in the United States since trading moved from coffee houses and curbs into exchanges (the American Stock Exchange did not move indoors until 1921). The pace of change accelerated in the mid-1970s with the passage of the U.S. Securities Acts Amendments of 1975, which precluded fixed commissions and mandated the development of a national market system. London's Big Bang in 1986 also precluded fixed commissions, broadened competition between dealers and brokers, and further spurred the globalization of trading. More recently, the NYSE and Nasdaq have completed a conversion from fractional to decimal prices under the pressure of the SEC. Technological developments, inter-market competition, and regulation will no doubt continue to reshape securities markets around the world. However, achieving meaningful change in market structure is not an easy task; much remains to be learned about how best to structure a technologically sophisticated, hybrid market that efficiently services the varied needs of diverse participants.

NOTE

1. This material is modified from an equivalent entry from: *The New Palgrave Dictionary of Money and Finance,* by Peter Newman. Reprinted with permission of Palgrave Macmillan. Copyright Σ Newman, Peter.

REFERENCES

Amihud, Y., Ho, T. and Schwartz, R.A. (eds.) (1985). *Market Making and the Changing Structure of the Securities Industry*. Lexington, MA: Lexington Books.

Cohen, K., Maier, S., Schwartz, R.A., and Whitcomb, D. (1979). "Market makers and the market spread: a review of recent literature." *Journal of Financial and Quantitative Analysis,* 14: 813–835.

Cohen, K., Maier, S., Schwartz, R.A., and Whitcomb, D. (1986). *The Microstructure of Securities Markets.* Englewood Cliffs, New Jersey: Prentice-Hall.

Christie, W.G. and Schultz, P.H. (1994a). "Why do NASDAQ market makers avoid odd-eighth quotes?" *Journal of Finance,* 49: 1813–1840.

Christie, W.G., Harris, J., and Schultz, P.H. (1994b). "Why did NASDAQ market makers stop avoiding odd-eighth quotes?" *Journal of Finance,* 49: 1841–1860.

Handa, P. and Schwartz, R.A. (1996)."Limit order trading." *Journal of Finance,* 51: 1835–1861.

Ho, T. and Stoll, H. (1983). "The dynamics of dealer markets under competition." *Journal of Finance,* 38: 1053–1074.

Neuberger, A. and Schwartz, R.A. (1990). "Current developments in the London equity market." *Finanzmarkt und Portfolio Management*, 3: 281–301.

Pagano, M. and Schwartz, R.A. (2003). "A closing call's impact on market quality at Euronext Paris." *Journal of Financial Economics,* 68: 439–484.

Schwartz, R.A. and Francioni, R. (2004). *Equity Markets in Action: The Fundamentals of Market Structure and Trading*. New Jersey: John Wiley.

Seguin, P. (1991). "Transactions reporting, liquidity and volatility: an empirical investigation of national market system listing." Paper given at Western Finance Association Meetings, Jackson Hole, Wyoming, June.

US Securities and Exchange Commission (SEC) (2000). NYSE Rulemaking: Notice of filing of proposed rule change to rescind exchange rule 390; Commission request for comment on issues related to market fragmentation. Release No. SR-NYSE-99–48.

Chapter 39

ACCOUNTING SCANDALS AND IMPLICATIONS FOR DIRECTORS: LESSONS FROM ENRON

PEARL TAN, *Nanyang Technological University, Singapore*
GILLIAN YEO, *Nanyang Technological University, Singapore*

Abstract

We analyze the Enron case to identify the risk factors that potentially led to its collapse and specific issues relating to its aggressive accounting and highlight the lessons for independent directors. In Enron, the interactions between external stimuli, strategies, corporate culture, and risk exposures possibly created an explosive situation that eventually led to its demise. Much of the post-Enron reforms have been directed towards regulating the roles and responsibilities of executive directors and auditors. However, the role of independent directors has received relatively lesser attention. Independent directors should analyze the risks of their companies and understand the pressures that arise from market conditions and firm-specific policies and incentive structures. They also need to close the information gap between executive directors and themselves. A post-Enron era also requires independent directors to change their focus. Traditionally, independent directors have to strike a difficult balance between maximizing returns and minimizing risks. Independent directors may now have to focus on the management of risks, the design and functioning of an effective corporate governance infrastructure, and the moderation of the power bases of dominant executives. Practically, they may also have to reduce the number of independent director appointments to enable them to focus more effectively on a fewer companies.

Keywords: corporate governance; independent directors; risks; incentives; accounting scandals; special purpose entity; hedging; volatility; Sarbanes–Oxley Act; audit committee

39.1. Introduction

The recent spate of accounting scandals raises serious concerns about the opportunistic use of accounting procedures and policies to camouflage fundamental problems in companies. The series of corporate collapses also highlight the failure of corporate governance mechanisms to prevent and detect accounting irregularities. The convergence of several factors, including competitive pressures, conflicts of interest, lack of market discipline, and inherent limitations of accounting standards resulted in an explosive situation whereby managers use aggressive accounting practices to present financial statements that do not reflect economic reality. In this essay, we analyze the Enron case with the objective of determining the risk factors that potentially led to its collapse and specific issues relating to its aggressive accounting and highlight the lessons to be learnt for corporate governance from the perspective of an independent director.

39.2. The Competitive Environment and Incentives for Aggressive Accounting

Enron was formed as a result of merger of two companies in 1985. The merger was funded by debt and pressure had existed from the start for the new company to reduce its debt burden. At about the same time, deregulation of the natural energy industry exposed Enron to substantial operating and price risks arising from the increase in gas supply and volatility in spot prices. However, deregulation also increased opportunities for more flexible and innovative contracts to be drawn up between the producer and buyers. To survive, Enron had to capitalize on these opportunities and became a primary market player through its development of the idea of a Gas Bank. Under this scheme, Enron facilitated the market for energy contracts by buying gas from suppliers and selling to buyers. In acting as an intermediary, Enron guaranteed both the supply and the price, and assumed the related risks in return for transaction fees. Innovations were subsequently extended to markets for basic metals, pulp and paper, and broadband products. Its diversification strategy also included investments in other countries in South America, Europe, and Asia. The business and geographical diversification created new risks for Enron. Its heavy investment in projects such as broadband network assets would pay off only in the long term. However, an immediate debt burden from these acquisitions placed pressure on Enron's balance sheet that was already weighed down by existing debt (Powers et al., 2002).[1]

Although Enron began as an operator of energy-related assets, by the end of the 1990s, the firm had divested a significant portion of its physical assets in what is known as an "asset light strategy" (Permanent Subcommittee on Investigations of the Committee of Governmental Affairs, 2002)[2] and was primarily focused on its trading and financial activities relating to physical energy

commodities. Effectively, the company was transformed from a natural gas supplier into an energy trader and intermediary. It offered specialist services in price risk management strategies and market-making activities. Its dominance in the market for energy contracts gave Enron a first-mover advantage in exploiting information economies of scale. However, the lucrative profits it enjoyed attracted other entrants to the industry and Enron's profit margins began to erode by the end of 2000. Further, as a trader, Enron was compelled to maintain an investment grade rating in order to lower its counter-party risk.

Against this backdrop of competitive pressures, Enron's senior management developed incentive schemes that turned the firm environment into a highly competitive internal market place. An internal ranking system administered by the company's Performance Review Committee became a means of allocating bonus points and determining dismissals. The entire process was described as a "blood sport" (Chaffin and Fidler, 2002) and former employees believed that the basis for reward was largely determined by whether a deal could be reported as revenue or earnings rather than commitment to the company's core values of Respect, Integrity, Communication, and Excellence. Enron's annual incentive awards and the long-term incentive grants are closely tied to company performance measures and stock prices. The annual incentive bonus was pegged to a percentage of recurring after-tax profit, while its long-term incentive grants provided for accelerated vesting provided Enron achieved performance targets linked to compounded growth in earnings-per-share and cumulative shareholder returns.[3] A Senate report on the Enron collapse concluded that Enron's Board of Directors approved lavish and excessive executive compensation and failed to stem the "cumulative cash drain" arising from its incentive schemes.[4]

Hence, Enron appeared to react to risk by creating an environment that generated new risk exposures through its business strategies and reward system that focused on short-term results. Figure 39.1 summarizes the competitive pressures at Enron.

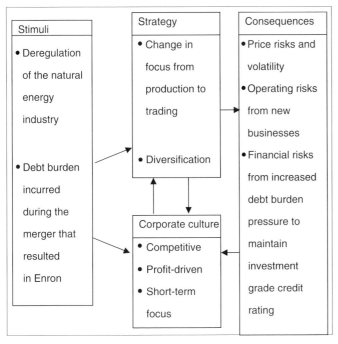

Figure 39.1. Competitive pressures at Enron

39.3. Aggressive Accounting Practices

Enron's accounting practices resulted in removing the liabilities of its balance sheet, improving profitability, and reducing profit volatility. These desired accounting effects were achieved through structuring numerous complex and "innovative" transactions. Many of these transactions involved dealing with special purpose entities that Enron set up in partnership with related parties. The investigating Senate Committee described these practices as "high-risk accounting." The manner in which certain transactions were reported was deemed to be at variance with their true economic substance. The main question that underlies these practices relates to the issue of whether Enron had retained the risks that were purportedly transferred to the special purpose entities.

39.3.1. Effectiveness of "Hedging" Transactions

An example included the entering into transactions that were purported to hedge the volatility of its "marked to market" investments. The hedging

transactions were entered into between Enron and a special purpose entity (SPE).[5] A hedge is effective only if a loss suffered by a hedged party is transferred out to an outside party. In its first hedging transaction, Enron transferred its own stock to the SPE in exchange for a note. The intention of the hedge was to transfer losses to the SPE, through the exercise of an option, should the stock price of a profitable "merchant" investment decline. The SPE purported to take on the risk of price volatility of the investment and to compensate Enron for the loss on its investments.

However, cash was available to the SPE only if the latter sold the Enron stock. Since the SPE was financed by Enron's stock, the transaction was effectively a self-hedging arrangement as the creditworthiness of the SPE was tied to Enron's fortunes. When Enron's stock fell in value in late 2000 and early 2001, the SPE faced a liquidity crisis and could not honor its obligations under the option. Hence, the "hedge" was ineffective because the counter-party's risk was inextricably intertwined with Enron's risk and the hedge did not constitute a true economic hedge.

39.3.2. Control and Risks Relating to Unconsolidated Entities

There are two broad approaches in accounting for an SPE. If an SPE is controlled by an investing company, the assets and liabilities of the SPE are consolidated entirely on to the investing company's balance sheet. Alternatively, if it is not under the investing company's control, it is treated as an investment in a separate entity, with off-balance sheet treatment of the SPE's assets and liabilities. Under applicable accounting rules in the United States, an SPE could receive off-balance-sheet treatment only if independent third-party investors contributed at least 3 percent of the SPE's capital. Some of Enron's dealings raised serious questions about whether this rule was effectively met.

For example, from 1997 to 2001, Enron did not consolidate an SPE called Chewco. In 1997, Enron and the California Public Employees' Retirement System (CalPERS) were joint venture partners in an off-balance sheet investment vehicle called Joint Energy Development Limited Partnership (JEDI). To enable CalPERS to cash out its investment in JEDI in order to invest in a larger Enron venture, Andrew Fastow, the then Chief Financial Officer at Enron, and others at Enron formed an SPE called Chewco to buy CalPERS' interest in JEDI. Thus, Enron was able to continue accounting for JEDI as an off-balance-sheet entity on the basis that the holdings by Enron staff members and related parties constitute outside capital at risk. According to SEC investigations,[6] Fastow, secretly controlled Chewco. Hence, a serious question arose as to whether Enron, through a related party, had effective control over major operating and financial policies of Chewco. Further, Enron and its related SPEs provided guarantees and cash collateral on bank funding to Chewco, indicating that equity at risk was effectively borne by Enron rather than independent third parties. In November 2001, both Enron and its auditors, Andersen, concluded that Chewco was an SPE without sufficient outside equity and should have been consolidated. The retroactive consolidation of Chewco from 1997 through 2001 had an astounding effect on the financial statements. Profits decreased by a total of $405 million over the period of restatement and additional debt of $711 million was recognized on the balance sheet in 1997.[7]

39.4. The Role of Corporate Governance

Theoretically, Enron had in place an impressive array of corporate governance mechanisms. Outside directors were well respected and highly qualified individuals in the fields of accounting, finance, and law. The Board of Directors had several committees to review various aspects of the company's policies and operations. There was separation of the offices of the Chairman and Chief Executive Officer. The external auditors were a Big Five accounting firm. However, following the company's massive financial collapse, serious doubts

arose as to the effectiveness of these institutional arrangements. The Senate Investigating Committee found that the Enron's Board failed to safeguard Enron shareholders and contributed to the collapse of the company by allowing Enron to engage in high-risk accounting, inappropriate conflict of interest transactions, extensive undisclosed off-balance-sheet activities, and excessive executive compensation.[8] Further, the Board was also found to have failed to ensure the independence of the company's external auditor, Andersen who provided internal audit and consulting services as well.[9]

Many valuable lessons can be learnt from the Enron case to prevent the derailing of the effective functioning of governance mechanisms. We focus our discussion on the role of independent directors. Much of the post-Enron reforms have been directed towards regulating the roles and responsibilities of executive directors and auditors. However, the role of independent directors has received relatively less attention than that of other corporate governance agents. We discuss below some implications of the Enron collapse on the role of independent directors.

(i) What is the primary role of independent directors? The multiple roles that independent directors have to undertake require them to strike a difficult balance between maximizing returns and minimizing risks. Their purview is wide, ranging from activities that have a "profit" focus to others that have a "defensive" focus. Independent directors potentially find themselves in an identity crisis. For example, if an independent director has to operate within an Enron-type environment, the director is confronted with an aggressive risk-taking internal environment. The question arises as to whether the independent director should act as a thorn in the managers' flesh or go with the flow of an aggressive managerial style for the sake of profit maximization?

The lesson from Enron is very clear that it does not pay to sacrifice the defensive role when risk factors are overwhelming and the long-run survival of the company is at stake. While post-Enron legislation such as the Sarbanes–Oxley Act of 2002 is primarily directed towards establishing mandates for insiders, audit committee board members and external auditors, much less is said about the responsibilities of independent directors *per se*. However, the implicit responsibilities of independent directors are clearly reinforced by laws that impose fiduciary duties on directors to act in good faith, with reasonable care, and in the best interest of the corporation and its shareholders. The Conference Board also reiterates directors' role to monitor management and to ensure their ethical and legal compliance (The Conference Board, 2003).[10]

Hence, independent directors owe a primary duty of care to outside investors. Their priority should be towards establishing and ensuring a corporate environment and infrastructure wherein managerial stewardship is executed without compromising the long-run interests of the firm and its stakeholders. They, more than anyone else, are best placed to limit the excesses of a dominant Chief Executive.

(ii) Independent directors have to bridge the information gap between executive directors and themselves. The Conference Board emphasizes that directors need to understand, among other things, the business strategies they approve, the risks and vulnerabilities arising from the strategies, growth opportunities, debt levels, and company's capital allocation of the companies under their purview.[11] Following the Enron experience, independent directors are well advised to understand the internal dynamics, managerial incentives, and power bases within the corporate environment and to adopt a healthy skepticism of strategies that potentially advance managerial interests over that of external investors. They should be keenly aware of the threats posed by dominant Chief Executive Officers and key personnel and the risks of opportunistic managerial behaviour.

(iii) Greater commitment in terms of time and effort are expected of independent directors to meet the governance objective. Independent directors must take a proactive role in governance and not rely solely on external auditors, legal counsel, or key executives to provide them the necessary assurance. For example, when the Enron Board was asked why they moved so quickly in their approval of an unusual hedging transaction, the response was that the company had obtained a fairness opinion from an outside accounting firm.[12] On another proposal, the Board relied on the company's legal counsel to advise if anything was amiss on a particular memorandum. Had the directors reviewed the memorandum for themselves, they would have noted that key company executives were involved in the arrangement that gave rise to conflicts of interest.[13] Interviewed Board members told the investigating Senate Subcommittee members that they assumed that the then Chief Executive Officer had actively reviewed and approved the fairness of the unusual business proposals and the compensation controls.[14] Enron's directors were also found to have knowingly allowed Enron's use of "high-risk" accounting without enforcing restraint.[15] Hence, the Senate Report underscores the principle that evidence of a suspect transaction or activity that is known to a director must be questioned and examined diligently and thoroughly, regardless of the views of other experts.

The implications for independent directors are enormous. The days when an independent director held several of such appointments concurrently are likely to be over. Independent directors may have to be selective in choosing appointments so as not to spread themselves too thinly. They must also be prepared to commit resources and time and change the mindset that their appointment is a "part-time" one. They may also have to assess the risks of companies to determine if they are willing to undertake the fiduciary responsibility of monitoring such a company.

39.5. Conclusion

The Enron case has painful lessons for the business community. A seemingly successful company was apparently derailed through the use of highly risky transactions and aggressive accounting that temporarily boosted profits and reduced debt. The question arises as to why the corporate guardians of Enron did not prevent these transactions from occurring. Following Enron and other accounting scandals, a re-examination needs to be carried out of the role and responsibilities of independent directors. This paper suggests that significantly greater challenges are posed to independent directors in a post-Enron world to understand more of the risks, accounting practices, and managerial opportunism existing in the companies under their purview and to take a more proactive role in governance, which inevitably requires a substantial commitment of their time and resources.

NOTES

1. Hereinafter referred to as the "Powers Report."
2. Hereinafter referred to as the "Senate Report," p. 7.
3. Proxy Statement Pursuant to Section 14(a) of the Securities Exchange Act of 1934, 2 March 2001, EDGARPlus(R).
4. The Senate Report, p. 3.
5. Details of the hedging transactions are found in The Powers' Report, pp. 13–15.
6. Securities and Exchange Commission, Litigation Release 17762, 2 October 2002.
7. The Powers' Report, p. 42.
8. The Senate Report, p. 11.
9. The Senate Report, p. 54.
10. Hereinafter referred to as The Conference Board Report.
11. The Conference Board Report, p. 9.
12. The Senate Report, p. 27.
13. The Senate Report, p. 28.
14. The Senate Report, pp. 30–31.
15. The Senate Report, pp. 14–24.

REFERENCES

Chaffin, J. and Fidler, S. (2002). "The Enron Collapse." *Financial Times*, London, 9: 30.

Permanent Subcommittee on Investigations of the Committee of Governmental Affairs.(2002). United States Senate, The Role of the Board of Directors in Enron's Collapse Report, 107–170.

Powers, Jr. W.C. , Troubh, R.S., and Winokur, Jr. H.R. (2002). "Report of investigation by the special investigative committee of the board of directors of enron Corp."

Securities and Exchange Commission. (2002). "Litigation Release No. 17762."

The Conference Board (2003). "Commission on public trust and private enterprise."

Chapter 40

AGENT-BASED MODELS OF FINANCIAL MARKETS

NICHOLAS S. P. TAY, *University of San Francisco, USA*

Abstract

This paper introduces the agent-based modeling methodology and points out the strengths of this method over traditional analytical methods of neoclassical economics. In addition, the various design issues that will be encountered in the design of an agent-based financial market are discussed.

Keywords: agent-based models; computer simulation; bounded rationality; heterogeneous agents; learning; co-evolution; complex adaptive system; artificial intelligence; neural networks; classifiers; genetic algorithms; genetic programming

40.1. Introduction

The sort of phenomena that are interesting in finance and yet difficult to investigate analytically involve the complex interactions among many self-interested heterogeneous boundedly rational agents acting within the constraints imposed by either formal or informal institutions or authorities. To outrival their opponents, each and every agent must continually evolve to adapt to changes that may arise either from exogenous perturbations to the environment or endogenous transitions caused by agents changing their strategies or modifying their behaviors as they learn more about the behaviors of the other agents and the environment they reside in. A good example of such complex adaptive systems is the stock market.

A natural way to study a complex adaptive system like the stock market is to use an agent-based model which entails simulating the stock market on a computer from the bottom up with a large number of interacting heterogeneous boundedly rational artificial agents that are created to mimic the traders in the stock market. Once the environment of the stock market and the behaviors of the agents are specified and the initial state of the model is set, the dynamics of the model from the initial state forward will be driven entirely by agent–agent interactions, and not by some exogenously determined systems of equations. Hence, if any macroscopic regularity emerges from the model, it must be a product of the endogenous repeated local interactions of the autonomous agents and the overall institutional constraints. This is the spirit of the agent-based modeling approach.

What makes the agent-based modeling methodology particularly appealing? To begin with, analytical tractability is not an issue since this approach relies on computer simulations to understand the complex model. Quite the reverse, it is inconceivable how one could obtain closed form solutions of a model as complex as the stock market without first diluting drastically the authenticity of the model. Although analytically tractable heterogeneous agent rational expectations models have been around, the complexity and realism that are captured in agent-based models are beyond the reach of those analytical models.

For instance, consider the problem that a decision maker faces when the outcome is contingent on the decisions to be made by all the participating heterogeneous decision makers, each with their own unique preferences and quirks and private information that are not directly observable by the other decision makers. This decision problem is inherently ill defined and cannot be solved through mathematical deduction or analytical modeling. In real life, when confronted with such an ill-defined situation, decision makers often rely on the rules of thumb that they have distilled from years and years of experience to guide them in their decision-making. This decision making process is formally known as inductive reasoning and it can be captured naturally with the agent-based approach by running computer simulations of a large number of interacting artificial agents who make decisions using rules of thumb that they distill from their repeated interactions with each other.

The ability to build more realistic models with the agent-based method often allows agent-based models to reveal a much richer set of behaviors that are embedded in a system which may otherwise be overlooked by traditional equation-based models. For instance, Parunak et al. (1998) in comparing the differences between equation-based modeling and agent-based modeling of a supply network have found that equation-based model fails to produce many of the rich effects, such as memory effect of backlogged orders, transition effects, or the amplification of order variation, which are observed in an agent-based model of the same supply network. In addition, various agent-based models (Farmer and Joshi, 2000; Johnson et al., 2001; LeBaron et al., 1999; Tay and Linn, 2001) have been successful in accounting for real financial markets phenomena such as market crashes, mean reversion, relatively high level of trading, technical trading, excess volatility, and volatility clustering. These are phenomena that analytical representative agent models of financial markets have tolled to explain without much success.

Another serious shortcoming of analytical representative agent models of financial markets is that by design these models do not specify the dynamic process that will need to happen in order to arrive at the equilibrium or equilibria that are characterized in these models. Consequently, for models that produce multiple equilibria, it is unclear which equilibrium among the multiple equilibria agents would converge on. In contrast, the events that unfold in a computer simulation of an agent-based model are completely transparent, and can be recorded hence providing the modeler a means to go back in the time line of evolution to understand how certain equilibrium or other global regularities came into existence.

The agent-based methodology therefore offers important advantages over the traditional analytical tools of neoclassical economics as it allows a researcher to obtain more germane results. Needless to say, the use of computer simulations as a tool for studying complex models has only became feasible in recent years because of the availability of fast and cheap computing power. Although the agent-based modeling methodology is still in its infancy, there is already a considerable literature on agent-based models. Leigh Tesfatsion at the Iowa State University maintains a website at *http://www.econ.iastate.edu/tesfatsi/ace.htm* to facilitate access to the extensive resources related to the agent-based modeling methodology, and to keep researchers in this field abreast of the latest developments.

In the introductory remarks on her website, Tesfatsion observes that agent-based research may generally be organized according to one of the following four research objectives: (1) empirical understanding, (2) normative understanding, (3) qualitative insight and theory generation, and (4) methodological advancement. The first objective focuses on seeking answers that are established on the repeated interactions of agents to explain the emergence of global regularities in agent-based models. Some examples of global regularities in financial markets are mean reversion and volatility clustering. Researchers in this group are interested in understanding if certain types of observed global regularities can be attributed to certain types of agent-based worlds. The second objective concerns using agent-based models as laboratories to aid in the discovery and design of good economic policies or good institutional structures. Researchers with this objective in mind are interested in using agent-based models to evaluate whether certain economic policies or institutional designs and processes will promote socially desirable outcomes over time among agents that are driven solely by their self interests. Tesfatsion phrased the third objective as "How can the full potentiality of economic systems be better understood through a better understanding of their complete phase portraits (equilibria plus basins of attraction)?" Unlike analytical models, the causal mechanisms in agent-based models are not direct and are very difficult to discern because of the complex nature of the interactions among the agents and between the agents and the environment. The goal here is to use the phase portraits as a means to enrich our understanding of the causal mechanism in these systems. The fourth objective addresses issues related to improving the methods and tools used by agent-based researchers.

For someone who is just starting out in this line of research, it is worthwhile to begin by reading "A Guide for Newcomers to Agent-based Modeling in the Social Sciences" by Axelrod and Tesfatsion which is available on the homepage of Tesfatsion's website. In addition, it is beneficial to read the survey articles written by Hommes (2004), Duffy (2004), LeBaron et al. (1999), LeBaron (2000, 2004a), and Tesfatsion (2002) and a book by Batten (2000) that provides an overview of agent-based models and offers some historical perspectives of this methodology.

The next section discusses the design issues that will be encountered in the design of an agent-based model. This discussion benefited greatly from the insights that LeBaron has provided in his excellent overviews of the various design issues (LeBaron, 2000, 2001c, 2004a).

40.2. Design Considerations

A typical agent-based model is made up of a set of autonomous agents that encapsulate the behaviors of the various individuals in a system we are interested in studying and the investigation involves simulating on a computer the interactions of these agents over time. Accordingly, there are two important design considerations in the development of an agent-based model – the design of the agents and the design of the environment.

How naive or sophisticated the agents should be modeled really depends on the objective of the research. For instance, if the research objective is to understand how certain market structures affect the allocative efficiency of a market independent of the intelligence of the agents as in Gode and Sunder (1993), then one can simply model the agents as naive "zero intelligence" agents. Zero intelligence agents are agents that are not capable of formulating strategies or learning from their experience; hence their behaviors will be completely random. Gode and Sunder populated their double auction market with zero intelligence agents that are designed to submit their bids and asks at random over a predefined range and remarkably they discover that zero intelligence agents when subjected to a budget constraint are able to allocate the assets in the market at over 97 percent efficiency. The lesson to be learned here is that not all macroscopic regularities that emerge from agent-based models are necessarily consequences of the actions taken by the agents as they evolve and learn from their interactions. In this case, the high level of allocative efficiency that is attained in a double auction market is due to the unique structure of the market itself.

However, in many agent-based models, the objective is to investigate the outcome of the interactions among many heterogeneous agents that are designed to mimic their counterparts in the real world. In these models, the key design issues related to the design of the agents are the agents' preferences and their decision-making behaviors.

Agents could have either myopic or intertemporal preferences. The latter is more realistic but will make the model much more complex. As we have alluded to earlier, the decision problem that the agents face is usually ill defined, and thus cannot be solved by deductive reasoning. A reasonable solution is to assume that the agents rely on inductive reasoning to arrive at a decision (see Arthur, 1994, 1999; Rescher, 1980). Inductive reasoning or induction is a means for finding the best available answers to questions that transcend the information at hand. In real life, we often have to draw conclusions based upon incomplete information. In these instances, logical deduction fails because the information we have in hand leaves gaps in our reasoning. In order to complete our reasoning, we fill those gaps in the least risky, minimally problematic way, as determined by plausible best-fit considerations. Consequently, the conclusions we draw using induction are suggested by the data at hand rather than logically deduced from them.

Inductive reasoning follows a two-step process: possibility elaboration and possibility reduction. The first step involves creating a spectrum of plausible alternatives based on our experience and the information available. In the second step, these alternatives are tested to see how well they answer the question at hand or how well they connect the existing incomplete premises to explain the data observed. The alternative offering the "best fit" is then accepted as a viable explanation. Subsequently, when new information becomes available or when the underlying premises change, the fit of the current alternative may degrade. When this happens a better alternative will take over.

How can inductive reasoning be implemented in an agent-based financial market model? Arthur (1994, 1999) envisions inductive reasoning in a financial market, taking place as follows. Initially, each agent in the market creates a multitude of decision-making rules (this corresponds to the possibility elaboration step discussed above). Next, the decision-making rules are simultaneously tested for their effectiveness based on some cri-

teria. Finally, effective decision-making rules are retained and acted upon in buying and selling decisions. Conversely, unreliable rules are dropped (this corresponds to the possibility reduction step). The rules that are dropped are then replaced with new ones in the first step and the process is carried out repeatedly to model how individuals learn inductively in a constantly evolving financial market.

Some examples of criteria that have been used for appraising the effectiveness of the decision rules includes utility maximization, wealth maximization, and forecast errors minimization. Once a decision has been made on a criterion for evaluating the decision-making rules, the next task is to decide the length of historical data to be used in computing the criterion. Although many agent-based models tend to allow the agents to adopt identical history length, this is not necessary. It is in fact more realistic to permit agents in the same model to adopt different history length as in LeBaron (2001a,b).

To take the modeling to the next step, decision will have to be made concerning what the decision making rules look like and how they are to be generated in the models? One possibility is to model the decision-making rules after actual trading strategies used in real financial markets. The benefit of this approach is that the results are likely to be tractable and precise and it will also shed light on the interaction among these actual trading strategies. However, this approach does not allow the agents any flexibility in modifying the strategies or developing new strategies. This could impose ad hoc restrictions on the model's dynamics. Some common tools that have been employed to allow the agents more degrees of freedom in structuring and manipulating the decision making rules as they learn are artificial neural networks (LeBaron, 2001a), genetic programming (Chen and Yeh, 2001), and classifiers that are evolved with genetic algorithms (LeBaron et al., 1999). Even with these artificial intelligence tools, the modeler will need to predefine a set of information variables and functional forms to be used in the strategies or decision-making rules. Although these tools can successfully mimic the inductive reasoning process described earlier, it is not known if any of these tools indeed faithfully represent the inductive reasoning used by actual human traders. It is also unclear at this juncture whether this issue matters. Another related decision that has to be made by the modeler concerns whether the agents should be allowed to learn only from their own experiences or from the collective experience of all the agents in the model. The latter is known as "social learning."

We will turn our attention next to the design of the financial market environment. Most agent-based models simplify the environment to a market with one risky asset and one risk-free asset. Clearly, this is an oversimplification of actual financial markets, but there are good reasons for doing so. Given that the agent-based methodology is new and researchers barely comprehend the implications of this methodology, it is prudent for them to begin by exploring what the new method can reveal about the dynamics in a fairly simple market environment. Moreover, doing so also facilitates comparisons with results from well-known neoclassical models of a market with one risky asset and one risk-free asset.

Another key design issue concerns the design of the trading mechanism that has a direct influence on how prices are determined in the market and how the market is cleared. LeBaron (2004a) observes that most of the agent-based models employ one of the following four designs for trading mechanism. The simplest trading mechanism is one that allows mutually beneficial trades to be consummated between agents that meet at random. Though this trading mechanism is quite simple, it bears some resemblance to the trades conducted on the floor of the Chicago futures and options exchanges and over the telephone in the foreign exchange markets. But for markets where the market makers play an important role in filling the buy and sell orders, this mechanism would not be an adequate representation. A second trading mechanism, which is more sophisticated

than the previous one is an analytical market-clearing device akin to one espoused in Grossman (1976). This device provides a closed form solution for the market-clearing price hence enabling the agent-based markets to be cleared analytically each period. A critical advantage of this design is that it avoids having to deal with the difficult issue of explicitly modeling the decision-making behaviors of the risk-adverse market maker. Unfortunately, this advantage is also a serious shortcoming in that this is not a realistic picture of what is happening in real markets that trade continuously and are rarely in equilibrium. The third trading mechanism attempts to address this issue. It assumes that agents submit trade orders to buy (D_t) and sell (S_t) at a price, p_t, which is announced beforehand by a market maker. The market maker then appraises the aggregate of the orders submitted by the agents, and adjusts next period price by a fixed fraction of the excess demand or supply according to $p_{t+1} = p_t + \alpha(D(p_t) - S(p_t))$. Granted that this adaptive price process may be a more reasonable model of how prices adjust in real markets, the problem with this mechanism is that it does not address how the market maker manages the imbalance between demand and supply in the market. Moreover, there is no guidance on how the parameter value for α should be determined and certain α values may in fact cause the market to deviate far from the market clearing price for a substantial period. The most sophisticated and also the most realistic trading mechanism is one that either models the market maker explicitly or implements an order book system that can accept and cross out the buy and sell orders from agents according to some defined procedure (Audet et al., 2001). The only downside of this approach is that the design of the agent-based model is much more complicated as many details at the institutional as well as the agent level will need to be clearly specified. But, this is inevitable if the objective is to simulate realistic market microstructure behavior.

To sum up, there are many design questions that need to be addressed in the development of an agent-based model and there is yet no clear guidance on how best to address these questions. Inevitably, design decisions will have to be made however arbitrary these decisions may be but it is important to keep in mind that the choices made by the designer may ultimately have important consequences on the results.

REFERENCES

Arthur, W.B. (1994). "Inductive reasoning and bounded rationality." *American Economic Review*, 84(2): 406.

Arthur, W.B. (1999). "Complexity and the economy." *Science*, 284(5411): 107.

Audet, N., Gravelle, T., and Yang, J. (2001). "Optimal market structure: does one shoe fit all?" *Technical Report*. Ottawa, CA: Bank of Canada.

Batten, D.F. (2000). *Discovering artificial economics: How agents learn and economies evolve*. Boulder, CO: Westview Press.

Chen, S.-H and Yeh, C.-H. (2001). "Evolving traders and the business school with genetic programming: a new architecture of the agent-based artificial stock market." *Journal of Economic Dynamics and Control*, 25: 363–394.

Duffy, J. (2006). "Agent-based models and human subject experiments," in K.L. Judd and L. Tesfatsion, (eds.), *Handbook of Computational Economics Volume 2: Agent-Based Computational Economics, Handbooks in Economics Series*. Amsterdam: Elsevier North-Holland.

Farmer, J.D. and Joshi, S. (2000). "The price dynamics of common trading strategies." Santa Fe Institute Working Paper 00-12-069, Santa Fe, New Mexico.

Gode, D.K. and Sunder, S. (1993). "Allocative efficiency of markets with zero intelligence traders." *Journal of Political Economy*, 101: 119–137.

Grossman, S.J. (1976). "On the efficiency of competitive stock markets where traders have diverse information." *Journal of Finance*, 31(2), 573.

Hommes, C.H. (2006). "Heterogeneous agent models in economics and finance." In K.L. Judd. and L. Tesfatsion (eds.) *Handbook of Computational Economics Volume 2: Agent-Based Computational Economics, Handbooks in Economics Series*. Amsterdam: Elsevier North-Holland.

Johnson, N.F., Lamper, D., Jeffries, P., Hart, M.L., and Howison, S. (2001). "Application of multi agent games to the prediction of financial time-series." *Physica A*, (299): 222–227.

LeBaron, B., Arthur, W.B., and Palmer, R. (1999). "Time series properties of an artificial stock market." *Journal of Economic Dynamics and Control*, 23:(9,10), 1487–1516.

LeBaron, B. (2000). "Agent-based computational finance: suggested readings and early research." *Journal of Economic Dynamics and Control*, 24(5–7): 679–702.

LeBaron, B. (2001a). "Empirical regularities from interacting long and short memory investors in an agent-based stock market." *IEEE Transactions on Evolutionary Computation*, 5: 442–455.

LeBaron, B. (2001b). "Evolution and time horizons in an agent-based stock market." *Macroeconomic Dynamics*, 5(2): 225–254.

LeBaron, Blake (2001c). *A builder's guide to agent-based financial markets*. Technical Report, International Business School, Brandeis University, Waltham, MA.

LeBaron, B. (2006). "Agent-based computational finance," in K.L. Judd and L. Tesfatsion, (eds.), *Handbook of Computational Economics Volume 2: Agent-Based Computational Economics, Handbooks in Economics Series*. Amsterdam: Elsevier North-Holland.

Parunak, H., Savit, R., and Riolo, R.L. (1998). "Agent-based modeling vs. equation-based modeling: a case study and users' guide." In MABS, Sichman, C. and Gilbert (eds.) *Multi-agent systems and Agent-based Simulation*. Berlin: Springer-Verlag.

Rescher, N. (1980). *Induction: An essay on the Justification of Inductive Reasoning*. Pittsburgh: University of Pittsburgh Press.

Tay, N.S.P. and Linn, S.C (2001). "Fuzzy inductive reasoning, expectation formation and the behavior of security prices." *Journal of Economic Dynamics and Control*, 25(3,4): 321–361.

Tesfatsion, L. (2002). "Agent-based computational economics: growing economies from the bottom up." *Artificial Life*, 8(1): 55–82.

Chapter 41

THE ASIAN BOND MARKET

KHAIRY TOURK, *Illinois Institute of Technology, USA*

Abstract

One major factor that led to the 1997 Southeast Asian financial crisis was the reliance of the afflicted nations on heavy borrowing from western banks. The crisis has shown the massive need for establishing a regional bond market. Given the huge foreign reserves held by Asian central banks, at present, it is crucial to create a vehicle in order to preserve Asian capital within the region.

Recent progress has been made in the direction of creating regional bond markets in the areas of Asian Bond Fund (ABF) that deals in foreign currency and Asian Basket Currency (ABC) bonds that deals in local currency.

The past few years have seen major improvements in the issuance of Asian government bonds. Yet, the area of corporate bonds in the region still remains clearly underdeveloped due to the lack of credit ratings at investment-grade. Addressing the issue of ratings is one of the real challenges that must be overcome before the Asian region could have a viable bond market.

Keywords: Executive Meeting of East Asia and Pacific (EMEAP) Central Banks; Takatashi Ito; Thansim Shinawatra; First Asian Bond Fund (ABF-1); ABC bond Corporation; The Asian Bond Market Initiative (ABMI); credit enhancement; Colletaralized Bond Obligation (CBO); Securitized Asian Corporate Bonds; International Rating Agencies

41.1. Introduction

Before the Southeast Asia financial crisis, the standard works on the role of capital markets in economic growth (Goldsmith, 1965, 1985; Hakansson, 1992; McKinnon, 1971, 1991) had focused mainly on the *equity* markets. Thus, the establishment of bond market in emerging nations has not received the attention it deserves in the finance literature.[1] For decades, the emerging economies in Asia had grown rapidly without the presence of an active bond market (Dalla et al., 1995; Emery, 1997; Levine, 1997; Sheng, 1994; Yam, 1997). In these economies, bond markets are very small relative to equity markets and the banking system.[2] One of the reasons that enticed Asian firms to borrow heavily from western banks before 1997 was the lack of an Asian bond market.[3] A major consequence of the crisis was to breathe life into the concept of setting up an Asian bond market in order to enhance financial stability (Alba, 1999; Rhee, 2003; Tourk, 2004).

A viable bond market gives the society a true measure of the opportunity cost of funds. In the absence of such market there is a loss of an important signal to channel savings into proper investments.[4] Another drawback is the distortion of the incentives for risk taking which raises the specter of a banking crisis.[5]

Overdependence on bank borrowing means that banks can extract rents from the borrowers as the cost of borrowing is higher than the case where firms have the option of accessing funds from a bond market.[6] Long-term investment is also biased under bank-centered loans since banking institutions tend to offer loans for periods that are significantly shorter than the life span of long-term bonds.

The concept of an Asian bond market is not a new one. The original idea was proposed by the Asian Development Bank, which in the early 1990s issued dollar denominated "Dragon Bonds."[7] The target of these bonds was the Asian investor. Unfortunately, the bonds did not succeed in attracting enough demand because of their low liquidity.

After 1997, the idea of an Asian bond as a vehicle to preserve long-term Asian capital within the region was a direct response to the financial crisis. The new initiative was taken by Japan's Ministry of Finance (MOF). It was supported by the United States. Thanks to the enthusiastic promotion by the Thai Prime Minister Thansin Shinawatra, the Asian bond market has become a reality. He floated the idea in October 2002, at the East Asian Economic Summit organized by the World Economic Forum. Stemming from this, an Asian Bond Fund was established in June 2003 by the head of central banks in the region.

The *raison d'etre* of the fund is for Asian governments and other entities to issue bonds in order to reinvest part of the region's savings in Asia itself (Oh, 2003; Sonakul, 2000]. "Since bond rating and settlement is to be handled within the region, the use of dollar bonds will become unnecessary. Eventually it should be possible to issue bonds denominated in regional currency or a basket of regional currencies."[8]

Developing local bond market (Mungthin, 2000) is important in reducing the Asian countries exposure to maturity and exchange rate risks and "sudden stops" in the availability of international capital.[9] The benefits include an increase in the efficiency of allocating surplus funds and the retention of Asian capital. In 2004, central banks of Asia held roughly $1.1 trillion of US Treasuries. In just two years beginning at the start of 2002, the dollar dropped around 26 percent against a basket of six major currencies.[10]

For Asian corporations, they benefit from the diversification of funding sources (i.e. less reliance on borrowing from domestic banks) and improving transparency, leading to better corporate governance. Another advantage is that it would give Asian governments more policy instruments to stabilize their financial markets.[11]

The Asian Bond Market has taken two forms: first an Asian bond market led by East Asia-Pacific (EMEAP) Central Banks and the second is represented by the Asian Bond Market Initiative (ABMI), proposed in 2002 by Japan's MOF, and under the supervision of the ASEAN + 3 finance ministers.

41.2. The Asian Bond Market launched by EMEAP Central Banks

At the beginning of 2005, the foreign exchange reserves in the Asian regions were around $2 trillion dollars, which equals more than 50 percent of the world's reserves.[12] These Asian resources could be channeled into banking, as well as other types of finance,[13] to enable Asian nations to create wealth in each other's economy. Thus, the necessity to establish an infrastructure for bond markets, both primary and secondary. Recent progress has been made in the direction of creating regional bond markets in the areas of Asian Bond Fund (ABF) that deals in *foreign* currency and Asian Basket Currency (ABC) bonds that deals in *local* currency.[14]

The first Asian bond fund (ABF-1) was launched in June 2003 by the central banks of the eleven countries who are members of EMEAP.[15] It consists of $1 billion worth of foreign reserves, which is being invested in a basket of *dollar-denominated* bonds issued in eight Asian economies[16] by sovereign and quasi-sovereign entities in the EMEAP countries, except in Japan, Australia, and New Zealand. The Bank of International Settlements (BIS) will be managing the fund. It has been indicated that the 11-member group plan to consider extending ABF investments to bonds denominated in *Asian* currencies. In December 2004, a second fund was launched with $2 billion in governments' capital to invest in corporate debt issued in local currencies.[17]

41.3. The Asian Bond Market Initiative (ABMI)

The Asian Bond Market Initiative (ABMI) is focused on the creation of a proper environment where access by a wider variety of issuers to the regional bond markets is facilitated (Taniguchi, 2003). Since summer of 2003, working groups representing the ASEAN + 3 finance ministers have defined specific subjects to be reported on to the ASEAN + 3 finance ministers meeting in 2004.[18]

One important step in the creation of proper environment is for the government to establish a benchmark yield curve to serve as the risk-free rate for the pricing of other securities.[19] A program of regular issues at appropriate maturities (e.g., three month, six month, one year, three years, five years, and eventually ten years) should be set up.[20] The interest rate on government bond should be market-determined. It must be kept in mind that minimizing the cost of government borrowing may be in conflict with the development of this market-determined rate. Thus, the government should refrain from any manipulation of the bond market (i.e. requiring some institutions to hold government debt, devising preferential tax treatment for public sector debt) with the purpose of reducing the cost of its borrowing. Doing that would negatively affect the efficiency of the bond market and lead to distortions in the allocation of capital.[20]

41.4. The ABC Bond Corporation

The creation of the ABC bond corporation, dealing in local currency, is the result of a Japanese MOF initiative. One major benefit of the ABC government bonds is that they represent a benchmark for the region. Ito (2003a,b) proposed the establishment of this corporation in order to serve as a depository for financial assets supplied by participating governments in the form of local currency denominated government bonds.

For the ABC government bonds to be priced correctly, it is important that the public sector should be vigorously involved in establishing a deep domestic bond market. Governments must cooperate to issue standardized bonds that can be put into depository to form a standardized basket (i.e. standardized maturity; standardized interest rate calculation, pre-announced coordinated issuance schedule, interest payment methods, depository location).[21] To reduce the weight of the dollar in Asian foreign reserves, ABC bonds that are issued offshore will be treated as foreign reserves.

In the first phase, the ABC Bond Corporation would issue bonds that match the value of the assets. In the second phase, the Corporation may issue bonds that match the value of corporate bonds denominated in various Asian currencies. As such, the ABC Bond Corporation operates along the same lines as a Special Purpose Vehicle (SPV) with asset-backed securities. It is here that the private sector can establish a corporate bond market and asset-backed securities denominated in the basket currency. Corporate bonds are brought into the depository, just like government bonds, and ABC corporate bonds can be issued. The benchmark yield is provided by the ABC sovereign bonds. Because the credit risk is higher, the yield would also be higher. Furthermore, as these bonds can now be sold in the region at large, instead of one country alone, this would reduce the issuing costs. Another advantage is the direct relationship between investors and borrowers.

One major attraction of issuing ABC bonds is that they will diversify currency risk. Firms exporting in the Asian region will issue liabilities that match their revenue streams denominated in the local currencies. By being less dependent on bank loans they will be less affected by banking crisis.[22]

The ABC Bond Corporation operates as an issuer of bonds to be bought by Asian institutional investors. Expected buyers of the ABC bonds include Asian central banks and pension funds. They also includes institutional investors, both Asian and foreign. This is different from the ABF, which serves as an investment vehicle for Asian central banks, acting as a buyer of dollar denominated bonds issued by Asian borrowers.

It should be kept in mind that since pension funds and central banks tend to have passive investment strategies, both the ABF and ABC invested bonds might not be powerful enough instruments in the promotion of market liquidity on the secondary market.[23]

41.5. Credit Enhancement

As explained above, the bonds issued by the ABC Bond Corporation match the value of the underlying assets of this entity, which are denominated in government bonds of various Asian currencies. Even though pledged bonds are backed by full faith and credit of participating Asian governments, the question of credit enhancement comes into play because international rating agencies view various governments differently with respect to credit risk. The enhancement could be either *internal* or *external*.

The most used form of internal enhancement is through the restructuring of the distribution of pooled cash flows to create a new instrument called a Collateralized Bond Obligation (CBO). Under this system, two tranches of ABC bonds could be issued: senior bonds with higher credit rating and lower yields and subordinate bonds with lower credit rating but higher yields.[24]

External enhancement includes third party guarantees provided by official financial institutions (e.g. Development Bank of Singapore, ADB, JBIC), letters of credit by leading international commercial banks and bond insurance provided by monoline bond companies.[25]

In order to transform Asian corporate bonds from speculative-grade assets to investment-grade assets, Asian governments, Asian banks, and Asian credit insurers could offer full or partial guarantees on the issuer. This will facilitate the issuance of credit insurance by top-rated insurers to bond issuers with poor credit ratings. Asian governments could also play an important role in strengthening a system of Asian-based credit insurers.[26]

41.6. Securitized Asian Corporate Bonds

The past few years have seen major improvements in the issuance of Asian government bonds. Yet, the area of corporate bonds in the region still remains clearly underdeveloped (Claessens et al., 1998) due to the lack of credit ratings at investment-grade.

One way to raise the quality of Asian corporate bonds to investment-grade assets is to pool the bonds together making them securitized corporate bonds. A large asset pool of this kind can be listed and traded on the exchange or in the OTC market. This has the advantage of satisfying the market demand for high-yield assets with credit protection. These assets are considered safe because top-rated credit insurers insure the cash flows from the bonds.

So far, Asian securitization has developed very slowly in the region.[27] At present, the investor base for Asian corporate bonds is extremely narrow. While credit enhancement would increase the participation of both Asian institutional and international investors, there is also a need to attract *individual* investors to be active participants in Asian debts. In this regard, the government policies could be important in developing bonds of smaller par value that the general public is enticed to invest in.

Another policy is government support of mutual funds that invest primarily in Asian *corporate* bonds. An encouraging development is the establishment of the Asian bond fund whose objective is to invest in Asian debt securities. It was established in May 2003, by nine Asian governments, where each contributed up to 1 percent of its foreign reserve to the fund. These governments consist of Thailand, China, Japan, Hong Kong SAR, South Korea, Singapore, Indonesia, Malaysia, and the Philippines. It has been suggested that in order to encourage the participation of individual investors,[28] the government bond fund can be further securitized to become either a closed or open-ended fund.[29] Assets in the fund must be insured in order to minimize the credit risk of individual investors. Due to its large market capitalization and prospective large number of investors, both institutional and individual, the liquid government bond fund can flourish into an actively traded asset capable of nurturing a number of financial derivatives. Such derivatives would enable international investors and credit insurers to hedge the credit and market risk in Asia. In short, the Asian governments can play a crucial role in asset securitization that would transform sovereign and corporate debts into attractive investment vehicles for the general public.[30]

41.7. Efficient Financial Intermediaries

An integral part of creating bond markets is the development of an efficient pension and insurance systems. The main advantage of the financial intermediaries, such as pension funds and insurance companies, is the ability to invest in financial instruments other than government bonds. Creditworthy Asian corporations would be able to borrow long-term.

In addition to expanding the finance choices for the private sector, many governments in Asia might find it preferable to develop a yield curve in order to meet their budget deficit obligations. Except for Japan, which has a well-developed bond market, there are still many barriers that must be overcome before it becomes a reality in other parts of Asia.[31] The barriers include weak financial institutions, restrictive investment eligibility requirements, and antiquated transfer, trust, title, and tax policies.[32]

Another major difficulty is the reluctance of international rating agencies[33] to analyze the credit worthiness of Asian corporations. Many of these corporations are family owned and there is a lack of information regarding their financial standing. Thus, poor credit ratings, as assessed by the dominant international rating agencies, are one of the main reasons preventing Asian corporations of issuing unsecured bonds.[34]

To conclude, the challenge facing Asia is to set up a deep and broad bond market.[35] One difficulty

is that each country's emerging economy is relatively small. The region has many national currencies. This is in contrast to the Europe where the combined bond market denominated in euro is now poised to rival the American dollar-denominated market.[36] Another related challenge is the present dominant role played by the American currency as a large number of Asian currencies remain tied to the American dollar. On the positive side, the region is witnessing the rise of a plethora of Free Trade Agreements.[37] Asian central banks are in control of huge foreign exchange reserves. This bodes well for the eventual creation of an East Asian monetary union and the introduction of a single currency, most probably in the distant future. In fact, the concept of ABC bonds might be looked upon as antecedent to an Asian common currency.

Acknowledgment

The author is indebted to Junji Nakagawa, Yoshinori Shimizu, and Akira Suehiro for valuable insights. I am grateful for stimulating discussions with Omar Farooq, Qi Liang, Sonia Sheikh, Ryusuke Shimizu, Kumiko Sakaim, Nariatsu Tanaka, and Bjorn Thunstrom. Special thanks to Yasuyo Mori for providing excellent secretarial help. The usual *caveat* applies.

NOTES

1. Arnoud Boot and Angan Thakor, " Financial System Architecture", *Review of Financial Studies*, Vol. 10, no. 3, pp. 693–733.
2. Richard J. Herring and Nathporn Chatusripitak, "The Case of the Missing Markets: The Bond Market and Why It Matters for Financial Development." *Asian Development Bank Institute, Working Paper 11*, Tokyo. July 2000, p.1.
3. At the end of 2001, the total outstanding amount issued by Asian emerging borrowers in local and international capital markets showed rapid increase, reaching $1.1 trillion. According to the IMF, in comparison with other regions, "emerging Asia has issued less international bonds (13 percent of the

Asian total outstanding), more government bonds in local markets, but not so dominating (50 percent), and a large private sector share: 20 percent for financial institutions and 17 percent for corporate. The composition of the Asian bond markets is thus similar to that of mature bond markets: domestic governments bonds account for 49 percent, financial institutions 22 percent, corporate 11 percent, and international bonds 18 percent. By contrast, Latin America has issued more international bonds (32 percent – mainly by sovereign borrowers) and government bonds in local markets (55 percent), leaving a small share for the private sector (13 percent). Similarly, EMEA (Eastern Europe, Middle East, Africa) has also issued more international bonds (23 percent) and government bonds in local markets (73 percent), with a negligible share of 4 percent for the private sector." Huan Q Tran and Jorge Roldos "Asian Bond Markets, The Role of Securitization and Credit Guarantees" *The 2nd ASEAN Central Bank Governor's Meeting*, Bangkok – 8,9/6/2003, p.2.

4. For example, lacking such signal, firms would overinvest if their internal rate of return is too low, as happened in many emerging economies in Asia during the 1990s.

5. This is particularly true when banks are undercapitalized. In such cases, making a write down in a loan renegotiation might result in violating capital adequacy standards. To avoid declaration of default, some banks might find it expedient to continue funding borrowers with negative present value projects. This exposes the banking system to liquidity shock. Without a bond market, banks do not have the option of selling bonds in a secondary market. Thus, they are likely to accept large losses on the sale of bad loans.

6. Richard J. Herring and Nathporn Chatusripitak, op. cit. pp. 2125.

7. These dragon bonds were simultaneously issued in more than two Asian markets. The markets included the "dragon" economies of Singapore and Hong Kong. Hisatsugu Nagao, "Market for Asian bonds taking shape", *The Nikkei Weekly*, November 24, 2003, p. 39.

8. Taniguchi Makoto, "Time for an East Asian economic Zone", *Japan Echo*, December 2003, p. 34.

9. Hung Q. Tran and Jorge Roldos, "Asian Bond Markets, The Role of Securitization and Credit Guarantees", *The 2nd ASEAN Central Bank Governor's Meeting*, Bangkok – 8,9/6/2003, p. 1.

10. William Pesek Jr. "Dollar skeptics in Asia have prominent company ", *International Herald Tribune*, February 3, 2005, p. B4.

11. Nils H. Hakansson, "The Role of Corporate Bond Market in an Economy – and in avoiding crisis", Working Paper, University of California, Berkeley.

12. At the end of March 2003, China, Hong Kong SAR, Japan, Korea, Singapore, Taipei, Thailand held $662 billion worth of U.S. treasury securities. This represented 50 percent of total foreign holdings of these securities and 20 percent of total outstanding treasury securities. These reserves are highly excessive with respect to the seven East Asian nations import needs and exchange rate management. Lim Hug Kiang, 2003, "East Asian Capital Markets: Challenging Times", A keynote address delivered at the *Euromoney 10th Asia-Pacific Issuers & Investors Forum*, March 18, 2003, Singapore, cited in S Ghon Rhee, "The Structure and Characteristics of East Asian Bond Markets, *Second Annual Conference of the PECC Finance Forum*, on Issues and Challenges for Regional Financial Cooperation in the Asia-Pacific, Hua Hin, Thailand, July 8–9, 2003, p. 9.

13. According to one analyst, the 1997 crisis would have completely different consequences had the Asian region allocated 15 percent of its accumulated reserves toward the capital account crisis. S. Ghon Rhee, *Second Annual Conference of the PECC Finance Forum*, op. cit., p. 6.

14. This section draws heavily on S. Ghon Rhee, *Second Annual Conference of the PECC Finance Forum*, op. cit. pp. 9–12.

15. The eleven EMEAP consists of China, Hong Kong, Indonesia, South Korea, Malaysia, Philippines, Singapore, Thailand, Japan, Australia, and New Zealand.

16. The eight economies are those of China, Hong Kong, Indonesia, South Korea, Malaysia, Philippines, Singapore, and Thailand.

17. Steven Glain, "Asia Creeping Unification", *Newsweek*, February 7, 2005, p. 32.

18. Hisatsugu Nagao, op. cit. p. 39.

19. In practice, government issues provide the benchmark for estimating term structure of interest rate. These issues are approximately default risk-free in domestic currency terms.

20. Richard J. Herring and Nathporn Chatusripitak, op. cit. p. 25.

21. Takatoshi Ito, Asian Basket Currency (ABC) Bonds, February 2003.

22. Takatoshi Ito, "Promoting Asian Basket Currency (ABC) Bonds," RCAST, University of Tokyo, March 1, 2003.

23. For the trade-off between liquidity and foreign exchange risk in the case of basket-denominated bonds, see Oiji Ogawa and Junko Shimizu, "Bond issuers' trade-off for common currency basket denominated bonds in East Asia," *Journal of Asian Economics*, Vol. 15, 2004, pp. 719–738.

24. This type of senior/subordinated bond issue was extremely popular in the post crisis period in Korea. See Gyutaeg Oh, Daekeun Park, Jaeha Park and Doo Yong Yang, 'How to Mobilize the Asian Savings within the Region: Securitization and Credit Enhancement for the Development of East Asia's Bond Market', *Korea Institute for International Economic Policy Working Paper* 03–02, 2003.

25. Many monoline bond insurance companies operate in the United States and Europe providing municipal bond insurance and pool insurance.

26. The first regional bond insurance company was established by the Asian Development Bank (ADB) in Singapore in 1995. This company was named as the Asian Securitization and Infrastructure Assurance Ltd (ASIA Ltd). Its owners consist of a diverse group consisting of financial institutions, ADB member countries, insurance companies in addition to others. Primarily, ASIA Ltd offers credit insurance to infrastructure projects of developing nations. Richard Yan Ki Ho and Chak Sham Michael Wong, "Road Map for Building the Institutional Foundation for Regional Bond Market in East Asia", *Second Annual Conference of the PECC Finance Forum*, op. cit. p. 21.

27. Korea has been an exception, being relatively active in this field. Korea set up a system of Primary Collateralized Bond Obligation in the year 2000. This program was introduced via the Korea Credit Guarantee Fund. In Hong Kong, the Mortgage Corporation, a subsidiary of the Hong Kong Monetary Authority, deals with mortgage securitization. Korea has enacted the Securitization Act in order to provide a workable legal system to facilitate the securitization of banks' nonperforming loans in addition to restructuring the balance sheet of financially troubled corporations.

28. For the benefit of institutional investors, the Hong Kong Monetary Authority issues Exchange Fund Bills and Notes. They are akin to U.S. treasury securities. The Authority started to issue smaller Exchange Fund Notes of around $7000 per contract in 2000. These notes are popular among the general public.

29. Richard Yan Ki Ho and Chak Sham Michael Wong, "Road Map for Building the Institutional Foundation for Regional Bond Market in East Asia", *Second Annual Conference of the PECC Finance Forum*, op. cit. p. 26.

30. During the South East Asian Crisis, the Hong Kong government took a pro-active stand against the attacks of global hedge funds speculators. To protect the stock market, the "equities purchased at that time were securitized to become a fund known as Tracker Fund. All the units of the Fund were later sold to both institutional and individual investors." Richard Yan Ki Ho and Chak Sham Michael Wong, "Road Map for Building the Institutional Foundation for Regional Bond Market in East Asia", *Second Annual Conference of the PECC Finance Forum*, op. cit., p. 26.

31. In 2003, Japan had a $5 trillion market, which is roughly equal to its gross domestic product. China, on the other hand, has less than $450 billion in issues outstanding representing 32 percent of its GDP.[1] Marshall Mays and Michael Preiss, "Asia must put its savings to work", *Financial Times*, November 7, 2003, p. 15.

32. Marshall Mays and Michael Preiss, op. cit., p. 15.

33. In the long term there is a need to establish Asian rating agencies. Practically however, it will take a few decades before the dominance of international rating agencies could be seriously challenged.

34. It has been estimated that for Asian corporations with less favorable credit ratings, the funding costs of issuing unsecured Asian corporation bonds could be higher than 18 percent. This is why many corporations in Asia prefer to acquire collateral pledged bank loans at an interest rate varying between 5 and 10 percent. Richard Yan Ki Ho and Chak Sham, Michael Wong, "Road Map for Building the Institutional Foundation for Regional Bond Market in East Asia", *Second Annual Conference of the PECC Finance Forum*, op. cit. p.16.

35. A deep market means the bond quantity can be sold without moving prices against the seller. Breadth signifies the diversity of participants and the heterogeneity of their responses to new information.

36. Richard J. Herring and Nathporn Chatusripitak, op. cit. p. 27.

37. A free trade area is formed when a group of nations agree to eliminate tariffs between themselves, but maintain their external tariffs on imports from the rest of the world.

REFERENCES

Alba, P., Hernandez, L., and Klingebiel, D. (1999). "Financial liberalization and the capital account: Thailand 1988–1997." Working Paper, World Bank.

Allen, F. and Gale, D. (2000). *Comparing Financial Systems*. Cambridge, MA: The MIT Press.

APEC (1999). "Compendium of sound practices, guidelines to facilitate the development of domestic bond markets in apec member economies." *Report of the Collaborative Initiative on Development of Domestic Bond Markets.*

Boot, A. and Thakor, A. "Financial system architecture." *Review of Financial Studies*, 10(3): 693–733.

Castellano, M. (1999). "Japanese foreign aid: a lifesaver for East Asia?" *Japan Economic Institute*, 12 February 1999, 6A, 5.

Claessens, S., Djankov, S., Fan, J.P.H., and Lang, L.H.P. (1998). "Corporate diversification in East Asia: The role of ultimate ownership and group affiliation." Working Paper, World Bank.

Dalla, I., Khatdhate, D., Rao, D.C.K., Kali, Jun, L., and Chuppe, T. (1995). "*The Emerging Asian Bond Market.*" Washington, DC: The World Bank.

Emery, R.F. (1997). *The Bond Markets of Developing*. East Asia, Boulder, Colorado: Westview Press.

Goldsmith, R. (1965). *The Flow of Capital Funds in the postwar Economy*, Chapter 2. New York: National Bureau of Economic Research.

Goldsmith, R. (1985). *Comparative National Balance Sheets: A Study of Twenty Countries, 1688–1978.*, Chicago: University of Chicago Press.

Hakansson, N.H. (1992). "Welfare economics of financial markets." In J. Eatwell, M. Milgate and P. Newman (eds.) *The New Palgrave Dictionary of Money and Finance*, volume 3. London: MacMillan Press, pp. 790–796.

Hakansson, N.H. (1999). "The role of corporate bond market in an economy – and in avoiding crisis." Working Paper, University of California, Berkeley.

Herring, R.J. and Chatusripitak, N. (2000). "The case of the missing markets: the bond market and why it matters for financial development." *Asian Development Bank Institute*. Working Paper 11, Tokyo, July 2000, 23–25.

Ho, R.Y.K and Wong, C.S.M. (2003). "Road map for building the institutional foundation for regional bond market in East Asia." *Second Annual Conference of the PECC Finance Forum*, on Issues and

Challenges for Regional Financial Cooperation in the Asia-Pacific, Hua Hin, Thailand, 8–9 July, 21.

Ito, T. (2003a). "Promoting Asian Basket Currency (ABC) bonds." RCAST, University of Tokyo, 1 March 2003.

Ito, T. (2003b). "Asian Basket Currency (ABC) Bonds," February 2003.

Kiang, L.H. (2003). East Asian capital markets: challenging times, A keynote address delivered at the *Euromoney 10th Asia-Pacific Issuers & Investors Forum*, 18 March, Singapore.

Levine, R. (1997). "Financial development and economic growth: views and agenda." *Journal of Economic Literature*, 36: 688–726.

Mays, M. and Preiss, M. (2003). "Asia must put its savings to work." *Financial Times*, 7: 15.

McKinnon, R.I. (1971). *Money and Capital in Economic Development*. Washington, DC: The Brookings Institution.

McKinnon, R.I. (1991). *The Order of Economic Liberalization: Financial Control in the Transition to a Market Economy*. Baltimore: Johns Hopkins University Press.

Mungthin, N. (2000). "Thai Bond market development (in Thai)." Bank of Thailand.

Nagao, Hisatsugu (2003). "Market for Asian bonds taking shape." *The Nikkei Weekly*, 24 November, 39.

Oh, G., Park D., Park, J., and Yang, D.Y. (2003). "How to mobilize the asian savings within the region: securitization and credit enhancement for the development of East Asia's bond market." *Korea Institute for International Economic Policy*. Working Paper, 3 February 2003.

Ogawa, O. and Shimizu, J. (2004). "Bond issuers' trade-off for common currency basket denominated bonds in East Asia." *Journal of Asian Economics*, 15: 719–738.

Pesek, W. Jr. (2005). "Dollar skeptics in Asia have prominent company." *International Herald Tribune*, 3 February 2005, B4.

Rhee, S.G. (2003). "The structure and characteristics of East Asian bond markets." *Second Annual Conference of the PECC Finance Forum*, on Issues and Challenges for Regional Financial Cooperation in the Asia-Pacific, Hua Hin, Thailand, 8–9 July, 21.

Sheng, A. (1994). "Future directions for Hon Kong's debt market," Speech at the First Annual Pan-Asia Bonds Summit, 29–30 November.

Sonakul, M.R.C.M. (2000). "Keynote address on the Occasion of the ADB Conference on Government

Bond Market and Financial Sector Development in Developing Asian Economies." Manila, 28–30 March.

Taniguchi, T. (2003). "Asian bond market initiative." A keynote speech delivered at the ASEAN+3 High-Level Seminar on *Fostering Bond Markets in Asia*. March, Tokyo, *Japan*, 30.

Tourk, K. (2004) "The political economy of east Asian economic integration." *Journal of Asian Economics*, 15(5): 843–888.

Tran, H.Q. and Roldos, J. (2003). "Asian bond markets, the role of securitization and credit guarantees." *The 2nd ASEAN Central Bank Governor's Meeting*, Bangkok, 8, 2.

Yam, J. (1997). "Development of the debt market, keynote address at the asian debt conference," *http://www.info.gov.hk/hkma/eng/speeches/speechs/joseph/speech_140797b.htm*, 14 July.

Chapter 42

CROSS-BORDER MERGERS
AND ACQUISITIONS

GERALDO M. VASCONCELLOS, *Lehigh University, USA*
RICHARD J. KISH, *Lehigh University, USA*

Abstract

Cross-border mergers and acquisitions have shown tremendous growth over time primarily due to a desire to circumvent tariffs and nontariff barriers arising from arms-length international trade and taxes; to obtain new options for financing; to access technology; and to distribute research and development costs over a broader base. Several factors put in place to moderate this growth include protecting key industries, limiting controlling interest levels, and restricting remittances of profits and dividends. This paper focuses on cross-border mergers and acquisitions, and their financial and economic (both macro and micro) underpinnings, which affect their direction and magnitude. In general terms, empirical analysis supports the fact that both a host country's and the foreign country's stock and bond prices are major causal factors that influence cross-border mergers and acquisitions.

Keyword: acquisition; barriers; cross-border; diversification; international; mergers; multinational; synergy; takeovers; tariffs; undervaluation

One of the remarkable developments that accompanied the vigorous growth in international trade in the post-World War II era has been an unabated increase in international direct investment. This phenomenon, including its theoretical underpinnings, benefits and costs, has been the subject of voluminous research. In addition, many studies have examined the attendant questions of the host country attitudes toward international direct investment. Extant research suggests that some of the main benefits of international direct investment can be found in the avoidance of tariffs and nontariff barriers to arms-length international trade, in tax incentives usually associated with efforts to attract foreign investment to a particular country or region within a country, in the ability to tap different markets for short-term and long-term capital, and in the possibility of obtaining quicker and cheaper access to superior technology, as well as the ability to spread out the output of a multinational corporation's own research and development efforts over a broader market base. On the other hand, risks and constraints affecting international direct investment include closed sectors or industries, limitations on the acquisition of a controlling interest in a foreign company, limitations on remittances of profits and dividends, limitations on cross-border mergers and acquisitions and, in some extreme cases, the possibility of expropriation.

The countries affiliated with the Organization for Economic Cooperation and Development (which includes all the major advanced market economies) lead this impressive growth in international direct investment. The outward direct investment flows are in general larger than the inward flows.

The reason is that OECD countries invest in non-OECD countries, generally less developed ones. The inward flows of foreign direct investment (FDI) in OECD countries come almost exclusively from other OECD countries, that is to say, other major industrial countries. For example, during the 1980s, the United States was the major recipient of flows of international direct investment, followed by Europe and Canada in more modest terms. Japan was the main source of flows of international direct investment. This helps to explain why the United States gave up its position as the world's largest creditor nation to become the world's largest debtor in less than a decade. In the same period of time, Japan became one of the largest creditors. The direct investment flows, however, explain only one part of these transformations. The rest of the explanation is found in portfolio investments and their reallocations.

The acquisition of a foreign firm is one of the fastest methods of entering into a foreign market. In the late 1980s and the 1990s, this method seemed especially attractive to businesses wanting to become involved in the evolving European market. As a result, there was a surge of foreign takeovers in the European Union during this period. This demonstrated that businesses had confidence in the E.U., forming a single internal market in the long run. In fact, many of these acquisitions took place before national barriers came down. The rationale for this may be attributed in part to a growing concern that a unified Europe could translate into a more protectionist "Fortress Europe." Many foreign companies believed that the only way to participate in a unified Europe was to quickly become an insider. Acquisitions subsided after the initial surge that took place in the late 1980s, due to the creation of natural barriers to entry for outsiders. Many mergers and acquisitions were taking place within the E.U., creating larger, more efficient European businesses and effectively producing fewer opportunities for foreign companies. By the early 1990s, however, acquisitions

of European firms were on the rise again due to two primary factors: (1) a need to complete the restructuring that had begun in the 1980s and that could not be done by European firms alone; and (2) regulatory changes that enabled hostile takeovers to occur more easily. But this rise in U.S. acquisitions of E.U. companies was followed by a rise in E.U. acquisitions of U.S. firms, a cycle that seem to exist within many areas of the world economy.

International direct investment, therefore, takes place in basically two forms: *de novo* entry or mergers and acquisitions. This review focuses on cross-border mergers and acquisitions, their financial and economic underpinnings, and the factors, which affect their direction and magnitude. FDI is an integral part of the developed capital markets. The significant rise in the number of cross-border mergers and acquisitions across time warrants a better understanding of the factors affecting these activities. For example, the publicity in the 1980s surrounding foreign acquisition activity in the United States created public concern over American firms being acquired by foreign entities, leading to a significant number of studies examining the wealth effects of foreign acquisitions and capital markets factors that affect acquisition activity. Since the early 1980s, the direction of the flow of cross-border acquisitions has shifted many times. During one time period, U.S. companies were acquiring foreign firms at a higher rate than they were being acquired, but by the end of the 1990s, foreign companies reversed this direction to become the predominant acquirer again. The cycle continues to this day, although of different durations. Studies done on acquisition activity between the U.S. and Britain (Vasconcellos et al., 1990), between the U.S. and Japan (Kish and Vasconcellos, 1993), between Canada and the U.S. (Vasconcellos and Kish, 1996), and between the U.S. and Europe (Vasconcellos and Kish, 1998) explore macroeconomic variables that contributed to this phenomenon.

42.1. Macroeconomic Factors

42.1.1. Favorable Acquisition Factors

Although there are a number of factors favoring acquisition activity, we focus on four of these factors: (1) exchange rates; (2) diversification; (3) economic conditions in the host country; and (4) technology and human resources within the acquiring firm.

42.1.1.1. Exchange Rates

One view on exchange rates revolves around the fact that while there seems to exist a relationship between exchange rates and acquisition activity, there is no evidence that a change in the exchange rate improves the position of foreign acquirers relative to their host counterparts. The argument is that when the host country's currency depreciates, the host country becomes a cheaper place for any firm to do business – foreign or domestic. Thus, the relationship between foreign acquisitions and exchange rates, contending that improved capital mobility facilitates equalized, risk-adjusted returns on international investments, is minimized. Another line of argument is that a depreciated host country's currency increases FDI in the host country's businesses. The reverse also holds true, i.e. if the host currency is strong, there should be a pause in the foreign acquisition of host firms and an upward trend in the home country's acquisitions of foreign firms.

42.1.1.2. Diversification

Given a firm's preferred risk-return position, international diversification by way of acquisition improves the risk-return tradeoff. This reasoning is based on the assumption that the covariance of returns across economies, even within the same industries, is likely to be smaller than within a single economy. The prospective acquiring company must first decide on its desired levels of risk and return. Only then should it attempt to identify countries, industries, and specific firms, which fall within its risk class. In addition, by acquiring an ongoing foreign concern, companies may be able to circumvent tariff and nontariff barriers (i.e. quotas, voluntary restraint agreements, etc.), which attempt to protect the domestic industries and contribute to market segmentation. This action improves the risk-return tradeoff by lowering the level of unsystematic risk.

42.1.1.3. Current Economic Conditions in the Home Country

Adverse economic conditions in the home country, such as a slump, recession, or capital constraint may cause firms to concentrate on their domestic business while temporarily delaying strategic international moves. Once the economy rebounds, cross-border acquisitions are likely to again become a means for increasing demand and levels of diversification.

42.1.1.4. Acquisition of Technological and Human Resources

There are cases where a firm falls behind in the level of technological knowledge necessary to compete efficiently in its industry. If a firm is unable or unwilling to develop the required technology through research and development, it may attempt to acquire a foreign firm, which is technologically more advanced. Such an acquisition allows a firm to gain a foothold in a foreign country's market, and it may transfer the acquired technology back home, in order to strengthen its position in the domestic market. Some of the firms engaging in cross-border acquisitions are either transnational firms or striving to become one. Transnational firms are able to behave like a local company in foreign markets, tapping into human and technological resources, while possessing the leverage of a larger, diversified entity. Indeed, this strategy provides significant diversification and allows the company to realize competencies in many markets.

42.1.2. Unfavorable Acquisition Factors

The factors discussed thus far generally tend to encourage firms to make cross-border acquisitions. In contrast, other variables that often serve to restrain cross-border movement include unavailability of information, inefficient management, monopolistic power, and government restrictions and regulations.

42.1.2.1. Unavailability of Information

The contention is that information about a prospective target firm is crucial in the decision-making process of an acquiring firm. Timely and accurate information include: current market share figures; comparisons with the competition; current sales; cash flow forecasts; and company specific strengths and weaknesses. However, foreign firms may not disclose these or other relevant figures. Thus, if the necessary information to make an accurate analysis is not available, the prospective acquiring firm may be forced to delay or discontinue its plans, even though the foreign firm appears to be an attractive target on the surface. Otherwise, failure to come up with an accurate analysis may prove harmful, or possibly devastating, to the acquiring firm. However, information effects are not always harmful, such as when the acquirer may be able to obtain information not available to other market participants.

42.1.2.2. Inefficient Management

The inefficiency argument centers on the acquiring firm being able to replace incompetent or inefficient management within the acquired firm in order to better utilize the firm's assets. The hope is that the new management will be able to increase the efficiency of the acquired firm and generate a higher return. A drawback of this action is the cost of replacing inefficient management. The negative aspects of the inefficiencies argument apply to the resistance that may materialize from the foreign managers who are left in place after the shake-up, emerging in the form of negative attitudes directed at the "outsiders" taking over the firm.

42.1.2.3. Monopolistic Power

Synergy arguments in defense of domestic or cross-border acquisitions are based on the economies of scale supposedly derived from horizontal mergers,

economies of scope associated with vertical mergers, or the gains from acquiring monopolistic power. However, if monopolistic or even oligopolistic power is attained by a firm or a group of firms (a difficult position in most developed countries due to the threat of antitrust action), then entry to the industry becomes more difficult for any competitor, domestic or foreign. In addition, a monopolist is much more likely to resist a takeover. Some of the barriers to entry that make cross-border acquisitions difficult include: R&D outlays; capital expenditures necessary to establish a plant; and product differentiation, sometimes tied to large advertising expenditures.

42.1.2.4. Government Restrictions and Regulations

Most governments have some form of takeover regulations in place. In many instances, government approval is mandatory before acquisition by a foreign business can occur. In addition, government restrictions may exist on capital repatriations, dividend payouts, intra-company interest payments, and other remittances. Although these restrictions seem to be more prevalent in less developed countries, even in the developed markets, regulatory actions have been used to discourage acquisition activity. For example, the William's Amendment within the U.S. market increased the difficulty and costs of completing tender offers. The Tax Reform Act of 1986 has also been cited as a factor in the increased acquisition transactions between U.S. sellers and foreign buyers. However, foreign buyers from countries with tax treaties with the host country are not subject to home taxes in repatriated earnings and, therefore, should be on equal footing with their host counterparts. Research in this area shows that most of the tax effects are industry-specific.

42.2. Microeconomic Factors

New relationships between the economic agents of different countries have come into existence with the ever-increasing globalization of markets. For example, the volume of cross-border mergers and acquisitions (M&A's) involving U.S. companies has increased in both the number of transactions and the dollar value for both net bidders and net targets. The exact motivations for cross-border M&A activity are many, including macroeconomic factors, firm-specific financial characteristics, corporate strategic moves, political motives, the possibility of a *good buy,* and/or the synergistic potential from the merged firms.

International merger and acquisition waves capture the attention of not only the business press but also of academia and policymakers. The effects of this merger-mania are felt by many (i.e. managers, stockholders, intermediaries, and consumers), and the dollar amounts are considerably high. To gain a better understanding of the characteristics of firms involved in the international market for corporate control, we now focus our attention on the firm-specific financial variables of both foreign companies and the host country's companies and the role that these variables have on the probability of the acquisition.

The composition of cross-border merger and acquisitions has changed over time. Contrary to the pattern in the 1970s, we have seen an increase in the relative proportion of U.S. targets and foreign acquirers in the 1980s and 1990s, with a slowdown in the first decade of the twentieth century. Among the most important factors in the past have attracted foreign firms to the U.S. market for corporate control are: (a) growth potential and accessibility to the U.S. market; (b) availability of high technology and highly skilled labor force; (c) relative easy access to financial markets; (d) undervaluation of some companies' stock; (e) relatively limited government intervention, and (f) currency fluctuations.

42.2.1. Undervaluation

The growing web of interdependencies in the global economy has developed new relationships between economic agents of different countries. Some existing international mergers and acquisitions research focuses primarily on wealth transfers.

For instance, Doukas and Travlos (1988), besides offering an excellent review of this literature, contrasts the returns to shareholders from U.S. and non-U.S.-based firms expanding into foreign markets. Conn and Connell (1990) also include an extensive literature review of mergers and acquisitions within their empirical study of wealth transfers between the U.S. and British firms, as they expand into each other's markets.

Undervaluation revolves from the existence of product and service market imperfections that cause frictions in the global market (such as transaction costs and costs associated with barriers to entry), contributing to favor the acquisition of a company already operating. This is because the amount paid for an existing company, as compared to the replacement cost of its assets, more than compensates for the costs that could have been incurred had the foreign firm started with brand new facilities. Thus, in order to minimize the acquisition costs, foreign firms attempt to follow the same pattern of analysis as their domestic counterparts and search for undervalued and/or mismanaged companies as targets for their acquisitions. This is the basic premise of the empirical study undertaken by Gonzalez et al. (1998a,b), among others.

From the target firm's viewpoint, undervaluation is described as the likelihood of a host country's firm becoming a target increasing when the firm is perceived as being undervalued. Assuming that the takeover decision is motivated by the same stimuli that encourage firms to grow internally, a number of research studies utilize Tobin's "q" ratio as a predictor of takeover targets. High abnormal returns, experienced by acquirers before the merger, are consistent with a high "q" ratio, signaling to the companies that it is time to expand. Nevertheless, the conclusion is that the effect of the "q" ratio is not always significant and that these effects vary over time and across countries.

Furthermore, under the assumption that the financial market rewards well-managed firms, it is commonly interpreted that a "q" greater than 1 is a proxy for good management. Conversely, a ratio less than one is viewed as evidence of poor management. Thus, well-managed bidders benefit substantially from tender offers, but more so when they take over poorly managed targets. Well-managed targets benefit less from tender offers than poorly managed targets. The total takeover gain is highest for tender offers by well-managed bidders, which acquire poorly managed targets. This target undervaluation implies that there is an inverse relationship between the probability of a host country's company being acquired and the Tobin's q. The empirical research provides support for this view.

From the bidding firm's viewpoint, undervaluation is shown as the likelihood of a foreign firm bidding for a host country's company increasing when the firm is perceived as being overvalued. Therefore, the relationship between the ratio of market value to replacement cost of assets of foreign firms to the likelihood of these companies acquiring a host country's companies is supported (i.e. there is a positive relationship between the likelihood of a foreign firm bidding for a host country's company and the ratio of market value to replacement cost of the foreign firm). Research results show the existence of direct relation between the possibility of a foreign firm bidding for a host country's firm and the Tobin's q of the overseas firm.

In sum, this research empirically validates undervaluation as a predictor of M&A activity within the international setting. The results support the existence of an inverse relationship between the probability of a host country's firm becoming a target of a foreign company and the Tobin's q ratio (i.e. undervalued host country's companies are more likely to be targets of foreign companies). This is consistent with the domestic market for corporate control.

If we relate these findings to Lang et al.'s (1989) conclusions from the domestic marketplace, then we observe positive abnormal returns for foreign companies upon the announcement of the foreign firms taking over a poorly managed host country's firms. A firm's overvaluation is proxied by a Tobin's q greater than 1. Lang et al. (1989) found positive abnormal returns when a firm with a Tobin's q greater than 1 (well-managed firm) acquired an undervalued company. Furthermore, foreign acquirers and host country's targets typically belong to the same industrial sectors. This can be interpreted as foreign companies reducing acquisition costs by acquiring undervalued firms as foreign firms trying to use their business knowhow to enhance the efficiency of the host country's targets.

Management inefficiency implies that the more inefficient is a firm's management, the greater is the probability of the firm becoming a target. Examples of variables used (in addition to the Tobin's q) to gauge management efficiency are the return on equity and sales growth. When the management is inefficient, both variables tend to show a negative relationship with the probability of an acquisition. Management inefficiency complements undervaluation reasoning. This interpretation is based on the premise that management fails to use the resources of the company up to their full potential. Thus, management inefficiency implies the existence of an inverse relationship between the ratio return on equity and growth and also the probability of the host country's company becoming a target of foreign firm. Therefore, the low return on equity and growth are manifestations of low quality management and are supported in the literature, implying that the probability that a host country's company will be taken over by a foreign firm is higher in case of greater inefficiency of the management of the domestic company.

42.2.2. Synergy Hypothesis

Much of the finance and accounting literature analyzing merger and acquisition activity is focused on the existence of synergy as a source of takeover gains within the domestic marketplace. Examples of the synergy identified that can transcend international borders include economies of scale, improved production techniques, increased market share, and more profitable use of existing assets.

This suggests the existence of a direct relationship between the perceived degree of *ex-ante* synergy and the number of host country's firms acquired by foreign companies. The possibility of obtaining economies of scale, improving production techniques, increasing market share, and otherwise squeezing more profits out of existing assets are major assumptions made by the proponents of the effects from synergy. Before a merger, firms are assumed to be operating at levels of asset utilization that fall short of achieving their true potentials. Thus, the management of the bidding company could improve the performance of both the target and the expanded firm, whether on the domestic or international level.

In an extensive literature review of the sources of gains in mergers and acquisitions, Jensen and Ruback (1983) document support for the gains to the target firms' shareholders. The basic assumption within their review is that shareholders play a passive role in any takeover activity, relying on the existence of good management who, through sound investment decisions, will be able to maximize the shareholders' wealth. The consensus within their review of studies shows that the stock price of the target firm goes up at the time surrounding the announcement date. Moreover, the majority of the empirical studies of the takeover gains rely upon event study methodology to conclude that synergy is one of the main motives behind merger and acquisition activity. But event studies are primarily a measure of the reaction of a particular economic variable (e.g. stock prices) to the event of interest (e.g. the merger or acquisition announcement) measured *ex-post*. In addition, this methodology often impairs the distinction among alternative sources of gains. In other words, this methodology is not able to identify which components of the present value of net cash flows have changed.

The fact that these studies look at the efficiency gains from mergers and acquisitions (i.e. via synergy) *ex-post* might be impairing their ability to disentangle the true gains from synergy from the existence of market imperfections. Another limita-

tion is that the event study methodology fails to account for the long-term effects of the takeover. Therefore, it is very difficult to distinguish the real sources of gains. An alternative *ex-ante* methodology is that synergy in mergers is measured by adding the acquisition premium to the difference between replacement costs and market value of the target firm (i.e. Tobin's q).

Relying on the relationship between the merger premium and the extent that replacement costs exceeds market value, a proxy successfully used the finance literature tests the effect of synergy. To measure the existence of *ex-ante* synergy, literature relies on the relationship between market value and replacement cost of the target assets. This difference is then related to the premium paid in the takeover transaction. Thus, synergy shows up as a direct relationship between the perceived degree of *ex-ante* synergy and the number of host country's targets of foreign acquisitions. Assuming that the market for corporate control is competitive, a change in value of the firm is equal to the difference between the replacement cost of the assets of the target firm and the market value of those assets, plus the premium paid in the acquisition or merger.

Although synergy is a factor in many but not all merger activities, it is only one of the many hypotheses used to explain all merger activity. Other related merger hypotheses include management inefficiency, goodwill, and barriers to entry. For example, foreign companies often acquire a host country's companies to get around market frictions that might increase the cost of doing business in the host country. Empirical studies document the relationship between merger and acquisition activity and the presence of frictions in the market as proxied by the existence of goodwill and barriers to entry in a particular industry. Typically, the degree of goodwill and barriers to entry show a direct relationship with the probability of acquisition. One factor used to proxy goodwill is advertising expenses. The documented trend is that the higher the proportion of advertising expenses to net sales, the larger the number of customers that have some knowledge about the product or service of the firm. Alternatively, the proportion of research and development expenses to net sales is used as a proxy for barriers to entry. The higher the proportion of research and development expenses to net sales in a particular industry, the more difficult it is to enter in the industry. Thus, there is a direct relationship between the ratio of research and development expenses to net sales of a host country's firms and the probability of these firms being a target of an overseas company. But the results are not conclusive as to what is the impact of barriers to entry and goodwill in the probability of a host country's company becoming a target. Thus, it appears that the foreign firms acquired undervalued host country's companies based on what these overseas acquirers think they can put in play to improve the operations of the host firms and not necessarily on what the host companies offer to these foreign companies in terms of reducing barriers to entry or the existence of an already established customer base.

42.2.3. Maximizing the value of the firm

Under the assumption that the goal of corporate managers is the maximization of shareholders' wealth, the process of cross-border mergers and acquisitions flows from the neoclassical theoretical framework of maximization of the value of the firm. If the acquisition of a host country's company is a project with a net present value larger than zero, then there is an increase in the shareholders' wealth of the acquiring company. For instance, the empirical analysis by Vasconcellos et al. (1990), using a capital budget framework, measures the feasibility of a proposed foreign acquisition. Although their research was carried out on the influence of financial variables (used in the capital budgeting process) on the difference between American acquisitions of British firms and British acquisitions of American firms, some of these findings can be generalized for all cross-border M&A activity. For example, the exchange rate has a significant positive impact on the acqui-

sition differential. In other words, foreign firms may acquire a host country's firms because of the relatively lower foreign currency value of the host country's currency (the host country's currency was "cheap"). The Kish and Vasconcellos (1993) study of cross-border acquisitions between the United States and Japan conclude that the stock prices and the costs of debt financing are the major contemporaneous causal factors; whereas exchange rates only had significance as a predictor of trends in acquisitions. Thus, generalities to fit all situations do not appear to exist. Most of the companies involved in cross-border M&As establish a sort of acquisition screening. This screening process involves country-specific and firm-specific screening variables (i.e. per capita GDP, market share of the target, etc.). The general conclusion is that the internationalization of the firm is a value-enhancing phenomenon.

The net present value (NPV) analysis assumes that the managers of the foreign firms bidding for the host country's companies decide to make the acquisition only when the decision has a positive impact on the shareholders' wealth of the foreign company. The net present value criteria assume a positive relationship between the factors affecting the NPV criterion and the likelihood of a foreign firm acquiring a host country's company. Another frequently argued view is that a relatively large and stable ("mature") host country's companies are more likely to go overseas than the average host's firms. Thus, the mature firm argument states that a host country's bidders in the cross-border merger and acquisition market are more likely to be mature firms.

Cross border M&A research start from the assumption that in the international market for corporate control, firms decide about an acquisition project using essentially the same decision-making framework that the firms would use for internal projects. Research supports the net present value approach and the assumption that the management of the foreign firm will undertake projects that have a positive impact on the wealth of its shareholders. The empirical research shows the existence of a positive relationship between the factors affecting the NPV criterion and the likelihood of a foreign firm acquiring a host country's firms.

Foreign firms also seem to be more likely to acquire a host country's companies with high debt capacity. A substantial debt capacity can be utilized to reduce the cost of the acquisition through debt financing at relatively low cost, whereas a high debt to equity ratio could increase the cost of new debt financing. Foreign firms are more likely to acquire a host country's companies with relatively high liquidity, as evidenced by the importance of the current ratio in the literature. In addition, host country's companies with relatively low price of stock to earnings are more probable to be acquired, serving as evidence that the managers of foreign companies acquiring host country's companies make their merger and/or acquisition decisions pursuing the maximization of the foreign companies shareholders' wealth.

In addition to examining the financial characteristics of the host country's targets from cross-border M&A, the same analysis for the host country's bidders in the global takeover market hes been summarized. The reasons for a host country's FDI have been widely discussed in the literature. The motivations leading to host country's FDI include product market imperfections, institutional imperfections (i.e. differentials in tax laws), and limitations of the domestic market.

Jensen (1988) argues that firms with free cash flows will be likely bidders in the takeover market. Thus, mature firms in a host country are more likely to be bidders in the cross-border M&A market. Normally, a company follows a life cycle that is closely connected to product line development. A mature firm has a relatively stable financial profile and may face two options: to become "better" or to get "bigger" In order to become "bigger," these companies may attempt to go overseas.

The following financial variables proxy for identifying mature companies relative to the industry: net sales growth, size of total assets, price-earnings ratio, and free cash flow. There is an inverse rela-

tionship between both the growth and the price–earnings ratio of a host country's firm and the probability of this firm becoming a bidder in the global market for corporate control. Furthermore, there is direct association between both the size and free cash flow of a host country's company relative to the industry and the likelihood of this company becoming a bidder for a foreign firm. In addition, foreign firms with a "Tobin's q" greater than 1 are more likely to acquire a host country's companies. This is consistent with Jensen's (1988) conclusions. Relatively high "Tobin's q" firms may have enough resources to invest in the acquisition of other firms. The exchange rate does not have a strong impact on the probability of acquisition of a host country's company. For example, a very strong dollar during the first half of the 1980s and a weak dollar the second half failed to impact the number of U.S. companies acquired or acquiring in that they were on average the same. There are alternative (and not mutually exclusive) explanations for the difference on the importance attributed to the exchange rate. First, most of the studies found in the literature examining the difference between the number of host country's acquisitions of foreign companies versus the number of foreign acquisitions of host country's firms report inconsistent results. Second, the exchange rate could affect the timing of the acquisition but not the acquisition decision itself. The other possibility is that there are different time periods being studied. Also found was that the foreign firms have a relatively high return on equity when compared to the industry average. Since return on equity is used as a proxy for management efficiency, the conclusion is that foreign companies with above average efficiency in their countries have a higher likelihood of acquiring a host country's firms.

The combined results on "Tobin's q" for the host country's targets and foreign bidders mirror the domestic case of mergers and acquisitions. That is, high "Tobin's q" foreign bidders had positive abnormal returns when they acquired targets with "Tobin's q" < 1. Research supports the shareholders' wealth maximization theory as applied to the investment decision of whether or not to acquire a host country's companies. Finally, the host country's companies going overseas are "mature" companies with large amounts of assets, considerable free cash flows, and low growth. The fact that the host country's companies acquiring foreign companies have an average low price to earnings ratio may be interpreted as a move of the management of these host country's companies to attempt to maximize its shareholders' wealth by signaling to the market that the increase in globalization of the company's operations is a risk reduction event due to diversification.

42.3. An Analytical View of Cross-Border Mergers and Acquisitions

The feasibility of a foreign acquisition can be evaluated first like any other project, with specific attention to peculiar characteristics. Capital budgeting analysis can be applied to determine whether the NPV of the acquisition is positive. Consider the following capital budgeting framework, as applied to a foreign acquisition:

$$\text{NPV}_{\text{FA}} = -I_{\text{FA}} + \sum_{t=1}^{n} \frac{\text{CF}_{\text{FA},t}}{(1 + k_{\text{FA}})^t} + \frac{\text{SV}_{\text{FA},n}}{(1 + k_{\text{FA}})^n}$$

$$(42.1)$$

where NPV_{FA} is the net present value of a foreign acquisition; I_{FA} the initial outlay of a foreign acquisition; k_{FA} the required return on the foreign acquisition; CF_{FA} the cash flows to the acquirer; SV the salvage value to the acquirer; t the $=$ time period and n the number of periods in which the project is expected to exist.

As with any project, the variables above should incorporate any tax implications so that the net present value reflects after-tax cash flows. In addition, all cash flows should be measured from the acquirer's perspective and in the acquirer's home currency.

Breaking the general NPV equation into its components can identify the factors that influence a firm's attraction to a prospective foreign acquirer. The following discussion identifies the specific factors, which affect a foreign acquisition's initial outlay, periodic cash flows, and salvage value. The initial outlay (I_{FA}) can be broken down into three components, as shown below:

$$I_{\text{FA}} = E_{\text{h}} + D_{\text{h}} + D_{\text{f}}(ER_{\text{f}}) \qquad (42.2)$$

where E_{h} the equity in the home currency; D_{h} borrowed funds in the home currency; D_{f} the borrowed funds in the foreign currency; and $ER_{\text{f},t}$ the exchange rate of foreign currency at the time the foreign funds were borrowed.

To measure the entire initial outlay in terms of the home currency, any foreign funds borrowed by the acquiring firm must be translated into the home currency. Moreover, some firms may cover the entire initial outlay from any one of the above components.

The relevant cash flows in the analysis of cross-border mergers and acquisitions are those received by the acquiring firm. These cash flows are determined by: (1) the after-tax foreign cash flows generated; (2) the percentage of those after-tax cash flows to be remitted to the acquirer; and (3) the exchange rates at the time the after-tax foreign cash flows are remitted. Then, the after-tax cash flows received by the acquiring firm can be described as:

$$\text{CF}_{\text{FA,t}} = (\text{CF}_{\text{f},t})(1 - \text{R}_{\text{f},t})(\text{ER}_{\text{f},t}) \qquad (42.3)$$

where $\text{CF}_{\text{f},t}$ is the foreign cash flows generated during period t; $R_{\text{f},t}$ the proportion of cash flows retained by the (then) foreign subsidiary to support future operations; and $ER_{\text{f},t}$ the exchange rate of the foreign currency at the time cash flows are remitted to the acquiring firm.

The salvage value from the acquirer's perspective as of time $n(\text{SV}_{\text{FA},n})$ is determined by the anticipated foreign market value of the acquired business at time $n(\text{MV}_{\text{f}},\text{n})$, and the prevailing exchange rate at the time of the planned sale, as described below:

$$\text{SV}_{\text{FA},n} = (\text{MV}_{\text{f},n})(\text{ER}_{\text{f},n}) \qquad (42.4)$$

Note that the foreign value may represent a liquidation value or a going concern value, whichever is likely to be higher.

Integrating the detailed expressions for the initial outlay, periodic cash flows, and salvage value, a comprehensive expression for the NPV analysis of a foreign acquisition can be written as follows:

$$
\begin{aligned}
\mathrm{NPV_{FA}} = & -I_{\mathrm{FA}} + \sum_{t=1}^{n} \frac{\mathrm{CF_{FA},}_{t}}{(1 + k_{\mathrm{FA}})^{t}} + \frac{\mathrm{SV_{FA},}_{n}}{(1 + k_{\mathrm{FA}})^{n}} \\
= & -\left[E_{\mathrm{h}} + D_{\mathrm{h}} + D_{\mathrm{f}}(ER_{\mathrm{f}}) \right] \\
& + \sum_{t=1}^{n} \frac{\left[(\mathrm{CF_{f},}_{t})(1 - \mathrm{R_{f},}_{t})(\mathrm{ER_{f},}_{t}) \right]}{(1 + k_{\mathrm{FA}})^{t}} \\
& \frac{\left[(\mathrm{MV_{f},}_{n})(\mathrm{ER_{f},}_{n}) \right]}{(1 + k_{\mathrm{FA}})^{n}}
\end{aligned}
\tag{42.5}
$$

When expressed as in Equation (42.5), the capital budgeting approach provides a valuable framework for explaining the influence of several factors regarding the feasibility of foreign acquisitions.

In conclusion, the phenomenon of cross-border mergers and acquisitions has shown vitality in the last two decades and the trend appears set to continue in the new century. For example, the UNCTAD's *World Investment Report, 2000* reported that the overall value of the flow of cross-border mergers and acquisitions was $151 billion in 1991 and increased to $720 billion in 1999. In addition, the annual growth rates of these flows are shown to be 26.4 percent for 1986–1990, 23.3 percent for 1991–1995, and 46.9 percent for 1996–1999. Moreover, the quickly evolving single European market in the late 1980s and early 1990s encouraged many non-European firms to establish a presence in Europe before the barriers to entry intensified. Consequently, by the mid-1990s U.S. FDIs in the European Union increased by approximately 200 percent from the early 1980s. In general terms, empirical analysis supports the fact that both a host country's and the foreign country's stock prices are a major causal factor that influence cross-border mergers and acquisitions. Bond yields are also shown to be major causal factors. This implies that bond yields may be one of the final negotiating points in the decision to consummate an acquisition. Finally, the exchange rate does not consistently acquire significance for all countries. Thus, the exchange rate can only serve as a predictor of trends in acquisitions.

REFERENCES

Conn, R.L. and Connell, F. (1990). "International mergers: returns to U.S. and British firms." *Journal of Business Finance and Accounting*, 17(5): 689–712.

Doukas, J. and Travlos, N.G. (1988). "The effect of corporate multinationalism on shareholders' wealth: evidence from international acquisitions." *Journal of Finance*, 43: 1161–1175.

Gonzalez, P., Vasconcellos, G.M., and Kish, R.J. (1998a). "Cross-border mergers and acquisitions: the undervaluation hypothesis." *Quarterly Review of Economics and Finance*, 38(1): 25–45.

Gonzalez, P., Vasconcellos, G.M., and Kish, R.J. (1998b). "Cross-border mergers and acquisitions: the synergy hypothesis." *The International Journal of Finance*, 10(4): 1297–1319.

Jenson, M. (1988). "Takeovers: their causes and consequences." *Journal of Economics Perspectives*, 2(1): 21–48.

Jensen, M., and Ruback, R.S (1983). "The market for corporate control the scientific evidence." *Journal of Financial Economics*, 11: 5–50.

Kish, R.J. and Vasconcellos, G.M. (1993). "An empirical analysis of factors affecting cross-border acquisitions: US–Japan." *Management International Review*, 33(3): 222–245.

Lang, L.H., Stulz, R.M., and Walking, R.A. (1989). "Managerial performance, Tobin's Q, and the gain from successful tender offers." *Journal of Financial Economics*, 24: 137–154.

Madura, J., Vasconcellos, G.M., and Kish, R.J. (1991). "A valuation model for international acquisitions." *Management Decision*, 29(4): 31–38.

United Nations Conference on Trade and Development (UNCTAD). (2000). *World Investment Report 2000: Cross-Border Mergers and Acquisitions and Development*. New York and Geneva, Switzerland.

Vasconcellos, G.M. and Kish, R.J. (1996). "Factors affecting cross-border mergers and acquisitions: the

Canada–US experience." *Global Finance Journal*, 7(2): 223–238.

Vasconcellos, G.M. and Kish, R.J. (1998). "Cross-border mergers and acquisitions: the European–US experience." *Journal of Multinational Financial Management*, 8: 431–450.

Vasconcellos, G.M., Madura, J. and Kish, R.J. (1990). "An empirical investigation of factors affecting cross-border acquisitions: the United States vs. United Kingdom experience." *Global Finance Journal*, 1(3): 173–189.

Chapter 43

JUMP DIFFUSION MODEL

SHIU-HUEI WANG, *University of Southern California, USA*

Abstract

Jump diffusion processes have been used in modern finance to capture discontinuous behavior in asset pricing. Various jump diffusion models are considered in this chapter. Also, the applications of jump diffusion processes on stocks, bonds, and interest rate are discussed.

Keywords: Black–Scholes model; jump diffusion process; mixed-jump process; Bernoulli jump process; Gauss–Hermite jump process; conditional jump dynamics; ARCH/GARCH jump diffusion model; affine jump diffusion model; autoregressive jump process model; jump diffusion with conditional heteroskedasticity.

43.1. Introduction

In contrast to basic insights into continuous-time asset-pricing models that have been driven by stochastic diffusion processes with continuous sample paths, jump diffusion processes have been used in finance to capture discontinuous behavior in asset pricing. As described in Merton (1976), the validity of Black–Scholes formula depends on whether the stock price dynamics can be described by a continuous-time diffusion process whose sample path is continuous with probability 1. Thus, if the stock price dynamics cannot be represented by stochastic process with a continuous sample path, the Black–Scholes solution is not valid. In other words, as the price processes feature big jumps, i.e. not continuous, continuous-time models cannot explain why

the jumps occur, and hence not adequate. In addition, Ahn and Thompson (1986) also examined the effect of regulatory risks on the valuation of public utilities and found that those "jump risks" were priced even though they were uncorrelated with market factors. It shows that jump risks cannot be ignored in the pricing of assets. Thus, a "jump" stochastic process defined in continuous time, and also called as "jump diffusion model" was rapidly developed.

The jump diffusion process is based on Poisson process, which can be used for modeling systematic jumps caused by surprise effect. Suppose we observe a stochastic process S_t, which satisfies the following stochastic differential equation with jump:

$$dS_t = a_t \, dt + \sigma_t \, dW_t + dJ_t, \quad t \geq 0, \tag{43.1}$$

where dW_t is a standard Wiener process. The term dJ_t represents possible unanticipated jumps, and which is a Poisson process. As defined in Gourieroux and Jasiak (2001), a jump process $(J_t, t \in R^+)$ is an increasing process such that

(i). $J_0 = 0$,

(ii). $P[J_{t+dt} - J_t = 1 | J_t] = \lambda_t \, dt + o(dt)$,

(iii). $P[J_{t+dt} - J_t = 0 | J_t] = 1 - \lambda_t \, dt + o(dt)$,

where $o(dt)$ tends to 0 when t tends to 0, and λ_t, called the intensity, is a function of the information available at time t. Furthermore, since the term dJ_t is part of the unpredictable innovation terms we make $E[\Delta J_t] = 0$, which has zero mean during a finite interval h. Besides, as any predictable part of the jumps may be can be included in the drift component α_t, jump times $\tau_j, j = 1, 2, \ldots$. vary by some discrete and random amount. Without loss of generality, we assume that there are k possible types of jumps, with size a_i, $i = 1, 2, L$, and the jumps occur at rate λ_t that may depend on the latest observed S_t. As soon as a jump occurs, the jump type is selected randomly and independently. The probability of a jump of size a_i, occuring is given by p_i. Particularly, for the case of the standard Poisson process, all jumps have size 1. In short, the path of a jump process is an increasing stepwise function with jumps equal to 1 at random rate $D_1, D_2, \ldots, D_t, \ldots,$.

Related research on the earlier development of a basic Poisson jump model in finance was by Press (1967). His model can be motivated as the aggregation of a number of price changes within a fixed-time interval. In his paper, the Poisson distribution governs the number of events that result in price movement, and the average number of events in a time interval is called intensity. In addition, he assumes that all volatility dynamics is the result of discrete jumps in stock returns and the size of a jump is stochastic and normally distributed. Consequently, some empirical applications found that a normal Poisson jump model provides a good statistical characterization of daily exchange rate and stock returns. For instance, using Standard & Poor's 500 futures options and assuming an underlying jump diffusion, Bates (1991) found systematic behavior in expected jumps before the 1987 stock market crash. In practice, by observing different paths of asset prices with respect to different assets, distinct jump diffusion models were introduced into literature by many researchers. Therefore, in this chapter, we will survey various jump diffusion models in current literature as well as estimation procedures for these processes.

43.2. Mixed-Jump Processes

The total change in asset prices may be comprised of two types of changes:

1. Normal vibrations caused by marginal information events satisfying a local Markov property and modeled by a standard geometric Brownian motion with a constant variance per unit time. It has a continuous sample path.

2. Abnormal vibrations caused by information shocks satisfying an antipathetical jump process defined in continuous time, and modeled by a jump process, reflecting the nonmarginal impact of the information.

Thus, there have been a variety of studies that explain too many outliers for a simple, constant-variance log-normal distribution of stock price series. Among them, Merton (1976) and Tucker and Pond (1988) provide a more thorough discussion of mixed-jump processes. Mixed-jump processes are formed by combining a continuous diffusion process and a discrete-jump process and may capture local and nonlocal asset price dynamics.

Merton (1976) pioneered the use of jump processes in continuous-time finance. He derived an option pricing formula as the underlying stock returns are generated by a mixture of both continuous and the jump processes. He posited stock returns as

$$\frac{dS}{S} = (\alpha - \lambda k)dt + \sigma dZ + dq \qquad (43.1)$$

where S is the stock price, α the instantaneous expected return on the stock, σ^2 the instantaneous variance of the stock return conditional on no arrivals of "abnormal" information, dZ the standardized Wiener process, q the Poisson process assumed independent of dZ, λ the intensity of the Poisson process, $k = \varepsilon(Y - 1)$, where $\tilde{Y} - 1$ is the random variable percentage change in stock price if the Poisson event occurs; ε is the expectation operator over the random variable Y. Actually, Equation (43.1) can be rewritten as

$$\frac{dS}{S} = (\alpha - \lambda k)dt + \sigma dZ$$

$$\text{if the Poisson does not occur} \qquad (43.2)$$
$$= (\alpha - \lambda k)dt + \sigma dZ + (Y - 1),$$
$$\text{if the Poisson occurs}$$

Therefore, the option return dynamics can be re-written as

$$\frac{\mathrm{d}W}{W} = (\alpha_w - \lambda k_w)\mathrm{d}t + \sigma_w \mathrm{d}Z + \mathrm{d}q_w \qquad (43.3)$$

Most likely, α_w is the instantaneous expected return on the option, σ_ω^2 is the instantaneous variance of the stock return conditional on no arrivals of "abnormal" information, q_w is an Poisson process with parameter λ assumed independent of $\mathrm{d}Z$, $k_w = \varepsilon(Y_w - 1)$, $(Y_w - 1)$ is the random variable percentage change in option price if the Poisson event occurs, ε is the expectation operator over the random variable Y_w. The Poisson event for the option price occurs if and only if the Poisson event for the stock price occurs. Further, define the random variable, X_n, which has the same distribution as the product of n independently and identically distributed random variables. Each of n independently and identically distributed random variables has the identical distribution as the random variable Y described in Equation (43.1). As a consequence, by the original Black–Scholes option pricing formula for the no-jump case, $W(S, \tau; E, r, \sigma^2)$, we can get the option price with jump component

$$F(s, \tau) = \sum_{n=1}^{\infty} \frac{\mathrm{e}^{-\lambda\tau}(\lambda\tau)^n}{n!} \left[\varepsilon_n \{ W(SX_n \mathrm{e}^{-\lambda k\tau,\tau}; E, \sigma^2, r) \} \right]$$

$$(43.4)$$

Generally speaking, W satisfies the boundary conditions of partial differential equation (see Oksendal, 2000), and can be rewritten as a twice continuously differentiable function of the stock price and time, $W(t) = F(S, t)$. Nevertheless, Equation (43.4) still not only holds most of the attractive features of the original Black–Scholes formula such as being regardless of the investor preferences or knowledge of the expected return on the underlying stock, but also satisfies the Sharpe–Linter Capital Asset Pricing model as long as the jump component of a security's return is uncorrelated with the market. In other words, the mixed-jump model of Merton uses the CAPM

to value options written on securities involving jump processes.

Also, Tucker and Pond (1988) empirically investigated four candidate processes (the scaled-t distribution, the general stable distribution, compound normal distribution, and the mixed-jump model) for characterizing daily exchange rate changes for six major trading currencies from the period 1980 to 1984. They found that the mixed-jump model exhibited the best distributional fit for all six currencies tested. Akgiray and Booth (1988) also found that the mixed-diffusion jump process was superior to the stable laws or mixture of normals as a model of exchange rate changes for the British pound, French franc, and the West German mark relative to the U.S. dollar. Thus, both theoretical and empirical studies of exchange rate theories under uncertainty should explicitly allow for the presence of discontinuities in exchange rate processes. In addition, the assumption of pure diffusion processes for exchange rates could lead to misleading inferences due to its crude approximation.

43.3. Bernoulli Jump Process

In the implementation of empirical works, Ball and Torous (1983) provide statistical evidence with the existence of log-normally distributed jumps in a majority of the daily returns of a sample of NYSE-listed common stocks. The expression of their Poisson jump diffusion model is as Equation (43.1), and jump size Y has posited distribution, $\ln Y \sim N(\mu, \delta^2)$.

Ball and Torous (1983) introduced the Bernoulli jump process as an appropriate model for stock price jumps. Denote X_i as the number of events that occur in subinterval i and independent distributed random variables. By stationary independent increment assumption,

$$N = \sum_{i=1}^{n} X_i,$$

where N is the number of events that occur in a time interval of length t. Besides, define $h = t/n$ for any arbitrary integer n and divide $(0, t)$ into n equal subintervals each of length h. Thus, X_i satisfies

$\Pr[X_i = 0] = 1 - \lambda h + O(h)$

$\Pr[X_i = 1] = \lambda h + O(h) \quad \text{for } i = 1, 2, \ldots, n$

$\Pr[X_i > 1] = O(h)$

For large n, X_i has approximately the Bernoulli distribution with parameter $\lambda h = \lambda t/n$. As a result, N has the binomial distribution, approximately, i.e.

$$\Pr[N = k] \cong \binom{n}{k}\left(\frac{\lambda t}{n}\right)^k \left(1 - \frac{\lambda t}{n}\right)^{n-k} \quad k = 0, 1, 2, \ldots, n.$$

Now, assume that t is very small, they can approximate N by the Bernoulli variate X defined by

$P[X = 0] = 1 - \lambda t,$

$P[X = 1] = \lambda t.$

The advantage of the Bernoulli jump process is that more satisfactory empirical analyses are available. The maximum likelihood estimation can be practically implemented and the unbiased, consistent, and efficient estimators that attain the Cramer–Rao lower bound for the corresponding parameters. Moreover, the statistically most powerful test of the null hypothesis $\lambda = 0$ can be implemented. Obviously, a Bernoulli jump process models information arrivals and stock price jumps. This shows that the presence of a jump component in common stock returns can be possessed well. As a consequence, Vlaar and Palm (1993) combined the GARCH (1,1) and Bernoulli jump distribution to account for skewness and leptokurtosis for weekly rates of the European Monetary System (EMS). Das (2002) considered the concept of Bernoulli approximation to test the impact of Federal Reserve actions by Federal Funds' rate as well. (See Section 43.9.2 and Section 43.5, respectively.)

43.4. Gauss–Hermite Jump Process

To ensure the efficiency properties in valuing compound option, Omberg (1988) derived a family of jump models by employing Gauss–Hermite quadrature.

Note that $t = 0$ and $t = T$ are the current time and expiration date of the option, respectively, and $\Delta t = T/N$. Consider a compound option that can only be exercised at the N interval boundaries $t_k = T - k\Delta t$, $k = 0, \ldots, N$. Let $C_k(S)$ be the value of the compound option at time t_k, the current value of the compound option is then $C_N(S)$; the value of an actual contingent claim with optimal exercise possible at any time is $\lim N \to C_N(S)$. The compound option can be recursively valued by

$$C_{k+1}(S) = \max\left\{EV_{k+1}, \, \mathrm{e}^{-r}\Delta t E\left[C_k(S_k; S)\right]\right\},$$

where EV_{k+1} is the immediate exercise value at time t_{k+1}. Since $S(t)$ is an unrestricted log-normal diffusion process from t_k to t_{k+1},

$$E[C_k] = \int_{-\infty}^{\infty} \phi(z) C_k\left(Se^{\mu'\Delta t + z\sigma\sqrt{(\Delta t)}}\right)\mathrm{d}z, \qquad (43.5)$$

where z is an independent sample from a normal distribution with mean zero and variance one, $\phi(z)$ is its density function, and $\mu' = r - \sigma^2/2$ for a risk-neutral valuation. A jump process approximation to the above with n jumps takes the form

$$E[C_k] \cong \sum_{j=1}^{n} p_j C_k(Se^{u}j), \, p_j \le 0 \, \text{for } j = 1, \ldots, n,$$

$$\sum_{j=1}^{n} p_j = 1, \, u_j = \mu'\Delta t + z_j\sigma\sqrt{(\Delta t)}$$

So, Omberg (1988) considers to use Gaussian integration to approximate an intergral of the form as in Equation (43.5). For example, for the intergral,

$$I = \int_a^b w(x)f(x)\mathrm{d}x,$$

we can approximate this equation by a weighted average of the function $f(x)$ at n points $\{x_1, \ldots, x_n\}$. Let $\{w_i\}$ and $\{x_j\}$ are selected to maximize the degree of precision m^*, which is a integration rule, i.e. if the integration error is zero for all polynomials $f(x)$ of order m^* or less. $\{P_j(x)\}$

is the set of polynomials with respect to the weighting function $w(x)$,

$$\int_a^b w(x)P_i(x)P_j(x)\mathrm{d}x = 0, \quad \text{for } i \neq j,$$

$$\int_a^b w(x)P_j^2(x)\mathrm{d}x = \gamma_j \neq 0, \quad \text{for } i = j,$$

Thus, the optimal evaluation points $\{X_j\}$ are the n zeros of $P_n(x)$ and the corresponding weights $\{w_j\}$ are

$$w_j = \frac{-(a_{n+1,\,n+1}/a_{n,\,n})\gamma_n}{P_n'(x_j)P_{n+1}(x_j)} > 0.$$

The degree of precision is $m^* = 2n - 1$. If the weighting function $w(x)$ is symmetric with regard to the midpoint of the interval $[a, b]$, then $\{x_j\}$ and $\{w_j\}$ are the Gaussian evaluation points $\{x_j\}$ and weights $\{w_j\}$, respectively. Particularly, the above procedure is called Gauss–Hermite quadrature to approximate the integration problem. What is shown in Omberg (1988) is the application of Gauss–Hermite quadrature to the valuation of a compound option, which is a natural way to generate jump processes of any order n that are efficient in option valuation. Thus, the Gauss–Hermite jump process arises as an efficient solution to the problem of replicating a contingent claim over a finite period of time with a portfolio of assets. With this result, he suggested the extension of these methods to option valuation problems with multiple state variables, such as the valuation of bond options in which the state variables are taken to be interest rates at various terms.

43.5. Jumps in Interest Rates

Cox et al. (1985a) proposed an influential paper that derived a general equilibrium asset pricing model under the assumption of diffusion processes, and analyzed the term structure of interest rate by it. Ahn and Thompson (1988) applied Cox, Ingersoll, and Ross's methodology to their model, which is driven by jump diffusion processes, and

investigated the effect of jump components of the underlying processes on the term structure of interest rates. They differ from the model of Cox et al. (1985) when they consider the state variables as jump diffusion processes. Therefore, they suggested that jump risks may have important implications for interest rate, and cannot be ignored for the pricing of assets. In other words, they found that Merton's multi-beta CAPM does not hold in general due to the existence of jump component of the underlying processes on the term structure of interest rate. Also, Breeden's single consumption beta does not hold, because the discontinuous movements of the investment opportunities cannot be fully captured by a single consumption beta. Moreover, in contrast with the work of Cox et al. (1981) providing that the traditional expectations theory is not consistent with the equilibrium models, they found that traditional expectations theory is not consistent with the equilibrium models as the term structure of interest rate is under the jump diffusion process, since the term premium is affected by the jump risk premiums. Das (2002) tested the impact of Federal Reserve actions by examining the role of jump-enhanced stochastic processes in modeling the Federal Funds rate. This research illustrated that compared to the stochastic processes of equities and foreign exchange rates, the analytics for interest rates are more complicated. One source of analytical complexity considered in modeling interest rates with jumps is mean reversion. Allowing for mean reversion included in jump diffusion processes, the process for interest rates employed in that paper is as follows

$$\mathrm{d}r = k(\theta - r)\mathrm{d}t + \upsilon \mathrm{d}z + J\mathrm{d}\pi(h), \tag{43.6}$$

which shows interest rate has mean-reversing drift and two random terms, a pure diffusion process and a Poisson process with a random jump J. In addition, the variance of the diffusion is υ^2, and a Poisson process π represents the arrival of jumps with arrival frequency parameter h, which is defined as the number of jumps per year. Moreover, denote J as jump size, which can be a constant or with a probability distribution. The diffusion and Poisson processes are independent of each other as well as independent of J.

The estimation method used here is the Bernoulli approximation proposed in Ball and Torous (1983). Assuming that there exists no jump or only one jump in each time interval, approximate the likelihood function for the Poisson–Gauss model using a Bernoulli mixture of the normal distributions governing the diffusion and jump shocks.

In discrete time, Equation (43.6) can be expressed as follows:

$$\Delta r = k(\theta - r)\Delta t + v\Delta z + J(\mu, \gamma^2)\Delta \pi(h),$$

where v^2 is the annualized variance of the Gaussian shock, and Δz is a standard normal shock term. $J(\mu, \gamma^2)$ is the jump shock with normal distribution. $\Delta \pi(q)$ is the discrete-time Poisson increment, approximated by a Bernoulli distribution with parameter $q = h\Delta t + O(\Delta t)$, allowing the jump intensity q to depend on various state variables conditionally. The transition probabilities for interest rates following a Poisson–Gaussian process are written as (for s > t):

$$f\left[r(s)|r(t)\right] = q\exp\left(\frac{-(r(s) - r(t) - k(\theta - r(t))\Delta t - \mu)^2}{2(v_t^2\Delta t + \gamma^2)}\right)$$

$$\frac{1}{\sqrt{(2\pi(v_t^2\Delta t + \gamma^2))}}$$

$$+ (1 - q)\exp\left(\frac{-(r(s) - r(t) - k(\theta - r(t))\Delta t)^2}{2v_t^2\Delta t}\right)$$

$$\frac{1}{\sqrt{(\pi v_t^2\Delta t)}},$$

where $q = h\Delta t + O(\Delta t)$. This is an approximation for the true Poisson–Gaussian density with a mixture of normal distributions. As in Ball and Torous (1983), by maximum-likelihood estimation, which maximizes the following function L,

$$L = \prod_{t=1}^{T} f\left[r(t + \Delta t)|r(t)\right],$$

we can obtain estimates that are consistent, unbiased, and efficient and attain the Cramer-Rao

lower bound. Thus, they obtain the evidence that jumps are an essential component of interest rate models. Especially, the addition of a jump process diminishes the extent of nonlinearity although some research finds that the drift term in the stochastic process for interest rates appears to be nonlinear.

Johannes (2003) suggested the estimated infinitesimal conditional moments to examine the statistical and economic role of jumps in continuous-time interest rate models. Based on Johannes's approach, Bandi and Nguyen (2003) provided a general asymptotic theory for the full function estimates of the infinitesimal moments of continuous-time models with discontinuous sample paths of the jump diffusion type. Their framework justifies consistent nonparametric extraction of the parameters and functions that drive the dynamic evolution of the process of interest. (i.e. the potentially nonaffine and level dependent intensity of the jump arrival being an example). Particularly, Singleton (2001) provided characteristic function approaches to deal with the Affine jump diffusion models of interest rate. In the next section, we will introduce affine jump diffusion model.

43.6. Affine Jump Diffusion model

For development in dynamic asset pricing models, a particular assumption is that the state vector X follows an affine jump diffusion (AJD). An affine jump model is a jump diffusion process. In general, as defined in Duffie and Kan (1996), we suppose the diffusion for a Markov process X is 'affine' if

$$\mu(y) = \theta + \kappa y$$

$$\sigma(y)\sigma(y)' = h + \sum_{j=1}^{N} y_j H^{(j)},$$

where $\mu: D \to R^n$ and $\sigma: D \to R^{n \times n}$, θ is $N \times 1$, κ is $N \times N$, h and $H^{(j)}$ are all $N \times N$ and symmetric. The X's may represent observed asset returns or prices or unobserved state variables in a dynamic pricing model, such as affine term structure models. Thus, extending the concept of 'affine' to the case of affine jump diffusions, we can note

that the properties for affine jump diffusions
are that the drift vector, "instantaneous" covariance matrix, and jump intensities all have affine
dependence on the state vector. Vasicek (1977) and
Cox et al. (1985) proposed the Gaussian and
square root diffusion models which are among
the AJD models in term structure literature. Suppose that X is a Markov process in some state
space $D \subset R^n$, the affine jump diffusion is

$$dX_t = \mu(X_t)dt + \sigma(X_t)dW_t + dZt,$$

where W is an standard Brownian motion
in R^n, $\mu : D \to R^n$, $\sigma : D \to R^{n \times n}$, and Z is a
pure jump process whose jumps have a fixed prob-
ability distribution v on and arriving intensity
$\{\lambda(X_t) : t \geq 0\}$, for some $\lambda : D \to [0, \infty)$.

Furthermore, in Duffie et al. (2000), they suppose that X is Markov process whose transition
semi-group has an infinitesimal generator of levy
type defined at a bounded C^2 function $f : D \to R$
with bounded first and second derives by

$$\wp f(x) = f_x(x)\mu(x) + \frac{1}{2} tr \left[f_{xx}(x)\sigma(x)\sigma(x)^T \right] + \lambda(x).$$

It means that conditional on the path of X, the
jump times of Z are the jump times of a
Poisson process with time varying intensity
$\{\lambda(X_s) : 0 \leq s \leq t\}$, and that the size of the jump
of Z at a jump time T is independent of
$\{X_s : 0 \leq s \leq T\}$, and has the probability distribution v. Consequently, they provide an analytical
treatment of a class of transforms, including
Laplace and Fourier transformations in the setting
of affine jump diffusion state process.

The first step to their method is to show that the
Fourier transform of X_t and of certain related
random variables are known in closed form.
Next, by inverting this transform, they show how
the distribution of X_t and the prices of options can
be recovered. Then, they fix an affine discount
rate function $R : D \to R$. Depending on coefficients
(K, H, L, ρ), the affine dependence of μ, $\sigma\sigma^T$, λ, R
are determined, as shown in p.1350 of Duffie et al.
(2000). Moreover, for $c \in C^n$, the set of n-tuples of
complex numbers, let $\theta(c) = \int_{R^n} \exp(c.z)dv(z)$.

Thus, the "jump transform" θ determines the
jump size distribution. In other words, the "coefficients" (K, H, l, θ) of X completely determine its
distribution. Their method suggests a real advantage of choosing a jump distribution v with an
explicitly known or easily computed jump transform θ. They also applied their transform analysis
to the pricing of options. See Duffle et al. (2000).
Furthermore, Singleton (2001) developed several
estimation strategies for affine asset pricing models
based on the known functional form of the conditional characteristic function (CCF) of discretely
sampled observations from an affine jump diffusion model, such as LML-CCF (Limited-information estimation), ML-CCF (Maximum likelihood
estimation), and GMM-CCF estimation, etc. As
shown in his paper, a method of moments estimator based on the CCF is shown to approximate the
efficiency of maximum likelihood for affine diffusion models.

43.7. Geometric Jump Diffusion Model

Using Geometric Jump Diffusion with the instantaneous conditional variance, V_t, following a mean
reverting square root process, Bates (1996) showed
that the exchange rate, $S(\$/\text{deutschemark(DM)})$
followed it:

$$dS/S = (\mu - \lambda \bar{k})dt + \sqrt{V}dZ + kdq$$
$$dV = (\alpha - \beta V)dt + \sigma_v \sqrt{V}dZ_v$$
$$Cov(dZ, dZ_v) = pdt$$
$$Pr(dq = 1) = \lambda dt$$
$$\ln(1 + k) \sim N\left(\ln(1 + \bar{k}) - \frac{1}{2}\delta^2, \delta^2\right),$$

where μ is the instantaneous expected rate of appreciation of the foreign currency, λ is the numbers
of jumps in a year, k is the random percentage
jump conditional on a jump occurring, and q is a
Poisson counter with intensity λ.

The main idea of this model illustrated that
skewed distribution can arise by considering nonzero average jumps. Similarly, it also discusses that
excess kurtosis can arise from a substantial jump

component. In addition, this geometric jump diffusion model can see a direct relationship between the magnitude of conditional skewness and excess kurtosis and the length of the holding period as well.

43.8. Autoregressive Jump Process Model

A theory of the distribution of stock returns was derived by Bachelier (1900) and expanded using the idea of Brownian motion by Osborne (1959). However, the empirical works generally concluded that the B-O model fits observed returns rather poorly. For example, a casual examination of transactions data shows that assumption of a constant interval between transactions is not strictly valid. On the other hand, transactions for a given stock occur at random times throughout a day which gives nonuniform time intervals Also, the notion of independence between transaction returns is suspect. Niederhoffer and Osborne (1966) showed that the empirical tests of independence using returns based on transaction data have generally found large and statistically significant negative correlation. Thus, it is reasonable to model returns as a process with random time intervals between transaction and serial correlation among returns on individual trades. Accordingly, an autoregressive jump process that models common stock returns through time was proposed by Oldfield et al. (1977). This model consists of a diffusion process, which is continuous with probability 1 and jump processes, which are continuous with probability 1. The jump process is assumed to operate such that a jump occurs at each actual transaction, and allows the magnitudes of jumps to be autocorrelated. In addition, the model relies on the distribution of random time intervals between transactions. They suppose the dollar return of a common stock over a holding period of length s is the result of a process, which is a mixture process composed of a continuous and jump process,

$$\frac{dP}{P} = \alpha dt + \beta dW + z d\pi, \qquad (43.7)$$

where P stands for share price, dW is the increment of a Wiener process with zero mean and unit variance, z is the percent change in share price resulting from a jump, $d\pi$ is a jump process (when $d\pi = 1$, a jump occurs; when $d\pi = 0$, no jump occurs) and $d\pi$ and dW are assumed to be independent. Jump amplitude is independent of $d\pi$ and dW, but jumps may be serially correlated. s is the elapsed time between observed price P_{t+s} and P_t. The number of jumps during the interval s is N, and $Z(i)$ are the jump size where $Z(0) = 1$ and $Z(i) \geq 0$ for $i = 1, \ldots, N$. And the solution for Equation (43.7) is

$$P(t + s) = P(t) \cdot Z(0) \cdot Z(1) \ldots Z(N) \cdot \exp \\ \{(\alpha - \beta^2/2)s + \beta\sqrt{(s)}W\} \qquad (43.8)$$

Divide Equation (43.8) by $P(t)$ and take natural logarithms, then

$$\ln[P(t+s)/P(t)] = (\alpha - \beta^2/2)s \\ + \beta\sqrt{(s)}W +]\sum_{i=1}^{N} \log Z(i). \qquad (43.9)$$

According to the Equation (43.9), we can see the third term of Equation (43.9) is the jump process. If $N = 0$ then $\ln[P(t+s)/P(s)]$ is normally distributed with mean $(\alpha - \beta^2/2)s$ and variance $\beta^2 s$. If the $\ln Z(i)$ are assumed to be identically distributed with mean μ and finite variance σ^2, a general form of joint density for $\ln Z(i)$ can be represented by:

$$f(\ln Z(1), \cdots, \ln Z(N)) = \int_{-\infty}^{\infty} f(\ln Z(1), \cdots, \\ \ln Z(N), W) dW,$$

with :

$$E[\ln Z(i)] = \mu, \quad \text{for} \quad i = 1, \cdots, N,$$

$$\text{Var}[\ln Z(i)] = \sigma^2, \quad \text{for} \quad i = 1, \cdots, N,$$

$$\text{Cov}[\ln Z(i), \ln Z(i-j)] = \rho_j \sigma^2, \quad \text{for } j \geq 0.$$

where ρ_j is the correlation between $\ln Z(i)$ and $\ln Z(i-j)$. The index i represents the jump number while the index j denotes the number of lags between jumps. The startling feature of this general joint density is the autocorrelation among jumps. Hence, some major conclusions are drawn from the data analysis: (1).

A geometric Brownian motion process or a subordinated process does not alone describe the sample data very well. (2). Stock returns seem to follow an autoregressive jump process based on the sample means and variances of transaction returns. (3). In contrast to the previous empirical work which is not sufficiently detailed to determine the probability law for transaction returns, the probability density for the time intervals between jumps is gamma.

43.9. Jump Diffusion Models with Conditional Heteroscedasticity

43.9.1. Conditional Jump Dynamics

The basic jump model has been extended in a number of directions. A tractable alternative is to combine jumps with an ARCH/GARCH model in discrete time. It seems likely that the jump probability will change over time. Ho et al. (1996) formulate a continuous-time asset pricing model based on the work of Chamnerlain (1988), but include jumps. Their work strongly suggested that both jump components and heteroscedastic Brownian motions are needed to model the asset returns. As the jump components are omitted, the estimated rate of convergence of volatility to its unconditional mean is significantly biased. Moreover, Chan and Maheu (2002) developed a new conditional jump model to study jump dynamics in stock market returns. They present a discrete-time jump model with time varying conditional jump intensity and jump size distribution. Besides, they combine the jump specification with a GARCH parameterization of volatility. Consider the following jump model for stock returns:

$$R_t = \mu + \sum_{i=1}^{t} \phi R_{t-i} + \sqrt{h_t} z_t + \sum_{k=1}^{n_t} Y_{t,k}, \quad (43.10)$$

$$z_t \sim NID(0,1), \quad Y_{t,k} \sim N(\theta_t, \delta^2).$$

Define the information set at time t to be the history of returns, $\Phi_t = \{R_t, \cdots, R_1\}$ The conditional jump size $Y_{t,k}$, given Φ_{t-1}, is presumed to be independent and normally distributed with mean θ_t and variance δ^2. Denote n_t as the discrete counting process governing the number of jumps that arrive between $t-1$ and t, which is distributed as a Poisson random variable with the parameter $\lambda_t > 0$ and density

$$P(n_t = j | \Phi_{t-1}) = \frac{\exp(-\lambda_t)\lambda_t^j}{j!}, \quad j = 0, 1, 2, \cdots. \quad (43.11)$$

The mean and variance for the Poisson random variable are both λ_t, which is often called the jump intensity. The jump intensity is allowed time-varying. h_t is measurable with respect to the information set Φ_{t-1} and follows a GARCH(p,q) process,

$$h_t = w + \sum_{i=1}^{q} \alpha_i \varepsilon_{t-i}^2 + \sum_{i=1}^{p} \beta_i h_{t-i},$$

where $\varepsilon_t = R_t - \mu - \sum_{i=1}^{p} \phi_i R_{t-i}$. ε_t contains the expected jump component and it affects future volatility through the GARCH variance factor. Moreover, based on a parsimonious ARMA structure, let λ_t be endogenous. Denote the following ARJI(r,s) model:

$$\lambda_t = \lambda_0 + \sum_{i=1}^{r} \rho_i \lambda_{t-i} + \sum_{i=1}^{s} \gamma_i \xi_{t-i}$$

$\lambda_t = E[n_t | \Phi_{t-1}]$ is the conditional expectation of the counting process. ξ_{t-i} represents the innovation to λ_{t-i}. The shock jump intensity residual is

$$\xi_{t-i} = E[n_{t-i} | \Phi_{t-i}] - \lambda_{t-i}$$
$$= \sum_{j=0}^{\infty} j P(n_{t-i} = j | \phi_{t-i}) - \lambda_{t-i}. \quad (43.12)$$

The first term of Equation (43.12) is average number of jumps at time $t - i$ based on time $t - i$ information. Therefore, xi_{t-i} represents the unpredictable component about the conditional mean of the counting process n_{t-i}. Moreover, having observed R_t, let $f(R_t|n_t = j, \Phi_{t-1})$ denote the conditional density of returns given that j jumps occur and the information set Φ_{t-1}, we can get the ex-post probability of the occurrence of j jumps at time t, with the filter defined as

$$P(n_t = j|\Phi_t) = \frac{f(R_t|n_t = j, \Phi_{t-1})P(n_t = j|\Phi_{t-1})}{P(R_t|\Phi_{t-1})},$$
$$j = 0, 1, 2, \cdots,$$
(43.13)

where, the definition of $P(n_t = j|\Phi_{t-1})$ is the same as Equation (43.11). The filter in Equation (43.13) is an important component of their model of time varying jump dynamics. Thus, the conditional density of return is

$$P(R_t|\Phi_{t-1}) = \sum_{j=0}^{\infty} f(R_t|n_t = j, \Phi_{t-1})P(n_t = j|\Phi_{t-1}).$$
(43.14)

Equation (43.14) shows that this model is nothing more than a discrete mixture of distribution where the mixing is driven by a time varying Poisson distribution. Therefore, from the assumption of Equation (43.10), the distribution of returns conditional on the most recent information set and j jumps is normally distributed as

$$f(R_t|n_t = j, \Phi_{t-1}) = \frac{1}{\sqrt{2\pi(h_t + j\delta_t^2)}} \times \exp$$
$$\left(-\frac{(R_t - \mu - \sum_{i=1}^{l} \phi_i R_{t-i} - \theta_t j)^2}{2(h_t + j\delta_t^2)} \right).$$

Equation (43.13) includes an infinite sum over the possible number of jumps n_t. However, practically, they consider truncating the maximum number of jumps to a large value τ, and then they set the probability of τ or more jumps to 0. Hence, the first way to choose τ is to check Equation (43.11) to be equal to 0 for $j \geq \tau$. The second check on the choice of τ is to investigate $\tau > \tau$ to make sure that the parameter estimate does not change.

The ARJI model illustrates that conditional jump intensity is time varying. Suppose that we observe $\xi_\tau > 0$ for several periods. This suggests that the jump intensity is temporarily trending away from its unconditional mean. On the other hand, this model effectively captures systematic changes in jump risk in the market. In addition, they find significant time variation in the conditional jump intensity and the jump size distribution in their application for daily stock market returns. Accordingly, the ARJI model can capture systematic changes, and also forecast increases (decreases) in jump risk into the future.

43.9.2. ARCH/GARCH Jump Diffusion Model

As described in Drost et al. (1998), there exists a major drawback of Merton's (1976) model which implies that returns are independent and identically distributed at all frequencies that conflict with the overwhelming evidence of conditional heteroscedasticity in returns at high frequencies, because all deviations from log normality of observed stock returns at any frequency can be attributed to the jumps in his model. Thus, several papers consider the size of jumps within the models that also involve the conditional heteroscedasticity.

Jorion (1988) considered a tractable specification combining both ARCH and jump processes for foreign exchange market:

$$\ln(P_t/P_{t-1})|t-1 = \mu + \sqrt{(b_t)}z + \sum_{i=1}^{n_t} \ln(Y_t),$$
$$b_t = E_{t-1}(\sigma_t^2) = \alpha_0 + \alpha_1(x_{t-1} - \mu)^2$$

in which α_1 is the autoregressive parameter inducing heteroskedasticity and the distribution of x_t is conditional on information at $t-1$ and define x_t as the logarithm of price relative $\ln(Pt/P_{t-1})$. A jump size Y is assumed independently log normally distributed, $\ln Y \sim N(\theta, \delta^2)$, n_t is the actual number of jumps during the interval. z is a standard normal deviate. Consequently, his results reveal that exchange rate exhibit systematic discontinuities even after allowing for conditional heteroskedasticity in the diffusion process. In brief, in his work, the maximum likelihood estimation of a mixed-jump diffusion process indicates that ignoring the jump component in exchange rates can lead to serious mispricing errors for currency options. The same findings also can be found in Nieuwland et al. (1991) who allow for the model with conditional heteroscedasticity and jumps in exchangerate market. Also, an application of a GARCH jump mixture model has been given by Vlaar and Palm (1993). They point out that the GARCH specification cum normal innovation cannot fully explain the leptokurtic behavior for high-frequency financial data. Both the GARCH specification and the jump process can explain the leptokurtic behavior. Hence, they permit autocorrelation in the mean higher-order GARCH effect and Bernoulli jumps.

A weak GARCH model can be defined as a symmetric discrete-time process $\{y_{(h)t}, t \in h\,\grave{A}\}$ with finite fourth moment and with parameter $\zeta_h = (\phi_h, \alpha_h, \beta_h, \kappa_h)$, if there exists a covariance-stationary process $\{\sigma_{(h)t, t \in h\alpha}\}$ with

$$\sigma^2_{(h)t+h} = \phi_h + \alpha_h y^2_{(h)t} + \beta_h \sigma^2_{(h)t}, \quad t \in h\,\grave{A}$$

and we denote $\kappa_h = \dfrac{E y^4_{(h)t}}{(E y^2_{(h)t})^2}$ as the kurtosis of the process.

Roughly speaking, the class of continuous-time GARCH models can be divided into two groups. One is the GARCH diffusion in which the sample paths are smooth and the other, where the sample paths are erratic. Drost and Werker (1996) developed several properties of discrete-time data that are generated by underlying continuous-time processes that accommodate both conditional heteroscedasticity and jumps. Their model is as follows. Let $\{Y_t, t \geq 0\}$ be the GARCH jump diffusion with parameter vector $\zeta_h = (\phi_h, \alpha_h, \beta_h, \kappa_h)$ and suppose α_{h_0} for some $h_0 > 0$. Then, there exists $\omega \in (0, \infty)$, $\theta \in (0, \infty)$, $\phi \in (0, \infty)$, $v \in (0, \infty)$ and c_h and κ_h are given by

$$c_h = \frac{4\{\exp(-h\theta) - 1 + h\theta\} + 2h\theta\left\{1 + \dfrac{v + 2h\theta}{v\phi(2 + \phi)}\right\}}{1 - \exp(-2h\theta)},$$

$$\kappa_h = 3 + \frac{v}{h\theta} + 3v\phi(2 + \phi)\frac{\exp(-h\theta) - 1 + h\theta}{(h\theta)^2},$$

such that ζ_h (with $|\beta_h| < 1$) is determined by

$$\psi_h = h\omega\{1 - \exp(-h\theta)\},$$

$$\alpha_h = \exp(-h\theta) - \beta_h, \quad \frac{\beta_h}{1 + \beta_h^2} = \frac{c_h \exp(-h\theta) - 1}{c_h\{1 + \exp(-2h\theta)\} - 2},$$

where θ is the time unit and scale is denoted by ω. ϕ and v are slope parameters and ϕ will denote slopes in the $(\alpha_h . \beta_h)$ plane, while v determines the slope of the kurtosis at very high frequencies. Drost et al. (1998) employed the results of Drost and Werker (1996), which stated that for GARCH diffusion at an arbitrary frequency h, the five discrete-time GARCH parameters can be written in terms of only four continuous-time parameters, i.e an over identifying restriction in GARCH diffusion, for proposing a test for the presence of jumps with conditional heteroscedasticity, which is based on the following Theorem 1.

Theorem 1. Let $\{Y_t : t \geq 0\}$ be a continuous-time GARCH diffusion. Then $\theta > 0$ and $\lambda \in (0,1)$ is defined by

$$\theta = -\ln(\alpha + \beta)$$

$$\lambda = 2\ln^2(\alpha + \beta)\left\{\frac{\{1 - (\alpha + \beta)^2\}(1 - \beta)^2}{\alpha - \alpha\beta(\alpha + \beta)}\right.$$

$$\left. + 6\ln(\alpha + \beta) + 2\ln^2(\alpha + \beta) + 4(1 - \alpha - \beta)\right\}$$

$$\kappa = 3 + 6\frac{\lambda}{1 - \lambda}\frac{\exp(-\theta) - 1 + \theta}{\theta^2}$$

Thus, we set up the null and alternative hypotheses:

$H_0 : \{Y_t : t \geq 0\}$ is a GARCH diffusion model and $H_1 : \{Y_t : t \geq 0\}$ is a GARCH jump diffusion model.

From Theorem 1, by simple calculation, we yield the relation between functions K and κ:

$$K(\alpha, \beta, \kappa) = \kappa - \kappa(\alpha, \beta) = 0$$

for GARCH diffusion. Furthermore, in Drost and Werker (1996), they showed that $K(\alpha, \beta, \kappa)$ will be strictly larger than 0 for any GARCH jump diffusion model. As a result, H_0 is equivalent to $K(\alpha, \beta, \kappa) = 0$ and H_1 is equivalent to

$K(\alpha, \beta, \kappa) > 0$. In other words, this test can be viewed as the kurtosis test for presence of jumps with conditional heteroscedasticity. As well, it indicates the presence of jumps in dollar exchange rate.

43.10. Other Jump Diffusion models

As shown in Chacko and Viceira (2003), the jump diffusion process for stock price dynamics with asymmetric upward and downward jumps is

$$\frac{\mathrm{d}S_t}{S_t} = \mu \mathrm{d}t + \sigma \mathrm{d}Z + [\exp(J_u) - 1]\mathrm{d}N_u(\lambda_u)$$
$$+ [\exp(-J_d) - 1]\mathrm{d}N_d(\lambda_d).$$

$[\exp(J_u) - 1]\mathrm{d}N_u(\lambda_u)$ and $[\exp(-J_d) - 1]\mathrm{d}N_d(\lambda_d)$ represent a positive jump and a downward jump, respectively. $J_u, J_d > 0$ are stochastic jump magnitudes, which implies that the stock prices are non-negative, $\lambda_d, \lambda_u > 0$ are constant, and also determine jump frequencies. Furthermore, the densities of jump magnitudes,

$$f(J_u) = \frac{1}{\eta_u} \exp\left(-\frac{J_u}{\eta_u}\right) \quad \text{and}$$

and

$$f(J_d) = \frac{1}{\eta_d} \exp\left(-\frac{J_d}{\eta_d}\right)$$

are drawn from exponential distributions. Note that μ and $\cdot\sigma$ are constants.

To estimate this process, they provide a simple, consistent procedure – spectral GMM by deriving the conditional characteristic function of that process.

REFERENCES

Ahn, C.M. and Howard, E.T. (1988). "Jump diffusion processes and the term structure of interest rates." *Journal of Finance*, 43(1): 155–174.

Akgiray, V. and Booth, G.G. (1988). "Mixed diffusion-jump process modeling of exchange rate movements." *Review of Economics and Statistics*, 70(4): 631–637.

Amin, K.L. (1993). "Jump diffusion option valuation in discrete time." *Journal of Finance*, 48(5): 1833–1863.

Bachelier, L. (1900). "Theory of speculation." in P. Costner (ed.) *Random Character of Stock Market Prices*. Cambridge: MIT Press, 1964, reprint.

Ball, C.A. and Torous, W.N. (1983). "A simplified jump process for common stock returns." *Journal of Financial and Quantitative analysis*, 18(1): 53–65.

Ball, C.A. and Torous, W.N. (1985). "On jumps in common stock prices and their impact on call option pricing." *Journal of Finance*, 40(1): 155–173.

Bandi, F.M. and Nguyen, T.H. (2003). "On the functional estimation of jump-diffusion models." *Journal of Econometrics*, 116: 293–328.

Bates, D.S. (1991). "The crash of '87: was it expected? The evidence from options markets." *Journal of Finance*, 46(3): 1009–1044.

Bates, D.S. (1996). "Jumps and stochastic volatility: exchange rate processes implicit in Deutsche Mark options." *Review of Financial Studies*, 46(3): 1009–1044.

Beckers, S. (1981). "A note on estimating the parameters of the diffusion-jump model of stock returns." *Journal of Financial and Quantitative Analysis*, XVI(1): 127–140.

Chacko, G. and Viceria, L.M. (2003). "Spectral GMM estimation of continuous time processes." *Journal of Econometrics*, 116: 259–292.

Chamberlain, G. (1988). "Asset pricing in multiperiod securities markets." *Econometrica*, 56: 1283–1300.

Chan, W.H. and Maheu, J.M. (2002). "Conditional jump dynamics in stock market returns," *Journal of Business and Economic Statistics*, 20(3): 377–389.

Clark, P.K. (1973). "A subordinated stochastic process model with finite variance for speculative prices." *Econometrica*, 41(1): 135–155.

Cox, J.C., Ingersoll, J.E. Jr., and Ross, S.A. (1981). "A re-examination of traditional hypotheses about the term structure of interest rate." *Journal of Finance*, 36: 769–799.

Cox, J.C., Ingersoll, J.E. Jr., and Ross, S.A. (1985a). "An intertemporal general equilibrium model of asset prices." *Econometrica*, 53: 363–384.

Cox, J.C., Ingersoll, J.E. Jr., and Ross, S.A. (1985b). "A theory of the term structure of interest rate." *Econometrica*, 53: 385–407.

Das, S.R. (2002). "The surprise element: jumps in interest rates." *Journal of Econometrics*, 106: 27–65.

Duffie, D. and Kan, R. (1996). "A yield-factor model of interest rate." *Mathematical Finance*, 6: 379–406.

Duffie, D., Pan, J., and Singleton, K. (2000). "Transform analysis and asset pricing for affine jump diffusion." *Econometrica*, 68: 1343–1376.

Drost, F.C. and Werker, B.J.M. (1996). "Closing the GARCH gap: continuous time GARCH modeling," *Journal of Econometrics*, 74: 31–57.

Drost, F.C., Nijman, T.E., and Werker, B.J.M. (1998). "Estimation and testing in models containing both jumps and conditional heteroscedasticity." *Journal of Business and Economic Statistics*, 16(2).

Gourieroux, C. and Jasiak, J. (2001). "Financial econometrics," 1st edn. New Jersey: Princeton University Press.

Ho, M.S., Perraudin, W.R.M., and Sorensen, S.E. (1996). "A continuous time arbitrage pricing model." *Journal of Business and Economic Statistics*, 14(1): 31–42.

Hull, J.C. (2000). "Option, futures, other derivatives", 4th edn. New Jersey: Prientice Hall.

Jarrow, R.A. and Rosenfeld, E.R. (1984). "Jumps risks and the intertemporal capital asset pricing model." *Journal of Business*, 57(3): 337–351.

Johannes, M. (2004). "The statistical and economic role of jumps in continuous time interest rate model", *Journal of Finance*, 59: 227–260.

Johnson, Timothy C. (2002) "Volatility, momentum, and time-varying skewneww in foreign exchange returns," *Journal of Business and Economic Statistics*, Vol 20, No 3, 390–411.

Jorion, P. (1988). "On jump processes in the foreign exchange and stock market." *Review of Financial Studies*, 1(4): 427–445.

Lawler, G.F. (2000). "Introduction to stochastic processes." Boca Raton : Chapman and Hall/CRC.

Merton, R.C. (1973). "An intertemporal capital asset pricing model." *Econometrica*, 41(5): 867–887.

Merton, R.C. (1976). "Option pricing when underlying stock returns are discontinuous." *Journal of Financial Economics*, 3: 125–144.

Neftci, S.N. (2000). "An introduction to the mathematics of financial derivatives," 2nd edn. New York: Academic press.

Niederhoffer, V. and Osborne, M.F.M. (1966). "Market making and reversal on the stock exchange." *Journal of the American Statistical Association*, 61: 897–916.

Nieuwland, F.G.M.C., Verschoor, W.F.C., and Wolff, C.C.P. (1991). "EMS exchange rates." *Journal of International Financial Markets, Institutions and Money*, 2: 21–42.

Oksendal, B. (1998). "Stochastic differential equations," 5th edn. New York: Springer.

Oldfield, G.S., Rogalski, R.J., and Jarrow, R.A. (1977). "An autoregressive jump process for common stock returns." *Journal of Financial Economics*, 5: 389–418.

Omberg, E. (1988). "Efficient discrete time jump process models in option pricing." *Journal of Financial and Quantitative Analysis*, 23(2): 161–174.

Osborne, M.F.M. (1959). "Brownian motion in the stock market." *Operations Research*, 7: 145–173.

Press, S.J. (1967). "A compound events model for security prices." *Journal of Business*, 40(3): 317–335.

Singleton, K. (2001). "Estimation of affine asset pricing models using the empirical characteristic function." *Journal of Econometrics*, 102(1): 111–141.

Tucker, A.L. and Lallon, P. (1988). "The probability distribution of foreign exchanges: tests of candidate processes." *Review of Economics and Statistics*, 70: 638–647.

Vasicek, O. (1977). "An equilibrium characterization of the term structure." *Journal of Financial Economics*, 5: 177–188.

Vlaar, P.J.G. and Palm, F.C. (1993). "The Message in weekly exchange rates in the European monetary system: mean reversion, conditional heteroscedasticity, and jumps." *Journal of Business and Economic Statistics*, 11(3): 351–360.

Chapter 44

NETWORKS, NODES, AND PRIORITY RULES

DANIEL G. WEAVER, *Rutgers University, USA*

Abstract

In the United States, the same stock can be traded at different locations. In the case of listed stocks, each location is a node in national network called the Intermarket Trading System (ITS). Unlisted stocks also trade at different nodes on the National Association of Securities Dealers Automated Quotation (NASDAQ) network. Each node of these two networks may have rules for breaking queuing ties among competing orders. Orders may be routed on the networks according to official rules (as with ITS) or order preferencing arrangements (both networks). This paper examines the impact of priority rules on individual markets and networks. The development of the ITS and NASDAQ networks as well as the relevant literature is discussed. I conclude that network priority rules improve market quality if they result in consolidated markets.

Keywords: networks; nodes; priority rules; preferencing; consolidated; fragmented; market quality; Intermarket Trading System; NYSE; NASDAQ

Assume that an investor wants to sell 100 shares of stock and a number of people are willing to buy it. Who should get to buy the 100 shares? If asked, the average person would say, the trader offering the highest price. What if there is more than one trader offering the same price? The average person would answer the trader who quoted the price first.

However, many times, the trader quoting the best price first does not get to trade. An understanding of the determinants of trade sequencing (called priority rules) will assist investors in designing trading strategies. This paper will review the different types of priority rules as well as the literature on the subject.

Related to priority rules is the concept of order routing. The average person conceives of a market for stock as a single entity. While it is true that Microsoft is a The National Association of Securities Dealers Automated Quotation (NASDAQ)-listed stock, the NASDAQ system is only one node in a network, any one of which could execute a trade for Microsoft. Similarly, there are more than a handful of markets in the United States that trade New York Stock Exchange (NYSE)-listed GE. The markets for both Microsoft and GE can be thought of as networks with multiple nodes. Each node may or may not have similar priority rules to the other nodes in the network.

In addition, networks may have priority rules that govern the routing of orders within the network (as does the network for NYSE stocks) or may not have network-wide priority rules (this is the case on NASDAQ). In fact, recently, the U.S. Securities and Exchange Commission (SEC) and derivatively Congress have begun addressing the issue of whether networks should have priority rules. The SEC has proposed imposing network-wide priority rules on NASDAQ, while some market forces have tried to convince the Congress that not only should NASDAQ not have network-wide priority rules, they have also lobbied to eliminate NYSE-listed network priority rules.

From the brief discussion just presented, it is clear that a submitted order faces a maze of routing and priority rules. Therefore, this paper will address these issues in hopes of shedding light on the relevant factors in designing an optimal network with regard to network routing and node priority rules.

In the following section, I shall discuss different types of priority rules in use in markets today as well as the literature on the subject. In Section 44.2, I will present a history of how the networks for NYSE-listed and NASDAQ stocks developed, which includes routing rules. In the Section 44.3, I will discuss the current political and regulatory environment concerning stock networks. I will also discuss whether networks benefit from priority rules. In the final section, I conclude.

44.1. Priority Rules

Markets and network nodes use a variety of priority rules to match buyers with sellers.[1] Typically, price takes the highest priority: The buyer willing to pay the most is entitled to trade with the next seller willing to sell at the buyer's bid price and vice versa. However, if there is a tie in which more than one buyer is willing to buy at a different price, markets use a variety of different rules to decide who gets to purchase from the next seller. Here is a sample of the different secondary rules:[2]

Time priority represents a first-come, first-served model. The first order submitted at a given price is the first one to be filled. The American Stock Exchange, Paris Bourse, Tokyo Stock Exchange, and Toronto Stock Exchange Computer-Assisted Trading System (CATS) prior to 1996 used some variation of this method. However, it is by no means clear that time priority is the most desirable second-

ary priority rule for a market. Indeed, few financial markets use pure time priority.[3]

Class priority gives priority to certain classes of traders over others. For example, on the Toronto Stock Exchange the Registered Trader has a higher priority than orders on the book in that he or she can participate in certain incoming trades up to half the minimum guaranteed fill. On the NYSE, however, the specialist cannot trade ahead of the limit order book. In a dealer market such as the old NASDAQ system (prior to the new order handling rules), dealers could take priority over customer orders – even if customer orders at a better price – because the customers have no means of bypassing the intermediaries. We will discuss dealer priority in more depth later in the paper.

Random priority randomly assigns an order among the traders willing to trade at a given price. Each floor trader willing to trade at a given price has an equal probability of filling the next order. This is effectively what happens in the "open outcry" method found in floor-based futures trading pits such as the Chicago Board of Trade.

Sharing or *pro rata priority* is also a common practice on many trading floors including the Stock Exchange of Hong Kong and the old Toronto Stock Exchange floor-based system. A sharing priority rule could allocate equal shares to each order on the book. Alternatively, the allocation could be proportional to the total size of a member's orders on the book (pro rata sharing.) However, even if a trading floor has a time priority rule, it may be virtually impossible to determine who was first. For example, a large order may arrive at a trading venue where there are several traders willing to fill the order. Therefore, a large order may be *de facto* shared among many traders.

Size priority grants priority to orders based on their size. Priority could be granted to the largest order, which has the advantage of giving traders an incentive to place larger orders.[4] Alternatively, priority could be granted to the order that matches the incoming order in size. This minimizes the number of trade tickets to be processed. A variation of this secondary priority rule is used on the New York Stock Exchange.

Exposure priority grants priority to orders that are revealed to other market makers and reduces the priority for those traders who want to hide their orders. On the old CATS system and the Paris Bourse, traders can hide a portion of their orders from exposure on the electronic systems.

These different secondary priority rules have strong implications for the ways that investors compete to obtain an order fill. In a pure time priority market, an investor who is the first to put in a bid at a higher price is first in line to fill the next market sell order. With random or sharing priority there is much less incentive to pay up by bidding higher. This is because there is a positive probability that a trader can obtain a fill, within the same time to execution as bidding higher, by merely matching existing quotes.

Therefore, it can be seen that priority rules can have an impact on market quality. For example, in systems with time as the secondary priority rule, traders have incentives to improve on the price since merely matching a current best price puts them at the back of the queue. This could lead to narrower spreads. Similarly, in systems where public orders take priority over market maker or specialist orders, there will be more public orders submitted. This can lead to more liquidity being supplied.

44.2. Literature on Priority Rules

Cohen et al. (1985) find support for the notion that time priority leads to more price competition and, hence, narrower spreads. They use a simulated queuing model to show that systems that do not enforce time priority have wider spreads relative to those that enforce time priority.

Angel and Weaver (1998) and Panchapagesan (1998) compare market quality and investor behavior differences between systems that use time priority as their secondary rule with systems that use pro rata sharing. In particular, Angel and Weaver examine the 29 July 1996 switch from time to sharing priority for stocks in the Toronto Stock Exchange's (TSX) CATS. Panchapagesan also examines the TSX but compares a matched sample of CATS stocks with stocks traded on the TSX floor. During Panchapagesan's sample period the TSX floor used sharing priority rules while CATS used time priority.

Both studies find that a sharing priority rule results in less price competition compared with a time priority rule. They also find that a sharing priority rule results in more gaming behavior by investors in an attempt to get their orders filled. For example, a sharing priority rule encourages investors to submit larger orders and then cancel them when their desired volume is filled. Panchapagesan (1998) additionally concludes that the lack of price competition in sharing priority rule systems results in wider bid ask spreads than under time priority.

Cordella and Foucault (1999) develop a theoretical model of dealer competition and also conclude that spreads will be wider under a random allocation rule than under a price/time priority system. The intuition is that under a random allocation rule dealers can always match other dealers' quotes without losing priority.

Harris (1994) addresses the relationship between priority rules, tick size, and depth.[5] Harris points out that large ticks and time priority protect traders that place limit orders. If a trader wants to trade ahead of another in a time priority rule system, he or she must improve on the price. A large tick makes obtaining precedence costly.[6] Harris then argues that time priority encourages traders to quote more size, which leads to greater quoted depth.

Two points are evident from the above discussion. First, traders will change their behavior as rules change. Second, the behavior of these traders impacts market quality and hence the terms of trade for unsophisticated traders.

44.3. Networks

Thus far, the discussion of priority rules has assumed that there is a single market for stocks. That is markets are consolidated. What if there are multiple markets? In this section, I will discuss networks of markets and how priority rules may apply to them. I will also consider the development of two major network structures: one for listed stocks such as those on the NYSE and another for over-the-counter (OTC) stock.

44.3.1. The Network for Listed Stocks

During the first half of the twentieth century, the role of regional stock exchanges changed and their number decreased dramatically. When regional stock exchanges like the Boston Stock Exchange were first established, there was poor telecommunications in the United States and travel was expensive. As a result, it was very difficult for investors away from a company's headquarters to find out anything about the company. Therefore, regional stock exchanges were established as a place to trade local companies. As telecommunications improved and travel became less expensive, it became easier to find out about companies located in distant geographic locations. As companies grew, they switched listed on the American or New York Stock Exchanges where they could obtain the prestige of a national listing.

So, the regional exchanges experienced a dramatic drop in listings. Perhaps to provide another source of revenue, local traders began trading NYSE-listed stocks. Multiple trading venues for the same NYSE-listed stock led to frequent differences in prices across markets. Stories are abound of traders paying for open phone lines between the NYSE and one of the regional stock exchanges so that they could capitalize on the discrepancies. Over time, Congress observed that prices for NYSE-and Amex-listed stocks varied widely across the exchanges that traded them. This led to the passage of the Securities Act Amendments of 1975 in which Congress ordered the SEC to create a National Market System (NMS) that, in part, would allow investors to execute trades on markets that displayed the best price.

After deliberation, on 26 January 1978, the SEC issued the Exchange Act Release No. 14416 that required markets to create a network that would "permit orders for the purchase and sale of multiple-traded securities to be sent directly from any qualified market to another such market promptly and efficiently."[7] Two months later, the American, Boston, NYSE, Pacific, and Philadelphia Stock Exchanges submitted a "Plan for the Purpose of Creating and Operating an Intermarket Communications Linkage." This became known as the Intermarket Trading System (ITS).

The ITS allowed exchanges to route orders to each other. It was in effect an e-mail system in which the specialist on an exchange could ask a specialist on another exchange if they would be willing to trade at their quoted price.[8] A few months later, the SEC also created the Consolidated Quote System (CQS), which collected the best quoted prices to sell (called the offer) and buy (called the bid) securities. The CQS then constructed the best bid and offer (BBO) and disseminated it to the exchanges and data vendors who disseminated it to the public.

Although the ITS established a network and a method for routing orders, there initially was no rule indicating under what circumstances participants were to route orders to another exchange. Nor was the OTC market a part of the linkage. The NASDAQ traded many NYSE and Amex stocks. After the passage of the Securities Act Amendments of 1975, they began work on a Computerized Automated Execution System (CAES) to interface with ITS. Finally, on 28 April 1981, the SEC issued an order requiring that CAES become a part of ITS.

That same month, the SEC issued Securities Exchange Act Release No. 17703 that prohibited ITS/CAES participants from executing orders at prices inferior to those displayed on another network node. This requirement became known as the trade through rule and established a network-wide priority system for investor orders. The rule requires an exchange to either match a better price or route the order to the exchange displaying the better price.

The effect of the trade through rule was and is to establish price as the first priority rule across the ITS network. In turn, each regional exchange (a node) has its own priority rules.[9] So, an order reaching any node of the ITS network was first subject to a network-wide price priority rule and then the node's priority rules.

44.3.2. The Network for OTC Stocks

In the previous section, I discussed how a network for exchange-listed stocks developed. While exchanges list many stocks in the United States, the majority of stock issued are traded OTC, so-called because you went to your broker's office and purchased them at the front counter. In the early part of the twentieth century, there was no organized way to buy and sell OTC stocks and so many times investors or brokers resorted to newspaper ads to accomplish the task.

In 1913, the National Quotation Bureau was formed by two businessmen who collected and published daily quotations from dealers of securities in five different cities. Their publication became known as the Pink Sheets because of the color of the paper they were printed on. For each stock the Pink Sheets listed the brokers trading the stock and representative quotes. The quotes were old, but at least brokers had a list of other brokers who were interested in trading a particular stock issue. Brokers would contact those listed in the Pink Sheets to get current quotes. Because of the large number of listed brokers for some stocks and the amount of time necessary to call each one, a rule was developed over time that required brokers to contact at least three (but not all) of the brokers listed on the Pink Sheets in order to try and find the best price for customers. Due to the lack of continuous investor interest in OTC stocks, the market developed as a dealer market who would act as intermediaries between investors – buying and selling stocks to earn a profit.

The vast majority of stock issues (but not stock volume) were traded this way for almost 60 years. As companies grew, they typically listed on an exchange. Over time, though telecommunications improved and the Pink Sheets expanded their coverage to nationwide. This increased the number of dealers making markets in a particular stock and made the goal of finding investors the best price more difficult. So, in 1971, the National Association of Securities Dealers (NASD) created an automated quotation system with the acronym NASDAQ for trading the more active OTC issues. The system allowed dealer members to input contemporaneous quotations for stocks they made a market in. NASDAQ was similar in its aggregating function to the CQS for listed stocks. Brokers still needed to telephone dealers to trade. And NASDAQ was a dealer market. While the exchanges established prices based on a combination of public limit orders and specialist quotes, NASDAQ displayed *dealer* quotes.[10,11]

Initially, NASDAQ dealers could ignore customer limit orders. Customers learned that limit orders were not executed and did not submit them. In 1994, an investor sued his broker and as a result NASDAQ established a rule which came be known as Manning I. The rule prevented NASDAQ dealers from trading through *their* customer limit orders at better prices – much like ITS trade through rules do.[12] However, after the passage of Manning I, NASDAQ dealers could still trade at the same price as customer limit orders they held, i.e. there was no public order priority rule. This was in contrast to the exchanges that had public priority rules. NASDAQ customers were still reluctant to submit limit orders. A year later, another rule, Manning II, gave public limit orders priority, but only within a dealer firm. In other words, a customer submitting a limit order to Dealer X could still see trades occurring at other dealers at the same price as the customer's limit order. Thus, Manning II still discouraged public limit order submission and as a result they were not a major supplier of liquidity on the NASDAQ market.

So it can be seen that although NASDAQ was a network of dealers, it had no market-wide priority rules as did the exchanges. In addition, proprietary

trading systems were established that allowed
NASDAQ dealers to trade between themselves at
prices that were better than the best quotes on
NASDAQ. Like it had for exchanges, Congress
and the SEC acted and established a method for
investors to access the best quoted prices. However, the landscape for NASDAQ stocks in the
1990s was different than that for exchange listed
stocks in 1975. While a number of exchanges were
trading the same stocks in 1975, there were really
only two players for NASDAQ stocks by the mid-
1990s. Other than NASDAQ itself, where dealers
traded with the public, the only other place NAS-
DAQ stocks were traded was on a proprietary
system called Instinet.[13]

Most, if not all, NASDAQ dealers also were
already connected to Instinet; so, rather than create a new network, the SEC required that Instinet
quotes be made part of the BBO for NASDAQ
stocks. The Order Handling Rules (OHR), enacted
in early 1997, also required NASDAQ dealers to
expose customer limit orders to the public by including them in their quotes. Rather than specifically including Instinet into the calculation of the
BBO, the SEC generalized the rule to include *any*
system for displaying limit orders for NASDAQ
stocks. These systems were referred to as Electronic Communications Networks (ECNs) and a
number of new systems were established in anticipation of the OHR or shortly after its passage.

These ECNs unleashed the potential of public
limit orders. After the OHR, spreads dropped dramatically with most of the drop attributed to public
limit orders competing with dealer quotes.[14] ECNs
grew in market share from around 20 percent in 1997
to 80 percent today. The OHR created a much larger
network of systems than ITS ever faced. At the time
of the OHR, the SEC did not require a trade through
rule for the NASDAQ/ECNs network as it did
for ITS.

44.3.3. Do Networks Need Priority Rules?

During 2004 the SEC proposed Regulation NMS.
Part of the rule proposes to extend the ITS trade

through rule to NASDAQ. On 10 February 2004,
Congressman Richard Baker sent SEC Chairman
William Donaldson a letter calling the ITS trade
through rule "antiquated" and calling for its complete repeal. Congressman Baker suggested that
execution speed was just as important as price
and that investors should be allowed to choose
whether they wanted price or speed to be the primary routing rule.

There is support for Congressman Baker's
position in the academic literature. For example
Hatch et al. (2001) compare trade executions for
NYSE-listed stocks between different nodes on
the ITS/CAES network. They find that investors
receive better prices on the NYSE, but the regional exchanges offer more speed of execution
and larger execution sizes. In addition, Battalio
et al. (2002) examined limit orders execution.
They find that at-the-inside limit orders do better
on regional exchanges in terms of speed of execution (perhaps due to shorter queues) than on
NYSE, but quote improving limit orders do better
on the NYSE where they execute faster and more
profitably.

Congressman Baker's letter then raises the question: Do networks need priority rules? On its face, it
would seem obvious that investors should be
allowed to send orders wherever they choose. However, overall market quality must be balanced
against the needs of individual traders. If the needs
of the individual do not cause harm to the overall
population then the individual should be allowed to
route orders as they wish. If however, the overall
population of traders is harmed by the choices of
the individual then the needs of the majority outweigh the individual's needs.

A similar argument is used to justify nonsmok-
ing areas. While an individual aware of smoking's risks has the right to smoke, the impact of
second-hand smoke on nonsmokers is such that
nonsmokers will be harmed if smokers exercise
their right to smoke around them. Therefore,
various laws have been enacted to protect nonsmokers from the harmful affects of second-hand
smoke. The greater good comes down on the side

of providing nonsmokers with a smoke-free environment.

Following the smoking analogy, the ability of traders to choose their priority rules should be weighed against overall market quality. For this purpose, the literature on consolidation and fragmentation becomes useful. In a consolidated market, order flow is concentrated in a single location. In a fragmented market, order flow is split up between multiple locations. The number of choices between consolidated and fragmented is a continuum not a bifurcation.

A number of papers have been written on the subject of fragmented versus consolidated markets. They generally conclude that consolidated markets offer better market quality than fragmented markets. For example, Madhavan (2000) developed a theoretical model that shows that fragmented markets have higher volatility than consolidated markets. Wei and Bennett (2003) find empirical support for Madhavan's conjecture. In particular, they find that stocks that switch from the fragmented NASDAQ to the comparatively consolidated NYSE, experience a reduction in spread and volatility.[15] Barclay et al. (2003) examined stock price and volume around quarterly expirations of the S&P 500 futures contract (so called witching days). They found that NYSE prices are more efficient than NASDAQ prices. They attributed the superior performance of the NYSE to the larger degree of order flow consolidation found there relative to NASDAQ.

Battalio et al. (1998) examined Merrill Lynch's decision to route all orders for NYSE-listed stocks to the NYSE rather than to a regional exchange where they could effectively internalize the order flow. They found that, consistent with other studies, the NYSE routing decision resulted in investors obtaining better prices and spreads narrowing.

Murphy and Weaver (2003) examined the TSX rule that require brokers receiving market orders of 5000 shares or less, to either improve on price or send the order to the TSX for execution against limit orders. Following the adoption of the rule, the affected stocks experienced an immediate increase in depth and reduction in spread.[16] In addition to the TSX, many other exchanges around the world have so-called concentration rules.

Therefore, the extant literature suggests that overall market quality is higher in consolidated versus fragmented markets. The NYSE market share of its listed stocks is around 80 percent and they display the best price over 90 percent of the time. Therefore the market for NYSE stocks can be considered relatively consolidated. Although never empirically tested, there appears to then be a link between percentage of the time a market displays the best price and its market share. So the ITS network price priority rule may be the mechanism that causes the consolidation of NYSE stocks. If orders are routed away from the NYSE to another exchange or market maker then the market for NYSE stocks will become more fragmented. The academic literature suggests that an increase in fragmentation will result in wider spreads and higher volatility. It has been shown, time and time again, that investors factor execution costs into their required cost of supplying funds to firms.[17] Therefore, higher execution costs will translate into higher costs of capital for firms and stock prices will fall.

Figure 44.1 illustrates the relationship between execution costs and stock prices.[18] On 11 April 1990, the TSX enacted rules that resulted in effective execution costs rising by about 0.25 percentage points. Within a week, prices declined by over 6 percent.

It can, therefore, be concluded that a network priority rule based on price results in improved market quality. Although a direct empirical link can only be proven by examining what happens if the network price priority rule is removed, logical inferences can be drawn from examining the behavior of those traders that supply liquidity to the market. The following section discusses the behavior of limit order traders who are the major supplier of liquidity on the NYSE.[19]

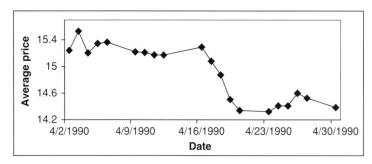

Figure 44.1.   Average daily prices of stocks in our sample for April 1990

44.3.4. Liquidity Supplied by Limit Order Traders

There is an old adage that "liquidity begets liquidity." In other words, limit order traders will submit limit orders where market orders exist. It is similar to the fact that the more traffic exists on a highway, the more gas stations will exist. If the traffic goes away so will the gas stations. Similarly, if market orders get routed away from the venue with the best price, limit orders will leave that venue as well. There will be less price competition and, as a result, spreads will widen.

Limit orders are shock absorbers for liquidity events. Without limit orders to absorb trades from liquidity demanders, large orders will increasingly push prices away from current prices.[20] While it may be argued that price impact is a fact of life for institutions, small traders who submit order in the same direction, but just behind the large order may suffer financial loss. The small order will execute at an inferior price before sufficient liquidity can be sent to the market by traders. It can then be seen that thin markets are more susceptible to liquidity event volatility than deeper markets.[21] Thus, markets with more depth are desirable.

The TSX market concentration rules best illustrate the above points. Prior to the adoption of the rule, it was common practice for member firms to execute market orders and marketable limit orders from the member's own inventory (called internalization). Limit order traders realized that even if they had the best quoted price, many orders would never reach them and they would not get timely executions.[22] The TSX adoption of its concen-tration rules caused more market and marketable limit orders to be submitted to the exchange where they could execute against limit orders. The increase in order flow to the exchange caused more limit order traders to compete for the order flow. This, in turn, resulted in narrower spreads and more quoted depth.

This section of the paper suggests that networks without priority rules discourage limit order submission which results in higher effective execution costs for the average investor. A few large players may benefit from the absence of a network priority rule, but it will be at the expense of the majority of long-term investors. Therefore, it can be seen that overall market quality benefits from network priority rules.

44.3.5. A Final Note on the Need for Speed

In the current drive to eliminate priority rules for the ITS network, the most common reason cited is a desire to get a trade done quickly – perhaps in a second or less. Is this advantageous? Perhaps examining a graph of a random stock on a random day would help. Figure 44.2 is the graph representing all trades in Juniper Inc. (JNPR) for 3 February 2003 from 10:00 AM until 10:01:30 AM.

It can be seen that getting an order filled at 10:00:51 compared to 10:00:52 may save you $0.02 on that trade. However, if we examine JNPR over the entire day it can be seen that prices fluctuated by $0.20 over the day, a factor of 10. So, price changes over small-time increments are much smaller than over longer increments (Figure 44.3). In that case,

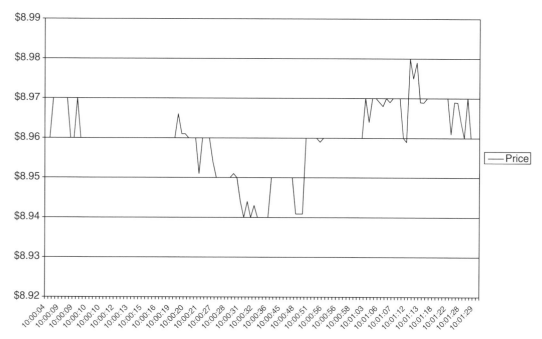

Figure 44.2. JNPR 3 February 2003 10:00 to 10:01:30 AM

what type of trader benefits from small price changes and, hence, needs speed? The answer is arbitrageurs and hedge funds. As mentioned earlier, if we allow orders to be routed for other than best price, then limit order traders will reduce the amount of liquidity they supply, increasing execution costs. It can then be seen that this "need for speed" benefits the few at the expense of the many.

Figure 44.3. Juniper corporation 3 February 2003

44.4. Conclusion

In this paper, I have considered priority rules as they apply to individual markets (nodes) and networks. The literature on priority rules suggests that the adoption of some priority rules can improve market quality within a node. After a discussion of the development of the ITS and NASDAQ networks, I consider whether network priority rules matter. Since a network's priority rules (or routing rules) can result in a concentration of orders, I discuss the literature on consolidated versus fragmented markets. I conclude that network priority rules improve the market quality if they result in consolidated markets. This further suggests that the current price priority rule on ITS should, therefore, be retained and extended to the NASDAQ network as proposed by the SEC.

NOTES

1. See Domowitz (1993) for taxonomy of many of the different rules found in different markets.
2. The following list is taken from an unpublished paper I co-authored with James Angel entitled "Priority Rules."
3. For example, on the old TSE CATS system, time priority did not expire, while on the Amex time priority lasts only until the next trade.
4. Note that size priority is different than pro rata sharing in that an entire incoming order may go to a single trader as opposed to be shared.
5. Tick size is the minimum price increment.
6. Assume a $0.125 tick size. Then in order to step ahead of an existing buy order, a trader must be willing to pay $12.50 more for each 100 shares he obtains. If the tick is only $0.01 then that same trader must only pay $1.00 more for each 100 shares he obtains.
7. Exchange Act Release No. 14416 at 4358.
8. A specialist is the designated primary dealer on a stock exchange. They have complete knowledge of all investor orders and generally have obligations to maintain orderly markets.
9. NASDAQ will be discussed in the next section.
10. Limit orders are orders to buy or sell a security at a specified price or better. Public customers submit limit orders, specialists and NASDAQ market makers submit quotes.
11. The quotes are predominately based on public orders. As evidence of this, consider that during 2003, NYSE specialists were involved in less than 20 percent of all trades.
12. The NASDAQ trade, through rule, only applied to an individual broker. That is, Broker X was not allowed to trade through any customer of Broker X, but was not prevented from trading through customer limit orders held by Broker Y.
13. The Midwest Stock Exchange traded some NASDAQ stocks, but was a distant third in market share.
14. see Barclay et al. (1998).
15. They use a Herfindahl–Hirschman Index as well as the number of nodes trading a stock to measure the degree of fragmentation before and after the switch to the NYSE and find that the gains in spread width and volatility are greater for firms experiencing more fragmentation prior to the decision to list on the NYSE.
16. The findings of Murphy and Weaver also suggest that TSX members eventually began using order routing technology that allowed them to capitalize on the TSX crossing priority rule. This action dampened the impact of consolidation and spreads widened again.
17. See Amihud (2002), Amihud and Mendelson (1986) and Amihud et al. (1997), among others.
18. Taken from Madhavan et al.(2004).
19. Recall that NYSE specialists are involved in less than 20 percent of all trades.
20. Assume that there are 100 shares offered at $19, 200 at $19.05, 100 at $19.10, and 300 at $19.15. A market order to buy 500 shares will take out the sell orders from $19 to $19.15, leaving the best offer at $19.15 until new offers to sell arrive. This is sometimes referred to at walking the book.
21. Assume a deeper market of 600 shares offered at $19. Then a 500 share order will not move the price.
22. Recall that a similar situation existed on NASDAQ before the adoption of the OHR.

REFERENCES

Amihud, Y. (2002). "Illiquidity and stock returns: Cross-sectional and time-series effects." *Journal of Financial Markets*, 5: 31–56.
Amihud, Y. and Mendelson, H. (1986). "Asset pricing and the bid-ask spread." *Journal of Financial Economics*, 17: 223–250.

Amihud, Y., Mendelson, H., and Lauterbach, B. (1997). "Market microstructure and securities values: evidence from the Tel Aviv Stock Exchange." *Journal of Financial Economics,* 45: 365–390.

Angel, J. and Weaver, D. (1998). "Priority Rules!" Working Paper, Rutgers University.

Barclay, Michael J., William G. Christie, Jeffrey H. Harris, Eugene Kandel, and Paul H. Schultz, 1999, The effects of market reform on the trading costs and depths of Nasdaq Stocks, *Journal of Finance,* 54, 1–34.

Barclay, M.J., Hendershott, T., and Jones, C.M. (2003). "Which witches better? A cross-market comparison of extreme liquidity shocks." Working Paper, University of Rochester.

Battalio, R., Greene, J., and Jennings, R. (1998). "Order flow distribution, bid-ask spreads, and liquidity costs: Merrill Lynch's decision to cease routinely routing orders to Regional Stock Exchanges." *Journal of Financial Intermediation,* 7: 338–358.

Battalio, R., Greene, J., Hatch, B., and Jennings, R. (2002). "Does the limit order routing decision matter?" *Review of Financial Studies,* 15(1): 159–194.

Cohen, K., Conroy, R., and Maier, S. (1985). "Order flow and the quality of the market," in Amihud, Ho, and Schwartz (eds.) *Market Making and the Changing Structure of the Securities Industry.* MA: Lexington Books.

Cordella, T. and Foucault, T. (1999). "Minimum price variations, time priority and quote dynamics." *Journal of Financial Intermediation,* 8(3): 141–173.

Domowitz, I. (1993). "A taxonomy of automated trade execution systems." *Journal of International Money and Finance,* 12: 607–631.

Harris, L. (1994). "Minimum price variations, discrete bid-ask spreads, and quotation sizes." *Review of Financial Studies,* 7: 149–178.

Hatch, B., Battalio, R., and Jennings, R. (2001). "Post-reform market execution quality: multidimensional comparisons across market centers." *The Financial Review,* 36(3): 123–151.

Madhavan, A. (2000). "Consolidation, fragmentation, and the disclosure of trading information." *Review of Financial Studies,* 8(3).

Madhavan, Ananth, David Porter, and Daniel Weaver, 2005. "Should Securities Markets be Transparent?" *Journal of Financial Markets.* 8: 265–287.

Murphy, A. and Weaver, D. (2003). "Order flow consolidation and market quality: an empirical investigation." Working Paper, Manhattan College.

Panchapagesan, V. (1998). "What if time priority is not enforced among traders?" Working Paper, Washington University.

Wei, L. and Bennett, P. (2003). "New York stock market structure, fragmentation and market quality – evidence from recent listing switches." Working Paper, New York Stock Exchange.

Chapter 45

THE MOMENTUM TRADING STRATEGY

K.C. JOHN WEI, *Hong Kong University of Science and Technology, Hong Kong*

Abstract

A strategy that buys past winners and simultaneously sells past losers based on stock performance in the past 3 to 12 months is profitable in the U.S. and the European markets. This survey paper reviews the literature on the momentum strategy and the possible explanations on the momentum profitability.

Keywords: past winners; past losers; momentum strategy; individual momentum; industrial momentum; international momentum; underreaction; overreaction; overconfidence; self-attribution; valuation uncertainty; conservatism; representative heuristic; gradual information diffusion

45.1. Introduction

"Trend is your friend" is a very popular saying in Wall Street since the inception of stock markets. However, whether this momentum trading strategy that is based on buying past winners and selling past losers is really profitable was controversial until recently. Jegadeesh and Titman (1993) were the first to comprehensively test the profitability of the momentum trading strategy based on the past 3-to 12-month performance. They document that momentum strategies implemented in the U.S. market from 1965 to 1989 generated a positive profit of about one percent per month over 3-to 12-month holding periods. In their recent follow-up study, Jegadeesh and Titman (2001) find that momentum strategies continued to be profitable after 1990 with past winners outperforming past losers by about the same magnitude as in the earlier period.

Rouwenhorst (1998) studied individual stock momentum with a sample of stocks listed on 12 European exchanges during the period from 1978 to 1995. The results demonstrate that momentum profits of about one percent per month are not limited to a particular market, but instead they are present in all 12 markets in the sample. Rouwenhorst (1999) also finds that momentum strategies are profitable although not to the same degree in 20 emerging markets. Chui et al. (2002) examine the profitability of momentum strategies in eight different Asian countries: Hong Kong, Indonesia, Japan, Korea, Malaysia, Singapore, Taiwan, and Thailand. Their evidence indicates that the momentum effect is present in all of the Asian countries except Korea and Indonesia but it is generally weak and is statistically significant only for Hong Kong, Malaysia, Singapore, and Thailand for the pre-crisis period. Interestingly, they find that the Common Law/Civil Law distinction provides an indicator of whether or not a market exhibited a momentum effect prior to the financial crisis. Asness et al. (1996), Chan et al. (2000), and Richards (1997) document that momentum strategies are profitable when implemented on stock market indices.

Recently Moskowitz and Grinblatt (1999) find that industry momentum strategies, which advocate buying stocks from past winning industries and selling stocks from past losing industries, appear to be highly profitable. This industry momentum accounts for much of the profitability of individual stock momentum strategies in the United States. Once returns are adjusted for industry effects, momentum profits from individual equities are significantly weaker, and for the most part are statistically insignificant. However, Grundy and Martin (2001) have a different view on the contribution of industries to individual momentum profits. They argue that a one-month interval between the ranking period and the holding period has a pivotal role in the conclusion that industry momentum strategies are profitable. Industry momentum strategies are significantly profitable only when the ranking period is contiguous to the holding period as documented by Moskowitz and Grinblatt (1999). However, given a one-month interval between the two periods, industry momentum strategies cannot earn significant profits. Grundy and Martin (2001) conclude that industry effects are not the primary cause of the individual momentum profitability. Liu and Wei (2004) document that industries in 12 European markets, like their counterparts in the U.S. market, also explain the profitability of individual momentum strategies. Specifically, past winner industries outperform past loser industries by more than one percent per month. However, unlike their counterparts in the U.S. market, industries cannot solely explain the profitability of individual momentum strategies in 12 European markets. In addition, industry momentum strategies can still earn significant profits even with a one-month interval between the formation and holding periods.

45.2. The Implementation of Momentum Strategies

To show how to implement a momentum strategy, we use a momentum strategy that is based on the past six-month performance with a six-month holding period an illustration. Specifically, to form momentum portfolios, at the end of each month all securities in each of the samples are ranked in ascending order based on the past six-month cumulative returns with dividends. The

securities in the bottom 10 percent (or 20 percent or 30 percent) are assigned to the loser (denoted as "L") portfolio, while those in the top 10 percent (or 20 percent or 30 percent) are assigned to the winner (denoted as "W") portfolio. These portfolios are value-weighted using the market capitalization of the security at the end of the ranking month as the weight. Each of these portfolios is held for six months.

To reduce the effect of nonsynchronous trading and the bid–ask bounce, Jegadeesh and Titman (1993) suggest that we measure returns on these portfolios one month after the ranking takes place. If a security has any missing returns during the holding period, we replace them with the corresponding value-weighted market returns. If the returns on the security are no longer available, we rebalance the portfolio in the month the security is deleted from our database. Excess returns on a security are calculated as the returns on that security minus the risk-free rate, which we assume is equal to the one-month government short-term rate, such as the U.S. Treasury bill rate.

To increase the power of our tests, we construct overlapping portfolios. The winner (loser) portfolio is an overlapping portfolio that consists of the "W" ("L") portfolios in the previous six months. The returns on the winner (loser) portfolios are the simple average of the returns on the six "W" ("L") portfolios. For instance, the January return on the winner portfolio is the simple average of the January returns on the "W" portfolios that are constructed from June to November in the previous year. The momentum portfolio we examine is the zero-cost, winner-minus-loser portfolio.

45.3. Explanations of Momentum Profits

Jegadeesh and Titman (2001) discuss three potential explanations for the profitability of momentum strategies and examine the performance of momentum portfolios over longer horizons in order to differentiate between these hypotheses. The three explanations include: (1) stock prices underreact to information, (2) there is a delayed overreaction to information, and (3) the profits are generated from cross-sectional differences in expected returns.

The first two explanations are consistent with some recent behavioral models. For example, the underreaction explanation is consistent with the Barberis, Shleifer, and Vishny (1998) model where a "conservatism bias" can lead investors to underreact or underweight new information. In the case with a pure conservatism bias, once the information is fully incorporated in prices, there is no predictability in stock returns. In this case, the expected post-holding period returns are zero.

There are a number of behavioral models that are consistent with a delayed overreaction. Barberis et al. (1998) also discuss this possibility and describe what they call the "representative heuristic," which suggests that investors may overly extrapolate a firm's past extraordinary earning growths into the future, and hence overreact to positive (or negative) information that is preceded by positive (or negative) information. In addition, Daniel et al. (1998) argue that delayed overreaction can arise because of "self-attribution (or cognitive) bias." That is, investors tend to become more overconfident when their stock picks become winners and take more aggressive positions that push up the prices of winners above their fundamental values. Finally, Hong and Stein (1999) propose a model with two groups of investors: informed investors and technical traders, who do not fully take into account the actions of each other. As a result, information is incorporated slowly into stock prices, providing a potential profit opportunity for technical traders. These traders, however, tend to push prices of past winners above their fundamental values. In each of these behavioral models, prices tend to eventually overreact to information and then reverse when prices eventually revert to their fundamentals. All these behavioral models predict the expected post-holding period returns to be negative.

The third explanation is consistent with an efficient market where stocks have different expected rates of return because of different risk exposures. In particular, Conrad and Kaul (1998) emphasize that there would be some evidence of momentum even if there were no time-series variation in expected returns since stocks with high-(low) expected returns would be expected to have the highest (lowest) returns in adjacent periods. This explanation suggests that the profits from a momentum strategy should be the same in any post-ranking period.

To test these competing hypotheses, we normally examine the post-holding period returns of momentum portfolios beyond the first year after formation, typically up to five years. The empirical evidence from the U.S. (Jegadeesh and Titman, 2001) and Asian markets (Chui et al., 2002) appears to support the delayed overreaction explanation. That is, the returns on the momentum portfolio eventually reverse to negative 2–5 years after formation. In addition, Fama and French (1996) find that the Fama–French (1993) three factors cannot explain the momentum profits in the United States.

45.4. Momentum Profits and Firm Characteristics

Firm characteristics such as book-to-market ratios, market capitalization, and turnover have shown to have the ability to predict the cross section of expected stock returns in the United States. Behavioral models also predict that momentum profits are related to firm characteristics.

The overconfidence model by Daniel, Hirshleifer, and Subrahmanyam (1998) suggests that momentum profits arise because investors are overconfidence. Daniel and Titman (1999) argue that overconfidence is likely to influence the perception of investors relatively more, when they analyze fairly vague and subjective information, and use book-to-market ratios as a proxy for information vagueness. Consistent with their hypothesis, they find that momentum profits are negatively related to the firm's book-to-market ratio in the U.S. market. Chui et al. (2002) also find similar results for Asian markets.

Trading volume or turnover could also proxy for information vagueness. As suggested by asymmetric information models (see for example, Blume et al., 1994), trading volume reflects investors' disagreement on a stock's intrinsic value. The more vague the information used to value the firm, the more disagreement among the investors, and hence, the greater the trading volume. Therefore, the momentum effect should be stronger for firms with high trading volume or turnover. Lee and Swaminathan (2000) find that momentum profits are indeed higher for firms with high turnover ratios in the U.S. market. Chui et al. (2002) also find similar results for Asian markets.

In contrast, Hong and Stein (1999) predict that stocks with slow information diffusion should exhibit stronger momentum. Hong et al. (2000) provide tests that support this prediction. In particular, except for the very smallest decile stocks, the profitability of momentum investment strategies declines sharply with firm size. Hong et al. (2000) also look at momentum profits and analyst coverage and find that holding size fixed-momentum strategies work better for stock with low analyst coverage. In addition, they find that the effect of analyst coverage is greater for stocks that are past losers than for stocks that are past winners. They conclude that their findings are consistent with the gradual information diffusion model of Hong and Stein (1999).

Acknowledgment

The author would like to acknowledge financial support from the Research Grants Council of the Hong Kong Special Administration Region, China (HKUST6233/97H).

REFERENCES

Asness, C.S., Liew, J.M., and Stevens, R.L. (1996). "Parallels between the cross-sectional predictability of stock returns and country returns." Working Paper, Goldman Sachs Asset Management.

Barberis, N., Shleifer, A., and Vishny, R. (1998). "A model of investor sentiment." *Journal of Financial Economics*, 49: 307–343.

Blume, L., Easley, D., and O'Hara, M. (1994). "Market statistics and technical analysis: The role of volume." *Journal of Finance*, 49: 153–181.

Chan, K., Hameed, A., and Tong, W. (2000). "Profitability of momentum strategies in the international equity markets." *Journal of Financial and Quantitative Analysis*, 35: 153–172.

Chui, A.C.W., Titman, S., and Wei, K.C.J. (2002). "Momentum, legal system, and ownership structure: an analysis of Asian stock markets." Working Paper, University of Texas at Austin.

Conrad, J. and Kaul, G. (1998). "An anatomy of trading strategies." *Review of Financial Studies*, 11: 489–519.

Daniel, K.D. and Titman, S. (1999). "Market efficiency in an irrational world." *Financial Analysts Journal*, 55: 28–40.

Daniel, K., Hirshleifer, D., and Subrahmanyam, A. (1998) "Investor psychology and security market under-and overreactions." *Journal of Finance*, 53: 1839–1886.

Fama, E.F. and French, K.R. (1993). "Common risk factors in the returns on stocks and bonds." *Journal of Financial Economics*, 33: 3–56.

Fama, E. and French, K. (1996). "Multifactor explanations of asset pricing anomalies," *Journal of Finance*, 51: 55–84.

Grundy, B.D., and Martin J.S. (2001). "Understanding the nature of the risks and the source of the rewards to mementum investing," *Review of Financial Studies*, 14: 29–78.

Hong, H. and Stein, J.C. (1999). "A unified theory of underreaction, momentum trading and overreaction in asset markets." *Journal of Finance*, 54: 2143–2184.

Hong, H., Lim, T. and Stein, J.C. (2000). "Bad news travels slowly: size, analyst coverage, and the profitability of momentum strategies." *Journal of Finance*, 55: 265–295.

Jegadeesh, N. and Titman, S. (1993). "Returns to buying winners and selling losers: Implications for stock market efficiency." *Journal of Finance*, 48: 65–91.

Jegadeesh, N. and Titman, S. (2001). "Profitability of momentum strategies: an evaluation of alternative explanations." *Journal of Finance*, 56: 699–720.

Lee, C.M.C. and Swaminathan, B. (2000). "Price momentum and trading volume." *Journal of Finance*, 55: 2017–2069.

Liu, S. and Wei, K.C.J. (2004). "Do industries explain the profitability of momentum strategies in European markets?" Working Paper, Hong Kong University of Science and Technology.

Lu, C. and Shen, Y. (2005). "Do REITs pay enough dividends?" Unpublished working paper, Department of Finance, Yuan Ze University.

Moskowitz, T.J. and Grinblatt, M. (1999). "Do industries explain momentum?" *Journal of Finance*, 54: 1249–1290.

Richards, A.J. (1997). "Winner-loser reversals in national stock market indices: Can they be explained?" *Journal of Finance*, 52: 2129–2144.

Rouwenhorst, K.G. (1998). "International momentum strategies." *Journal of Finance*, 53: 267–284.

Rouwenhorst, K.G. (1999). "Local return factors and turnover in emerging stock markets," *Journal of Finance*, 55: 1439–1464.

Chapter 46

EQUILIBRIUM CREDIT RATIONING AND MONETARY NONNEUTRALITY IN A SMALL OPEN ECONOMY

YING WU, *Salisbury University, USA*

Abstract

This paper modifies the well-known Mundell–Fleming model by adding equilibrium credit rationing as well as imperfect asset substitutability between bonds and loans. When the representative bank's backward-bending loan supply curve peaks at its profit-maximizing loan rate, credit rationing can be an equilibrium phenomenon, which makes credit-dependent capital investment solely dependent upon the availability of customer market credit. With credit rationing, an expansion in money and credit shifts the IS curve as well as the LM curve even in a small open economy under a regime of fixed exchange rates, and the magnitude of offset coefficient between domestic and foreign asset components of high-powered money is less than one. In contrast, if there is no credit rationing, imperfect asset substitutability between bonds and loans per se cannot generate the real effect of money in the same model.

JEL classification: E51 F41

Keywords: credit rationing; monetary policy; capital flow; Mundell–Fleming model; monetary neutrality; open market operation; IS-LM curves; offset coefficient; monetary base; small open economy

46.1. Introduction

Is money non-neutral in a small open economy with international capital mobility and a fixed exchange rate regime? Can monetary policy affect real output in these circumstances? The answer to these questions is widely construed to be negative because the money supply has lost its role of a nominal anchor in this case.[1] In the orthodox money view, it is the interest rate that serves as the channel through which monetary policy affects the real sector of an economy; however, because the interest rate channel of monetary policy is highly correlated with exchange rates, and because the monetary authority commits to the maintenance of the fixed exchange rate, the consequent foreign exchange intervention by the monetary authority using official reserves necessarily washes out any real effect of the monetary policy that it has previously initiated. The same approach is used in most of the existing literature on small open economies, such as the traditional IS/LM analysis, which holds a lopsided view of bank liabilities and bank loans. Other than influencing interest rates via manipulating deposits (a money asset and bank liability), banks have no active leverage to play with; the role of bank loans escapes unnoticed since bank loans are grouped together with other nonmonetary assets such as bonds.

In contrast to the money view, the credit view of monetary transmission mechanism rejects the notion that all nonmonetary assets are perfect substitutes. According to the credit view, due to information asymmetries between borrowers and lenders in financial markets, banks can play a particular role in reducing information costs. It is financial intermediation that can help a firm with risk-sharing, liquidity, and information services; as a result, a large number of firms have in fact become bank dependent. Furthermore, although a rise in the loan rate increases, *ceteris paribus*, the bank's expected return by increasing interest payment when the borrower does not default, it lowers the bank's expected return by exacerbating adverse selection and moral hazard problems, and thus raising the probability of default. Hence, the bank's loan supply curve can be backward-bending, and credit rationing may occur as an equilibrium phenomenon.[2] Credit rationing *per se* makes monetary credit availability rather than interest rates in order to be the conduit for the real effect of money, therefore providing a major theoretical underpinning for the effectiveness of monetary policy under fixed exchange rates.

This paper begins with a study of the loan market setting with asymmetric information as a microfoundation for consumption and investment, and further develops a macromodel of a small open economy under a fixed exchange rate regime with perfect capital mobility in the bond market and imperfect asset substitutability between bonds and loans. As far as the credit view is concerned, this paper in spirit is close to Bernanke and Blinder (1988), who address the credit channel of monetary policy in a variant of the IS/LM model. They differ in several regards, however. Unlike Bernanke and Blinder, the model in this paper incorporates the possibility of equilibrium credit rationing while maintaining the assumption of imperfect substitutability of bank loans and bonds. With imperfect substitutability between bonds and bank loans, this paper nests both credit-rationed and credit-unrationed equilibrium regimes. Additionally, by placing the credit channel of monetary policy in

the setting of a small open economy, this chapter allows the possibility to explore the relevance of the "monetary policy ineffectiveness" proposition in the existing mainstream small-open-economy literature.

Partly based on Wu (1999) by drawing on its microeconomic foundation setting, this study has made important and substantial revisions to its macroeconomic analysis. With the credit availability channel, this study shows that money in the fixed exchange rate model is not completely endogenous by appealing to the asymmetry between customer market credit and auction market credit under equilibrium credit rationing.[3] Incorporating bank credit into the fixed exchange rate model leads to two fundamental changes. First, it extends the scope for monetary policy to affect economy from the standard interest rate channel to the one including the bank lending channel and balance sheet channel as well; the latter two conduits can be independent of changes in interest rates. Second, and more importantly, monetary policy will no longer be deemed impotent since it can directly "shift" the goods market as well as money market equilibrium schedules in such a way that the targeted real effect could be achieved while the fixed exchange rate is sustained.

The next section presents the analytical structure of bank behavior and credit market; the following two sections explore how credit market conditions determine macroeconomic equilibrium in an open-economy IS/LM framework, and demonstrate the real impacts of monetary shocks through its credit channel, respectively. The final section concludes the study.

46.2. Bank Behavior and Credit Market

It is well known that due to the credit risk associated with adverse selection and moral hazard problems a banking firm has an inverse U-shaped loan supply curve with a backward-bending portion. This section essentially modifies the pedagogical model in Christopher and Lewarne (1994) by extending the spectrum of bank investment into the portfolio selection between bonds and loans.

The representative banking firm is assumed to hold exactly the required amount of reserves, and allocate all of its excess reserves between the two bank assets: bonds and loans. Thus, it chooses loans, l, subject to its balance sheet identity, to maximize its profits from lending

$$\Pi = \theta(\rho)l\rho + b_{\mathrm{b}}r - dr - \frac{\gamma}{2}l^2$$
$$\text{s.t. } b_{\mathrm{b}} + l = (1-k)d,$$

(46.1)

where ρ is the loan rate, $\theta(\rho)$ the probability of loan repayment, γ the cost parameter of servicing loans, b_{b} denotes bonds held by the banking firm, r is the interest rate on bond, d represents total deposits, and k is the required reserve ratio for deposits.

Here, the low-risk or risk-free interest rate on bond holding is assumed to be the same as the interest cost of taking in deposits. Thus, deposits and bonds are perfectly substitutable assets to depositors so that they pay the same expected return per dollar. The key characteristic of the bank profit is that the repayment probability depends on the loan rate. Following the existing literature on equilibrium credit rationing, an increase in the loan rate makes it more likely for borrowers to default, hence the repayment probability is a decreasing function of the loan rate.[4] In addition, the representative bank takes the flow of deposits as given when making its portfolio decisions. Substituting the balance sheet identity into the bank's objective function and maximizing it with respect to l yields the banking firm's loan supply curve

$$l^S = \frac{\theta(\rho)\rho - r}{\gamma}.$$

(46.2)

Several implications of the loan supply curve can be derived. First, the loan supply curve is backward bending. The co-movement of the loan rate and loan volume hinges on the elasticity of the odds of repayment with respect to the loan rate. Only when the repayment probability is inelastic can a positive relationship exist between the loan rate and loan volume. To be specific, consider

a linear repayment probability $\theta(\rho) = \phi - \psi\rho$, where ϕ is the autonomous repayment probability determined by noninterest factors such as the liquidity of balance sheet positions, and ψ measures the sensitivity of the repayment probability to the loan rate $(0 < \psi < \phi \leq 1)$. Figure 46.1 depicts the loan repayment probability function. In the case of linear loan repayment probability function, the loan volume supplied increases with the loan rate until the loan rate achieves $\phi/2\psi$, after which a higher loan rate actually reduces the loan volume. In Figure 46.1, the loan rate at which the loan supply curve begins to bend backward points to the repayment probability halfway to its maximum within the possible range.

Substituting $\theta(\rho) = \phi - \psi\rho$ into (46.2) and differentiating (46.2) with respect to r, ϕ, ψ, and γ produces the responses of loan supply to the parameters of servicing loans. In particular, an increase in the bond interest rate, r, *ceteris paribus*, makes bond holding more attractive; accordingly, banks will reduce loans and hold more bonds. Another interpretation for the decrease of bank loans is based on the equivalence between the bond interest rate and the deposit rate: the higher the interest expenses of raising loanable funds by issuing deposits, the higher the economic cost of making loans. Next, banks tend to issue more loans when the autonomous repayment probability, ϕ, is higher, for example due to borrowers' increased net worth,. In addition, the larger the sensitivity of the repayment probability to the loan interest rate, ψ, the more deteriorating the problems of adverse selection and moral hazard, thus it is more likely for credit rationing to occur. Finally, an increase in the cost of servicing loans, γ, also tends to reduce loans as long as the expected return per dollar of loans exceeds the corresponding real opportunity cost.

Applying the envelope theorem to the representative bank's profit function in Equation (46.1) while incorporating Equation (46.2) and $\theta(\rho) = \phi - \psi\rho$ generates the following marginal bank profit with respect to the loan rate:

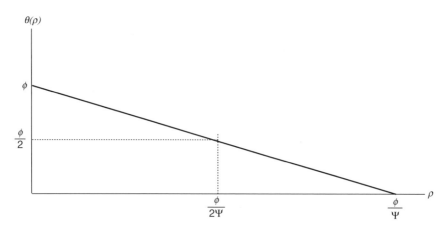

Figure 46.1. Loan repayment probability

$$\frac{d\Pi(\rho)}{d\rho} = \frac{1}{\gamma}[2\psi^2\rho^3 - 3\psi\phi\rho^2$$

$$+ (2\psi r + \phi^2)\rho - \phi r].$$

(46.3)

The bracket term on the RHS of Equation (46.3) is a cubic expression but two of the three roots are degenerated solutions at which loans are zero, respectively; thus the only feasible root for Equation (46.3) is $\rho^* = \phi/2\psi$, at which the bank's expected profits are maximized. Recall that the bank's loan supply curve peaks exactly at the same loan rate as the profit-maximizing loan rate here. Therefore, the result suggests the existence of equilibrium credit rationing. Further, the result for profit-maximizing loans also imply that the loan interest rate exceeds the bond interest rate such that $\rho > \sqrt{r/\psi} > r$, which captures the existence of risk premium of bank lending, and therefore signifies the imperfect substitutability between loans and bonds.

Moving from the representative bank to the aggregate banking system, the aggregated bank balance sheet identity shows $B_b + L + R = D$, where B_b represents the bonds held by banks, D denotes deposits, and L is the volume of loans. For simplicity, currency is abstracted from the model. The required reserve of the banking system, R, constitutes the monetary authority's liabilities, or high-powered money, H, which are generated by its acquisition of bonds (B_a) and foreign exchange (F). The high-powered money in this framework is composed of exclusively required reserves; the money supply can be expressed by H/k.

Suppose there are n banks, with the representative bank's supply of loans specified in Equation. (46.2) aggregating, and which generates the total supply of loans. A structural view of the aggregated balance sheet of banks suggests that if banks allocate a fraction of their excess reserves into loans and the rest into bonds, the aggregate supply of loans is given by $\varepsilon(1 - k) \cdot (H/k)$, where ε represents the ratio of loans to excess reserves. Accordingly, the share of loans in excess reserves must characterize the banks' loan-making behavior and it is thus actually a function of the same set of variables that determine aggregate supply of loans.

$$L^S = \varepsilon(\rho, r, \phi, \psi, \gamma, n)\left(\frac{1 - k}{k}\right)H,$$

(46.4)

$$? - + - - +$$

where the symbols underneath each of the arguments in $\varepsilon(\bullet)$ denote the signs of the partial derivatives associated with them. For simplicity, it is assumed that bank credit is the only debt instrument for firms to finance their investment; investment demand and the demand for bank loans are taken to be equal.[5] Thus, aggregate demand for loans is negatively related to the loan interest rate, and its standard linear form is

$$L^D = \alpha - \beta\rho. \tag{46.5}$$

Indeed, as demonstrated by the existing literature on markets in disequilibrium, the loan market may or may not be at the market-clearing equilibrium.[6] Nevertheless, unlike disequilibrium economics, the loan quantity traded in the market is not uniformly characterized by the minimum of demand and supply sides. Loan rationing can arise in an unrestricted market setting flawed only by plausible information asymmetries; the loan rate can always freely adjust to a level consistent with market forces driven by the profit-maximization incentives. Therefore, credit rationing could exist at the profit-maximizing loan rate, $\rho^* = \phi/2\psi$, and sustain as an equilibrium phenomenon. The excess demand fails to drive the loan rate upward because the associated credit risk would reduce banks' profits; however, if at the same loan rate there is an excess supply, the loan interest rate will adjust downward to clear the loan market, since holding excess reserves does not add to profits at all.

Consider the demand for and supply of loans specified in Equations (46.4) and (46.5), respectively, then the equilibrium interest rate in the loan market is given by

$$\rho = \begin{cases} \dfrac{\phi}{2\psi}, & \text{if } L^D \geq L^S \text{ at } \dfrac{\phi}{2\psi}; \\[2mm] \min(\rho_1, \rho_2 | L^D = L^S), & \text{if } L^D < L^S \text{ at } \dfrac{\phi}{2\psi}, \end{cases} \tag{46.6}$$

where ρ_1 and ρ_2 are the two roots of the quadratic equation given by $L^D = L^S$. Recall that $\rho^* = \phi/2\psi$ is the loan rate that corresponds to the maximum quantity of loans. If an excess supply exists at ρ^*, L^D must cross L^S once at a loan rate below ρ^* and once at a loan rate above ρ^*. Since ρ^* is the profit-maximizing loan rate, the bank has no incentive to raise the loan rate to any level above ρ^*, and credit is then rationed at the equilibrium. On the other hand, the profit-maximizing loan rate is not attainable if there is excess supply at ρ^*, since

the bank cannot force the firms to borrow in excess of the amount that maximizes their profits. It follows that if a bank cannot maximize its profit at ρ^* due to deficient demand, the best attainable outcome for the bank is to allow a downward adjustment in the loan rate until the loan market clears. Therefore, the loan quantity traded is at the market-clearing equilibrium level if the market interest rate of loans is below the banks' desired level, ρ^*; otherwise, it would be determined by supply at the profit-maximizing loan rate.

46.3. Macroeconomic Equilibrium

Assume that investment is solely dependent on the availability of bank credit, and investment demand is equivalent to the demand for loans. Based on the analytical results in the preceding section, there is an implicit positive relationship between the interest rates on loans and bonds, which can be explicitly expressed as $\rho = \lambda(r)$. If credit demand is not rationed in the loan market, we have $I(\rho) \equiv L^D[\lambda(r)]$, with $I' = L'^D \lambda' < 0$, however, with credit rationing, investment demand is totally determined by the aggregate supply of loans.

46.3.1. Case for Credit Rationing

With credit rationing, the quantity of loans effectively traded is given by L^S as specified in Equation (46.4). In this case, the monetary authority can help loosen credit rationing through open market purchases: the nonbank public, which sells bonds to the monetary authority deposits the proceeds into banks, and the loan supply increases with the deposits. The rationing situation improves and the resulting increase in output increases money demand, and thus imposes upward pressure on the interest rate and the exchange value of the domestic currency. This in turn relieves the money market of the adjustment burden resulting from the monetary authority's commitment to the fixed exchange rate under the circumstances of open market purchases. Therefore, following the monetary authority's open market purchases, although there are market forces to purchase foreign bonds, which leads the monetary authority to sell foreign reserves, the authority's operation on foreign reserves does not fully sterilize its open-market operation on domestic bonds so that its net effects are to expand loans and increase output.

Credit rationing enhances originally existing imperfect asset substitutability between bonds and loans, and lending to domestic capital investment under rationing is expected to be more preferable for holding foreign bonds. Without losing generality, a thought experiment could be to assume credit movement to be "segmented" in such a way that the goods market takes only credit expansion from open-market purchases on domestic bonds whereas it is asset portfolio adjustment rather than disinvestments in real capital goods that responds to any credit contraction from open-market sales on foreign bonds.[7] Hence, grouping Equation (46.4) with the equilibrium conditions of the goods market and the money market yields the following simple macroeconomic models:

$$Y = C(Y) + \varepsilon \left(\frac{1-k}{k} \right) B_a + X(Y, eP^f) \qquad (46.7)$$

$$B_a + F = kl(Y, r^f). \qquad (46.8)$$

Note that the domestic price level is normalized at unity since price rigidity applies to the short-run macroeconomic model. Besides the derivatives property of L^S stipulated in (Equation (46.4)), the other relevant derivatives in the above model satisfy the following conditions: $C' > 0$, $X'_Y < 0$, $i_Y > 0$, and $l'_r < 0$. Equation (46.7) is the private-sector-only IS equation with the presence of the loan market in an open economy, where $C(\cdot)$ is consumption function, $\varepsilon[(1-k)/k]B_a$ is the supply of loans available to investment from the monetary authority's open market purchases, $X(\cdot)$ is the net export function, e is the domestic currency price of foreign exchange, and P^f is the foreign price level. Equation (46.8) represents the "monetary" version of the open-economy LM equation (or the balance-of-payments equation). r^f is the foreign

interest rate on bonds, which equals to r by perfect capital mobility in the bond market, and $l(\cdot)$ is the demand for money, increasing in income and decreasing in the interest rate.

There are three endogenous variables when credit rationing exists in the loan market: income Y, loan quantity L, and the international reserve component in the monetary base F. These are determined simultaneously in three equations (Equations (46.4), (46.7), and (46.8)). Although money is partly endogenous due to perfect capital mobility in the bond market and the monetary authority's commitment to maintain fixed exchange rates, the endogeneity of money is not complete due to the credit channel of monetary transmission mechanism, and thus money is not completely neutral. Changes in the money supply serve to shift not only the LM curve but also the IS curve, so that the responsive change in money does not totally wash out the real effect generated by the monetary change associated with open-market purchases. Therefore, the credit channel rescues monetary policy from the charge of impotency.

46.3.2. Case for Nonrationing of Credit

In the regime in which loans are not rationed, both the loan quantity and the loan interest rate are endogenous variables in addition to income and the international reserves of the central bank. The general equilibrium system consists of the loan supply Equation (46.4), the monetary version of the balance-of-payments Equation (46.8), and two other basic equations given below:

$$Y = C(Y) + (\alpha - \beta\rho) + X(Y, eP^f) \qquad (46.9)$$

$$\alpha - \beta\rho = \varepsilon(\rho, r, \phi, \psi, \gamma, n) \left(\frac{1-k}{k} \right) (B_a + F) \qquad (46.10)$$

Equation (46.9) is the standard IS equation, unlike the credit-rationing counterpart in Equation (46.7), the interest rates play a role in the determination of income. In Equation (46.10), its LHS is the demand for loans, and the RHS the supply of loans. Equations (46.4), (46.8), (46.9), and (46.10) implicitly determine the equilibrium values of Y, L, ρ, and F.

46.4. Comparative Static Analysis

The present section examines the responses of the equilibrium income, loan quantity, loan interest rate, and international reserve component of the monetary base to a monetary shock initiated through an open-market operation conducted by the monetary authority. These impacts vary with the rationing of credit.

Consider the credit-rationing model. Differentiating Equations (46.4), (46.7), and (46.8) with respect to L^S, Y, F, and B_a produces the following results:

$$\frac{dL^S}{dB_a} = \frac{kl_Y\left(\varepsilon\frac{1-k}{k}\right)^2}{1-C'-X'} > 0 \qquad (46.11)$$

$$\frac{dY}{dB_a} = \frac{\varepsilon\left(\frac{1-k}{k}\right)}{1-C'-X'} > 0 \qquad (46.12)$$

$$\frac{dF}{dB_a} = -1 + kl_Y\frac{\varepsilon\left(\frac{1-k}{k}\right)}{1-C'-X'} < 0 \qquad (46.13)$$

Under the fixed exchange rate system, changes in the official international reserves mirror the status of the balance of payments. Starting from the open-market purchase on the part of the monetary authority, the money supply (bank deposits) increases and multiplies through the money multiplier $1/k$ as high-powered money B_a increases. Banks usually tend to make more loans due to an expanded volume of deposits, and the increased loans relax the credit constraint facing the economy so that income rises, as measured in Equations (46.11) and (46.12). Finally, transaction demand for money also increases as a result of increased income but the generated money demand via the credit channel is less than the initial increase in money supply, i.e. the money created by the central bank outpaces the growth of money demand. The resulting excess supply of money must

be spent on the purchase of foreign goods or financial assets. As the domestic residents exchange their domestic money for foreign money, the central bank loses international reserves and the money account of the balance of payment moves into a deficit ($dF < 0$). The consequent money contraction will sustain until the disequilibrium in the money market disappears and the balance of payments is back to equilibrium at the foreign interest rate, r^f.

Examining Equation (46.13) suggests that the credit channel per se plays a role to preserve the legacy of monetary policy. The increase in money demand generated from the credit-driven income expansion minimizes the adjustment burden that has fallen upon the official international reserves, so that the absolute value of the offset coefficient is less than 1 and monetary control is not completely lost.[8] The economics reasoning and the pertinent empirics suggest that the second term on the RHS of Equation (46.13) is a positive fraction, and in that term a large credit multiplier, $\varepsilon \cdot (1-k)/k$, serves to reduce the magnitude of the offset coefficient given by Equation (46.13). Hence, the stronger the credit channel is, the more legacy of monetary policy can be reserved. However, without considering the credit channel, the endogenous change in foreign reserves would completely offset the initial change in the credit brought about by the central bank's open-market operations, and then the traditional result of monetary neutrality would follow.

Figure 46.2 summarizes the analytical results in a four-quadrant diagram. Quadrant I depicts the IS-LM-BP curves in the traditional general equilibrium framework, with the initial credit-rationing equilibrium as shown in Quadrant III, and Quadrant II depicts the linearized implicit function $\rho = \lambda(r)$. Consider an expansionary monetary policy initiated by the open market purchase. The LM curve shifts rightward initially to the position of the dashed line, causing the IS curve to shift in the same direction through the credit channel. This is reflected in Quadrant III by the downward shift of the aggregate loan supply curve, with the loan interest rate remaining at the profit-maximizing

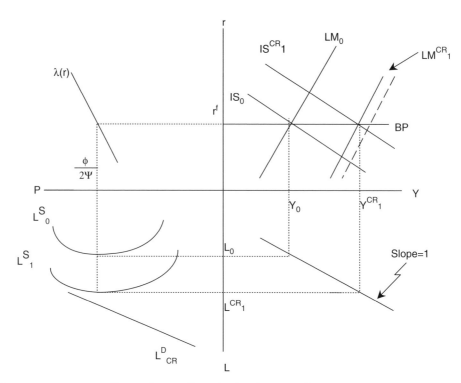

Figure 46.2. Monetary non-neutrality under credit rationing in a small open economy with a fixed exchange rate

equilibrium level. Due to the tight credit market, the resulting increase in loans directly translates into the corresponding increase in income at the full scale, as depicted in Quadrant IV.[9] The increased money demand mitigates the excess supply pressure on the money account of the balance of payments, though the equilibrium in the money market and foreign exchange market still entails a reduction of official international reserves held by the central bank. As a result, although the LM curve shifts backward away from its initial post-shock position as given by the dashed line, it does not shift all the way back to LM_0; instead, LM_1^{CR} meets IS_1^{CR} at Y_1^{CR} under the circumstances.

Now let us turn to the situation in which there is no credit rationing. Differentiating Equations (46.4), (46.8), (46.9), and (46.10) with respect to L, Y, ρ, F, and B_a generates the following comparative static results:

$$\frac{dL}{dB_a} = 0, \qquad (46.14)$$

$$\frac{dY}{dB_a} = 0, \qquad (46.15)$$

$$\frac{d\rho}{dB_a} = 0, \quad \text{and} \qquad (46.16)$$

$$\frac{dF}{dB_a} = -1. \qquad (46.17)$$

As shown by the comparative static results in Equations (46.14) through (46.17), there is a sharp contrast between the cases of credit rationing and nonrationing of credit in terms of monetary neutrality and the effectiveness of monetary policy. In the absence of credit rationing, the credit channel can only operate through its impact on the loan interest rate. Nevertheless, the loan interest rate is directly related to the world interest rate through $\rho = \lambda(r)$, and the world interest rate cannot be influenced by a small open economy's monetary authority. Following an open-market purchase, once the domestic interest rate tends to decline from the level of the world interest rate, and thus the exchange rate may deviate from its par accordingly, the monetary authority is obliged to contract money and credit by selling its foreign reserves until the asset prices restore their initial equilibrium levels, therefore rendering the intended monetary expansion ineffective.

46.5. Conclusion

This paper has demonstrated that equilibrium credit rationing plays a role in preserving the legacy of monetary policy even under a fixed exchange rate regime with perfect international capital mobility. Under equilibrium credit rationing, credit-dependent investment transmits a monetary shock into changes in real income, and thus transaction demand for money, therefore sharing the adjustment burden of maintaining the fixed exchange rate, which would otherwise completely fall upon the official international reserves. The magnitude of offset coefficient becomes less than 1 since any expansion of domestic credit and its real effect is only partially offset by the associated monetary contractions happening through international financial portfolio investment. The degree of retained monetary autonomy depends on the magnitude of the credit multiplier under rationing.

When there exists equilibrium credit rationing, monetary contractions resulting from the monetary authority's endogenous open-market sale of foreign assets will take a conduit of portfolio disinvestments rather than real capital disinvestments. Therefore, the asymmetry between domestic real capital investment (customer market credit) and financial portfolio investment (auction market credit) in responding to impulses of open-market operations holds the key for monetary nonneutrality.

In contrast, incorporating credit market without credit rationing into analysis fails to rescue monetary policy from its neutrality in a small open economy committed to fixed exchange rates. The assumption of imperfect substitutability *per se* between auction market credit (bonds) and customer market credit (bank loans) is insufficient

for monetary autonomy in the Mundell–Fleming model, though it is adequate for the modified IS-LM type model (Bernanke and Blinder, 1988) in which the features of small open economy and fixed exchange rates do not appear.

NOTES

1. This line of analysis can be traced back to Fleming (1962) and Mundell (1963).
2. In their influential paper, Stiglitz and Weiss (1981) provide information-based analysis of equilibrium credit rationing. Blinder and Stiglitz (1983) further argue that monetary policy works through bank credit for there are no close substitutes for it at least as far as most medium and small firms with relatively high risk are concerned. For a comprehensive review of the credit view literature, see Kashyap and Stein (1993).
3. It is shown indeed in my earlier paper (Wu, 1999) that monetary policy can have real effects in both credit-rationing regime and the market-clearing regime if the central bank's foreign exchange reserves are independent of open-market operations. While considering the endogeneity of the monetary base, Ramírez (2001) argues that "monetary policy is still ineffective in influencing output under a fixed exchange rate, even with an operative credit channel." Nevertheless, in response to Ramírez (2001), this paper shows particularly how credit-rationing channel can save monetary policy from being charged with impotence even in a small open economy with complete capital mobility and fixed exchange rates.
4. As shown by Stiglitz and Weiss (1981) and others, the loan rate and intermediary charges may have both an adverse selection effect and a moral hazard effect on the risk of a pool of loans. Raising the loan rate shifts the mix of borrowers toward riskier firms and their projects to be financed by loans, thus reducing the lender's expected return. As a result, the intermediary may maximize its expected profits by setting an interest rate at a level that results in an excess demand for bank credit.
5. More generally, the demand side of the loan market is influenced by the interest rates on the two credit instruments, loans and bonds, as well as aggregate income, see Bernanke and Blinder (1988).
6. For studies on disequilibrium markets under price rigidity, see Barro and Grossman (1971), and Muellbauer and Portes (1978), among others.

7. Although the assumption of perfect capital mobility rules out the possibility of "home bias" that would otherwise explain the asymmetry between holding of domestic assets and holding of foreign assets, it is credit rationing that holds the key for the real effect of monetary policy here.

8. Some studies have provided the evidence for a certain degree of monetary autonomy under fixed exchange rates. For example, Cumby and Obstfeld (1983) and Rennhack and Mondino (1988) find that structural estimates of offset coefficients are less than one. Also, using Granger causality tests for a number of countries, Montiel (1989) and Dowla and Chowdhury (1991) report that some domestic financial aggregates like money and credit Granger-cause domestic real output.

9. For simplicity, the income multiplier effect is ignored here.

REFERENCES

Barro, R.J. and Grossman, H.I. (1971). "A general disequilibrium model of income and employment." *American Economic Review*, 61: 82–93.

Bernanke, B. and Blinder, A. (1988). "Credit, money, and aggregate demand." *American Economic Review (Paper and Proceedings)*, 78: 435–439.

Blinder, A.S. and Stiglitz, J. (1983). "Money, credit constraints, and economic activity." *American Economic Review (Papers and Proceedings)*, 73: 297–302.

Christopher, J.W. and Lewarne, S. (1994). "An expository model of credit rationing." *Journal of Macroeconomics*, 16(3): 539–545.

Cumby, R.E. and Obstfeld, M. (1983). "Capital mobility and the scope for sterilization: mexico in the 1970s," in P.A. Armella, R. Dornbusch, and M. Obstfeld (eds.) *Financial Policies and the World Capital Market*. Chicago: University of Chicago Press, pp. 245–276.

Dowla, A. and Chowdhury, A. (1991). "Money, credit, and real output in the developing economies." Unpublished. Department of Economics, Marquette University.

Fleming, J.M. (1962). "Domestic financial policies under fixed and floating exchange rates." *International Monetary Fund Staff Papers*, 9: 369–379.

Kashyap, A. and Stein, J. (1993). "Monetary policy and bank lending." Working Paper No. 4317, National Bureau of Economic Research.

Montiel, P.J. (1989). "Empirical analysis of high-inflation episodes in Argentina, Brazil and Israel." *IMF Staff Papers*, 36: 527–549.

Muellbauer, J. and Portes, R. (1978). "Macroeconomic models with quantity rationing." *Economic Journal*, 88: 788–821.

Mundell, R.A. (1963). "Capital mobility and stabilization under fixed and flexible exchange rates." *Canadian Journal of Economics and Political Science*, 29: 475–485.

Ramírez, C.D. (2001). "Even more on monetary policy in a small open economy." *International Review of Economics and Finance*, 10(3): 399–405.

Rennhack, R. and Mondino, G. (1988). *Capital Mobility and Monetary Policy in Colombia*. Working Paper No. 88/77, International Monetary Fund (August).

Stiglitz, J. and Weiss, A. (1981). "Credit rationing in markets with imperfect information." *American Economic Review*, 71: 393–410.

Wu, Y. (1999). "More on monetary policy in a small open economy: a credit view." *International Review of Economics and Finance*, 8(2): 223–235.

Chapter 47

POLICY COORDINATION BETWEEN WAGES AND EXCHANGE RATES IN SINGAPORE

YING WU, *Salisbury University, USA*

Abstract

Singapore's unique experience in macroeconomic management involves the government's engagement in a tripartite collective bargaining and its influence on the macroeconomic policy game in wages and exchange rates in response to inflation and output volatility. The period from the mid-1980s to mid-1990s features the policy game with a Nash equilibrium in the level of wages and exchange rates and a non-Nash equilibrium in wage growth and exchange rate appreciations. Based on the empirical evidence in this period, the models used in this study suggests that wage and exchange-rate policies are a pair of complements both at their levels (Nash equilibrium) and at their percentage changes (non-Nash equilibrium).

Keywords: wages; effective exchange rates; collective bargaining; Nash equilibrium; National Wages Council; Monetary Authority of Singapore; unit labor cost; macroeconomic stabilization; inflation; unemployment

47.1. Introduction

Adverse supply shocks often pose a dilemma for the Keynesian approach to aggregate demand management: implementing expansionary monetary and fiscal policies tend to exacerbate inflation, whereas the laissez-faire policy stance is conducive to acute and prolonged unemployment before the economy restores its natural rate level of output. As an alternative means to avoid the predicament and cope with demand shocks as well as supply shocks, appropriate labor market policies, including wage policy, are recently gaining importance in macroeconomic management.[1] Nevertheless, wages tend to be sticky downward and it becomes difficult to attempt to reduce them due to the existence of strong labor unions or laws prohibiting such measures. The idea of instituting an agreement by unions and corporations to link wage growth with productivity growth, though attractive, often faces great political and economic challenges when it is put in practice.[2] Accordingly, in general, there is a dearth of research on the effectiveness of wage policy in an environment where other aggregate demand policies exist.

Singapore is an ideal case for the study of the effectiveness and dynamics of wage and exchange-rate polices, not only because it has actively deployed wage policy in combination with exchange-rate policy for more than two decades but also because it has maintained a remarkable record of sustained economic growth with low inflation in a small open economy.[3] As a highly opened small economy, Singapore faces the challenges of "imported" foreign inflation as well as the wage-push inflation that results from rapid economic growth and labor shortage. The exchange rate and wage movements naturally become the two inter-related key factors in maintaining macroeconomic stability. Specifically, the wage policy manipulated by a tripartite collective bargaining institution known as the National Wages Council (NWC) has actually acted as an important complement to the country's exchange-rate policy controlled by the Monetary Authority of Singapore (MAS) (Otani and Sassanpour, 1988; Wu, 1999).

The NWC is made up of representatives from the government, labor unions, and employer fed-erations. Its main function is to select a wage pol-icy that is not only agreeable by all three parties but also compatible with macroeconomic targets. Although the NWC's wage recommendations only sketch a guideline for negotiations between em-ployers and employees, both public and private sectors usually accept and implement them rather smoothly. The resulting collective bargaining agreements often extend to nonunion workers as well. Labor unions in Singapore actively promote sound economic policies to their members and support restraints when needed. In this way, the wage council helps to reduce the frictions that information asymmetry and costly bargaining often cause in supply-side adjustments.[4] In coord-ination with the NWC's endeavor in achieving orderly wage settlements, the Monetary Authority of Singapore (MAS), as the other key player in Singapore's macroeconomic management, chooses the optimal exchange rate variation to cope with the dual inflationary pressures (i.e. the imported inflation and the inflation pushed by labor short-ages) and to maintain the economy's competitive-ness.

With its focus on the role of collective bargain-ing in macroeconomic management in Singapore, this study attempts to model the policy game of wage and exchange rate policies between the NWC and the MAS. The study starts with an analysis of the behavior of wage and exchange rate levels in the policy game and its empirics. It then further derives the MAS's exchange-rate response function and the NWC's wage response function in terms of

percentage changes of the two policies, and ana-lyzes two interplay patterns of the two response functions: the Nash game and the non-Nash game. For the non-Nash game, the study calibrates the analytical outcome in each of the three poten-tial scenarios of the economy: inflation, recession, and the "Goldilocks" scenario (neither inflation-ary nor recessionary), and compares the simulation results with the actual quarterly growth paths under the two policy rules for the period from 1987:1 to 1996:4.

47.2. Complementarity of Wages and Exchange Rates

This section presents a policy-game model of wages and exchange rates at their levels.[5] For analytical simplicity, consider a composite product traded internationally under the purchasing power parity. Suppose that workers (employees) exert their influence in cooperation with the government and employers rather than through militancy. Wages are negotiated between firms and workers for each period. The representative firm hires workers to produce output q according to a pro-duction function $q(L) = L^\phi (0 < \phi < 1)$. In wage negotiations, the right-to-manage model is used, whereby workers bargain with employers for de-sired wages and employers choose employment at the negotiated wage level.[6]

Let W be the nominal wage, E the nominal exchange rate measured as units of the domestic currency per unit of a foreign currency, P^f the price of the tradable good in the foreign currency, L^* the level of employment demanded as a func-tion of the real wage W/EP^f, i.e. $L^*(W/EP^f)$, and r the alternative source of income in real terms (unemployment compensation, for example) when the negotiating parties fail to agree upon W. Add-itionally, a constant-elasticity-of-substitution func-tion $U(x) = x^{1-\gamma}/(1 - \gamma)$ $(0 < \gamma < 1)$ determines a representative worker's increasing and concave utility of the earned real income x. Denote the gain to the firm from agreeing to any given wage by $G_F(W; EP^f)$ and the similar gain to workers by

$G_L(W; EP^f, r)$, respectively. The role of the NWC is to incorporate any exchange-rate policy signal into the wage settlement process and guide the two negotiating parties to choose a wage level to maximize the generalized Nash product, a weighted geometric average of the gains to workers and to firms:

$$\{G_F(W; EP^f)\}^s \{G_L(W; EP^f, r)\}^{1-s}$$
$$\equiv \left\{ EP^f q \left[L^* \left(\frac{W}{EP^f} \right) \right] - WL^* \left(\frac{W}{EP^f} \right) \right\}^s$$
$$\left\{ L^* \left(\frac{W}{EP^f} \right) \left[U \left(\frac{W}{EP^f} \right) - U(r) \right] \right\}^{1-s}$$

(47.1)

where $s(0 < s < 1)$ is a weight reflecting the relative bargaining strength of workers. The variation of s traces out all the negotiated wages between the reservation level and the monopoly level in a Nash bargaining.

The first-order optimality condition determines the negotiated wage as

$$w = e + p^f + (1 - \phi)s + \frac{\phi}{1 - \gamma} + \ln r,$$

(47.2)

where the lower case variables denote their logarithms and the last two parametric terms are the result of Taylor's approximation. Equation (47.2) gives the wage negotiator's reaction function, which predicts the unit elasticities of wages with respect to the exchange rate and to the foreign price level, respectively. Furthermore, the Nash bargaining wage is greater the larger the workers' bargaining power (s), the higher the productivity (ϕ), the greater the unemployment compensation (r), and the greater the elasticity of marginal utility (γ).

Since employment is determined by the firms' demand for labor at the negotiated level of real wage, aggregate output, Y, is a decreasing function of the real wage. Let L^A be aggregate employment and $F(L^A)$ aggregate output. Since the Cobb–Douglas production function determines aggregate output, it then follows that $Y = F(L^A (w - e - p^f)) \equiv h(w - e - p^f) = (w - e - p^f)^{\phi(\phi - 1)}$, with $h' = F'L^{A'} < 0$ and $h'' = F''L^{A'} + F'L^{A''} > 0$.

The monetary-fiscal authority has a loss function, Ω, which involves a cost associated with the inflation rate, $\pi \equiv De + Dp^f$ (D is the first-order difference operator) and the deviations of the current account from its target level, $\Theta > 0$ (See Wu (1999) for the detailed derivation of current account balance, CA).

$$\Omega = \frac{a}{2} \pi^2 - (CA - \Theta).$$

(47.3)

The current account surplus, unlike inflation, is favorable to the government so that a negative weight is attached to the second term in the loss function.[7] Inflation costs rise at an increasing rate with the rate of inflation, and the coefficient $a > 0$ measures the authority's intolerance of inflation. The authority's problem is to choose the exchange rate to minimize the loss function (Equation (47.3)). The associated first-order condition is

$$a(De + Dp^f) + \frac{1 - c}{1 + \psi} h'(w - e - p^f) + \frac{\psi}{1 + \psi} \tau\lambda = 0,$$

(47.4)

where c is the marginal propensity to consume with respect to changes in disposable income, λ the weight for changes in the exchange rate in the balance payment account as opposed to changes in real foreign reserves ($0 < \lambda < 1$), and τ^{-1} is the sensitivity of exchange rate appreciation with respect to the balance of payments ($\tau^{-1} < 0$); in addition,

$$-1 < \psi \equiv \frac{\beta}{1 - \lambda} \left[\frac{d}{\theta} - (\rho - r) \right] < 0,$$

where β is offset coefficient between domestic and foreign components of the monetary base ($0 < \beta < 1$), θ the proportion of CPF liabilities invested in government securities, d the marginal propensity to consume with respect to changes in real private saving, r the real interest rate on the government debt, and ρ the real rate of return on the debt-financed government overseas investment. Equation (47.4) implicitly determines the government's reaction function of the exchange rate to changes in the wage level, which, in turn, influences the wage that wage negotiators in the private sector demand. Therefore, the reaction function also indirectly conveys a signal of the government preference about the desired wage level with respect to the optimal exchange rate.

The wage-negotiators' reaction function (47.2), with the unemployment compensation parameter r being normalized to unity, and the government's reaction function (47.4) jointly determine the static equilibrium (e^*, w^*). The corresponding dynamic system in the neighborhood of (e^*, w^*) is

$$\dot{e} = g_1(e, w)$$
$$= -a(De + Dp^f)$$
$$\qquad - \frac{1-c}{1+\psi} h'(w - e - p^f) - \frac{\psi}{1+\psi} \tau \lambda, \qquad (47.5)$$

$$\dot{w} = g_2(e, w) = e - w + p^f + (1 - \phi)s + \frac{\phi}{1 - \gamma} \qquad (47.6)$$

where $\dot{e}$ and $\dot{w}$ are the time derivatives of e and w. The dynamic system of the exchange rate and wages is stable as long as inflation is so expensive that a depreciation increases inflation costs more than strengthens competitiveness, that is,

$$a > \frac{1-c}{1+\psi} h''. \,^{8}$$

The empirical analysis with a vector error correction (VEC) model below demonstrates the robustness of the negative relationship between the exchange rate and wages obtained from comparative statics.

There are three variables: the logarithm of unit labor costs of all sectors (LULC,); the logarithm of the nominal effective exchange rate (LNEER); and the logarithm of the import price (LIMP) index compiled using the US dollar prices. The quarterly data are from the *International Financial Statistics*, ranging from 1980:1 to 1997:1. The augmented Dickey–Fuller test suggests that the three variables are all $I(1)$ sequences.[9] The model is set with four-quarter lags by the conventional criteria, and the Johanson cointegration test suggests that there are

exactly two cointegrating equations. Formally, after depressing the lagged difference terms, the estimated vector error correction model with four-period lags can be written as

$$DY_t = \alpha \beta' Y_{t-1} + \ldots + \varepsilon_t, \qquad (47.7)$$

where $DY_t = (DLULC_t, DLNEER_t, DLIMP_t)'$, $Y_{t-1} = (LULC_{t-1}, LNEER_{t-1}, LIMP_{t-1}, 1)'$, α is a 3×2 matrix of the speed-of-adjustment parameters estimated as $[\alpha_1 \alpha_2 \alpha_3]'$ with $\alpha_1 = (-0.10, -0.01)$, $\alpha_2 = (-0.03, -0.18)$, and $\alpha_3 = (0.09, 0.07)$, β is a 4×2 matrix of the normalized cointegrating vectors given by $[\beta_1 \beta_2]$ with $\beta_1 = (1, 0, -1.05, 0.09)'$, and $\beta_2 = (0, 1, 1.06, -9.46)'$, and $\varepsilon_t = (\varepsilon_{t,LULC}, \varepsilon_{t,LNEER}, \varepsilon_{t,LIMP})'$ is the vector of white-noise disturbances.

The estimated cointegrating coefficients in the matrix β are significant with wide margins even at 1 percent significance level. According to the two cointegration equations, responding to an increase of 1 percentage in import prices, wages increase by 1.05 percent and the exchange rate decreases by 1.06 percent in the long run. It follows that the purchasing power of wages in Singapore, measured in a basket of foreign currencies, has been rising in terms of imported goods. Derived from the two estimated cointegrating equations, the deterministic long-run equilibrium relationship can be described as

$$LULC = 9.28 - 0.99 LNEER. \qquad (47.8)$$

Equation (47.8) says that on average, each percentage of wage growth goes hand in hand with an approximately equal percentage of the Singapore currency appreciation vis-à-vis a basket of foreign currencies. The estimated speed-of-adjustment coefficients in α reflect the dynamic adjustment mechanism and support the robustness of the long-term equilibrium relationship. Suppose that one-unit positive shock in import prices results in a negative deviation in the unit labor cost and a positive deviation in the exchange rate from the previous period's stationary equilibrium, respectively. In response to the disequilibrium errors, the growth of unit labor cost increases by 10 percent as suggested by the first adjustment coefficient in α_1 and the appreciation rate increases by 18 percent as suggested by the second adjustment coefficient in α_2. Both the speed-of-adjustment coefficients are significant at 1 percent level and convergent as well.[10]

47.3. Policy Games in Wage Growth and Exchange Rate Appreciation

This section explicitly models the tripartism between employers, union workers, and the government as the institutional foundation to form the NWC objective function.[11] Employers as a whole concern themselves with the competitiveness of their products in the world market, which hinges highly upon relative unit labor cost. Union workers, on the other hand, are interested in maintaining a balance between employment and the growth of real income. Unlike the groups of union workers and employers, the government targets healthy macroeconomic performance characterized by a balance between inflation and unemployment.

The growth rate of ULC (g_{ULC}) is a weighted average of the wage-growth rate (g_w) and the inflation rate (π): $g_{\mathrm{ULC}} = (1 - \theta)g_\mathrm{w} + \theta\pi$, where the weight θ is actually the parameter in a power function of labor productivity.[12] Denote the growth rate of foreign unit labor cost by $g_{\mathrm{ULC}^\mathrm{f}}$, then the expression $[(1 - \theta)g_\mathrm{w} + \theta\pi + g_{\mathrm{NEER}} - g_{\mathrm{ULC}^\mathrm{f}}]$ describes the evolution of relative unit labor costs. Formally, the NWC chooses the growth rate of wages to minimize its loss function

$$\mathrm{Loss}_{\mathrm{NWC}} = \alpha_1[(1 - \theta)g_\mathrm{w} + \theta\pi + g_{\mathrm{NEER}} - g_{\mathrm{ULC}^\mathrm{f}}]$$
$$+ \alpha_2\left[\frac{1}{2}(U - \hat{U})^2 + \frac{\gamma}{2}(\pi - \hat{\pi})^2\right]$$
$$+ \alpha_3[\beta(g_\mathrm{w} - \pi) + U]$$

$$(47.9)$$

where $\hat{U}$ and $\hat{\pi}$ are the rates of unemployment and inflation targeted by the government, β the union workers' loss weight of real income relative to unemployment, γ the government's loss weight of

inflation relative to unemployment, and α_1, α_2, α_3 represent the three weights associated with the loss functions of employers, the government, and union workers, respectively (these α's are the proxy parameters for the NWC participants' bargaining power). Note that $\gamma > 0$, $\beta < 0$, $\alpha_i > 0$, and $\Sigma\alpha_i = 1$. The first term in (47.9) describes the cost to employers of deteriorating the relative unit labor cost, the second term represents the cost to the government when the unemployment rate and the inflation rate are off their targets, and the last term characterizes the cost to union workers when the real wage-growth rate falls or the unemployment rate rises.

The resulting optimal wage-growth rate responds to changes in economic conditions according to the following rule of reaction:

$$g_\mathrm{w} = \frac{A_1}{A_0} + \frac{A_2}{A_0}\pi_{\mathrm{Nop}} + \frac{A_3}{A_0}g_{\mathrm{NEER}} + \frac{A_4}{A_0}g_{\mathrm{w}-2}$$
$$+ \frac{A_5}{A_0}\pi_{-2} + \frac{A_6}{A_0}\pi_{\mathrm{OP}-2} + \frac{A_7}{A_0}g_{\mathrm{w}-3}$$
$$+ \frac{A_8}{A_0}\pi_{-3} + \frac{A_9}{A_0}\mathrm{CPFC} + \frac{A_{10}}{A_0}\hat{U} + \frac{A_{11}}{A_0}\hat{\pi}$$

$$(47.10)$$

where $A_j(j = 0,1,\ldots,11)$ are the functions of the structural parameters in the inflation equation, the unemployment-rate equation, and the unit-labor-cost growth equation; and the relative weights in the NWC's loss function (Equation (47.9)). The values of these coefficient functions (A_j's) are sensitive to the model's economic structure.

The other policy-game player, the MAS, manipulates the exchange rate to improve the tradeoff between the imported inflation and the international competitiveness of Singapore's goods and services,[13] which depends upon the real effective exchange rate, i.e. the relative unit labor cost in this article. Although the benefits of currency depreciation to the export sector can be lost to imported inflation and the resulting wage-price spiral that builds up in the medium-term horizon of three or more years,[14] maintaining a strong currency is detrimental to the export sector in the short run.

Let g_E be the actual real appreciation rate, which equals $(1 - \theta)g_\mathrm{w} + \theta\pi + g_{\mathrm{NEER}} - g_{\mathrm{ULC}^\mathrm{f}}$, $\hat{g}$ the real appreciation rate targeted by the MAS, and δ the weight loss of the deviation of the inflation rate from its target relative to the deviation of real appreciation. The MAS selects the nominal appreciation rate, g_{NEER}, to minimize its loss function:

$$\text{Loss}_{\text{MAS}} = \frac{1}{2}(g_E - \hat{g}_E)^2 + \frac{\delta}{2}(\pi - \hat{\pi})^2 \quad (47.11)$$

The first-order condition generates the MAS' rule of reaction:

$$g_{\text{NEER}} = \frac{B_1}{B_0} g_{\text{ULC}^f} + \frac{B_2}{B_0} g_w + \frac{B_3}{B_0} g_{w-2} + \frac{B_4}{B_0} \pi_{-2}$$
$$+ \frac{B_5}{B_0} \pi_{\text{NOP}} + \frac{B_6}{B_0} \pi_{\text{OP}-2} \quad (47.12)$$
$$+ \frac{B_7}{B_0} \hat{g}_E + \frac{B_8}{B_0} \hat{\pi}$$

where B_k's $(k = 0, 1, \ldots, 8)$ are functions of the structural parameters and weights as A_j's in Equation (47.10).

In this model, the Nash game requires that a policy-making institution react to the optimal policy move made by the other policy-making institution as well as to the state of the economy. At the equilibrium, each institution's policy response is the best not only for the economy but also for the optimal policy of the other institution. Simultaneously solving the system of two non-Nash policy response functions, i.e. Equations (47.10) and (47.12) with the estimated structural coefficients, produces the Nash equilibrium characterized by the Nash appreciation rate of NEER (g^*_{NEER}) and Nash wage-growth rate (g^*_w) (both in their implicit forms) below:

$$g^*_w = f(\pi_{\text{NOP}}, g_{\text{ULC}^f}, \pi_{\text{OP}-2}, g_{w-2}, \pi_{-2},$$
$$g_{w-3}, \pi_{-3}, CPFC, \hat{g}_E, \hat{U}, \hat{\pi}) \quad (47.13)$$

$$g^*_{\text{NEER}} = h(\pi_{\text{NOP}}, g_{\text{ULC}^f}, \pi_{\text{OP}-2}, g_{w-2},$$
$$\pi_{-2}, g_{w-3}, \pi_{-3}, CPFC, \hat{g}_E, \hat{U}, \hat{\pi}) \quad (47.14)$$

In contrast, the non-Nash game simply takes feedback from the state of the economy over a set of current and lagged state variables. Under this rule, any policy variable under the control of one institution does not react to a policy variable under the control of the other institution, i.e. only the currently observed appreciation rate enters the NWC's reaction function, whereas only the currently observed wage growth rate enters the MAS's reaction function. By estimating the structural coefficients in the non-Nash policy response functions for the NWC and MAS (i.e. Equations (47.10) and (47.12)) the non-Nash game can be reduced to one in which the policy sensitivity depends only on the weighting parameters and policy targets.[15]

The stability of Nash equilibrium depends on whether the recursive relations determined by Equations (47.10) and (47.12) will yield a damped or an explosive time path of oscillation once the Nash equilibrium is disturbed. As shown in Wu (2004), the MAS response function (47.12) with estimated structural parameters is negatively sloped (for a reasonable value range of δ) and the similarly estimated NWC response function (47.10) is positively sloped and then the stability condition for the Nash equilibrium requires that the NWC response function be flatter than the MAS response function in the policy space (g_{NEER}, g_w). This condition is not satisfied, however. It, therefore, follows that with the appropriate estimates of structural parameters the Nash equilibrium is not stable and it is more meaningful to concentrate on the non-Nash equilibrium.

47.4. Complementarity of Non-Nash Wage Growth and Exchange-Rate Appreciation

Fixing the policy targets and assigning different values to the relative weights α_i, β, and γ makes it possible to simulate the computable time-paths of the non-Nash optimal appreciation rate, g_{NEER}, and the non-Nash optimal wage growth rate, g_w, over different economic scenarios. The purpose of simulation is to mimic non-Nash policy strategies and thus examine their sensitivity to the game-players' bargaining parameters and the policy stance.

There are three economic scenarios for simulation. In the benchmark case of Goldilocks economy (scenario 1), employees are equally concerned with real wage decline and unemployment ($\beta = -1$). The deviations from the government's targeted inflation rate are equally penalized as those from the targeted unemployment rate ($\gamma = 1$). And the MAS weights equally the deviations of the real exchange rate and inflation rate from their targeted levels ($\delta = 1$). In addition, the targeted rates of inflation and unemployment are, respectively, set at 2 and 3 percent, approximately, to reflect their long-term trend in the period; the targeted rate of real effective exchange-rate appreciation is chosen as 3 percent based on an eight-year moving average since 1988; and the targets specified above continue to apply to the other two economic scenarios. In a recession (scenario 2), the threat of recession prevents employees from demanding too much of real wage growth so that β falls in its absolute value ($\beta = -0.8$). The government's and the monetary authority's inflation weights assume a smaller value compared with the Goldilocks economy ($\gamma = \delta = 0.8$). The third scenario concerns an inflationary economy in which the monetary and fiscal authority weighs inflation more than the targeted real competitiveness ($\delta = 1.2$). In the NWC's loss function, the government's inflation target now also takes a greater weight than the unemployment target ($\gamma = 1.2$), and meanwhile, the inflation threat naturally raises the employees' concern with their real income ($\beta = -1.2$).

How do the growth rate of wages and the appreciation rate of exchange rates work together in Singapore? Table 47.1 presents the correlation coefficients between the NEER appreciation rate and non-Nash wage growth rate in all the three simulated scenarios as well as the actually observed correlation coefficient.[16] As in Table 47.1, all the simulation-based correlation coefficients are positive for the non-Nash regime. It follows that the two policies are complements in a non-Nash environment. Instead of responding optimally to each other, the non-Nash strategies work in such a way

Table 47.1. Correlation between Wage Growth and NEER Appreciation

		Non-Nash Game Simulation		
	Actual	Scenario 1	Scenario 2	Scenario 3
Correlation Coefficient	0.644	0.588	0.646	0.520

that at least one strategy acts independently without taking into consideration the intended target of the other. Hence, the two strategy variables tend to be relatively impartial in balancing and achieving their own targets. Furthermore, the observed positive correlation between actual wage growth and actual exchange-rate appreciation also matches the pattern for the simulated non-Nash outcome; it does so especially in scenario 2.[17]

47.5. Concluding Remarks

Singapore government's commitment to and continuous participation in the annual tripartite collective bargaining over wage growth signifies the effectiveness of the NWC's adaptable stance and flexible wage policy in smoothing out business cycles, which detracts from the conventional wisdom on wage rigidity and its macroeconomic implications. This paper explores the manner in which Singapore policymakers deploy wage policy in coordination with its exchange-rate policy to achieve macroeconomic stability. The theoretical result from the Nash bargaining in the level of wages and exchange rates suggests that in the long run, wages increase one percentage point for about every percentage point appreciation in the exchange rate, which is well supported by the cointegration and error-correction analysis.

Furthermore, for the period studied, Singapore's tripartite collective bargaining (through NWC) in the growth rate of wages seems to have followed the non-Nash game practice as opposed to the Nash game, as the latter is unstable. A number of structural factors could have actually prevented the NWC from optimally reacting to the best move made by the MAS, such as asymmetry in the decision-making frequency (high frequency on the part of MAS vs. the low frequency on the part of NWC), asymmetric information between policy players as well as their overlapping interests, or simply any barrier in the institutional structure that makes a full-fledged interaction between policy players unrealistic. Both the non-Nash rule simulation and actual observations indicate that the Singapore dollar exchange rate appreciation has acted as a complement to wage growth. Indeed, Singapore currency has exhibited a clear trend of appreciation vis-à-vis a basket of foreign currencies during economic upturns while the growth of labor earnings are rising and a trend of depreciation during economic downturns while the wage growth are declining.

NOTES

1. In the euro area, particularly the familiar policy instruments like the exchange rate and money supply have ceased to be available at the national level while fiscal policy is also often constrained by the straitjacket that the budget deficit cannot exceed 3 percent of GDP, which renders more room for national wage policies (Calmfors, 1998; Wu, 1999; Lawler, 2000; Karadeloglou et al., 2000; Abraham et al., 2000).
2. The Council of Economic Advisers to the President in the US explicitly implemented income policies by imposing the general guidepost for wages from 1962 to 1965 for example (see Perry, 1967;Schultz and Aliber, 1966). The guidepost implicitly remained in practice from time to time in the 1970s as well. In the UK, the 1980s and 1990s saw a resurgence of interest in income policies due to rising unemployment. For an argument for wage policy, see Hahn (1983, p.106).
3. The average annual GDP growth in Singapore over the last decade was greater than 7.5 percent, with an inflation rate of about 2 percent per year.
4. Singapore's system of national wage council has distinguished itself from the centralized collective bargaining in European countries in three aspects. First, unlike the intermittent European government involvement in wage negotiations, the Singapore

government has continuously committed to its participation in the yearly tripartite wage-policy dialogue and agreements since the NWC was formed in 1972. Second, the smooth cooperation between union and nonunion workers and the NWC's effective tripartite coordination resulted in relatively small wage drifts (wage increases beyond those agreed upon in the central negotiations), which are in sharp contrast to the large wage drifts in Europe. Third, serving endogenously as an integrated part of Singapore's macroeconomic management strategy, the NWC has reduced government reliance on exogenous instruments such as fiscal policy and other nonwage income policies, whereas many European governments normally approach interventions from outside the labor market.
5. For a longer and more detailed version of the model discussed in this section, see Wu (1999). The author gratefully acknowledges the permission granted by Blackwell Publishing in this regard.
6. For the right-to-manage model, see Nickell and Andrews (1983) and Oswald (1985).
7. For a similar formulation of the loss function, see Barro and Gordon (1983), and Agénor (1994).
8. The mathematical results of dynamics as well as comparative statics are available from the author upon request.
9. The augmented Dicky–Fuller values for LULC, LNEER, and LIMP are all below the 10 percent MacKinnon critical value in absolute terms.
10. With one standard-deviation innovation in import prices (LIMP) leading to a positive response of unit labor cost (LULC) and a negative response of the exchange rate (LNEER), both responses peak almost simultaneously at the fourteenth quarter after the shock; after that, both of them show a tendency to decay. Consistent with the cointegrating relationship discussed earlier, the pattern in which the wage response mirrors inversely the exchange rate response holds uniformly for all the possible orderings of the Choleski decomposition.
11. With kind permission of Springer Science and Business Media, the author has drawn on a longer version of Wu (2004) in the writings of this section and the next.
12. For the modeling and econometric specification of unit labor cost equation as well as price equation and unemployment equation, see the appendices in Wu (2004).
13. See Teh and Shanmugaratnam (1992) and Carling (1995) for the analyses of Singapore's monetary policy via exchange-rate targeting.

14. See Low (1994).
15. See Wu (2004).
16. For a given simulated scenario, the correlation coefficient does not vary with different bargaining cases because the parameters that reflect bargaining power are constant over time and they do not appear in the coefficients of any time-series variables in either Equation (47.10) or Equation (47.12).
17. Clearly, scenario 2 (recession) cannot characterize the 1987–1995 period in Singapore. The closest match of the simulated correlation with actual correlation in the scenario only suggests that there are some similarities between a recession period with low inflation or deflation and a high-growth period with low inflation. However, the simulation that is based almost exclusively on inflation-related parameters cannot distinguish one from the other.

REFERENCES

Agénor, P.R. (1994). "Credibility and exchange rate management in developing countries." *Journal of Development Economics*, 45(1): 1–16.

Abraham, F., De Bruyne, K., and Van der Auwera, I. (2000). "Will wage policy succeed in euro-land? The case of Belgium." *Cahiers Economiques de Bruxelles*, 0(168): 443–480.

Barro, R.J. and Gordon, D.B. (1983). "Rules, discretion and reputation in a model of monetary policy." *Journal of Monetary Economics*, 12: 101–121.

Calmfors, L. (1998). "Macroeconomic policy, wage setting, and employment – what difference does the EMU make?" *Oxford Review of Economic Policy*, 14(3): 125–151.

Carling, R.G. (1995). "Fiscal and monetary policies," in K. Bercuson (ed.) *Singapore: A Case Study in Rapid Development, IMF Occasional Paper 119*. Washington, DC: International Monetary Fund.

Hahn, F.H. (1983). *Money and Inflation*. Cambridge, MA: The MIT Press.

Karadeloglou, P., Papazoglou, C., and Zombanakis, G. (2000). "Exchange rate vs. supply-side policies as anti-inflationary devices: a comparative analysis for the case of Greece." *Archives of Economic History*, 11: 47–61.

Lawler, P. (2000). "Union wage setting and exchange rate policy." *Economica*, 67: 91–100.

Low, V. (1994) "The MAS model: structure and some policy simulations," in *Outlook for the Singapore Economy*. Singapore: Trans Global Publishing, pp. 20–32 (Chapter 3).

Nickell, S.J. and Andrews, M. (1983). "Unions, Real Wages and Employment in Britain, 1951–79." *Oxford Economic Papers*, 35(Supplement): 183–206.

Oswald, A.J. (1985). "The economic theory of trade unions: an introductory survey." *Scandinavian Journal of Economics*, 87(2): 160–193.

Otani, I. and Sassanpour, C. (1988). "Financial, exchange rate, and wage policies in Singapore, 1979–86." *International Monetary Fund Staff Papers*, 35(3): 474–495.

Perry, G.L. (1967). "Wages and the guideposts." *American Economic Review*, 57(3): 897–904.

Schultz, G.P. and Aliber, R.Z. (1966). *Guidelines: Formal Controls and Marketplace*. Chicago: University of Chicago Press.

Teh, K.P. and Shanmugaratnam, T. (1992). "Exchange rate policy: philosophy and conduct over the past decade," in L. Low and M.H. Toh (eds.) *Public Policies in Singapore: Changes in the 1980s and Future Signposts*. Singapore: Times Academic Press.

Wu, Y. (1999). "Macroeconomic cooperation of exchange rate and wage movements under quasi-sterilization: Singapore experience." *Pacific Economic Review*, 4(2): 195–212.

Wu, Y. (2004). "Singapore's collective bargaining in a game of wage and exchange rate policies." *Open Economies Review*, 15(3): 273–289.

Chapter 48

THE LE CHATELIER PRINCIPLE OF THE CAPITAL MARKET EQUILIBRIUM

CHIN-WEI YANG, *Clarion University of Pennsylvania, USA*
KEN HUNG, *National Dong Hwa University, Taiwan*
JOHN A. FOX, *The Fox Consultant Incorporated, USA*

Abstract

This paper purports to provide a theoretical underpinning for the problem of the Investment Company Act. The theory of the Le Chatelier Principle is well-known in thermodynamics: The system tends to adjust itself to a new equilibrium as far as possible. In capital market equilibrium, added constraints on portfolio investment on each stock can lead to inefficiency manifested in the right-shifting efficiency frontier. According to the empirical study, the potential loss can amount to millions of dollars coupled with a higher risk-free rate and greater transaction and information costs.

Keywords: Markowitz model; efficient frontiers; with constraints; without constraints; Le Chatelier Principle; thermodynamics; capital market equilibrium; diversified mutual funds; quadratic programming; investment company act

48.1. Introduction

In the wake of a growing trend of deregulation in various industries (e.g. utility, banking, and airline), it becomes more and more important to study the responsiveness of the market to the exogenous perturbations as the system is gradually constrained. According to the law of thermodynamics, the system tends to adjust itself to a new equilibrium by counteracting the change as far as possible. This law, the Le Chatelier's Principle, was applied to economics by Samuelson (1949, 1960, 1970), Silberberg (1971, 1974, 1978), and to a class of spatial equilibrium models: linear programming, fixed demand, quadratic programming, full-fledged spatial equilibrium model by Labys and Yang (1996). Recently, it has been applied to optimal taxation by Diamond and Mirrlees (2002).

According to subchapter M of the Investment Company Act of 1940, a diversified mutual fund cannot have more than 5 percent of total assets invested in any single company and the acquisition of securities does not exceed 10 percent of the acquired company's value. This diversification rule, on the one hand, reduces the portfolio risk according to the fundamental result of investment theory. On the other hand, more and more researchers begin to raise questions as to the potential inefficiency arising from the Investment Company Act (see Elton and Gruber, 1991; Roe, 1991; Francis, 1993; Kohn, 1994). With the exception of the work by Cohen and Pogue (1967), Frost and Savarino (1988), and Loviseck and Yang (1997), there is very little evidence to refute or favor this conjecture.

Empirical findings (e.g. Loviscek and Yang, 1997) suggest that over 300 growth mutual funds evaluated by Value Line shows that the average weight for the company given the greatest share of a fund's assets was 4.29 percent. However, the Le Chatelier's Principle in terms of the Investment Company Act has not been scrutinized in the literature of finance. The objective of this paper is to investigate the Le Chatelier Principle applied to the capital market equilibrium in the framework of the Markowitz portfolio selection model.

48.2. The Le Chatelier Principle of the Markowitz Model

In a portfolio of n securities, Markowitz (1952, 1956, 1959, 1990, 1991) formulated the portfolio selection model in the form of a quadratic programming as shown below

$$\min_{x_i x_j} v = \sum_{i \in I} x_i^2 \sigma_{ii} + \sum_{i \in I} \sum_{j \in J} x_i x_j \sigma_{ij} \qquad (48.1)$$

$$\text{subject to} \sum_{i \in I} r_i x_i \geq k \qquad (48.2)$$

$$\sum_{i \in I} x_i = 1 \qquad (48.3)$$

$$x_i \geq 0 \; \forall i \in I, \qquad (48.4)$$

where x_i = proportion of investment in security i
  σ_{ii} = variance of rate of return of security i
  σ_{ij} = covariance of rate of return of security i and j
  r_i = expected rate of return of security i
  k = minimum rate of return of the portfolio
  I and J are sets of positive integers
The resulting Lagrange function is therefore

$$L = v + \lambda \left(k - \sum r_i x_{ij} \right) + \gamma \left(1 - \sum x_i \right) \qquad (48.5)$$

The solution to the Markowitz is well-known (1959). The Lagrange multiplier of constraint from Equation (48.2) assumes the usual economic interpretation: change in total risk in response to an infinitesimally small change in k while all other decision variables adjust to their new equilibrium levels, i.e. $\lambda = dv/dk$. Hence, the Lagrange multiplier is of utmost importance in determining the shape of the efficiency frontier curve in the capital

market. Note that values of x_{is} are unbounded between 0 and 1 in the Markowitz model. However, in reality, the proportion of investment on each security many times cannot exceed a certain percentage to ensure adequate diversification. As the maximum investment proportion on each security decreases from 99 percent to 1 percent, the solution to the portfolio selection model becomes more constrained, i.e. the values of optimum xs are bounded within a narrower range as the constraint is tightened. Such impact on the objective function v is straight forward: as the system is gradually constrained, the limited freedom of optimum xs gives rise to a higher and higher risk level as k is increased. For example, if parameter k is increased gradually, the Le Chatelier Principle implies that in the original Markowitz minimization system, iso-risk contour has the smallest curvature to reflect the most efficient adjustment mechanism:

$$\text{abs}\left(\frac{\partial^2 v}{\partial k^2}\right) \leq \text{abs}\left(\frac{\partial^2 v^*}{\partial k^2}\right) \leq \text{abs}\left(\frac{\partial v^{**}}{\partial k^2}\right), \qquad (48.6)$$

where v^* and v^{**} are the objective function (total portfolio risk) corresponding to the additional constrains of $x_i \leq s^*$ and $x_i \leq s^{**}$ for all i and $s^* > s^{**}$ represent different investment proportions allowed under V^* and V^{**}, and abs denotes absolute value. Via the envelope theorem (Dixit, 1990), we have

$$\begin{aligned} d\{L(x_i(k),k) &= v(x_i(k))\}/dk = \partial\{L(x_i,k) \\ &= v(x_i(k))\}/\partial k \qquad (48.7) \\ &= \lambda | x_i = x_i(k) \end{aligned}$$

hence Equation (48.6) can be rewritten as

$$\text{abs}\left(\frac{\partial \lambda}{\partial k}\right) \leq \text{abs}\left(\frac{\partial \lambda^*}{\partial k}\right) \leq \text{abs}\left(\frac{\partial \lambda^{**}}{\partial k}\right) \qquad (48.8)$$

Equation (48.8) states that the Lagrange multiplier of the original Markowitz portfolio selection model is less sensitive to an infinitesimally small change in k than that of the model when the constraints are gradually tightened. Note that the Lagrange multiplier λ is the reciprocal of the slope of the efficiency frontier curve frequently drawn in investment textbooks. Hence, the original

Markowitz model has the steepest slope for a given set of x_is. However, the efficiency frontier curve of the Markowitz minimization system has a vertical segment corresponding to a range of low ks and a constant v. Only within this range do the values of optimum xs remain equal under various degrees of constraints. Within this range constraint Equation (48.2) is not active, hence the Lagrange multiplier is 0. As a result, equality relation holds for Equation (48.8). Outside this range, the slopes of the efficiency frontier curve are different owing to the result of Equation (48.8).

48.3. Simulation Results

To verify the result implied by the Le Chatelier, we employ a five-stock portfolio with $x_i \leq 50$ percent

and $x_i \leq 40$ percent. The numerical solutions are reported in Table 1. An examination of Table 1 indicates that the efficiency frontier curve is vertical and all optimum xs are identical between $0.001 \leq k \leq 0.075$. After that, the solutions of xs begin to change for the three models. Note that the maximum possible value for x_4 remains 0.4 throughout the simulation for $k > 0.075$ for the model with the tightest constraint $x_i \leq 0.4$. In the case of $x_i \leq 0.5$, a relatively loosely constrained Markowitz system, all the optimum values of decision variables remain the same as the original Markowitz model between $0.01 \leq k \leq 0.1$. Beyond that range, the maximum value of x_4 is limited to 0.5. As can be seen from Table 1, the total risk v responds less volatile to the change in k in the original unconstrained Markowitz system than

Table 48.1.

LEAST-CONSTRAINED SOLUTION (Original Markowitz Model)						SOLUTION WITH $x_i \leq 0.5$						SOLUTION WITH $x_i \leq 0.4$					
K(%)	$v(10^{-5})$	$x_1\%$	$x_2\%$	$x_3\%$	$x_4\%$	$x_5\%$	$v(10^{-5})$	$x_1\%$	$x_2\%$	$x_3\%$	$x_4\%$	$x_5\%$	$v(10^{-5})$	$x_1\%$	$x_2\%$	$x_3\%$	$x_4\%$	$x_5\%$
1	257.2	39.19	0	31.87	28.94	0	257.2	39.19	0	31.87	28.94	0	257.2	39.19	0	31.87	28.94	0
2	257.2	39.19	0	31.87	28.94	0	257.2	39.19	0	31.87	28.94	0	257.2	39.19	0	31.87	28.94	0
3	257.2	39.19	0	31.87	28.94	0	257.2	39.19	0	31.87	28.94	0	257.2	39.19	0	31.87	28.94	0
4	257.2	39.19	0	31.87	28.94	0	257.2	39.19	0	31.87	28.94	0	257.2	39.19	0	31.87	28.94	0
5	257.2	39.19	0	31.87	28.94	0	257.2	39.19	0	31.87	28.94	0	257.2	39.19	0	31.87	28.94	0
6	257.2	39.19	0	31.87	28.94	0	257.2	39.19	0	31.87	28.94	0	257.2	39.19	0	31.87	28.94	0
7	260.8	35.02	0	32.6	32.38	0	260.8	35.02	0	32.6	32.38	0	260.8	35.02	0	32.6	32.38	0
7.5	274.8	30.54	0	32.77	36.69	0	274.8	30.54	0	32.77	36.69	0	274.8	30.54	0	32.77	36.69	0
8	299.3	25.82	0	33.27	40.91	0	299.3	25.82	0	33.27	40.91	0	300.5	24.91	0	34.55	40	5.39
8.5	333.1	21.65	0	33.26	43.63	1.45	333.1	21.65	0	33.26	43.63	1.45	340.2	20.42	0	35.34	40	4.24
9	371.2	17.82	0	32.92	45.73	3.53	371.2	17.82	0	32.92	45.73	3.53	387.7	15.93	0	36.13	40	7.94
9.5	413.2	14.05	0	32.53	47.64	5.79	413.2	14.05	0	32.53	47.64	5.79	443	11.44	0	36.92	40	11.64
10	459	9.68	0.58	32.17	49.59	7.98	459	9.68	0.58	32.17	49.59	7.98	506.2	6.95	0	37.71	40	15.34
10.5	508.3	4.83	1.96	31.44	51.56	10.2	509.5	4.25	2.1	32.23	50	11.42	576.7	1.23	1.93	37.7	40	19.15
11	560.9	0	3.53	30.46	53.55	12.46	567.5	0	2.66	32.03	50	15.31	656.5	0	0.21	36.45	40	23.34
11.5	619.9	0	1.34	27.91	55.8	14.95	637.4	0	0	30.39	50	19.62	751.7	0	0	31.79	40	28.22
12	687.5	0	0	24.31	58.11	17.58	724.5	0	0	25.39	50	24.62	866.3	0	0	26.79	40	33.22
12.5	765.4	0	0	19.02	60.68	20.3	826.7	0	0	20.52	50	29.48	995.2	0	0	21.91	40	38.09
13	854.3	0	0	13.73	63.2	23.07	949.7	0	0	15.53	50	34.48						
13.5	954	0	0	8.45	65.72	25.83	1086.8	0	0	10.65	50	39.45						
14	1064.6	0	0	3.16	68.25	28.59	1243.3	0	0	5.73	50	44.28						
14.5	1309.1	0	0	0	55.63	44.37	1417.7	0	0	0.79	50	49.21						
15	2847.3	0	0	0	20	80												
15.29	4402	0	0	0	0	100												

that in the constrained systems. In other words, the original Markowitz minimization system guarantees a smallest possible total risk due to the result of the Le Chatelier's Principle: a thermodynamic system (risk-return space) can most effectively adjust itself to the parametric change (temperature or minimum rate of return of a portfolio or k) if it is least constrained.

48.4. Policy Implications of the Le Chatelier's Principle

As shown in the previous section, the efficiency frontier curve branches off to the right first for the most binding constraint of $x_i \leq s^{**}$. Consequently, the tangency point between the efficiency frontier curve and a risk-free rate on the vertical axis must occur at a higher risk-free rate. As the value of maximum investment proportion for each stock s decreases, i.e. the constraint becomes more binding; there is a tendency for the risk-free rate to be higher in order to sustain an equilibrium (tangency) state. Second, one can assume the existence of a family of isowelfare functions (or indifference curves) in the v–k space. The direct impact of the Le Chatelier Principle on the capital market equilibrium is a lower level of welfare measure due to the right branching-off of the efficiency frontier curve. In sum, as the constraint on the maximum investment proportion is tighter, the risk-free rate will be higher and investors in the capital market will in general experience a lower welfare level. In particular, the 5 percent rule carries a substantial cost in terms of shifting of the efficiency frontier to the right. The study by Loviscek and Yang (1997) based on a 36-security portfolio indicates the loss is about 1 to 2 percentage points and the portfolio risk is 20 to 60 percent higher. Given the astronomical size of a mutual fund, 1 to 2 percentage point translates into millions of dollars potential loss in daily return. Furthermore, over diversification would incur greater transaction and information cost, which speaks against the Investment Company Rule.

48.5. Conclusion

In this paper, we apply the Le Chatelier Principle in thermodynamics to the Markowitz's portfolio selection model. The analogy is clear: as a thermodynamic system (or the capital market in the v–k space) undergoes some parametric changes (temperature or minimum portfolio rate of change k), the system will adjust most effectively if it is least constrained. The simulation shows that as the constraint becomes more and more tightened, the optimum investment proportions are less and less sensitive. Via the envelope theorem, it is shown that investors will be experiencing a higher risk-free rate and a lower welfare level in the capital market, if a majority of investors in the capital market experience the same constraint, i.e. maximum investment proportion on each security. Moreover, the potential loss in daily returns can easily be in millions on top of much greater transaction and information costs.

REFERENCES

Cohen, K.J. and Pogue, J.A. (1967). "An empirical evaluation of alternative portfolio selection models." *Journal of Business*, 40: 166–189.

Diamond, P. and Mirrlees, J.A. (2002). "Optimal taxation and the Le Châtelier principle." Working Paper Series, MIT Dept of Economics.

Dixit, A.K. (1990). *Optimization in Economic Theory*, 2nd edn. New York: Oxford University Press.

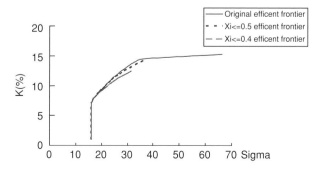

Figure 48.1. Efficent Frontier

Elton, E.J. and Gruber, M.J. (1991). *Modern Portfolio Theory and Investment Analysis*. New York: John Wiley.

Francis, J.C. (1993). *Management of Investment*. New York: McGraw-Hill.

Frost, P.A. and Savarino, J.E. (1988). "For better performance, constrain portfolio weights." *Journal of Portfolio Management*, 14: 29–34.

Kohn, M.G. (1994). *Financial Institutions and Markets*. New York: McGraw-Hill.

Labys, W.C. and Yang, C.-W. (1996). "Le Châtelier principle and the flow sensitivity of spatial commodity models," in J.C.J.M. van de Bergh and P. Nijkamp and P. Rietveld (eds.) *Recent Advances in Spatial Equilibrium Modeling: Methodology and Applications*. Berlin: Springer, pp. 96–110.

Loviscek, A.L. and Yang, C.-W. (1997). "Assessing the impact of the investment company act's diversification Rule: a portfolio approach." *Midwest Review of Finance and Insurance*, 11(1): 57–66.

Markowitz, H.M. (1952). "Portfolio Selection." *The Journal of Finance*, 7(1): 77–91.

Markowitz, H.M. (1956). "The optimization of a quadratic function subject to linear constraints." *Naval Research Logistics Quarterly*, 3: 111–133.

Markowitz, H.M. (1959). *Portfolio Selection*. New York: John Wiley.

Markowitz, H.M. (1990). *Mean-Variance Analysis in Portfolio Choice and Capital Markets*. Oxford: Basil Blackwell.

Markowitz, H.M. (1991). "Foundation of portfolio theory." *Journal of Finance*, XLVI(2): 469–477.

Roe, M.J. (1991). "Political element in the creation of a mutual fund industry." *University of Pennsylvania Law Review*, 1469: 1–87.

Samuelson, P.A. (1949). "The Le Châtelier principle in linear programming." *Rand Corporation Monograph*.

Samuelson, P.A. (1960). "An extension of the Le Châtelier principle." *Econometrica*, 28: 368–379.

Samuelson, P.A. (1972). "Maximum principles in analytical economics." *American Economic Review*, 62(3): 249–262.

Silberberg, E. (1971). "The Le Châtelier Principle as a corollary to a generalized envelope theorem." *Journal of Economic Theory*, 3: 146–155.

Silberberg, E. (1974). "A revision of comparative statics methodology in economics, or how to do economics on the back of an envelope." *Journal of Economic Theory*, 7: 159–172.

Silberberg, E. (1978). *The Structure of Economics: A Mathematical Analysis*, New York: McGraw-Hill.

Value Line (1994). *Mutual Fund Survey*. New York: Value Line.

Chapter 49

MBS VALUATION AND PREPAYMENTS

C.H. TED HONG, *Beyond Bond Inc., USA*
WEN-CHING WANG, *Robeco Investment Management, USA*

Abstract

This paper not only provides a comparison of recent models in the valuation of mortgage-backed securities but also proposes an integrated model that addresses important issues of path-dependence, exogenous prepayment, transaction costs, mortgagors' heterogeneity, and the housing devaluation effect.

Recent research can be categorized into two frameworks: empirical and theoretical option pricing. Purely empirically derived models often consider estimation of the prepayment model and pricing of the mortgage-backed security as distinct problems, and thus preclude explanation and prediction for the price behavior of the security. Some earlier theoretical models regard mortgage-backed securities as default-free callable bonds, prohibiting the mortgagors from exercising the default (put) option, and therefore induce bias on the pricing of mortgage-backed securities. Other earlier models assume homogeneity of mortgagors and consequently fail to address important issues of premium burnout effect and the path-dependence problem.

The model proposed is a two-factor model in which the housing price process is incorporated to account for the effect of mortgagor's default and to capture the impact of housing devaluation. Default is correctly modeled in terms of its actual payoff through a guarantee to the investors of the security such that the discrepancy is eliminated by assuming mortgage securities as either default-free or unin-sured. Housing prices have been rising at unsustainable rates nation wide, especially along the coasts, suggesting a possible substantial weakening in house appreciation at some point in the future. The effect of housing devaluation is specifically modeled by considering the possibility that the mortgagor might be restrained from prepayment even if interest rates make it advantageous to refinance.

Mortgagors' heterogeneity and the separation of exogenous and endogenous prepayments are explicitly handled in the model. Heterogeneity is incorporated by introducing heterogeneous refinancing transaction costs. The inclusion of heterogeneous transaction costs not only captures premium burnout effect but also solves the path-dependence problem. Finally, the model separates exogenous prepayment from endogenous prepayment, and estimates their distinct magnitudes from observed prepayment data. This construction provides a better understanding for these two important components of prepayment behavior. The generalized method of moments is proposed and can be employed to produce appropriate parameter estimates.

Keywords: MBS valuation; option pricing theory; exogenous and endogenous prepayments; housing devaluation effect; devaluation trap; transaction costs of refinancing and default; generalized method of moments; path dependency; premium burnout effect; heterogeneity

49.1. Introduction

The main objective of this paper is to gain a better understanding of the valuation of mortgage-backed securities. Mortgage-backed securities have attracted unprecedented investor interest over the last decade, spurring tremendous growth in the market for this important financial instrument. There are over $7.7 trillion worth of residential mortgage loans outstanding, an amount far exceeding the size of the corporate debt market. Approximately $5.1 trillion worth of securitized mortgage-backed securities and CMOs are outstanding, and well over $1.8 trillion new mortgage-backed securities and whole loans pools are issued each year for the past three years.[1] Mortgage-backed securities are extensively held by every class of institutional investor, including commercial banks, saving institutions, insurance companies, mutual funds, and pension plans.

An in-depth study of the valuation of mortgage-backed securities is of interest to financial economists because mortgage-backed securities have unique characteristics that are distinct from other contingent claims, such as monthly amortization, negative convexity, premium burnout, and path-dependence. This paper examines recent developments in the area of valuing mortgage-backed securities and proposes a model that accommodates these factors affecting the price of mortgage-backed securities.

The core issue in valuing mortgage-backed securities is the modeling of the prepayment behavior of mortgagors in the pool backing the security. Continuous-time option pricing methodology has been a popular method in the mortgage-backed securities valuation because of the obvious parallel between the call option and the right of a mortgagor to prepay. In order to model the mortgagors' prepayment behavior more realistically, recent theoretical models have added modifications to the original stock option pricing theory framework. The first of these modifications broadly accounts for prepayment due to reasons exogenous to financial consideration, such as moving and job changes. The second group of modification addresses transaction costs. The third considers heterogeneity among mortgagors, and the fourth group discusses the separation of exogenous prepayment and endogenous prepayment.

The observation that homeowners clearly do not prepay as objectively as option pricing models imply has motivated many researchers to add prepayment functions that allow prepayments for reasons that are exogenous to purely financial considerations. Such research includes the work of Dunn and McConnell (1981a,b), and Brennan and Schwartz (1985), and most of the prepayment functions have been arbitrary. The main drawback of adding an arbitrary prepayment function is that it does not aid in the identification of the factors responsible for prepayment behavior. Identifying these factors would go a long way toward enhancing the explanatory power of the model.

Applying the option pricing theory to the valuation of residential mortgage-backed securities, one can see a departure from the perfect market assumption when homeowners face transaction costs upon refinancing or defaulting. For this reason, Dunn and Spatt (1986) and Timmis (1985) add homogenous refinancing transaction costs in their models to adjust the prepayment speeds from those implied in the frictionless economic environment. Kau et al. (1993) also add the transaction cost of default in their modeling of the probability of default for residential mortgages.

Addressing mortgagors' heterogeneity is a more complex matter. Many earlier models assumed homogeneity among mortgagors to avoid complexity in the pricing process. However, the assumption of mortgagors' homogeneity fails to address the issue of premium burnout which is an important empirical effect of homeowner heterogeneity. And this assumption also results in a path-dependent problem when numerically solving the optimal refinancing strategies backwards. The premium burnout effect is the tendency of prepayments from premium pools to slow down over time, with all else held constant. If a large number of mortgagors have already prepaid, those remaining are likely to have a relatively low probability of prepaying. Conversely, the smaller the number of previous prepayments, the higher the probability of prepaying by the remaining mortgagors. The aforementioned path-dependent problem occurs because any mortgage pool contains a group of mortgagors who behave differently in their prepayment decisions: these mortgagors differ in their willingness or ability to prepay their loans under favorable circumstances. As a result, without knowing either the type of mortgagor or the entire path of interest rates from origination, backward optimization is not applicable because there is no way of knowing whether the earlier prepayment exercise is optimal.

Johnston and Van Drunen (1988), and Davidson et al. (1988) improve on the homogenous transaction cost model by introducing heterogeneous transaction models. They assume that different homeowners face different levels of refinancing transaction costs. In addition to the ability to capture the premium burnout, the inclusion of heterogeneous transaction costs also solves the path-dependent problem encountered when pooling individual mortgagors, who behave differently in their prepayment decisions.

Another common problem in existing models is the lack of differentiation between exogenous prepayment and endogenous prepayment. This lack of distinction between the two thereby precludes explanation of the interrelation between these important behavioral components. Endogenous prepayment refers to any prepayment decision that occurs in response to changes in underlying economic processes, such as the interest rate. Stanton (1990) incorporates an endogenous decision parameter that enables separate estimations of endogenous prepayment and prepayment for exogenous reasons. As a result, the explanatory power of the model is improved. In addition to the inclusion of the previously discussed modifications, our model introduces two adjustments. One is the treatment of mortgagors' right to default in the content of mortgage-backed securities valu-

ation. And the other is the impact of the housing prices on prepayment behavior.

Although default has been modeled as a put option in the models of residential mortgages or commercial mortgage-backed securities, many earlier models have not incorporated it in the valuation of residential mortgage-backed securities. This is because government agency guarantees lead to the perception that securities are default-free. Default should be taken into consideration because there is a payoff difference between a guaranteed mortgage-backed security and a default-free security. The payoff from a guarantee in the event of default is the par amount rather than the market value of the security, thus producing an asymmetric return for investors.

In modeling default, we expand previous default-free models into a default-risky model in which the housing price process is included as a second-state variable. Default is explicitly modeled in terms of its actual payoff through a guarantee to the investors of the residential mortgage-backed security. This is in contrast to models for individual mortgages or commercial mortgages in which mortgages are neither insured nor guaranteed. Consequently, the payoff in the event of default in these cases is the value of the house. By correctly modeling the effect of default, our model reduces the discrepancy from assuming mortgage-backed securities as either default-free or uninsured.

The housing price process is incorporated in the model not only to account for the effect of default on security price, but also to determine its impact on the prepayment behavior of mortgagors. The effect of housing prices on prepayment is specifically modeled by considering the possibility that the mortgagor might be restrained from prepaying even if interest rates make it advantageous to refinance. This is because housing prices have fallen to the extent that the mortgagor is no longer qualified for refinancing.

The model we propose not only captures the fundamental characteristics of the mortgagors' prepayment behavior but it also combines parametric heterogeneity and variability of the decision parameter to the extent that our model can come closer than previous models in describing empirical prepayment behaviors.

49.2. The Model

The central issue in valuing mortgage-backed securities is the treatment of prepayment uncertainty. The valuation model of mortgage-backed securities proposed here is based on the continuous-time option pricing methodology. This methodology treats the right of a mortgagor to prepay as a call option and the right to default as a put option. Modifications to the assumption of perfect capital markets and the principle that borrowers act to minimize the market cost of their mortgages are required to portray mortgagors' actual prepayment behavior in a more realistic manner.

According to Dunn and McConnell (1981) and Brennan and Schwartz (1985), we allow mortgagors to prepay for reasons exogenous to purely financial considerations. In contrast to their models that assume arbitrary exogenous prepayment functions, our model utilizes the proportional hazard function and can be estimated from observable prepayment data.

To account for the fact that homeowners face transaction costs when they prepay or default on their mortgages, we follow Johnston and Van Drunen (1988). Consequently, we add heterogeneous refinancing transaction costs in our models to adjust the prepayment speeds from those implied in the frictionless economic environment. Following Kau et al. (1993), we also add the transaction cost of default in modeling the effect of default.

Default has been modeled as a put option in the valuation of residential mortgages or commercial mortgage-backed securities. However, many models have not incorporated default in the valuation of residential mortgage-backed securities because government agency guarantees lead to the perception that securities are default-free. Moreover, there is a significant difference between the payoff of a guaranteed mortgage-backed security and that of a default-free security. The payoff from

insurance in the event of default is the par amount rather than the market value of the security, producing an asymmetric return for investors.

Kau and associates (1992) develop a two-factor model for both prepayment and default only in the context of evaluating individual mortgages, where mortgages are considered as uninsured. As discussed in the Chapter 49, the payoff from uninsured mortgages is the value of the house when the mortgage is defaulted. In our model, the payoff to the investor from default is explicitly modeled as insured mortgages. This eliminates the potential bias in the pricing of mortgage-backed securities.

A significant relationship between observed prepayment and housing prices data pointed out by Richard (1991) leads us a final adjustment of the two-factor model. The housing price process is brought in not only to account for the effect of default on security price, but also to determine its restraining effect on mortgagors' refinancing decisions.

Figure 49.1 outlines these differences between one-and two-factor models and the innovations presented in this study.

In the one-factor model, the prepayment decision responds to the level of interest rates. The two-factor model adds two additional termination outcomes that follow from the level of housing prices. At very low housing prices, the mortgagors may default regardless of the interest rate in order to cut their losses. Finally, the mortgagor might be restrained from prepaying even if interest rates make it advantageous to refinance. This occurs when the housing prices fall to the extent that the new loan cannot cover the costs of refinancing.

In addition to capturing these fundamental characteristics of the mortgagor's termination behavior, this model aggregates the underlying pool of mortgages according to the heterogeneity of transaction costs. And it is the specification of heterogeneous transaction costs that also solves the path-dependent problem displayed by pooled mortgages.

The following first section pertains to the modeling of termination decisions affected by exogenous

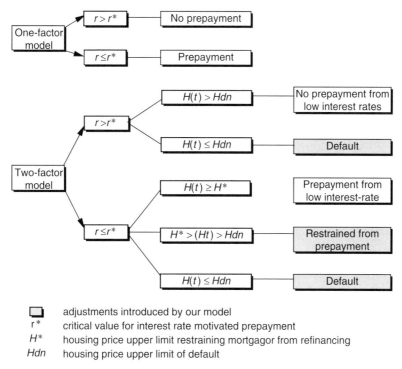

adjustments introduced by our model
r^* critical value for interest rate motivated prepayment
H^* housing price upper limit restraining mortgagor from refinancing
Hdn housing price upper limit of default

Figure 49.1.   Model trees

and endogenous factors, housing prices, and trans-action costs. The later section introduces our model, which is a two-factor pricing framework that pro-vides exact security prices given underlying interest rate and housing prices processes, and precludes arbitrage opportunities.

49.2.1. Modeling Issues

49.2.1.1. Exogenous Prepayment

In practice, exogenous reasons for termination in-clude factors such as relocation, death, divorce, or natural disasters. Exogenous prepayments are also known as turnover prepayments. A hazard function is used to model exogenous prepayment as follows:

$$\pi(t) = \lim_{\delta t \to 0^+} \frac{\text{Pr(Exogeneous prepayment in}(t, t + \delta t)|}{\delta t}$$

$$(49.1)$$

There are numerous parametric methods used in the analysis of duration data and in the modeling of aging or failure processes. We use the exponen-tial distribution in the model for its simplicity. The

distribution is characterized by the constant haz-ard function

$$\pi(t) = \pi, t \geq 0 \text{ and } \pi > 0. \qquad (49.2)$$

The probability that an individual has not prepaid for exogenous reasons until time t is given by the survival function $S(t)$,

$$S(t) = \mathrm{e}^{-\pi(t)} = \mathrm{e}^{-\pi t}, t \geq 0 \qquad (49.3)$$

49.2.1.2. Endogenous Termination

A mortgage is terminated when mortgagors either prepay or default on their mortgages. Any termin-ation which affects the cash flows passed through to the investors will have an impact on the price of the mortgage-backed securities. Throughout the model, endogenous termination is defined as any rational termination decision that occurs in re-sponse to underlying economic processes rather than personal considerations.

We assume that mortgagors maximize their cur-rent wealth, or equivalently, minimize their liabil-ities. Mortgagors' liabilities can be thought of as composed of three parts. The first part consists of owing the scheduled streams of cash flows associated with the mortgage. The second part constitutes their option to prepay at any time, which is equivalent to possessing a call option. And the third part consists of mortgagor's option to default, which functions as a put option. Option pricing theory is, therefore, an appropriate method for determining the value of mortgagors' mortgage liability.

A model of mortgage pricing should incorporate both refinancing transaction costs and default transaction costs in order to more accurately portray the decision-making processes of mortgagors. Although including transaction costs causes the resulting termination strategy to deviate from the perfect market assumption, the strategy still remains rational.

In order to derive the magnitude of endogenously determined termination, we follow Stanton (1990) and introduce ρ, which measures the frequency of mortgagors' termination decisions. The time between successive decision points is described as an exponential distribution. If we let T_i be one such decision point, and T_{i+1} the next, then

$$\Pr(T_{i+1} - T_i > t) = e^{-\rho t} \qquad (49.4)$$

If mortgagors are continually re-evaluating their decisions, then the parameter ρ takes on a value of infinity. If mortgagors never make endogenous termination decisions and only terminate for exogenous reasons, then ρ takes on a value of zero. If ρ takes on a value between these limits, then this signifies that decisions are made at discrete times, separated on average by $1/\rho$.

Given this specification, the magnitude of endogenized termination can be estimated and studied. The contribution of this device is to separate the magnitude of endogenized termination from that of exogenous termination. It also serves to help understand the actual termination behavior of mortgagors. Without this specification, it would be difficult to know the proportion of termination from endogenous optimization decisions and the proportion due to exogenous factors.

Utilizing the definitions from Sections 49.2.1.1 and 49.2.1.2, we notice that the optimal exercise strategy immediately leads to a statistical representation of the time to terminate for a single mortgagor. If termination is due exclusively to exogenous factors, then the termination rate is π and the survival function is defined as in Equation (49.4). When termination occurs for endogenous reasons, the probability that the mortgagor terminates in a small time interval, δt, is the probability that the mortgagor neither prepays for exogenous reasons nor makes a rational exercise decision during this period. This survival function can be approximated by

$$S(t) = \begin{cases} e^{-\pi \delta t} \cdot e^{-\rho \delta t} = e^{-(\pi+\rho)\delta t} & \text{if endogenous termination} \\ e^{-\pi \delta t} & \text{if no endogenous termination} \end{cases}$$
$$(49.5)$$

49.2.1.3. Transaction Costs and Aggregation of Heterogeneous Mortgages

The cash flows that accrue to the investor of a mortgage-backed security are not determined by the termination behavior of a single mortgagor, but by that of many mortgagors within a pool. To cope with the path-dependent problem caused by the heterogeneity within a pool of mortgages, we assume that the different refinancing transaction costs each mortgagor faces is the only source of heterogeneity. Although the costs of initiating a loan vary among different types of mortgages, some of the most common costs borrowers face include credit report, appraisal, survey charges, title and recording fees, proration of taxes or assessments, hazard insurance, and discount points.

The transaction costs of individual mortgagors are drawn from a univariate discrete distribution, which allows for underlying heterogeneity in the valuation of the mortgage-backed security. A better way to choose the underlying distribution that represents this heterogeneity would be to look at summary statistics of transaction costs actually incurred by mortgagors when they refinanced. A discrete rectangular distribution is chosen for its simplicity and the task of determining which distribution improves the fit is left for future research.

The value of the security is equal to the expected value of the pool of mortgages weighted by the proportions of different refinancing transaction cost categories. Suppose that each X_i (the refinancing transaction costs faced by mortgagor i) is drawn from a discrete rectangular, or uniform distribution

$$\Pr(x = a + ih) = M^{-1}, \quad i = 1, \ldots, M \quad (49.6)$$

Various standard forms are in use. For this application, we set $a = 0$, $h = RM^{-1}$, so that the values taken by x are $RM^{-1}, 2RM^{-1}, \ldots, R$. The upper bound R of the transaction cost is set at 10 percent. The distribution for the transaction costs is then defined as:

$$\Pr\left(x = i\frac{0.1}{M}\right) = M^{-1}, \quad i = 1, \ldots, M \quad (49.7)$$

In principle, given any initial distribution of transaction costs, it is possible to value a mortgage-backed security backed by a heterogeneous pool of mortgages in a manner similar to the valuation of a single mortgage. If the value of individual mortgages is known, then the value of the pool is the sum of these individual values. When the value of individual mortgages is not known, but a distribution of transaction costs is generated that accounts for heterogeneity, the expected value of a pool of mortgages is the sum of the transaction cost groups times the probability of their occurrence in the pool.

Recall from Section 49.1.2 that for a given transaction cost X_i and state of the world, if any mortgagor finds it optimal to terminate, the hazard rate is the sum of the exogenous prepayment rate, π, and the endogenized termination rate, ρ. If it is not optimal to terminate, the hazard rate falls back to the background exogenous prepayment rate π.

Models that neither permit the estimation of ρ nor consider exogenous factors in the prepayment decision imply that $\rho = \infty$ and $\pi = 0$, and the single-transaction cost level predicts that all mortgages will prepay simultaneously. Adding heterogeneous transaction costs addresses the problem of path dependence, however, keeping the same parameter values still does not permit hesitation in the prepayment decision. Although prepayment rates fluctuate, in reality, they do tend to move fairly smoothly. The effect of setting ρ to a value other than ∞ is to permit a delay even when it is optimal to prepay. And prepayment need not occur at all if interest rates or housing prices change such that it is no longer optimal. The actual value of ρ determines how fast this drop occurs. Thus, combining parametric heterogeneity and variability of the parameter ρ would allow the model to come closer than previous rational models to describe empirical prepayment behavior.

49.2.2. A Model for Pricing Mortgage-Backed Securities

49.2.2.1. Termination Decision of a Single Mortgagor

The following is a model of rational prepayment behavior of mortgages that extends the rational prepayment models of Stanton (1990) and Kau and associates (1993). Mortgagors may terminate their mortgages for endogenous financial reasons that include interest rates and housing prices, or for exogenous reasons. They also face transaction costs, which are used to differentiate mortgagors and solve the path-dependent problem. Mortgagors choose the strategy that minimizes the market value of the mortgage liability.

The following assumptions are employed:

1. Trading takes place continuously and there are no taxes or informational asymmetries.
2. The term structure is fully specified by the instantaneous riskless rate $r(t)$. Its dynamics are given by.

$$dr = \kappa(\mu_r - r)dt + \sigma_r\sqrt{r}dz_r \quad (49.8)$$

3. The process to capture the housing price is assumed to follow a Constant Elasticity of Variance (CEV) diffusion process

$$dH = \mu_H H dt + \sigma_H H^{\gamma/2} dz_H, \qquad (49.9)$$

where μ_H, $\sigma_H > 0$, $0 < \gamma < 2$, and $\{z_H(t), t \geq 0\}$ is a standard Wiener Process, which may be correlated with the process $\{z_r(t), t \geq 0\}$. When $\gamma = 2$, the process is lognormal.

The underlying state variables in the model are the interest rate $r(t)$ and the housing price $H(t)$. By applying the arbitrage argument, the value of the ith mortgage liability $V^i(r, H, t)$ satisfies the following partial differential equation:

$$\frac{1}{2}\sigma_r^2 r V_{rr}^i + \rho\sigma_r\sigma_H \sqrt{r}H^{\gamma/2} V_{rH}^i$$

$$+ \frac{1}{2}\sigma_H^2 H^\gamma V_{HH}^i + [\kappa(\mu_r - r) - \lambda r]V_r^i$$

$$+ rHV_H^i + V_t^i - rV^i$$

$$= 0, \qquad (49.10)$$

where λr represents factor risk premium.

The value of the mortgage liability is also required to satisfy the following boundary conditions:

1. At maturity T, the value of a monthly amortization bond is equal to the monthly payment:

$$V^i(r, H, T) = MP$$

2. As r approaches infinity, the payoff of the underlying mortgage bond approaches zero:

$$\lim_{r\to\infty} V^i(r, H, t) = 0$$

Figure 49.2 summarizes the remaining conditions, which establish the boundaries of the various circumstances affecting the termination decision.

3. At any time t, the mortgage value satisfies the following conditions:

Let $V^i(r, H, t^+) = V^i(r, H, t+1) + MP$, then

$$V^i(r,H,t) = \begin{cases} V^i(r,H,t^+) & \text{if } H(t) > Hdn \text{ and } U(t)(1+X_i) > \\ & V_i(r, H, t^+) \text{ if continued} \\ U(t) & \text{if } H(t) > Hdn \text{ and } V^i(r,H,t^+) \geq \\ & U(t)(1+Xi) \text{ if refinanced} \\ U(t) & \text{if } H(t) \leq Hdn \text{ if defaulted} \end{cases}$$

where $U(t)$ is the principal remaining at time t. Hdn is the boundary of default, defined as the housing price times the cost of default, or $Hdn = (V^i r, H, t^+)/(1+d)$. X_i is the prepayment transaction costs for individual i and d is the transaction cost of default for all individuals. This boundary condition defines the default and refinancing regions in Figure 49.2. When housing prices fall so low that they are exceeded by the default cost-adjusted mortgage value, the mortgagor will exercise their put option by defaulting. The refinancing region describes a situation in which

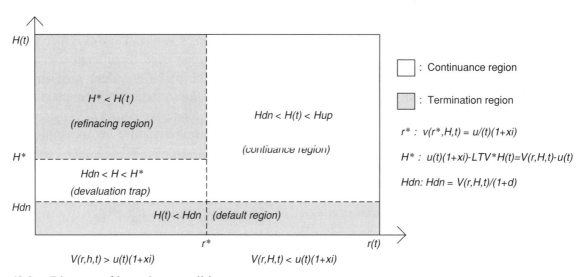

Figure 49.2. Diagram of boundary conditions

the interest rate falls to the point where the mortgage value is greater than the refinancing cost-adjusted unpaid principal. In this case, the mortgagor exercises the call option by refinancing their loan. The value of the mortgage liability takes on the value of unpaid principal $U(t)$ unadjusted by transaction costs $(1 + X_i)$, because the refinancing costs are collected by the third party who services the mortgage.

4. To improve on the previous model, we have included the effect of housing prices on the termination decision

$$V^i(r, H, t) = V^i(r, H, t^+) \text{ if } H^* > H(t)$$
$$> Hdn \text{ and } V^i(r, H, t^+) \geq U(t)$$
$$(1 + Xi) \text{ if restrained,}$$

where LTV is the loan-to-value ratio and H^* is determined at

$$U(t) + (1 + Xi) - LTV * H(t)$$
$$= V^i(r, H, t) - U(t). \tag{49.11}$$

This condition encompasses the devaluation trap. The devaluation trap occurs when housing prices fall between H^* and Hdn, where the costs of refinancing exceed its benefits. The mortgagor will be unable to refinance their loan, even though interest rates are advantageous, because they will have to pay the difference out of their pocket. And since the housing price remains above the default threshold, the mortgagor continues the mortgage. The present value of costs is determined by the left-hand side of Equation (49.11), that is the difference between the unpaid principal plus refinancing transaction cost and the new loan amount, which is the housing price times the loan-to-value ratio. The benefit of refinancing is given by the right-hand side of Equation (49.11), i.e. the mortgage value minus the unpaid principal. The role of the loan-to-value ratio is important in determining the size of the devaluation trap. The higher loan-to-value ratios result in decreases in the range of the devaluation trap.

Working back one month at a time, we can value the ith mortgage liability $V^i(r, H, t)$ by solving Equation (49.10), given boundary condition 1 through 4. Given π and ρ, we can also calculate the probability that the mortgage is terminated in month t. Denote P_e the probability of termination if only exogenous prepayment occurs. Denote P_r the probability of termination if it is endogenous conditions that lead to a decision to terminate in month t. According to the survival function Equation (49.5), these termination probabilities are given by

$$P_r = 1 - e^{-(\pi+\rho)/12} \text{ if endogenous termination}$$

$$P_e = 1 - e^{-\pi/12} \text{ if no endogenous termination}$$

We can now calculate the expected value of a single mortgage liability. That is

$$V^i(r, H, t) = \begin{cases} (1 - P_r)V^i(r, H, t^+) + P_r U(t) \\ \text{(if endogenous termination)} \\ (1 - P_e)^i(r, H, t^+) + P_e U(t) \\ \text{(if no endogenous termination)} \end{cases}$$

49.2.2.2. Valuation of a Pool of Mortgages

To determine the value of the mortgage-backed security at any time t, as mentioned above, we can simply take the expected value of pooled mortgage liabilities

$$V(r, H, t) = \sum_{i=1}^{M} V^i(r, H, t) \times P(X_i = x)$$
$$x \in (0, 0.1] \tag{49.12}$$

49.3. Estimation

A model for valuing mortgage-backed securities was described that permits the determination of the security's price for given parameter values describing exogenous and endogenous factors that contribute to the termination decision. The next logical step would be to estimate these parameter values from prepayment data. In this sector, the generalized method-of-moment technique is proposed for the estimation, where the termination probability at any given time t is required for equating the population and sample moments. In order to accomplish this, we must determine the model in terms of the probability rather than in terms of the dollar value of the security.

49.3.1. Determination of the Expected Termination Probability

In addition to equating the population and sample moments when the generalized method-of-moment technique is employed for the estimation, the calculation of termination probability is useful because it can also be utilized to determine the expected cash flows for any other mortgage-related securities, such as collateralized mortgage obligations. We first restate the procedure for determining the price in order to provide a comparison to the procedure for determing termination probability.

49.3.1.1. Procedure for Determining the Security Price

In this model, the uncertain economic environment a homeowner faces is described by two variables: the interest rate and the housing price. The term structure of the interest rate is assumed to be generated from the stochastic process described in Equation (49.8) and the process of the housing prices is represented in Equation (49.9). Assuming perfect capital markets, the present value $V^i(r, H, t)$ of the mortgage contract at time t is of the form

$$V^i(r, H, t) = \tilde{E}_t \left[e^{-\int_t^T r(t)dt} \bar{V}^i(T) \right], \qquad (49.13)$$

where $\bar{V}^i(T)$ is the terminal value of the mortgage liability at expiration date T. This equation states that the value of the mortgage is equivalent to the discounted-expected-terminal payoff under the risk-neutral measure. By Girsanov's theorem, under certain circumstances, the change in measure merely

produces a change in drift in the underlying diffusions. Consequently, one must substitute the risk-adjusted processes for the actual stochastic processes in Equations (49.8) and (49.9), which in this case are

$$dr = (\kappa\mu_r - (\kappa + \lambda)r)dt + \sigma_r d\tilde{z}_r \qquad (49.14)$$

and

$$dH = rHdt + \sigma_H d\tilde{z}_H. \qquad (49.15)$$

When the housing price process is transformed to its risk-adjusted form, the actual required rate of return on the house μH drops out of the equation. Therefore μH does not influence the mortgage and default option values. We know that the mortgage value $V^i(r, H, t)$ satisfies the partial differential equation specified in Equation (49.10). And thus, with the appropriate terminal and boundary conditions, the value of the mortgage is determined by solving this partial differential equation (PDE) backwards in time.

49.3.1.2. Deriving the Expected Termination Probability of Mortgage i

In order to implement the parameter estimation, we are now concerned with the actual occurrence of termination instead of the dollar value of the mortgage. We begin the derivation of termination probability with the following definition:

$$
\begin{aligned}
P^i(r, H, t) = \text{Pr}(\,&(r(\tau), H(\tau), \tau) \\
&\in \text{termination region of mortgage } i, \text{ for some} \\
&\tau > t, \text{ given}(r(t), H(t), t) = (r, H, t))
\end{aligned}
$$
$$(16)$$

where (r, H, t) are the interest rate and housing price at current time t, while $P^i(r, H, t)$ is the probability that termination ever occurs beyond the current situation. The general theory of stochastic processes allows that such a probability satisfies the Kolmogorov backward equation

$$
\begin{aligned}
\frac{1}{2}\sigma_r^2 r P_{rr}^i &+ \rho\sigma_r\sigma_H\sqrt{r}H^{\gamma/2}P_{rH}^i + \frac{1}{2}\sigma_H^2 H^\gamma P_{HH}^i \\
&+ \kappa(\mu_r - r)P_r^i + \mu_H P_H^i + P_t^i = 0
\end{aligned}
$$
$$(17)$$

To describe the boundary and terminal conditions, we denote Ω for the part of (r,H,t) space outside the termination region, while $\partial\Omega$ forms the termination boundary. Using this notation, we have the terminal and boundary conditions

$$P^i(r,H,T) = \begin{cases} 1/M & \text{if } (r,H,t) \in \partial\Omega, t \in (o, T) \\ 0 & \text{otherwise} \end{cases}$$

(49.18)

These conditions merely state the obvious principle that termination has a probability of $1/M$ if the conditions lead to a decision to terminate and has a probability of zero if the mortgage continues. One might recall that a pool of the mortgagors is segregated according to a discrete uniform distribution with M groups. Hence, if the environment is within the termination region, the probability of termination of any given mortgage group is $1/M$, rather than one.

The determination of probability of termination does not involve discounting, and as such the non-homogeneous rV^i term from Equation (49.10) is excluded from Equation (49.17). Considering we are concerned with the actual incidence of termination and not the dollar value of the termination option, the real process in Equations (49.8) and (49.9) are used for $r(t)$ and $H(t)$ rather than the risk-adjusted processes. Therefore, μH is required when the probability of termination is calculated although μH has no effect on the dollar value of mortgage liability. Solving the valuation problem from Equation (49.10) gives the index result of the termination region $\partial\Omega$, which consequently enters into the terminal conditions of Equation (49.17). These conditions are treated as a fixed-boundary problem in the solving of Equation (49.17), rather than as a free-boundary problem as in the solving of Equation (49.10).

Solving Equation (49.17) subject to the boundary conditions in Equation (49.18) yields the termination probability at any grid (r, H, t, X_i) for the individual mortgage liability i, called P_{it}. Recalling that the hazard rate for mortgage i from Equation (49.5) takes on a value of π if it is not optimal to

terminate for endogenous reasons, and takes on a value of $(\pi + \rho)$ otherwise, and thus the expected termination probability for mortgage i, P_{it}^*, is calculated as

$$P_{it}^* = P_e(1 - P_{it}) + P_r P_{it}.$$

(5.19)

49.3.1.3. Determination of the Expected Termination Level of Pool j

Since the distribution of the refinancing transaction cost X_i is independent of the underlying stochastic processes, the expected termination for any given pool j is calculated by counting the proportion of terminations in each transaction cost group. If we denote P_{jt}^* as the expected termination probability for a given pool j, then

$$P_{jt}^* = \sum_{i=1}^{M} P_{it}^* = \sum_{i=1}^{M} P_e(1 - P_{it}) + P_r P_{it}$$

$$= P_e\left(1 - \sum_{i=1}^{M} P_{it}\right) + P_r \sum_{i=1}^{M} P_{it}$$

(49.20)

Equation (49.20) permits us to calculate the expected termination probability for a given pool j without having to calculate the expected probability of each individual mortgage i.

49.3.2. Estimation Approach

49.3.2.1 Generalized Method of Moments (GMM)

The generalized method of moments procedure set out by Hansen (1982) and Hansen and Singleton (1982) has been widely used in financial market applications and in labor market application. The procedure is a limited-information method analogous to two-stage least squares. GMM provides a means of estimating parameters in a model by matching theoretical moments of the data, as a function of the parameters, to their sample counterparts.

The usual way of proceeding is to identify error functions of the parameters and observable data which have an expectation of zero, conditional on the information available at the time the data are observed. That is, if we let θ_0 denote the true vector of parameter values, there are error functions $e_{it}(\theta_0)$, $i = 1, 2, \ldots, M$, satisfying the orthogonality conditions

$$E[e_{it}(\theta_0)|I_t] = 0, \qquad\qquad (49.21)$$

where e_{it} is a function of the parameters and of data up to and including time t and I_t is the information set at time t. This equation states that these error functions have a mean zero conditional on the information set at time t, when the functions are evaluated at the true parameter value. The implication is that the errors must be uncorrelated with the variables in the information set I_t, and thus, if z_{jt} is a finite dimensional vector of random variables that are I_t measurable, then by the law of iterated expectations

$$E[e_{it}(\theta_0)z_{jt}] = 0. \qquad\qquad (49.22)$$

If e is a $M \times T$ matrix, and z is $N \times T$, this can be rewritten as

$$E[g_t(\theta_0)] = 0, \qquad\qquad (49.23)$$

where g is the $MN \times T$ matrix formed by taking the direct product of e and z. This equation is the basis for the GMM technique. Suppose the sample counterpart of this set of population moments is the MN-vector valued function $g_T(\theta)$, which is defined by

$$g_T(\theta)_i = \frac{1}{T}\sum_{t=1}^{T} g_{it}(\theta). \qquad\qquad (49.24)$$

The usual GMM estimation procedure involves minimizing a quadratic form of the type

$$Q_T(\theta) = g_T(\theta)' W g_T(\theta), \qquad\qquad (49.25)$$

where W is some positive-definite weighting matrix. This is usually done in two steps. First, take W to be the identity matrix and perform one minimization. Next calculate W_T, the sample estimator of

$$W_0 = (E[g_t(\theta_0)g_t(\theta_0)'])^{-1}, \qquad\qquad (49.26)$$

and use this as the weighting matrix in the second stage. As long as $W_T \to W_0$ almost surely, then the asymptotic variance matrix of the GMM estimator is

$$\sum_0 = \frac{1}{T}[(E[\partial g_t(\theta_0)'/\partial\theta])W_0(E[\partial g_t(\theta_0)/\partial\theta'])]^{-1} \qquad (49.27)$$

In addition, the statistic $TQ_T(\hat{\theta})$, which is sample size times the minimized value of the objective function, $g_T(\theta)' W g_T(\theta)$, is distributed as a chi-squared random variable with degrees of freedom equal to the dimension of $g_t(\theta 0)$ less the number of estimated parameters. This statistic provides a test of the over-identifying restrictions.

49.3.2.2. Moment Restrictions

The typical moment condition to use is the expectation of the difference between the observed prepayment level and its expected value, defined appropriately, equal zero. If we denote φ_{it} for the proportion of pool i prepaying in month t. The expected value of φ_{it}, t conditional on the information set at time t follows from above, assuming that the distribution of transaction costs among the mortgages remaining in the pool is known. If the termination probability of pool i at time t is P_{it}^*, then

$$E[\varphi_{it}|I_t] = P_e(1 - P_{it}^*) + P_r P_{it}^*, \qquad (49.28)$$

where $P_r = 1 - e^{-(\pi+\rho)\delta t}$, $P_e = 1 - e^{-\pi\delta t}$ are previously defined and P_{it}^* is calculated from the previous section.

It is possible to calculate unconditional moment conditions by multiplying these conditional moment conditions in Equation (49.28) and appropriate elements of the information set. Define the residual for pool i at time t as

$$e_{it} = \varphi_{it} - \bar{\varphi}_{it}. \qquad\qquad (49.29)$$

This satisfies the following expression:

$$E[e_{it}(\theta_0)|I_t'] = 0, \qquad\qquad (5.30)$$

where I_t' is a subset of the full information set at time t, which includes the interest rate path. Given this, it is possible to create more moment conditions as above. If z_{jt} is an element of I'_t, then $E[e_{it}z_{jt}] = 0$. However, z_{jt} may not be any variable that gives information about the actual sequence of prepayments. For example, setting z_{jt} equal to a lagged value of the prepayment level is not valid because the expected residual may be correlated with lagged prepayment levels. The implication of this is that there will be positive serial correlation in the residuals e_{it}. Hence, if the residuals are stacked in the usual way, averaging across time periods, one will have to deal with this serial correlation in calculating the appropriate standard errors for the GMM estimators.

To avoid the issue of serial correlation, the residuals can be stacked by averaging across pools, instead. Under the null hypothesis of independent pools, this way of stacking will result in no correlation between the contemporaneous residuals from different pools. Therefore, by assuming that the mortgages are drawn from a well-behaved underlying distribution, the sample estimator W_T is still a consistent estimator of the optimal weighting matrix W_0, and the usual asymptotic standard error results are valid.

49.4. Conclusion

The valuation model of mortgage-backed securities proposed here is a model that extends the rational option pricing approach used by previous authors. This model is able to capture many important empirical regularities observed in prepayment behavior that have previously been modeled successfully using only purely empirically derived prepayment models. However, in these purely empirical models, estimation of the prepayment behavior and the valuation of a mortgage-backed security are often treated as completely separate problems. This model prevents *ad hoc* integration of the estimation of prepayment and the valuation of a mortgage-backed security, and links these two into a structured model. Therefore, this model can address economic questions that are beyond the

scope of purely empirical models, while possessing a simple reduced form representation that allows estimation using observed prepayment data.

This integrated model captures the fundamental characteristics of a mortgage-backed security, such as exogenous prepayment, endogenous prepayment, transaction costs of refinancing and default, heterogeneity among mortgagors, and the issue of path dependence. In addition, the treatment of embedded options, the prepayment (call) option and the default (put) option, are modeled with care to accommodate more realistic aspects of a mortgagor's behavior. In particular, the payoff from the incident of default is modeled as an insured mortgage, so that the potential discrepancy in the pricing of the mortgage backed security is eliminated.

Another important innovation of the model is the explicit modeling of the housing devaluation effect that was the prevailing phenomenon in the early 1990s due to declined home prices. Over last several years, housing prices have been rising at unprecedented rates. A correction in the housing market is likely to occur in the near future and trigger a devaluation-induced prepayment slowdown. The term used for the devaluation effect is "devaluation trap" because the effect is activated only when housing prices fall to a degree at which the costs of refinancing exceed its benefits. The mortgagors are trapped and unable to refinance their loans even though interest rates are advantageous, because the new loans entitled from devaluated houses are no longer sufficient to cover the costs of refinancing.

Two constituents allow this model to come closer than previous models in describing empirical prepayment and price behavior. These are the incorporation of mortgagors' heterogeneity and the delaying of the rational prepayment decisions of mortgage holders. The heterogeneity of mortgagors is accomplished by introducing heterogeneous refinancing transaction costs. And the mortgagors' prepayment decisions are assumed to occur at discrete intervals rather than continuously, as was assumed with previous rational models. Hence, these two combined factors produce smoother prepayment behavior as observed in the actual data, and allow the model to generate prices that exceed par without requiring excessive transaction costs.

It is known that utilizing maximum likelihood as a means of estimating the parameters in parametric hazard models of prepayment is problematic, given the constitution of available prepayment data. Thus, by utilizing an alternative approach, the generalized method of moments, the model parameters can be estimated. This approach overcomes the problems associated with maximum likelihood in this setting.

NOTE

1. Taken from the Federal Reserve Bulletin, Inside MBS & ABS, and UBS.

BIBLIOGRAPHY

Becketti, S. and Morris, C.S. (1990). "The prepayment experience of FNMA mortgage backed securities." *Monograph Series in Finance and Economics*, Saloman Center, New York University.

Black, F. and Scholes, M. (1973). "The pricing of options and corporate liabilities." *Journal of Political Economy*, 81: 637–654.

Brennan, M. and Schwartz, E. (1978). "Finite difference methods and jump processes arising in the pricing of contingent claims: a synthesis." *Journal of Financial and Quantitative Analysis*, 13: 461–474.

Brennan, M. and Schwartz, E. (1985). "Determinants of GNMA mortgage prices." *AREUEA Journal*, 13: 209–228.

Buser, S.A. and Hendershott, P.H. (1983). "Pricing default-free fixed-rate mortgages." *Housing Finance Review*, 3: 405–429.

Cox, J.C., Ingersoll, J.E. Jr., and Ross, S.A. (1985a). "An intertemporal general equilibrium model of asset prices." *Econometrica*, 53: 363–384.

Cox, J.C., Ingersoll, J.E. Jr., and Ross, S.A. (1985b). "A theory of the term structure of interest rates." *Econometrica*, 53: 385–407.

Cunningham, D. and Hendershott, P.H. (1984). "Pricing FHA mortgage default insurance." *Housing Finance Review*, 13: 373–392.

Davidson, A.S., Herskovitz, M.D., and Van Drunen, L.D. (1988). "The refinancing threshold pricing model: an economic approach to valuing MBS." *Journal of Real Estate Finance and Economics*, 1: 117–130.

Dunn, K.B. and McConnell, J.J. (1981a). "Valuation of GNMA mortgage-backed securities." *Journal of Finance*, 36: 599–616.

Dunn, K.B. and McConnell, J.J. (1981b). "A comparison of alternative models of pricing GNMA mortgage backed securities." *Journal of Finance*, 36: 471–483.

Dunn, K.B. and Spatt, C.S. (1986). "The effect of refinancing costs and market imperfections on the optimal call strategy and pricing of debt contracts." Working Paper, Carnegie-Mellon University.

Epperson, J., Kau, J., Keenan, D., and Muller, III W. (1985). "Pricing default risk in mortgages." *Journal of AREUEA*, 13: 261, 272.

Hansen, L.P. (1982). "Large sample properties of generalized method of moments estimators." *Econometrica*, 50: 1029–1054.

Hansen, L.P. and Singleton, K.J. (1982). "Generalized instrumental variables estimators of nonlinear rational expectations models." *Econometrica*, 50: 1269–1286.

Hendershott, P. and Van Order, R. (1987). "Pricing mortgages: an interpretation of the models and results." *Journal of Financial Service Research*, 1: 77–111.

Johnson, E.T. and Van Drunen, L.D. (1988). "Pricing mortgage pools with heterogeneous mortgagors: empirical evidence." Working Paper, University of Utah.

Kau, J.B. and Kim, T. (1992). "Waiting to default: the value of delay." Working Paper, University of Georgia.

Kau, J.B., Keenan, D.C., Muller, III W.J., and Epperson, J.F. (1992). "A generalized valuation model for fixed rate residential mortgages." *Journal of Money, Credit and Banking*, 24: 279–299.

Kau, J.B., Keenan, D.C., and Kim, T. (1993). "Transaction costs, suboptimal termination, and default probabilities." Working Paper, University of Georgia.

Kau, J.B., Keenan, D.C., Muller, III W.J., and Epperson, J.F. (1993). "The valuation at origination of fixed rate mortgages with default and prepayment," forthcoming. *The Journal of Real Estate Finance and Economics*.

Lawless, J.F. (1982). *Statistical Models and Methods for Lifetime Data*. New York: John Wiley.

Merton, R. (1973). "Theory of rational optional pricing." *Bell Journal of Economics and Management Science*, 4: 141–183.

Pearson, N.D. and Sun, T. (1989). "A test of the Cox, Ingersoll, Ross Model of the term structure of interest rates using the method of maximum likelihood." Working Paper, Stanford University.

Richard, S.F. (1991). "Housing prices and prepayments for fixed-rate mortgage-backed Securities." *Journal of Fixed Income*, 54–58.

Richard, S.F. and Roll, R. (1989). "Prepayments on fixed-rate mortgage-backed securities." *Journal of Portfolio Management*, 15: 73–82.

Schwartz, E.S. and Torous, W.N. (1989). "Prepayment and the valuation of mortgage-backed securities." *Journal of Finance*, 44: 375–392.

Stanton, R. (1990). "Rational prepayment and the valuation of mortgage-backed securities." Working Paper, Stanford University.

Tauchen, G. (1986). "Statistical properties of generalized method of moments estimators of structural parameters obtained from financial market data." *Journal of Business and Economic Statistics*, 4: 397–416.

Timmis, G.C. (1985). "Valuation of GNMA mortgage-backed securities with transaction costs, heterogeneous households, and endogenously generated prepayment rates." Working Paper, Carnegie-Mellon University.

Titman, S. and Torous, W. (1989). "Valuing commercial mortgages: an empirical investigation of the contingent claims approach to pricing risky debt." *Journal of Finance*, 44: 345–373.

Wang, W. (1994). "Valuation of mortgage-backed securities." Working Paper, Columbia University.

Chapter 50

THE IMPACTS OF IMF BAILOUTS IN INTERNATIONAL DEBT CRISES

ZHAOHUI ZHANG, *Long Island University, USA*
KHONDKAR E. KARIM, *Rochester Institute of Technology, USA*

Abstract

The roles played by the IMF in international debt crises have long been considered controversial among both academics and policy makers. This study reviews the role of IMF bailouts in international debt crises. The literature shows that there is a statistically significant positive wealth transfer from the IMF to the international bank creditors during major event announcements. Further, the evidence indicates the existence of market informational efficiency and different pricing behavior of different groups of international bank creditors. A pertinent future research topic would be to examine whether IMF introduces the moral hazard problem into the international financial markets.

Keywords: event studies; IMF bailout; equity prices; bank returns; international debt crisis; market efficiency; currency crisis; LDC loans

50.1. Introduction

"The roles played by the IMF in international debt crises have long been controversial among both academics and policy makers" (Zhang, 2001, p. 363). Financial crises in emerging markets and their contagion effects on the global financial system over the last two decades or so – Mexico, Argentina, Brazil, and Chile in 1982–83, Brazil in 1987, Mexico in 1990–1991 and again in 1994–

1995, Argentina in 1995, Southeast Asia and Russia from 1997 to 1998, and the Brazilian crisis along with the U.S. Congressional debate over the increase in IMF quotas during 1997–1998 – have put the IMF under an intense spotlight in the global financial environment.

The current 182-member-country IMF was founded in July 1944 "in the hope that establishing a permanent forum for cooperation on international monetary problems would help avoid the competitive devaluation, exchange restrictions, and other destructive economic policies that had contributed to the Great Depression and the outbreak of war" (Fischer, 1998). The institution has evolved through the years along with a changing international financial community. Although the current role of the IMF is being challenged from both sides, by those who denounce it and those who want to expand it (Fischer, 1999), the IMF's objectives remain the same as when it was established.[1]

Who needs IMF bailouts? Two sharply opposing views confront each other. Criticisms of IMF policies can be found in David Malpass (1997, 1998), Shultz et al. (1998), Schuler (1998), Sacks and Thiel (1998), and in Wall Street Journal editorial articles (Editorial Articles, 1998a–c; 6 April, 15 April, 23 April), etc. Some even assert that the IMF caused the crises and therefore should be abolished. On the contrary, former U.S. Treasury Secretary Robert Rubin, Federal Reserve

Chairman Greenspan (1998), former Treasury Secretary Summers (1998), and Rockefeller (1998), etc. argue that IMF loans are not only necessary but also the IMF needs to be strengthened.

The central discussion surrounding IMF bailouts is about the potential moral hazard problem in the international debt markets,[2] or put more explicitly, socializing costs versus privatizing gains. The negative views toward the IMF hold that bailout packages encourage imprudent lending behavior and that has resulted in a large amount of bad investments. There are opinions that these bad investments are largely responsible for the financial meltdowns in the troubled Asian countries. At the same time, the Western creditor banks are avoiding the negative ramifications of their bad investments in those countries by propping up their equity values with bailouts from the IMF using member countries' (both debtors and creditors) taxpayers funds. Arguably, those international bank creditors and troubled countries' domestic banks should bear the negative consequences caused by their imprudent lending and investments. As put in Radelet and Sachs (1998, pp. 51–52):

> The mechanics of the IMF loans merit special attention, ... the (IMF) loan packages had the direct function of providing the central bank with resources to support the payment of debts falling due, while limiting the adverse effects of such repayments on the exchange rate. In the case of Korea, the linkage between the loan package and the repayment of the foreign debts was direct and fairly automatic ...

The supportive views toward IMF bailouts mainly emphasize the insurance against the spread of the Asian crisis to other regions, i.e. containing the contagion effects. The following quote is again from Radelet and Sachs (1998, p. 52):

> The IMF has emphasized that the lending packages were intended to support stabilization, not merely to bail out foreign financial institutions. It had hoped that its role as a quasi lender of last resort would sufficiently restore market confidence that Asian governments would not need

> to draw down the full package of loans. If exchange rates could be stabilized and default avoided, the thinking presumably ran, private lending would revive ...

According to this view, the IMF can deal with those troubled governments as a neutral, nonpolitical party; can contain social costs in those troubled countries as well as the danger of causing regional security problems; and can exert leverage to restructure those countries' economic systems toward a free-market system, therefore affecting and leading political systems toward more democratic ones.[3,4]

While it is easy to understand why some people have a certain view of IMF bailouts, the role or the existence of the IMF itself, and the conditions the IMF enforces on bailout recipients are not well differentiated in the current discussions. The negative view toward bailouts sometimes claims that the existence of the IMF bailouts fosters imprudent lending behavior that in turn contributes to the development of currency crises. However, this view does not give the IMF credit for the condition that they lay out when they make a bailout to a country in crisis. Like the Federal Reserve's discount window policy, if the benefits of obtaining the funds are not as good as they look (i.e. the banks' books must be checked as a condition for obtaining the loan), then the incentives of committing moral hazard would be greatly reduced. The condition of the bailouts is nothing else but the counterparts of the incentives of committing moral hazard.

The following argument against the international critics of the IMF with regard to the moral hazard problem is extracted from Stanley Fischer's address[5]:

> To begin with, the notion that the availability of IMF programs encourages reckless behavior by those countries is far-fetched: no country would deliberately court such a crisis even if it thought international assistance would be forthcoming. The economic, financial, social, and political pain is simply too great; nor do countries show any desire to enter IMF programs unless they absolutely have to.

This point is further supported by the initial reluctance of South Korea to ask for the IMF bailout,[6] China's accelerated reforms in its financial sector to avoid similar crisis, and other similar arguments.

50.2. Literature Review

Event studies of international debt crises are abundant in the finance literature. These studies can be categorized according to several criteria. Based on subject matter, one group of studies (Cornell and Shapiro, 1986; Bruner and Simms, 1987; Smirlock and Kaufold, 1987) examines the impact of the "emergence" of less developed countries' (LDC) loan problems on the value of firms. Another group of studies analyzes the impact on firm values when the "solutions" to the LDC loan problems are proposed. The literature in this second group can be further divided into two subgroups according to whether the solutions are "direct" resolutions of the crises (Demirguc-Kunt and Huizinga, 1993; Madura et al., 1993; Unal et al., 1993; Zhang, 2001; Zhang and Karim, 2004), or "indirect" workouts of the crises (Billingsley and Lamy, 1988; Musumeci and Sinkey, 1990). Based on whether events "cluster" or not, or in other words, whether event windows are overlapping due to the characteristics of the occurrence of events, the event study methodology is also different. The clustering event analysis requires the estimation of the cross-sectional correlation between firms by employing multivariate analysis, such as in Smirlock and Kaufold (1987), Zhang (2001), and Zhang and Karim (2004). The more traditional nonclustering event studies use simple portfolio aggregation approaches, such as Fama et al. (1969).

Billingsley and Lamy (1988) studied the impact of the regulation of international lending on bank stock prices with regard to the U.S. legislative events in 1983. In the wake of the Mexican moratorium in August 1982, the United States passed the International Lending Supervision Act (ILSA), and increased the U.S. quota in the IMF by $8.5 billion in 1983. While previous studies reveal that the impact of the passage of the ILSA on bank stock prices is negative, Billingsley and Lamy (1988) carried the study further to include the impact of the introduction of the Act in the Congress on bank stock returns. More importantly, the joint impact of the passage of the Act and the increase of the IMF quota for the United States were studied and found to be positive, though the perceived benefit of a greater IMF quota is diminished by the ILSA impact. Also, they find that the risk to the banking industry is decreased as a result of the legislative events. The authors assert that the economic significance of the legislative changes to bank stockholders depends on the perceived trade-off between the benefits of increased IMF subsidization of international loan risk and the reduced opportunity to pursue such risks under the ILSA.

The related hypotheses are: one, that investors did not perceive any of the considered legislative events to include economically material information; two, that investors did not view the exposed banks differently from nonexposed banks due to the legislative changes. They find that the United States support of the IMF event produced a daily positive excess return of about 1 percent for the stockholders, while the cumulative effect of the introduction of the ILSA has a negative impact on the stockholders as predicted. Both events were tested on the whole sample basis.

They also find that the nonexposed banks did not react significantly to the greater U.S. support of the IMF, while the exposed banks reacted in a vigorously positive manner. The "introduction" of the ILSA had no impact on either of the two subsamples. But the "passage" of the ILSA had a significant negative impact on exposed banks while there was no impact on nonexposed banks. Also, a significantly positive relationship was found to exist between the individual BHC stockholders' reactions and the extent of BHCs' Latin American loan exposures for both the passage of the IMF quota increase and the passage of the ILSA.

Demirguc-kunt and Huizinga (1993) studied the impact of "direct" official credits to debt countries on returns of foreign-exposed banks. The purpose of the paper is to infer from the movement of bank stock prices the implicit transfer of official funds (loan to the debtor countries) back to the foreign commercial banks that made the loans in the first place. Four different types of events were tested.

From October 1982 to February 1983, the IMF made loan commitments to Argentina, Mexico, Chile, and Brazil, The main result is that the stock market did not change significantly in light of the IMF loan commitments, as market investors anticipated larger commitments to the indebted neighboring countries after the commitment to Argentina was made.[7] And even in Argentina's case, only two banks enjoyed significantly positive returns over the 3-day event period.

The hypotheses for zero coefficients are rejected for the exposed banks and for all banks together, as expected. But they also were rejected at the 10 percent level for nonexposed banks. This points to possible contagion. However, the hypothesis that the event parameters are equal is rejected for all three groups of banks, indicating that investors knew at least some information about each individual bank's exposure level. This, on the contrary, implies the rational pricing hypothesis. In general, the test results are not always consistent with each other and few significant results are obtained. The obscure results may be attributed to mismatching the data selection with the event periods. All three groups of banks are categorized by using the exposure data till the end of 1988. The tests could be very misleading when the actual data used were dated several years later. Also, the study left unexplained how market investors knew information about individual bank's exposures without getting it as public information.

The IMF's direct resolution of the Asian crisis in 1997 consists of clustering events that can be analyzed by conducting multivariate analyses. The IMF's bailout of South Korea in December 1997 is considered as an event that simultaneously affected all firms related cross-sectionally. The IMF's direct involvement in the global financial crisis from mid-1997 to early 1999 spurred a great deal of discussion among political leaders and

economists worldwide as to whether the policies of (actions by) the IMF were appropriate to solve the crisis, and whether the existence of the institution itself was necessary at all.

Zhang (2001) examines whether the IMF bailout of South Korea in early December 1997 produced significantly positive abnormal returns in the equity values of the lending institutions. If significant positive abnormal returns occurred, then we can infer that IMF bailouts are probably generating "extra" positive wealth for the private shareholders, since potential losses without the bailouts are assumed to have negative impact on the equity values of creditors.

Zhang also examines the contagion pricing notion versus the rational pricing notion. More specifically, it is to examine whether equity prices of banks with similar foreign exposure features respond to their foreign exposure levels equally cross sectionally. If so, then equity prices change with exposure levels proportionally, which indicates the existence of rational pricing in international debt markets.

The abnormal returns of the individual banks are aggregated cross sectionally into the three portfolios based on the three bank subgroups in the study: the South Korean exposed bank group, the foreign but non-South Korean exposed bank group, and the pure domestic lending bank group. Because of the clustering of the event announcements, multivariate analysis is employed to adjust for the variance estimation to take into consideration the cross-sectional correlation between the banks in each portfolio and between portfolios. Significantly positive abnormal returns are found for the three different bank groups on the event dates, except in one case.

The event impacts on the different bank groups are different. The South Korean exposed bank group experienced the largest positive gains among the three groups, while the foreign but non-South Korean exposed bank group did not outperform the pure domestic lending bank group. This latter result may be attributed to the fact that the lack of unison of the geographical distribution of the foreign exposure among this group of banks renders the direct comparison of their respective foreign exposures less meaningful. For banks that had no or an insignificant amount of emerging market exposure, their equity behavior may be closer to that of domestic banks than to the South Korean exposed banks.

The empirical evidence here clears the controversy regarding whether the IMF generated a wealth transfer in its bailout of South Korea in late 1997. The focus of the future discussion is not whether the IMF has generated a wealth transfer from the public funds to the private shareholders, but whether this could be avoided and how?

Zhang and Karim (2004) test the informational efficiency of financial markets related to the IMF bailout of South Korea. Informational efficiency is defined as how fast the news of the bailout announcements is incorporated into the equity pricing of U.S. banks that lend in the international debt markets. If the news of the bailout announcements were incorporated into equity prices immediately, then the abnormal returns of the foreign exposed banks would be significant on event dates but insignificant on nonevent dates. Because the IMF bailout happened in international debt markets, foreign exposed banks were directly involved, and the foreign exposure variable should be directly related to their return changes. Thus, the existence of informational efficiency can be inferred by observing whether the coefficient estimate of the foreign exposure variable is significant in terms of equity pricing on both the event and nonevent days. It has been shown in the literature that the foreign exposure variable has been the most important variable in studying equity responses in international debt crises. Presumably, if the market is informationally efficient, then the foreign exposure variable should be incorporated into the equity pricing, and its coefficient estimate is significant on the event dates, but the variable should not be incorporated into the equity pricing, and its coefficient estimate is insignificant on the nonevent dates.

For the foreign exposed banks, the mean abnormal returns tend to be significant on event dates but insignificant on nonevent dates. This evidence indicates that the news of bailout announcements was incorporated into the equity pricing immediately. There was no delay or lag effect reflected in the foreign exposed banks' equity prices. This supports the existence of market informational efficiency during the IMF bailout of South Korea in late 1997. Also, a quadratic cross-sectional regression model is employed to further examine this question by studying whether the equity returns changed proportional to the exposure levels. The CAR model on the main event date and the cumulative regression of ARs on both event dates are significant at the 5 percent level, while the CAR models on nonevent dates are not significant. The evidence indicates that the market is informationally efficient during the IMF bailout of South Korea in late 1997 as investors incorporated the foreign exposure into pricing their bank equities rapidly and proportionally. There is a significant positive relationship between the banks' equity prices and their respective exposure levels on the event days. This relationship is not shown on the nonevent dates. The empirical evidence here indicates that the banks' foreign exposure information seems to be either publicly available to the markets, or investors are able to get access to this type of information.

50.3. Suggestions For Future Research

Existing literature has tried to answer the question of whether there is a potential wealth transfer from the IMF to the private shareholders of international bank creditors resulting from IMF bailouts. A more pertinent question, which is also the central debate of all the bailout events, is left unanswered. This is the issue of a potential moral hazard problem in international financial markets. The test of moral hazard requires the testing of structural risk changes before and after a bailout event. The existence of the moral hazard problem is indicated if the risk structure changes that occur after the event are significant.

While the foreign exposure variable is probably the most important variable in this type of study, the exposure data for a specific country are not available all the time. Also, due to the lack of data reporting unison, the foreign exposure examined in the literature cannot be specified according to detailed geographical locations either. The test results would certainly be improved if such data were to become available in the future.

The results would be more complete if other international lenders could be examined simultaneously along with U.S. bank creditors.

On the methodology side, while it is common to use a two-index market model in bank studies to provide the parameter estimates, which are used in the event window to calculate the abnormal returns, the significance of the contribution and the depth of the effect of the second index (usually a stationary interest rate index), in addition to the market index, needs further exploration. In other words, whether the results are sensitive to the omission of the second index or to an alternative interest rate index deserves more research effort. Also, autocorrelation is often assumed to be zero in the literature. The complexity of incorporating autocorrelation into the models so far has prevented this type of analysis being carried out in event studies. While this may not cause serious problems, the incorporation of autocorrelation into the variance estimation should give more accurate results and inferences.

Further, a random coefficient model can be employed in the estimation window to allow for any possible structural changes before the underlying event window. If multiple coefficients are obtained, then the most recent one should be used in the event window analysis. This step is especially necessary when the length of the estimation window is long.

Acknowledgment

The authors are grateful to Richard L. Peterson and Carl H. Stem for their very valuable suggestions and comments. Remaining errors are ours.

NOTES

1. See the IMF's Articles of Agreement online at: http://www.imf.org/external/pubs/ft/aa/index.htm.
2. Radical differences also exist as to whether the Asian countries' markets have been opening enough or whether the countries should strengthen the free-market aspects of their economies before they open further. Related discussions also focus on the transparency and regulation issues in those troubled countries (Camdessus, January 16, 1998a).
3. For example, Summers (1998) said that: "The IMF has a unique ability to provide apolitical, conditional finance . . . in the context of strong reforms."
4. Camdessu's (January 22, 1998b) address at Transparency International: "The IMF helps members impose the management of their public resources and establish a stable and transparent regulatory environment for private sector activity, a *sine qua non* for economic efficiency and the eradication of corruption."
5. Same as endnote 1.
6. The influential *Dong-A Ilbo* newspaper claims: "The party is over, Korea's international standing has shamefully crashed," extracted from "Out of Our Hands," Lee, 1997, *Far Eastern Economic Review*, p. 81.
7. Another explanation would be that banks were not required to publish their developing country exposures at that time. This made it much more difficult for the investors to respond in any meaningful way.

REFERENCES

Billingsley, R.S. and Lamy, R.E. (1988). "The regulation of international lending: IMF support, the debt crisis, and bank stockholder wealth." *Journal of Banking and Finance*, 12: 255–274.

Bruner, R.F. and Simms, J.M. (1987). "The international debt crisis and bank security returns in 1982." *Journal of Money, Credit and Banking*, 19(1): 46–55.

Camdessus, M. (1998a). "An Address at the Press Conference in Kuala Lumpur," 16 January, http://www.web.org.

Camdessus, M. (1998b). "The IMF and Good Governance." addressed in Paris on 21 January, http://www.imf.org/external/np/speeches

Cornell, B. and Shapiro, A. (1986). "The reaction of bank stock prices to the international debt crisis." *Journal of Banking and Finance*, 10: 55–73.

Demirguc-Kunt, A. and Huizinga, H. (1993). "Official credits to developing countries: implicit transfers to the banks." *Journal of Money, Credit, and Banking*, 25: 76–89.

Editorial Article (1998a). "What's an IMF for?" *The Wall Street Journal*, 6 April, 14.

Editorial Article (1998b). "The IMF Crisis." *The Wall Street Journal*, 15 April, 22.

Editorial Article (1998c). "IMFonomics." *The Wall Street Journal*, 23 April, 18.

Fama, E.F., Fisher, E.L., Jensen, M., and Roll, R. (1969). "The adjustment of stock prices to new information." *International Economic Review*, 1–21.

Fischer, S. (1998). "The Asian Crisis: A View from the IMF", addressed in Washington, DC on 22 January, http://www.imf.org/external/np/speeches

Fischer, S. (1999). "On the Need for an International Lender of Resort." an address to AEA/AFA joint luncheon meeting in New York, 3 January, http://www.imf.org/external/np/speeches

Greenspan, A. (1998). "Remarks by Greenspan." at the Annual Convention of the American Society of Newspaper Editors, in Washington, DC, on 2 April, *WSJ* Interactive Edition.

Lee, C. (1997). "The Next Domino?" *Far Eastern Economic Review*, 20: 14–16.

Madura, J., Tucker, A.L. and Zarruk, E.R. (1993). "Market reaction to the thrift bailout." *Journal of Banking and Finance*, 17(4): 591–608.

Malpass, D. (1997). "Break the IMF shackles." *The Wall Street Journal*, 26 September, 15.

Malpass, D. (1998). "The road back from devaluation." *The Wall Street Journal*, 14: 16.

Musumeci, J.J. and Sinkey, J.F. Jr. (1990). "The international debt crisis, investor contagion, and bank security returns in 1987: The Brazilian experience." *Journal of Money, Credit, and Banking*, 22: 209–220.

Rockefeller, D. (1998). "Why we need the IMF?" *The Wall Street Journal*, 1 May, 17.

Radelet, S. and Sachs, J. (1998). "The East Asian financial crisis: diagnosis, remedies, prospects." *Brookings Papers on Economic Activity*, 1: 1–90.

Sacks, D., and Thiel, P. (1998). "The IMF's big wealth transfer." *The Wall Street Journal*, 13 March, 14.

Schuler, K. (1998). "A currency board beats the IMF Rx." *The Wall Street Journal*, 18 February, 19.

Shultz, G., Simon, W., and Wriston, W. (1998). "Who needs the IMF." *The Wall Street Journal*, 3 February, 15.

Smirlock, M. and Kaufold, H. (1987). "Bank foreign lending, mandatory disclosure rules, and the reaction of bank stock prices to the mexican debt crisis." *Journal of Business*, 60(3): 77–93.

Summers, L. (1998). "Why America needs the IMF." *The Wall Street Journal*, 27 March, 16.

Unal, H., Demirguc-Kunt, A., and Leung, K. (1993). "The Brady Plan, 1989 Mexican debt-reduction agreement, and bank stock returns in United States and Japan." *Journal of Money, Credit and Banking*, 410–429.

Zhang, Z. (2001). "The impact of IMF term loans on U.S. Bank creditors' equity values: an event study of South Korea's case." *Journal of International Financial Markets, Institutions and Money*, 11: 363–394.

Zhang, Z. and Karim, K.E. (2004). "Is too-big-to-fail policy effective for US Banks in an international currency crisis?" *Review of Pacific Basin Financial Markets and Policies*, 7: 311–333.

PART III: Appendix

Appendix A

DERIVATION OF DIVIDEND DISCOUNT MODEL

I. Summation of Infinite Geometric Series

Summation of geometric series can be defined as:

$$S = A + AR + AR^2 + \cdots + AR^{n-1} \quad \text{(A1)}$$

Multiplying both sides of equation (A1) by R, we obtain

$$RS = AR + AR^2 + \cdots + AR^{n-1} + AR^n \quad \text{(A2)}$$

Subtracting equation (A1) by equation (A2), we obtain

$$S - RS = A - AR^n$$

It can be shown

$$S = \frac{A(1 - R^n)}{1 - R} \quad \text{(A3)}$$

If R is smaller than 1, and n approaches to ∞, then R^n approaches to 0 i.e.,

$$S_\infty = A + AR + AR^2 + \cdots + AR^{n-1} + \cdots + AR^\infty, \quad \text{(A4)}$$

then,

$$S_\infty = \frac{A}{1 - R} \quad \text{(A5)}$$

II. Dividend Discount Model

Dividend Discount Model can be defined as:

$$P_0 = \frac{D_1}{1 + k} + \frac{D_2}{(1 + k)^2} + \frac{D_3}{(1 + k)^3} + \cdots \quad \text{(A6)}$$

Where P_0 = present value of stock price per share
D_t = dividend per share in period t ($t = 1$, 2, ...,n)

If dividends grow at a constant rate, say g, then, $D_2 = D_1(1 + g)$, $D_3 = D_2(1 + g) = D_1(1 + g)^2$, and so on.

Then, equation (A6) can be rewritten as:

$$P_0 = \frac{D_1}{1 + k} + \frac{D_1(1 + g)}{(1 + k)^2} + \frac{D_1(1 + g)^2}{(1 + k)^3} + \cdots \quad \text{or,}$$

$$P_0 = \frac{D_1}{1 + k} + \frac{D_1}{(1 + k)} \times \frac{(1 + g)}{(1 + k)} + \frac{D_1}{(1 + k)}$$

$$\times \frac{(1 + g)^2}{(1 + k)^2} + \cdots \quad \text{(A7)}$$

Comparing equation (A7) with equation (A4), i.e., $P_0 = S_\infty$, $\frac{D_1}{1+k} = A$, and $\frac{1+g}{1+k} = R$ as in the equation (A4).

Therefore, if $\frac{1+g}{1+k} < 1$ or if $k > g$, we can use equation (A5) to find out P_0
i.e.,

$$P_0 = \frac{D_1/(1 + k)}{1 - [(1 + g)/(1 + k)]}$$

$$= \frac{D_1/(1 + k)}{[1 + k - (1 + g)]/(1 + k)}$$

$$= \frac{D_1/(1 + k)}{(k - g)/(1 + k)}$$

$$= \frac{D_1}{k - g} = \frac{D_0(1 + g)}{k - g}$$

Appendix B

DERIVATION OF DOL, DFL AND DCL

I. DOL

Let P = price per unit

V = variable cost per unit

F = total fixed cost

Q = quantity of goods sold

The definition of DOL can be defined as:

DOL(Degree of operating leverage)

$$= \frac{Percentage\ Change\ in\ Profits}{Percentage\ Change\ in\ Sales}$$

$$= \frac{\Delta\ EBIT/EBIT}{\Delta Sales/Sales}$$

$$= \frac{\{[Q(P-V)-F]-[Q'(P-V)-F]\}/[Q(P-V)-F]}{(P\times Q - P\times Q')/(P\times Q)}$$

$$= \frac{[Q(P-V)-Q'(P-V)]/[Q(P-V)-F]}{P(Q-Q')/P\times Q}$$

$$= \frac{(Q-Q')(P-V)/[Q(P-V)-F]}{P(Q-Q')/P\times Q}$$

$$= \frac{(Q-Q')(P-V)}{Q(P-V)-F} \times \frac{P\times Q}{P(Q-Q')}$$

$$= \boxed{\frac{Q(P-V)}{Q(P-V)-F}}$$

$$= \frac{Q(P-V)-F+F}{Q(P-V)-F} = \frac{Q(P-V)-F}{Q(P-V)-F} + \frac{F}{Q(P-V)-F}$$

$$= 1 + \frac{F}{Q(P-V)-F}$$

$$\boxed{= 1 + \frac{Fixed\ Costs}{Profits}}$$

II. DFL

Let i = interest rate on outstanding debt $\left.\right\}$ iD = interest payment on dept

D = outstanding debt

N = the total number of shares outstanding

τ = corporate tax rate

$EAIT = [Q(P-V)-F-i\text{D}](1-\tau)$

The definition of DFL can be defined as:

DFL (Degree of financial leverage)

$$= \frac{\Delta\ EPS/EPS}{\Delta\ EBIT/EBIT} = \frac{(\Delta\ EAIT/N)/(EAIT/N)}{\Delta\ EBIT/EBIT}$$

$$= \frac{\Delta\ EAIT/EAIT}{\Delta\ EBIT/EBIT}$$

$$= \frac{\dfrac{[Q(P-V)-F-i\text{D}](1-\tau)-[Q'(P-V)-F-i\text{D}]}{(1-\tau)[Q(P-V)-F-i\text{D}](1-\tau)}}{\dfrac{[Q(P-V)-F]-[Q'(P-V)-F]}{[Q(P-V)-F]}}$$

$$= \frac{\dfrac{[Q(P-V)](1-\tau)-[Q'(P-V)](1-\tau)}{[Q(P-V)-F-i\text{D}]-(1-\tau)}}{\dfrac{[Q(P-V)-Q'(P-V)]}{[Q(P-V)-F]}}$$

$$= \frac{[(Q-Q')(P-V)](1-\tau)}{[Q(P-V)-F-i\text{D}](1-\tau)} \times \frac{Q(P-V)-F}{(Q-Q')(P-V)}$$

$$= \boxed{\frac{Q(P-V)-F}{Q(P-V)-F-i\text{D}}} \left(= \frac{EBIT}{EBIT-i\text{D}}\right)$$

III. DCL (degree of combined leverage)

$$= DOL \times DFL$$

$$= \frac{Q(P-V)}{Q(P-V)-F} \times \frac{Q(P-V)-F}{Q(P-V)-F-i\text{D}} = \boxed{\frac{Q(P-V)}{Q(P-V)-F-i\text{D}}}$$

Appendix C

DERIVATION OF CROSSOVER RATE

Suppose there are 2 projects under consideration. Cash flows of project A, B and B – A are as follows:

Period	0	1	2	3
Project A	−10 500	10 000	1000	1000
Project B	−10 500	1000	1000	12 000
Cash flows of B – A	0	−9000	0	11 000

Based upon the information the table above we can calculate the NPV of Project A and Project B under different discount rates. The results are presented in table C1.

Table C1. NPV of Project A and B under Different Discount Rates

Discount rate	NPV (Project A)	NPV (Project B)
0%	1500.00	3500.00
5%	794.68	1725.46
10%	168.67	251.31
15%	−390.69	−984.10
20%	−893.52	−2027.78

NPV(B) is higher with low discount rates and NPV(A) is higher with high discount rates. This is because the cash flows of project A occur early and those of project B occur later. If we assume a high discount rate, we would favor project A; if a low discount rate is expected, project B will be chosen. In order to make the right choice, we can calculate the crossover rate. If the discount rate is higher than the crossover rate, we should choose project A; if otherwise, we should go for project B. **The crossover rate, R_c, is the rate such that NPV(A) equals to NPV(B).**

Suppose the crossover rate is R_c, then

$$NPV(A) = -10{,}500 + 10{,}000/(1 + R_c) + 1{,}000/(1 + R_c)^2 + 1{,}000/(1 + R_c)^3 \tag{C1}$$

$$NPV(B) = -10{,}500 + 1{,}000/(1 + R_c) + 1{,}000/(1 + R_c)^2 + 12{,}000/(1 + R_c)^3 \tag{C2}$$

$$NPV(A) = NPV(B)$$

Therefore,

$$\begin{aligned} &-10{,}500 + \frac{10{,}000}{1 + R_c} + \frac{1{,}000}{(1 + R_c)^2} + \frac{1{,}000}{(1 + R_c)^3} \\ &= -10{,}500 + \frac{1{,}000}{1 + R_c} + \frac{1{,}000}{(1 + R_c)^2} + \frac{12{,}000}{(1 + R_c)^3} \end{aligned}$$

Rearranging the above equation (moving all terms on the LHS to the RHS), we obtain (C3)

$$\begin{aligned} 0 = &[-10{,}500 - (-10{,}500)] + \left[\frac{1{,}000}{1 + R_c} - \frac{10{,}000}{1 + R_c}\right] \\ &+ \left[\frac{1{,}000}{(1 + R_c)^2} - \frac{1{,}000}{(1 + R_c)^2}\right] + \left[\frac{12{,}000}{(1 + R_c)^3} - \frac{1{,}000}{(1 + R_c)^3}\right] \end{aligned} \tag{C3}$$

Solving equation (C3) by trial and error method for R_c, R_c equals 10.55%.

Using the procedure of calculating internal rate of return (IRR) as discussed in equations (C1), (C2), and (C3), we calculate the IRR for both Project A and Project B. The IRR for Project A and B are 11.45% and 10.95% respectively. From this information, we have concluded that Project A will perform better than Project B without consideration for change of discount rate. Therefore, the IRR decision rule cannot be used for capital budgeting decisions when there exists an increasing or decreasing net cash inflow. This is so called "The Timing Problem" for using the IRR method for capital budgeting decisions.

Appendix D

CAPITAL BUDGETING DECISIONS WITH DIFFERENT LIVES

I. Mutually Exclusive Investment Projects with Different Lives

The traditional NPV technique may not be the appropriate criterion to select a project from mutually exclusive investment projects, if these projects have different lives. The underlying reason is that, compared with a long-life project, a short-life project can be replicated more quickly in the long run. In order to compare projects with different lives, we compute the NPV of an infinite replication of the investment project. For example, let Projects A and B be two mutually exclusive investment projects with the following cash flows.

Year	Project A	Project B
0	100	100
1	70	50
2	70	50
3		50

By assuming a discount rate of 12 percent, the traditional NPV of Project A is 18.30 and the NPV of Project B is 20.09. This shows that Project B is a better choice than Project A. However, the NPV with infinite replications for Project A and B should be adjusted into a comparable basis.

In order to compare Projects A and B, we compute the NPV of an infinite stream of constant scale replications. Let NPV (N, ∞) be the NPV of an N-year project with NPV (N), replicated forever. This is exactly the same as an annuity paid at the beginning of the first period and at the end of every N years from that time on. The NPV of the annuity is:

$$NPV(N, \infty) = NPV(N) + \frac{NPV(N)}{(1+K)^N} + \frac{NPV(N)}{(1+K)^{2N}} + \cdots$$

In order to obtain a closed-form formula, let $(1/[(1 + K)^N]) = H$. Then we have:

$$NPV(N, t) = NPV(N)(1 + H + H^2 + \cdots + H^t) \quad (D1)$$

Multiplying both sides by H, this becomes

$$H[NPV(N, t)] = NPV(N)(H + H^2 + \cdots + H^t + H^{t+1}) \quad (D2)$$

Subtracting equation. (D2) from equation. (D1) gives:

$$NPV(N, t) - (H)NPV(N, t) = NPV(N)(1 - H^{t+1})$$

$$NPV(N, t) = \frac{NPV(N)(1 - H^{t+1})}{1 - H}$$

Taking the limit as the number of replications, t, approaches infinity gives:

$$\lim_{t \to \infty} NPV(N, t) = NPV(N, \infty)$$

$$= NPV\left[\frac{1}{1 - [1/(1 + K)^N]}\right]$$

$$= NPV(N)\left[\frac{(1 + K)^N}{(1 + K)^N - 1}\right] \quad (D3)$$

Equation (D3) is the NPV of an N-year project replicated at constant scale an infinite number of times. We can use it to compare projects with different lives because when their cash-flow streams are replicated forever, it is as if they had the same (infinite) life.

Based upon equation (D3), we can calculate the NPV of Projects A and B as follows:

For Project A

$NPV(2, \infty)$

$= NPV(2)\left[\dfrac{(1+0.12)^2}{(1+0.12)^2 - 1}\right]$

$= (18.30)\left[\dfrac{1.2544}{0.2544}\right]$

$= 90.23$

For Project B

$NPV(3, \infty)$

$= NPV(3)\left[\dfrac{(1+0.12)^3}{(1+0.12)^3 - 1}\right]$

$= 20.09\left[\dfrac{1.4049}{0.4049}\right]$

$= 69.71$

Consequently, we would choose to accept Project A over Project B, because, when the cash flows are adjusted for different lives, A provides the greater cash flow.

Alternatively, equation (D3) can be rewritten as an equivalent annual NPV version as:

$$K \times NPV(N, \infty) = \frac{NPV(N)}{Annuity\ factor} \quad (D4)$$

where the annuity factor is

$$\frac{1 - 1/(1+K)^N}{K}$$

The decision rule from equation (D4) is equivalent to the decision rule of equation (D3).

The different project lives can affect the beta coefficient estimate, as shown by Meyers and Turnbull (1977). For empirical guidance for evaluating capital-investment alternatives with unequal lives, the readers are advised to refer Emery (1982).

II. Equivalent Annual Cost

Equation (D4) can be written as:

$$NPV(N) = K \times NPV(N, \infty) \times Annuity\ Factor \quad (D5)$$

Corporate Finance by Ross, Westerfield, and Jaffe (2005, 7th edn, p. 193) has discussed about Equivalent Annual Cost. The Equivalent Annual Cost (C) can be calculated as follows:

$$NPV(N) = C \times Annuity\ Factor \quad (D6)$$

From equation (D5) and (D6), we obtain

$$C = K \times NPV(N, \infty) \quad (D7)$$

Assume company A buys a machine that costs $1000 and the maintenance expense of $250 is to be paid at the end of each of the four years. To evaluate this investment, we can calculate the present value of the machine. Assuming the discount rate as 10 percent, we have

$$NPV(A) = 1000 + \frac{250}{1.1} + \frac{250}{(1.1)^2} + \frac{250}{(1.1)^3} + \frac{250}{(1.1)^4}$$
$$= 1792.47 \quad (D8)$$

Equation (D8) shows that payments of (1000, 250, 250, 250, 250) are equivalent to a payment of 1792.47 at time 0. Using equation (D6), we can equate the payment at time 0 of 1792.47 with a four year annuity.

$$1792.47 = C \times A_{0.1}^4 = C \times 3.1699$$
$$C = 565.47$$

In this example, following equation (D3), we can find

$$NPV(N, \infty) = 1749.47 \times (1+0.1)^4/[(1+0.1)^4 - 1]$$
$$= 5654.71$$

Then following the equation (D7), we obtain

$$C = K \times NPV(N, \infty) = 0.1 \times 5654.71 = 565.47$$

Therefore, the equivalent annual cost C is identical to the equivalent annual NPV as defined in equation (D4).

Appendix E

DERIVATION OF MINIMUM-VARIANCE PORTFOLIO

If there is a two security portfolio, its variance can be defined as:

$$\sigma_p^2 = w_D^2 \sigma_D^2 + w_E^2 \sigma_E^2 + 2 w_D w_E \text{Cov}(r_D, r_E) \qquad \text{(E1)}$$

where r_D and r_E are the rate of return for security D and security E respectively; w_D and w_E are weight associated with security D and E respectively; σ_D^2 and σ_E^2 are variance of security D and E respectively; and $\text{Cov}(r_D, r_E)$ is the covariance between r_D and r_E.

The problem is choosing optimal w_D to minimize the portfolio variance, σ_p^2

$$\underset{w_D}{Min} \ \sigma_P^2 \qquad \text{(E2)}$$

We can solve the minimization problem by differentiating the σ_p^2 with respect to w_D and setting the derivative equal to 0 i.e., we want to solve

$$\frac{\partial \sigma_p^2}{\partial w_D} = 0 \qquad \text{(E3)}$$

Since, $w_D + w_E = 1$ or, $w_E = 1 - w_D$

therefore, the variance, σ_p^2, can be rewritten as

$$\begin{aligned}
\sigma_p^2 &= w_D^2 \sigma_D^2 + w_E^2 \sigma_E^2 + 2 w_D w_E \ \text{Cov}(r_D, r_E) \\
&= w_D^2 \sigma_D^2 + (1 - w_D)^2 \sigma_E^2 + 2 w_D (1 - w_D) \ \text{Cov}(r_D, r_E) \\
&= w_D^2 \sigma_D^2 + \sigma_E^2 - 2 w_D \sigma_E^2 + w_D^2 \sigma_E^2 + 2 w_D \ \text{Cov}(r_D, r_E) \\
&\quad - 2 w_D^2 \text{Cov}(r_D, r_E)
\end{aligned}$$

Now, the first order conditions of equation (E3) can be written as

$$2 w_D \sigma_D^2 - 2 \sigma_E^2 + 2 w_D \sigma_E^2 + 2 \ \text{Cov}(r_D, r_E) - 4 w_D \ \text{Cov}(r_D, r_E) = 0$$

Rearranging the above equation,

$$w_D \sigma_D^2 + w_D \sigma_E^2 - 2 w_D \ \text{Cov}(r_D, r_E) = \sigma_E^2 - \text{Cov}(r_D, r_E)$$
$$\left[\sigma_D^2 + \sigma_E^2 - 2\text{Cov}(r_D, r_E) \right] w_D = \sigma_E^2 - \text{Cov}(r_D, r_E)$$

Finally, we have

$$\boxed{ w_D = \frac{\sigma_E^2 - \text{Cov}(r_D, r_E)}{\sigma_D^2 + \sigma_E^2 - 2\text{Cov}(r_D, r_E)} }$$

Appendix F

DERIVATION OF AN OPTIMAL WEIGHT PORTFOLIO USING THE SHARPE PERFORMANCE MEASURE

Solution for the weights of the optimal risky portfolio can be found by solving the following maximization problem:

$$\underset{w_D}{Max}\, S_p = \frac{E(r_p) - r_f}{\sigma_p}$$

where $E(r_p)$ = expected rates of return for portfolio P

r_f = risk free rates of return

S_p = sharpe performance measure, and

σ_p as defined in equation (E1) of Appendix E

We can solve the maximization problem by differentiating the S_p with respect to w_D, and setting the derivative equal to 0 i.e., we want to solve

$$\frac{\partial S_p}{\partial w_D} = 0 \tag{F1}$$

In the case of two securities, we know that

$$E(r_p) = w_D\, E(r_D) + w_E\, E(r_E) \tag{F2}$$

$$\sigma_p = \left[w_D^2\sigma_D^2 + w_E^2\sigma_E^2 + 2w_D\, w_E\, \text{Cov}(r_D, r_E)\right]^{1/2} \tag{F3}$$

$$w_D + w_E = 1 \tag{F4}$$

From above equations (F2), (F3), and (F4), we can rewrite $E(r_p) - r_f$ and σ_p as:

$$\begin{aligned}
E(r_p) - r_f &= w_D\, E(r_D) + w_E\, E(r_E) - r_f \\
&= w_D\, E(r_D) + (1 - w_D)\, E(r_E) - r_f \quad \text{(F5)} \\
&\equiv f(\mathbf{w_D})
\end{aligned}$$

$$\begin{aligned}
\sigma_p &= \left[w_D^2\, \sigma_D^2 + w_E^2\, \sigma_E^2 + 2w_D w_E\, \text{Cov}(r_D,\, r_E)\right]^{1/2} \\
&= \big[w_D^2\, \sigma_D^2 + (1 - w_D)^2\, \sigma_E^2 + 2w_D(1 - w_D) \\
&\quad \text{Cov}(r_D,\, r_E)\big]^{1/2} \\
&\equiv g(\mathbf{w_D}) \tag{F6}
\end{aligned}$$

Equation (F1) becomes

$$\begin{aligned}
\frac{\partial S_p}{\partial w_D} &= \frac{\partial[f(w_D)/g(w_D)]}{\partial w_D} \\
&= \frac{f'(w_D)g(w_D) - f(w_D)g'(w_D)}{[g(w_D)]^2} = 0 \tag{F7}
\end{aligned}$$

where $f'(w_D) = \dfrac{\partial f(w_D)}{\partial w_D} = E(r_D) - E(r_E)$ (F8)

$$\begin{aligned}
g'(w_D) &= \frac{\partial g(w_D)}{\partial w_D} \\
&= \frac{1}{2} \times \big[w_D^2\sigma_D^2 + (1 - w_D)^2\sigma_E^2 + 2w_D(1 - w_D) \\
&\qquad\qquad\qquad\qquad \text{Cov}(r_D, r_E)\big]^{1/2 - 1} \\
&\quad \times \big[2w_D\sigma_D^2 + 2w_D\sigma_E^2 - 2\sigma_E^2 + 2\text{Cov}(r_D, r_E) \\
&\qquad\qquad\qquad\qquad - 4w_D\, \text{Cov}(r_D, r_E)\big] \\
&= \big[w_D\sigma_D^2 + w_D\sigma_E^2 - \sigma_E^2 + \text{Cov}(r_D, r_E) \\
&\qquad\qquad\qquad\qquad - 2w_D\, \text{Cov}(r_D, r_E)\big] \\
&\quad \times \big[w_D^2\sigma_D^2 + (1 - w_D)^2\sigma_E^2 + 2w_D(1 - w_D) \\
&\qquad\qquad\qquad\qquad \text{Cov}(r_D, r_E)\big]^{-1/2} \tag{F9}
\end{aligned}$$

From equation (F7),

$$f'(w_D)g(w_D) - f(w_D)g'(w_D) = 0, \text{ or } f'(w_D)g(w_D)$$
$$= f(w_D)g'(w_D)$$

(F10)

Now, plugging $f(w_D)$, $g(w_D)$, $f'(w_D)$, and $g'(w_D)$ [equations (F5), (F6), (F8), and (F9)] into equation (F10), we have

$$[E(r_D) - E(r_E)]$$
$$\times \left[w_D^2\sigma_D^2 + (1-w_D)^2\sigma_E^2 + 2w_D(1-w_D)\text{Cov}(r_D,r_E)\right]^{1/2}$$
$$= [w_DE(r_D) + (1-w_D)E(r_E) - r_f]$$
$$\times \left[w_D\sigma_D^2 + w_D\sigma_E^2 - \sigma_E^2 + \text{Cov}(r_D,r_E)\right.$$
$$\left. - 2w_D\text{Cov}(r_D,r_E)\right]$$
$$\times \left[w_D^2\sigma_D^2 + (1-w_D)^2\sigma_E^2 + 2w_D(1-w_D)\right.$$
$$\left.\text{Cov}(r_D,r_E)\right]^{-1/2}$$

(F11)

Multiplying by $\left[w_D^2\sigma_D^2 + (1-w_D)^2\sigma_E^2 +2w_D\right.$
$\left.(1-w_D)\text{Cov}(r_D,r_E)\right]^{1/2}$ on both sides of equation
(F11), we have

$$[E(r_D) - E(r_E)]$$
$$\times \left[w_D^2\sigma_D^2 + (1-w_D)^2\sigma_E^2 + 2w_D(1-w_D)\text{Cov}(r_D,r_E)\right]$$
$$= [w_DE(r_D) + (1-w_D)E(r_E) - r_f]$$
$$\times \left[w_D\sigma_D^2 + w_D\sigma_E^2 - \sigma_E^2 + \text{Cov}(r_D,r_E) - 2w_D\text{Cov}(r_D,r_E)\right]$$

(F12)

Rearrange all terms on both hand sides of equation
(F12), i.e.,

Left hand side of equation (F12)

$$[E(r_D) - E(r_E)]$$
$$\times \left[w_D^2\sigma_D^2 + (1-w_D)^2\sigma_E^2 + 2w_D(1-w_D)\text{Cov}(r_D,r_E)\right]$$
$$= [E(r_D) - E(r_E)]$$
$$\times \left[w_D^2\sigma_D^2 + \sigma_E^2 - 2w_D\sigma_E^2 + w_D^2\sigma_E^2 + 2w_D\text{Cov}(r_D,r_E)\right.$$
$$\left. - 2w_D^2\text{Cov}(r_D,r_E)\right]$$

$$= [E(r_D) - E(r_E)] \times \{w_D^2[\sigma_D^2 + \sigma_E^2 - 2\text{Cov}(r_D,r_E)]$$
$$+2w_D\left[\text{Cov}(r_D,r_E) - \sigma_E^2\right] + \sigma_E^2\}$$
$$= [E(r_D) - E(r_E)] \times \{w_D^2[\sigma_D^2 + \sigma_E^2 - 2\text{Cov}(r_D,r_E)]\}$$
$$+[E(r_D) - E(r_E)] \times \{2w_D\left[\text{Cov}(r_D,r_E) - \sigma_E^2\right]\} + [E(r_D)$$
$$-E(r_E)]\times\sigma_E^2 = [E(r_D) - E(r_E)]\times[\sigma_D^2 + \sigma_E^2$$
$$-2\text{Cov}(r_D,r_E)]w_D^2 + 2[E(r_D) - E(r_E)]$$
$$\times\left[\text{Cov}(r_D,r_E) - \sigma_E^2\right]w_D + [E(r_D) - E(r_E)] \times \sigma_E^2$$

Right hand side of equation (F12)

$$[w_DE(r_D) + (1-w_D)E(r_E) - r_f] \times [w_D\sigma_D^2 + w_D\sigma_E^2$$
$$- \sigma_E^2 + \text{Cov}(r_D,r_E) - 2w_D\text{Cov}(r_D,r_E)]$$
$$= [w_DE(r_D) + E(r_E) - w_DE(r_E) - r_f] \times [w_D\sigma_D^2$$
$$+ w_D\sigma_E^2 - 2w_D\text{Cov}(r_D,r_E) - \sigma_E^2 + \text{Cov}(r_D,r_E)]$$
$$= \{w_D[E(r_D) - E(r_E)] + [E(r_E) - r_f] \} \times \{w_D[\sigma_D^2$$
$$+ \sigma_E^2 - 2\text{Cov}(r_D,r_E)] + \text{Cov}(r_D,r_E) - \sigma_E^2\}$$
$$= w_D[E(r_D) - E(r_E)] \times w_D[\sigma_D^2 + \sigma_E^2 - 2\text{Cov}(r_D,r_E)]$$
$$+ w_D[E(r_D) - E(r_E)] \times [\text{Cov}(r_D,r_E) - \sigma_E^2]$$
$$+ [E(r_E) - r_f] \times w_D[\sigma_D^2 + \sigma_E^2 - 2\text{Cov}(r_D,r_E)]$$
$$+ [E(r_E) - r_f] \times [\text{Cov}(r_D,r_E) - \sigma_E^2]$$
$$= [E(r_D) - E(r_E)] \times [\sigma_D^2 + \sigma_E^2 - 2\text{Cov}(r_D,r_E)]w_D^2$$
$$+ [E(r_D) - E(r_E)] \times [\text{Cov}(r_D,r_E) - \sigma_E^2]w_D$$
$$+ [E(r_E) - r_f] \times [\sigma_D^2 + \sigma_E^2 - 2\text{Cov}(r_D,r_E)]w_D$$
$$+ [E(r_E) - r_f] \times [\text{Cov}(r_D,r_E) - \sigma_E^2]$$

Subtracting $[E(r_D) - E(r_E)][\sigma_D^2 + \sigma_E^2 - 2\text{Cov}$
$(r_D,r_E)]w_D^2$ and
$[E(r_D) - E(r_E)][\text{Cov }(r_D,r_E) - \sigma_E^2]w_D$ from both
hand sides of equation (F12), we have

$$[E(r_D) - E(r_E)] \times [\text{Cov}(r_D,r_E) - \sigma_E^2]w_D$$
$$+ [E(r_D) - E(r_E)] \times \sigma_E^2$$
$$= [E(r_E) - r_f] \times [\sigma_D^2 + \sigma_E^2 - 2\text{Cov}(r_D,r_E)]w_D$$
$$+ [E(r_E) - r_f] \times [\text{Cov}(r_D,r_E) - \sigma_E^2] \tag{F13}$$

Moving all the terms with w_D on one side and
leaving the rest terms on the other side from equation (F13), we have

$$[E(r_D) - E(r_E)] \times \sigma_E^2 - [E(r_E) - r_f]$$
$$\qquad \times [Cov(r_D, r_E) - \sigma_E^2]$$
$$= [E(r_E) - r_f] \times [\sigma_D^2 + \sigma_E^2 - 2Cov(r_D, r_E)]w_D$$
$$\qquad - [E(r_D) - E(r_E)] \times [Cov(r_D, r_E) - \sigma_E^2]w_D$$

$$\text{(F14)}$$

Rearrange equation (F14) in order to solve for w_D, *i.e.*,

$$[E(r_D) - E(r_E) + E(r_E) - r_f] \times \sigma_E^2$$
$$\qquad - [E(r_E) - r_f]Cov(r_D, r_E)$$

$$= \{[E(r_E) - r_f]\sigma_D^2 + [E(r_E) - r_f]\sigma_E^2$$
$$\qquad - [E(r_E) - r_f][2Cov(r_D, r_E)] - [E(r_D)$$
$$\qquad - E(r_E)]Cov(r_D, r_E) + [E(r_D) - E(r_E)]\sigma_E^2\}w_D$$
$$= \{[E(r_D) - r_f]\sigma_E^2 + [E(r_E) - r_f]\sigma_D^2 - [E(r_D)$$
$$\qquad - r_f + E(r_E) - r_f]Cov(r_D, r_E)]\}w_D$$

Finally, we have the optimum weight of security D as

$$w_D = \frac{[E(r_D) - r_f]\sigma_E^2 - [E(r_E) - r_f]Cov(r_D, r_E)}{\begin{array}{c}[E(r_D) - r_f]\sigma_E^2 + [E(r_E) - r_f]\sigma_D^2 \\ -[E(r_D) - r_f + E(r_E) - r_f]Cov(r_D, r_E)\end{array}}$$

Appendix G

APPLICATIONS OF THE BINOMIAL DISTRIBUTION TO EVALUATE CALL OPTIONS

In this appendix, we show how the binomial distribution is combined with some basic finance concepts to generate a model for determining the price of stock options.

What is an Option?

In the most basic sense, an **option** is a contract conveying the right to buy or sell a designated security at a stipulated price. The contract normally expires at a predetermined date. The most important aspect of an option contract is that the purchaser is under no obligation to buy; it is, indeed, an "option." This attribute of an option contract distinguishes it from other financial contracts. For instance, whereas the holder of an option may let his or her claim expire unused if he or she so desires, other financial contracts (such as futures and forward contracts) obligate their parties to fulfill certain conditions.

A *call option* gives its owner the right to buy the underlying security, a *put option* the right to sell. The price at which the stock can be bought (for a call option) or sold (for a put option) is known as the exercise price.

The Simple Binomial Option Pricing Model

Before discussing the binomial option model, we must recognize its two major underlying assumptions. First, the binomial approach assumes that trading takes place in discrete time, that is, on a period-by-period basis. Second, it is assumed that the stock price (the price of the underlying asset) can take on only two possible values each period; it can go up or go down.

Say we have a stock whose current price per share S can advance or decline during the next period by a factor of either u (up) or d (down). This price either will increase by the proportion $u-1 \geq 0$ or will decrease by the proportion $1-d$, $0 < d < 1$. Therefore, the value S in the next period will be either uS or dS. Next, suppose that a call option exists on this stock with a current price per share of C and an exercise price per share of X and that the option has one period left to maturity. This option's value at expiration is determined by the price of its underlying stock and the exercise price X. The value is either

$$C_u = Max(0, uS - X) \qquad (G1)$$

or

$$C_d = Max(0, dS - X) \qquad (G2)$$

Why is the call worth Max $(0, uS - X)$ if the stock price us uS? The option holder is not obliged to purchase the stock at the exercise price of X, so she or he will exercise the option only when it is beneficial to do so. This means the option can never have a negative value. When is it beneficial for the option holder to exercise the option? When the price per share of the stock is greater than the price per share at which he or she can purchase the stock by using the option, which is the exercise price, X. Thus if the stock price uS exceeds the exercise price X, the investor can exercise the option and buy the stock. Then he or she can immediately sell it for uS, making a profit of $uS - X$ (ignoring commission). Likewise, if the stock price declines to dS, the call is worth Max $(0, dS - X)$.

Also for the moment, we will assume that the risk-free interest rate for both borrowing and lending is equal to r percent over the one time period and that the exercise price of the option is equal to X.

To intuitively grasp the underlying concept of option pricing, we must set up a *risk-free portfolio* – a combination of assets that produces the same return in every state of the world over our chosen investment horizon. The investment horizon is assumed to be one period (the duration of this period can be any length of time, such as an hour, a day, a week, etc.). To do this, we buy h share of the stock and sell the call option at its current price of C. Moreover, we choose the value of h such that our portfolio will yield the same payoff whether the stock goes up or down.

$$h(uS) - C_u = h(dS) - C_d \qquad (G3)$$

By solving for h, we can obtain the number of shares of stock we should buy for each call option we sell.

$$h = \frac{C_u - C_d}{(u - d)S} \qquad (G4)$$

Here h is called the *hedge ratio*. Because our portfolio yields the same return under either of the two possible states for the stock, it is without risk and therefore should yield the risk-free rate of return, r percent, which is equal to the risk-free borrowing and lending rate, the condition must be true; otherwise, it would be possible to earn a risk-free profit without using any money. Therefore, the ending portfolio value must be equal to $(1 + r)$ times the beginning portfolio value, $hS - C$.

$$(1 + r)(hS - C) = h(uS) - C_u = h(dS) - C_d \qquad (G5)$$

Note that S and C represent the beginning values of the stock price and the option price, respectively.

Setting $R = 1 + r$, rearranging to solve for C, and using the value of h from Equation (G4), we get

$$C = \left[\left(\frac{R - d}{u - d} \right) C_u + \left(\frac{u - R}{u - d} \right) C_d \right] / R \qquad (G6)$$

where $d < r < u$. To simplify this equation, we set

$$p = \frac{R - d}{u - d} \text{ so } 1 - p = \left\{ \frac{u - R}{u - d} \right\} \qquad (G7)$$

Thus we get the option's value with one period to expiration

$$C = \frac{pC_u + (1 - p)C_d}{R} \qquad (G8)$$

This is the binomial call option valuation formula in its most basic form. In other words, this is the binomial valuation formula with one period to expiration of the option.

To illustrate the model's qualities, let's plug in the following values, while assuming the option has one period to expiration. Let

$X = \$100$

$S = \$100$

$U = (1.10)$, so $uS = \$110$

$D = (0.90)$, so $dS = \$90$

$R = 1 + r = 1 + 0.07 = 1.07$

Table G.1. Possible Option Value at Maturity

Today Stock (S)	Option (C)		Next Period (Maturity)
		$uS = \$110$	$C_u = Max(0, uS - X)$ $= Max(0, 110 - 100)$ $= Max(0, 10)$ $= \$10$
$\$100$	C		
		$dS = \$90$	$C_d = Max(0, dS - X)$ $= Max(0, 90 - 100)$ $= Max(0, -10)$ $= \$0$

First we need to determine the two possible option values at maturity, as indicated in Table G.1.

Next we calculate the value of p as indicated in Equation (G7).

$$p = \frac{1.07 - 0.90}{1.10 - 0.90} = 0.85 \text{ so } 1 - p = \frac{1.10 - 1.07}{1.10 - 0.90}$$
$$= 0.15$$

Solving the binomial valuation equation as indicated in Equation (G8), we get

$$C = \frac{0.85(10) + 0.15(0)}{1.07}$$
$$= \$7.94$$

The correct value for this particular call option today, under the specified conditions, is \$7.94. If the call option does not sell for \$7.94, it will be possible to earn arbitrage profits. That is, it will be possible for the investor to earn a risk-free profit while using none of his or her own money. Clearly, this type of opportunity cannot continue to exist indefinitely.

The Generalized Binomial Option Pricing Model

Suppose we are interested in the case where there is more than one period until the option expires. We can extend the one-period binomial model to consideration of two or more periods.

Because we are assuming that the stock follows a binomial process, from one period to the next it can only go up by a factor of u or go down by a factor of d. After one period the stock's price is either uS or dS. Between the first and second periods, the stock's price can once again go up by u or down by d, so the possible prices for the stock two periods from now are uuS, udS, and ddS. This process is demonstrated in tree diagram (Figure G.1) given in Example G.1 later in this appendix.

Note that the option's price at expiration, two periods from now, is a function of the same relationship that determined its expiration price in the

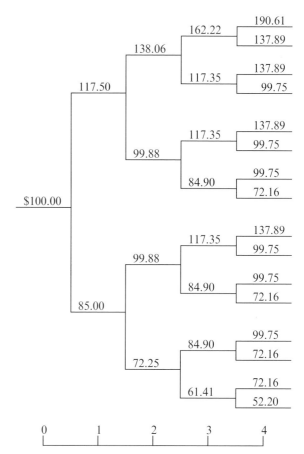

Figure G.1. Price Path of Underlying Stock *Source:* Rendelman, R.J., Jr., and Bartter, B.J. (1979). "Two-State Option Pricing," *Journal of Finance* 34 (December), 1906.

one-period model, more specifically, the call option's maturity value is always

$$C_T = [0, S_T - X] \tag{G9}$$

where T designated the maturity date of the option.

To derive the option's price with two periods to go ($T = 2$), it is helpful as an intermediate step to derive the value of C_u and C_d with one period to expiration when the stock price is either uS or dS, respectively.

$$C_u = \frac{pC_{uu} + (1 - p)C_{ud}}{R} \tag{G10}$$

$$C_d = \frac{pC_{du} + (1 - p)C_{dd}}{R} \tag{G11}$$

Equation (G10) tells us that if the value of the option after one period is C_u, the option will be worth either C_{uu} (if the stock price goes up) or C_{ud} (if stock price goes down) after one more period (at its expiration date). Similarly, Equation (G11) shows that the value of the option is C_d after one period, the option will be worth either C_{du} or C_{dd} at the end of the second period. Replacing C_u and C_d in Equation (G8) with their expressions in Equations (G10) and (G11), respectively, we can simplify the resulting equation to yield the two-period equivalent of the one-period binomial pricing formula, which is

$$C = \frac{p^2 C_{uu} + 2p(1-p)C_{ud} + (1-p)^2 C_{dd}}{R^2} \quad \text{(G12)}$$

In Equation (G12), we used the fact that $C_{ud} = C_{du}$ because the price will be the same in either case.

We know the values of the parameters S and X. If we assume that R, u, and d will remain constant over time, the possible maturity values for the option can be determined exactly. Thus deriving the option's fair value with two periods to maturity is a relatively simple process of working backwards from the possible maturity values.

Using this same procedure of going from a one-period model to a two-period model, we can extend the binomial approach to its more generalized form, with n periods maturity

$$C = \frac{1}{R^n} \sum_{k=0}^{n} \frac{n!}{k!(n-k)!} p^k (1-p)^{n-k}$$
$$Max[0, u^k d^{n-k} S - X] \quad \text{(G13)}$$

To actually get this form of the binomial model, we could extend the two-period model to three periods, then from three periods to four periods, and so on. Equation (G13) would be the result of these efforts. To show how Equation (G13) can be used to assess a call option's value, we modify the example as follows: $S = \$100$, $X = \$100$, $R = 1.07$, $n = 3$, $u = 1.1$ and $d = 0.90$.

First we calculate the value of p from Equation (G7) as 0.85, so $1 - p$ is 0.15. Next we calculate the four possible ending values for the call option after three periods in terms of $Max[0, u^k d^{n-k} S - X]$.

$$C_1 = [0, (1.1)^3 (0.90)^0 (100) - 100] = 33.10$$
$$C_2 = [0, (1.1)^2 (0.90)(100) - 100] = 8.90$$
$$C_3 = [0, (1.1)(0.90)^2 (100) - 100] = 0$$
$$C_4 = [0, (1.1)^0 (0.90)^3 (100) - 100] = 0$$

Now we insert these numbers (C_1, C_2, C_3, and C_4) into the model and sum the terms.

$$C = \frac{1}{(1.07)^3} \left[\frac{3!}{0!3!}(0.85)^0 (0.15)^3 \times 0 \right.$$

$$+ \frac{3!}{1!2!}(0.85)^1 (0.15)^2 \times 0$$

$$+ \frac{3!}{2!1!}(0.85)^2 (0.15)^1 \times 8.90$$

$$\left. + \frac{3!}{3!0!}(0.85)^3 (0.15)^0 \times 33.10 \right]$$

$$= \frac{1}{1.225} \left[0 + 0 + \frac{3 \times 2 \times 1}{2 \times 1 \times 1}(0.7225)(0.15)(8.90) \right.$$

$$\left. + \frac{3 \times 2 \times 1}{3 \times 2 \times 1 \times 1} \times (0.61413)(1)(33.10) \right]$$

$$= \frac{1}{1.225} [(0.32513 \times 8.90) + (0.61413 \times 33.10)]$$

$$= \$18.96$$

As this example suggests, working out a multiple-period problem by hand with this formula can become laborious as the number of periods increases. Fortunately, programming this model into a computer is not too difficult.

Now let's derive a binomial option pricing model in terms of the cumulative binomial density function. As a first step, we can rewrite Equation (G13) as

$$C = S\left[\sum_{k=m}^{n}\frac{n!}{k!(n-K)!}p^K(1-p)^{n-k}\frac{u^k d^{n-k}}{R^n}\right]$$
$$-\frac{X}{R^n}\left[\sum_{k=m}^{n}\frac{n!}{k!(n-k)!}p^k(1-p)^{n-k}\right]$$

(G14)

This formula is identical to Equation (G13) except that we have removed the Max operator. In order to remove the Max operator, we need to make $u^k d^{n-k}S - X$ positive, which we can do by changing the counter in the summation from $k = 0$ to $k = m$. What is m? It is the minimum number of upward stock movements necessary for the option to terminate "in the money" (that is, $u^k d^{n-k}S - X > 0$). How can we interpret Equation (G14)? Consider the second term in brackets; it is just a cumulative binomial distribution with parameters of n and p. Likewise, via a small algebraic manipulation we can show that the first term in the brackets is also a cumulative binomial distribution. This can be done by defining $P' \equiv (u/R)p$ and $1 - P' \equiv (d/R)(1 - p)$. Thus

$$P^k(1-p)^{n-k}\frac{u^k d^{n-k}}{R^n} = p'^k(1-p')^{n-k}$$

Therefore the first term in brackets is also a cumulative binomial distribution with parameters of n and p'. Using Equation (G10) in the text, we can write the binomial call option model as

$$C = SB_1(n, p', m) - \frac{X}{R^n}B_2(n, p, m) \qquad (G15)$$

where

$$B_1(n, p', m) = \sum_{k=m}^{n}C_k^n p'^k(1-p')^{n-k}$$
$$B_2(n, p, m) = \sum_{k=m}^{n}C_k^n p^k(1-p)^{n-k}$$

and m is the minimum amount of time the stock has to go up for the investor to finish *in the money*

(that is, for the stock price to become larger than the exercise price).

In this appendix, we showed that by employing the definition of a call option and by making some simplifying assumptions, we could use the binomial distribution to find the value of a call option. In the next chapter, we will show how the binomial distribution is related to the normal distribution and how this relationship can be used to derive one of the most famous valuation equations in finance, the Black-Scholes option pricing model.

Example G.1

A Decision Tree Approach to Analyzing Future Stock Price

By making some simplifying assumptions about how a stock's price can change from one period to the next, it is possible to forecast the future price of the stock by means of a decision tree. To illustrate this point, let's consider the following example.

Suppose the price of Company A's stock is currently $100. Now let's assume that from one period to the next, the stock can go up by 17.5 percent or go down by 15 percent. In addition, let us assume that there is a 50 percent chance that the stock will go up and a 50 percent chance that the stock will go down. It is also assumed that the price movement of a stock (or of the stock market) today is completely independent of its movement in the past; in other words, the price will rise or fall today by a random amount. A sequence of these random increases and decreases is known as a **random walk**.

Given this information, we can lay out the paths that the stock's price may take. Figure G.1 shows the possible stock prices for company A for four periods.

Note that in period 1 there are two possible outcomes: the stock can go up in value by 17.5 percent to $117.50 or down by 15 percent to $85.00. In period 2 there are four possible outcomes. If the stock went up in the first period, it can go up again to $138.06 or down in the second period to $99.88. Likewise, if the stock went down in the first period, it can go down again to $72.25 or up in the second period to $99.88. Using the same argument, we can trace the path of the stock's price for all four periods.

If we are interested in forecasting the stock's price at the end of period 4, we can find the average price of the stock for the 16 possible outcomes that can occur in period 4.

$$\bar{P} = \frac{\sum_{i=1}^{16} P_i}{16} = \frac{190.61 + 137.89 + \cdots + 52.20}{16} = \$105.09$$

We can also find the standard deviation for the stock's return.

$$\sigma_P = \left[\frac{(190.61 - 105.09)^2 + \cdots + (52.20 - 105.09)^2}{16}\right]^{1/2}$$

$$= \$34.39$$

$\bar{P}$ and σ_P can be used to predict the future price of stock A.

PART IV: References

REFERENCES

A

1 Abel, A.B. (1990). "Asset prices under habit formation and catching up with the Joneses". *American Economic Review* 80: 38–42.

2 Abraham, F., Karolien De, B., and Van der, A.I. (2000). "Will wage policy succeed in Euro-land? The case of Belgium". *Cahiers Economiques de Bruxelles* n°(168): 443–480.

3 Abuaf, N., and Jorion, P. (1990). Purchasing power parity in the long run. *Journal of Finance* 45: 157–174.

4 Acharya, V.V., and Carpenter, J.N. (2002). "Corporate bond valuation and hedging with stochastic interest rates and endogenous bankruptcy". *Review of Financial Studies* 15: 1355–1383.

5 Adler, M., and Bernard D. (1983). "International portfolio selection and corporation finance: A synthesis". *Journal of Finance* 38: 925–984.

6 Admati, A., and Pfleiderer, P. (1997). "Performance benchmarks: Does it all add up?" *Journal of Business*.

7 Admati, A., Bhattacharya, S., Ross, S., and Pfleiderer, P. (1986). "On timing and selectivity". *Journal of Finance* 41: 715–730.

8 Admati, A.R., and Paul, C.P. (1988). "A theory of intraday trading patterns". *Review of Financial Studies* 1: 3–40.

9 Agénor, P. R. (1994). "Credibility and exchange rate management in developing countries". *Journal of Development Economics* 45(1): 1–16.

10 Agrawal, A., and Ralph A.W. (1994). "Executive careers and compensation surrounding takeover bids". *Journal of Finance* 49(3): 985–1014.

11 Agrawal, A., Jeffery, J., and Gershon, N.M. (1992). "The post-merger performance of acquiring firms: A re-examination of an anomaly". *Journal of Finance* 47(4): 1605–1621.

12 Ahn, C.M., and. Thompson, H.E. (1988). "Jump diffusion processes and the term structure of interest rates". *Journal of Finance* 43(1): 155–174.

13 Ahn, D.H., Cao, H.H., and Stephane, C. (2003). Portfolio Performance Measurement: A No Arbitrage Bounds Approach, Working Paper, University of Alberta.

14 Ahn, D.H., Cliff, M., and Shivdasani, A. (2003). Long-Term Returns of Seasoned Equity Offerings: Bad Performance or Bad Models? Working Paper, Purdue University.

15 Ahn, D.H., Conrad, J., and Robert F.D. (2003a). "Risk adjustment and trading strategies". *Review of Financial Studies* 16: 459–485.

16 Ahn, D.H., Conrad, J., and Robert, F.D. (2003b). Basis Assets, Working Paper, University of North Carolina.

17 Ahn, H.J., Charles Q.C., and Hyuk, C. (1998). "Decimalization and competition among stock markets: Evidence from the Toronto stock exchange cross-listed securities". *Journal of Financial Markets* 1: 51–87.

18 Aitken, M., Brown, P., Buckland, C., Izan, H.Y., and Walter, T. (1995). Price Clustering on the Australian Stock Exchange, Working Paper, University of Western Australia.

19 Akerlof, G. (1970). "The Market for 'Lemons,' Qualitative Uncertainty and the Market Mechanism". *Quarterly Journal of Economics* 84: 488–500.

20 Akgiray, V., and Booth, G. G. (1988) "Mixed diffusion-jump process modeling of exchange rate movements". *Review of Economics and Statistics* 70(4): 631–637.

21 Alba, P., Hernandez, L., and Klingebiel, D. (1999). Financial Liberalization and the Capital Account: Thailand 1988–1997, Working Paper, World Bank.

22 Albo, W.P., and Henderson, R.A. (1987). Mergers and Acquisitions of Privately-held Businesses, Canadian Cataloguing in Publication Data.

23 Albuquerque, R., Bauer, G., and Schneider, M. (2004). International Equity Flows and Returns: A Quantitative Equilibrium Approach. NBER Working Paper.

24 Alexander, S.S. (1961). "Price movements in speculative markets: trends or random walks". *Industrial Management Review* 2: 7–26.

25 Allais, M. (1953). Le Comportement de l'homme rationnel devant le risque: Critique des postulates

et axioms de l'école Americaine. *Econometrica* 21: 503–564.

26 Allen, F., and Douglas, G. (2000). Comparing Financial Systems, Cambridge, MA: The MIT Press.

27 Allen, L., and Peristiani, S. (2004). Conflicts of Interest in Merger Advisory Services. Baruch College, Working Paper.

28 Altman, E.I. (1968). "Financial ratios, discriminant analysis, and the prediction of corporate bankruptcy". *Journal of Finance* 23: 589–609

29 Altman, E.I. (1971). Corporate Bankruptcy in America, New York: Lexington Books.

30 Altman, E.I. (1983). Corporate Financial Distress: A Complete Guide to Predicting, Avoiding, and Dealing with Bankruptcy, New York: John Wiley & Sons.

31 Altman, E.I., and Robert, O.E. (1978). "Financial applications of discriminant analysis: A clarification". *Journal of Quantitative and Financial Analysis* 13(1): 185–195.

32 Altman, E.I., Robert, G.H., and Paul, N. (1977). "Zeta analysis: A new model to identify bankruptcy risk of corporations". *Journal of Banking and Finance* 1: 29–54.

33 Amemiya, T. (1981). "Qualitative response models: A survey". *Journal of Economic Literature* 19(4): 1483–1536.

34 Amihud, Y. (2002). "Illiquidity and stock returns: Cross-sectional and time-series effects". *Journal of Financial Markets* 5: 31–56.

35 Amihud, Y., and Haim, M. (1986). "Asset pricing and the bid-ask spread". *Journal of Financial Economics* 17: 223–250.

36 Amihud, Y., and Mendelson, H. (1980). "Dealership market: market making with inventory". *Journal of Financial Economics* 8: 31–53.

37 Amihud, Y., Haim, M., and Beni, L. (1997). "Market microstructure and securities values: Evidence from the Tel Aviv Stock Exchange". *Journal of Financial Economics* 45: 365–390.

38 Amihud, Y., Ho, T., and Schwartz, R.A. (eds.), (1985). Market Making and the Changing Structure of the Securities Industry. Lexington: Lexington Books.

39 Amin, K.L. (1993). "Jump diffusion option valuation in discrete time". *Journal of Finance* 48(50): 1833–1863.

40 Amram, M.H., and Nalin, H.K. (1999). "Real Options". Harvard Business School Press 11: 11–31.

41 Amsterdam; New York and Oxford: Elsevier, North-Holland (1995).

42 Andersson, H. (1999). "Capital Budgeting in a Situation with Variable Utilization of Capacity – An Example from the Pulp Industry". *SSE/EFI*, Working Paper.

43 Ang, J.S., and Jess, H.C. (1981). "Corporate bankruptcy and job losses among top level managers". *Financial Management* 10(5): 70–74.

44 Angel, J. (1998). How Best to Supply Liquidity to a Small-Capitalization Securities Market, Working Paper, Georgetown University.

45 Angel, J., and Daniel, W. (1998). Priority Rules! Working Paper, Rutgers University.

46 Anonymous. (1998). "IMFonomics". *The Wall Street Journal* 18.

47 Anonymous. (1998). "The IMF Crisis". *The Wall Street Journal* 22.

48 Anonymous. (1998). "What's an IMF for?" *The Wall Street Journal* 14.

49 Anson, M., Frank, J.P., Fabozzi, J., Chouray, M., and Chen, R.R. (2004). Credit Derivatives Instruments, Applications, and Pricing. New York: John Wiley & Sons, Inc.

50 APEC. (1999). Compendium of Sound Practices, Guidelines to Facilitate the Development of Domestic Bond Markets in APEC member Economies. Report of the Collaborative Initiative on Development of Domestic Bond Markets.

51 Arrow, K. (1965). Aspects of the Theory of Risk Bearing. Helsinki: Yrjo Jahnssonin Sattio.

52 Arrow, K.J. (1971). Essays in the Theory of Risk Bearing. Chicago: Markham Publishing Company.

53 Arthur, W.B. (1994). "Inductive reasoning and bounded rationality". *American Economic Review* 84(2): 406.

54 Arthur, W.B. (1999). Complexity and the economy. *Science* 284(5411): 107.

55 Arzac, E.R., Schwartz, R.A., and Whitcomb, D.K. (1981). "A theory and test of credit rationing: Some further results". *American Economic Review* 71: 735–777.

56 Asian Basket Currency (ABC) Bonds, February 2003.

57 Asness, C.S., Liew, J.M, and Stevens, R.L. (1996). Parallels between the cross-sectional predictability of stock returns and country returns. Working Paper, Goldman Sachs Asset Management.

58 Asquith, P., Beatty, A., and Weber, J. (2002). Performance pricing in debt contracts, Working Paper, Penn State University and MIT.

59 Asquith, P., Robert G.R., and Scharfstein, D. (1994). "Anatomy of financial distress: An

examination of junk bond issuers". *Quarterly Journal of Economics* 109(3): 625–658.

60 Audet, N., Gravelle, T., and Yang, J. (2001). Optimal market structure: Does one shoe fit all? Technical report, Ottawa, CA : Bank of Canada.

61 Avner, A. (1985). "Geberic stocks: An old product in a new package". *Journal of Portfolio Management*.

62 Azzi, C.F., and Cox, J.C. (1976). "A theory and test of credit rationing: comment". *American Economic Review* 66: 911–917.

B

1 Bachelier, L. (1900). Theory of speculation. In: Costner, P. (ed.), (1964). The Random Character of Stock Market Prices. Cambridge: MIT Press reprint.

2 Bacidore, J. (1997). "The impact of decimalization on market quality: An empirical investigation of the Toronto Stock Exchange". *Journal of Financial Intermediation* 6: 92–120.

3 Bacidore, J., Battalio, R., and Jennings, R. (2001). Order submission strategies, liquidity supply, and trading in pennies on the New York Stock Exchange, Working Paper, Indiana University.

4 Bacidore, J., Battalio, R., Jennings, R., and Farkas, S. (2001). Changes in order characteristics, displayed liquidity, and execution quality on the NYSE around the switch to decimal pricing, Working Paper, the New York Stock Exchange.

5 Bagehot, W. (1971). "The only game in town". *Financial Analysts Journal* 27: 12–14, 22.

6 Baillie, R.T., and Bollerslev, T. (1990). "A multivariate generalized ARCH approach to modeling risk premia in forward foreign exchange rate markets". *Journal of International Money and Finance* 9: 309–324.

7 Bakashi, G., and Zhiwu, C. (1998). Asset Pricing Without Consumption or Market Portfolio Data, Working Paper, University of Maryland.

8 Ball, C.A., and Torous, W.N. (1983). "A simplfied jump process for common stock returns". *Journal of Financial and Quantitative analysis* 18(1): 53–65.

9 Ball, C.A., and. Torous, W.N. (1985). "On jumps in common stock prices and their impact on call option pricing". *Journal of Finance* 40(1): 155–173.

10 Ball, C.A., Torous, W.N., and Tshoegl, A.E. (1985). "The degree of price resolution: The case of the gold market". *Journal of Futures Markets* 5: 29–43.

11 Ball, R.B., and Brown, P. (1968). "An Empirical Evaluation of Accounting Income Numbers". *Journal of Accounting Research* 6: 159–178.

12 Bandi, F.M., and Nguyen, T.H. (2003). "On the functional estimation of jump-diffusion models". *Journal of Econometrics* 116: 293–328.

13 Banerji, S., Chen, A.H., and Mazumda, S.C. (2002). "Universal banking under bilateral information asymmetry". *Journal of Financial Services Research* 22(3): 169–187.

14 Bansal, R., and Viswanathan, S. (1993). "No arbitrage and arbitrage pricing: A new approach". *Journal of Finance* 48: 1231–1262.

15 Bansal, R., Hsieh. D., and Viswanathan, S. (1993). "A new approach to international arbitrage pricing". *Journal of Finance* 48: 1719–1747.

16 Barberis, N., Shleifer, A. (2003). A Survey of Behavioral Finance. In: Stulz, R. (ed.), Handbook of the Economics of Finance. North Holland, Ch. 18.

17 Barberis, N., Shleifer, A. (2003). Behavioral Finance, Handbook of the Economics of Finance. In: George M. Constantinides, Milton Harris, and Rene M. Stulz (eds.), Chapter 18, North Holland: Elsevier Science Publishers.

18 Barberis, N., Shleifer, A., and Vishny, R. (1998). "A model of investor sentiment". *Journal of Financial Economics* 49: 307–343.

19 Barclay, M.J., Christie, W., Harris, J., Kandel, E., and Schultz, P. (1999). "Effects of market reform on the trading costs and depths of Nasdaq stocks". *Journal of Finance* 54: 1–34.

20 Barclay, M.J., Hendershott, T., and Jones, C.M. (2003). Which Witches Better? A Cross-Market Comparison of Extreme Liquidity Shocks, Working Paper, University of Rochester.

21 Barnea, A., Haugen, R., and Senbet, L. (1980). "A rationale for debt maturity structure and call provisions in an agency theoretic framework". *Journal of Finance* 35: 1223–1234.

22 Barnett, M. (1999). "Day trading can damage your wealth". *The Industry Standard* 19.

23 Barnett, M. (1999). "Individual Investors are Becoming Institutions". *Industry Standard* 33–34.

24 BarNiv, R., and Hathorn, J. (1997). "The Merger or Insolvency Alternative in the Insurance Industry". *Journal of Risk and Insurance* 64(1): 89–113.

25 Barro, R.J. and. Gordon, D.B. (1983). "Rules, discretion and reputation in a model of monetary policy". *Journal of Monetary Economics* 12: 101–121.

26 Barro, R.J., and Grossman, H.I. (1971). "A general disequilibrium model of income and employment". *American Economic Review* 61: 82–93.

27 Barth, J.R., Brumbaugh, R.D. Jr., and Wilcox, J. (2000). "Glass-Steagall repealed: Market forces compel a new bank legal structure". *Journal of Economic Perspective:* 191–204.

28 Barth, J.R., Caprio, G., and Levine, R. (2004). "Bank regulation and supervision: What works best?" *Journal of Financial Intermediation* 13(2): 205–248.

29 Barth, J.R., Caprio, G., and Levine, R. (2005). Rethinking Bank Regulation and Supervision: Till Angels Govern. Cambridge University Press.

30 Bartlett, W.W. (1989). Mortgage-Backed Securities: Products, Analysis, Trading. NJ: Prentice Hall, Englewood Cliffs.

31 Bates, D.S. (1991). "The crash of '87: was it expected ? The evidence from options markets". *Journal of Finance* 46(3): 1009–1044.

32 Bates, D.S. (1996). "Jumps and stochastic volatility: Exchange rate processes implicit in Deutsche Mark options". *Review of Financial Studies* 46(3): 1009–1044.

33 Battalio, R., Greene, J., and Jennings, R. (1998). "Order flow distribution, bid-ask spreads, and liquidity costs: Merrill Lynch's decision to cease routinely routing orders to regional stock exchanges". *Journal of Financial Intermediation* 7: 338–358.

34 Battalio, R., Greene, J., Hatch, B., and Jennings, R. (2002). "Does the limit order routing decision matter?" *Review of Financial Studies* 15(1): 159–194.

35 Batten, D.F. (2000). Discovering Artificial Economics: How Agents Learn and Economies Evolve. Boulder, CO: Westview Press.

36 Baum, C.F., Barkoulas, J.T., and Caglayan, M. (2001). "Nonlinear adjustment to purchasing power parity in the post-Bretton Woods era". *Journal of International Money and Finance* 20: 379–399.

37 Baysinger, B., and Butler, H. (1985). "The role of corporate law in the theory of the firm". *Journal of Law and Economics* 28: 179–191.

38 Beatty, A., Dichev, I.D., Weber, J. (2002). The role and characteristics of accounting-based performance pricing in private debt contracts, Working Paper, Penn State University, University of Michigan, and MIT.

39 Beaver, W. (1966). "Financial Ratios as Predictors of Failure". *Journal of Accounting Research* 4 (Supplement): 71–111.

40 Bebchuk, L. (1992). "Federalism and the corporation: The desirable limits on state competition in corporate law". *Harvard Law Review* 105: 1435–1510.

41 Bebchuk, L., and Cohen, A. (2002). Firms' decisions where to incorporate, Discussion, Paper No. 351. Cambridge, Mass: Harvard Law School, Olin Center for Law, Economics, and Business. www.law.harvard.edu/programs/olin_center.

42 Bebchuk, L., and Ferrell, A. (1999). "Federalism and corporate law: The race to protect managers from takeovers". *Columbia Law Review* 99: 1168–1199.

43 Bebchuk, L.A., and Cohen, A. (2003). "Firms' decisions where to incorporate". *Journal of Law and Economics* 46: 383–425.

44 Beck, T., Demirguc-Kunt, A., and Maksimovic, V. (2004). "Bank competition and access to finance: International evidence". *Journal of Money, Credit, and Banking* 36: 627–649.

45 Becker, C., Ferson, W., Myers, D., and. Schill, M. (1999). "Conditional Market timing with Benchmark investors". *Journal of Financial Economics* 52: 119–148.

46 Becker, G. (1998). "You want high retruns? Brace yourself for high risk". *Business Week* 15.

47 Becker, G., and. Murphy, K.M. (1988). "A theory of rational addiction". *Journal of Political Economy* 96: 675–700.

48 Beckers, S. (1981). "A note on estimating the parameters of the diffusion-jump model of stock returns". *Journal of Financial and Quantitative Analysis* XVI(1): 127–140.

49 Becketti, S. and Morris, C.S. (1990). The Prepayment Experience of FNMA Mortgage Backed Securities, Monograph Series in Finance and Economics, Saloman Center, New York University.

50 Beebower, G., Kamath, V., and Surz, R. (1985). Commission and transaction costs of stock market trading, Working Paper, SEI Corporation, 28 pp.

51 Beja, A. (1971). "The structure of the cost of capital under uncertainty". *Review of Economic Studies* 4: 359–369.

52 Bekaert, G., and Hodrick, R.J. (1993). "On biases in the measurement of foreign exchange risk premiums". *Journal of International Money and Finance* 12: 115–138.

53 Benartzi, S., and Thaler, R. (1995). "Myopic loss aversion and the equity premium puzzle". *The Quarterly Journal of Economics* 110(1): 73–92.

54 Benartzi, S., and Thaler, R. (1999). "Risk aversion or myopia? Choices in repeated gambles and

retirement investments". *Management Science* 45(3): 364–381.

55 Benartzi, S., and Thaler, R. (2001). "Naive diversification strategies in retirement savings plans". *American Economic Review* 91(1): 79–98.

56 Benninga, S., and Protopapadakis, A. (1983). "Nominal and real interest rates under uncertainty: The Fisher theorem and the term structure". *The Journal of Political Economy* 91(5): 856–867.

57 Bensaid, B., Lesne, J.-P., Pages, H., and Scheinkman, J. (1992). "Derivative asset pricing with transactions costs". *Mathematical Finance* 2: 63–86.

58 Berger, A.N., and Hannan, T.H. (1989). "The price-concentration relationship in banking". *The Review of Economics and Statistics* 71: 291–299.

59 Berger, A.N., and Udell, G.F. (1990). "Collateral, loan quality and bank risk". *Journal of Monetary Economics* 25: 21–42.

60 Berger, A.N., and Udell, G.F. (1995). "Relationship lending and lines of credit in small firm finance". *Journal of Business* 68: 351–381.

61 Berk, J. (1995). "A critique of size-related anomalies". *Review of Financial Studies* 8: 275–286.

62 Bernanke, B., and Blinder, A. (1988). "Credit, money, and aggregate demand". *American Economic Review* 78: 435–439.

63 Bernhardt, D., and. Hughson, E.N. (1996). "Discrete pricing and the design of dealership markets". *Journal of Economic Theory* 71.

64 Bernstein, P. (1987). Liquidity, stock markets, and market makers. *Financial Management* 16: 54–62.

65 Bernstein, P. (2003). "Real estate matters". *The Journal of Portfolio Management: Special Real Estate Issue* 1 pp.

66 Besanko, D., and Thakor, A.V. (1987). "Collateral and rationing: Sorting equilibria in monopolistic and competitive credit markets". *International Economic Review* 28: 671–690.

67 Bessembinder, H. (1999). "Trade execution costs on Nasdaq and the NYSE: A post-reform comparison". *Journal of Financial and Quantitative Analysis* 34: 387–407.

68 Bessembinder, H. (2002). "Trade execution costs and market quality after decimalization". *Journal of Financial and Quantitative Analysis*.

69 Bessembinder, H. (2003). "Trade execution costs and market quality after decimalization". *Journal of Financial and Quantitative Analysis*.

70 Bessembinder, H. (2004). "Quote-based competition and trade execution costs in NYSE-listed stocks". *Journal of Financial Economics*.

71 Bessembinder, H., and Kaufman, H. (1997). "A comparison of trade execution costs for NYSE and Nasdaq-listed stocks". *Journal of Financial and Quantitative Analysis* 32: 287–310.

72 Best, M.J., and Grauer, R.R. (1991). "On the sensitivity of mean variance efficient portfolios to changes in asset means: Some analytical and computational results". *The Review of Financial Studies* 4(2): 315–342.

73 Bester, H. (1985). "Screening vs. rationing in credit markets with imperfect information". *American Economic Review* 57: 850–855.

74 Bester, H. (1987). "The role of collateral in credit markets with imperfect information". *European Economic Review* 31: 887–899.

75 Bester, H. (1994), "The role of collateral in a model of debt renegotiation". *Journal of Money Credit and Banking* 26: 72–86.

76 Bhattacharya, S. (1981). "Notes on multiperiod valuation and the pricing of options". *Journal of Finance* 36: 163–180.

77 Bhattacharya, S., and Pfleiderer, P. (1983). A note on performance evaluation, Technical report 714, Stanford University Graduate School of Business.

78 Bhattcharya, S., and Chiesa, G. (1995)."Proprietary information, financial intermediation, and research incentives". *Journal of Financial Intermediation* 4: 328–357.

79 Bhide, A.V. (2000). The Origin and Evolution of New Business. Oxford University, England.

80 Biais, B., Hillion, P., and Spatt, C.S. (1995). "An empirical analysis of the limit order book and the order flow in the Paris Bourse, *Journal of Finance* 50(5)

81 Bierwag, G.O. (1977). "Immunization, duration, and the term Structure of interest rates". *Journal of Financial and Quantitative Analysis* 725–741.

82 Bierwag, G.O. (1987a). Duration Analysis, Managing Interest Rate Risk, Cambridge. MA : Ballinger Publishing Company.

83 Bierwag, G.O. (1987b). "Bond returns, discrete stochastic processes, and duration". *Journal of Financial Research* 10.

84 Bierwag, G.O. (1996). "The Ho-Lee binomial stochastic process and duration". *The Journal of Fixed Income* 6(2): 76–87.

85 Bierwag, G.O. (1997). Duration Analysis: A Historical Perspective, Document, School of Business, Miami International University.

86 Bierwag, G.O., and Kaufman, G.G. (1977). "Coping with the risk of interest-rate fluctuations: A note". *Journal of Business* 364–370.

87 Bierwag, G.O., and Kaufman, G.G. (1985). "Duration gaps for financial institutions". *Financial Analysts Journal* 68–71.

88 Bierwag, G.O., and Kaufman, G.G. (1988). "Duration of non-default free securities". *Financial Analysts Journal* 44(4): 39–46; published as a monograph to members of the Institute of Chartered Financial Analysis. (July/August)

89 Bierwag, G.O., and Kaufman, G.G. (1992). "Duration gaps with futures and swaps for managing interest rate risk at depository institutions". *Journal of Financial Services Research* 5(3): 217–234.

90 Bierwag, G.O., and Kaufman, G.G. (1996). "Managing interest rate risk with duration gaps to achieve multiple targets". *Journal of Financial Engineering*.

91 Bierwag, G.O., and Khang, C. (1979). "An immunization strategy is a maximin strategy". *Journal of Finance* 389–399.

92 Bierwag, G.O., and Roberts, G.S. (1990). "Single factor duration models: Canadian tests". *Journal of Financial Research* 13: 23–38.

93 Bierwag, G.O., Corrado, C., and. Kaufman, G.G. (1990). "Macaulay durations for bond portfolios". *Journal of Portfolio Management*.

94 Bierwag, G.O., Corrado, C., and Kaufman, G.G. (1992). "Durations for portfolios of bonds priced on different term structures". *Journal of Banking and Finance* 16(4): 705–714.

95 Bierwag, G.O., Fooladi, I., and Roberts, G. (1993). "Designing and immunization portfolio: Is m-squared the key?" *Journal of Banking and Finance*, 1147–1170.

96 Bierwag, G.O., Kaufman, G.G., and Khang, C. (1978). "Duration and bond portfolio analysis: an overview". *Journal of Financial and Quantitative Analysis* 671–679.

97 Bierwag, G.O., Kaufman, G.G., and Latta, C. (1987). "Bond portfolio immunization: Tests of maturity, one- and two - factor duration matching strategies". *Financial Review*.

98 Bierwag, G.O., Kaufman, G.G., and Toevs, A. (1982b). Empirical Tests of Alternative Single Factor Duration Models, Paper Presented at Western Finance Association, Portland, Oregon.

99 Bierwag, G.O., Kaufman, G.G., and Toevs, A. (1983a). "Bond portfolio immunization and stochastic process risk" *Journal of Bank Research* 13:282–291.

100 Bierwag, G.O., Kaufman, G.G., and Toevs, A. (1983b). "Immunization strategies for funding multiple liabilities". *Journal of Financial and Quantitative Analysis* 18: 113–124.

101 Bierwag, G.O., Kaufman, G.G., and Toevs, A.T. (1982a). "Single factor duration models in a discrete general equilibrium framework". *The Journal of Finance* 37: 325–338.

102 Bierwag, G.O., Kaufman, G.G., Schweitzer, R., and Toevs, A. (1981). "The art of risk management in bond portfolios". *Journal of Portfolio Management* 7: 27–36.

103 Billingsley, R.S., and Lamy, R.E. (1988). "The regulation of international lending-IMF support, the debt crisis, and bank stockholder wealth". *Journal of Banking and Finance* 12: 255–274.

104 Birnbaum, M.H. (1999). The Paradoxes of Allais, stochastic dominance, and decision weights. In: J. Shanteau, B. A. Mellers, and D. A. Schum (eds.), *Decision science and technology: Reflections on the contributions of Ward Edwards*. Boston, MA: Kluwer Academic Publishers.

105 Birnbaum, M.H., and McIntosh, W.R. (1996). "Violations of branch independence in choices between gambles". *Organizational Behavior and Human Decision Processes* 67: 91–110.

106 Black, F. and Scholes, M. (1973). "The pricing of options and corporate liabilities". *Journal of Political Economy* 81: 637–659.

107 Black, F., (1971). "Capital market equilibrium with restricted borrowing". *Journal of Business* 45: 444–454.

108 Black, F., Jensen, M.C, and Scholes, M. (1972). The Capital Asset Pricing Model: Some Empirical Tests. In: M.C. Jensen (ed.), *Studies in the Theory of Capital Markets*. New York: Praeger Publishers, Inc.

109 Blinder, A.S. (1987). "Credit rationing and effective supply failures". *The Economic Journal* 97: 327–352.

110 Blinder, A.S., and Stiglitz, J. (1983). "Money, credit constraints, and economic activity". *American Economic Review* 73: 297–302.

111 Blum, M. (1974). "Failing company discriminant analysis". *Journal of Accounting Research* 12(1): 1–25.

112 Blume, L., Easley, D., and O'Hara, M. (1994). "Market statistics and technical analysis: The role of volume". *Journal of Finance* 49: 153–181.

113 Bodie, Z. (1996). "What the pension benefit guarantee corporation can learn from the federal savings and loan insurance corporation". *Journal of Financial Services Research*, 10 (March), 83–100.

114 Bolton, P., and Scharfstein, D. (1996), "Optimal debt structure and the number of creditors". *Journal of Political Economy* 104: 1–25.

115 Boot, A., and Thakor, A. (2000). "Financial system architecture". *Review of Financial Studies* 10(3): 693–733.

116 Boot, A.W. (2000). "Relationship banking: What do we know?" *Journal of Financial Intermediation* 9: 7–25.

117 Boot, A.W., and Thakor, A.V. (2000). "Can relationship banking survive competition?" *Journal of Finance* 55: 679–713.

118 Boot, A.W., Thakor, A.V., and Udell, G.F. (1991). "Collateralized lending and default risk: Equilibrium analysis, policy implications and empirical results". *Economic Journal* 101: 458–472.

119 Boyle, P., and Vorst, T. (1992). "Option pricing in discrete time with transactions costs". *Journal of Finance* 47: 271–293.

120 Bradley, C.M. (2000). "A historical perspective on deposit insurance coverage". *FDIC-Banking Review* 13(2): 1–25.

121 Bradley, M. (1980). "Interfirm tender offers and the market for corporate control". *Journal of Business* 53(4): 345–376.

122 Bradley, M., Capozza, D., and Seguin, P. (1998). "Dividend policy and cash-flow uncertainty". *Real Estate Economics* 26: 555–580.

123 Bradley, M., Desai A., and Han Kim, E. (1983). "The rationale behind interfirm tender offers: information or synergy". *Journal of Financial Economics* 11(4): 183–206.

124 Branson, W.H. (1988). "Comments on political vs. currency premia in international real interest differentials: A study of forward rates for 24 countries". By Frankel, J.A., and MacArthur, A.T., *European Economic Review* 32: 1083–1114.

125 Braun, P., Ferson, W.E., and George, M. (1993). "Constantinides, time nonseparability in aggregate consumption: international evidence". *European Economic Review* 37: 897–920.

126 Brealey, R.A. and. Myers, S.C. (1988). Principals of Corporate Finance, 3rd ed., New York, NY: McGraw-Hill.

127 Brealey, R.A., Myers, S.C., and. Marcus, A.J (2001). Fundamentals of Corporate Finance, 3rd ed., New York: McGraw-Hill Companies, Inc.

128 Breeden, D. (1979). "An intertemporal asset pricing model with stochastic consumption and investment opportunities". *Journal of Financial Economics* 7: 265–296.

129 Brennan, M., and Schwartz, E. (1978). "Finite difference methods and jump processes arising in the pricing of contingent claims: A synthesis". *Journal of Financial and Quantitative Analysis* 13: 461–474.

130 Brennan, M., and Schwartz, E. (1985). "Determinants of GNMA mortgage prices". *AREUEA Journal* 13: 209–228.

131 Brennan, M.J., and Kraus, A. (1978) "Necessary conditions for aggregation in securities markets". *Journal of Financial and Quantitative Analysis* 407–418.

132 Brennan, M.J., and Schwartz, E. (1979). "A continuous time approach to the pricing of bonds". *Journal of Banking and Finance* 3: 133–155.

133 Brennan, M.J., and Schwartz, E.S. (1985). "Evaluating natural resource investment." *Journal of Business* 58: 135–157.

134 Brennan, M.J., and Subrahmanyam, A. (1996). "Market microstructure and asset pricing: On the compensation for illiquidity in stock returns". *Journal of Financial Economics* 41(3): 441–464.

135 Brennan, Michael J., and Schwartz, E.S. (1983). Duration, Bond Pricing, and Portfolio Management. In: Kaufman, G.G., Bierwag, G. O., and Toevs, A. (eds.), Innovations in Bond Portfolio Management, Duration Analysis and Immunization, Proceedings from the Ashland Conference, 1981, Greenwich, Conn: JAI PRESS, Inc.

136 Brent, R.P. (1971). Algorithms for Minimization without Derivatives. Prentice-Hall.

137 Brigham, E.F., and Daves, P.R. (2004). Intermediate Financial Management, 8th edition Mason, Ohio: Thomson Southwestern Publishing 617–620.

138 Brigham, E.F., and Houston, J. (2001). Fundamentals of Financial Management. 9th ed., Orlando, FL: Harcourt.

139 Britten-Jones, M., (1999). "The sampling error in estimates of mean efficient portfolio weight". *The Journal of Finance* 54(2): 655–671.

140 Brockman, P., and Dennis, C. (2000). "Informed and uninformed trading in an electronic, order-driven environment". *Financial Review* 125–146.

141 Broome, L.L., and Markham, J.W. (2000). "Banking and insurance: Before and after the Gramm-Leach-Bliley Act". *Journal of Corporation Law* 25(4): 723–785.

142 Brotherton-Ratcliffe (1994). "Monte Carlo Monitoring". *Risk* 53–58.

143 Brown, D.T., James, C.M., and Mooradian, R.M. (1993). "The information content of distressed restructurings involving public and private debt claims". *Journal of Financial Economics* 33(1): 93–118.

144 Brown, D.T., James, C.M., and Mooradian R.M. (1994). "Asset sales by financially distressed firms". *Journal of Corporate Finance* 1(2): 233–257.

145 Brown, S., Laux, P., and Schachter, B. (1991). "On the existence of an optimal tick size". *Review of Futures Markets* 10: 50–72.

146 Brueggeman, W., and Fisher, J. (2001). Real Estate Finance and Investments, McGraw-Hill, IRWIN.

147 Bruner, R.F., and Simms, J.M. (1987). "The international debt crisis and bank security returns in 1982". *Journal of Money, Credit and Banking* 19(1): 46–55.

148 Bulow, J., and Shoven, J. (1978). "The bankruptcy decision". *The Bell Journal of Economics* 9(2): 437–456.

149 Burgess, R.C., and Johnson, K.H. (1976). "The effects of sampling fluctuations on required inputs of security analysis". *Journal of Financial and Quantitative Analysis* 11: 847–854.

150 Burmeister, E., and McElroy, M.B. (1988). "Joint estimation of factor sensitivities and risk premia for the arbitrage pricing theory". *Journal of Finance* 43(3): 721–733.

151 Buser, S.A., and Hendershott, P.H. (1983). "Pricing default-free fixed-rate mortgages". *Housing Finance Review* 3: 405–429.

152 Busse, J. (1999). "Volatility timing in mutual funds: Evidence from daily returns". *Review of Financial Studies*.

C

1 Calmfors, L. (1998). "Macroeconomic policy, wage setting, and employment – what difference does the EMU make?" *Oxford Review of Economic Policy* 14(3): 125–151.

2 Camdessus, M. (1998). "The IMF and Good Governance". Addressed in Paris on January 21, http://www.imf.org/external/np/speeches.

3 Camdessus, M. (1998). An address at the press conference in Kuala Lumpur, January 16, http://www.web.org.

4 Campbell, J. (1987). "Stock returns and the term structure". *Journal of Financial Economics* 18: 373–399.

5 Campbell, J. (1996). "Understanding risk and return". *Journal of Political Economy* 104: 298–345.

6 Campbell, J., and Shiller, R. (1991). "Yield spreads and interest rate movements: A bird's eye view". *Review of Economic Studies* 58: 495–514.

7 Campbell, J., Lo, A., and MacKinley, A. (1997). The Econometrics of Financial Markets. Princeton, NJ: Princeton University Press.

8 Campbell, J.Y. (1987). "Stock returns and the term structure". *Journal of Financial Economics* 18: 373–399.

9 Campbell, J.Y. (1991). "A variance decomposition for stock returns". *Economic Journal* 101: 157–179.

10 Campbell, J.Y. (1993). "Intertemporal asset pricing without consumption data". *American Economic Review* 83: 487–512.

11 Campbell, J.Y., and Cochrane J.H. (1999). "By force of habit: A consumption-based explanation of aggregate stock market behavior". *Journal of Political Economy* 107: 205–251.

12 Campbell, J.Y., Lo, A., and MacKinlay, A.C. (1997). The Econometrics of Financial Markets. Princeton, NJ: Princeton University Press.

13 Caouette, J.B., Altman E.I., and Narayanan, P. (1998). Managing Credit Risk: The Next Great Financial Challenge. New York: John Wiley & Sons.

14 Carey, M., Post, M., and Sharpe, S.A. (1998). "Does corporate lending by banks and finance companies differ? Evidence on specialization in private debt contracting". *Journal of Finance* 53: 845–878.

15 Carhart, M.M. (1997). "On persistence in mutual fund performance". *Journal of Finance* 52: 57–82.

16 Carling, R.G. (1995). Fiscal and monetary policies, In: Bercuson, K. (ed.), Singapore: A Case Study in Rapid Development, IMF Occasional Paper 119. Washington DC: International Monetary Fund.

17 Carow, K.A., and Randall, A.H. (2002). "Capital market reactions to the passage of the financial services modernization act of 1999". *Quarterly Review of Economics and Finance* 42(3): 465–485.

18 Carpenter, J., Dybvig, P.H., and Farnsworth, H. (2000). Portfolio Performance and Agency, Working Paper. St. Louis: Washington University.

19 Carrera, J.M. (1999). "Speculative attacks to currency target zones: A market microstructure approach". *Journal of Empirical Finance* 6: 555–582.

20 Cary, W. (1974). "Federalism and corporate law: Reflections upon delaware". *Yale Law Journal* 83: 663–707.

21 Castellano, M. (1999). "Japanese foreign aid: A lifesaver for east asia?". *Japan Economic Institute* 6A: 5.

22 Chacko, G., and Viceria L.M. (2003). "Spectral GMM estimation of continuous time processes". *Journal of Econometrics* 116: 259–292.

23 Chakravarty, S., Harris, S., and Wood, R. (2001a). Decimal Trading and Market Impact, Working Paper, University of Memphis.

24 Chakravarty, S., Harris, S., and Wood, R. (2001b). Decimal Trading and Market Impact: The Nasdaq Experience, Working Paper. University of Memphis.

25 Chamberlain, G. (1983). "Funds, factors and diversification in arbitrage pricing models". *Econometrica* 51: 1305–1324.

26 Chamberlain, G. (1988). "Asset pricing in multiperiod securities markets". *Econometrica* 56: 1283–1300.

27 Chamberlain, G., and Rothschild, M. (1983). "Arbitrage, factor structure and mean variance analysis on large asset markets". *Econometrica* 51: 1281–1304.

28 Chambers, D.R., Carleton, W.T., and McEnally, R.W. (1988). "Immunizing default-free bond portfolios with a duration vector". *Journal of Financial and Quantitative Analysis* 23(1): 89–104.

29 Chan, K., Hameed, A., and Tong, W. (2000). "Profitability of momentum strategies in the international equity markets". *Journal of Financial and Quantitative Analysis* 35: 153–172.

30 Chan, K.C., and Chen, Nai-fu (1988). "An unconditional test of asset pricing and the role of firm size as an instrumental variable for risk". *Journal of Finance* 63: 431–468.

31 Chan, W.H., and Maheu, J.M. (2002). "Conditional jump dynamics in stock market returns". *Journal of Business and Economic Statistics* 20(3): 377–389.

32 Chan, Y., and Kanatas, G. (1985). "Asymmetric valuations and the role of collateral in loan agreements". *Journal of Money Credit and Banking* 17: 84–95.

33 Chance, D.M. (1990). "Default risk and the duration of zero coupon bonds". *Journal of Finance* 45(1): 265–274.

34 Chance, D.M. (1991). An Introduction to Options and Futures, 2nd ed. Orlando, FL: Dryden.

35 Chang, E.C. and Lewellen, W.G. (1984). "Market timing and mutual fund investment performance". *Journal of Business* 57: 55–72.

36 Chang, Jow-ran, and Hung, Mao-wei (2000). "An international asset pricing model with time-varying hedging risk". *Review of Quantitative Finance and Accounting* 15: 235–257.

37 Chang, Jow-ran, Errunza, V., Hogan, K., and Hung, Mao-wei (2004). "Disentangling exchange risk from intertemporal hedging risk: Theory and empirical evidence". *Euorpean Financial Management* 11(2): 173–194.

38 Chatterjee, S. (1986). "Types of synergy and economic value: The impact of acquisitions on merging and rival firms". *Strategic Management Journal* 7(2): 119–139.

39 Chen, N., Roll, R., and Ross, S. (1986). "Economic forces and the stock market". *Journal of Business* 59: 383–403.

40 Chen, Nai-fu, Copeland, T., and Mayers, D. (1987). "A comparison of single and multifactor performance methodologies". *Journal of Financial and Quantitative Analysis* 22: 401–417.

41 Chen, Nai-fu. (1983). "Some empirical tests of the theory of arbitrage pricing". *Journal of Finance* 38: 1393–1414.

42 Chen, Shu-Heng., and Yeh, Chia-Hsuan (2001). "Evolving traders and the business school with genetic programming: A new architecture of the agent-based artificial stock market". *Journal of Economic Dynamics and Control* 25(3/4): 363.

43 Chen, Son-Nan, and Lee, Cheng-Few (1981). "The sampling relationship between Sharpe's performance measure and its risk proxy: Sample size, investment horizon and market conditions". *Management Science* 27(6): 607–618.

44 Chen, Son-Nan, and Lee, Cheng-Few (1984). "On measurement errors and ranking of three alternative composite performance measures". *Quarterly Review of Economics and Business* 24: 7–17.

45 Chen, Son-Nan, and Lee, Cheng-Few (1986). "The effects of the sample size, the investment horizon and market conditions on the validity of composite performance measures: A generalization". *Management Science* 32(11): 1410–1421.

46 Chen, Y. (2003). On Conditional Market Timing of Hedge Fund Manager's Working Paper, Boston College.

47 Chen, Y., Ferson, W., and Peters, H. (2004). Measuring the Timing Ability of Fixed-Income Mutual Funds, Working Paper. Boston College.

48 Chen, Z. (1995). "Financial innovation and arbitrage pricing in frictional economies". *Journal of Economic Theory* 65: 117–135.

49 Chen, Z., and Knez, P.J. (1996). "Portfolio performance measurement: Theory and applications". *Review of Financial Studies* 9: 511–556.

50 Cheung, Y.W., and Lai, K.S. (1993). "Long-run purchasing power parity during the recent float". *Journal of International Economics* 34: 181–192.

51 Cheung, Y.W., and Lai, K.S. (1998). "Parity reversion in real exchange rates during the post-Bretton Woods period". *Journal of International Money and Finance* 17: 597–614.

52 Cheung, Y.W., and Wong Clement, Y.P. (2000). "A survey market practitioners' view on exchange rate dynamics". *Journal of International Economics* 51: 401–423.

53 Chiang, T.C. (1988). "The forward rate as a predictor of the future spot rate - a stochastic coefficient approach". *Journal of Money, Credit and Banking* 20: 210–232.

54 Chiang, T.C. (1991). "International asset pricing and equity market risk". *Journal of International Money and Finance* 10: 349–364.

55 Chiang, T.C., and Trinidad, J. (1997). "Risk and international parity conditions: A synthesis from consumption-based models". *International Economic Journal* 11: 73–101.

56 Cho, C.D., Eun, C.S., and Senbet, L.W. (1986). "International arbitrage pricing theory: An empirical investigation". *Journal of Finance* 41: 313–330.

57 Chopra, V.K. (1991). "Mean variance revisited: Near optimal portfolios and sensitivity to input variations". *Russell Research Commentary*.

58 Chopra, V.K., and Ziemba, W.T. (1993). "The effect of errors in mean, variances and covariances on optimal portfolio choice". *Journal of Portfolio Management* 19: 6–11.

59 Chordia, T., Roll, R., and Subrahmanyam, A. (2002). "Order imbalance, liquidity, and market returns". *Journal of Financial Economics* 65: 111–131.

60 Chretien, S., and Cliff, M. (2001). "Assessing Asset Pricing Models With A Returns Decomposition, Working Paper, Purdue University.

61 Christie, W., and Schultz, P. (1994). "Why do Nasdaq market makers avoid odd-eighth quotes?" *Journal of Finance* 49: 1813–1840.

62 Christie, W.G., and Schultz, P.H. (1994a). "Why do NASDAQ market makers avoid odd-eighth quotes?" *Journal of Finance* 49: 1813–1840.

63 Christie, W.G., Harris, J., and Schultz, P.H. (1994b). "Why did NASDAQ market makers stop avoiding odd-eighth quotes?" *Journal of Finance* 49: 1841–1860.

64 Christopher, J.W., and Lewarne, S. (1994). "An expository model of credit rationing". *Journal of Macroeconomics* 16(3): 539–545.

65 Christopherson, J.A., Ferson, W., and Glassman, D.A. (1998). "Conditioning manager alpha on economic information: Another look at the persistence of performance". *Review of Financial Studies* 11: 111–142.

66 Chu, Q.C., Lee, C.F., and Pittman, D.N. (1995). "On the inflation risk premium". *Journal of Business, Finance, and Accounting* 22(6): 881–892.

67 Chui, A., and Kwok, C. (1998). "Cross-autocorrelation between A shares and B shares in the Chinese stock market". *Journal of Financial Research* 21: 333–354.

68 Chui, A.C.W., Titman, S., and John Wei, K.C. (2002). Momentum, Legal System, and Ownership Structure: An Analysis of Asian Stock Markets, Working Paper, Austin: University of Texas.

69 Chung, K., Chuwonganant, C., and McCormick, T. (2004). "Order preferencing and market quality on Nasdaq before and after decimalization". *Journal of Financial Economics* 71: 581–612.

70 Chung, K., Van-Ness, B., and Van-Ness, R. (2001). Are Nasdaq Stocks More Costly to Trade than NYSE Stocks? Evidence after Decimalization, Working Paper, Kansas State University.

71 Chung, K.H., and Chuwonganant, C. (2000). Tick Size and Trading Costs: NYSE vs. Nasdaq, Working Paper, Buffalo University.

72 Claessens, S., Djankov, S., Fan, J.P.H., and Lang, L.H.P. (1998). "Corporate Diversification in East Asia: The Role of Ultimate Ownership and Group Affiliation". Working Paper, World Bank.

73 Clark, P.K. (1973). "A subordinated stochastic process model with finite variance for speculative prices". *Econometrica* 41(1): 135–155.

74 Cochrane, J.H. (1996). "A cross-sectional test of an investment based asset pricing model". *Journal of Political Economy* 104: 572–621.

75 Cochrane, J.H. (2001). Asset Pricing. Princeton and Oxford: Princeton University Press.

76 Coco, G. (1999). "Collateral and heterogeneity in risk attitudes and credit market equilibrium". *European Economic Review* 43: 559–574.

77 Coggin, T.D. (1998). "Long-term memory in equity style index". *Journal of Portfolio Management* 24(2): 39–46.

78 Cohen, K., Conroy, R., and Maier, S. (1985). Order flow and the quality of the market. In: Amihud, Ho, and Schwartz, (eds.), Market Making and The Changing Structure of the Securities Industry (Lexington, Mass).

79 Cohen, K., Maier, S., Schwartz, R.A., and Whitcomb, D. (1979). "Market makers and the market spread: A review of recent literature". *Journal of Financial and Quantitative Analysis* 14: 813–835.

80 Cohen, K., Maier, S., Schwartz, R.A., and Whitcomb, D. (1986). The Microstructure of Securities

Markets. Englewood Cliffs, New Jersey: Prentice-Hall.

81 Cohen, K.J., and Pogue, J.A. (1967). "An empirical evaluation of alternative portfolio selection models". *Journal of Business* 40: 166–189.

82 Cohen, K.J., and Schwartz, R.A. (1989). An electronic call market: Its design and desirability. In: Lucas, H., and Schwartz, R.A. (eds.), The Challenge of Information Technology for the Securities Markets: Liquidity, Volatility, and Global Trading. pp. 15–58.

83 Coleman, A.D.F., Esho, N., and Sharpe, I.G. (2002). Do Bank Characteristics Influence Loan Contract Terms, Working Paper, University of New South Wales.

84 Compbell, J.Y., and Shiller R. (1988). "Stock prices, earnings and expected dividends". *Journal of Finance* 43: 661–676.

85 Conn, R.L., and Connell, F. "International mergers: Returns to U.S. and British Firms". *Journal of Business Finance and Accounting* 17(5): 689–712.

86 Connor, D. (1984). "A unified beta pricing theory". *Journal of Economic Theory* 34: 13–31.

87 Connor, G. (1984). "A Unified beta pricing theory". *Journal of Economic Theory* 34: 13–31.

88 Connor, G., and Korajczyck, R. (1988). "Risk and return in an equilibrium APT: Application of a new test methodology". *Journal of Financial Economics* 21: 255–290.

89 Connor, G., and Korajczyk, R.A. (1986). "Performance measurement with the arbitrage pricing theory: A new framework for analysis". *Journal of Financial Economics* 15: 373–394.

90 Conrad, J., and Kaul, G. (1988). "Time-variation in expected returns." *Journal of Business* 61(4): 409–425.

91 Conrad, J., and Kaul, G. (1989). "Mean reversion in short-horizon expected returns". *Review of Financial Studies* 2: 225–240.

92 Conrad, J., and Kaul, G. (1998). "An anatomy of trading strategies". *Review of Financial Studies* 11: 489–519.

93 Constantinides, G.M. (1978). "Market risk adjustment in project valuation". *Journal of Finance* 33: 603–616.

94 Constantinides, G.M. (1982). "Intertemporal asset pricing with heterogeneous consumers and without demand aggregation. *Journal of Business* 55: 253–267.

95 Constantinides, G.M. (1990). "Habit formation: A resolution of the equity premium puzzle". *Journal of Political Economy* 98: 519–543.

96 Constantinides, G.M., and Duffie, D. (1996). "Asset pricing with heterogenous consumers". *Journal of Political Economy* 104: 219–240.

97 Cooper, J. (2001). "Hey, chicken littles, the sky isn't falling". *Business Week* 12: 43.

98 Cooper, K., Groth, J., and Avera, W. (1985). "Liquidity, exchange listing, and common stock performance". *Journal of Economics and Business* 37(1): 19–33.

99 Cooper, R., and Ross, T.W. (2002). "Bank runs: Deposit insurance and capital requirements". *International Economic Review* 43(1): 55–72.

100 Copeland, T., and Antikarov, V. (2001). Real Options: A Practitioner's Guide, New York: Texere.

101 Copeland, T.E., and Mayers, D. (1982). "The value line enigma (1965–1978): A case study of performance evaluation issues". *Journal of Financial Economics* 10: 289–321.

102 Copeland, T.E., and Weston, J.F. (1988). Financial Theory and Corporate Policy, 3rd ed., Reading: Addison-Wesley.

103 Copeland, T.E., Weston, J.F., and Shastri, K. (2005). Financial Theory and Corporate Policy, 4th ed., Upper Saddle River, NJ: Pearson Addison Wesley.

104 Cordella, T., and Foucault, T. (1999). "Minimum price variations, time priority and quote dynamics". *Journal of Financial Intermediation* 8(3).

105 Cornell, B. (1979). "Asymmetric information and portfolio performance measurement". *Journal of Financial Economics* 7: 381–390.

106 Cornell, B. (1989). "The impact of data errors on measurement of the foreign exchange risk premium". *Journal of International Money and Finance* 8: 147–157.

107 Cornell, B., and Shapiro, A. (1986). "The reaction of bank stock prices to the international debt crisis". *Journal of Banking and Finance* 10: 55–73.

108 Cosslett, S.R. (1981). Efficient estimation of discrete-choice models. In: Manski, C.F., and McFadden, D. (eds.), Structural Analysis of Discrete Data with Econometric Applications, London: MIT Press. pp. 51–111.

109 Coughenour, J., and Harris, L. (2003). Specialist Profits and the Minimum Price Increment, Working Paper.

110 Counsell, G. (1989). "Focus on workings of insolvency act". *The Independent* 4th April.

111 Covitz, D., and Heitfield, E. (1999). Monitoring, moral hazard, and market power: A model of bank lending, Finance and Economics Discussion Series 37, Board of Governors of the Federal Reserve System.

112 Cox, J., and Ross, S. (1976). "The valuation of options for alternative stochastic processes". *Journal of Financial Economics* 3: 145–166.

113 Cox, J.C., and Ross, S.A. (1976). "The valuation of options for alternative stochastic processes". *Journal of Financial Economics* 3: 145–166.

114 Cox, J.C., Ingersoll, J.E., and Ross, S.A. (1985). "A theory of the term structure of interest rates". *Econometrica* 53: 385–408.

115 Cox, J.C., Ingersoll, Jr., J.E., and Ross, S.A. (1985a). "An intertemporal general equilibrium model of asset prices". *Econometrica* 53: 363–384.

116 Cox, J.C., Ingersoll, Jr., J.E., and Ross, S.A. (1985b). "A theory of the term structure of interest rates". *Econometrica* 53: 385–407.

117 Cox, R., Ingersoll, J., and Ross, S. (1981). "A re-examination of traditional hypotheses about the term structure of interest rate". *Journal of Finance* 36: 769–799.

118 Cragg, J.G., and Malkiel, B.G. (1982). Expectations and the Structure of Share Prices. Chicago: University of Chicago Press.

119 Cramer, J.S. (1991). The Logit Model: An Introduction for Economists. Kent: Edward Arnold.

120 Cranley, R., and Patterson, T.N.L. (1976). "Randomization of number theoretic methods for multiple integration". *SIAM Journal of Numereical Analysis* 13: 904–914.

121 Cumby, R. (1990). "Consumption risk and international equity returns: Some empirical evidence". *Journal of International Money and Finance* 9: 182–192.

122 Cumby, R., and Glen, J. (1990). "Evaluating the performance of international mutual funds". *Journal of Finance* 45: 497–521.

123 Cumby, R.E. (1990). "Consumption risk and international equity returns: Some empirical evidence". *Journal of international Money and Finance* 9: 182–192.

124 Cumby, R.E., and Obstfeld, M. (1983). Capital mobility and the scope for sterilization: Mexico in the 1970s. In: Armella, P.A., Dornbusch, R., and Obstfeld, M. (eds.), Financial Policies and the World Capital Market. Chicago: University of Chicago Press, pp. 245–276.

125 Cunningham, D., and Hendershott, P.H. (1984). "Pricing FHA mortgage default insurance". *Housing Finance Review* 13: 373–392.

D

1 Dahlquist, M., and Soderlind, P. (1999). "Evaluating portfolio performance with stochastic discount factors". *Journal of Business* 72: 347–384.

2 Daines, R., and Klausner, M. (2001). "Do IPO charters maximize firm value? An empirical examination of antitakeover defenses in IPOs". *Journal of Law Economics and Organization* 17: 83–120.

3 Dalla, I., Khatdhate, D., Rao, D.C., Kali, K., Jun, L., and Chuppe, T. (1995). The Emerging Asian Bond Market. Washington DC: The World Bank.

4 Damodaran, A. (1997). Corporate Finance: Theory and Practice. John Wiley & Sons.

5 Daniel, K., Grinblatt, M., Titman, S., and Wermers, R. (1997). Measuring mutual fund performance with characteristic based benchmarks". *Journal of Finance* 52: 1035–1058.

6 Daniel, K., Hirshleifer, D., and Subrahmanyam, A. (1998). "Investor psychology and security market under- and overreactions". *Journal of Finance* 53: 1839–1886.

7 Daniel, K.D., and Titman, S. (1999). "Market efficiency in an irrational world". *Financial Analysts Journal*, 55: 28–40.

8 Das, S.R. (2002). "The surprise element: Jumps in interest rates". *Journal of Econometrics* 106: 27–65.

9 Davidson, A.S., Herskovitz, M.D., and Van Drunen, L.D. (1988). "The refinancing threshold pricing model: An economic approach to valuing MBS". *Journal of Real Estate Finance and Economics* 1: 117–130.

10 De Santis, G., and Gerard, B. (1997). "International asset pricing and portfolio diversification with time-varying risk". *Journal of Finance* 52: 1881–1912.

11 De Santis, G., and Gerard, B. (1998). "How big is the premium for currency risk?" *Journal of Financial Economics* 49: 375–412.

12 De Santis, G., Litterman, B., Vesval, A., and Winkelmann, K. (2003). Covariance matrix estimation in Modern Investment Management, B. Litterman and the Quantitative Resources Group, Goldman Sachs Asset Management, Hoboken, NJ: Wiley.

13 Deakin, E.B. (1976). "Distributions of financial accounting ratios: Some empirical evidence". *Accounting Review* 51(1): 90–96.

14 DeBondt, W., and Thaler, R. (1985). "Does the stock market overreact?" *Journal of Finance* 40: 793–805.

15 Degryse, H., and Ongena, S. (2001). *Bank relationships and firm profitability, Financial Management* 30: 9–34.

16 Dekker, T.J. (1969). Finding a zero by means of successive linear interpolation. Constructive Aspects of The Fundamental Theorem of Algebra in Dejon and Henrici.

17 Demirgüç-Kunt, A., and Detragiache, E. (2000). "Does deposit insurance increase banking system stability?" International Monetary Fund Working Paper: WP/00/03.

18 Demirgüç-Kunt, A., and Kane, E.J. (2002). "Deposit insurance around the globe: Where does it work?" *Journal of Economic Perspectives* 16(2): 178–195.

19 Demirgüç-Kunt, A., and Sobaci, T. (2001). "Deposit insurance around the world". *The World Bank Economic Review* 15(3): 481–490.

20 Demirguc-Kunt, A., and Huizinga, H. (1993). "Official credits to developing countries: Implicit transfers to the banks". *Journal of Money, Credit, and Banking* 25: 76–89.

21 Dennis, S., Nandy, D., and Sharpe, I.G. (2000). "The determinants of contract terms in bank revolving credit agreements". *Journal of Financial and Quantitative Analysis* 35: 87–110.

22 Dennis, S.A., and Mullineaux, D.J. (2000). "Syndicated loans". *Journal of Financial Intermediation* 9: 404–426.

23 Derman, E., Ergener, D., and Kani, I. (1995). "Static options replication". *The Journal of Derivatives* 2(4): 78–95.

24 Detemple, J., and Murthy, S. (1997). "Equilibrium asset prices and no-arbitrage with portfolio constraints". *Review of Financial Studies* 10: 1133–1174.

25 Detragiache, E., Garella, P.G., and Guiso, L. (2000). "Multiple versus single banking relationships, theory and evidence". *Journal of Finance* 55: 1133–1161.

26 Diamond, D.W., and Dybvig, P.H. (2000). "Bank runs, deposit insurance, and liquidity". *Federal Reserve Bank of Minneapolis Quarterly Review* 24(1): 14–23.

27 Diamond, P., and Mirrlees, J.A. (2002). "Optimal Taxation and the Le Chatelier Principle". MIT Dept of Economics Working Paper Series.

28 Dixit, A.K. (1990). Optimization in Economic Theory, 2nd ed., Oxford University Press.

29 Dodd, P. (1980). "Merger proposals, management discretion and stockholder wealth". *Journal of Financial Economics* 8: 105–137.

30 Dodd, P., and Leftwich, R. (1980). "The market for corporate charters: 'Unhealthy Competition' versus federal regulation". *Journal of Business* 53: 259–282.

31 Dodd, P., and Ruback, R. (1977). "Tender offers and stockholder returns: An empirical analysis". *Journal of Financial Economics* 5(3): 351–374.

32 Doherty, J. (1997). For Junk Borrowers, Pre-Funded Bonds Pick Up Steam, But They May Pose Greater Risk Than Zeros. Barrons, December, MW15.

33 Dominguez Katherine M.E. (2003). "Book Review: Richard K. Lyons, The Microstructure Approach to Exchange Rates, MIT Press, 2001". *Journal of International Economics* 61: 467–471.

34 Domowitz, I. (1993). "A taxonomy of automated trade execution systems". *Journal of International Money and Finance* 12: 607–631.

35 Domowitz, I., and Hakkio, C.S. (1985). "Conditional variance and the risk premium in the foreign exchange market". *Journal of International Economics* 19: 47–66.

36 Donaldson, G. (1961). Corporate Debt Capacity: A Study of Corporate Debt Policy and the Determination of Corporate Debt Capacity. Boston: Division of Research, Harvard Graduate School of Business Administration.

37 Doukas, J., and Travlos, N.G. (1988). "The effect of corporate multinationalism on shareholders' wealth: Evidence from international acquisitions". *Journal of Finance* 43: 1161–1175.

38 Dowla, A., and Chowdhury, A. (1991). Money, Credit, and Real Output in the Developing Economies. Department of Economics, Marquette University.

39 Doyle, J.T. (2003). Credit risk measurement and pricing in performance pricing-based debt contracts. Working Paper, University of Michigan.

40 Drezner, Z. (1992). "Computation of the multivariate normal integral". *ACM Transactions on Mathematical Software* 18: 470–480.

41 Drost, C.F., and Werker, B.J.M. (1996). "Closing the GARCH gap: Continuous time GARCH modeling". *Journal of Econometrics* 74: 31–57.

42 Drost, C.F., Nijman, T.E., and Werker, B.J.M. (1998). "Estimation and testing in models containing both jumps and conditional heteroscedasticity". *Journal of Business and Economic Statistics* 16(2).

43 Duan, C., William, T.L., and Lee, C. (2003). "Sequential capital budgeting as real options: The case of a new DRAM chipmaker in Taiwan". *Review of Pacific Basin Financial Markets and Policies* 6: 87–112.

44 Duffie, D., and Kan, R. (1996). "A yield-factor model of interest rate". *Mathematical Finance* 6: 379–406.

45 Duffie, D., and Singleton, K.J. (2003). Credit Risk: Pricing, Measurement and Management. New Jersey: Princeton University Press.

46 Duffie, D., Pan, J. , and Singleton, K. (2000). "Transform analysis and asset pricing for affine jump diffusion". *Econometrica* 68: 1343–1376.

47 Duffy, J. (2004). Agent-based models and human subject experiments. In: Judd, K.L., and Tesfatsion, L. (eds.), Handbook of Computational Economics II. Elsevier.

48 Dumas, B., and Solnik, B. (1995). "The world price of foreign exchange risk". *Journal of Finance* 50: 445–479.

49 Dunn, K.B., and McConnell, J.J. (1981). "A comparison of Alternative models of pricing GNMA mortgage backed securities". *Journal of Finance* 36: 471–483.

50 Dunn, K.B., and McConnell, J.J. (1981). "Valuation of GNMA mortgage-backed securities". *Journal of Finance* 36: 599–616.

51 Dunn, K.B., and Singleton, K.J. (1986). "Modelling the term structure of interest rates under nonseparable utility and durability of goods". *Journal of Financial Economics* 17: 27–55.

52 Dunn, K.B., and Spatt, C.S. (1986). The Effect of Refinancing Costs and Market Imperfections on the Optimal Call Strategy and Pricing of Debt Contracts Working Paper, Carnegie-Mellon University.

53 Dybvig, P., and Ingersoll, J. (1982). "Mean variance theory in complete markets". *Journal of Business* 55: 233–252.

54 Dybvig, P., and Ross, S. (1985), "Yes, the APT is testable". *Journal of Fiance* 40: 1173–1183.

55 Dybvig, P., and Ross, S. (1986). "Tax clienteles and asset pricing". *Journal of Finance* 41: 751–762.

56 Dybvig, P., and Ross, S. (1987). Arbitrage. In: Eatwell, J., Milgate, M., and Newman, P. (eds.), The New Palgrave: A Dictionary of Economics. New York: Stockton Press., Vol. 1, pp. 100–106.

57 Dybvig, P.H. (1983). "An explicit bound on individual assets' deviations from APT pricing in a finite economy". *Journal of Financial Economics* 12: 483–496.

E

1 Easley, D., Hvidkjaer, S., and O'Hara, M. (2002). "Is information risk a determinant of asset returns?" *Journal of Finance* 57: 2185–2221.

2 Easley, D., Kiefer, N., O'Hara, M., and Paperman, J. (1996). "Liquidity, information, and infrequently traded stocks". *Journal of Finance* 51: 1405–1436.

3 Easterbrook, F., and Fischel, D. (1983). "Voting in corporate law". *Journal of Law and Economics* 26: 395–427.

4 Easterbrook, F.H. (1984). "Two agency-cost explanations of dividends". *American Economic Review* 74(4): 650–659.

5 Economides, N., and Schwartz, R.A. (1995). "Electronic call market trading". *Journal of Portfolio Management* 10–18.

6 Economides, N., and Siow, A. (1988). "The division of markets is limited by the extent of liquidity". *American Economic Review* 78: 108–21.

7 Edwards, W. (1955). "The prediction of decisions among bets". *Journal of Experimental Psychology* 50: 201–214.

8 Edwards, W. (1962). "Subjective probabilities inferred from decisions". *Psychology Review* 69: 109–135.

9 Eichenbaum, M.S., Hansen, L.P., and Singleton, K.J. (1988). "A time series analysis of representative agent models of consumption and leisure choices under uncertainty". *Quarterly Journal of Economics* 103: 51–78.

10 Eisenbeis, R.A. (1977). "Pitfalls in the application of discriminant analysis in business, finance, and economics". *The Journal of Finance* 32(3): 875–900.

11 Eisenbeis, R.A., and Avery, R.B. (1972). Discriminant Analysis and Classification Procedure: Theory and Applications. Lexington, Mass: DC Heath and Co.

12 Elgers, P. (1980). "Accounting-based risk predictions: A re-examination". *The Accounting Review* 55(3): 389–408.

13 Elton, E.J., and Gruber, M.J. (1984). Modern Portfolio Theory and Investment Analysis, 2nd ed. New York: Wiley.

14 Elton, E.J., and Gruber, M.J. (1991). Modern Portfolio Theory and Investment Analysis. New York: John Wiley.

15 Elton, E.J., and Gruber, M.J. (1995). Modern Portfolio Theory and Investment Analysis, 5th ed. John Wiley & Sons.

16 Emery, R.F. (1997). The Bond Markets of Developing East Asia. Boulder, Colorado: Westview Press.

17 Engel, C. (1996). "The forward discount anomaly and the risk premium: A survey of recent evidence". *Journal of Empirical Finance* 3: 123–192.

18 Epperson, J., Kau, J., Keenan, D., and Muller, W. III (1985). "Pricing default risk in mortgages". *Journal of AREUEA* 13: 261, 272.

19 Epstein, L.G., and Zin, S.E. (1989). "Substitution, risk aversion and the temporal behavior of asset returns: A theoretical approach". *Econometrica* 57: 937–970.

20 Epstein, L.G., and Zin, S.E. (1991). "Substitution, risk aversion, and the temporal behavior of consumption and asset returns: An empirical analysis". *Journal of Political Economy* 99: 263–286.

21 Esty, B., and Megginson, W. (2003). "Creditor rights, enforcement, and debt ownership structure: Evidence from the global syndicated loan market". *Journal of Financial and Quantitative Analysis* 38(1): 37–59.

22 Evans, J.L., and Archer, S.H. (1968). "Diversification and reduction of dispersion: An empirical analysis". *Journal of Finance* 23: 761–767.

23 Evans, M. (2001). "FX trading and exchange rate dynamics". *NBER* Working paper 8116.

24 Evans, M., and Lyons, R.K. (2002). "Order flow and exchange rate dynamics". *Journal of Political Economy* 110: 170–180.

25 Evans, M.D.D. (1994). "Expected returns, time-varying risk and risk premia". *Journal of Finance* 49(2): 655–679.

26 Ezzamel, M., Mar-Molinero, C., and Beecher, A. (1987). "On the distributional properties of financial ratios". *Journal of Business Finance and Accounting* 14(4): 463–481.

F

1 Fabbozzi, F.J. (2000). Bond Markets, Analysis and Strategies, 4th ed., Englewood Cliffs, NJ: Prentice Hall, pp. 61–68.

2 Falloon, W. (1993). Southern exposure, risk. 6: 103–107.

3 Fama, E., and French, K. (1988). "Permanent and temporary components of stock prices". *Journal of Political Economy* 96: 246–273.

4 Fama, E., and French, K. (1989). "Business conditions and expected returns on stocks and bonds". *Journal of Financial Economics* 25: 23–49.

5 Fama, E., and French, K. (1996). "Multifactor explanations of asset pricing anomalies". *Journal of Finance* 51: 55–84.

6 Fama, E.F. (1965). "The behavior of stock market price". *Journal of Business* 38(1): 34–105.

7 Fama, E.F. (1970). "Efficient capital markets: A review of theory and empirical work". *Journal of Finance* 25(2): 383–417.

8 Fama, E.F. (1975). "Short-term interest rates as predictors of inflation". *American Economic Review* 65: 269–282.

9 Fama, E.F. (1976). Foundations of Finance. New York: Basic Books.

10 Fama, E.F. (1984). "Forward and spot exchange rates". *Journal of Monetary Economics* 14: 319–338.

11 Fama, E.F. (1991). "Efficient capital markets II". *Journal of Finance* 46(5): 1575–1617.

12 Fama, E.F. (1996). "Multifactor portfolio efficiency and multifactor asset pricing". *Journal of Financial and Quantitative Analysis* 31(4): 441–465.

13 Fama, E.F., and Blume, M. (1966). "Filter rules and stock market trading profits". *Journal of Business* (Special Supplement) 39: 226–241.

14 Fama, E.F., and French, K.R. (1988). "Dividend yields and expected stock returns". *Journal of Financial Economics* 22: 3–25.

15 Fama, E.F., and French, K.R. (1993). "Common risk factors in the returns on stocks and bonds". *Journal of Financial Economics* 33: 3–56.

16 Fama, E.F., and French, K.R. (1996). "Multifactor explanations of asset pricing anomalies". *Journal of Finance* 51: 55–87.

17 Fama, E.F., and MacBeth, J.D. (1973). "Risk, return and equilibrium: Empirical tests". *Journal of Political Economy I* 81: 607–636.

18 Fama, E.F., and Schwert, G.W. (1997). "Asset returns and inflation". *Journal of Financial Economics* 5: 115–146.

19 Fama, E.F., Fisher, E.L., Jensen, M., and Roll, R. (1969). "The adjustment of stock prices to new information". *International Economic Review* 10: 1–21.

20 Fama, E.F., Lawrence, F., Jensen, M.C., and Richard, R. (1969). "The adjustment of stock prices to new information". *International Economic Review* 5: 1–21.

21 Farmer, J.D., and Joshi, S. (2000). The price dynamics of common trading strategies. Santa Fe Institute Working Paper 00-12-069, Santa Fe, New Mexico.

22 Farnsworth, H., Ferson, W.E., Jackson, D., and Todd, S. (2002). "Performance Evaluation with stochastic discount factors". *Journal of Business* 75: 473–504.

23 Farrell, C. (2000). "Online or off, the rules are the same". *Business Week* 148–149.

24 Ferson, W., and Qian, M. (2004). Conditional Performance Evaluation revisited. Charlottesville, VA: Research Foundation Monograph, CFA Institute.

25 Ferson, W., and Schadt, R. (1996). "Measuring Fund Strategy and Performance in Changing Economic Conditions". *Journal of Finance* 51: 425–462.

26 Ferson, W., and Warther, V.A. (1996). "Evaluating fund performance in a dynamic market". *Financial Analysts Journal* 52(6): 20–28.

27 Ferson, W., Henry, T., and Kisgen, D. (2004). "Evaluating government bond fund performance with stochastic discount factors". Working Paper, Boston College.

28 Ferson, W.E. (1983). "Expectations of real interest rates and aggregate consumption: Empirical tests". *Journal of Financial and Quantitative Analysis* 18: 477–497.

29 Ferson, W.E. (1989). "Changes in expected security returns, risk and the level of interest rates". *Journal of Finance* 44: 1191–1217.

30 Ferson, W.E. (1995). Theory and Empirical Testing of Asset Pricing Models. In: Jarrow, M. and Ziemba (eds.), Handbooks in Operations Research and Management Science. Elsevier, Chapter 5 in Finance 145–200.

31 Ferson, W.E. (2003). Tests of multifactor pricing models, volatility bounds and portfolio performance. In: Constantinides, G.M., Harris, M., and Stulz, R. (eds.), Handbook of the Economics of Finance. Elsevier Science.

32 Ferson, W.E., and Constantinides, G.M. (1991). "Habit persistence and durability in aggregate consumption: empirical tests". *Journal of Financial Economics* 29: 199–240.

33 Ferson, W.E., and Foerster, S.R. (1994). "Finite sample properties of the generalized methods of moments tests of conditional asset pricing models". *Journal of Financial Economics* 36: 29–56.

34 Ferson, W.E., and Harvey, C.R. (1991). "The variation of economic risk premiums". *Journal of Political Economy* 99: 385–415.

35 Ferson, W.E., and Harvey, C.R. (1992). "Seasonality and consumption based asset pricing models". *Journal of Finance* 47: 511–552.

36 Ferson, W.E., and Harvey, C.R. (1993). "The risk and predictability of international equity returns". *Review of Financial Studies* 6: 527–566.

37 Ferson, W.E., and Harvey, C.R. (1999). "Economic, financial and fundamental global risk in and out of EMU". *Swedish Economic Policy Review* 6: 123–184.

38 Ferson, W.E., and Jagannathan, R. (1996). Econometric Evaluation of Asset Pricing Models. In: Maddala, G.S., and Rao, C.R. (eds.), Handbook of Statistics: Vol. 14: Statistical Methods in Finance, Chapter 1: 1–30. North Holland.

39 Ferson, W.E., and Khang, K. (2002). "Conditional performance measurement using portfolio weights: Evidence for pension funds". *Journal of Financial Economics* 65: 249–282.

40 Ferson, W.E, and Korajczyk, R.A. (1995). "Do arbitrage pricing models explain the predictability of stock returns?" *Journal of Business* 68: 309–349.

41 Ferson, W.E., and Merrick, J.J. (1987). "Nonstationarity and stage of the business cycle effects in consumption-based asset pricing relations". *Journal of Financial Economics* 18: 127–146.

42 Ferson, W.E., and Schadt, R.W. (1996). "Measuring fund strategy and performance in changing economic conditions". *Journal of Finance* 51: 425–461.

43 Ferson, W.E., and Siegel, A.F. (2001). "The efficient use of conditioning information in portfolios". *Journal of Finance* 56: 967–982.

44 Ferson, W.E., and Siegel, A.F. (2003). "Testing Portfolio Efficiency with Conditioning Information". Working Paper, Boston College.

45 Ferson, W.E., Foerster, S.R., and Keim, D.B. (1993). "General tests of latent variable models and mean variance spanning". *Journal of Finance* 48: 131–156.

46 Ferson, W.E., Henry, T., and Kisgen, D. (2003). "Evaluating government bond performance with stochastic discount factors". Working Paper, Boston University.

47 Ferson, W.E., Sarkissian, S., and Simin, T. (1999). "The alpha factor asset pricing model: A parable". *Journal of Financial Markets* 2 (February): 49–68.

48 Ferson, W.E., Sarkissian, S., and Simin, T. (2003). "Spurious regressions in Financial Economics?" *Journal of Finance* 58: 1393–1414.

49 Field, L. and Karpoff, J. (2002). "Takeover defenses of IPO firms". *Journal of Finance* 57: 1857–1889.

50 Firth, M. (1980). "Takeovers, shareholder returns, and the theory of the firm". *Quarterly Journal of Economics* 94(2): 235–260.

51 Fischer, S. (1998). "The Asian Crisis: A View from the IMF", addressed in Washington, DC http://www.imf.org/external/np/speeches.

52 Fischer, S. (1999). "On the Need for an International Lender of Resort," An address to AEA/AFA joint luncheon meeting in New York. http://www.imf.org/external/np/speeches.

53 Fishburn, P.C. (1964). Decision and Value Theory. New York: Wiley.

54 Fishburn, P.C. (1978). "On Handa's 'new theory of cardinal utility' and the maximization of expected return". *Journal of Political Economy* 86: 321–324.

55 Fisher L. (1966). "Some New Stock-Market Indexes". *Journal of Business* 39(1): 191–225 (Part 2).

56 Fisher, E., and Park, J. (1991). "Testing purchasing power parity under the null hypothesis of cointegration". *Economic Journal* 101: 1476–1484.

57 Fisher, L., and Weil, R.L. (1971). "Coping with the risk of market-rate fluctuations: Returns to bondholders from naive and optimal strategies". *Journal of Business* : 408–431.

58 Fishman, M.J. (1989). "Preemptive bidding and the role of the medium of exchange in acquisitions". *Journal of Finance* 44(1): 41–57.

59 Flannery, M. (1986). "Asymmetric information and risky debt maturity choice". *Journal of Finance* 41: 18–38.

60 Flannery, M.J. and C.M. James, (1984). "The effect of interest rate changes on the common stock returns of financial institutions". *The Journal of Finance*, 39: 1141–1153.

61 Fleissig, A.R., and Strauss, J. (2000). "Panel unit root tests of purchasing power parity for price indices". *Journal of International Money and Finance* 19: 489–506.

62 Fleming, J.M. (1962). "Domestic financial policies under fixed and floating exchange rates". *International Monetary Fund Staff Papers* 9: 369–379.

63 Fletcher, J., and Forbes, D. (2004). "Performance evaluation of UK unit trusts within the stochastic discount factor approach". *Journal of Financial Research* 27: 289–306.

64 Fong, H.G., and Vasicek, O. (1983). Return maximization for immunized portfolios. In: Kaufman, G.G., Bierwag, G.O., and Toevs, A. (eds.), Innovations in Bond Portfolio Management, Duration Analysis and Immunization, The Ashland Conference, 1981, Greenwich, CT: Jai Press.

65 Fong, H.G., and Vasicek, O.A. (1984). "A risk minimizing strategy for portfolio immunization". *Journal of Finance* 34: 1541–1546.

66 Fooladi, I., and Roberts, G. (1992). "Bond portfolio immunization: Canadian tests". *Journal of Economics and Business* 44: 3–17

67 Fooladi, I., and Roberts, G. (2004). "Macrohedging for financial institutions: beyond duration". *Journal of Applied Finance* 14(1): 11–19.

68 Fooladi, I., Roberts, G., and Skinner, F. (1997). "Duration for bonds with default risk". *Journal of Banking and Finance* 21: 1–16.

69 Foster, D., Smith, T., and Whaley, R. (1997). "Assessing goodness-of-fit of asset pricing models: The distribution of the maximal R-squared". *Journal of Finance* 52: 591–607.

70 Foster, G. (1986). Financial Statement Analysis, 2nd ed. New Jersey: Prentice-Hall.

71 Francis, J.C. (1980). Investments: Analysis and Management, 3rd ed. New York: McGraw-Hill Book Company.

72 Francis, J.C. (1993). Management of Investment. New York: McGraw-Hill.

73 Francis, J.C., and Ibbotson, R. (2002). Investments: A Global Perspective. Upper Saddle River. NJ: Pearson Education.

74 Frankel, J.A. (1979). "On the mark: A theory of floating exchange rates based on real interest differential". *American Economic Review* 69: 610–622.

75 Frankel, J.A., and Froot, K.A. (1987). "Using survey data to test standard propositions regarding exchange rate expectations". *American Economic Review* 77: 133–153.

76 Frankel, J.A., and MacArthur, A.T. (1988). "Political vs. currency premia in international real interest differentials: A study of forward rates for 24 international real interest differentials: A study of forward rates for 24 countries". *European Economic Review* 32: 1083–1114.

77 Frankel, J.A., and Schmukler, A.L. (2000). "Country funds and asymmetric information". *International Journal of Finance and Economics* 5: 177–195.

78 Frankfurter, G.M., Phillips, H.E., and Seagle, J.P. (1971). "Portfolio selection: the effects of uncertain means, variances, and covariances". *Journal of Financial and Quantitative Analysis* 6(5): 1251–1262.

79 Fratianni, M., and Wakeman, L.M. (1982). "The law of one price in the Eurocurrency market". *Journal of International Money and Finance* 3: 307–323.

80 Frecka, T.J., and Hopwood, W.S. (1983). "The effects of outliers on the cross-sectional distributional properties of financial ratios". *The Accounting Review* 58(1): 115–128.

81 French, K.R., and Richard, R. (1986). "Stock return variances: The arrival of information and the reaction of traders". *Journal of Financial Economics* 17: 5–26.

82 Frenkel, J.A. (1981). "The collapse of purchasing power parities during the 1970s". *European Economic Review* 16: 145–165.

83 Friedman, M., and Savage, L.J. (1948). "The utility analysis of choices involving risk". *Journal of Political Economy* 56: 279–304.

84 Friend, I., and Blume, M.E. (1970). "Measurement of portfolio performance under uncertainty". *American Economic Review* 60: 561–575.

85 Froot, K.A., and Thaler, R.H. (1990). "Anomalies: foreign exchange". *Journal of Economic Perspective* 4: 179–192.

86 Frost, P.A., and Savarino, J.E. (1988). "For better performance, constrain portfolio weights". *Journal of Portfolio Management* 14: 29–34.

87 Fudenberg, D., and Tirole, J. (1986). "A 'Signal-Jamming' theory of predation". *Rand Journal of Economics* 17(3): 366–376.

88 Funk, S.G., Rapoport, A., and Jones, L.V. (1979). "Investing capital on safe and risky alternatives: An experimental study". *Journal of Experimental Psychology: General* 108: 415–440.

G

1 Gallinger, G.W., and Healey, P.B. (1991). Liquidity Analysis and Management, 2nd ed. Reading, Massachusetts: Addisonn-Wesley Publishing Company.

2 Garcia, G. (1999). "Deposit insurance: A survey of actual and best practices". International Monetary Fund Policy Working Paper: WP/99/54.

3 Garcia, G. (2000). "Deposit insurance and crisis management". International Monetary Fund Policy Working Paper: WP/00/57.

4 Garden, M.J., and Mills, D.L. (1994). Managing Financial Institution, 3rd ed. New York: The Dryden Press.

5 Garman, M., and Ohlson, J. (1981). "Valuation of risky assets in arbitrage-free economies with transactions costs". *Journal of Financial Economics* 9: 271–280.

6 Genty J., and De La Garza, J. "A generalized model for monitoring accounts receivable". *Financial Management* (Winter Issue) 23–38.

7 Genz, A. (1992). "Numerical computation of the multivariate normal probabilities". *Journal of Comput. Graph. Stat.* 1: 141–150.

8 Genz, A. (1999). "Comparison of Methods for the Computation of Multivariate Normal Probabilities". Working Paper.

9 Geske, R. (1977). "The valuation of corporate liabilities as compound options". *Journal of Financial and Quantitative Analysis* 12: 541–552.

10 Geske, R. (1979). "The valuation of compound options". *Journal of Financial Economics* 7: 63–81.

11 Gibbons, M. (1982). "Multivariate tests of financial models: A new approach". *Journal of Financial Economics* 10: 3–27.

12 Gibbons, M.R., and Ferson, W.E. (1985). "Testing asset pricing models with changing expectations and an unobservable market portfolio". *Journal of Financial Economics* 14: 217–236.

13 Gibbons, M.R., Ross, S.A., and Shanken, J. (1989). "A test of the efficiency of a given portfolio". *Econometrica* 57: 1121–1152.

14 Gibbs, P.A. (1993). "Determinants of corporate restructuring: The relative importance of corporate governance, takeover threat, and free cash flow" '. *Strategic Management Journal* 14(Special Issue): 51–68.

15 Gibson, S., Singh, R., and Yerramilli, V. (2002). "The effect of decimalization on the components of the bid-ask spreads". Working Paper, Cornell University.

16 Gilson, S.C. (1989). "Management turnover and financial distress". *Journal of Financial Economics* 25(2): 241–262.

17 Gilson, S.C., and Vetsuypens, M.R. (1993). "CEO compensation in financially distressed firms: An empirical analysis". *Journal of Finance* 48(2): 425–458.

18 Gilson, S.C., John, K., and Lang, L.H.P. (1990). "Troubled debt restructurings: An empirical study of private reorganisation of firms in default". *Journal of Financial Economics* 27(2): 315–353.

19 Gimein, M. (1999). "Playing the Net Stock Game". *The Industry Standard* 20–21.

20 Giovannini, A., and Jorion P. (1987). "Interest rates and risk premia in the stock market and in the foreign exchange market". *Journal of International Money and Finance* 6: 107–124.

21 Giovannini, A., and Weil, P. (1989). "Risk aversion and intertemporal substitution in the capital asset pricing model". *NBER*: 2824.

22 Glascock, J., and Hughes, W.T. (1995). "NAREIT identified exchange listed REITs and their performance characteristics, 1972–1990". *Journal of Real Estate Literature* 3(1): 63–83.

23 Glassman, J., and Hassett, K. (1998). "Are stocks overvalued? Not a chance". *The Wall Street Journal*.

24 Gode, D.K., and Sunder, S. (1993). "Allocative efficiency of markets with zero intelligence traders". *Journal of Political Economy* 101: 119–137.

25 Godfrey, M.D., Granger, C.W.J., and Oskar, M. (1964). "The random walk hypothesis of stock market behavior". *Kyklos* 17: 1–30.

26 Goetzmann, W.N., Ingersoll, J., and Ivkovic, Z. (2000). "Monthly measurement of daily timers". *Journal of Financial and Quantitative Analysis* 35: 257–290.

27 Gogoi, P. (2000). "Rage against online brokers". *Business Week*: EB98–EB102.

28 Gokey, T.C. (1994). "What explains the risk premium in foreign exchange returns?" *Journal of International Money and Finance* 13: 729–738.

29 Goldsmith, R. (1688–1978). Comparative National Balance Sheets: A Study of Twenty Countries. Chicago: University of Chicago Press.

30 Goldsmith, R. (1965). The Flow of Capital Funds in the postwar Economy, Chapter 2. New York: National Bureau of Economic Research.

31 Goldstein, M., and Kavajecz, K. (2000). "Eighths, sixteenths and market depth: Changes in tick size and liquidity provision on the NYSE". *Journal of Financial Economics* 56: 125–149.

32 Gonzalez, P., Vasconcellos, G.M., and Kish, R.J. (1998). "Cross-border mergers and acquisitions: The synergy hypothesis". *The International Journal of Finance* 10(4): 1297–1319.

33 Gonzalez, P., Vasconcellos, G.M., and Kish, R.J. (1998). Cross-border mergers and acquisitions: The undervaluation hypothesis". *Quarterly Review of Economics and Finance* 38(1): 25–45.

34 Goodhart, C., and Curcio, R. (1992). "Asset price discovery and price clustering in the foreign exchange market". Working paper, London School of Business.

35 Goodman, L.S., and Cohen, A.H. (1989). "Payment-in-kind debentures: An innovation". *Journal of Portfolio Management* 15: 9–19.

36 Gordon, M. (1962). The investment, financing and valuation of the firm, Irwin, Homewood, IL.

37 Gordon, M.J., Paradis, G.E., and Rorke, C.H. (1972). "Experimental evidence on alternative portfolio decision rules". *The American Economic Review* 52: 107–118.

38 Gorman, W.M. (1953). "Community preference fields". *Econometrica* 21: 63–80.

39 Gottesman, A.A., and Roberts, G.S. (2004). "Maturity and corporate loan pricing". *Financial Review* 38: 55–77.

40 Gottesman, A.A., and Roberts, G.S. (2005). "Loan rates and collateral". Working Paper, York University.

41 Goudie, A.W., and Meeks, G. (1982). "Diversification by Merger". *Economica* 49(196): 447–459.

42 Gourieroux, G., and Jasiak, J. (2001). Financial Econometrics, 1st ed., Princeton University Press, NJ. Hull, J.C., (2000). Option, Futures, other Derivatives, 4th ed. NJ: Prientice Hall,

43 Goyal, A., and Welch, I. (2003). "Predicting the equity premium with dividend ratios". *Management Science* 49(5): 639–654.

44 Granger, C.W.J. (1969). "Investigating causal relations by econometric models and cross-spectral methods". *Econometrica* 37: 424–438.

45 Grant, D. (1977). "Portfolio performance and the 'cost' of timing decisions". *Journal of Finance* 32: 837–846.

46 Green, C.J., Maggioni, P., and Murinde, V. (2000). "Regulatory lessons for emerging stock markets from a century of evidence on transactions costs and share price volatility in the London Stock Exchange". *Journal of Banking & Finance* 24: 577–601.

47 Greene, W.H. (1997). Econometric Analysis, 3rd ed. New Jersey: Prentice-Hall.

48 Greenspan, A. (1998). Remarks by Greenspan, at the Annual Convention of the American Society of Newspaper Editors, Washington, DC: WSJ Interactive Edition.

49 Gregory, A. (1997). "An examination of the long run performance of UK acquiring firms". *Journal of Business Finance* 24(7 and 8): 971–1002.

50 Grinblatt, M., and Titman, S. (1983). "Factor pricing in a finite economy". *Journal of Financial Economics* 12: 497–508.

51 Grinblatt, M., and Titman, S. (1987). "The relation between mean-variance efficiency and arbitrage pricing". *Journal of Business* 60: 97–112.

52 Grinblatt, M., and Titman, S. (1989). "Mutual fund performance: An analysis of quarterly portfolio holdings". *Journal of Business* 62: 393–416.

53 Grinblatt, M., and Titman, S. (1989). "Portfolio performance evaluation: Old issues and new insights". *Review of Financial Studies* 2: 393–421.

54 Grinblatt, M., and Titman, S. (1993). "Perform-ance measurement without benchmarks: An exam-ination of mutual fund returns". *Journal of Business* 60: 97–112.

55 Grinblatt, M., Titman, S., Wermers, R. (1995). "Momentum strategies, portfolio performance and herding: A study of mutual fund behavior". *American Economic Review* 85: 1088–1105.

56 Gropp, R., and Vesala, J. (2001). "Deposit Insurance and Moral Hazard: Does the Counterfactual Mat-ter?" European Central Bank Working Paper, 47.

57 Grossman, S., and Shiller, R.J. (1982). "Consump-tion correlatedness and risk measurement in econ-omies with nontraded assets and heterogeneous information". *Journal of Financial Economics* 10: 195–210.

58 Grossman, S.J. (1976). "On the efficiency of com-petitive stock markets where traders have diverse information". *Journal of Finance* 31(2): 573.

59 Grossman, S.J. (1988). "An analysis of the impli-cations for stock and futures price volatility of program trading and dynamic hedging strategies". *Journal of Business*, 61: 275–298.

60 Grossman, S.J., and Miller, M. (1988). "Liquidity and market structure". *Journal of Finance* 43: 617–633.

61 Guedes, J., and Opler, T. (1996). "The determin-ants of the maturity of new corporate debt issues". *Journal of Finance* 51: 1809–1833.

H

1   Hadar, J., and Russell, W. (1969). "Rules for ordering uncertain prospects". *American Economic Review* 59: 25–34.

2   Hahn, F.H. (1983). Money and Inflation, Cam-bridge, Massachusetts: The MIT Press.

3   Hakansson, N.H. (1992). Welfare Economics of Financial Markets. In: Eatwell, J., Milgate, M., and Newman, P. (eds.), The New Palgrave Diction-ary of Money and Finance, London: MacMillan Press, 3: 790–796, 1999. "The Role of Corporate Bond Market in an Economy – and in avoiding crisis", Working Paper, University of California, Berkeley.

4   Halpern, P. (1983). "Corporate acquisitions: A theory of special cases? A review of event studies applied to acquisitions". *Journal of Finance* 38(2): 297–317.

5   Hamer, M.M. (1983). "Failure prediction: Sensi-tivity of classification accuracy to alternative stat-istical methods and variable sets". *Journal of Accounting and Public Policy* 2(4): 289–307.

6   Hampton, J.J. (1989). Financial Decision Making: Concepts, Problems, and Cases, 4th ed., New Jer-sey: Prentice-Hall.

7   Handa, P., and Schwartz, R.A. (1996). "Limit order trading". *Journal of Finance* 51: 1835–1861.

8   Hannan, T.H. (1997). "Market share inequality, the number of competitors, and the HHI: An examination of bank pricing". *Review of Industrial Organization* 12: 23–35.

9   Hanoch, G., and Levy, H. (1969). "The efficiency analysis of choices involving risk". *Review of Eco-nomic Studies* 36: 335–346.

10 Hansen, L.P. (1982). "Large sample properties of generalized method of moments estimators". *Econ-ometrica* 50: 1029–1054.

11 Hansen, L.P., and Hodrick, R.J. (1980). "Forward exchange rates as optimal predictors of future spot rates: An econometric analysis". *Journal of Polit-ical Economy* 88: 829–853.

12 Hansen, L.P., and Hodrick, R.J. (1983). Risk averse speculation in the forward foreign exchange market. In: Frenkel, J. (ed.), An Econometric An-alysis of Linear Models, Exchange Rates and Inter-national Macroeconomics, University of Chicago Press, Chicago, IL.

13 Hansen, L.P., and Jagannathan, R. (1991). "Impli-cations of security market data for models of dynamic economies". *Journal of Political Economy* 99: 225–262.

14 Hansen, L.P., and Jagannathan, R. (1997). "As-sessing specification errors in stochastic discount factor models". *Journal of Finance* 52: 591–607.

15 Hansen, L.P., and Richard, S.F. (1987). "The role of conditioning information in deducing testable restrictions implied by dynamic asset pricing models". *Econometrica* 55: 587–613.

16 Hansen, L.P., and Singleton, K.J. (1982). "Gener-alized instrumental variables estimation of nonlinear rational expectations models". *Econome-trica* 50: 1269–1285.

17 Hansen, L.P., and Singleton, K.J. (1983). "Sto-chastic consumption, risk aversion and the tem-poral behavior of asset returns". *Journal of Political Economy* 91: 249–266.

18 Hara, C. (2000). "Transaction costs and a redun-dant security: Divergence of individual and social relevance". *Journal of Mathematical Economics* 33: 497–530.

19 Harhoff, D., and Korting, T. (1998). "Lending relationships in Germany: Empirical evidence

from survey data". *Journal of Banking and Finance* 22: 1317–1353.

20 Harrington, J.E. (1986). "Limit pricing when the potential entrant is uncertain of its cost function". *Econometrica*. 54(2): 429–438.

21 Harris, L. (1994). "Minimum price variations, discrete bid-ask spreads, and quotation sizes". *Review of Financial Studies* 7: 149–178.

22 Harris, L. (1997). Decimalization: A review of the arguments and evidence, Working Paper, University of Southern California.

23 Harris, L. (1999). Trading in pennies, A survey of the issues, Working Paper, University of Southern California.

24 Harrison, M., and Kreps, D. (1979). "Martingales and arbitrage in multi-period securities markets". *Journal of Economic Theory* 20: 381–408.

25 Hart, P.E., and Clarke, R. (1980). Concentration in British Industry 1935–75. London: Cambridge University Press.

26 Harvey, C.R. (1989). "Time-varying conditional covariances in tests of asset pricing models". *Journal of Financial Economics* 24: 289–318.

27 Harvey, C.R. (1991). "The world price of covariance risk". *Journal of Finance* 46: 111–157.

28 Hasbrouck, J., and Schwartz, R.A. (1988). "Liquidity and execution costs in equity markets". *Journal of Portfolio Management* 14(3): 10–17.

29 Hatch, B., Battalio, R., and Jennings, R. (2001). "Post-Reform Market Execution Quality: Multidimensional Comparisons Across Market Centers". *The Financial Review* 36: 3.

30 He, Y., and Wu, C. (2003a). "Price rounding and bid-ask spreads before and after the decimalization". *International Review of Economics and Finance*, forthcoming.

31 He, Y., and Wu, C. (2003a). "The post-reform bid-ask spread disparity between Nasdaq and the NYSE". *Journal of Financial Research* 26: 207–224.

32 He, Y., and Wu, C. (2003b). "What Explains the Bid-Ask Spread Decline after Nasdaq Reforms?" *Financial Markets, Institutions & Instruments* 12: 347–376.

33 He, Y., and Wu, C. (2003b). The Effects of Decimalization on Return Volatility Components, Serial Correlation, and Trading costs, Working Paper.

34 He, Y., Wu, C., and Chen, Y.M. (2003). "An explanation of the volatility disparity between the domestic and foreign shares in the chinese stock markets". *International Review of Economics and Finance* 12: 171–186.

35 Helwege, J. (1996). "Determinants of saving and loan failures: estimates of a time-varying proportional hazard function". *Journal of Financial Services Research* 10: 373–392.

36 Helwege, J., and Turner, C.M. (1999). "The slope of the credit yield curve for speculative-grade issuers". *Journal of Finance* 54: 1869–1884.

37 Hendershott, P., and Order, R.V. (1987). "Pricing mortgages: An interpretation of the models and results". *Journal of Financial Service Research* 1: 77–111.

38 Henderson, J.M., and Quandt, R.E. (1980). MicroEconomic Theroy: A Mathematical Approach, 3rd ed., McGraw-Hill, Apprendix, pp. 363–391.

39 Hendriksson, R., and Merton, R.C. (1981). "On market timing and investment performance. II. Statistical procedures for evaluating forecasting skills". *Journal of Business* 54: 513–533.

40 Henriksson, R.D. (1984). "Market timing and mutual fund performance: An empirical investigation". *Journal of Business* 57: 73–96.

41 Heron, R., and Lewellen, W. (1998). "An empirical analysis of the reincorporation decision". *Journal of Financial and Quantitative Analysis* 33: 549–568.

42 Herring, R.J., and Chatusripitak, N. (2000). "The Case of the Missing Markets: The Bond Market and Why It Matters for Financial Development". Asian Development Bank Institute, Working Paper 11, Tokyo. pp. 23–25.

43 Hester, D.D. (1979). "Customer relationships and terms of loans: Evidence from a pilot survey". *Journal of Money, Credit and Banking* 11: 349–357.

44 Hicks, J.R. (1939). Value and Capital, Clarendon Press, Oxford (2nd ed. in 1946).

45 Hindy, A. (1995). "Viable prices in financial markets with solvency constraints". *Journal of Mathematical Economics* 24: 105–136.

46 Hirshleifer, D., and Titman, S. (1990). "Share tendering strategies and the success of hostile takeover bids". *Journal of Political Economics* 98(2): 295–324.

47 Hlawka, E.M. (1962). "Zur Angenäherten Berechnung Mehrfacher Integrale". *Monatsh. Math.* 66: 140–151.

48 Ho, M.S., Perraudin, W.R.M., and Sorensen, S.E. (1996). "A continuous time arbitrage pricing model". *Journal of Business and Economic Statistics* 14(1): 31–42.

49 Ho, R.Y.K., and Wong, C.S.M. (2003). "Road Map for Building the Institutional Foundation for Regional Bond Market in East Asia." Second Annual Conference of the PECC Finance Forum, on Issues

and Challenges for Regional Financial Cooperation in the Asia-Pacific, Hua Hin, Thailand, p. 21.

50 Ho, T., and Stoll, H. (1983). "The dynamics of dealer markets under competition". *Journal of Finance* 38: 1053–1074.

51 Ho, T., Schwartz, R.A., and Whitcomb, D. (1985). "The trading decision and market clearing under transaction price uncertainty". *Journal of Finance* 40(1): 21–42.

52 Ho, T.S.Y., and Lee, S.B. (2004). The Oxford Guide to financial Modeling. New York: Oxford University Press.

53 Hodrick, R., and Zhang, X. (2001). "Evaluating the specification errors of asset pricing models". *Journal of Financial Economics* 62: 327–376.

54 Hodrick, R.J. (1987). The Empirical Evidence on the Efficiency of Forward and Futures Foreign Exchange Markets. New York: Harwood Academic.

55 Hodrick, R.J., Ng, D.T.C., and Sengmueller, P. (1999). "An International Dynamic Asset Pricing Model". *International Tax and Public Finance* 6: 597–620.

56 Homan, M. (1989). A Study of Administrations Under The Insolvency Act 1986: The Results of Administration Orders Made in 1987, London: ICAEW.

57 Hommes, C.H. (2004). Heterogeneous agent models in economics and finance. In: Judd, K.L., and Tesfatsion, L. (eds.), Handbook of Computational Economics II, Elsevier.

58 Hong, H., and Stein, J.C. (1999). "A unified theory of underreaction, momentum trading and overreaction in asset markets". *Journal of Finance* 54: 2143–2184.

59 Hong, H., Lim, T., and Stein, J.C. (2000). "Bad news travels slowly: Size, analyst coverage, and the profitability of momentum strategies". *Journal of Finance* 55: 265–295.

60 Hopewell, M.H., and Kaufman, G.G. (1973). "Bond Price Volatility and Term to Maturity: A Generalized Respecification". *American Economic Review*, 749–753.

61 Howard, C.T., and D'Anton, L.J. (1984). "A Risk Return Measure of Hedging Effectiveness". *Journal of Finance and Quantitative Analysis*, 1984: 101–112.

62 Hu, J. (2002). "Real Estate Securitization: Learning from the U.S. Experience", presented at Real Estate Securitization Seminar hosted by Council for Economic Planning and Development, Taiwan.

63 Hu, X. (1997). "Macroeonomic uncertainty and the risk premium in the foreign exchange market". *International Journal of Finance and Finance* 16: 699–718.

64 Huang, R., and Stoll, H. (1996). "Dealer versus auction markets: A paired comparison of execution costs on Nasdaq and the NYSE". *Journal of Financial Economics* 41: 313–357.

65 Huang, R.D. (1990). "Risk and parity in purchasing power". *Journal of Money, Credit and Banking* 22: 338–356.

66 Huberman, G., Kandel, S.A., and Stambaugh, R.F. (1987). Mimicking Portfolios and Exact Arbitrage Pricing". *Journal of Finance* 42: 1–10.

67 Hudson, J. (1987). "The Age, Regional and Industrial Structure of Company Liquidations". *Journal of Business Finance and Accounting* 14(2): 199–213.

68 Hui, B., and Heubel, B. (1984). Comparative liquidity advantages among major U.S. stock markets. DRI Financial Information Group Study Series No.84081.

69 Hull, J.C. (1997). Options, Futures, and Other Derivatives, 3rd ed., Prentice Hall.

70 Hull, J.C. (2002). Options, Futures and Other Derivatives, 5th ed., Upper Saddle River, NJ: Pearson Education.

I

1 Ibbotson, R.G., and Sinquefield, R.A. (1999). Stocks Bonds, Bills, and Inflation. Yearbook, Ibbotson Associates, Chicago.

2 Ingersoll, J.E., Skelton, J., and Weil, R.L. (1978). "Duration forty years later". *Journal of Financial and Quantitative Analysis* 621–650.

3 Isard, P. (1995). Exchange Rate Economics. Cambridge University Press.

4 Ito, T. (2003). Promoting Asian Basket Currency (ABC) Bonds, RCAST, University of Tokyo.

J

1 Jacoby, G. (2003). "A duration model for defaultable bonds". *Journal of Financial Research* 26: 129–146.

2 Jacoby, G., and Roberts, G. (2003). "Default- and call-adjusted duration for corporate bonds". *Journal of Banking and Finance* 27: 2297–2321.

3   Jagannathan, R., and Wang, Z. (1996). "The conditional CAPM and the cross-section of expected returns". *Journal of Finance* 51: 3–54.

4   Jagannathan, R., and Wang, Z. (2002). "Empirical evaluation of asset pricing models: A comparison of sdf and beta methods". *Journal of Finance* 57: 2337–2367.

5   Jagannathan, R., Georgios, S., and Wang, Z. (2002). "Generalized method moments: Applications in finance". *Journal of Business and Economic Statistics* 20: 470–481.

6   Jarrow, R., and Maureen, O'Hara (1989). "Primes and scores: An essay on market imperfections". *Journal of Finance* 44: 1263–1287.

7   Jarrow, R.A., and Rosenfeld, E.R. (1984). "Jumps risks and the intertemporal capital asset pricing model". *Journal of Business* 57(3): 337–351.

8   Jeffery, F., and Andrew, R. (1995). "Empirical Research on Nominal Exchange Rates". *Handbook of International Economics* 3: 1689–1729.

9   Jegadeesh, N., and Titman, S. (1993). "Returns to buying winners and selling losers: Implicataions for stock market efficiency". *Journal of Finance* 48: 65–91.

10 Jegadeesh, N., and Titman, S. (2001). "Profitability of momentum strategies: An evaluation of alternative explanations". *Journal of Finance* 56: 699–720.

11 Jensen, M. (ed.), (1972). Studies in the Theory of Capital Markets, Praeger Publishers.

12 Jensen, M., and Meckling, W. (1976). "Theory of the firm: Managerial behavior, agency costs, and ownership structure". *Journal of Financial Economics* 3: 305–360.

13 Jensen, M., and Richard, S.R. (1983). "The market for corporate control the scientific evidence". *Journal of Financial Economics* 11: 5–50.

14 Jensen, M.C. (1968). "The performance of mutual funds in the period 1945–64". *Journal of Finance* 23: 389–416.

15 Jensen, M.C. (1969). "Risk, the pricing of capital assets, and the evaluation of investment portfolios".0 *Journal of Business* 42: 167–247.

16 Jensen, M.C. (1986). "Agency costs of free cash flow, corporate finance, and takeovers". *American Economic Review* 76(2): 323–329.

17 Jensen, M.C., and Richard, S.R. (1983). "The market for corporate control: The scientific evidence". *Journal of Financial Economics* 11(1–4): 593–638.

18 Jensen, M.C., and William, H.M. (1976). "Theory of the firm: Managerial behaviour, agency cost and ownership structure". *Journal of Financial Economics* 3: 305–360.

19 Jenson, M. (1988). "Takeovers: Their causes and consequences". *Journal of Economics Perspectives* 2(1): 21–48.

20 Jiang, C., and Chiang, T.C. (2000) "Do foreign exchange risk premiums relate to the volatility in the foreign exchange and equity markets?" *Applied Financial Economics* 10: 95–104.

21 Jiang, W. (2003). "A nonparametric test of market timing". *Journal of Empirical Finance* 10: 399–425.

22 Jobson, J.D., and Robert, K. (1982). "Potential performance and tests of portfolio efficiency". *Journal of Financial Economics* 10: 433–466.

23 Johannes, M. (2003). "The statistical ena economic role of jumps in continuous time interest rate models". *Journal of Finance*, forthcoming.

24 John, K., Larry, H.P.L., and Jeffry, N. (1992). "The voluntary restructuring of large firms in response to performance decline". *Journal of Finance* 47(3): 891–917.

25 John, K., Lynch, A.W., and Puri, M. (2003). "Credit ratings, collateral and loan characteristics: Implications for yield". *Journal of Business* (July).

26 Johnson, K.H., and Donald S.S. (1974). "A note on diversification and reduction of dispersion". *Journal of Financial Economics*, 365–372.

27 Johnson, K.H., and Richard C.B. (1975). "The effects of sample sizes on the accuracy of E-V and SSD efficient criteria". *Journal of Financial and Quantitative Analysis* 10: 813–848.

28 Johnson, N.F., Lamper, D., Paul, J., Hart, M.L., and Howison, S. (2001). "Application of multi-agent games to the prediction of financial time-series". *Physica A* 299: 222–227.

29 Johnson, T.C. (2002). "Volatility, momentum, and time-varying skewneww in foreign exchange returns". *Journal of Business and Economic Statistics* 20(3): 390–411.

30 Johnston, E.T., and Van Drunen, L.D. (1988). "Pricing mortgage pools with heterogeneous mortgagors: Empirical evidence". Working Paper, University of Utah.

31 Jones, C., and Lipson, M. (2001). "Sixteenths: Direct evidence on institutional trading costs". *Journal of Financial Economics* 59: 253–278.

32 Jones, C.M. (2002). "A century of stock market liquidity and trading costs, working paper, Columbia University". *Journal of Political Economy* 111(3): 642–685.

33 Jones, J., Lang, W., and Nigro, P. (2000). "Recent trends in bank loan syndications: Evidence for 1995 to 1999". Working Paper, Office of the Controller of the Currency.

34 Jorian, P., and Sweeney, R.J. (1996). Mean reversion in real exchange rates. *International Journal of Finance and Economics* 15: 535–550.

35 Jorion, P. (1986). "Bayes-Stein estimation for portfolio analysis". *Journal of Financial and Quantitative Analysis*, 21(3): 279–292.

36 Jorion, P. (1988). "On jump processes in the foreign exchange and stock market". *Review of Financial Studies* 1(4): 427–445.

37 Joshua, C., and Stephen, F. (2002). "The Enron Collapse". London: Financial Times, p. 30.

38 Jouini, E., and Hedi, K. (1995a). "Martingales and arbitrage in securities markets with transaction costs". *Journal of Economic Theory* 66: 178–197.

39 Jouini, E., and Hedi, K. (1995b). "Arbitrage in securities markets with short-sales constraints". *Mathematical Finance* 5: 197–232.

40 Joy, M.O., and Tollefson, J.O. (1975). "On the financial applications of discriminant analysis". *Journal of Financial and Quantitative Analysis* 10(5): 723–739.

41 Judge, G.G., Griffiths, W.E., Hill, R.C., Helmut, L., and Lee, T.C. (1985). The Theory and Practice of Econometrics. New York: John Wiley and Sons.

K

1 Kagel, J.H., and Roth, A.E. (1995). Handbook of Experimental Economics. Princeton, NJ: Princeton University Press.

2 Kahneman, D., and Tversky, A. (1979). "Prospect theory of decisions under risk". *Econometrica* 47(2): 263–291.

3 Kale J., and Noe, T.H. (1990). "Risky debt maturity choice in a sequential game equilibrium". *Journal of Financial Research* 13: 155–166.

4 Kan, R., and Zhou, G. (1999). "A critique of the stochastic discount factor methodology". *Journal of Finance*, 54: 1221–1248.

5 Kandel, S., and Robert, F.S. (1989). "A mean variance framework for tests of asset pricing models". *Review of Financial Studies* 2: 125–156.

6 Karadeloglou, P., Christos, P., Zombanakis, G. (2000). "Exchange rate vs. supply-side policies as anti-inflationary devices: A comparative analysis for the case of Greece". *Archives of Economic History* 11: 47–61.

7 Karels, G.V., and Prakash, A.J. (1987). "Multivariate normality and forecasting of business bankruptcy". *Journal of Business Finance & Accounting* 14(4): 573–595.

8 Kashyap, A., and Stein, J. (1993). Monetary Policy and Bank Lending. *NBER* Working Paper No. 4317.

9 Kau, J.B., and Kim, T. (1992). Waiting to Default: The Value of Delay, Working Paper, University of Georgia.

10 Kau, J.B., Keenan, D.C., and Kim, T. (1993). Transaction Costs, Suboptimal Termination, and Default Probabilities, Working Paper, University of Georgia.

11 Kau, J.B., Keenan, D.C., Muller III, W.J., and Epperson, J.F. (1985). "Rational pricing of adjustable rate mortgages". *AREUEA Journal* 117–128.

12 Kau, J.B., Keenan, D.C., Muller III, W.J., and Epperson, J.F. (1987). "The valuation and securitization of commercial and multifamily mortgages". *Journal of Banking and Finance* 525–546.

13 Kau, J.B., Keenan, D.C., Muller III, W.J., and Epperson, J.F. (1990a). "Pricing commercial mortgages and their mortgage-backed securities". *Journal of Real Estate Finance and Economics* 3(4): 333–356.

14 Kau, J.B., Keenan, D.C., Muller III, W.J., and Epperson, J.F. (1990b). "The valuation and analysis of adjustable rate mortgages". *Management Science* 36: 1417–1431.

15 Kau, J.B., Keenan, D.C., Muller III, W.J., and Epperson, J.F. (1992). "A generalized valuation model for fixed rate residential mortgages". *Journal of Money, Credit and Banking* 24: 279–299.

16 Kau, J.B., Keenan, D.C., Muller III, W.J., and Epperson, J.F. (1993). "Option theory and floating rate securities with a comparison of adjustable- and fixed-rate mortgages". *Journal of Business* 66(4): 595–617.

17 Kau, J.B., Keenan, D.C., Muller III, W.J., and Epperson, J.F. (1993). "The valuation at origination of fixed rate mortgages with default and prepayment". *The Journal of Real Estate Finance and Economics,* Article 1(Abstract), 11(1): 5–36.

18 Kau, J.B., Keenan, D.C., Muller III, W.J., and Epperson, J.F. (1995). "The valuation at origination of fixed-rate mortgages with default and prepayment". *Journal of Real Estate Finance and Economics* 11: 5–36.

19 Kaufman, G.G. (1984). Measuring and Managing Interest Rate Risk: A Primer, Economic Perspec-

tive, Federal Reserve Bank of Chicago (January-February), pp. 16–29.

20   Kaul, G. (1987). "Stock returns and inflation: The role of the monetary sector". *Journal of Financial Economics* 18(2): 253–276.

21   Kazemi, H. (2003). Conditional Performance of Hedge Funds, Working paper, Amherst: University of Massachusetts.

22   Keasey, K., and Watson, R. (1987). "Non-financial symptoms and the prediction of small company failure: A test of the argenti hypothesis". *Journal of Business Finance & Accounting*, 14(3): 335–354.

23   Keasey, K., and Watson, R. (1991). "Financial distress prediction models: A review of their usefulness". *British Journal of Management* 2(2): 89–102.

24   Keeley, R.H., Punjabi, S., and Turki, L. (1996). "Valuation of early-stage ventures: Option valuation models vs. traditional approach". *Entrepreneurial and Small Business Finance* 5: 115–138.

25   Kelly, S. (1998). "A binomial lattice approach for valuing a mining property IPO". *Quarterly Review of Economics and Finance* 38: 693–709.

26   Kemna, A.G.Z. (1993). "Case studies on real options". *Financial Management* 22: 259–270.

27   Kendall M.G. (1953). "The analysis of economic time-series, part I: Prices". *Journal of the Royal Statistical Society* 96 (Part I): 11–25.

28   Kennedy, P. (1991). "Comparing classification techniques". *International Journal of Forecasting* 7(3): 403–406.

29   Kennedy, P. (1992). A Guide to Econometrics, 3rd ed. Oxford: Blackwell.

30   Kiang, L.H. (2003). East Asian Capital Markets: Challenging Times, A keynote address delivered at the Euromoney 10th Asia-Pacific Issuers & Investors Forum, Singapore.

31   Kim, H., and McConnell, J. (1977). "Corporate mergers and co-insurance of corporate debt". *Journal of Finance* 32(2): 349–365.

32   Kim, M., Nelson, C.R., and Startz, R. (1991). "Mean reversion in stock returns? A reappraisal of the statistical evidence". *Review of Economic Studies* 58: 515–528.

33   Kim, T. (1978). "An assessment of performance of mutual fund management". *Journal of Financial and Quantitative Analysis*, 13(3): 385–406.

34   Kish, R.J., and Vasconcellos, G.M. (1993). "An empirical analysis of factors affecting cross-border acquisitions: U.S.-Japan". *Management International Review* 33(3): 222–245.

35   Klein, R.W., and Bawa, V.S. (1976). "The effect of estimation risk on optimal portfolio, choice". *Journal of Financial Economics* 3: 215–231.

36   Klemkosky, R.C. (1973). "The bias in composite performance measures". *Journal of Financial and Quantitative Analysis* 8: 505–514.

37   Koch, T.J., and MacDonald, S.S. (2003). Bank Management, 5th ed. Thomson/South-Weston.

38   Kocherlakota, N. (1990). "Disentangling the coefficient of relative risk aversion from the elasticity of intertemporal substitution: An irrelevance result". *Journal of Finance* 45: 175–190.

39   Kohn, M.G. (1994). Financial Institutions and Markets. New York: McGraw-Hill.

40   Korajczyk, R.A. (1985). "The pricing of forward contracts for foreign exchange". *Journal of Political Economy* 93: 346–368.

41   Korajczyk, R.A., and Viallet, C. (1989). "An empirical investigation of international asset pricing". *Review of Financial Studies* 2: 553–585.

42   Korajczyk, R.A., and Viallet, C.J. (1992). "Equity risk premia and the pricing of foreign exchange risk". *Journal of International Economics* 33: 199–220.

43   Korobov, N.M. (1957). "The approximate calculation of multiple integral using number-theoretic methods". *Dokl. Akad. Nauk SSSR* 115: 1062–1065.

44   Koskela, E. (1983). "Credit rationing and non-price loan terms". *Journal of Banking and Finance* 7: 405–416.

45   Kosowksi, R. (2001). Do mutual funds perform when it matters most to investors? US mutual fund performance and risk in recessions and booms 1962–1994, Working Paper, London School of Economics.

46   Kreps, D., and Porteus, E. (1978). "Temporal resolution of uncertainty and dynamic choice theory". *Econometrica* 46: 185–200.

47   Kroll, Y., and Levy, H. (1992). "Further tests of separation theorem and the capital asset pricing model". *American Economic Review* 82: 664–670.

48   Kroll, Y., Levy, H., and Rapoport, A. (1988a). "Experimental tests of mean-variance model for portfolio selection". *Organizational Behavior and Human Decision Processes* 42: 388–410.

49   Kroll, Y., Levy, H., and Rapoport, A. (1988b). "Experimental tests of the separation theorem and the capital asset pricing model". *American Economic Review* 78: 500–519.

50   Krugman, P. (1978). "Purchasing power parity and exchange rate, another look at the evidence". *Journal of International Economics* 8: 397–407.

51 Kryzanowski, L., Lalancette, S., and Minh Chau To (1997). "Performance atrribution using an APT with prespecified factors". *Journal of Financial and Quantitative Analysis* 32.

52 Kshirsagar, A.M. (1971). Advanced Theory of Multivariate Analysis, New York: Marcel Dekker.

53 Kuo, H.C., Wu, S., Wang, L., Chang, M. (2002). "Contingent fuzzy approach for the development of banks Credit-granting Evaluation Model". *International Journal of Business* 7(2): 53–65.

54 Kyle, A. (1985). "Continuous auctions and insider trading". *Econometrica* 53: 1315–1335.

L

1 Labys, W.C., and Chin-Wei, Y. (1996). "Le Chatelier principle and the flow sensitivity of spatial commodity models". In: van de Bergh, J.C.J.M., Nijkamp, P., and Rietveld, P. (eds.), Recent Advances in Spatial Equilibrium Modeling: Methodology and Applications, Berlin: Springer, pp. 96–110.

2 Lang, L.H., Rene, M.S., and Ralph, A.W. (1989). "Managerial performance, Tobin's Q, and the gain from successful tender offers". *Journal of Financial Economics* 24: 137–154.

3 Langetieg, T.C. (1978). "An application of a three-factor performance index to measure stockholder gains from merger". *Journal of Financial Economics* 6: 365–383.

4 Laplante, M. (2003). Mutual fund timing with information about volatility, Working paper, University of Texas at Dallas.

5 Larson, H., and Gonedes, N. (1969). "Business combinations: An exchange-ratio determination model". *Accounting Review* 720–728.

6 Lawler, G.F. (2000). Introduction to Stochastic Processes, Boca Raton: Chapman and Hall/CRC.

7 Lawler, P. (2000). "Union Wage Setting and Exchange Rate Policy". *Economica* 67: 91–100.

8 Lawless, J.F. (1982). Statistical Models and Methods for Lifetime Data, New York: John Wiley.

9 LeBaron, B. (2000). "Agent-based computational finance: Suggested readings and early research". *Journal of Economic Dynamics and Control* 24(5–7): 679.

10 LeBaron, B. (2001a). "Empirical regularities from interacting long and short memory investors in an agent-based stock market". *IEEE Transactions on Evolutionary Computation* 5: 442–455.

11 LeBaron, B. (2001b). "Evolution and time horizons in an agent-based stock market". *Macroeconomic Dynamics* 5(2): 225–254.

12 LeBaron, B. (2001c). A Builder's Guide to Agent-Based Financial Markets. Technical Report. International Business School. Waltham, MA: Brandeis University.

13 LeBaron, B. (2002a). Calibrating an Agent-Based Financial Market. Technical Report, International Business School, Waltham, MA: Brandeis University.

14 LeBaron, B. (2002b). "Short-memory traders and their impact on group learning in financial markets". *Proceedings of the National Academy of Science* 99: 7201–7206.

15 LeBaron, B. (2004a). Agent-based Computional Finance, In: Judd, K.L., and Tesfatsion, L. (eds.), Handbook of Computational Economics II. Elsevier.

16 LeBaron, B. (2004b). Building the Santa Fe artificial stock market. In: Francesco, L., and Alessandro, P. (eds.), Agent-based Theory, Languages, and Experiments, Routledge Publishing.

17 LeBaron, B., Arthur, W.B., and Palmer, R. (1999). "Time series properties of an artificial stock market". *Journal of Economic Dynamics and Control* 23: (9–10): 1487.

18 Lee, C. (1997). "The Next Domino?" *Far Eastern Economic Review* 20: 14–16.

19 Lee, C.F. (1976). "Investment horizon and functional form of the capital asset pricing model". *Review of Economics and Statistics* 58: 356–363.

20 Lee, C.F. (1985). Financial Analysis and Planning: Theory and Application. Addison-Wesley.

21 Lee, C.F., and Finnerty, J.E. (1990). Corporate Finance: Theory, Method, and Applications. Orlando, FL: Harcourt Brace Jovanovich.

22 Lee, C.F., and Jen, F.C. (1978). "Effects of measurement errors on systematic risk and performance measure of a portfolio". *Journal of Financial and Quantitative Analysis* 13: 299–312.

23 Lee, C.F., and Kau, J.B. (1987). "Dividend payment behavior and dividend policy of REITs". *The Quarterly Review of Economics and Business* 27: 6–21.

24 Lee, C.F., and Rahman, S. (1990). "Market timing, selectivity and mutual fund performance: An empirical investigation". *Journal of Business* 63: 261–287.

25 Lee, C.F., Chen, G.M., and Rui, Oliver M. (2001). "Stock returns and volatility on China's stock markets". *The Journal of Financial Research* 24: 523–544.

26 Lee, C.F., Finnerty, J.E., and Norton, E.A. (1997). Foundations of Financial Management. St. Paul, MN: West

27 Lee, C.F., Finnerty, J.E., and Wort, D.H. (1990). Security Analysis and Portfolio Management. Glenview, IL: Scott, Foresman/Little Brown.

28 Lee, C.F., Lee, J.C., and Lee, A.C. (2000). Statistics for Business and Financial Economics, 2nd ed. Singapore: World Scientific.

29 Lee, C.F., Newbold, P., Finnerty, J.E., and Chu, C.C. (1986). "On accounting-based, market-based, and composite-based beta predictions: methods and implications". *Financial Review* 51–68.

30 Lee, C.F., Wu, C., and Wei, K.C.J. (1990). "The heterogeneous investment horizon and the capital asset pricing model: Theory and implications". *Journal of Financial and Quantitative Analysis* 25: 361–376.

31 Lee, C.M.C., and Swaminathan, B. (2000). "Price momentum and trading volume". *Journal of Finance* 55: 2017–2069.

32 Lee, S.W., and Mullineaux, D.J. (2001). The size and composition of commercial lending syndicates, Working Paper, University of Kentucky.

33 Lehmann, B.N., and Modest, D.M. (1987). "Mutual fund performance evaluation: A comparison of benchmarks and benchmark comparisons". *Journal of Finance* 42: 233–265.

34 Lehmann, B.N., and Modest, D.M. (1988). "The empirical foundations of the arbitrage pricing theory". *Journal of Financial Economics* 21: 213–254.

35 Leibowitz, M.L., and Weinberger, A. (1981). "The uses of contingent immunization". *Journal of Portfolio Management* (Fall): 51–55.

36 Leibowitz, M.L., and Weinberger, A. (1982). "Contingent immunization, part I: Risk control procedures". *Financial Analysts Journal* (November-December): 17–32.

37 Leibowitz, M.L., and Weinberger, A. (1983). "Contingent immunization, part II: Problem areas". *Financial Analysts Journal* (January-February): 35–50.

38 Leigh, R., and North, D.J. (1978). "Regional aspects of acquisition activity in british manufacturing industry". *Regional Studies* 12(2): 227–245.

39 Leshno, M., and Levy, H. (2002). "Preferred by 'All' and preferred by 'Most' decision makers: Almost stochastic dominance". *Management Science*.

40 Lettau, M., and Ludvigson, S. (2001). "Consumption, aggregate wealth and expected stock returns". *Journal of Finance* 56: 815–849.

41 Lettau, M., and Ludvigson, S. (2001). "Resurrecting the (C)CAPM: A cross-sectional test when risk premia are time-varying". *Journal of Political Economy* 109(6): 1238–1287.

42 Lev, B., and Sunder, S. (1979). "Methodological issues in the use of financial ratios". *Journal of Accounting and Economics* 1(3): 187–210.

43 Levhari, D., and Levy, H. (1977). "The capital asset pricing model and investment horizon". *Review of Economics and Statistics* 59: 92–104.

44 Levine, R. (1989). "The pricing of forward exchange rates". *Journal of International Money and Finance* 8: 163–180.

45 Levine, R. (1997). "Financial development and economic growth: Views and agenda". *Journal of Economic Literature* 36: 688–726.

46 Levy, H. (1972). "Portfolio performance and investment horizon". *Management Science* 18(12): B645–B653.

47 Levy, H. (1992). "Stochastic dominance and expected utility: Survey and analysis". *Management Science* 38(4): 555–593.

48 Levy, H. (1997). "Risk and return: An experimental analysis". *International Economic Review* 38: 119–149.

49 Levy, H. (1998). Stochastic Dominance: Investment Decision Making Under Uncertainty. Boston, MA: Kluwer Academic Publishers.

50 Levy, H., and Levy, M. (2002c). "Arrow-Pratt risk aversion, risk premium and decision weights". *The Journal of Risk and Uncertainty* 25: 265–290.

51 Levy, H., and Levy, M. (2004). "Prospect theory and mean-variance analysis". *The Review of Financial Studies* 17: 1015–1041.

52 Levy, H., and Markowitz, H.M. (1979). "Approximating expected utility by a function of mean-variance". *American Economic Review* 69: 308–317.

53 Levy, H., and Wiener, Z. (1998). "Stochastic dominance and prospect dominance with subjective weighting functions". *Journal of Risk and Uncertainty* 16: 147–163.

54 Levy, M., and Levy, H. (2001). "Testing the risk-aversion: A stochastic dominance approach". *Econom. Lett.* 71: 233–240.

55 Levy, M., and Levy, H. (2002a). "Prospect theory: Much ado about nothing?" *Management Science* 48: 1334–1349.

56 Levy, M., and Levy, H. (2002b). "Experimental test of prospect theory value function". *Organizational Behavior and Human Decision Processes* 89: 1058–1081.

57 Levy, M., Levy, H., and Solomon, S. (2000). Microscopic Simulation of Financial Markets:

From Investor Behavior to Market Phenomena. San Diego, CA: Academic Press.

58   Lewellen, W.G. (1971). "A pure financial rationale for the conglomerate merger". *Journal of Finance* 26(2): 521–537.

59   Lewellen, W.G. (1972). "Finance subsidiaries and corporate borrowing capacity". *Financial Management* 1(1): 21–31.

60   Lin, L., and Piesse, J. (2004). "Financial risk assessment in takeover and the change of bidder shareholders' wealth". *International Journal of Risk Assessment & Management* 4(4): 332–347.

61   Lin, L., and Piesse, J. (2004). "The identification of corporate distress in UK industrials: A conditional probability analysis approach". *Applied Financial Economics*, 14: 73–82.

62   Lin, W.T. (2002). "Computing a multivariate normal integral for valuing compound real options". *Review of Quantitative Finance and Accounting* 18: 185–209.

63   Lintner J. (1956). "Distribution and incomes of corporations among dividends, retained earnings and taxes". *American Economic Review* 97–113.

64   Lintner J. (1965). "Security prices, risk, and maximal gains from diversification". *Journal of Finance* 20: 587–615.

65   Lintner, J. (1965). "The valuation of risk assets and the selection of risky investments in stock portfolios and capital budgets". *Review of Economics and Statistics* 47: 13–37.

66   Lippman, S.A., and McCall, J.J. (1986). "An operational measure of liquidity". *American Economic Review* 76(1): 43–55.

67   Litner, J. (1965). "The valuation of risk assets and the selection of risky investment in stock portfolios and capital budgets". *Review of Economics and Statistics* 47: 13–47.

68   Litterman, B., (2003), and the Quantitative Resources Group, Goldman Sachs Asset Management (2003), *Modern Investment Management*, Hoboken, NJ: Wiley.

69   Litzenberger, R.H., and Ramaswami, K. (1979). "The effects of personal taxes and dividends on capital asset prices: Theory and empirical evidence". *Journal of Financial Economics* 7(2).

70   Litzenberger, R.H., and Ramaswami, K. (1980). "Dividends, short selling restriction, tax induced investor clienteles and market equilibrium". *Journal of Finance* 35(2).

71   Litzenberger, R.H., and Ramaswami, K. (1982). "The effects of dividends on common stock prices tax effects or information effect". *The Journal of Finance* XXXVII(2).

72   Liu, S., and John Wei, K.C. (2004). "Do Industries Explain the Profitability of Momentum Strategies in European Markets?" Working paper, Hong Kong University of Science & Technology.

73   Lo A.W., and MacKinlay A.C. (1988). "Stock market prices do not follow random walks: Evidence from a simple specification test". *Review of Financial Studies* 1(1): 41–66.

74   Lo, A., and MacKinlay, A.C. (1990). "Data snooping biases in tests of financeial asset pricing models". *Review of Financial Studies* 3: 431–468.

75   Lo, A.W. (1986). "Logit versus discriminant analysis: A specification test and application to corporate bankruptcies". *Journal of Econometrics* 31(3): 151–178.

76   Lo, A.W. (1991). "Long-term memory in stock market prices". *Econometrica* 59(5): 1279–1313.

77   Long, J. (1974). "Stock prices, inflation, and the term structure of interest rates". *Journal of Financial Economics* 1: 131–170.

78   Long, J. (1990). "The numeraire portfolio". *Journal of Financial Economics* 26: 29–70.

79   Lothian, J.R., and Taylor, M.P. (1997a). "The recent float from the perspective of the past two centuries". *Journal of Political Economy* 104: 488–509.

80   Lothian, J.R., and Taylor, M.P. (1997b) "Real exchange rate behavior". *Journal of International Money and Finance* 16: 945–954.

81   Loviscek, A.L., and C-W.,Y. (1997). "Assessing the impact of the investment company act's diversification rule: A portfolio approach". *Midwest Review of Finance and Insurance* 11(1): 57–66.

82   Low, V. (1994). "The MAS model: Structure and some policy simulations. In Outlook for the Singapore Economy, Chapter 3, Singapore: Trans Global Publishing, pp. 20–32.

83   Lu, C., and Yangpin, S. (2004). Do REITs pay enough dividends? Unpublished working paper, Department of Finance, Yuan Ze University.

84   Lucas, R.E., Jr. (1978). "Asset prices in an exchange economy". *Econometrica* 46: 1429–1445.

85   Lucas, R.E., Jr. (1982) "Interest rates and currency prices in a two-country world". *Journal of Monetary Economics* 10: 335–360.

86   Luce, R.D. (2000). Utility of Gains and Losses: Measurement-Theoretical and Experimental Approaches. Mahwah, NJ: Erlbaum.

87 Luehrman, T.A. (1998). "Investment opportunities as real options: Getting started on the numbers". *Harvard Business Review* (July–August): 51–67.

88 Luehrman, T.A.(1998). "Strategy as Portfolio of Real Options". *Harvard Business Review* (September–October): 89–99.

89 Luttmer, E. (1996). "Asset pricing in economies with frictions". *Econometrica* 64: 1439–1467.

90 Lynch, A.W., Wachter, J., and Walter, B. (2004). Does Mutual Fund Performance Vary Over the Business Cycle. Working Paper, New York University.

91 Lyness, J.N., and Gabriel, J.R. (1969). "Comment on a new method for the evaluation of multidimensional integrals". *J. Chem. Phys.* 50: 565–566.

92 Lyons, R.K. (2001). The Microstructure Approach to Exchange Rates. MIT Press.

M

1 MaCardle, K.F., and Viswanathan, S. (1994). "The direct entry versus takeover decision and stock price performance around takeovers". *Journal of Business* 67(1): 1–43.

2 Macaulay, F. (1938). Some Theoretical Problems Suggested by the Movement of Interest Rates, Bond Yields, and Stock Prices in the U.S. since 1856 New York: National Bureau of Economic Research.

3 Macaulay, F.R. (1938). Some Theoretical Problems Suggested by the Movement of Interest Rates, Bonds, Yields, and Stock Prices in the United States since 1856. National Bureau of Economic Research, New York: Columbia University Press, pp. 44–53.

4 Machina, M.J. (1994). "Review of generalized expected utility theory: The rank-dependent model". *Journal of Economic Literature* 32: 1237–1238.

5 MacKinlay, A.C. (1995). "Multifactor models do not explain deviations from the CAPM". *Journal of Financial Economics* 38: 3–28.

6 Maddala, G.S. (1983). Limited-dependent and Qualitative Variables in Econometrics. Cambridge: Cambridge University Press.

7 Madhavan, A. (2000). "Consolidation, fragmentation, and the disclosure of trading information". *Review of Financial Studies* 8(3).

8 Madhavan, A., David, P., and Daniel W. (2004). "Should securities markets be transparent?" *Journal of Financial Markets.*

9 Madura, J., Geraldo, M.V., and Richard, J.K. (1991). "A valuation model for international acquisitions". *Management Decision* 29(4): 31–38.

10 Madura, J., Tucker, A.L., and Zarruk, E.R. (1993). "Market reaction to the thrift bailout". *Journal of Banking & Finance* 17(4): 591–608.

11 Majd, S., and Robert, S.P. (1987). "Time to build option value, and investment decisions". *Journal of Financial Economics* 18: 7–27.

12 Malatesta, P.H. (1983). "The wealth effect of merger activity and the objective functions of merging firms". *Journal of Financial Economics* 11: 155–181.

13 Malpass, D. (1997). "Break the IMF Shackles". *The Wall Street Journal* p. 15.

14 Malpass, D. (1998). "The Road Back from Devaluation". *The Wall Street Journal* p. 16.

15 Mamaysky, H., Matthew, S., and Hong, Z. (2003). Estimating the Dynamics of Mutual Fund Alphas and Betas. Yale School of Organization and Management.

16 Maness, T.S., and John, T.Z. (1998). Short Term Financial Management, Fort Worth, Texas: The Dryden Press.

17 Manne, H.G. (1965). "Mergers and the market for corporate control". *Journal of Political Economy* 73(2): 110–120.

18 Manski, C.F., and Daniel, L. McFadden (1981). Alternative estimators and sample designs for discrete choice analysis. In: Manski, C.F., and McFadden, D.L. (eds.), Structural Analysis of Discrete Data with Econometric Applications, London: MIT Press. pp. 2–50.

19 Mark, N.C. (1988)."Time-varying betas and risk premia in the pricing of forward foreign exchange contracts". *Journal of Financial Economics* 22: 335–354.

20 Markowitz, H. (1959). "Portfolio selection: Efficient diversification of investments". New York: John Wiley.

21 Markowitz, H.M. (1952a). "Portfolio selection". *Journal of Finance* 7: 77–91.

22 Markowitz, H.M. (1952b). "The utility of wealth". *Journal of Political Economy* 60: 151–156.

23 Markowitz, H.M. (1956). "The optimization of a quadratic function subject to linear constraints". *Naval Research Logistics Quarterly* 3: 111–133.

24 Markowitz, H.M. (1987). Mean variance analysis, Portfolio choice and capital markets. New York: Basil Blackwell.

25 Markowitz, H.M. (1990). Mean-Variance Analysis in Portfolio Choice and Capital Markets. Basil: Blackwell.

26 Markowitz, H.M. (1991). "Foundation of portfolio theory". *Journal of Finance* XLVI(2): 469–477.

27 Marks, S., and Olive, J.D. (1974). "Discriminant functions when covariance matrices are unequal". *Journal of the American Statistical Association* 69(346): 555–559.

28 Marschak, J. (1938). "Money and the theory of assets". *Econometrica*, 6: 311–325.

29 Marston, R.C. (1997)."Tests of three parity conditions: Distinguishing risk premia and systematic forecast errors. *Journal of International Money and Finance* 16: 285–303.

30 Martin, D. (1977)."Early warning of bank failure: A logit regression approach". *Journal of Banking And Finance* 1(3): 249–276.

31 Mays, M., and Preiss, M. (2003). "Asia must put its savings to work". *Financial Times* 7: 15.

32 McDonald, B., and Michael, H.M. (1984). "The functional specification of financial ratios: An empirical examination". *Accounting And Business Research* 15(59): 223–228.

33 McDonald, R. (2002). *Derivatives Markets*. Addison Wesley.

34 McDonald, R., and Daniel, S. (1984). "Option pricing when the underlying asset earns a below-equilibrium rate of return: A note". *Journal of Finance* 39: 261–265.

35 McDonald, R., and Daniel, S. (1985). "Investment and the valuation of firms when there is an option to shut down". *International Economic Review* 26: 331–349.

36 McDonald, R.L. (2002). *Derivatives Markets*. Boston, MA: Pearson.

37 McKinnon, R.I. (1971). Money and Capital in Economic Development. Washington DC : The Brookings Institution.

38 McKinnon, R.I. (1991). The Order of Economic Liberalization: Financial Control in the Transition to a Market Economy. Baltimore : Johns Hopkins University Press.

39 McLean, B. (1999). "Net stocks have their seasons too". *Fortune* 6: 305–308.

40 McLeay, S. (1986). "Students and the distribution of financial ratios". *Journal of Business Finance & Accounting* 13(2): 209–222.

41 McNamee, M. (2000). "Trading online: It's a jungle out there". *Business Week*, pp. 168–169.

42 Meese R. (1990) . "Currency fluctuations in the post-Bretton Woods era". *The Journal of Economic Perspectives* 4(1): 117–134.

43 Meese R., and Rogoff, K. (1983). "Empirical exchange rate models of the seventies". *Journal of International Economics* 14: 3–24.

44 Mehra, R., and Prescott, E.C. (1985). "The equity premium: A puzzle". *Journal of Monetary Economics* 15: 145–161.

45 Melnik, A., and Plaut, S. (1986). "Loan commitment contracts, terms of lending, and credit allocation". *Journal of Finance* 41: 425–435.

46 Mensah, Y. (1983). "The differential bankruptcy predictive ability of specific price level adjustments: Some empirical evidence". *Accounting Review* 58(2): 228–246.

47 Merton, R. (1973). "Theory of rational optional pricing". *Bell Journal of Economics and Management Science* 4: 141–183.

48 Merton, R.C. (1973). "An intertemporal capital asset pricing model". *Econometrica* 4(5): 867–887.

49 Merton, R.C. (1974). "On the pricing of corporate debt: The risk structure of interest rates". *Journal of Finance* 29: 449–470.

50 Merton, R.C. (1976). "Option pricing when underlying stock returns are discontinuous". *Journal of Financial Economics* 3: 125–144.

51 Merton, R.C. (1980). "On estimating the expected return on the market: An exploratory investigation". *Journal of Financial Economics* 8: 323–362.

52 Merton, R.C., and Roy, D.H. (1981). "On market timing and investment performance II: Statistical procedures for evaluating forecasting skills". *Journal of Business* 54: 513–534.

53 Michaud, R.O. (1989)."The markowitz optimization enigma: Is 'optimized' optimal ?" *Financial Analysis Journal* 45: 31–42.

54 Milgrom, P., and John, R. (1982). "Limit pricing and entry under incomplete information: An equilibrium analysis". *Econometrica* 50(2): 443–460.

55 Milgrom, P., and John, R. (1992). Economics, Organisation and Management, New Jersey: Prentice-Hall.

56 Miller M., and Modigliani, F. (1961). "Dividend policy, growth and the valuation of shares". *Journal of Business* 43: 411–432.

57 Miller M.H. and Orr, D. (1968). "A model of the demand for money". *Quarterly Journal of Economics* 80: 413–435.

58 Miller, R.E., and Gehr, A.K. (1978). "Sample size bias and Shape's performance measure: A note". *Journal of Finance and Quantitative Analysis* 943–946.

59 Mintel International Group Ltd. "Online Trading Market – US Report", December 1, 2002.

60 Mishkin, F.S. (1984). "Are real interest rates equal across countries: An empirical investigation of international parity conditions". *Journal of Finance* 39: 1345–1357.

61 Mitchell, M.L., and Kenneth, L. (1990). "Do bad bidders become good targets?" *Journal of Political Economy* 98(2): 372–398.

62 Modigliani, F., and Leah, M. (1997). "Risk-adjusted performance: How to measure it and why". *Journal of Portfolio Management* 23: pp. 45–54.

63 Modigliani, F., and Merton, H.M. (1963). "Corporate income taxes and the cost of capital". *American Economic Review* 53(3): 433–443.

64 Modigliani, F., and Merton, M. (1958). "The cost of capital, corporation finance and the theory of investment". *American Economic Review* 48: 261–297.

65 Montiel, P.J. (1989). "Empirical analysis of high-inflation episodes in Argentina, Brazil and Israel". *IMF Staff Papers* 36: 527–549.

66 Moore, A. (1962). "A statistical analysis of common stock prices". Ph.D. thesis, Graduate School of Business, University of Chicago.

67 Morgan, J.P. (1994). Introduction to Riskmetrics. New York: J.P. Morgan.

68 Moskowitz, T.J., and Mark, G. (1999). "Do industries explain momentum?" *Journal of Finance* 54: 1249–1290.

69 Mossin, J. (1966). "Equilibrium in a capital asset market". *Econometrica* 34(4): 768–783.

70 Muellbauer, J., and Richard, P. (1978). "Macroeconomic models with quantity rationing". *Economic Journal* 88: 788–821.

71 Mullaney, T. (2001). "What's an investor to do?" *Business Week*. pp. EB14–EB15.

72 Mundell, R.A. (1963). "Capital mobility and stabilization under fixed and flexible exchange rates". *Canadian Journal of Economics and Political Science* 29: 475–485.

73 Mungthin, N. (2000). "Thai bond market development (in Thai)". Bank of Thailand.

74 Murphy, A., and Daniel, W. (2003). Order Flow Consolidation and Market Quality: An Empirical Investigation. Working Paper, Manhattan College.

75 Musumeci, J.J., and Sinkey, J.F., Jr. (1990). "The international debt crisis, investor contagion, and bank security returns in 1987: The Brazilian experi-ence". *Journal of Money, Credit, and Banking* 22: 209–220.

76 Myers, S. (1977). "The determinants of corporate borrowing". *Journal of Financial Economics* 5: 147–176.

77 Myers, S.C. (1968). "Procedures for capital budgeting under uncertainty". *Industrial Management Review* 9(3): 1–19.

78 Myers, S.C. (1984). "Finance theory and financial strategy". *Interface* 14: 126–137.

79 Myers, S.C. (1984). "The capital structure puzzle". *Journal of Finance* 39: 575–592.

80 Myers, S.C. (1987). "Finance theory and financial strategy". *Midland Corporate Finance Journal* 5: 6–13.

N

1 Nagao, H. (2003). "Market for Asian bonds taking shape". *The Nikkei Weekly*, p.39.

2 Nasdaq (2001). The impact of decimalization on the Nasdaq stock market, prepared by Nasdaq Research Department.

3 Nawalkha, S.K., and Donald, R.C. (1997). "The M-Vector model: Derivation and testing of extensions to M-square". *Journal of Portfolio Management* 23(2): 92–98.

4 Neftci, S.N. (2000). An Introduction to the Mathematics of Financial Derivatives. 2nd ed., New York : Academic press.

5 Neuberger, A., and Schwartz, R.A. (1990). "Current developments in the London equity market". *Finanzmarkt und Portfolio Management* 3: 281–301.

6 Newey, W.K., and West, K.D. (1987). "A simple, positive semi-definite, heteroskedasticity and auto-correlation consistent covariance matrix". *Econometrica* 55: 703–708.

7 Nickell, S.J., and Andrews, M. (1983). "Unions, real wages and employment in Britain, 1951–79". *Oxford Economic Papers* 35(Supplement): 183–206.

8 Niederhoffer, V., and Osborne, M.F.M. (1966). "Market making and reversal on the stock exchange". *Journal of the American Statistical Association*, 61: 897– 916.

9 Nieuwland, F.G.M.C., Verschoor, W.F.C., and Wolff, C.C.P. (1991). "EMS exchange rates". *Journal of International Financial Markets, Institutions and Money* 2: 21–42.

10 NYSE (2001). Comparing bid-ask spreads on the NYSE and NASDAQ immediately following

NASDAQ decimalization, prepared by NYSE Research Department.

O

1   O/ksendal, B. "Stochastic differential equations". 5th ed., New York: Springer.
2   Odean, T. "Are investors reluctant to realize their losses". *Journal of Finance* 53: pp. 1775–1798.
3   Ogawa, O., Junko S. (2004). "Bond issuers' trade-off for common currency basket denominated bonds in East Asia". *Journal of Asian Economics* 15: pp. 719–738.
4   Ogden, J.P., Frank, C.J., and Philip, F. O'Connor (2003). Advanced Corporate Finance: Policies and Strategies. Upper Saddle River , NJ: Prentice Hall.
5   Oh, G., Park, D., Park, J., and Yang, D.Y. (2003). "How to mobilize the Asian savings within the region: Securitization and credit enhancement for the development of East Asia's bond market". *Korea Institute for International Economic Policy Working Paper 03-02.*
6   Ohlson, J.A. (1980). "Financial ratios and the probabilistic prediction of bankruptcy". *Journal of Accounting Research* 18(1): pp. 109–131.
7   Oldfield, G.S., Rogalski, R.J., and Jarrow, R.A. (1977). "An autoregressive jump process for common stock returns". *Journal of Financial Economics* 5: 389–418.
8   Omberg, E. (1988). "Efficient discrete time jump process models in option pricing". *Journal of Financial and Quantitative Analysis* 23(2): 161–174.
9   Opiela, N. (2000). "Online trading: Opportunity or obstacle?" *Journal of Financial Planning* pp. 54–60.
10 Osborne, M. (1959). "Brownian motion in the stock market". Operations Research 7: 145–173.
11 Oswald, A.J. (1985). "The economic theory of trade unions: An introductory survey". *Scandinavian Journal of Economics* 87(2): 160–93.
12 Otani, I., and Cyrus, S.(1988). "Financial, exchange rate, and wage policies in Singapore, 1979–86". *International Monetary Fund Staff Papers* 35(3): 474–495.
13 Ozenbas, D., Schwartz, R.A., and Wood, R., (2002). "Volatility in U.S. and European equity markets: An assessment of market quality". *International Finance* 437–461.

P

1   Pagano, M., and Schwartz, R.A. (2003). "A closing call's impact on market quality at Euronext Paris". *Journal of Financial Economics* 68: 439–484.
2   Palepu, K.G. (1986). "Predicting takeover targets: A methodological and empirical analysis". *Journal of Accounting and Economics* 8(1): pp. 3–35.
3   Pamepinto, S. (1988). Reincorporation: 1988 background report, Investor Responsibility Research Center Report, Washington, DC.
4   Panchapagesan, V. (1998). What If Time Priority Is Not Enforced Among Traders? Working Paper, Washington University.
5   Panyagometh, K., Roberts, G.S., and Gottesman, A.A. (2004). The Relation between Performance Pricing Covenants and Corporate Loan Spreads. Working Paper, York University.
6   Parunak, H.V.D., Robert S., and Rick, L.R. (1998). Agent-based modeling vs. equation-based modeling: A case study and users' guide. In: Sichman, MABS, Conte, and Gilbert (eds.), Multiagent systems and Agent-based Simulation Berlin: Springer-Verlag.
7   Pastena, V., and William, R. (1986). "The merger bankruptcy alternative". *Accounting Review* 61(2): pp. 288–301.
8   Pastor, L., and Stambaugh, R.F. (2003). Liquidity risk and expected stock returns.
9   Patel, J. (1990). "Purchasing power parity as a long run relation". *Journal of Applied Econometrics* 5: 367–379.
10 Patrick, P.J.F. (1932). "A comparison of ratios of successful industrial enterprises with those of failed firms". *Certified Public Accountant* October, November, and December, pp. 598–605, 656–662, and 727–731, respectively.
11 Paye, B., and Allan, T. (2003). How stable are financial prediction models? Evidence from US and International Stock Market Data, working paper, San Diego: University of California.
12 Payne, R. (1999). Informed Trade in Spot Foreign Exchange Markets: An Empirical Investigation. Typescript, London School of Economics.
13 Pearson, N.D., and Sun, T. (1989). A Test of the Cox, Ingersoll, Ross Model of the Term Structure of Interest Rates Using the Method of Maximum Likelihood. Working Paper, Stanford University.
14 Peel, M.J., and David, A.P. (1987). "Some further empirical evidence on predicting private company failure". *Accounting and Business Research*, 18(69): pp. 57–66.

15 Peel, M.J., and Nicholas, W. (1989). "The liquid-ation/merger alternative: Some results for the UK corporate sector". *Managerial and Decision Economics* 10(3): pp. 209–220.

16 Pennachi, G.G. (1991). "Identifying the dynamics of real interest rates and inflation: Evidence using survey data". *Review of Financial Studies* 4(1): 53–86.

17 Permanent Subcommittee on Investigations of the Committee of Governmental Affairs, United States Senate, The Role of the Board of Directors in Enron's Collapse, Report 107–70, July 8, 2002.

18 Perry, G.L. (1967). Wages and the Guideposts. American Economic Review, 57(3): 897–904.

19 Pesaran, M.H., and Alan, T. (1995). "Predictability of stock returns: Robustness and economic significance". *Journal of Finance* 50: 1201–1228.

20 Pesek, Jr., William, Jr. (2005). "Dollar skeptics in Asia have prominent company". *International Herald Tribune* p.B4.

21 Peters, E.E. (1991). Chaos and Order in the Capital Markets: A New View of Cycles, Prices and Market Volatility. New York: John Wiley & Sons, Inc.

22 Peterson, M.A., and Rajan, R.G. (1995). "The effect of credit market competition on lending relationships". *Quarterly Journal of Economics* 110: 403–444.

23 Pethokoukis, J. (1999). Forget the Cyclone. The Net Ride is Scarier. *U.S. News & World Report* p. 55.

24 Pethokoukis, Ja. (1999). "The Young and the Fearless". *Business Week*, 1: pp. 63–64.

25 Pickles, E., and Smith, J.L. (1993). "Petroleum property valuation: A binomial lattice implementation of option pricing theory". *Energy Journal* 14: 1–26.

26 Pindyck, R.S. (1993). "Investments of uncertain cost". *Journal of Financial Economics* 34: 53–76.

27 Plott, C.R. (1979). "The application of laboratory experimental methods to public choice". In: Russell, C.S. (ed.), Collective Decision Making, Washington: Resources for the Future.

28 Pontiff, J., and Schall, L. (1998). "Book-to-market as a predictor of market returns". *Journal of Financial Economics* 49: 141–160.

29 Pozzolo, A.F. (2002). Collateralized Lending and Borrowers' Riskiness, Working Paper, Banca d' Italia.

30 Pratt, J.W. (1964). "Risk aversion in the small and in the large". *Econometrica* 32: 122–136.

31 Prelec, D. (1998). "The probability weighting function". *Econometrica* 66: 497–527.

32 Prescott, E.S. (2002). "Can risk-based deposit insurance premiums control moral hazard?" *Federal Reserve Bank of Richmond Economic Quarterly* 88(2): pp. 87–100.

33 Press, S.J. (1967). "A compound events model for security prices". *Journal of Business* 40(3): 317–335.

34 Preston, M.G., and Baratta, P. (1948). "An experimental study of the auction-value of uncertain outcomes". *American Journal of Psychology, 61*: 183–193.

35 Prisman, E. (1986)."Immunization as a MaxMin Strategy: A New Look". *Journal of Banking and Finance* 10: 493–504.

36 Prisman, E. (1986). "Valuation of risky assets in arbitrage free economies with frictions". *Journal of Finance* 41: pp. 293–305.

37 Prisman, E.Z., and Marilyn, R.S. (1988). "Duration measures for specific term structure estimations and applications to bond portfolio immunization". *Journal of Banking and Finance* 12(3): 493–504.

Q

1 Quiggin, J. (1982). "A theory of anticipated utility". *Journal of Economic Behavior and Organization* 3: 323–343.

2 Quiggin, J. (1993). Generalized expected utility theory: The rank dependent model. Boston, MA: Kluwer Academic Publishers.

R

1 Radcliffe, R.C. (1989). Investment: Concepts, Analysis, Strategy. 3rd ed. Glenview, IL: Scott, Foresman/Little Brown.

2 Radcliffe, R.C. (1990). Investment: Concepts, Analysis, and Strategy. 3rd ed. Glenview, IL: Scott, Foresman and Company.

3 Radelet, S., and Sachs, J. (1998). "The East Asian financial crisis: Diagnosis, remedies, prospects". *Brookings Papers on Economic Activity* 1: 1–90.

4 Rajan, R.G. (1992). "Insiders and outsiders: The choice between informed and arm's-length debt". *Journal of Finance* 47: 1367–1400.

5 Ramírez, C.D. (2001). "Even more on monetary policy in a small open economy". *International Review of Economics and Finance* 10(3): 399–405.

6 Rapoport, A. (1984). "Effects of wealth on portfolio under various investment conditions". *Acta Psychologica* 55: 31–51.

7 Reardon, T. (2000). "The Price is right". *Accountancy*, May, p. 81.

8 Redington, F.M. (1952). "Review of the principles of life office valuation". *Journal of the Institute of Actuaries* 78: 286–340.

9 Rees, Bill (1990). Financial Analysis. London: Prentice Hall.

10 Reilly, F.K. (1986). Investments. 2nd ed. Chicago, IL: The Dryden Press.

11 Rendelman, R.J., and Bartter, B.J. (1979). "Two-Stat option pricing". *Journal of Finance* 34, September.

12 Rennhack, R., and Guillermo, M. (1988). "Capital Mobility and Monetary Policy in Colombia". Working Paper no. 88/77, International Monetary Fund (August).

13 Rescher, N. (1980). Induction: An Essay on the Justification of Inductive Reasoning. Pittsburgh: University of Pittsburgh Press.

14 Rhee, S.G. (2003). "The Structure and Characteristics of East Asian Bond Markets". Second Annual Conference of the PECC Finance Forum, on Issues and Challenges for Regional Financial Cooperation in the Asia-Pacific, Hua Hin, Thailand, July 8–9, p.21.

15 Richard, S.F. (1991). "Housing prices and prepayments for fixed-rate mortgage-backed securities". *Journal of Fixed Income* (December): 54–58.

16 Richard, S.F., and Roll, R. (1989). "Prepayments on fixed-rate mortgage-backed securities". *Journal of Portfolio Management* 15: 73–82.

17 Richards, A.J. (1997). "Winner-loser reversals in national stock market indices: Can they be explained"? *Journal of Finance* 52: 2129–2144.

18 Roberts, H.V. (1959). "Stock market 'patterns' and financial analysis: Methodological suggestions". *Journal of Finance* 14: 1–10.

19 Robinson, R.J., and Shane, P.B. (1990). "Acquisition accounting method and bid premia for target firms". *The Accounting Review*, 65(1): 25–48.

20 Rockefeller, D. (1998). "Why we need the IMF"? *The Wall Street Journal* May 1, p. 17.

21 Roe, M.J. (1991). "Political element in the creation of a mutual fund industry". *University of Pennsylvania Law Review* 1469: 1–87.

22 Rogoff, K. (1996). "The purchasing power parity puzzle". *Journal of Economic Literature*, 34: 647–668.

23 Roll, R. (1977). "A critique of the asset pricing theory's tests - part 1: On past and potential testability of the theory". *Journal of Financial Economics* 4: 129–176.

24 Roll, R. (1977). "An analytic valuation formula for unprotected American call options on stocks with known dividends". *Journal of Financial Economics* 5: 251–258.

25 Roll, R. (1978). "Ambiguity when performance is measured by the securities market line". *Journal of Finance* 33: 1051–1069.

26 Roll, R. (1979). Violations of purchasing power parity and their implications for efficient international commodity market. In Sarnat, M., and Szego, G.P. (eds.), International Finance and Trade, Cambridge, MA: Ballinger.

27 Roll, R. (1986). "The hubris hypothesis of corporate takeovers". *Journal of Business*, 59(2): 197–216.

28 Roll, R. (1992). "Industrial structure and the comparative behavior of international stock market indexes". *Journal of Finance* 47: 3–41.

29 Roll, R. (1996). "U.S. Treasury inflation-indexed bonds: the design of a new security". *The Journal of Fixed Income* 6(3): 9–28.

30 Roll, R., and Ross, S.A. (1980). "An empirical investigation of the arbitrage pricing theory". *Journal of Finance* 33: 1073–1103.

31 Roll, R., and Solnik, B. (1979). "On some parity conditions encountered frequently in international economics". *Journal of Macroeconomics* 1: 267–283.

32 Roll, R.R. (1984). "A simple implicit measure of the effective bid-ask spread in an efficient market". *Journal of Finance* 39: 1127–1140.

33 Romano, R. (1985). "Law as a product: Some pieces of the reincorporation puzzle". *Journal of Law, Economics, and Organization* 1(2):225–283.

34 Romer, D. (1993). "Rational asset-price movements without news". *American Economic Review* 83: 1112–1130.

35 Ross, S. (1976). Return, risk and arbitrage. In Ballinger, Friend, I., and Bicksler, J. (Eds.), Risk and Return in Finance. Cambridge, MA, pp. 189–218.

36 Ross, S. (1977). Risk, return and arbitrage. In: Ballinger, Friend, I., and Bicksler, J. (Eds.). Risk and Return in Finance, Cambridge, Massachusetts.

37 Ross, S. (1978). "A simple approach to the valuation of uncertain income streams". *Journal of Business* 51: 453–475.

38 Ross, S.A. (1976). "The arbitrage theory of capital asset pricing." *Econometrica*.

39 Ross, S.A. (1976). "The arbitrage pricing theory of capital asset pricing". *Journal of Economic Theory* 13: 341–60.

40 Ross, S.A. (1977). "The determination of financial structure: The incentive signalling approach". *Bell Journal of Economics* 8(1): 23–70.

41 Ross, S.A., Westerfield, R.W., and, Jefferey Jaffe (2002). Fundamentals of Corporate Finance. 6th ed. New York, NY: McGraw-Hill/Irwin.

42 Ross, S.A., Westerfield, R.W., and, Jefferey Jaffe (2004). Corporate Finance. 7th ed. New York, NY: McGraw-Hill/Irwin.

43 Ross, S.A., Westerfield, R.W., and, Jeffrey F Jaffe. (2002). Corporate Finance. 6th ed., New York: McGraw-Hill Companies Inc.

44 Ross, S.A., Westerfield, R.W., and Jeffrey Jaffe. (2005). Corporate Finance. 7th ed., Irwin McGraw Hill, Homewood, Ill, 87.

45 Rothschild, M., and Stiglitz, J. (1970). "Increasing risk. I. A definition". *Journal of Economic Theory* 2: 225–243.

46 Rouwenhorst, K.G. (1998). "International momentum strategies". *Journal of Finance* 53: 267–284.

47 Rouwenhorst, K.G. (1999). "Local return factors and turnover in emerging stock markets". *Journal of Finance* 55: 1439–1464.

48 Rozeff, M. (1982). "Growth, beta and agency costs as determinants of dividend payout ratios". *Journal of Financial Research* 5: 249–259.

49 Rubinstein, M. (1974). "An aggregation theorem for securities markets". *Journal of Financial Economics* 1: 225–244.

50 Rubinstein, M. (1976). "The valuation of uncertain income streams and the pricing of options". *Bell Journal of Economics and Management Science* 7: 407–425.

51 Rubinstein, M. (1985). "Alternative paths for portfolio insurance". *Financial Analyst Journal* 41(July/August): 42–52.

52 Rubinstein, M., and Leland, H.E. (1981). "Replacing options with positions in stock and cash". *Financial Analysts Journal* 37 (July/August) : 63–72.

53 Ryder, H.E., Jr., and Heal, G. M. (1973). "Optimal growth with intertemporally dependent preferences". *Review of Economic Studies* 40: 1–31.

S

 1 Samuelson, P. (1970). Economics. 8th ed. New York: McGraw-Hill.

 2 Samuelson, P.A. (1945). "The effect of interest rate increases on the banking system". *American Economic Review* 35: 16–27.

 3 Samuelson, P.A. (1945). "The effects of interest rate increases on the banking system". *American Economic Review* (March), 16–27.

 4 Samuelson, P.A. (1949). "The le chatelier principle in linear programming". *Rand Corporation Monograph* August.

 5 Samuelson, P.A. (1960). "An extension of the le chatelier principle". *Econometrica* (April): 368–379.

 6 Samuelson, P.A. (1972). "Maximum principles in analytical economics". *American Economic Review* 62(3): 249–262.

 7 Samuelson, P.A. (1994). "The long term case for equities". *Journal of Portfolio Management* 21: 15–24.

 8 Samuelson, R.J. (1986). "How companies grow stale". *Newsweek* September, 8: 45.

 9 Sarkissian, S. (2003). "Incomplete consumption risk sharing and currency premiums". *Review of Financial Studies* 16: 983–1005.

10 Saunders, A., (2000). Financial Institutions Management. 3rd ed. Irwin/McGraw Hill, Boston, Chapters 8, 9 and 18.

11 Saunders, A., and Allen, L. (2002). Credit Risk Measurement: New Approaches to Value at Risk and Other Paradigms. 2nd ed. John Wiley and Sons.

12 Saunders, A., and Cornett, M. M. (2003). Financial Institutions Management. 5th ed. New York, NY: Irwin/McGraw-Hill.

13 Saunders, A., and Cornett, M. M. (2004). Financial Markets and Institutions, IRWIN/McGraw-Hill, 645–667.

14 Schall, L.D. (1971). "Firm financial structure and investment". *Journal of Financial and Quantitative Analysis* 6(3): 925–942.

15 Schall, L.D. (1972). "Asset valuation, firm investment, and firm diversification". *Journal of Business* 45(1): 11–28.

16 Scholes, M. (1969). A Test of the Competitive Hypothesis: The Market for New Issues and Secondary Offering. Ph.D. thesis, Graduate School of Business, University of Chicago.

17 Scholes, M., and Williams, J. (1977). "Estimating beta from nonsynchronous data". *Journal of Financial Economics* 5: 309–327.

18 Schroder, M. (1989). "Computing the constant elasticity of variance option pricing formula". *Journal of Finance* 44(1): 211–218.

19 Schuler, K. (1998). "A currency board beats the IMF Rx". *The Wall Street Journal* February 18, p. 19.

20 Schultz, G.P., and Aliber, R.Z. (1966). Guidelines: Formal Controls and Marketplace. Chicago: University of Chicago Press.

21 Schumpeter, J.A. (1939). Business Cycles: A Theoretical, Historical, and Statistical Analysis of the Capitalist Process. New York: McGraw-Hill.

22 Schwartz, E.S., and Torous, W.N. (1989). "Prepayment and the valuation of mortgage-backed securities". *Journal of Finance* 44: 375–392.

23 Schwartz, R.A., and Francioni, R. (2004). Equity Markets in Action: The Fundamentals of Market Structure and Trading. John Wiley & Sons.

24 Schwert, G.W. (2003). Anomalies and market efficiency. In Constantinides, G.M., Harris, M., and Stulz, R. M. (eds.), Handbook of the Economics of Finance (North Holland, Amsterdam).

25 Securities and Exchange Commission, Litigation Release 17762, October 2, 2002.

26 Seguin, P. (1991). Transactions reporting, liquidity and volatility: an empirical investigation of national market system listing. Paper given at Western Finance Association Meetings, Jackson Hole, Wyoming, June.

27 Seth, A. (1990). "Value creation in acquisitions: A Re-examination of performance issues". *Strategic Management Journal* 11: 99–115.

28 Shailer, G. (1989). "The predictability of small enterprise failures: Evidence and issues". *International Small Business Journal* 7(4): 54–58.

29 Shanken, J. (1982). "The arbitrage pricing theory: Is testable"? *Journal of Finance* 37(5): 1129–1140.

30 Shanken, J. (1985). "Multivariate tests of the zero-beta". *Journal of Financial Economics* 14: 327–348.

31 Shanken, J. (1987). "Multivariate proxies and asset pricing relations: Living with the roll critique". *Journal of Financial Economics* 18: 91–110.

32 Shanken, J. (1990). "Intertemporal asset pricing: An empirical investigation". *Journal of Econometrics* 45: 99–120.

33 Sharma, M. (2000). "The growth of web-based investment". *Information Systems Management* Spring, pp. 58–64.

34 Sharpe, W.F. (1964). "Capital assets prices: A theory of market equilibrium under conditions of risk". *Journal of Finance* 19: 425–442.

35 Sharpe, W.F. (1966). "Mutual fund performance". *Journal of Business Supplement on Security Prices* January: 119–138.

36 Sharpe, W.F. (1967). "A linear programming algorithm for mutual fund portfolio selection". *Management Science* March pp. 499–510.

37 Sharpe, W.F. (1977). The capital asset pricing model: A muti-beta interpretation. In: Levy, H., and Sarnat, M. (eds.), Financial Decision Making Under Uncertainty. New York: Academic Press.

38 Sharpe, W.F. (1984). "Factor models, CAPM's and the APT". *Journal of Portfolio Management* 11: 21–25.

39 Shefrin, H., and Statman, M. (1993). "Behavioral aspect of the design and marketing of financial products". *Financial Management* 22(2): 123–134.

40 Sheng, A. (1994). "Future Directions for Hon Kong's Debt Market," Speech at the First Annual Pan-Asia Bonds Summit, November 29–30

41 Shrieves, R., and Stevens, D. (1979). "Bankruptcy avoidance as a motive for merger". *Journal of Financial and Quantitative Analysis* 14(3): 501–515.

42 Shultz, G., Simon, W., and Wriston, W. (1998). "Who needs the IMF". *The Wall Street Journal* February 3, p. 15.

43 Shumway, T. (2001). "Forecasting bankruptcy more accurately: A simple hazard model". *Journal of Business* 74(1): 101–124.

44 Silberberg, E. (1971). "The le chatelier principle as a corollary to a generalized envelope theorem". *Journal of Economic Theory* 3: 146–155.

45 Silberberg, E. (1974). "A revision of comparative statics methodology in economics, or how to do economics on the back of an envelope". *Journal of Economic Theory* 7: 159–172.

46 Silberberg, E. (1978). The Structure of Economics: A Mathematical Analysis. New York: McGraw-Hill Book Company.

47 Simin, T. (2002). The (poor) Predictive Performance of Asset Pricing Models. working paper, The Pennsylvania State University.

48 Sims, C.A. (1980). "Macroeconomics and reality". *Econometrica* 48:1–48.

49 Singh, A. (1971). Take-overs: Their Relevance to the Stock Market and the Theory of the Firm. Cambridge: University Press.

50 Singleton, K.J. (1990).Specification and estimation of intertemporal asset pricing models. In: Friedman, E., and Hahn, F. (eds.), Handbook of Monetary Economics. North Holland.

51 Singleton, K.J. (2001). "Estimation of affine asset pricing models using the empirical characteristic function". *Journal of Econometrics* 102(1): 111–141.

52 Sinkey, J.F., Jr. (1992). Commercial Bank Financial Management in the Financial Services Industry. 4th ed. New York, NY: Macmillian.

53 Smirlock, M., and Kaufold, H. (1987). "Bank foreign lending, mandatory disclosure rules, and the

reaction of bank stock prices to the Mexican debt crisis". *Journal of Business* 60(3): 77–93.

54 Smith, G. (1999). "Day of reckoning for day-trading firms"? *Business Week* January 18, pp. 88–89

55 Smith, G. (1999). "Valuing those internet stocks". *Business Week* Feb. 8, p. 87.

56 Smith, V.L. (1976). "Experimental economics: Induced value theory". *American Economic Review Proceedings* 66: 274–279.

57 Smith, V.L. (1982). "Microeconomic systems as an experimental science". *The American Economic Review* 72: 923–955.

58 Sofianos, G. (2001). Trading and market structure research. Goldman Sachs.

59 Solnik, B. (1974). "An equilibrium model of the international capital market". *Journal of Economic Theory* 8: 500–524.

60 Solnik, B. (1978). "International parity conditions and exchange risk". *Journal of Banking and Finance* 2: 281–293.

61 Solnik, B. (1982). "An empirical investigation of the determinants of national interest rate differences". *Journal of International Money and Finance* 3: 333–339.

62 Solnik, B. (1993). "The unconditional performance of international asset allocation strategies using conditioning information". *Journal of Empirical Finance*.

63 Sonakul, M.R.C. M. (2000). Keynote Address on the Occasion of the ADB Conference on Government Bond Market and Financial Sector Development in Developing Asian Economies. Manila, 28–30 March.

64 Song, M.H., and Ralph, A.W. (2000). "Abnormal returns to rivals of acquisition targets: A test of 'Acquisition Probability Hypothesis' ". *Journal of Financial Economics* 55: 143–171.

65 Soto, G.G. (2001). "Immunization derived from a polynomial duration vector in the Spanish bond market". *Journal of Banking and Finance* 25: 1037–1057.

66 Stallworthy, E.A., and Kharbanda, O.P. (1988). Takeovers, Acquisitions and Mergers: Strategies for Rescuing Companies in Distress. London: Kogan Page Limited.

67 Stambaugh, R. (1982). "On the exclusion of assets from tests of the two parameter model". *Journal of Financial Economics* 10: 235–268.

68 Stambaugh, R.S. (1999). "Predictive regressions". *Journal of Financial Economics* 54: 315–421.

69 Standard and Poor's, 2004, Corporate defaults in 2003 recede from recent highs, Standard and Poor's, January.

70 Stanton, R. (1990). Rational Prepayment and the Valuation of Mortgage-Backed Securities. Working Paper, Stanford University.

71 Starks, L. (1987). "Performance incentive fees: an agency theoretic approach". *Journal of Financial and Quantitative Analysis* 22: 17–32.

72 Steen, N.M., Byrne, G.D., and Gelbard, E.M. (1969). "Gaussian quadratures for integrals". *Mathematics of Computation* 23: 169–180.

73 Stiglitz, J. (1972). "Some aspects of the pure theory of corporate finance: bankruptcies and takeover". *The Bell Journal of Economics and Management Science* 3(2): 458–482.

74 Stiglitz, J., and Andrew Weiss (1981). "Credit rationing in markets with imperfect information". *American Economic Review* 71: 393–410.

75 Storey, D.J., Keasey, K., Watson, R. and Pooran Wynarczyk (1987). The Performance Of Small Firms. Bromley: Croom-Helm.

76 Strahan, P.E. (1999). Borrower Risk and the Price and Nonprice Terms of Bank Loans. Working Paper, Federal Reserve Bank of New York.

77 Stulz, R.M. (1981). "A model of international asset pricing". *Journal of Financial Economics* 9: 383–406.

78 Stulz, R.M. (1986). "Asset pricing and expected inflation". *Journal of Finance* 41: 209–223.

79 Su, D. (1999). "Ownership restrictions and stock prices: Evidence from Chinese markets". *Financial Review* 34: 37–56.

80 Su, D., and Fleisher, B.M. (1999). "Why does return volatility differ in Chinese stock markets". *Pacific-Basin Finance Journal* 7: 557–586.

81 Sullivan, M.J., Jensen, M.R.H. and Hudson, C.D. (1994). "The role of medium of exchange in merger offers: Examination of terminated merger proposal". *Financial Management* 23(3): 51–62.

82 Summers, L. (1998). "Why America needs the IMF". *The Wall Street Journal*, March 27, p.16.

83 Sun, Q., and Tong, W. (2000). "The effect of market segmentation on stock prices: The China syndrome". *Journal of Banking and Finance* 24: 1875–1902.

84 Sundaresan, S.M. (1989). "Intertemporally dependent preferences and the volatility of consumption and wealth". *Review of Financial Studies* 2: 73–89.

85 Sunders, A., and Allen, L. (2002). Credit Risk Measurement. New York: John Wiley & Sons.

86 Svensson, L.E.O. (1989). "Portfolio choice with non-expected utility in continuous time". *Economics Letters* 30: 313–317.

87 Swalm, R.O. (1966). "Utility theory – Insights into risk taking". *Harvard Business Review* 44: 123–136.

T

1 Taniguchi, T. (2003). Asian Bond Market Initiative. A keynote speech delivered at the ASEAN+3 High-Level Seminar on "Fostering Bond Markets in Asia". Tokyo, *Japan Echo* p. 30.

2 Tauchen, G. (1986). "Statistical properties of generalized method of moments estimators of structural parameters obtained from financial market data". *Journal of Business and Economic Statistics* 4: 397–416.

3 Tay, N.S.P., and Linn, S.C. (2001). "Fuzzy inductive reasoning, expectation formation and the behavior of security prices". *Journal of Economic Dynamics and Control* 25(3/4): 321.

4 Taylor, M. (1988). "An empirical examination of long run purchasing power parity using cointegration techniques". *Applied Economics* 20: 1369–1381.

5 Taylor, M.P. (1995)."The economics of exchange rates". *Journal of Economic Literature* 83: 13–47.

6 Teh, K.P., and Shanmugaratnam, T. (1992). "Exchange Rate Policy: Philosophy and Conduct over the Past Decade". In: Low, L., and Toh, M.H. (eds.), *Public Policies in Singapore:* Changes in the 1980s and Future Signposts. Singapore: Times Academic Press.

7 Tehranian, H., Travlos, N., and Waegelein, J. (1987). "The effect of long-term performance plans on corporate sell-off induced abnormal returns". *Journal of Finance* 42(4): 933–942.

8 Tesfatsion, L. (2002). "Agent-based computational economics: Growing economies from the bottom up". *Artificial Life* 8(1): 55.

9 Thaler, R.H. (1999). "The end of behavioral finance". *Financial Analysts Journal* 12–17.

10 The Conference Board (2003). Commission on Public Trust and Private Enterprise.

11 Thornton, E. (2000). "Take that, cyber boy". *Business Week* 58–59.

12 Timmis, G.C. (1985). Valuation of GNMA Mortgage-Backed Securities with Transaction Costs, Heterogeneous Households, and Endogenously Generated Prepayment Rates, Working Paper, Carnegie-Mellon University.

13 Titman, S., and Torous, W. (1989). "Valuing commercial mortgages: An empirical investigation of the contingent claims approach to pricing risky debt". *Journal of Finance* 44: 345–373.

14 Tobin, J. (1958). "Liquidity preference as behavior toward risk". *Review of Economic Studies* 25: 65–86.

15 Tourk, K. (2004). "The political economy of east Asian economic integration". *Journal of Asian Economics* 15(5): 843–888.

16 Tran, H.Q., and Roldos, J. (2003). Asian Bond Markets, The Role of Securitization and Credit Guarantees. The 2nd ASEAN Central Bank Governor's Meeting, Bangkok, p. 2.

17 Travlos, N.G. (1987). "Corporate takeover bids, methods of payment, and bidding firms' stock returns". *Journal of Finance* 42(4): 943–963.

18 Treacy, W.F., and Carey, M.S. (1998). Credit risk rating at large U.S. banks, Federal Reserve Board Bulletin.

19 Treynor, J., and Black, F. (1973). "How to use security analysis to improve portfolio selection". *Journal of Business* 46: 66–86.

20 Treynor, J., and Mazuy, K. (1966). "Can mutual funds outguess the market?" *Harvard Business Review* 44: pp. 131–136.

21 Treynor, J.L. (1965). "How to Rate Management of Investment Funds". *Harvard Business Review* pp. 63–75.

22 Trigeorgis, L. (1993a). "The nature of option interactions and the valuation of investment with multiple real options". *Journal of Financial and Quantitative Analysis* 28: 1–20.

23 Trigeorgis, L. (1993b). "Real options and interactions with financial flexibility". *Financial Management* 25: 202–224.

24 Trigeorgis, L. (1994). Options in Capital Budgeting: Managerial Flexibility and Strategy in Resoure Allocation. Cambridge, MA: MIT Press.

25 Trigeorgis, L. (1996). Real Options: Managerial Flexibility and Strategy in Resource Allocation. Cambridge, MA: MIT Press.

26 Trigeorgis, L., and Mason, S.P. (1987). "Valuing managerial flexibility". *Mildland Corporate Journal* 5: 14–21.

27 Tucker, A.L., and Pond, L. (1988). "The probability distribution of foreign exchanges: Tests of candidate processes". *Review of Economics and Statistics* 70: 638–647.

28 Tversky, A., and Kahneman, D. (1981). The framing of decisions and the psychology of choice. *Science* 211: 453–480.

29 Tversky, A., and Kahneman, D. (1992). Advances in prospect theory: Cumulative representation of uncertainty. *Journal of Risk and Uncertainty* 5: 297–323.

U

1 U.S. Securities and Exchange Commission (SEC), 2000. Disclosure of order routing and execution practices, Release No. 34-43084, July 28.

2 U.S. Securities and Exchange Commission (SEC), 2000. Release No. SR-NYSE-99-48, NYSE Rule-making: Notice of filing of proposed rule change to rescind exchange rule 390; Commission request for comment on issues related to market fragmentation.

3 Unal, H., Demirguc-Kunt, A., and Leung, K.W. (1993). "The Brady plan, 1989 Mexican debt-reduction agreement, and bank stock returns in United States and Japan". *Journal of Money, Credit & Banking* 25: 410–429.

4 United Nations Conference on Trade and Development (UNCTAD). *World Investment Report 2000: Cross-Border Mergers and Acquisitions and Development*. 2000. New York, and Geneva, Switzerland.

5 Utton, M.A. (1982). The Political Economy of Big Business. Oxford: Martin Robertson.

V

1 Value Line (1994). Mutual Fund Survey. New York: Value Line.

2 Van Horne, J.C. (1986). Financial Management and Policy. 7th ed., New Jersey: Prentice-Hall.

3 Vasconcellos, G.M., and Kish, R.J.(1996). "Factors affecting cross-border mergers and acquisitions: The Canada - U.S. experience". *Global Finance Journal* 7(2): 223–238.

4 Vasconcellos, G.M., and Kish, R.J. (1998). "Cross-border mergers and acquisitions: The European-U.S. experience". *Journal of Multinational Financial Management* 8: 431–450.

5 Vasconcellos, G.M., Jeff, M., and Kish, R.J. (1990). "An empirical investigation of factors affecting cross-border acquisitions: the United States vs. United Kingdom experience". *Global Finance Journal* 1(3): 173–189.

6 Vasicek Oldrich, A. (1973). "A note on using cross-sectional information in bayesian estimation of security betas". *Journal of Finance* 28: 1233–1239.

7 Vasicek, O. (1977). "An equilibrium characterization of the term structure". *Journal of Financial Economics* 5: 177–188.

8 Viscusi, W.K. (1989). "Prospective reference theory: Toward an explanation of the paradoxes". *Journal of Risk and Uncertainty* 2: 235–264.

9 Vlaar, P.J.G., and Palm, F.C. (1993). "The Message in weekly exchange rates in the European monetary system: Mean reversion, conditional heteroscedasticity, and jumps". *Journal of Business and Economic Statistics* 11(3): 351–360.

10 Vogelstein, F. (1999). "A Virtual Stock Market". *U.S. News & World Report* pp. 47–48.

11 Vogelstein, F. (1999). "Online Traders Beware!" *U.S. News & World Report* pp. 41–42.

12 Von Neuman, J., and Morgenstern, O. (1944). Theory of games and economic behavior. Princeton, NJ: Princeton University Press.

13 Von Neumann, J., and Morgenstern, O. (1947). Theory of games and economic behavior. 2nd ed., Princeton: Princeton University Press.

14 Von Thadden, E.L. (1992). The commitment of finance, duplicated monitoring, and the investment horizon, ESF-CEPR Working Paper in Financial Markets 27.

W

1 Wagner, W.H., and Sie, T.L. (1971). "The effect of diversification on risk". *Financial Analysts Journal* November–December: 48–53.

2 Wagster, J.D. (1996). "Impact of the 1988 Basle Accord on international banks". *Journal of Finance* 51: 1321–1346.

3 Wakker, P.P. (2003). "The data of Levy and Levy (2002), Prospect theory: Much ado about nothing? actually support prospect theory". *Management Science*.

4 Wakker, P.P., Erev, I., and Weber, E.U. (1994). "Comonotonic independence: The critical test between classical and rank-dependent utility theories". *Journal of Risk and Uncertainty* 9: 195–230.

5 Walker, I.E. (1992). Buying A Company in Trouble: A Practical Guide, Hants: Gower Publishing Company Limited.

6 Wang, W. (1994). Valuation of Mortgage-Backed Securities. Working Paper, Columbia University.

7 Waud, R.N. (1970). "Public interpretation of federal discount rate changes: Evidence on the 'announcement effect' ". *Econometrica* 38: 231–250.

8 Weber, J. (1999). "The Market: Too High? Too Low?" *Business Week*, pp. 92–93.

9 Wei, Li, and Paul, B. (2003). New York Stock Market Structure, Fragmentation and Market Quality – Evidence from Recent Listing Switches, Working paper, New York Stock Exchange.

10 Weil, P. (1989). "The equity premium puzzle and the risk free rate puzzle". *Journal of Monetary Economic* 24: 401–421.

11 Wermers, R. (1997). Momentum Investment Strategies of Mutual Funds, Performance Persistence, and Survivorship Bias. Working paper. University of Colorado.

12 Weston, J. (2000). "Competition on the Nasdaq and the impact of recent market reforms". *Journal of Finance* 55: 2565–2598.

13 Weston, J.F., and Eugene F.B. (1990), Essentials of Managerial Finance. 9th ed., London: Dryden Press.

14 Whalen, G. (1991), "A proportional hazard model of bank failure: An examination of its usefulness as an early warning tool". *Economic Review* First Quarter, 20–31.

15 Wheatley, S. (1989). "A critique of latent variable tests of asset pricing models". *Journal of Financial Economics* 23: 325–338.

16 White, H. (1980). "A heteroscedasticity-consistent covariance matrix estimator and a direct test for heteroscedasticity". *Econometrica* 48: 55–68.

17 Whittington, G. (1980). "Some basic properties of accounting ratios". *Journal of Business Finance & Accounting* 7(2): 219–232.

18 Wilcox, D.W. (1998). "The introduction of indexed government debt in the United States". *The Journal of Economic Perspectives* 12(1): 219–227.

19 Wilde, L. (1980). In the case of laboratory experiments in economics. In: Pitt, J. (ed.), The Philosophy of Economics, Dordrecht, Holland: Reidel.

20 William C.P., Jr., Troubh, R.S., and Winokur, Jr., H.R. (2002). Report of Investigation by the Special Investigative Committee of the Board of Directors of Enron Corp.

21 Wilmarth, A.E. Jr. (2002). "The transformation of the U.S. financial services industry, 1975–2002: Competition, consolidation and increased risks". *University of Illinois Law Review* (2): 215–476.

22 Wilson, R.B. (1968). "The theory of syndicates". *Econometrica* 36: 119–131.

23 Wood, D., and Piesse, J. (1988). "The Information Value of Failure Predictions in Credit Assessment". *Journal of Banking and Finance* 12: 275–292.

24 Wu, Y. (1999). "Macroeconomic cooperation of exchange rate and wage movements under quasi-sterilization: Singapore experience". *Pacific Economic Review* 4(2): 195–212.

25 Wu, Y. (1999). "More on monetary policy in a small open economy: A credit view". *International Review of Economics and Finance* 8(2): 223–235.

26 Wu, Y. (2004). "Singapore's collective bargaining in a game of wage and exchange rate policies". *Open Economies Review* 15(3): 273–289.

27 Wyatt Company, 1988, Directors and officers liability survey, Chicago, IL.

Y

1 Yaari, M. (1987). "The dual theory of choice under risk". *Econometrica* 55(1): 95–115.

2 Yam, J. (1997). "Development of the Debt Market, Keynote Address at the Asian Debt Conference". http://www.info.gov.hk/hkma/eng/speeches/speechs/joseph/speech_140797b.htm, July 14.

Z

1 Zaremba, S.K. (1966). "Good lattice points, discrepancy and numerical integration". *Ann. Mat. Pura Appl.* 73: 293–318.

2 Zavgren, C.V. (1985). "Assessing the vulnerability to failure of American industrial firms: A logistic analysis". *Journal of Business, Finance and Accounting* 12(1): 19–45.

3 Zavgren, C.V. (1988). "The association between probabilities of bankruptcy and market responses – A test of market anticipation". *Journal of Business Finance & Accounting* 15(1): 27–45.

4 Zhang, P.G. (1997). Exotic Options: A Guide to Second Generation Option. Singapore: World Scientific.

5 Zhang, Z. (2001). "The impact of IMF term loans on U.S. bank creditors' equity values: An event study of South Korea's case". *Journal of International Financial Markets, Institutions and Money* 11: 363–394.

6 Zhang, Z., and Karim, K.E. (2004). The Reaction of Bank Stock Prices to the IMF Term Loans in the International Currency Crisis in 1997, Working paper.

7 Zheng, L. (1999). "Is money smart? A study of mutual fund investors' fund selection ability". *Journal of Finance* 54: 901–933.

8 Zhou, G. (1991). "Small samples tests of portfolio efficiency". *Journal of Financial Economics* 30: 165–191.

9 Zion, D., and Carache, B. (2002). The Magic of Pension Accounting, Credit Suisse First Boston.

10 Zmijewski, M.E. (1984). "Methodological issues related to the estimation of financial distress prediction models". *Journal of Accounting Research* 22(Supplement): 59–82.

PART V: Index

SUBJECT INDEX

AUTHOR INDEX

Khang, Chulsoon, 426, 780
Khang, Kenneth, 391, 413, 790
Kharbanda, Om Prakash, 554, 811
Khatdhate, Deena, 662, 786
Kiang, Lim Hug, 662, 799
Kiefer, Nicholas, 438, 788
Kim, E. Han, 552, 781
Kim, Han, 553, 799
Kim, Myung, 383, 799
Kim, T., 476, 742, 798–799
Kisgen, Darren, 391, 414, 790
Kish, Richard J., 674–675, 793, 799, 813
Klausner, Michael, 455, 786
Klein, R.W., 462, 799
Klemkosky, Robert C., 476, 799
Klingebiel, Daniela, 662, 775
Knez, Peter J., 413, 783
Koch, Timonthy J., 799
Kocherlakota, Narayana, 335, 799
Kohn, Meir G., 728, 799
Kondury, Kali, 662, 786
Korajczyck, R., 373, 785
Korkie, Robert, 374
Korobov, Nikolai Mikhailovich, 582, 799
Korting, T., 434, 794
Kose, John, 2
Koskela, E., 434, 799
Kosowksi, Robert, 414, 799
Kraus, Alan, 373, 781
Kreps, D., 335, 374, 414, 511, 602, 795, 799
Kroll, Y., 539, 799
Krugman, P., 357, 799
Kryzanowski, Lawrence, 392, 800
Kshirsagar, Anant M., 489, 800
Kulatilaka, Nalin H., 581
Kuo, Hsien Chang, 800
Kwok, Chuck, 438, 784
Kyle, Albert, 438, 800

L

Labys, Walter C., 728, 800
Lai, K.S., 356, 783
Lalancette, Simon, 392, 800
Lamper, David, 654, 797
Lamy, Robert E., 749, 780
Lang, Larry H., 674, 800
Lang, W., 434, 798
Langetieg, Terence C., 553, 800
Laplante, Mark, 392, 800
Larson, H., 800
Latta, Cynthia, 426, 780
Lau, Sie Ting, 476
Lauterbach, Beni, 699

Laux, Paul, 441, 782
Lawler, G.F., 688, 800
Lawler, Phillip, 723, 800
Lawless, J.F., 742, 800
LeBaron, Blake, 654, 800
Lee, Alice C., 801
Lee, Charles, 582, 750, 788, 800
Lee, Charles M.C., 703, 201
Lee, Cheng F., 363, 374, 392, 438, 475–476, 519, 622, 784, 800–801
Lee, John C., 801
Lee, S.W., 434, 801
Lee, Sang Bin, 500, 511, 796
Lee, Tsoung Chao, 489, 798
Leftwich, Richard, 455, 787
Lehmann, B.N., 374, 414, 801
Lehmann, Bruce, 392
Lehn, Kenneth, 553
Leibowitz, M.L., 427, 801
Leigh, Roy, 553, 801
Leland, H.E., 809
Leshno, M., 539, 801
Lesne, Jean-Philippe, 602, 779
Lettau, Martin, 383, 414, 801
Leung, Kwok-Wai, 813
Lev, Baruch, 489, 801
Levhari, David, 475, 801
Levine, R., 306, 312, 357, 662, 778, 801
Levy, H., 476, 539, 794, 799, 801, 810
Levy, M., 539, 801
Lewarne, Stephen, 714, 784
Lewellen, Wilbur G., 553, 589, 783, 802
Liew, John M., 703, 776
Lim, Terence, 703, 796
Lin, Lin, 489, 553, 802
Lin, William T., 582, 802
Linn, Scott C., 654, 812
Lintner, J., 335, 374, 463, 589, 622, 802
Lippman, Steven A., 633, 802
Lipson, Marc, 442, 797
Litner, John, 476, 802
Litterman, B., 462–463, 786, 802
Litzenberger, Robert H., 476, 802
Liu, Shuming, 703, 802
Lo, A., 382–383, 782, 802
Long, J., 374, 414, 802
Lothian, J.R., 357, 802
Loviscek, Anthony L., 728, 802
Low, Vincent, 723, 802
Lu, Chiuling, 519, 704, 802
Lucas, R.E. Jr., 357, 802
Luce, R.D., 802
Ludvigson, S., 383, 414, 801
Luehrman, Timothy A., 803